THE

WAR OF THE REBELLION:

A COMPILATION OF THE

OFFICIAL RECORDS

OF THE

UNION AND CONFEDERATE ARMIES.

PREPARED, UNDER THE DIRECTION OF THE SECRETARY OF WAR, BY

The late Lieut. Col. **ROBERT N. SCOTT**, Third U. S. Artillery.

PUBLISHED UNDER THE SUPERVISION OF

Lieut. Col. **HENRY M. LAZELLE**, Twenty-third U. S. Infantry.

PURSUANT TO ACTS OF CONGRESS.

SERIES I—VOLUME XXII—IN TWO PARTS.

PART I—REPORTS.

WASHINGTON:
GOVERNMENT PRINTING OFFICE.
1888.

PREFACE.

By an act approved June 23, 1874, Congress made an appropriation "to enable the Secretary of War to begin the publication of the Official Records of the War of the Rebellion, both of the Union and Confederate Armies," and directed him "to have copied for the Public Printer all reports, letters, telegrams, and general orders not heretofore copied or printed, and properly arranged in chronological order."

Appropriations for continuing such preparation have been made from time to time, and the act approved June 16, 1880, has provided "for the printing and binding, under direction of the Secretary of War, of 10,000 copies of a compilation of the Official Records (Union and Confederate) of the War of the Rebellion, so far as the same may be ready for publication, during the fiscal year"; and that "of said number, 7,000 copies shall be for the use of the House of Representatives, 2,000 copies for the use of the Senate, and 1,000 copies for the use of the Executive Departments."*

This compilation will be the first general publication of the military records of the war, and will embrace all official documents that can be obtained by the compiler, and that appear to be of any historical value.

* Volumes I–V distributed under act approved June 16, 1880. The act approved August 7, 1882, provides that—

"The volumes of the Official Records of the War of the Rebellion shall be distributed as follows: One thousand copies to the Executive Departments, as now provided by law. One thousand copies for distribution by the Secretary of War among officers of the Army and contributors to the work. Eight thousand three hundred copies shall be sent by the Secretary of War to such libraries, organizations, and individuals as may be designated by the Senators, Representatives, and Delegates of the Forty-seventh Congress. Each Senator shall designate not exceeding twenty-six, and each Representative and Delegate not exceeding twenty-one of such addresses, and the volumes shall be sent thereto from time to time as they are published, until the publication is completed. Senators, Representatives, and Delegates shall inform the Secretary of War in each case how many volumes of those heretofore published they have forwarded to such addresses. The remaining copies of the eleven thousand to be published, and all sets that may not be ordered to be distributed as provided herein, shall be sold by the Secretary of War for cost of publication, with ten per cent. added thereto, and the proceeds of such sale shall be covered into the Treasury. If two or more sets of said volumes are ordered to the same address, the Secretary of War shall inform the Senators, Representatives, or Delegates who have designated the same, who thereupon may designate other libraries, organizations, or individuals. The Secretary of War shall report to the first session of the Forty-eighth Congress what volumes of the series heretofore published have not been furnished to such libraries, organizations, and individuals. He shall also inform distributees at whose instance the volumes are sent."

The publication will present the records in the following order of arrangement:

The **1st Series** will embrace the formal reports, both Union and Confederate, of the first seizures of United States property in the Southern States, and of all military operations in the field, with the correspondence, orders, and returns relating specially thereto, and, as proposed, is to be accompanied by an Atlas.

In this series the reports will be arranged according to the campaigns and several theaters of operations (in the chronological order of the events), and the Union reports of any event will, as a rule, be immediately followed by the Confederate accounts. The correspondence, &c., not embraced in the "reports" proper will follow (first Union and next Confederate) in chronological order.

The **2d Series** will contain the correspondence, orders, reports, and returns, Union and Confederate, relating to prisoners of war, and (so far as the military authorities were concerned) to State or political prisoners.

The **3d Series** will contain the correspondence, orders, reports, and returns of the Union authorities (embracing their correspondence with the Confederate officials) not relating specially to the subjects of the *first* and *second* series. It will set forth the annual and special reports of the Secretary of War, of the General-in-Chief, and of the chiefs of the several staff corps and departments; the calls for troops, and the correspondence between the National and the several State authorities.

The **4th Series** will exhibit the correspondence, orders, reports, and returns of the Confederate authorities, similar to that indicated for the Union officials, as of the *third* series, but excluding the correspondence between the Union and Confederate authorities given in that series.

ROBERT N. SCOTT,
Major Third Art., and Bvt. Lieut. Col.

WAR DEPARTMENT, *August* 23, 1880.

Approved:

ALEX. RAMSEY,
Secretary of War.

CONTENTS.

CHAPTER XXXV.

CONTENTS OF PRECEDING VOLUMES.

VOLUME I.

VOLUME II.

VOLUME III.

VOLUME IV.

VOLUME V.

VOLUME VI.

VOLUME VII.

VOLUME VIII.

VOLUME IX.

VOLUME X—IN TWO PARTS.

VOLUME XI—IN THREE PARTS.

VOLUME XII—IN THREE PARTS, AND SUPPLEMENT.

VOLUME XIII.

VOLUME XIV.

VOLUME XV.

VOLUME XVI—IN TWO PARTS.

CHAPTER XXVIII.

VOLUME XVII—IN TWO PARTS.

CHAPTER XXIX.

VOLUME XVIII.

CHAPTER XXX.

VOLUME XIX—IN TWO PARTS.

CHAPTER XXXI.

VOLUME XX—IN TWO PARTS.

CHAPTER XXXII.

VOLUME XXI.

CHAPTER XXXIII.

CHAPTER XXXIV.

OPERATIONS IN MISSOURI, ARKANSAS, KANSAS, THE INDIAN TERRITORY, AND THE DEPARTMENT OF THE NORTHWEST.

November 20, 1862–December 31, 1863.

PART I.

REPORTS .... Nov. 20, 1862–Dec. 31, 1863.
CORRESPONDENCE, ETC .... Nov. 20, 1862–Dec. 31, 1862.

SUMMARY OF THE PRINCIPAL EVENTS.*

Nov. 20-23, 1862.—Reconnaissance toward Van Buren and Fort Smith, Ark.
24, 1862.—Skirmish at Beaver Creek, Mo.
24-26, 1862.—Expeditions from Greenfield into Jasper and Barton Counties, Mo.
25, 1862.—Skirmish at Pitman's Ferry, Ark.
Skirmish near Cane Hill, Ark.
25-29, 1862.—Expedition to Yellville, Ark.
26, 1862.—Brig. Gen. James G. Blunt, U. S. Army, assumes command of the District of Kansas.
26-29, 1862.—Affairs in Jackson and La Fayette Counties, Mo.
27, 1862.—Skirmish at Carthage, Mo.
27-Dec. 5, 1862.—Expedition from Helena, Ark., to Grenada, Miss.†
28, 1862.—Engagement at Cane Hill, or Boston Mountains, Ark.
Brig. Gen. Washington L. Elliott, U. S. Army, temporarily in command of the Department of the Northwest.
30-Dec. 6, 1862.—Expedition from Rolla to the Ozark Mountains, Mo., and skirmishes.
Dec. 2, 1862.—Skirmish at Saline, Ind. T.
4, 1862.—Attack by citizens on Indian prisoners at Mankato, Minn.
4- 6, 1862.—Operations about Cane Hill, and skirmish (December 6) at Reed's Mountain, Ark.
4-12, 1862.—Operations in the Cherokee country, Ind. T.
6, 1862.—Skirmish at Parkersville, Mo.
7, 1862.—Battle of Prairie Grove, Fayetteville, or Illinois Creek, Ark.

* Of some of the minor events noted in this "Summary," no circumstantial reports are on file.
† For reports, see Series I, Vol. XVII, Part I, pp. 528-541.

Dec. 9, 1862.—Skirmish at Mudtown, Ark.
9–15, 1862.—Expedition from Ozark, Mo., into Marion County, Ark.
14, 1862.—Affair near Helena, Ark.
15, 1862.—Skirmish at Neosho, Mo.
17–21, 1862.—Expedition from New Madrid to Clarkton, Mo.
20, 1862.—Skirmish near Cane Hill, Ark.
21, 1862.—Skirmish at Van Buren, Ark.
21–23, 1862.—Expedition from Fayetteville to Huntsville, Ark.
22, 1862.—Troops of the Department of the Missouri operating on the Mississippi River embodied in the Thirteenth and Fifteenth Army Corps, Department of the Tennessee.
23, 1862.—Skirmish on the Saint Francis Road, near Helena, Ark.
23–31, 1862.—Operations in the Sugar Creek Hills, Mo.
28, 1862.—Skirmish at Dripping Springs, and capture of Van Buren, Ark.
New Madrid, Mo., evacuated by the Union forces.
30, 1862.—Skirmish at La Grange, Ark.
31, 1862–Jan. 25, 1863.—Marmaduke's expedition into Missouri.
Jan. 1, 1863.—Affair near Helena, Ark.
2, 1863.—Skirmish at Cane Hill, Ark.
Reoccupation of New Madrid, Mo., by Union forces.
[illegible]– 6, 1863.—Scout from Ozark, Mo., to Dubuque, Ark.
4–11, 1863.—Expedition against, and capture of, Arkansas Post, Ark.*
6, 1863.—Capture of the steamer Jacob Musselman, opposite Memphis.
Affair near Linn Creek, Mo.
8–10, 1863.—Scout from Elk Horn to Berryville, Ark.
9–12, 1863.—Expedition from Huntsville to Buffalo River, Ark.
10, 1863.—Skirmish at Carrollton, Mo.
11, 1863.—Skirmish at Wood Creek, Mo.
Capture of the steamer Grampus No. 2, opposite Memphis.
12, 1863.—Skirmish at Lick Creek, near Helena, Ark.
13, 1863.—Skirmish at Carthage, Mo.
13–19, 1863.—Expedition from Helena up the White River, and capture of Saint Charles, Clarendon, Devall's Bluff, and Des Arc, Ark.
14, 1863.—The "Southwestern Army" (Confederate) constituted, under command of Lieut. Gen. E. Kirby Smith.
—, 1863.—Skirmish near Maysville, Ark.
15, 1863.—Burning of Mound City, Ark.
18, 1863.—Skirmish in the Cherokee country, Ind. T.
21, 1863.—Skirmish near Columbia, Mo.
22, 1863.—Maj. Gen. U. S. Grant, U. S. Army, commanding Department of the Tennessee, assumes command of all the troops in Arkansas within reach of his orders.
23–27, 1863.—Scout from Fayetteville to Van Buren, Ark.
26, 1863.—Skirmish at Mulberry Springs, Ark.
27, 1863.—Affair at Bloomfield, Mo.
29, 1863.—Brig. Gen. Thomas J. McKean, U. S. Army, assumes command of the District of Northern Missouri.
Feb. 2– 3, 1863.—Skirmishes at Vine Prairie, on White Oak River, and near the mouth of Mulberry River, Ark.
2–13, 1863.—Scouts and skirmishes in and about Mingo Swamp, Mo.
4, 1863.—Skirmish at Batesville, Ark.
5, 1863.—Skirmish in Pope County, Ark.
Skirmish on Bear Creek, Johnson County, Mo.

---

* For reports, see Series I, Vol. XVII, Part I, pp. 698–796.

Feb 5-12, 1863.—Scout from Fayetteville to the Arkansas River, and skirmishes at Threlkeld's Ferry and near Van Buren, Ark.

8, 1863.—Skirmish near Independence, Mo.

9, 1863.—The "Southwestern Army" (Confederate) extended to embrace the Trans-Mississippi Department.

10, 1863.—Skirmish on Sarcoxie Prairie, Mo.

12, 1863.—Skirmish near Frog Bayou, Ark.

13, 1863.—Maj. Gen. John Pope, U. S. Army, resumes command of the Department of the Northwest.

15, 1863.—Skirmish near Arkadelphia, Ark.

17-19, 1863.—Attack on the steamer Hercules and burning of Hopefield, Ark.

19-22, 1863.—Scout in Barton and Jasper Counties, Mo.

20, 1863.—Skirmish near Fort Halleck, Dak.

27, 1863.—Maj. Gen. Sterling Price, C. S. Army, ordered to the Trans-Mississippi Department.

28, 1863.—Skirmish near Fort Gibson, Ind. T.

Mar. 1- 2, 1863.—Capture of, and skirmish near, Bloomfield, Mo.

2, 1863.—Skirmish at Neosho, Mo.

3, 1863.—Raid by guerrillas on Granby, Mo.

5, 1863.—Skirmish opposite Fort Smith, Ark.

5-12, 1863.—Expedition from Helena up the Saint Francis and Little Rivers, and skirmish at Madison, Ark.

5-13, 1863.—Operations in Newton and Jasper Counties, Mo., and skirmish (9th) near Sherwood.

6, 1863.—Skirmish on White River, Ark.

6-10, 1863.—Expedition from Helena to Big and Lick Creeks, Ark., and skirmishes.

7, 1863.—Lieut. Gen. E. Kirby Smith, C. S. Army, assumes command of the forces west of the Mississippi.

9-15, 1863.—Expedition from Bloomfield, Mo., to Chalk Bluff, Ark., and to Gum Slough, Kennett, Hornersville, etc., Mo., and skirmishes.

10, 1863.—Maj. Gen. Edwin V. Sumner, U. S. Army, assigned to command of the Department of the Missouri.

18, 1863.—Lieut. Gen. Theophilus H. Holmes, C. S. Army, assumes command of the District of Arkansas.

19, 1863.—Skirmish on Frog Bayou, Ark.

19-23, 1863.—Scout toward, and affair (21st) near, Doniphan, Mo.

22, 1863.—Skirmish at Blue Springs, near Independence, Mo.
Skirmish near the head of White River, Ark.

24-Apr. 1, 1863.—Scout from Bloomfield to Scatterville, Mo.

27, 1863.—Skirmish with Indians on the Rio Bonita, Dak.

28, 1863.—Guerrilla attack on steamer Sam. Gaty.

29-Apr. 5, 1863.—Scouts from Fayetteville, Ark.

30, 1863.—Skirmish at "The Island," Vernon County, Mo.
Skirmishes at Tahlequah, Ind. T.
Skirmish at Cross Hollow, Ark.

31, 1863.—Skirmish at Clapper's Saw-Mill, Crooked Creek, Ark.
Skirmish at Owensville, Mo.

Apr. 1, 1863.—Maj. Gen. Francis J. Herron, U. S. Army, supersedes Brig. Gen. John M. Schofield in command of the Army of the Frontier.
Skirmish at Chalk Bluff, Ark.
Skirmish near Clarendon, Ark.

1- 5, 1863.—Scout from Linden to White River Mo.

—, 1863.—Skirmishes in Carroll County, Mo.

2, 1863.—Skirmish on Little Rock Road, Ark.
Affair in Jackson County, Mo.

Apr. 3– 8, 1863.—Scout from Carrollton to Yellville, Ark., and skirmishes.
5, 1863.—Scouts from Fayetteville, Ark.
8, 1863.—Skirmish in Saint Francis County, Ark.
9, 1863.—Skirmish at Sedalia, Mo.
Skirmish on White River, Ark.
10, 1863.—Expedition from Humboldt to Cottonwood, Kans.
11, 1863.—Skirmish at Webber's Falls, Ind. T.
Skirmish near Squirrel Creek Crossing, Colo.
17, 1863.—Skirmish on White River, Mo.
17–May 2, 1863.—Marmaduke's expedition into Missouri.
18, 1863.—Action at Fayetteville, Ark.
Scout through Shannon County, Mo.
18–21, 1863.—Scout from Salem to Sinking Creek, Current River, and Big Creek, Mo.
19–20, 1863.—Scout near Neosho, Mo.
20, 1863.—Affair at Bloomfield, Mo.
21–May 2, 1863.—Expedition from Lake Spring, Mo., to Chalk Bluff, Ark.
23, 1863.—Skirmish at Independence, Mo.
25, 1863.—Skirmish at Webber's Falls, Ind. T.
26, 1863.—Skirmish at Elm Springs, Ark.
30, 1863.—Skirmish at Fort Gibson, Ind. T.
May 1, 1863.—Skirmish at La Grange, Ark.
3, 1863.—Expedition on the Santa Fé Road, Mo.
3–11, 1863.—Scout in Cass and Bates Counties, Mo.
4, 1863.—Operations about Lexington, Mo.
5– 9, 1863.—Scout from Fort Scott, Kans., to Sherwood, Mo., and skirmishes.
6–15, 1863.—Scout between the White and Saint Francis Rivers, Ark.
6–19, 1863.—Scout from Creek Agency, Ind. T., to Jasper County, Mo., including skirmishes at Martin's House, Centre Creek, and near Sherwood, and destruction of Sherwood.
9, 1863.—Skirmish in Stone County, Mo.
11, 1863.—Skirmish at Mount Vernon, Ark.
Skirmish at Taylor's Creek or Crowley's Ridge, Ark.
12, 1863.—Skirmish at Bloomfield, Mo.
13–18, 1863.—Scout from Newtonia to French Point and Centre Creek, Mo., and skirmishes.
14, 1863.—Skirmish at Fort Gibson, Ind. T.
15, 1863.—Skirmish at Fort Smith, Ark.
Skirmish at Big Creek, near Pleasant Hill, Mo.
16, 1863.—Skirmish near Carthage, Mo.
18, 1863.—Affair at Hog Island, Bates County, Mo.
19, 1863.—Skirmish near Richfield, Clay County, Mo.
20, 1863.—Action near Fort Gibson, Ind. T.
21, 1863.—Operations of guerrillas on Santa Fé Road, near Kansas City, Mo.
21–30, 1863.—Scout from Cassville, through Northwestern Arkansas, into Newton and Jasper Counties, Mo., including skirmishes (22d) at Bentonville and (26th) near Carthage.
22, 1863.—Skirmish at Fort Gibson, Ind. T.
23, 1863.—Skirmish at Hartville, Mo.
23–26, 1863.—Expedition from Helena to near Napoleon, Ark., and skirmish near Island No. 65, Mississippi River.
24, 1863.—Maj. Gen. John M. Schofield, U S. Army, supersedes Maj. Gen. Samuel R. Curtis in command of the Department of the Missouri.

May 25, 1863.—Skirmish at Polk's Plantation, near Helena, Ark.
26, 1863.—Skirmish at Mountain Store, Mo.
Skirmish at Bush Creek, Mo.
28, 1863.—Skirmish near Fort Gibson, Ind. T.
29, 1863.—The Enrolled Militia of Missouri placed under command of Major General Schofield.
—, 1863.—Affair near Patterson, Mo.
June 1, 1863.—Skirmishes near Rocheport, Mo.
Skirmish near Doniphan, Mo.
Affair at Waverly, Mo.
4, 1863.—Skirmish at Fayetteville, Ark.
6, 1863.—Skirmish near Shawneetown, Kans.
6-20, 1863.—Operations about Fort Gibson, Ind. T., including skirmish (16th) on Greenleaf Prairie.
8, 1863.—Skirmish at Cole Camp, Mo.
Affair near Fort Scott, Kans.
9, 1863.—District of the Frontier constituted, under command of Maj. Gen. James G. Blunt, U. S. Army.
District of the Border constituted, under command of Brig. Gen. Thomas Ewing, jr.
11, 1863.—Scout to Jacksonport, Ark.
16-Sept. 13, 1863.—The Sioux Expedition, Dakota.
17, 1863.—Skirmish near Westport, Mo.
Affair near Wellington, Mo.
18, 1863.—Skirmish near Rocheport, Mo.
20-23, 1863.—Scouts from Waynesville, Mo.
23, 1863.—Skirmish at, and destruction of, Sibley, Mo.
Skirmish near Papinsville, Mo.
Attack on Pawnee Agency, Nebr.
25, 1863.—Skirmish at Madison, Ark.
27-28, 1863.—Skirmishes at Carthage, Mo.
30, 1863.—Skirmish near Hudson's Ford, Neosho River.
July 1- 2, 1863.—Engagement at Cabin Creek, Ind. T.
3, 1863.—Scout from Salem, Mo., and skirmish.
4, 1863.—Attack on Helena, Ark.
Skirmish at Cassville, Mo.
Affair in the Black Fork Hills, Mo.
7, 1863.—Skirmish near Drywood, Mo.
Skirmish with Indians at Grand Pass, Idaho.
10, 1863.—Skirmish at Florence, Mo.
11, 1863.—Skirmish at Stockton, Mo.
—, 1863.—Skirmish near Cross Hollow, Ark.
12, 1863.—Skirmish near Switzler's Mill, Chariton County, Mo.
17, 1863.—Engagement at Elk Creek, near Honey Springs, Ind. T.
18-26, 1863.—Scout from Cassville, Mo., to Huntsville, Ark., etc.
20, 1863.—Skirmish at Cabin Creek, Ind. T.
24, 1863.—Maj. Gen. Sterling Price, C. S. Army, supersedes Lieut. Gen. Theophilus H. Holmes in command of the District of Arkansas.
Skirmish in Dade County, Mo.
25, 1863.—Skirmish at Brownsville, Ark.
27, 1863.—Affair near Cassville, Mo.
27-29, 1863.—Expedition from Baxter Springs to Grand River, Kans.
28, 1863.—Skirmish at Marshall, Mo.
28, 1863.—Skirmish near High Grove, Mo.

July —, 1863.—Expedition from Greensborough to Helena, Ark.
28–30, 1863.—Scout from Newtonia to Oliver's Prairie, Mo.
30, 1863.—Skirmishes near Elm Springs, Ark.
Skirmish near Lexington, Mo.
Skirmish near Marshall, Mo.
Aug. 1, 1863.—Skirmish at Taylor's Farm, on the Little Blue, Mo.
Affair at Round Ponds, near Castor River, Mo.
1–Sept. 14, 1863.—Advance of the Union forces upon Little Rock, Ark., etc.
2, 1863.—Skirmish at Stumptown, Mo.
—, 1863.—Scout from Pocahontas, Ark., to Patterson, Mo.
5, 1863.—Maj. Gen. Frederick Steele, U. S. Army, assumes command of the army, to take the field from Helena, Ark.
6– 9, 1863.—Scout from Greenfield to Golden Grove and Carthage, Mo.
Scout from Lexington to vicinity of Hopewell, Mo.
6–10, 1863.—Expedition from Fort Scott, Kans., to Clear Lake, Mo.
6–11, 1863.—Scout from Houston to Spring River Mills, Mo., and skirmishes.
7, 1863.—Skirmish at New Madrid, Mo.
8, 1863.—Affair on Clear Creek, near Ball Town, Mo.
9, 1863.—Skirmish at Garden Hollow, near Pineville, Mo.
9–18, 1863.—Scout from Cape Girardeau to Ash Hill and Poplar Bluff, Mo., and skirmish (13th) at Ash Hill.
10, 1863.—Skirmish at Dayton, Mo.
11, 1863.—Maj. Gen. Frederick Steele, U. S. Army, assumes command of all troops in Arkansas north of the Arkansas River.
12–16, 1863.—Scout from Houston to Jack's Fork, Mo., and skirmish (14th).
13, 1863.—Skirmish at Pineville, Mo.
13–Sept. 11, 1863.—Expedition against Indians in Dakota.
14, 1863.—Skirmish at West Point, Mo.
Skirmish near Sherwood, Mo.
Skirmish near Wellington, Mo.
Skirmish near Jack's Fork, Mo.
15, 1863.—Skirmish at Bentonville, Ark.
17–26, 1863.—Expeditions from Cape Girardeau and Pilot Knob, Mo., to Pocahontas, Ark.
20–28, 1863.—Quantrill's raid into Kansas, and pursuit by Union forces.
22–23, 1863.—Skirmishes at Pocahontas, Mo.
23, 1863.—Skirmish at Fayetteville, Ark.
Scout on Bennett's Bayou, Mo., and skirmishes.
25, 1863.—Skirmish near Waynesville, Mo.
Skirmish near Independence, Mo.
25–28, 1863.—Scout from Sedalia, and skirmish (26th) at Clear Fork, Mo.
26, 1863.—Skirmish at Perryville, Ind. T.
28–Sept. 7, 1863.—Expedition from Lexington into La Fayette, Johnson, Cass, and Henry Counties, Mo.
29, 1863.—Skirmish at Texas Prairie, Mo.
30, 1863.—Skirmish at Washington, Ark.
31, 1863.—Skirmish on the Marais des Cygnes, Kans.
Sept. 1, 1863.—Occupation of Fort Smith, Ark., by the Union forces.
Skirmish at Jenny Lind, Ark.
Action at Devil's Backbone, or Backbone Mountain, Ark.
4, 1863.—Affair at Quincy, Mo.
4– 5, 1863.—Skirmishes at Bentonville, Flint Creek, Hog-Eye, and Round Prairie, Ark.

Sept. 4- 7, 1863.—Scout from Cold Water Grove to Pleasant Hill and Big Creek, Mo., and skirmishes.
4-24, 1863.—Scout from Fort Lyon, Colo., to Fort Larned, Kans.
5, 1863.—Skirmish near Maysville, Ark.
6, 1863.—Attack on train between Fort Scott, Kans., and Carthage, Mo.
Skirmish in Hutton Valley, Mo.
7, 1863.—Skirmish at Bear Skin Lake, Mo.
7-19, 1863.—Expedition from Springfield, Mo., into Arkansas and Indian Territory, and skirmish (15th) near Enterprise, Mo.
7-30, 1863.—Expedition to Big Lake, Mississippi County, Ark.
9, 1863.—Skirmish at Webber's Falls, Ind. T.
11, 1863.—Skirmish at Waldron, Ark.
12, 1863.—Affair near Houston, Texas County, Mo.
Skirmish at Dardanelle, Ark.
13, 1863.—Attack on, and skirmish near, Salem, Mo.
13-21, 1863.—Scout from Fort Larned to Booth's Ranch, Arkansas River, Kans.
15, 1863.—Skirmish near Enterprise, Ark.
Skirmish in Jackson County, Mo.
15-18, 1863.—Scout from Greenfield, Mo.
16, 1863.—Affair at Brownsville, Ark.
17, 1863.—Skirmish on Horse Creek, Mo.
20, 1863.—Skirmish at Hornersville, Mo.
22-25, 1863.—Scout in La Fayette County, Mo., and skirmishes.
22-Oct. 26, 1863.—Shelby's raid in Arkansas and Missouri.
23, 1863.—Skirmish near Bayou Meto Bridge, Ark.
25, 1863.—Lieut. Gen. Theophilus H. Holmes, C. S. Army, resumes command of the District of Arkansas.
26, 1863.—Skirmish at Cassville, Mo.
27, 1863.—Skirmish at Newtonia, Mo.
27-28, 1863.—Scout in Bates County, Mo.
29-Oct. 26, 1863.—Expeditions from Pilot Knob, Mo., to Oregon County, Mo., and Pocahontas, Ark.

Oct. 1, 1863.—Skirmish at Elizabethtown, Ark.
2, 1863.—Skirmish at Carthage, Mo.
Skirmish at Vance's Store, Ark.
3- 7, 1863.—Operations in Bates and Vernon Counties, Mo.
4, 1863.—Skirmish near Widow Wheeler's, southwest of Neosho, Mo.
5, 1863.—Skirmish near Syracuse, Mo.
6, 1863.—Action at Baxter Springs, Ark.
Skirmish at Waldron, Ark.
7, 1863.—Skirmish at Evening Shade, Ark.
Skirmish at Ferry's Ford, Ark.
Skirmish in the Choctaw Nation, Ind. T.
7-10, 1863.—Scout in Spring River country, Ark.
7-17, 1863.—Expedition from Sedalia to Marshall, Mo.
10, 1863.—Skirmish at Tulip, Ark.
11, 1863.—Skirmish at Brazil Creek, Choctaw Nation, Ind. T.
11-14, 1863.—Demonstration against Fayetteville, Ark.
12, 1863.—Skirmish at Webber's Falls, Ind. T.
Skirmish at Tulip, Ark.
Affair at McGuire's, near Fayetteville, Ark.
12-16, 1863.—Scout from Fort Garland, Colo., and killing of outlaw Espanoza.
14, 1863.—Skirmish near Man's Creek, Shannon County, Mo.
15, 1863.—Skirmish on Creek Agency, Ind. T.

Oct. 19, 1863.—Affair on Honey Creek, Mo.
21, 1863.—Affair in Greenton Valley, near Hopewell, Mo.
22, 1863.—Mutiny at Bloomfield, Mo.
25, 1863.—Action at Pine Bluff, Ark.
26, 1863.—Skirmish at King's House, near Waynesville, Mo.
26–Nov. 12, 1863.—Scout from Cape Girardeau to Doniphan, Mo., and Pocahontas, Ark.
27, 1863.—Skirmish at Tulip, Ark.
27–Nov. 15, 1863.—Expedition from Cape Girardeau to Clarkton, Mo.
28, 1863.—Skirmish at Clarksville, Ark.
29, 1863.—Affair near Warsaw, Mo.
Skirmish at Ozark, Ark.
29–Nov. 5, 1863.—Scout from Pilot Knob to Alton and Doniphan, Mo.
30, 1863.—Skirmish at Fourteen-mile Creek, Ind. T.

Nov. 2, 1863.—Brig. Gen. John McNeil, U. S. Army, assumes command of the District of the Frontier.
Skirmish in Bates Township, Ark.
4, 1863.—Skirmish near Lexington, Mo.
4– 6, 1863.—Skirmishes at and near Neosho, Mo.
4– 9, 1863.—Scout from Houston to Jack's Fork, Mo.
4–19, 1863.—Scouts in Reynolds, Shannon, and Oregon Counties, Mo.
5, 1863.—Skirmish at Neosho, Mo.
7–13, 1863.—Expedition from Fayetteville to Frog Bayou, Ark., and skirmishes (9th) near Huntsville and (10th) near Kingston.
9, 1863.—Skirmish in the Choctaw Nation, Ind. T.
10–18, 1863.—Expedition from Benton to Mount Ida, Ark., and skirmish (11th) at Caddo Gap.
Expedition from Springfield, Mo., to Huntsville, Carrollton, and Berryville, Ark., and skirmishes.
—, 1863.—Expedition into Arkansas, and skirmish.
11, 1863.—Skirmish at Fouché-le-Faix Mountains, Ark.
Skirmish at Greenleaf Prairie, Ind. T.
12, 1863.—Skirmish at Roseville, Ark.
Skirmish at Greenleaf Prairie, Ind. T.
13, 1863.—Skirmish at Mount Ida, Ark.
14–17, 1863.—Expedition from Helena, Ark.
15, 1863.—Skirmish in Newton County, Ark.
17–27, 1863.—Scouts about Houston, Mo.
18, 1863.—Skirmishes on Shoal and Turkey Creeks, Jasper County, Mo.
19, 1863.—Skirmish at Dr. Green's Farm, near Lawrenceville, Ark.
21, 1863.—Affair at Jacksonport, Ark.
22, 1863.—Affair near Houston, Mo.
23–29, 1863.—Scouts from Houston, Mo.
23–Dec. 18, 1863.—Expedition from Springfield to Howell, Wright, and Oregon Counties, Mo.
24, 1863.—Skirmish at Clarksville, Ark.
24–28, 1863.—Scouts from Salem to Bushy and Pigeon Creeks, Gladen Valley, and Dry Fork, Mo.
25, 1863.—Skirmish in Crawford County, Ark.
Skirmish on the Big Piney, near Houston, Mo.
Scout in the vicinity of Waynesville, Mo.
Raid on Farmington, Mo.
26, 1863.—Skirmish near Woodson, Mo.
—, 1863.—Scout from Neosho to Shoal and Turkey Creeks, Mo.
29–30, 1863.—Attack on Bloomfield, Mo., and pursuit of the Confederates to Brown's Ferry, Ark.

Dec. 1, 1863.—Skirmish near Benton, Ark.
Skirmish near Devall's Bluff, Ark.
Affair with Ponca Indians.
2- 7, 1863.—Scout from Waldron to Mount Ida, Caddo Gap, and Dallas, Ark.
4, 1863.—Skirmish with Indians at Niobrara, Nebr.
5-13, 1863.—Reconnaissance from Little Rock, and skirmish (8th) at Princeton, Ark.
9-14, 1863.—Scouts from Waldron down Dutch Creek, Ark.
9-19, 1863.—Scouts from Houston, Mo.
11, 1863.—Brig. Gen. S. B. Maxey, C. S. Army, assigned to command of the Indian Territory.
11-13, 1863.—Scout from Waldron to Dallas, Ark.
12, 1863.—Skirmish at Devall's Bluff, Ark.
13, 1863.—Skirmish at Meriwether's Ferry, Bayou Boeuf, Ark.
14, 1863.—Skirmish at Caddo Mill, Ark.
16, 1863.—Demonstration on Fort Gibson, Ind. T.
Skirmish near Springfield, Mo.
16-31, 1863.—Scout from Fayetteville, Ark., including skirmishes (23d) at Stroud's Store and (25th) on Buffalo River.
18, 1863.—Skirmish near Sheldon's Place, Barren Fork, Ind. T.
19-20, 1863.—Scout from Lexington, Mo.
23, 1863.—Skirmish at Jacksonport, Ark.
23-25, 1863.—Attack on Centreville, Mo., and pursuit of the Confederates, including skirmish (25th) at Pulliam's.
24-29, 1863.—Scout from Cassville, Mo.
26, 1863.—Skirmish near Fort Gibson, Ind. T.
26-28, 1863.—Scout from Salem, Mo.
26, 1863-Jan. 2, 1864.—Scout from Forsyth, Mo., to Batesville, Ark.
29, 1863.—Attack on Waldron, Ark.
31, 1863.—Skirmish in Searcy County, Mo.

GENERAL REPORTS.

No. 1.—Maj. Gen. Henry W. Halleck, U. S. Army, General-in-Chief, of operations in the Departments of the Missouri and of the Northwest, November 25, 1862–November 15, 1863.

No. 2.—Maj. Gen. John M. Schofield, U. S. Army, commanding Department of the Missouri, of operations May 24–December 10, 1863.

No. 3.—Lieut. Gen. E. Kirby Smith, C. S. Army, commanding Trans-Mississippi Department, of operations March 7, 1863–February 21, 1864.

No. 4.—Brig. Gen. William Steele, C. S. Army, of operations in the Indian Territory in 1863.

No. 1.

Report of Maj. Gen. Henry W. Halleck, U. S. Army, General-in-Chief, of operations in the Departments of the Missouri and of the Northwest, November 25, 1862–*November* 15, 1863.

HEADQUARTERS OF THE ARMY,
Washington, D. C., November 25, 1863.

SIR: In compliance with your orders, I submit the following summary of military operations since my last annual report:

* * * * * * *

DEPARTMENT OF THE MISSOURI.

The withdrawal to Missouri of a large part of our forces in Arkansas, as stated in my last annual report, left the frontier of the former exposed to raids, of which the rebels were prompt to take advantage. Marmaduke, with the advance of Hindman's rebel army, moved forward with the purpose of entering the southwest of Missouri. Before the enemy could concentrate his forces for battle, Brigadier-General Blunt, by forced marches, encountered him at Cane Hill, in the Boston Mountains. A running fight took place on the 28th of November, 1862, in which the enemy was defeated with a heavy loss. Our casualties were 4 killed and 36 wounded.

Four days after the combat of Cane Hill, it was ascertained, from reliable information, that Hindman's army had crossed the Arkansas River, and formed a junction with Marmaduke at Lee's Creek, 15 miles north of Van Buren, to which point the latter had retreated after the action of the 28th of November.

The united rebel force was believed to be very much greater than our own, of which two divisions were more than 100 miles in the rear. Immediately upon learning General Blunt's danger from an overwhelming attack of the enemy, General Herron, by forced marches (110 miles in three days), arrived at Fayetteville, Ark., early on the morning of the 7th of December. Soon after, we encountered the enemy in force at Prairie Grove, while attempting a flank movement to get between Blunt and the approaching succor, designing to crush both in succession. This skillfully devised project was fortunately frustrated by the valor and endurance of Herron's divisions, which stoutly held their ground till about 2 o'clock in the afternoon, when Blunt's forces arrived upon the field, and the engagement became general along the entire line, and continued to be fiercely contested until dark. During the night the enemy retreated across the Boston Mountains. Although the rebels suffered much more severely than ourselves, we purchased the victory with the loss of 167 killed, 798 wounded, and 183 missing, making a total loss of 1,148, of which 953 were of Herron's divisions.*

Early in January, 1863, a rebel force, estimated at from 4,000 to 6,000, under Marmaduke, moved upon Lawrence Mills, and proceeded, by way of Ozark, to the attack of Springfield, Mo., to which place our small force, consisting chiefly of militia, convalescents, and citizens, was compelled to fall back. This miscellaneous garrison, of only about 1,000 men, obstinately defended the place most of the day of the 8th of January, with the loss of 14 killed, 145 wounded, and 5 missing—in all, 164. Under cover of the night the enemy withdrew, and our force was too feeble to make a vigorous pursuit. Another skirmish took place at Hartville on the 11th, in which our loss was 7 killed and 64 wounded. We captured 27 prisoners.

The season was now so far advanced and the roads so impassable that further operations could not be carried on by either party.

On the 15th of July, Major-General Blunt crossed the Arkansas River, near Honey Springs, Ind. T., and on the 16th [17th] attacked a superior force of rebels under General Cooper, which he completely routed, the enemy leaving their killed and wounded on the field. Our loss was 17 killed and 60 wounded, while that of the enemy was 150 killed (buried by our men), 400 wounded, and 77 prisoners taken, besides 1 piece of artillery, 200 stand of arms, and 15 wagons.

After several skirmishes with the enemy, General Blunt descended the Arkansas River, and, on the 1st of September, occupied Fort Smith, Ark.

The main body of our troops in the Department of the Missouri had, in the early part of the season, been sent to re-enforce General Grant

* But see revised statement, pp. 84–86.

before Vicksburg. Taking advantage of this reduction of force, the enemy moved against Helena, and attacked that place on the 4th of July. After a severe engagement, he was defeated by Major-General Prentiss, with a heavy loss in killed and wounded and 1,100 prisoners. Our loss in killed, wounded, and missing was only about 250.*

As soon as Vicksburg had capitulated, Major-General Steele was sent with a force to Helena, with instructions to form a junction with Brigadier-General Davidson, who was moving south from Missouri, by Crowley's Ridge, and drive the enemy south of Arkansas River. This junction being effected, General Steele established his depot and hospitals at Devall's Bluff, and on the 1st of August advanced against the enemy, who fell back toward Little Rock. After several successful skirmishes he reached the Arkansas River, and threw a part of his force upon the south side to threaten the enemy's communications with Arkadelphia and take his defenses in reverse. The rebels, on seeing this movement, destroyed what property they could, and, after a slight resistance, fled in disorder, pursued by our cavalry; and on the 10th of September our troops took possession of the capital of Arkansas. Our loss in killed, wounded, and missing did not exceed 100. We captured 1,000 prisoners, and such public property as the rebels had not time to destroy. After the capture of Little Rock, and while our cavalry were driving the main force of the rebels south, the enemy attempted to recapture Pine Bluff, but was repulsed with heavy loss. On the 28th of October our troops occupied Arkadelphia, the enemy retreating to Red River.

A large part of the military force in the Department of the Missouri has been employed during the past year in repelling raids and in repressing the guerrilla bands of robbers and murderers who have come within our lines or been organized in the country. Most of these bands are not authorized belligerents under the laws of war, but simply outlaws from civilized society. It is exceedingly difficult to eradicate these bands, inasmuch as the inhabitants of the country, sometimes from disloyalty and sometimes from fear, afford them subsistence and concealment. They usually hide themselves in the woods, and, being well mounted, move rapidly from one point to another, supplying themselves by the way with provisions and fresh horses. They rob and murder wherever they go. In the recent raid of one of these bands into Kansas, they burned the city of Lawrence and murdered the inhabitants without regard to age or sex, committing atrocities more inhuman than those of Indian savages.

These are the terrible results of a border contest, incited at first for political purposes, and since increased in animosity by the civil war in which we are engaged, till all sense of humanity seems to have been lost in the desire to avenge with blood real or fancied grievances. This extraordinary condition of affairs on that frontier seems to call for the application of a prompt and severe remedy.

It has been proposed to depopulate the frontier counties of Missouri, and to lay waste the country on the border so as to prevent its furnishing any shelter or subsistence to these bands of murderers. Such measures are within the recognized laws of war; they were adopted by Wellington in Portugal, and by the Russian armies in the campaign of 1812; but they should be adopted only in case of overruling necessity. The execution of General Schofield's order on this subject has been suspended, and it is hoped that it will not be necessary hereafter to renew it.

---

* See p. 390.

DEPARTMENT OF THE NORTHWEST.

As soon as the season was sufficiently advanced for a campaign against the Indians, General Pope sent a column, under Brigadier-General Sibley, up the Mississippi River to near our northern boundary, and thence across the country to the Missouri; and another of cavalry, under Brigadier-General Sully, from Sioux City up the latter river to cut off the retreat of the hostile Indians whom General Sibley might drive before him from Minnesota and Eastern Dakota. Unfortunately these movements were not well timed, and no junction was effected. A portion of the savages driven north took refuge within British territory, where our troops were not permitted to follow them. Some fled westward, and were overtaken by General Sibley near Missouri Coteau, where he encountered a force of Minnesota and Dakota warriors, estimated at from 2,200 to 2,500. In the engagements which followed at Big Mound and Dead Buffalo Lake, the Indians were completely routed, with a heavy loss in killed and wounded, and in the destruction of their provisions and means of transportation. Our loss was 5 killed and 4 wounded. The savages who escaped crossed to the west side of the Mississippi, and General Sibley reached that river, about 40 miles below Fort Clarke, on the 29th of July, having marched a distance of some 600 miles from Saint Paul.

On the 3d of September, General Sully encountered and defeated, at White Stone Hill, about 130 miles above the Little Cheyenne, a body of Indians, a part of whom had previously been engaged against Sibley's column. The savages were defeated with a heavy loss in killed and wounded and 156 prisoners. Our loss was 20 killed and 38 wounded.*

With these operations the present Indian campaign was terminated. Recent hostilities in Idaho may render it necessary to send a military expedition into that Territory early in the spring.

* * * * * * *

All of which is respectfully submitted.

H. W. HALLECK,
General-in-Chief.

Hon. E. M. STANTON,
Secretary of War.

No. 2.

Report of Maj. Gen. John M. Schofield, U. S. Army, commanding Department of the Missouri, of operations May 24–December 10, 1863.

HEADQUARTERS DEPARTMENT OF THE MISSOURI,
Saint Louis, Mo., December 10, 1863.

COLONEL: I have the honor to submit a general summary of military operations in this department since the 24th of May, 1863, when I assumed this command.

At that time active operations against the organized force of the enemy in Arkansas had been suspended until the opening of the Mississippi should give us a new base and a new line of operations, by which it would be practicable to operate in the interior of Arkansas. There was no immediate employment for the troops of this department

---

* But see revised statement, p. 561.

except the ordinary police duties in Missouri, Kansas, and among the Indian tribes in the Western Territories.

The effective troops in the department at that time consisted of 14,248 infantry, 15,509 cavalry, and thirteen batteries of artillery, distributed as follows, viz: The Army of the Frontier, distributed along the southern border of Missouri and Kansas, and in the Indian Territory as far south as Fort Gibson, 5,011 infantry, 3,826 cavalry, and four batteries of artillery. Troops doing police duty in Missouri, 5,657 infantry, 9,200 cavalry, and six batteries. In Kansas, 3,506 infantry, 1,343 cavalry, and two batteries. In Nebraska, 392 cavalry. In Colorado, 74 infantry, 748 cavalry, and one battery.

In addition to the above, the Governor of Missouri had commenced the organization of nine regiments of militia, styled "provisional regiments," intended for continuous active service. A portion of this militia had been in active service for a considerable length of time, but not under the orders of the department commander, and not acting in concert with the United States troops. At my suggestion, the Governor placed these nine regiments under my command; whereupon the War Department gave me authority to supply them with everything necessary to their efficiency, and they became a real addition to the effective force in the department, making my entire force 36,816 men effective.

With a view to the commencement of active operations as soon as practicable, I reorganized the Army of the Frontier, uniting all the cavalry and adding to it, forming a division of cavalry 6,000 strong, with a proper proportion of artillery, under Brig. Gen. J. W. Davidson, and forming the infantry into a single division, with three batteries, under Maj. Gen. F. J. Herron, intending to send the infantry and artillery by water to a new base on the river, and let the cavalry march overland, as soon as General Grant's operations should enable me to commence an aggressive movement.

This reorganization had but commenced, when, on the 2d day of June, I received a dispatch from the General-in-Chief, directing me to send all the force I could spare to the aid of General Grant at Vicksburg. Accordingly I immediately dispatched eight regiments of infantry and three batteries, under Major-General Herron, and subsequently sent in the same direction three more regiments of infantry, in all 8,000 men Also to enable Brig. Gen. [A.] Asboth, commanding at Columbus, to meet an expected attack, I sent him from New Madrid, on the 30th of July, 1,300 men, and to Major-General Rosecrans, commanding Department of the Cumberland, a regiment of cavalry and two regiments of infantry, 2,400 men, making a total of forces transferred from my department of 11,700 men and three batteries.

This great reduction of the force before considered necessary for defensive purposes, left me very weak in Missouri and Kansas, and, occurring at the season favorable for guerrilla operations, exposed these States to the depredations of guerrillas, from which they continued to suffer more or less until the success of my main force in Arkansas, and that of the detachments operating in Missouri and Kansas, rendered it impossible for them to longer exist in these States.

The capture of Vicksburg and Port Hudson by the forces under Generals Grant and Banks on the 4th and 8th of July, respectively, opened the way for active operations in Arkansas, and enabled General Grant to return to me the troops I had sent him. I inclose herewith copies of correspondence with General Grant on that subject, which, together with orders from the General in-Chief, resulted in his sending (including the force already at Helena) a force of about 8,000 infantry and five batteries, to form, with troops to be sent from Missouri, an expedition against the enemy in Arkansas. At my request, Maj. Gen. Frederick Steele was sent to command this force. At the same time I sent the cavalry division, under Brigadier-General Davidson, with orders to move south, through the eastern part of Arkansas, and effect a junction with the force at Helena. Copy of instructions to General Davidson is inclosed herewith, marked A [Nos. 5 and 6]; also copy of instructions for General Steele, marked B [No. 9].

General Davidson reached Wittsburg, on the Saint Francis River, on the 28th day of July, without encountering any considerable force of the enemy, and opened communication with General [L. F.] Ross, then commanding at Helena, General Steele not having arrived at that time.

On the 10th day of August, General Steele had completed the organization of his forces, and commenced his advance, via Clarendon, on White River; thence up that river to Devall's Bluff, where he established his base of operations. Considerable time was consumed here in fortifying, establishing depot for supplies, hospital for the sick, who had become frightfully numerous, and in making other necessary preparations for a further advance. These preparations were completed on the 1st day of September.

The enemy, under Sterling Price, occupied an intrenched position 3 miles east of Little Rock, covered by cavalry outposts at Bayou Meto and Ashley's Mills. His force was estimated at about 16,000 men, with thirty-eight pieces of artillery. General Steele's effective force was about 13,000 men, with fifty-three pieces of artillery.

Steele advanced, with the main body of his infantry, against the enemy's position, while the cavalry, under Davidson, crossed the Arkansas River 7 miles below Little Rock, encountering the rebel cavalry, under Marmaduke, defeated him after a sharp engagement, and marched upon the town. Price, finding his position turned, hastily abandoned his intrenchments, retreated across the river, destroying his bridges, and escaped from the town before the arrival of our cavalry. Davidson's division entered Little Rock at dark in the evening of the 10th of September.

The enemy retired toward Arkadelphia, pursued the next day about 20 miles by a considerable force of cavalry and artillery, under command of Col. Lewis Merrill, U. S. Volunteers, but with no very important results.

For the details of these operations, resulting in the capture of Little Rock, and subsequent pursuit of the enemy, I respectfully refer to reports heretofore forwarded.

Since the capture of Little Rock, the time has been chiefly employed in perfecting communications, including repair of the railroad to Devall's Bluff, the fortification of Little Rock, and the occupation of points necessary to the security of the Arkansas River as a line of defense, and in preparation for an advance to Red River as soon as General Banks' operations should justify. The cavalry of General Steele's command has been actively employed during the time against the enemy's cavalry, and with considerable success in the capture of prisoners, arms, and other property.

On the 25th day of October, Marmaduke, with about 2,500 cavalry and twelve pieces of artillery, attacked a force of about 800 cavalry of the Fifth Kansas and the First Indiana Cavalry, and nine pieces of artillery, under Colonel [P.] Clayton, of the Fifth Kansas Cavalry, at Pine Bluff. The fight was sharp, lasted five hours, and resulted in a decisive victory to our troops.

Some cavalry, sent from Little Rock and Camden, under Lieutenant-Colonel [H. C.] Caldwell, Third Iowa Cavalry, pursued the rebel cavalry to Arkadelphia, captured that place, with a number of prisoners and some property. Colonel Clayton's and Lieutenant-Colonel Caldwell's reports were forwarded on the 19th instant.

On the 9th of June, I made a division of the former District of Kansas, the one embracing the northern portion of Kansas and the border counties of Missouri, the other the southern portion of Kansas, the Indian Territory, and Western Arkansas.

Major-General [J. G.] Blunt was placed in command of the latter district, and Brigadier-General [Thomas] Ewing, [jr.,] of the former, with his headquarters at Kansas City, as near as possible to the center of the disturbed portion of his district.

The troops placed under General Ewing's command were selected with reference to their fitness for that special service, as far as practicable at that time.

On the 11th day of June, General Blunt assumed command at Fort Gibson, Ind. T., at that time occupied by a small force, mostly Indians, under command of Col. William A. Phillips. All troops had been withdrawn from Western Arkansas some time before.

On the 20th of July, General Blunt reported that he was threatened by a force about 15,000 strong, under Cabell and [D. H.] Cooper, and asked for re-enforcements. His force at that time amounted to about 3,000 men, of whom about one-half were Indians. I sent him about 1,500 men from Southwest Missouri, under Colonel [W. F.] Cloud, of the Second Kansas Cavalry, which force reached Fort Gibson on the 22d of August. General Blunt crossed the Arkansas River to attack the enemy, but they retreated without a general engagement.

On the 1st of September, Colonel Cloud's brigade came up with the enemy's rear, about 16 miles southeast of Fort Smith, and, after a short skirmish, routed them, with a loss of 8 killed and wounded on our side and 20 to 30 on that of the enemy, and capturing 40 prisoners.

General Blunt, with the First Arkansas Infantry, occupied Fort Smith on the same day without opposition—ten days before the capture of Little Rock. Since that time we have held, without difficulty, the line of the Arkansas River, and our cavalry have operated as far south as Arkadelphia.

The border of Kansas and Missouri has been the scene of the most revolting hostilities during the past two years. The summer just ended has been no exception to this rule. A band of outlaws, numbering sometimes as high as 500 men, have infested the thickly wooded fastnesses in the western counties of Missouri, from which to prey upon the unarmed people. These brigands were aided in every way, whether willingly or unwillingly, by the large majority of the inhabitants of those counties, making it impossible, with any reasonable force, to drive them out or capture them.

On the 19th of August, the brigands secretly assembled to the number of about 300, near the border of Kansas, marched rapidly upon the town of Lawrence, and attacked it at dawn of day, when the people were least prepared for defense. No resistance whatever was offered. The town was robbed and burned, and the unarmed people murdered in the most fiendish manner. Probably no act of the war has been so barbarous in its whole details as this. I refer you to the report of Brigadier-General Ewing, forwarded to Washington on the 4th of September, for full details of the operations of his troops in pursuit of the murderers. The excitement among the people of Kansas, resulting from the massacre at Lawrence, was necessarily intense. For a time it threatened a serious difficulty, from the desire of a large portion of the people to enter Missouri to avenge the crime that had been perpetrated upon one of their fairest towns. Wiser counsels, however, prevailed, and the excitement passed off without further trouble. To guard against the probability of the recurrence of such a calamity, I recommended to His Excellency the Governor of Kansas to adopt the system which had been established in Missouri a year before, of organizing and arming all the militia of the State, thus placing every town, at least, in condition to defend itself from any guerrilla attack. This suggestion was as promptly adopted, and the State soon made secure.

For some time previous to the Lawrence massacre, the necessity of adopting some measures more vigorous than any before adopted to rid the border counties of the brigands who had so long infested them had been discussed, and I had directed General Ewing to remove the families of all guerrillas and all those who were known to aid them, and also the slaves of all disloyal persons living in those counties, it having been shown satisfactorily that a main object of the guerrilla bands was to protect their disloyal friends in the possession of their slaves, and that they were encouraged and supported for this purpose. After the massacre at Lawrence, General Ewing deemed this measure not adequate, and ordered a total depopulation of the district which was then the chief haunt of the guerrillas. After a protracted visit to the border, and as full an examination of the case as I could make, I modified General Ewing's order so far as to preserve, as far as possible, all property in the depopulated district, and approved the order. The measure, though very severe, seemed necessary at the time, and I believe the result has proved the wisdom of it. The guerrillas soon found it impossible to live where before they had roamed almost at will. Large numbers of them were killed, and the remainder driven beyond the Arkansas River. Since the rebels have all been driven out, I have directed that all the loyal people of those counties be permitted to return to their homes, and that they be armed and organized into companies. I believe there will be no difficulty hereafter in preserving peace in that district. In the retreat of the enemy from Little Rock and Fort Smith, several small bands of guerrillas were left in the northern part of Arkansas, and two or three still remained in Missouri.

About the last of September, a detachment of rebel cavalry, from 600 to 800 strong, under command of Shelby, left Price's army, near Arkadelphia, in Arkansas, moved north, and crossed the Arkansas River a short distance below Fort Smith. After crossing, Shelby moved rapidly toward Huntsville, which place he reached September 30, and moved thence via Bentonville, Ark., cutting the telegraph line as he passed; thence through Pineville to Neosho, Mo., where he attacked and captured two companies of Missouri militia.

Shelby was joined in Arkansas by Brooks and other guerrilla leaders, and in Missouri by Quantrill, Jackman, and others, with all the guerrillas in Western Missouri. These increased his force to about 2,000 men. Passing rapidly through Greenfield and Warsaw, he succeeded in destroying the La Mine Bridge, on the Pacific Railroad, and reached the town of Boonville, on the Missouri River. Up to this time he succeeded in entirely eluding the troops sent to intercept him, and passed north of them. At Boonville he was overtaken by Brig. Gen. E. B. Brown, with about 1,500 men, and pursued to Marshall, skirmishing continually. At Marshall, Shelby made a stand, and a sharp fight ensued, lasting five hours, and resulting in a total defeat of the rebels. They scattered in all directions and fled toward Arkansas, hotly pursued by General Brown's troops. Subsequently, the chase was taken up by Colonel Weer, then by General Ewing, and finally by General McNeil, who continued the pursuit until the remnant of Shelby's force had crossed the Arkansas River. The pursuit was attended with numerous skirmishes, always favorable to our troops, and resulted in a loss to the enemy of more than half his force, two pieces of artillery (all he had), all his ammunition, baggage, and plunder.

Quantrill, Jackman, and other guerrilla leaders, who have been the curse of Missouri and Kansas during the past two years, were driven out with Shelby, or about the same time, leaving behind them a state of peace and security to which the people have long been strangers.

I respectfully refer to accompanying reports for details of these operations.* They exhibit a degree of energy and endurance on the part of our troops worthy of all commendation.

Military operations in the Territories of Nebraska and Colorado have not been of special importance. The Indians in those Territories, although occasionally manifesting a hostile disposition, have thus far remained quiet, and the troops on the frontier have proven amply sufficient to protect the people and important public interests. Several of the tribes have recently manifested an unusual hostile feeling, and have given evidence of a combination for war upon the white settlers. Timely measures have been instituted to prevent actual hostilities, if possible, and to meet them with an adequate force, if necessary.

Of the numerous skirmishes and engagements within the last five months, twenty-eight have been reported, showing a loss on our side of 159 killed, 311 wounded, and 200 prisoners; and on that of the enemy 643 killed, 697 wounded, and 856 prisoners. To the enemy's loss must also be added the large number of desertions, consequent upon his defeat.

Measures have been taken to secure prompt and accurate reports hereafter of all engagements and skirmishes, and in future reports details will be given more explicitly. The total effective force now in the department is about 36,800 men, including troops returned to me by General Grant, re-enforcements received from Major-General Pope's department, and new organizations of white and colored troops recruited since the 31st of May. It does not exceed that of the 24th of May, when the honor of the command was conferred upon me. Yet it has repossessed, and now securely holds, over 60,000 square miles more of territory.

I have not deemed it necessary in this report to refer to matters not of a purely military character. The perplexing subjects, of a semi-political character, which are inseparably connected with this command, have been the subject of correspondence from time to time with the General-in-Chief and the War Department, and the Government is fully informed of all that has transpired.

I have the honor to be, very respectfully, your obedient servant,

J. M. SCHOFIELD,
Major-General.

Col. E. D. TOWNSEND,
Assistant Adjutant-General, Washington, D. C.

[Inclosure No. 1.]

HEADQUARTERS DEPARTMENT OF THE MISSOURI,
Saint Louis, June 25, 1863.

Brigadier-General DAVIDSON, *Commanding First Cav. Div., Arcadia:*

GENERAL: I desire you to carry out the plan of operations discussed by us during our interview at your headquarters on the 23d instant, with as little delay as practicable.

---

* See September 22–October 26, Shelby's raid in **Arkansas and Missouri**, p. 621.

The immediate object of this expedition is to keep open the river between New Madrid and Memphis, and secure safe navigation for our transports, until the fall of Vicksburg shall place us in condition to carry the war into the interior of Arkansas. To accomplish this I propose the following plan, in substance the same as that discussed by us, viz: Your division of cavalry to move down Crowley's Ridge, make a demonstration against Price's infantry, supposed to be at or near Jacksonport, and attack Marmaduke's cavalry along the ridge, and between that and the river. This, I presume, will compel him to withdraw from the river and mass his troops in your front; perhaps also to make, or attempt, a junction with Price's infantry. If so, the immediate object will be accomplished.

If the enemy concentrate his force and offer you battle, you will be compelled to act with much caution. Your force being only cavalry and artillery, you may be unable to cope with the enemy's combined force; but I presume you can easily beat his entire cavalry. You may be able to bring on an engagement with the enemy's cavalry alone. If so, I shall look for the most fortunate and beneficial results. You may also be able, by operating upon the flank and rear of Price's position, to compel him to retire and leave Northeastern Arkansas entirely in your possession. In any event, endeavor to compel the enemy to keep his force so concentrated as to be unable to interfere with the navigation of the river, and, at the same time, hold yourself in such position as to prevent his making a raid into Missouri.

It is important for you to accomplish a decided result as soon as practicable, with a view to a change of your base of operations to some point on the river. To enable you to accomplish this change of base with certainty as soon as your success will justify it, I will keep a force of infantry and artillery ready to move with supplies for your division to some point down the river. So far as I have been able to learn, Osceola is probably the best point for you to communicate with from Crowley's Ridge, but it will probably be best to leave this for you to determine, after you have advanced into the country and obtained more accurate information.

Please communicate with me frequently, and give me full information, so that I may be able to act promptly and understandingly in supporting your movements.

I desire to keep the infantry here until your success shall remove all danger of any aggressive movement of the enemy in this direction.

Very respectfully, your obedient servant,

J. M. SCHOFIELD,
Major-General.

[Inclosure No. 2.]

HEADQUARTERS DEPARTMENT OF THE MISSOURI,
Saint Louis, July 8, 1863.

Maj. Gen. U. S. GRANT,
Commanding Army of Tennessee, Vicksburg, Miss.:

GENERAL: I congratulate you most heartily upon your glorious triumph at Vicksburg.

I desire, general, as soon as possible to commence active operations in Arkansas, now that you have removed the obstacle which has so long stood in our way, and forced us to remain comparatively idle. You are aware that since active operations in this department ceased last winter, nearly all the troops in my department, except those necessary for police duty, have been sent to re-enforce your army, with the understanding that, as soon as Vicksburg should fall, they, or a sufficient portion of them, would be sent back into my department. It occurs to me that the concentration of the rebel forces near the river, in the vicinity of Vicksburg, may force you to keep all your present forces on or near the river for some time to come. I do not desire to ask anything which will, in any way, embarrass your operations, but simply to inform you what I am prepared and desire to do, and to gain similar information from you so far as your operations affect mine, and thus be prepared to act promptly in harmony with you. It is very important, with reference to my department, to occupy the line of the Arkansas River as soon as possible. This can be done by the use of the Arkansas River, if it be navigable at this season, or, if not, then the White River as far as Devall's Bluff, and the railroad or even wagon road from that place to Little Rock. The force which will be required for this purpose will depend upon operations up the Ouachita and Red Rivers, but I presume will be in no case very large.

I have a cavalry division, full 5,000 strong, now operating in Southeast Missouri and Northeast Arkansas, which is ready to move across the country and join a force of infantry and artillery at any point on the Arkansas or White Rivers, as soon as you can send such force. I have also small bodies of troops in Southwest Missouri and the Indian country, ready to advance and occupy the country south of them as soon as we get possession of the Arkansas River.

I have directed the quartermaster in Saint Louis to send you 500 wagons and teams for your own operations, and will probably have enough left to supply the forces which are to operate in Arkansas.

Please inform me, general, what you will be able to do, and give me details as to time, &c., as far as possible.

I would like to suggest Major-General Steele as a suitable officer to command the force to be sent into Arkansas.

I am, general, very respectfully, your obedient servant,

J. M. SCHOFIELD,
Major-General.

[Inclosure No. 3.]

HEADQUARTERS DEPARTMENT OF THE TENNESSEE,
Vicksburg, Miss., July 15, 1863.

Maj. Gen. JOHN M. SCHOFIELD,
Commanding Department of the Missouri:

GENERAL: Your letter of the 8th instant is just received. In answer, I will give you a brief statement of the position of affairs here.

During the siege of Vicksburg, I had a large surplus of troops over what was required to make the investment complete. These troops occupied a line from Haynes' Bluff to Black River, across which Johnston would have to move to reach Vicksburg, or the rear of the investing army. Sherman commanded all these forces, and held them in readiness to move the moment Vicksburg should fall into our hands. Accordingly, on the 4th instant, he started. As soon as the city capitulated, I ordered the whole of Sherman's and Ord's corps, forming about two-thirds of the investing army, to move out and join Sherman. They started the night of the 4th. A portion of McPherson's corps was already with Sherman. This left me at this place but six small brigades. Hearing that the enemy was fortifying Yazoo City most vigorously, I sent two of them to that place. They captured it, with considerable stores, five or six pieces of artillery, and several hundred prisoners; but one of the gunboats accompanying the expedition being sunk by the explosion of a torpedo, I shall have to leave them there until the armament and machinery of the vessel can be got away. I have also sent a brigade to Natchez, to collect a large number of Texas cattle supposed to be there, destined for Johnston's army. This, you will see, leaves me no force to move with, until Sherman returns. When this will be it is hard to tell. Johnston commenced to fall back from the Big Black the moment he heard of the surrender of Vicksburg. As all his droves of cattle and wagon trains that fell back, via Canton, were ordered east to the Mobile and Ohio road, he could not have intended to make a determined stand. He drew all his troops, however, inside the intrenchments of Jackson, and remains there yet. Sherman has him closely invested, from the Pearl River on the north to the river on the south. By this an immense deal of rolling stock has been separated from the Confederacy, both north and south of Jackson, and the roads so completely destroyed as to render them forever useless. How long this siege will last it is impossible to say. When Johnston is driven from his position, however, I will have troops available for anything that will go to put down the rebellion. I suppose the Ninth Army Corps will have to be sent back to Burnside, and 10,000 to 12,000 effective men sent to Banks. But for the expedition you speak of, unless other orders should come from Washington, I will still have force enough.

Kirby Smith has been hovering around on the opposite side of the river, with his headquarters at Monroe, and his force scattered from Saint Joseph to Floyd. It has been my intention to pay him a call as soon as possible; but I now learn, and I believe reliably, that all his scattered forces are called in, and the whole are moving to Shreveport, La. The object of the move I don't see, unless it is to avoid being hurt.

I have not paid any special attention to the geography of the opposite side of the river, but suppose at this season of the year White River would have to be used as a base for supplies to reach Little Rock. The Arkansas can hardly be used until the fall rains set in.

You will see, from the foregoing statements, that I can give you nothing definite of future operations yet. As soon as I possibly can I will do so. Nothing like 500 wagons will be required with this army to prepare it for any move, and, should any be required, it would probably be only the wagons and harness, without the animals.

I am, general, very respectfully, your obedient servant,

U. S. GRANT,
Major-General.

[Inclosure No. 4.]

HEADQUARTERS DEPARTMENT OF THE MISSOURI,
Saint Louis, Mo., July 15, 1863.

COMMANDING GENERAL, *Helena, Ark.:*

GENERAL: I am informed by the General-in-Chief that you have been ordered to move against Price, who is reported to be somewhere between the Saint Francis and White River. I have sent a cavalry division, about 5,000 strong, under General Davidson, to co-operate with you.* He will move from Bloomfield, Mo., on the 17th instant. Will march down Crowley's Ridge, and endeavor to cut off Price's retreat across White River. He will carry supplies to last him until he can communicate with you at Helena or some other point. If you could send supplies for General Davidson's command by boat up the Saint Francis

---

*See Ross to Grant, July 18, Part II, p. 381, and Ross to Schofield, July 22, Part II, p. 387.

to Madison or Wittsburg, it would facilitate his operations. I am not aware whether this is practicable or not. In any event, I respectfully request you to assist General Davidson as far as in your power in opening communication with you and in obtaining supplies from Helena.

I can send you some wagons if you need them. Please advise me of your movements, and let me know if I can assist you in any way.

General Prentiss, I am informed, has left Helena, and I am unable to learn who is now in command.

Very respectfully, your obedient servant,

J. M. SCHOFIELD,
Major-General.

[Inclosure No. 5.]

HEADQUARTERS DEPARTMENT OF THE MISSOURI,
Saint Louis, July 15, 1863.

Brigadier-General DAVIDSON,
Cape Girardeau:

The force at Helena has been ordered to move on Price's rear. Your command should move forward as soon as possible to prevent his escape across the river. The plan you suggest in your letter of the 10th is very good; you should take supplies enough to last until you can draw from Madison or Helena. How soon can you move?

J. M. SCHOFIELD,
Major-General.

[Inclosure No. 6.]

HEADQUARTERS DEPARTMENT OF THE MISSOURI,
Saint Louis, July 15, 1863.

Brigadier-General DAVIDSON,
Bloomfield, Mo.:

I have written to Helena about your movement, and asked assistance for you in obtaining supplies at Madison or Wittsburg. If this cannot be done, you will have to draw from Helena. Take care in your movements to cover Pilot Knob and Rolla until Marmaduke is no longer in position to threaten those places. Port Hudson surrendered on the 7th, with 6,000 prisoners.

J. M. SCHOFIELD,
Major-General.

[Inclosure No. 7.]

HEADQUARTERS DEPARTMENT OF THE TENNESSEE,
Vicksburg, Miss., July 21, 1863.

Major-General SCHOFIELD,
Commanding Department of the Missouri:

GENERAL: I am sending, or will send, as soon as transportation can be provided, one division (about 5,000 effective men) to operate in Price's rear. These are the only troops I have not exhausted and worn down. In addition to these, there will probably be 3,000 more to spare from the garrison of Helena and from West Tennessee.

Johnston has been totally routed from Jackson, and will, no doubt, lose half his army from desertion, and the balance will be so broken down and demoralized that but little danger need be apprehended from them for the next sixty days.

My troops are not yet in from Jackson; no part of them. Should it be necessary to send more troops to Helena, I can send from here men to hold that place, and release the entire garrison to look after Price. Possibly this will be the better course to pursue.

I am, general, very respectfully, your obedient servant,

U. S. GRANT,
Major-General.

[Inclosure No 8.]

WASHINGTON, D. C., *July* 27, 1863.

Major-General SCHOFIELD:

The expeditionary corps in Arkansas will act under your general orders. General Grant will garrison Helena with his troops, so as to render present garrison available for the field.

H. W. HALLECK,
General-in-Chief.

[Inclosure No. 9.]

HEADQUARTERS DEPARTMENT OF THE MISSOURI,
Saint Louis, Mo., August 6, 1863.

Major-General HURLBUT,
Commanding Sixteenth Army Corps, Memphis, Tenn.:

GENERAL: Since the assignment of Major-General Steele to the command of the force which is to operate in Arkansas from Helena, I have not thought it necessary to enter much into detail concerning the plan of operations. From his previous campaign in Arkansas, General Steele is thoroughly acquainted with the country, and is also familiar with my views and those of the General-in-Chief regarding the true theory of operations in Arkansas.

The first object to be accomplished is, of course, the destruction of the rebel army as an organized force, and hence the movements of our troops must be guided very much by those of the enemy. In reference to this matter, I take it the commander in the field must be left to his own discretion, guided by the information he may be able to obtain from day to day.

The second object is to gain possession of, and permanently hold, as much of the State as practicable. For this purpose, the natural line of operations during the season of high water is the Arkansas River, and its permanent possession and use is of the greatest importance as a means of securing Missouri and Northern Arkansas against future rebel inroads. At this season we are compelled to use the White River instead of the Arkansas, and can use it to advantage only to a certain point, which is to be determined by the enemy's position and movements and the character of the wagon roads leading to and from it. I presume Clarendon or Des Arc will be the highest point to which the river can be used to advantage. But of this General Steele can judge more accurately than I can. On account of the short distance by land from Helena to either Clarendon or Des Arc, it will, no doubt, be much the best for the troops to march to the point selected, and be met there by gunboats and supplies. It may be advisable to send a small force of infantry, say, a brigade and a light battery, with the flotilla, to assist in capturing or dispersing any force that may be found along the river. I am not informed that there is any fortified place on the White River below Devall's Bluff, and presume there is none. No doubt the commanding officer at Helena has accurate information on this point. Should there be such a place below the point to which the boats are to ascend, of course an adequate force must be sent with the flotilla to capture it.

Having crossed White River, the important point to be gained is Little Rock. That or some point near it will, I presume, be defended obstinately. I am not informed to what extent it is fortified, if at all; but presume it will be found necessary to reduce some place of considerable strength on the Arkansas River, not far from Little Rock. This, I hope, will end the main part of the work to be done by our troops as a body in that part of the country. I presume the rebel army, being driven from the vicinity of Little Rock, will retreat to Arkadelphia, perhaps beyond. How far they may be pursued will depend upon contingencies which it is impossible to foresee, and must be left for the future to determine.

It is my desire to get possession of the whole length of the Arkansas River to Fort Smith, and open communication by that line with the troops now under General Blunt in the Indian Territory. This probably cannot be done for the present on account of the low stage of water above as well as below Little Rock; but in a comparatively short time the fall rains will make the river navigable to Fort Smith. We ought to be in condition to take advantage of high water as soon as it comes, to send supplies to Fort Smith, and make preparations for a winter campaign south and west of that point, as well as Little Rock.

On account of the unnavigable condition of the Arkansas during a large portion of the year, it is important to have easy communication from Little Rock to some point on White River. The rolling stock on the Little Rock and Memphis Railroad should be secured, if possible. Failing in this, the wagon road from Des Arc or Clarendon should be made practicable at all seasons.

I desire to obtain telegraphic communication with Little Rock as soon as possible after it shall be occupied by our troops. Presuming the line from Cairo to Memphis will soon be repaired and kept in order, the best line for my purposes will be directly from Little Rock to Memphis. This line can, I presume, be protected with very little difficulty. I will send a telegraph corps in time to construct it, as soon as they can be protected.

It was my intention, when General Davidson was ordered forward from Bloomfield, that he should preserve his connection with that place, and operate against the enemy's cavalry until the movements of the force from Helena should compel them to retreat, or cut them off, and enable him to destroy them. Meanwhile he would have protected my present line. His movement to Wittsburg, leaving Marmaduke so far in his rear, exposed my advanced posts to attack and capture, and compelled me to withdraw some of them, which was done in time to prevent any loss beyond the capture of a considerable train and its escort.

During the past few days the rebel cavalry has shown no disposition to advance farther in this direction, and perhaps their timidity may save us from the damage which they could easily inflict without any great danger to themselves. If General Steele's column moves soon, or General Davidson threatens Marmaduke while Steele is completing his preparations, nothing further will be probably necessary to prevent any movement of the enemy in this direction in greater force than I can take care of. General Davidson's movement to Wittsburg was doubtless caused by the belief that the column from Helena was to start immediately, and, hence, that his best plan was to join it as soon as possible. General Davidson is a most excellent and energetic officer, and has a splendid division of cavalry. I presume General Davidson has already reported to General Steele, and is now acting under his orders. If not, General Steele is authorized to assume command of General

Davidson's division, without reference to the conditions contained in my order to the latter, already transmitted. I will so inform General Davidson.

I believe, general, I have mentioned all that is essential for the present time, but will be glad to communicate with you further at any time if you will suggest any point upon which you desire my views.

I am, general, very respectfully, your obedient servant,

J. M. SCHOFIELD,
Major-General.

[Inclosure No. 10.]

HEADQUARTERS DEPARTMENT OF THE MISSOURI,
Saint Louis, Mo., August 7, 1863.

Brig. Gen. J. W. DAVIDSON,
Comdg. First Cav. Div., Dept. of the Missouri, via Helena, Ark.:

GENERAL: Under instructions from the General-in-Chief, General Grant has sent a force of infantry and artillery to Helena, for the purpose of operating against Price. General Steele is assigned to the command, and it is to act under the orders of General Hurlbut. My troops in that part of Arkansas are, for the time being, to form part of General Steele's command. Hence my dispatch to you of August 1, directing you to report to the officer commanding the expedition from Helena. How long this arrangement will last will, I presume, depend upon the success of the expedition and future demands for troops elsewhere. I have found it necessary to withdraw the force from Chalk Bluffs for the present, and have succeeded in preventing any further damage since the destruction of the train near Bloomfield, of which I telegraphed you.

Marmaduke does not seem inclined to risk any farther advance, I presume in consequence of your proximity to his flank and rear. I think you may now safely act directly with General Steele, or in such manner as he may direct, without special reference to the protection of my southern line in Missouri. You will, therefore, report to General Steele, if you have not already done so, and will hereafter act under his orders.

I understand that General Steele's force is still regarded as belonging to the command of General Grant, and that your division is to be regarded as temporarily attached; therefore you will continue to make your reports and returns to these headquarters; of course, furnishing duplicates to General Steele, if he desires them, as, doubtless, he will.

I hope, general, you will keep me fully advised of everything of interest connected with your operations.

Very respectfully, your obedient servant,

J. M. SCHOFIELD,
Major-General.

No. 3.

Report of Lieut. Gen. E. Kirby Smith, C. S. Army, commanding Trans-Mississippi Department, of operations March 7, 1863–February 21, 1864.

HEADQUARTERS TRANS-MISSISSIPPI DEPARTMENT,
Shreveport, La., November 14, 1863.

GENERAL: I have forwarded reports of General Taylor's operations in Lower Louisiana, from the commencement of the campaign to its successful termination by the retreat of General Banks to Berwick Bay.

In August I received reliable information that expeditions were organizing at Helena, Vicksburg, and New Orleans, under orders of General Grant, having Arkansas, Louisiana, and Texas for their objective points. I soon obtained corroborative proof that General Grant's whole disposable command was being employed in these preparations, and that an effective force of at least 80,000 would be at once thrown upon the department. A prearranged and predetermined plan for the occupation of the whole Trans-Mississippi Department, with all the machinery for State governments under Federal rule, was being perfected and carried into execution. Every effort was made with my limited means to prepare for the coming storm. The effective force at my disposal within the department was less than 30,000, and scattered from Fort Smith, Ark., to the Rio Grande. No concentration could be made without the sacrifice of vital interests. General Holmes, at Little Rock, and General Taylor, in Lower Louisiana, the two commands nearest each other and most easily concentrated, were each opposed by a superior force of the enemy, and were separated by 700 miles of land travel, over a country which, with our limited means of transportation, presented almost physical obstacles to the march of a large body of troops. Depots of provisions were collected on the lines of communication, and arrangements were made so that, in the event of falling back before superior forces, the enemy could be drawn into the interior, a rapid concentration effected, and his advancing columns taken in detail. Appeals were made to the people, and the Governors urged to increase and prepare their State organizations for immediate service. Some 8,000 men responded to the call in Texas; a few companies were raised in Arkansas, but little or nothing was effected in Louisiana. General Price was re-enforced by a brigade of infantry from Northern Louisiana. General Taylor was directed to concentrate his whole disposable force in the neighborhood of Alexandria, to march in either direction, as the developments of the enemy's plans might demand. In the latter part of August the advance from Helena was made, and Little Rock was occupied by the enemy on the 10th of September. General Price, though he overestimated the force opposed to him, had from his morning report less than 8,000 effective men, of which a large portion were indifferent and ill-armed cavalry. The enemy was superior in numbers and equipments, and, after his position and defenses were turned by the passage of the Arkansas below the city, General Price feared risking a general engagement, and fell back to the line of the Ouachita. All his material and stores were safely sent to the rear. The sickness of General Grant and the successes of General Bragg delayed and deranged the entire plans of the enemy on the Mississippi. The force collected at Vicksburg for operations in Louisiana was sent up the Mississippi to re-enforce the army of Rosecrans. The enemy's Texas column was being prepared on a grand scale. Two entire corps and a portion of a third, under General Banks, composed the command. The movement was to have been simultaneous with that from Vicksburg and Helena. Sabine Pass was to have been made the base of operations. The failure of the attack on that place on the 8th of September delayed the expedition; it was subsequently weakened by the re-enforcements sent Rosecrans.

About the 20th September, Ord's and Franklin's corps, commanded by General Banks in person, crossed Berwick Bay, and made preparations for a march by the coast road to Niblett's Bluff, on the Sabine. Though repeatedly urged by General Magruder to concentrate Taylor's command on his, and to make the defense on the Sabine, I replied that the enemy could never march successfully by the road proposed, with

Taylor on his flank and communications. Early in October, General Banks advanced from Berwick Bay with an immense supply train, a heavy artillery force, water tanks, &c., prepared for a long campaign, conquest, and permanent occupation. General Taylor concentrated to oppose his advance. He was instructed to throw every obstacle in the enemy's way, to contest every position. He was cautioned against risking a general engagement, but, whilst acting on the defensive, was directed to assume the offensive on every favorable occasion. Entire confidence was placed in his skill and the marked ability with which on every previous occasion he had handled the troops under his command. How far this confidence was well placed is seen by the result. Every foot of ground was contested; the enemy was forced to march with his whole command in hand, and did not reach Opelousas till the 23d November; worried, punished, held in check, his supplies were exhausted, and he was compelled to retreat, with the loss of over 2,000 killed, wounded, and prisoners.

The defenses and obstructions of the Lower Red River are being pushed with all the means at my disposal, and it is hoped they will be made so effective as to secure us the possession and navigation of the Red River this winter.

I am, general, very respectfully, your obedient servant,

E. KIRBY SMITH,
Lieutenant-General.

General S. COOPER,
Adjutant and Inspector General.

SHREVEPORT, LA., *August* 28, 1864.

SIR: I have the honor to report that the general commanding the department [E. Kirby Smith] has been sick for the last ten days, with an attack of acute dysentery. Being very weak, he directs me to write you as follows:

I was very much surprised at receiving your telegram informing me that no order was on file directing the infantry of my command to cross the Mississippi River. Your telegram implies that I should have followed the enemy's troops lately operating in this department, and that I was expected to so employ my force as to prevent him at least from re-enforcing the armies of Grant and Sherman. I beg leave to submit the following *resumé* of events which have transpired since my arrival in this department,* as also my plans for the last campaign, and the reasons why I was unable to detain longer the armies opposed to me.

Soon after I reached the department, and before I could become fully acquainted with the character and position of the troops, the operations against Vicksburg and Port Hudson absorbed all attention. Banks' first raid, in which he overpowered General Taylor at Camp Bisland, swept through the most productive portion of Louisiana, and caused the loss of our works controlling the navigation of the Red River and the Atchafalaya. This was subordinate to the investment of Port Hudson. I made the best disposition I could of my troops to aid in the relief of Vicksburg and Port Hudson. General Taylor, with Walker's division, drawn from Arkansas, and moved secretly up the Tensas, in transports, and landing a few miles from where Grant crossed the Mississippi River,

*General Smith assumed command March 7, 1863.

attempted a *coup de main* upon his communications. The enterprise succeeded, but did not produce the important results anticipated, Grant having previously acquired a base of supply upon the Yazoo River. General Taylor now moved into the La Fourche country, where he operated successfully in interrupting the navigation of the Mississippi River between Port Hudson and New Orleans. His position became perilous after the fall of Port Hudson, and he recrossed Berwick Bay. General Holmes reported that it was practicable for him to take Helena, and permission was given for him to attempt it. The position was unsuccessfully assailed on the 4th of July. The enemy subsequently advanced. General Price abandoned Little Rock, and our forces fell back to Camden.

In the fall of 1863 the enemy made two attempts upon Texas. In the first, he landed at the mouth of the Sabine, where, by the gallantry of a single company occupying a small fort, he was beaten, two of his gunboats captured, and his design frustrated. He then concentrated a column at Berwick Bay, in the season of low water, intending to proceed along the coast, drawing his supplies from its numerous inlets. I met this by placing Magruder's small force at the Sabine, holding Taylor on his flank. The latter, by avoiding a general engagement, while he harassed and menaced his communications, caused him to retire; when, by a brilliant rear-guard action, General Green punished him severely. Banks then commenced his series of grand maneuvers upon the whole length of the coast of Texas. General Green's division was transported to Galveston and the mouth of the Brazos, to meet a powerful force landed on Matagorda Peninsula. Throughout the winter, General Magruder was occupied in foiling the designs of the enemy, who numerically was greatly his superior. This brings me to the point of time when the spring campaign opened, and I beg you to remark the position of the opposing forces. My lines extended from the Indian Territory, through Arkansas, to the Mississippi, and down to the mouth of Red River; thence, by the Atchafalaya, to Berwick Bay, and from thence, by the coast, to the Colorado. A small body of troops was engaged in observing the enemy at Brownsville. My forces were massed in three principal bodies, to wit: Under Magruder, opposite Banks, on Matagorda Peninsula; under Price, confronting Steele; under Taylor, holding the Lower Red River. The immense transportation of the enemy admitted of his taking the initiative with his entire force, at any moment, against any portion of my extended lines, while my limited transportation, and the wide distances which separated my commands, made it impossible to effect rapid concentration, or assume the offensive. My only alternative was to wait the development of the enemy's plans, to retire before him until I effected my concentrations, and to endeavor to maneuver to throw the principal mass, if not my whole force, against one of his columns. As I wrote you in the fall of 1863, I was satisfied that the line of Red River would be the line of his principal attack, because, as I then said, the water arose so as to admit his powerful naval armament, in conjunction with the advance of his infantry column. In accordance with this view, I had established, last fall, subsistence and forage depots along the roads through the barren country between Texas and Red River, and between Camden and Natchitoches. I omitted to state that I had been obliged to keep a force in the Indian Territory to hold in check several thousand men under Thayer, at Fort Smith, and to cross Northern Texas, filled with disloyal people. The water in the beginning of February being in a stage to admit gunboats into Red River, General Banks suddenly transferred his force to New

Orleans and Berwick Bay, leaving but 6,000 or 8,000 men on Matagorda Peninsula, who subsequently joined him at Alexandria after the retreat from Mansfield.*

* * * * * * *

I am, sir, very respectfully, your obedient servant,

S. A. SMITH,

Medical Director General Hospitals, Dept. of Trans-Mississippi.

The PRESIDENT OF THE CONFEDERATE STATES.

No. 4.

Report of Brig. Gen. William Steele, C. S. Army, of operations in the Indian Territory in 1863.

AUSTIN, TEX., *February* 15, 1864.

SIR: Having been relieved of the command of the Indian Territory, at my own request, I think it proper to report a brief summary of the military operations in that Territory during the past year, giving, as accurately as may be, an account of such causes as have led to results not unapprehended on my part, nor so fortunate in their character as could have been desired. The facts necessary to a correct and intelligent understanding of the condition of affairs in the Indian Territory during the past year cannot be reported as fully as I could wish, owing to the possession of the records of my assistant adjutant-general's office having been retained by my successor in that command. I therefore report briefly such facts and circumstances as are to be derived from the limited data in the shape of private memoranda, &c., in my possession, and the recollection of myself and a few of the officers who served on my staff.

Early in the month of January, of the past year, in conformity with orders received from Lieutenant-General Holmes, commanding Trans-Mississippi Department, I reported to Major-General Hindman for duty in the Indian Territory, and, in accordance with instructions from the latter, proceeded without delay to Fort Smith, and, on or about January 8, 1863, assumed the command to which I had been assigned. I will premise by saying that I was fully and truthfully advised by Major-General Hindman of the exhausted condition of the country, as well as the undisciplined, ill-equipped, and demoralized state of the few troops over whom I was called to command. On my arrival at Fort Smith the appearance of everything was of the most gloomy description. The continuous occupation of the country by a large Confederate force from the beginning of the war had utterly exhausted its resources, and the retreat of General Hindman from that section immediately preceding my arrival had left the people desponding, hopeless, and, with a few honorable exceptions, thoroughly demoralized; insomuch that my anxiety and watchfulness was more taxed by the operations of traitors, deserters, and Union men, known in common as "jayhawkers" (who were in the majority), than by the movements of the enemy in my front.

The only force I found at Fort Smith was about 100 men, under Colonel [J. C.] Monroe, of the First Arkansas Cavalry, who had been sent temporarily to that point by General Hindman, and the remnant of Lane's (Texas) Partisan Rangers, under Lieutenant-Colonel [R. P.] Crump, num-

* Portion relating to operations in 1864, here omitted, will appear in proper sequence.

bering about 150 men, this being the entire number present for duty in a regiment originally consisting of fourteen full companies This regiment had not a change of clothing nor an average of a blanket to the man. About 1,500 inmates, in a wretched condition, were officially reported in the numerous hospitals in the place. The quartermaster and commissary departments throughout the Territory were found in the utmost confusion. The officers serving in those departments, as a general rule, had derived their appointments from General Hindman or General Pike, were without legal commissions, and, in many cases, had executed no bonds. To have displaced these would have stopped all operations; therefore, having no others to replace them, I was compelled to continue them on duty. Many of these staff officers were incompetent and negligent. Orders were issued and reissued demanding that their returns should be forwarded to headquarters without attaining the object sought. From Majors [Israel G.] Vore and [N. B.] Breedlove, quartermaster and commissary of subsistence, respectively, of Cooper's brigade, of some 6,000 men, on paper, returns were repeatedly called for, but never received. I may here also mention that I was unable to procure a single paper (nor did I ever receive one) in the way of a record, either in reference to previous military operations or the Indian superintendency.

The few stores left by General Hindman on his retreat had been stolen and scattered to all parts of the country. In the quartermaster's department there was neither transportation nor forage. The best efforts of the officer in charge of the commissary department were only productive of a very limited supply of poor beef and corn meal. Of the latter, there was but a few days' supply on hand, and, to obtain the necessary supply for the subsistence of the troops mentioned, and the hospitals, it became imperatively necessary to reopen the navigation of the Arkansas River.

I ascertained, on inquiry, that a considerable supply of flour, for the use of the Indian Department, had been purchased in Northern Texas by an agent sent by General Hindman for that purpose, but the deficiency in transportation and the condition of the roads forbade the hope of an adequate supply of breadstuffs from that quarter. The Arkansas River was, therefore, the only avenue for a supply left open to me, and this of corn. The territory on the northern side of the stream for a considerable distance was virtually in the possession of the enemy, whilst jayhawkers in considerable numbers were boldly depredating on both sides of the river between Little Rock and Fort Smith. Under these circumstances, I besought the lieutenant-general commanding to so dispose a sufficient force of cavalry along the north side of the river as to afford protection to such boats as might be employed in the transportation of corn. After no little delay and embarrassment, a sufficient supply of corn was thus obtained, not, however, until I was forced, through absolute want of subsistence, to send to Red River Speight's brigade, with a battery attached. The scarcity of forage and subsistence, together with the destitute condition of the command, involved the necessity, also, of ordering the remnant of Lane's regiment to a point at which there was a probability of subsistence, recruiting, reequipping, &c. Bass' [Texas] regiment, of Speight's brigade, numbering some 200 men, was kept at Fort Smith for police duty, &c. This regiment, as was the case with most of the other regiments composing Speight's brigade, was found to be greatly demoralized, and in a very short time after being put on duty exhibited an effective strength of less than 100 men, this depletion arising, in the main, from desertion.

The necessity of sending Speight's infantry brigade to the Red River, though deeply regretted at the time, was, nevertheless, imperative. Could I have retained that brigade at Fort Smith, I should have been enabled, in all probability, to have inaugurated the spring campaign from the line of the Arkansas River, and thus, perhaps, have materially changed the fortunes of war in that section of country. All of these many difficulties and embarrassments will be seen by reference to my official correspondence, to which I would most respectfully refer.

Prior to my arrival at Fort Smith, General Hindman had directed Brigadier-General Cooper, in command of the Indian Brigade, to adopt a universal system of furloughs. Very many of the Indian troops availed themselves of this privilege. There, however, remained quite a number who refused to accept furloughs, and whose subsistence, &c., added greatly to the then existing difficulties. Brigadier-General Cooper's official reports represented the troops under his command as being almost destitute of clothing; miserably equipped in all respects; poorly armed (many being without arms), and that it was impossible to subsist them on the line of the Arkansas River; hence I was under the necessity, also, of ordering this force to the southward. The alternative was thus presented to me either to proceed with the troops that had been ordered southward, and abandon the line of the Upper Arkansas, or remain in person at Fort Smith, and attempt, with the small force in garrison at that point, to hold possession of the place, and, to some extent, the line indicated, until such time as I should have it in my power to subsist such troops as were then in the country or as might be sent from other points. I determined, believing, as I did, that Fort Smith was the true strategic key to the Indian Territory, to adopt the latter course, trusting to the inclemency of the season and the waters of the Arkansas to shield me from an attack. During the winter the enemy made frequent raids, penetrating as far southward as the Arkansas, doing little other mischief than annoying and interrupting the river transportation. I became satisfied, however, that he had no design of attempting the permanent occupation of any point south of the Arkansas so long as our forces held possession of, and controlled, the navigation of the Lower Arkansas. Thus impressed, I ordered the main body of the troops in the Territory to encamp as near Red River as was convenient, in order, first, that they might be more readily subsisted, recruited, and equipped; and, second, that the available transportation might be used in accumulating supplies in the depots near the line of the Arkansas. I thus hoped to accumulate an ample supply of breadstuffs for the commencement of the spring campaign at the earliest day, the artillery and cavalry horses being meanwhile recruited on Red River, where an abundance of forage had been placed, under my direction, by Maj. A. S. Cabell, chief quartermaster.

In order to distract the attention of the enemy from an insight into these plans and operations, I resolved to have the enemy, then at Fayetteville, Ark., 55 miles northwest from Fort Smith, annoyed as much as possible, and to this end I gave every encouragement in my power to the formation of partisan companies. Colonel Monroe's First Arkansas Cavalry, about 400 strong, having been sent to my aid, I caused as frequent scouts to be made as it was possible for man and horse to endure. The greater portion of this cavalry was constantly employed watching over and defeating the operations of the numerous bands of jayhawkers who were committing daily deeds of violence and bloodshed.

The full force of the enemy in Northwestern Arkansas and the Cherokee country during the winter and early spring did not exceed 3,000, inclusive of Pin Indians. Of the latter, some 1,200 or 1,500 were in the service of the Federal Government. To subsist this force and obtain forage, the enemy was under the necessity of scattering it over a large extent of country. In Northwestern Arkansas he was unable to mount a force exceeding 500 men. These facts were repeatedly urged upon the lieutenant-general commanding, and a movement in the rear of this force urgently pressed. I became satisfied that if the enemy was permitted to remain in quiet and uninterrupted possession of the north side of the Arkansas River during the winter and spring, he would, in the exercise of his customary energy, throw forward in the direction of Fort Gibson such quantity of supplies as would suffice to attempt a flank movement on Fort Smith in that direction. General Marmaduke's cavalry force was then occupying the country in the vicinity of Batesville. A brigade of cavalry, under Colonel [C. A.] Carroll, occupied the country in the vicinity of Roseville. From Batesville to Fayetteville was but a short distance, and from Roseville to the same point the distance was not exceeding four or five days' march. Had Marmaduke's cavalry been thrown rapidly in the rear of the enemy at Fayetteville while Carroll marched upon the front, it is quite sure that the result would have been either his capture in detail or his entire abandonment of Northwestern Arkansas and the Indian country. I mean no disrespect to the lieutenant-general then commanding, in making these statements, yet justice to myself and the subsequent verification of the correctness of the views then entertained and repeatedly urged, demand that I should record them. Had the movement indicated been made (its successful issue, in my judgment, being beyond the peradventure of a doubt), I should have been enabled to have had in store, in depots on or near the Arkansas River, an ample supply of breadstuffs, while the country south of that stream abounded in beef cattle of the best quality. In short, I could have assumed the offensive from the line of the Arkansas River with a force fully rested and recruited, both as regards men and horses, considerably earlier in the spring than the enemy could have begun his movements from either Missouri or Kansas. The moral effect of such a condition of affairs upon the people of Arkansas and the Indian Territory and Northern Texas, and its influence upon operations then contemplated and subsequently consummated in the direction of Little Rock, remains, of course, only a subject of conjecture.

During the winter months I had caused workshops for the repair, &c., of arms and wagons (of which quite a number were fitted up from the *débris* found scattered about the garrison), as well as put in operation such other branches of industry necessary to the supply of the army as the resources of the country afforded.

Repeated requisitions for the supply of arms and ammunition remaining unfilled, I assumed the responsibility of sending an officer of my staff to Texas, with a view of making an endeavor to obtain the necessary supply of ammunition and arms, if possible, from that quarter. A greater portion of the ammunition obtained by this officer had to be transported from San Antonio to Bonham, Tex., in ox wagons. The delay incident to this means of transportation was of very material prejudice, especially so, as it was found impossible to procure a supply from any other quarter. I also procured some 500 stand of arms from this source, these being the only arms brought into the Territory during the period of my command, other than a few repaired arms.

I repeatedly urged upon General Cooper and the officer in command of Speight's brigade the necessity of straining every energy to the preparation of their commands for an advance movement at the earliest practicable period; and, in accordance with my orders, the march northward was begun by the entire force near Red River left under my command as soon as the condition of the roads, &c., would permit. Speight's brigade, together with West's battery (this being the only reliable battery then under my control), was ordered to Louisiana, after being some days on the march northward.

Notwithstanding this sudden and important depletion of my effective strength, I determined to make every effort to hold the line of the Arkansas, and, if possible, by means of a superior numerical force of cavalry operating upon the enemy's rear, compel him to abandon his hold on the north bank of that stream, at Fort Gibson, a point which he had strongly fortified and garrisoned with from 2,500 to 3,500 troops.

General Cooper, in conformity with my orders, moved forward with his brigade, consisting of two regiments of Texas cavalry (De Morse's and Martin's), with the bulk of the Indian troops, and a battery of three mountain howitzers and one small prairie rifle gun, to the vicinity of Fort Gibson. Fully apprised of the difficulties experienced by the enemy in regard to his supplies (he being under the necessity of transporting them in wagons for a distance of several hundred miles), and being regularly and correctly advised of the departure of his trains from Fort Scott and other depots to the northward, I made such dispositions as I flattered myself would effectually cut off supplies and re-enforcements. Cabell's brigade, which had been placed under my command a short time before, was moved forward to Fayetteville, with the design of operating upon the rear and lines of communication from that quarter, whilst General Cooper was instructed to avoid a general action, and operate with his available cavalry from the west. Attempts to effect this object were accordingly made. With the conduct and results of these expeditions I was wholly unsatisfied. The failure of the first expedition, under Colonel McIntosh, sent by General Cooper, was attributable, in my judgment, to the command of the expedition devolving upon an Indian officer, deficient in energy and capacity, and who did not enjoy the confidence of the white troops under his command.

A second expedition, under Col. Stand Watie, was sent to the west of Grand River and in rear of Fort Gibson, with the view of attacking a large train of the enemy and a number of re-enforcements, known to be *en route* for Gibson. General Cabell was ordered to co-operate in this movement, by way of Fayetteville. Col. Stand Watie came up with the enemy's train and made an attack upon it. He was, however, able to accomplish little, owing to the failure of a junction of the forces under Cabell and others sent to his assistance by General Cooper. General Cabell's failure and that of the forces sent by Cooper to form this junction, as designed, were officially ascribed to high waters intersecting their line of march.

The enemy having thus succeeded in getting into Gibson considerable re-enforcements and a quantity of supplies, assumed the offensive from that base of operations. An attack was made by General Blunt, commanding the Federal forces, on General Cooper, then encamped at Honey Springs, who, with twenty-four hours' notice of the enemy's approach, and with the knowledge that re-enforcements were *en route* to join him, gave battle upon the ground he occupied, and, having taken no steps to strengthen his position, was driven from it, after a short contest, with the loss of one howitzer and about 200 men in killed, wounded, and captured. General Blunt did not pursue, but contented himself with destroying some flour and a few broken wagons, &c. This battle was fought on the 17th July, the best portion of Cabell's brigade, with all of his artillery, being within hearing of the cannon and *en route* for the scene of action. In a few days (July 22) Cooper's and Cabell's brigades were concentrated about 25 miles in rear of the battle-ground, and by the 25th were placed in position at Prairie Springs, 15 miles from Fort Gibson, where I determined to await the arrival of a brigade from Texas, under command of Col. S. P. Bankhead, which I had been notified was ordered to report to me, and which was expected before the 10th of August. Upon the arrival of that brigade, it was my intention to take a position near enough to Fort Gibson to effectually prevent any further supplies or re-enforcements from going in. In a few days the desertions from Cabell's Arkansas brigade became alarming, without any apparent cause. They left by tens and hundreds (as many as 200 leaving in one night, several officers going with them). The weather at this time was good, and provisions (flour and beef) abundant; but another serious difficulty presented itself. The powder which had been received from Texas was found to be worthless when exposed to the slightest moisture, a night's heavy dew converting it into a paste. Under these circumstances, I determined to withdraw farther from the enemy, who might in a night's march attack us at any time, knowing, as he undoubtedly did, the condition of affairs with us, from several deserters who went to his lines. The whole force was accordingly withdrawn to the south side of the Canadian River, and Fort Smith being threatened by a force from Springfield, Mo., Cabell's brigade was posted within supporting distance of that place. My force being nearly all cavalry, and dependent entirely upon grass to subsist the animals, was necessarily much scattered; consequently, when a few days later the enemy was reported advancing in force, a move to the rear was made to a point where all could concentrate. The Creeks failed entirely to come to the point designated, and most of the Cherokees and several companies of Choctaws being absent, I found myself with not over 1,500 men, many of whom were unarmed (nearly all with indifferent arms), opposed to a force of 2,000 cavalry and about 3,000 infantry, the latter transported in 300 two-horse wagons. Instead, therefore, of risking an engagement, nothing was attempted but to keep the enemy in check until our supplies were moved to the rear. In this we were successful, nothing having been left to fall into the enemy's hands. He gratified his malice, however, by burning the little town of Perryville. From Perryville the enemy turned toward Fort Smith with a portion of his forces, where General Cabell contested his advance in an engagement of several hours' duration, most of his men behaving badly. A few hundred repulsed the attacking force, and then retired in the direction of Waldron.

Whilst retiring before the enemy, near Perryville, I again received notice that Bankhead's brigade was ordered to report to me. It was hurried forward in the direction of Fort Smith, to the support of General Cabell, who had been instructed to retire, in case of necessity, on the road this brigade advanced upon. It was expected that if General Cabell had been obliged to evacuate, this re-enforcement would have enabled him to regain his lost ground. General Cooper's brigade, composed of a few whites and several different tribes of Indians, could not be moved. General Cabell's movements, by the way of Waldron, prevented his junction with the re-enforcements at a time when the enemy, feeling secure, had scattered his forces and offered an easy conquest. General Cabell reported that he had received orders from Major-General Price, which orders were never sent me, and thus his brigade was in some way disconnected with my command. Acting Brigadier-General Bankhead remained several weeks near Fort Smith, cutting off small parties of the enemy. General Cooper, with his brigade, was, as soon as possible, advanced upon the line we had retired upon.

At this time I left General Cooper in command, for the purpose of having an interview with the commander of the Trans-Mississippi Department. On my return, I found that all the troops had been concentrated near North Fork Town, on the Canadian, and immediately after my arrival, and without consulting my wishes, General Cooper moved the whole slowly in the direction of Fort Smith, halting about 35 miles from that place, where I overtook him. The statements in regard to the enemy's force and position, sent to me during the few days previous to my arrival at his camp, had varied so much from day to day that I was in great uncertainty as to the best course to pursue. The troops had moved down with the expectation of a battle. I determined to attempt a surprise, upon learning that, owing to the annoyance given by the Choctaws, the enemy had no pickets on one road leading through the Arkansas Bottom, and gave orders accordingly, when General Cooper represented to me that he could not bring up his brigade of Indians to take the part assigned to them. I then thought of making the attack from another direction, where a prairie, with several roads leading from it to the enemy's position, would obviate the objection urged. To this plan General Cooper demurred, on the ground that the ponies of his Indians, having been without forage for several days, could not make the march in time. The distance was estimated at about 35 miles, to be traveled between 12 m. and daylight the next morning. Wishing to remove every objection, I moved my camp farther around to the south of Fort Smith, and to within 20 miles of that place, where I arrived on the 31st of October, having been delayed by a storm of rain and snow, and in cutting out a road through the Poteau Bottom. During this storm the various commanders of the regiments of Texas troops, composing the Second Brigade, came in a body to inform me of the suffering condition of their men from the want of proper clothing, and of their inability to keep the men together much longer under such circumstances. My force on the 31st of October, as I derived from inspectors' reports, was: Seminoles, 106; Chickasaws, 208; Creeks, 305; Choctaws, 1,024; Choctaw militia, 200, and whites, 999. Of the Indians, all but one regiment were armed with any kind of guns that could be obtained. Some were entirely without arms. The whole force was cavalry and artillery. General Gano arrived the next day with his escort and a portion of Howell's battery, making my whole force nearly 3,000, about two-thirds of which was composed of at least three different nations, speaking different languages, and under no kind of discipline. The enemy's scouts had discovered us; consequently all hope of a surprise was at an end. General McNeil had arrived at Fort Smith with re-enforcements. I believe that to have made an attack would only have ended in disaster. Under these circumstances, I withdrew the white troops, and directed General Cooper to keep up, with his Indian brigade, a desultory warfare, to prevent the enemy from foraging or moving about at will. The Texas brigade, Brigadier-General Gano commanding, was withdrawn, and found its clothing at Boggy Depot, from which point it was moved at once eastward near the Arkansas State line. At the time of withdrawing the Texas brigade, the whole command was out of flour or other breadstuffs; 4 small wagon loads only arrived just as we were retiring.

One of the most fruitful sources of embarrassment experienced in the command of the Indian country, and one which, instead of being repressed, constantly increased, was that of feeding the indigent Indians

The policy of feeding such Indians as had been driven from their homes, and whose country was in the occupation of the enemy, had been inaugurated prior to my arrival. The total failure of the crops throughout the entire Indian Territory had increased the number dependent upon the commissariat to many thousands. It became necessary to give these people bread or have them throw themselves upon the charity of the enemy, who lost no opportunity to gain ground by holding out liberal inducements of pardon, and of supplies of clothing and food. To resist the moral effect of these inducements held out by the enemy, I was compelled to yield with as much show of cheerfulness as possible to the very heavy demands that were made upon me, and, to meet these demands, large draughts were constantly being made upon stores accumu lated for military purposes.

An experience of twelve months in the command of the Indian country has convinced me that, with a few exceptions, the Indians are wholly unreliable as troops of the line. The officers, as a general rule, are ignorant, void of moral tone of character, and indisposed to enforce discipline among their men. Their allegiance to the Government seems to be regarded more in the light of a voluntary contribution on their part, susceptible of being withheld at their option, than the performance of an obligatory duty. In order to acquire the reputation derived from success, in the administration of the affairs of the Territory (according to the somewhat doubtful standard, success) it is necessary to pander to the opinions and sentiments of Indianized white men, and through such to coax and demagoguize with the Indians, rather than attempt the enforcement of discipline among the troops and system in the various departments. The ignorance of the main body of the Indians naturally subjects them to the influence for good or evil of a class of whites and educated half-breeds, who, living among them and having a knowledge of their language, feelings, prejudices, &c., find no difficulty in molding the masses to their generally interested views. I became satisfied that with those exercising the chief influence among the Indians there was a settled design to subordinate white officers and white troops to Indian officers and Indian troops.

In suggesting these views, I would take occasion to state that there are serving in the Indian country a few striking exceptions. Among these I may mention Col. Stand Watie, whom I found to be a gallant and daring officer, but, as was the case in all other instances among the Indian troops, without the slightest discipline in his regiment. For some time prior to making the movement in the direction of Fort Smith, already referred to, I had discerned a growing disinclination on the part of the Indian troops to serve under my command. The ingenuity of my defamers had been taxed to the utmost in giving circulation to the most reckless falsehoods. I was charged with a determination to take the white troops out of their country and abandon them to their fate; that I only awaited a favorable opportunity to go over to the enemy in person; that I was Northern-born, and had no true feeling of sympathy with the South. With another class of troops such calumnies could have been successfully met, and my influence as a commander not, perhaps, have been thereby materially impaired; but among the Indian troops, with the influences mentioned operating against me, the consequence will be patent. An improper and unjust construction was given to almost every step I deemed it necessary to take for the good of the service; in short, nothing seemed to have been left undone by designing men and knaves to excite the most violent prejudice and distrust on the part of the Indians. The dark side of my picture, painted in their own colors, was kept constantly presented to their view. Explanations of my official conduct were never attempted to be made by those whose implied duty it was to give me their aid and support. The Indian troops were also led to believe that I was illegally exercising the command of the Territory over Brigadier-General Cooper, who was represented as my superior in rank, and that he being an Indian officer, I was thereby trampling upon the rights, privileges, and wishes of the Indian troops.

Concluding from these reasons, and many more of a similar character that might be urged, that my influence and usefulness as a commanding officer were so much impaired as to render further attempts in the military administration of the country nugatory, and in view of the promotion of that harmony of action and unity of sentiment so necessary to success especially in the conduct of military operations, I respectfully asked of the lieutenant-general commanding to be relieved of duty in the Indian country.

I entered upon the command of the Indian Territory conscious of my inability, with the limited means at my command, to meet the demands and expectations of the country. I can only express my consciousness of having at least honestly and faithfully labored for the good of the service and the common good of the inhabitants of the country over which I exercised a command.

In conclusion, I would refer to the valuable assistance rendered me by my staff officers, Capt. J. F. Crosby, as adjutant-general; Maj. S. J. Lee, commissary; Maj. A. S. Cabell, chief quartermaster; Surg. E. R. Duval, medical director, and Lieut. B. G. Duval, aide-de-camp, and, during the absence of Captain Crosby, acting assistant adjutant-general; Lieutenant [J. J.] Du Bose, of Morgan's (Arkansas) infantry regiment, as acting ordnance officer. All of these officers displayed zeal, energy, ability, and, what I have found more rare, honesty.

I am, colonel, very respectfully, your obedient servant,

WM. STEELE,
Brigadier-General.

Lieut. Col. S. S. ANDERSON,
Assistant Adjutant-General.

NOVEMBER 20-23, 1862.—Reconnaissance toward Van Buren and Fort Smith, Ark.

Report of Brig. Gen. James G. Blunt, U. S. Army.

CAMP BABCOCK, ARK.,
November 24, 1862.

I have the honor to report that Lieutenant-Colonel [L. R.] Jewell, with a detachment of 600 men, sent on a reconnaissance in the direction of Van Buren and Fort Smith, returned last night. He met the enemy's pickets 15 miles this side of Van Buren, who retreated at his approach. Learning that a large force was at Van Buren, he deemed it prudent to proceed no farther, and returned. Information obtained from various sources, which I deem quite reliable, is that Hindman's, Marmaduke's, Cooper's, and Stand Watie's forces are at Van Buren and Fort Smith. Their entire force is estimated as high as 30,000; but I am quite sure it does not exceed 15,000 effective men, and probably not over 12,000.

If a small re-enforcement could be sent me, to enable me to leave a small force in the vicinity of Evansville, to protect my rear and line of communication from any flank movement that might be made by any small rebel force sent by some other route than the one upon which my column would move, I would not hesitate to attack them on the other side of the mountains, and do not doubt of my ability to occupy and hold Van Buren and Fort Smith, provided General Steele occupies the attention of General Holmes, so that re-enforcements cannot be sent from Little Rock.

JAS. G. BLUNT,
Brigadier-General.

Maj. Gen. SAMUEL R. CURTIS.

NOVEMBER 24-26, 1862.—Expeditions from Greenfield into Jasper and Barton Counties, Mo.

Report of Brig. Gen. Francis J. Herron, U. S. Army.

NOVEMBER 28, 1862.

Brigadier-General Brown reports the result of two expeditions sent from Greenfield, Mo. One under Major [G. W.] Kelly, Fourth Missouri State Militia, into Jasper County, encountered and dispersed Jackman's band of guerrillas, killing 1 lieutenant and 1 private, and capturing 6 prisoners, with their horses, arms, &c. Captain Roecker, of Major Kelly's command, had a hand-to-hand encounter with a rebel lieutenant, finally killing him. The other expedition, under Lieutenant Pritchard, met a portion of the same band near Lamar, in Barton County, dispersing them and killing 2. Quantrill, with 1,000 men, came up to within 10 miles of Newtonia, intending to surprise Colonel [J. F.] Philips, stationed at that place; but hearing of the re-enforcements sent there, has scattered his command, falling back into McDonald County. Colonel Philips is after him. The southwestern counties are swarming with guerrilla bands.

F. J. HERRON,
Brigadier-General.

Maj. Gen. SAMUEL R. CURTIS.

NOVEMBER 25, 1862.—Skirmish near Cane Hill, Ark.

Report of Brig. Gen. James G. Blunt, U. S. Army.

HDQRS. FIRST DIVISION, ARMY OF THE FRONTIER,
Camp Babcock, November 26, 1862.

GENERAL: I have the honor to report that General Marmaduke, with his entire command, followed about twenty-four hours in the rear of Lieutenant-Colonel [L. R.] Jewell, on his return from reconnoitering in the direction of Van Buren. He is now encamped at Cane Hill, 7,000 or 8,000 strong. A detachment sent from my command attacked a large reconnoitering party of the enemy yesterday, and scattered them. Spies who left their camp this morning inform me that General Hindman, with a large force of infantry, is expected to join them, when they will make an attempt to get north into Missouri. My supply train arrived this evening all right. I shall move on Marmaduke to-morrow morning, leaving my transportation at this point with a small guard. Shall strike him next morning at daylight, unless he runs. Hope to destroy him before he can be re-enforced by Hindman. Distance to Cane Hill is 30 miles. Can you not send a cavalry force to Pineville or Neosho to protect my supply trains, as detachments of the enemy, in considerable force, are hanging on my rear for the purpose of capturing or annoying them?

Very respectfully, your obedient servant,

JAS. G. BLUNT,
Brigadier-General, Commanding.

Brigadier-General SCHOFIELD,
Commanding Army of the Frontier.

NOVEMBER 25-29, 1862.—Expedition to Yellville, Ark.

REPORTS.

No. 1.—Maj. Gen. Samuel R. Curtis, U. S. Army.
No. 2.—Brig. Gen. Francis J. Herron, U. S. Army, with congratulatory dispatch

No. 1.

Report of Maj. Gen. Samuel R. Curtis, U. S. Army.

NOVEMBER 30, 1862.

GENERAL: General Herron telegraphs that the Yellville expedition, of which I wrote you, has returned. It was successful in destroying the saltpeter works, the arsenal, and the store-houses, with about 500 shot-guns and rifles. Sixty prisoners were taken, and over 100 horses. Their sick in the hospital were paroled, and the troops returned last evening, after traveling 250 miles in less than five days. The troops were the First Iowa, Tenth Illinois, and Second Wisconsin, commanded by Colonel [D.] Wickersham, of the Tenth Illinois.

SAML. R. CURTIS,
Major-General.

H. W. HALLECK,
General-in-Chief.

No. 2.

Report of Brig. Gen. Francis J. Herron, U. S. Army, with congratulatory dispatch.

ARMY OF THE FRONTIER,
Southwest Missouri, November 30, 1862.

The cavalry expedition sent by me to Yellville returned last night, having made the march of 250 miles in less than five days. It was a complete success, and not only have all the saltpeter works in that section and at Dubuque been destroyed, but the arsenal and store-houses of the rebels were burned. Sixty of Burbridge's command were taken prisoners; about 500 shot-guns and rifles at the arsenal were destroyed, and over 100 good horses brought out. The rebels have a large hospital at that place. and the inmates were paroled. The force usually congregated there is now south of West Plains. Our troops have left the place in such shape that I do not think the rebels will again attempt to make a depot. The expedition consisted of the First Iowa Cavalry, Tenth Illinois Cavalry, and one battalion of the Second Wisconsin, all under command of Colonel Wickersham, Tenth Illinois. This movement, with Blunt's victory at Cane Hill, effectually clears the north side of the mountains of all troops except guerrillas.

F. J. HERRON,
Brigadier-General.

Maj. Gen. SAMUEL R. CURTIS.

SAINT LOUIS, *December* 1, 1862.

Brigadier-General HERRON, *Springfield:*

I congratulate you and your cavalry on the success of the expedition to Yellville, Ark. Colonel Wickersham is especially deserving my thanks.

SAML. R. CURTIS,
Major-General.

NOVEMBER 26-29, 1862.—Affairs in Jackson and La Fayette Counties, Mo

Report of Col. James McFerran, First Missouri State Militia Cavalry.

HDQRS. FIRST MISSOURI STATE MILITIA CAVALRY,
Lexington, Mo., November 29, 1862.

SIR: On the 26th instant, pursuant to instructions received by telegraph from General Loan, through General [R. C.] Vaughan, directing my co-operation with him, I proceeded with all the available force that could be spared from this post, in pursuit of certain forces, said to be engaged committing depredations on the citizens of the counties of Jackson and La Fayette, in this State. We marched to Greenton, 12 miles from this post, and quartered for the night. In this vicinity the widow of Barker, who was murdered by the bushwhackers last summer, had been robbed the night previous of all the negroes and horses on the plantation by armed men unknown to the family.

The next morning we resumed our march in the direction of Pink Hill. On the march a man by the name of Grear was shot by our scouts for refusing to obey their summons to halt.

About 1 p. m. we entered the Independence road and found that Colonel [W. R.] Penick had just passed with 110 men, in the direction of Independence. We followed, and in the course of an hour overtook his command.

About 3 p. m. we came upon the Kansas forces, encamped at James' residence, and drawn up in line of battle, their right resting across the road at the end of a lane; their left extending in the rear of the buildings. They had their artillery, one 6-pounder, planted on their right, in position to rake the lane. A part of Colonel Penick's force marched into the lane, in range of the artillery and small-arms of the Kansas men, before I was aware of their proximity, the road at that point making a right angle.

As soon as I saw their position, I formed our forces on an elevation, and planted our artillery so as to command their position. Immediately after this the Kansas men broke ranks and stacked their arms, displaying the United States flag, whereupon a correspondence ensued between General Vaughan and Colonel [C. W.] Adams, in command of the Kansas forces, being the Twelfth Kansas Volunteers, a copy of which is herewith presented.* Before the correspondence closed, night had set in, and our men having been on the march and under arms since daylight in the morning, they were permitted to get quarters for the night at the different farm houses surrounding the position occupied by the forces during the day. During the night Colonel Adams was placed under arrest for disobedience of orders, and the command devolved upon the second in command, reported to be Lieutenant-Colonel [J. E.] Hayes. Thus matters stood until morning. Our forces consisted of detachments of my regiment, First Cavalry, Missouri State Militia; Second Battalion Cavalry, Missouri State Militia, under the command of Captain [R.] Smith; La Fayette Enrolled Missouri Militia, under the command of Colonel Neill, and the Ray Enrolled Missouri Militia, under the command of Lieutenant-Colonel [J. W.] Black, and Colonel Penick's command, numbering in all about 450 effective men, with three pieces of artillery. The Kansas forces numbered about 300 effective men.

At sunrise in the morning our forces again reoccupied the position of the evening before. Shortly after this the Kansas troops sent within our lines about 20 horses, and resumed their line of march toward Kansas. We had, however, taken the precaution to station a part of our forces in their advance, thus putting them on the offensive, and making them responsible for a collision, if one ensued, by their attempt to force our lines. As soon as they began their march we began the pursuit. Thus finding themselves surrounded, upon the demand of an officer, specially detailed for the duty, they delivered up all property claimed as belonging to citizens of Missouri, including negroes, after which they resumed their march to Kansas. The property turned over by them to General Vaughan consisted of about 100 horses and mules, 40 negroes, 6 ox-teams, and 1 two-horse team, loaded with household goods of great variety. This property was brought with us several miles as we returned. The negroes were turned out of the lines, and the property placed in the hands of discreet citizens, by direction of General Vaughan, to be delivered to the owners, upon application. Our forces continued their march, arriving at this post at about 8 p. m. on the 28th instant. Colonel [A. J.] Barr, of the Ray Enrolled Missouri Militia, came up to us with a re-enforcement of about 100 men, while the property was being delivered, and returned with us to this post.

After the arrest of Colonel Adams, Lieutenant-Colonel Hayes, being in command of the Twelfth Kansas, placed the major of said regiment under arrest, and was afterward arrested himself, for disobedience of orders, by General Vaughan. This placed the Twelfth Kansas under command of its senior captain. As far as I know or believe, the expedition of the Twelfth Kansas into this State was not in pursuit of guerrillas or other military forces of the enemy, no such forces being in the counties of La Fayette and Jackson at the time, and had not been for some time before. From the best evidence I could obtain, much of the property returned by the Twelfth Kansas to General Vaughan was taken by them from Union men. It is proper to state, however, that I was informed in some instances they had, to some extent, respected the rights

* See pp. 822–824.

of Union men. Thus the supremacy of the laws was vindicated, our officers and men doing their duty and observing good order throughout.

All of which is respectfully submitted.

Your obedient servant,

JAMES McFERRAN,
Colonel First Missouri State Militia Cavalry.

Maj. JAMES RAINSFORD,
Assistant Adjutant-General, Jefferson City, Mo.

NOVEMBER 28, 1862.—Engagement at Cane Hill, or Boston Mountains, Ark.

REPORTS.

No. 1.

Report of Maj. Gen. Samuel R. Curtis, U. S. Army, commanding Department of the Missouri.

NOVEMBER 29, 1862.

General Blunt, with his division, made a forced march and attacked the enemy yesterday morning at Cane Hill, Ark. The battle lasted for several hours. The enemy, under General Marmaduke, began to fall back about 1 o'clock, but retreated, fighting till sundown. The victory was complete. Our loss is not great. The enemy much more. Our forces camp on the battle-field. The enemy has retreated to Van Buren.

SAML. R. CURTIS,
Major-General.

H. W. HALLECK,
General-in-Chief.

No. 2.

Reports of Brig. Gen. James G. Blunt, U. S. Army, commanding division, with congratulatory orders.

CANE HILL, ARK., *November* 29, 1862.

GENERAL: Learning that a rebel force, under Marmaduke, 8,000 strong, was at Cane Hill, 40 miles north of Van Buren, Ark., and that General

Hindman was to join him to-day or to-morrow with a large force of infantry, for the purpose of making a desperate effort to enter Missouri, I determined to strike Marmaduke, and destroy him before re-enforcements arrived. Leaving my transportation in the rear, I made a forced march of 35 miles, with about 5,000 men, and attacked him about 10 o'clock this morning. Found him strongly posted on advantageous ground. After an engagement of about three hours, he commenced a retreat. Every foot of the ground was fought over and hotly contested. The fight continued until near sundown, when the enemy, finding that their artillery, which they were making every effort to get away, was about to be captured, sent Colonels Shelby and Emmett MacDonald with a flag of truce, for the ostensible purpose of caring for their dead and wounded, but with the real object of making good their retreat to Van Buren.

The casualties of the army I am unable to state with accuracy at this time, as we fought over 12 miles of ground. One of the rebel officers, under the flag of truce, stated to me that they had lost 60 in killed, among them a lieutenant-colonel. My loss is comparatively small. Among the wounded are Lieutenant-Colonel [L. R.] Jewell and Lieutenant [J. A.] Johnson, of the Sixth Kansas. Both of them, I fear, mortally. The enemy are badly whipped, and will probably not venture north of the Boston Mountains again this winter. If this part of the State is held, as it is their reliance for subsistence, having eaten out all in the valley of the Arkansas, they must soon retreat into Texas. I have sent for my teams to come up, and shall occupy a position at or near Cane Hill. The rebels had about ten days' rations of bread, cooked, and in little sacks behind their saddles, from which it is evident they intended making a desperate effort to force their way north.

JAS. G. BLUNT,
Brigadier-General, Commanding.

Maj. Gen. SAMUEL R. CURTIS.

CANE HILL, ARK., *December* 2, 1862.

General Marmaduke continued his flight all night, after the battle of the 28th, and is now in Van Buren. General Hindman was expected to re-enforce him at this place on the evening of that day. Prisoners, of whom I captured 25, state that Marmaduke's force was 11,000. They were compelled to abandon two pieces of artillery, disabled by my batteries. A number of their officers are killed, among them a Lieutenant-Colonel Monroe, of a Texas [Arkansas] regiment, and a Captain Martin, of an Arkansas [Missouri] regiment. The notorious Quantrill and his band were engaged in the fight, and, with Colonels Shelby and Emmett MacDonald, commanding the rear guard in the retreat across the Boston Mountains, they fought desperately. Some of Quantrill's men were killed and others taken prisoners.

My loss in killed is 5, and 4 mortally wounded, one of whom, Lieutenant-Colonel Jewell, Sixth Kansas, has since died. Lieutenant [A. H.] Campbell, Sixth Kansas, was taken prisoner. The loss of the enemy in killed is about 75. They carried most of their wounded off the field, and sent them to houses on the right and left of the road and battle-ground. All regret the leath of Lieutenant-Colonel Jewell, as he was a brave and gallant officer.

Two contrabands arrived to-day from Van Buren, who state that Hindman, with 12,000 infantry, crossed the Arkansas River from the south

Tuesday last, for the purpose of moving up to re-enforce Marmaduke, but have now all gone back to their hole.

My transportation has just come up. I occupy the same position held by Marmaduke when I attacked him, and intend holding it. They will not advance this side of the mountains, except with their combined forces; but I am prepared to meet them, and with my little army whip 25,000 of such chivalry. An officer who came inside of our lines under a flag of truce after night terminated the fighting, acknowledges that they were badly whipped and worse chased.

Lieutenant [J. A.] Johnson, Sixth Kansas, dangerously wounded; may possibly recover.

JAS. G. BLUNT,
Brigadier-General.

Maj. Gen. SAMUEL R. CURTIS.

HDQRS. FIRST DIVISION, ARMY OF THE FRONTIER,
Cane Hill, Ark., December 3, 1862.

GENERAL: I have the honor to report that, on November 26, while encamped at Lindsey's Prairie, 15 miles south of Maysville, I received reliable information that General Marmaduke, with a force estimated at 8,000 men, was at Cane Hill. I further learned that Marmaduke's command was the advance of Hindman's army, the remainder of which was expected to arrive at Cane Hill on the evening of the 28th. I immediately determined to attack Marmaduke, and, if possible, defeat him before the arrival of General Hindman with re-enforcements.

Early on the morning of the 27th, I ordered all of my transportation and commissary trains parked on Lindsey's Prairie, and, after detailing a sufficient guard for its protection, I commenced my march, with about 5,000 men and thirty pieces of artillery, the men taking with them four days' rations of hard bread and salt. The distance to be traveled to reach the enemy was 35 miles, of which 25 were made by 7 p. m. on the 27th, when the command bivouacked for the night. From that point I sent spies into the enemy's camp, and learned that their pickets were strongly posted on the main road (on which I was advancing), and that it could be easily defended.

I marched at 5 a. m. on the 28th, leaving that road and making a detour to the left, by a blind track; struck one that was obscure and unfrequented, and entered Cane Hill directly from the north. As I had anticipated, they had no pickets on this road, and I met no resistance until within half a mile of their camp. The enemy had learned, however, the night previous, that I was moving upon them, and were prepared for our reception. About 200 of the Second Kansas Cavalry, under Colonel [W. F.] Cloud, with two mountain howitzers, under Lieutenant [E. S.] Stover, were in the advance, which, with [J. W.] Rabb's battery and my staff and body guard, constituted the only force upon the ground, the main column having been delayed in ascending a mountain about 7 miles back to the rear. Of this fact I was not apprised until my advance was engaged. In passing down a gorge between two abrupt hills, their grand guard was encountered in considerable force. Dashing on, and driving them before us, a few hundred yards brought us to where the bluff on the right terminated, and in full view of the enemy, who were posted on the right of the road, on elevated ground, with timber in their rear, their guns in battery, bearing upon the road on which I was approaching, and from which they immediately opened a brisk fire. I at once ordered Rabb's battery into position, and also the two howitzers under Lieutenant [E. S.] Stover, when a fierce cannonading ensued, which lasted for the space of nearly an hour. My column not being up, I could do nothing more than engage in this artillery duel until it arrived, and the enemy, thinking, no doubt, that I had a large force on hand, did not venture from under the cover of their guns. Reconnoitering upon their left, I discovered an approach by which a force could be brought on their left flank and do them great damage, and, perhaps, capture their artillery.

I ordered Major [V. P.] Van Antwerp, of my staff, back to meet the Eleventh Kansas and Hopkins' battery, who were in the advance of the column, to bring them up on the double-quick, and send the battery, with six companies of the Eleventh, to follow me, with the object above named, and to take the other four companies to the support of Rabb's battery; but they were too far in the rear and the men too much fatigued by the march to reach me in time. Major Van Antwerp took the four companies down the road to Rabb's battery, the fire from which, as afterward appeared (although laboring under great disadvantage from the nature of the ground), had been very destructive on the enemy, compelling them to abandon their position and seek another, on a high ridge three-fourths of a mile farther south, where their reserve had been posted. To this point access was very difficult, as rugged ravines intervened, and it could only be approached by the road. Taking a position on high ground, facing them from the north, I opened upon them a destructive fire with my artillery, dismounting one of their guns and compelling them again to retire. For the third time they made a stand in the town, or, rather, on the south side of it, upon a commanding eminence running east and west, and a most admirable position for defense. Having now concentrated their entire force and selected this strong position, I felt assured that they had resolved on a desperate resistance, and made my arrangements accordingly; but, after getting my force across a deep and rugged ravine, and deploying them in position, ready to advance upon their long and well-formed line, I discovered, much to my disappointment, that they had again retired, and were in full retreat to the mountains, Tenney's battery coming upon the ground they had abandoned just in time to send a few shells into the rear of their retreating column, as they escaped under cover of the woods. As the men and horses of the enemy were fresh, and mine were worn down and exhausted by hard marching, it was difficult to follow them in their flight; yet the men, eager for the fray, strained every nerve.

For nearly 3 miles from the town, in the direction of Van Buren, the road runs through a valley, in which there are a few farms, alternating with low hills and ravines, covered with thick woods and brush. Over this road a running fight, with small-arms, took place, without much damage occurring to either party. Reaching a large mound at the base of the first mountain (the commencement of the Boston Mountains proper), the enemy placed his artillery upon it, in a position covering the road.

From this position he sought to prevent my force from proceeding up the valley and approaching the mountain. Directing two howitzers, under Lieutenant Opdyke, to the right, upon a by-road, they quickly obtained a good position on the enemy's flank, while Rabb's battery opened upon them in front. They were soon forced to abandon the high mound and seek the side and top of the mountain, where they made a determined resistance. Their artillery was posted on the crest of the mountain, while their mounted riflemen were dismounted, and their whole force massed upon the sides and top of the mountain, which was covered with scattered timber and but little underbrush. The nature of the ground was such that I could not use my artillery to any advantage, and the mountain could be taken in no other way except by storm. I accordingly ordered up the Second Kansas and dismounted them. They charged up the steep acclivity in the advance, under the command of Capts. S. J. Crawford and A. P. Russell, Major [J. G.] Fisk having been wounded by a piece of shell early in the day. Next followed the Third Indian Regiment (Cherokee), under the command of Colonel [W. A.] Phillips, and its other field officers, Lieutenant-Colonel Downing and Major [J. A.] Foreman, voluntarily assisted by Major Van Antwerp, of my staff, and the Eleventh Kansas, under the command of its field officers, Colonel [Thomas] Ewing, [jr.,] Lieutenant-Colonel [Thomas] Moonlight, and Major [P. B.] Plumb. The resistance of the rebels was stubborn and determined. The storm of lead and iron hail that came down the side of the mountain, both from their small-arms and artillery, was terrific; yet most of it went over our heads without doing us much damage. The regiments just named, with a wild shout rushed up the steep acclivity, contesting every inch of ground, and steadily pushing the enemy before them, until the crest was reached, when the rebels again fled in disorder. Four howitzers and Rabb's battery were now brought up the mountain and the pursuit renewed; the Third Indian and Eleventh Kansas Regiments, on the right and left of the road, advancing in line through the woods, while the four howitzers occupied the road in front, with the Second and Sixth Kansas and Rabb's battery in their rear. About every half mile the enemy made a stand, when the four howitzers and the Eleventh Kansas and Third Indian would as often put them to flight, leaving more or less of their dead and wounded behind them. Thus the fight continued for some 3 miles, until, on descending partially from the mountain into a valley, the Cove Creek road, leading from Fayetteville to Van Buren, was reached, at the point where it intersects the road from Cane Hill to the last-named place. At this point the enemy again brought his artillery into requisition. It was now near sundown, and darkness must soon put an end to the pursuit. Down the valley, in front of us, the ground appeared adapted to the use of cavalry to good advantage, and I determined to make an effort to capture their artillery, of which they had six pieces. A large force of their best cavalry was acting as rear guard, with a portion of their artillery just in front of them. Waiting for my cavalry to come up, I called for volunteers to make a charge. Three companies of the Sixth Kansas, nearest at hand, responded promptly to the call, and, under command of their three field officers, Colonel [W. R.] Judson, Lieutenant-Colonel [L. R.] Jewell, and Major [W. T.] Campbell, dashed on to the rear of the rebel column, cutting and shooting them down with sabers, carbines, and revolvers. The charge continued for about half a mile down the valley, to a point where it converged in a funnel shape, terminating in a narrow defile. At this point a large body of the enemy were in ambush in front and upon the flanks, where cavalry could not approach, with their battery also masked in front. As soon as the party we were pursuing had passed through the defile, they opened upon us a most destructive fire, which, for the moment, caused my men to recoil and give back, in spite of my own efforts and those of other officers to rally them; whereas, if they had, after receiving the enemy's fire, passed on 200 or 300 yards, we could have secured, in a moment more, what we so much coveted—the enemy's artillery. Emboldened by their success in defending the defile and checking our advance, they raised a wild yell and advanced toward us. With the aid of Colonel Judson, Major Campbell, and Captains [H. S.] Greeno and [D.] Mefford, I succeeded in rallying the three companies of the Sixth Kansas, who had suffered severely in the charge, and formed them across the valley, and the four howitzers, coming up at the same time and opening on the enemy with shell, soon forced them to retire. Yet they seemed determined to dispute the passage of the defile to which I have referred—a position admirably adapted for defense, and beyond which, as I afterward learned, there was a wide, open valley; hence their obstinate resistance at this point, in order to save their guns. I resolved, however, at all hazards to force my way through this gorge, and, as darkness was approaching and I had no time to get up infantry and send them out upon the flanks, I prepared to make an assault in front. Loading the four howitzers and one section of Rabb's battery with double canister, I ordered them up by hand, in battery, with the three companies of the Sixth Kansas with Sharps' carbines advancing in line in rear. I had directed that not a gun should be fired until I gave the word. When within about 400 yards of the enemy, who were defending the gorge, and as I was about to give the word to fire, an officer from General Marmaduke came galloping up with a white flag. On sending an officer to receive it, they requested the privilege of taking off their dead and wounded. Consideration for the fate of Lieutenant-Colonel Jewell, and others who had fallen upon the ground they then occupied, and whom I feared they might brutally murder, induced me to respect their flag of truce, convinced though I was at the time that it was a cowardly trick, resorted to to enable them to make good their retreat and save their guns. It being now dark, and my men entirely exhausted and without food, I considered further pursuit useless, and returned with my command to Cane Hill.

The casualties in my command were 4 killed and 36 wounded; 4 of them mortally, since dead. Among the latter was Lieutenant-Colonel Jewell, of the Sixth Kansas. He was a brave and gallant officer, whose noble example is worthy of emulation. Lieut. J. A. Johnson, of the same regiment, a daring and excellent young officer, received a desperate wound from a musket-ball, which passed entirely through his body; yet it is hoped he will recover. The enemy's loss is 75 killed; wounded not known, as they took a large portion of them away.

The officers and men of my command who took part in this engagement behaved, without exception, nobly.

To the following members of my staff, Maj. V. P. Van Antwerp, inspector-general; Capt. Lyman Scott, acting assistant adjutant-general; Lieut. J. Fin. Hill, aide-de camp, and Lieut. D. Whitaker, acting aide-de-camp, I am indebted for efficient and valuable services during the day.

I am, general, very respectfully, your obedient servant,

JAS. G. BLUNT,

Brigadier-General, Comdg. First Division, Army of the Frontier.

Maj. Gen. SAMUEL R. CURTIS,

Commanding Department of the Missouri.

SAINT LOUIS, *December* 1, 1862.

Brigadier-General BLUNT:

I tender you and the officers and men under your command my thanks for your gallantry and success in the battles of Old Fort Wayne and Cane Hill, Ark.

The District of Western Arkansas is added to your command.

SAML. R. CURTIS,

Major-General.

No. 3.

Report of Col. William F. Cloud, Second Kansas Cavalry, commanding brigade.

HDQRS. 3D. BRIG., 1ST DIV., ARMY OF THE FRONTIER,
Cane Hill, Ark., December 15, 1862.

SIR: I have the honor to make the following report of the part which the Third Brigade took in the action at this place and at the Boston Mountains on the 28th ultimo:

Moving, by your order, in the advance, I came upon the enemy's grand guard about 10 a. m., taking him by surprise. The first intimation he had of our proximity was a shell from Lieutenant Stover's Second Kansas (howitzer) Battery. Upon the dispersing of their guard, I saw their camp, which was upon a brushy hill, about one-half mile to our right and a little in advance.

Lieutenant Stover was immediately sent to the front, and with his battery did good work until the retreat of the rebels. Captain Rabb, with his Second Indiana Battery, took position upon the point of a hill in fair view of, but much lower than, the enemy's batteries, where he did good execution, and after nearly an hour's artillery duel the enemy moved his guns and joined the retreat, which had been commenced soon after the beginning of the engagement. I supported the batteries with four companies of the Second Kansas Cavalry (dismounted), under Major Fisk. The infantry had unfortunately halted about 2 miles to the rear without orders, and with it the whole column in its rear, else the guns of the enemy could have been taken, and also many prisoners. As it was, I was compelled to see the long files of the enemy (who were all mounted) retreat, and could not charge them.

At this time the remaining companies of the Second Kansas Cavalry came up, having passed the infantry upon hearing the firing, and soon after Captain Hopkins' Second Kansas (Trophy) Battery and the infantry made their appearance and reported.

The enemy having taken another position, with his artillery to protect his retreat, I ordered Captain Hopkins to drive him, which he did, assisted by a section of Rabb's Second Indiana Battery, under Sergeant Whicher. I then moved the column, for the purpose of getting an advantageous position upon the enemy's flank and rear, but was much retarded by hills, ravines, and brush. Soon, however, gaining the main road, the Third Brigade commenced the pursuit in earnest, taking position after position upon the hills overlooking and commanding the road through which the enemy were fleeing, thus keeping them lively until we reached the Boston Mountains, about 4 miles from the place of the first fight. Here, with battery placed upon a commanding hill, and well supported by a heavy force of cavalry in the wood, behind a cornfield and fence, the rebels made a determined stand, and seemed to have a hold from which they could not be driven.

I again dismounted the Second Kansas, and, assisted by Colonel [W. A.] Phillips, of the Second Brigade, and his Cherokees, together with Rabb's battery, the enemy were compelled to run, taking the road directly up the steep mountain side. Still he would place his guns and throw out heavy flanks of supporters, and still the Second Kansas, assisted by others and our mountain howitzers, would drive him.

While thus steadily forcing our way forward and the enemy back, the Eleventh Kansas Infantry made its appearance, and under the direction of its officers opened such a fire of musketry that the enemy hastened his retreat.

Thus we crossed the mountain, and, having entered the Cove Creek Valley, the enemy were charged by the Sixth Kansas Cavalry, of the First Brigade. Upon his making a determined stand, and for the time resisting successfully the cavalry, the Eleventh Kansas came up, as also did a section of Rabb's battery, under Lieutenant [W. W.] Haines, who had just placed his guns in a commanding position, and was ready to fire, when the enemy sent a flag of truce. I was ordered by you to meet it, which I did, and, in the *interim* which followed, night came on and hostilities ceased, I returning with my brigade to bivouac for the night.

I took with me in the morning Captain [A. P.] Russell and Company K, of the Second, and, passing over the ground occupied by the rebels, found them gone, and, burning a disabled gun carriage left by them, I returned to camp at this place, satisfied with the day's work.

Herewith I have the honor to transmit the reports of the various commanders of my brigade. Of the officers and men I am constrained to speak in the highest terms; all did their duty as soldiers.

W. F. CLOUD,
Colonel, Commanding Third Brigade.

Brigadier-General BLUNT,
Commanding Army of the Frontier.

ADDENDA.

Statement of killed and wounded at Cane Hill and upon Boston Mountains, November 28, *and in skirmishes to December* 15.

Command.	Killed.	Wounded.
2d Kansas Cavalry	1	8
11th Kansas	.....	8
1st Indian Home Guards	1	2
Rabb's [Indiana] battery	1	4
Total	3	22

No. 4.

Report of Maj. Albert C. Ellithorpe, First Indian Home Guards.

CANE HILL, ARK., *December* 1, 1862.

SIR: I have the honor to report that my regiment was engaged, during the battle of the 28th instant [ultimo], in a skirmishing fight over the hills and through the ravines and woods, a distance of about 4 miles. I found the men willing and eager to engage the enemy. All the company officers were prompt and at their posts. Lieutenants [A. F.] Bicking, [F.] Crafts, [F. J.] Fox, [S. C.] Hall, and [E. C.] Manning, proved themselves competent for the emergency. Adjutant [J. H.] Gillpatrick rendered efficient service throughout the day. I learn that 1 of our men only is killed and 2 slightly wounded.

I am, with respect, your obedient servant,

A. C. ELLITHORPE,
Major, Commanding.

Col. WILLIAM F. CLOUD,
Commanding Third Brigade.

No. 5.

Report of Lieut. Col. Owen A. Bassett, Second Kansas Cavalry.

HEADQUARTERS SECOND KANSAS VOLUNTEERS,
Boonsborough, Ark., December 2, 1862.

[SIR:] I have the honor to report that, on the evening of the 27th ultimo, I left Camp Babcock and marched in column, formed by the Third Brigade, in the place assigned, which was in the immediate rear of the Eleventh Kansas Infantry.

My command consisted of nine companies of cavalry: Company A, commanded by Lieutenant [J.] Johnston; Company C, by Captain [D. S.] Whittenhall; Company D, by Lieutenant [A.] Moore; Company E, by Captain [J.] Gardner; Company F, by Captain [H.] Cameron; Company G, by Captain [A. W.] Matthews; Company H, by Captain [A.] Gunther; Company I, by First Sergt. M. Enright, and Company K, by Captain [A. P.] Russell, numbering 337 enlisted men; one battery of light artillery (four pieces), the same captured by this regiment at Maysville on October 22, under command of Captain [H.] Hopkins, known as Company B, Second Kansas Volunteers, and one section of mountain howitzers, under command of Lieutenant [E. S.] Stover, Second Kansas Volunteers.

On the evening of the 27th, I went into camp 10 miles north of Cane Hill, and received orders to march next morning at 5 a. m.

Moved on the morning of the 28th, at 5 o'clock. I was ordered to send a portion of my force in advance, and accordingly I sent Companies C, I, and G to the head of the column, under command of Major [J. G.] Fisk, and with the rest of my regiment took the same position assigned to me the day previous, Captain Gunther having been detailed by yourself as field officer of the day, leaving Company H in command of Lieutenant Ballard.

About 10 a. m., Captain Whittenhall, at the head of the column as advance guard, surprised and captured 3 of the enemy's pickets and killed 1. Major Fisk hurried forward, and at the foot of the hill, about one-half mile north of Boonsborough, came upon a party of the enemy's cavalry drawn up in a lane leading to the village. He formed line, and Lieutenant Stover, coming up with his howitzers, opened upon them with good effect. The enemy was drawn up in force on a hill to the right front of Major Fisk's line, and with three pieces of artillery opened fire. Lieutenant Stover immediately turned his howitzers to bear upon them. Rabb's Second Indiana Battery coming up, Major Fisk moved a portion of his force to the rear, over the brow of the hill, dismounted it, and ordered the men to lie down and hold themselves as a support to Rabb's battery. The remainder he sent to reconnoiter the enemy's position. Just after making this disposition of his battalion, the major received a severe wound on the top of his head by a piece of shell, which tore away the top of his hat-crown and knocked him down. He recovered in a few minutes, and remained in command for a full hour afterward.

When the first shot was fired by the enemy, I was still in rear of the Eleventh Kansas Infantry, which had halted 2 miles back, but immediately passed that regiment by file to their right and left flanks, through timber and underbrush; brought up my men to the brow of the hill in rear of Major Fisk's position, where I found General Blunt, and, under his orders, I sent Captain [S. J.] Crawford, with Companies A and D, to occupy a hill to the right and front of Major Fisk's position.

At the same time, Captain Cameron, commanding Company F, was sent to a hill still farther to the right of the position occupied by Captain Crawford, and Captain Gardner, commanding Company E, to the right of the position taken by Captain Cameron. Lieutenant [D. E.] Ballard and Captain Russell, with their companies, remained on the hill to support Rabb's battery.

I rode over to where Captain Cameron was stationed, and discovered the enemy in full retreat from the timber on the hill, where they had made a stand, and sent word to General Blunt, communicating to him what I had discovered, and caused Companies A, C, D, F, G, and I to move forward to the front and right, and soon afterward, under direction of Colonel Cloud, skirmished through the timber the enemy had lately occupied; passed out on their trail to the top of the hill I had discovered them retreating over, and awaited there for Captain Hopkins' battery to come up, which, arriving soon after, opened fire on the retreating column, about three-fourths of a mile distant, and upon a section of the enemy's battery on a hill about 1 mile distant. With such precision was the round shot thrown from the gun handled by Corporal Sawyers that the enemy retreated with their pieces immediately.

Companies H and K, left in support of Rabb's battery, having been relieved by the Eleventh Kansas Infantry, came up to the support of Captain Hopkins' battery, under command of Major Fisk, whom I ordered to report to the surgeon to have his wound dressed, and, with the other companies under my command, moved forward to the right front over the chain of hills, where I remained for half an hour inactive.

General Blunt coming up, I moved forward to the town of Newberry, 1 mile south of Boonsborough, and there, under direction of Colonel Cloud, dashed down the road, across the valley to the heights opposite, and pressed the enemy's rear closely to the foot of the mountain, 5 miles from where the fight first commenced. Companies F, G, and I had, by some means, become separated from me in the woods. The enemy had made a stand, placing their artillery upon a high point, and stationed their cavalry at the foot of the hill. I sent Companies C, A, and D forward through the brush, under command of Captain Crawford, to drive back the cavalry, and a sharp skirmish took place, lasting for several minutes, when the enemy gave way and retreated up the hill, taking position behind his artillery. I here drew in my skirmishers, ordered them to mount and remain under cover. The enemy's artillery opening, Lieutenant Stover, having arrived, opened fire with his howitzers, and, the enemy soon afterward withdrawing his artillery, I started with my men up the hill. Having gained the point which the enemy had just abandoned, I dismounted my men, and ordered them to skirmish. At this time Captain Russell came up and took position on the right, and, with Companies C, D, A, and K, I moved forward to the second bench, when Company C returned to their horses and mounted. Captain Russell, commanding Company K, pressed forward in advance of everything else around the base of the rocky ledge, just below the summit, along which runs the main road, and Companies A and D pressed on up and over the summit, under my immediate command, and returned into the road about 1 mile from the foot of the hill. I halted to let the Eleventh and Thirteenth Kansas Infantry and Sixth Kansas Cavalry pass; collected my regiment, and moved forward about 2 miles farther into a field, and encamped for the night.

My loss during the day amounted to 1 killed and 4 wounded, my regiment maintaining the advance from the first opening of the fight, at 11

a. m., until 3.30 p. m., following the enemy's retreating column for a distance of about 6 miles. It is unnecessary for me to say more than this for the courage and bravery displayed by the men under my command. I could not discriminate if I desired.

I have the honor to be, very respectfully, your obedient servant,

OWEN A. BASSETT,
Lieutenant-Colonel, Commanding Second Kansas Volunteers.

Lieut. B. S. BASSETT,
A. A. A. G., Third Brig., First Div., Army of the Frontier.

No. 6.

Report of Capt. Henry Hopkins, Second Kansas Cavalry, commanding battery.

HEADQUARTERS HOPKINS' BATTERY,
Boonsborough, Ark., December 1, 1862.

SIR: I respectfully submit the following report of the part the battery under my command took in the engagement at Cane Hill, Ark., November 28, 1862:

In compliance with orders received November 28, 1862, the battery marched at 8 a. m. the following day, forming the rear of the column of the Second Kansas Cavalry. After a march of 20 miles south, in the direction of Cane Hill, Ark., I was ordered to bivouac, and move again at 5 o'clock the next morning.

Marching at the hour specified, in the direction of Cane Hill for 10 miles, the report of artillery was heard in the direction of the enemy. Moving as rapidly as the troops in front of me would permit, I was ordered to take position on an eminence, 1 mile northwest of the town. Finding that the enemy had changed their position farther south, I was ordered to occupy a point one-half mile to the front. From this position I proceeded to shell the woods below and in my front, where a body of the enemy's cavalry was moving. Immediately to the left a rebel battery was discovered posted on a high hill. I directed the fire of my guns upon it, dislodging and forcing it to retire. It appeared shortly afterward in the main road, passing through the town. Again changing the direction of fire, shell were thrown with evident effect, the enemy retreating behind the hills to the left of Boonsborough. I was ordered to move in that direction, and obeyed as rapidly as the nature of the ground would permit; but, owing to the steepness of the hills, could not take a position that would at all prove effectual in harassing the enemy in his retreat. First Lieut. John F. Aduddell commanded the right, and owing to the absence of Lieut. B. S. Bassett, who was acting assistant adjutant-general, Third Brigade, Sergeant McLain commanded the left section.

Considering the short period of time the battery has been in my possession, the officers and men show a good degree of proficiency as artillerists, and in this engagement their conduct is entitled to much praise.

Respectfully, your obedient servant,

H. HOPKINS,
Captain Second Kansas Cavalry, Commanding Battery.

Lieut. S. K. CROSS,
Acting Adjutant, Second Kansas Cavalry.

No. 7.

Report of Col. Thomas Ewing, jr., Eleventh Kansas Infantry.

CAMP CANE HILL, *Benton Co., Ark., December* 1, 1862.

COLONEL: In compliance with your order of this date, I submit the following report of the part taken by the Eleventh Regiment of Kansas Volunteers in the engagements of the 28th ultimo, commonly called in camp the battles of Cane Hill and Boston Mountains:

At 5 o'clock on the morning of that day we left bivouac, about 15 miles north of the scene of the first engagement. We marched rapidly until about 10 o'clock, halting then about fifteen minutes to rest, and to enable many who had fallen out of the ranks from fatigue to come up. Here we heard the booming of cannon, indicating that Rabb's battery (which, with four companies of the Second Kansas Cavalry, had hurried forward 4 or 5 miles in advance of us) was engaged with the enemy. We hastened on at quick step and double-quick, alternately—the left wing, under Major Plumb, passing down the hill to the battery, and the right forward to the hill north of and overlooking the town of Boonsborough; to which latter place Rabb's and Hopkins' batteries, accompanied by the left wing of my regiment, presently came. Here we remained in supporting distance of the batteries while they were engaged on the right, and Colonel [William] Weer's brigade on the left, in driving the enemy from the town and the hills adjacent to and south of it; thence, by order, we accompanied Rabb's battery through the fields and woods to Kidd's Mills, and thence, by the Fayetteville and Fort Smith road, to the foot of the east range of the Boston Mountains, about 5 miles from the point where the fight began. Here the battery was delayed in ascending the mountain, and we left it, and hurried to the summit, where a large part of the Third Indian and some of the Second Kansas were engaged with the enemy in a fire of musketry and howitzers. Forming there with the Indians a line of battle, varying from a quarter to a half a mile in extent, we advanced through the woods, joined by a part of a company of the Sixth Kansas, engaging in an irregular musketry fight with the enemy, who slowly retreated along the hill-sides and ravines upon and on both sides of the road. Here were killed Colonel [J. C.] Monroe, commanding Fagan's Texas [Arkansas] Cavalry, Captain Martin, of the Arkansas [Missouri] Cavalry, and others.

The engagement here lasted about an hour, when, the enemy drawing off out of sight and range, I collected and formed my regiment in a clearing on the left of the road, and was at once again ordered forward. Taking the road, we pushed on about 4 miles, to within supporting distance of the batteries and near the scene of the last engagement, where we were halted by order of General Blunt, and whence, after nightfall, we returned 6 miles to get our blankets, and bivoucked.

I take pleasure in saying that, although the regiment was never before under fire, there was no lack of spirit or courage evinced by any officer or private belonging to it. The march had been severe up to 11 o'clock, when we reached the field, and, being almost uninterrupted from that until 9 o'clock at night, it taxed beyond their power of endurance the strength of about one-third of the men, who fell out from time to time utterly exhausted. The entire march of my regiment that day was not less than 34 miles. We had no man killed; 4 were wounded.

I am, colonel, your obedient servant,

THOMAS EWING, JR.,
Colonel Eleventh Regiment Kansas Volunteers, Commanding.

Col. WILLIAM F. CLOUD, *Comdg. 3d Brig., 1st Div., Army Frontier.*

No. 8.

Report of Col. Charles A. Carroll, C. S. Army, commanding Arkansas Cavalry Brigade.

HEADQUARTERS ARKANSAS CAVALRY BRIGADE,
Camp near Dripping Springs, Ark., November 29, 1862.

CAPTAIN: In compliance with General Orders, No. —, of even date, I have the honor to make the following report of the conduct of the forces of my command in the engagement of the 28th instant; but in justice to my command beg leave to state that, having inspected the brigade on the 27th instant, I had only 200 effective men for duty and 317 non-effective men. The non-effective men were composed of the sick and men whose horses were in bad condition. Of the non-effective force, 60 men were on duty as pickets, picketing the roads from our encampment to the Line road west of us, and 100 men were detailed as escort for the trains of the division, which were ordered to the rear on the 27th instant, leaving me 389 men to represent my brigade, while the muster-rolls call for 1,700. With but few sick, the brigade is thus diminished by the condition of the horses, which are worn down, having been constantly on the move for six weeks, and for the want of forage and shoeing. Of the mountain howitzer battery attached to my brigade, and commanded by First Lieutenant Hughey, only one section was serviceable.

After being notified of the approach of the enemy, at 8 p. m. on the 27th instant, the men were kept under arms and the horses saddled until the opening of the enemy's artillery north of us, in the direction of Colonel Shelby's camp, on the morning of the 28th instant, at about 9 o'clock, when orders were received to move my command rapidly to the front. After moving about 1 mile, I received orders to place the battery on an eminence to the right, commanding the road leading north, with the two regiments in line of battle perpendicular to the road, supporting the battery, my own regiment on the right, under Lieutenant-Colonel Johnson, and Colonel [J. C.] Monroe's regiment on the left of the road. The eminence occupied by my battery was commanded by the heights north and northwest of us, from which points the artillery of the enemy were firing; and although they had the range of my battery, they were at too great a distance to be affected by our light metal. I was then ordered to the rear. After moving 1 mile, I was directed to move rapidly to the rear and select some good position. In a few minutes, however, further orders were received to continue moving to the rear until otherwise ordered. Having moved half a mile beyond the summit of the mountain on the Cane Hill and Cove Creek road, I received orders to halt and occupy a position. I countermarched the command beyond the summit of the mountain, and took position commanding the Cane Hill road, with the regiment under Lieutenant-Colonel Johnson supporting the battery, and Colonel Monroe's regiment 200 yards to the right of Lieutenant-Colonel Johnson's regiment. The fire of the enemy's artillery at this time was continuous and incessant on the rear of Colonel Shelby's command. I was ordered to throw out Colonel Monroe's regiment as skirmishers, but before the order could be obeyed I was ordered to move my command to the rear, and soon thereafter ordered to take command of all the forces in my advance, which separated me to some extent from my own brigade. Soon after passing the pinnacle of the mountain, Colonel Monroe, who was marching in rear of my regiment, received the enemy at short range, and retired, as previously directed

Such was the nature of the ground from the top of the mountain to Cove Creek, a distance of 1½ miles, that but few advantageous positions could be found. Just before reaching Cove Creek, Captain Stanley's company, of my regiment, was ordered to an eminence commanding the road on which the enemy were to travel, with orders to fire upon them with deliberation, and to retire immediately thereafter. After reaching Cove Creek, Captains Gordon and Carroll, with their respective companies, of my regiment, were directed to occupy an eminence on the right of the road. The captains fired upon the enemy and retired, as directed. From this point on down Cove Creek, I selected suitable positions and placed detachments of my regiment and Colonel Shelby's brigade. At a point 2 miles below the junction of the Cane Hill and Cove Creek roads, I ordered Lieutenant-Colonel Johnson, with five companies of my regiment and about 200 men of Colonel Thompson's regiment, Colonel Shelby's brigade, to an eminence immediately over the road, with instructions to let the enemy's advance pass them before firing. Immediately in rear of this point, Colonel Monroe formed with 86 men in the valley below. At this time the enemy was pushing the rear with great energy, and made it necessary for the companies left ambushed to receive them to retire very rapidly after firing. The captains of my own command, who have reported to me, state that they obeyed orders, receiving the enemy at close distance, the men behaving, almost without exception, with great bravery. When the rear retired past the position occupied by Lieutenant-Colonel Johnson and Colonel Thompson, they were followed very closely by a detachment of the enemy's cavalry, a much larger number halting just before reaching the position above referred to. A lieutenant-colonel of the enemy's force was severely wounded by one of the volleys fired by the men under Lieutenant-Colonel Johnson. At this time the confusion below the position above referred to of our retiring men was disgraceful, and every effort made by officers to halt them futile, the cry extending down the line that our friends had gorged the road and were being sabered mercilessly by the enemy. Just then the roar of shot-guns from the eminence occupied by Lieutenant-Colonel Johnson and Colonel [G. W.] Thompson threw the enemy's advance in confusion, when they were immediately charged by Colonel Monroe, and after the third effort driven for the first time during the day, which gave time for collecting and forming the scattered men, hitherto rapidly moving to the rear. The enemy here concluded, notwithstanding the superior weight and quantity of their artillery and their superior force, outnumbering ours more than ten to one, to risk nothing against the positions of which we were availing ourselves, and at once retired about sunset.

The conduct of the officers and men of my command throughout the entire day, and almost without an exception, evidenced entire coolness and determined bravery, as did the officers and men of Colonel Shelby's brigade, of whom I assumed command and placed in position. I would be glad to speak of them more particularly if my personal acquaintance with these officers was such as to do so without a report from them.

I will take occasion to remark that the retiring fight, lasting from 9 o'clock in the morning until sunset, over a rugged and narrow road, with but a scanty supply of ammunition, pursued by a greatly superior force, moving from position to position with an astonishing rapidity, was well calculated to have confused, and, indeed, demoralized men well drilled and disciplined, and it is, indeed, astonishing that troops without drill should have evinced a nerve so steady, a courage so cool. In moving the battery from the first position taken in the morning, the carriage of one of the pieces was so badly broken as to render impossible the moving of it by horses. Notwithstanding the gun thus dismantled was under a galling fire of the enemy's artillery, shells bursting by the minute around it, the cannoneers dismounted, and, under the direction of their officers, bore the piece, crippled but triumphant, to the rear. Just before reaching the second position taken by my brigade, as alluded to in the above report, Captain Shoup, the commander, and Lieutenant Halliburton, of the battery, met me. The captain at once took command of his company. There was now but one serviceable gun of the four-gun battery, which was placed in position frequently during the day with a skill and energy deserving a more substantial battery. After passing some little distance beyond the top of the mountain, this gun was placed in position and opened on the enemy. Notwithstanding the energy with which it was handled, it was dismantled by the enemy's artillery, the carriage being broken to pieces by their heavy shot. This casualty was followed by a cavalry charge made with great energy. The officers, unwilling to leave any trophy in the hands of their country's enemy, took the gun from the shattered carriage and bore this, too, to the rear. I cannot but commend the pride and bravery of the men here evidenced.

The loss the brigade sustained is as follows: Colonel Monroe's regiment, 3 men slightly wounded, 4 horses killed and 1 wounded; Lieutenant-Colonel Johnston's regiment, 5 men were wounded and 2 men are missing; Captain Shoup's battery, 3 men were wounded and 4 horses killed.

I am, captain, very respectfully, your obedient servant,

CHAS. A. CARROLL,
Colonel, Commanding Brigade.

Capt. E. G. WILLIAMS,
Asst. Adjt. Gen., 4th Div., 1st Corps, Trans-Mississippi Army.

No. 9.

Report of Col. Joseph O. Shelby, commanding Fourth Missouri Cavalry Brigade (Confederate).

CAMP DRIPPING SPRINGS, ARK., *December* 1, 1862.

CAPTAIN: Being called upon for a report of the action of this brigade in the Cane Hill fight, I inclose the same, as follows:

My brigade consisted of the following regiments: First, commanded by [B. F.] Gordon; Second, by [B. G.] Jeans; Third, by [G. W.] Thompson; also Elliott's scouts and Quantrill's famous company, in command of First Lieutenant Gregg. Having had due notice (eighteen hours previous) by the general commanding that the enemy were advancing, we endeavored to be on the alert, but I must confess (though it may reflect somewhat upon myself) that the enemy, by his skillful management, fell upon me sooner than I would have desired, considering that a portion of our division was encamped some distance in my rear and I had but little time to give them the notice required; yet I had sufficient time to place my men in their proper positions and await the coming of the hated foe.

Between the hours of 9 and 10 a. m., Friday, November 28, he rapidly advanced and unlimbered his guns, and sent his iron missiles in search of the "rebels." We had expected him (the enemy) to advance either on the Cincinnati or Fayetteville road, our position covering both. Bledsoe, in command of the artillery, consisting of two iron 6-pounders, had his guns so arranged as to cover each road; that is, one piece bearing on the Cincinnati road and the other covering the Fayetteville road. Having notice of the approach of the enemy on the Fayetteville road, I ordered all the regiments to mount and form, knowing that their advance on that route gave them an advantage over my position which could not be overlooked. If they forced a passage down the main road, we would be cut off from assistance in the rear and be deprived of the Cane Hill and Cove Creek road, thereby preventing our passage over the mountain, the route our train had taken. The gun covering the Fayetteville road occupied an elevated position, the hill descending to its foot about 300 yards. Here, waiting for the enemy to advance, I took my position at the gun, which was so masked as not to be seen by him. Thus waiting, and in no little suspense, he (the enemy) soon showed himself with a four-gun battery, supported by infantry close up. He opened rapidly, but the smoke of his guns had not cleared away before Bledsoe's gun responded and continued to respond, showing to the naked eye that it was sending death in every shot to our heartless invaders. I soon discovered that they were not disposed to flank us on our right, and for the protection of our batteries I ordered all the regiments to dismount, placing Gordon on our right, Jeans in the center, and Thompson on our extreme left. By this time I had received satisfactory information from the Cincinnati road, which convinced me that there was no move by the enemy on that route, and I immediately ordered Captain Bledsoe to move the gun that covered the Cincinnati road to a point which secured a cross-fire on the batteries playing upon us. I should mention here that by this time they had at least twelve guns bearing upon our position, and then the artillery fight commenced in earnest, lasting at this point about one hour and a half.

During this time Gordon, Jeans, and Thompson lay close up to the guns, anxiously awaiting the charge of the invader, while [Maj. B.] Elliott's scouts and Quantrill's company sat quietly on their steeds awaiting his further coming; but as long as the enemy could confine himself to the artillery fight at long range he was content, but in the mean time General Marmaduke, after surveying the position, and I having notified him that a heavy body of infantry was endeavoring to flank me on the left, I received orders to fall back, which I did, by ordering Colonel Jeans to mount his men and directing Bledsoe to withdraw his piece, at the same time ordering Lieutenant [R. A.] Collins, who was in charge of the piece that commanded the Fayetteville road, to keep a steady fire on the enemy until I could mount and form all my regiments, which he did, pouring a murderous fire upon them, driving them at one time back from their guns. I will here mention that no man ever evinced more courage or executed his orders more cheerfully or promptly than Lieutenant Collins on that occasion. Captain Bledsoe, Sergeant Bledsoe, Lieutenants Connor and Anson, and, in fact, all of this battery, have the thanks of the entire brigade for their gallant conduct upon this trying occasion. I then ordered Colonel Thompson to mount his regiment, which was done in the best order, moving the piece under Bledsoe by the right to the rear; Thompson's regiment followed, after which came Jeans, the Collins gun following, covered by Gordon's regiment. I could not, if disposed, speak too highly of the conduct of the officers and men of this brigade in making the above move, it being executed under a terrible fire; but others witnessed it, and say men never gave way in better order. After falling back about half a mile, we found the remainder of this division formed and ready to protect us. By order of the general we took position on the hill, bringing our guns in battery back of the village of Newburg, there awaiting and expecting to witness brilliant charges from the foe; but, as before, he depended on dislodging us with his long-range guns. Here the naked eye could see General Blunt's columns of cavalry and infantry pouring over the hills in our front, and advancing slowly and cautiously to the attack. It was a splendid sight—flaunting banners, serried ranks, as the long lines came gleaming on;

> Ere yet the life-blood, warm and wet,
> Had dimmed a glistening bayonet!

Being satisfied that with our small force and short-range guns we could not cope with him, we withdrew to the Boston Mountains, where we placed one of Bledsoe's guns in position, and there awaited his advance. We were not allowed to tarry long, for they soon reached the foot of the mountain, commenced placing their batteries in position, and opened fire. Our gunners were eager and ready. The work again commenced, and at short range. We then exhausted all of our artillery ammunition, and from that cause had to push our guns ahead, which we did, and did safely. I had ordered Lieutenant Gregg at that point over to the right, but finding the enemy were making a move still to his right, I withdrew him, and had him to form back on the main road to await further orders. Immediately on top of the mountain I had a part of Colonel Thompson's command, under Major [M. W.] Smith, formed to receive the enemy, and a little to the rear of Smith, on the right, I had one company of Elliott's scouts, commanded by Captain Martin. Smith and Martin calmly awaited the coming of the enemy, and as they came charging up the hill in solid columns, they poured a deadly fire on them, which sent them staggering down the mountain. By this time I had other detachments formed but a short distance in the rear (Smith and Martin falling back and loading), who fired on them with much effect, being in easy gun-shot. Martin, having his men ready and formed, delivered once more a terrible fire, but in so doing this brigade suffered a terrible loss in the death of the gallant and heroic Martin. He fell, as he lived, fighting for his home and fireside, "with his back to the field and his feet to the foe."

> Ah! soldier, to your honored rest,
> Your truth and valor bearing;
> The bravest are the tenderest,
> The loving are the daring!

The enemy pushing us about this time with all the force he could urge on, and the ground being of such a nature as not to allow us to form by regiments or squadrons, I was compelled to detach companies and form them on both sides of the road, receive and fire on the enemy, load, form, and reform, using in that manner every company in the regiments of this brigade. We fought them in this manner about three hours, never once allowing them to reach our rear in sufficient numbers to capture any of the men.

I will likewise mention that [Col. Emmett] MacDonald's men were at the same time equally as active in their efforts to retard the movements of the enemy. I noticed also with much pleasure the gallant conduct of Captain Shoup, who commanded his little howitzer well and delivered his fire with great coolness, effect, and precision. With this battery was a brave and fighting driver, who was conspicuous for his daring and the readiness with which he obeyed all orders.

Captains Webb and Snook, of Colonel Jeans' regiment, were both wounded while gallantly leading their men on the enemy.

I cannot close this report without speaking in high terms of the coolness and daring of Lieutenant McCoy, of your escort, and Lieutenant Conkling, of Thompson's regiment. They, with the prestige and glory of Shiloh still hanging to their garments, were in the thickest of the fight.

Our men fought them well, and while the enemy evinced great desperation, our command showed a determination and coolness that their officers have reason to be proud of, contending, as they were, with vastly superior numbers, the sight of which did not in the least discourage them.

About sunset the enemy made the last and desperate charge, led by Colonel [L. R.] Jewell, in person. Colonels Thompson's and Jeans' men received him with a fire the effect of which will ever be remembered by Jewell's regiment. In that charge Jewell fell, mortally wounded. Upon the fall of Jewell, Colonel Gordon, with a portion of his regiment and a portion of Colonel Jeans', under Captain Jarrett, charged the Federals hotly and fiercely, sending them back in perfect confusion, and thus ending a hard day's fight.

It is not necessary for me to state the casualties of this brigade, as they have already been reported to you; but I will here mention that the officers and men of this brigade executed promptly, cheerfully, and willingly every order that was given; were easily rallied; held all positions assigned them, and fell back when ordered, only to form and reform and fire again.

Elliott and his scouts were to be seen performing their duty on all occasions.

Lieutenant Gregg, of Quantrill's command, and his company had been held in reserve by me during the greater part of the fight, so that when suitable ground was obtained a grand charge might be made. The position was taken, this stone-wall company formed, Gregg at its head, the light of the battle on his face, but, fortunately or unfortunately, the enemy checked pursuit just before coming to where they crouched like lions in their lairs.

I will also here speak favorably of Captains Brewster (my adjutant), Nichols, Edwards, St. Clair, and Page, for the service they performed relative to their various duties.

Many others I could call your attention to for their gallant conduct, among whom are Philip Wilder, of your own escort; Lieutenants Moorman and Buffington, of Gordon's; but as the general commanding was everywhere upon the field, he saw as much, perhaps more than myself.

I close this report with the proud satisfaction of knowing that we did our duty, and are anxious once more to meet the enemy in a fair field and an open fight.

Respectfully,

JO. O. SHELBY,
Colonel, Commanding Missouri Cavalry Brigade.

Capt. E. G. WILLIAMS,
Asst. Adjt. Gen., Fourth Division, First Army Corps.

No. 10.

Report of Col. Emmett MacDonald, Missouri Cavalry.

CAMP DRIPPING SPRINGS, ARK.,
November 30, 1862.

CAPTAIN: I have the honor to submit the following report of the part my command took in the late battle in the Boston Mountains:

On November 28, I received orders about 9 o'clock in the morning to prepare for action, as the enemy was engaging Colonel Shelby's command about 1 mile in my advance. I at once moved forward at a rapid pace with my command, and took position northwest of Kidd's Mill, near Cane Hill. My position being much exposed, the enemy poured a heavy volley of grape upon my ranks, while another battery threw shell in my rear and front continually, but without killing or wounding a man. In the mean time Colonel Shelby had fallen back with his brigade. At this time I received orders to fall back and form south of Boonsborough, where Colonels Shelby and [C. A.] Carroll were posted. The enemy appeared at this point in great force. A large body of infantry moved rapidly upon our left and front. Here a general engagement seemed imminent; but the enemy appeared in such large force I was again ordered to fall back, which I did, fighting the enemy at every point, whether the position suited or not, until, reaching the mountain, a halt was ordered for one desperate resistance. I took position upon the right; Colonel Shelby the center. I immediately advanced upon the enemy, when a sharp engagement ensued. Our firing was so constant and well directed that he seemed completely checked; but long lines of infantry and cavalry again appeared, re-enforcing him, until it seemed that all Yankeedom had turned out. Feeling confident that my men would not flinch, I determined to meet them, while Colonel Shelby was preparing to receive them in the center. Here they charged us again and again, but they were driven back until our rear moved farther up the mountains. In this way we fought them over the mountains and 3 miles down Cove Creek, fighting at one point, falling back, forming, and fighting again. Their number being five or six times greater than ours, and they knowing the fact, they pressed us hard, and finally charged us with drawn sabers, when a hand-to-hand conflict ensued. So very few of them were left that charged, they finally drew off their forces and retreated back toward the mountain.

During the entire engagement Companies A and B fought nobly. No company of officers and men ever fought better. Captain Harrison, commanding Company A, and First Lieutenant Yonts, Company B, and the lieutenants in both companies, deserve much praise.

Privates and officers acted well throughout the entire engagement.

I lost in the engagement the following:

Command.	Killed.	Wounded.	Missing.
Company A:			
Officers	......	1	......
Privates	4	6	......
Company B:			
Officers	......	2	......
Non-commissioned officers	......	1	1
Privates	1	2	3
Company C:			
Privates	......	2	......
Company D:			
Non-commissioned officers	......	2	......
Privates	......	1	......
Total	5	17	4

Respectfully,

EMMETT MACDONALD,
Colonel, Commanding Missouri Cavalry.

F. B. DAVIDSON, *Adjutant.*

NOVEMBER 30–DECEMBER 6, 1862.—Expedition from Rolla to the Ozark Mountains, Mo., and skirmishes.

Report of Col. John M. Glover, Third Missouri Cavalry.

HEADQUARTERS ROLLA DISTRICT,
Rolla, Mo., December 8, 1862.

SIR: I have the honor to report that, having heard of several hundred rebels supposed to be encamped on the headwaters of the Current River, on the 30th ultimo, with parts of Companies A and B, Third Missouri Cavalry, and part of Company H, Ninth Missouri Cavalry, Captains [James T.] Howland, [Albert D.] Glover, and [John] Ing in command, consisting of 130 men (being all the force that could be spared from here at the time), I proceeded in quest of the enemy.

On the 2d instant had a collision with a light force of the enemy in the gorges of the Ozark. The impetuosity of my officers and men soon dispersed them in the mountains, killing 4 and capturing 2, with 4 horses. We marched 200 miles in seven days, finding no considerable force, having not a man injured in my command. I returned to these headquarters on the 6th instant.

Your obedient servant,

J. M. GLOVER,
Colonel, Commanding District.

Maj. H. Z. CURTIS,
Assistant Adjutant-General.

DECEMBER 4–6, 1862.—Operations about Cane Hill, and skirmish (December 6) at Reed's Mountain, Ark.

REPORTS.*

No. 1.—Brig. Gen. James G. Blunt, U. S. Army, commanding Army of the Frontier.
No. 2.—Lieut. Col. Owen A. Bassett, Second Kansas Cavalry.
No. 3.—Capt. Amaziah Moore, Second Kansas Cavalry, of skirmish at Reed's Mountain.
No. 4.—Capt. Joel Huntoon, Eleventh Kansas Infantry, of skirmish at Reed's Mountain.

No. 1.

Report of Brig. Gen. James G. Blunt, U. S. Army, commanding Army of the Frontier.

CANE HILL, ARK., *December* 6, 1862.

GENERAL: The enemy (25,000 strong) yesterday attempted to force my position, but the advance was driven back into the mountains. This morning they made an attack upon my outposts upon two roads, driving in my pickets upon one of them about 3 miles, who, upon being re-enforced, again drove the enemy back. It is my opinion that the demonstrations this morning were to cover their retreat, as they were felling timber during all of that night, possibly to obstruct the road and prevent my artillery and cavalry following them. I have been holding

* See also battle of Prairie Grove, December 7, 1862, pp. 67-158 (reports of Blunt, Cloud, Hindman, Marmaduke, Shelby, and Monroe).

them in check four days, determined to hold my position until re-enforcements could arrive. General Herron's advance cavalry will reach here to-night, and expect his whole command to reach me to-morrow night. Can you inform me what rebel forces there are defending Little Rock, and if any Federal forces are making a demonstration in that direction? It is important that I should have the information, to govern my future movements.

JAS. G. BLUNT,
Brigadier-General.

Maj. Gen. SAMUEL R. CURTIS.

No. 2.

Report of Lieut. Col. Owen A. Bassett, Second Kansas Cavalry.

HEADQUARTERS SECOND KANSAS VOLUNTEERS,
In the Field, December 10, 1862.

SIR: I have the honor to report that, in obedience to instructions received from yourself, I detailed a scouting party from my regiment under command of Captain [A. P.] Russell, consisting of Companies A, D, and I, 10 men from Company C, 10 from Company E, and 10 from Company F, numbering 147 men.

Captain Russell left camp with this force at about 4 p. m. on the 4th instant, and the following is his report to me:

CAMP OF THE SECOND REGIMENT KANSAS VOLUNTEERS,
Cane Hill, Ark., December 5, 1862.

Lieut. S. K. CROSS,
Acting Regimental Adjutant:

I have the honor to report that, pursuant to orders received on the afternoon of the 4th instant, with a detachment of 147 men from the Second Kansas Volunteers, I left camp to reconnoiter, and, if possible, to discover the position and movements of the enemy. About 2 miles from camp I sent Lieutenant [H. L.] Moore with about 60 men (Companies A and D) down what is known as the Mount Air road, while I proceeded with the remainder of the party in the direction of the Cove Creek road. I came into the Cove Creek road at Price's old headquarters, 9 miles southeast of camp, where our advance pickets are posted, and, after following this road about 6 miles, the advance discovered a fire, supposed to be that of the enemy's pickets. After reconnoitering, I became satisfied that it was either a very strong picket or the advance of the main force of the enemy, and concluded to wait until daylight before proceeding any farther. I posted a picket, and, with the remainder of my men, fell back half a mile and formed line in a field. In this position, every man standing by his horse, I remained until the morning of the 5th, when just before sunrise my picket was fired on by the enemy, and at once retired. I then sent forward about 30 men dismounted, as skirmishers, under charge of Lieutenant [J. M.] Mentzer, holding the others mounted in line as reserve. A brisk skirmish ensued, lasting for several minutes, when, seeing a movement made to flank me, I withdrew the skirmishers and fell back about 4 miles, where I again formed line and remained nearly two hours. Seeing nothing further of the enemy, I returned to camp, reaching it about 3 p. m.

Respectfully,

AVRA P. RUSSELL,
Captain, Commanding Detachment.

Lieutenant Moore returned to camp about 3 a. m. on the 5th instant, and reported to me that he proceeded down the mountain road to within a short distance of the junction with the Cove Creek road, where he expected to rejoin Captain Russell, when he discovered the enemy's camp fire, ranged up and down the creek valley, as he estimated, for a distance of 2½ or 3 miles, and reconnoitered their camp, driving in their pickets from the south.

At daylight on the morning of the 5th, I sent Lieutenant [B. B.] Mitchell with Company K to re-enforce the pickets at Price's old headquarters, desiring him if necessary to support Captain Russell, and about 8 a m., by your order, started with the remainder of my men to re-enforce Captain Russell. Having proceeded about 7 miles, I met him upon the mountain, returning, when he stated to me the substance of his report. Considering it unnecessary at that time to proceed any farther, I sent Captain [A. W.] Matthews to re-enforce the pickets and sent 20 men from Company E to report to Lieutenant Mitchell, ordering him to scout eastwardly on the Wire road, and returned with the rest of my men to where you had the Third Brigade drawn up in line of battle.

About 12 m. I ordered Captain [J.] Gardner to take Company C, under command of Lieutenant [W. M.] Hook, and post a picket east of Price's old headquarters, on the Wire road.

About sunset of that day, I received word from Captain Gardner that he found it impracticable to station a picket on the Wire road, from the fact that the enemy were occupying it with their scouting parties, and had accordingly re-enforced Captain Matthews and sent in the old picket of the night before.

At 9 p. m. of the same day, Lieutenant Mitchell returned to camp, reporting that he had been on the Wire road; met the enemy's scouting parties, and remained at Hawkeye until dark.

About 6 a. m. next morning, the enemy attacked the picket under Captain Gardner, and the following is his report to me:

CAMP OF THE SECOND REGIMENT KANSAS VOLUNTEERS,
Boonsborough, Ark., December 6, 1862.

Lieut. S. K. CROSS,
Acting Regimental Adjutant:

I have the honor to report that on the afternoon of the 5th instant I re-enforced Captain Matthews, who commanded the picket at Price's old headquarters, at the junction of the Cove Creek and Cane Hill roads. Having sent in the old pickets, my force consisted of Company G, commanded by Captain Matthews, and Company C, by Lieutenant Hook.

About 6 a. m. this morning, the enemy advanced with considerable force, attacking me in front and on both flanks, bringing my men under a very heavy fire. I retired slowly, keeping up a skirmishing fire for 2 miles, when I formed line and drove the enemy back. I maintained this position for half an hour or more, and then retired to the foot of the mountain, and awaited the arrival of re-enforcements.

Captain Matthews lost 1 man, Corpl. John Dower, killed, and Private Thomas Martin, of Company C, received a severe wound in the arm.

Respectfully,

JOHN GARDNER,
Captain, Commanding Pickets.

At 6 a. m., in obedience to your instructions, I sent Captain [H.] Cameron and Lieutenant [S. K.] Cross, with 50 men, and Lieutenant [E. S.] Stover, with his howitzers, to re-enforce the pickets, and they joined Captain Gardner soon after he had retired to the foot of the mountain, and started with the rest of my mounted force about sunrise for the same purpose.

Arriving within half a mile of the foot of the mountain, I formed the First Battalion, under command of Captain [S. J.] Crawford, in line of battle, and formed the Second Battalion in line half a mile to the rear, and remained in this position until 11 a. m., awaiting the approach of the enemy, who was occupying the mountain about three-quarters of a mile in advance of Captain Crawford. The road up the mountain side is very steep, and near the summit runs a ledge of rocks.

Having received re-enforcements of about 100 Indians, under command of Lieutenant [A. F.] Bicking, I sent him to reconnoiter on my left flank, and at the same time moved the First Battalion forward to the foot of the mountain, and the Second Battalion to the ground previously occupied by the First, and in this position remained until about 2 p. m., at which time you came up, and, under your direction, Companies A and C were dismounted and sent as skirmishers up this side of the mountain, under command of Captain Crawford. They proceeded as far as the ledge of rocks, exchanging but a few shots with the enemy, who retired at their approach.

Colonel [Thomas] Ewing, [jr.,] Eleventh Kansas Infantry, came up with four companies of his regiment, and he sent Company H, under Captain [J.] Huntoon, up the mountain to the ledge of rocks where they were concealed, and a few skirmishers were thrown forward to draw the advance of the enemy into ambush. Failing in this, Companies A and C were withdrawn and mounted.

Colonel Ewing and yourself returned with three companies of the infantry to the main line. I then ordered Captain Gunther to take command of Companies E and I, as a picket for the night, and he posted 6 men at the ledge of rocks, posting his reserve at the foot of the mountain. Captain Huntoon then withdrew his company and stationed it in the rear of the reserve picket, and soon afterward the outpost discovered the enemy approaching in force, and, coming under a severe fire, they retired slowly. Captain Gunther went immediately forward with his reserve to their support, and reoccupied the ledge of rocks. Soon afterward I sent Captain Huntoon forward with his company to re-enforce Captain [A.] Gunther, and sent Companies A and D forward, dismounted, under command of Captain Crawford, instructing him to hold the ground, if possible. Brisk firing was opened on both sides.

The enemy, with a regiment of cavalry, charged upon our lines, but, our men reserving their fire until they advanced within 20 yards from their protected position, then poured in a well-directed volley, throwing the enemy's line in confusion, driving them back. The enemy approached again, but with more caution, and the fight became general along the entire line, lasting for more than three-quarters of an hour. The enemy was driven back, our men firing the last shot. The superior force of the enemy, and the demonstrations made by them upon our flanks, compelled Captain Crawford to retire to the foot of the hill. By this time it being dusk, and the enemy not advancing, Captain Gunther posted his pickets at the foot of the hill, and soon afterward Major [P. B.] Plumb re-enforced me with five companies of the Eleventh Kansas Infantry, occupying the ground where I had my First Battalion stationed in the forenoon. About 9 p. m. I ordered Captain Moore, with Companies F and H, to re-enforce Captain Gunther's picket.

I stationed Companies K and D near Major Plumb's position, and Companies C and G at the junction of the mountain road with the Cane Hill and Cove Creek road, and sent Company A to reconnoiter down the mountain road, where they remained until morning. At sunrise the next morning, Companies C, D, and G came forward to the advance, and firing again commenced between the pickets. I sent Captain Gunther, with 20 men, upon a high point to my right, to overlook and discover the movement of the enemy. At 9 o'clock he reported that the enemy had withdrawn his force toward Cove Creek, which he estimated at one regiment of cavalry and two regiments of infantry. I immediately sent forward skirmishers, who soon reported that the enemy's column had retired. I then sent Lieutenant-Colonel [S. H.] Wattles, who had re-enforced me with 200 Indians, up to the valley to my left, and ordered Major Plumb, with his infantry, and Lieutenant Stover, with his howitzers, to report to you. I sent Captain Cameron, with his company, to reconnoiter the mountains to my left, and prepared to pursue the enemy with my cavalry, when I received orders from you to march toward Fayetteville, on the road by way of Ross' Mill, as rear guard to the column which was then moving in that direction.

My loss in the action of the night of the 6th was Privates Albert Payne, of Company A, and Sylvanus Heberling, of Company I, both severely wounded. Captain Huntoon had [several men] wounded; names unknown.

I have since ascertained, from officers and soldiers of the rebel army, that the force sent up there to attack me that night consisted of one regiment of cavalry, under Colonel Shelby, two regiments of infantry, one under command of Colonel Hunter and the other under command of ——— ———, and Tilden's battery, the whole under command of Brigadier-General Frost; but meeting, as they did, with such unexpected and well-timed resistance, did not attempt to follow us.

The rebel loss was 10 killed and 27 wounded.

During the night of the 6th the wheels of the enemy's battery were muffled, and it was taken back to Cove Creek.

I have been thus explicit in detailing the events of nearly three days from the fact that it has been definitely ascertained, since the occurrence of the same, that it was a part of the enemy's plan to divide his force at Price's old headquarters, sending one part up, through Cane Hill, to attack this division of the army and drive it back, and to send the rest up the Cove Creek road to the rear, to intercept and cut off retreat, and, also, because it required extreme vigilance and watchfulness on the part of the officers and men, testing their courage and bravery, their willingness to endure fatigue, and their skill in checking the advance of a foe.

Captain Huntoon, with his company (H, Eleventh Kansas Infantry), behaved in an admirable manner, standing firm and unflinching, though for the first time under fire. To Captain [A.] Moore, who was left in command of the advance during the night, should be awarded more than ordinary praise for his vigilance in the discharge of his duty. To D. B. Smith, esq., of Leavenworth, I tender my acknowledgments for valuable services and gallant conduct as volunteer aide during the 6th and 7th instant. To the officers and soldiers who were with me during the various skirmishes and maneuvers here recounted, my thanks are tendered.

As an appropriate designation for the affair on the evening of the 6th, I most respectfully suggest "The action of Reed's Mountain."

I have the honor to be, very respectfully, your obedient servant,

OWEN A. BASSETT,
Lieutenant-Colonel, Commanding.

Col. WILLIAM F. CLOUD,
Commanding Third Brigade, First Division.

No. 3.

Report of Capt. Amaziah Moore, Second Kansas Cavalry, of skirmish at Reed's Mountain.

CAMP NEAR CANE HILL, ARK., *December* 11, 1862.

COLONEL: The picket guard, commanded by Captain [A.] Gunther, composed of detachments from Companies I and C, having been attacked by the enemy with a force of cavalry, I ordered Captain [J.] Huntoon to re-enforce the guard with Company H, of the Eleventh Regiment. The guard was posted upon a rocky eminence on the Cove Creek road, about 3 miles from this encampment.

I formed my line across the road, below the bluff, concealing my men as much as the nature of the ground would permit from the view of the enemy. A desultory fire had for some time been kept up by Captain [A.] Gunther, who had been obliged to abandon his ground, although gallantly contested.

A forward movement soon regained the ground we had lost, and drove the enemy back, but he immediately returned and attacked us with great fury. He was received with a vigorous fire, the men loading and firing rapidly and with great steadiness. The enemy, failing to drive me from my position, charged gallantly up to my line, but was repulsed with considerable loss. Falling back beyond the reach of our pieces, he rallied a second time and came down upon the line in splendid style, discharging his pieces at full speed. During this impetuous charge a part of my force fell back, but were soon rallied, and held the ground against the enemy.

In the mean time, having sent for re-enforcements, Captain and Acting Major [S. J.] Crawford came forward with Companies A and D, under command of Lieutenants [J.] Johnston and [H. L.] Moore, and formed upon the right. It now became evident that the enemy had been re-enforced, and was preparing for another desperate charge. Infantry were seen moving down upon the right flank, and shots were fired from the ravine upon the left. Nevertheless, the line remained firm, and repulsed the enemy's charge most gallantly. The enemy having effected a flank movement, a change of position became necessary, which was accomplished in good order and without loss.

The enemy's loss has since been ascertained to be 21 killed and wounded, and 12 horses dead upon the field. My loss is 4 wounded, 1 severely.

I take this occasion to speak in the highest terms of the bravery and good conduct of Captain Huntoon, of the Eleventh Regiment, and of Captain Gunther, of the Second Regiment. The men, with scarcely an exception, fought gallantly, and many instances of great personal daring were observed.

Very respectfully, &c.,

A. MOORE,
Captain, and Field Officer of the Day.

Col. WILLIAM F. CLOUD,
Commanding Third Brigade.

No. 4.

Report of Capt. Joel Huntoon, Eleventh Kansas Infantry, of skirmish at Reed's Mountain.

On the morning of the 6th of December, 1862, Company H, of the Eleventh Kansas Infantry, marched with a detachment of that regiment from line of battle, near Cane Hill, Ark., to the foot of the Boston Mountains, at which place Company H was ordered to relieve the advance, stationed near the top of the mountain, which was composed of a detachment of the Second Kansas Cavalry. The company remained at this station until about 12 o'clock, when we were ordered to withdraw to the foot of the mountain.

Soon after, the advance of the enemy appeared in sight, on the brow of the mountain, and the company was again ordered forward. Having deployed in line of skirmishers, we advanced and drove the enemy beyond the old advance position, when, the enemy appearing in force, we retired to the point we had occupied in the morning, and formed, being protected by a ledge of rocks, where we repulsed the advancing enemy, who retreated out of range of our guns and formed with a large force.

Captain [S. J.] Crawford, of the Second Kansas Cavalry, at this time came up with a detachment of his regiment, and assumed command. A second charge was now made by the enemy, but was repulsed with loss.

The enemy being again re-enforced, a third charge was made, with the determination to carry the position, but they were driven back with heavy loss.

The superior force of the enemy enabled them to outflank our small advance, which they were doing, when Captain Crawford ordered the advance to retire to the foot of the mountain. Company H was ordered to guard a road coming down the mountain, where it remained during the night of the 6th. On the morning of the 7th, it was ordered to join the regiment *en route* for the battle-field of Prairie Grove.

This was the first time that Company H was under heavy fire, and I feel it my duty, as well as a pleasure, to say that every man stood up to the work faithfully, and did his duty as became an American citizen fighting the enemies of his country.

JOEL HUNTOON,
Captain Company H, Eleventh Kansas Volunteer Infantry.

DECEMBER 4-12, 1862.—Operations in the Cherokee Country, Indian Territory.

Report of Col. Stand Watie, First Cherokee Regiment.

SCULLYVILLE, C. N., *December* 19, 1862.

GENERAL: On Wednesday morning, December 3, I received an order from you inclosing instructions from Major-General Hindman to proceed to the neighborhood of Evansville, and, if possible, open a communication with the pickets of the Confederate army on the Line road. I therefore notified you, by express, that I would be at Peyton's Spring, 4 or 5 miles from Evansville, on Friday evening (5th), to meet with the detachment from Fort Coffee.

Thursday evening (4th), I took a line of march with about 400 men for the place designated; halted at Dwight Mission until daylight.

In the morning sent out scouts on each side of the road; met with Pin Indians in small parties at various places on that day, killing several. Arrived at Peyton's Spring that evening after dark. The detachment from Fort Coffee, under Lieutenant-Colonel [S. N.] Folsom, had not yet arrived.

Early next morning (Saturday, the 6th) sent a scout to Evansville, in order to communicate with the pickets of our army; found none, but on entering the town discovered a Federal scout going out; learned from the citizens that our pickets had not been there since the Monday before (December 1); sent to the neighborhood of the Dutch Mills; was not able to learn anything of our army. The enemy were then in force at Cane Hill and had pickets near the Dutch Mills. I remained in that vicinity until late that evening, when I considered it prudent to retire down Lee's Creek and communicate with Colonel Folsom, which I did that night about 5 miles from camp (Peyton's Spring). The detachment under Colonel Folsom consisted of about 150 dismounted Choctaws, Captain Gatlin's company of Texas Rangers, and detachment of Bryan's battalion, under Captain Miller, the whole amounting to 200 men.

On Sunday morning I sent a scout to the Line road, but found no pickets on that road; same day cannonading was heard at a distance. That evening marched back to the camp at Peyton's Spring.

Monday morning took possession of Dutch Mills and notified General Hindman of the fact. Not being able to hear anything reliable from our army, Captain Wells was dispatched Tuesday morning to communicate with General Hindman, supposed to be somewhere near Cane Hill; moved my camp nearer the Line; kept a company at the Dutch Mills.

On Wednesday evening (10th) received information, considered reliable, that the Pins were concentrating at Manus', 10 miles from my camp, with the intention of attacking us the next night.

Early next morning I moved upon them; soon dispersed them into the mountains without any damage to our men, with the exception of three horses shot. We did not follow them far into the mountains. Three Pins were killed and 1 wounded. Quite a number of them were in uniform, thought to be soldiers. Sutler tickets were found in possession of some that were killed previous to that fight.

Friday (the 12th), I moved back my command in the direction of Webber's Falls, in compliance with orders from you, Colonel Folsom's detachment having been previously ordered to fall back with the train in the direction of Fort Coffee.

On the day of the battle at Prairie Grove the enemy sent his trains on a different route from the Dutch Mills.

On the expedition we killed 10 Pins and took 3 prisoners. One being quite young and another badly wounded, were released.

Respectfully,

STAND WATIE,
Colonel, Commanding, &c.

Brig. Gen. D. H. COOPER.

DECEMBER 7, 1862.—Battle of Prairie Grove, Fayetteville, or Illinois Creek, Ark.

REPORTS.

No. 1.—Maj. Gen. Samuel R. Curtis, U. S. Army, commanding Department of the Missouri.

No. 2.—Brig. Gen. James G. Blunt, U. S. Army, commanding Army of the Frontier, with congratulations from General Curtis.

No. 3.—Return of Casualties in the Army of the Frontier.

No. 4.—Col. John M. Richardson, Fourteenth Missouri State Militia, Cavalry.

No. 5.—Col. William Weer, Tenth Kansas Infantry, commanding Second Brigade, First Division.

No. 6.—Maj. Henry H. Williams, Tenth Kansas Infantry.

No. 1.

Reports of Maj. Gen. Samuel R. Curtis, U. S. Army, commanding Department of the Missouri.

SAINT LOUIS, MO., *December* 9, 1862—3 p. m.

My forces and the Army of the Frontier united near Fayetteville in the midst of a hard-fought battle. General Blunt had sustained his position at Cane Hill till Saturday night, when the enemy, 25,000 strong, under General Hindman, attempted a flank movement on his left to prevent the arrival of General Herron's forces, which have been approaching for four days by forced marches. Sunday, about 10 a. m., the enemy attacked General Herron near Fayetteville, who, by gallant and desperate fighting, held him in check for three hours, until General Blunt's division came up and attacked him in the rear. The fight continued desperate until dark. Our troops bivouacked on the battle-field, while the enemy retreated across the Boston Mountains. The loss on both sides is heavy, but much the greater on the side of the enemy, our artillery creating terrible slaughter in their greater numbers. The enemy had great advantage in position. Among the enemy's killed were Colonel Steen, formerly brigadier-general, Missouri State Guard. Both Generals Herron and Blunt deserve special commendation for their gallantry in the battle of Fayetteville, Ark.

SAML. R. CURTIS,
Major-General, Commanding.

Major-General HALLECK,
General-in-Chief.

DECEMBER 10, 1862.

Further details are received from Generals Blunt and Herron from the battle-ground of Prairie Grove, near Fayetteville, Ark. Our loss in killed and wounded is now estimated at 1,000;* that of the enemy at over 2,000. The rebels left many of their dead and most of their wounded for us to care for. Extensive hospitals will be improvised in Fayetteville. Prisoners returned report the enemy 28,000 strong. Their artillery was much crippled. We took four caissons, filled with ammunition, and a large number of small-arms. General Blunt moves forward to-day to Cane Hill, General Herron remaining at Prairie Grove, burying the dead and providing for the wounded. The enemy muffled their wheels and moved off in the night, continuing their retreat to Van Buren, probably crossing Arkansas River. Colonel [S.] McFarland, Nineteenth Iowa, is killed. Colonel [J. C.] Black, Thirty-seventh Illinois; Major [W. G.] Thompson, Twentieth Iowa, and a large number of subaltern officers, wounded. It was a hard-fought battle and complete victory.

SAML. R. CURTIS,
Major-General.

H. W. HALLECK,
General-in-Chief, Washington, D. C.

No. 2.

Reports of Brig. Gen. James G. Blunt, U. S. Army, commanding Army of the Frontier, with congratulations from General Curtis.

ARMY OF THE FRONTIER,
In the Field, near Fayetteville, Ark., December 8, 1862.

GENERAL: This place, on yesterday, was the scene of a hard-fought and bloody field, resulting in a complete victory to the Army of the Frontier. The rebel forces, under Generals Hindman, Marmaduke, Parsons, and Frost, numbered 25,000. My whole force in the field did

---

* See pp. 84-86.

not exceed 8,000. I had been holding the enemy on the Boston Mountains for two days, skirmishing with their advance and holding them in check until General Herron could come up with re-enforcements.

On the 7th, they drove in my outposts; got possession of the road, by which they commenced a flank movement on my left during the night, while they made a heavy feint in front. Their object was to cut off communication between myself and General Herron, who was to be at Fayetteville at daylight. They attacked General Herron at about 10 a. m., who, by gallant and desperate fighting, held them in check for three hours, until I came up and attacked them in the rear. The fighting was desperate on both sides, and continued until it was terminated by the darkness of the night. My command bivouacked on their arms, ready to renew the conflict at daylight in the morning; but the enemy had availed themselves of the night to retreat across the Boston Mountains. The loss on both sides has been heavy. My loss in killed is small in proportion to the number of wounded The enemy's loss, compared with ours, is at least four to one. My artillery made terrible destruction in their ranks. They had greatly the advantage in numbers and position, yet Generals Marmaduke and Hindman acknowledged to me, in an interview under a flag of truce, that they had been well whipped. Among the enemy's killed was Colonel Steen, formerly brigadier-general of the Missouri State Guard. The Nineteenth and Twentieth Iowa, Thirty-seventh Illinois, and Twenty-sixth Indiana Regiments, of General Herron's division, suffered severely. General Herron deserves great credit for the promptness with which he re-enforced me by forced marches from near Springfield, as also for his gallantry upon the field.

JAS. G. BLUNT,
Brigadier-General, Commanding.

Maj. Gen. SAMUEL R. CURTIS.

—

PRAIRIE GROVE, ARK.,
December 9, 1862.

The enemy did not stop in their flight until they had crossed the Boston Mountains, and are probably, ere this, across the Arkansas River. I shall move my advance to-day to Cane Hill. I shall establish a general hospital at Fayetteville. Shall I not extend the telegraph to that place? The enemy's killed and wounded between 1,500 and 2,000; a large proportion of them killed. One hundred of their wounded have died since the battle, and a large proportion of others are wounded mortally, showing the terrible effect of my artillery. My casualties will be about 200 killed and 500 wounded. Most of the wounded will recover. The enemy have left their wounded on my hands, and most of their dead uncared for. They are being buried by my command. Hindman admitted his force to be 28,000. Major Hubbard, who was a prisoner with them all day of the fight, counted twenty regiments of infantry and twenty pieces of artillery. They had no train with them, and muffled the wheels of their artillery in making their retreat. Four caissons, filled with ammunition, were taken from the enemy. The Twentieth Regiment Wisconsin Volunteers, in addition to those mentioned yesterday, suffered severely in charging one of the enemy's batteries, which they took, but were unable to hold.

JAS. G. BLUNT,
Brigadier-General.

Maj. T. J. WEED,
Assistant Adjutant-General, Fort Leavenworth.

HEADQUARTERS ARMY OF THE FRONTIER,
Rhea's Mills, Ark., December 20, 1862.

GENERAL: I have the honor to report that, on the 2d instant, and four days subsequent to the battle of Cane Hill, or Boston Mountains, of November 28, I obtained reliable information that the entire force of infantry and artillery of General Hindman's army had crossed the Arkansas River and joined General Marmaduke at Lee's Creek, 15 miles north of Van Buren, to which point the latter had retreated after the battle of the 28th ultimo. I further learned that the united forces under General Hindman's command numbered between 25,000 and 30,000 men, and that he designed advancing upon me in case I did not attack him south of the mountains.

Determined to hold my position at Cane Hill, unless driven from it by a superior force, I immediately telegraphed to the Second and Third Divisions to come to my support by forced marches. I may here mention that I had no knowledge of the whereabouts of these two divisions, except from rumor, and had not been apprised of their movements or locality for a period of over two weeks. My telegraphic dispatch reached General Herron, commanding the Second and Third Divisions, on the 3d, who promptly responded to my order, keeping me advised, by telegraph from Elkhorn, of his progress. The Second and Third Brigades of the First Division, with my headquarters, were at Cane Hill; the First Brigade at Rhea's Mills, 8 miles north, where a large supply train, just arrived from Fort Scott, was halted. My pickets were advanced 6 miles beyond Cane Hill, on the road leading to Van Buren, and a strong outpost of the Second Kansas established where that road intersects the Cove Creek road, running from Fayetteville to Van Buren, and which road passes about 6 miles east of Cane Hill.

On the morning of the 5th instant, this outpost was attacked by a large force of rebel cavalry, but they were repulsed and driven back some 6 miles through the mountains. Expecting that the same demonstration would be repeated on the next morning, I directed Colonel [W. F.] Cloud, commanding the Third Brigade, to strengthen this post by the addition of 100 cavalry and two howitzers, to be at the outpost at daybreak. In consequence of this order not being promptly carried out, and the support not arriving at the time directed, the pickets, on being attacked about daylight by a superior force, were compelled to retire some 3 miles, when, support having reached them, they held the ground during the day, with continual skirmishing, in which several of my men were wounded and a number of the enemy killed.

The enemy had now got possession of the Cove Creek and Fayetteville road, and I learned about 8 p. m. that a force of about 10,000 had advanced beyond the junction of the Cove Creek road with the Cane Hill and Van Buren road, and were massed upon the mountain in front of my outpost, while the remainder of the rebel army was below the junction of the roads just named, about 3 miles in rear of their advance. The Third Brigade, under Colonel Cloud, was ordered to bivouac for the night on their arms upon the ground south of the town that I had selected to make a stand upon in case I was attacked in front.

It was now evident that a general engagement must take place next day, and my apprehensions were that with their superior numbers they would make a feint in front, while with their main force they would make a flank movement on my left, by the Cove Creek road, to intercept General Herron before he could reach me from Fayetteville, which point he was expected to reach by daylight on the morning of the 7th.

About 9 p. m. of the 6th, I received a note from Colonel [M. La Rue] Harrison, of the First Arkansas Cavalry, who had been ordered down from Elkhorn at the same time that General Herron started from Wilson's Creek, informing me that he had arrived at Illinois Creek, 8 miles north of Cane Hill, with 500 men, and that his horses and men were so tired that he did not think he could move farther until Monday, the 8th. Whether his regard for the Sabbath or the fear of getting into a fight prompted him to make such a report to me, I am unable to say; but, judging from his movements that he was not a man upon whom to place much reliance on the battle-field, I ordered him to proceed by daybreak to Rhea's Mills, to guard the transportation and supply trains at that point, the First Brigade having been ordered to join me at Cane Hill. Had he, instead of making unnecessary delay, promptly obeyed that order, he would not have had a portion of his command and transportation captured by General Marmaduke's advance, as occurred on the morning of the 7th.

At about 10 p. m. of the 6th, Colonel [D.] Wickersham, with about 1,600 cavalry, of the Second Wisconsin, First Iowa, Tenth Illinois, and Eighth Missouri Regiments, who, at my request, had been sent forward by General Herron, arrived at Cane Hill. I had, as I have before remarked, considerable apprehension that a flank movement would be attempted on my left during the night. I therefore determined to send a cavalry force across on a road called the Hog-eye road, running from the north part of Cane Hill east to the Telegraph road, and crossing the Cove Creek and Fayetteville road about 4 miles north of the junction of the latter with that running from Cane Hill to Van Buren, already referred to, and from which my outpost had been driven in the morning.

A Colonel [J. M.] Richardson, of the Fourteenth Missouri State Militia, who had arrived during the day with about 150 men, importuned me to be detailed for this service, recommending himself as a brave man, eager for a fight. Committing the folly of taking him upon his own recommendation, I furnished him 100 additional men, making his force 250. Endeavoring to impress upon him the importance of the trust with which he was confided, and stating that I expected the enemy would advance up the Cove Creek road during the night, I directed him to proceed east on the Hog-eye road to the crossing of the Cove Creek and Fayetteville road, to select the best position for defense, sending his pickets down the road toward the enemy, and, if their column approached in that direction, to resist their advance to the last extremity, and notify me promptly of their movements. How I was deceived in sending the wrong man on so important a service, the sequel will show.

At daylight on Sunday morning, I had the transportation of the Second and Third Brigades, of the First Division, hitched up, ready to move to Rhea's Mills, should circumstances render it necessary, and the Second Brigade was ordered to the front, south of the town, where the Third Brigade had bivouacked during the night, the First Brigade and Colonel Wickersham's brigade of cavalry being stationed about 1½ miles in the rear, on the north side of the town, where the Hog-eye road intersects that between Cane Hill and Fayetteville, and where it was possible the enemy might attempt to come in upon my rear.

About 7 o'clock, with my staff, I proceeded to the front. On arriving there, I learned that the enemy were still in considerable force upon the mountain, and so soon as it became sufficiently light they threw several shots from their artillery at my advance outpost, which was replied to by two of my 12-pounder mountain howitzers, without any damage to either party. I directed Colonel [W. F.] Cloud to withdraw his troops on the outposts, with the view of drawing them out and ascertaining their force and design. Upon my advance falling back, the rebels came forward a short distance and formed in line of battle, their right resting on the mountain, their left extending down the valley, and presenting a front of half a mile. It now became evident that their demonstration in front was only a feint, and that their main force had gone by the Cove Creek road, for the purpose of intercepting communication between General Herron and myself, and, notwithstanding that I had received no intelligence from Colonel Richardson, upon whom I had relied to watch this movement, I determined to act accordingly. I immediately ordered the transportation to Rhea's Mills, by a road leading directly north over the mountain, guarded by the Third Indian Regiment (Colonel Phillips), keeping the bottom road on the right, leading to the same point, and also the Fayetteville road, open for the movement of troops. I ordered Colonel Wickersham, with his cavalry, to move rapidly in the direction of Fayetteville and form a junction with General Herron. He was followed by General [Frederick] Salomon's brigade, and the Second and Third Brigades were withdrawn from the front and directed to move rapidly on the Fayetteville road.

As soon as I determined on this disposition of the forces under me, I sent two messenger parties with dispatches to General Herron, apprising him of my movements, and what I believed to be those of the enemy, and urged him to press forward as rapidly as possible, that we might form a junction of our forces before Hindman could get between us, and also directing him to send his train to Rhea's Mills. Neither of these dispatches reached him, the messengers being cut off by Marmaduke's advance.

At about 10 a. m., and after the whole of the First Division was in motion toward Fayetteville, I received the first intelligence from Colonel Richardson, who coolly informed me that the rebel forces had been moving up the Cove Creek and Fayetteville road since midnight, and he judged, from the noise, that several batteries of artillery had passed. I afterward learned that Colonel Richardson, instead of obeying my orders, had only gone to within 2 miles of the Cove Creek road, sending a light picket to the crossing, which was driven back by the advance of the rebel column to where the remainder of the party had halted, and where the valiant colonel was content to remain until 9 o'clock the next morning, listening to the tramp of the rebel army, and not even notifying me of the fact until the rear of their column had passed. The conduct of Colonel Richardson in this instance, upon whose vigilance and strict compliance with orders depended the safety and success of my command, is, to say the least, deserving of the severest censure.

On learning that Hindman's forces had passed north, I ordered Colonel Judson, with his regiment (cavalry) and two 12-pounder mountain howitzers, to proceed rapidly on the same road by which I had sent Colonel Richardson the previous night, and to attack and harass them in the rear, which order he executed with promptness and gallantry, attacking them in the rear with his howitzers and following them 2 or 3 miles, until they made a stand in such force as to compel him to withdraw his command.

Moving with my staff in advance of the First Division, on reaching a point some 3 miles north of Cane Hill, where a road to the left leads to Rhea's Mills, I learned that Colonel Wickersham, who was in the advance with the cavalry, and had been instructed to proceed directly on the Fayetteville road, and furnished with a guide, instead of doing so had taken the left-hand road to the mills. Not deeming it prudent, under all the circumstances, to separate my command, I was compelled to follow the same road, in order to get my forces concentrated. On coming up with Colonel Wickersham, I ordered him to proceed in the direction of Fayetteville with all of his cavalry, and endeavor to open communication with General Herron. I also sent forward Major [E. A.] Calkins, with the Third Wisconsin Cavalry, for the same purpose. But a few minutes elapsed after Colonel Wickersham had started with his command, when I heard the discharge of artillery in a northeast direction, and immediately moved rapidly, with the Second and Third Brigades, in the direction of the firing, leaving the First Brigade (General Salomon's) to guard the trains at Rhea's Mills. It was now between 12 and 1 o'clock. The distance to where the firing was heard was about 5 miles, by an obscure road, leading through a valley, with strips of prairie and brush alternating across it. The firing between General Herron's command and the rebel forces was confined to artillery, which, as I approached the field, became more rapid.

At 1.45 o'clock I came upon the field, in advance of the First Division, when a hasty reconnaissance discovered the enemy in superior force, strongly posted upon elevated ground, behind timber, with the Fayetteville road (on which he had advanced) running through it northeast and southwest. On the north and in front of the enemy's lines was an open valley, divided into large fields, a portion of them cultivated in corn. At the east end of this valley General Herron, with the Second and Third Divisions, was engaged with the enemy, having met their advance early in the day and driven them back to that position.

For the details of the engagement between the rebels and the Second and Third Divisions, under General Herron, up to the time when I came upon the field, I refer you to the report of that gallant officer.

The road on which my column was advancing entered the valley at its western extremity and in front of the left wing of the enemy. They had no intimation of my approach on that road, until a large force of their infantry, which, for the purpose of flanking General Herron's division and overwhelming it by superior numbers, had been massed upon their left, was suddenly confronted by the troops of the First Division, when the engagement soon became general along their entire line.

At about 2 o'clock the fire from the artillery of the First Division was commenced by Rabb's battery, which opened a cross-fire upon two rebel batteries and a heavy body of infantry that were fronting and engaged with General Herron's division. A few moments later and Tenney's battery of Parrott guns came into position on the right and Hopkins' battery on the left of Captain [J. W.] Rabb's. The fire from all three of these batteries was first directed to the enemy's right, where two batteries of the rebels and a heavy body of their infantry were engaged with the Second and Third Divisions. Shell and case-shot from these eighteen pieces were hurled upon the enemy's right with terrible effect. The rebel artillery and infantry, being driven from this position under cover of the wood, the three batteries above named ceased firing, when the infantry of the Second and Third Divisions advanced upon the enemy's right, and the fire of musketry was opened on both sides with great vigor. The Twentieth Wisconsin and Nineteenth Iowa gallantly charged the rebel batteries and drove the enemy from their guns, but were unable to hold them, in consequence of being overwhelmed by a superior force.

The Twenty-sixth Indiana and Thirty-seventh Illinois subsequently charged the same batteries with the same result.

Observing that the enemy had now thrown a large force upon my center and right, I directed the infantry of the First Division to enter the wood and engage them, which order was executed with promptness, Colonel [William] Weer leading the Tenth and Thirteenth Kansas Regiments of his brigade upon the right; a portion of the Second Kansas (dismounted), under command of Capt. S. J. Crawford; the right wing of the Eleventh Kansas, under Colonel [Thomas] Ewing, jr., and the First Indian, under Colonel [S. H.] Wattles, upon the left; the Twentieth Iowa Regiment advancing upon the left of the Indians, the left wing of the Eleventh Kansas, under Lieutenant-Colonel [T.] Moonlight, supporting Rabb's and [H.] Hopkins' batteries. The First Iowa, Tenth Illinois, Eighth Missouri, and the First Battalion of the Second Wisconsin Cavalry, under Colonel Wickersham, and the Third Wisconsin Cavalry, under Major Calkins, were directed to proceed to my extreme right to watch any flank movement of the enemy that might be attempted in that direction, and also to guard the road leading to Rhea's Mills, and prevent communication being cut off with the First Brigade (General Salomon's).

The contest by this time (about 3 p. m.) had become vigorous and determined. The entire infantry of the three divisions, and also a portion of the Second Kansas (dismounted), were engaged in the wood with the rebel infantry, three times their number. The rattling of musketry, uninterrupted for fully three hours, was terrific. The contending armies swayed to and fro, each alternately advancing and retiring. Some rebel sharpshooters, firing from the windows of a house situated in the edge of the wood and a little to my left, were evidently directing their compliments specially to myself and staff. I directed Captain Rabb to open upon it with shell, and in a few moments the house was in flames.

While the infantry was vigorously contesting every inch of ground, I directed Lieutenant [E S.] Stover, with two 12-pounder mountain howitzers, to advance into the wood, which he promptly did, taking position on a little knoll on the right of the Eleventh Kansas, and directing his guns across a small field, where a heavy force of rebels were massed. He poured into them his canister and shell until his ammunition was exhausted and his horses shot down, being compelled to bring away his guns by hand. I then directed Lieutenant [M. D.] Tenney to advance his battery to the edge of the wood, on the left of the Eleventh Kansas, taking position about 200 yards in front of the rebel ranks. From his six 10-pounder Parrott guns he opened on them with terrible effect, driving them back with great slaughter.

Learning that a heavy force was massing on my right with a view of turning my flank, I immediately withdrew Tenney's battery, and proceeded with it to an open field on the right, at the same time directing the infantry to withdraw from the wood, in order to draw the enemy from under cover and within range of my artillery. On reaching the open field on their right, just alluded to, I discovered the entire division of General Frost advanced to the edge of the timber, and about 200 yards distant. They opened upon us a fierce fire from Enfield rifles, and were in the act of throwing down the fence to make an assault on the battery, which had no support except my own staff and body guard; but Lieutenant Tenney, with commendable promptness, wheeled his guns into position, when their destructive fire of canister and shell soon sent the rebel hordes back under cover of the wood. At the same time a fire from the two mountain howitzers, attached to the Third Wisconsin Cavalry, was directed upon them, farther on my right, with good effect. It was here that the rebel General Steen fell. A few minutes after this last repulse of the enemy by Lieutenant Tenney, a rebel battery of ten guns, supported by a heavy body of infantry, opened from their extreme left, when, bringing his guns to bear in that direction, he, in less than ten minutes, silenced their battery, dismounting two of their guns and driving them from the position with a severe loss. While this attempt was being made to charge my artillery on the right, the same demonstration was made upon Rabb's and Hopkins' batteries, the enemy following up my infantry as they retired from the wood, and with a wild shout rushed out from under cover of the trees, when the two batteries, supported by the infantry of the Eleventh Regiment, belched forth a perfect storm of canister, producing immense slaughter in their ranks and compelling them again to retire. As darkness approached, the fire, which from both artillery and musketry had been terrific and uninterrupted for over three hours, gradually ceased along the whole line, and my command bivouacked upon their arms, ready to renew the conflict at early dawn.

I could not tell with any certainty the extent of the damage done the enemy, but knowing that they had a force greatly superior to mine in numbers, I felt assured that they would give us battle again in the morning, and made my arrangements accordingly.

My wounded were all cared for during the night, the transportation and supply trains of the whole army sent to Fayetteville, and General Salomon's brigade, which had been left at Rhea's Mills, ordered to the field; ammunition was brought up and distributed, some refreshments obtained for the men, and everything was in readiness to renew the battle at the first dawn of day; but daylight revealed the fact that the enemy had availed themselves of the night to retreat across the Boston Mountains. Their transportation had been left south of the mountains, and their retreat thereby made unincumbered and stealthily. I am assured by my men who were prisoners with them, as well as by deserters from their ranks, that they tore up the blankets of their men to muffle the wheels of their artillery.

Just before daylight I received a note from General Hindman, under a flag of truce, requesting a personal interview, to make provision for caring for his dead and wounded. On meeting him, I soon became satisfied that no other force was there, except his staff and escort and a party left to take care of the wounded, and that his forces had commenced retreating early the previous night.

On looking over the battle-field in the morning, it soon became evident that the enemy had been most roughly handled, and that our artillery had made fearful slaughter in their ranks. Though many had been already carried away, their dead lay strewn over its whole extent.

The entire Federal loss is: Killed, 167; wounded, 798; missing, 183; total, 1,148.* Of the missing, the greater portion were taken prisoners, and have been since exchanged. The enemy's loss in killed and wounded cannot fall short of 3,000, and will probably much exceed that number, as many of them, not severely wounded, were taken to Van Buren. Their loss in killed upon the ground will reach 1,000, the greater number of whom have been buried by my command. The entire force of Federal troops engaged did not exceed 7,000, about 3,000 cavalry not

---

* But see revised statement, p. 86.

having been brought into action. The enemy's force, according to their own admission, was 28,000, and all well armed, mostly with the Enfield rifle.

Many instances of individual gallantry and daring occurred during the day, for an account of which I refer you to the reports of regimental, brigade, and division commanders. As the immediate commander of the First Division, I deem it but justice to say of Col. William Weer, commanding the Second Brigade, that he behaved throughout with great gallantry, leading his men into the thickest of the fight. The same is true of Colonel [T. M.] Bowen and Maj. H. H. Williams, commanding regiments in the same brigade. Capt. S. J. Crawford, of the Second Kansas Cavalry, who commanded a battalion of that regiment that fought on foot, displayed great gallantry, as did also the lamented Capt. A. P. Russell, who fell, mortally wounded. Col. Thomas Ewing, Lieutenant-Colonel Moonlight, and Major Plumb, of the Eleventh Kansas, gave evidence of their high qualities as gallant officers. To Captains Rabb and Hopkins and Lieutenants Tenney and Stover, who served their artillery with such terrible and destructive effect upon the enemy's ranks, too much praise cannot be awarded. All did their duty well and nobly. Men of Kansas, Missouri, Iowa, Wisconsin, Illinois, and Indiana mingled their blood upon the same field, and for the same worthy cause. For their deeds of valor upon the field of Prairie Grove, their native States may well be proud of them.

I cannot close this report without availing myself of the occasion to express my thanks to Brig. Gen. F. J. Herron for the promptness with which he responded to my order to re-enforce me, as also for the gallantry displayed by him upon the field. His conduct is worthy of emulation and deserving of the highest praise.

To the members of my staff, Maj. V. P. Van Antwerp, inspector-general; Capt. Oliver Barber, chief commissary; Capt. Lyman Scott, jr., acting assistant adjutant-general, and Lieuts. J. Fin. Hill, H. G. Loring, G. M. Waugh, D. Whittaker, and C. H. Haynes, aides-de-camp, who were in the saddle, and with me constantly from before daylight in the morning until the close of the action after dark, I am indebted for efficient and valuable services on the field. Made a special target by the rebel troops, in obedience to the notorious address of their commander (General Hindman), issued on the eve of battle, and a printed copy of which, over his signature, each of them carried upon his person, "to shoot down my mounted officers," they were saluted wherever they rode by a perfect storm of balls from the enemy's guns.

I have the honor to be, general, very respectfully, your obedient servant,

JAS. G. BLUNT,
Brigadier-General, Commanding.

Maj. Gen. SAMUEL R. CURTIS,
Commanding Department of the Missouri.

[Inclosure No. 1.]

HDQRS. FIRST CORPS, TRANS-MISS. ARMY, *December* 9, 1862.

Brig. Gen. JAMES G. BLUNT,
Commanding U. S. Forces in the Field:

GENERAL: I send, in charge of Colonel O'Kane, C. S. Army, who bears this flag, the medicines and hospital stores and one of the ambulances, captured by my troops in the engagement of the 7th instant. The other ambulance was broken down and left on the roadside.

Colonel O'Kane also takes ambulances and supplies for my wounded at Prairie Grove.

On yesterday, during our interview, one of my officers notified me that men of your command were removing arms from the battle-field. I called your attention to the fact, and you at once gave to Brigadier-General Herron, of your command, an order to prevent such conduct. This action of yours was perfectly satisfactory and proper, the field of battle being in my possession, and your officers and men being upon it only by virtue of the truce granted by me at your request. I hoped there would be no similar ground of complaint, but information has been given me that Brigadier-General Herron, the officer to whom you gave the order, did in person, at a part of the field where there were but few of my men and many of yours, require my men, who were there collecting arms, to lay them down, under a threat to arrest them, the arms so taken from my men numbering between 50 and 60. I request their return by the bearer of this.

I have the honor to be, general, very respectfully, your obedient servant,

T. C. HINDMAN,
Major-General, Commanding.

[Inclosure No. 2.]

HDQRS. ARMY OF THE FRONTIER, *December* 10, 1862.

Maj. Gen. T. C. HINDMAN,
Commanding Confederate Forces:

GENERAL: Your communication of December 9, under flag of truce by Colonel O'Kane, is received. I had already sent to the surgeon in charge of the Confederate hospital 5,000 rations complete, for use of your wounded, and had tendered the use of my ambulances to send them to such place as they might select as a general hospital.

In response to your complaint of General Herron's men gathering up the arms upon the battle-field, I have the honor to inform you that you have an entire misapprehension of the nature of the flag of truce referred to. It is true I sent a surgeon with ambulances to your lines to gather up any wounded I might have on the ground occupied by you. This is a privilege I would not deny an enemy, even during an engagement, without being accompanied by a flag of truce.

It is true, however, that you seized upon this pretext as the occasion for sending me, under flag of truce, three communications, the last one asking a personal interview. This, as I then suspected, and as has since proven satisfactorily to be the case, was to enable you to make good your retreat, which was commenced early in the night, the precaution having been taken by you to tear up your blankets and muffle the wheels of your artillery, that you might move stealthily away.

I had no other intention than that my ambulances should return before morning, and expected to renew the battle at daybreak. Had I not ascertained the fact about daylight, previous to your requesting an interview for the purpose of making arrangements to care for the dead and wounded, that your forces had stolen away during the night, I should not have granted it, but would have attacked you at early dawn, notwithstanding that your forces, occupying a strong position of your own choosing, outnumbered mine as three to one.

That you should claim the right to carry off the arms from the field by the men you had detailed, under flag of truce, to bury your dead, is not only simply preposterous, but very ridiculous.

I only directed General Herron to keep his men in the rear while our personal interview lasted, and it was in compliance with your earnest and repeated request that I gave you six hours to secure your own personal safety and that of your staff and body guard, which time I have learned you made good use of, instead of the thirty-six hours that you petitioned for, and which I refused, to enable your whole army to stampede to Van Buren. A flag of truce, which should always be respected by belligerents, is a thing too sacred to be abused, as has been the case of late by the Confederate forces under your command; not only in the instance referred to, clearly to cover the retreat of your defeated army, but also at the battle of Cane Hill, on November 28, when your artillery was on the very point of being captured. Just in time to save the rear of your retreating column from being annihilated, and to enable him to retire under cover of the night, and obtain possession of one of his guns that had been disabled and thrown into a creek, an officer from General Marmaduke, upon that occasion, came galloping up with a flag of truce.

In this connection also I may call your attention to the flag of truce sent with Captain Stanley to my camp, near Maysville, which resulted in no benefit to either army, other than to enable your flag-bearer to spy out my force and position, which I trust was entirely satisfactory to him.

Still another instance that may be mentioned, where this privilege has been abused, is that of a party sent under a flag of truce, with Major [J. M.] Hubbard, of the First Missouri Regiment, and Lieutenant Bassett, of the Second Kansas, who were taken prisoners during the battle of the 7th instant, to Cane Hill, Cincinnati, and Fayetteville, with the ostensible object of conducting them within my lines, but with the actual purpose of ascertaining whether a portion of my forces was not at some of the points named. This may have been considered by you as strategy, or, perhaps, that other thing, called chivalry. If the latter, it is not of the kind that I have so often heard discussed as being the boast of the South, or else it must have become of late wofully deteriorated.

Whatever method you may adopt, I do not propose to avail myself of a flag of truce to cover a retreat, or to ascertain the enemy's position. Notwithstanding that I am in an enemy's country, and labor under every disadvantage in obtaining information, it shall never be said of me, when this contest has closed, that I have violated any of the prescribed rules of civilized warfare. I avail myself of this occasion to inform you that, after we had agreed to consider sick and wounded soldiers, as well as those connected with the hospital department, as not being prisoners of war, when a portion of your forces retreated through Cane Hill, on the night of the 7th instant, they not only paroled my sick left there, but robbed them of their clothes and hospital supplies.

I must also call your attention to the fact that several of my men were brutally murdered by your command after they fell, wounded, upon the field, which one of your officers vouches for. Such conduct contrasts very unfavorably with the kind treatment that has been extended by my command to your wounded, whom you were compelled to leave upon the battle-field.

I have the honor to be, very respectfully, your obedient servant,

JAS. G. BLUNT,
Brigadier-General, Commanding.

P. S.—If you claim the field of Prairie Grove, as your communication complaining of General Herron's taking away arms would seem to indicate, may I be permitted to ask why you did not remain there? And will you be so kind as to grant the privilege of staying there to that portion of my command now encamped on the battle-field?

[Inclosure No. 3.]

HEADQUARTERS FIRST CORPS, TRANS-MISSISSIPPI ARMY,
December 10, 1862.

Brig. Gen. JAMES G. BLUNT,
Commanding U. S. Forces in the Field:

GENERAL: I send you herewith, under flag of truce, by Captain Rathbun, C. S. Army, a copy of the report of Captain Garrett, of my command, who was left by me on the 8th instant in charge of the burying party on the battle-field of Prairie Grove. The conduct of men of your command, as described in this report, is atrocious. I will not insult you by asking its disavowal, but I demand that you take such measures as will allow the performance of the rites of burial toward my dead upon the field they won, according to your own admission, and from which my troops were only withdrawn by reason of their utter lack of subsistence. A burial party goes back with this flag to execute the orders previously given on that subject.

I inclose to you, also, the report of Brigadier-General Marmaduke, C. S. Army, and report of Colonel Shelby, C. S. Army, commanding brigade, for your further information upon the subject of arms taken by men of your command, referred to in my former letter of yesterday, sent under flag of truce by the hands of Colonel O'Kane. As I remarked to you during our conference on the 8th instant, I desire and intend in all things to conform to all the usages of civilized war. It is necessary that you should do the like, in order that I may be enabled fully to carry out that desired intention. I inclose you a list of the prisoners paroled by me on the field during the engagement. I ask that an equal number of my men, if any, captured by your forces be returned to me by Captain Rathbun.

Very respectfully, &c.,

T. C. HINDMAN,
Major-General, Commanding.

[Inclosure No. 4.]

HEADQUARTERS ARMY OF THE FRONTIER,
Rhea's Mills, Ark., December 11, 1862.

Maj. Gen. T. C. HINDMAN,
Commanding Confederate Forces:

GENERAL: I am just in receipt of your communication of December 10, under flag of truce, with Captain Rathbun, C. S. Army. An equivalent, under the cartel, will be sent to your lines without delay, for those you released on parole, as per statement of General Frost. In answer to your second reference to the matter of General Herron's men removing arms from the battle-field of Prairie Grove, I refer you to my letter of yesterday, in reply to yours of the 9th instant. Your remarks about the "battle-field won by your men, as admitted by me," is considered here as a very good joke.

I send back with the flag of truce the men you sent to complete burying your dead. I have had this matter properly attended to, and directed General Herron to detail a party to go over the ground again and bury such as had not yet been discovered. The number of your dead was so great, and being mostly in the timber and brush, the task of burying them has been quite an arduous one; hence the delay.

I must again call your attention to the abuse that is being made of flags of truce. I have never had occasion to send a flag of truce to your lines, yet I have received several when no legitimate object was to be obtained by the party sending them. Hereafter flags of truce will only be sent or received by me, except for the exchange of prisoners, as already mutually agreed upon at our interview on the 8th instant, and also to enable you to send supplies, medical officers, and hospital attendants to your wounded within my lines. When I send scouting and reconnoitering parties to ascertain the position of the enemy, I send them under the flag of my Government, and not with a white flag. I desire that you should do the same.

I avail myself of this opportunity to express to you my thanks for the very flattering description of the troops under my command, as contained in your address of December 4, to your soldiers upon the eve of battle. Your instructions to your soldiers to pick off my officers smacks very strongly of chivalry, and when they are especially directed to pick off mounted officers, I consider them as complimentary to myself.

I have the honor, general, to be, most respectfully, your obedient servant,

JAS. G. BLUNT,
Brigadier-General, Commanding.

[Inclosure No. 5.]

HEADQUARTERS CAVALRY DIVISION,
Dripping Springs, Ark., December 11, 1862.

Brig. Gen. JAMES G. BLUNT, U. S. Army,
Commanding Forces in the Field:

GENERAL: By direction of Major-General Hindman, I have to send under a flag of truce medicines and ambulances to the battle-ground at Prairie Grove, for the use of the Confederate wounded there. Please give them all the assistance in your power, and oblige,

Very respectfully, your obedient servant,

J. S. MARMADUKE,
Brigadier-General, C. S. Army, Commanding.

[Inclosure No. 6.]

HEADQUARTERS FIRST CORPS, TRANS-MISSISSIPPI ARMY,
December 12, 1862.

[General BLUNT:]

GENERAL: I send the bearer, Lieutenant Lawrence, to the battlefield, for the purpose of making a plat of it and the approaches to it. I request that you grant him the privilege, under such restrictions and obligations as you may see proper to impose. This courtesy to me on your part, if extended to me, will be reciprocated whenever occasion may offer.

I have the honor to be, &c.,

T. C. HINDMAN,
Major-General, Commanding.

[Indorsement.]

HEADQUARTERS ARMY OF THE FRONTIER,
Rhea's Mills, Ark., December 14, 1862.

[General HINDMAN:]

Your request, contained within, is a very modest one, and will be granted, provided you allow me to send an artist to your present camp to sketch it and the approaches leading thereto. Such little courtesies must be reciprocated.

Respectfully, your obedient servant,

JAS. G. BLUNT,
Brigadier-General, Commanding.

[Inclosure No. 7.]

GENERAL FIELD ORDERS, No. 2.

HDQRS. ARMY OF THE FRONTIER,
Rhea's Mills, Ark., December 12, 1862.

The general commanding takes this occasion to express his heartfelt thanks to the officers and soldiers of his command for their gallantry at the battle of Prairie Grove, on Sunday, the 7th instant, which crowned the Army of the Frontier with complete success and a brilliant victory.

When it is considered that the enemy we engaged outnumbered us as three to one; that they were inspired by the confidence of success, and stimulated by the most urgent appeals to their passions and prejudices; that they possessed the advantage of being in their own country, and familiar with every road, hill, and mountain pass; that they possessed every advantage in positions, which were of their own choosing, you have every reason to be proud of having participated upon that bloody field. No battle during the present war has been more determined and bloody, and never was there a field upon which, considering the number of troops engaged and the time occupied, the slaughter was as great.

The results of your victory cannot be overestimated. The stake was an important one. With your defeat, Western Arkansas, Missouri, Kansas, and the Indian country would have been the prey of the rebel army. Your victory has virtually ended the war north of the Arkansas River. For these results you are entitled to the plaudits of a grateful country.

To the Second and Third Divisions, for the promptness with which they responded to my request to re-enforce me, and the unparalleled marching done by them to reach me before support would be too late, as well as for the gallantry displayed by them upon the field upon that memorable day, the highest praise is justly due.

Although we have cause to rejoice over our victory, yet we cannot but feel saddened at the loss of our brave comrades who have fallen by our side, and to condole with those to whose homes grief has been brought, by the loss in battle of those friends that were dear; but while we drop the tear of sympathy over their gaves, we cannot forget that their death was a noble sacrifice to sustain their country's flag, and that they died such a death as every true soldier and patriot would choose to die.

Your noble conduct upon the field of Prairie Grove, as also upon other occasions, gives evidence of your invincibility, and assures me that, whatever emergency may arise, you will be equal to the task.

JAS. G. BLUNT,
Brigadier-General, Commanding.

[Inclosure No. 8.]

HEADQUARTERS FIRST CORPS, TRANS-MISSISSIPPI ARMY,
In the Field, December 4, 1862.

SOLDIERS: From the commencement to the end of the battle, bear constantly in mind what I now urge upon you:

First. Never fire because your comrades do; nor because the enemy does; nor because you happen to see the enemy; nor for the sake of firing rapidly. Always wait till you are certainly within the range of your gun, then single out your man, take deliberate aim, as low down as the knee, and fire.

Second. When occasion offers, be certain to pick off the enemy's officers, especially the mounted ones, and to kill his artillery horses.

Third. Do not shout, except when you charge the enemy. As a general thing, keep silent, that orders may be heard. Obey the orders of your officers, but pay no attention to idle rumors or the words of unauthorized persons.

Fourth. Do not stop with your wounded comrades; the surgeons and infirmary corps will take care of them; do you go forward and avenge them.

Fifth. Do not break ranks to plunder. If we whip the enemy, all he has will be ours; if not, the spoil will be of no benefit to us. Plunderers and stragglers will be put to death upon the spot. File-closers are especially charged with this duty. The cavalry in rear will likewise attend to it.

Remember that the enemy you engage has no feeling of mercy or kindness toward you. His ranks are made up of Pin Indians, free negroes, Southern tories, Kansas jayhawkers, and hired Dutch cut-throats. These bloody ruffians have invaded your country; stolen and destroyed your property; murdered your neighbors; outraged your women; driven your children from their homes, and defiled the graves of your kindred. If each man of you will do what I have here urged upon you, we will utterly destroy them. We can do this; we must do it; our country will be ruined if we fail. A just God will strengthen our arms and give us a glorious victory.

T. C. HINDMAN,
Major-General, Commanding.

HEADQUARTERS ARMY OF THE FRONTIER,
In the Field, Rhea's Mills, Ark., December 12, 1862.

GENERAL: The enemy's loss in killed and wounded at the battle of Prairie Grove, on the 7th instant, was much greater than was at first supposed. It will not fall short of 3,000, and not less than 1,000 killed. Dead bodies in great numbers were found scattered through the woods for three days after the battle; some of them 10 miles from the scene of conflict, who had been carried to the rear by their comrades, and there left to die. Their wounded are badly mangled, and many of them must die. My artillery was worked upon them with terrible effect. They were left entirely destitute of subsistence, and would have starved had I not provided for them. For our kind treatment they appear very grateful.

My last advices from Hindman's command is that it was near Van Buren. Their flight across the mountains was precipitate and without order. Their defeat has greatly demoralized their army, and hundreds are throwing down their arms and coming into my lines daily.

My wounded are well cared for and doing well.

Respectfully,

JAS. G. BLUNT,
Brigadier-General, Commanding.

Maj. Gen. SAMUEL R. CURTIS,
Commanding Department of the Missouri.

[DEPARTMENT OF THE MISSOURI,]
December 10, 1862.

Brigadier-General BLUNT,
Prairie Grove, Ark.:

The country is rejoicing over the victory of Prairie Grove. I congratulate you and General Herron on your glorious success, and thank you and the officers and soldiers of the Army of the Frontier for a victory that will carry despair into the hearts of our foes and gladness to the friends of liberty throughout the country.

SAML. R. CURTIS,
Major-General.

No. 3.

Return of Casualties in the Army of the Frontier.

[Compiled from nominal lists of casualties, returns, &c.]

Command.	Killed.		Wounded.		Captured or missing.		
	Officers.	Enlisted men.	Officers.	Enlisted men.	Officers.	Enlisted men.	Aggregate.
FIRST DIVISION.							
Brig. Gen. JAMES G. BLUNT.*							
First Brigade.							
Brig. Gen. FREDERICK SALOMCN.							
6th Kansas Cavalry	.....	.....	.....	.....	.....	1	1
9th Kansas Cavalry†	.....	.....	.....	.....	.....	.....	.....
3d Wisconsin Cavalry†	.....	.....	.....	.....	.....	.....	.....
9th Wisconsin Infantry‡	.....	.....	.....	.....	.....	.....	.....
Total First Brigade	.....	.....	.....	.....	.....	1	1
Second Brigade.							
Col. WILLIAM WEER.							
3d Indian Home Guard Infantry	.....	1	.....	1	.....	.....	2
10th Kansas Infantry	.....	6	4	59	.....	.....	69

* Senior officer in command of all the troops engaged.
† No loss reported.
‡ Not in action.

Return of Casualties in the Army of the Frontier—Continued.

Command.	Killed.		Wounded.		Captured or missing.		
	Officers.	Enlisted men.	Officers.	Enlisted men.	Officers.	Enlisted men.	Aggregate.
***Second Brigade*—Continued.**							
13th Kansas Infantry	......	8	3	40	......	5	56
Kansas Light Artillery, 1st Battery	......	1	......	10	......	......	11
Total Second Brigade	......	16	7	110	......	5	138
Third Brigade.							
Col. WILLIAM F. CLOUD.							
1st Indian Home Guard Infantry	......	2	......	4	......	......	6
2d Kansas Cavalry	......	3	1	21	......	......	25
11th Kansas Infantry	......	3	1	28	......	......	32
Indiana Light Artillery, 2d Battery	......	......	......	8	......	......	8
Kansas Light Artillery, Hopkins' battery *	......	......	......	......	......	......	......
Total Third Brigade	......	8	2	61	......	......	71
Total First Division	......	24	9	171	......	6	210
SECOND DIVISION.							
Col. DANIEL HUSTON, JR.							
First Brigade.							
Col. JOHN G. CLARK.							
2d Illinois Light Artillery, Battery A †	......	......	......	......	......	......	......
26th Indiana Infantry	......	25	8	167	......	1	201
7th Missouri Cavalry	2	3	......	6	2	129	142
Total First Brigade	2	28	8	173	2	130	343
Second Brigade.							
Col. WILLIAM MCE. DYE.							
37th Illinois Infantry	......	8	2	56	2	6	74
20th Iowa Infantry	1	8	5	35	......	......	49
6th Missouri Cavalry, 2d Battalion	......	......	......	1	2	28	31
1st Missouri Light Artillery, Battery F †	......	......	......	......	......	......	......
Total Second Brigade	1	16	7	92	4	34	154
Total Second Division	3	44	15	265	6	164	497
THIRD DIVISION.							
Brig. Gen. FRANCIS J. HERRON. ‡							
First Brigade.							
Lieut. Col. HENRY BERTRAM.							
10th Illinois Cavalry §	......	......	......	2	......	......	2
1st Iowa Cavalry §	......	......	......	1	......	......	1
1st Missouri Light Artillery, Battery L	......	1	......	2	......	......	3
2d Wisconsin Cavalry, 1st Battalion §	......	......	......	......	......	......	......
20th Wisconsin Infantry	2	48	11	143	......	13	217
Total First Brigade	2	49	11	148	......	13	223

* Manned by Company B, Second Kansas Cavalry; afterward designated Third Kansas Battery. No loss reported.

† No loss reported.

‡ Also in command of the Second and Third Divisions combined.

§ Temporarily organized, with the Eighth Missouri Cavalry, of the Second Brigade, as a cavalry brigade, under Col. Dudley Wickersham.

Return of Casualties in the Army of the Frontier—Continued.

Command.	Killed.		Wounded.		Captured or missing.		
	Officers.	Enlisted men.	Officers.	Enlisted men.	Officers.	Enlisted men.	Aggregate.
Second Brigade.							
Col. WILLIAM W. ORME.							
94th Illinois Infantry	......	1	1	30	......	2	34
19th Iowa Infantry	3	42	5	140	1	2	193
8th Missouri Cavalry*	......	1	......	3	......	9	13
1st Missouri Light Artillery, Battery E	......	2	......	6	......	......	8
Total Second Brigade	3	46	6	179	1	13	248
Total Third Division	5	95	17	327	1	26	471
ESCORT.							
1st Missouri Cavalry (Battalion)	......	......	......	5	3	10	18
UNATTACHED.							
1st Arkansas Cavalry	......	4	......	4	1	46	55
14th Missouri State Militia, Cavalry †	......	......	......	......	......	......	......

RECAPITULATION.

First Division	......	24	9	171	......	6	210
Second Division	3	44	15	265	6	164	497
Third Division	5	95	17	327	1	26	471
Escort	......	......	......	5	3	10	18
Unattached	......	4	......	4	1	46	55
Total Army of the Frontier	8	167	41	772	11	252	1,251

OFFICERS KILLED.—Seventh Missouri Cavalry: Maj. Eliphalet Bredett and Capt. William McKee. Nineteenth Iowa: Lieut. Col. Samuel McFarland and Lieuts. Thomas Johnson and Loammi M. Smith. Twentieth Iowa: Lieut. Harrison Oliver. Twentieth Wisconsin: Capt. John McDermott and Lieut. Thomas Bintliff; Capt. John Weber and Lieut. George W. Root died of wounds.

No. 4.

Report of Col. John M. Richardson, Fourteenth Missouri State Militia, Cavalry.

HDQRS. FOURTEENTH REGT. CAV., MISSOURI STATE MILITIA,
December 15, 1862.

COLONEL: A standing order requires reports to be made to the State headquarters of the part taken by the State troops in all scouts, skirmishes, and battles. In compliance with that order, I have the honor to submit, through the hands of General E. B. Brown, the following report:

On the 3d instant, I received from General Brown an order directing

* See note (§) on p. 85.

† No loss reported.

me to proceed immediately with all the available force at Cassville and report to Brigadier-General Blunt, commanding Army of the Frontier. The order was received at 8 p. m., and at 9 o'clock the troops marched, traveling without tents or camp equipage. I had with me 100 men of the First Battalion of my regiment and 28 men from the First Arkansas Cavalry.

At 9 p. m. of the 5th, I reported to General Blunt, having traveled 73 miles in three days.

On the morning of the 6th, General Blunt ordered me to proceed with my troops from Cane Hill down the Cove Creek road to ascertain if the enemy were approaching. On reaching the divide between the waters of White River and Cove Creek, I ordered Captain [S. H.] Julian, with his company, to proceed in advance, to fire on an approaching enemy, and then retreat in haste to the rear of the main column. The captain had not proceeded far before he commenced sending back prisoners, a strong indication we were in close proximity to the rebel forces. He directed the guard bringing in the third prisoner to inform me that he had driven in the rebel picket, and had, 300 yards in his front, a rebel camp, the part he could see containing not less than 2,000 men, and that he was awaiting orders. Upon interrogating the prisoner, I was informed that my command was in less than a mile of a rebel camp containing 18,000 men; that it contained six brigades and six brigade generals, among whom were Parsons, Steen, Marmaduke, Shelby, &c., and that Hindman was to be up that night; that the enemy were moving up the mountain, taking the Chute, the direct road to Cane Hill. My force not being strong enough to harass the camp, after consulting Majors [J.] Sullivan and Fitch, Captain Julian was ordered to return. Contrary to my expectation, the rebel cavalry did not follow, and I returned to report to General Blunt a large rebel force within 6 miles of his headquarters. The reason we were not followed, the enemy supposed us to be a reconnaissance in force, not less than three regiments of cavalry.

On the 7th, General Blunt directed me to take my own battalion (100 strong), Captain [T.] Conkey, of the Third Wisconsin Cavalry, and proceed on the same road as the day previous. Before reaching the Hog-eye Junction, on the Cove Creek road, I met Captain Coleman, of the Ninth Kansas, with 30 men, who reported that the enemy had driven him from the junction, and were marching up the Cove Creek road in great force. A messenger was immediately dispatched to General Blunt to report the fact. The enemy being in possession of the junction, and my position being unfavorable, my force only numbering 166 men, and having good reason to believe the enemy were marching on Cane Hill, I fell back a mile, took a strong position, intending to check and delay their advance as long as possible. The enemy not coming up, Captain Julian was sent forward to ascertain their movements. That prompt and efficient officer soon reported to me the enemy were not marching on Cane Hill, but were moving on the road in the direction of Fayetteville. That fact I immediately reported to General Blunt. The general ordered Colonel [W. R.] Judson to report to me with three squadrons of the Sixth Kansas Cavalry, two howitzers, and to direct me to proceed to the junction and attack the enemy. Colonel Judson requested me to take charge of the howitzers, as my men were suitably armed to defend them. Not knowing which ranked, we agreed to jointly command the detachment. We proceeded to the junction, drove in the enemy's pickets just as their rear was passing. Taking into consideration the reason of General Blunt's order, we followed up and harassed the enemy for 5 miles, firing on them and taking several prisoners. About 3 miles from

Prairie Grove we found the enemy drawn up in line to resist our advance. They had, to oppose our progress, ten regiments of infantry, two batteries of artillery, and about 1,500 cavalry. Our force, numbering 316 men, was drawn up within 300 yards of the enemy's line. We commenced the attack with the howitzers, the enemy returning our fire with a volley of musketry and one small piece of artillery. Their aim was too high, the balls passing harmlessly over our heads. Being unable to maintain our position, we fell back with our force. Colonel Judson, at my request, consented I should command the rear. We were greatly astonished that the enemy did not follow. They, however, believing we were the advance of General Blunt's whole force, declined accepting our invitation to leave their strong position. We kept this half of the enemy's force in line until they heard General Blunt's guns on their left, thereby preventing them from throwing their whole force (28,000 strong) upon the tired troops of Brigadier-General Herron.

General Hindman, who commanded the Confederate force, as a military man has been underrated by our side. Being unwilling to contend with our force united, his feint, marching up the mountain on the Chute road, as if intending to attack General Blunt in front at Cane Hill, and then marching down during the night, taking the road to Fayetteville, intending to fall on the fatigued troops of General Herron (who were on a forced march to re-enforce General Blunt), crush them out, and then turn, and, with his immense army, work on General Blunt at his leisure, indicates military genius of a high order. The movement was executed with that promptness which generally insures success, but General Blunt deceived the enemy. With the force of Colonel Judson and myself, only 316 strong, he caused them to believe he was coming up on their rear, held a large part of their army off General Herron, and made his attack at a point not expected by the enemy.

I feel it my duty to bear testimony to the ability and soldierly conduct of Colonel Judson and his officers, and of Captains Coleman and Conkey; also to the Kansas troops for great kindness toward us; they received us as brothers and fought with us as true soldiers. The conduct of my own officers and men affords me great pleasure. They were willing to undergo any hardship and fatigue to aid their brethren in arms and advance the interest of the country.

The courage and discipline of the men, the promptness and ability of the officers, justified me, when we were about to retreat before so large a force, in asking of Colonel Judson the post of honor for them and myself.

I am, sir, very respectfully, your obedient servant,

JOHN M. RICHARDSON,
Colonel Fourteenth Cavalry, Missouri State Militia.

Col. WILLIAM D. WOOD,
Adjutant-General, Missouri.

No. 5.

Report of Col. William Weer, Tenth Kansas Infantry, commanding Second Brigade, First Division.

HDQRS. 2D BRIG., 1ST DIV., ARMY OF THE FRONTIER,
Camp at Cane Hill, Ark., December 12, 1862.

SIR: Having just received the reports of the subordinate commanders, I hasten to submit to the general commanding an account of the part taken by this brigade in the battle of Prairie Grove, Washington County, Arkansas, on Sunday, December 7.

The Third Indian Regiment (Cherokee) had, previously to the action, been ordered to protect the train, some miles distant, so that we went into the engagement as follows: Tenth Kansas Regiment, Maj. H. H. Williams commanding, 387 men (Company I being absent on detached service); First Kansas Battery, Lieut. Marcus D. Tenney commanding, 96 men; Third Indian Regiment, Adjutant Gallaher commanding, 44 men; Thirteenth Kansas Regiment, Col. Thomas M. Bowen commanding, 375 men. Total number of men engaged, 902.

We entered the field upon the enemy's left, General Herron being then engaged some distance in our front, and immediately received an order to hurry forward to his assistance. The battery was placed in advance, the infantry marching by the right flank in its rear. The hurrying forward had just commenced, the head of the battery having entered an orchard, when a shower of bullets was sent at it from an adjoining thicket on the right. Fearing for its safety, and surprised at this unexpected reception, so far distant from where General Herron was engaged, the Tenth Kansas was hurried into the thicket to clear it. They had hardly entered before they were subjected to a terrific fire, but fortunately with little loss. The battery moved forward into a meadow out of reach of small-arms, while the Tenth Kansas continued moving and driving the enemy, but were soon again involved in a severe contest. Thereupon the Thirteenth Kansas and the fragment of the Third Indian were moved forward into the timber to the assistance of the Tenth. A line of battle was formed under the brow of a gentle declivity. Some detachments from the Second Kansas Cavalry, dismounted, and the right wing of the Eleventh Kansas Regiment came to our help during the fight, and a continuous firing, with but slight intermission, was kept up until dark. The line was as follows: The Indians upon the right, under Lieutenant [William] Gallaher, as skirmishers; next, to the left, the Tenth Kansas, under Major Williams; next, a detachment of Second Kansas, under Lieutenant-Colonel [O. A.] Bassett; next, the Thirteenth Kansas, under Colonel Bowen; next, the right wing of the Eleventh Kansas, under Colonel Ewing, and, next and last, upon the left, a small detachment of the Second Kansas, under Captain [S. J.] Crawford.

The firing was general and very rapid, with occasional lulls, during which we several times attempted to pass the brow of the hill and engage the enemy in close quarters. We were as often repulsed by the rain of bullets. At one time two mountain howitzers, under Lieutenant [E. S.] Stover, Second Kansas, came to our assistance and did splendid execution.

About dark, and while making a final attempt tc pass over the brow of the hill, the enemy arose in the timber with loud yells, surrounding us on all sides, and charged. The air was thick with bullets, and nothing saved us from annihilation but the protection afforded by the brow of the hill. They must have been heavily re-enforced; and so overpowering were their numbers that we were compelled to yield before the charge and fall back. At this time, about dark, Rabb's battery, on our left, and Lieutenant Tenney, with First Kansas Battery, on our right, saved us from destruction. Their firing was so rapid and well directed that the enemy was compelled to fall back, and we marched from the field in good order. We were engaged from 3 p. m. until dark. Our whole line of battle could not have numbered over 1,200, and with this force we engaged, as we afterward learned, General Frost's whole division and two Mississippi regiments, &c., and, with the aid of the batteries above named, his final re-enforcements. Our safety even at the commencement of the action must be attributed to the fact that our weakness was concealed from the enemy by our position, and that many of their men were unwilling conscripts. The desperate charge made by him at night by so large a force was evidently intended to cover his retreat.

The damage done the enemy far exceeded our loss. As this was the first time most of the men were under fire, great credit is due them for the pertinacity with which they clung to their position or rallied when broken. There were some disgraceful exceptions, but it is hoped that upon a fresh field they will show themselves worthy soldiers.

I desire to express my grateful acknowledgment to Colonel Ewing, of the Eleventh Kansas; Lieutenant-Colonel Bassett and Captain Crawford, of the Second Kansas; Lieutenant Stover, commanding the two howitzers, and Captain Rabb, commanding battery, their officers and men, for their valuable assistance, courage, and zeal. Due credit will doubtless be given them in reports from the proper commanders.

I cannot be too earnest in my commendations of Colonel Bowen, commanding the Thirteenth Kansas; Major Williams, commanding the Tenth Kansas, and Lieutenant Tenney, commanding the First Kansas Battery; all of my own brigade. Their daring, skill, and active endeavors, in the rallying and management of their men amid storms of bullets, deserve not only honorable mention, but a place upon the record of those who merit promotion.

Though not immediately under my personal supervision, I am credibly informed that Adjutant Gallaher and his handful of Cherokees did noble service in protecting the right flank of the Tenth Kansas, under Captain [M.] Quigg.

The accompanying reports from regimental commanders will give the names of those receiving at their hands special mention.

The conduct of Lieutenant Tenney and his battery was under the immediate eye of the general commanding. Their destructive and rapid fire has even extorted high encomiums from the enemy. I desire to officially call the attention of the general to the condition of this battery, and would respectfully state that it is due to the valor, skill, and patient labor of Lieutenant Tenney that the proper steps be taken to place him as its captain (he having for a long time been discharging the functions of that office), and that the meritorious officers under him be promoted.

To my adjutant, Lieut. J. K. Hudson, of the Tenth Kansas, I cannot award too high praise. He was my solitary aide, and was everywhere at duty's call, carrying orders, cheering and rallying the men. His worthy qualities in camp, as well as upon the field, entitle him to promotion.

I trust that the merits of several non-commissioned officers and privates will not hereafter be overlooked in granting commissions.

We lost 16 killed, 117 wounded, and 5 missing; total, 138.

Very respectfully, your obedient servant,

WM. WEER,
Colonel, Commanding.

Lieutenant-Colonel MOONLIGHT,
Chief of Staff.

No. 6.

Report of Maj. Henry H. Williams, Tenth Kansas Infantry.

HEADQUARTERS TENTH REGIMENT KANSAS VOLUNTEERS,
Rhea's Mills, Ark., December 10, 1862.

LIEUTENANT: I have the honor to submit the following report of the part taken by the Tenth Kansas Volunteers in the battle of Prairie Grove, Washington County, Arkansas, on Sunday, the 7th instant:

The regiment entered the grove on the enemy's left, by order of the colonel commanding the brigade, about 3 p. m. Upon entering the timber, which was very dense, I ordered Company B, Captain [M.] Quigg, to deploy as skirmishers to find the enemy. The regiment had but just formed, and the skirmishers advanced 30 yards, before the enemy opened fire upon us, and the regiment was immediately engaged under a terrible fire, which lasted for half an hour, when, by order of General Blunt, I withdrew the regiment to the open ground adjoining the timber; but after a few moments' respite we moved again to the front, about 30 yards in advance of our former position, obliquing our line of battle to the right, as the rebels had moved a large force to their left, extending far beyond our right. Our line at this time was in a hollow or depression in the ground, and the command, by lying down, escaped the most of the leaden rain which was hurled at them, by more than three times their number of the rebels, for an hour and a half. Exposed to a deadly fire during that time from the front and both flanks, it seems to me almost a miracle that the command was not annihilated.

About sunset the rebels charged with two regiments upon and turned our right flank, and I ordered the regiment to retreat, which it did in good style, to the open ground in our rear.

In the mean time the First Kansas Battery, Lieutenant Tenney commanding, which was in our rear, opened upon the rebels, obliquely across our right, with canister, which checked the force of the rebels extending beyond our right, and sent them in disorder to the brush. The Tenth then formed on the right of the battery, when the rebels commenced playing upon us with a battery which they had planted on their extreme left, but it was quickly silenced by a few well-directed shots from Tenney's battery. By this time, it being quite dark, both parties ceased firing and the engagement was ended.

Lieutenant [J. A.] Phillips, regimental adjutant, and all the officers of the line present, behaved with gallantry, and attended to their duties with promptness and decision. The non-commissioned officers and privates also, with a very few exceptions, behaved nobly, and obeyed every command promptly, and with a coolness worthy of veterans.

I remain, your obedient servant,

H. H. WILLIAMS,
Major, Commanding Tenth Kansas Volunteers.

Lieut. J. K. HUDSON,
A. A. A. G., Second Brig., First Div., Army of the Frontier.

No. 7.

Report of Col. William F. Cloud, Second Kansas Cavalry, commanding Third Brigade.

HDQRS. 3D BRIG., 1ST DIV., ARMY OF THE FRONTIER,
Cane Hill, Ark., December 15, 1862.

SIR: I have the honor to make the following report of the part taken by my brigade in the action at Prairie Grove on the 7th instant:

Having passed Friday and Saturday, the 5th and 6th, in skirmishing with the enemy upon the Boston Mountains, and lying in line of battle during the night of the 6th, I received your order to march toward Rhea's Mills at 9 a. m. of the 7th, and marched in the rear of the Second Brigade until within a mile of the mills, when, hearing heavy firing to the right, I moved in that direction, by your order, and reached the battle-field, where General Herron was engaging the enemy, under General Hindman, at 2 p. m., in advance. I found the enemy occupying a ridge of timber, thus concealed from view, and General Herron occupying the open field in front. By your order, I placed Rabb's battery in position in the open field, and Hopkins' Second Kansas (trophy) Battery at his left, and under their fire the rebel battery was soon silenced. Lieutenant Stover, with his Second Kansas Battery, also did good execution.

The right wing of the Eleventh Kansas Infantry, under Colonel Ewing, was ordered to enter the wood in front, to attack the rebels.

The left wing, under Lieutenant-Colonel Moonlight and Major Plumb, stood by the guns. The Second Kansas (dismounted), under Lieutenant-Colonel Bassett and Captain Crawford, and the First Indian, under Lieutenant-Colonel Wattles and Major Ellithorpe, and Stover's battery, I also sent into the wood in front. The Twentieth Iowa, of General Herron's command, also formed upon my left and entered the wood.

While the front was thus occupied by the infantry, the artillery ceased. Soon the entire line was engaged, and, from the heavy firing, severe work was evidently going on.

Upon the left, the enemy was evidently very strong. The Twentieth Iowa, overpowered by numbers, retired from the wood to the fence at the foot of the ridge, firing rapidly upon the enemy, who swarmed upon the crest. Directing my batteries, they fired over the heads of the Iowa boys, driving the rebels back with heavy loss. Still they pressed on, under cover of the wood, from our left to our right, causing my infantry to fall back to the fence, and giving my batteries opportunity to work, which they did successfully, driving the enemy up the hill into their cover. The infantry would then advance. Still, it was evident that the enemy had superior numbers; and, as the wood to their left had been abandoned, I rode forward to order the Eleventh to retire to the fence permanently, when Colonel Ewing, anticipating my order, retired his command just in time to save it from a heavy flank movement.

The enemy, now strongly re-enforced, pressed down in numbers to the fence at the foot of the hill, and, pouring a shower of rifle-balls upon us, took position within 200 yards of the batteries.

In this fire three of my orderlies were hit, but with spent balls. It now became evident that the enemy intended a demonstration upon my batteries, with the hope of their capture.

I then ordered the left wing of the Eleventh forward, when they advanced impatiently to the front, firing rapidly. The batteries met them also with case, canister, and shell. The enemy seemed determined to succeed, and, as my entire command was within close rifle-shot, I ordered the batteries to retire, firing, which they did; the infantry also retired slowly. Having obtained a position beyond their short-range guns, we continued the conflict until dark, when, not being able longer to see the enemy, firing ceased. My brigade then moved across the valley to the high ground, and bivouacked for the night. In the morning the enemy were gone.

During the entire conflict, I had the proud satisfaction of watching my command, and am happy to notice the conduct of the field officers of the First Indian, Lieutenant-Colonel Wattles and Major Ellithorpe; of Colonel Ewing, of the Eleventh, and the captains and lieutenants, and of Sergeant Enright, commanding Company I, of the Second, and especially of Captain Crawford, who was in command of the First Battalion, who are all worthy of their brave commands. These officers went into the thickest of the fight, and staid there until, by order or of necessity, the whole line fell back to more effective positions.

Of Captain Rabb's Second Indiana Battery, Captain Hopkins' Second Kansas (trophy) Battery, and Lieutenant Stover's Second Kansas (howitzer) Battery, I cannot speak in too high terms. Their batteries opened the fire, continued during and ended the fight, and the numbers of killed and wounded of the enemy in front of the batteries testify to their skill.

The hard marching of my command necessarily reduced its numbers, so that my effective force was much smaller than would have been expected.

My loss, though small, is severely felt. I had 8 killed and 59 wounded, of which about 8 are considered mortal. Among the latter was Captain [A. P.] Russell, since dead, who was a good and brave soldier, and a true and gallant friend. His loss is mourned by the entire command.

Herewith I have the honor to transmit the reports of the various commanders of my brigade.

I have the honor to be, general, your obedient servant,

W. F. CLOUD,
Colonel, Commanding Third Brigade.

Brig. Gen. JAMES G. BLUNT,
Commanding Army of the Frontier.

No. 8.

Report of Lieut. Col. Stephen H. Wattles, First Indian Home Guards.

HDQRS. FIRST REGIMENT INDIAN HOME GUARDS,
Cane Hill, Ark., December 12, 1862.

SIR: Your order of this date, requiring me to report to your headquarters the part which my command took in the action at Prairie Grove, on the 7th instant, has been received.

Soon after daylight, we were ordered to take position at the base of Boston Mountains, on the road where the small-arms were first brought into play in the running fight of the 28th ultimo. We remained in that position until the enemy abandoned the hill, and the cannonading commenced at Prairie Grove, when we rapidly marched for the scene of conflict. On our way, at Price's Barracks, about 2 miles from Cane Hill, a flanking party put to flight about 40 of the enemy's mounted men, who were watching our movements about 50 rods from our road.

On arriving at the battle-ground, we dismounted and entered the wood on the left of the center, with the Eleventh Kansas Volunteers on our right and an Iowa regiment on our left, and rapidly penetrated to the line of battle of the enemy, which gave way on our approach. At this time the Iowa regiment gave our left the partial effect of a volley. This fire in front and rear forced us to retrace our steps, but we rallied and formed again on the first little eminence in the edge of the wood, after a five-minute panic. On account of the retreat of the Iowa regiment from this place, we were ordered to the support of Captain Allen's battery, through the corn-field. All the companies in the command were engaged, except Company B, which was on detached service.

Major Ellithorpe and all the other white officers were particularly active and efficient during the whole day.

Of the Indian officers, Captain Jon-neh, of the Uches, and Capt. Billy Bowlegs, of the Seminoles, and Captain Tus-te-nup-chup-ko, of Company A (Creek), are deserving of the highest praise.

Our loss was 2 killed and 4 wounded, as far as reported, but the Indians entertain a prejudice against speaking of dangerous occurrences in battle, and report no wounds but such as the necessities of the case demand.

Your obedient servant,

STEPHEN H. WATTLES,
Lieutenant-Colonel, Comdg. First Indian Home Guards.

Col. WILLIAM F. CLOUD,
Comdg. Third Brigade, First Division, Army of the Frontier.

No. 9.

Report of Lieut. Col. Owen A. Bassett, Second Kansas Cavalry.

HEADQUARTERS SECOND KANSAS VOLUNTEERS,
In the Field, December 12, 1862.

SIR: I have the honor to report that, in obedience to your orders, I left my position, 5 miles south of Newburg, at 11 a. m. on the 7th instant, and moved toward Rhea's Mills, as rear guard to the column formed by the Second and Third Brigades. About an hour previous to receiving your orders to march, I had directed Major Plumb, commanding four companies of the Eleventh Kansas Infantry, that had been sent to my support the night previous, and Lieutenant Stover, commanding section of mountain howitzers, to report to you. Captain [H.] Hopkins, of my regiment, commanding battery, had already reported to you, and I had sent Captain [H.] Cameron to reconnoiter the mountains to my left.

Accordingly I had under my command Company A, commanded by Lieutenant [J.] Johnston; Company C, by Captain [D. S.] Whittenhall; Company D, by Captain [A.] Moore; Company E, by Captain [J.] Gardner; Company G, by Captain [A. W.] Matthews; Company H, by Captain [A.] Gunther; Company I, by First Sergt. Morris Enright; Company K, by Captain [A. P.] Russell, numbering 12 officers and 332 enlisted men. In addition thereto, I had with me Captain [S. J.] Crawford, assisting me in the field, 3 staff officers, and 2 of the non-commissioned staff. On my arrival at Boonsborough, I was delayed half an hour or more by the removal of the sick. I arrived at within 1½ miles of Rhea's Mills, where I came up with the rear of the column, and just then received word that a battle was being fought, 5 miles east, on the Fayetteville and Cove Creek road, and moved at once in that direction with all possible speed. My progress was much impeded from the fact that I was in rear of two brigades; the roads lay most of the way through lanes and thick underbrush, and it became necessary for me to pass through the fields, throwing down fences for that purpose, and through the tangled undergrowth, without the benefit of roads or paths. On my way to the battle-ground I passed the Tenth, Eleventh, and Thirteenth Regiments of Kansas Infantry, First Regiment of Indian Home Guards, Captain Rabb's, Captain Hopkins', and Lieutenant Tenney's batteries, and halted my regiment within range of the enemy's left flank in the woods about — p. m. A few minutes later I moved to the left out through the woods into a corn-field, where I formed line of battle on the right of our lines and opposite the enemy's left flank, where I, by your suggestion, dismounted my men and moved forward with them into the woods I had just left. I sent Companies E and I, under command of Captain Crawford, to take position on the left of the Eleventh Kansas Infantry, and placed Companies C, A, G, D, K, and H on the right of the Thirteenth Kansas Infantry, under a heavy fire of the enemy's musketry at long range. Lieutenant [E. S.] Stover took position with his howitzers in an interval made for him in the Thirteenth Kansas Infantry, where he opened fire upon the enemy with canister at short range with good effect. Captain Hopkins with his battery took position on the left of Captain Rabb's battery, where he remained until dark. The enemy hurling his masses of infantry upon our left flank, having compelled one or two regiments on the left of Captain Crawford's battalion to give way, charging obliquely on our lines from right to left, pouring volley after volley of musketry into our ranks, more than decimating them, it required all the nerve and courage that Captain Crawford was able to infuse into his men, by his brilliant example and courageous bearing, to enable them to withstand the shock. The enemy, however, bringing up heavy reenforcements, compelled Companies E and I to fall back, leaving the left to be held by the Eleventh Kansas Infantry. Lieutenant Stover with his howitzers was obliged to retire, his gunners and horses being too much exposed in their advanced position; and soon afterward, and just about dark, the infantry on my left retiring, I withdrew my men, they being unable longer to withstand the severe fire of the enemy. I ordered them remounted, and about an hour after dark received orders to retire to the rear of the field I was occupying, and bivouacked for the night.

The officers and men under my command behaved gallantly during the entire action. The commanding officers of squadrons already mentioned encouraged their men by their coolness and bravery, and I regret to say that Captain Russell fell, severely wounded, at the head of his company. Lieutenants Ballard, Moore, Mentzer, and Hook displayed more than ordinary courage. Lieutenant [B. B.] Mitchell, commanding a number of dismounted men in support of Captain Hopkins' battery, and Lieutenant Aduddell, second in command of that battery, did their duty. I desire to call especial attention to the manner in which Captain Hopkins with his company handled the captured battery. Although having but four weeks' experience with that arm of the service, their coolness and the well-directed fire of their pieces would have reflected credit upon veterans.

Before closing this report, I desire to add that Capt. John Gardner has my thanks for holding his position so long on the extreme left, while opposing, with his men, more than twenty times his number; and to Sergeant Enright, who commanded the second company from the left, the same are tendered.

To my staff officers, Lieutenants [S. K.] Cross, [C. L.] Gorton, and [L. H.] Wood, I am under obligations for valuable services; and I cannot pass unnoticed Sergeants Remiatte, Bailey, and Vangender, who acted in the capacity of orderlies.

The loss sustained by my regiment was 3 killed and 21 wounded, 16 of them severely.*

I have the honor to be, colonel, very respectfully, your obedient servant,

OWEN A. BASSETT,

Lieutenant-Colonel, Commanding Second Kansas Volunteers.

Col. WILLIAM F. CLOUD, *Commanding Third Brigade.*

No. 10.

Report of Capt. Henry Hopkins, Second Kansas Cavalry, commanding battery.

HEADQUARTERS HOPKINS' BATTERY,
Rhea's Mills, Ark., December 10, 1862.

SIR: I respectfully submit the following report of the part taken by the battery under my command in the battle of Prairie Grove, Ark., December 7, 1862, and the series of skirmishes preceding that action:

Information having been received on the 3d of December that the enemy was advancing in force from the south, the battery was ordered to take position in advance of the main line, where it remained until the morning of the 7th, rendering some assistance in checking the enemy on the Newburg road.

About 10 a.m., December 7, in obedience to orders, I moved the battery into the position assigned it in column north to Rhea's Mills, and thence, 5 miles east, to Prairie Grove, where the Second and Third Divisions, Army of the Frontier, under Brigadier-General Herron, were engaging the enemy, under General Hindman, who, during the night of the 6th, had flanked the First Division, commanded by Brigadier-General Blunt, passing 12 miles to the left and rear.

Having been ordered into position in an open field, on the left of the First Division, I opened fire with shot and shell on the enemy, occupying a position on a densely wooded rise of ground, and drove him back. At this time the only support for my battery was a detachment of dismounted cavalry, not exceeding 25, under command of Lieutenant [B. B.] Mitchell, Second Kansas Cavalry. Shortly afterward the enemy again advanced in greater force, moving obliquely along our front, threatening the left flank. In conjunction with Rabb's battery, which was some distance on my right, I opened a heavy fire again upon the enemy, and was supported by a regiment of Iowa troops, which had been driven back by the advancing column. The enemy appeared to be massing his forces for a charge, and just at sunset moved impetuously forward, but, by well-directed and rapid discharges of spherical case and canister, their advance was checked, and the battery slowly retired, firing with prolonges attached. Night coming on, firing ceased and the troops bivouacked on the field. The next morning it was known that the enemy had fallen back. By good fortune there were no casualties in my command.

Respectfully, your obedient servant,

H. HOPKINS,

Captain Second Kansas Cavalry, Commanding Battery.

Lieut. S. K. CROSS,
Acting Adjutant, Second Kansas Cavalry.

---

* But see revised statement, p. 85.

No. 11.

Report of Col. Thomas Ewing, jr., Eleventh Kansas Infantry.

HDQRS. ELEVENTH REGIMENT KANSAS VOLUNTEERS,
Camp at Cane Hill, Ark., December 12, 1862.

COLONEL: In compliance with your order of this date, I submit a report of the part taken by the Eleventh Regiment of Kansas Volunteers in the late battle of Prairie Grove.

At 1 p. m. of the 7th instant, as the Third Brigade reached Rhea's Mills, in march from Boston Mountains, the sound of cannon was heard from the battle-field, 5 miles east of the mills. By your order I followed with my regiment close after Rabb's battery, in its rapid drive to the field, losing out of the ranks about 50 men, who were unable to keep pace with the command. As the battery took position, I sent the left wing of my regiment, with Lieutenant-Colonel Moonlight and Major [P. B.] Plumb, to its left, while, with the adjutant and sergeant-major of the regiment, I marched the right wing to the right of the battery. Thence I was immediately ordered by General Blunt to move with the five companies composing that wing, and form in line of battle with the left of the Thirteenth Regiment; which being done, we moved through the orchard and field adjacent to it, to the road on the hillside, about 600 yards from where we left the battery. Here a musketry engagement ensued with the enemy, who were about 200 yards in advance of us, under cover of the crest of the hill. Two howitzers of the Second Kansas took position at the blacksmith shop, in front of my right, and played effectively upon the enemy for half an hour, and then withdrew for want of ammunition. The musketry fire nearly ceased when the howitzers commenced playing, but was renewed when they withdrew.

When the engagement had lasted here about an hour, I noticed that the First Indian Regiment, which had entered the wood about 300 yards to the left of me, had been driven out, and were fleeing toward the battery, which fact I at once communicated to Colonel [William] Weer, commanding Second Brigade, under whose orders I was then acting. In about five minutes afterward I was ordered to advance, and did so, in line, with the Thirteenth Regiment on my right, and three companies of the Second Kansas (dismounted), who had formed upon my left. When within about 25 yards of the crest of the hill, the enemy appeared in overwhelming numbers, advancing over the hill on our left and front, and poured on us a tremendous fire. My command remained, steadily holding their ground, until they had fired four rounds, when, seeing that the three companies of the Second Kansas had withdrawn, and finding that the enemy's force in our front, left, and rear was strong, and near enough to surround and overwhelm us, I ordered my command to fall back, which they did, firing. I then attempted to form again in the road on the hillside, but the enemy was too close upon us to render such formation practicable or the position tenable. I then ordered them to fall back, and formed them in the orchard lane, near the edge of the wood and at the foot of the hill, where they were partially sheltered by the broken fences forming the lane.

In this new position we remained three-quarters of an hour, hotly engaged with the enemy, who swarmed in great numbers in the orchard and about the farm-house, out-buildings, and straw-piles adjacent, under cover of which they had apparently intended to move upon Rabb's battery, which had advanced to within 200 yards of the wood.

A little after dark, when the enemy's fire and our own had ceased over the whole field, I withdrew my command in good order from the hillside, and returned to the prairie, where the rest of the First Division of the army lay.

My command suffered less than might have been expected, owing to our position being at all times lower than that of the enemy, who generally overshot. I led into action in my right wing 291 officers and men, and had 3 killed, and 3 mortally, 12 severely, and 11 slightly, wounded. The loss was greatest in Companies I and C, because they were on the left of my line and were subjected to the heaviest of the flank fire.

I am happy to say that my command obeyed my orders implicitly, and without faltering in advancing and in reforming and holding the several lines. It were unfair to specially name any, where all did nobly; but I cannot close my report without reference to Private William Grigsby, of Company I, who was mortally wounded in the action, and who, though detailed as teamster when the battle began, found a substitute to drive his team, that he might go to the field and share with his friends its dangers.

I inclose herewith a report of Lieutenant-Colonel Moonlight of the part taken by the left wing of my regiment, under his command, in the engagement.

I am, colonel, very respectfully, yours,

THOMAS EWING, JR.,
Colonel Eleventh Regiment Kansas Volunteers, Commanding.

Col. WILLIAM F. CLOUD,
Comdg. Third Brigade, First Division, Army of the Frontier.

No. 12.

Report of Lieut. Col. Thomas Moonlight, Eleventh Kansas Infantry.

HDQRS. ELEVENTH REGIMENT KANSAS VOLUNTEERS,
Rhea's Mills, Ark., December 11, 1862.

SIR: I have the honor to report officially the part the left wing of your regiment (my command) took in the engagement of the 7th instant, known as Prairie Grove.

I was detailed with my command to support Rabb's Indiana battery, and when it took position, about 300 yards in front of the enemy, I formed on its left flank. Shortly afterward the battery changed position, and I formed on its right, a few paces in rear.

About sundown, when the enemy, with overwhelming numbers, charged our infantry in the wood in front, they fell back, so as to give our batteries an opportunity to play on the enemy, which they did in beautiful style. I moved up my command in a line with Rabb's guns, the better to resist the enemy's charge, for it was evident they intended charging the battery.

I would here state that I kept my command flat on the ground (very much against their wish), the better to shelter them from the enemy's fire. At this time there was a complete shower (so to speak) of bullets. One man of Company K and two of Company E were here wounded; one since dead—Private Judge.

The battery was ordered to retire, firing, and I conformed to the movement, the command retiring in excellent order.

I was ably assisted during the engagement by Major Plumb, of the regiment, who was ever at his post, proving himself a soldier of the right stamp.

The companies composing my command were H, Captain [J.] Huntoon; E, Captain [E. G.] Ross; K, Captain [J. M.] Allen; G, Captain [N. A.] Adams, and B, Captain Anderson.

Every officer and soldier behaved throughout with judgment and gallantry, and it would be impossible for me to make any selections as to bravery or soldierly conduct, for all were equally determined to excel on these points. The trouble was to keep them back with the battery, as the duty assigned us required me to do.

Very respectfully, your obedient servant,

THOS. MOONLIGHT,
Lieut. Col. Eleventh Regiment Kansas Vols., Comdg. Left Wing.

Col. THOMAS EWING, Jr.,
Commanding Eleventh Regiment Kansas Volunteers.

No. 13.

Report of Capt. John W. Rabb, Second Indiana Battery.

HDQRS. SECOND BATTERY, INDIANA VOLUNTEERS,
Camp at Rhea's Mills, December 10, 1862.

SIR: I have the honor to make the following report of the part my command took in the late engagement of Prairie Grove:

On the morning of the 7th instant we were in position on the Boston Mountains, south of Cane Hill, expecting an attack from the enemy, as our pickets were engaged. About 10 a. m. I received orders from you to fall back toward Rhea's Mills, as the enemy were evidently attempting to flank us by passing up the Fayetteville road. The First Brigade, under General Salomon, held the advance in falling back. The Second Brigade, under Colonel Weer, followed, while the Third Brigade followed the Second. The Second Kansas Cavalry brought up our rear, preceded by the First Indian Home Guard. My battery was placed just in advance of the Indians.

Our brigade arrived within a mile of Rhea's Mills about 2 p. m., when heavy firing was heard about 4 miles to the right, upon the Fayetteville road. You immediately ordered me to take the advance of the Third Brigade and proceed rapidly to the scene of action. I marched under your direction across the country, followed by the other commands of the Third Brigade, a distance of 3 miles, where we came upon the enemy, stationed in force upon a commanding hill, covered with timber. By your order, I brought my battery into position in a meadow, and immediately opened fire upon the batteries of the enemy. Lieutenant Tenney's battery was placed in position upon my right, and Captain Hopkins' on my left and rear. Our infantry and cavalry were posted in supporting distance, to the rear. In less than half an hour the rebel batteries were silenced. I then directed my fire upon the infantry of the enemy that were advancing from the left toward our right. An order came at this time for Lieutenant Tenney's battery to join Colonel Weer's brigade.

In a few moments the infantry and cavalry (the latter dismounted) of your brigade were ordered to engage the enemy and draw them from the cover of the wood. My batteries ceased firing for a short time. Five companies of the Eleventh Kansas, under Lieutenant-Colonel [T.] Moonlight, remained in the open field as a support to my battery.

The Twentieth Iowa Regiment, Col. [W.] McE. Dye's brigade, General Herron's command, advanced into the wood upon my left, but, after fifteen minutes' firing, was driven back, when I opened upon the enemy, firing shell over the heads of the Twentieth Iowa. In a few minutes our infantry drove the rebels to the edge of the wood, when I again, by your order, opened fire upon them. A heavy musketry fire was then brought to bear upon my command. I answered with canister. For fifteen minutes my men stood firm, firing their pieces with terrible precision, making roads in the ranks of the enemy, which were quickly filled by fresh men from the rear. Three times they advanced in heavy force upon the battery, but were driven back to the wood with heavy loss. Finding that we were too near the wood, you ordered me to fire, retiring a distance of 100 yards. This order was successfully complied with, notwithstanding several men had been wounded and horses killed and disabled.

In our new position, by your order, I threw several shell into a straw pile, near the edge of the timber, around which large bodies of the enemy swarmed. The straw was soon ignited, and again we opened with canister for about fifteen minutes. My guns were worked rapidly, making sad havoc in the ranks of the enemy, who retreated to the wood. I gave them a few shell as a parting salute, when darkness closed upon us, and we rested upon the field. In about two hours we removed to a better position, where we rested for the night.

During the heat of the engagement the five companies of the Eleventh Kansas, commanded by Lieutenant-Colonel Moonlight, stood manfully at their posts, and, when it appeared that the enemy were about to charge upon me, rushed forward and assisted in driving the enemy back.

I need hardly report to you that every officer, non-commissioned officer, and private of my command behaved manfully during the whole engagement. Lieutenants [H.] Espey and [W. W.] Haines and Sergeant [J. S.] Whicher, commanding sections, rendered me great assistance in the management of the battery. Sergeant [G. B.] Sink, when 2 of his men were wounded, took the company colors, and still superintended his piece while bearing aloft the Stars and Stripes. Corpl. Samuel Mullen and Private [J.] Warren Dibble were severely wounded early in the engagement, yet remained at their posts until its close. I had 4 horses killed, 5 badly wounded, and 7 slightly wounded. The carriages of the battery bear marks of the storm of bullets and buckshot poured upon us.*

I am, most respectfully, your obedient servant, &c ,

JOHN W. RABB,

Captain, Commanding Second Battery, Indiana Volunteers.

Col. WILLIAM F. CLOUD,

Commanding Third Brigade, Army of the Frontier.

No. 14.

Reports of Brig. Gen. Francis J. Herron, U. S. Army, commanding Second and Third Divisions.

HDQRS. 2D AND 3D DIVS., ARMY OF THE FRONTIER,
Battle-field, Prairie Grove, December 9, 1862.

[SIR :] General Blunt has undoubtedly informed you of the battle of yesterday. Hindman moved in to the east of Blunt, with his entire

*Nominal list of casualties shows 8 men wounded.

force (25,000 men), intending to cut off my command. I had sent forward to Blunt all my cavalry, having left six regiments of infantry, three batteries, and about 500 cavalry.

General Marmaduke opened on my advance at 7 a. m. with a heavy cavalry force, but I forced them back to Illinois Creek, 8 miles from Cane Hill. At this point they took a strong position with infantry and artillery, and tried to prevent my crossing; but, by cutting roads through the woods, I got the batteries into position, and at 9.30 o'clock opened on them with eighteen guns, bringing forward my infantry, crossing the creek, and getting them into position under cover of my artillery. From this hour until 7 o'clock in the evening the fighting was furious.

General Blunt arrived within 1 mile of my right at 4 p. m., opening on the enemy's left. Learning definitely that he was on the ground, I ordered the infantry to charge the enemy's batteries. The Nineteenth Iowa and Twentieth Wisconsin did it gallantly, taking a whole battery, but were afterward overwhelmed and forced to leave it. Colonel Huston, commanding Second Division, then charged the same battery with the Thirty-seventh Illinois and Twenty-sixth Indiana, retaking it a second time, but, after holding it half an hour, were compelled to give way. The fighting was constant and furious throughout the entire day.

I met General Blunt late in the evening, and we arranged the attack for morning; but daylight found the rebels gone.

Their loss is from 600 to 700 killed and 2,500 wounded. Ours is probably 250 killed and 700 wounded in the Second and Third Divisions.* Lieutenant-Colonel [S.] McFarland, Nineteenth Iowa, is killed, and Colonel [J. C.] Black, Thirty-seventh Illinois, Major [W. G.] Thompson, Twentieth Iowa, and a large number of line officers wounded. The prisoners state that General Steen and 5 colonels were killed. We captured four caissons full of ammunition and a large number of small-arms. Their artillery was knocked to pieces by our batteries, and Major [J. M.] Hubbard, who was a prisoner with them, reports seeing piece after piece sent off entirely disabled. The working of Murphy's and Foust's batteries excelled anything I ever witnessed.

General Blunt and myself had an interview with Hindman and Marmaduke, and I consider the former just what you stated of him. We are camped on the battle-field. General Blunt moves to-morrow to Cane Hill, while I occupy this ground.

F. J. HERRON,
Brigadier-General, Commanding Second and Third Divisions.

Maj. Gen. SAMUEL R. CURTIS,
Saint Louis, Mo.

PRAIRIE GROVE, ARK.,
December 11, 1862.

One of my spies, who came to the battle-field with Hindman's troops, and retreated with them to Dripping Springs, has just come in. He reports the rebel loss at 2,500 killed and wounded, including a very large number of officers. Brigadier-General Steen, of Missouri, was killed, and some 6 or 7 field officers are in the hospital within our lines. Two batteries were so much damaged by the firing from Foust's and Murphy's guns as to be entirely worthless, and several guns were hauled off

* See revised statement, p. 86.

in wagons. All of their artillery horses were left dead on the field and the caissons taken away by mules in the night. Hindman's entire force was here, and from personal observation I can say they were well clothed and well armed. My divisions took over 60 prisoners, including 2 commissioned officers, during the fight, and all refuse to be exchanged, except 12. Over 150 have come in since the battle, and the report is that hundreds are coming back on the road to give themselves up. The greater proportion of the dead have been left by them unburied, and were buried to-day by my order. The advance had arrived at Van Buren, and the rumor was they were all going to Little Rock. The loss in my division is heavy, and will almost reach 1,000 killed and wounded. For four hours the fighting was the most desperate I ever witnessed, and within a space of two acres 250 of our own and the enemy's dead were found. The victory is more complete and decisive than I had imagined. The Iowa regiments fought nobly, the Nineteenth particularly distinguishing itself. We mourn the loss of Lieutenant-Colonel [Samuel] McFarland, and several other officers of that regiment, killed. The Twentieth Wisconsin, Twenty-sixth Indiana, and Thirty-seventh Illinois fought nobly. The battle-field is on the road from Fayetteville to Cove Creek, and just half way between the former place and Cane Hill. General Blunt has moved to Rhea's Mills, while I occupy the battle-field. I am strengthening my line with Springfield, and will have it safe to-morrow. Have established a hospital at Fayetteville, and removed all our sick and wounded to it. If Steele could take Little Rock, now is our best opportunity to open the Arkansas River. I hope you will let us do it.

F. J. HERRON,
Brigadier-General.

Maj. Gen. SAMUEL R. CURTIS.

HDQRS. 2D AND 3D DIVS., ARMY OF THE FRONTIER,
Prairie Grove, Ark., December 12, 1862.

GENERAL: After leaving Wilson's Creek, in accordance with the orders from General Blunt and yourself, I moved my command by forced day marches, the distance being too great for day and night movements, and, traveling at the rate of 35 miles per day, reached Fayetteville Sunday morning, the 7th, at 3 o'clock. Resting one hour, I pushed on, and, when 6 miles south of the town, my advance (Major Hubbard, with two companies of the First Missouri Cavalry) met the First Arkansas and Seventh Missouri Cavalry coming back in great disorder.

At Cross Hollow General Blunt had sent me an order to send on all my cavalry, which I did, sending all that was with the Third Division, and sending back for what was with the Second Division to come up and pass me. The cavalry of the Third Division started from Cross Hollow on Saturday, the 6th, at 10 a. m., reaching Cane Hill about 10 o'clock the same night. The cavalry from the Second Division passed me and traveled until 12 o'clock at night, stopping half way between Fayetteville and Cane Hill to feed and start at daylight. They encamped with the First Arkansas, this regiment having been ordered forward by General Blunt. Just at daylight they were attacked by a heavy cavalry force, under Marmaduke, and after several rounds were stampeded. They came back on me 6 miles south of Fayetteville, at 7 a. m., closely pursued by at least 3,000 cavalry. It was with the very greatest difficulty that we got them checked, and prevented a general stampede of the battery horses; but after some hard talking, and my finally shooting one cowardly whelp off his horse, they halted. I at once formed a battery and two regiments of infantry and checked Marmaduke.

Taking one section of artillery, four companies of infantry, and some cavalry, I pushed on, driving them 4 miles, to Illinois Creek, where I found the whole force in position, and the strongest one I had ever seen. I crossed the creek with one of my staff to reconnoiter, keeping every one else out of sight, and, after getting a view of the ground and surrounding country, determined at once to attack. I learned the whole force had slipped past Blunt, and was between us, and knew that by opening the fight I could bring him up. Getting two pieces of Cole's over, I felt their position, they opening on me with twelve pieces from different positions. I then withdrew the section, and ordered Murphy's battery to cut a road through the wood, crossing the creek half a mile below, getting it into a fair position opposite the enemy's center. Colonel Huston's division (the Second) I ordered to the same place, throwing two regiments to the right of the battery and one to its left. I had divided the battery, placing the halves 600 yards apart.

This movement was entirely concealed, and not visible to the enemy until the two half batteries were run out to the edge of the brush by hand. I then ordered Colonel [W. W.] Orme, with the Second Brigade of the Third Division, to cross his battery at the regular crossing, dividing it and opening fire at once, and to hold his infantry in rear and at the edge of the brush, at the same time ordering Lieutenant-Colonel [H.] Bertram, with the First Brigade, Third Division, to follow up Orme, dividing his battery the same way, and forming his infantry to the right of Orme.

At 10 o'clock all was ready, and Murphy opened. The other batteries crossed under cover of Murphy's fire, getting into shape and opening up magnificently, so that I had in ten minutes eighteen pieces hard at work; or, as they afterward styled it, six full batteries. This brought out the fire of all their guns, twenty-two in number, and for the next eight hours it was hot work. About half an hour after the firing commenced, they threw a heavy body of infantry on my left and endeavored to force it back, but I ordered the Nineteenth Iowa and Twentieth Wisconsin to charge them, which they did in gallant style, pushing on for 1,000 yards and capturing a battery of four pieces, but such a mass of the enemy came upon them they were compelled to leave it. The infantry fighting was continuous from 11 until 5 o'clock.

At 4 o'clock a battery opened about 1 mile to the right of my right flank, throwing two shells into my line of skirmishers. At first I thought the rebels had worked around me, but, upon making a reconnaissance in person, I discovered it to be Blunt's advance, whereupon I sent him word to change his fire. For two hours Blunt had a severe artillery fight, and at 6.30 o'clock the firing closed. I was then about 1,000 yards in advance of the creek crossed in the morning, with Murphy's battery still in a high position in the rear. We lay on our arms that night, the pickets within 50 yards of each other.

At 3 a. m. I formed my line ready to open, and while doing so saw a flag of truce approaching. It proved to be General Marmaduke and staff, with a communication for General Blunt, in answer, they said, to one he had sent them. I held them, and sent the document to Blunt, whose quarters were 1 mile from me. He returned by my adjutant-general a verbal reply, which they refused to accept, and I visited Blunt in person, telling him that I thought they had left the field. He returned a written reply, with which I started them; but hardly had it disappeared beyond their pickets until another flag came, asking a personal interview with Blunt. This the general granted, and at 7 o'clock called for me to accompany him. I saw what was up, and, before starting, ordered two regiments to advance through the brush on my left and occupy the hill where the enemy were posted. This they did, the rebel pickets retiring before them. During the interview, Hindman was informed of it, and asked Blunt to withdraw them. He referred the matter to me, and I refused.

At 10 o'clock the interview ended, Blunt having given Hindman until 5 p. m. to bury his dead. They immediately sent forward two regiments of cavalry for that purpose, but instead of doing it they commenced gathering up arms, &c. I went then in person and notified both colonels that any of their men found gathering or carrying off arms, or at anything else than burying the dead, I would hold them as prisoners of war. This had the desired effect, and we thus secured the arms on the field in spite of the flag of truce.

My two divisions, the Second and Third, fought splendidly, while the artillery firing of Murphy's, Foust's, and Backof's batteries was the finest thing I ever witnessed. The artillery horses of the enemy lie dead, four and six in a heap, wherever their batteries were placed. On less than two acres of ground laid 300 of our own and the rebel dead. It was terrible—terrific in the extreme.

The loss in my own immediate division (Third) is 483 killed and wounded; in the Second, Colonel Huston commanding, 350 killed and wounded, making a total, in my two divisions, of almost 850.* The loss in General Blunt's division is about 150 killed and wounded.* I have established a post hospital at Fayetteville, and removed all my wounded to that point, as has General Blunt.

We want sanitary goods badly. Lieutenant-Colonel McFarland, of the Nineteenth Iowa, was killed in the first charge, with 5 captains and a large number of lieutenants of the Nineteenth Iowa and Twentieth Wisconsin Regiments. In the second charge, made by the Twenty-sixth Indiana and Thirty-seventh Illinois, Lieutenant-Colonel Black, of the Thirty-seventh, and his adjutant, were both badly wounded, and the adjutant, with several captains and lieutenants of the Twenty-sixth Indiana, killed. Major Thompson, Twentieth Iowa, was also badly wounded. Five of my body guard were wounded and 12 horses killed.

At one time, while passing from the right to the left through an open field, they opened two pieces on me from a distance of 300 yards, killing 2 horses of my body guard and wounding 1 man. The head was shot off the horse immediately in rear of me. I can assure you it was hot work.

The rebel loss in killed and wounded is not less than 2,500 men, while by desertion it will be from 5,000 to 8,000. They are fleeing in every direction. Of over 60 prisoners taken during the fight, not over 12 will go back, as they positively refuse to be exchanged.

I am now occupying the battle-field, while General Blunt is at Rhea's Mills, 5 miles west. Two of his brigades are at Cane Hill. We have assisted the rebels in moving all their wounded to Cane Hill, and have furnished them five days' rations. Had it not been for us they would have starved to death.

We have as trophies, captured during the fight, four caissons, filled with good ammunition and everything in good style. We have also about 400 stand of good arms, gathered on the field; this is clear gain.

---

* See revised statement, p. 86.

In regard to General Blunt, I would say that he is, beyond question, a good fighting man. Last evening I spent with him at Rhea's Mills. Major Van Antwerp is here, and makes a very efficient officer.

In conclusion, general, permit me to say that you have here a good, reliable army, but there are some officers that must be cleared out. They are worse than worthless. It was a narrow escape getting rid of Colonel Wright.

With kind regards to Mrs. Curtis, Major Harry, and others, I am, very respectfully, your friend,

F. J. HERRON,
Brigadier-General.

Maj. Gen. SAMUEL R. CURTIS,
Commanding.

HDQRS. 2D AND 3D DIVS., ARMY OF THE FRONTIER,
Battle-field of Prairie Grove, Ark., December 19, 1862.

GENERAL: In reviewing the operations of the 7th instant, I must necessarily commence my report a few days previous to that date.

On the morning of December 3, I was encamped, with the Second and Third Divisions of the Army of the Frontier, at Wilson's Creek, Mo., and there received your dispatch announcing the advance of the rebel forces under General Hindman, and ordering me to move forward, with my command, to your support, at Cane Hill, Ark. Within three hours after the receipt of your dispatch, the Third Division was in motion, the Second soon following.

Reaching Elkhorn on the evening of the 5th instant, I there received your order to send forward all my cavalry to you, and, in obedience thereto, I ordered forward Colonel Wickersham, with the Tenth Illinois, First Iowa, Eighth Missouri, and First Battalion Second Wisconsin Cavalry, all of which reached you safely.

On Sunday morning, the 7th instant, at 4 o'clock, I arrived at Fayetteville, having marched all night, and was pushing rapidly forward, expecting to join you by 10 o'clock of the same day, when, 6 miles south of Fayetteville, my advance, consisting of two companies of the First Missouri Volunteer Cavalry, under Maj. J. M. Hubbard, discovered a body of cavalry falling back on the road in great disorder. It proved to be the First Arkansas and Seventh Missouri Cavalry, that were moving forward to join you, and had been attacked by a large force of rebel cavalry, under General Marmaduke, near Illinois Creek, 10 miles from Cane Hill. After some effort, the retreating cavalry were checked and reformed; but in holding the rebel advance, the First Battalion First Missouri Cavalry was severely handled and Major Hubbard taken prisoner. Here the rebels formed in line of battle, but on opening fire upon them with a section of Battery E, First Missouri Artillery, they were soon put to flight, and driven back 4 miles, to Illinois Creek. Here I discovered the enemy in position directly in front on each side of the road, occupying a high ridge, about three-quarters of a mile from the ford of the creek, covered with timber and thick underbrush.

Wishing to feel the position of the enemy, I ordered the Ninety fourth Illinois Infantry, with a section of Battery E, First Missouri Light Artillery, across the creek, and opened fire upon them. Their batteries were in good position, commanding the ford of the creek, and, having excellent range, compelled my advance to fall back, it being impossible to move my command across the ford under their fire.

I then ordered Colonel Huston, commanding the Second Division, to cut a road through the timber, and move Battery F (Captain Murphy), First Missouri Artillery, to a point on the south side of the creek, and half a mile from the regular ford, my intention being to draw the fire of the enemy, to enable my infantry to cross the creek at the ford. The movement was entirely successful, the battery dividing, getting into position, and opening fire on the enemy before they discovered the movement. Under cover of its fire, I ordered forward the batteries of Captain Backof, Lieutenant Foust, and Lieutenant Borris, supported by the Nineteenth Iowa, Twentieth Wisconsin, and Ninety-fourth Illinois Infantry. So rapidly was the order obeyed that the whole eighteen pieces were at work before the enemy could obtain our range. The fire was rapidly replied to by the rebel batteries, which had every advantage in position; but so accurate was the firing that in one hour nearly all their batteries were silenced.

During this time I had formed the infantry, the Second Division, Colonel Huston commanding, occupying the right, and the Third Division, under my immediate command, the left of my position. It required but a short time to satisfy myself that the rebels were present in largely superior force, and I immediately determined to give them the best fight I could until you could come up with additional forces. The enemy making a movement of their infantry toward my left, I ordered forward the Second Brigade of the Third Division, under Col. W. W. Orme, to the base of the ridge occupied by them, and, while their attention was attracted by the fire of the Second Brigade, I moved up the First Brigade, under command of Lieutenant-Colonel Bertram. The batteries advanced across the open field with the infantry, pouring in a terrible fire of grape and canister. When within 100 yards of the ridge, the Twentieth Wisconsin and Nineteenth Iowa Infantry were ordered to charge a battery placed near a farm house, on the edge of the hill. The charge was made in gallant style, the enemy driven back, and the battery taken, but the ground could not be held. Regiment after regiment of infantry was hurled upon them, and they were compelled to fall back. This was followed by a charge of the rebels *en masse* upon the batteries of Captains Foust and Backof, and Lieutenant Borris. Never was there more real courage and pluck displayed, and more downright hard fighting done, than at this moment by the above-named batteries. Advancing to within 100 yards of the guns, the rebels received a fire that could not be withstood, and retreated in disorder, receiving, as they ran, a terrible fire, causing great slaughter among them.

For the management of his battery and the soldier-like qualities displayed by Captain Foust, Company E, First Missouri Light Artillery, at this time especially, he deserves very great credit. Colonel Huston was then instructed to move one of his brigades from the right to the support of the center.

Arriving at the point and discovering the rebel infantry again moving down the hill, Colonel Huston ordered the Twenty-sixth Indiana and Thirty-seventh Illinois Regiments to charge them, which they did, Colonel Huston leading them in person. It was a repetition of the first charge; the same battery was captured, the enemy again driven back, and we, in turn, compelled to abandon the position by force of numbers.

About this time (2.30 p. m.) a battery opened some distance from my right, which I soon discovered to be from your division. With the knowledge that you had really arrived, a new spirit was infused in my command, now almost worn out by the severe work, and they went at it again with increased vigor. When your column moved up, the Second Brigade of the Second Division, Col. William McE. Dye commanding, also advanced on your left, having a severe fight in the timber, and driving the enemy from the hillside. From this hour until dark the firing was steady and terrific, the batteries of the First Division firing the last round.

My command slept on their arms nearly 1,000 yards in advance of the position occupied in the morning, and ready to renew the fight at daybreak. The arrangement for attack on the 8th; the flight of the enemy during the night; the trickery of the rebel Generals Hindman and Marmaduke, are all known to you. Night alone saved them from capture.

I have as captures four caissons complete, and filled with ammunition; a number of sets of artillery harness, caisson wheels, and about 300 stand of arms. I regret to state that my loss was very severe. Lieutenant-Colonel McFarland, who led the Nineteenth Iowa in the first charge, a true man and gallant soldier, sleeps his last sleep. Lieutenant-Colonel Black, Thirty-seventh Illinois; Major Thompson, Twentieth Iowa, and a large number of line officers, are wounded. Major Bredett, of the Seventh Missouri Cavalry, a brave and noble soldier, was killed in the early part of the battle. My troops all did well. Iowa, Illinois, Wisconsin, Indiana, and Missouri, side by side, proved by the truest test their loyalty and love of country.

Colonel Huston, commanding Second Division, was always in the front and did valuable service. Colonels Orme, Clark, McE. Dye, and Bertram, commanding brigades, were with their commands in the thickest of the fight, and performed their duties well.

I must especially mention the working of Murphy's, Foust's, Backof's, and Borris' batteries. The former fired his guns with the precision of a sharpshooter, while the others worked their pieces gallantly in the midst of a terrible infantry fire.

My cavalry, the First Iowa, Eighth Missouri, Tenth Illinois, and Second Wisconsin, having been with you during the day, I know but little of the parts taken by them. They have on other fields proved themselves worthy of the name of American soldiers, and I have no doubt sustained it while with you.

Maj. J. M. Hubbard and his command, the fighting battalion of the First Missouri Cavalry, gallantly held in check the rebel advance in the early part of the day, and on this occasion officers and men have added to their already high reputation.

To Capt. William Hyde Clark, my assistant adjutant-general, who had for three days been carried sick in an ambulance, but mounted that morning to be with me during the battle, I am much indebted for services on the field, and also to Captain Littleton, commissary of subsistence; Captain Brewster, Lieutenants Pettit, Shiras, and Douglas, of my staff, for their conduct and assistance throughout the battle.

There were many instances of individual courage and bravery that I should like to mention, but will have to refer you to the reports of brigade commanders. Of Lieutenant-Colonel Black, Thirty-seventh Illinois Infantry, I must say that a braver man never went upon the battle-field, and he has on this occasion added to the laurels won at Pea Ridge.

In conclusion, general, let me say for the Second and Third Divisions that they had marched 110 miles in three days to join you, and that they came upon the field weak in numbers, on account of the severity of the march, 3,500 men being all that I had engaged.*

I am, very truly, your obedient servant,

F. J. HERRON,
Brigadier-General, Commanding Second and Third Divisions.

Brig. Gen. JAMES G. BLUNT,
Commanding Army of the Frontier.

[Inclosure.]

HDQRS. 2D AND 3D DIVS., ARMY OF THE FRONTIER,
Prairie Grove, Ark., December 10, 1862.

FELLOW SOLDIERS: It is with pride and pleasure that I am enabled to congratulate you on the victory so recently achieved over the enemy. Meeting their combined forces, vastly your superiors in numbers; armed and equipped in the most efficient manner, contrary to what we had been led to believe; marshaled by their ablest generals; posted in a strong position of their own selection, prepared and ready to attack us; entertaining toward us feelings of hatred and fiendish passion, evoked by infamous lies, which even rebel generals should have disdained to utter, you, fellow soldiers, after a forced march of over 100 miles in less than three days, weary, exhausted, and almost famishing, animated only by that feeling of patriotism that induced you to give up the pleasures and comforts of home to undergo the dangers and hardships of the field, did most gallantly meet, fight, and repulse the enemy. Your fellow soldiers elsewhere; your friends and relatives at home; your fellow citizens, and your country, as they learn of the splendid service of the artillerymen; of the determined daring and brillant charges of the infantry, will render you that praise and honor which is justly your due. Iowa, Illinois, Indiana, Wisconsin, and Missouri, your native States, are proud of their noble sons. I, who witnessed your gallant daring in every encounter, in behalf of your country and myself, tender you grateful thanks for the services you have rendered.

While we drop a tear, therefore, for those who have fallen, and sympathize with those who are yet suffering, let us not forget to render thanks to the Beneficent Giver of all blessings for the success that has thus far attested the truth and right of our glorious cause.

F. J. HERRON,
Brigadier-General, Commanding Second and Third Divisions.

No. 15.

Report of Col. Daniel Huston, jr., Seventh Missouri Cavalry, commanding Second Division.

HDQRS. SECOND DIVISION, ARMY OF THE FRONTIER,
Prairie Grove, Ark., December 9, 1862.

SIR: I have the honor to forward herewith a report of the part taken by the division under my command in the action of the 7th instant.

After a rapid march of 66 miles from Camp Lyon, accomplished in two and a half days, the division reached Cross Hollow at 7 o'clock on the evening of the 6th instant, and there remained until 12 midnight,

---

*For summary of casualties, here omitted, see pp. 85, 86.

when the march was resumed, arriving in Fayetteville at sunrise on the morning of the 7th.

I had intended to await at Fayetteville the arrival of the trains, in order to allow the men to procure breakfast, much needed after their long and toilsome night march. Before the arrival of the trains afforded opportunity for so doing, a message from General Blunt, with an indorsement thereon by the general commanding, was received, urging me to bring forward my division as rapidly as possible. Without a moment's delay I put my column in motion, and before noon had united with the Third Division on the bank of Illinois Creek, in front of the enemy.

Very soon after my arrival, by direction of the commanding general, I brought forward Battery F (Murphy's), First Missouri Light Artillery, and, dividing it into half batteries, placed the three pieces of the right half, under Lieutenant Marr, at a point in the open field, affording a good command of the enemy's position.

The left half, under the immediate command of Captain Murphy himself, I placed in a more commanding position, about 400 yards from there to the right, upon higher ground. In compliance with an order received from the commanding general, I then directed Captain Murphy to open the attack, which he did in gallant style, followed by the batteries of the Third Division, posted on lower ground in front.

I had meanwhile placed the Thirty-seventh Illinois Infantry as a support to protect the battery on the right, and the Twentieth Iowa Infantry on the left, with the Twenty-sixth Indiana Infantry 100 yards in the rear and center, under cover of a thick growth of young wood, as a reserve. Occupying this position, the battery did superb execution, and, in conjunction with the other battery of my command and those of the Third Division, silenced all those the enemy brought forward, as soon as their position could be ascertained. The enemy's batteries being silenced, I was ordered to move forward two infantry regiments of my division to the support of the infantry of the other division, which were falling back, after a desperate assault of the enemy's position, on the ridge. I brought forward the Twenty-sixth Indiana and the Thirty-seventh Illinois at double-quick.

Finding, on my arrival at the foot of the ridge, that the other regiments had fallen back so far, and were so badly cut up that it was necessary to give them time to reform, I ordered the two regiments to move up the hill to assault the position of the enemy, strongly posted on the crest of the ridge. Throwing out a company of skirmishers from each to cover their front, both regiments moved steadily and compactly forward till they reached a point 75 to 100 yards beyond the crest of the ridge, when the skirmishers commenced firing upon the enemy, of whom comparatively few could be seen. Suddenly the infantry of the enemy, which had been lying down, concealed by the thick brush and leaves, rose up in one overwhelming number and poured in a deadly, galling fire, which was withstood and returned for a time by our troops with the coolness and firmness of veteran soldiers. The preponderance of numbers on the part of the enemy was so great that the infantry was eventually forced to retire in some little confusion; but they soon reformed in good order, taking a position about 250 yards from the foot of the ridge, which they maintained until the close of the action. The two regiments had lost nearly one-third their number in killed and wounded in the desperate assault. All these operations took place under my immediate supervision.

During this time the Twentieth Iowa Infantry, which had formed the left support of Murphy's battery, was, by some mistake in conveyance of an order, without my knowledge brought into action beyond the extreme right of the line. The movements of this regiment took place beyond my immediate sphere of observation, but it is only necessary for me to say that it was led by Col. William McE. Dye, an old, tried, and gallant soldier, and that Iowa's sons will always be in the front of battle.

For a detailed report of the operations of the regiment, I refer you to the official report of Colonel Dye, herewith inclosed.

Murphy's battery, from different positions, at distances from 500 to 1,000 yards from the enemy's lines, which it occupied as occasion required, continued throughout the engagement to pour a terrible fire into their ranks, nobly sustaining the reputation of its chief, and the regiment to which it belongs. The first section of the Peoria Light Battery, Lieutenant Borris commanding, consisting of one 6-pounder field piece and of one 12-pounder howitzer, when the infantry regiments of the division moved forward, was ordered to a point upon the left of Foust's battery, of the Third Division, about 800 yards from the enemy's position on the ridge, where he opened a very destructive fire upon their line; particularly upon two houses, behind which they had taken shelter. This position Lieutenant Borris maintained during the greater portion of the engagement. Owing to the momentary repulse of the infantry, I ordered the section to be removed a short distance to the rear. I soon, however, ordered it back to its old position, where it continued firing while any sign of the enemy appeared.

The Seventh Missouri Cavalry and two companies of the Sixth Missouri Cavalry, under command of Major [E.] Bredett, of the Seventh Missouri Cavalry, were ordered, on the day previous to the battle, to proceed to Cane Hill, and there report to General Blunt. Early on the morning of the 7th instant, when within 4 miles of General Blunt's camp, while feeding their horses, Major Bredett's command was surrounded by a force of 3,000 of the enemy's cavalry, with a battery of artillery, and, after a short engagement, was dispersed, losing a considerable number in killed, wounded, and prisoners.

Among the missing is Major Bredett (since found dead), commanding the Seventh Missouri Cavalry, a gallant and accomplished soldier, whose loss is severely felt. The only officer known to be killed was Capt. William McKee, Company D, Seventh Missouri Cavalry, a brave man, who fell in the full performance of his duty.

The scattered fragments of the Seventh Missouri Cavalry were reformed later in the day, and, under the command of Captains Love and Rockwell, brought into action in support of the Peoria battery. Two companies of the Second Battalion, First Missouri Cavalry, under command of Major [C.] Banzhaf, forming the general escort of the division, were placed upon the extreme left to watch the enemy, and toward the close of the day were ordered to the rear to protect the trains. Major Banzhaf rendered efficient service during the day as aide-de-camp to myself and the general commanding.

After the regiments were reformed and the batteries placed in the last-named positions, night soon closed the engagement. The exhausted troops, wearied by their long marches and the toils of the day, and almost famished by an abstinence of thirty-six hours from food, lay down on their arms, ready for a renewal of the fight on the coming day, which the retreat of the enemy during the night prevented.

The officers and men of my division conducted themselves during the entire engagement in a manner which meets my approval, and does credit to themselves and the States to which they belong.

Among those whose conduct fell under my special observation, and whom I would bring to the favorable notice of the commanding general, are Colonel [J. G.] Clark, of the Twenty-sixth Indiana Volunteers; Lieutenant-Colonel [J. C.] Black, of the Thirty-seventh Illinois Volunteers, and Adjt. Dela Hunt, of the Twenty-sixth Indiana, the two latter of whom were severely wounded; also Lieutenant Chandler, assistant adjutant-general of the division, who was conspicuous everywhere upon the field, rendering most invaluable assistance, being the only officer on my staff present during the engagement.

Under the energetic superintendence of Surg. F. G. Porter, medical director of the division, the medical corps of the division were active and unceasing in their efforts to relieve the wounded, performing their duties in an admirable manner.

I have the honor to inclose herewith reports of the commanders of brigades, regiments, battalions, and batteries composing the division.

I am, very respectfully, your obedient servant,

DANL. HUSTON, JR.,
Colonel 7th Mo. Vol. Cav., Comdg. 2d Div., Army of the Frontier.

Capt. WILLIAM HYDE CLARK,
A. A. G., Second and Third Divisions, Army of the Frontier.

No. 16.

Report of Col. John G. Clark, Twenty-sixth Indiana Infantry, commanding First Brigade.

HDQRS. 1ST BRIG., 2D DIV., ARMY OF THE FRONTIER,
Prairie Grove, Ark., December 14, 1862.

SIR: I have the honor to state the part taken in the action of Sunday, December 7, by the First Brigade, Second Division, Army of the Frontier.

The Seventh Missouri Volunteer Cavalry, forming a part of the brigade, was ordered forward on the morning of the 6th instant, and I did not see them again until after the battle. About 10 a. m. I was ordered forward from Fayetteville, Ark., where we had halted to allow the men to get rations from the wagons, and, by rapid marching, reached the field of action (about 10 miles distant) at 1 p. m. As soon as we reached the ground, the section of the Peoria battery attached to my brigade was ordered into position, and, by the consent of Colonel Huston, commanding the division, I assumed command of my own regiment, the Twenty-sixth Indiana Volunteer Infantry.

The regiment was at that time ordered on the left of the Thirty-seventh Illinois Volunteers, which formed the extreme right of the line of battle Soon after, the Thirty-seventh Illinois and the Twenty-sixth Indiana were ordered forward, and moved to the left of the line, where they were ordered to charge the enemy, who were strongly posted on a hill covered with timber. My regiment succeeded in reaching a point some 75 yards beyond the crest of the hill, but was overpowered by being outnumbered two to one, and driven back in considerable disorder, but rallied before they were beyond the reach of the fire of the enemy. The regiment was then ordered to fall back, and take position on the main road, where it remained until the next morning.

The regiment had in the ranks at the commencement of the action 445 men, of whom ——*

The conduct of the regiment was all I could expect under the circumstances, and I cheerfully attest to the bravery and good conduct of both officers and men.

Very respectfully, your obedient servant,

JOHN G. CLARK,
Colonel, Commanding First Brigade, Second Division.

Col. DANIEL HUSTON, JR., *Commanding Second Division.*

No. 17.

Report of Lieut Herman Borris, Battery A, Second Illinois Light Artillery.

CAMP AT PRAIRIE GROVE, ARK.,
December 8, 1862.

SIR: In compliance with an order from Colonel Huston, commanding Second Division, Army of the Frontier, I have the honor to make the following report:

My section (first section Peoria Light Artillery), entered, with other troops from the First Brigade, Second Division, under command of Colonel Clark, the field of battle at noon on the 7th instant. The battle had then commenced. I took possession of a place on our left, on the main road, about 600 yards from the enemy, so as to bring the section in an echelon position with the other batteries of our army. Here I commenced firing, and kept it up until about 4.30 o'clock, when a charge of our infantry was repelled, which compelled them to retreat toward my position. I ceased firing, but renewed the fire as soon as our infantry was covered against my artillery. I had scarcely fired two rounds per piece when the battery in front of me (Captain Cole's battery) left their position and passed by me. The other artillery on the right of my section did the same. The confusion was great. While the whole line of battle was going to retreat, I limbered up to the rear and tried to get a favorable position, which would allow me to keep back the foe. In this I succeeded, after I had crossed a creek 200 yards in rear of my last position. The enemy having given up the pursuit, Colonel Huston then ordered the batteries back, and gave my section a position in an open field, about 900 yards from the enemy's line. After having fired there a few rounds, the colonel ordered my section to its first position, where I commenced firing again, and kept it up until I ran short of ammunition. The men, without exception, have fulfilled their duties as soldiers and good artillerymen. I have fired during the whole engagement 320 rounds.

I brought into action, rank and file, 40 men, from whom are killed, wounded, or missing, none. My horses are well, with the exception of two, which are slightly wounded by pieces of shell, but not rendered unserviceable. The pieces, caissons, and the harness are in good condition.

I have the honor to be, very respectfully, your obedient servant,

H. BORRIS,
Lieutenant, Commanding First Section Peoria Battery.

Colonel CLARK,
Comdg. First Brigade, Second Division, Army of the Frontier.

---

*Summary of casualties, omitted, embodied in revised statement, p. 85.

No. 18.

Report of Capt. Milton H. Brawner, Seventh Missouri Cavalry.

HDQRS. SEVENTH MISSOURI VOLUNTEER CAVALRY,
Prairie Grove, Ark., December 11, 1862.

SIR: I have the honor to report that the detachment of Seventh Missouri Volunteer Cavalry, ordered forward from Camp Sigel on the morning of the 6th of December, under command of Major Bredett, marched in a southwesterly direction with the utmost rapidity, passing through Fayetteville (a distance of 46 miles) at dark. Advancing 4 miles, a short halt was ordered, for the purpose of resting the worn-out men and horses.

At 2 a. m., December 7, the command again moved forward, and at daylight, when within 4 miles of Cane Hill, halted to feed. While feeding (with bridles off and girths loosened), a cavalry troop (part of the Eighth Missouri Cavalry) passed through the lane in which we were feeding. When nearly through they were assailed by a volley of small-arms, fired by an unseen foe (concealed by thick underbrush and corn-fields), which threw them into great disorder, they retreating through our column, causing great confusion. Major Bredett at this juncture behaved with great coolness and bravery, using his utmost exertion to rally and form the men. The line was twice formed, but the enemy pouring in heavy volleys on our front, left, and rear, the retreat was sounded. As it afterward appeared, the detachment was surrounded by the entire brigade of the rebel General [Colonel] Emmett MacDonald, supported by a battery, getting into position to open on us when the retreat was sounded. The command, after getting out of the lane, retreated in every direction, quite a number running into the rebel lines, being killed or captured.

Among the missing I mention with deep sorrow the name of Major [E.] Bredett; and among the killed Capt. William McKee, who lost his life while gallantly trying to cut his way out. When fairly outside the rebel lines, the command was again collected and marched to the battle-field, and reported to Adjutant-General Chandler, who assigned it to duty as support to the Peoria battery, posted under his direction. The command remained on the field during the entire engagement, supporting the above-named battery.

I inclose report of First Lieutenant [L.] Bunner, who, with his company, formed the advance guard and was cut off from the detachment. I also inclose a list of the losses sustained by the Seventh Missouri Cavalry.*

Very respectfully, your obedient servant,

M. H. BRAWNER,
Captain Company A, Seventh Missouri Volunteer Cavalry.

Col. JOHN G. CLARK, *Comdg. 1st Brig., 2d Div., Army of the Frontier.*

No. 19.

Report of Lieut. Lafayette Bunner, Seventh Missouri Cavalry.

CAMP ON THE BATTLE-FIELD,
Prairie Grove, Ark., December 9, 1862.

SIR: I have the honor to report that, on the morning of the 7th instant, Company M, Seventh Cavalry Missouri Volunteers, was ordered

* Embodied in revised statement, p. 85.

to the front as advance guard to the regiment, then marching toward Cane Hill. Just after daylight, and when about 5 miles from Cane Hill, I ordered a halt, the regiment appearing to have done the same about three-fourths of a mile to my rear. After waiting a reasonable time for the regiment to come up, and hearing several pistol reports, I moved back, with the main guards, supposing you were feeding and preparing to breakfast. Upon nearing the place where I supposed the regiment to be, I discovered a body of mounted men, the most of whom were clothed in Federal uniforms, and a majority wearing the regulation overcoat, in line directly in my front. I moved up and discovered they were strangers, but, taking them to be the First Arkansas Cavalry, approached to within 50 paces of their line, when they opened fire on me. I cried out, "Cease firing; we are friends." They fired more vigorously. I continued crying to cease until a body of infantry appearing, convinced me I was not among friends, but confronted by a body of rebels. I then withdrew, surprised to find an enemy instead of friends, who, events have shown, came in between me and my regiment (which had halted farther back) through a by-way, and was reported to me by my orderly, just before passing that point, as my own regiment, distant 200 yards from my rear.

In the hope of being able to force my way through and rejoin my regiment, I advanced and engaged them; but learning from men of my command, whom I had placed as lookouts on the mountains, they were trying to outflank and surround me, I drew off, with a loss of 1 man severely wounded, and 1 horse killed and 4 disabled.

I next desired to ascertain their strength. With this view, I divided my command into squads, dispersed them right and left, with orders to advance cautiously, glean what they could of the enemy's strength, and report. Ascertaining they numbered several hundred, I immediately dispatched a messenger with this intelligence to General Blunt. Learning afterward they were in force with artillery, I reported with my command to General Blunt. I then joined a force of General Blunt's command, proceeding to Rhea's Mills. While on the way, hearing fighting at this point, I left them, hastened hither, and placed myself and company under command of Major Rich, commanding a battalion of the Eighth Cavalry Missouri Volunteers, and remained on the field until the close of the action, sustaining some loss.

I am, very respectfully, your obedient servant,

LAFAYETTE BUNNER,
First Lieut. Seventh Cav. Missouri Vols., Comdg. Company M.

Capt. M. H. BRAWNER,
Seventh Cavalry Missouri Volunteers, Comdg. Regiment.

No. 20.

Report of Col. William McE. Dye, Twentieth Iowa Infantry, commanding Second Brigade.

HDQRS. 2D BRIG., 2D DIV., ARMY OF THE FRONTIER,
Battle-field of Prairie Grove, Ark., December 10, 1862.

SIR: In obedience to the circular from division headquarters, dated on the 8th instant, I have the honor to make the following report of the part taken by this brigade in the engagement of the 7th instant:

The brigade is composed of the Thirty-seventh Illinois Infantry, under command of Lieut. Col. [John] Charles Black; Twentieth Iowa Volunteer Infantry, under command of Lieut. Col. J. B. Leake; Second Battalion, Sixth Missouri Cavalry, under Maj. Samuel Montgomery, and Battery F, First Missouri Volunteer Light Artillery, under command of Capt. David Murphy.

The brigade moved by forced marches for about eighty consecutive hours, during the last thirty-one of which it passed a distance of about 52 miles. On the day of the battle there were absent from the brigade two companies of cavalry, *en route* to join General Blunt—one company at Springfield and the other company guarding the train, with orders to force up all stragglers lounging around it; also one company from each of the infantry regiments guarding the train, in addition to the old guard of 100 infantry, who were a part of the train guard. This, with the sick and stragglers, diminished the brigade to a total fighting force of 644, and aggregate, 694, infantry; Maj. Samuel Montgomery, of the Sixth Missouri Cavalry (stripped necessarily of his companies one by one), and Battery F.

The Second Brigade was directed to take a position on the extreme right. Captain Murphy's battery occupied the most commanding position in the vicinity. Three guns, under the command of Lieut. John [L.] Matthaei, occupied the right, and three guns, under the immediate command of Lieut. James Marr, occupied the left, of the line; the first supported by the Thirty-seventh and the second by the Twentieth, both regiments being well under cover; the former with a defensive crotchet of two companies on the right flank to prevent a surprise, &c., from that direction through the thicket; the latter, with a small detachment thrown to the right and rear, to assist in securing the brigade from surprise.

At 1.30 p. m., Lieutenant Marr, seconded by Lieutenant Matthaei, opened our side of the contest, and elicited a spirited reply. After about three-fourths of an hour's remarkable artillery practice, during which time new rebel batteries were being constantly exposed, only to be silenced, the Thirty-seventh Illinois debouched, and, in battle-line, to the music of their own voices, moved to an advanced position, far in front of its battery. About fifteen minutes afterward, Lieutenant Marr's artillery, with its support, was directed to advance to a certain position. In doing so we found it necessary, as the battery to our left was moving, to take position to its right, from which the battery opened on a rebel one within 300 yards (which was being brought into position in the road near the white house), and, by a few well-directed shots, prevented its opening upon us. What remained of the battery moved to its left under cover (white house), which necessitated the moving of ours to a new position to the right.

While doing this, the general commanding ordered the battery to return to a position near that of the half battery under Lieutenant Matthaei. The Twentieth being a new regiment under fire, and without orders to return with the battery, I assisted it into a position from which it could assume the offensive or defensive at pleasure, making its movements secondary to those of other parts of the line. This regiment, instead of the Thirty-seventh, now occupied the extreme right of the advanced position.

My special attention was from this time forward directed to the movements of this regiment, remaining at times with it, and then in a position from which I could see and make its movements conform to those of the infantry on its left. Under a sharp fire the regiment in gallant style threatened a strong position of the enemy, and, when commanded, retired with the order of old soldiers. It continued from this position to annoy the enemy with remarkable effect, by assaulting and retiring, until the appearance of a large body of advancing men on our right, when it retired to a more defensible position to cover the flank.

From this point I dispatched messengers to learn what forces were moving toward us, and learned that it was General Blunt's advance. This information I immediately communicated to the commanding general (Herron). I also sent General Blunt what information was necessary as to our position. The firing, which, previous to his appearance, was waging severe on the left, in which the Thirty-seventh was engaged, now began to wane. The enemy, who evidently had endeavored to overpower our left before his arrival, now was massing his forces against General Blunt's.

I immediately sent General Blunt word, as we were near him, and there appeared at the time nothing else to do, that the Twentieth would move in conjunction with his forces. By a stoutly contested fight the forces advanced to the crest of the hill (with the assistance of General Blunt's well-directed artillery), and maintained this corner-stone to the enemy's position until he, under cover of a feint of moving one regiment against our left, had withdrawn his forces from there and thrown them in overwhelming numbers against us. The fire was galling. General Blunt's Indians commenced retiring, and I directed the Twentieth to retire gradually and take a covered position under the hill. In doing so, General Blunt's artillery, from as yet an unopened battery, commenced, as he informed me he would do, to deal destruction into the ranks of the advancing foe, and, under the immediate surpervision of General Herron, Murphy's battery soon opened on the same spot. The Twentieth continued its fire against this force as long as there was an enemy within sight, and then, under the fatigues of the day, retired to rest on arms. Some firing continued on General Blunt's extreme right for a short time after this, and night then dropped a veil over the bloody scene.

At the commencement of the battle, the Thirty-seventh Illinois advanced without order from or through me. The brigade was entirely broken up by orders, which never reached us, and the parts sent to widely separated portions on the field.

Finding that orders were constantly being sent directly to officers under my command, I soon abandoned all hope of harmonizing the movements of the brigade, as such, with those of other bodies, and devoted the greater part of my attention to the movements of the Twentieth Iowa.

For these reasons I must respectfully refer to the reports of junior commanders for information as to the conduct of their respective commands, where not immediately under my eyes, and also for details.

The Thirty-seventh Illinois, as will be seen by Major [H. N.] Frisbie's report, claims to have captured and spiked a battery of three guns; to have captured one regimental color from the enemy, and to have carried within our lines the regimental flag of the Twentieth Wisconsin, which had been left on the field.

There were many guns, &c., picked up, but as yet I have not received a list of the property, all of which I directed to be turned over to the quartermaster.

Although the troops of the brigade did, at least, their part in the charges on the left, as well as on the right, with General Blunt, yet they did not suffer as severely as some others. They moved with regularity amid danger.

The brigade lost ——.*

The report of Major Montgomery, Sixth Missouri Cavalry, is inclosed. The loss of his battalion was, before the general engagement, when *en route* to join General Blunt: Prisoners: Commissioned officers, 2; non-commissioned officers, 4; privates, 16 (the 10 officers having since been paroled). Missing: Privates, 8. Wounded: Privates, 1.

Before closing this report, I should, as a duty, publish the recreant. I am delighted to say that I found none on the field. However much the hot contest of musketry tends to confuse the ideas, every man's mind appeared to be open for the reception and execution of orders. The very keystone to discipline and success was exhibited in the midst of thickening danger to an extent few new troops could hope to rival and none to excel.

Lieut Col. [John] Charles Black, Thirty-seventh Illinois, with the ardor of youth and the discretion of riper years, gallantly moved his regiment under heavy fire with perfect order, and continued in command after being severely wounded, until, exhausted by suffering, he was obliged to turn the regiment over to Maj. H. N. Frisbie, who, by his skill and coolness, gained for himself and regiment a reputation worthy of the State from which he hails.

Lieut. Col. J. B. Leake, of the Twentieth Iowa, with unsurpassing bravery, moved his regiment in advance and retreat with a confidence and devotion truly to be admired. Major [W. G.] Thompson, with the enthusiasm of one devoted to his regiment and cause, continued by his brave example to encourage the men, until, near the close, with remarkable thoughtfulness, under severe suffering, he reported personally to me that he regretted to leave the field. Under such officers the Twentieth Iowa more than sustained the reputation of the State.

To Captain Murphy's battery, reared under his strict but just discipline, we are particularly indebted as an army. His characteristic concentration to duty has, in his battery, made for him a reputation of which all might be proud. The equanimity of Lieutenant Marr and careful attention of Lieutenant Matthaei are qualities possessed in such a degree by them that they can be discovered on the battle-field, even among the ruins of the enemy's artillery.

Lieut. C. S. Lake, acting assistant adjutant-general, and orderlies did important and dangerous service, with perfect satisfaction to myself and to those to whom they carried and delivered the orders.

It required heroism in Major Montgomery and the officers and soldiers of the train to remain complacently (but necessarily) inactive while the battle was raging.

In the accompanying reports will be found the names of those mentioned for good conduct. Our men behaved so well that it required but ordinary exertions on the part of officers to be successful. The fortunate have our congratulations, the wounded our sympathy, and the fallen our envy.

I am, sir, very respectfully, your obedient servant,

WM. McE. DYE,
Colonel, Commanding Brigade.

Lieut. J. G. CHANDLER,
Actg. Asst. Adjt. Gen., Second Div., Army of the Frontier.

---

* Embodied in revised statement, p. 85.

No. 21.

Report of Lieut. Col. John Charles Black, Thirty-seventh Illinois Infantry.

HDQRS. THIRTY-SEVENTH ILLINOIS VOL. INFANTRY,
Fayetteville, Ark., December 10, 1862.

COLONEL: I have the honor of submitting the following report of the marches of the Thirty-seventh Illinois prior to the late engagement, and also of the part borne by the regiment in the battle of Prairie Grove:

On December 4, at 3 a. m., we marched from Camp Lyon, near Crane Creek, some 25 miles south of Springfield, and encamped on Flat Creek at 4 p. m., having made 20 miles.

Reveille was ordered at 2 a. m., and the regiment marched at 4 a. m., December 5, passing through Cassville and Keytesville to within 3 miles of the Arkansas line, making 23 miles.

We started the next morning (December 6) at 5 o'clock, and marched to Cross Hollow, 28 miles, by 1.30 p. m. Resting until 12 midnight, we started for Fayetteville, Ark., distant 16 miles, and arrived there at sunrise December 7. A halt of one and a half hours was ordered, to get breakfast and snatch a few moments of much-needed sleep. We were speedily aroused by the cannon of General Herron's advance, skirmishing with the enemy, some 12 miles in advance. Moving rapidly forward, we reached the Illinois Creek, and, crossing it, took position on the battle-field of Prairie Grove at 12 m. of December 7, having made the tremendous march of 66 miles in thirty-six hours, after marching 43 miles in the two preceding days.

By your order, I took post on the extreme right, supporting half of Captain Murphy's battery (F, First Missouri Light Artillery), moving up under cover of a dense *chaparral* until abreast of our position, and then advancing to the edge of the brush, by the left flank, in line of battle. A halt was ordered and the men ordered to lie down. In five minutes the ball was opened by the artillery on either side, and a fierce cannonade was kept up for an hour. So completely were the men exhausted that I saw them sleeping quietly around, paying no heed to the fierce missiles.

At the end of an hour we were ordered to advance into the open field. A cheer was given, and we moved out a short distance, and remained stationary for some fifteen minutes, when I was ordered by Colonel Huston, commanding the Second Division, to advance the regiment down the slope to the support of the batteries of the Third Division.

Scarcely had this position been reached before Colonel Huston again ordered our advance against the hill, on which the center of the enemy was posted in unknown strength, and from which two regiments had just been driven with heavy loss. Throwing out Company A on the right and Company I on the front and left, as skirmishers, I ordered a charge up the hill. It was executed in fine style, the men advancing steadily and swiftly up to the edge. The firing of the skirmishers in front announced the enemy close at hand. Clearing the edge, we stood face to face with them, their numbers overwhelming (5,000 or 6,000 strong, as it was subsequently proved), one column moving by left-oblique upon our left and the right of the Twenty-sixth Indiana, another moving direct upon our right. They moved in column *en masse*, with guns at a ready. The firing began first upon the left, and in a few minutes was general along the entire line. But, pressed by overwhelming numbers, the right of the Twenty-sixth gave way after most gallantly contesting the ground. My skirmishers about the same time reported the enemy's artillery posted on our right. Thus overwhelmed, the only hope from annihilation was the bayonet or retreat. The bayonet could not be used; directly in front of us was a rail fence, and it could not have been passed and we reformed before the enemy would have been upon us; so, reluctantly, I ordered a retreat. Not a man had moved from his post till that order. Falling back some 300 yards, they reformed in the rear of the batteries.

In this charge and retreat, Captain [G. R.] Bell, of Company G, was wounded, doing splendid duty with his men. Lieutenant [F. J.] Abbey, Company I, and Lieutenant [N. B.] Hicks, Company K, were taken prisoners, they not receiving the order to retreat until too late to execute it. I was too seriously wounded to retain the command, and so, turning it over to Major [H. N.] Frisbie, I left the field; not, however, until the regiment was reformed and had again commenced its fire. I refer you to Major Frisbie for a continuation of this report.

To Major Frisbie and Adjutant Bandy my thanks are due for the calm, fearless manner in which they conveyed and executed my commands.

All officers and men stood nobly at their posts. The hand of death has snatched a brave, true man from our midst—Lieutenant Johnson, Company D, who fell, mortally wounded, at a subsequent movement of the fight. I sorrow for him, and beg leave to pay the last tribute I can to a soldier and a friend—a word of praise and a tear of mingled pride and sorrow for his gallant death. All who fell, fell nobly. Those who serve on, may envy their fate.

I have the honor to be, very respectfully,

[JOHN] CHAS. BLACK,
Lieutenant-Colonel, Commanding Thirty-seventh Illinois.

Col. W. McE. Dye,
20th Iowa Vols., Comdg. 2d Brig., 2d Div., Army of the Frontier.

No. 22.

Report of Lieut. Frederick J. Abbey, Thirty-seventh Illinois Infantry.

BATTLE-FIELD, PRAIRIE GROVE, ARK.,
December 10, 1862.

MAJOR: In compliance with your direction, I have to report that on the advance of the regiment to the foot of the hill, which we stormed, and the throwing out of Company I as skirmishers, I took my position on the left of the line, when the regiment fell back. As we reached the fence, and at the same time heard the cry to halt, I lay where I was, supposing the regiment had halted, and under cover of the fence. On discovering that the regiment had fallen still farther back, I saw it was impossible for me to follow. I then emptied my revolver at them and loaded again. At that time I was surrounded, and, presenting my pistol, demanded protection, which was guaranteed me, and then I surrendered. I was hurried to the rear and paroled the camp for the night. I was paroled the next morning until exchanged. Pledged secrecy as to all I saw and learned of their strength and position.

FRED. J. ABBEY,
First Lieutenant, Company I, Thirty-seventh Regiment.

Maj. H. N. Frisbie,
Commanding Thirty-seventh Illinois Infantry.

P. S.—I surrendered my sword, belt, and revolver, which they did not return.

No. 23.

Report of Lieut. Col. Joseph B. Leake, Twentieth Iowa Infantry.

HDQRS. TWENTIETH REGT. IOWA VOLUNTEER INFANTRY,
Camp at Prairie Grove, Ark., December 9, 1862.

I have the honor to report the part taken by the Twentieth Regiment of Iowa Infantry in the battle of Prairie Grove, fought on the 7th instant. I think it necessary, in order to have full justice done to the regiment, to state by what marches it arrived upon the field.

On the morning of December 4, at 4 o'clock, we left Camp Lyon, 22 miles from Springfield, Mo., on the road to Cassville, and marched to the Three Widows, 12 miles from Cassville, and on the following day we moved at 5 a. m., and marched through Cassville and Keytesville to camp, 2 miles from Keytesville.

On the morning of the 6th instant we moved at 5 o'clock, and, passing Elkhorn and Sugar Creek, arrived at Cross Hollow about 5 p. m. Bivouacked till 10 o'clock, and again commenced the march. Marched all night. Passed through Fayetteville, and halted for breakfast about 1 mile beyond.

After remaining one hour, we marched on rapidly until we arrived upon the field of battle, about 12 m. of the 7th instant, thus having marched a distance of 100 miles in eighty consecutive hours, the last 57 miles of which we passed over in thirty-one consecutive hours.

Very many of my command marched with shoes so much worn that their feet were on the ground, and were badly bruised and cut up by the stony roads. A few had been supplied with boots at Camp Lyon, which fitted them so illy that their feet became much blistered and inflamed by the continuous marching. A few of these last mentioned carried their boots and marched in their bare feet to the scene of action.

Under these circumstances we went into the engagement with only 270 enlisted men and 23 officers. I neglected to mention, however, that before moving from our halting-place near Fayetteville, having learned of the capture of a portion of the train of the First Arkansas Cavalry a few miles beyond, I was ordered to detail a company, under a reliable officer, to protect our train, for which duty I assigned Company B, under the command of Captain [E.] Coulter, so that Company B was deprived the privilege of being present at the engagement, except 3, who joined other companies.

Pursuant to orders, the regiment was drawn up in line of battle in an open field to the right of the road, a short distance from the creek, and 50 yards in the rear of the Thirty-seventh Illinois. After remaining in this position a few minutes, we moved forward by the right flank, following the Thirty-seventh Illinois, wading the creek, and formed in line of battle in the rear of and supporting three pieces of Battery F, First Missouri Light Artillery, and under shelter of the hill upon which the battery was in position. Immediately after forming in line, I was ordered to throw out a party of skirmishers to protect our right flank and rear from surprise, for which service I detailed 20 men of Company A, under the command of First Lieutenant [C. L.] Drake, of that company.

At or near 2 p. m. the battery was moved forward, and we moved forward in line of battle to the middle of the field on the right of the main road and in front of the white house, on the road to the top of the hill. By order of Colonel Dye, I immediately moved the regiment to the right, into the adjoining field and in front of the orchard, to check a movement of the enemy on our right flank. Here we were exposed to the fire of the enemy for a short time, which we returned, advancing a short distance toward them. At this time a force appeared on our right, advancing down the valley. I was ordered to fall back behind the fence in our rear, which was executed in good order, under fire. I then threw out Companies A and F, under the command of Captains [E. N.] Bates and [N. M.] Hubbard, from the right wing, as skirmishers.

Shortly after, a cavalry force appeared upon our right and rear. The skirmishers were directed to assemble on the battalion, and, by order of Colonel Dye, I changed front toward the force approaching, which was done in good order in the rear of the fence running perpendicular to the one from which we moved. It having been ascertained that the forces approaching were re-enforcements, under command of General Blunt, I was directed and did immediately move the regiment to the position behind the fence from which we had changed our front. General Blunt having taken position on our right in the middle of the field, I was ordered to move forward in support of his Indians. Skirmishing, I moved forward in line of battle rapidly across the field, obliquing to the left, across the orchard fence, at the foot of the hill; drove the enemy's skirmishers through the orchard, and advanced beyond the fence, through the wood, a short distance. The left wing being more severely engaged, the right had passed farther in advance, through the wood, where some of the Indians came running back through the wood to the right, gesticulating violently and pointing toward the direction whence they came.

At this moment an officer shouted to me that we were firing on friends. I gave the order to cease firing, and rode toward the left, fearing that the troops on our left might have ascended the hill and advanced to our front, when I saw directly in front of us a mass of troops moving down upon us. At almost the same instant they fired a volley, under which the left wing recoiled to nearly the orchard fence, where they promptly rallied at my command and renewed the firing with great rapidity and, I think, effect.

At this moment I received orders to retire behind the fence at the foot of the hill, and hold it, which movement was promptly executed by the regiment in good order, climbing the fence under a galling fire and lying down under it, continuing the fire between the fence-rails.

The moment we crossed the fence the orchard was shelled by the battery of General Blunt's forces on the right, in the field, and that under command of Captain Murphy and Lieutenant Marr, in position at the point from which we entered the action, from the combined efforts of which, and our own firing, the enemy were driven from the orchard. They remained in large force about the house and stone wall, firing from under their protection upon our extreme left wing. It was here our heaviest loss occurred.

As soon as the enemy were driven from the orchard, I was ordered to retire in good order from the fence and form in the middle of the field. As we commenced to retire, Major Thompson was wounded, and the left wing, not receiving the order promptly, remained a little too long, and retired precipitately nearly to the fence from which we advanced. I rode down, and at the command they returned and formed at the place designated.

In the mean time the right wing, being much exposed, had moved into the adjoining field, under the protection of the battery on the right, and at this time, receiving the order to retire to the fence again, I formed the line behind the fence, in rear of the battery, and moved by the left flank along it to our original position. This ended our active participation in the contest.

We remained on our arms at the fence during the night, and the next morning before daylight I formed the line of battle and awaited the renewal of the action.

After daylight, seeing no movement of the enemy in front, I ordered arms to be stacked, and awaited further orders. The enemy had fled, and the battle was over.

Our loss in killed was 1 commissioned officer and 8 enlisted men; wounded, 5 commissioned officers and 35 enlisted men, a list of whom is herewith transmitted.*

The men acted throughout the action bravely and with entire self-possession, retiring under fire repeatedly, and rallying with the utmost promptness at the word of command. I do not think there was a moment when they were not under control of their officers.

I would be glad to mention instances of personal heroism which passed under my own notice, but, when all acted with equal bravery, I fear I would injure others by merely noticing those which happened to pass under my own eyes. Of the conduct of the officers of companies, I can only say that it was all that could be expected or hoped for from men who were gallantly offering up their lives in a cause in which their whole hearts were engaged.

I was assisted in the discharge of my duties as commander of the regiment by Major Thompson, who, although exposed to the hottest of the fire on the left wing, conducted himself with great gallantry and self-possession, and who, fortunately for the regiment, was not wounded until near the close of the action, and, though suffering great pain, did not leave the field until the command was safely withdrawn from under the fire of the enemy. The conduct of the chaplain, Rev. U. Eberhart, deserves particular mention for his activity and zeal in assisting in the removal of the wounded from the field, and his unremitting attention to their wants in the hospitals. I would do great injustice to a gallant officer did I forbear to most highly commend the conduct of Lieut. J. C. McClelland, the acting adjutant, who assisted me on horseback during the entire engagement.

Permit me to remark, in closing, that I consider the regiment much indebted for their escape with so little loss from the orchard to the prompt and intelligible manner in which the timely orders of Colonel Dye, commanding brigade, were transmitted to me, at the most imminent risk of life, by yourself and James W. Cliff, and Thomas H. Henderson, Sixth Missouri Cavalry, acting under your direction.

I remain, most respectfully, &c.,

J. B. LEAKE,
Lieutenant-Colonel, Commanding Twentieth Iowa.

Lieut. C. S. LAKE,
Actg. Asst. Adjt. Gen., 2d Brig., 2d Div., Army of the Frontier.

No. 24.

Report of Maj. Samuel Montgomery, Sixth Missouri Cavalry.

HDQRS. SECOND BATT. SIXTH MISSOURI CAV. VOLS.,
[*December* —, 1862.]

SIR: I beg leave respectfully to make the following report of the operations of the battalion under my command from the 6th instant to the present time, and incidents and casualties, so far as known:

I was ordered to detail two of my squadrons, on the 6th instant, to

---

*Embodied in revised statement, p. 85.

report to the officer commanding the Seventh Missouri Cavalry. Companies A and L reported immediately to that officer, and moved rapidly in the direction of Cane Hill. When about 2 miles from this camp they were surrounded by an overwhelming force of cavalry, while feeding, about daylight on the 7th instant. All of the two squadrons effected their escape, except 29 non-commissioned officers and privates, together with Capt. John H. Paynter and Lieutenant Stockstill, of Company A. Twenty of the enlisted men are known to have been captured. The remaining 9 are supposed to be killed or wounded. Captain Paynter and Lieutenant Stockstill have since been paroled, and have returned to camp. Company D, the only remaining company of my command during this time, was on duty as rear guard. Of the captured and missing men, Company A lost ——.*

SAML. MONTGOMERY,
Major, Commanding Battalion.

Lieut. C. S. LAKE,
Asst. Adjt. Gen., 2d Brig., 2d Div., Army of the Frontier.

No. 25.

Report of Capt. David Murphy, Battery F, First Missouri Light Artillery.

BATTLE-FIELD, *December* 8, 1862.

COLONEL: I have the honor to report that, on the morning of the 7th instant, hearing cannonading to the front, I ordered cannoneers to take equipments and prepare for action. About 12.30 p. m. I received orders from Colonel Huston, commanding Second Division, to move to the front of the brigade with my battery, and take position on the right of the division. After a brief consultation, it was decided to place the right half battery there, and I was allowed to move the left half battery 400 yards to the right, upon a more commanding position. As soon as everything was in readiness, I was ordered to open the attack. The order was anticipated, however, by the enemy; they being in position, fired a blank cartridge for the purpose of finding the strength and position of our artillery. Lieutenant [J.] Marr, under your immediate supervision, replied with the right half battery. This was the signal agreed upon by General Herron, commanding, and was responded to nobly by every piece in our lines. Leaving Lieutenant [J. L.] Matthaei in charge of the left half battery, and seeing that both chiefs were sustaining their well-earned reputation as artillerists, I rode down to the left of the line, and found Captain [J.] Foust, commanding Company E, Captain [F.] Backof, commanding Company L, First Missouri Light Artillery, and Lieutenant [H.] Borris, commanding section Peoria Light Artillery, hard at work, advancing with their respective batteries to the attack. Anxious to come to close quarters with my battery, I rode back to the right and met you advancing with Lieutenant Marr's half battery, which took position within 300 yards of a rebel battery. The fire was so well directed that the enemy retired, minus caissons, horses, and one piece disabled. Lieutenant Marr was ordered to return, and form on the right of Lieutenant Matthaei, who had, from his commanding position, a fine opportunity of testing the qualities of our rifled cannon.

My battery was now together, and it was truly a gratifying sight to

---

* Nominal list omitted. See p. 85.

me to witness the magnificent practice of my officers and men. Wherever a rebel battery disclosed its position, my gunners directed their fire upon it; and I am proud to say that one or two rounds from each piece was sufficient to cause the enemy to limber to the rear and "skedaddle." When the infantry were repulsed, I directed my fire over their heads into the pursuing enemy. The enemy were checked.

The battle had now been raging fiercely for three hours, when a battery was discovered upon our right flank, blazing away like fury. I ordered the right half battery to change front forward on the right piece, and was ready to give the new comer a warm reception, when an orderly arrived and reported General Blunt on our right. This, of course, saved us the necessity of opening on our new friend.

My fire was now directed, under the immediate supervision of General Herron, upon new formations of the enemy, who were endeavoring to make a demonstration upon our left. Their flag was soon shot down, and I ceased firing, not wishing to waste ammunition. This was at 4.30 p. m. In three hours and a half, 450 percussion shells were sent screeching into the enemy's lines, and 60 solid shot from my battery. I am satisfied that there is somebody hurt. Let those who witnessed the skill and coolness of my officers and men sound their praise. I forbear. Suffice it to say, however, that I am proud of them; proud of my regiment, and proud to claim that I belong to the Second Division, Army of the Frontier.

I am, very respectfully, your obedient servant,

DAVID MURPHY,
Captain Company F, First Missouri Light Artillery.

C. S. LAKE,
Asst. Adjt. Gen., 2d Brig., 2d Div., Army of the Frontier.

No. 26.

Report of Col. Dudley Wickersham, Tenth Illinois Cavalry, commanding First Brigade, Third Division.

HDQRS. FIRST BRIG., THIRD DIV., ARMY OF THE FRONTIER,
In Camp at Prairie Grove, December 8, 1862.

GENERAL: I have the honor to report that, in obedience to Brigadier-General Herron's orders, received at Sugar Creek on the morning of the 7th [6th] instant, I reached your command at Cane Hill at 9 p. m. that evening, after a very fatiguing march of 50 miles, my men weary and horses jaded and worn out from the long, rapid, and continuous marching of the previous three days. Later that evening my command received provisions and forage enough to satisfy their needy wants, through the kindly offices of Colonel Weer, to whom, through you, I beg to return my grateful acknowledgments.

Next morning [December 7], as ordered, my command was formed in line of battle in the field east and adjacent to the old camping ground of the rebels at Cane Hill, and from thence, as ordered, I marched it to Rhea's Mills, being first re-enforced by the Ninth Kansas Cavalry and a section of howitzers from the Third Wisconsin Cavalry, both under the immediate command of Colonel Lynde, where, about noon, your order directing me to open communication and effect a junction with the forces under Brig. Gen. F. J. Herron, then supposed to be engaging the enemy somewhere between Fayetteville and Cane Hill, was received.

In conformity thereto, I proceeded with my command on the old Fayetteville road, in the order hereinafter mentioned, consisting of two battalions First Iowa Cavalry, Col. James O. Gower, commanding; two battalions Tenth Illinois Cavalry, and their two sections 2-pounder steel howitzers, Lieut. Col. James Stuart commanding; two squadrons First Battalion Second Wisconsin Cavalry, Maj. William H. Miller commanding, and about 400 of the Eighth Missouri Volunteer Cavalry, Colonel [W. F.] Geiger commanding. When it had reached a point just as you enter the woods, the prairie stretching out to the left and front, and about three-fourths of a mile from the point of intersection of this road and the Cane Hill road, my advance fired into some 30 of the enemy's pickets, who fled and disappeared in the woods without returning the fire I then deployed skirmishers into the woods from the front, and detailed an additional squadron from the First Iowa Cavalry as advance guard. When the advance guard reached Marr's house, say one-half mile from the attack just mentioned, it received a heavy fire from the enemy, who were posted there in force, forming their left wing, luckily injuring but one man, whose name will be found at the close of this report. My command closed up rapidly to the aid of the advance, and formed in close column of squadrons. The firing by this time became general between the advance, supported by another squadron of the First Iowa Cavalry, and the enemy. At this juncture a section of the 2-pounder howitzers was ordered to their support; ere they arrived, their movements being characterized with no delay, the enemy had fallen back some 150 yards. The howitzers proceeded some 100 yards down the road in advance of my forces, and there received a terrible fire from the enemy, wounding Corpl. Levi Cassity, of Company B, Tenth Illinois Cavalry, destroying one of his arms, and Private E. McCarty, of Company G, of same regiment, both belonging to the front gun, the former in command thereof. Corporal Cassity's horse was killed, and both of the horses attached to the gun wounded. The others, beholding this, fell back with the remaining gun to the head of the column, then at Marr's house, and opened into the enemy's ranks with several rounds of canister, killing 30 men.

Finding at this time that our infantry was hotly engaging the enemy from a position a short distance in my front, from an open meadow adjacent to a corn-field on my left, I left with my command to support them; when, just before reaching them, I received your order to give way to the left, to permit your battery to come to their relief, and your further order to support said battery.

Just prior to these changes, Lieutenant ——— (name unable to learn), with 20 men from Companies L and M, First Iowa Cavalry, volunteered to rescue the missing gun—a perilous task, speedily and meritoriously accomplished. The enemy had not taken it from the field, having been driven back immediately, subsequent to delivering their fire upon it, by the galling fire of my howitzer. Here an individual act of heroism became known, and is worthy of mention, namely, Corporal Cassity was still with the gun, having refused to desert it.

After the formation in the field, my command met with no further attacks, and, in accordance with your orders, received after a general engagement had commenced between your battery, sustained by your infantry, and the enemy's forces, fell back 1½ miles on the road toward Rhea's Mills; and, still later, by your orders, formed a part of the escort to Fayetteville of the commissary and baggage trains of your command, the rear thereof reaching that place on the evening of the 8th instant. I then reported with my command to Brig. Gen. F. J. Herron, finding you were beyond him.

Let me remark, in concluding, that the troops of my command are deserving of mention for the cool, unflinching spirit they evinced during the attack upon them. Not a man wavered, and during the short suspension of firing, intervening after the general attack on my front, when all was suspense and uncertainty, their bearing was soldierly in every regard.

Inclosed I beg you to find a recapitulation of the casualties.*

I have the honor to remain, general, with every consideration of respect, very respectfully, your obedient servant,

D. WICKERSHAM,

Colonel, Commanding Cavalry Brigade, Army of the Frontier.

Brig. Gen. JAMES G. BLUNT,
Commanding Army of the Frontier.

No. 27.

Report of Col. James O. Gower, First Iowa Cavalry.

HEADQUARTERS FIRST IOWA CAVALRY,
Camp, Prairie Grove, Washington Co., Ark., December 10, 1862.

CAPTAIN: I have the honor to report that, at 6 o'clock on the morning of the 6th instant, in obedience to orders, with the First and Third Battalions of the First Iowa Cavalry, comprising an available force of 500 men, Lieutenant-Colonel [P. G.] Bryan, with the Second Battalion, being detailed as rear guard for the wagon train of the Third Division, I moved from camp on Sugar Creek, Benton County, Arkansas, and, after marching eighteen consecutive hours, reached the headquarters of Brigadier-General Blunt, at Cane Hill, near Boonsborough, Washington County, Arkansas, at 12 o'clock on the night of the 6th instant.

On the morning of the 7th instant, I marched with my command to Rhea's Mills, 8 miles, thence south 5 miles, to Prairie Grove, as advance guard for General Blunt's division, and encountered the enemy at 2.30 p. m., posted in the timber. Squadrons L and M, being in advance, were fired upon, but no one injured. Lieut. R. M. Reynolds, with 20 men from Company A, being thrown out as skirmishers, were fired upon by the enemy, and one man of Company A, Private William H. Fortune, severely wounded in the right shoulder, this being the only casualty to the regiment.

The several squadrons being formed in line of battle in the timber, maintained their position for one hour against the continual fire of the enemy, during which time Lieutenant [J. M.] Simeral, of Company L, with 20 men, retook from the enemy one howitzer, lost by the Tenth Illinois Cavalry.

Upon the arrival of General Blunt's division, at 4 p. m., I was ordered to the support of Captain Rabb's battery, and moved my command eastwardly to a large corn-field near the battery, where I remained until 5 p. m., when, by orders, I moved 1½ miles on the road to Rhea's Mills, and took position, standing to horse until daylight of the 8th instant, when, in obedience to orders, I moved my command northwardly 4 miles, and accompanied, as rear guard, the wagon train of General Blunt's division to a camp 1½ miles west of Fayetteville, where I remained until

---

* Embodied in revised statement, pp. 85, 86.

daylight on the morning of the 9th instant, when, as advance guard to the same train of wagons, I marched to Rhea's Mills, thence south 7 miles, to the present camp.

I am, very respectfully, your obedient servant,

JAMES O. GOWER,
Colonel First Iowa Cavalry.

Capt. WILLIAM HYDE CLARK,
Asst. Adjt. Gen., Third Division, Army of the Frontier.

No. 28.

Report of Maj. William H. Miller, Second Wisconsin Cavalry.

HDQRS. FIRST BATTALION, SECOND WISCONSIN CAVALRY,
Camp of Prairie Grove, Ark., December 9, 1862.

CAPTAIN: I have the honor to submit the following report, pursuant to orders received from Colonel Wickersham, commanding First Brigade, Third Division, to which brigade my command was attached. We marched from Camp Curtis, near Wilson's Creek, on the 3d of December at 12 m.; encamped for the night on Crane Creek, resuming our march next morning (December 4), arriving and encamping for the night on Crane Creek, near Cassville. December 5, we marched to Sugar Creek. December 6, with the cavalry of the brigade in advance, made a forced march, separating ourselves from balance of the division; reached Cane Hill; joined General Blunt's forces at 11 p. m. Sunday, December 7, at daylight, we were ordered to a position on the field, making a few slight preparations for battle, and remaining until 9 a. m., when we were ordered forward on the road leading in direction of Fayetteville. We marched until 1 p. m., and halted at Rhea's Mills. At 1.30 we marched to the battle-field, arriving and taking a position on right of cavalry; deployed as skirmishers, watching the enemy on that flank, pursuant to orders received from General Blunt. We remained in the position until recalled at the close of the battle. During the day a few slight demonstrations were made upon us by small numbers of the enemy, but without effect. No casualties occurred.

Yours, to command,

WM. H. MILLER,
Major, Comdg. First Batt. Second Wisconsin Vol. Cavalry.

WILLIAM HYDE CLARK,
Asst. Adjt. Gen., Second and Third Divs., Army of the Frontier.

No. 29.

Report of Lieut. Col. Henry Bertram, Twentieth Wisconsin Infantry.

HDQRS. 1ST BRIG., 3D DIV., ARMY OF THE FRONTIER,
December 9, 1862.

GENERAL: I have the honor to report that, on the 7th instant, after being ordered by you to place that portion of the First Brigade under my charge into position, the order was promptly executed by Battery L, First Missouri Light Artillery, supported by the Twentieth Wisconsin Volunteer Infantry, advancing across the creek. After playing the battery for about thirty minutes, doing good execution, I observed the enemy's fire to slacken. I then ordered the Twentieth Regiment Wisconsin Volunteer Infantry to move cautiously forward. They advanced about 500 yards across an open field; here I ordered them to lie down under cover.

Receiving information that a heavy force of the enemy was threatening my left flank, I immediately changed front to the left. The Nineteenth Iowa and Ninety-fourth Illinois Infantry following up the movement, brought us *en échelon*, the Twentieth Regiment leading on the right. After the execution of this movement, I observed a battery of the enemy, supported by infantry, trying to get into position in my front. I immediately ordered the Twentieth Wisconsin to charge the battery, which was done in gallant style, Major [H. A.] Starr leading. After taking the battery, the regiment advanced under a heavy fire to the brow of the hill, where they met a heavy force of the enemy's infantry, some four or five regiments, advancing, which poured a terrific fire into the Twentieth Regiment Wisconsin Infantry, and obliged them to fall back, which they did in good order, destroying what they could while falling back of the battery taken before. The Twentieth fell back in good style across an open field to a fence, where they reformed and remained until the firing ceased for the day.

Officers and men behaved nobly, and stood fire like veterans.

I regret the loss of the Twentieth Wisconsin is heavy. As far as I have been able to ascertain, it amounts to 49 killed, 148 wounded, and 8 missing.*

In conclusion, I cannot help but bring to your favorable notice the gallant behavior of Major Starr, in immediate command of the Twentieth Wisconsin, and also Adjutant [H. V.] Morris, of the Twentieth, for the cool and prompt manner in which they executed my orders. Captain Backof's battery (L) behaved nobly, and did good execution, although exposed for a time to a heavy fire of the enemy's infantry.

I have the honor to be, your obedient servant,

HENRY BERTRAM,
Lieut. Col. 20th Wisconsin Vols., Comdg. Portion of 1st Brigade.

Brigadier-General HERRON,
Comdg. Second and Third Divisions, Army of the Frontier.

No. 30.

Report of Capt. Frank Backof, Battery L, First Missouri Light Artillery.

CAMP AT ILLINOIS CREEK, ARK.,
December 9, 1862.

COLONEL: The undersigned would respectfully report to you the part his command took in the battle of December 7.

About 8 a. m., December 7, I took position a few miles from Fayetteville, Ark., in a corn-field, at the same time that two companies of your command drove the enemy back. After waiting for some time for an attack, I was ordered to move position 2 miles, to Illinois Creek; crossed the creek, and took position to the right of the road, at the farm, by

* But see revised statement, p. 85.

your order. After silencing the enemy's battery on the hill in front of us, I advanced 200 yards, flanked on the left by the Twentieth Wisconsin Volunteers and by the Ninety-fourth Illinois on the right, and sustained an effectual artillery fire at the enemy's position (which they moved several times) for three hours. In the same time you made a charge with your infantry on the hill and through the woods surrounding; meanwhile the shells of my battery did great execution amongst the enemy. After the great loss of your regiment in a charge on the hill and the pursuit of the enemy, having given them a few rounds of canister, and being without support, we were unable to hold our position, and retreated to the first position, two of our pieces being disabled; but the infantry having rallied again, we advanced about 100 yards from our first position and kept it.

Our loss was 1 man killed and 2 wounded; 8 horses killed, and 1 piece and 1 caisson disabled.

It is my duty to mention on this occasion the good behavior of my men, and especially of the chiefs of sections and pieces; and I return my sincerest thanks to you, colonel, for the effectual support of your command.

I am, colonel, very respectfully,

F. BACKOF,
Commanding Battery L, First Missouri Light Artillery.

Colonel BERTRAM,
Twentieth Wisconsin Volunteers.

No. 31.

Report of Col. William W. Orme, Ninety-fourth Illinois Infantry, commanding Second Brigade.

HDQRS. 2D BRIG., 3D DIV., ARMY OF THE FRONTIER,
Camp, Prairie Grove, Ark., December 10, 1862.

CAPTAIN: In compliance with General Orders, No. 35, issued from the headquarters of the general commanding the Second and Third Divisions, Army of the Frontier, I have the honor to report that in the late action at Prairie Grove, on December 7, I had under my command the Nineteenth Iowa and the Ninety-fourth Illinois Volunteer Infantry Regiments and Battery E, First Missouri Light Artillery. The Eighth Missouri Cavalry, having been detached from my command and sent forward to General Blunt the day before the engagement, was not with me during the fight.

The Nineteenth Iowa was commanded by Lieut. Col. Samuel McFarland. The Ninety-fourth Illinois was commanded by Lieut. Col. John McNulta. Battery E, First Missouri Light Artillery, was commanded by First Lieut. Joseph Foust.

When I reached Illinois Creek, under orders from General Herron, I advanced the infantry across the creek, the Ninety-fourth Illinois on the left of the road and the Nineteenth Iowa on the right of the road, placing both regiments under cover of the bluffs of the stream. Immediately afterward the battery was ordered across the creek, and placed in position on the high ground to the left of the road.

At the ford of the creek the enemy's batteries were in full view, about half a mile distant in the road, on a rising ground, at the foot of a hill.

Skirmishers were sent forward from both regiments. The enemy's batteries were opened upon us. The firing was very accurate, the shells falling on the right and in the rear of the Ninety-fourth Illinois; but they were soon silenced and compelled to retire their batteries to a less exposed position, from which they fired only at intervals. The Twentieth Wisconsin Infantry, having advanced on the right of the Nineteenth Iowa, I sent out three companies of the Nineteenth Iowa as skirmishers, and ordered the remaining seven companies to advance and support the Twentieth Wisconsin, which was now moving forward through an open field on the right of the road, and at the same time I ordered the Ninety-fourth Illinois to advance through the brush to an open field on the left. Here the Ninety-fourth received the first fire from the enemy, which was hotly returned, and the enemy fell back to a position under cover of the fence.

Meanwhile the Nineteenth Iowa had received and returned the fire of the enemy, and now advanced steadily up the hill to the left of the white house, and across the orchard back of the house to a fence, behind which the enemy in greatly superior force were concealed. As it approached, the enemy rose up and poured in a most severe and destructive fire upon it, and the Twentieth Wisconsin having already commenced to fall back in disorder, the Nineteenth Iowa was unable to hold its position, and was compelled to fall back across the orchard, when Lieutenant-Colonel McFarland fell, shot through the body. Major [D.] Kent then took command and rallied a portion of his men, who had fallen back to the right of the battery, near the position of the Ninety-fourth Illinois. This detachment he left in command of Captain Roderick, while he was engaged in rallying the remainder of his men.

Meanwhile the three companies of the Nineteenth Iowa which were sent out as skirmishers had been advanced to the right of the battery, up to a corn-field, when they were attacked by a superior force of the enemy's cavalry, which they drove back, and continued to advance near to the foot of the hill, when they were met by a greatly superior force of infantry and cavalry, which they dispersed.

I then ordered them to fall back to the corn-field, in order to give the artillery a chance to shell the wood, where they remained until ordered to join the regiment. The battery meanwhile had been actively and effectually engaged in throwing shot and shell wherever it was most needed; changing its position to the front and to the left as circumstances required, and, as the enemy were making great efforts to turn our left wing, the battery took position in the wheat-field on the left of the road, supported by the Ninety-fourth Illinois on the left, outside of the fence.

After the Nineteenth Iowa and Twentieth Wisconsin were driven back, the rebels poured down in large numbers on our left, but were twice repulsed with heavy slaughter by the Ninety-fourth Illinois and the well-served canister from Battery E. But the rebels continuing to menace our left flank in large force, and the battery being so far advanced, with no support but the Ninety-fourth Illinois, which was kept continually engaging the enemy, the battery and the infantry regiment were ordered to fall back. The battery, from loss of horses, was compelled to leave one of its caissons on the field, but it was brought away by a squad of the Ninety-fourth Illinois, under the personal direction of Lieutenant-Colonel McNulta. The battery fell back across the road, and the Ninety-fourth Illinois also fell back to the road in good order.

The three companies of skirmishers of the Nineteenth Iowa were brought out to the road by my direction, when they came up in perfect order, under command of Lieut. Richard Root, acting adjutant of the regiment. The different portions of the Nineteenth Iowa then fell back and formed in line across the creek.

As the sun set, the firing on both sides closed, the infantry resting on their arms, without camp-fires during the whole night.

At 3 o'clock on the morning of the 8th, by order of the general commanding, I formed the Nineteenth Iowa and Ninety-fourth Illinois in line, where they, respectively, took position on the night of the 7th. Soon after sunrise on the morning of the 8th, I ordered forward a company of the Ninety-fourth Illinois as skirmishers, advancing them up the hill occupied by the rebels the evening before; and by direction of the general I also ordered the Nineteenth Iowa and Twentieth Wisconsin to follow the company of skirmishers, and post themselves on the hill, where they remained until ordered back to go into camp.

I regret to announce the death of Lieut. Col. Samuel McFarland, commanding the Nineteenth Iowa, who fell while gallantly leading his men in the charge on the rebels on the hill.

I cannot speak too highly of the gallant conduct of the officers and men of the Nineteenth Iowa, for, after being repulsed with great loss by an overwhelming force of the enemy, they rallied and brought from the field the colors of the Twentieth Wisconsin Regiment. Captain [S. F.] Roderick, of the Nineteenth Iowa, deserves especial mention for meritorious conduct. He gathered together some 70 men of his regiment, after it was broken and scattered; rallied them around the regimental colors, and, under my direction, formed them on the left of the Ninety-fourth Illinois, where they did good service, and only retired from the field when ordered to fall back. Lieut. Richard Root, acting adjutant of the regiment, is also entitled to honorable mention. By direction of his commanding officer, and at the request of the captains, he took charge of the three companies of skirmishers, and maneuvered them with great bravery and skill.

Too much praise cannot be accorded to the officers and men of Battery E, First Missouri Light Artillery; and Lieutenants Foust, [C. L.] Edwards, and [J. B.] Atwater are entitled to honorable notice for their gallant conduct and the signal ability with which they managed their battery. The Ninety-fourth Illinois behaved well. The safety of our left wing depended in a great measure upon their efforts. They withstood every attack on our left, and repulsed the enemy with heavy loss.

The intrepid bearing of Lieut. Col. John McNulta inspired his men with courage; and when the battery retired, leaving one of its caissons on the field, he took a squad of his men and in person brought it from the field.

Iowa and Illinois may still continue to view with pride the heroic conduct of their volunteers, for on the field of Prairie Grove, as on all other battle-fields of the war, these soldiers have fought side by side, winning fresh laurels and proudly maintaining the high honor of their respective States.

I cannot close this report without making honorable mention of my adjutant, Lieut. Hudson Burr. He fearlessly visited every part of the field bearing my orders, and aiding very much in rallying the men when their regiments had been repulsed.

One of my orderlies, Private George Wilkerson, of Company E, Eighth Missouri Volunteer Cavalry, is entitled to notice for the fearless discharge of his duties. He was with me during the whole engagement, until late in the afternoon, when he was wounded in the left arm while riding by my side.

I have annexed hereto a statement of the killed, wounded, and missing of the brigade.* I also inclose herewith the reports of the different regiments and detachments of my command.

I have the honor to be, captain, respectfully, yours, &c.,

WM. W. ORME,
Colonel, Commanding Second Brigade, Third Division.

Capt. WILLIAM HYDE CLARK,
Assistant Adjutant-General, Second and Third Divisions.

No. 32.

Report of Lieut. Col. John McNulta, Ninety-fourth Illinois Infantry.

HDQRS. NINETY-FOURTH ILLINOIS VOL. INFANTRY,
Camp, Prairie Grove, Ark., December 8, 1862.

SIR: I hereby submit the following report of the part taken by my command in the battle of Prairie Grove on the 7th instant:

My men were very much fatigued and foot-sore, being marched, as you are aware, nearly 100 miles. They endured all the privations, loss of sleep, short rations, &c., with commendable firmness and patience; and, when a prospect of being speedily brought to face the enemy was presented to them, forgot their suffering, and responded with the promptness of fresh troops to the orders to prepare for immediate action. Although scarcely able to walk, from their sore and blistered feet, they formed in line of battle and awaited with anxiety the order to advance.

Companies A and K were deployed as skirmishers, under my special supervision, on the base and the side of the mountain on the left, the regiment occupying the left of the line of battle. The regiment was then ordered forward, with two pieces of artillery, by General Herron. They moved on the double-quick nearly a mile in advance of the line of battle, already formed. The battery being already planted, our regiment was placed as its support while they shelled the woods down the valley in our advance. No response being given by the enemy, the battery was limbered and the regiment again ordered to advance, accompanied by General Herron and body guard and two pieces of Battery E, First Missouri Artillery.

Companies B, C, and D were then deployed to our left as skirmishers, under the command of Major [R. G.] Laughlin. They, covering the valley to our left, crossed the creek and advanced to the fence, in view of the enemy's line, which was formed in the rear of the fence on the other side of the field. The regiment in the mean time, marching by the road, crossed the creek at the ford, and was formed in line on the left of the ford under cover. The skirmishers were then ordered to rally on the command. Company A was placed as flankers on our left, and the regiment awaited further orders. Soon after, the firing of the artillery commenced, when orders were received from Colonel [W. W.] Orme to take our position in line of battle on the extreme left. I then changed our front and engaged the enemy on our left, opening the infantry engagement of the day and receiving their first fire. I then moved by the left flank farther to the left in the wood, and formed in line of battle within 200 yards of the enemy's line, where we again drew their fire; but in a few moments the enemy fell back from our front over the brow of the hill.

---

*Nominal list omitted. See p. 86.

The advantage thus gained was not followed up, on account of an order being received from Colonel Orme to support Battery E at all hazards. Our line was again withdrawn and formed in the rear. I again formed the line in the same position formerly occupied, the enemy reforming their right with increased numbers. We again opened fire upon them, when they again withdrew.

The right of our line having fallen back to a new line, about 200 yards to the rear, the battery also being withdrawn to the same line, I then formed my line on that point, under immediate orders from General Herron, bringing with me a caisson left on the field by Battery E. I then formed my regiment on the road near the ford, and, under orders from General Herron, held it there during the night. My regiment, as I believe, received the first infantry fire of the enemy, and were the last to leave the field.

The officers and men of my command behaved more like veterans than new troops in their first battle. Where so much courage was shown it is difficult to speak of some and not of others; yet, when such instances of gallantry are displayed as were shown by some of the officers and men of my command, I deem it proper to mention the names of those who made themselves most conspicuous by their conduct during the engagement. Much credit is due Maj. R. G. Laughlin, for the energy and perseverance he has displayed on not only this, but on all important occasions. His efforts in carrying out all orders and encouraging the men to deeds of bravery, by his personal example, had a most beneficial effect, and on this, as upon all other occasions, he showed himself possessed of all the qualifications that are essential to the officer and man. Brave and cool in danger, and firm in the administration of discipline, he has shown himself competent to fill the position he occupies, or any that may be assigned him, with honor to himself and credit to the service.

In my efforts to carry out orders delivered to me, and in the performance enjoined by myself, I was nobly seconded by the line officers of my command, who, with one or two exceptions, were active and efficient, and did honor to themselves and to the regiment.

In this connection I would mention particularly Captain [A. T.] Briscoe, Company A, who acted with his company as skirmishers, and did us good service; Captain [J. M.] Burch, of Company K, who managed his command admirably, and, by his coolness and courage under fire and general good conduct, gave evidence of fine military attainments; Captain [J. L.] Routt, of Company E, although quite unwell, was cool, collected, and rendered extraordinary service by encouraging and stimulating his men, and Captain [J. C.] McFarland, Company B, also displayed coolness and courage of a high order. I must not fail to speak of Captain [J. P.] Orme, of Company H, who, although the youngest officer in command, distinguished himself during the whole engagement. Lieutenant [G.] Hayes, of Company K, was prominent for his activity in the discharge of his duty, and showed by his conduct prominent soldierly qualities. Lieutenant [W. W.] Elder, of Company B, I am sorry to say, was severely wounded, and we lose for a time the services of a reliable and faithful officer. Great praise is due to Sergeants Haywood, Company K; Minier, Company I; Rouie, Company A; Grier, Company C; J. S. Martin, Company B, and Orderly Sergeant Bishop, Company D, for their gallant conduct on the field and efficient service rendered in their respective positions. Color-Sergeants Stipp and McKenzie are deserving of the highest praise for the manner in which they performed their duties in the responsible positions which they occupied.

The color-guard also stood nobly to their posts, and suffered no danger to drive them from the discharge of duty. Corpl. A. C. Stewart is worthy of particular mention for the coolness and bravery he displayed throughout the day. Also Privates William H. Carter, of Company C, and William Clark, of Company A, were conspicuous for the prompt and efficient manner in which they discharged their duty.

I desire, in addition, to make mention of the regimental staff. Drs. Ross and Stewart proved themselves most efficient officers in their department; Dr. Stewart remained upon the field with his attendants, and, as each man fell, he was taken up, his wounds examined, and treated in the best possible manner without delay; Lieut. M. L. Moore, and his faithful assistant, Sergt. R. S. McEntyre, in attending to the wants of the regiment. Chaplain R. E. Guthrie proved himself to be a soldier in every sense of the word, and eminently qualified to fill the position he occupies. He was on the field throughout the whole engagement, encouraging the men on in their good work, calling on them to trust in God, do their duty, and fire low, and using such other expressions as were calculated to inspire with courage. I am under personal obligations to Lieut. George B. O'Keson, acting adjutant, for the prompt assistance rendered by him upon the field, and the coolness and courage he displayed in executing all orders given him and seeing that all commands were carried out promptly.

All of which is most repectfully submitted.

Your obedient servant,

J. McNULTA,

Lieutenant-Colonel, Comdg. Ninety-fourth Illinois Vol. Infantry.

Lieut. HUDSON BURR,

A. A. A. G., Second Brig., Third Div., Army of the Frontier.

No. 33.

Report of Maj. Daniel Kent, Nineteenth Iowa Infantry.

HEADQUARTERS NINETEENTH IOWA VOLUNTEERS,
Camp, Prairie Grove, December 10, 1862.

COLONEL: I have the honor of reporting to you the part taken by the Nineteenth Regiment in the late battle of the 7th instant.

The Nineteenth Regiment, 500 strong, was ordered into line of battle at 12 m., Lieutenant-Colonel [S.] McFarland in command. By order of Colonel Orme, three companies were detached and deployed as skirmishers. The companies were A, B, and C, and, owing to the circumstances, Lieutenant [R.] Root, acting adjutant of the regiment, was ordered to take command, which was done. The skirmishers advanced under a heavy fire to a corn-field on the right of Battery E, First Missouri Light Artillery, and were ordered to hold it at all hazards, which was done, until ordered to fall back and form in line of battle. The regiment was then ordered to advance to the left of the white house on the hill, to support the Twentieth Wisconsin Infantry, which was hotly engaged. The Nineteenth, led by Lieutenant-Colonel McFarland, advanced up the hill steadily, and across the orchard back of the house, when the Twentieth Wisconsin gave way. The Nineteenth still advanced to the fence adjoining the wood, when the enemy, who lay concealed, arose to their feet, three regiments deep, pouring a destructive fire on us from three sides, which caused the regiment to waver and fall back to the battery, on the left of the road leading up the hill. Lieutenant-Colonel McFarland here fell, shot through the body. I then took command, and rallied what was left of the regiment, as the regiment met with a severe loss in the charge. I then left the men I had rallied in charge of Captain [S. F.] Roderick, of Company K, and went to rally some scattered troops. Colonel Orme then rode up and ordered Captain Roderick to fall in and rally with the Ninety-fourth Illinois, which he did, led by Colonel Orme in person, driving the enemy back with great slaughter, and holding their position until ordered to fall back and reform.

In the retreat of the Twentieth Wisconsin, the color-bearer was shot, letting fall the colors, when the enemy made a desperate effort to get them, but a portion of the Nineteenth Iowa rallied and got possession of and carried them off the field.

In making out the report, it is with pleasure I can say that the officers and men behaved nobly and fought desperately, as if the fate of the battle depended on them alone. I will mention especially Captain Roderick, of Company K, whom I left in charge of some scattered troops; also Captain [T. W.] Richmond, of Company H, and Captain [A. M.] Taylor, of Company G; also Lieutenant [W. S.] Brooks, of Company D, who brought the colors off the field, and in doing so was badly wounded. Others are equally meritorious, but too numerous to mention at present.

The report of the detachment of skirmishers I send to you as received:

SIR: Having been ordered to take command of the three companies of skirmishers on the 7th instant, the day of battle, I advanced them to the right of Battery E, First Missouri Light Artillery, when the right wing, under Captain Bruce, was attacked by a superior force of the enemy; but a few well-directed shots drove them back. I would here notice the bravery of Captain Bruce and the men under him. After advancing up near the wood, the enemy came out of cover, showing a heavy body of infantry and two battalions of cavalry. They met with a warm reception from the right, under Captain Bruce, which made them scatter. At this time I received an order from Colonel Orme to fall back to the corn-field, so as to let the battery shell the wood, which was done in good order, and held until ordered by you to join the regiment.

R. ROOT,
Lieutenant, Commanding Skirmishers.

Major KENT,
Commanding Nineteenth Iowa Volunteers.

On the morning of the 8th instant was ordered into line at 6 o'clock, and advanced across the creek and formed a line of battle, and advanced up through the timber, on the left of the Twentieth Wisconsin. Was then ordered to occupy the fence east of the house. Did so, crossing part of the ground that was fought over the day before. Occupied the position until ordered to fall back, so as to let both sides have a chance to collect their dead. Selected an advantageous piece of ground, and occupied it until ordered into camp.*

I remain, yours, respectfully,

D. KENT,
Major, Commanding Nineteenth Iowa Volunteers.

Col. W. W. ORME,
Comdg. Second Brig., Third Div., Army of the Frontier.

---

* Summary of casualties, here omitted, is embodied in revised statement, p. 86.

No. 34.

Report of Lieut. Joseph Foust, Battery E, First Missouri Light Artillery.

BATTLE-FIELD OF PRAIRIE GROVE, ARK.,
December 8, 1862.

COLONEL: I have the honor to report that, on the morning of the 7th instant, while on the march from Fayetteville to Illinois Creek, the enemy having attacked our advance, I was ordered by you to take a position on the left of the road.

After reconnoitering and finding no enemy on the east side of the creek in force, I was ordered by you to send one section to the front, to report to General Herron. I ordered Lieut. C. L. Edwards to take one section, and report accordingly. He advanced, shelling the wood until he arrived at the east bank of the creek, which he was ordered to cross and open upon the enemy, who was visible in force, about three-fourths of a mile to the front. The position of the enemy's batteries having been ascertained, he was ordered by General Herron to retire. At the same time I was ordered to advance with the remainder of the battery to the front. Arriving at the ford of the creek, I was ordered to halt out of sight of the enemy, and to advance and open the battery upon a signal to be given from Captain Murphy's battery.

We went into action at the signal, under a terrible fire from the enemy while crossing the ford. About the third round the enemy's guns were silenced. Another battery on our left having got our range, we were compelled to change position to the front.

I would state, however, that I went on to the field with orders to take such positions as would afford the greatest advantage over the enemy. The same orders were extended to my officers by myself. Each one taking command of a section, we acted independently, but supported each other. The enemy was about to turn our left flank with an overwhelming force, when Lieutenant Edwards took a position on the extreme left with his section, while Lieutenant [J. B.] Atwater and myself kept up a heavy fire. I then ordered my section to the same position, Lieutenant Atwater covering my advance. The latter then took a position beside me. We were now within 150 yards of the enemy's line, supported on the left by the Ninety-fourth Illinois Infantry.

At this time the enemy attempted to charge our lines, when the whole battery opened on them with canister, and they fell back in confusion. The infantry attempted to charge the hill, but were repulsed by an overwhelming force of the enemy, when we again forced them back with canister. Again the infantry attempted to carry the hill, but were driven back the second time, when we covered their retreat once more with canister, driving the enemy back again to the wood. The enemy seeing the battery without support, made a great effort to take it, but were driven back by the battery. Colonel Huston having ordered us off the field, in consequence of our canister having been exhausted, the battery retired in good order, with the exception of one caisson, which could not be brought off on account of the horses and men being killed or disabled. It was finally brought off by Lieutenant-Colonel McNulta, of the Ninety-fourth Illinois Infantry.

After receiving fresh supplies of ammunition, we again advanced to the front, and continued the action until night closed the contest. During the engagement we fired 562 rounds of shot, shell, and canister.

Our loss was 2 men killed and 6 wounded; 8 horses killed and 11 wounded.

I can make no exceptions to the conduct of both officers and men, as under the most galling fire each one was at his post, and not one man wavered.

I have the honor to be, your most obedient servant,

JOSEPH FOUST,
First Lieut., Comdg. Company E, First Missouri Light Artillery.

Col. W. W. ORME,
Comdg. Second Brig., Third Div., Army of the Frontier.

No. 35.

Report of Capt. Amos L. Burrows, First Missouri Cavalry.

HDQRS. FIRST BATTALION FIRST MISSOURI CAVALRY,
Camp at Prairie Grove, Ark., December 9, 1862.

CAPTAIN: General Orders requiring it, I herewith beg leave to submit the following as my report of the part taken by this battalion in the action of December 7:

I left Fayetteville at 4 o'clock on the morning of the 7th instant with three companies (I, H, and L), Company I, Capt. J. M. Adams, being detailed as immediate body guard. Company H, commanded by Lieutenant [G. W.] Hanna, and Company L, escort to the general, were sent out as advance guard, commanded by Maj. J. M. Hubbard. We marched on without interruption until within 8 miles of Cane Hill, when we saw a large body of the First Arkansas and Seventh Missouri Cavalry on the retreat. We undertook to stop them, and, finding it being of no use, Major Hubbard ordered the fence to be thrown down on the left-hand side of the road, and drew up in line of battle in the wheat-field, and instructed the First Arkansas and Seventh Missouri Cavalry to form in our rear. They partially did so, but, having several shots fired at our line by the enemy, they broke and fled. The enemy came down the road within 200 yards; filed off right and left of the road to flank us. Major Hubbard saw that their numbers were too great to contend with, and gave the order to retreat. We started across the field to the mountain, some 3 miles distant, in order to divert the enemy from coming down on the infantry before they were prepared for it.

Having so many fences to cross, our progress was much impeded, and having to cross a lane, the enemy came up on our rear and commenced firing. Major Hubbard, in trying to cross the fence, was compelled to surrender, when the command devolved upon myself. I immediately commanded the head of the column to the right, in order to get to the mountain quicker. The enemy continued to follow us until we reached the foot of the mountain. During the time we lost 1 lieutenant and 10 men, taken prisoners, and 3 men wounded.

When we arrived at the foot of the mountain, we met about 200 stragglers from the First Arkansas and Seventh Missouri Cavalry. I told them to fall into ranks. I formed them into line of battle immediately, to make a stand if they followed us any farther. But they discontinued the pursuit, and we struck off through the fields to the main road, coming into the road in the rear of the infantry. I immediately marched to the front and reported to General Herron, when I was ordered to skirmish on our left flank and find out the position of the enemy. After going some 600 yards, we found the enemy drawn up in line of battle in a corn-field, about 300 yards in advance of us. I reported the same to

General Herron, when we were ordered to skirmish on the right flank. We skirmished our right flank until we got on the west side of the Illinois River, where we found the enemy strongly posted, some half mile in advance. We immediately formed on the right of Battery E, First Missouri Light Artillery, when our artillery opened, being immediately replied to by the enemy. The shells coming rather close, we were ordered to fall back to give place to the infantry, who had by that time come up to the support of the battery.

I retired some 200 yards farther to the right, and sent out skirmishers to protect our right flank, when I was ordered to throw out skirmishers on our left flank. We followed up the west side of the river about 1 mile; discovered no trace of the enemy, when I was ordered to keep my command in readiness for further orders, when I was ordered by Colonel Orme, commanding Second Brigade, Third Division, to advance as skirmishers on the left flank of the Ninety-fourth Illinois Infantry.

After coming out of the brush we received a heavy volley from the enemy's right flank, posted behind a fence in the edge of the timber, when we retired and gave room for the Ninety-fourth Illinois to charge them, which poured in a deadly volley into their ranks. I immediately went back and reported to General Herron for further orders, when I was ordered to move with my command down the valley, to ascertain if the enemy were trying to get in our rear to attack the baggage train. I went down 4 miles. Seeing no signs of the enemy, I again reported to the general, and, it being dark, I was ordered to camp at the general's headquarters.*

AMOS L. BURROWS,
Captain Company L, First Battalion, First Missouri Vol. Cav.

No. 36.

Reports of Maj. Gen. Thomas C. Hindman, C. S. Army, commanding First Corps, Trans-Mississippi Army, including preliminary skirmishes.

BATTLE-FIELD AT PRAIRIE GROVE, ARK.,
Camp 23 miles west of Van Buren, December 9, 1862.

I threatened the enemy's right and front at Cane Hill; moved on his left to cut off re-enforcements, which I attacked and drove back, and then took position at Prairie Grove, and fought the whole army with the following result: My loss is about 350 killed, wounded, and missing. The Federal loss was about 1,000 killed and wounded, about 300 prisoners (including a large number of officers), a train of 20 wagons, and 4 stand of colors. We hold the battle-field. A flag has this moment been sent in by the enemy, asking a truce of twelve hours to bury his dead and care for his wounded. I have granted it.

T. C. HINDMAN.

Major-General HOLMES.

HEADQUARTERS FIRST CORPS, TRANS-MISSISSIPPI ARMY,
Camp near Fort Smith, Ark., December 25, 1862.

COLONEL: I marched from near Van Buren on the 3d instant with 9,000 infantry, 2,000 cavalry, and 22 pieces of artillery. Lack of shoes

* Casualties embodied in revised statement, p. 86.

and arms prevented me from taking my entire force. My intention was to attack Brigadier-General Blunt, on Cane Hill, reported to have between 7,000 and 8,000 men and 30 cannon. I expected, as stated at the time in dispatches to department headquarters, to return immediately after the engagement, having barely ammunition enough for one battle, and not sufficient subsistence and forage for seven days at half rations. These meager supplies had been accumulated with extreme difficulty by hauling in wagons of the general train and regiments 80 miles, my transportation being very limited, the country around me entirely exhausted, and the river too low for navigation. These facts had made it certain that I must soon retire the greater part of my force toward Little Rock; hence it seemed important for the security of what was to be left that Blunt was to be driven from his position.

Cane Hill is a ridge of perhaps 8 miles length and 5 miles width, in the southwest part of Washington County, Arkansas, just beyond the north base of the Boston Mountains. Three villages are built upon it (Russellville, Boonsborough, and Newburg), which almost blend with each other, covering a distance, as the road to Fayetteville runs, of 3 or 5 miles. The enemy's main body was about Newburg. The distance from Van Buren to Newburg is 45 miles. The intermediate country is a rugged and sterile range of mountains. The roads across it are gathered together at Van Buren, on the south side, and at Fayetteville, on the northern. These places are from 50 to 65 miles apart, according to the route traveled. There are four principal roads; one bends to the right and east with the valley of Frog Bayou, crosses the mountains, then follows the West Fork of White River and strikes Fayetteville from the southeast; another, known as the Telegraph road, proceeds for the most part upon ridges directly north; the third leaves the Telegraph road 12 miles above Van Buren, runs along the Cherokee line to Evansville, and there branches through the Cane Hill country to Fayetteville, its main trunk going north, by Cincinnati and Maysville, to Fort Scott; the fourth turns to the left from the Telegraph road at Oliver's, 19 miles above Van Buren, follows the valley of Cove Creek to the foot of the mountains, and, after crossing, passes through a succession of defiles, valleys, and prairies, reaching Fayetteville from a southwesterly direction. At Morrow's, 15 miles above Oliver's, the Cove Creek road sends a branch direct to Newburg, 7 miles distant. Eight miles above Morrow's it is crossed by a road leading from Hog-eye, 5 miles east on the Telegraph road, to Newburg. Two miles beyond this it sends a branch to Rhea's Mills, to Maysville, which crosses the Cane Hill and Fayetteville road at the distance of 2 miles from the Cove Creek road. This crossing is 7½ miles from Newburg and 12½ miles from Fayetteville. Two miles and a half above this crossing the Cove Creek road and the Cane Hill and Fayetteville unite. There is a road from Newburg, by Rhea's Mills, to this junction, the distance by that route being about 2 miles greater. The accompanying map* may serve to make this description more intelligible.

Marmaduke's cavalry division formed my advance, moving on the Telegraph road, with detachments on those east and west of it. Colonel Watie's Cherokee regiment was ordered to the vicinity of Evansville, instructed, when the firing should commence, to move forward and occupy certain mills in the Cane Hill region, and to attack the enemy's train if retired toward Cincinnati. The balance of my force moved on the Telegraph road, and bivouacked at Oliver's on the night of the 4th.

---

*Not found.

There I received information that a re-enforcement of 3,000 or 4,000 men had arrived on Cane Hill, making Blunt's force fully equal to mine.

On the 5th, instead of getting to Morrow's, as I had expected, we went but little farther than half way, in consequence of some of those apparently unavoidable delays to which troops so ill-provided as ours are liable.

On the 6th we reached Morrow's. In the morning of that day, Marmaduke's advance (under Col. J. O. Shelby) encountered the enemy's cavalry and drove them back beyond Morrow's to within 2 miles of Newburg. There, from the crest of the mountain to its base, about sunset a sharp engagement occurred, in which Col. J. C. Monroe and his brigade of Arkansas cavalry (who had relieved Shelby) greatly distinguished themselves, charging a superior force of the enemy's cavalry with boldness and vigor, breaking his ranks, and only ceasing to pursue when recalled. I had previously ordered forward Hunter's regiment of Missouri infantry, of Parsons' brigade, of Frost's division, to hold the ground which the cavalry might gain. This order was promptly executed. The regiment was in possession of the heights and defiles that might be used for annoying us before the skirmish had ceased. To make sure of this advantage, the remainder of Parsons' brigade was thrown forward to the same position.

This being the situation of affairs, the several commanders of divisions were assembled on the night of the 6th, to receive final instructions, when I learned a further re-enforcement of from 4,000 to 6,000 infantry and 2,000 cavalry, with 30 cannon, under Brigadier-General Herron, was then at Fayetteville, on the way to Cane Hill, making forced marches. It had been my intention to throw Marmaduke's cavalry by the Cove Creek road and its Maysville branch upon the enemy's left and rear, while scattered in front by the road leading from Morrow's to Newburg. It now seemed evident that that plan would simply cause the retirement of Blunt upon his re-enforcements, without accepting battle till after the junction should be effected. There was a possibility that I might, by adopting a different plan, destroy the re-enforcements and afterward fight the main body upon equal terms. To withdraw without fighting at all, would discourage my own troops and so embolden the enemy as to insure his following me up. His sudden concentration of troops justified the opinion that a movement against me was intended in any event. Influenced by these considerations, I determined to risk an engagement.

At 12 p. m., after replenishing his camp-fires, Parsons moved back to Morrow's, Monroe remaining in position on the crest of the mountain, instructed to dismount and skirmish as infantry at daylight, so as to deceive the enemy and detain him at Newburg as long as possible, and, when he should commence retreating, to press him vigorously. The trains were ordered by a cross route to the Telegraph road and then to Hog-eye, guarded by 100 cavalry and the disabled men of the infantry, of whom there was, unfortunately, a considerable number. These arrangements left me for the fight less than 10,000 men of all arms.

The order was given to march forward at 3 a. m. on the 7th, on the Cove Creek road and its Maysville branch to the Cane Hill and Fayetteville road. The command was not in motion till nearly 4 o'clock, and then the route proved so excessively bad, and the detentions so frequent from the breaking of artillery harness and debility of the battery animals, that the infantry failed to march above 2 miles an hour. A little before sunrise, Marmaduke discovered the cavalry of Herron's command moving on the Cane Hill and Fayetteville road toward Newburg. Making his dispositions rapidly and with excellent judgment, he attacked them in front and flank, routed them completely, killed and wounded many, captured over 200, with the train of a regiment, and pursued the fugitives 5 miles in the direction of Fayetteville to the line of battle formed by Herron's infantry. My infantry was yet far in rear, but moving up as rapidly as possible. When the head of the column at length reached the Cane Hill and Fayetteville road, Parsons' brigade was put in position, facing toward Newburg, to resist any movements of the enemy from that direction, a regiment of cavalry thrown toward that place to reconnoiter, and the balance of the force ordered forward, with instructions to attack the re-enforcements at once; Marmaduke in advance, Shoup next, then Frost. I remained with Parsons' brigade, hoping to get some reliable intelligence of the enemy at Newburg. Receiving none, at 11 a. m. I went forward about 2 miles and overtook the marching column. It was painful to observe the exhaustion of the men. They had marched nearly 15 miles. None of them had eaten since the preceding day. The rations of all had been insufficient for over thirty days. Many, overcome with fatigue, had been left on the roadside. Brigadier-General Shoup met me, and stated that Marmaduke was falling back before the enemy's infantry, which was advancing, and that he had therefore put his division in position to resist attack. I found the position taken by General Shoup an exceedingly strong one. It was upon the edge of a hill, densely wooded, descending abruptly to Crawford's Prairie, half a mile in width, which encircled all its northern half. Five hundred yards in rear was another prairie. Between the two, on the right and left, a skirt of woods connected the timber of the hill with that beyond. The Cane Hill and Fayetteville road cuts the center of this hill, passing by Prairie Grove Church, which is upon its summit. A cross-road from the Cane Hill and Fayetteville to the Cove Creek road passes also immediately by the church, dividing the south prairie from the growth upon the hill. By the time I had completed my reconnaissance of the ground, a regiment of Federal cavalry, with two pieces of artillery, opened fire upon the captured train and prisoners, that had been ordered toward Morrow's, and also upon a hospital established by my medical director for the treatment of the wounded of the Federal cavalry. No loss ensued, and this force retired rapidly upon observing Parsons' brigade. Shortly after, dense columns of smoke in the direction of Rhea's Mills and between there and Newburg indicated that Blunt had retreated hastily, destroying his stores, and was moving to unite with Herron. I immediately ordered forward Parsons' brigade. Blunt's advance soon appeared on the farther side of Crawford's Prairie. The interval of time in which I might have attacked Herron was past. Circumstances did not permit me to avail myself of it, for the manifest reason that at the favorable moment the rear of my column could not be where the head of it was. Evidently the combined forces of Blunt and Herron would speedily attack me. I made such arrangements as seemed best to meet that contingency. The line of battle determined on was nearly in the form of a horseshoe, conforming to the shape of the hill. Only Shoup's division and Shelby's brigade, of Marmaduke's division (the latter dismounted), were at first placed upon that line, filling the center and right opposite the line taken by Herron, which was upon the farther side of Crawford's Prairie, on a bluff that rose up steeply behind a stream flowing into Illinois River. Frost's division, to which had been added the brigade of Texans, with Clark's Missouri regiment, commanded by Brigadier-General Roane, was held in reserve to await the movements of Blunt. MacDonald's regiment of Missouri cavalry and Lane's regiment of Texas cavalry (the latter commanded by Lieut. Col. R. P. Crump) were held in readiness to meet any attempt upon the flanks. About 12 o'clock the enemy opened with artillery, to which ours began responding, but this I prohibited.

At 1 p. m., aided by a tremendous artillery fire, the infantry of Herron's command advanced against the position held by Shoup and Marmaduke. It was permitted to approach within 60 yards, and then, as it charged, making gallantly past one of our batteries, and having it a moment in possession, Fagan's Arkansas brigade, part of McRae's brigade, and the Missourians, under Shelby, delivered a terrific fire from their shot-guns, rifles, and muskets, and charged the enemy furiously. Hawthorn's regiment of Arkansians retook the battery. The Federals broke and fled. Our men pursued them far into the prairie. The slaughter was great, the earth in many places strewn with Federal wounded and dead. Very soon the attack was renewed, a little farther to my right, with great vigor and determination. I ordered Shaver's Arkansas brigade, of Frost's division, to the support of General Shoup. The enemy was again repulsed with heavy loss, and retired in confusion.

Blunt had now formed line of battle 2,000 yards to the front and left of Shoup, and commenced advancing. I ordered Frost's division forward on the left of Marmaduke's. The thick undergrowth on that flank rendered it difficult to execute the movement, which was further embarrassed by the well-directed and determined fire of the enemy's batteries. There was, however, no confusion. By the time Frost's division was in line, the enemy was nearly across the prairie, and our skirmishers engaged his almost as soon as deployed. His attack was directed against Parsons' brigade. It was fierce and prolonged, but ended in his being driven back in disorder with heavy losses. One of Marmaduke's regiments and one of Roane's (both Missourians) shared the honor of this brilliant achievement. The enemy now brought up all his artillery, many pieces of which were rifled, and endeavored to shake our troops by playing upon the entire line for nearly an hour. Then he attacked with all his infantry, at the same time threatening the extreme left with a heavy cavalry force and attempting to turn the right. MacDonald's Missouri cavalry defeated him in the last maneuver. Lane's Texas cavalry and Roane's brigade deterred him from seriously assailing the left, and Shoup's division, Shelby's brigade, of Marmaduke's division, and Parsons' and Shaver's brigades, of Frost's division, gloriously repulsed him in his desperate attacks upon their lines. He again fled beyond the prairie, leaving his dead and wounded, and the colors of several of his regiments, in our hands, besides a number of prisoners. Some of these were ascertained to be of Totten's division, which had arrived upon the field, still further increasing the disparity of forces.

In the midst of this struggle information reached me that a considerable body of Federal cavalry was approaching Hog-eye, to which place I ordered my trains. I directed the wagons retired on the Telegraph road to Oliver's. This was done without loss. A furious cannonade was kept up by the enemy until near sunset; then a last attack of his infantry was directed against the line held by Frost. This was a most determined effort to retrieve the fortunes of the day. It signally failed, and the enemy paid dearly in killed and wounded for the attempt. At dark the battle closed, leaving us masters of every foot of the ground on which it was fought.

Our loss in killed was 164; wounded, 817; missing, 336. The enemy left not less than 400 dead on the field, and his wounded certainly exceeded 1,500. The number of prisoners in our hands was 275, including

9 officers. We also captured 5 Federal flags and over 500 small-arms, with 23 wagons containing clothing and camp and garrison equipage. Invoices of this property have been forwarded.

Of all the troops engaged on our side, Adams' Arkansas regiment alone dishonored itself. It was well armed, ably commanded, and surrounded by good soldiers from the same State, setting it an example of courage and patriotism; but, after delivering a single fire, the greater part of the men broke ranks, threw down their arms, and shamefully fled, many of them even deserting to the enemy. The field and staff officers who had been appointed rallied about 75 around the colors, and these did much to redeem the reputation of the regiment. With but few exceptions, the company officers exerted no influence. The other troops displayed the greatest courage, constancy, and enthusiasm. There was no place of shelter upon any portion of the field. Wounds were given and deaths inflicted by the enemy's artillery in the ranks of the reserves as well as in the front rank. During five hours, shell, solid shot, grape and canister, and storms of bullets swept the entire ground. Many gallant officers, and many soldiers equally brave, fell dead or wounded, but their comrades stood as firm as iron. Volunteers maintained their reputation. Conscripts rose at once to the same standard, and splendidly refuted the slanders put upon them by the class of exempts.

Generals Frost, Shoup, and Marmaduke, commanding divisions; Generals Roane, Fagan, Parsons, and McRae, and Colonels Shaver and Shelby, commanding brigades, did their duty nobly. I strongly commend them to the lieutenant-general commanding the department. Generals Shoup and Marmaduke do not appear to have been confirmed as brigadiers. They fully merit the honor. Had the authorities, whose consent is requisite, been present at Prairie Grove or at Shiloh, where these gallant officers equally distinguished themselves, the act of confirmation could not be delayed. The reports of the division commanders and their subordinates are forwarded herewith. Especial attention is invited to them. They embody many valuable details and specify instances of courage and good conduct on the part of field, staff, and company officers and enlisted men which I will not be expected otherwise to mention here.

I had with me the following staff: Col. R. C. Newton, chief of staff; Maj. J. P. Wilson, assistant adjutant-general; Lieut. S. B. Reardon, aide-de-camp; Lieut. R. W. Lee, aide-de-camp, acting chief of ordnance; Col. D. Provence, acting chief of artillery; Col. A. S. Dobbin and Maj. E. C. Boudinot, volunteer aides-de-camp; Surg. J. M. Keller, medical director. All of them were constantly under fire. They displayed great coolness and disregard of danger in the discharge of their duties. This was the second bloody battle in which Colonel Newton and Major Wilson served on my staff. In both they evinced the same high qualities. The confirmation of their rank has been fairly won at Shiloh and at Prairie Grove. I present this subject specially to the department commander, with the case also of Lieutenant [McK. A.] Hammett, all being of the number of assignments made by me while commanding the Trans-Mississippi District.

Considering the strength of my command, as compared with the enemy; considering that my men were destitute of food, their wagons 30 miles in rear, and not to be brought forward without imminent danger of being lost; that my small supply of ammunition was reduced far below what would be necessary for another day's fighting, and that my battery animals were literally dying of starvation, and could not be foraged in the presence of a superior force of the enemy, I determined to retire, and gave the necessary orders for that purpose. Cavalry was extended along both sides of the Cove Creek road, distant 2 or 3 miles from it, from near Prairie Grove to the mountains, and scouts were thrown upon all routes leading toward the enemy's position. The prisoners and captured property were removed. At 12 o'clock the rear guard of the infantry had passed out of hearing. I remained with Marmaduke's cavalry on the field, occupying the line held at dark, caring for our wounded and dead, and collecting the arms which the enemy had abandoned in his frequent flights before our men.

A Federal officer, under flag, brought the following letter:

HEADQUARTERS FEDERAL FORCES,
On the Field, December 7, 1862.

Commanding Officer, Confederate Forces:

GENERAL: The bearer, Dr. Parker, visits your lines with flag of truce for the purpose of caring for my wounded.

JAS. G. BLUNT,
Brigadier-General, Commanding.

The bearer of the flag indicated twelve hours from sunrise next day as the desired period of truce. To this I acceded, detaining the Federal officer, and notifying General Blunt immediately of the fact. Receiving no written reply, and the bearer of my first note not returning, I again gave him the same information. He replied as follows:

HEADQUARTERS FEDERAL FORCES,
In the Field, December 8, 1862—6 a. m.

Maj. Gen. T. C. HINDMAN,
Commanding Confederate Forces:

I have the honor to acknowledge your second note, under flag of truce, and express to you my regards for the privilege granted of entering your lines to care for my wounded, which is in accordance with the usages of civilized warfare. Instead of returning a written reply, as, perhaps, I should have done, I sent an unarmed party with ambulances, accompanied by commissioned officers, to meet General Marmaduke, and to be by him conducted within your lines.

I have the honor to be, general, your obedient servant,

JAS. G. BLUNT,
Brigadier-General, Commanding.

General Blunt's officer had submitted a proposition, as by authority, that surgeons, hospital nurses, and attendants on the sick and wounded, should not in any cases be regarded as prisoners, but released unconditionally. This was not in such shape as to be conclusive. I therefore requested that General Blunt should meet me personally next day. He assented, and we met about 10 a. m. on the 8th. The result of the conference was the adoption of the proposition before referred to, with the additional stipulation that ambulances and hospital trains, medicines, and medical and hospital stores should be exempt from capture.

About 12 m. I withdrew Marmaduke's command, and overtook the infantry that night at Morrow's. The return to our former camp was attended with no incident worthy to be reported. After a battle the mind naturally passes in review all the circumstances connected with it. I hope the expression here of such reflections as now present themselves to me will not be deemed improper. Undoubtedly there are serious defects in our military system. Chief among these is the rule of electing to the lowest commissioned office and promoting to those above in companies and regiments. It combines mobocracy and primogeniture in such proportions that it seems almost a miracle that anything of discipline or efficiency survives. As a substitute, I would propose this, that whenever a vacancy does occur in a company or regiment, an examining board of three capable officers be appointed by the division or corps commanders; that, without regard to rank or restriction to the command, all persons desiring the vacant place be invited to appear before the board within a given time to be examined as to character and qualification, and that the board recommend and the division or corps commander immediately assign to duty the one found best qualified and most meritorious, conditioned that he shall not draw pay till the assignment be approved by the War Department. As auxiliary to this, division or corps commanders should be authorized to order before a similar board any regimental or company officer deemed incapable, neglectful, or otherwise unfit, and, on the report of the board against him, to suspend him from duty and cause the place to be immediately filled, as in the case of any other vacancy, and on the approval of the proceedings by the War Department. The delinquent officer should invariably be put in the ranks as a private soldier. I would apply these provisions to all the staff officers of corps, divisions, brigades, and regiments, with the further regulation that persons assigned to staff duty, where bond is required by law, may execute the same before the commander of the division or corps. Great delays and detriment to the service result from the existing arrangements as to that matter.

Next in importance is the subject of the pay of the troops. Poor men almost invariably make up our armies. Their wives and children, left without protection, are exposed to absolute suffering unless the men are regularly and adequately paid. No troops that I have known during the war have been paid with anything like promptness. Immense arrearages are now due the men of this corps. Their families are in great suffering. The consequence is that very many desertions have occurred. If arrearages could be at once discharged, the evil would be checked. If the pay of the soldier was not only promptly given him, but made sufficient in amount to support his family as it should be, desertions would be unknown. This subject involves the fate of the Confederacy. Notions of false economy ought to be discarded in considering it. The conscript act ought to be revised. Every man between sixteen and sixty, who is able to serve the Confederacy in the army, whether in the ranks or as an artisan or mechanic, laborer, teamster, cook, hospital attendant, or in any other capacity, ought to be put in service without regard to avocation or other plea. There ought to be no exemption whatever, except in the case of absolute and permanent physical disability. If by this means more soldiers are raised than necessary, it would be a very just and humane policy to grant furloughs to the old soldiers and put the young conscripts in their places. If the men out of the army are "the people," these ideas may fail of popular approval. That, however, in no way affects their merits.

Under the same supposition, the last suggestion I have to make will be still more decidedly unpopular. It will be odious in the eyes of speculators, extortioners, refusers of Confederate money, evaders of conscription, deserters, harborers of deserters, spies, marauders, federalists, and that less respectable class who regard these others as the people, and pander to them for their votes. The obnoxious suggestion is, a vigorous and determined system of martial law, covering all classes of evil-doers mentioned above, and compelling them, by stern and swift punishment, either to leave the Confederacy or to bear their due part of the burdens of the war. Without martial law, loyal citizens and the fighting soldiers of the country, their wives and children, are literally the prey of the basest of the population. The civil laws, State organizations, rights on paper, and penalties on statute-books, are inert and powerless to help them. A living, active, fearless assertion and enforcement of martial law alone can do it. If much longer delayed, that remedy itself will come too late.

Respectfully,

T. C. HINDMAN,
Major-General, Commanding.

Lieut. Col. S. S. ANDERSON,
Assistant Adjutant-General, Trans-Mississippi Department.

—

HEADQUARTERS TRANS-MISSISSIPPI DEPARTMENT,
Little Rock, Ark., December 24, 1862.

Maj. Gen. T. C. HINDMAN,
Comdg. First Corps, Trans-Mississippi Army, in the Field:

GENERAL: I have the pleasure of acknowledging the receipt, at the hands of Lieutenant Hammett, acting assistant adjutant-general of your corps, of the three stand of colors captured by your army from the enemy at Prairie Grove Church on the 7th instant.

I am, general, very respectfully, your most obedient servant,

S. S. ANDERSON,
Assistant Adjutant-General.

No. 37.

Report of Brig. Gen. John S. Marmaduke, C. S. Army, commanding Fourth Division, including preliminary skirmishes.

HDQRS. FOURTH DIVISION, TRANS-MISSISSIPPI ARMY,
Clarksville, Ark., December 16, 1862.

COLONEL: I have the honor to report herewith the part taken by my division in the battle of Prairie Grove and the skirmishes preceding.

In obedience to orders received from Major-General Hindman, I moved my division early Wednesday morning, December 3, from Dripping Springs in the direction of the enemy, at Cane Hill, as follows: Carroll's brigade—reduced to about 500 effective men—under the command of Colonel [J. C.] Monroe, on the Line road; Shelby's brigade, under Colonel Shelby—about 1,100 effective men—beyond Oliver's, on the Cove Creek road; [Emmett] MacDonald, with his brigade—about 700 effective men—to Oliver's, on the Wire road, each guarding with strong pickets and scouts all approaches from the northward.

On Thursday, the several brigades moved forward a few miles on the roads named.

On Friday [5th instant], Monroe's command marched across and formed junction with Shelby on the Cove Creek road, some 10 miles above Oliver's. MacDonald pressed forward some 10 miles on the Wire road; Shelby on the Cove Creek road. The two latter brigades engaged the enemy's pickets to-day and drove them back.

Friday night, Shelby's advance met the Federal pickets in strong force near Morrow's.

Early Saturday morning [6th instant], before daylight, he dismounted his brigade, and with skill and vigor rapidly drove them back and beyond the crest of Boston Mountains. The enemy made a stubborn resistance, but were compelled to retire to within 2 miles of their main force.

During Friday night, MacDonald's command was withdawn to form junction with the main cavalry force on the Cove Creek road, leaving, however, a strong picket (100 men) to watch the Wire road.

On Saturday morning, Shelby, relieved by an infantry command, was withdrawn from the front to cook and rest.

About 2 p. m. Saturday, it being reported that the Federals were retreating from Cane Hill, I received orders from the major-general commanding to press the enemy vigorously on the Cane Hill road, and to move forward rapidly on the Cove Creek road to cut off the enemy's retreat. Monroe moved rapidly forward on the Cane Hill road, engaged, charged, and drove back a superior force of the enemy, and continued to drive them until he received orders from me to cease advancing, to picket, and watch all approaches in that direction.

The conduct of Colonel Monroe, who charged at the head of this brigade, and of the officers and men under his command in this affair, was gallant in the extreme.

Shelby and MacDonald pressed forward on the Cove Creek road until orders were received to halt.

The brigades bivouacked in their present positions until 3 p. m. Sunday morning, when, in obedience to orders, I ordered Monroe to threaten and press the enemy vigorously on the Cane Hill road, while Shelby and MacDonald were moved forward on the Cove Creek road to its intersection with the Fayetteville and Cane Hill road, where the advance of Shelby arrived about daylight. Here I learned that re-enforcements, under General Herron, from Springfield, Mo., were some half mile off in the direction of Fayetteville, moving toward Cane Hill. I ordered Shelby to dismount a part of his brigade, and, with the artillery under Bledsoe, to hold the road—to resist the enemy coming from either direction—and with the remainder of his force to move up the Fayetteville road and attack the re-enforcements. At the same time I ordered MacDonald, with his whole command, to move rapidly and strike the enemy in flank and rear. Promptly, vigorously, skillfully, and successfully were these commands executed. The Federal cavalry were charged and routed wherever found. They fled panic-stricken, and were pursued some 5 miles up to the Federal infantry, formed in line of battle some 5 or 6 miles from Fayetteville.

In the charge some 50 or 60 Federals were killed, about 300 were taken prisoners, among them several officers; a number of horses and cavalry equipments, small-arms, and several wagons loaded with clothing and camp equipage were captured. As soon as the head of the infantry column came up, I ordered the cavalry held in reserve to mount; Colonel [G. W.] Thompson's regiment to march toward Cane Hill to determine the enemy's movements in that direction; the remainder to move in the direction of Fayetteville, to join the main cavalry force, which I had ordered to be reformed after the long and desperate charge and pursuit, and to await further orders. I now received orders from General Hindman in person to move against the Federal re-enforcements. I ordered Shelby's brigade forward. After crossing the Illinois River and advancing about 1½ miles, I found the enemy in position and in force—infantry, artillery, and cavalry. The enemy opened upon Shelby with artillery, and soon began to advance. I ordered him to retire upon the infantry, which I found posted upon a high and commanding hill. Shelby's brigade, after falling back deliberately under fire to the infantry, were dismounted, and, under a murderous fire of shot, shell, and small-arms, fought as infantry during the rest of the battle, gallantly holding the center of the line of battle. As the enemy advanced upon Shelby, I ordered MacDonald to retire around to the foot of the hill, and watch the movements of the enemy from the north and west. Subsequently, finding the enemy attempting to turn our right flank, I ordered MacDonald to move his command to the extreme right, to dismount his men, and repel any attack in that direction. It was gallantly done.

Monroe, in obedience to orders, attacked the enemy at daylight on Sunday morning, and, by his daring and skill, kept the enemy in the belief, until 10 a. m., that the attack was to be made in that direction. Upon the enemy retreating, he pursued and formed a junction with the main force about sunset on the battle-field. From early morn until night the brave men of my division (on horse and afoot) fought the foe, and were everywhere victorious. The serried columns of Federals again and again came forward to meet their fate—death or defeat. Never did they gain one inch of ground nor even partial success. All orders were promptly and properly obeyed, and the conduct of both officers and men was chivalrous, and deserves the highest commendation. I must specially mention the skill and daring of Colonels Shelby, Monroe, and MacDonald, each commanding brigade. Shelby was wherever duty and danger called him, and rendered most distinguished service.

For a more detailed report of the conduct of the several brigades and regiments and of the brave officers and men under my command, I respectfully refer you to the reports of the brigade commanders, inclosed herewith.

The following officers of my staff were with me during the engagement: Captain [E. G.] Williams, assistant adjutant-general; Captain [Henry] Ewing, inspector-general; Major [R. H.] Smith, division quartermaster; Dr. [C.] Peyton, chief surgeon, and Colonel [A. W.] Slayback, division ordnance officer. I desire to bring them to your notice for the prompt and perfect execution of all their duties and my orders, their daring and efficiency under every danger. Major Smith and Colonel Slayback were particularly exposed in the discharge of their duties, and participated in the gallant charges and encouraged others to deeds of coolness and courage. I beg also to bring to your favorable notice Mr. C. O. Bell and my two orderlies, Stafford and Cook, who were with me during the engagement.

Very respectfully,

J. S. MARMADUKE,
Brigadier-General, Commanding.

Col. R. C. NEWTON,
Assistant Adjutant-General and Chief of Staff.

No. 38.

Report of Col. Joseph O. Shelby, Missouri Cavalry (Confederate), commanding Fourth Missouri Cavalry Brigade, including preliminary skirmishes.

CAMP BELOW VAN BUREN, ARK.,
December 11, 1862.

GENERAL: I have the honor to report the following as the part taken by my brigade in the battle of Prairie Grove, and also the skirmishes preceding it, as required by you in a previous order:

On the morning of December 5, my advance, consisting of Company F, commanded by Captain Rathbun, First Regiment, met a largely superior force of the enemy, and, after a sharp little fight, drove him back in great confusion. I then strengthened my advance, took other precautions against the increasing danger (for we were nearing the enemy's lines), and moved northward again slowly but surely.

When your order was received to cut off, if possible, the enemy's pickets, I immediately ordered Major [B.] Elliott's battalion of scouts to make a forced march across the mountains for that purpose; but, owing to the darkness of the night, the rugged and almost impassable road, and the ignorance of the guide, the expedition failed in its essential points.

During the day of the 5th, a large scout, well acquainted with both country and roads, made a close swoop almost to our camp, but immediately sending forward Colonel [Beal G.] Jeans in command of the Second Regiment, they took the road at a gallop, nor ceased pursuit until the enemy was driven some 10 miles in a running fight.

During this engagement I had the First Regiment, Lieutenant-Colonel [B. F.] Gordon, and the Third, Colonel [G. W.] Thompson, dismounted and formed as support to Bledsoe's battery, now in position, with lighted port-fires and eager gunners, keen for the fray that grew fainter and fainter as Colonel Jeans pushed them hard and heavily, until the grand old mountains gave no murmur back, and all was silent, cold, and still.

Early, very early, on the morning of the 6th, I had my brigade under arms, and sending forward three companies as my advance, with the other three regiments dismounted and close up, I drove in the enemy's pickets with great rapidity and execution, although he made three different stands and fought me three times. This advance of three companies was under the charge of Major [M. W.] Smith, who, by his prompt deploying of skirmishers, his quiet self-possession, and his determined coolness, evinced much bravery and skill. The men were this morning keen for a fight, and went furiously up the steep and rugged mountain at a double-quick for miles. After being relieved by a regiment of infantry, I returned with my brigade to camp, where three days' rations were cooked, some little sleep obtained by the men, and again we were marching northward.

After encamping, and upon learning the near proximity of the enemy, I doubled my guards, threw out infantry skirmishers in every direction, under the charge of trusty officers, and lay down with the conscious satisfaction that neither Federal, Kansas jayhawker, nor Pin Indian could surprise us, and if they came they would meet with a bloody and hospitable welcome, for I had ordered my entire brigade upon the slightest alarm to form rapidly as infantry and to sleep upon loaded arms.

Upon the eventful morning of the 7th, long before the full round moon had died in the lap of the dawn; long before the watching stars had grown dim with age, my brigade was saddled, formed, and their steeds champing frosted bits in the cold, keen air of a December morning, ready and eager for the march. After advancing rapidly and without intermission for several hours, I struck their trail, hot with the passage of many feet, reeking with the foot-prints of the invader. It needed no command now to close up. There was no lagging, no break in serried ranks, no straggling from the line, but each man grasped his gun with the strong, firm grasp and the strange, wild looks of heroes and born invincibles. After riding hard for about an hour, my advance came full upon the foe, and, with the mad, fierce whoop of men who have wrongs to right and blood to avenge, they dashed on and away at the *pas de charge*. Rapidly and in splendid style Colonel Jeans, by my command, rushed on to follow up the attack, while Colonels Thompson's and Gordon's regiments were dismounted and formed in the dry bed of a creek, and so stationed that they could resist an attack either from the east or west. With these two regiments was one piece of Bledsoe's two-gun battery; the other I had sent thundering down the road to support Colonel Jeans. With the Second Regiment of my brigade I also threw forward Captain Quantrill's company, under First Lieutenant Gregg, and Major [B.] Elliott's battalion of scouts, who, joining in the wild halloa, pressed forward eagerly and fiercely, driving the frightened Federals before them like chaff before the winds of heaven. Still the rout continues.

Tramp, tramp, along the land they ride,
Splash, splash, along the lea;
The scourge is red, the spur drops blood,
The flashing pebbles flee!

The fight grows intensely interesting, and my men, feeling the inspiration of the scene, dash on and on, taking prisoners, capturing guns, colors, horses, mules, and every form and variety of clothing, left in the desperate flight of the terror-[stricken] enemy. It was only when I deemed further pursuit not only imprudent, but highly dangerous, that I called off my troops and proceeded to avail myself of the now substantial fruits of the victory, bought with but scarcely any effusion of blood.

At this time Lieutenant [J. E.] Corder, with 20 men, whom I had left on picket when I turned from the main Fayetteville road, came up for orders, he having been driven from his position there by a largely superior force. I ordered him to improvise his men as teamsters and drive the captured train rapidly to the rear, which they did, and did safely.

In this brilliant and dashing charge, Lieutenant Gregg and company sustained their high renown for chivalric courage and daring, capturing, among many other articles, three standards, one of them regimental.

Major Elliott, with his bold scouts, did good work, and it was while leading a headlong charge, five lengths ahead of his best and bravest, that his horse fell with his gallant rider, injuring him quite severely, though not fatally.

The three companies of my advance in this fight were commanded by Major [David] Shanks, which were followed by three more, commanded by Lieutenant-Colonel [Charles A.] Gilkey, within easy supporting distance. When the enemy were first found he was in line. The charge was ordered, and Colonel Jeans, Major Elliott, and Lieutenant Gregg rushed their commands straight at the foe. They broke and fled precipitately, followed by the three commands furiously to $1\frac{1}{2}$ miles beyond Illinois Creek, where, drawn up in line to dispute further progress, was a regiment of Federal cavalry. This was hotly charged, broken, routed, and Major [J. M.] Hubbard, the arch fiend of many a midnight foray and murder, was taken prisoner. When I found that large masses of Federal infantry were marching up to support their cavalry, I fell back with this command to the position first occupied by me. Again advanced to within sight, formed and sent out skirmishers all along my front and flanks, holding this position until ordered by you to fall back, which I did, retiring under fire. In the final dispositions of the day, I formed the First Regiment on the extreme right and the Second Regiment on the left, both covering batteries, and both within supporting distance of each other, the Third Regiment having previously been sent to ascertain the position of the enemy in the direction of Cane Hill, which they did, meeting their pickets, engaging them, and, after a sharp little fight, driving them back. They held their position thus gained until ordered to return and cover the rear of General Parsons. Captain Quantrill's company, commanded by First Lieutenant Gregg, was assigned to Colonel Gordon, who had now divided his regiment, leaving four on the right, under Major [George R.] Kirtley, leading the other four on the left, in person, in conjunction with Colonel Jeans, of the Second Regiment, and Major Elliott, of the scouts. The Third Regiment, Colonel Thompson, after returning from its successful reconnaissance, was ordered to the front, on the left of Bledsoe's battery, dismounted. The battle now began with terrific fury. All along the lines the near fire of the infantry rose, crash upon crash, the dense smoke filling the air and the wild powder gloom getting darker and darker. This terrible fire soon rippled out in one vast, mighty wave of bullets, that circled and roared like a storm at sea, varied incessantly by the thunder of impatient cannon and the yell of exultant and furious combatants. On the right, four regiments of Federal infantry formed in the open field, and came up in splendid order, with flaunting banners and waving pennons, the light of battle on their faces and their steps proud with the thoughts of an easy victory. My skirmishers were steadily driven in, and down to meet them like an avalanche our own infantry swept. They met, the shock was terrible, but, broken and rent, our boys drove them back and followed at the charge. Again and again they returned to the fight, and again and again were they repulsed with great slaughter. The four companies under Major Kirtley were now ordered to dismount and join the mad *mêlée*. It was done, and they stood shoulder to shoulder and eyes to the front. Now the enemy, gathering all his remaining strength, came back again with unbroken front and steady step. This conflict was intensely hot. Our men drove them from the woods, drove them across the opening directly in our front, and even drove them beyond their batteries, causing them to limber up and change position. In this charge Major Kirtley led the four companies detached from the First Regiment with much skill and coolness. On the left, the remainder of my brigade was attacked by a largely superior force of cavalry and artillery with much vigor and determination. They fought them as cavalry, and drove them back with heavy loss, although I had not a single piece of artillery to cover my attack or meet the batteries of the enemy.

During all the day I had noticed the terrible efficiency of the enemy's batteries, and saw that they were handled with remarkable skill and effect, and thinking it prudent—nay, absolutely necessary—to change the position of some of our guns, I ordered Captain Bledsoe to bring his battery to the brow of the hill, in the center, and draw their fire, while the other guns could be removed without any unnecessary exposure. This move was executed by Bledsoe in keeping with his hitherto high reputation, and once more, with gathered strength, our batteries opened on the foe. Now, on the left of Captain Bledsoe's battery, the Third Regiment was formed, dismounted, and never did men stand a more terrible and well-directed fire, and that, too, without flinching or giving back an inch. When the final struggle came, when General Parsons met the shock of Blunt's entire command, this regiment formed with him, and fought with great effect and intrepidity, for the dead and wounded Federals, lying stretched out in their gory beds, "thick as autumnal leaves in Vallombrosa," can well attest the fury and courage with which the Missourians [fought] shoulder to shoulder and side by side. Colonel Thompson, Lieutenant-Colonel [John C.] Hooper, Major Smith, the captain of each respective company, were amid their men, and did great good by their true and heroic bearing. Now the combat thickens all along the lines, and death, with its black banner on the breeze, nerves each heart and cheers them on to the rough, red fray. Bledsoe was there amid his guns, all dirt-begrimed and powder-blackened, plying his lurid torch where balls would send or powder search, and never once during that long, hot day were they silent, except when going nearer and nearer to the foe. Colonel Jeans, Lieutenant-Colonel Gordon, and Lieutenant Gregg were also on the left, where the fire was getting hotter and hotter, and with the pilot's weary eyes steered their commands safely through the breakers, white with the fire of deadly cannon, and painted with all the dread and gloom of ghastly war. On the right, that part of my command under Major Kirtley had returned from a successful charge, under your immediate eye, and when the dark and weird shadows of night had closed over earth and sky and the dead and wounded, reports of a well-won and well-fought battle came cheerily up from all parts of the field, and I drew my command together calmly and cautiously, knowing that the day in all its bearings was ours. Night had closed the march of death, and the idle breeze now gave no murmur back to tell of what had been passing but a few brief moments before, when—

Our bugles sang truce and the night cloud had lowered,
And the sentinel stars kept their watch in the sky;
When thousands had sunk to the earth overpowered,
The weary to sleep and the wounded to die.

I dismounted my entire command, moved them as infantry to the road leading directly down to the house at the foot of the hill and behind the batteries there stationed, and ordered them to bivouac without fires, with guns in their hands, and determination in their hearts. Down upon the cold, hard earth, without a murmur, without a word spoken above a whisper, they lay, with longing eyes stretched far away northward, thinking of home and the morrow, and another glorious day. When my command was thus formed, I covered my entire front and flanks with picked and vigilant scouts and keen and daring skirmishers, cautioning them to move lightly, step noiselessly, look well and truly about them, and report constantly and frequently. This done, and well done; and no enemy, however insidious or in what guise presented, could have approached to within 300 yards at the nearest to my lines.

When your order came to withdraw my forces and light fires all along my front, I communicated it to the commanders of each command, and not until the fires were lighted, the command withdrawn, and three companies sent back as skirmishers, drew in my well-tried and trusty scouts. My command now, with saddled steeds in readiness, slept with bridle in hand, in line of battle, awaiting any orders you might communicate through me to them, ever on the alert, and ready at the slightest call.

I cannot close this report without speaking in the highest terms of Capt. Westley Roberts, commanding the only rifled battery we had. He took position about 3 o'clock on the brow of the hill just above the house, and for two mortal hours bore that storm of shot and shell without a murmur, and it was [only] when further delay were suicide did he move to a less exposed position. Captain Bledsoe, with his two iron guns, the hero of many a well-fought field, stood and fought, and fought and stood, towering above the press, his clarion voice ringing ever proudly, defiantly, and his smoking guns thundering the mad requiem and belching the wild lullaby of the hated invaders. I would also call your special attention to the knightly bearing and conduct of David Shanks, major of the Second Regiment. Whether amid the crash and clatter of the headlong charge, whether leading the cold and cautious advance, or cheering on his regiment where blue coats and saber-crossed hats went down like apple-blossoms in a sweet May wind, he was ever the same—brave, kind, humane, chivalric, devoted, daring; now three lengths ahead of his best and bravest, and now speaking the quick, keen words of hope and courage. Lieut. Col. [B.] Frank Gordon, of the gallant First, was there among his men, ever where the fire was heaviest and hottest, leading them on to glory, and showing by his actions that Missourians know their rights, and, knowing, dare maintain them. Lieutenant-Colonel Gilkey, Lieutenant-Colonel Hooper, and all my officers behaved in a most gallant and praiseworthy manner, never seeming to mind the tempest of shot and shell bursting all around them. My adjutant (Captain Brewster) was ever with me, brave and daring, carrying orders and forming regiments as if on dress-parade. I will here also state that I noticed with much pleasure the adjutant of the First Regiment, John [N.] Edwards, who was actively engaged in watching the movements of the enemy upon every corner, and with his regiment aiding and cheering them on to victory or death. Also my young orderly, Jimmy Clark, behaved admirably; his fair, boyish face lit up with the halo of battle, and his voice mingling with the rage and roar of the cannon. My aides (also Corder and [L.] Shindler) deserve special mention for their good behavior. Captain [John] Jarrett, of the Second Regiment, bore himself on this eventful day with marked bravery, capturing with his own hand Major Hubbard, of the old First Missouri (Federal) Cavalry, a man well known in that State as a daring and dashing officer. I would also speak in the most favorable terms of Maj. George R. Kirtley, of the First Regiment, and Lieutenant Gregg, Major Elliott, of the scouts, and, indeed, of every officer of my command.

When your final orders came to retire from the field, the theater of high and knightly deeds, I detailed Captain [J. M.] Garrett, commanding Company E, of the First Regiment, to remain with his company to bury our dead, and then marched my entire brigade southward.

The substantial fruits of the victory are 12 standards, 32 wagons, some 400 or 500 stand of arms, about 300 prisoners, besides quantities of clothing, commissary stores, quartermaster's supplies, negroes, horses, mules, and every variety and description of articles a corrupt Government can furnish to hired freebooters and cut-throats and thieves. I need not, general, speak further of my command. You were ever on the field, ever under fire, and saw for yourself the actions and behavior of my men, and whether you lead them in Arkansas, Missouri, or Mississippi, you will constantly find them worthy of your utmost confidence and respect.

I have, general, the honor to be, your obedient servant,

JO. O. SHELBY,

Colonel, Commanding Fourth Missouri Cavalry Brigade.

Brig. Gen. J. S. MARMADUKE, *Commanding Cavalry Division.*

No. 39.

Report of Col. J. C. Monroe, Arkansas Cavalry, commanding brigade, including skirmish at Reed's Mountain.

HEADQUARTERS CARROLL'S BRIGADE,
Camp near Van Buren, on Arkansas River, December 10, 1862.

CAPTAIN: In compliance with General Orders, No. —, I make the following report of the part taken by the forces under my command in the engagements on the 6th and 7th instant:

I had in my command about 400 effective men, of which number there were 150 on picket duty the evening of the 6th and the morning of the 7th. At 3 p. m. (6th) I was ordered forward to cover the front of an infantry regiment under the command of General Parsons. After passing the regiment of infantry, I threw out a line of skirmishers on either side of the road. I then moved forward cautiously, feeling for the enemy; found him at the foot of the mountain in strong position, where I engaged him. After twenty-five minutes' heavy firing, I was forced to retire. I then ordered up my whole command, and formed them in line of battle behind the hill, out of range of the enemy's guns. I then sent two companies around to attack the enemy's right flank, and at the same time made a vigorous charge in front. The enemy held his position until we were in 10 paces of him, when he broke and fled in confusion. I would have pursued him were it not for the nature of the ground, which was so rugged that it was impossible to ride over. It was now dark, and I moved back about half a mile, leaving a strong picket on the ground.

My loss in killed and wounded was 15—3 killed and 12 wounded; 1 killed and 10 wounded from the regiment commanded by Major Thomson, and 2 killed and 2 wounded from the regiment commanded by Major Johnson.

During the night I was informed that the whole force, except my command, would move by way of Cove Creek road. I was ordered to remain in my present position and engage the enemy at daylight. I dismounted all the men in both regiments who had long-range guns, deployed them as skirmishers, moved forward and commenced skirmishing with the enemy just after daylight, which was kept up until cannonading was heard in the direction of Fayetteville, when the enemy retired, and I moved slowly and cautiously in the direction of Cane Hill. On arriving at Cane Hill, I found no enemy there except some sick and convalescents, who had been left behind by the enemy. These I paroled, except one Pin Indian, who could not speak English. I also found one negro who had been acting as teamster. I found in the hospital a surgeon's sack filled with lint, bandages, medicines, &c., and a case of dental instruments, which I brought away. There was also at Cane Hill a few commissary and quartermaster's stores, but I could get no wagons to send them to the rear. I left Cane Hill at dark, and arrived on the battle-ground at 9 p. m., after the battle had ceased.

J. C. MONROE,
Colonel, Commanding Brigade.

No. 40.

Report of Col. Emmett MacDonald, Missouri Cavalry (Confederate), commanding brigade.

HEADQUARTERS MACDONALD'S CAVALRY BRIGADE,
Van Buren, Ark., December 11, 1862.

CAPTAIN: I have the honor to submit to you the following report of the part my brigade took in the battle of Prairie Grove, Ark.:

On the morning of the 7th instant, I was ordered to march in column on the Cove Creek and Fayetteville road. After having proceeded on that road for 10 miles, I was ordered to take a right-hand road; that the enemy was right in my front. I at once directed my course north-westerly, and succeeded in getting between the enemy and Fayetteville. Discovering the enemy behind a rail fence and in the brush, I ordered up Captain West's battery, which was in the rear. In the mean time I discovered the enemy was forming to charge me. I at once divided my force in two columns, intending to attack the enemy in front and flank, and ordered charge. The charge was led gallantly by Colonels [R. P.] Crump and [M. L.] Young. While running on the enemy, they ran up two white flags. Thinking it a signal for surrender, I ordered my command to cease firing, and galloped up toward the enemy and found they were retreating. I repeated my order of charge, and my command dashed in upon them, scattering them in all directions. There were some 50 or 60 threw down their arms and surrendered at once. My command, never stopping to take prisoners, continued the pursuit within 6 miles of Fayetteville. The road was strewn with guns, pistols, sabers, wagons, and all descriptions of camp and garrison equipage that the enemy deserted in their wild panic. We charged through woods, over creeks, and through open fields, no obstacle seeming to impede the valor and impetuosity of my gallant command, only a remnant of the Yankee brigade escaping in the fastnesses of the Boston Mountains. I then ordered a recall of my troops from the pursuit.

After having fallen back for about 2 miles, I found the main body of my command formed behind a protection, in front of a large force of the enemy's infantry and artillery. I then, in company with Lieutenant-Colonel Crump, made a reconnaissance, and found the enemy strongly posted in a skirt of timber. Learning that our infantry was a long distance behind, I dismounted 75 of my men and sent them out as skirmishers, deceiving the enemy, while I withdrew my command, and, falling back across the Illinois, I was then ordered by General Marmaduke to take position on the left of the Fayetteville road. We remained in line of battle for some time, expecting the approach of the enemy for some three hours.

In the mean time Captain West's battery was ordered up to a strong position on my right. I then sent out a portion of my command, under command of Capt. William P. Saufley, of Colonel Crump's Texas regiment, to scout on the left flank.

In the mean time the enemy formed a line of battle in the open field in my front, and I opened upon them with my artillery. This artillery duel lasted for some time. I was then ordered to move my cavalry force upon the Cane Hill road, which order was immediately obeyed. Having moved but a short distance, General Marmaduke ordered me on the extreme right, to outflank and charge the enemy, and, in conjunction with Generals Shoup's and Fagan's gallant commands, succeeded in compelling the enemy to fall back rapidly. I was then ordered by General Hindman to move a portion of my command on the extreme left, which order was immediately obeyed, and that portion of the command put in charge of Lieutenant-Colonel Young, whose accompanying report you will find inclosed within.

These positions were occupied until night put an end to the battle. I was then ordered to move my command to the field near General Hindman's headquarters. I was ordered then to picket the right flank of the army. During the night the enemy asked for an armistice of twelve hours, for the purpose of burying their dead.

At sunrise the next morning I was ordered to bring up the rear of the army, which I did, carrying off the field some 400 of the enemy's arms, and conveyed them to our camp at Oliver's.

For the list of casualties of this almost bloodless victory, I refer you to the within inclosed reports of Colonels Young and Crump.

From the beginning to the end of the fight, whether in the headlong charge or quietly standing 'neath the leaden hail, they all, without a single exception, evinced the most unflinching courage and intrepidity.

I would call your attention particularly to the daring chivalry of Colonels Young and Crump, and Major [G. W. C.] Bennett.

I also extend my thanks to my aide, Lieut. John P. Bull, for the cool and gallant manner in which he carried my orders during the whole battle.

To Captain Tholt, of Colonel Young's command, and Lieutenant Gregg, commanding Quantrill's men, I return my thanks for services and gallant deeds upon the battle-field.

I would also return my thanks to all the officers and men in my brigade for obedience to all my orders, especially my acting orderlies—Estes, Yetee, Theyer, and Tate—for their coolness and bravery during the entire day; and, captain, in conclusion, allow me to say the cavalry has proven itself one of the most effective arms of the service, and this battle is another evidence that it is the soul wins battles and not arms or numbers.

Respectfully, yours,

EMMETT MACDONALD,
Colonel, Commanding Cavalry Brigade.

Captain [E. G.] WILLIAMS.

No. 41.

Report of Lieut. Col. M. L. Young, MacDonald's cavalry.

HEADQUARTERS MACDONALD'S CAVALRY BRIGADE,
FOURTH DIVISION, TRANS-MISSISSIPPI ARMY,
Camp on Cove Creek, Ark., December 9, 1862.

COLONEL: I have the honor to report that on the 7th instant I attacked the enemy's cavalry, consisting of one regiment Arkansas and one of Missouri, near Prairie Grove. I charged the enemy upon the right; Colonel Crump's Texas cavalry pierced the center. The enemy, panic-stricken, fled from the field, leaving all their baggage, commissary and quartermaster's stores behind them. A running fight was kept up for several miles, scattering guns, pistols, horses, blankets, haversacks, knapsacks, saddles, gloves, overcoats, and, in fact, everything that would make a soldier comfortable. These were all picked up by regiments who came up in my rear. Forty or fifty of the enemy were killed and a large number wounded. My regiment and Colonel Crump's captured 40 wagons with teams, about 200 prisoners, 300 stand of arms, 60 sabers, and 150 pistols. The wagons and goods were the kind our troops most needed, such as blankets, overcoats, shirts, drawers, and also a large supply of commissary stores. Colonel Shelby, with two pieces of artillery, was captured by the enemy. The colonel, with his guns, was liberated by our troops.

In the general engagement I was posted upon the extreme left. Company B, commanded by Captain [W. H.] Frazier, with one company of Colonel Crump's Texas cavalry, was sent as skirmishers upon our left, when they were fired upon by the enemy's artillery. The guns were charged and the horses killed; but the guns could not be held, as there was no infantry near to support them.

My command was divided during the day, and a portion of them engaged the enemy with credit and much success on several occasions.

Officers and men behaved gallantly on every occasion during the engagement.

The following is a list of casualties:

Whole number engaged	202
Whole number wounded	2
Whole number missing	3
Whole number horses killed	3

Respectfully,

M. L. YOUNG,
Lieutenant-Colonel, Commanding MacDonald's Cavalry.

F. B. DAVIDSON, *Adjutant.*

No. 42.

Report of Lieut. Col. R. P. Crump, First Texas Partisan Cavalry.

CAMP ON COVE CREEK, ARK.,
December 9, 1862.

COLONEL: I have the honor to report that on the morning of the 7th instant we attacked the enemy's cavalry near Prairie Grove Church, supposed to be 600 strong, composed of the First Kansas and First Arkansas Regiments. Lieutenant-Colonel Young charged on the right, quartered on the left; my command penetrated the center, completely routing him, pursuing him, and keeping up a running fight for 5 miles, killing about 40, capturing about 200 prisoners, including Major Hubbard, 40 wagons, and several negroes, 200 stand of arms, and 200 horses. We also had the pleasure of recapturing Colonel Shelby and his battery of light artillery, who had been previously taken by the enemy. The wagons were loaded with boots, shoes, hats, arms, sugar, coffee, rice, flour, hams, tobacco, cigars, tents, and camp equipage.

Accompanying this you will find a list* of killed, wounded, and missing, with the other casualties of the regiment.

The officers and men, without exception, behaved most gallantly.

Respectfully,

R. P. CRUMP,
Lieutenant-Colonel, Comdg. First Texas Regt. Partisan Rangers.

Col. EMMETT MACDONALD.

No. 43.

Report of Capt. Henry C. West, commanding battery.

IN CAMP NEAR OLIVER'S STORE,
December 9, 1862.

COLONEL: In compliance with your orders, I prepared to march on the morning of the 7th instant, at 2 o'clock, and at 2.30 o'clock I reported

---

*List shows 444 men engaged; 2 killed, 17 wounded, and 4 missing.

at your headquarters, and from there I proceeded with the brigade until within some 4 miles of Cane Hill, where I received orders from you to proceed along the road on which we were marching, and learned that you had pushed ahead to attack a body of the enemy. After arriving at the Cane Hill and Fayetteville road, I was ordered into battery by General Marmaduke, and prepared for action. I remained in this position until the arrival of the main body of the army, when I was ordered by General Hindman to limber up and proceed with it. On arriving at Prairie Grove, I was ordered by General Marmaduke to report to General Fagan, as I could not operate with the cavalry. Having done so, I was at once ordered into battery near the foot of the battle hill, near the white house, on the road.

About 3 p. m., when the enemy began to advance, General Shoup ordered me to open fire, which I did. I had been engaged but a short time when General Shoup in person ordered me to cease firing. Captain [W. D.] Blocher's battery ceasing about the same time, several of the enemy's batteries turned upon my position. After remaining thus silently for some time, the enemy having perfect range of my position, I asked General Shoup if I had not better change to a new one, and he ordered me to do so. I moved off on the road leading to the left of the main road, and came back into the main road on the south side of the hill. I was proceeding up the road when met by Colonel Shelby, who said I had better go to the rear, as it was impossible for me to get in a position to do any good. Major [W. E.] Woodruff, [jr.,] (chief of artillery) coming up at the same time, Colonel S. [Shelby] told him the same, and he, Major W. [Woodruff], ordered me to countermarch and go to the rear and remain until further orders.

I proceeded to the field where General Hindman was, and refilled my chests. Directly after, General H. [Hindman] ordered me with one section of my battery to report immediately to General Roane, who was on the extreme left, which I did, and immediately General Roane's line advanced, I on his left, advancing with him until arriving at the open field, when I at once went into battery and opened fire upon the enemy, and I continued firing until all firing ceased at nightfall. I then reported to General Roane for further orders, and was ordered to return to the remainder of my battery, which I did at General Hindman's headquarters, and there I remained until the line of march was taken up about midnight. Below I give the list of casualties of my battery:

	Killed.	Wounded.	Missing.
Non-commissioned officers	2		
Privates	1	3	1
Total	3	3	1

Respectfully submitted.

HENRY C. WEST,
Captain, Commanding Battery.

Col. EMMETT MACDONALD,
Commanding Cavalry Brigade.

DECEMBER 9-15, 1862.—Expedition from Ozark, Mo., into Marion County, Ark.

REPORTS.

No. 1.—Brig. Gen. Egbert B. Brown, U. S. Army.
No. 2.—Capt. Milton Burch, Fourteenth Missouri State Militia Cavalry.

No. 1.

Report of Brig. Gen. Egbert B. Brown, U. S. Army.

SPRINGFIELD, MO., *December* 18, 1862.

I have the honor to report a successful scout of Captain Burch, Fourteenth Missouri State Militia, with 40 men of his regiment and company Enrolled Missouri Militia, into Arkansas, burning and destroying the saltpeter works of the Confederate Government, including 5 buildings, 1 engine, 26 large kettles, 6 tanks, blacksmiths' and carpenters' shops and tools; $6,000 worth of saltpeter, packed, which was to have been moved in two days; capturing 500 barrels of jerked beef, together with a full supply of other provisions for the winter, and returning, without a casualty, with 42 prisoners, their arms, horses, and equipments. The affair is the more creditable, as a large force of the enemy was encamped within a few miles of the works; but so rapid and secret were the movements of Captain Burch that they were unapprised of them until he had accomplished the duty assigned him, and returned in safety. This is the fourth equally important and successful scout of Captain Burch in the past few months, besides numbers of smaller affairs. These are the same works reported to have been destroyed by Colonel Wickersham about a month since. The destruction was not complete, as they were again in full operation. The works cost the Confederate Government $30,000. They are now destroyed. The engine, tanks, and kettles were broken with sledges, and buildings burned. The cave is sufficiently roomy to work 100 men.

E. B. BROWN,
Brigadier-General.

Maj. Gen. SAMUEL R. CURTIS.

No. 2.

Report of Capt. Milton Burch, Fourteenth Missouri State Militia Cavalry.

OZARK, MO., *December* 18, 1862.

SIR: I have the honor of reporting to you, for the information of the commanding general, the results of a scout, commanded by me, in Marion County, Arkansas.

By permission from Captain [S. A.] Flagg, commanding this post, I took command of 40 men, composed of detachments from Companies D, F, G, and H, Second Battalion Fourteenth Regiment Missouri State Militia Cavalry, and, on the morning of the 9th instant, marched for Lawrence's Mill, a distance of 35 miles. I arrived at the mill early in the night, and remained there till noon of the 10th, waiting for forage. During the time, I held a consultation with the officers of my command and those of the enrolled militia stationed at the mill, in regard to the direction we should take. It had been my intention to make an expedition into the White River country below Dubuque, where it is said a band of marauders have a considerable number of horses. These marauders I wished to destroy or drive out, and to capture their horses; but, having received information that a rebel captain by the name of Mooney, with 75 men, were encamped at Tolbert's Ferry, on White River, 60 miles from us, I resolved, with the advice of the other officers, to go and capture them. I received a re-enforcement of 60 men from the enrolled militia at the mill, and marched 20 miles in the direction of Tolbert's Ferry.

The march was continued on the morning of the 11th, but, instead of keeping the road, I bore to the eastward, and marched through the wood, under the guidance of an excellent woodman by the name of Willoughby Hall. I arrived within 8 miles of the ferry by dusk, and stopped to feed and rest in the dense forest, near an out of the way corn-field. During the time of our stay at this place, I sent Lieut. John R. Kelso, with 8 men, to capture some rebel pickets that I supposed would be found at the house of a rebel by the name of Brixy. Lieutenant Kelso soon returned, having found and captured 2 rebels, with their guns, and 1 horse. From these prisoners I learned that Captain Mooney's men had temporarily disbanded, and were not to assemble again for two days. I felt a little disappointed upon the reception of this intelligence, but I determined to proceed and make a dash upon a band of armed rebels that I learned were at the saltpeter cave, on the other side of White River, 7 miles from Captain Mooney's house. At midnight my little band emerged from the dark wood, where we had been resting, and silently wound along the hills in the direction of Captain Mooney's. Lieutenant Kelso led the advance, and, by the most excellent management, succeeded in capturing 7 or 8 rebels, who lived near the road, without giving any alarm to the country around. Just before day we captured a rebel recruiting officer by the name of Mings, formerly a lieutenant-colonel. At the break of day we reached Captain Mooney's residence. We took him, with one other man, together with 15 stand of small-arms, most of which we destroyed, not being able to carry them. We also recaptured 8 horses, which had been taken from the enrolled militia stationed at Lawrence's Mill.

I remained here to feed and await the arrival of a party that I had sent out, with orders to meet at this point. They soon came in, bringing several prisoners. I then sent Captain [P. T.] Green, of the enrolled militia, back with the prisoners, 17 in number, and 25 men as an escort. I then divided the rest of my command into two divisions, sending one, under command of Captain [J. H.] Sallee, accompanied by Lieutenant Bates, formerly of the Sixty-fourth Illinois, to march up the river on this side, and to await in concealment till I began the attack with the other division, which was to cross and approach from the other side.

It was just noon when we arrived at the cave. The rebels were at their dinner, all unconscious of our approach. When at last they discovered us, they mistook us for a company of their own men which they were expecting, and they did not discover their error until we were in half pistol shot of them. I ordered them to surrender, which they did, without firing a gun.

They numbered 23, of whom 3 were left, being unable to travel. Their arms were mostly shot-guns and rifles, which I ordered to be destroyed. We also captured 4 mules and 2 wagons. The wagons, however, we could not bring away; also 3 horses were taken. I ordered the saltpeter works to be destroyed, which was effectually done. These are gigantic works, having cost the rebel Government $30,000. Captain McNamar, who was in command, stated that in three days they could have had $6,000 worth of saltpeter ready for use. These works, although reported as destroyed at the time of the burning of Yellville, had been unmolested since early last spring, when they were slightly injured by a detachment from General Curtis' army. The works being destroyed, and learning that a party of Burbridge's command was hourly expected, I thought better to retire, as I was already encumbered with prisoners. I marched nearly all night through the dark woods, the rain pouring down upon us in torrents.

On the next day we advanced as far as Little North Fork, which was not fordable. Here we remained till the morning of the 13th, when we crossed and reached Lawrence's Mills.

On the 15th we reached this place, having been absent seven days. We traveled 225 miles; captured 42 prisoners; destroyed 40 stand of small-arms; also captured 12 horses and 4 mules, and destroyed $30,000 worth of machinery, &c., and all without any loss whatever on my side.

In conclusion, I must say a word in praise of the brave men under my command. Often without any food, except parched corn, and no shelter from the chilling rains; deprived of sleep, and weary from long night marches, not a murmur was heard. Every hardship was borne with cheerfulness, and every danger met with the utmost coolness. The enrolled militia officers, Captains Sallee, Green, and [J. F.] Huffman, all did their duty well. Lieutenant Bates, of the Sixty-fourth Illinois, showed himself a brave soldier. Lieutenant Warren, of Company F, also deserves favorable notice. As to Lieutenant Kelso, his reputation as an intrepid soldier and skillful officer is too well known to require any comment at this time. These, major, I think, are all the facts worthy of notice.

I am, very respectfully, your obedient servant,

MILTON BURCH,
Captain, Commanding Expedition.

Maj. JAMES H. STEGER,
Assistant Adjutant-General.

DECEMBER 14, 1862.—Affair near Helena, Ark.

REPORTS.

No. 1.—Brig. Gen. Willis A. Gorman, U. S. Army, commanding Eastern District of Arkansas.

No. 2.—Maj. Henry P. Hawkins, Sixth Missouri Cavalry.

No. 1.

Report of Brig. Gen. Willis A. Gorman, U. S. Army, commanding Eastern District of Arkansas.

HEADQUARTERS EASTERN DISTRICT OF ARKANSAS,
Helena, [Ark.,] December 15, 1862.

MAJOR: On yesterday morning, a little after daylight, the Texas Rangers made a dash at our outpost picket, 4 miles from this place, and captured 23, including 1 commissioned officer, all belonging to the Sixth Missouri Cavalry.

I find this whole command extremely loose in doing picket and all other guard duty. I will correct it, or dismiss, with the approval of the Government, one officer after another in disgrace, until the remedy is effective.

I am, major, your obedient servant,

W. A. GORMAN,
Brigadier-General, Commanding.

Maj. H. Z. CURTIS,
Assistant Adjutant-General, Department of the Missouri.

No. 2.

Report of Maj. Henry P. Hawkins, Sixth Missouri Cavalry.

HEADQUARTERS SIXTH MISSOURI CAVALRY,
Helena, [Ark.,] December 14, 1862.

CAPTAIN: I have the honor to submit the following report of the capture of the picket guard on Saint Francis road, furnished from my command, in compliance with Special Orders, No. 95, from Headquarters First Brigade, Second Division, Army of the Eastern District of Arkansas, and dated December 13, 1862:

The picket guard was detailed from Company E of my command. The picket guard consisted of 1 commissioned officer, 4 non-commissioned officers, and 21 privates. They relieved the pickets at the regular picket station, about 4 miles from this camp, at 3 p. m. of the 13th instant. At 8 this a. m. Private Hugh Roark reported to me that the lieutenant commanding the picket guard and 23 enlisted men, with horses, arms, and equipments complete, were surprised and captured by a band of guerrillas at daylight this morning, near the residence of a citizen named Turner. Most of the horses and horse equipments were the private property of the soldiers captured.

Immediately on receipt of the above information, I ordered Capt. F. A. Millert and 25 enlisted men of Company F, my command, to replace the picket guard captured this morning. I reported the capture of the picket guard at headquarters First Brigade, and at headquarters Second Division, immediately after the receipt of the above information. Having learned (not officially) that the Army of the Eastern District of Arkansas had just been reorganized, and that Brig. Gen. C. C. Washburn was commanding all the cavalry at this point, I respectfully submit the facts for your consideration as reported to me by Captain Millert.

Mr. Turner stated that the guard was captured by Texas Rangers; but the negroes on his plantation stated that they are acquainted with Captain Anderson, and that they saw him (Anderson) this morning talking with Mr. Turner; they state, also, that, about 9 o'clock last night (13th instant), they heard a large body of troops moving through the corn-field near Mr. Turner's residence.

I am informed that Mr. Turner has a guard of two United States soldiers, with United States horses, arms, and equipments, at his house.

That guard, or the Government property in their possession, was not molested, although Captain Anderson and his men saw the guards, and even captured one or two men of the picket guard in Mr. Turner's door-yard.

One of Mr. Turner's guards informed Capt. F. A. Millert that he also heard a body of troops moving through the corn-field last night about 9 o'clock, but he did not inform the officer commanding the picket guard, neither did he take, or cause to be taken, any steps to inform the picket guard of the danger surrounding them. The guard witnessed the capture of our men from the front door of Mr. Turner's house. He says the men were very much scattered; they had just come up to the regular picket station; the pickets had not yet been stationed for the day. The picket guard at night retires about 1 mile from the position they occupy during the day. They had just halted, had unbridled their horses, and were feeding when attacked from the rear.

The enlisted men captured have seen and done hard service, and would not have been taken prisoners if the lieutenant had done his duty. For the men I have sympathy; for the officer, contempt; and respectfully recommend that he may be mustered out of the service of the United states.

Respectfully, your obedient servant,

HENRY P. HAWKINS,
Major, Commanding Sixth Missouri Cavalry.

Capt. WILLIAM H. MORGAN,
Assistant Adjutant-General.

DECEMBER 17-21, 1862.—Expedition from New Madrid to Clarkton, Mo.

Report of Capt. Hubert F. Peebles, Thirty-second Iowa Infantry.

HEADQUARTERS,
New Madrid, Mo., December 22, 1862.

I have the honor to submit the following report of the operations of the forces under my command in the late expedition to Clarkton, Mo.:

The command consisted of Captain [J.] Hutchinson, Second Lieutenant [A.] Dowd, and 40 men of Company I; First Lieutenant [H. C.] Raymond, and 57 men of Company C; Chaplain Coffin, and Surgeon Waters. The command left New Madrid at about 8 a. m. December 17, and went as far as Weaversville, a distance of 22 miles, the first day. Little River, at this place, is from 2 to 5 feet deep at the ford, the bridge having been destroyed some time since, by order of Major Jones, then in command at New Madrid; the width of the ford is some 5 rods. We were obliged to ferry the men across in a small skiff. The roads, notwithstanding the recent heavy rains, were in excellent condition to this point. The Plank road begins at Weaversville and runs to Clarkton, a distance of 12 miles, through a swamp.

At daylight on the 18th, we continued our march, and arrived at Clarkton the same evening. We found the roads almost impassable; culverts, to the number of some 20, had all been destroyed, and the teams were obliged to pass around them, going down the bank into the water and mud to the depth of from 3 to 5 feet. The bridge across New River,

4 miles from Clarkton, we also found destroyed, and we were compelled to cross in the small skiff which we had brought from Weaversville. The horses and teams were obliged to ford a distance of 200 yards. The bridges and culverts could be repaired at small expense, as the foundation works are in very good condition. We halted about 1 mile from Clarkton, and rested until after dark, keeping close guard that no one should carry intelligence of our approach. Soon after dark, we marched into town, and immediately surrounded every house, placed our pickets on all the avenues of approach, and commenced our search for prisoners. Captain McDonald was found at the house of ———, and arrested. Learning that Captain Pankey was at home on a furlough, Captain Hutchinson was dispatched with a detachment of men, and soon returned with him as prisoner.

On the following morning three expeditions were organized—one of 15 men, under command of Chaplain Coffin, who went south toward Kennett, some 5 miles, and took prisoner Quartermaster-Sergeant Sebecker; he also secured several valuable horses belonging to rebels. One detachment of 15 men, under command of Captain Hutchinson, went north from Clarkton, and returned with Captain Page and one Montgomery and his son Lentz, as prisoners, all of whom were engaged in the guerrilla service; he also took several valuable horses. Another detachment of 15 horsemen, under command of Captain Peebles, went to Halkolm's Island and to the Saint Francis River, to the Arkansas border. The last-mentioned detachment took Surgeon Bartlett and considerable rebel property. We could hear of depredations committed by small bands of guerrillas, but we were unable to meet any of them. I learned that a band of from 100 to 200 guerrillas were making their headquarters at Chalk Bluff, on the Saint Francis River.

Depredations are frequently committed by guerrillas in the vicinity of Clarkton, and the perpetrators flee to Chalk Bluff, and thence across the river into Arkansas. A force stationed at the bluff would do much toward restoring quiet and safety to the law-abiding citizens of Southeastern Missouri. Many of the citizens claim to be loyal.

The result of our expedition was the taking prisoners of 2 captains, 1 surgeon, and 1 quartermaster-sergeant, all of the Regular Confederate Army; 1 captain and 3 privates in the guerrilla service. Besides the prisoners, we took 15 horses, some valuable ones; one mule team, wagon, harness, &c.; 40 head of cattle, and several stand of small-arms. Could the expedition have been absent several days longer, much additional good might have been accomplished.

On the 20th we returned from Clarkton to Weaversville, and on the 21st arrived at New Madrid, all the men in better health and spirits than when they started.

I would make honorable mention of Captain Hutchinson, Chaplain Coffin, Lieutenants Raymond and Dowd for the prompt and faithful manner in which they discharged the duties devolving upon them.

I am glad to bear witness that every man in the command acted throughout as becomes a patriot soldier battling for a just cause.

All of which is respectfully submitted.

H. F. PEEBLES,
Captain Company C, Commanding.

Col. JOHN SCOTT,
Comdg. Thirty-second Regiment Iowa Volunteer Infantry.

DECEMBER 21-23, 1862.—Expedition from Fayetteville to Huntsville, Ark.

Report of Lieut. Col. James Stuart, Tenth Illinois Cavalry.

HEADQUARTERS TENTH ILLINOIS CAVALRY,
Fayetteville, Ark., December 23, 1862.

COLONEL: In obedience to your orders of the 21st instant, I proceeded, in command of detachments of the First Arkansas Cavalry, Eighth Missouri Cavalry, and Tenth Illinois Cavalry, to Huntsville, Ark., to attack a party of the enemy reported in that locality. On arriving at that point a little after daybreak on the morning of the 22d, I found the enemy, 150 strong, had been in there all night of the 18th, and committed depredations on all the Union families in that vicinity, more especially that of Judge Murphy, the ladies of whose family they stripped of everything but what was on their bodies, leaving them in a destitute condition. After leaving Huntsville some of them proceeded down the War Eagle Creek, others toward Carrollton, scattering all through the country in small parties of twos and threes. I caught 15 stragglers from the rebel army and paroled them; they had all left the army immediately after the battle of Prairie Grove.

I would likewise beg to state, for the information of the general commanding, that the road leading through the mountains from Ozark, Van Buren, and Clarksville passes direct through Huntsville, and from Huntsville leading north there is one road which strikes the Wire road at Mud Town, one at Cross Hollows, one at Elk Horn, one at Keytesville, Mo., and one at Cassville, Mo., making five different roads which a rebel party might choose from on arriving at Huntsville if they desired to molest our line of communication with Springfield, Mo., and from inquiry I find that each of the points mentioned is as near to them from Huntsville as it is to us at Fayetteville. Consequently the necessity, in my opinion, of having a strong force of cavalry stationed at that point, as there is no other route the enemy can cross the Boston Mountains until they get about 100 miles east of that gap.

I would likewise state that forage is plentiful in that vicinity.

I am, sir, very respectfully, your obedient servant,

JAMES STUART,
Lieutenant-Colonel Tenth Illinois Cavalry, Comdg. Expedition.

DECEMBER 23, 1862.—Skirmish on the Saint Francis road, near Helena, Ark.

Report of Brig. Gen. Willis A. Gorman, U. S. Army.

HEADQUARTERS DISTRICT OF EASTERN ARKANSAS,
Helena, Ark., December 23, 1862.

The enemy's cavalry attacked and ambushed our outpost picket on the Saint Francis road, and killed 2 and wounded 16, captured none. We pursued them at once, and so closely that they only escaped by scattering in all directions through the wood. The boldness of the Texas cavalry is becoming highly important, and if I send 2,000 cavalry to open up communication with General Grant, as he specially requests, these Texans will venture still more; but it can only cause annoyance.

I am, major, your obedient servant,

W. A. GORMAN,
Brigadier-General, Commanding.

Maj. H. Z. CURTIS,
Assistant Adjutant-General.

DECEMBER 23-31, 1862.—Operations in the Sugar Creek Hills, Mo.

Report of Maj. Edward B. Eno, Eighth Missouri State Militia Cavalry.

HEADQUARTERS,
Newtonia, Mo., December 31, 1862.

GENERAL: I have the honor to make the following condensed statement of the operations of my command during the ten days past:

On the evening of the 23d instant, I started with 80 men for the purpose of dispersing several gangs of guerrillas known to harbor among the Sugar Creek Hills. After riding hard two nights and days, we had succeeded in finding three different camps of from 20 to 50 men each. These were broken up, 10 prisoners taken, 12 horses, with saddles, bridles, &c., 2 wagons, 1 tent, marked "Sixth Kansas Volunteers," together with a quantity of blankets, kettles, pans, &c. It was impossible to completely surprise them, as there are none but rebels and rebel sympathizers living in the country, and though the immediate results of the scout were but small, I have discovered their "licks" in that section, and will find much less difficulty in exterminating them. Scouts are kept out constantly after them, with orders to show them no mercy.

On the night of the 28th instant, a party of guerrillas came to the house of Mrs. Joy, a Union lady, who has been robbed of almost everything, and carried off her negro girl. I immediately started a party, under command of Captain [B. A.] Reeder, but failed to find the perpetrators of the outrage, they having dispersed and taken to the brush. I have seized upon a slave belonging to the Mr. Adams who is in the brush and said to be one of the robbers, and have notified his family that the negro shall be held until Mrs. Joy's is returned.

Sugar Creek, Shoal Creek, Indian Creek, Center Creek, and Jones' Creek, at distances from 5 to 15 miles of the post, are full of these outlaws, but 8 of them having been shot in the last two weeks, and the continual scouting after them, has made them much less daring than heretofore. It will take some little time, but I am determined to root them out, stem and branch, and, if horse-flesh and ammunition do not fail me, will do it.

The block-house and stockade are progressing rapidly, and the force engaged in the work is being daily increased, as per orders. Will send full drawings of the fort per next messenger.

I am, general, very respectfully, your obedient servant,

E. B. ENO,
Major, Commanding Post.

Brig. Gen. E. B. BROWN,
Comdg. Southwest District of Missouri, Springfield, Mo.

DECEMBER 28, 1862—Skirmish at Dripping Springs and capture of Van Buren, Ark.

REPORTS.

No. 1.

Report of Maj. Gen. Samuel R. Curtis, U. S. Army.

DECEMBER 29, 1862.

The Army of the Frontier, under Generals Blunt and Herron, moved over Boston Mountains on Saturday. Advanced without halting to Van Buren; drove the enemy across the Arkansas; killed and wounded a few; took three steamboats, camp equipments, and 100 prisoners. The march of 45 miles, with all arms of service, over the mountains and through the deep mud of the valley was a most arduous and gal lant affair.

SAML. R. CURTIS,
Major-General.

H. W. HALLECK, *General-in-Chief, Washington, D. C.*

No. 2.

Reports of Brig. Gen. James G. Blunt, U. S. Army.

HEADQUARTERS ARMY OF THE FRONTIER,
Van Buren, Ark., December 28, 1862.

GENERAL: The Stars and Stripes now wave in triumph over Van Buren. On learning that Hindman had been re-enforced and contemplated making another attempt to force his way to Missouri, I determined to make the attack upon him.

Leaving my transportation north of the mountains, I marched with 8,000 of my best troops and thirty pieces of artillery, from Prairie Grove at 8 o'clock yesterday morning upon this place; distance, 50 miles. At 10 o'clock this morning my advance came upon two regiments of rebel cavalry at Dripping Springs, 8 miles north of the river. Dashing upon them with 3,000 cavalry and four mountain howitzers, a brisk running fight took place, which was kept up into the town, resulting in the capture of all their transportation—40 wagons, with six-mule teams, camp and garrison equipage, 100 prisoners, a large amount of ammunition; four steamers and the ferry-boat were also captured. The latter, in attempting to cross the river with rebel troops, was shelled from the howitzer. When in the middle of the river the boats were disabled and a number of the men killed. The remainder jumped overboard and swam to the shore. Three large steamers, heavily laden with Government supplies, had got up steam and attempted to escape down the river, but were pursued by the cavalry 5 miles and brought to by the fire of their carbines, and returned back to the levee. The enemy then brought their artillery to the opposite bank of the river and commenced shelling the town, for the purpose of driving out my cavalry, but resulting in no other damage than the destruction of some buildings; my artillery, coming up soon, silenced their batteries. Quite a number of the enemy have been killed during the day's operations. The only casualties on our side are 5 or 6 men slightly wounded. My long-range guns are now shelling the rebel camp across the river, 5 miles below this place. If the enemy does not retire during the night, I shall endeavor to cross my troops over the river in the morning and offer them battle.

JAS. G. BLUNT,
Brigadier-General.

Maj. Gen. SAMUEL R. CURTIS.

HEADQUARTERS ARMY OF THE FRONTIER,
Van Buren, Ark., December 30, 1862.

The enemy retreated during the night of the 28th in the direction of Arkadelphia. About 600 sick and wounded Confederates were abandoned at Fort Smith, with instructions to take care of themselves. I sent a small force to Fort Smith to destroy two steamers there, but the rebels had saved us the trouble by burning them before they retreated. The four steamers captured at Van Buren, also the ferry-boat, were burned by my order. Last night as much of the sugar and other supplies as I had transportation to remove were landed. The remainder, including about 13,000 bushels of corn, shipped from Little Rock for the rebel army, shared the fate of the boats. As it is impossible to sustain an army here, for the want of forage and supplies, until they can be brought up the river, or the animals subsist upon grass, I shall therefore commence moving my troops back to-day north of the mountains.

Dispatch just received from Colonel [W. A.] Phillips, whom I had sent with 1,200 men to the Indian Territory, dated Fort Gibson, the 27th, informs me that he has driven and pursued the forces of Cooper and Stand Watie across the Arkansas River, and destroyed the rebel fortifications, barracks, and commissary buildings at Fort Davis. Colonel McIntosh and the rebel Creeks are desirous of laying down their arms and unite their destinies again with the Federal Government. The same feeling also manifested by the Choctaws.

Respectfully,

JAS. G. BLUNT,
Brigadier-General, Commanding.

Maj. T. J. WEED, *Asst. Adjt. Gen., Fort Leavenworth, Kans.*

No. 3.

Reports of Brig. Gen. Francis J. Herron, U. S. Army.

HDQRS. 2D AND 3D DIVS., ARMY OF THE FRONTIER,
Van Buren, Ark., December 29, 1862.

We have bearded the tricky rebel, General Hindman, in his den. Yesterday morning we left north side of mountains, General Blunt taking Cove Creek road and I taking Telegraph road. It was a terrible trip. We formed junction at daylight this morning, and pushed the cavalry into Van Buren without halting. Two regiments of cavalry were encamped at Dripping Springs and showed fight, but after killing a few and wounding some, they left, crossing the river on two boats at the wharf. We captured two boats and the ferry-boat, the transportation of two regiments, and 100 prisoners, including several officers. It is a good joke on Hindman. He is across the river, 5 miles from here, with his whole force. We claim the country to the Arkansas River.

F. J. HERRON,
Brigadier-General.

Maj. Gen. SAMUEL R. CURTIS.

—

HEADQUARTERS SECOND AND THIRD DIVISIONS,
Prairie Grove, Ark., December 31, 1862.

GENERAL: Some days after the battle of Prairie Grove, General Blunt and myself decided upon an expedition to Van Buren, but the weather was such as to prevent any movement at that time. On Christmas night we met and arranged the details, fixing the starting time on the morning of the 27th instant. The impression was given to the troops that a demonstration was to be made in the direction of Huntsville, and with that idea preparations were made.

At daybreak on the 27th, we moved out of camp, with picked men of the whole command, General Blunt going from Cane Hill, by the Cove Creek route, while I took the Telegraph or mountain road. We marched all of that day and until 3 o'clock the next morning, crossing the mountains successfully, and forming a junction at Oliver's Store, 18 miles from the river. Getting information in regard to their camps, pickets, &c., General Blunt instructed me to advance all my cavalry, leaving Huston, with the infantry and artillery, to follow up. The general and myself pushed on with the advance guard, striking their first picket 3 miles from Oliver's. After firing upon us, they ran, we following them into the camp at Dripping Springs. Here a regiment was formed in line, but our cavalry charged and drove them in great disorder, capturing wagons, tents, and all their camp equipage complete. On we traveled, chasing them through the streets of Van Buren, to the great surprise and astonishment of the citizens, who had heard nothing of our coming. They made three attempts to check us between Dripping Springs and Van Buren, but were driven every time. The last 10 miles was traveled in one hour, the whole cavalry force going in at a gallop.

Arriving on the hill overlooking the town, we found three steamboats leaving the wharf and the ferry, making good time over the river. We chased them with the cavalry, overtaking the first one a mile below town, and, by a well-directed fire of musketry, brought her to. Colonel Cloud followed the other two 10 miles, capturing both, and bringing them back to the wharf. They were all loaded with corn and other stores. In the mean time the cavalry were scouring the country, and wagons were being brought in from every direction.

About 2.30 o'clock (we had arrived at 12 o'clock) a battery opened on the town from the opposite side of the river, and shelled the town for an hour. One of our men was killed and 5 wounded. General Blunt and myself made a narrow escape. We soon hurried up a long-range battery, and drove them off. The transaction was diabolical, to say the least of it, the town being full of women and children. At least 100 shells were fired into the houses, doing great damage, only one citizen being hurt that I know of. We remained there over night and until dark the next night, moving the command back to Dripping Springs.

The captures are numerous. After feeding all the corn we could, there remained between 15,000 and 20,000 bushels, which we destroyed, also burning the three boats captured—the ferry-boat and two boats that were laid up at the wharf. We have over 50 six-mule teams taken; 250 head of fine cattle, and a large number of horses, &c. The camp equipage was all destroyed, and the wagons loaded with Government sugar and brought with us. The telegraph operator, instruments, and official dispatches of Hindman were taken. I will send the telegrams to you; they are a curiosity.

Hindman's whole force was encamped within 5 miles, on the south bank of the river. They at once evacuated Fort Smith; destroyed all their stores on hand and burned two steamboats, and traveled, leaving 4,000 sick in a very destitute condition. The divisions of Frost, Shoup, Roane, and Fagan retreated in great confusion, each one taking the first road they came to, and without any plan for concentrating. They are demoralized and broken up, and I think this section is rid of Hindman. My opinion is they will go to Marshfield, in Texas, and cross over to Vicksburg. I also think Little Rock will be abandoned, and a new demonstration will cause them to abandon the whole line of the Arkansas River. I would like to be at Helena with a good division just at this time, and have a chance to operate. We cannot subsist on the river until the mouth is opened, there being nothing above Little Rock. Hindman has told the people on the river that all was well; that it was an impossibility for us to cross the mountains; that, if we did, he would never let one man get back, &c. This demonstration has done more to demoralize the army, to create a distrust in the leaders, and to satisfy the people that we can accomplish what we undertake, than anything done in this quarter. They are ready and willing to give it up.

The march down and back was terrible. We crossed the mountains in the night, and was more of a contract than I had yet got. It required 12 horses to draw the artillery over, and sometimes 50 men on a rope, in addition. The feat, however, was accomplished without losing anything.

I left Van Buren at 7 o'clock on the evening of the 29th, and met General Schofield 10 miles north of that place. He returned to Prairie Grove without visiting Van Buren, and to-day assumed command of the army. General Blunt returned to Rhea's Mills, and I am still at Prairie Grove.

I sent you to-day a Fort Smith paper, containing a flattering notice of Judge Tibbetts, of Fayetteville, and the obituary of Governor Claib. [F.] Jackson.

The army is in excellent health and condition, but need shoes badly. Somehow they cannot be had.

Hoping that one little column of your forces have wound up the year in a manner to suit you, I remain, very truly, yours,

F. J. HERRON.

Maj. Gen. SAMUEL R. CURTIS, *Saint Louis, Mo.*

No. 4.

Report of Maj. Charles Banzhaf, First Missouri Cavalry.

HDQRS. SECOND BATTALION, FIRST MISSOURI CAVALRY,
Fayetteville, Ark., January 2, 1863.

SIR: I have the honor to transmit to you herewith the particulars of the operations of Company E, First Missouri Cavalry, under command of Capt. Irving W. Fuller, at Van Buren, on Sunday, December 28, 1862.

Supposing a portion of the enemy to have retreated toward the southeast part of the town, I dispatched Captain Fuller and his command, while yet one-half mile this side of Van Buren, to make a charge on said part of the town, the result of which I give in Captain Fuller's own language, as follows:

After riding about 1½ miles, we overtook and captured 3 six-horse teams loaded with ammunition, which were placed under guard and sent to be reported to General Blunt. Proceeding down the road, we succeeded in capturing, in all, 27 wagons and teams, loaded with baggage, camp and garrison equipage, and, discovering the steamer Rose Douglass in the Arkansas River retreating down the river with all speed, we brought her to by firing at her with our carbines, and succeeded in capturing her, and her whole cargo, consisting of 4,300 bushels of corn, 6 hogsheads of sugar, a quantity of molasses, &c., which was handed over to General Herron. We also took 21 prisoners, all soldiers, and, except the teamster, with their arms and accouterments.

Captain Fuller and his command returned to town with the steamer on the morning of December 29, 1862.

I take pleasure in calling your attention to the gallantry and efficiency displayed by Captain Fuller and his command, and the daring exhibited throughout the engagement.

I am, very respectfully, your most obedient servant,

CHAS. BANZHAF,
Major First Missouri Cavalry.

Col. DANIEL HUSTON, JR.,
Commanding Second Division, Army of the Frontier.

No. 5.

Report of Maj. Gen. T. C. Hindman, C. S. Army.

HEADQUARTERS HINDMAN'S DIVISION,
Little Rock, [Ark.,] February 15, 1863.

COLONEL: After the battle of Prairie Grove, having returned south of the mountains, I found it impossible to forage Marmaduke's cavalry in Northwest Arkansas, and accordingly ordered him to Lewisburg, 100 miles below Van Buren. My force being thus reduced and continuing to diminish in strength daily by desertions and a frightful increase of sickness, the latter caused by the unprecedented hardships to which the men had been exposed, the former resulting principally, in my opinion, from the non-payment of the troops and the consequent sufferings of their families, I decided that it was unadvisable to keep my main body on the north side of the river, and, therefore, crossed it to the south side, and went into camp in the vicinity of Fort Smith. One of Fagan's infantry regiments, with a section of artillery, remained at Van Buren, and one regiment of cavalry, under Lieut. Col. R. P. Crump, was posted at Dripping Springs, 9 miles north of that place, instructed to picket at Oliver's, 19 miles north, and at corresponding points on all other roads leading toward the enemy, scouting actively on each road, and keeping up constant patrols by day and night between the several picket stations.

On the 21st of December, the lieutenant-general commanding the department, who was then at my headquarters, instructed me to move my command, except Roane's and Cooper's brigades of Texas and Indian troops, to Lewisburg, it being no longer possible to maintain them where I was.

On the 23d of December, I gave orders for the removal of the sick and such public stores as would not be necessary to the troops that were to remain, and that all wagon trains and boats on the way up with supplies should be stopped about Clarksville. Fagan's division was ordered to march on the 26th and Frost's division on the 28th.

In the interval between the issuance and execution of these orders, desertions from the Texas infantry, under General Roane, increased to such an extent that I deemed it best to break up that brigade and distribute the regiments among the Missouri and Arkansas troops, and substituted Shaver's Arkansas brigade to be left for defending the Indian country.

On December 28, at 10 a. m., Lieutenant-Colonel Crump reported to me by courier that the enemy was advancing on the Cove Creek road in heavy force of cavalry, infantry, and artillery. A few minutes afterward, Brigadier General Cooper, who was at Scullyville, in the Choctaw Nation, 15 miles from Fort Smith, reported to me by courier that a Federal cavalry force of three or four regiments, with artillery, under Colonel Phillips, had crossed to the south side of the river, at Fort Gibson, on the preceding day. Immediately after, I received information by telegraph from a detachment of cavalry posted at Borland's, 35 miles below Van Buren, on the north side of the river, covering the roads from Fayetteville to Ozark and Clarksville, that a regiment of Federal cavalry was within 20 miles of that position, moving south.

Fagan's division was on the march, 25 miles below; Frost's was 10 miles below; Shaver's brigade, less than 1,000 strong, with one battery, was 2 miles below, in camp.

General Cooper was ordered to retire southward upon his depots of supplies, the nearest of which was Johnson's Station, on the Canadian, about 90 miles from Fort Smith. Shaver's brigade was put under arms, and moved forward to the river opposite Van Buren. Frost was ordered back to Shaver's position, detaching enough artillery and infantry to hold the crossing at Strain's, 6 miles below Van Buren; and orders were given to remove by boat and wagon, as rapidly as possible, the public property at Van Buren and Fort Smith. At the same time I telegraphed General Marmaduke, at Lewisburg, to move northward and strike the enemy in flank or rear.

At 11.05 o'clock, being one hour and five minutes after the first notice of the enemy's advance, the Federal cavalry and light artillery were in Van Buren. As they approached the landing, West's battery, of Shaver's brigade, drove them back, killing and wounding several. Skirmishing continued there till nearly sunset, when the Federal infantry appeared, and two batteries of heavy rifled pieces opened from the commanding heights in and above the town. Meanwhile a cavalry force pursued and captured Colonel Crump's train and part of a train laden with supplies for my wounded at Cane Hill, and also captured three steamboats, the Notre, which had grounded on a bar 1 mile below Van Buren, and the Key West and Rose Douglass, which had been ordered down, but had stopped for some cause unknown on the south side of the river, opposite Strain's Landing. This was before there was time for Frost's detachment to reach that point. The steamers Eva and Arkansas, being still above Van Buren, were burned by my orders, after transferring to wagons all their freight for which I had transportation.

About dark, artillery firing commenced at Strain's Landing, between Frost's detachment, posted there, and a Federal force on the opposite side, having field pieces of large caliber. It continued during two hours, when the enemy retired. I had now removed all the public stores for which I had transportation. My whole force did not exceed 4,000. That of the enemy in and near Van Buren was not less than 7,000. His cavalry, moving on both my flanks, might soon get entirely in my rear. I therefore determined to retire all my command southward, and cross the river near Clarksville, unite with Fagan, and there take position. This intention was carried out without any occurrence that need be reported.

I forward herewith the reports of my staff officers,* showing the losses of public property at Van Buren and Fort Smith. All is reported as lost which was not actually brought away by them, though a considerable quantity of these stores has since been recovered.

The report of Lieutenant-Colonel Crump and his officers commanding pickets, scouts, &c., is forwarded also.*

I likewise forward herewith Brigadier-General Marmaduke's report of his expedition into Missouri, under the order telegraphed him by me on December 28.

Respectfully,

T. C. HINDMAN,
Major-General, Commanding.

Col. S. S. ANDERSON,
Assistant Adjutant-General.

DECEMBER 28, 1862—Evacuation of New Madrid, Mo.

REPORTS.†

No. 1.—Col. John Scott, Thirty-second Iowa Infantry, with communications from Brig. Gen. Thomas A. Davies, U. S. Army.

No. 2.—Extract from proceedings of a Special Commission, and letter from Col. John Scott, Thirty-second Iowa Infantry.

No. 1.

Reports of Col. John Scott, Thirty-second Iowa Infantry, with communications from Brig. Gen. Thomas A. Davies, U. S. Army.

FORT PILLOW, *January* 1, 1863.

GENERAL: On the 27th ultimo, I received orders to destroy public property and remove the detachment to Fort Pillow. On the 28th this was accomplished. I was much disappointed, and feared you would be also; but the order was peremptory from General Davies, and General Fisk informed me that General Davies had authority from you.

The detachment is now here. As far as I can see, we are of no use here. There is no artillery here, and the works are much extended. With a few pieces the place might be held against a large force. As it is, an attack from a largely superior force would be fatal. I know, of course, nothing of the policy that sent me here in such haste. I do know, how-

* Not found.

† See also in "Correspondence, etc.," Part II, Curtis to Davies and Halleck, December 29, 1862; to Halleck, December 31, 1862, and January 3 and February 11, 1863, and Carr to Curtis, January 3, 1863. The post was reoccupied on or before December 31, 1862.

ever, that my regiment is divided, and that I would be pleased to have it united.

When at New Madrid and Cape Girardeau, I felt that we were in the same neighborhood; now we are certainly not neighbors, and are embarrassed by being in two departments. It is not my place to suggest either the when or the where, but only my wish, that, if consistent with the public welfare, it would be remembered as a kindness could we again be brought together.

Your most obedient servant,

JOHN SCOTT,
Colonel Thirty-second Iowa Infantry.

Maj. Gen. SAMUEL R. CURTIS,
Saint Louis, Mo.

[Indorsement.]

SAINT LOUIS, MO., *January* 5, 1863.

The abandonment of Fort Pillow [New Madrid] must be punished. General Carr reports that he communicated different orders to Colonel Scott. He should have obeyed Carr, not Davies, and must be arrested.

SAML. R. CURTIS,
Major-General.

COLUMBUS, *January* 12, 1863.

Brigadier-General CARR, *Saint Louis:*

SIR: I hear you have placed Colonel Scott under arrest for evacuating New Madrid.

The circumstances of the case were these: Colonel Scott happened to be in Columbus during the excitement along the river, and information, such as was supposed reliable, reached here that New Madrid was threatened by a very large [force] under Thompson and Jeffers; that Fort Pillow was in like manner threatened, as was true, by Van Dorn.

I called General Tuttle and General Fisk to my office, and we carefully looked over the ground, and agreed that the force at New Madrid was insufficient to stand a heavy attack, and the six pieces (siege guns) then in position, if they fell into the hands of the enemy, would, in the present position of the army below, prove almost fatal to us, we having no gunboats or forces to displace them immediately.

As a precaution, which we deemed bound to take, it was determined to evacuate New Madrid and couple the armament and re-enforce Fort Pillow. I had great hesitancy in giving the order, the troops not being under my command; but on the assurance of General Fisk that it would be all right, and that General Curtis would approve of it (not knowing that you commanded the district), I gave the order to Colonel Scott to evacuate New Madrid, spike the guns with soft iron, and destroy the ammunition, which, I understand, was done.

I took the ground we would be blamable to allow any chance, however remote, to be embraced by the enemy to capture any heavy ordnance on the river at this particular juncture.

I think the position is a correct one, and I hope this explanation will relieve Colonel Scott, at least, from any blame. We acted according to our best judgment in the premises.

I am, general, very respectfully,

THOS. A. DAVIES,
Brigadier-General, Commanding.

COLUMBUS KY., *January* 15, 1863.

Brigadier-General CARR, *Saint Louis, Mo.:*

GENERAL: On the 12th of January I wrote you a communication respecting the evacuation of New Madrid, and, as dispatches sometimes miscarry, I send you duplicate.*

I have to add that the telegram to General Curtis, in the following words, needs some explanation:

> Colonel Scott sends me back word to-day that Jeff. Thompson and Jeffers were within 10 miles of him with a force; that he could not have held the place.

Colonel Scott has since told me that he did not send me such a message, which is, no doubt, true. It was brought to me by the captain of the steamer O'Brien, a boat owned by Government, who was at Island 10 the morning of the evacuation, who said that it was a verbal message from Colonel Scott. The boat is now at New Madrid delivering supplies, and, when the captain returns, will investigate the source of information and send you a statement. The only point in the affair where Colonel Scott is in fault, it seems to me, was in not reporting to you the order; but I am sure, from the little knowledge I have of him, that such failure was owing to ignorance of military rule. I reported the order to Major-General Curtis, not knowing that you was his immediate commanding officer.

The extent of property destroyed was six secesh gun carriages and platforms and some secesh ammunition, which, I was informed, had just been sent there from Island No. 10. The siege guns can be unspiked by a few hours' work.

There is any quantity of gun carriages lying about Columbus and at Island 10, which I can send you to New Madrid if you desire at any time to remove the siege guns at that place.

I also inclose you a copy of my order to Colonel Scott.

I am, general, very respectfully,

THOS. A. DAVIES,
Brigadier-General, Commanding.

WASHINGTON, D. C., *January* 26, 1863.

Maj. Gen. SAMUEL R. CURTIS,
Saint Louis, Mo.:

GENERAL: The Secretary of War directs that you investigate and report upon the facts of the destruction of the ordnance and ordnance stores at New Madrid, and also report whether the officer in command should not be dismissed from the service. This may either be done by yourself in person or by a board of officers appointed by you for that purpose.

Very respectfully, your obedient servant,

H. W. HALLECK,
General-in-Chief.

---

* See p. 174.

No. 2.

Extract from proceedings of a Special Commission, and letter from Col. John Scott, Thirty-second Iowa Infantry.

PROCEEDINGS OF A SPECIAL COMMISSION WHICH CONVENED AT SAINT LOUIS, MO., BY VIRTUE OF THE FOLLOWING SPECIAL ORDER:

SPECIAL ORDERS, No. 30. } HDQRS. DEPARTMENT OF THE MISSOURI, *Saint Louis, February* 3, 1863.

* * * * * * *

VII. Pursuant to authority from the General-in-Chief,* a Special Commission is hereby constituted, to consist of the following officers, viz: Brig. Gen. W. K. Strong, U. S. Volunteers; Col. J. L. Geddes, Eighth Iowa Infantry; Col. Albert G. Brackett, Ninth Illinois Cavalry, whose duty it shall be to investigate and report upon the facts of the destruction of the ordnance and ordnance stores at New Madrid about the 27th of December, 1862. The Commission will also report as to the culpability of the officer or officers responsible, and whether or not he or they should be dismissed the service of the United States.

The Commission will sit at such post or place as they shall see fit, or will move from post to post as the necessity of the service may require, and will sit without regard to hours.

By command of Major-General Curtis:

H. Z. CURTIS,
Assistant Adjutant-General.

* * * * * * *

SAINT LOUIS, MO.,
February 26, 1863—11 a. m.

Commission met pursuant to adjournment. Present, all the members. The proceedings of yesterday were then read by the recorder.

The Commission, after mature deliberation, find the following facts:

That on the 28th day of December, A. D. 1862, six iron siege guns were spiked at New Madrid, Mo.; six gun carriages and platforms were burned, and a quantity of ammunition destroyed. The loss to the Government, aside from the loss of the ammunition, the value of which is not ascertained, was about $350 or $450. A set of barracks were on the same day burned at New Madrid, but this was purely the result of an accident. No other Government property was destroyed.

The ordnance and ordnance stores above mentioned were destroyed by men of the garrison of New Madrid, under command of Col. John Scott, of the Thirty-second Regiment Iowa Volunteer Infantry, commanding post. This was done by virtue of an order which Colonel Scott received from Brig. Gen. Thomas A. Davies, commanding District of Columbus; and although Colonel Scott was not under the direct command of Brigadier-General Davies, he did right under the circumstances in obeying Brigadier-General Davies' order, and not only did his duty, but is honorably acquitted of all blame.

Brig. Gen. Thomas A. Davies, U. S. Volunteers, commanding at that time the District of Columbus, gave Col. John Scott the order, and is responsible for it. The post at Columbus, he had good reason to suppose, was in imminent danger of capture by the rebel forces, and he acted the part of a prudent and faithful officer in crippling the arma-

---

* See Halleck to Curtis, January 26, 1863, in "Correspondence, etc.," Part II, p.

ment at New Madrid, Mo., and removing the United States troops from that place to Fort Pillow. He is not only free from culpability, but is honorably acquitted of all blame.

Neither Brig. Gen. Thomas A. Davies, U. S. Volunteers, nor Col. John Scott, Thirty-second Regiment of Iowa Volunteers, should be dismissed the service of the United States.

There being no further business to transact, the Special Commission adjourned *sine die*.

WM. K. STRONG,
Brigadier-General U. S. Volunteers, President.

ALBERT G. BRACKETT, *Colonel Ninth Illinois Cavalry, Recorder.*

Findings approved.

SAML. R. CURTIS,
Major-General.

HEADQUARTERS POST OF COLUMBUS,
Columbus, Ky., September 1, 1863.

COLONEL: A Military Commission, of which Brig. Gen. W. K. Strong was president, was convened in Saint Louis in February last, by order of Major-General Halleck, to investigate as to the evacuation of New Madrid and destruction of property there and at Island No. 10.

Grave charges were preferred against me, as commanding officer, for the evacuation of New Madrid, under alleged "pretended orders," and I was in arrest for two months. On the finding of that Commission, I was ordered to duty by General Curtis, but the finding was not made public, nor has been to this time, to my knowledge.

Feeling that my arrest was an outrage, and that the Commission fully justified my action, I deem myself entitled to a copy of the finding. I have applied for it heretofore in vain.

I respectfully ask that the major-general commanding the department will secure me a copy of the finding of said Commission.

Your most obedient servant,

JOHN SCOTT,
Colonel Thirty-second Iowa Infantry, Commanding Post.

Col. JOHN A. RAWLINS, *Assistant Adjutant-General.*

[Indorsements.]

HEADQUARTERS DEPARTMENT OF TENNESSEE,
Vicksburg, Miss., September 14, 1863.

Respectfully forwarded to Headquarters of the Army, Washington, D. C., with the request that, if deemed proper, Colonel Scott be furnished with a copy of such part of the proceedings as interest him.

U. S. GRANT,
Major-General.

OCTOBER 3, 1863.

I see no objection to the Adjutant-General furnishing Colonel Scott with the opinion of the court of inquiry in his case.*

H. W. HALLECK,
General-in-Chief.

---

* Copy was furnished.

DECEMBER 31, 1862–JANUARY 25, 1863.—Marmaduke's expedition into Missouri.

SUMMARY OF THE PRINCIPAL EVENTS.

Dec. 31, 1862.—Marmaduke's command moves from Lewisburg, Ark.
Jan. 2, 1863.—Skirmish at White Spring, Boston Mountains, Ark.
6, 1863.—Skirmish at Fort Lawrence, Beaver Station, Mo.
7, 1863.—Ozark, Mo., captured by Confederate forces.
8, 1863.—Engagement at Springfield, Mo.
9, 1863.—Garrison at Hartville, Mo., surrendered to Confederate forces.
11, 1863.—Engagement at Hartville, Mo.
25, 1863.—Marmaduke's command reaches Batesville, Ark.

REPORTS.

No. 1.—Maj. Gen. Samuel R. Curtis, U. S. Army, commanding Department of the Missouri, of engagement at Springfield, Mo.
No. 2.—Brig. Gen. Egbert B. Brown, U. S. Army, of engagement at Springfield, Mo.
No. 3.—Brig. Gen. Colly B. Holland, Missouri Militia, of engagement at Springfield, Mo.
No. 4.—Col. Benjamin Crabb, Nineteenth Iowa Infantry, of engagement at Springfield, Mo.
No. 5.—Brig. Gen. Fitz Henry Warren, U. S. Army, of engagement at Hartville, Mo.
No. 6.—Lieut. Col. Cornelius W. Dunlap, Twenty-first Iowa Infantry, of engagement at Hartville, Mo.
No. 7.—Capt. Milton Burch, Fourteenth Missouri State Militia Cavalry, of skirmish at Fort Lawrence, Beaver Station, Mo.
No. 8.—Brig. Gen. John S. Marmaduke, C. S. Army, commanding expedition.
No. 9.—Return of Casualties in Marmaduke's command.
No. 10.—Col. Joseph O. Shelby, Missouri Cavalry (Confederate), commanding brigade.
No. 11.—Col. J. C. Porter, Missouri Cavalry (Confederate), commanding brigade.
No. 12.—Maj. G. W. C. Bennett, MacDonald's Missouri Cavalry (Confederate).

No. 1.

Reports of Maj. Gen. Samuel R. Curtis, U. S. Army, commanding Department of the Missouri, of engagement at Springfield, Mo.

SAINT LOUIS, MO., *January* 8, 1863.

Rebels came to outskirts of Springfield at 1 o'clock, and immediately began shelling the town with two cannon. Our troops responded from fort. Nothing decisive. Have directed General [E. B.] Brown to hold out as long as possible. At last accounts the Army of the Frontier was moving east, to cover Springfield.

SAML. R. CURTIS,
Major-General.

Maj. Gen. H. W. HALLECK,
General-in-Chief.

SAINT LOUIS, MO., *January* 8, 1863.

Fight closed at dark. We hold all the forts. Enemy occupy southwest corner of town. General Brown wounded in shoulder. Marmaduke is said to command, and has a large force. They fight for bread. Our troops behaved well. Our cavalry made a gallant charge. Expect the fight to be resumed in the morning.

SAML. R. CURTIS,
Major-General.

Maj. Gen. H. W. HALLECK,
General-in-Chief.

JANUARY 8, 1863—9 p. m.

General BROWN, *Springfield:*

You and your troops are heroes. I hope God will spare you strength for to-morrow. I expect a desperate effort early in the morning. All the troops, especially the cavalry, should be ready. Herron started with two divisions eastward from Fayetteville on the 6th. He will soon be behind or near the foe. Don't weary in well doing. The eyes of the country are on you. Your general feels for you deeply. God grant you success.

SAML. R. CURTIS,
Major-General.

JANUARY 12, 1863.

General BROWN, *Springfield:*

Dispatch of the 11th, via Sedalia, received. Your gallant and successful defense of Springfield has added to the glory of the 8th January. The troops and people of Springfield who participated in your efforts have given imperishable proof of their loyal devotion to our cause and country, and the State of Missouri will cherish your memory.

SAML. R. CURTIS,
Major-General.

SAINT LOUIS, MO., *January* 12, 1863.

Governor GAMBLE, *Jefferson City, Mo.:*

All right in Springfield. The enemy got nothing but a good thrashing and one gun. It is not true that enrolled militia went over to the enemy. They fought like heroes. Our troops, 700 strong, attacked the enemy at Hartville Saturday, and drove him 5 miles, but were finally obliged to fall back. Rebels will have to move fast to get away from some of my advancing columns. The telegraph is again open to Lebanon, which we still hold all safe. All my trains are safe. General Brown has lost an arm, and I fear his wound is dangerous.

SAML. R. CURTIS,
Major-General.

No. 2.

Reports of Brig. Gen. Egbert B. Brown, U. S. Army, of engagement at Springfield, Mo.

SPRINGFIELD, *January* 8, [1863]—10 a. m.

GENERAL: The enemy's advance is on James, 7 miles from here, on the Ozark road. I have our iron 6 and 12 pounder guns and howitzers, which I mounted last night, in addition to two brass 6-pounders at Fort No. 1. A lieutenant of artillery and some enlisted men have been put in charge of them. The convalescents in hospitals, employés of quartermaster, commissary, and ordnance, and citizens of all ages are being armed. The militia are coming in, and by 12 o'clock I shall have 2,000 men in arms. The brick buildings are being pierced for musketry, and I shall have the wooden ones, if attacked. Fifty thousand rations have been removed to the forts. The trains from the west arrived in the night, and those coming from the east have been sent back to Lebanon. I shall fight as long as I can, in hopes re-enforcements will reach me in time to save the stores. I give you all my plans, as I have no doubt the enemy is in force, and will attack me.

E. B. BROWN.

[Maj. Gen. SAMUEL R. CURTIS.]

SPRINGFIELD, MO., *January* 8, 1863.

GENERAL: Our fight has been confined to skirmishing on the open ground south of the town, and cannonading from one of the forts at long range. I have thought best to await the attack until the last moment, as the demonstration looks like a feint, while the real attack is reserved for another point. The enemy have not shown over 500 infantry, two pieces of artillery, and about 1,000 mounted men. Our men are behaving well.

E. B. BROWN,
Brigadier-General.

Maj. Gen. SAMUEL R. CURTIS,
Commanding Department of the Missouri.

SPRINGFIELD, MO., *January* 8, 1863—3 p. m.

The enemy are crowding the fighting, but my men are behaving well. Rapid musketry firing in the bush close to the town, on the south. I am holding the strong positions, and as night is closing, the enemy must fight me as I want to, or not to-night. They are fighting for bread.

E. B. BROWN,
Brigadier-General.

Maj. Gen. SAMUEL R. CURTIS,
Commanding Department of the Missouri.

SPRINGFIELD, MO., *January* 8, 1863—11.50 p. m.

GENERAL: The firing at this post has just ceased. The attack was made at 10.10 this morning. The fight lasted thirteen hours, under the command of General Marmaduke, C. S. Army, with 5,000 picked mounted infantry and two pieces rifled field artillery, drawn by ten horses each.

The expedition was fitted in this manner on the Arkansas River for the special service of the capture of Springfield, with its forts and large depots of stores. They moved with great rapidity, marching the last 50 miles in twenty-four hours, skirmishing with my scouting parties almost the entire distance. He moved right up, and immediately commenced the fight by cannonading the town without having given a moment's time to move the sick and the helpless women and children. Our artillery consisted of two old iron 12-pounder howitzers, one iron 6-pounder gun (rudely mounted, one of them on old wagon wheels and without the ordinary equipments for artillery, hand-spikes and wedges having to take the place of elevating screws), and two 6-pounder brass guns at Fort No. 1. The balance of our force consisted of the following-named commands and detachments of commands: Third Missouri State Militia Cavalry, commanded by Col. W. King (453); Fourth Missouri State Militia Cavalry, commanded by Col. George H. Hall (289); Eighteenth Iowa Volunteer Infantry, commanded by Lieut. Col. Thomas Z. Cook (378); Second Battalion Fourteenth Missouri State Militia Cavalry, commanded by Lieut. Col. John Pound (223); Seventy-fourth Regiment Enrolled Missouri Militia, commanded by Capt. Green B. Phillips; 48 convalescents, organized by Dr. S. H. Melcher, and stragglers commanded by Col. B. Crabb and Captain McAfee (447). Total force, 2,099.

General, these troops acted like heroes. I am too weak from the loss of blood to dictate more.

Very respectfully, your obedient servant,

E. B. BROWN,
Brigadier-General.

Maj. Gen. SAMUEL R. CURTIS,
Commanding Department of the Missouri.

I will add to the general's dispatch that he was treacherously shot from a secesh residence, while leading a charge of his body guard when the day seemed to be lost.

JAS. H. STEGER,
Assistant Adjutant-General.

***Return of Casualties in the Union forces engaged at Springfield, Mo., January* 8, 1863.**

[Compiled from nominal lists of casualties, returns, &c.]

Command.	Killed.		Wounded.		Captured or missing.		Aggregate.
	Officers.	Enlisted men.	Officers.	Enlisted men.	Officers.	Enlisted men.	
General staff			1				1
18th Iowa Infantry		5	4	42		1	52
3d Missouri State Militia Cavalry		1		4			5
4th Missouri State Militia Cavalry		1		10			11
14th Missouri State Militia Cavalry		3	1	15		3	22
74th Missouri Enrolled Militia		2	4	46		1	53
"Quinine Brigade" *		2	1	13			16
Citizen Volunteers				5			5
Total		14	11	135		5	165

* A force (so styled) composed of convalescents from the hospitals, and representing various regiments.

No. 3.

Report of Brig. Gen. Colly B. Holland, Missouri Militia, of engagement at Springfield, Mo.

HDQRS. FOURTH DIST., ENROLLED MISSOURI MILITIA,
Springfield, January 11, 1863.

COLONEL: I have the honor to submit the following report:

On the evening of the 7th instant, Brig. Gen. E. B. Brown, commanding Southwestern District of Missouri, received intelligence from a scouting party, composed of detachments of the Fourteenth Missouri State Militia and Seventy-third Regiment Enrolled Missouri Militia, under command of Captain [M.] Burch, that a large force of the enemy, said to be 6,000 strong, under command of General Marmaduke, were moving on Lawrence's Mill, Taney County, from Dubuque, Ark., with the intention of attacking this place, to capture the depot of arms and stores, and to destroy all communication with the Army of the Frontier and Saint Louis.

Immediately orders were dispatched by me to Colonel [J. W.] Johnson, Twenty-sixth Regiment; Colonel [Henry] Sheppard, Seventy-second Regiment; Colonel [Marcus] Boyd, Seventy-fourth Regiment Enrolled Missouri Militia, to call in all their furloughed men and concentrate them immediately at this post; also to detached companies in Dade and Lawrence Counties.

In the course of the night information was received confirming the report of the enemy's advance. At daylight on the 8th, the troops stationed at Ozark arrived, reporting the enemy had arrived and burned their post, and by 10 a. m. our pickets were attacked, and he appeared on the edge of the prairie southeast of town.

The enemy at once planted his battery and commenced firing upon the town and Fort No. 4, commanding the approach from the south; while the cavalry, consisting of detachments of the Third, Fourth, and Fourteenth Missouri State Militia, were formed on the left of the fort, and charged on the enemy's right.

General Brown formed his line of battle, with detachments of cavalry on the left, southeast of town, a detachment of the Eighteenth Iowa Infantry on their right, Fort No. 4, mounting two guns, garrisoned with Company C, Colonel Boyd's Seventy-fourth Regiment Enrolled Missouri Militia, Captain [G. B.] Phillips, and convalescent soldiers, commanded by Lieutenant [J.] Hoffman, of the First Missouri Artillery, connected with the Army of the Frontier, and a brick college, inclosed on three sides with palisades, used for a military prison, being the center; Colonel Sheppard's regiment Enrolled Missouri Militia Infantry to the right of the college, flanked on his right by detachments of cavalry, with Fort No. 1 about one-half mile to the rear, being the extreme right, which was garrisoned by the Eighteenth Iowa and citizens.

The skirmishing with cavalry on our left, with artillery firing, continued with but trifling loss until 2 p. m., when the enemy extended his left, and advanced his right and whole line toward Fort No. 4. After some sharp fighting, he was repulsed from the fort, but succeeded in capturing one piece of artillery, which, in charge of a small detachment of the Eighteenth Iowa, was advanced too far to the front, the horses being killed and the men compelled to retire with heavy loss. Upon the repulse from Fort No. 4, the enemy combined his attack upon our right wing, composed of Colonel Sheppard's regiment, when the hardest and most decisive fighting of the day took place. This regiment maintained its ground for more than an hour against overwhelming numbers of the enemy's whole infantry, assisted by three pieces of artillery. The two guns from Fort No. 4 played upon the enemy during the latter part of the time with considerable effect.

Colonel Sheppard was compelled to fall back in the direction of Fort No. 1, taking advantage of the scattered houses to continue the fight as they retired. After falling back some 300 yards, they were rallied, and made a spirited charge upon the enemy, driving them back south of the Fayetteville road, being assisted on their left by a detachment of Iowa troops, under Col. B. Crabb.

The enemy succeeded in gaining possession of the college building, a strong position, enabling their sharpshooters to check our farther advance until night closed the contest.

Late in the day, Maj. A. C. Graves, of my staff, brigade commissary, who was acting as aide-de-camp, was mortally wounded, shot by a musket ball in left breast; Lieut. D. J. McCrosky, Company A, Seventy-second Regiment Enrolled Missouri Militia, killed; Maj. John Hornbeak wounded in arm; Lieut. W. F. Lane, Company E, Seventy-second Regiment, leg broken; Sergeants Burling and Campbell killed, and Sergeant Rainey mortally wounded.

Annexed in hand is a statement of killed, wounded, and missing of my command.*

I take pleasure in reporting the valuable aid afforded me by members of my staff on the field, Majors Sheppard, Bishop, Graves, and Clarke; also volunteer aide, Lieutenant Matthews, of Eighth Missouri Cavalry Volunteers.

I am proud to report the bravery of my command, being raw troops, who have been greatly maligned by enemies of the Union and some politicians of the State, and can assure the Commander-in-Chief of their readiness to defend the Constitution and support the Government of the United States and this State, not only with words, but by the sacrifice of their lives, as they have so abundantly proved by their conduct on the now still more memorable day—the 8th of January.

Very respectfully, your obedient servant,

C. B. HOLLAND,

Brig. Gen., Comdg. Fourth Dist., Enrolled Missouri Militia.

Col. WILLIAM D. WOOD,

Acting Adjutant-General, Missouri.

No. 4.

Report of Col. Benjamin Crabb, Nineteenth Iowa Infantry, of engagement at Springfield, Mo.

HEADQUARTERS SOUTHWESTERN DISTRICT OF MISSOURI,
Springfield, Mo., January 10, 1863.

GENERAL: Owing to the illness of General Brown, and by his request, I have the honor to submit the following report of an engagement at this place, on the 8th instant, between the Federal forces, commanded by Brigadier-General Brown, and a rebel force, under the command of General Marmaduke:

On Wednesday, the 7th instant, about 3 p. m., General Brown received the first information that the enemy, estimated from 4,000 to 6,000 strong, had forced our troops to abandon Lawrence's Mill; that

---

* See revised statement, p. 181.

they had burned the mill and block-house there, and were rapidly approaching this place by the way of Ozark.

Not having a force sufficient at that place to contend with the enemy, they were ordered to fall back on this place, with instructions to destroy what Government property they could not carry with them, which order was promptly executed.

The enemy entered Ozark a few minutes after our forces had evacuated it. They destroyed the block-house, and then continued their march on this place. Messengers were dispatched to the various stations around Springfield to send in re-enforcements, and the Enrolled Missouri Militia was ordered into service.

The night of the 7th was spent in making preparations to meet the enemy. Under the supervision of Lieutenant [J.] Hoffman, of Backof's First Missouri Light Artillery, two 12-pounder iron howitzers and one 6-pounder piece were mounted on wheels, as temporary carriages, taken to the blacksmith shop, repaired, and rolled into the fort, No. 4, by daylight of the 8th instant.

Dr. S. H. Melcher mustered some 300 convalescents from the various hospitals, who were armed and equipped; also near 100 soldiers, who had recently been discharged from the same, under command of Captain McAfee, were armed, and many loyal citizens turned out willingly, and were armed, to fight in the defense of their homes.

At an early hour on the morning of the 8th, about 200 or 300 of the Enrolled Missouri Militia reported for duty. Scouting parties were sent to the south and southeast, for the purpose of ascertaining the whereabouts of the enemy and report their movements. At 10 a. m. of the 8th, the scouts and pickets on the south of the town were fired upon, and driven in by the advance of the enemy. They were soon discovered, some 2 or 3 miles off, formed in line of battle, and advancing slowly across the prairie from the direction of Ozark. About one-half of their command was dismounted, acted as infantry, supporting a battery of some three pieces of artillery (one piece rifled), which formed their center, while their right and left wings were formed of heavy bodies of cavalry.

In this manner, with skirmishers and sharpshooters thrown forward, they advanced steadily and slowly, occasionally halting and firing shot from their rifled piece, apparently trying the range and feeling their way. The cavalry, under the command of Colonel [W.] King, Third Missouri State Militia, and Colonel [G. H.] Hall, Fourth Missouri State Militia, were ordered forward to meet the advancing foe. By order, several houses were burned south of the fort, to prevent the enemy from occupying them, and that the artillerymen and riflemen in the fort could have an unobstructed view of their approach. As the enemy continued to advance, the firing became more frequent. Our artillery opened fire upon them as soon as they came within range of our guns. Our cavalry gradually retired within supporting distance of the fort. The artillery and riflemen in the fort drove back the enemy's sharpshooters. The firing gradually increased until about 1 p. m., when the forces on both sides were fiercely engaged.

Colonel King was ordered to charge with his regiment the enemy's right. He drove them back, when they turned their artillery and sharpshooters upon him. At this time Colonel Hall, with the Fourth Missouri State Militia Cavalry, by order, moved forward and engaged their center, fighting with coolness and bravery, entitling them to high honor.

The cavalry being exposed in the open field to the fire of the enemy's artillery and infantry, and fearful they would be cut to pieces, they were ordered to retire under protection of the fort, which order was executed promptly and in good order, bringing with them their wounded. The enemy threw forward a regiment of cavalry on our left, which was promptly checked by the Second Battalion Fourteenth Missouri State Militia Cavalry, under command of Lieutenant-Colonel Pound. Meantime the enemy were busy with their artillery throwing shot and shell at the fort and into the houses occupied by our troops. Our artillery, before mentioned, under command of Lieutenant Hoffman, and one field piece, under command of Captain Landis, Eighteenth Iowa Infantry, were driving back the enemy's center; but the firing from the guns inside the fort, though well aimed, was not sufficiently rapid, owing to their being manned by volunteers, with only 5 artillery soldiers at the three pieces.

The enemy about 2 p. m. massed their forces and advanced on our center and right. Captain [J. A.] Landis, with his piece of artillery, was ordered to advance to the front and right of the fort, which order he promptly executed. He was supported by parts of three companies of the Eighteenth Iowa, under their respective commanders, Captains [W. R.] Blue, [J.] Van Meter, and [W.] Stonaker. This piece of artillery, owing to some mistake in the delivery of the order, was placed in a very exposed position. The enemy, perceiving this, made a desperate charge upon it with overwhelming numbers, killing the horses and driving back the support; captured it after a hard and bloody contest. Captains Blue and Van Meter fell, mortally wounded, and Captain Landis and many of their brave comrades fell, severely wounded, while some were killed.

It was now between 2 and 3 p. m. The enemy had captured one piece of artillery; at the same time had taken possession of an unfinished stockade fort that had been used as a prison, and were pressing hard on our center and right. The "Quinine Brigade," which was placed under my command, and which up to this time was stationed in various brick buildings in and around the center of town, was ordered to move to the front and attack the enemy. I had the honor to lead them in person, assisted by Lieutenants [R.] Root, of the Nineteenth Iowa; [S. A.] Wilson, Eighteenth Iowa, and [W. F.] Bodenhammer, Twenty-fourth Missouri Volunteers.

We advanced to the front and west of the fort, and took a position behind a fence and about 50 to 75 yards from the rebels, who were likewise posted behind fences and in and around a house to our front. After fighting for nearly one hour, the enemy gave way and fled precipitately from this part of the field.

In the mean time they were making strong efforts to turn our right, and, after being driven from our center, threw their main force forward for that purpose, when they were met by the Seventy-second Regiment Enrolled Missouri Militia, under the command of Colonel Sheppard; the "Quinine Brigade," under the command of Lieutenants Root, Wilson, and Bodenhammer and Captain [C. B.] McAfee, who repulsed them. There were also engaged at this time the Third and Fourth Missouri State Militia Cavalry and the Second Battalion Fourteenth Missouri State Militia, and five companies of the Eighteenth Iowa, two of which had recently come to our support, under the command of Captain [W. H.] Evans. The enemy had gained possession of several houses, and were pouring into our ranks volley after volley of musketry while they were endeavoring to dislodge them. The cause became desperate; the enemy were pressing hard upon our brave men, and they were yielding before the overwhelming numbers brought against them, when General Brown and staff rode forward to encourage them, when he was treacherously shot from a house by some hidden foe, and fell from his horse. He immediately remounted, but was unable to remain in his saddle, and was carried off the field.

This was about 4 p. m., when I received an order from the general to take command, which I immediately complied with. The fighting at this time was hard. It was one continual roar of musketry and artillery. The enemy had advanced to a point beyond the range of the small-arms of the fort; but the artillery continued to pour a heavy fire of shot and shell into their midst, which would cause them to falter, but they would again and again rally. The stockade fort, which they had previously taken possession of, gave them great protection, and in and around which they would mass their forces, and from which they would make their charges. They would drive our men, and then in turn be driven back.

A little after 5 o'clock they made the most desperate effort that they had made during the day to drive back our forces by throwing their whole force upon our center and right wing, but mainly upon the center. A part of the Seventy-second Enrolled Missouri Militia, Fourth Missouri State Militia Cavalry (dismounted), the Second Battalion Fourteenth Missouri State Militia Cavalry (dismounted), part of five companies of the Eighteenth Iowa Infantry, and the "Quinine Brigade," amounting, in all, to about 800 men, had to oppose the major part of the rebel army, amounting to three or four times their own number; but our troops met them promptly, and fought them most gallantly for nearly one-half hour, when a part of our lines began to give back.

At this critical time, an officer commanding a company in the Second Battalion Fourteenth Missouri State Militia, ordered his men to horse (as I was afterward informed), and the whole battalion came running in great confusion to the rear, and took to horse. I tried in vain to rally them; they seemed panic-stricken. This caused a partial giving way among the other troops. I had no difficulty in rallying them, and they went again into the fight.

It was now near dark, and the enemy were making an additional demonstration on our left. By this time Lieutenant-Colonel Pound, commanding, had succeeded in reforming the Second Battalion Fourteenth Missouri State Militia. I ordered him to advance on the enemy's right, which order he promptly executed. The enemy fired but a few rounds, and again retired, leaving us in full possession of this part of the field.

Five additional companies of the Eighteenth Iowa, under the command of Lieut. Col. Thomas Z. Cook, came to the rescue, whooping and cheering, which gave fresh courage to our brave men, who immediately drove the enemy before them and back into the stockade fort. Colonel Cook's troops arrived too late to take an active part in the engagement. Darkness coming on, the firing gradually ceased, after which all was quiet, save an occasional firing from the artillery. The enemy, under cover of the darkness, withdrew from the field, carrying away part of their dead and wounded. I expected them to renew the attack on the following morning.

On the morning of the 9th, they appeared in full force to the east, and about 1 mile from town. Preparations were made to receive them. A cavalry force was sent forward to engage them and check their advance; but they declined another engagement and retired in haste. We did not have a sufficient force to pursue them. We did not have at any one time during the day more than 900 to 1,000 men engaged. The enemy had some 4,000 men, under the command of General Marmaduke, [Colonels] Shelby, Gordon, Gilkey, Elliott, MacDonald, and others, with three pieces of artillery, who came with the full expectation of an easy conquest. They had invited their friends in the country to come and bring their wagons, promising them all the booty they could carry; but, thanks to a kind Providence, brave hearts, and strong arms, they were most signally defeated in their designs of plunder.

The Seventy-second Regiment, Enrolled Missouri Militia, under the command of Col. Henry Sheppard, fought well and faithfully during the entire contest. Companies A, C, F, G, and H, of the Eighteenth Iowa, numbering 156 men, fought as Iowa boys know how to fight. Their heavy loss and bloody record is proof of their valor. The "Quinine Brigade," made up of men from Iowa, Illinois, Wisconsin, and other States, fought like heroes, Spartans, and veterans, as their respective commanders report. All the troops, with but few exceptions, did their duty.

I cannot forbear to say that to the vigilance of General Brown, his promptness in preparing to meet the enemy, and to his coolness, courage, and personal supervision of the troops in battle, while under his command, we are in a great measure indebted for our success. He has by his conduct endeared himself to those under his command.

Lieut. Richard Root, Company K, Nineteenth Iowa, who arrived during the fight; Lieut. S. A. Wilson, Company I, Eighteenth Iowa; Captain McAfee and Lieutenant Bodenhammer, who were in command of the "Quinine Brigade;" Capt. W. H. Evans, of Company F, Eighteenth Iowa; Dr. Whitney, of the Fourth Missouri State Militia Cavalry, who took a gun and fought, and the Rev. Mr. Wynes, post chaplain, who, in the face of the enemy, assisted in removing the wounded from the battle-field, deserve great praise for their gallant conduct during the engagement.

I am under many obligations to Major Steger and Lieutenants Campion and Blodgett, members of General Brown's staff, for the efficient service they rendered me. There are many other officers and men deserving of honorable mention.

We lost 14 killed, 144 wounded, and 4 missing, making a total of killed, wounded, and missing of 162.* The enemy's loss cannot be definitely ascertained. Their own estimates of their losses range from 200 to 300 killed and wounded. Among their slain is a major.

We captured several prisoners, and among them are 2 commissioned officers. We buried a part of their dead, and have some 60 to 80 of their wounded to take care of.

I send herewith attached a detailed report of the killed, &c.

I have the honor to remain, your most obedient servant,

B. CRABB,
Colonel, Commanding.

Maj. Gen. SAMUEL R. CURTIS,
Commanding Department of the Missouri.

No. 5.

Reports of Brig. Gen. Fitz Henry Warren, U. S. Army, of engagement at Hartville, Mo.

HEADQUARTERS,
Houston, Mo., January 12, 1863—5 a. m.

My force of 1,000 men attacked Marmaduke's column, 1,500 strong, 7 miles west of Hartville, toward Springfield (2 a. m., January 11). The

---

* But see revised statement, p. 181.

enemy were repulsed, and retreated upon Hartville, where the rebels were re-enforced by Porter, Burbridge, and Greene, 3,500 strong, with five pieces of artillery. They had a most obstinate fight, until sunset, when our force fell back toward Lebanon in perfect order. Our losses are heavy, but the enemy's much greater. Captain [G. D.] Bradway, of Company E, Third Missouri Cavalry, is the only officer reported killed. I move toward Hartville at 6 o'clock this morning, with 500 men and two pieces of artillery, although barely able to keep my saddle. The infantry in wagons. Our artillery, under Lieutenant [William] Waldschmidt, did fine execution, while the enemy's was badly served, and did us but little damage. Colonel Merrill, of the Twenty-first Iowa, was wounded. I can give no further particulars of casualties.

FITZ HENRY WARREN,
Brigadier-General.

Maj. Gen. SAMUEL R. CURTIS,
Saint Louis, Mo.

HEADQUARTERS,
Houston, Mo., January 14, 1863.

The battle at Hartville is developed into a brilliant victory. Lieutenant-Colonel [C. W.] Dunlap, with a portion of the Twenty-first Iowa, held the field two hours after the enemy retreated, and Lieutenant [F.] Dale, of same regiment, with 17 men, bivouacked on the fighting-ground, and received the flags of truce in the morning. [J. C.] Porter is reported dead of his wounds. Colonels Hinkle [?] and [G. W.] Thompson, Major [George R.] Kirtley, Captain [C. M.] Turpin, and 2 lieutenants are killed, and Captain [L. J.] Crocker and 2 other captains wounded. We captured 2 surgeons, 1 lieutenant, and 38 privates. Lieutenant-Colonel Dunlap and Lieutenant [J. H.] Alexander, of the Twenty-first Iowa, are wounded, in addition to those already reported. Colonel [S.] Merrill and command are within 10 miles of camp. The whole force will be concentrated to-day.

General Marmaduke sends this message by a citizen prisoner: "Tell General Warren his men fought like tigers"—a generous tribute to as brave soldiers as ever bore muskets.

FITZ HENRY WARREN,
Brigadier-General.

Maj. Gen. SAMUEL R. CURTIS,
Saint Louis, Mo.

HEADQUARTERS,
Houston, Mo., January 14, 1863.

All information by scouting parties sent out confirms me in the opinion expressed yesterday, that the enemy are in rapid retreat toward Arkansas. The force at Hartville consisted of three brigades, General Marmaduke in command, with from 4,000 to 5,000 men. Their loss in killed, wounded, and prisoners will not fall below 250 or 300, including Brig. Gen. [Colonel] Emmett MacDonald killed, and Porter badly wounded. The conduct of our officers and men was admirable.

FITZ HENRY WARREN,
Brigadier-General.

Maj. Gen. SAMUEL R. CURTIS,
Saint Louis, Mo.

HEADQUARTERS,
Houston, Mo., January 16, 1863.

COLONEL: I have the honor to report the operations of my force against the combined troops of General Marmaduke and [Colonel] MacDonald and Colonel Porter.

Immediately on the receipt of a copy of the telegram from Brigadier-General Brown, commanding at Springfield, January 9, informing Major-General Curtis of the advance of a column of 6,000 rebels toward Springfield, I ordered Colonel [S.] Merrill, of the Twenty-first Iowa, senior officer, to move with 700 men—infantry, cavalry, and one section of artillery—by a forced march to Springfield, to report to the commanding officer there. My own health incapacitated me from the fatigue of the expedition. For greater speed and progress, I sent with them a heavy transportation train for use of the infantry.

They reached Hartville at 6 a. m. Saturday, and learned that Porter's column had passed through, taking the Marshfield road. Here Colonel Merrill was re-enforced by 180 men of the Third Iowa and Third Missouri Cavalry, under command of Captain [T. G.] Black, Third Missouri Cavalry, sent by me to overtake and join them. The command pushed on some miles toward Springfield, and halted for supper and rest on Wood's Fork.

No indications of the enemy were observed until reveille was sounded at 2 o'clock Sunday morning, when our scouts reported the advance of a heavy column in the direction of Springfield. Our position was a most unfavorable one, being an open space on the margin of the river, with high swells of ground, covered with timber and brush, surrounding. The command was thrown into line of battle, and skirmishers sent out to dispute the advance.

Brisk firing was kept up for an hour, during which Captain [G. D.] Bradway, Company E, Third Missouri Cavalry, was killed, when the enemy fell back in a southerly direction. This was a most favorable movement for us. Had they made a stand with their combined forces, they would have completely enveloped the command and cut them to pieces.

Sending out a pursuing force of cavalry, Colonel [S.] Merrill resumed his march on the Hartville road, and soon discovered that the rebel force was swinging round and moving on Hartville by the old Springfield road. The cavalry were promptly ordered to a trot and the artillery thrown to the front, while the infantry came up on double-quick in gallant style. Colonel Merrill's dispositions were made with great judgment and coolness. The artillery took position on a favorable elevation west of the court-house; the Ninety-ninth Illinois formed the right, flanked on the left by the Twenty-first Iowa, both in a cover of low brush, while the left, composed of detachments of the Third Iowa and Third Missouri Cavalry, dismounted, extended in an attenuated line on the Lebanon road, also screened by a sparse undergrowth.

Our artillery opened fire at 11 o'clock. The position of their troops was, 1,000 thrown out $3\frac{1}{2}$ miles on the Houston road; 1,000 held the lower approach from Springfield; 1,000 rested on the Gasconade, south of town, covered by a high bluff, while 2,500 to 3,000 were in the open field in front of our lines, and occupying the court-house and the dwellings of the town. Their artillery (five pieces) was in battery on a high bluff east of town, and to occupy it they used a road cut out by my order for the same purpose during my former occupancy of Hartville.

The officers in command were General Marmaduke and [Colonel] Mac

Donald, and Colonels Porter, Thompson, Burbridge, Shelby, Hinkle [?], Jeffers, and Campbell.

The battle opened after the fire of artillery by a charge of Jeffers' cavalry, 700 strong, on our whole line. The infantry, lying flat, held themselves with great coolness until the line was in easy range, when they fired with great accuracy and threw the whole force into utter confusion.

From this time until 4.30 o'clock the firing was incessant; but smaller bodies of men were brought out, and although at times both flanks and the center were heavily pressed, no large columns were moved up. Our men held their cover and did fine execution, while the artillery shelled the enemy from the court and other houses.

At this time, 3 p. m., had we had a reserve of 500 men we could have broken their line and compelled their retreat in disorder; but every man was required to hold our only avenue of retreat, the Lebanon road, where our communication was constantly threatened. The enemy commenced falling back, as I am informed by Lieutenant [J. D.] Brown, Third Iowa Cavalry (taken prisoner while reconnoitering at Wood's Fork during the first fight), at 3 o'clock, and the retreat became general at twilight.

In the mean time, our artillery ammunition being nearly spent, Colonel Merrill, ignorant of their movement, ordered the detachments to fall back on the Lebanon road, which they did in perfect order with their whole transportation, losing not even a musket or a cartridge-box.

Our loss, as by statement appended herewith, is 7 killed, 64 wounded, 5 prisoners, and 2 missing. Theirs is larger in men and officers. From subsequent details, I am satisfied it will exceed 300 in killed and wounded, besides 2 lieutenants and 27 privates prisoners. Among the killed, whose bodies were recognized at Hartville, are Brig. Gen. [Colonel] Emmett MacDonald, Colonels Thompson and Hinkle [?], Major Kirtley, Captain Turpin, and two lieutenants (names not known), Colonel Porter, mortally wounded (since dead), Captain Crocker, well known in Western Missouri, and two other captains severely wounded. One piece of their artillery was dismounted and abandoned. They retreated toward Houston, but on Monday changed their direction and moved rapidly south to the North Fork of White River, at the mouth of Indian Creek, where they paroled and released Lieutenant Brown and other prisoners.

General Marmaduke several times on the march expressed his wonder at the bravery of our troops, repeating, "Why, lieutenant, your boys fought like devils!" I cannot sufficiently express my admiration of their conduct. The Twenty-first Iowa and Ninety-ninth Illinois were never before under fire, yet not a single man or officer flinched. Nothing could have been finer than their steadiness and discipline. The Third Iowa and Third Missouri Cavalry are equally cool and determined, but they have before seen dangerous service. Where all were so brave, I am embarrassed to distribute commendation. To Colonel Merrill, in command of the force, I am under high obligations for his prudent firmness and good disposition. Lieutenant-Colonel Dunlap, Twenty-first Iowa, was conspicuous, much exposed, and wounded. He is worthy of high praise. Lieutenant-Colonel [L.] Parke, commanding Ninety-ninth Illinois, and Major [E. A.] Crandall, of the same corps, won honor and did their whole duty. Major [G.] Duffield, commanding the cavalry force, is also to be mentioned in warm terms; but Captain [T. G.] Black, in command of the Third Missouri Cavalry, made himself a most enviable reputation. Thirteen shot-holes in his coat sufficiently indicate where he was—in the hottest of the fire. I respectfully commend him to your attention and that of Governor Gamble, for one of the vacant field commissions in his regiment, which he has so nobly earned. I should be unjust did I omit to name Captain [J. A.] Lennon, of the same regiment, who, at the head of his company, held a most exposed post, and had several narrow escapes from sharpshooters concealed in the brush. But the artillery saved the battle. Lieutenant [W.] Waldschmidt's gunnery was superb and his coolness astonishing. The enemy's Parrott gun got his range, and fired with great precision, compelling him to change the position of his pieces constantly.

A courier reached Houston, giving me the information of the engagement at 3 o'clock Monday morning. I at once moved with 500 men to Hartville, supposing the enemy still in force. Arriving within 7 miles at 4 p. m., my reconnoitering parties brought me intelligence that they were retreating in the direction of Houston. Sending back a courier with orders to Lieutenant-Colonel Caldwell, in command, to hold the place until I could re-enforce him, I countermarched in all haste, through mud and rain, and reached Houston that evening, finding all quiet.

Colonel Merrill's force rejoined me Thursday, and I am now once more concentrated.

Hoping that our conduct will meet the approbation of the general commanding, I am, colonel, very respectfully, your obedient servant,

FITZ HENRY WARREN,
Brigadier-General, Commanding.

Col. N. P. CHIPMAN,
Chief of Staff, Saint Louis, Mo.

[Inclosure.]

Return of Casualties in the engagement at Hartville, Mo., January 11, 1863.

Command.	Killed.	Wounded.	Paroled.	Missing.	Total.
99th Illinois	1	29	......	1	31
3d Iowa Cavalry	......	......	4	1	5
21st Iowa	3	18	1	......	22
3d Missouri Cavalry	3	14	......	......	17
2d Missouri Artillery, Battery L	......	3	......	......	3
Total	7	64	5	2	78

OFFICERS KILLED.—Ninety-ninth Illinois: Lieut. Thomas A. Hubbard, died of wounds. Third Missouri Cavalry: Capt. George D. Bradway.

No. 6.

Report of Lieut. Col. Cornelius W. Dunlap, Twenty-first Iowa Infantry, of engagement at Hartville, Mo.

LEBANON, MO., *January* 22, 1863.

GENERAL: In obedience to your order of to-day, I send you a full report of the battle of Hartville, on the 11th instant:

With 800 men and two pieces of artillery, under Colonel Merrill, we left Houston Friday noon to re-enforce Springfield.

Sunday morning about 4 o'clock we encountered the rebel army, under General Marmaduke, 9 miles beyond Hartville, on the Springfield road.

A brisk fire of artillery and some skirmishing among the cavalry ensued, and continued until about 8 o'clock, when the enemy withdrew, and, as we soon learned, took a circuitous route toward Hartville. Our forces immediately started for the same point. We took 30 or 40 prisoners in this engagement, from whom we learned that Marmaduke had with him something over 5,000 men, having been joined by Porter and Greene since his attack on Springfield.

Both armies arrived at Hartville at the same time (a little before 11 a. m.), and took positions on opposite sides of the town. Our line formed the arc of a circle, close to the place, on the brow of a row of hills, sheltered by underbrush and small trees. The Twenty-first Iowa Infantry occupied the center, and Ninety-ninth Illinois the right, and dismounted Third Iowa Cavalry and Third Missouri Cavalry the left. Our artillery, Lieutenant Waldschmidt commanding, opened on the enemy immediately with shell. When he had fired a few rounds, the rebels commenced replying briskly. In a few moments their cavalry dismounted and charged upon us along our whole line, but, receiving repeated and heavy volleys from our forces, they gave way and fled to the other side of the town, leaving many dead and wounded behind them. Fresh troops came to their aid, and they again charged upon us in force, and were each time handsomely repulsed with great loss on their part. In one instance they charged upon our artillery, in heavy force, with mounted cavalry, but were driven back in confusion by the cross-fire of the Ninety-ninth Illinois and Twenty-first Iowa Infantry. Charges were repeatedly made, and as often repulsed, and a heavy and destructive fire of artillery and musketry maintained until about the middle of the afternoon, our troops having manifestly the best of the fight.

Finding that the town was full of rebel sharpshooters, who were very annoying to us, I sent a request to Colonel Merrill to have the artillery turned upon them. Not being able to find him, I ordered Lieutenant Waldschmidt to shell the town, and clear the court-house and other places of rebels. He immediately turned his pieces upon the town with good effect, but, after firing a few shots, retired from his position. About the same time firing ceased on both my right and left, and, supposing that a strategic movement was going on, I increased the force of my fire, in order to attract the attention of the rebels while the other commands changed their positions. In about half an hour, not hearing anything from our troops, I sent men out to look for them, who soon returned and reported that our forces had all left the field. In what direction they had gone I could not ascertain.

Finding myself deserted and without orders (I had received no orders and seen no commanding officer since I got into position in the forenoon), I determined to hold my position, at least until dark, in order to conceal from the enemy the absence of most of our forces and keep him ignorant of my own weakness. I had only 250 men of the Twenty-first Iowa. I threw squads of men to the right and left, with orders to maintain rapid firing. After this they charged upon our front three times, in one instance coming up in four ranks, and were every time repulsed, thrice at the point of the bayonet. A continued running fire was carried on between the charges.

Half an hour before sundown, much to our satisfaction, the enemy commenced falling back and retreating over the opposite hills in a southerly direction. They were so near that we could distinctly hear the orders of their officers and see every movement. They began to move off rapidly; seeing which I increased my fire, in order, as much as possible, to hurry their retreat. By sundown their whole army was in full retreat, and their rear guard followed, leaving us in full possession of the field. Paroled prisoners report that Marmaduke did not halt a moment from this time until noon of the next day, and then only for a few moments.

My men all acted finely, and were cool and active when they learned that they were left alone in front of a rebel horde of 5,000 men. I remained on the field about three-quarters of an hour, and gathered up what things we could. It was a cold night, and my men had been forty hours with but a few moments' sleep and nothing to eat. Our rations, blankets, and overcoats were with the train, and I sent in pursuit of it, supposing we should find it a few miles from the place. My horse was shot in the early part of the fight, and no horse was left with us by which I could send out a messenger to ascertain the whereabouts of the train.

I found our train and the forces next morning encamped on the Lebanon road. The colonel commanding having gone on with most of the cavalry the night before, I took command of the brigade, and put it in motion for Lebanon, the nearest point then to us.

The rebels sent in a flag of truce the next morning, with a party to take care of their wounded and bury their dead, the number of which I think will amount to 200 killed, among whom are Colonel Emmett MacDonald, Colonel Porter, and other important officers, and about 300 wounded.

The number of our killed and wounded is comparatively small, owing to our sheltered position and the height of the enemy's fire.

Our troops all behaved nobly, and did fine execution while they were left on the field, and were surprised at being withdrawn.

The battle of Hartville began about 10.45 a. m. and lasted until nearly sundown. The firing was continuous and rapid on both sides during the whole time. The last half of the battle was fought by the Twenty-first Iowa alone, and resulted in a signal victory to our arms and in driving Marmaduke with thinned ranks back into Arkansas.

Having with pleasure obeyed your orders to report the particulars of this battle, I remain, general, very respectfully, your obedient servant,

C. W. DUNLAP,

Lieutenant-Colonel, Comdg. Twenty-first Iowa Volunteers.

Major-General CURTIS.

No. 7.

Report of Capt. Milton Burch, Fourteenth Missouri State Militia Cavalry, of skirmish at Fort Lawrence, Beaver Station, Mo.

SPRINGFIELD, *January* 16, 1863.

COLONEL: I submit for your investigation my report of a scout, of which I had the honor, by permission from General Brown, to command. The object of the scout was to destroy a powder-mill situated on Crooked Creek, Carroll County, Arkansas; likewise to break up some parties of guerrillas that were organizing in the vicinity of the powder-mill.

I started from Ozark on the morning of the 4th of January with 100 men, belonging to the Second Battalion Fourteenth Regiment Missouri State Militia, for Dubuque, Marion County, Arkansas, by the way of the Beaver Station, Lawrence's Mill, expecting to get some re-enforcements there. I proceeded with my command within 4 miles of the post, to rest my horses and feed. I then proceeded to the station, after resting and feeding, and requested co-operation of the Enrolled Missouri Militia, through Major [William] Turner, to which he was willing to comply, but, owing to their provisions not coming in, they could not start with me; but the major promised to send all the men he could spare, under the command of Captain Green, after me to catch up with me that night (4th of January), to a point on Big Creek, 6 miles from Dubuque, known as the Widow Fisher's, to which place I proceeded. I there captured 2 rebel prisoners, who gave me information that a rebel force, 6,000 strong, under the command of General Marmaduke, had left Dubuque that morning *en route* for this place. I immediately dispatched a messenger back to the Beaver Station, with instructions for Major Turner to dispatch forthwith to Ozark. I then started with my command back to the Beaver Station, expecting to meet Captain Green with a re-enforcement of Enrolled Missouri Militia from the Beaver Station, but did not. As my guide was not very well acquainted with the country and the roads, I took the main road leading from the Beaver Station, and, Captain Green being well acquainted with the country, took a near road and missed me. I arrived at the Beaver Station about 4 o'clock on the morning of the 6th. I then asked the major if he was in a condition to fall back; he replied that he had no transportation. I then ordered scouts out on different roads to give intimation of the enemy's approach. I dismounted my men for the purpose of resting, as we had not been out of our saddles for twelve hours, and accomplished a march of 60 miles. I then went to take a little rest, and see that the boys had everything in readiness for moving to Ozark, as I was fearful the enemy would reach there before me. I therefore ordered my men into the saddle again, it being now daylight, and we started for Ozark. We had not proceeded far before the enemy's infantry opened upon the picket guard southeast of the station. I then ordered a halt, with the intention of gaining and occupying the block-house; but before we could make the point the enemy was in possession of the block-house and all the ground around the block-house. I then ordered my men to move by the head of column to the right, under a smart fire from the rebels. There was also a detached force of the enemy coming up Big Beaver with the intention of cutting off our retreat. I started for Ozark, leaving the main road and taking a right-hand road. Hearing that a portion of the enemy had gone up Little Beaver with the intention of cutting us off from Ozark, I traveled slowly, using precaution against surprise, and arrived at Ozark about 10 o'clock of the night of the 6th. I then ordered all the baggage to be conveyed across the river on the road to Springfield, which was promptly complied with, and waited for further orders, which orders I received for us to fall back to Springfield.

Respectfully, your most obedient servant,

MILTON BURCH,

Capt., Comdg. Company H, 14th Cavalry, Missouri State Militia.

Colonel CRABB.

No. 8.

Report of Brig. Gen. John S. Marmaduke, C. S. Army, commanding expedition.

HDQRS. FOURTH DIV., FIRST CORPS, TRANS-MISS. DEPT.,
Batesville, Ark., January 18, 1863.

COLONEL: In obedience to instructions from Major-General Hindman, I marched from Lewisburg, Ark., December 31, 1862, via Yellville, Ark., to strike the enemy in rear or flank, with 1,600 men, under Shelby, and 270 men, under MacDonald. Before marching, I telegraphed to Lieutenant-General Holmes if it would not be best to move up the troops under Colonel White, to co-operate in the movement; to which he consented, and the order was given. Colonel [J. C.] Porter, with 600 men, moved forward to this purpose.

En route, in the Boston Mountains, Shelby attacked 60 tories and deserters; killed 12 and captured 27. MacDonald surprised and captured and burned Fort Lawrence, on Beaver Creek, Mo. Of its garrison, killed 10, captured 17, and routed the rest—about 250; captured 200 horses, 300 stand of arms, 10 wagons, and a quantity of quartermaster and commissary stores. Shelby captured and burned the fort at Ozark. The garrison fled. With Shelby and MacDonald, I attacked Springfield, Mo., and, after eight hours' hard fighting, driving the Yankees before me and into their strongholds, I captured one piece of artillery (6-pounder), a stockade fort, a large part of the town, which the Yankees burned as they retired. At dark the fighting ceased; the greater part of the town, the fort, and many of the dead and wounded Federals in my possession. The Federal force there was 4,200. My loss was 20 killed and 80 wounded. Yankee loss much greater. I did not deem it best to renew the attack, and the next day marched toward Rolla. The Federals scattered and fled before me. I burned the forts at Sand Spring and Marshfield. After passing Marshfield, I formed a junction with Porter, who had burned the forts at Hartville and Hazlewood. All the forts burned were well-built works, generally large block-houses, with stockade and good earthworks around; so strong that 100 brave men, well armed, could defy 1,000 infantry or cavalry. After joining Porter, I marched southeasterly, making my way toward Arkansas. At Hartville I met, fought, and drove in the direction of Lebanon 1,500 infantry and 500 cavalry, under General Merrill. The battle was desperate. My loss was 15 killed and 70 wounded. Of the former, was the brave MacDonald, Lieutenant-Colonel Wimer, Major Kirtley, and other brave officers and men. The Federal loss was also heavy. The enemy sent in a flag to bury their dead. At this place I captured a caisson with ammunition, a number of small-arms, and about 150 great-coats, which the Yankees left as they ran off.

I continued my march, and reached here to-day. Will to-morrow morning commence crossing White River at this place and 12 miles below. Both men and horses are worn out, and need rest. A detailed report of the expedition I will forward at the earliest moment.

Respectfully, &c.

J. S. MARMADUKE,
Brigadier-General, Commanding.

Col. R. C. NEWTON.

HDQRS. FOURTH DIV., TRANS-MISSISSIPPI DEPARTMENT,
Camp near Batesville, Ark., February 1, 1863.

SIR: I have the honor to submit the following report of the expedition under my command into Missouri, made in obedience to General Hindman's order to move, if possible, rapidly, and strike the enemy in rear or flank, in order to withdraw the heavy masses (infantry, cavalry, and artillery), under Blunt, then moving toward the Arkansas River, back into Missouri:

Immediately upon the receipt by telegraph of the order, I proceeded to put my command in readiness to march. To execute the order, I determined at least to threaten Springfield, and operate in the country between there and Rolla, and create the impression that the force was sufficiently large to take and hold the country.

On the morning of December 31, 1862, at daylight, Col. J. O. Shelby, with his Missouri brigade, about 1,600 effective men, some without horses; Col. J. C. Monroe, commanding Carroll's Arkansas brigade, about 500 effective men, and Col. Emmett MacDonald, with his Missouri battalion, about 270 effective men, marched from camp near Lewisburg, the two latter with orders to march via Clinton to Yellville. Shelby, by a route more westerly to same point, moved on different route, on account of scarcity of forage.

On the morning of December 31, after the troops were on the march, I received orders to detach Carroll's brigade from the expedition and order it to operate against the enemy then at Van Buren Creek. The order was obeyed. Previous to the moving of this column, I had ordered (by consent of Lieutenant-General Holmes) Col. J. C. Porter to take command of White's Missouri cavalry brigade, at Pocahontas, and to march with his entire effective force north and west, and make junction with the troops from Lewisburg at Hartville, January 9, 1863. The distance from Lewisburg to Hartville was about 200 miles; from Pocahontas to Hartville about 140 miles; both routes difficult, mountainous, and barren. Colonel Porter with his brigade, about 700 effective men, marched from Pocahontas January 2, 1863. Shelby, *en route* to Yellville, in the Boston Mountains, surprised about 100 jayhawkers (tories and deserters), killed a large number, and captured 27. The vigor with which his troops attacked and pursued those scoundrels terrified them, and broke up, for a time at least, the lawless bands in this part of the mountains. Shelby and MacDonald reached Yellville January 4, 1863. From Yellville this column moved northward, crossing (fording) White River at Dubuque.

On the night of January 6, MacDonald with his men marched to destroy Fort Lawrence, on Beaver Creek, Mo., some 17 miles to the right of my line of march. At daylight, MacDonald stormed the work; 300 of the enemy abandoned the fort and fled in wild fright and disorder. A number of them were killed and some 20 taken prisoners and paroled. The fort, arms, ammunition, wagons, mules, horses, quartermaster's and commissary stores were destroyed, save the little which MacDonald in his forced marches could carry with him.

On the evening of January 6, from scouts and other sources, I learned that Springfield, with its rich army stores, was weakly garrisoned, though strongly fortified, and, if surprised, I thought it could be captured. I determined to attack it. Dispatched to Colonel Porter, by different couriers, my plans, and ordered him to move to my support as rapidly as possible; Shelby to move forward in the direction of Springfield, through Ozark, a fortified town, garrisoned by 400 militia; MacDonald by way of Fort Lawrence to Springfield. The courier to Porter failed to meet him till January 10, too late. Shelby, destroying the fort and stores at Ozark, the enemy fleeing before him, and arriving on the 8th of January, at early dawn, in front of Springfield, rapidly and judiciously made preparation for the attack, dismounting the greater part of his brigade to fight as infantry. The delay necessary to reconnoiter, and for the arrival of MacDonald, who had made the detour (some 35 miles) via Fort Lawrence, deferred the engagement till 10 a. m. Shelby's brigade, on the right in line of battle, stretched from the Rolla to the main Ozark road; MacDonald's command, except one company dis mounted, on Shelby's left. When the struggle began, horse by horse, the advance of the whole line was steady and determined. MacDonald, with his brave little command, made a desperate and successful charge upon the enemy's right. Just then Shelby, seizing the opportune moment, vigorously supported MacDonald (sorely pressed), and the entire line, with a wild shout, rushed to the terrible charge at the double-quick, driving before them the frightened foe, who fled, abandoning all stores, stockade, fort, and a piece of artillery. This gallant charge was not, however, without the sad loss of a number of brave men. During the day's engagement, as the enemy retired, they burned much of Springfield. Night closed upon the combatants, and stopped the carnage.

During the night of the 8th, Maj. R. H. Smith, division quartermaster, a gallant officer, volunteered to take a few picked men and bear orders to Porter to re-enforce me. He was unable to find him.

On the morning of the 9th, I deemed it best not to renew the attack, for the reason that the enemy had been re-enforced; that my troops, from forced marches, sleepless nights, and the hard-fought battle of the 8th, were not in condition for another desperate struggle. I addressed a letter, under flag of truce, to General Brown, commanding at Springfield, stating that my wounded were left in charge of competent surgeons and attendants, and asking from him a proper treatment to all. A little after sunrise the column moved eastward on the Rolla road. Shelby camped at Sand Spring, a fortified post, which he burned; MacDonald at Marshfield, a fortified town; the forts and stores he destroyed. The Federals (militia) fled from both places toward Rolla.

January 10, a junction was made with Porter near Marshfield, who had captured the militia (some 50) and destroyed the forts at Hartville, and had also burned the fortifications at Hazlewood.

On the night of the 10th, the column was put in motion toward Hartville. A little before daylight the advance encountered a Federal force coming from Austin, via Hartville, to Springfield, and hearing that a strong cavalry force was in my rear, I deemed it best not to put myself in battle between the two forces, but to turn the force in my front and fight them, after I had secured, in case of defeat, a safe line of retreat. This I did, by making a detour 7 miles, and fought the enemy (2,500 Iowa, Illinois, Michigan, and Missouri troops) at Hartville.

The Federal position at Hartville was a very strong one, and the battle hotly contested for several hours, till the enemy gave way and retreated rapidly and in disorder, leaving the dead and wounded, many arms, ammunition, and clothing on the field and in my possession.

I have established a hospital, leaving surgeons and attendants sufficient to take care of the dead and wounded, Confederate and Federal. Here fell the chivalrous MacDonald, Lieutenant-Colonel Wimer, and Major Kirtley (noble men and gallant officers), and other officers and men equally brave and true. Here, too, was seriously wounded Col. J. C. Porter, a brave and skillful officer. He was shot from his horse at the head of his troops.

After the battle of Hartville, my division marched toward Batesville. The march was a long and most trying one, over rough, rock roads, through rain and snow and icy mountain streams, and a country laid waste by the Federals, furnishing neither food for man nor horse. The command reached Batesville January 25, and commenced crossing (by ferry) White River. The camp was established on the south bank of the river.

The expedition was an extremely hazardous and trying one. On leaving Lewisburg and Pocahontas, the men were indifferently armed and equipped, thinly clad, many without shoes and horses, marched without baggage wagons or cooking utensils, carrying all they had on their horses, and subsisting as best they could on the country through which they marched. The horses were worn by continued and active service of many months; were, for the most part, unshod, very poor, and unfit for any service. At least 200 of the command abandoned their horses on the roadside to die, and waded many a weary mile through the snow and deep mud, some barefooted, yet they encountered every danger willingly and endured all fatigues cheerfully. On the battle-field, in the camp, on the march by day and night, they proved themselves worthy of the great cause for which we are fighting.

For a more detailed account of the conduct of the several corps and regiments, and, more especially, of the brave officers and men so honorably mentioned, to whom I beg to call your favorable consideration, I refer you to the reports of Colonels Shelby and Porter and Major Bennett, submitted herewith.

Lieutenant [R. A.] Collins, and the officers and men under him, and a part of Bledsoe's battery rendered distinguished services both at Springfield and Hartville. Lieutenant Collins deserves promotion and a battery of his own. I hope he may get it speedily. I have, on other occasions, had the pleasure to speak of the skill, vigor, and bravery of Col. Jo. Shelby. I can only say that his conduct on this expedition, on and off the battle-field, fully sustained his splendid reputation, and merits for him speedy promotion, which I earnestly recommend. I beg, also, to call to the favorable notice of the general Col. J. C. Porter, commanding brigade, Major Bennett, commanding MacDonald's battalion, and the following officers of my staff who were with me during this expedition, and who bravely did their whole duty, to wit: Capt. Henry Ewing, acting adjutant and inspector general; Maj. R. H. Smith, quartermaster; Col. A. W. Slayback, ordnance officer; Capt. Thomas W. Newton, aide-de-camp, and Maj. Charles C. Rainwater, acting division commissary of subsistence.

My loss was 33 killed, 203 wounded, and 29 missing. The loss of the Federals was about 300 prisoners captured (paroled), and a very heavy loss in killed and wounded at Springfield and Hartville. A detailed report of my killed, wounded, and missing is sent herewith.

In conclusion, I think I may safely state that the object of the expedition was fully accomplished, and more. Blunt's Army of the Frontier countermarched rapidly to save Springfield; a long chain of forts, strong in themselves, built at great expense and labor, which overawed and kept in subjection the country, were razed to the ground, and the heart of the people revived again at the presence of Confederate troops.

Very respectfully,

J. S. MARMADUKE,
Brigadier-General, Commanding.

Col. R. C. NEWTON, *Chief of Staff, First Corps, Trans-Miss. Dept.*

[Indorsement.

HEADQUARTERS TRANS-MISSISSIPPI DEPARTMENT,
Little Rock, Ark., February 8, 1863.

Respectfully forwarded.

This expedition was gotten up by General Hindman to divert the enemy from their attack on Van Buren, and to force them to retire from the valley of the Arkansas. It was perfectly successful, and made them fall back into Missouri. General Marmaduke's conduct and management was gallant and excellent, and I earnestly recommend that the acting appointment of brigadier-general, under which he is now serving, may be at once confirmed. This is the more necessary as he is the only officer I have who is fitted for a large cavalry command.

Very respectfully,

TH. H. HOLMES,
Lieutenant-General.

Col. R. C. NEWTON,
Chief of Staff, First Corps, Trans-Mississippi Department.

No. 9.

Return of Casualties in Marmaduke's command, January 2-11, 1862.

Command.	Killed.			Wounded.			Missing.			Aggregate.	Remarks.
	Officers.	Enlisted men.	Total.	Officers.	Enlisted men.	Total.	Officers.	Enlisted men.	Total.		
Shelby's brigade:											
1st Regiment, Lieutenant-Colonel Gordon.	1	2	3	7	34	41	....	....	....	44	Springfield, January 8.
	2	....	2	4	27	31	....	....	....	33	Hartville, January 11.
2d Regiment, Lieutenant-Colonel Gilkey.	1	7	8	4	24	28	....	3	3	39	Springfield.
	....	3	3	6	12	18	....	1	1	22	Hartville.
3d Regiment, Col. G. W. Thompson.	....	3	3	1	11	12	1	5	6	21	Springfield.
	....	....	....	1	6	7	1	1	2	9	Hartville.
1st Battalion, Major Elliott.	....	1	1	....	....	....	....	....	....	1	White Spring, January 2.
	....	....	....	....	1	1	....	....	....	1	Springfield.
	....	....	....	1	2	3	....	....	....	3	Hartville.
Total *	4	16	20	24	117	141	2	10	12	173	
Porter's brigade:											
Burbridge's regiment	1	....	1	2	8	10	....	....	....	11	Hartville.
Greene's regiment	1	3	4	4	18	22	....	....	....	26	
Jeffers' regiment	....	1	1	1	4	5	....	....	....	6	
Total	2	4	6	7	30	37	....	....	....	43	
MacDonald's regiment	....	5	5	7	16	23	....	17	17	45	Springfield.
	1	....	1	....	....	....	....	....	....	1	Hartville.
Total	1	5	6	7	16	23	....	17	17	46	
Grand total	7	25	32	38	163	201	2	27	29	262	

No. 10.

Report of Col. Joseph O. Shelby, Missouri Cavalry (Confederate), commanding brigade.

HEADQUARTERS SHELBY'S CAVALRY BRIGADE,
Camp Carter, January 31, 1863.

GENERAL: On the last day of December, 1862, when the old year was dying in the lap of the new, and January had sent its moaning

* The nominal list from which Shelby's casualties are compiled bears the following indorsement:

"The orderly sergeants were without their rolls, and their reports were made from memory and guess-work. Some others wounded and killed, but cannot get their names for the want of the rolls."—W. J. MCARTHUR, *Captain and Assistant Adjutant-General.*

winds to wail the requiem of the past, my brigade, consisting of the First Regiment, Lieutenant-Colonel [B. F.] Gordon; Second Regiment, Lieutenant-Colonel [C. A.] Gilkey; Third Regiment, Colonel [G. W.] Thompson; the scouts, Major Elliott, and Captain Quantrill's old company, under First Lieutenant Gregg, were on the march for foray on the border's side.

The day was auspicious; a bright red sun had tempered the keen air to pleasantness, and cheered the mounted soldiers with the hopes of a gay and gallant trip. The first two days' march was long and comfortable; the third the rain commenced, cold and chilling, and continued without intermission for three days, the grand old mountains standing bare against the dull and somber sky, their heads heavy with the storms of centuries. The men suffered much, but, keeping the bright goal of Missouri constantly in sight, spurred on and on quite merrily.

For two days all went well. The third day my advance, consisting of Major [B.] Elliott's scouts, came suddenly upon about 100 notorious bushwhackers and deserters, who fired upon them quite stubbornly; but upon dismounting several companies of Colonel Gilkey's regiment, in conjunction with Elliott's battalion, and following them in their almost inaccessible retreat, 20 were killed, about the same number wounded, and many prisoners taken, and this murdering, robbing, jayhawking band broken up completely and effectually. Thus the skirmish of White Spring, successful as it was, proved to be the prelude of the victories of Springfield and Hartville. The rain commenced now in earnest, and for three days its cold, merciless peltings were endured by the men without a murmur, although the sky was dark and barren as a rainy sea, and the keen northeast wind pierced the thin clothing of the men with icy breath.

The 4th, 5th, and 6th were spent in long and cold forced marches, varied somewhat by Colonel MacDonald's successful sally upon Fort Lawrence and your advance upon the fortified town of Ozark. Five miles from this place, by your order, I halted my brigade, and gave them time to forage their animals and cook something for themselves, which they did, and were again in marching order by 9.30 o'clock. At this place, and before we started to attack Ozark, I sent Major Elliott and his scouts and two companies from Lieutenant-Colonel Gilkey's regiment to gain a position in the rear of the town, on the road leading north, and cut off their retreat. He gained the position thus indicated, but gained it too late, for the Federals had left in hot haste long before Major Elliott could have possibly got around them. Upon arriving in close proximity to Ozark, and not being satisfied as to its evacuation, I dismounted the half of each regiment composing the brigade, formed them as infantry, and, feeling my way along slowly and cautiously, with numerous skirmishers, I soon found that the nest was there and it was warm, but the birds had flown, and nothing remained to do but apply the torch to fort and barracks. Soon the red glare of flames burst out upon the midnight sky, and the cold, calm stars looked down upon the scene. Several prisoners were here taken, and any quantity of commissary stores, but, having no transportation, all, except a small portion consumed by the men, were destroyed, and by 12 o'clock we were again marching northward. It was an intensely cold night, that of the 7th, and the frost hung heavy and chill on the garments of my devoted brigade, marching on to the stronghold of the enemy with a determination in their hearts rarely surpassed.

The sun came up on the morning of the 8th like a ball of fire, and the day was gloomy and chill; but Springfield loomed up before us in the distance like a beautiful panorama, and the men, catching the inspiration of the scene, forgot all their trials and hardships, and were eager for the rough, red fray. With flaunting banners, and all the pomp and circumstance of war, the Federals had marched gaily out to meet us, and taken their position in our front. I had dismounted, meanwhile, the First and Third Regiments, and was forming them as infantry, holding Lieutenant-Colonel Gilkey's command mounted until the position of the enemy was perfectly understood and all his motions thoroughly seen. When the plan of action had been decided upon, I then dismounted Lieutenant-Colonel Gilkey's regiment and formed them as infantry, holding in reserve as cavalry Major Elliott's scouts and Lieutenant Gregg's company. Then forming my lines, I rapidly moved my brigade to the open plain south and southeast of the town, rested for a moment, making the final dispositions, and taking breath for the crisis. Major Elliott and Lieutenant Gregg were on the right flank, watching and skirmishing with the enemy there, and over the level earth squadrons of horse swept gaily and fantastically. 'Twas a bright and beautiful scene. There lay the quiet town, robed in the dull, gray hue of the winter, its domes and spires stretching their skeleton hands to heaven, as if in prayer against the coming strife, and, drawing near and nearer, long black lines came gleaming on, while the sun shone out like a golden bar, uncurling its yellow hair on earth and sky, stream and mountain, and lent the thrilling picture a sterner and fiercer light. My skirmishers advanced steadily, and now continual shots in front tell that the enemy are found and pressed sorely. On the extreme left you have organized Colonel MacDonald's regiment into a storming party and sent it at the fort, and they could be plainly seen winding over the crest of the hill and moving rapidly to the attack. MacDonald has met the enemy and is driving them, but they soon re-enforced, and would in turn compel him to retreat. I saw the crisis, and ordered Lieutenant-Colonel Gordon and Lieutenant-Colonel Gilkey to charge with their regiments, to support MacDonald. Gallantly it was done, and as gallantly sustained. At the command, a thousand warriors sprang to their feet, and, with one wild Missouri yell, burst upon the foe; officers mix with men in the mad *mêlée*, and fight side by side; some storm the fort at the headlong charge, others gain the houses from which the Federals had just been driven, and keep up the fight, while some push on after the flying foe. The storm increases and the combatants get closer and closer.

> I heard the cannon's shivering crash,
> As when the whirlwind rends the ash;
> I heard the muskets deadly clang,
> As if a thousand anvils rang!

In this charge a regiment of Federals, just sent from their main fort, were scattered and driven back, and their entire force forced into their heavy earthworks, surrounded by rifle-pits and other obstructions.

I cannot fail, in this connection, to speak of the daring charge of Capt. L. J. Crocker, of Company K, First Regiment; Lieut. William [H.] Ferrell, of Company F, same regiment, and about a dozen other reckless spirits from Gordon's and Gilkey's regiments, upon one piece of artillery, supported by a battalion of Iowans, but who fled after a sharp, hot rally, and suffered their gun and caisson, filled with valuable ammunition, to be borne in triumph to the rear. The battle thickens; Colonel Thompson, who had been stationed on the right with his regiment, and who did not participate in the charge, but who was watching and foiling the movements of a large body of cavalry in that direction, was now ordered up, and advanced with spirit and alacrity. The battery which accompanied the expedition from Lewisburg, commanded by Lieut. Richard A. Collins, and consisting of one rifled piece and one smooth-bore 6-pounder, was advanced, one piece being brought up into the very town, and opening at point-blank range with grape and canister. The Federals re-enforced largely, and came back with cavalry and artillery, and a hot, desperate conflict ensued; one side struggling to hold the position gained, the other to drive them from it. Bravely my fighting brigade meets the onset, and stubbornly they resist; blow falls on blow, shot follows shot. Lieutenant-Colonel Gordon leads the gallant First, and they never fail. Major [D.] Shanks, and Lieutenant-Colonel Gilkey, and Colonel Thompson are piloting their regiments, bravely and well, and the contest rages, and the wild death-dance goes merrily on.

Still Collins plies his lurid torch,
Where balls will rend or powder scorch;
Still Shanks and Gordon, side by side,
Like veteran heroes stem the tide.

This stern, sanguinary fight was kept up for hours, and even into the night the roar of artillery and small-arms was incessant. On the right, Lieutenant [F. M.] Scott made a bold and daring charge, breaking the first line of Federals in splendid style, and only retiring when accumulating numbers made it madness to advance.

About 3 o'clock I had Major Elliott's scouts dismounted and brought up in the town, forming in rear of and supporting Collins' iron 6-pounder, which moved along the various streets as unconcerned as if peace were made and he was firing a salute over the joyous event, although he was constantly exposed and always in range of minie musketry.

Night came down with weary, brooding wings, laid her dark brow across the cloudy sky, and threw her sable mantle over fort and wall and house and men, checking the bloody strife, and calming the furious passions that had been at war all day. I drew my brigade off calmly and cautiously, formed them in and around the heavy stockade, threw out trusty skirmishers, and prepared to pass the night as best I could, although it was very cold, and the men had no fires, save the smouldering fragments of consumed houses, burned by the terrified enemy at our first approach. When all was quiet, Collins, with his iron 6-pounder and a small support, made a promenade upon the principal streets of the city. Acting upon the principle of the Irishman at a Donnybrook fair, who, whenever he saw a head, hit at it, so this little party, whenever a light appeared, fired at it, and it served not only to encourage our tired soldiers, but it told to the foe, with thunder tones, that we were still victors, proud and defiant. The men lay on their arms until about 2 o'clock in the morning, when I deemed it best, as they were suffering greatly from cold and hunger, to withdraw, which was done quietly and in order, some of Colonel MacDonald's command and Major Elliott's scouts picketing my flanks and front. My brigade suffered seriously in the attack upon Springfield, but it covered itself all over with glory, and won imperishable laurels. There the heroic John W. Buffington, second lieutenant of Company H, First Regiment, ahead of his best and bravest, fell, almost leading a forlorn hope.

Oh! smooth the damp hair over his brow;
It is pale and white, and ghastly now;
And hide the wounds in his gory breast,
For his soul has fled to its final rest.

In the charge beyond the stockade, after that had been won, and almost upon the enemy's guns, H. S. Titsworth, captain of Company H,

First Regiment, fell, badly wounded, and has since died. The South had no nobler champion, our cause no braver defender, and he, with Major [Samuel] Bowman, of Lieutenant-Colonel Gilkey's regiment, and Lieutenant Buffington form an illustrious trio—three of the grand "immortal names that were not born to die." Peace to their ashes! When the warfare of the world is over, when time strikes records with eternity, and mortality is paling beyond the sunset shore, and the billows of dissolution are white with the wrecks of the universe, these deathless spirits will rise beautiful from their urns of death and chambers of decay, and join the noble band of Southern martyrs that have fallen "with their backs to the field and their feet to the foe."

After the men had all breakfasted the next morning, after ammunition had been distributed, and a leisurely forming of the brigade effected, we started from the scene of a hard-fought battle. The mission had been accomplished; two forts had been captured, a piece of artillery taken, several hundred prisoners paroled, considerable commissary stores destroyed, and we, after making almost a circuit of the town with floating banners and waving pennons, left it alone in its glory, because all had been done that could be done.

Friday, the 9th, moved east with my brigade on the Rolla road, and camped for the night at Sand Spring, where your escort and Lieutenant Scott had fired a Federal fort.

The 10th, we marched through Marshfield, and after burning the fort there, which was done by Colonels MacDonald and Thompson, and after forming a junction with Colonel Porter's command, we camped again for the night, but with orders issued to move at 3 o'clock upon the enemy, as our scouts had brought information of their close proximity.

After a brisk, stiff gallop for several hours this quiet Sunday morning of the 11th, Colonel Porter, leading the advance, came upon them, and formed to fight, waiting in line until my brigade came up, which it did in splendid spirits. After maneuvering for a while, at your order we marched hurriedly to the town of Hartville, and found the enemy in position. My brigade was immediately dismounted and formed for the attack, and Collins stationed on a commanding hill with his three-gun battery. Lieutenant-Colonel Gordon held the left, Lieutenant-Colonel Gilkey the center, and Colonel Thompson the right, the other portions of your division being disposed by your immediate command. Almost immediately after dismounting, I threw out skirmishers, and advanced the whole line upon the town and upon the woods beyond, knowing that within the dark shades of the timber the crouching Federals were waiting for the spring. After gaining the town, and just upon entering the woods, the brigade received a terrible and well-directed fire, which was so sudden that it almost became a surprise. The men stood all its fury well, and it was not until the tornado had passed did they begin to waver; some fell back, it is true; some stood firm, and others crouched behind obstructions that sheltered them; but the left of the First Regiment closed in on them, and the fight raged evenly there. Gordon fell back a little with his regiment, formed their lines anew, and marched again upon the foe. Shanks, with three companies on the right, covered Porter's artillery, and fought long and well. Thompson gets away from the noise and confusion of the start, and comes up sternly on the right. Gordon advances his regiment on the left again, and death's black banner is waving there, and his best and bravest are falling round him. Gilkey comes up to Gordon's aid, and Shanks and Thompson are doing all that men can do to stem the tide. Maj. George R. Kirtley, of the First, and Capt. C. M. Turpin, of Company I, First also, are dead. Captains Dupuy,

Burkholder, Jarrett, and Webb, of the Second, are wounded. Captain Garrett, First Sergt. William Buckley, and Private C. [B.] Bullard, of Company G, all of the First Regiment, and all lion-hearted, are badly wounded, and more are falling. Gordon's ensign is shot down, but Lieutenant Corder, of Company C, catches the fallen beacon, and the banner of the bars waves again high over the lurid light of the fight. Collins' battery is busy with its work of death, and his men stand nobly to their posts. But the conflict wanes, and Federals are retreating. I drew off my brigade, mounted them, and left Gordon's regiment to bring up the rear. No pursuit was attempted, for the condition of horses and men forbade it, and prudence demanded we should fall back nearer to our base, which began on the night of the 11th and continued until the evening of the 20th, suffering from cold, hunger, fatigue, rain, snow, and all the ills our exposed condition presented. The trip, general, will be a memorable one. The enemy thought that your division, broken down and demoralized, was hibernating on the banks of the Arkansas, and could do nothing. What will be their surprise to learn that this same division, after marching 300 miles on unshod and miserable horses, hurled itself upon their Gibraltar of the Southwest, terrified them into burning commissary and quartermaster's stores, caused them to evacuate forts, which were burned, frightened Rolla into hysterics, gave the militia of the surrounding country the nightmare for months to come, and woke a thrill in Southern hearts that will prove seed for the harvest. During the march from Hartville to Batesville, the men suffered much, and some in my brigade are badly frozen, yet the cause demanded the sacrifice, and it was made.

I cannot close this report without calling your attention to the brave and gallant manner in which Lieutenant Collins handled his battery, assisted by Lieutenant [Jacob D.] Connor and Sergeants [F. L.] Wayman and [Joseph] Cooper. They deserve a separate battery. Lieutenant-Colonels Gordon and Gilkey, Colonel Thompson, Majors Smith and Shanks, Adjutants [Eli] Hodge, Edwards, and [George M.] Winship did their duty well and nobly, and can be greeted as "Well done, good and faithful servants."

Captain Crocker, of Company K, First Regiment, fell at Hartville badly wounded, and my brigade is thereby deprived of as gallant, as heroic a spirit as ever drew sword for the battles of the right. The officers and men of my command, with but few exceptions, answered all my expectations, and will do to rely upon when "Greek meets Greek." I am also indebted to the valuable assistance of my adjutant, Capt. W. J. McArthur, who, always cool and collected, moved the various regiments without the slightest mistake. In closing my report of this adventurous foray, you will pardon the pride I manifest in speaking of the heroic examples and conduct of many of my men and officers. Captain Dupuy, of the Second Regiment, brave, and tender of heart as a woman, fell, badly wounded, and has lost a leg. The chivalrous Captain [Washington] McDaniel, of Major Elliott's scouts, in that grim charge of Hartville, fell, with a bullet through his dauntless breast, just as the Federals retreated and a few faint notes of victory came pealing on the air. Lieutenant Royster, of the First Regiment, and Captains [H. D.] Stengle and D. A. Williams, of the Second Regiment, showed a bravery and heroism worthy of all praise, and poor Royster was left behind badly wounded. Thomas Smart, private, also of same regiment, who was killed, left behind a name bright as the hills that girt the shores of paradise. In the First Regiment, Privates Bushrod Corder, Christopher Moorman, Harvey Plattenburg, James Gordon, and many others particularly distinguished themselves. Maj. George R. Kirtley and Capt. James M. Garrett, of the First, have left behind them immortal names—names that are too bright to die. My young orderly, Jimmy Chark, displayed a venturesome courage and bravery worthy of the most favorable notice, and was always where I needed him, in his place. My volunteer aide, Captain Waters, was of great assistance, always brave, cool, collected, and daring; wherever the fire was heaviest there he was, and never flinched. My quartermaster and commissary, Majors [G. D.] Page and [John B.] Dale, were always with me, rendering valuable assistance by their great coolness and attention. To those ladies of Little Rock who so kindly remembered my brigade, their thanks are especially due, and under the folds of their starry banners many a noble heart was fired and many a proud step fell quicker when their silken folds caught each warrior's eye.

Yours, respectfully,

JO. O. SHELBY,
Colonel, Commanding Cavalry Brigade.

Brigadier-General MARMADUKE,
Commanding Cavalry Division.

No. 11.

Report of Col. J. C. Porter, Missouri Cavalry (Confederate), commanding brigade.

HDQRS. PORTER'S BRIG., MISSOURI CAV., C. S. ARMY,
Camp Allen, February 3, 1863.

SIR: In obedience to your order, I, on the 2d day of January, 1863, detached from my command (then encamped at Pocahontas, Randolph County, Arkansas), the effective men of my command, numbering in the aggregate 825 men, and proceeded westward with said detachment through the counties of Lawrence and Fulton, in the State of Arkansas. Arriving at or near the northwestern corner of Fulton County, I learned of a considerable force of Federals stationed at Houston, in Texas County, Missouri. I therefore continued my march farther to the west, going farther west than I had anticipated. Arriving at a point nearly due south of the town of Hartville, in the county of Wright, State of Missouri, I changed my course northward, and in the direction of said town (Hartville). However, before changing my course to the north, on account of the roughness of the roads and the impossibility of having my horses shod, I was compelled to order about 125 of my men back to camp, as being unable to proceed farther, for want of shoes on their horses, leaving my detachment only 700 strong. No incident of importance occurred worthy of note up to this time, save that my men so well behaved that I was enabled to surprise all citizens along the road, and enabled me to capture some of the worst jayhawkers that infested the country.

The men of my command seemed well satisfied, and all things went well, notwithstanding the hardships all were compelled to undergo on account of shortness of provisions and clothing.

On the morning of the 9th of January, 1863, we neared the town of Hartville, Wright County, Missouri, at which point I learned that a company of the enrolled militia of Missouri were stationed. Putting my command in order, I detached a company as advance guard, ordering them to reconnoiter to ascertain the position, and, as far as possible, the strength of the enemy. Following my advance, I found, upon approaching the town, that the enemy, 40 strong, had surrendered to my advance without firing a gun. Before approaching the town, however, I ordered the detachment of Colonel Burbridge's regiment, under command of Lieut. Col. John M. Wimer, to support Captain Brown's battery, the rest of my command, Lieutenant-Colonel Campbell and Colonel Jeffers, marching under my immediate command. Upon the surrender of the town, we took 35 (militia) prisoners and 2 United States soldiers and some citizens, and destroyed the fortifications, with 200 stand of arms, finding no commissary or quartermaster's stores or trains.

Remaining in Hartville until 8 p. m. of the 9th of January, and receiving no orders from you, as I had anticipated, I concluded to march upon Lebanon by way of Hazlewood, and immediately dispatched a messenger informing you of my plans.

At 8 p. m. of the 9th of January, I moved my command upon the road to Marshfield, some 6 miles, and bivouacked till sunrise on the morning of the 10th of January, when I ordered Lieutenant-Colonel Wimer to proceed with his command to the town of Hazlewood. In obedience to my orders, Colonel Wimer proceeded to Hazlewood, and, finding the place evacuated by the enemy, forthwith burned the block-house, and rejoined my command some two hours after I had met the balance of my command; joined yours about 4 miles from the town of Marshfield.

At 3 p. m. (10th) my command was ordered back 3 miles, upon the road leading to Hartville, to encamp. At 11 p. m., same night, I received orders to proceed with my command to Hartville, at which hour I moved my command in the direction of said town, sending in advance the detachment of Colonel Burbridge's regiment under command of Lieutenant-Colonel Wimer, to take possession of and operate the mill at Hartville, following with the rest of my command, to wit, Lieutenant-Colonel Campbell, Colonel Jeffers, and Captain Brown's two-gun battery.

The advance, under Lieutenant-Colonel Wimer, when within 5 miles of the town of Hartville (at 3 a. m., 11th of January), were fired upon by Federal pickets, upon which Colonel Wimer fell back a short distance, dismounted his command, and formed in line of battle, immediately after which a scout of Federal cavalry advanced upon Colonel Wimer's command. Arriving very near, they were fired upon by Colonel Wimer's command, killing 2, and killing and wounding several horses.

Upon receiving information of the enemy in front, I ordered Colonel Wimer to skirmish with the enemy, and fall back gradually upon my command, at the same time ordering Captain Brown's guns in position in the center, with Colonel Campbell on the right and Colonel Jeffers on the left; also dispatching a courier to you. I continued my advance as skirmishers until daylight and your arrival, the enemy during the time shelling to the right and left of my line, slightly wounding one of my men in the leg. Whilst the advance, under Lieutenant-Colonel Wimer, were falling back upon my line, the sharpshooters of Colonel Campbell, by mistake, fired upon and wounded 2 of Lieutenant-Colonel Wimer's command.

At 7 a. m. (11th January), I was ordered to fall back and follow your command, which I did, however, keeping my battery (Captain Brown) in position for a time, when I perceived Federal cavalry advance up the road, when I ordered Captain Brown to open on them; upon which Captain Brown fired two rounds, dispersing them, doing no other damage to them. Captain Brown then limbered up his guns and fell back with the other command. After marching, per order, until about 1 p. m., we again neared the town of Hartville. I was then ordered to dismount my command and place Captain Brown's battery in position on the left. Before having completed or carried out the last order, I received information that the enemy were in full retreat from the town of Hartville, and at the same time an order to remount my command and pursue the enemy. On arriving at the court-house with the head of my column, I found the enemy formed in the brush just above town, within 50 yards of my command. Immediately upon perceiving the enemy in position, I ordered my men to dismount; but the enemy poured upon us such a heavy volley of musketry that my command was compelled to fall back somewhat in disorder, I being at the same time wounded in leg and hand. I ordered my adjutant to report the fact to you. Having, at the same time that I ordered my command to dismount, ordered Captain Brown's battery to take position near the head of my column, after Captain Brown took position as ordered, he was compelled, for want of ammunition (his ammunition being carried off by his horses stampeding) and a galling fire of the enemy, to retire, leaving his pieces on the field, which were afterward brought off by a part of Colonel Greene's and Burbridge's men. Lieutenant-Colonel Wimer was shot dead whilst leading the detachment of Colonel Burbridge's regiment. Colonel Jeffers, without fear, led his men through the fight. The detachment of Colonel Greene's regiment was gallantly led by Lieutenant-Colonel [L. C.] Campbell, assisted by Major [L. A.] Campbell. I would do great injustice did I make distinction among my officers present on that occasion, all having displayed great gallantry. My men, I must say, acquitted themselves with honor, almost without exception. Our loss foots up 6 killed and 38 wounded. I would here mention that Captain [George R.] McMahan and 50 of Lieutenant-Colonel Campbell's men destroyed the block-house and stockade at Dallas, the enemy fleeing before him.

On our return march from Missouri, my men and officers displayed great energy in undergoing the fatigues and privations necessary. Arrived at Camp Sallado, January 20, 1863.

Respectfully,

JO. C. PORTER,
Colonel, Commanding Porter's Brigade.

General MARMADUKE.

No. 12.

Report of Maj. G. W. C. Bennett, MacDonald's Missouri Cavalry (Confederate.)

HEADQUARTERS MACDONALD'S CAVALRY REGIMENT,
Camp Horton, January 29, [1863.]

CAPTAIN: I have the honor to submit the following report of the part this regiment has taken in the late expedition to Missouri:

Pursuant to General Orders, No. —, this regiment took up its line of march from Lewisburg, on the 31st of December, 1862, for Yellville, via Clinton, and camped on the evening of the same day on Wolfe Creek,

23 miles from Lewisburg. Nothing of interest transpired during this day's march.

On the next morning, January 1, we marched at daylight. Arrived at, and encamped 1 mile beyond, Clinton, 28 miles from our previous camp.

The next day's march was to an old camp-ground, within 8 miles of Burnville.

Marched 25 miles January 3. Captured H. H. Thompson, a deserter from Colonel Matlock's Arkansas regiment. Camped on Buffalo Creek, 16 miles from our former camp.

Upon the afternoon of the 4th of January, we arrived at Yellville, having marched 20 miles. Being in the land of jayhawkers, our camp guards were regularly mounted, and scouts kept out to prevent a surprise. On arriving at Yellville, Colonel MacDonald received your General Orders, No. —, ordering him to have his command in readiness to march at sunrise on the morning of January 5, 1863, about 25 miles in the direction of Springfield, via Dubuque.

We camped, on the evening of the 5th, near Sugar Loaf, Ark., where a general court-martial was ordered and held, for the trial of Private H. H. Thompson or any other prisoners we might have in our possession. The finding of the court-martial being "not guilty," and the findings and proceedings being confirmed, by your order the prisoner was released and ordered to report back to his regiment.

On the morning of the 6th, we marched toward Dubuque, and encamped on Beaver Creek, 23 miles from Sugar Loaf, at 4 p. m. You sent for Colonel MacDonald and myself, and ordered us, verbally, to move our command at 10 o'clock in the direction of Fort Lawrence, 22 miles from our encampment, and attack the fort at night or in the morning, as Colonel MacDonald thought best.

The march was attended with much suffering from cold. The men were, however, buoyed up and kept in excellent spirits in expectation of a fight on the coming morning. At daybreak on the morning of the 7th, we arrived at an eminence overlooking Major Turner's domicil, where we dismounted, and, hitching our horses, prepared to charge the enemy on foot. Slowly and quietly we crept along, until within 20 steps of the picket fires, when we were discovered by the pickets, two of whom were killed while attempting to alarm the fort. The remaining one we captured, and, without stopping, pushed on to storm the fort. What was our surprise, on arriving in sight, to find 500 well-armed and well-equipped troops fleeing from an almost impregnable fort, before our little squad of 250 men. The fort and surrounding buildings were taken and in flames in ten minutes after the first gun was fired, destroying their commissary and quartermaster's stores and what medical stores we were unable to carry with us, of the value, I suppose, of $15,000, about 100 head of horses, and 5 wagons. The horses were, however, very inferior, nearly all worthless. Among the captures were about 300 stand of arms (Belgian rifles and Minie muskets), with 6 boxes fine cartridges. On account of having no transportation, we were compelled to bury the arms. The fort consisted of a two-story log building, 12 inches thick. The logs were dovetailed, and were very closely fitted together. The second story projected over the first. The building was about 150 feet long and 40 wide, with port-holes for musketry extending around the entire building, and mortised on the inside for the purpose of turning the muskets in any direction. The other buildings, some eight or ten in number, were used for barracks. We captured also 14 prisoners, who were paroled on the field. Their names I give in my summary. At 10 a. m. we moved toward Ozark, traveling some 45 miles, and camped, at 12 o'clock that night, 5 miles from Ozark. At 4 o'clock in the morning we moved on in the direction of Springfield; passed through Ozark at daylight, and arrived in front of Springfield at 10 a. m. on the morning of the 8th of January, 1863. The line of battle being formed, Colonel MacDonald received an order from you to occupy the left of Colonel Shelby's brigade, resting upon the Telegraph road, and the extreme left of the line. He was also ordered to send out lookouts and skirmishers to prevent a flank movement of the enemy, and ascertain any movement of the enemy. In a few minutes one of the lookouts discovered a considerable body of infantry formed directly in our front. He was ordered to dismount the men and dislodge them. When dismounted, he marched them through the thick underbrush as quietly as possible; but our movements were discovered, and they retired to their trenches. Colonel MacDonald was then ordered to oblique his command to the right, as he was too far to the left; and just as we emerged from the brush, Major Smith came galloping down with orders for us to move directly to the front, toward the houses; that there was a considerable body of infantry behind the houses and fences. As soon as Colonel MacDonald drew the men in line, he ordered the charge, routed the enemy, and took possession of the houses. As soon as we arrived at the houses, we were charged by a body of Federal cavalry on the left. Just at this time Colonel Shelby, with his command, moved rapidly forward on my right, and, had it not been for this gallant movement of Colonel Shelby, our command would have suffered more severely than it did. We immediately opened a brisk fire upon the cavalry, and it fled in confusion. We then moved from house to house and from fence to fence, the enemy flying before us, until we arrived at the fort, which, in connection with Colonel Shelby's command, we occupied the rest of the day. We advanced twice, occupying the houses in front of the fort; but the enemy being largely re-enforced, we found we could not hold them without an unnecessary loss of life, and we returned inside the palisades, where the hard fight continued until after dark. Though entirely successful in my attempt to drive the enemy from the houses and fences, I am sorry to record the loss of some of my best officers and men.

In my summary I give an account of the killed, wounded, and missing sustained in the engagement.

At about 8 o'clock, Colonel MacDonald was ordered to move his command and camp them upon the farm of John S. Phelps, distant 2 miles from the scene of action. The men here bivouacked for the night, and, building large fires from the fine oak fence rails of mine host Phelps, and with a plentiful supply from the richly stored larder of Mrs. Phelps, regaled themselves after the hard day's fight.

On the morning of the 9th, we moved out on and marched some 20 miles upon the Rolla road, when we left Colonel Shelby's command and took a right-hand road leading to Marshfield. Upon this day's march we captured some 6 or 8 prisoners, who were turned over to General Marmaduke; tore down the telegraph wires, and captured one two-mule wagon, with 1,600 pounds of flour; several horses, equipments, &c., which I mention in my summary. We there separated from Colonel Shelby's command, they taking the road to Sand Spring, we marching on Marshfield, distant 11 miles, where the militia were fortified. Our advance entered the town about 7 p. m., and took possession. Here we found rich stores, suitable to the wants of our men, consisting of boots, shoes, hats, caps, socks, gloves, &c. We also captured 6 prisoners, who were paroled on the succeeding morning, and a quantity of fine arms and ammunition. The name and regiment to which the prisoners belong I give in my summary. This fort was built of heavy oak boards, and in arrangement very similar to Fort Lawrence. Besides the fort, they had stockades or piles driven in the ground and dirt thrown up against it from the outside. On the succeeding morning we were ordered to march, and moved about 8 o'clock. After making a circuit of some 8 or 10 miles, we again returned to Marshfield, and, marching through, proceeded to camp, some 7 miles distant. At this point we formed a junction with Colonel Porter's command. Here we received orders to move the next morning at 1 o'clock, and march in the rear of Colonel Porter's command. About 4.30 o'clock, Colonel Porter's advance encountered the enemy's pickets at a point on the road about 5 miles from Hartville, and a considerable volley of musketry was fired. We were ordered up on double-quick, dismounted, and formed on the extreme left of Colonel Porter's line, where we remained until between daylight and sunrise, when we were ordered to remount and move in the rear of Colonel Shelby's command, taking a left-hand road that intersected the Hartville and Vera Cruz road, about 4 miles from Hartville. At this point the entire column countermarched, moving directly toward Hartville. After moving in this direction about 1 mile, I received orders, through Captain [W. J.] McArthur, of Colonel Shelby's command, to take a right-hand road, and moved rapidly with my command to a point where this road intersected the Houston and Hartville road, 1½ miles east of Houston, and to remain there until further orders. I was placed there for the purpose of cutting off the retreat of the enemy and their baggage trains. I had no engagement with the enemy, with the exception of picket fighting. A small body of the enemy's cavalry, from his right wing, made a movement in a southeasterly direction, and were fired into by my pickets, killing 1 and capturing 6 prisoners. We sustained no loss. These prisoners were afterward turned over to, and paroled by, Captain [Henry] Ewing. I remained here until dark, when I was ordered to return and fall in with the main column. At the point on the Vera Cruz road, where we countermarched, Colonel MacDonald, being in the rear, became separated from his command. He followed the main column to the field of battle. During this engagement he fell, mortally wounded in the thigh. Of his action on this occasion, others who were present have a better right to speak than myself. Surely none that knew him will pretend to say he did not die gallantly battling with the enemy—bravely fighting for his country and his country's cause. During my connection with the army I have never known a kinder-hearted man—a braver officer or soldier. Let us drop one tear upon the grave of the departed hero, and pass on to renewed victories and to avenge his death.

We camped the night of the 11th, 7 miles from Hartville, and bivouacked on an open prairie until sunrise, when I was ordered to report at your headquarters in person for orders. I was ordered to fall in rear of the entire command, with one piece of artillery, commanded by Lieutenant Collins.

I detached one company as rear guard, and, without any incidents of interest, arrived in camp about 4 p. m. On the evening of the 12th, marched 17 miles. I sent back, about 4 miles, a heavy picket. The next day I again brought up the rear with the same piece of artillery; marched 23 miles. About 3 o'clock in the afternoon of the 13th, a heavy rain commenced and continued all night. Lieutenant Collins informed me his horses were unable to proceed farther, and, learning camp was still 12 miles ahead, I thought it best to halt my command, and did so. The men were without rations for themselves and horses, and, notwithstanding the rain was falling in torrents, I did not hear a murmur from one of my command; on the contrary, they were cheerful. I again picketed the road some 5 miles in the rear. On the morning of the 14th, I again moved my command, and rejoined the main column about 11 a. m. At about 12 m. of the 14th, I again received orders to move about 9 miles and camp in the vicinity of Captain Howard's. During the night there was a heavy snow-fall, and in the excessive cold several of my men were frost-bitten. They bore it, however, heroically, not a murmur escaping the lips of a single man. On the morning of the 15th, I was ordered to march in rear of Colonel Shelby and in advance of Colonel Porter, which I did, camping about 3 p. m.; marched 15 miles. That night I received orders to march in advance of the whole column, which was executed on the morning of the 16th at 3 o'clock, marching 25 miles. This was the most severe march we experienced on the whole expedition. Some 20 or 25 of my men were severely frost-bitten. That night I received verbal orders to move my command and subsist my command separately, and would receive my orders at Magness' Ferry. I moved at sunrise and marched 18 miles, and camped near Mr. Williams', 2½ miles from Hookran. On the night of the 17th, I received an order from you, dated Hookran, January 17, ordering me to march my command as rapidly as possible, and take the most energetic measures to bring forward every Confederate soldier, all of which was executed, marching about 20 miles, camping 4 miles from Sulphur Rock. On the morning of the 18th, we marched at sunrise, and arrived at Magness' Ferry at about 11 a. m. We immediately commenced crossing, though, with the facilities offered, it was a slow process. We completed the crossing about 10 o'clock on the morning of the 19th, and camped 1 mile from the White River, on the south side.

In conclusion, I am glad to say this regiment displayed all the courage, patience, and endurance during the march, in camp, or on the field of battle which has always rendered it a command of which Napoleon himself might be proud. Where all did so nobly it is difficult and needless to particularize, and hence I shall forbear. The officers and men are now, and have been during the entire trip, in excellent spirits, ready and willing to bear all for their country, whenever and wherever called.

Respectfully submitted.

G. W. C. BENNETT,
Major, Comdg. MacDonald's Missouri Regiment of Cavalry.

JANUARY 1, 1863.—Affair near Helena, Ark.

Report of Brig. Gen. Willis A. Gorman, U. S. Army.

HDQRS. DIST. OF EAST. ARK., *Helena, Ark., January* 3, 1863.

GENERAL: On January 1, the Texas Rangers, with 25 or 30 men, about sunrise made a dash upon my pickets again, where 26 men and 1 commissioned officer were on duty, and, without the least resistance or the firing of a gun, disgracefully surrendered and were taken off. They belonged to the Twenty-eighth Iowa, a new regiment, but a short time in the service. The officer must be disgracefully dismissed from the service, and I trust you will order that the men, when they return under parole, as they probably will in a few days, shall be ordered on duty again and put in the front of the first fight, and if ever captured again let them be hung, as they deserve. There are strong suspicions that they surrendered to be paroled, that they might get home. They were all sitting down and lying around, shamefully neglecting their duty.

About four days previous to this they attacked our cavalry pickets from an ambuscade in the dense woods; killed 2 and wounded 16. These belonged to the Sixth Missouri Cavalry, and behaved handsomely. None were captured. I am still occupying Friar's Point with the Twenty-ninth Wisconsin Regiment, 100 cavalry, and two pieces of artillery.

General Sherman's troops, on the way down the Mississippi, wantonly burned much property. The general arrested the guilty parties, had them tried promptly, and seven of them shot. I am not advised to what regiment or command they belonged. This is the first execution for plundering, marauding, or burning property that has occurred in our army during the war. I regret to say that this army has acquired an unenviable reputation for plundering, robbing, and burning property. The discipline is improving. When I took command it seemed to me the most undisciplined mob I ever came in contact with. The *matériel* is splendid, but the political demagogues among the line officers are enough to damn the best army on God's footstool. I found colonels giving leaves of absence, men and officers slipping off home on boats, and all manner of breaches of discipline and order. I have had thorough inspections of infantry, artillery, and cavalry, commissary and quartermaster's departments, transportation, and all public property. I have had drills and reviews of every arm of the service. If I had thirty days' pretty weather, I would set up this army in as fine style as need be.

I am, general, very respectfully, your obedient servant,

W. A. GORMAN,
Brigadier-General, Commanding.

Major-General CURTIS,
Commanding Department of the Missouri, Saint Louis, Mo.

JANUARY 2, 1863.—Reoccupation of New Madrid, Mo., by Union forces.

Report of Col. D. Henry Hughes, Thirty-eighth Iowa Infantry.

NEW MADRID, MO., *January* 3, 1863.

GENERAL: I occupied this post with my regiment yesterday. We found the guns spiked, gun carriages burned, and magazine blown up, filling the works with *débris*. The defenses proper are but little injured. No opposition was made to my landing, the few guerrillas in the place scattering to the country. From the best intelligence I hear, there is no large body of the enemy within 30 miles, but several bands of from 100 to 250, which, united, would make considerable force. I would suggest, general, that we need a company or two of cavalry to scour the country and pick up information, capture chiefs of guerrilla bands, &c. We also need a battery of light artillery. If it is a possible thing, I would like to have them furnished immediately.

I am, general, your obedient servant,

D. H. HUGHES,
Colonel, Commanding Thirty-eighth Iowa Infantry.

Brigadier-General FISK.

JANUARY 8-10, 1863.—Scout from Elkhorn to Berryville, Ark.

Report of Col. John F. Philips, Seventh Missouri State Militia Cavalry.

HEADQUARTERS,
Elkhorn, Ark., January 10, 1863.

GENERAL: I have the honor to report that night before last I sent out, under Captain [T. W.] Houts, of Company A, about 75 men in the direction of Berryville. He has just returned, 6 a. m. Near Berryville he surprised and killed a gang of 10 bushwhackers. They were clothed and armed with Federal uniforms and arms, and mounted on good horses, all of which fell into our hands, except one or two horses killed in the *mêlée*. One man made his escape; wounded, however. The scout entered Berryville. No force there. All is quiet, as far as can be learned, to the east of that point.

I send dispatch from Springfield, which explains itself. Marmaduke's force is reported at 6,000. Our trains on Rolla road are in danger. I send a squad to examine telegraph lines.

Very respectfully, &c.,

JNO. F. PHILIPS,
Colonel, Commanding.

Brigadier-General SCHOFIELD,
Commanding Army of the Frontier.

[Inclosure.]

HEADQUARTERS, *January* 9, 1863.

Brigadier General HERRON:

GENERAL: I believe the enemy have decamped, and taken the old Saint Louis road. We whipped them yesterday. General Brown is wounded. I have sent a force to watch them.

Yours,

B. CRABB,
Colonel, Commanding Forces and Post.

JANUARY 9-12, 1863.—Expedition from Huntsville to Buffalo River, Ark.

Report of Maj. Joseph W. Caldwell, First Iowa Cavalry.

HEADQUARTERS FIRST IOWA CAVALRY,
Camp at Carrollton, Ark., January 13, 1863.

GENERAL: I have the honor to report that, in compliance with instructions received from you, I left camp at Huntsville, Ark., on the morning of the 9th instant, at 8 o'clock, with a detachment of the First Regiment Iowa Cavalry, numbering 300 officers and men, and proceeded toward Kingston, Ark., where I arrived at 2 p. m. of said day, when I received important information of the movements of the enemy, which I immediately conveyed to you by dispatch.

The guides who accompanied me not being acquainted with the region of country beyond Kingston, where your instructions required that I should go, I procured new guides at the above-named place, and proceeded on the road 4 miles beyond Kingston. It being 4 p. m., and learning that the road before me was a winding one, through wild mountains, utterly devoid of habitations, I bivouacked for the night, and threw out on all the roads in the vicinity strong guards.

Early in the evening the picket guard on the eastern road captured 3 men and 14 head of horses and mules, owned by an individual called Parson Rodgers, who confessed to me that he was engaged in buying horses and mules and selling them to the army of the so-called Confederate States, this being the third lot he had purchased.

During the night Capt. J. D. Jenks and Corporal Ramsey, of Company D, First Iowa Cavalry, having in charge 3 prisoners, captured while on picket, and being on their way to camp with them, were halted on the road by some unknown person or persons, who demanded that they surrender, which was promptly refused; whereupon the party was fired upon, without injury, however, to any one, and the fire instantly returned by Captain Jenks, killing 1 man, whose name was ascertained to be Allen Basham. Captain Jenks and Corporal Ramsey succeeded in reaching camp safely with 2 of the 3 prisoners, 1 of the prisoners escaping during the encounter.

At 4 o'clock on the following morning I had the column in motion, and by daylight reached the salpeter works on Buffalo River, 14 miles from Kingston, where I completely surprised the small force there employed, and captured 17 out of 20; the lieutenant in charge and 2 men being engaged at work in the timber a short distance from the buildings, succeeded in making good their escape.

The buildings, fourteen in number, very extensive, entirely new and of good workmanship, together with two steam-engines, three boilers, seven large iron kettles, weighing, according to the bill for the same, found on the premises, 800 pounds each, besides half a ton of saltpeter, a large fire-proof iron safe (Hall's patent), three Concord wagons, two carts, and all the appurtenances of a first-class establishment of this character, were completely destroyed by fire and otherwise.

After remaining at this place about six hours, I moved my command to a point 4 miles below, on Buffalo River, and sent a detachment of 100 men, under the command of Captains [Alexander G.] McQueen and [David C.] Dinsmore, of the First Iowa Cavalry, to destroy an establishment of similar character. The working party, having a lookout posted on an elevated point on the mountains, escaped, but the detachment took possession of the works, which consisted of several frame buildings, entirely new, with four large iron kettles, in full operation, all of which were destroyed.

In the mean time I captured, in the valley and mountains skirting the Buffalo River, some 20 prisoners, all notorious outlaws, and a like number of horses.

Having been entirely successful in accomplishing all that was assigned to me, without casualty to any of my command, I started on my return, and recrossed the mountains in the night time, arriving in camp, at Carrollton, Ark., on the evening of January 12, delivering my prisoners, to the number of 39, and 39 horses and mules, to Lieutenant-Colonel [Elias B.] Baldwin, of the Eighth Missouri Cavalry, provost-marshal of the Third Division, Army of the Frontier.

Very respectfully, your obedient servant,

J. W. CALDWELL,
Major First Iowa Cavalry.

Brig. Gen. F. J. HERRON,
Commanding Third Division, Army of the Frontier.

JANUARY 12, 1863.—Skirmish at Lick Creek, near Helena, Ark.

Report of Lieut. James B. Bradford, Second Wisconsin Cavalry.

HELENA, ARK., *January* 13, 1863.

COLONEL: I have the honor to state that, by order of Col. Powell Clayton, of the Fifth Kansas Cavalry, commanding the expedition which left Helena, Ark., on Sunday, January 11, for White River, I was detailed by Col. Thomas Stephens, commanding Second Wisconsin Cavalry, to convey dispatches to the commanding officer at Helena, Ark., and was furnished with a command, consisting of 1 sergeant and 24 men, for that purpose from the Second Wisconsin Cavalry.

The command left Big Creek, the camp of the above-named regiment (a point 18 miles west of Helena, on the Saint Charles road, I believe), on Monday, January 12, at 3 p. m. A small party of rebels having been reported to me as seen a short distance in the advance, I used the utmost caution, keeping 3 men well in advance, but in sight of myself and command.

On arriving at a point called Lick Creek, about 6 miles east of Big Creek and 12 miles from Helena, I found that the bridge across said creek, constructed by the Federal troops the day previous, had been destroyed. Thinking it necessary that I should advance as rapidly as possible, I immediately gave orders to cross the creek at a ford a short distance from the bridge. I had succeeded in crossing about 10 of the command (including myself and sergeant), and while on the east bank superintending the crossing of the balance (the ford being very deep and muddy), we were attacked by a body of rebel cavalry from the west side of the creek, supposed to be about 75 strong. Before crossing the creek, having reasons to believe that we might be attacked at that point, some of the command had examined a road and the surroundings leading into the one upon which I had advanced at a distance of about 40 rods from the creek. They reported that no enemy were visible. I now think that the above-mentioned cavalry were secreted in the woods between the roads.

On being attacked, those of the command who had crossed the creek immediately commenced pouring a very effective fire (with their revolvers, not having any carbines) into the enemy, and succeeded in unhorsing 5 or 6 of them. We continued to fire until our revolvers were exhausted of their loads, when my men commenced to retreat, having seen that those who were in the creek and on the west bank were either killed, wounded, or prisoners.

I succeeded in rallying those remaining of the command after retreating about 30 rods, and commanded them to reload their revolvers and endeavor to assist those who were on the east side of the creek unhorsed or wounded; but, while preparing to load, we were fired upon by a party of about 30 men, commanding us at the same time to surrender. The said men were concealed about 4 rods north of the road leading to Helena. Not deeming it safe to attack (our arms being unloaded), and their party numbering at least four to one of my command, I gave the order to follow, and succeeded in passing the enemy, after receiving two volleys from them at a distance of about 10 and 4 rods. I immediately pursued my way to Helena with what remained, consisting of myself, sergeant, and 3 privates. We succeeded in securing 4 horses and equipments belonging to those who had been unhorsed, and brought them to Helena, at which point we arrived at 7 p. m., when I immediately reported myself and command, and delivered the dispatches as ordered.

At about 10 o'clock on the same evening, four more of the command reported at Helena, having succeeded in evading the second ambush by taking a circuit to the right, their firing on the advance having warned them of the position of the rebels.

On this day, January 13, about 10 a. m., one more man came in, having remained secreted in the neighborhood of the fight until evening, when he succeeded in making his way to Helena, and reported that, as well as he could judge, he saw about 9 or 10 of our men taken prisoners, and supposed that the balance were either killed or wounded.

It gives me pleasure to state that the men under my charge behaved admirably.

I am, very respectfully, your obedient servant,

JAMES B. BRADFORD,
Lieutenant and Reg. Com. of Sub., Second Wisconsin Cav.

Col. CYRUS BUSSEY, *Commanding Post at Helena, Ark.*

P. S.—Since writing the above, 5 paroled prisoners have reported to me, who state that our loss was 1 killed, 2 badly wounded, besides several slightly, making 14 who have returned. Captains Cawley and Clifford, commanding rebels, admit that they were 200 strong, and that they lost 1 lieutenant killed; also others killed and wounded, which my men corroborate.

JANUARY 13-19, 1863.—Expedition from Helena up the White River, Ark., and capture of Saint Charles, Clarendon, Devall's Bluff, and Des Arc, Ark.

*Reports of Brig. Gen. Willis A. Gorman, U. S. Army.**

HEADQUARTERS DISTRICT OF EASTERN ARKANSAS,
Saint Charles, White River, January 14, 1863.

GENERAL: General McClernand's attack and capture of Post Arkansas, with about 6,000 prisoners, 13 guns, and all their stores and munitions of war, has been heretofore reported to you. I arrived at this place last night, and found the place evacuated, they having left day before yesterday evening, carrying away, by a little steamer, two 8-inch siege guns, and six light pieces. Their train and infantry left by land at the same time. I have started the cavalry in pursuit of their train, but I think they have burned one bridge, which will prevent its capture. I have left one regiment of infantry, one battery of six guns, two companies of cavalry, and the iron-clad gunboat Cincinnati here, as a temporary garrison. I proceed at once, with the iron-clad gunboat Saint Louis and the remainder of the command, to Devall's Bluff, where I hope to overtake their little steamer with their artillery aboard, before they can carry it off by railroad from Devall's Bluff to Little Rock. No accident has occurred, and all is going well. I expect to meet 1,500 of my cavalry at Clarendon. I shall try and communicate with our forces at Batesville, if they are there.

I am, general, respectfully, &c.,

W. A. GORMAN,
Brigadier-General, Commanding.

Maj. Gen. SAMUEL R. CURTIS,
Commanding Department of the Missouri.

---

* For reports of Lieut. Commander John G. Walker, U. S. Navy, commanding naval forces, see Annual Report of the Secretary of the Navy, December 7, 1863.

HEADQUARTERS DISTRICT OF EASTERN ARKANSAS,
Devall's Bluff, January 18, 1863.

GENERAL: On yesterday we took, and my command now occupy, this point. I found the railroad from here to Little Rock in good running order, a train having been here the day before we arrived. They have 2 locomotives, 2 passenger cars, and 12 platform cars. Three of the latter we have here.

I captured here two 8-inch Columbiads in good order, with carriages complete; 90 new Enfield rifles, and 25 prisoners, including a master's mate of the rebel Navy.

Our approach was sudden and rapid, and on arriving in sight two companies of infantry, who were here busily engaged in getting the two large guns on the cars, ran at once and scattered into the woods. My infantry, which had been landed below and sent to their rear, caught all except those who took the Des Arc road and concealed themselves in the woods. My cavalry was landed at once, and penetrated the road 7 miles on the Little Rock road, until the mud and water became utterly impassable. I started a gunboat and some infantry early this morning up the river to Des Arc, where I hope to capture a train engaged in transporting supplies to Little Rock, and perhaps a quantity of corn, oats, and other forage.

Hindman with his forces are at Little Rock, having arrived there last Monday [12th]. General Henry [E.] McCulloch is believed to be at Pine Bluff. General Hawes, with three regiments of cavalry and six pieces of light artillery, was ordered to re-enforce Post Arkansas, and started last Sunday [11th] on a forced march, but only got as far as Hicks' railroad station, 3 miles from Brownsville, and is supposed now to be on the west side of the Arkansas.

All the forces of the enemy except two, or possibly three, companies of bushwhackers are west of the Arkansas River, and the people are running their stock and negroes toward Texas. It seems to be quite sure that their army does not intend to fight at Little Rock.

If it were possible for me to get cavalry across this low, marshy country to Brownsville and Little Rock, I would start them at once; but this is utterly impracticable at present. The snow is now 4 or 5 inches deep, and melting, and Grand Prairie is one vast sheet of water, precluding the least possible hope of getting across to Little Rock with either infantry, artillery, or cavalry until the rainy season is over and the country, which is a vast level plain, dries off. If it were possible to get cavalry across the prairie, the enemy would cut the bridges over the Bayou Metoe and smaller streams, now much swollen, and stop our progress.

In obedience to your orders, I sent a force of cavalry, 1,200 strong, from Helena to Clarendon. Since their arrival at Clarendon the rain has fallen to such an extent as to fill the vast bayous, &c., to such proportions as to make it a serious question whether I shall be able to save the horses, as I have not sufficient transportation to take them out by water, and forage cannot be had, for like causes, except by the river.

General McClernand has ordered me to send him General Fisk's brigade, which I will have to do, as General Grant has authority to take him. I will, therefore, be compelled to leave this point and go below, as I shall be so crippled as to leave me utterly powerless. I was weakened before by the withdrawal of one regiment at New Madrid and one at Memphis, and then was required to have a garrison of 2,000 men at Helena. I have left a regiment of 800 infantry, two companies of cavalry, and one battery at Saint Charles, and now I am called on to part with my largest brigade, at least 3,500 strong, making a draft in all of 6,400 men on me, leaving me less than 5,000 effective infantry.

By the junction of Hawes, Hindman, McCulloch, and Holmes, at or near Little Rock, the enemy's forces will equal, if not exceed, 25,000.

General McClernand informs me that the Arkansas River is not yet safely navigable, and says that he has been ordered to Napoleon at once.

I am, general, very truly, your obedient servant,

W. A. GORMAN,
Brigadier-General, Commanding.

Maj. Gen. SAMUEL R. CURTIS,
Commanding Department of the Missouri.

HEADQUARTERS DISTRICT OF EASTERN ARKANSAS,
Devall's Bluff, January 18, 1863.

GENERAL: The gunboats Romeo and Rose, with my forces, under Colonel [W. T.] Spicely, Twenty-fourth Indiana Infantry, entered Des Arc on yesterday at 4 p. m.; seized the post-office and telegraph office, and captured 70 prisoners, none escaping; several thousand bushels of Government corn, 70 small-arms, and 200 rounds 6-pounder ammunition, the same captured by the enemy when they took the Blue Wing. A large number of letters from the post-office has fallen into our hands.

I find that there are two or three companies, under Major Chrisman, at Cotton Plant, but poorly armed, and now they are cut off from all support, and I have destroyed all their ferries across White River up to Des Arc, and I may send an expedition to Batesville to hunt the Blue Wing and capture or burn her. Thus you see the expedition to Des Arc is a handsome success.

It is very annoying to find that I cannot cross the flats to Little Rock from here, and still more so to find my strongest brigade taken from me just at this time, leaving me powerless for efficient service.

I am, general, truly, yours,

W. A. GORMAN,
Brigadier-General, Commanding.

Maj. Gen. SAMUEL R. CURTIS,
Commanding Department of the Missouri.

HEADQUARTERS DISTRICT OF EASTERN ARKANSAS,
Saint Charles, Ark., January 20, 1863.

GENERAL: The expedition up the White River, under my command, has proved a complete success. At Saint Charles I captured a large amount of forage, corn, &c., with some prisoners. At Devall's Bluff I took two 8-inch columbiads, with carriages, all in complete order; 25 prisoners, with 70 new Enfield rifles, some stores, tents, &c.; destroyed three cars, the railroad depot, tore up the railroad track, and burned two railroad bridges, one 90 and the other 200 feet in length. At Des Arc we captured 100 prisoners, several hundred rounds of fixed 6-pounder ammunition, several thousand bushels of Government corn, a large rebel mail, and destroyed their telegraph.

All the force of the enemy in this part of the State have crossed the Arkansas to Little Rock. They have driven their negroes and carried their property, supplies, and munitions south of the Arkansas, toward Arkadelphia.

I should have gone direct to Little Rock if it had been practicable to cross the sea of mud and water intervening between that place and Devall's Bluff, but this is impossible at the present. Furthermore, my orders were such as to compel my immediate return.

I am now returning to Helena, in order to fit out a force to assist in the expedition against Vicksburg. I shall perform that duty with all possible dispatch.

I am, general, very respectfully, your obedient servant,

W. A. GORMAN,
Brigadier-General, Commanding.

Maj. Gen. SAMUEL R. CURTIS,
Commanding Department of the Missouri.

JANUARY —, 1863.—Skirmish near Maysville, Ark.

Report of Col. William A. Phillips, Third Indian Home Guard, commanding brigade.

HDQRS. 3D BRIG., 1ST DIV., ARMY OF THE FRONTIER,
Camp Curtis, January 15, 1863.

GENERAL: I have just this moment heard from my commissary, Captain Heath. I start an escort toward Fayetteville to meet him.

We have had 4 inches of snow.

Quite a spirited little affair occurred between a detachment of my command, under Captain [H. S.] Anderson, of the Third Indian Regiment, and a force of some 200 rebels, or bushwhackers, under Colonel Livingston and Captains Timon and Fry Smith. It took place 12 miles south of this, and was very well managed, our force moving on them in three separate columns, and, when the enemy broke, they ran from the first into the second, and finally into the third. Not less than 25 or 30 rebels must have been killed or disabled. Captain Smith (formerly of Jasper County, Missouri) was killed by Lieutenant Whitlow, and 7 others were killed on the spot of the attack. The enemy was pursued until his broken fragments were lost in the woods.

There has evidently been an attempt to organize a force either to take Neosho or menace the trains. I sent a party to Hildebrand's Mill, 20 miles southwest.

With respect,

WM. A. PHILLIPS,
Colonel, Commanding Third Brigade.

General SCHOFIELD,
Commanding Army of the Frontier.

JANUARY 21, 1863.—Skirmish near Columbia, Mo.

Report of Col. Joseph B. Douglass, Sixty-first Enrolled Missouri Militia.

HDQRS. SIXTY-FIRST REGT. ENROLLED MISSOURI MILITIA,
Columbia, Mo., January 22, 1863.

SIR: Late yesterday evening a body of troops under my command, whilst on a scout, and some 9 miles from my headquarters, found a Confederate camp, with tents and all necessary appurtenances thereto, containing 8 Confederate captains. The camp was situated in a very brushy country; consequently they escaped from their tent, my men following, and eventually succeeded in capturing 4 of them, after a brief resistance. We got all their arms, camp equipage, &c. The lateness of the attack prevented us from capturing the whole of them. My men camped on the ground, and are scouring the country in the vicinity to-day. We also succeeded in capturing 2 of Porter's men last night in addition.

I regret to say that 2 of my bravest troops got seriously wounded in the fight before we captured the 4 rebel captains. They never surrendered until they had exhausted all their shots, they being armed with double-barreled shot-guns, in addition to navy revolvers.

You can now see why I object to this indiscriminate release of bad men from prison, and why you should not permit banished men to return here.

I am, sir, very respectfully, your obedient servant,

J. B. DOUGLASS,
Colonel, Commanding.

General SAMUEL R. CURTIS,
Commanding Department of the Missouri.

JANUARY 23-27, 1863.—Scout from Fayetteville to Van Buren, Ark.

REPORTS.

No 1.—Col. M. La Rue Harrison, First Arkansas Cavalry.
No. 2.—Lieut. Col. James Stuart, Tenth Illinois Cavalry.

No. 1.

Report of Col. M. La Rue Harrison, First Arkansas Cavalry.

FAYETTEVILLE, ARK., *January* 27, 1863.

GENERAL: On Friday [23d], I sent from this post a scout, under Lieut. Col. James Stuart, of the Tenth Illinois Cavalry, composed of 90 men of the First Arkansas Cavalry, under Capt. Charles Galloway, and 40 men, with two howitzers, of the Tenth Illinois Cavalry. The scout crossed Boston Mountains, at the head of Frog Bayou, on Saturday morning [24th], and entered Van Buren the same evening about 7 o'clock.

On Sunday morning our men captured the steamer Julia Roan, and took from it 175 Confederate prisoners. About 50 were captured in the town and 75 more on the route. Over 200 were released on parole, subject to exchange for Federal prisoners. Colonel Stuart's command was fired on, without effect, by a company of rebel infantry stationed on the south side of the river. Our loss, none; the enemy, 6 killed and several wounded.

Lieutenant-Colonel Stuart arrived at this post with his command this evening at 6 o'clock.

M. LA RUE HARRISON,
Colonel, Commanding Post.

Maj. Gen. SAMUEL R. CURTIS,
Commanding Department of the Missouri.

No. 2.

Report of Lieut. Col. James Stuart, Tenth Illinois Cavalry.

HEADQUARTERS TENTH ILLINOIS CAVALRY,
Fayetteville, Ark., January 28, 1863.

GENERAL: I have the honor to report, for your information, that I proceeded from this place on a scout to Van Buren, Ark., in command of 150 men of the Tenth Illinois Cavalry and First Arkansas Cavalry, on the 23d instant, by the way of the Frog Bayou road, and arrived at Van Buren on the 24th.

I received information that a steamboat had gone up the river to Fort Smith for men and stores for the enemy. On my arrival at Van Buren, I placed a patrol guard on the bank of the river to watch for the boat, and with the remaining portion of my command patrolled the town, taking 25 Confederate soldiers prisoners, who were on their way to Fort Smith with their arms, horses, &c. About half an hour after daybreak the next morning, the boat was reported coming down the river, and I made my arrangements to receive her. I brought her opposite the levee, and found 1 lieutenant, 1 surgeon, and 246 men on board, on their way to Little Rock. Part of the men were sick. I paroled all of them, and allowed the boat to proceed. I inclose herewith a list* of all the prisoners taken and paroled during my scout, namely, 3 lieutenants and 246 men. I likewise ascertained that General Steele, of Texas, was in command at Fort Smith, with from 400 to 500 men. A skeleton brigade of Texas troops had passed up through there two days before, who had ninety days' furlough to go to Texas and recruit up. I am likewise informed from a reliable source that the Choctaw, Creek, and Cherokee Nations are anxious to join our forces. All they want is a nucleus to form on.

I had quite a lively skirmish with a small body of the enemy across the river, at Van Buren, on the 25th, but soon dispersed them with one of my howitzers, which I had along. Several of the enemy were seen to fall from their horses, and, I presume, were either killed or wounded. None of my men were hit, although the bullets fell thick for a short time.

After remaining in Van Buren from the evening of the 24th instant until 10 o'clock on the 26th, I started for the post, at which place I arrived on the evening of the 27th instant.

Your obedient servant,

JAMES STUART,
Lieutenant-Colonel Tenth Illinois Cavalry.

[Maj. Gen. JOHH M. SCHOFIELD.]

JANUARY 27, 1863.—Affair at Bloomfield, Mo.

Congratulatory orders from Brigadier-General Carr.

GENERAL ORDERS, No. 4. } HEADQUARTERS SAINT LOUIS DISTRICT,
Saint Louis, Mo., February 2, 1863.

The brigadier-general commanding the district has heard with pleasure of the affair of the 27th ultimo, in which Colonel [James] Lindsay, Sixty-

* Not found.

eighth Regiment Enrolled Missouri State Militia, with about 250 of his men and two small pieces of artillery, provided at private expense, dashed into the town of Bloomfield, Mo., capturing a large number of the enemy, with their horses, equipments, arms, and stores, thus completely routing and breaking up the troublesome band of guerrillas which have for a long time infested that neighborhood.

The officers and men of the Sixty-eighth Regiment Enrolled Missouri Militia engaged in this affair have the thanks of the brigadier-general commanding, and he hopes their example, when occasion requires, will be emulated, not only by the Enrolled Missouri Militia, but by all the troops in his command.

By order of Brigadier-General Carr:

R. M. ELLIOTT,
Lieutenant and Acting Aide-de-Camp.

FEBRUARY 2-3, 1863.—Skirmishes at Vine Prairie, on White Oak River, and near the mouth of Mulberry River, Ark.

Reports of Col. M. La Rue Harrison, First Arkansas Cavalry.

HEADQUARTERS,
Post Fayetteville, Ark., February 6, 1863.

GENERAL: Inclosed I send you copies of Captain [Charles] Galloway's report of the late scout, and also my letter of instructions to him. Captain G. [Galloway] disobeyed my orders in two particulars: First, he went to Ozark before going to the canebrake, at mouth of Mulberry; second, he did not surround the canebrake, but took his command toward Fayetteville, allowing Captain [R. E.] Travis, a junior captain, to make the attack, unsupported, on 30 rebels at Therilkyl's Ferry. Captain Galloway's reputation as a commander of scouts; his thoroughness as a soldier and a man, and his success (in the main) on this and other scouts, have induced me not to place him under arrest, but to reprimand him in the place of it. If Captain G. [Galloway] had followed my instructions implicitly, the whole Mankins gang could and would have been taken in. Everything was really as my map and instructions represented. Captain Galloway's excuse for going to Ozark first, is set forth in his report (the hope of capturing a steamer and 100 rebels in Ozark). The disobedience in that particular brought him in contact with 180 rebels, and he gained a brilliant victory. His excuse for not surrounding the canebrake is, that Captain Travis' spies reported no rebels in the cane (nearly all having crossed the river the day before), and that he allowed Captain T. [Travis] to go with 8 men to take in a party of 5 at Farmer's. That the party proved (as I had told him) to be Mankins' gang; and the attack on 30 men in a log-house by 8 from without was foolhardy, and that Captain T. [Travis] should have reconnoitered and notified the command before making the attack.

Subsequent to Captain Galloway's report comes the complete final particulars of Captain Travis' assault. Captain Travis drove every one of the rebels from the house, but did not know it at the time he retreated. He was not killed, but was brought out by the citizen who was employed to bury him, and is now likely to recover. Two of the other men were killed, 1 severely wounded, and 1 taken prisoner. The rebels left some of their horses and most of their arms, which were picked up and taken off by the Union men who went to bury the dead.

Captain Galloway has always been one of my best officers; a truly brave, worthy, and patriotic man, and, though he took this course with the advice and sanction of other officers in his command, I am satisfied such a thing will not be repeated; and I hope my lenity to him will be sanctioned by you, on account of his former services and many good qualities.

I remain, general, your obedient servant,

M. LA RUE HARRISON,
Colonel First Arkansas Cavalry, Commanding Post.

Maj. Gen. JOHN M. SCHOFIELD,
Commanding Army of the Frontier.

P. S.—Permit me to say, in addition, that Lieutenant-Colonel Stuart never sent me his official report of scout to Van Buren, nor the list of prisoners, as ordered; consequently, I am unable to give you a written report of that scout, although it was wholly planned and sent out by me. I learn that Lieutenant-Colonel Stuart has sent you a report. I think it should be returned.

—

HEADQUARTERS,
Post Fayetteville, Ark., February 9, 1863.

GENERAL: On Saturday, January 31, I sent Capt. C. [Charles] Galloway, Company E, First Arkansas Cavalry, in command of 81 men, to Huntsville, to protect the citizens of that place in holding a Union convention, and to assist in organizing companies for the First Arkansas Infantry, Colonel [James M.] Johnson.

On the 31st a large and enthusiastic meeting was held there; nearly 1,000 said to be present. Addresses were made by Colonel Johnson and Captain Searle, of the Tenth Illinois Cavalry. From Huntsville I ordered Captain Galloway to proceed, with his command, to the Arkansas River.

On Monday morning, February 2, he entered Ozark, but, finding no enemy, proceeded up the river, on the stage road, toward Van Buren. At the White Oak River, 7 miles west of Ozark, our advance guard, under Lieutenant [James] Roseman, was attacked by a steamboat escort of 180 men of Colonel Dorsey's rebel cavalry. Shots were exchanged, and our advance fell back to a commanding position, and formed on Captain Galloway's main column. The rebels charged upon them with a yell like that of the Indians. When within about 150 yards, a volley from our rifles brought them to a stand. After thirty minutes' severe fighting, the enemy retreated in disorder, carrying their dead and wounded with them. The enemy lost 8 killed and 15 or 20 wounded; also 6 horses killed and a large number disabled. Captain Galloway lost 2 horses killed and had 1 man slightly wounded. He followed the rebels westward for 10 miles, scattering them completely. On Monday night he encamped near the mouth of Little Frog Bayou Creek, and returned toward Fayetteville on Tuesday.

On Tuesday morning a small reconnoitering party (7 men), under Capt. Robert E. Travis, Company M, First Arkansas Cavalry, attacked 30 rebels of Mankins' gang in a log-house in the canebrake near the mouth of Mulberry River, and fought there for nearly half an hour.

The rebels retreated, leaving most of their horses and arms on the ground. Captain Travis' party were so much crippled in the fight as to be unable to take any advantage of the affair, and left the ground. A Union citizen took some men, went and buried the dead, brought off the wounded, and picked up the rebel arms and captured their horses.

The attack was the most daring one of any I have heard of since the commencement of the war. The party consisted of Capt. R. E. Travis, Company M, First Arkansas Cavalry (severely wounded in the right hip), and Sergts. W. P. Clark (unhurt), P. Asbill (unhurt), and Noel G. Rutherford, Company D, First Arkansas Cavalry (taken prisoner); Sergt. Benjamin Hooper, Company M, First Arkansas Cavalry (unhurt); Private Giles Loften, Company D, First Arkansas Cavalry (unhurt; was not in the action; held the horses 80 rods distant); Privates Edgar White, Oscar White, and James R. Williamson, Company I, Tenth Illinois (2 killed instantly and 1 died of wounds). The prisoners taken by this scout were 1 captain, 2 lieutenants, and 2 privates paroled and 7 brought in.

I am, colonel, your most obedient servant,

M. LA RUE HARRISON,

Colonel First Arkansas Cavalry, Commanding Post.

LORENZO THOMAS,

Adjutant-General, U. S. Army.

FEBRUARY 2-13, 1863.—Scouts and skirmishes in and about Mingo Swamp, Mo.

REPORTS.

No. 1.—Lieut. Col. Bazel F. Lazear, Twelfth Missouri State Militia Cavalry.
No. 2.—Maj. F. W. Reeder, Twelfth Missouri State Militia Cavalry.

No. 1.

Report of Lieut. Col. Bazel F. Lazear, Twelfth Missouri State Militia Cavalry.

JACKSON, MO., *February* 14, 1863.

SIR: I have the honor to report that Captain [Levi E.] Whybark, Company F, Twelfth Missouri State Militia Cavalry, with 50 men of the different companies of the regiment, returned yesterday from a scout to Mingo Swamp, and reports killing 3 and wounding 2 more of the band of General McGee. This has been one of the worst bands of guerrillas that has infested Southeast Missouri, making their headquarters in the swamps. They have been a terror to the whole country. I inclose you a note, addressed to McGee by two Confederate captains,* showing you in what light they were looked upon by Confederate officers. There are not more than three of the notorious ones of the gang left; their names are Hetterbrand, Cowan, and Dixon. There are two of the gang now in the guard-house here, who were slightly wounded. Their names are Spain and Bradaway. The last deserves particular notice. He was a notorious outlaw in California. Since he returned, and before this, he

---

* Not found.

was a notorious counterfeiter here, and nigger thief, and for the last five months he has been connected with McGee's band of guerrillas, which they are in every sense of the word. I am sorry they are prisoners on my hands, as they should have been shot on the spot. There are other bands of this character in the county below here, and it was concerning these bands that I wished to see the commanding general; but the breaking up of our regiment has interfered with my arrangements, and I am sorry for these poor Union people, who never have been properly protected, as they should have and might have been; and if the authorities could see the downcast and saddened countenances of Union men here, they, I think, would hesitate about breaking up and sending off this regiment. For my own part, I think injustice has been done me and my men; but I am too good a soldier to disobey any order coming to me from my superior officers.

I hope you will pardon me for alluding to this matter in this report, but justice to this section demands that attention should be called to the state of affairs here, and I hope you will not allow all protection to be taken from these people.

Very respectfully, &c.,

B. F. LAZEAR,

Lieut. Col., Comdg. Twelfth Missouri State Militia Cavalry.

Captain DYER,

Assistant Adjutant-General, Saint Louis District, Mo.

No. 2.

Report of Maj. F. W. Reeder, Twelfth Missouri State Militia Cavalry.

JACKSON, MO., *February* 7, 1863.

COLONEL: Pursuant to your order, I proceeded, on the 2d instant, to Dallas, Mo., for the purpose of killing, capturing, and dispersing such bands of outlaws and rebels as infest the vicinity of Dallas and Mingo Swamp.

After arriving in Dallas with my command, detachments of the different companies at this post, I was joined by detachments from the companies stationed at Fredericktown and Patton, and at once sent out four scouts to capture the notorious McGee and his outlaws, said to be harboring around that place. These scouts brought in three of the outlaws, from whom I learned that McGee had started the day previous toward Bloomfield, carrying with him a number of stolen horses and arms, as well as four Union citizens as prisoners. I waited until the evening of the 3d instant, when the last scout came in, bringing twenty-five saddles, buried by the rebels some two months since, and which, on account of lack of transportation, as well as their total worthlessness, I ordered to be burned.

Resolving to overtake McGee, with his band, the next day, and to push on to Bloomfield through the Mingo Swamp, I allowed the men and horses to rest till next morning, and started after these outlaws. Regardless of the advice of those who had for a long time been residents within the said swamp, and who pronounced the passage through the same at this time of the year an impossibility, as the ground would be frozen, and the water below would, consequently, recede from beneath, I determined to risk it, and went on. When you add to all this the circumstance that a violent snow-storm set in as we started, which lasted without intermission till the next day, as well as the uncertainty of finding a road through that swamp, you can form an idea of the obstacles presented to us.

Arriving within 4 miles of the swamp (at Bollinger's Mills), I left the light wagon, with the provisions we carried along, with orders to return. We here crossed the Castor River, which most of my men had to swim, and I took 40 of the best horses and men and pushed rapidly forward, having heard that McGee with 35 of his men had passed there that morning. I left Captain [William T.] Hunter with the rest of the command (50 men) to follow slowly. After a sharp trot of 10 miles, we suddenly came to the house of S. Cato, a man who had been harboring these outlaws for a long time, and perceiving a considerable number of men feeding their horses, we dashed upon them before a single one had the chance to escape. They were at once recognized as McGee's band, and as our approach was as sudden as it was unexpected, they fled in confusion across the large corn-field in the center of which the house of Cato stood. My men now were in their element, and whilst others quickly tore down the fence of the corn-field, the rest surrounded it, and within fifteen minutes we had exterminated the whole band. We took no prisoners from amongst them, as I had previously given the order not to do so. We counted 9 killed, amongst them McGee; 20 mortally wounded, and 3 slightly, the latter of whom we brought in. We did not lose a man. Besides, we captured some 25 horses and equipments, many of which have already been identified as having been stolen by them from Union men, and some arms, all of which are ordered to be turned over by different commanders of companies to the quartermaster. Not having time to bury the dead and attend to the crippled and dying, I left them to the tender care of their good friends, of whom there are plenty close by; and, being meanwhile joined by Captain Hunter, I pushed on to Bloomfield, which town I entered amidst a terrible snow-storm at midnight. Although we at once surrounded the town and every house in it, we did not capture more than 8 prisoners, some of whom, being on furlough from the so-called Confederate Army, were paroled, and ordered to report to this post at the end of each month. Adjutant Macklind will hand in their names. All the rumors I heard of a force of 200 or 300 being at that place, and of a still larger force 40 miles below, at Four Mile, are without the slightest foundation, and the only reliable information I obtained was that [W. L.] Jeffers, with 2,000 men, was at Epsom Bottom, 150 miles below Bloomfield, and that he was preparing to join General Holmes at Pocahontas. I quartered my men, who had been without food since morning, at the different houses in the town, and having sufficiently refreshed the horses, I returned through the swamp the next morning by a different route than the one I came, with the hope of getting a few more of them, should there be any.

On my route back I divided my command into six parties, with orders to thoroughly scour the country and meet me at Dallas the next day. We returned here on the 7th instant, having accomplished our object and restored peace to a part of the country to which McGee for the last year has been a terror. Officers and men behaved admirably throughout the scout. They bore the severe hardships of fatigue, hunger, and cold, through the most desolate part of Missouri, and a march in the midst of a most violent snow-storm, with alacrity and without a murmur, and so well did they do their duty that it would be injustice almost for me to mention any particular name. Those, however, who were the most conspicuous for their gallant conduct were First Lieutenant [Thomas H.] Macklind, acting adjutant; Captain [William C.] Bangs, commanding Company G; Lieutenant Pope [Erich Pape], Company A;

Lieutenant Charveaux, and our guide, Private William Massey, a member of Company D, of this regiment, who truly guided us the different routes through the swamp as to elicit the admiration of all. I ought also to mention Sergt. Jesse Green, of the Sixty-eighth Ohio Regiment Infantry Volunteers, who volunteered to accompany the expedition, and who, whilst acting as sergeant-major, proved himself very efficient and trustworthy.

I have the honor to be, colonel, very respectfully, your obedient servant,

F. W. REEDER,
Major Twelfth Missouri State Militia Cav., Comdg. Expedition.

Lieut. Col. B. F. LAZEAR,
Comdg. Twelfth Missouri State Militia Cavalry, Jackson, Mo.

FEBRUARY 4, 1863.—Skirmish at Batesville, Ark.

Report of Brig. Gen. John W. Davidson, U. S. Army.

WEST PLAINS, MO., *February* 7, 1863.

The dash on Batesville has accomplished all it was intended. Express is just received from Colonel [G. E.] Waring, commanding my cavalry division. He drove Marmaduke's forces out of Batesville the night of the 4th instant, killing and wounding many and capturing some prisoners, among them Colonel Adams. Waring says Captain [G. C.] Rose, Fourth Missouri Cavalry, led the charge into Batesville most gallantly. Such of the enemy as could not crowd into the ferry-boats swam the river. Marmaduke's entire force is on the other side, and the pickets were exchanging shots on the morning of the 5th. Waring has remounted his men from the country. Of course, as the expedition was only intended as a reconnaissance and a forage, it has its full instructions to return carefully. I am sending a fresh battalion to act as its rear guard. I am moving back to our new position, and you may rely on my keeping myself ready to move at twenty-four hours' notice. I am sending dragoons to see what Leeper did at Van Buren. I have two good ferry-boats there.

J. W. DAVIDSON,
Brigadier-General.

Major-General CURTIS.

FEBRUARY 5-12, 1863.—Scout from Fayetteville to the Arkansas River, and skirmishes at Threlkeld's Ferry and near Van Buren, Ark.

REPORTS.

No. 1.—Col. M. La Rue Harrison, First Arkansas Cavalry.
No. 2.—Lieut. Col. James Stuart, Tenth Illinois Cavalry.

No. 1.

Report of Col. M. La Rue Harrison, First Arkansas Cavalry.

FAYETTEVILLE, *February* 12, 1863.

GENERAL: Lieutenant-Colonel Stuart has just returned from scout to Arkansas River. One hundred men crossed the river near mouth of

Frog Bayou; had a skirmish with Carroll's command, and scattered them. They marched 10 miles into the country on the other side; destroyed the rebel camp and burned their stores; attacked and routed a part of Carroll's command on this side the river, 8 miles east of Van Buren, killing several. [C. A.] Carroll was attempting to cut off Stuart's return, or attack Fayetteville in his absence, but has been foiled in the attempt. About 40 prisoners were taken. Our loss is 1 prisoner and 1 drowned. Quite a number of horses, mules, and arms have fallen into our hands. Lieutenant-Colonel Stuart's official report shall be forwarded immediately.

M. LA RUE HARRISON,
Colonel, Commanding Post.

Maj. Gen. SAMUEL R. CURTIS.

No. 2.

Report of Lieut. Col. James Stuart, Tenth Illinois Cavalry.

HEADQUARTERS TENTH ILLINOIS CAVALRY,
Fayetteville, Ark., February 14, 1863.

GENERAL: I have the honor to report that I left Fayetteville, Ark., on the 5th instant, on a scout to the Arkansas River, in command of 100 men of the Tenth Illinois Cavalry and 125 men of the First Arkansas Cavalry.

On arriving at the river, 4 miles below the mouth of Frog Bayou, I learned that a small force of the enemy was encamped 3 miles below, at Threlkeld's Ferry. I immediately procured some skiffs and had others constructed, with which I ferried over 100 of my command, with orders to surround their camp and attack them. At the same time I moved down on the north side of the river, with two small howitzers, to destroy their log buildings, in case the enemy should take to them for defense; but, through the indiscretion of a small party I had placed on the road leading to the ferry to cut off communication with the enemy, the movement was discovered, which enabled many of them to escape my command.

We had quite a lively engagement, killing several of the enemy, and taking 7 prisoners. My loss, 1 man drowned (Private Douglass, First Arkansas Cavalry). I proceeded thence 12 miles up the river, and captured 30 bales of cotton, which had been turned over by the Confederate States provost-marshal to a man named A. Waddell. I had the same transported by Government teams, which accompanied me to Fayetteville, and placed in a vacant church, by direction of Colonel Harrison.

On the 10th instant, while moving along the Ozark Stage road, about 8 miles east of Van Buren, and near the fork of the Frog Bayou and Stage roads, I was attacked by about 100 of the enemy, who were quickly routed by Capt. William A. Chapin and 50 men of the Tenth Illinois Cavalry, who made a prompt and gallant charge, dispersing the enemy in every direction. I afterward ascertained that it was a party of Colonel Carroll's men, taking down the telegraph wire along the road. I ascertained that this was the only force on this side of the river above Clarksville.

During the scout I took 21 Confederate soldiers prisoners, also horses, mules, arms, &c. I inclose herewith list * of paroled prisoners.

I am, general, very respectfully, your obedient servant.

JAMES STUART,
Lieutenant-Colonel Tenth Illinois Cavalry, Commanding.

Maj. Gen. JOHN M. SCHOFIELD,
Commanding Army of the Frontier.

FEBRUARY 8, 1863.—Skirmish near Independence, Mo.

Report of Col. W. R. Penick, Fifth Missouri State Militia Cavalry.

HDQRS. FIFTH MISSOURI STATE MILITIA CAVALRY,
Independence, Mo., February 11, 1863.

GENERAL: On the 8th instant I sent a detachment of 50 men from Companies C, D, and F, of my command, in charge of Lieut. D. A. Colvin, of Company C, in pursuit of a guerrilla camp, of which I had information. My scout came up with the enemy about 2 p. m., and a running fight commenced, which lasted about thirty minutes. My men killed 8 of the guerrillas, wounded 2, and the remainder, some 4 or 5, escaped in the woods. Captured all their arms and horses, and lost 1 man in the skirmish. To try the fighting qualities of the negro, I sent a contraband along, at his own request. My officers and men agree that his fighting propensities are splendid; he was wounded severely in the right shoulder; he expresses his willingness to again fight the bushwhackers as soon as he is able.

Very respectfully,

W. R. PENICK,
Colonel Fifth Missouri State Militia Cavalry.

Maj. Gen. SAMUEL R. CURTIS,
Commanding Department of the Missouri.

FEBRUARY 15, 1863.—Skirmish near Arkadelphia, Ark.

Report of Col. M. La Rue Harrison, First Arkansas Cavalry.

MARCH 9, [1863.]

Captain Brown, a Union man from Arkadelphia, has just arrived. Had 83 men in the mountains of Washita River, near Arkadelphia, and was attacked by 300 rebels on Sunday, the 15th of February last. The fight lasted from sunrise till noon, when the rebels were completely routed. with a loss of 16 killed and 12 wounded. Captain Brown lost 2 killed and 4 wounded. Captain Brown brought in some recruits for the First Arkansas Infantry.

Captain Vanderpool came in yesterday from Newton County with 200 Union men, mostly recruits for the volunteer service.

M. LA RUE HARRISON,
Colonel, Commanding Post.

Maj. Gen. SAMUEL R. CURTIS,
Commanding Department of the Missouri.

---

* Not found.

FEBRUARY 17-19, 1863.—Attack on the steamer Hercules and burning of Hopefield, Ark.

REPORTS.

No. 1.

Report of Maj. Gen. Stephen A. Hurlbut, U. S. Army, commanding Sixteenth Army Corps.

HEADQUARTERS SIXTEENTH ARMY CORPS,
Memphis, Tenn., February 20, 1863.

SIR: Three days since the rebel guerrillas at Hopefield surprised the tow-steamer Hercules, which had gone into the Arkansas shore in a dense fog, killed 1 of the crew, and burned the boat and a barge of coal. It having been ascertained that Hopefield is a mere shelter for guerrillas, I ordered the place burned, which was done on yesterday; 16 or 17 horses were captured, which no person there would own, quite a number of cavalry saddles, and other evidences of the haunts of the guerrillas. One barn blew up, in burning, with a quantity of concealed powder.

I have stopped all communication with Arkansas for the present. I have consulted with General Veatch as to the possibility of barricading the streets and roads leading into Memphis, and we unite that it can only be effectually done by cutting the bridges across Gayoso Bayou on such roads as may be selected. This, however, will leave outside of barricades a large portion of the suburbs of Memphis. With the immense depots and hospitals here, both for the Army and the Navy, and the certainty that this point is to be a base of supplies, it will require, in my judgment, an entire division to cover this city so as to prevent the terrible smuggling which is now going on. The effects of it are perfectly demoralizing; bribery and corruption seem to go into every branch of service, and the actual cases of which proof can be made are only, I am afraid, symptoms of a widespread disease.

I have sure information that [R. V.] Richardson's guerrillas have been supplied with revolvers from this city. I propose, to-day, to forbid any arms whatever being exposed or kept for sale in the command.

Major Mudd, supported by two regiments of General Quinby's command, made a dash on Blythe, and captured 12 [guerrillas], and ran the rest off to Coldwater; but they come back as fast as our troops are withdrawn.

As soon as the roads become decent, I think of putting a brigade in near Horn Lake, in the country infested by the guerrillas, and let them eat them out. The country is rich in forage and provisions.

Colonel Webster informs me that the railroad will be completed to-day or to-morrow. It will soon be broken up again, somewhere in

Obion County, I think. The cavalry expedition south starts to-day or to-morrow. I have heard nothing of importance from Dodge or from the Tennessee.

Respectfully,

S. A. HURLBUT,
Major-General.

Lieut. Col. JOHN A. RAWLINS,
Assistant Adjutant-General.

No. 2.

Report of Brig. Gen. James C. Veatch, U. S. Army, commanding District of Memphis.

HEADQUARTERS DISTRICT OF MEMPHIS,
Memphis, Tenn., February 21, 1863.

CAPTAIN: In obedience to the orders of Major-General Hurlbut, I sent four companies of the Sixty-third Illinois Volunteers, under command of Capt. Joseph K. Lemon, on board of the steamer Mill Boy, at 10 a. m. on the 19th instant, with orders to proceed, under convoy of the gunboat Cricket, to the village of Hopefield, on the Arkansas shore, and to burn every house in the place.

This duty was promptly performed, and Captain Lemon reported to me, with his entire command, on his return from the expedition at 5 p. m. on the same day. A lot of horses and mules were found in a stable, unclaimed. They were brought over, and all delivered to Captain Walker, post quartermaster, to be held by him, subject to the claim of loyal owners, with one exception, which will be seen by reference to the report of Captain Lemon, here attached. I also append a copy of the order of Major-General Hurlbut, under which I acted, and a copy of instructions given to the officer commanding the expedition, and ask that they be considered a part of this report.

Very respectfully, your obedient servant,

JAMES C. VEATCH,
Brigadier-General.

Capt. HENRY BINMORE,
Assistant Adjutant-General, Sixteenth Corps.

[Inclosures.]

HEADQUARTERS DISTRICT OF MEMPHIS,
Memphis, Tenn., February 19, 1863.

Commanding Officer of Expedition to Hopefield, Ark.:

SIR: By the within orders of Major-General Hurlbut, you are required to destroy the village of Hopefield.

You will be vigilant and careful, and see that your men commit no depredations nor offer any insults to the inhabitants.

Keep your guard well posted, so that no lurking band of guerrillas shall be allowed to approach without your knowledge.

As soon as you have executed the general's orders, you will return with your command, and report to these headquarters.

By order of Brig. Gen. James C. Veatch:

F. W. FOX,
Assistant Adjutant-General.

SPECIAL ORDERS, No. 10. } HEADQUARTERS SIXTEENTH ARMY CORPS, *Memphis, Tenn., February* 18, 1863.

* * * * * * *

IV. Brig. Gen. J. C. Veatch will detail four companies, under a field officer, with 40 rounds of ammunition, who will proceed to-morrow, under convoy of the gunboat Cricket, to Hopefield, on the Arkansas shore. Upon landing at Hopefield, the place will be immediately covered by guards. The residents will be allowed one hour to remove their effects, after which every building will be burned, and the troops will return, reporting to General Veatch.

* * * * * * *

By order of Major-General Hurlbut:

HENRY BINMORE,
Assistant Adjutant-General.

No. 3.

Report of Capt. Joseph K. Lemon, Sixty-third Illinois Infantry.

CAMP SIXTY-THIRD REGT. ILLINOIS VOL. INFANTRY,
District of Memphis, Tenn., February 20, 1863.

SIR: In compliance with your orders, I proceeded with four companies of the above-named regiment, viz, Company C, commanded by Captain [W. M.] Boughan; Company D, commanded by Lieutenant [J.] Isaminger; Company E, commanded by Captain [H. H.] Walser; Company F, commanded by Lieut. A. Davis, and the gunboat Cricket, to Hopefield, Ark.; placed a strong guard around the village, and, after giving the inhabitants one hour's notice of the destiny of their village, the lighted torch was applied and the place was consumed. There were no depredations committed, neither were any insults offered to the inhabitants. In the livery stables I found 15 head of horses, 9 mules, and 10 saddles, and, as they were said to be owned by citizens of Arkansas, I took them under charge. I turned over 15 head of horses and 9 mules to the quartermaster, Captain Walker. One fine horse was kept by Lieutenant Cook, of General Hurlbut's staff, by order of Major-General Hurlbut.

Very respectfully, your obedient servant,

JOSEPH K. LEMON,
Captain, Commanding Expedition.

Brig. Gen. J. C. VEATCH.

No. 4.

Report of Capt. J. H. McGehee, Arkansas Cavalry, including destruction of the Steamers Jacob Musselman and Grampus No. 2.

CAMP OF UNATTACHED COMPANY, ARKANSAS CAVALRY,
Marion, Ark., March 2, 1863.

COLONEL: In obedience to orders received from the major-general commanding the Trans-Mississippi District, to proceed to the county of Crittenden, Arkansas, for the purpose of scouting and burning cotton in that country, and annoying the enemy on the Mississippi River.

I have the honor to report that I marched from Austin, Ark., and proceeded to the Mississippi River, burning all cotton as I went which was liable to fall into the hands of the enemy.

On the 6th day of January, I captured the steamboat Jacob Musselman, opposite Memphis, lying at the Arkansas shore; ran her to Bradley's Landing, 15 miles above that point, where I captured another boat (flat-boat) loaded with stock. After taking what was valuable on the steamer Jacob Musselman, and the stock off of the flat-boat, I burned them both.

On the 11th day of January, I captured the steamboat Grampus No. 2, just off the wharf at Memphis; run her to Mound City, 5 miles above Memphis, and burned her. There were with the Grampus 5 coal boats, which were turned loose in the river when she was captured, and floated down and sunk.

On the 17th of February, I captured the steam tug Hercules opposite Memphis, and 7 coal boats, which were with her, and burned them on the spot, being unable to run them off, owing to the terrific fire from the gunboats which were lying at the Memphis wharf.

On the 16th of February, I captured a flat boat, 30 miles below Memphis, laden with medicine, &c.; she had on board the following articles, to wit: 600 ounces of quinine, 200 ounces of morphine, 6 pounds of opium, 5 pounds of ipecac, 5 navy repeaters, 450 rounds of navy cartridges, 3,000 percussion caps, and 6 pairs of gauntlets.

I am, colonel, your obedient servant,

J. H. McGEHEE,
Captain, Commanding Company.

Col. R. C. NEWTON,
Assistant Adjutant-General.

FEBRUARY 19-22, 1863.—Scout in Barton and Jasper Counties, Mo.

Report of Maj. Edward B. Eno, Eighth Missouri State Militia Cavalry.

HEADQUARTERS,
Newtonia, Mo., February 22, 1863.

COLONEL: In compliance with your request, made to me at Sherwood on the 18th instant, I have to report that, on the 19th instant, I dispatched Captain Reeder, with 30 men and the worn-out horses, in charge of corpse of one of my men, who died the night previous, back to this post, instructing him to proceed by route which would cross your line of march from Shoal Creek to Fidelity. Captain Reeder reached this post without any incident worthy of remark.

With the balance of my command, I marched down Centre Creek; thence up Spring River to Carthage, where I encamped on the night of the 19th. Here I learned that the Enrolled Missouri Militia from Bower's Mills had overtaken Livingston, with about 60 men, 6 miles distant, on Dry Fork of Spring River; had fought him a little, and came charging back through Carthage, swearing because they did not catch him. My conjecture relative to his rendezvous was correct; but, on hearing of my scout being below on Spring River, he ran directly north, about Lamar. Knowing that Captain Moore's scouts, from Fort Scott, would be in that neighborhood on the 20th, I concluded to march back to Jenkins' and Jones' Creeks. We took the brush and creek until within a quarter of a mile of that misnomer, Fidelity; then charged into the place, came upon a small party of the rascals, wounded 1, captured 3; the balance escaped, our horses being too tired to overtake them. Thence, I divided my command again, and beat the brush of Jones' and Jenkins' Creeks, up-stream. Not finding anything, we encamped on Jones' Creek, sending out parties up and down the creek during the night.

If the Wisconsin scout does not come across Livingston and cut him up, he will go down to the border and harbor at mouth of Shoal Creek again, provided he does not conclude to leave the country altogether. Many of the best friends of this guerrilla chief solemnly own to me that they see and fully appreciate the injury he is doing the country, and they talk seriously of presenting a petition to him to leave.

I hope the happiest results from the extensive scout just made in that region; if not so immediately successful as we could have wished, it has made the country uncomfortably hot for guerrillas, and must convince them of our determination to hunt them down.

Hoping to hear from you soon, and that you met with more success than myself, I am, colonel, very truly, your obedient servant,

E. B. ENO,
Major, Commanding Sub-district.

Col. WILLIAM F. CLOUD, *Springfield, Mo.*

FEBRUARY 20, 1863.—Skirmish near Fort Halleck, Dak.

Report of Capt. Asaph Allen.

FORT HALLECK, DAK., *February* 27, 1863.

SIR: On the 19th, a report came to me that the Ute Indians had broken up the station at Pass Creek, driven off the mail stock, cut up the harness, and committed other depredations. I started Lieutenant Brandley, with all the available force here (not having but 20 horses at the post), after them. He overtook and killed some of them, and was badly wounded by a ball through the left arm. He shot the Indian through the head. I brought my herd of horses in and went out myself, and hunted the hounds three days.

On the night of the 24th, Mr. Kerr, superintendent of the overland stage line, came to Fort Halleck, reporting a new trail of Indians 20 miles west. I started Sergeant Williams, with 35 men, at 12 o'clock at night, in pursuit. I could not go, as Major Adams, paymaster, was here to pay the troops. The party came in sight of the Indians about 9 o'clock the next morning. The Indians had some 10 miles the start. The chase resulted in the recovery of a portion of the stolen stock, but could not overtake the Indians, although the party followed them until night, the day being the stormiest that I ever saw. I do not think that the Indians will trouble the stage line for the present, but expect that they will favor it with a call in the spring. I have sent men up the road to the different stations.

I am, sir, with respect, your obedient servant,

A. ALLEN,
Captain, Commanding Fort Halleck.

General JAMES CRAIG,
Commanding District of Nebraska.

MARCH 1-2, 1863.—Capture of, and skirmish near, Bloomfield, Mo.

Report of Lieut. Frederick R. Poole, adjutant Second Missouri State Militia Cavalry.

HDQRS. SECOND MISSOURI STATE MILITIA CAVALRY,
Bloomfield, Mo., March 3, 1863.

COLONEL: I have the honor to report that, after leaving your camp on White Water, on the night of the 28th of February, I proceeded, in command of the advance guard, for the purpose of surprising a party of rebels reported to be in Bloomfield. On arriving at Castor River, I found it impassable, owing to the destruction of the bridge and the high stage of water; but being determined to prosecute your orders, I swam my command, and shortly after daylight had the town completely invested. I succeeded in capturing the rebel provost-marshal, R. Seckel (with all his official documents), and 20 others, nearly all of whom were Confederate soldiers. A Confederate officer, who was on recruiting service, in madly endeavoring to escape after firing upon me as I advanced, was instantly killed from his horse. From documents found upon his person, he seems to have been a Lieut. J. D. Brazeau, formerly from Saint Louis. I took a number of horses, guns, ammunition, &c. We marched during the night about 35 miles, and, notwithstanding the fatigue and cold the men had to undergo in traveling such a distance, and having to swim a deep and rapid river, I never heard a murmur, the motto "Down with the traitors" actuating every breast.

Next morning, learning that a camp of rebels were within 15 miles of this post, I selected 20 of my best horses, and proceeded down the Arkansas road 15 miles in the direction of Chalk Bluff, when I came upon their picket, who precipitately fled, being well mounted. I overtook them, 3 in number, quite near the camp. I called upon them to halt and surrender, but they continued to fly. I then commenced firing, and killed 2 of them, and took the other a prisoner. Upon hearing the firing, the rebels, 50 strong, under Cooper, as I was informed, fled in every direction, leaving their arms, &c.

I cannot express my gratitude to the men who accompanied me in both cases; suffice it to say they are model soldiers, and as brave as they are true.

I am, colonel, very respectfully, your obedient servant,

FRED. R. POOLE,
Adjutant.

Col. JOHN MCNEIL,
Commanding Second Missouri State Militia Cavalry.

MARCH 3, 1863.—Raid by guerrillas on Granby, Mo.

Report of Maj. Edward B. Eno, Eighth Missouri State Militia Cavalry.

HEADQUARTERS,
Newtonia, Mo., March 4, 1863.

MAJOR: I have to report that, on the night of the 3d instant, the guerrilla chief, Livingston, with 100 men, dashed into Granby, where 25 men of my battalion were stationed. The patrol guard, 2 men, were captured, disarmed, and probably killed, as nothing has since been heard of them. Two other soldiers, who were attending upon a sick family a short distance outside the stockade, were captured, and, unarmed as they were, begging for their lives, were shot down in their tracks. Livingston passed rapidly out, without venturing to attack the squad in the stockade.

Very respectfully, your obedient servant,

E. B. ENO,
Major, Commanding Sub-district.

Maj. JAMES H. STEGER,
Assistant Adjutant-General, Springfield, Mo.

MARCH 5-12, 1863.—Expedition from Helena up the Saint Francis and Little Rivers, and skirmish at Madison, Ark.

Report of Col. Powell Clayton, Fifth Kansas Cavalry.

HEADQUARTERS FIFTH KANSAS REGIMENT,
Camp Vandever, March 13, 1863.

COLONEL: In accordance with Special Orders, No. —, brigade headquarters, and subsequent orders from Brigadier-General [B. M.] Prentiss, I proceeded with my command, composed of 50 infantry (Twenty-fourth Indiana Volunteers), 25 cavalry (Third Iowa Volunteers), and one section of the Second Ohio Battery (6-pounders), on board the steamer Hamilton Belle, up the Saint Francis River, starting on Friday, March 5, at 9 a. m. Nothing of interest occurred until we arrived at Madison, a small country town situated at a point where the Memphis and Little Rock Railroad crosses the Saint Francis River. We arrived at this point a little after daylight, and, from the nature of the river, we were entirely concealed from observation from the town until we arrived within a few hundred yards of it. Here we completely surprised a rebel force of about 75 strong, who fled in great confusion as the boat touched the landing, leaving behind everything except the clothing they had upon their persons. My infantry and cavalry landed with the greatest possible celerity, and pursued them in every direction, capturing and bringing to the boat 27 of their number. Of course, everything they left behind fell into our hands, consisting of arms, horses, horse equipments, blankets, &c.

Having instructions from General Prentiss to capture, if possible, the steamer Miller, which was said to be somewhere in Little River near its mouth, I therefore continued up the Saint Francis until I came to the mouth of that river; thence up the same for about 25 miles, when I reached the Miller, which, to my disappointment, I found in a sunken condition. The point where the Miller lay was about 250 miles from Helena, and believing that before I could return the rebels would probably collect all available troops together at some favorable point to dispute my passage, I seized, at different points and from different persons, sixty-four bales of cotton, out of which I had constructed very efficient breastworks, not only for the protection of the men, but for the protection of the boat in case they should bring artillery to bear upon us.

Upon my return, I captured, near the mouth of Little River, 3 men engaged in contraband trade. I found in their possession 13 barrels of salt, 2 barrels of flour, 80 ounces of quinine, and a large amount of percussion-caps. At Wittsburg I captured 15 hogsheads of sugar, and received information that the enemy had collected in considerable force at Madison, and had blockaded the river. Arriving within about 2 miles of Madison, I discovered a load of cotton placed upon a conspicuous point on a high, sloping bank. Believing it to be a trap, I ordered the artillerymen to drop a few shells into the thick underbrush a short distance back of the cotton bales. I soon discovered, farther up on the slope, a large number of saddled horses, which convinced me that my suspicions were well founded.

I continued the shelling process, and, coming within nearer range, I swept the underbrush with canister. I then landed as rapidly as possible my entire force, leaving about one-half on the river bank by the boat as a reserve. The balance deployed as skirmishers and soon came upon the enemy, who had been previously scattered by our artillery. A running fight ensued, which resulted in the enemy retreating to the hills, leaving 4 of their dead upon the field.

In this skirmish Lieutenant [William C.] Niblack, of the Third Iowa Cavalry, received a severe buck-shot wound in the left breast while gallantly leading his cavalry. No other one on our side sustained any injury.

After securing the cotton used as a bait and some horses captured upon the field, I proceeded to Madison, where I found the river blockaded by means of a chain drawn between the piers of the railroad bridge. I landed above the bridge and sent out skirmishers to reconnoiter and cover the operations of a working party sent to remove the blockade. A little skirmishing ensued, and we captured 1 prisoner. My working party soon reported a safe passage through the blockade. I called in my skirmishers and without much difficulty cleared the bridge, which was no sooner accomplished than a heavy volley saluted us from a canebreak on the right, where the enemy were posted behind log breastworks. After about 25 rounds from our field pieces, the enemy retreated in great confusion, and we experienced no further interruption between that point and Helena, where we arrived on the morning of the 12th, it being the seventh day out.

I cannot but speak in the highest terms of the manner in which the officers and men of the different detachments conducted themselves throughout. It was truly gratifying and well worthy of imitation.

We captured in all 46 prisoners, 10 of whom I paroled on account of being short of subsistence. The balance I have turned over to the provost-marshal-general.

The following is a list of captured property (contraband) and property seized for military purposes:

Cotton	bales	4
Sugar	hogsheads	15
Salt	barrels	13
Flour	do	2
Bacon	pounds	500
Horses		23
Mules		3
Quinine	ounces	80
Shot-guns, rifles, &c., about		30
Percussion-caps		500

Sixty bales of cotton seized for military purposes, claimants of which were permitted to return with the expedition to represent their claims.

Having nothing further to report, I am, colonel, very respectfully, your obedient servant,

POWELL CLAYTON,
Colonel, Commanding.

MARCH 5-13, 1863.—Operations in Newton and Jasper Counties, Mo., and skirmish (9th) near Sherwood.

Report of Capt. David Mefford, Sixth Kansas Cavalry.

CAMP SALOMON, MO., *March* 14, 1863.

SIR: Agreeably to your order, I left camp on March 5, with a detachment of the Sixth Kansas Cavalry, comprising Company A, Lieutenant [Thomas J.] Darling; Company C, Lieutenant [Richard L.] Phillips, and Company H, Lieutenant Campbell, in command of the respective companies, and proceeded to Newtonia, Newton County, a distance of 25 miles, and encamped for the night.

Next morning (Friday) [6th] I went to Granby; scouted Shoal Creek thoroughly in that vicinity, and proceeded to Neosho.

Left Neosho Saturday morning early; scouted the country north and encamped at Savilla, a little village containing about a dozen houses, and each house containing several rebel sympathizers. Lost a valuable horse that night.

Sunday [8th] I went to Diamond Grove, about 5 miles from Savilla, and searched the woods thoroughly, but without any satisfactory result. Then moved down Turkey Creek and went to Sherwood, in Jasper County, a distance of 18 miles. Found a trail, but could get no information as to what troops had passed. It being nearly night, I remained in the town until 3 a. m. Monday. Followed up the trail a short distance, when my advance ran into a picket. Shots were exchanged, in which Sergeant Fountain, non-commissioned staff, was severely, though not dangerously, wounded in the face. The rebel picket was also wounded, but not fatally. Searched the woods and found the camp, which had contained about 70 or 80 men, judging from appearances, which the noted Tom Livingston had left in great haste, cutting halters and ropes, &c. The bush being so thick it was impossible to follow them. I moved out on the edge of Turkey Creek timber and proceeded about 2 miles, and, seeing several men in a little bend of prairie, the advance went in pursuit, and after a chase of three-fourths of a mile they were suddenly turned upon by Livingston's whole force and obliged to fall back to the main command, still pursued. Seeing them repulsed, I quickly formed my men behind a clump of trees and bushes, dismounted them, and sent them in on foot. The enemy coming within 90 or 100 yards, firing commenced, lasting but a few minutes, the enemy retreating precipitately.

I had 1 man wounded in the leg. Injury sustained by the rebels not known, but, from the appearance of the woods, must have been considerable in horses. I sent Company H in the woods as skirmishers, and found the trail again; but, considering it useless to try to follow them, turned my course toward Neosho, which place I reached at sundown.

I remained in Neosho Tuesday, getting my horses shod, &c.

Wednesday [11th] morning I was furnished with 40 Indians as scouts by Captain [A. C.] Spillman, Third Indian Regiment, commanding post. Found the trail and followed it for 35 miles, and encamped at Crawford Seminary, Ind. T. Took it up next morning and continued to follow it until about 2 p. m. Thursday, without getting any information as to his whereabouts. My men being without rations, and horses run down with hard marching and no forage, I abandoned the pursuit and turned my course toward camp. I marched to Savilla that night.

Next morning [13th], being ready to mount, I heard firing half a mile from camp. I sent the Indians in the woods as flankers, and took the main road, with the Sixth Kansas. Came upon two men of Company A, who stated that three of them had been to a house outside the lines to get their breakfast, and, in returning, were fired into, taken prisoners, and disarmed, and one of their number was badly wounded and left on the ground, where I found him in a few minutes. I scoured the woods thoroughly with Indians and whites, but could find no one. I procured a wagon and sent the wounded man to Neosho under escort of the Indians, and proceeded to camp, which I reached at 9 p. m. Friday, the 13th, being out nine days. I issued an order, the first day out, strictly prohibiting men from leaving the command without the consent of a commissioned officer, which order was disobeyed in several instances by those men of Company A, who were disarmed.

D. MEFFORD,
Captain Company H, Sixth Kansas, Commanding Detachment.

Col. W. R. JUDSON,
Commanding First Brig., First Div., Army of the Frontier.

MARCH 6-10, 1863.—Expedition from Helena to Big and Lick Creeks, Ark., and skirmishes.

Report of Brig. Gen. Benjamin M. Prentiss, U. S. Army.

HEADQUARTERS DISTRICT OF EASTERN ARKANSAS,
Helena, Ark., March 11, 1863.

GENERAL: On the morning of the 6th instant I dispatched Major [Samuel] Walker, of the Fifth Kansas Cavalry, with about 500 men of different regiments, in search of a camp of rebels said to be between Big and Lick Creeks, and he reports to me that he arrived at Lick Creek on the 8th instant, and after hunting in vain for an enemy, he sent Major Winslow to one crossing of Big Creek and went himself to the other, at both of which he encountered small parties of rebels, killing 1, taking 1 prisoner, and destroying their ferry-boats. One man of the Fourth Iowa Cavalry was shot from his horse while on picket, and Lieutenant [Joseph] McCarty and Sergeant Orcutt, Fifth Kansas, were taken prisoners. He reports Lieutenant Cleaveland, of Parsons' rebel regiment, killed; also 2 of Wetherby's men, and says he took 4 prisoners, and that, having scoured the country well between Big and Lick Creeks, is satisfied that there is no large party there. A force of rebels is reported to be at Cotton Plant. The major speaks in high terms of the conduct of his officers and men.

I have the honor to be, very respectfully,

B. M. PRENTISS,
Brigadier-General.

Major-General MCCLERNAND,
Commanding Thirteenth Army Corps.

MARCH 9-15, 1863.—Expedition from Bloomfield, Mo., to Chalk Bluff, Ark., and to Gum Slough, Kennett, Hornersville, etc., Mo., and skirmishes.

Report of Col. John McNeil, Second Missouri State Militia Cavalry.

HDQRS. SECOND REGT. MISSOURI STATE MILITIA CAV.,
Bloomfield, Mo., March 16, 1863.

GENERAL: I have the honor to report that I left this post on Monday, the 9th instant, with 500 men of my command and two mountain howitzers, two days' small rations with hard bread, no tents for either officers or men, and 5 wagons, lightly loaded. We arrived at Chalk Bluff the next morning, having traveled over 40 miles of such roads as only the swamps of the earthquake region of Missouri can turn out.

On our arrival at that point, at 9 a. m., we found that the advance party, which we had sent forward to feel the enemy, had failed to get the ferrymen to cross, and had been exchanging shots across the river for some two hours. We deployed skirmishers, and tried to move the force covering the ferry-boat, but they were well posted and stuck to their position with a determination worthy of a better cause. By bringing up our howitzers, we drove them out with canister and shell, and after three hours' fighting were able to cover a party of five brave volunteers who swam the river, seized the boat, and brought it over. We soon crossed three companies, who succeeded in clearing the hills, burning their store of corn, all the buildings, and a large ferry-boat which was being constructed. In this affair we had 2 men wounded, Blacksmith William J. Dryden, of Company E, and Private Cicero G. Davis, of Company H.

Having thus cut off their exit by this ferry, we marched, at 4 o'clock next morning, against Thompson's fort, at Gum Slough, 23 miles distant.

We came to the slough at about noon. The slough is about 500 yards across, with a narrow road cut through a dense cypress swamp, with water girth-deep all the way across. We drove from this slough 30 well-armed men, a party under Lieutenant [Frederick R.] Poole pursuing them 11 miles, killing 4 and capturing 5 of them.

The fort of General Thompson was at the opposite side of the slough, commanding the road. It consisted of a parallelogram 90 paces on its main face, with a salient angle on its main face, and one of its interior faces to command the encampment and ditch. We could have shelled them out of it from across the slough, or even have ridden over their works.

To our great chagrin, we found the fort without defenders, the garrison having evacuated it on hearing the report of my guns the day before. They had swum the slough, and taken to the island of Saint Francis River, intending to cross into Arkansas in Thompson's mosquito fleet of dug-outs. We were advised that these canoes were in Varney's River, an arm of the Saint Francis, and Lieutenant Poole, with 7 men, pushed on in advance to capture and destroy them. When he got to the river, 8 miles beyond Kennett, he found the canoes gone, the main body of the fugitives having left the night before.

We encamped at Kennett that night, and the succeeding two days scoured the country; captured over 60 of the enemy, including 2 captains and 2 lieutenants; destroyed or took away about 250 guns, of all kinds, and captured 65 horses and mules, subsisting entirely on the country, which abounded in forage, good bacon, and corn bread. We scoured Holcombe, Ten-Mile, Buffalo, Horse, and Two-Mile Islands, the scouts traveling sometimes 40 miles a day, often crossing from one island to another in dug-outs and scouting on foot all day. We thus drove the whole force of Thompson and Clark out of the State into Arkansas, or into their hiding places in the jungles and among the cypress trees of the swamps.

The war steed of General Thompson, which proved to be a mare heavy with foal, fell into our hands, and the last that was heard of this doughty hero he was floating down the Saint Francis, the solitary tenant of a dug-out, quite drunk and very melancholy. Upon information that a large force had arrived at Chalk Bluff, and were felling trees into the river, and that the company I had posted at Four Mile, a small village 4 miles from the ferry, had fallen back 6 miles, I marched toward Bloomfield, making 46 miles by 9 p. m., and encamped in a good position on the direct road from the Bluff to Bloomfield. The regiment marched into Bloomfield yesterday at 9 a. m. The command had marched 184 miles in six days, besides numerous scouts both at night and day.

We had 2 men wounded by the fire of the enemy at Chalk Bluff, and 2 accidentally; only 1 man on the sick report from other causes, thus proving that the field is more healthy than quarters. I administered the oath to over 100 citizens, and could have done so to many times that number had they not been scared off by extravagant reports of our killing unarmed and innocent persons. The covers being on our guidons, for it rained most of the time, they were taken for black flags, and the story that we were marching under that peculiarly Southern emblem widely circulated. Rape and murder were charged on us, causing the men to flee to the swamps. The women alone stood their ground, either not believing the charge or not fearing the consequences. I have promised protection to the loyal and law-abiding, and forgiveness for the past to those sincerely tired of rebellion, and disposed to be at peace with their neighbors, and announced that the rule for the future is, that where a Union man cannot live in peace a secessionist shall not live at all. A better state of feeling is fast obtaining among this simple-minded people, and the timely display of force is begetting confidence in the power of the Government. When our operations can be extended to clearing Crawley Ridge, in Arkansas, we may hope for peace in these counties.

I take pleasure in commending the zeal and devotion to duty that has characterized the officers and men under me on this expedition. Major [Hiram M.] Hiller, commanding the First Battalion, Captain [Josephus] Robbins, the Second, and Captain Sells, the Third, were constant and unremitting in duty. First Lieutenant [Amos P.] Wright, of Company L, and Second Lieut. Joseph H. Cell, of Company K, were always active and efficient. Sergt. Darius Dennis, Company E; Sergt. Hewlit H. McIlhany, Company G; Bugler Hiram H. Swasey, Company A, and Privates John W. Dryden, Company K, and William J. Dryden, Company E, attested courage of the highest order in charges and pursuits, everywhere riding down and sabering their foes. Sergt. H. H. McIlhany, of Company G; Corpl. George Rose, of Company B; Privates Samuel Knox and George McConnel, Company A, and James T. Hoover, Company F, I would make especial mention of for their gallantry in swimming the Saint Francis on a dismal, cold, and bleak day, and, under the fire of the enemy, seizing the ferry-boat and bringing it across. Such a devotion to duty should not go unrewarded. I have thanked them in orders, desiring that their names should be borne as they deserve on the durable records of their regiments.

I cannot close this report without particular mention of the gallant bearing and valuable services of Lieutenant Poole, regimental adjutant, on this expedition. A fine cavalry officer and a spirited soldier, he has given my men an example of dash and daring throughout this whole expedition that cannot but be highly beneficial to the regiment. I respectfully commend him for promotion.

Our horses are now resting, and will soon be again fit for duty.

I have the honor to be, your obedient servant,

JOHN McNEIL,
Colonel, Commanding.

Brig. Gen. J. W. DAVIDSON,
Commanding District of Saint Louis, Mo.

MARCH 19, 1863.—Skirmish on Frog Bayou, Ark.

Report of Col. M. La Rue Harrison.

FAYETTEVILLE, ARK., *March* 23, 1863.

A reconnoitering party of 9 men, under Captain Whiteford, sent out by me a few days ago, attacked 20 rebels of Captain Wright's company, at Bill Young's, on Frog Bayou, 18 miles north of the Arkansas River, on Thursday morning [19th]. Our men killed and mortally wounded 10; killed 3 horses and disabled 5. They completely routed the rebels, taking most of their blankets and arms. Captain Wright is reported mortally wounded. Captain Whiteford returned last night without the loss of a man.

M. LA RUE HARRISON,
Colonel, Commanding Post.

Major-General CURTIS.

MARCH 19–23, 1863.—Scout toward, and affair (21st) near, Doniphan, Mo.

Report of Lieut. Frederick R. Poole, Adjutant Second Missouri State Militia Cavalry.

HDQRS. SECOND MISSOURI STATE MILITIA CAVALRY,
Bloomfield, March 23, 1863.

SIR: I have the honor to report that, in accordance with your instructions, I left this post on the evening of the 19th instant, for the purpose of making a tour of reconnaissance west of the Saint Francis River. For this purpose, I took with me 75 men, 25 of whom I left at Williams' Crossing, on the Saint Francis River, under command of Lieutenant [J.] Donahoo, to guard two ferry-boats, one of which I captured on the Mingo, and the other at Punches' Crossing, on the Saint Francis, together with several canoes, all of which I floated down stream to the point above indicated, about three-fourths of a mile south of the junction of the Mingo with the Saint Francis River.

Shortly after daylight next morning, I crossed my party, arriving that evening at Poplar Bluff. Here we were enthusiastically hailed by the few inhabitants that remain, and who express more Union sentiment, and are more truly loyal, than any people I have yet met with in Southeast Missouri.

Aware of the small force at my disposal, and being now 40 miles from any support, I deemed it prudent to withdraw from town, and encamp at the foot of the bridge over Blackwater River, on the east side of the village, there holding a position that no enemy could well force. Not being able to ascertain any information relative to the reported advance of Marmaduke's army, I resolved to push still farther in the direction of Pocahontas, until I could meet his advance or capture his pickets, or strike his trail in case he had moved north.

About 1 o'clock next day [21st], I surprised a picket, consisting of 5 men, who fled at our approach. They were stationed about 20 miles from Poplar Bluff, at the junction of the Pitman's Ferry and Doniphan roads. I captured 3 of the pickets and killed the remaining 2. I will here state that the two who were killed had good horses, and exhibited a degree of bravery worthy of a better cause. Being well mounted, myself and Captain [Perry D.] McClanahan, commanding Company C, of this regiment, soon took the lead of our men and each singled out his man and pursued him. Several pistol shots were exchanged during the chase, and not until we were within 3 miles of Doniphan could we get fairly up with them. Here my antagonist shot my horse, and at the same instant I killed his; both horses fell together, and we (my butternut friend and myself) rolled over and over, when he broke loose and attempted to get away on foot, but I soon caught him and put an end to the desperado.

At some little distance I found my friend McClanahan, standing over the remains of him he pursued. We were both exhausted, and had to wait until our party came up.

I must make special notice of Corporal Blurton, of Company B, for his zeal and bravery throughout.

From the pickets captured, I learned that Marmaduke's main force was still encamped in the vicinity of Batesville, and that Jeffers', Clark's, and Lewis' men were acting as his advance guard, making their regular reports to him, and being guided and instructed from his headquarters. One of the prisoners captured was lately from Little Rock, Ark., and seemed to have been acting in the capacity of postmaster, as the inclosed package of communications, found upon his person, will indicate.

The road from Bloomfield to the Saint Francis is tolerably good, passing over gentle ridges and plateaus, or glades, through which levees have been constructed, with the necessary culverts. A train of artillery, in good weather, could easily pass over, with some repairs being done to the bridge over Lick Creek. I would calculate the distance at about 18 miles. Forage very scarce.

From the Saint Francis to Poplar Bluff the roads are excellent, with the exception of about 1 mile through the Blackwater bottom, passing over a high, barren, and uncultivated ridge.

A couple of thousand bushels of corn might be collected at Poplar Bluff from the farms on the Blackwater bottom. This is all an army could depend upon. It must be nearly 20 miles from Williams' Crossing, on the Saint Francis, to Poplar Bluff. From Poplar Bluff to Pitman's Ferry it must be about 35 miles, and about an equal distance to Doniphan. The roads are good and practicable for trains or artillery. But few cultivated farms, and forage very scarce.

The telegraph constructed by General Steele has been completely destroyed and strewn carelessly along the road. I had several horses thrown by it in the charge, and some of the riders seriously injured.

Before concluding this hurried report, I would state that, in the neighborhood of Pitman's Ferry, I found Saint Louis newspapers of a more recent date than we could obtain at Bloomfield, thus clearly demonstrating that the rebels are in direct communication with that city.

My command arrived safely at this post at 1 a. m., having been absent four entire days. We took with us but a limited supply of hard bread; marched 150 miles during that time without either tent or blanket, and during the entire trip I never heard a murmur.

I am, colonel, very respectfully, your obedient servant,

FRED. R. POOLE,
Regimental Adjutant.

Col. JOHN MCNEIL,
Commanding Southeastern Expedition.

MARCH 22, 1863.—Skirmish at Blue Springs, near Independence, Mo.

Report of Col. William R. Penick, Fifth Missouri State Militia Cavalry.

HDQRS. FIFTH MISSOURI STATE MILITIA CAVALRY,
Independence, Mo., March 23, 1863.

GENERAL: Yesterday a detachment of 50 men, composed of the Fifth Regiment and artillery company, under command of Capt. H. B. Johnson, met with a superior force of guerrillas about 12 miles from this post, and were driven back, with a loss of 9 killed, 3 wounded, and 6 missing. The loss of the enemy I have not yet ascertained. The guerrillas, as usual, have scattered all over the county in twos, threes, &c. It will be impossible for United States soldiers to drive them out of this county unless the Government can afford to send ten soldiers for one guerrilla. The only way to get them out is to destroy all subsistence in rocky and brushy parts of the country, and send off their wives and the children; also the wives and children of sympathizers who are aiding and abetting them.

Very respectfully,

W. R. PENICK,
Colonel Fifth Missouri State Militia Cavalry.

Maj. Gen. SAMUEL R. CURTIS,
Saint Louis, Mo.

[Indorsement.]

HEADQUARTERS DEPARTMENT OF THE MISSOURI,
Saint Louis, March 28, 1863.

Respectfully referred to Brigadier-General Loan, who will take all possible means to suppress the rebels consistent with orders from Washington.

SAML. R. CURTIS,
Major-General.

MARCH 22, 1863.—Skirmish near the head of White River, Ark.

Report of Col. M. La Rue Harrison.

FAYETTEVILLE, ARK., *March* 26, 1863.

On Sunday last a party of 35 men (25 soldiers and 10 citizens) sent out to assist the beef contractor in getting in his stock, were attacked from three directions, near the head of White River, by a rebel scout of 200 men from Clarksville, led by Major McConnell, said to be of Brooks' regiment. Our men lost: Killed, 3 soldiers and 1 citizen; wounded, 1 citizen; prisoners, 7 soldiers and 8 citizens; escaped, 14 soldiers and 1 citizen. The scout was informed of their whereabouts by a treacherous citizen. The disaster is half owing to carelessness in not putting out pickets. Major McConnell is known to have been shot dead from his horse while leading the charge. If our cavalry could get horses, they would not be half so liable to such disasters. At present all escorts have to be sent out dismounted.

M. LA RUE HARRISON,
Colonel Commanding Post.

Major-General CURTIS.

MARCH 24–APRIL 1, 1863.—Scout from Bloomfield to Scatterville, Mo.

Report of Maj. William H. Torrey, First Wisconsin Cavalry.

HDQRS. FIRST WISCONSIN CAVALRY VOLUNTEERS,
Post Bloomfield, Mo., April 2, 1863.

GENERAL: Left Bloomfield March 24, 1863, at 6 a. m., with detachment of First Wisconsin Cavalry, Second Missouri State Militia Cavalry, and one mountain howitzer. Arrived within 1½ miles this side of Chalk Bluff at 4 p. m. the same day; found the enemy in possession of the bluffs, skirmishing with our pickets; learned their force to be two companies. Immediately sent 8 miles for tools to build a raft, and 6 miles for a canoe; could not get the canoe for high water. Built the raft next morning above the bluffs, and crossed with 70 men. The enemy attempted to prevent our crossing, but were driven back by the howitzer; found one of the enemy dead on the bank. Marched around to the bluffs, surprised the picket, mortally wounding 2 men; learned from them that Colonel Preston was in camp, 1 mile from the bluffs, with 400 men. Recrossed the river.

Next morning [26th], crossed over with 100 men, and commenced swimming horses; found it impossible to get them across; the water was so cold and the current so strong that the horses would not leave the shore. Crossed the men back to the Missouri shore, and commenced building a foot-bridge, which was completed the next day at 3 p. m. Immediately commenced crossing the men and horses, swimming the horses beside the bridge. Completed the crossing next day [28th] at 8 a. m., and started for Scatterville. Marched 7 miles, and heard that the enemy were in camp 5 miles west of us the day before; took a guide and started across the ridge; found the camp vacant. The tracks in the road indicated that considerable force had moved toward the bluffs that morning; followed them 3 miles, and met the enemy returning. Captain [Henry] Harnden, with his company (the advance guard), charged upon them, capturing several and putting the rest to flight. Learned from the prisoners that Colonel Preston had moved down toward Pocahontas, 20 miles. Camped that night 7 miles from the bluffs.

Next morning [29th], at 2 o'clock, marched in pursuit; came into his camp at 7 a. m.; learned that he had left for Jonesborough the afternoon previous. Halted one hour and a half for breakfast and feed for horses; then marched 5 miles to Scatterville, and from there to Chalk Bluff, and recrossed the river with some difficulty, the water rising rapidly.

Next day [30th], marched to West Prairie, camped, and from there to this place, April 1, 1863. Captured property, 12 horses and 11 guns; prisoners, 11.

Respectfully submitted.

W. H. TORREY,
Major, Commanding Detachment.

Brigadier-General MCNEIL.

MARCH 28, 1863.—Guerrilla attack on Steamer Sam. Gaty.

Report of Maj. Gen. Samuel R. Curtis, U. S. Army.

HEADQUARTERS,
Saint Louis, Mo., April 3, 1863—8 p. m.

A band of guerrillas took steamer Sam. Gaty, and murdered several

soldiers and 9 contrabands.* General Loan telegraphs that Colonel King, in pursuit, had two fights yesterday with guerrillas, totally routing them, mortally wounding their chief.

SAML. R. CURTIS, *Major-General.*

Maj. Gen. H W. HALLECK, *General-in-Chief.*

MARCH 29-APRIL 5, 1863.—Scouts from Fayetteville, Ark.

Report of Lieut. James Roseman, First Arkansas Cavalry.

HEADQUARTERS,
Post Fayetteville, Ark., April 5, 1863.

COLONEL: I am instructed by the colonel commanding post to say that your dispatch was received late last evening. Six of our wagons leave to-morrow for Cassville, to bring back the revolvers, cartridges, &c., sent down by Major Corning to that post. Eight more wagons, escorted by the batterymen, go direct to Springfield, there to obtain in part the supplies so much needed at this post.

Our scouts have all been called in, and all are now in but one. They have been remarkably successful the past week. Captain [John T.] Worthington and Lieutenant [Joseph S.] Robb, of the First Arkansas Cavalry, returned on Friday evening from a week's trip, in which they were so fortunate as to leave 22 dead rebels in their track. They entirely cleared out MacFarlane's band, and he is reported killed. The loss on our side was 1 man wounded.

Captain [James R.] Vanderpool, of the infantry, returned yesterday from a scout to Newton and Carroll Counties. He had several fights with rebel bands, and succeeded in killing 19 in all, with the loss of 1 wounded. One scout is still out, but will be in in a few days. Positions have been selected for fortifications, and the work will be commenced without delay.

Respectfully, your obedient servant,

JAMES ROSEMAN, *Lieutenant and Post Adjutant.*

MARCH 31, 1863.—Skirmish at Clapper's Saw-Mill, Crooked Creek, Ark.

REPORTS.

No. 1.—Col. William Weer, Tenth Kansas Infantry, commanding First Division, Army of the Frontier.

No. 2.—Lieut. Col. Richard H. White, Third Wisconsin Cavalry.

No. 1.

Report of Col. William Weer, Tenth Kansas Infantry, commanding First Division, Army of the Frontier.

HEADQUARTERS FIRST DIVISION,
Carrollton, Ark., April 1, 1863.

As per my last telegraph, I sent yesterday, at 3 p. m., Lieutenant-Colonel White, Third Wisconsin Cavalry, with a detachment of his regiment,

---

* See also Loan to Curtis, March 29, in "Correspondence, etc.," Part II, p. 183.

with minute instructions as to route and mode of attack against the enemy on Crooked Creek. He just reports to me that he surprised their camp, 400 strong, under a Colonel Woodson, about 10 o'clock last night; captured their picket, fired into their camp, taking them by complete surprise; some of the enemy wounded, but loss not known, owing to the darkness. Captured arms, wagons, mules, camp and garrison equipage, &c., and our loss none. Enemy fled, and Colonel White yet in pursuit, in a southeasterly direction. Captured muster-rolls and correspondence. They are part of the Confederate Army, and under a Colonel [W. H.] Brooks, commanding Second Division, headquarters at Clarksville, Ark. A letter from him states that he had sent a force, under a Colonel [J. F.] Hill, from Clarksville into this country, who was no doubt with the force on Crooked Creek. The correspondence discloses great exertions to obtain recruits, promising that all deserters will be pardoned if they return. Forage is as yet abundant, and if a force was sent to take care of Marmaduke, I could feel my way still farther south. The troops at Fayetteville should be sent into this country.

Your obedient servant,

WM. WEER,
Colonel, Commanding Division.

Major-General SCHOFIELD.

(Forwarded, April 3, by Lieut. Luke O'Reilly, to Major-General Herron.)

No. 2.

Report of Lieut. Col. Richard H. White, Third Wisconsin Cavalry.

HEADQUARTERS THIRD WISCONSIN CAVALRY,
Camp at Clapper's Saw-Mill, on Crooked Creek,
Carroll County, Arkansas, March 31, 1863.

COLONEL: Pursuant to orders, I started this afternoon, at 3 o'clock, from camp near Carrollton, taking a southeasterly road, toward Crooked Creek. On the road I learned that the camp of the enemy was at the steam-mill, where I am now in bivouac. On the road several men, running from the houses at the approach of the advance guard, were chased and fired at, but only one taken with arms. Reaching a point about three-fourths of a mile from the creek, I received information that on the opposite bank of the creek a picket of the enemy was stationed. Sending Captain Horn, with the advance guard, by a left-hand road (crossing the creek more below), into the rear of the same, I moved on, and, as expected, the picket retreated, and was taken by the party in ambush without a shot being fired. One of the so-captured men jumped from his horse and could not be found in the thicket. I therefore concluded to march right up on the enemy's camp, in order to prevent their being warned.

At 10 p. m. I reached the house of Mr. Clapper, where the officers of the command were assembled in council of war, as I afterward learned. A pistol fight took place, which probably alarmed the camp earlier than intended. I therefore moved on toward the camp, which was only a quarter of a mile farther in the timber, and in plain sight, a large field in front of it giving an opportunity for bringing howitzers into action. I ordered the same to the front, drawing the cavalry up in line on the right and left and rear of the same, and threw a few shells into the enemy's encampments.

The complete stampede thereby caused being immediately followed by a spirited cavalry charge, the darkness of the night in the timber can only explain the fact that all but one (wounded) made good their escape. A great many arms, some wagons, mules, and cattle, cooking utensils, &c., were left on the ground. The pursuit was continued for about 2 miles, when I returned to the camp.

The force routed is reported to have numbered 400, under command of Colonel Woodson, of the Confederate Army. To-morrow I intend to follow them up to Bluff Spring, about 12 miles farther southeast. I found a sufficient forage for my command at this place, but am unable to report any particulars about forage in the country.

I have the honor, colonel, to be, your most obedient servant,

RICHARD H. WHITE,
Lieutenant-Colonel, Commanding Third Wisconsin Cavalry.

Col. CHARLES E. SALOMON, *Commanding Brigade.*

APRIL 1-5, 1863.—Scout from Linden to White River, Mo.

Report of Maj. Henry Suess, Seventh Missouri State Militia Cavalry.

HEADQUARTERS,
Linden, Mo., April 5, 1863.

COLONEL: I have the honor to report to you a successful scout made by Capt. M. U. Foster, of Company G, with 41 men, south. I ordered him, April 1, on a reconnaissance south as far as Talbot's Ferry, or as far south as he should find it safe to go. Captain Foster, returned this evening, reports: Passed Lawrence's Mill to head of Little Fork, passing down that stream to White River, where he crossed and fell in with 3 armed guerrillas, who were killed on the spot. Then, recrossing the river, he traveled southeast some 25 miles. Near the mouth of Sister Creek, he happened to fall upon a Capt. John McClure, a noted guerrilla, who was killed in the attempt to run away. Then visiting the saltpeter works, 2 others, that had been stealing and robbing on a large scale from Union people, were served like the rest, they attempting to escape. Reports about 200 of Shaver's men at Yellville; Shaver at Little Rock. These men are not stationary, but act as rangers. The conscript law is being enforced there, but with no success. It is rumored there that Marmaduke is preparing for another raid in this direction.

Van Zandt, former clerk of Taney County court, and a noted rebel, was killed by the Enrolled Missouri Militia a few days ago. Another scout of Captain [Elias] Slocum, Company H, returned just now, having been about 45 miles east-southeast, passing Haywood and Cowskin without making any discoveries. He reports forage so scarce in that region that I shall remain here, hoping that this command may go to the land of plenty some time. We are on short rations of corn. The health of my command is excellent.

I am, very respectfully, your obedient servant,

HENRY SUESS,
Major Seventh Missouri State Militia Cavalry.

Col. WILLIAM F. CLOUD,
Commanding District of Southwest Missouri.

P. S.—Will you permit me to send about two companies to Yellville? In surprising that place at daybreak, we might gain an easy victory there.

APRIL —, 1863.—Skirmishes in Carroll County, Mo.

Report of Col. M. La Rue Harrison, commanding Fayetteville, Ark.

[APRIL 3, 1863.]

Capt. J. I. Worthington is just in from scout in Carroll County; has had four skirmishes with bushwhackers, and killed 22 and taken 7 prisoners. Captain McFarlane reported killed, and Captain Walker is a prisoner. Guerrilla Captain Smith was also killed. Scout consisted of Companies H and L, First Arkansas Cavalry. They lost 1 man wounded, but not dangerously.

M. LA RUE HARRISON,
Colonel, Commanding Post.

Major-General CURTIS,
Commanding Department of the Missouri.

(Sent by Curtis to Halleck, same date.)

APRIL 11, 1863.—Skirmish near Squirrel Creek Crossing, Colo.

Report of Lieut. Col. George L. Shoup, Third Colorado Cavalry.

SQUIRREL CREEK CROSSING, COLO.,
April 11, 1863.

SIR: I have the honor to report that at daylight this morning I surprised and captured a small camp of guerrillas. The loss of the guerrilla band is 1 man killed and 2 taken prisoners; one of the prisoners is shot through the leg. They (the guerrillas) were in camp about 10 miles east of this place. I have no clew to the whereabouts of other desperadoes.

I left Pueblo the day after the detachment that you ordered to Colorado City. I went direct to Colorado City. I there learned that the detachment had taken the Cherry Creek road. I left Colorado City yesterday morning. Procured Mr. Templeton (about 12 m.) as guide. Found the detachment at Smith's saw-mill. Left there at 4 p. m., and arrived here about dark. Soon after dark, I discovered a camp-fire, that I supposed to be near by. I detailed Sergeant Rigsby and 4 others to reconnoiter the camp. Sergeant Rigsby and party returned about 12 o'clock at night. He reported the camp to be 10 miles distant. He saw in camp 1 man and 2 mules. He saw other camp-fires beyond, but did not visit them.

I took Sergeant Rigsby, Corporal Wood, and 9 others, and rode rapidly to and passed the camp visited in the forepart of the night by Sergeant Rigsby. Finding a good place to leave my horses, I took 3 men with me; visited the other fires, but found them to be burning logs that had taken fire from the burning prairie. I then returned to the camp visited by Sergeant Rigsby, and made a reconnaissance myself. I could tell nothing of their number. Their position was a good one, among large rocks, in a cañon. Day was breaking, and I decided to charge their camp from below and above, that there might be no chance for them to escape. The charge was made with the result above stated. I asked them who they were, and demanded them three different times to surrender. I did not fire on them until one of them raised his gun on Sergeant Rigsby. William Waggle was killed; John Rily shot through the leg; William Way is a prisoner.

You will be generous enough to overlook this soiled letter, the only piece of paper that I could procure. I will take the prisoners to Colorado City, and there await your orders.

I am, colonel, truly, your obedient servant,

G. L. SHOUP,
Lieutenant-Colonel of Volunteers.

Col. J. M. CHIVINGTON,
Commanding District of Colorado.

APRIL 17, 1863.—Skirmish at White River, Mo.

Reports of Maj. David McKee, Seventh Missouri Cavalry.

CASSVILLE, MO., *April* 18, 1863.

SIR: I sent Captain Humphrey out on a scout with 50 men in the White River country, 18 miles from here. He sent a squad of 20 men to reconnoiter near Relleford's Mill; they were attacked by a band of 80 or 100 rebels, and had a running fight for about 4 miles. Eight of our men are missing; 3 of them were killed; the others' horses gave out, and I think they must have taken to the bushes. I sent out re-enforcement of 66 men about 2 o'clock this morning. Would it be convenient for you to send me a couple of companies of infantry? Our horses are run down, and it is impossible for me to keep up the telegraph patrol and forage, besides doing guard duty.

DAVID McKEE,
Major Seventh Missouri Volunteer Cavalry, Commanding Post.

Colonel CLOUD.

CASSVILLE, MO., *April* 18, 1863.

COLONEL: My scout, under command of Captain Humphrey, has returned. He reports the enemy at, or near, Moore's Mill, on White River, 200 strong, and he has reliable information that the enemy is in camp at Leashure, Wood Creek, 8 miles south of Moore's Mill, from 400 to 600 strong. They have been concentrating there for three days past, from all directions, to my own knowledge. From what I can learn, they intend making an attack on some military post. We lost 1 man killed that we know of, and 9 missing in all. We killed 1 rebel that they know of. We lost 9 horses. Captain Humphrey saw two companies of rebels, from 80 to 100 in each. A deserter came in. He reports the enemy about 600 strong. They are a part of Shelby's and Marmaduke's men. It is a matter of impossibility to keep the wire up. They cut it almost daily in front and rear of my patrol.

DAVID McKEE,
Major Seventh Missouri Volunteer Cavalry, Commanding Post.

Colonel CLOUD.

APRIL 17-MAY 2, 1863.—Marmaduke's Expedition into Missouri.

SUMMARY OF THE PRINCIPAL EVENTS.

April 20, 1863.—Skirmish at Patterson, Mo.
22, 1863.—Skirmish at Fredericktown, Mo.
24, 1863.—Skirmish at Mill, or Middle, Creek Bridges, Mo.
26, 1863.—Action at Cape Girardeau, Mo.
Skirmish near Jackson, Mo.
27, 1863.—Skirmishes at Jackson and near White Water Bridge, Mo.
29, 1863.—Skirmish at Castor River, Mo.
30, 1863.—Skirmish at Bloomfield, Mo.
May 1- 2, 1863.—Skirmishes at Chalk Bluff, Saint Francis River, Ark.

REPORTS.*

No. 1.—Maj. Gen. Samuel R. Curtis, U. S. Army, commanding Department of the Missouri, of action at Cape Girardeau and pursuit of Marmaduke, with Return of Casualties.

No. 2.—Brig. Gen. John W. Davidson, U. S. Army, of skirmishes at Patterson and Mill Creek.

No. 3.—Brig. Gen. John McNeil, U. S. Army, of action at Cape Girardeau and pursuit of Marmaduke.

No. 4.—Capt. Charles P. Meisner, Second Missouri Light Artillery, of action at Cape Girardeau and pursuit of Marmaduke.

No. 5.—Maj. Joseph W. Caldwell, First Iowa Cavalry, Glover's brigade, of skirmish at Chalk Bluff.

No. 6.—Col. Edwin Smart, Third Missouri State Militia Cavalry, of skirmish at Patterson.

No. 7.—Col. Oscar H. La Grange, First Wisconsin Cavalry, commanding brigade, of engagement at Chalk Bluff, Mo.

No. 8.—Col. R. R. Livingston, First Nebraska Infantry, of the pursuit of Marmaduke.

No. 9.—Lieut. Col. William Baumer, First Nebraska Infantry, of action at Cape Girardeau and pursuit of Marmaduke.

No. 10.—Lieut. Col. John F. Benjamin, Second Missouri State Militia Cavalry, of action at Cape Girardeau and pursuit of Marmaduke.

No. 11.—Brig. Gen. William Vandever, U. S. Army, commanding Second Division, Army of the Frontier, of the pursuit of Marmaduke.

No. 12.—Brig. Gen. Alexander Asboth, U. S. Army, commanding at Columbus, Ky., of co-operation with McNeil.

No. 13.—Brig. Gen. J. S. Marmaduke, C. S. Army, commanding expedition.

No. 14.—Col. G. W. Thompson, Sixth Missouri Cavalry (Confederate), commanding Shelby's brigade.

No. 15.—Capt. John M. Muse, First Missouri Infantry.

No. 16.—Col. John Q. Burbridge, Fourth Missouri Cavalry (Confederate), commanding brigade.

No. 17.—Lieut. Col. S. G. Kitchen, Missouri Cavalry Battalion (Confederate).

No. 18.—Col. George W. Carter, Twenty-first Texas Cavalry, commanding brigade.

No. 19.—Col. Colton Greene, Third Missouri Cavalry (Confederate), commanding brigade.

No. 20.—Asst. Surg. S. S. Harris, Jeffers' Missouri regiment (Confederate).

---

*See also communications from Buford, Curtis, Davidson, Herron, Phelps, and Tyler, April 20-May 2, in "Correspondence, etc.," Part II.

No. 1.

Reports of Maj. Gen. Samuel R. Curtis, U. S. Army, commanding Department of the Missouri, of action at Cape Girardeau and pursuit of Marmaduke, with return of casualties.

HEADQUARTERS,
Saint Louis, Mo., April 26, 1863—2.30 p. m.

Dispatch received from General [John] McNeil, dated 12 noon. Two gunboats had just arrived. Our troops in good spirits. General [William] Vandever left Fredericktown this morning with strong cavalry force to attack rebels in rear. Fifty miles to go, but will travel day and night. The firing heard at telegraph station, Jonesborough, has just ceased.

SAML. R. CURTIS,
Major-General.

Maj. Gen. H. W. HALLECK,
General-in-Chief.

SAINT LOUIS, MO.,
April 26, 1863—7.20 p. m.

General McNeil telegraphs, 2 p. m., from Cape Girardeau that the enemy had ceased firing and seem to be changing position to renew the attack. Some of my re-enforcements had arrived safely by steamer. There has been no further firing heard at railroad station. Every moment admits of Vandever's nearer approach in the enemy's rear. Our troops are behaving well.

SAML. R. CURTIS,
Major-General.

Maj. Gen. H. W. HALLECK,
General-in-Chief.

SAINT LOUIS, MO.,
April 26, 1863—9 p. m.

Another dispatch from Cape Girardeau to General Davidson, just received, asks the whereabouts of General Vandever, preparatory to a sortie. The repulse of rebels seems complete, as there is no new attack. Our long-range guns made great havoc in the rebel lines. Our loss is only 20 killed and wounded. The enemy may take advantage of the darkness to retreat before Vandever's cavalry arrives. So far we claim a decided victory.

SAML. R. CURTIS,
Major-General.

Maj. Gen. H. W. HALLECK.

SAINT LOUIS, MO.,
April 26, 1863—11.12 p. m.

I sent a small re-enforcement to McNeil last night, and the naval commander at Cairo sent two gunboats, which, I suppose, arrived there in the night. At 2 this a. m. General McNeil received, by flag of truce, a demand for a surrender within half an hour, signed, "By order of

General Sterling Price," which was declined. It has been said Price was coming up, but I doubt his being present. 11 a. m. firing just commenced.

SAML. R. CURTIS,
Major-General.

Maj. Gen. H. W. HALLECK, *General-in-Chief.*

SAINT LOUIS, MO., *April* 27, 1863.

General Vandever came on the enemy's rear near Cape Girardeau last night, attacked and routed him, taking a large number of prisoners, horses, arms, &c. The enemy retreated toward Bloomfield in great disorder, pursued by our victorious and combined forces of Generals Vandever and McNeil. I have telegraphed General Asboth at Columbus, asking him to strike a blow through New Madrid to prevent or embarrass their escape.

SAML. R. CURTIS,
Major-General.

Maj. Gen. H. W. HALLECK, *General-in-Chief.*

SAINT LOUIS, MO.,
April 28, 1863—9 p. m.

Generals Vandever and McNeil united in pursuit of rebels. Yesterday firing was heard from 10 p. m. to 3 a. m. The rebels destroyed bridge after crossing White Water, and retreated pell-mell beyond. Bridge was being repaired for further pursuit. They move west from New Madrid to intercept retreat going farther. No further particulars.

SAML. R. CURTIS,
Major-General.

Maj. Gen. H. W. HALLECK, *General-in-Chief.*

ADDENDA.

Return of Casualties in the Union forces operating against Marmaduke, April 17–May 2, 1863.

[Compiled from nominal lists of casualties, returns, &c.]

Command.	Killed.		Wounded.		Captured or missing.		
	Officers.	Enlisted men.	Officers.	Enlisted men.	Officers.	Enlisted men.	Aggregate.
37th Illinois *	1			1			2
1st Iowa Cavalry				6			6
32d Iowa						1	1
1st Missouri State Militia		1					1
2d Missouri Light Artillery, Battery D			1				1
3d Missouri Cavalry		2	3	10		2	17
3d Missouri State Militia Cavalry		12	2	5	2	39	60
1st Nebraska		2		7		1	10
1st Wisconsin Cavalry		5	1	8		8	22
Total	1	22	7	37	2	51	120

* Lieut. Joseph Eaton killed at Chalk Bluff, May 2.

No. 2.

Reports of Brig. Gen. John W. Davidson, U. S. Army, of skirmishes at Patterson and Mill Creek.

HEADQUARTERS SAINT LOUIS DISTRICT,
Saint Louis, Mo., April 21, 1863.

MAJOR: I have to report that the enemy (whose strength is variously estimated from 2,000 to 4,000, with two pieces of artillery, and under Marmaduke) drove Smart's regiment out of Patterson yesterday, one of my outposts, and that Smart has fallen back upon Pilot Knob. His loss is said to be 200 in killed, wounded, and missing.*

I suspend further report and opinion until all the details reach me. Appended are copies of my orders to Smart, preparing him for such possible contingency.

The remaining movable troops of the district are being rapidly put in position at the Knob, and Glover, with two regiments of cavalry and four pieces, has been ordered to ascertain the whereabouts of Marmaduke, as Smart has lost hold of him.

I am, sir, your obedient servant,

J. W. DAVIDSON,
Brigadier-General, Commanding.

Maj. H. Z. CURTIS,
Assistant Adjutant-General.

[Inclosures.]

SAINT LOUIS DISTRICT, *April* 11, 1863.

Colonel SMART, *Patterson, Mo.:*

Put pickets, of at least one company each, at Greenwood Valley and Reeves' Station, watching the crossings of the Black River between these points. Let them be in daily communication with you. Be vigilant where you are. Send good spies to Pitman's Ferry and Doniphan.

DAVIDSON,
Brigadier-General.

SAINT LOUIS DISTRICT, *April* 16, 1863.

Colonel SMART, *Patterson, Mo.:*

Keep your patrols well to the front, as ordered, examining well the line of the Black River, from Greenwood Valley to Reeves' Station. If the enemy come up in force, fall back to Pilot Knob. Report all occurrences at once by telegraph. Matthews has been ordered to join you from Jackson. Organize good spies, and send them out in your front.

DAVIDSON,
Brigadier-General.

SAINT LOUIS DISTRICT, *April* 16, 1863.

Colonel SMART, *Patterson, Mo.:*

Collect all the fire-arms in your neighborhood, except those in the armories of the Enrolled Militia, or in the hands of thoroughly loyal men, who will come into our lines on the advance of the enemy. Don't

---

* But see revised statement, p. 253.

keep any amount of ammunition on hand, nor subsistence on hand at Patterson. This hint is given you that you may feel your regiment is part of a movable force.

DAVIDSON,
Brigadier-General.

HEADQUARTERS SAINT LOUIS DISTRICT,
Saint Louis, Mo., April 28, 1863.

COLONEL: The details of the attack of the rebels on Mill Creek Bridge on the night of the 24th instant have just been received by me from Colonel [John F.] Tyler, commanding the troops on the Iron Mountain Railroad. The attack was repulsed by Captain [Isaac D.] Johnson, Twenty-fourth Missouri Volunteers, and Lieutenant [August] Haufbauer, First Missouri State Militia, with a loss on our side of 1 non-commissioned officer, Corporal Ochs, First Missouri State Militia, killed, and on that of the rebels of 3 dead on the ground and 12 wounded. The wounded were left in the neighborhood. I am having inquires made whether these men were part of Marmaduke's forces or military insurgents, in order to take the proper steps. At one time Mill Creek Bridge was set on fire, but was promptly extinguished by our men.

Very respectfully,

J. W. DAVIDSON,
Brigadier-General, Commanding.

Col. N. P. CHIPMAN, *Chief of Staff.*

No. 3.

Reports of Brig. Gen. John McNeil, U. S. Army, of action at Cape Girardeau and pursuit of Marmaduke.

CAPE GIRARDEAU, *April* 26, 1863—6 p. m.

GENERAL: I am attacked by 8,000 men under Marmaduke. I have repulsed them this afternoon. Expect to be stormed to-morrow. Can you send me two regiments of infantry and a field battery, with supply of ammunition? Answer.

Respectfully,

JOHN McNEIL,
Brigadier-General, Commanding.

General ASBOTH,
Commanding Columbus, Ky.

APRIL 26, 1863.

Two steamers with re-enforcements from you have arrived. I have already put them in the field. The first attack of the enemy has been brilliantly repulsed. He has ceased firing all arms, and now appears to be changing his position to attack our right flank. He will be well cared for in that direction. I have not yet used the gunboats, but am holding them in readiness. I think you may give yourself no concern about Cape Girardeau. Do me the favor to keep my family advised with the progress of events.

JOHN McNEIL,
Brigadier-General, Commanding Cape Girardeau.

Major-General CURTIS.

HEADQUARTERS MCNEIL'S BRIGADE,
April 28, 1863—10.45 p. m.

GENERAL: The enemy are building rafts at the river, and will probably cross to-night or toward morning, unless we shell them from the ford. This can only be done from a good defensible position, by guns of larger range than any now at the front. Can your rifled guns be forced up? Horses may be taken from the ranks, caissons lightened, and drivers urged to work up their guns and caissons.

With the artillery soon up, they are bagged. Please send to the rear to hurry up ammunition for Welfley's battery; it started from the Cape this morning.

I have the honor to be, general, your most obedient servant,

JOHN MCNEIL,
Brigadier-General.

General VANDEVER.

HEADQUARTERS MCNEIL'S BRIGADE,
April 28, 1863—2.30 p. m.

GENERAL: I have now halted the head of the column, in order to close up. Am taking fresh horses from the ranks, in order to keep Welfley's battery moving. The main army of the enemy in front, with eight pieces of artillery. They are inquiring for a road across the swamps. If I am fortunate in getting up my support, especially the light guns from your command, I shall cut them out of the center, and capture their artillery. The inclosed* was found torn up in a house this morning. We are entirely out of subsistence; please send us rapidly forward a share of the rations you received this morning. We are losing time waiting for support to our artillery.

JOHN MCNEIL.

General VANDEVER.

HEADQUARTERS MCNEIL'S BRIGADE,
April 28, 1863—12 p. m.

GENERAL: Both columns of the enemy met at and encamped at this place last night (4 miles from White Water), and are now moving in our advance, in the direction of Bloomfield. Marmaduke is in command. They have destroyed the bridge over Crooked Creek between this point and Williams' Ferry, so as to impede your advance. I will move forward and engage them as soon as I can reach them. We cannot be more than five hours behind their rear guard. If you can hurry up some of your artillery, well supported, I shall have no doubt but the pursuit will be successful; but I must be strong enough to protect my flanks. Please answer by return of courier.

JOHN MCNEIL,
[*Brigadier-General.*]

General VANDEVER.

FOURTEEN MILES FROM BLOOMFIELD,
May 1, 1863—6 a. m.

GENERAL: We are driving the enemy in front, and have peppered them from the howitzer battery. La Grange has discovered a small

* Not found.

party, say from 500 to 800, on the railroad cut, 4 miles in the rear and east of this road. This I suppose to be the party that went east from Bloomfield, or some other that has ventured down the prairie road. A regiment can take care of them.

I shall keep ahead, being sure that I am within 8 or 10 miles of the main force of our enemy. Hurry up, for victory is sure.

I have the honor to be, your obedient servant,

McNEIL,
Brigadier-General.

General VANDEVER.

HEADQUARTERS SUB-DISTRICT OF CAPE GIRARDEAU,
May 10, 1863.

GENERAL: I have the honor to report my return to this post, and to acknowledge receipt of your order to occupy it until further orders.

Capt. Anton Gerster, Topographical Engineers, is here inspecting the forts. I have already detailed an officer with a working party for his assistance.

The post ordnance officer has made a report of small-arm ammunition, and the ordnance sergeant of the regular service is directed to do the same. Requisitions for ammunition for the forts go forward by this mail.

I shall, as soon as I get matters arranged, forward my report of proceeding up to the time I reported to and was directed by orders of General Vandever. I am only waiting for reports of the officers of the different commands.

We took no transportation, guns, or stores from the enemy, and but few prisoners. The officers and men displayed on every occasion the most soldierly spirit, marching until both horse and man had to succumb to fatigue and want of rest and food. But our fatal error was in allowing the enemy to cross the Castor.

Please excuse the haste with which this letter is written.

I have the honor to be, your obedient servant,

JOHN McNEIL.

Brigadier-General DAVIDSON,
Commanding District of Saint Louis.

HEADQUARTERS SOUTHWEST DISTRICT,
Cape Girardeau, Mo., May 12, 1863.

GENERAL: I have the honor herewith to submit to you my report of the pursuit of General Marmaduke's forces from Cape Girardeau to Chalk Bluff, and also accompany it with the several reports of the brigade and regimental commanders.

On Monday, April 27, at 2 p. m., notwithstanding my men were worn out by their recent severe marches, and two days and nights of constant duty in preparing for the enemy, and finally defeating him on Sunday, I started in pursuit.

My force was composed of the First Wisconsin Cavalry, Colonel [O. H.] La Grange; Second Missouri State Militia, Lieutenant-Colonel [John F.] Benjamin; Welfley's battery, Lieutenant [Lawrence] Jacoby, and two detachments of Enrolled Missouri Militia, under Colonel [William H.] McLane and Lieutenant-Colonel Lee. The Enrolled Missouri Militia, however, were sent in the direction of Perry County, with instructions to move through the country, and, in case of my engaging at White Water, to pick up straggling detachments.

I left as garrison in the Cape the Thirty-seventh Illinois Infantry, the Thirty-second Iowa Infantry, and the First Nebraska Infantry. My men were in fine spirits, although but one day's rations and no equipage encumbered their movements or added to their comforts.

That afternoon we made 16 miles, reaching White Water. I had expected that General Vandever, by a forced march from Jackson, would have cut the enemy out from the bridge and placed him between our two columns, forcing him to general action, when our great superiority in artillery and better quality of troops must have given us a decided victory. I found the White Water Bridge had been thoroughly destroyed by the fleeing foe, just two hours in advance of me. Learning that General Vandever was encamped about 4 miles to the north of the bridge, and higher up the river, I there reported to him, and learned from him that the jaded condition of his horses had prevented his farther pursuit that day.

By 10 o'clock next morning, owing to the indefatigable exertions of the First Wisconsin, Colonel [O. H.] La Grange and Major [William H.] Torrey, the bridge was rebuilt, and General Vandever having assigned to me the advance, I hurried on and encamped after dark about 3 miles from the Castor River, having marched, over very bad roads, 32 miles.

At this point Lieut. F. R. Poole, my acting assistant adjutant-general, who was urging the advance, made a dashing charge upon a part of the enemy's rear with only 6 men, killing 2 of the Texans and capturing Lieutenant [William] Bast, of Thompson's regiment. I learned from a farmer near, whom I know to be loyal, that the main body of the enemy was at the Castor, and he supposed, from the recent rain, they would be unable to cross. Colonel [John M.] Glover, with the Third Missouri Cavalry and Welfley's battery, was pushed on to within 1½ miles of the river crossing, and I made every arrangement for an attack by early dawn, but received orders from the rear to halt until they had come up. I sent Colonel La Grange, with the First Wisconsin, to feel his way, and learned that the river was fordable and the enemy had been crossing all night, drowning several of their men, and were posted in the woods on the opposite bank and prepared to dispute our crossing. Captain [Perry D.] McClanahan's section of the Second Missouri State Militia advanced, afterward strengthened by Cole's section of long-range guns, under Lieutenant [Joseph B.] Atwater, and Colonel La Grange, First Wisconsin Cavalry, who soon drove the enemy from their position, the First Wisconsin doing excellent service as sharpshooters. I then fell back, and in the afternoon crossed the river, as per order received April 29, a copy of which is transmitted. The river in the mean time having risen, I am indebted to the exertions of Captain [William] Dawson and his company, Second Missouri State Militia, for being enabled to cross my artillery and ammunition with the necessary dispatch.

I pushed on toward Bloomfield, as far as obedience to the order would allow, when Colonel La Grange, who was leading an advance party, commenced skirmishing with the enemy's rear, driving them to within three-fourths of a mile of Bloomfield, where the enemy had taken position in some force. I at once hurried up to the support of La Grange, and posted the artillery on Walker's hill, within 1,000 yards of the enemy; recalled the skirmishers and opened fire. By dark the enemy was silenced, and I was in hopes the report of their being in strong position at Bloomfield and determined to make a stand would prove correct.

The men lay down that night in line of battle, and at 4 a. m. the First Wisconsin advanced and engaged the enemy, whose rear occupied the position of the night before. Opened on them with artillery at 5 a. m., and also on the town, forcing the enemy to a precipitate retreat, my advance entering the town at 10 a. m. from the north as they retired by the south, on Chalk Bluff road. My whole column was in full occupancy of the town before 11 o'clock. Here I was compelled to wait further orders.

In the afternoon there was assigned to me, by Brigadier-General Vandever, two brigades: The First Brigade—Third Missouri Cavalry, Third Missouri State Militia Cavalry, Third Iowa Cavalry, Thirteenth Illinois, Stange's section, Hauck's battery, Lindsay's section of Enrolled Missouri Militia, and the First Iowa Cavalry, Col. J. M. Glover commanding. The Second Brigade—First Nebraska Infantry, Second Missouri State Militia Cavalry, First Wisconsin Cavalry, and Welfley's battery, Colonel La Grange commanding.

I found the enemy had sent fatigue parties in advance, to construct a floating bridge with which to expedite their crossing the Saint Francis. The delays which had occurred satisfied me that it would be nearly impossible to bring the rebels to an engagement, the nature of the country between Bloomfield and Chalk Bluff being such that a strong rear guard could retard a heavy column with ease and almost impunity. Hoping that I could make the river in time to injure them, however, I notified the various corps of the change in order of assignment, with orders to march at 7 p. m., the Second Brigade, under Colonel La Grange, in the advance. We marched all night and came up with the enemy; attacked them at 5 a. m. on May 1; engaged them in constant succession, they taking position after position for 20 miles. Night found me in position 2 miles from Chalk Bluff.

Next morning, May 2, I advanced the artillery on the bluff—north side of river—the enemy having crossed; bridge being destroyed, and being posted on Chalk Bluff, south side of the river, advanced skirmishers to find their position. The enemy immediately opened with artillery and small-arms, which was as promptly replied to. Our artillery was admirably served, and our fire soon became terrific. The First Nebraska, the Thirty-seventh Illinois, part of the First Wisconsin, and Second Missouri State Militia performed admirably as skirmishers and sharpshooters, and finally drove the enemy, with heavy loss to them, from the bluff, when I received orders to fall back.

I deeply regret that despite the excellent quality of the force in pursuit, and the splendid and effective artillery placed at our disposition, Marmaduke was allowed to make a successful retreat into Arkansas, saving his guns and baggage, but trust that an examination of the reports made by the various brigade and regimental commanders will exonerate me from blame in the premises.

The loss I suffered will be seen from the report of Maj. William McClellan, surgeon of the general hospital at Cape Girardeau, also inclosed. I must make honorable mention of Colonel Glover and the Third Missouri Cavalry, who on all occasions conducted themselves as gallant soldiers, and particularly during our 20-mile engagement, when, with Lieutenant-Colonel [Robert] Carrick and the Third Missouri, they made a dashing charge on the enemy on May 1, for the purpose of taking their artillery, which would have been a complete success had the First Iowa, which was ordered to support the charge, got up in time. Welfley's battery, Lieutenant Jacoby, and Captain McClanahan's section, Second Missouri State Militia, deserve special mention for good conduct and execution done the enemy. The First Wisconsin, always zealous to be first in the fight, did admirable service in every position in which it was placed. The First Nebraska, as you will see by the brigade report, again sustained its well-earned reputation. Captain [Charles P.] Meisner, up to the time of his wound, acting as chief of artillery, discharged his duties fully up to the mark as a brave and good soldier.

I would also mention the volunteer members of my staff, who were ready at all times to discharge any and every duty assigned them, Col. W. R. Strachan, Lieutenant-Colonel Lee, Lieut. F. R. Poole, and Lieutenant [Tolbert C.] Ankeny.

I have the honor to be, your obedient servant,

JOHN McNEIL,
Brigadier-General, U. S. Volunteers.

Brig. Gen. J. W. DAVIDSON,
Commanding District of Saint Louis.

No. 4.

Reports of Capt. Charles P. Meisner, Second Missouri Light Artillery, of action at Cape Girardeau and pursuit of Marmaduke.

CAPE GIRARDEAU, MO., *May* 9, 1863.

GENERAL: I have the honor to lay before you the report of the artillery in the action at Cape Girardeau, Mo., April 26, 1863.

On my arrival from Saint Louis, on Saturday night, April 25, 1863, I was appointed by you chief of artillery. I entered upon duty immediately, and consulted Lieutenant-Colonel Baumer, First Nebraska Infantry, about his position and course of retreat, if needed. The position of artillery engaged was: Fort B, on a hill north of Jackson road, guarding same, 1,900 yards from where the Jackson road leads in to the woods, mounted with two 24-pounder barbettes and one 24-pounder siege gun. On a hill north of Fort B, guarding the Perryville road, were two 12-pounder howitzers, of Welfley's battery, stationed. On a hill southwest of Fort B, about 1,400 yards distant, was Lieutenant [Lawrence] Jacoby, of Welfley's battery, with two 12-pounder howitzers and two 12-pounder guns, protected by detachment of First Nebraska Infantry, under Lieutenant-Colonel Baumer. This position commands the Jackson and Bloomfield roads.

On the 26th of April, at 11 a. m., our pickets were driven in by the enemy on the Jackson road. As soon as the advance of the enemy came out of the woods, I opened fire on them with shell from Fort B. Lieutenant Jacoby, with his four pieces, followed; also the two howitzers north of Fort B; but these two being out of range, I stopped their firing. The enemy now planted four pieces of rifled 3-inch Parrott guns on the Jackson road, and opened fire on Fort B, without doing any harm. I now changed from shell to solid shot, and soon removed them, they moving southwardly toward the Bloomfield road. Now, about 12.30 p. m., Lieutenant-Colonel Baumer changed position to a hill north of his first position, and near the Jackson road, with two howitzers, under Lieutenant Jacoby, the two 12-pounder guns falling back onto Fort B. The enemy tried several times to flank us on the north, but as soon as they showed themselves they were driven back by the guns of Fort B and the two howitzers near the Perryville road. When the enemy withdrew their cannon from the Jackson road, I heard them fire from the southwest on Lieutenant-Colonel Baumer's position. I anticipated an attack on the Bloomfield road; then I went to Fort C, to be ready for them there; but they were held in check by Lieutenant-Colonel Baumer and the two howitzers, under Lieutenant Jacoby. At 2.30 p. m. the firing ceased, the enemy withdrawing. No loss to report. Beg leave to mention Sergt. George Voelker and Corporal Gier, Company D, Second Missouri Artillery, for firing their pieces with excellent precision.

I have the honor to be, sir, very respectfully, your obedient servant,

CHAS. P. MEISNER,
Capt. Company D, Second Missouri Artillery, Chief of Artillery.

Brig. Gen. JOHN MCNEIL, *Commanding.*

CAPE GIRARDEAU, MO., *May* 9, 1863.

GENERAL: I have the honor to lay before you also the actions of the artillery in the pursuit of the enemy from Bloomfield to Chalk Bluff.

Left Bloomfield at 12 m. on the night of the 30th of April. About 5 a. m. May 1, our advance drove in the enemy's pickets. At 5.30 the enemy had taken position, with two 6-pounders and two 3-inch rifled Parrott guns, on the first range of hills, called Crowley's Ridge. Lieutenant [Lawrence] Jacoby soon drove them, with shells, from their position. About 2 miles farther the enemy tried to make a stand, but Lieutenant Jacoby and Lieutenant [Joseph B.] Atwater, of Cole's battery, drove them off with a few shots. Then I ordered the two mountain howitzers, under Captain [Perry D.] McClanahan, to follow up with the advance. They fired several times on the enemy, when they broke and ran. About noon there was a charge made by Colonel [John M.] Glover, sustained by the two mountain howitzers. Then a charge of the brigade was made. At 4.30 p. m. the enemy made a stand again, about 1½ miles beyond Four Mile, and opened a heavy fire with four pieces of artillery and infantry. Captain [George] Hauck's battery took position. I was wounded in the foot by a grape-shot, and was obliged to fall to the rear.

No loss in the artillery by the enemy's fire. Private Preuzner, Company K, Second Missouri Artillery, Hauck's battery, fell, with his horse, and had a leg bruised.

I have the honor to be, sir, very respectfully, your obedient servant,

CHAS. P. MEISNER,
Capt. Company D, Second Missouri Artillery, Chief of Artillery.

Brig. Gen. JOHN MCNEIL, *Commanding.*

No. 5.

Report of Maj. Joseph W. Caldwell, First Iowa Cavalry, Glover's brigade, of skirmish at Chalk Bluff.

ROLLA, MO., *May* 15, 1863.

MAJOR: My attention has been called to an article in the Missouri Democrat of the — instant, in which the correspondent does great injustice to General Vandever and to the First Iowa Cavalry.

It is true, as stated, that General Vandever gave General McNeil two brigades. The first consisted, mainly, of the First Iowa Cavalry, 500 men, well armed and mounted, and not inferior to any equal number of men in the service in skill and bravery, and the Third Missouri Volunteer Cavalry, about 400 men, I think, not quite so well armed as the First Iowa, but, in other respects, as good soldiers. These last were commanded by Colonel [John M.] Glover, who, being the senior officer of the brigade, was placed in command of it. There were some other commands in the brigade, but the regiments above designated were the only ones engaged during the fight on May 1 until 2 or 3 p. m., with the exception of the artillery, which did good service. The First Iowa Cavalry was placed in advance.

On the evening of Thursday, 30th of April, when about 8 miles south of Bloomfield, being then in the night, we were halted, and remained until 2 a. m. Two squadrons of the First Iowa, under the command of Lieutenants [Thomas H.] Barnes and [David C.] McIntyre, both deserving the highest praise for their skill and bravery, were placed in the advance, and the column marched on. Between 3 and 4 a. m. the advance was fired on by the rear guard of Marmaduke. I sent word back to General McNeil, and received orders to halt the column until daylight.

At daylight the column moved on, until about sunrise, when the advance received the fire of Marmaduke's artillery and small-arms. The regiment dismounted, deployed as skirmishers, and drove the enemy before them. In the mean time the battery came up and shelled them, while retreating.

After the First Iowa had proceeded about 3 miles, it was relieved by the Third Missouri, who dismounted and drove the enemy in a similar manner, for about the same distance, during which the First Iowa was rallied, mounted, and led under full speed to relieve them again. Thus the two regiments alternated until 2 or 3 p. m.

On two or three occasions, when Colonel Glover was present with the First Iowa, he asserted that he intended to charge the scoundrels and take their artillery, and that he would do it with the Third Missouri, his own regiment, as they had good sabers, and he wanted them to have an opportunity of trying them. From the pertinacity with which he insisted that his regiment should make the charge, when it was no better armed than the First Iowa in any respect, induced the belief that he desired his command should monopolize the glory of the charge and the capture of the battery, and this belief was strengthened when I learned that the charge had been made at a time when, and a place where, it was utterly impossible for the First Iowa to reach the conflict in time to participate as supporters. The First Iowa had been deployed as skirmishers, with a line extending a half mile on either side of the road, with their horses some distance in the rear, and the enemy retreating under full speed to a favorable point for further resistance, entirely out of sight, when Colonel Glover's command charged by the line of skirmishers. The rally was at once sounded, the men drawn in from both sides of the road with all possible speed, mounted, and led on to the scene of the charge; but before they could possibly arrive (and they traveled as expeditiously as any troops could have done) the conflict was over, and the rebels again retreating at full speed.

There was no order whatever given, save there was a general conversational direction to push forward, and, when the charge should be made, to be ready to render any necessary support; but at the time the charge was made there was nothing from Colonel Glover to me indicating that he intended making the charge at that particular time. He had charged by us in the same manner before.

These facts are well known by Captain Thompson, who was aiding me in command of the regiment, Adjutant Donnell, and other officers of the regiment.

Will you be kind enough to set this matter right?

Truly, yours,

J. W. CALDWELL,
Major, Commanding Detachment First Iowa Cavalry.

LUCIEN J. BARNES,
Major and Assistant Adjutant-General.

No. 6.

Reports of Col. Edwin Smart, Third Missouri State Militia Cavalry, of skirmish at Patterson.

PILOT KNOB, *April* 21, 1863.

GENERAL: I could not communicate with you yesterday; the line was cut as soon as the engagement began, which was 6 miles from my post. I had a scout out on Black River, who found the enemy early yesterday morning, but they succeeded in cutting them off so that they could not communicate with me. The number of the enemy was between 1,500 and 3,000. I think they had six pieces of artillery. I could not ascertain who commanded the enemy. The attack began about 12 o'clock on Reeves' Station road, with a scout I had sent out in that direction. I then sent Major [Richard G.] Woodson on to re-enforce with a battalion, who held them in check, and skirmished them into town. This gave me time to load my train, and have it ready to move if I had to retreat. Before I left the town I destroyed what stores I could not bring away. Nothing fell into the hands of the enemy. The fight continued to Big Creek, about 8 miles this side of Patterson. The engagement was severe in the extreme. After fighting hand to hand at Big Creek, they had got in my front and attempted to cut off my retreat, but I forced my way and formed on this side the creek. But the enemy did not renew. My loss in killed, wounded, and missing in the action was about 50. I had scouts on the Van Buren, Greenwood Valley, and Bush Creek roads; also on the Reeves' Station road, which I heard from. I will send you an official report as soon as I can learn all the details. Major [Henry L.] McConnel* was wounded and fell into the hands of the enemy. I think his wound was mortal. My regiment fell back in good order, and are now together, except the scouts above mentioned. I had about 400 men in the engagement.

EDWIN SMART,
Colonel, Commanding Post.

Brig. Gen. J. W. DAVIDSON.

HDQRS. THIRD MISSOURI STATE MILITIA CAVALRY,
Pilot Knob, May 9, 1863.

GENERAL: I have the honor to submit the following report of an engagement near Patterson, Mo., on the 20th day of April, 1863, between

* Major McConnel resigned July 3, 1863.

a portion of my regiment and the Confederate forces, under the command of Marmaduke. Having information from my spies and scouts that a large rebel force was moving into Missouri from Batesville, Ark., I kept my front as well picketed as my limited force would permit, keeping scouting parties on Black River, at or near all the available fords on that stream, which was some 20 miles to the front of my post.

The rebel force approached in three columns from the Doniphan, Van Buren, and Pitman's Ferry roads, commanded, respectively, by Shelby, Greene, and Burbridge. They thus succeeded in capturing or cutting off my scouting parties, and preventing their communicating with me. Their immediate approach was not known until within 6 miles of Patterson, where they met and commenced an engagement with a scouting party, 20 in number, under the command of Captain Hunter. This party, making a strong resistance to their approach, compelled the enemy to commence a brisk cannonade.

I immediately ordered Major [Richard G.] Woodson to move out two companies (B and G) and meet the enemy; ascertain, as near as possible, their position and strength; skirmish them into town, detaining them as much as he could, in order to give time for preparations for defense, and, if necessary, to fall back. Major Woodson held his position, some 2 miles from town, until he discovered the enemy were about to outflank him, when he commenced falling back.

From his messenger I was able to learn that the enemy outnumbered my force at least seven to one, with five pieces of artillery; and knowing that it would be impossible to hold my position against such superior numbers, I determined to fall back, some 7 miles, to a point on the Pilot Knob road, known as Stony Battery, on Big Creek. All the wagons at the post were loaded with company property, quartermaster's, commissary, and hospital stores, and the remainder that could not be brought away was burned. I directed Lieutenant-Colonel Morsey to move on with the train to this point, and prevent the rebels obtaining possession of it if he endeavored to cut off my retreat. Major McConnel commanded the rear, and covered the retreat with Companies E and I, commanded, respectively, by Captain [George L.] Hewing and Lieutenant [James W.] Bradley. The major remained until the rebels came into town, when he moved off, followed by two regiments of Texas cavalry and two pieces of artillery, who soon came up, when the engagement began.

My men fought nobly, under the command of Captain Hewing, Lieutenants Bradley, [Warren C.] Shattuck, [Henry] Sladek, and [James A.] Blain, contesting their advance against overwhelming numbers. Arriving in the battery, I formed a line of battle to hold the enemy in check until the rear battalion, which had already suffered severely, could pass to the front. Soon after, hearing that Colonel Morsey was engaged in front with a force endeavoring to prevent his crossing the bridge, I pushed forward with Major Matthews' battalion to re-enforce; but the rebels, some 300 or 400 in number, made but little resistance to my force, and soon gave way and retired over the hill to my left. I then moved all my force across the creek, and formed, where I remained until near dark. The enemy did not again appear, but soon fell back to Patterson. All my command behaved well, and retired, when necessary, in good order.

Nothing fel into the hands of the enemy except the contents of three or four wagons, that broke down and were abandoned on the road. The rebel force numbered 3,000, with five pieces of artillery. My force was about 400, with no artillery.

The rebel loss in killed, as near as I can ascertain, was 28, besides a number of wounded.

I inclose herewith a correct list* of killed, wounded, and captured of my command.

I am, general, very respectfully, your obedient servant,

EDWIN SMART,
Colonel Third Missouri State Militia Cavalry.

Brig. Gen. J. W. DAVIDSON,
Commanding Saint Louis District.

No. 7.

Report of Col. Oscar H. La Grange, First Wisconsin Cavalry, commanding brigade, of skirmish at Chalk Bluff, Mo.

CAPE GIRARDEAU, MO., *May* 9, 1863.

GENERAL: In compliance with orders, the following report is respectfully submitted:

At 4 p. m., the Second Brigade was ordered to advance, and, if possible, engage the enemy north of the Saint Francis. After marching 6 miles, Lieutenant [Thomas] Bateman, Company L, First Wisconsin Cavalry, charged and drove the enemy's pickets within 3 miles of the river, and the Second Missouri State Militia Cavalry, [Lieutenant]-Colonel [John F.] Benjamin, dismounted and deployed as skirmishers, driving the front line of the enemy rapidly up the hill. General McNeil, Captain [Charles P.] Meisner, chief of artillery, and the colonel commanding were with our line of skirmishers, selecting a position for our artillery, when the enemy opened with grape and canister from a masked battery planted within 150 yards. Captain Meisner was severely wounded in the foot; but, owing to the wretched gunnery of the enemy and the peculiarities of the ground, no other injury was sustained. Lieutenant Bateman also received two heavy volleys of musketry at very short range without injury to a single man. At this time, Adjutant [Edward D.] Town, First Wisconsin Cavalry, displayed coolness worthy of a veteran. Our artillery, which had been ordered to advance, was thrown into confusion, but by his order fell back to a suitable position, and was well supported by the Third Iowa Cavalry, Lieutenant-Colonel [Henry C.] Caldwell. By order of the general commanding, the recall was sounded for our skirmishers, and had to be twice repeated before it was reluctantly obeyed. The cavalry was now formed for the support of the artillery, and welcomed by the cheers of all the troops. The gallant First Nebraska came to the front. Before dark their advance occupied the ground where Captain Meisner was wounded. During the night they discovered the enemy's picket posts, and early on the morning of the 2d, in connection with the First Iowa Cavalry, formed the advance of the movement that drove the remnant of the enemy across the Saint Francis, and even away from the shelter of its right bank. When it is remembered that the regiment had marched 90 miles in three days, we are at a loss whether to admire most its bravery in battle or its power of endurance.

Welfley's battery, which was admirably handled during this engagement, as usual, made terrible havoc among the rebels.

---

* See revised statement, p. 253.

By order of the general commanding, the brigade marched for Cape Girardeau on the morning of the 3d, and, notwithstanding the wretched state of the roads, arrived in good condition at noon on the 7th.

Very respectfully, your obedient servant,

O. H. LA GRANGE,
Colonel First Wisconsin Cavalry, Commanding Brigade.

General JOHN MCNEIL,
Commanding U. S. Forces, Cape Girardeau, Mo.

No. 8.

Report of Col. R. R. Livingston, First Nebraska Infantry, of the pursuit of Marmaduke.

SAINT LOUIS, *April* 30, 1863.

CAPTAIN: Having been instructed, on the night of the 25th instant, by order (copy of which I inclose, marked A), to take charge of the Thirty-seventh Regiment Illinois Volunteer Infantry, Captain Brown's company (G), Twenty-third Regiment Missouri Volunteer Infantry, and 20 men, under Lieutenant Ewing, Twenty-third Iowa, to see them shipped without delay to re-enforce the post of Cape Girardeau, then return to this post immediately after the attack had ceased, I have the honor to report as follows:

We arrived at Cape Girardeau on Sunday, 26th instant, at 2.50 p. m., just as the firing on both sides ceased for that day. I turned over my command to Brig. Gen. John McNeil, commanding forces at Girardeau, and was ordered by him to move with two companies of the Thirty-seventh Illinois Infantry, under Captain [Charles W.] Hawes, to report to Lieutenant-Colonel [William] Baumer, at Fort B, as the enemy were attempting to flank our right. Shortly afterward I received an order to take charge of my own regiment; but, finding the conduct of Lieutenant-Colonel Baumer, of the First Nebraska, all that could be desired, I, in the spirit of a soldier, permitted him to retain the command he had fought so gallantly previous to my arrival. Fearing a night attack, I went with General McNeil, and arranged a system of signals with two gunboats, then lying in the Mississippi River, opposite the town, by which they could direct their fire where it would be most effective. General McNeil, at my suggestion, also sent for re-enforcements to General Asboth, commanding at Columbus, Ky., whose promptness in forwarding the troops is deserving of all praise.

When daylight broke, the enemy had not appeared before our pickets, and two detachments of cavalry were sent out to feel them; but it was not before 11.30 a. m., the 27th instant, that the retrograde movement of the enemy toward Bloomfield was definitely ascertained; and at 2 p. m. two regiments of cavalry (First Wisconsin and Second Missouri), four guns of Welfley's battery, two mountain howitzers, and two companies of Colonel McLane's Missouri Militia moved out in pursuit, on the Bloomfield road. Arriving near Black Creek, the advance under Major [William H.] Torrey, First Wisconsin, drove a small force of the enemy from the bridge, which they had commenced to destroy, by tearing up plank and piling dry stakes in the bridge, preparatory to firing it. The bridge was speedily repaired, and we pushed on to the junction of the Jackson and Bloomfield roads, where we met the advance of General Vandever's column. There the column halted. Myself and a small party pushed forward to the bridge across White Water, about 1½ miles distant, and found the last span destroyed, the stringers being cut, the plank thrown in the river, and the up-stream post on the last bent cut in such a manner as to render it useless. To my great surprise, no further progress was made that day, our forces being ordered into camp at 6 p. m., with a demoralized and flying enemy only one hour ahead of us.

I left camp the next morning at 7.10 o'clock, at which time our forces had not yet pushed forward; and feeling convinced that so tardy a pursuit would certainly be a vain one, I returned to this post with all dispatch, knowing my services were needed here.

I would respectfully state that the enemy were confident of carrying and holding Cape Girardeau; that their battle cry was, "Hurrah now for McNeil!" and that, in their conversations with the peaceful citizens, they asked if Fayetteville had been attacked, stating that place and the Cape were to be struck at the same time, and that on Sunday, 3d of May next, Price, with 30,000 men, would attack Jefferson City, after which the forces at the Cape and that place were to make a combined attack on Saint Louis.

I refrain from giving you the particulars of the battle or the losses on either side, as competent authority will soon furnish the official report.

I am, captain, very respectfully, your obedient servant,

R. R. LIVINGSTON,
Col. 1st Regt. Nebraska Vol. Infty., Comdg. Post, Saint Louis, Mo.

Capt. H. C. FILLEBROWN,
Assistant Adjutant-General, District of Saint Louis, Mo.

[Inclosure A.]

SPECIAL ORDERS, No. 91. } HEADQUARTERS SAINT LOUIS DISTRICT,
Saint Louis, Mo., April 25, 1863.

* * * * * * *

XVIII. Col. R. R. Livingston, First Nebraska Infantry Volunteers, will proceed to Cape Girardeau, Mo. He will take command of all troops going down to that point. Upon his arrival, he will turn over the troops to the command of Brig. Gen. John McNeil.

By order of Brigadier-General Davidson:

HENRY C. FILLEBROWN,
Assistant Adjutant-General.

No. 9.

Reports of Lieut. Col. William Baumer, First Nebraska Infantry, of action at Cape Girardeau and pursuit of Marmaduke.

CAPE GIRARDEAU, *April* 28, 1863.

SIR: The undersigned respectfully submits to you the special description of the [part the] party under his command performed when attacked by the enemy on Cape Girardeau.

On the morning of the 24th of April, news came in from the scouts that the enemy was approaching this place with a force of about 8,000 men. The garrison of this place consisted then of about 350 men of the First Nebraska Infantry, two field pieces of Welfley's battery, one company of First Wisconsin Cavalry, Captain [George O.] Clinton, and Captain Meisner's artillery, Battery D, Second Missouri Artillery.

My idea was then to meet the enemy outside of the fortifications, and, by being overpowered, to fall back to Fort B, and from thence to Fort A, which place could be held against any force of the enemy.

The position selected by me (Captain [Thomas J.] Majors, First Nebraska, and Lieutenant [Adolphus] Stauber, Welfley's battery) was west of Cape Girardeau, about three-quarters of a mile from Fort B. The small number of the defending force allowed only to protect the northwestern part of the town, which commands all other places in and around town. The troops had made up their mind to defend the place to the last man, and never to surrender to the rebels.

On the evening of the 24th, General McNeil arrived and took command of the place. The general approved of my plan of defense, and ordered, on the 25th, Welfley's battery, consisting of six pieces, and part of the Thirty-second Iowa for the protection of the north and west side of the town. The position north, on the Perryville road, was very important, and the force of defense was two companies (F and G), First Nebraska, two field [pieces] of Welfley's battery, and three companies of the Thirty-second Iowa, all under the charge of Captain [Thomas J.] Weatherwax, First Nebraska. The central position was between the Bloomfield and Jackson roads, on a hill, which commands all approaches from the west, on which was placed four pieces of Welfley's battery, under Lieutenant [Lawrence] Jacoby, and five companies of the First Nebraska, commanded by Captain Majors. The first division of the First Nebraska Infantry (Companies B and D) were placed as skirmishers in advance, and, after twenty-four hours on duty, they were relieved by Companies I and C, of First Nebraska. Captain [H. H.] Ribble, Company I, was on the right of the skirmish line, on the Jackson road, where the attack of the enemy was first made on the morning of the 26th, at 10 a. m. The rebels were stopped by the fire of the pickets, who had orders to fall back on the battalion. Companies B and D were sent as a detachment on a hill, near the Jackson road, to act as skirmishers, and could do good service. The main attack was made northwest of the Jackson road. The guns of our position on the Perryville road fired first. Then, from the central position, and in the rear of the two outside positions, the guns of Fort B opened fire. The cross-fire of the artillery was so well directed, and the artillerists so much skilled and intrepid, that the enemy could not advance from the ambush. The five companies (C, I, K, E, and A) of First Nebraska did not give up one inch of ground in the face of the enemy, who were about ten to their one, and fired all their ammunition away. Never can soldiers perform their duty on the battle-field better or braver than did this small band of heroes. The enemy tried then to attack our right flank, on the Perryville road, when I moved two pieces of artillery on the hill, on the Jackson road, protected by Companies B and D, and their position was very destructive to the enemy. The left flank, on the Bloomfield road, was protected by the First Wisconsin Cavalry, Colonel [O. H.] La Grange, Lieutenant-Colonel [Henry] Pomeroy. Three of their companies dismounted and fought the enemy on foot with their carbines. Two mountain howitzers did also excellent service in dislodging a battery of the enemy. The position on Perryville road was strengthened by taking two more field pieces to the place; also the five companies of the First Nebraska, which were supplied with new ammunition. The firing against the enemy was still kept up from the position on the Jackson road and Fort B, until about 3 p. m., when the enemy fell back. Only small detachments were sent out to ascertain where the enemy had gone. Some of them went out as far as 3 miles. The artillery and infantry were under arms all night, ready to engage the enemy at any time. Meantime re-enforcements came up, and the rebels fell back faster than they came up. Every officer and man under my command behaved as soldiers, and displayed great courage and bravery. Every order was executed promptly, each officer and soldier discharging his duty; otherwise it would have been impossible for so small number of men to repulse an enemy with such great odds. In the first place, we had possession of a ground with the facility to assist one party through the other, and then the men had the determination not to give up the place, and would have died in fulfilling their duties before surrendering. Specially I would mention the name of Captain Majors, whose horse was shot from under him, whilst in command of the five companies in the central position; then Captain Ribble, who was first engaged with his company as skirmishers, and showed great bravery; also Captain Weatherwax, who had position on the Perryville road, from where the first shot was fired; also Lieutenant [Francis A.] McDonald, acting adjutant; quartermaster, Lieutenant [Charles] Thompson, Lieutenant Moore, and Sergeant Gillespie, who assisted me greatly in carrying orders and reports to the most dangerous places of the field. The battery (Welfley's), commanded by Lieutenant Jacoby, assisted by Lieutenant Stauber, deserve great praise for their skill and coolness in firing and rapidity in their movements.

List of killed and wounded: Killed, 3; wounded, 7.

I am, very respectfully, your obedient servant,

WILLIAM BAUMER,

Lieutenant-Colonel, Commanding First Nebraska Infantry.

Capt. WILLIAM R. STRACHAN,

Chief of Staff, Cape Girardeau, Mo.

HEADQUARTERS FIRST NEBRASKA INFANTRY,

Cape Girardeau, Mo., May 9, 1863.

SIR: The undersigned respectfully submits to you the following report of the march of the First Regiment Nebraska Infantry, ordered by General Vandever:

Marching orders received at regimental headquarters in the evening of the 28th of April, with information that the enemy were surrounded near Castor River, and to take three days' provisions and full supplies of ammunition, and to move on in forced marches. According to orders received, I started on the morning of 29th of April, at 5 o'clock, with all men of the regiment except those on extra and detached duty, the whole force amounting to 270 active soldiers. All regimental wagons and teams were ordered to accompany the regiment, and by this arrangement one-third of the men could ride at a time. The regiment encamped at Lakeville; marched at 2 o'clock in the morning; arrived at Castor River, crossed over, and marched as advance guard of column to Bloomfield, and arrived there at 10 o'clock in the morning on the 30th of April. In the afternoon, the regiment received orders to prepare for a night's march. The regiment started at 7 p. m.; marched until 3 a. m.; rested for one hour; continued the march and engaged the enemy's rear guard at 5 a. m., supporting Welfley's battery. The enemy retreating, were followed up by the regiment, and several skirmishes took place during the day of the 1st of May. In the evening, 3 miles from Saint Francis River, the regiment was ordered to the front to ascertain the enemy's position. Their position was soon discovered by the scouts of the First Nebraska Infantry, mounted on cavalry horses furnished from the cavalry on the field. The next day, May 2, the regiment marched as advance guard to the Saint Francis River. No artillery being up, we had to await their arrival before engaging the enemy. Four companies as advance were placed as line of skirmishers on the right of the main river road. Five companies, commanded by Captain Majors, were placed on the extreme left flank, a portion deployed as skirmishers. After the artillery firing and some sharpshooting, the order was received to march back to Bloomfield, which place the regiment reached on the evening of the 3d of May. From there orders were received to march to Cape Girardeau, Mo. Marched at 1 o'clock, May 4; arrived at Cape Girardeau at 4 p. m., May 5.

The soldiers of the First Nebraska Infantry, within seven days, marched 190 miles; were engaged with the enemy for fourteen hours; had only three days' rations for seven days; lost 2 men wounded, and had only 1 man on the sick report upon its arrival in camp.

They deserve the greatest praise for the willingness with which all the hardships were endured.

I am, respectfully, yours, truly,

WILLIAM BAUMER,
Lieutenant-Colonel, Commanding First Nebraska Infantry.

Capt. WILLIAM R. STRACHAN,
Chief of Staff, Cape Girardeau, Mo.

No. 10.

Report of Lieut. Col. John F. Benjamin, Second Missouri State Militia Cavalry, of action at Cape Girardeau and pursuit of Marmaduke.

CAPE GIRARDEAU, *May* 9, 1863.

GENERAL: The following is my report of the part this regiment took in the battle at this place on the 26th ultimo, and its subsequent march in pursuit of the enemy to Bloomfield, where it was assigned to the brigade of Colonel [O. H.] La Grange, First Wisconsin Cavalry:

At the time of the attack on this city, I occupied a position in front of and to the left of Fort C, the right resting on the Bloomfield road, the point where it was supposed the main force of the enemy would be concentrated; but as no demonstration was made upon this part of the town, we were at no time exposed to the enemy's fire. During the fight, however, Captain [Perry D.] McClanahan, Company C, with the two small howitzers attached to this regiment, was ordered to take position about midway between the Bloomfield and Jackson roads, supported by his company, from which he completely silenced the opposing artillery after firing a few rounds. After the retreat of the enemy, Major [H. M.] Hiller, with three companies of the First Battalion and the howitzers, was ordered to reconnoiter on the Jackson road, when, after following 5 miles, he found the enemy too strongly posted to be successfully assailed with his small force, and, night coming on, he returned.

On the following day, at 1 p. m., all the available part of the regiment joined the other forces that left here in pursuit of the enemy on the Bloomfield road, traveling that day to near the White Water without coming up with them. The bridge over that stream having been destroyed, we encamped for the night.

The bridge being sufficiently repaired by 10 a. m. the next day, I was ordered to the front and to pursue vigorously. A few miles brought us to their last encampment, which they had left but an hour and a half before; the camp-fires still burning. About 2 p. m., and when only fifteen minutes behind their rear guard, orders came to me to halt until further orders. An hour or more elapsed before I was ordered again to march, and the enemy, evidently being apprised of our near approach, as their scouts were seen taking observations from the high points in front, was enabled to get considerably the start of us again. About 5.30 p. m. I again came up with a party left to tear up a small bridge, and captured 2, with their horses. The balance of the party, having succeeded in destroying the bridge, escaped. I set all hands to work on the bridge, and had succeeded in getting it repaired so as to cross, and, when about to move, an order came from the rear to not move, whether the bridge was repaired or not, until ordered to do so. A picket guard was, however, sent ahead to Spring Hill, distant a mile or so, near where they surprised a party of 6, killing 1 and taking a lieutenant prisoner. They were not encountered again by us until after we reached Bloomfield, at which place I was put under the orders of Colonel La Grange, as before stated.

I am clearly of opinion that I could have captured many of the enemy if I had been suffered to pursue him without hinderance. The road passes through open woods, and bordered on one side by an impassable swamp most of the way. In attacking them on the march, the head of the column only could be engaged, and one regiment is as effective as a greater number. All accounts represented their rear guard as weak and the stragglers numerous.

I remain, general, very respectfully, your obedient servant,

J. F. BENJAMIN,
Lieutenant-Colonel, Commanding.

General JOHN MCNEIL,
Commanding Sub-district, Southeastern Missouri.

No. 11.

Reports of Brig. Gen. William Vandever, U. S. Army, commanding Second Division, Army of the Frontier, of the pursuit of Marmaduke.

PILOT KNOB, MO., *April* 23, 1863.

GENERAL: Just arrived with advance of 2,000 men. Main body will be in soon after noon. Hear nothing of an enemy toward Centreville or in that direction. Have parties out who will report to-day.

WM. VANDEVER,
Brigadier-General.

Major-Generals CURTIS and HERRON.

PILOT KNOB, *April* 23, 1863.

GENERAL: I have temporarily assumed command of the forces, and continue to head my orders as of the Second Division, Army of the Frontier. I have no additional news from the enemy. He was reported to be at Fredericktown last evening, 3,000 or 4,000 strong. No intelligence from there to-day.

WM. VANDEVER,
Brigadier-General.

Maj. Gen. FRANCIS J. HERRON, *Rolla.*

PILOT KNOB, MO., *April* 24, 1863.

GENERAL: Colonel Smart communicates that the enemy broke up their encampment in Fredericktown before his approach, and moved 3 miles out on Cape Girardeau road, where they formed, but had not encamped. Smart then retired to the Saint Francis bridge, and awaits orders. He believes this is the same force he encountered at Patterson, and that it does not exceed, at the utmost, 10,000. I have now available 2,500 cavalry and twelve pieces of artillery. Shall I move against the enemy at Fredericktown or not? The flag of truce is just leaving. I can move to-night, and attack in the morning, if you order it, giving the truce party the night to return here in.

WM. VANDEVER,
Brigadier-General.

Major-General CURTIS, *Saint Louis, Mo.*

HDQRS. SECOND DIVISION, ARMY OF THE FRONTIER,
Pilot Knob, Mo., April 24, 1863.

GENERAL: My latest intelligence from the enemy is up to 8 o'clock this morning at Fredericktown. Colonel Smart had approached within sight of the town, and found his pickets drawn in to the east side of the town, on the Cape Girardeau road. The colonel was reconnoitering the town, and I am in momentary expectation of further news from him.

From my examination of the approaches to this place, and from the best information I can get, I do not think an enemy would venture to attack us by the direct Fredericktown road, as a very small force, with one section of artillery, at the shut-in, 4 miles from here, can prevent the approach of almost any force.

If this locality is to be attacked from the direction of Fredericktown, the attack will come by the road from Farmington, which can be intersected about 10 miles from here by a route from Fredericktown, or the enemy, if he seeks the best road for travel, might even come round by Farmington. Nine miles from here we strike a point on the Farmington road, which is only 6 miles from Iron Mountain, over a good road. I infer from your dispatch of last night that infantry are on the way down, to be left at Iron Mountain, which is, I think, the best point to post them, for, should I ascertain that the enemy was advancing in force, I would not hesitate to move to meet him at the intersection of the road from here with the road from Iron Mountain to Farmington. Before this reaches you I shall probably have communicated other intelligence by telegraph.

I inclose a rough sketch of the country,* which I think more accurate than the maps as to roads. If further information from Colonel Smart is satisfactory, I will move on the enemy rapidly with my cavalry and artillery, but I would like the infantry you speak of sent to Iron Mountain quickly.

Very respectfully, your obedient servant,

WM. VANDEVER,
Brigadier-General.

Brig. Gen. J. W. DAVIDSON, *Saint Louis, Mo.*

---

* Not found.

PILOT KNOB, MO., *April* 24, 1863.

GENERAL: Your dispatch of last night,* directing movement, when I found the Iron Mountain road destroyed, &c., was received, but did not order a movement under present circumstances.

There is no force coming from Black River. The only force there is a few hundred, under Reves, in the vicinity of Patterson, jayhawking and robbing.

At 12.30 Colonel Smart had returned with one battalion to Saint Francis Bridge, leaving one battalion 6 miles beyond. He went within 1 mile of Fredericktown, and reports the enemy broke up their encampment in town, and withdrew 3 miles toward Cape Girardeau, where they halted and formed, but had not encamped. From all the information Colonel Smart can gather, he believes this to be the same force that was at Patterson, and does not exceed, at the utmost, 10,000.

I sent Lieutenant-Colonel Chandler, with two battalions of the Seventh Missouri Volunteer Cavalry, after the party threatening the bridges. He left at 10 this morning, moving via Farmington. Have not yet heard from him.

I telegraphed General Curtis my information from Colonel Smart, and asking if I should attack at Fredericktown to-morrow morning. Can there not be concert with McNeil? See dispatch to General Curtis and direct me. Flag of truce sent to Fredericktown to-day may delay the movement.

WM. VANDEVER,
Brigadier-General.

Brigadier-General DAVIDSON, *Saint Louis, Mo.*

FREDERICKTOWN, MO.,
April 25, 1863—7 p. m.

GENERAL: Just arrived. Marmaduke left yesterday in direction of Cape Girardeau. Camped last night 8 miles east of this. I am after him. Cannot McNeil co-operate? Remain here till morning.

Respectfully,

WM. VANDEVER,
Brigadier-General.

Brigadier-General DAVIDSON, *Saint Louis, Mo.*

NEAR FREDERICKTOWN, MO.,
April 25, 1863—11.20 p. m.

GENERAL: Yours received.† The party attacked bridges yesterday afternoon, and were repulsed with some loss. They are now trying to effect their retreat, and Chandler and Lisenby ought and I trust will annihilate them. Colonel Clark's regiment is on the bridges, I understand. All pursuing Marmaduke toward Cape Girardeau.

WM. VANDEVER,
Brigadier-General.

Major-General HERRON.

---

* See Addenda, p. 279.

† Not found.

HDQRS. SECOND DIVISION, ARMY OF THE FRONTIER,
Near White Water, Mo., April 27, 1863.

GENERAL: Came upon the enemy last evening at 9 o'clock, near Jackson, to which place they had fallen back after attacking Cape Girardeau. With the First Iowa Cavalry, I charged the enemy's camp, driving him beyond the town.

The enemy suffered in killed and wounded, and we captured a large number of horses and other property. I lost no men.

At 6 o'clock in the morning I entered the town and found the enemy posted in force 1 mile out on the Bloomington road. Opened upon him with artillery. He made no reply, but moved off, and I pursued. The enemy moved with baggage trains and artillery in front, defending his rear by strong bodies of cavalry. Five miles out on the Bloomington road he destroyed a bridge, which delayed me one hour. I crossed and came up with him again within 3 miles of the bridge over White Water, the enemy from 6,000 to 7,000 strong. The Third Iowa Cavalry were in advance, and had a severe skirmish with the enemy before the main body came up. The enemy here rallied in considerable force, but we drove him back, and pushed on to the bridge over White Water, which we could not reach in time to prevent him from crossing. After passing this bridge the enemy destroyed it. In the last encounter we had 1 man killed and 4 men wounded, one captain and 16 privates missing, probably captured, and 4 horses killed and 10 wounded. Our rations being entirely exhausted, I am obliged to pause a few hours for supplies to come up. There is a ford not far above, over which I will attempt to pass, unless I can repair the bridge within the course of the day.

General McNeil joined me with his force of cavalry. I feel justified in pressing the enemy until he is punished and driven out of the State.

WM. VANDEVER,
Brigadier-General.

Brigadier-General DAVIDSON, *Saint Louis, Mo.*

HDQRS. SECOND DIVISION, ARMY OF THE FRONTIER,
Camp, Six Miles from Bloomfield, Mo., April 29, 1863.

GENERAL: I am now at the Castor, 6 miles from Bloomfield. The enemy still retiring. I have made a temporary halt for the purpose of closing up the column. I will advance to Bloomfield this evening, and advise you further. We have had smart skirmishing this morning at the crossing of Castor, with some few casualties. In his retreat the enemy destroyed the bridges in his rear, which we have had to repair and rebuild. I think we have run him harder than he was ever run before.

Very respectfully, your obedient servant,

WM. VANDEVER,
Brigadier-General.

Brigadier-General DAVIDSON, *Saint Louis, Mo.*

P. S.—It is very important that the bridge across White Water should be well guarded. I respectfully suggest that the forces at Cape Girardeau attend to that, as it is within supporting distance from there. Would it not be well also to push down toward us from Pilot Knob a strong reconnoitering party? I would like to open my line of communication in that direction.

Respectfully, &c.,

WM. VANDEVER,
Brigadier-General.

HEADQUARTERS IN THE FIELD,
SECOND DIVISION, ARMY OF THE FRONTIER,
Bloomfield, April 30, 1863.

GENERAL: I crossed the Castor yesterday afternoon, in face of the enemy, with a large part of my command. The stream was considerably swollen, and fording was difficult. The enemy had destroyed all conveniences for crossing.

General McNeil, in command of the advance, pushed forward to within 1½ miles of this place, which was occupied by the enemy in force. The skirmishing in the evening was spirited, and the enemy retired beyond the town and assumed a position as if he intended to fight. This morning I crossed the balance of my forces, and upon moving forward the enemy again retreated.

The demonstrations in front appear to be merely for the purpose of protecting his rear while in retreat, and to draw us on. The enemy is retiring in the direction of Chalk Bluff, on the Saint Francis River, where he undoubtedly intends to cross. His trains and most of his artillery are ahead. I shall follow him up. This afternoon I again send General McNeil forward with a strong force. All accounts agree in the statement that the enemy is 7,000 or 8,000 strong, with ten pieces of artillery, but he seems to be much demoralized. The indications are that a portion of the enemy went west from here, toward Greenville; probably one brigade.

Not having received any communication from you since leaving Fredericktown, I am somewhat in doubt as to what your wishes and designs may be regarding operations in this district. I take the liberty of remarking that, if supported, an effectual advance can be speedily made into Arkansas. Forage is plenty in this direction.

Very respectfully, your obedient servant,

WM. VANDEVER,
Brigadier-General.

Brigadier-General DAVIDSON,
Saint Louis, Mo.

[Indorsement.]

MAY 2, 1863.

Respectfully inclosed for the general's reading.

Vandever's remark that, if supported, an effectual advance might be made into Arkansas, makes me think of my own situation last winter. With 9,000 splendid troops at my back, two gunboats and a boat-load of provisions on the White River would have enabled us to make an "effectual advance" also. I will at once send out from Pilot Knob to look out for the brigade which crossed toward Greenville. There is no apprehension for the Knob, even if part of the enemy should wheel that way, thinking we had robbed it of its troops.

Respectfully submitted.

J. W. DAVIDSON.

HDQRS. SECOND DIVISION, ARMY OF THE FRONTIER,
Chalk Bluff, May 2, 1863.

GENERAL: One hour ago I received your dispatch of the 30th ultimo,* per hands of Captain [R. H.] Brown, Twenty-third Missouri Volunteers. I was at the moment actively shelling the enemy across the river. I had

* See p. 281.

hoped to intercept him and capture his guns before crossing the Saint Francis, but his retreat was too precipitate. I have punished the enemy severely. A large number of dead and wounded strew the road. His rear guard fought us stubbornly all along the road from Jackson to this point, destroying bridges in their rear and adopting every means to retard our progress. Brigadier-General McNeil has greatly distinguished himself. Throughout the arduous pursuit, on account of his personal knowledge of the country, I assigned him the advance. This morning he had a horse shot from under him. Colonel [J. M.] Glover, commanding troops from Ironton, also deserves special mention for his undoubted bravery and skill. I would also call your special attention to the skill and bravery displayed by Colonel [O. H.] La Grange, of the First Wisconsin Cavalry, who commanded a brigade. Colonel [John C.] Black, Thirty-seventh Illinois Volunteers, brought a portion of his brigade gallantly into action this morning, and deserves special mention for his services. I regret to announce the loss to-day of Lieutenant [Joseph] Eaton, of the Thirty-seventh Illinois Volunteers, killed by the premature explosion of one of our own shells. Lieutenant-Colonel [Robert] Carrick, Third Missouri Volunteer Cavalry, slightly wounded. Captain Meisner, Second Missouri Artillery, chief of artillery, wounded in foot. Our whole loss in killed, wounded, and missing will not exceed 50. In obedience to your order, I am now moving to Bloomfield, from which place I will communicate further. I write this from the field almost before the sound of our artillery has ceased to echo along the valley of the Saint Francis, on the line between Arkansas and Missouri.

The officers and men of my command deserve the highest praise for courage and endurance displayed on the most arduous pursuit of an enemy which has characterized this war.

Thanking you most sincerely for kind expressions contained in your dispatch, I am, general, most respectfully, your obedient servant,

WM. VANDEVER,
Brigadier-General.

Maj. Gen. SAMUEL R. CURTIS,
Commanding Department.

HDQRS. SECOND DIVISION, ARMY OF THE FRONTIER,
Bloomfield, Mo., May 4, 1863.

GENERAL: I am thus far back from the pursuit of Marmaduke. I followed him to the Saint Francis River, at Chalk Bluff, which is a little beyond the Arkansas line, and drove him across, with heavy loss of men, though he contrived to save his guns. I fought him each day for a week, and kept him moving. It is two weeks to-day since I left you, and have marched in that time 275 miles, and fought the enemy wherever I could get at him. The roads have been in very bad condition, and, as the enemy destroyed bridges in his rear, we had to rebuild them as we went. I think I can challenge the events of the war to show a more earnest and persistent pursuit of an enemy. Of course, men and horses have suffered from fatigue, but the men are in the best of spirits, and feel to-day as though this little army could whip the whole Southern Confederacy. I am going to Cape Girardeau, and will there telegraph General Curtis for leave to come to Saint Louis, where I shall hope to meet you, for I think I can communicate some things which it appears to me have been overlooked.

This region of country is rich, and full of corn and cattle. An army passing this way need not suffer. If we give up this route to the enemy, it will enable him to approach Saint Louis nearer by land than he can by any other route, and subsist himself. A number of reasons occur to me which I could urge upon the general, verbally, better than I can in a communication, and I am anxious to see him with you.

From here the route is open to Pocahontas, Jacksonport, Batesville, or any point below on the White River. We are within reach of Crowley's Ridge, where there are abundance of supplies, and for operations against Little Rock it is the direct route. If Price is attempting to go to Missouri, we can turn his flank and get in his rear. A pontoon train, however, is necessary to operations down this way.

My orders upon the post at Girardeau about keeping us supplied with rations have not been complied with, and we are short. I am subsisting my men wholly on corn-meal and beef. I gather the corn in the country and grind it. I find plenty of beef. I shall be obliged to go to the Cape to refit. Dragging the artillery over heavy roads has pulled down the horses, and I must have some fresh ones; otherwise we are in good condition, except that our rations are not of the regular kind.

I have regretted every step of the way that you were not along with the rest of the Army of the Frontier, as I believe it was the opportune moment for driving the enemy south of the Arkansas River.

Pardon this hurried and ill-written communication, as I am much pressed at this time.

Very respectfully, your obedient servant,

WM. VANDEVER,
Brigadier-General.

Maj. Gen. FRANCIS J. HERRON,
Commanding Army of the Frontier.

HDQRS. SECOND DIVISION, ARMY OF THE FRONTIER,
Bloomfield, May 4, 1863.

GENERAL: In obedience to orders from department headquarters, I have fallen back to this point, after driving the enemy from the limits of the State.

I have already sent forward one brigade toward Cape Girardeau, and will follow with the rest as soon as practicable, except Colonel Glover's command, which I will dispatch direct from this point to Pilot Knob, instructing him to keep out strong reconnoitering parties in the direction of Greenville and Patterson, which places will be on his left flank.

Colonel Glover will start in the morning. [G.] Hauck's battery, which accompanied Colonel Glover from Pilot Knob, I have ordered to report for the time being to General [J.] McNeil, who will take it to the Cape. I was induced to do this for the reason that I desire Colonel Glover to move with celerity. He will have Captain [G.] Stange, with one section, and Colonel Lindsay, with two small pieces, along. Supplies have not been sent forward to me from Cape Girardeau, as I have ordered them. They are understood to be on the way, and I am compelled to go forward and meet them. My men are now subsisting on corn-meal and beef alone.

General McNeil will remain at Bloomfield until the morning of the 6th, when he will also move back to the Cape.

The portion of my command belonging to the Army of the Frontier proper I take with me to Cape Girardeau, that being the nearest point at which I can refit.

The entire march has been arduous in the extreme, taxing the energy, endurance, and bravery of officers and men to the fullest extent. Every duty has been performed with readiness and alacrity, and I feel it incumbent on me to move back with moderation, so as not to impair the efficiency of the heroic little army which I have the honor to command.

From the Cape I will endeavor to make a more detailed report. Herewith I send a full list of casualties.

In regard to the enemy's loss, I can only say that it must have been large. In one place, after a gallant charge made by Colonel Glover, with the Third Missouri Volunteer Cavalry, there were 19 of the enemy's dead piled together.

The engagement at Chalk Bluff, on the morning of the 2d, was also disastrous to the enemy, as at one time I played upon him with ten pieces of artillery, before he could get out of the bottom on the opposite side of the river.

On Sunday, the 26th ultimo, in the evening, I first struck the enemy, the First Iowa Cavalry charging his camp by moonlight, and, every day thereafter until the 2d instant, we fought him as he ran.

I have the honor to be, very respectfully, your obedient servant,

WM. VANDEVER,
Brigadier-General.

Brigadier-General DAVIDSON,
Saint Louis, Mo.

ADDENDA.

HEADQUARTERS ARMY OF THE FRONTIER,
Rolla, April 20, 1863.

General VANDEVER: [?]

GENERAL: Marmaduke is pushing on toward Pilot Knob, and at 9.30 this evening was within 16 miles of that place, with 4,000 men and six pieces of artillery.

General Curtis directs me to throw forward the cavalry to Centreville, and I have concluded to send you with the expedition. You will take all of your own cavalry, and I have ordered all of the cavalry in Third Division to report to you. Major Townsley's battalion, of First Missouri, will also join you in the morning. General Davidson is preparing to give them fight at Pilot Knob, and probably we can attack on the flank by way of Centreville

Should you find anything like forage at Salem or beyond that place, I will move forward the remainder of both divisions at once to support you.

You will take Foust's battery along. Let me know by return messenger how soon the cavalry can move. They should take fifteen days' rations, or as near it as possible. You had, probably, better see me before starting yourself.

Respectfully,

F. J. HERRON,
Major-General, Commanding.

[SAINT LOUIS, MO.,] *April* 23, 1863.

General VANDEVER, *Pilot Knob:*

Dispatch received.* You have made a gallant march. Have your

---

* Of same date. See p. 271.

men and horses ready for further efforts. The rebels must have no rest in Missouri. I am anxious about McNeil, who left Bloomfield when you left Rolla.

[SAML. R. CURTIS,]
Major-General.

SAINT LOUIS, MO., *April* 23, 1863.

Brigadier-General VANDEVER:

Your message received.* I wish you would have the Iron Mountain Railroad patrolled by cavalry on a side road as far as Irondale, 12 miles above the Knob, for the present, as the ground at the Knob is contracted. I want Tyler to go on with his defensive arrangements, as the cavalry will move as soon as the infantry arrive. Let me know if you are supplied with everything you want; if not, send up a staff officer for what you need. Even the short time you are there have drills twice a day by the troops that are not working, that the officers may be kept with their companies. I have ordered fifteen days' subsistence for 5,000 men; seven days' forage for 5,000 animals on hand. I think the enemy's aim is to get possession of some point of the river. Smart should get intelligence of McNeil, if possible. He certainly can test the enemy at Fredericktown, and he owes it to himself and his regiment to do it.

J. W. DAVIDSON,
Brigadier-General.

HEADQUARTERS DEPARTMENT OF THE MISSOURI,
Saint Louis, Mo., April 24, 1863.

Brigadier-General VANDEVER:

Major McConnel has been exchanged, and gives his account of the rebel force. Marmaduke has 5,000 or 6,000 and ten pieces of artillery, with no baggage. I think this is more than he has, and, no doubt, the troops are exhausted and weakened by marching. It seems to me they can be whipped badly by your forces anywhere. General McNeil is at Cape Girardeau; is also pretty strong in cavalry.

SAML. R. CURTIS,
Major-General.

[DEPARTMENT OF THE MISSOURI,]
April 24, 1863.

General McNEIL, *Cape Girardeau:*

Major McConnel, who was taken prisoner by Marmaduke, is released, and he tells me Marmaduke has some 6,000. Such reports should always be taken as extravagant. If you and Vandever could unite in a chase, you could soon drive him out of the State. I have so said to Vandever, who is still at Pilot Knob. Marmaduke acted as though he was moving on Saint Louis, but he expected to gobble you up, which shows a different direction.

[SAML. R. CURTIS,]
Major-General.

---

* Not found.

SAINT LOUIS, MO., *April* 25, 1863.

Brigadier-General VANDEVER, *Fredericktown:*

Will move toward you in the morning. Gunboats will reach you, from Cairo, to-night. Be ready, with your cavalry and light artillery, haversacks filled, to fight or pursue, as occasion may offer. My chief of artillery says you can, with your troops and guns, resist 15,000. Instruct your gunners always to try to hit enemy's guns cool and steady. General, the God of battles be with you.

SAML. R. CURTIS,
Major-General.

(Same to General McNeil, Cape Girardeau.)

SAINT LOUIS, MO., *April* 25, 1863.

General VANDEVER, *Fredericktown:*

General McNeil expects to be attacked at daylight to-morrow on both Jackson and Bloomfield roads, by two columns. I am sending him troops by water. If you can cut your way into Girardeau, to help, I think it would be well.

SAML. R. CURTIS,
Major-General.

SAINT LOUIS, MO., *April* 25, 1863.

General VANDEVER:

I would not, under the last information you have, leave Pilot Knob, for I have reports just in from McNeil. He says the enemy is moving on him from the southwest, 4,000 strong, and have driven in his outposts on the Fredericktown road and on the White Water.

J. W. DAVIDSON,
Brigadier-General.

SAINT LOUIS, MO.,
April 25, 1863—9 a. m.

General VANDEVER, *Pilot Knob, Mo.:*

Have you moved against the enemy? Official report from a reconnaissance sent by boat to the Cape shows the enemy at three points on the river: Neeley's Landing, 20 miles above the Cape; at Saint Mary's, and near Saint Genevieve. The idea seems to be that they want to seize boats for their stores, while they get off the lead at Fredericktown. It is left to your judgment whether you had better move on them with your cavalry and artillery, via Fredericktown.

J. W. DAVIDSON,
Brigadier-General.

HEADQUARTERS,
Saint Louis, Mo., April 25, 1863.

Brigadier-General VANDEVER, *Commanding:*

From what you can learn below, do you suspect the existence of co-operation in this city with Marmaduke by a plan to rise here coincident with his approach? I have warning of such, and have taken precaution.

J. W. DAVIDSON,
Brigadier-General.

HEADQUARTERS ARMY OF THE FRONTIER,
Rolla, Mo., April 25, 1863.

General VANDEVER:

I sent the infantry regiments of your division to Pilot Knob yesterday, to operate as Second Division, Army of the Frontier. I have scouts out to watch the bridges on Southwest Branch, Pacific road. Keep me posted. The probability is that I will move from there to Pilot Knob with balance of command, and take your transportation with me. We are reducing baggage and issuing shelter tents. Nothing new from Southwest.

F. J. HERRON,
Major-General, Commanding.

HEADQUARTERS,
Saint Louis, Mo., April 25, 1863.

General VANDEVER:

Dispatch* received. Exercise your own discretion. Bleed the enemy, if you can, and punish his impudence.

N. P. CHIPMAN,
Colonel and Chief of Staff.

HDQRS. SECOND DIVISION, ARMY OF THE FRONTIER,
Jackson, Mo., April 27, 1863.

Brig. Gen. JOHN MCNEIL:

General Vandever directs me to inform you that he is in pursuit of the fleeing enemy on the Bloomfield road, under the belief that they were escaping, via Dallas. Last night he attacked a camp of them 2½ miles west of here, ordering the First Iowa, under Major [Joseph W.] Caldwell, to charge them with saber and pistol. This was gallantly done by moonlight, and was entirely successful. Our prisoners number some 40 already, and more are being brought in. A large quantity of horses, saddles, and arms were secured.

The cannonading at the Cape yesterday was heard by our advance about noon yesterday, and under its influence we traveled yesterday 40 miles. Can you, by moving out on Bloomfield road, cut retreat?

Very respectfully,

LUCIEN J. BARNES,
Major and Assistant Adjutant-General.

HEADQUARTERS DEPARTMENT OF THE MISSOURI,
Saint Louis, Mo., April 30, 1863.

Brig. Gen. WILLIAM VANDEVER,
Bloomfield, Mo.:

GENERAL: I have just seen yours of the 28th to General Davidson, asking for your transportation, and saying you will occupy Bloomfield. There is nothing to be gained by an occupation of Bloomfield. If the rebels have got out of your reach, you will immediately fall back to Pilot Knob or Cape Girardeau, whichever is most convenient. I would rather you would be at Pilot Knob, where you can report to General Herron, and immediately to this place, with a view to completely repairing all damage arising from your recent hard and very successful campaign.

---

*Of April 24. See p. 272.

I have ordered a move out from New Madrid to cut off the rebel retreat, and before this reaches you I suppose all our efforts against Marmaduke will be at an end.

Tender my thanks, general, to the officers and soldiers of your command, for the energy, courage, and victories they have won. General McNeil's gallantry will deserve a separate and special notice. You have added to your former well-earned distinctions in the field, and your State and country are proud of such a soldier.

I remain, very truly, your friend and fellow-soldier,

SAML. R. CURTIS,
Major-General.

---

*Itinerary of the Second Division, Army of the Frontier, April 4–May 2, 1863.**

April 4–6.—Marched from Elk Creek to Camp Totten, 10 miles southwest of Rolla, 55 miles.

April 9.—Brig. Gen. William Vandever arrived and assumed command.

April 21–23.—Brigadier-General Vandever, with all the cavalry of the division and Battery E, First Missouri Artillery, marched to Pilot Knob to meet a cavalry raid under General Marmaduke.

April 26.—Moved on toward Cape Girardeau in pursuit of the enemy. Marched 40 miles, over bad roads considerable of the way. Within 5 miles of Jackson captured a few straggling rebels. Within 2½ miles of Jackson, at 9 p. m., found the enemy in some force. Sent the First Iowa Volunteer Cavalry, Major [Joseph W.] Caldwell, in with the saber by moonlight, and scattered a brigade of the enemy, making considerable captures of prisoners and horses; used artillery that the garrison at Cape Girardeau, General McNeil commanding, might be apprised of our presence and act accordingly. If they had moved out properly, Marmaduke would have been captured.

April 27.—The enemy, finding us in possession of his desired line of retreat via the Dallas pike, from which the First Iowa Cavalry had driven a brigade, was compelled to take the road due south from Jackson, which he did, destroying all bridges in his rear. We pursued him vigorously, skirmishing several times, killing a few and capturing some prisoners. Marched 15 miles; found the enemy had escaped over the White Water (not fordable), and destroyed one span of the bridge. Before leaving Jackson, a messenger was sent to Cape Girardeau, ordering General McNeil to move out rapidly on the Bloomfield road and get the road near White Water ahead of the enemy and cut off his retreat. Although General McNeil had but 9 miles to march, over a macadamized road, to do this, he did not reach the intersection until after the enemy had all passed and our troops arrived at the river. This was unfortunate, and guaranteed to the enemy his escape, unless perchance the Castor River should not be fordable, and we could compel him to fight before crossing that stream. The bridge over White Water was therefore ordered to be repaired, which was done early on the morning of the 28th, in the face of the enemy's rear guard.

April 28.—The command crossed the White Water and pushed through the desperate swamps for 5 miles to higher ground, and, on General McNeil having been recently stationed at Bloomfield, and his command knowing the country, was given the advance, with instruc-

---

* From "Record of Events," on return for month of April, 1863.

tions to pursue as rapidly as possible to the Castor. However, the enemy made good his escape over that river. Marched 26 miles.

April 29.—The crossing of Castor was successfully effected in the face of a strong rear guard of the enemy, and the advance of the command moved a few miles toward Bloomfield, skirmishing nearly all the way with the enemy and occasionally taking a few prisoners. The command did not all pass the river during the day, as it rose so as to be unfordable and one floating bridge had been swept away. Marched 8 miles, and captured Marmaduke's body-servant, Bill.

April 30.—Enough of the command having crossed the Castor, an advance was ordered, and the enemy was driven out of Bloomfield and the place occupied by our forces about noon. A command was organized from the most fresh troops to march at 9 p. m., under General McNeil, in pursuit of the enemy, who had taken the road to Chalk Bluff. There was still a faint hope that by pushing him hard he would be compelled to leave his artillery in our hands. Therefore the pursuit was continued, and early in May, after a few brilliant charges of his rear guard, Marmaduke was driven across the Saint Francis at Chalk Bluff and out of Missouri. In this pursuit and the attack on the enemy's rear, Col. John M. Glover, Third Missouri Volunteer Cavalry, distinguished himself with his regiment.

No. 12.

Reports of Brig. Gen. Alexander Asboth, U. S. Army, commanding at Columbus, Ky., of co-operation with McNeil.

HDQRS. SIXTH DIVISION, SIXTEENTH ARMY CORPS,
Columbus, Ky., April 26, 1863.

GENERAL: Lieutenant Livingston, aide-de-camp to Brigadier-General Montgomery, has just arrived from Cairo, and reports that heavy artillery firing commenced early this morning at Cape Girardeau, and has continued all day.

I would be glad to take the enemy in the rear, but my troops here are all provided with condemned arms, worthless in the field. The Bostona No. 2 is now at landing, with over 10,000 stand of good arms and ammunition, consigned to Capt. J. P. Harper, Memphis. Can I take 3,000 stand and ammunition for my troops, and will you give your consent to the movement proposed?

I will, in anticipation, take steps immediately to secure transportation.

ASBOTH,
Brigadier-General.

Major-General HURLBUT,
Memphis, Tenn.

MEMPHIS, *April* 26, 1863—11 p. m.

Brig. Gen. A. ASBOTH:

The commanding general directs that if you are sure there is a real attack, you will take 3,000 stand of arms and move up.

Respectfully,

HENRY BINMORE,
Assistant Adjutant-General.

HDQRS. SIXTH DIVISION, SIXTEENTH ARMY CORPS,
Columbus, Ky., April 27, 1863.

COLONEL: At the urgent solicitation of Brig. Gen. John McNeil, commanding at Cape Girardeau, I have this morning sent him two regiments of infantry, a section of artillery, and 100,000 rounds of ammunition for his command, with directions to send back the troops as soon as re-enforced by Brigadier-General Vandever, which he expected to-day. General McNeil wrote me that he had been attacked by Marmaduke, with four brigades, 8,000 men, and repulsed him, but would be attacked again.

As my troops here were all provided with condemned arms, I considered it necessary to take from a large lot of good arms on steamer Bostona No. 2, consigned to Captain Harper, Memphis, 3,000 Enfield rifled muskets, as alluded to in yesterday's telegram, and had my explanatory report ready to send by Bostona, but she left from the lower depot without orders or permission. The report will be sent by first boat.

ASBOTH,
Brigadier-General.

Lieutenant-Colonel BINMORE,
Assistant Adjutant-General, Memphis, Tenn.

ADDENDA.

SAINT LOUIS, *April* 27, 1863.

General ASBOTH:

My troops have routed the rebels near Cape Girardeau, and they retreated toward Chalk Bluff. Even a small additional force at New Madrid would admit of a successful move from that point. There is some trouble crossing Little River, but this makes it safe if the enemy goes down on the west side of Little River.

SAML. R. CURTIS,
Major-General.

SAINT LOUIS, *April* 27, 1863.

General ASBOTH:

If you can send force to Chalk Bluff, via New Madrid, you may take Marmaduke in flank, or cut off his retreat. Some artillery and cavalry would be necessary. The river swamp would be the proper base to hold, while light troops act toward Chalk Bluff and New Madrid. Infantry will co-operate.

SAML. R. CURTIS,
Major-General.

HDQRS. SIXTH DIVISION, SIXTEENTH ARMY CORPS,
Columbus, April 27, 1863.

GENERAL: I this morning sent two regiments of infantry, two companies of cavalry, a section of artillery, and 100,000 rounds of small-arm ammunition to Brigadier-General McNeil, at Cape Girardeau, being all in my power to accomplish, having no more infantry or artillery that can be sent, which I regret exceedingly. I will immediately secure transportation, and send six companies of cavalry to New Madrid, to operate as desired by you, as far as possible.

ASBOTH,
Brigadier-General.

Maj. Gen. SAMUEL R. CURTIS, *Saint Louis, Mo.*

HDQRS. SIXTH DIVISION, SIXTEENTH ARMY CORPS,
Columbus, April 28, 1863—2.15 p. m.

GENERAL: Six companies of the Fourth Missouri Cavalry, Major Langen commanding, left last evening for New Madrid, with orders to co-operate with the commander of that post. The rebels being repulsed from Cape Girardeau, I request that my troops sent yesterday morning may be immediately ordered back. An action is now going on in the direction of Charleston, the cannonading being very distinct. I hope my cavalry is at work, and I have ordered General Buford to inform General McNeil of their co-operation.

ASBOTH,
Brigadier-General.

Major-General CURTIS, *Saint Louis.*

SAINT LOUIS, *April* 28, 1863.

General ASBOTH:

GENERAL: Your troops sent to Cape Girardeau have started back. Accept my thanks for this and other favors. Press the New Madrid movement. The rebels made a stand for several hours yesterday, but finally retired and retreated toward Bloomfield. There must be a pretty strong force.

SAML. R. CURTIS,
Brigadier-General.

No. 13.

Report of Brig. Gen. J. S. Marmaduke, C. S. Army, commanding expedition.

HEADQUARTERS MARMADUKE'S DIVISION,
Jacksonport, Ark., May 20, 1863.

MAJOR: I have the honor to report, briefly, the movements of my division in the late expedition into Missouri.

My command consisted of the following brigades: Shelby's Missouri cavalry brigade, Greene's Missouri cavalry brigade, Carter's Texas cavalry brigade, and Burbridge's brigade, composed of Burbridge's Missouri cavalry regiment and Newton's Arkansas cavalry regiment. My whole strength was about 5,000 men, eight pieces of field artillery, and two light mountain pieces. Of this force about 1,200 were unarmed and 900 dismounted. Of those armed, the greater part had shot-guns; some were armed with Enfield rifles and Mississippi rifles, and some with common squirrel rifles. I carried with me the unarmed and dismounted men for two reasons: First, with the hope of arming and mounting them, and, second, knowing, from the great anxiety of all to go into Missouri, that, if left behind, many would probably desert, I therefore deemed it most advisable to take them with me, hoping to be able to arm and mount them. I concentrated my division on Eleven Points River, and intended marching in the direction of Rolla, but found it impossible to do so. The country for at least 100 miles was without forage or subsistence, it having been destroyed to prevent raids or army movements. I then determined to march to the east of Ironton, capture the outpost (a regiment) at Patterson, and strike [John] McNeil, who was at Bloomfield, with a force I estimated to be about 2,000, cavalry, infantry, and artillery. I anticipated that McNeil, on hearing of my move, would make forced marches to reach Ironton before I could cut him off. If successful in capturing McNeil's forces, I anticipated that my whole command could be well armed and finely mounted for vigorous action. It was impossible, on account of forage and subsistence, to march the whole division by one route on Patterson. And I furthermore desired to make demonstrations, as if a large force of infantry and cavalry were invading the State via Thomasville, Houston, and to the west of Rolla, expecting by this means to withdraw all their forces from Northern Arkansas and extreme Southwest Missouri, and at the same time throw the forces about Ironton, Patterson, and Bloomfield off their guard until I had gained a position to surprise or cut off the forces at Patterson and Bloomfield, and thence move northward between Saint Louis and Ironton, if I deemed it advisable. I divided the command into two columns: One under Shelby, composed of Shelby's and Burbridge's brigades, to march via Van Buren, Mo., and reach Patterson on the evening of April 20; the other, under Carter, composed of Carter's and Greene's brigades, to march via Doniphan and reach Patterson the same evening. Shelby had instructions to throw out scouts well to his left, to create the impression of a force moving northwesterly. I marched with Carter's column. His route was the shortest and most secret. With a part of his column I intended to surprise and capture Patterson, and from thence to strike McNeil.

About midnight April 19, when 30 miles distant from Patterson, Carter detached Lieutenant-Colonel [D. C.] Giddings—in command of his regiment (about 450 men), Reves' independent company of spies and guides, and two pieces of [J. H.] Pratt's battery—to move rapidly, cautiously, and secretly by a more direct and unfrequented route to surprise Patterson. When 12 miles from Patterson, about daylight, Colonel Giddings surprised and handsomely captured the whole Federal picket from Patterson—1 lieutenant and 24 men. He marched on, and could have successfully surprised the whole garrison, but that he moved too slowly; did not take sufficient risk for the nature of his expedition, and allowed his artillery to open when within 2 miles of the fort. The troops there (about 600 cavalry, under Colonel Smart) took the alarm, and precipitately fled to Pilot Knob, burning everything they could, but leaving behind a large supply of subsistence and some quartermaster's stores. Colonel Giddings pursued them vigorously for 7 miles, killing, wounding, and capturing a number. All the prisoners taken except those in hospital I paroled.

On the evening of the 20th, as ordered, the two columns entered Patterson. Colonel Shelby's column encountered a Federal picket from Patterson, and killed or captured 8 or 10 of them.

On the 21st, I ordered Carter's column to march against McNeil in the direction of Bloomfield, and Shelby's column to march on Fredericktown, supposing that McNeil would attempt to make his escape to Ironton. If he remained in Bloomfield, Carter would whip him, and if he attempted to get to Ironton, Shelby would capture him.

Shelby's column surprised Fredericktown on the morning of April 22, capturing dispatches ordering McNeil to Ironton. He was expected at Fredericktown on the 22d.

McNeil left Bloomfield on the 21st, abandoning and burning a large amount of quartermaster's and commissary stores *en route* for Pilot Knob via Dallas.

On the 22d, he learned of Shelby's column, and retreated hastily toward Cape Girardeau. Carter pursued him, hoping to prevent his reaching there, but was too late, owing to high water, marshes, and bad roads, besides having a longer route to march, with horses very much worn down by forced marches and want of forage. *En route* to Cape Girardeau, Carter with a small detachment of men charged and captured Captain [Stephen V.] Shipman and 40 men out of a guard of 60 men. I kept Shelby's column near Fredericktown, marching daily a few miles toward Cape Girardeau to catch McNeil if he marched toward Ironton, and to await information from Carter (whose dispatch bearers were captured by the enemy) and the junction of his column, and also to watch and learn of the movements of the Federals in the direction of Ironton. From Fredericktown I sent out a detachment of 90 men, under command of Captains [William T.] Lineback and [J. M.] Muse and Lieutenant [Josiah L.] Bledsoe, with instructions to burn and destroy the bridges over Big Creek, on the Iron Mountain and Saint Louis Railroad. They found a guard stationed at the point indicated of 250 or 300 men, whom they at once vigorously attacked, killing, wounding, and capturing several, and succeeded in leaving one of the three bridges in flames. This detachment afterward rejoined their command at Bloomfield, having accomplished their work in a dashing manner.

On the 25th, I received dispatches from Carter that he had pursued McNeil to within 4 miles of Cape Girardeau. I immediately ordered Shelby to make a night march (some 30 miles) to Cape Girardeau, in order to form a junction with Carter. On learning the Federal forces were in the fortifications, I deemed it unwise to attack and storm the place. I so informed Colonel Shelby, and ordered him on the Jackson and Cape Girardeau road, to make a demonstration against the enemy, while I withdrew Carter by the Bloomfield road, intending to unite the columns at Jackson. Shelby's demonstration amounted almost to an attack. I deemed it necessary to bring Carter's column up to his support. I moved rapidly toward Shelby's column, and on arriving found that Shelby had driven the enemy's pickets and advanced forces into their works; that the enemy were admirably posted, possessing great natural advantages in position, supported by four large forts mounted with heavy guns, field artillery, and about 3,000 infantry and cavalry. As soon as the two columns had united, I withdrew toward, and encamped them around Jackson.

On the night of the 26th, a force of about 3,500 cavalry and artillery, under General Vandever, attacked Newton's regiment, who were encamped on the Jackson and Fredericktown road. Newton's loss was 2 killed and 6 or 8 wounded or captured.

In the mean time McNeil had been heavily re-enforced by water.

On the morning of the 27th, I found myself between two forces—McNeil on the east and Vandever on the west—either outnumbering my force, and both prepared to attack me simultaneously. At daylight I ordered my forces in retreat southward via bridge over White Water, Bloomfield, and crossing of Saint Francis at Chalk Bluff. Vandever and McNeil, with their combined force, pursued me. My effective fighting force did not exceed 3,500. The enemy had about 8,000—4,500 cavalry, 3,500 infantry, and fifteen pieces of artillery. I anticipated no damage or trouble except in crossing Saint Francis River, which was much swollen, rapid, unbridged, and no ferry-boats on it. When I commenced my retreat, I ordered details of the unarmed and non-effective to proceed rapidly to Chalk Bluff, under charge of my division quartermaster, to construct rafts for crossing. My retreat was orderly and slow. Vandever and McNeil did not seem anxious for a fight. Light rear-guard fighting was of daily occurrence. Shelby's or Carter's brigades were habitually in the rear and always did their duty. On several occasions I offered battle when the advantages in position were greatly in my favor. My object was to give ample time to the bridge party.

My division reached Chalk Bluff the evening of May 1. I dismounted the greater part of my command, selected a strong position about 4 miles from the crossing, where I formed line of battle to resist the advance of the enemy till my wagons, horses, and artillery had crossed. A little before day I quietly withdrew the men, and by sun-up my whole command was safely across. The pursuit here ceased.

My loss in the expedition is some 30 killed, 60 wounded, and 120 missing (stragglers), perhaps captured. I gained on the raid about 150 recruits and a great improvement in the number and quality of horses. The Federal loss must have been at least five times as great as mine in killed and wounded. In every instance when he made the attack he was repulsed.

The officers and men deserve special mention for their bravery, steadiness, and endurance. At no time were they in the least demoralized, but were always willing, even anxious, to fight.

I submit herewith a report of the brigade commanders. I will forward as soon as prepared the names of the killed, wounded, and missing of my command; also a list of Federal prisoners paroled.

Very respectfully,

J. S. MARMADUKE,
Brigadier-General, Commanding.

Maj. W. B. BLAIR, *Assistant Adjutant-General.*

[Indorsement.]

HDQRS. DEPT. TRANS-MISS., *Shreveport, La., June* 4, 1863.

Respectfully forwarded. The expedition under General Marmaduke into Missouri was made more particularly on account of the scarcity of forage in Arkansas, it being deemed probable that he would be able to sustain himself, and thereby relieve Arkansas in a great degree of the large amount of forage it was supplying the army in that section.

E. KIRBY SMITH,
Lieutenant-General, Commanding.

ADDENDA.

Return of Casualties in Marmaduke's cavalry division during the expedition.

[Compiled from nominal lists.]

Command.	Killed.		Wounded.		Missing.		Aggregate.
	Officers.	Men.	Officers.	Men.	Officers.	Men.	
Shelby's brigade:							
Gordon's regiment	......	2	3	10	......	29	44
Jeans' regiment	......	1	1	9	......	3	14
Thompson's regiment	......	......	1	5	......	10	16
Elliott's battalion	......	......	......	2	......	......	2
Collins' battery	......	......	......	3	......	6	9
Carter's brigade:							
19th Texas (Burford's)	......	5	1	18	......	9	33
21st Texas (Carter's)	......	1	5	10	......	1	17
Morgan's squadron	......	1	......	3	......	......	4
Burbridge's brigade:							
Burbridge's regiment	......	......	1	6	......	......	7
Newton's regiment*	1	2	......	5	......	3	11
Kitchen's battalion	......	2	......	2	......	......	4
Total†	1	14	12	73	......	61	161

* Lieut. John Edwards accidentally killed.
† No report from Greene's brigade.

No. 14.

Report of Col. G. W. Thompson, Sixth Missouri Cavalry (Confederate), commanding Shelby's brigade.

HEADQUARTERS SHELBY'S BRIGADE,
May 15, 1863.

SIR: On the morning of April 18, last, while General Marmaduke's cavalry division of the army was *en route* for Missouri, I received orders from Col. Joseph O. Shelby to take command of the brigade formerly commanded by himself, and, in obedience to said orders, did take command. I now have the honor to submit the following report of the part taken by it on the last raid made into Missouri:

The troops composing this brigade are Lieutenant-Colonel [B. F.] Gordon's, Colonel [Beal G.] Jeans', and my own regiment, with Major Shanks' battalion, and Captain [R. A.] Collins' battery of four guns (two Parrott guns, one brass and one iron 6-pounder), the effective force numbering about 1,250 men.

Our route lay over a very barren country, almost destitute of provisions and forage, and save the arresting of a number of the enrolled militia, nothing of importance occurred until the morning of the 20th, when, after a forced march and to within some 8 miles of the village of Patterson, in [Wayne] County, Missouri, Maj. D. Shanks, with his battalion, forming the advance guard, surprised, and, after exchanging a few shots, captured the enemy's entire picket guard of 8 men, together with their arms and horses. Here Capt. Reck Johnson, a good and gallant man, was severely wounded. Learning there was but one picket stand between us and the town, and having so completely surprised their pickets, and, in fact, the entire country through which we passed, a complete surprise and capture of the Federal fort and forces was deemed certain. So elated were the troops of my command with the bright prospects before them, they moved with renewed energy and determination.

At 3 p. m. my advance arrived to within 3 miles of town, and to our chagrin and supreme annoyance we learned the enemy, having taken fright from some cause or other, had set fire to the town, and in terror fled in the direction of Ironton. Before reaching the town the dense columns of smoke but too plainly told the information received to be correct. On my arrival, I found General Marmaduke and the division under Colonel Carter occupying the place.

On the following morning, with my brigade in the rear, we crossed the Saint Francis River, *en route* for Fredericktown, Mo., which place we arrived at on the evening of the 22d, surprising the place, capturing the bogus "Gamble sheriff," telegraph operator, and a number of the enrolled tory militia.

On the night of the 23d, a detachment of 90 men, under Lieutenant [J. L.] Bledsoe, of Gordon's regiment, and Lieutenant [J. M.] Wills, of my own regiment (now commanded by Lieutenant-Colonel [J. C.] Hooper), all under command of the gallant Captain [J. M.] Muse, of the First Regiment Missouri Infantry, with instructions from Colonel Shelby, were sent on an expedition to the Iron Mountain Railroad for the purpose of destroying certain bridges over which said road passed. This I considered truly a hazardous enterprise, and one fraught with much peril and hardship, as the country through which they would have to pass was filled with bodies of tory militia, and all the bridges guarded by large bodies of infantry. However, after an absence of several days the command returned and reported having burned the extensive bridge over Mill Creek after a spirited fight, in which the frightened enemy were scattered in wild confusion. Our loss during this expedition was 1 killed and several wounded; that of the enemy several killed and many wounded. This I consider a most daring adventure, reflecting great credit upon both officers and men.

While encamped here and in the vicinity, quite a number of men were recruited for the service, and our scouts continued to bring in squads of the tory militia, who were generally paroled and set at liberty.

On the evening of the 25th, we again took up the line of march, which was continued throughout the entire night, and, as red-eyed morning peeped out of the cloud-curtained window of the east, our advance, under Major Shanks, entered the sleeping village of Old Jackson. Pushing on to a point 4 miles from town, the command was halted, where both men and horses partook of a hasty meal, during which time a heavy fall of rain drenched to the skin my weary men.

At about 8 o'clock, I received orders from Colonel Shelby to move my command, which was immediately executed, and, when arriving within 3 miles of Cape Girardeau, my advance, yet under command of Major Shanks, encountered and drove in, at a rapid pace, the enemy's pickets, nor gave up the chase until the enemy opened upon them with shot and shell from the commanding heights encircling and overlooking the town. At the base of this chain of hills, the sloping sides of which were open fields, over which ran the main road, I formed my command in line of battle in the following order, viz: Forming Major Shanks' battalion to the left of the road, and on the extreme left of the line, with his left resting upon the woods; upon his right rested my own regiment, while Captain Collins' battery wheeled into line, with one gun in the road and the other three into line in the small field to the right; Colonel Jeans, with his regiment dismounted, formed in the woods, with his left resting upon the battery, while Colonel Gordon, with his regiment also dismounted, formed the extreme right of my lines. Captain Collins' battery, although greatly exposed to a cross-fire from the enemy's heavy guns, gallantly maintained its position and thundered forth a reply searchingly inquisitive. The roar of artillery now became constant. The enemy's heavy guns from the forts on the apex of the hill overlooking our extreme left hurled their heavy shot and screaming shell furiously at our little battery, but with no other effect than slightly wounding 3 men and killing 3 battery horses. The enemy's skirmishers, occupying the woods in front of Colonels Jeans' and Gordon's regiments, opened upon them a brisk fire, but were almost instantly dislodged by the two regiments advancing at a charge, driving them, in wild disorder, across the open field and behind the crest of the hill. Here we captured several prisoners. My own regiment, having been dismounted, I now ordered around into position on Colonel Gordon's right, and moved the battery to a position in the corner of the woods and to the right of my regiment, it being supported on the right by Colonel [J. Q.] Burbridge's brigade. Again the firing became constant and terrific, as if the momentary lull only gave strength and vigor to the contest. The enemy's forts and batteries continued to play upon our battery for more than one hour without intermission, and now and then swept the woods with shell and shot, canister and grape, while the Minie balls came hissing a treble to the music of the roar.

During this severe contest, Major [Y. H.] Blackwell, Adjutant [John N.] Edwards, and Lieutenant [William H.] Ferrell, of Colonel Gordon's regiment, and Captain [H. M.] Woodsmall, of Colonel Jeans' regiment, fell, severely wounded, while gallantly leading and encouraging their men upon the field. My loss here was 3 killed and 35 wounded, the engagement lasting about two and one-half hours, when I received orders from Colonel Shelby to withdraw my forces, which was done quietly and in perfect order.

I may be permitted to remark here, in my judgment it would have been impossible to have taken the place without charging it in force, and to have done this, under the circumstances, would have been wanton butchery and slaughter. And here would I say, with a few exceptions, no body of men ever acted with more coolness or bravery than did the officers and men on this occasion. Every movement was skillfully executed and order promptly obeyed.

Falling back without annoyance, my command encamped for the night near Old Jackson, and on the following morning resumed our march, taking the Bloomfield road.

On the evening of the 28th, my command, forming the rear guard, crossed the Castor River by fording, it being very deep and rising from the heavy rains of the day. Here we found a large new bridge being constructed and an old pontoon floating moored to the bank, both of which we completely destroyed; and leaving Captains [D. A.] Williams and [W. P.] Norman, of my regiment, and Captain [G. B.] Webb, of Jeans' regiment, with their companies, under command of Major [M. W.] Smith, of my regiment, to guard the crossing, we encamped for the night 2 miles beyond.

Early the next morning, learning the enemy were following in force, I determined to contest their passage at the ford, and therefore took with me, to re-enforce the guards, the companies of my regiment commanded by Captains [John C.] Toney, [Isham J.] West, and [John T.] Crisp, and placed them at such points as I deemed the most advantageous. Before reaching the river, however, the advance of the enemy had approached and opened a brisk fire upon the guards, which was promptly returned, when heavy skirmishing became general along the lines, which continued about one hour, when the enemy opened upon us with two pieces of artillery, which was soon increased to four, and with which the woods skirting the bank of the stream in which my men lay concealed were raked by showers of grape and canister. Major [M. W.] Smith, having formed Captain Toney's company up the river and above the upper ford, and Captain [D. A.] Williams at the lower ford, with Captain [G. B.] Webb in the center, held Captain [W. P.] Norman's company mounted as a reserve, yet warmly engaged during most of the time. In this position we continued to hold our ground under a most galling fire, repeatedly driving the enemy beyond the range of our murderous fire during the time. The enemy, seemingly in a fit of desperation, ran their battery upon the high bank overlooking the stream, when a well-directed fire from Captain Toney's sharpshooters drove them in dismay out of sight, leaving several of their battery horses dead upon the ground. For three hours the contest continued, the chivalrous Major Smith, with the gallant officers and men under him, continuing to hold the fords, when I received an order from General Marmaduke to withdraw my forces and abandon it, which was done, losing only 1 man, dangerously wounded in the engagement. Loss of the enemy not known.

Moving quietly on, I continued with the rear until we crossed the bridge near Bloomfield, which I caused to be torn down and destroyed. On my arrival at Bloomfield, it having been determined to give them battle, a line was accordingly formed, my brigade dismounted and occupying the central and front positions on the sloping ridge adjacent to the house of Mr. ———, in the suburbs of the town, and commanding the main road, or entrance thereto. After putting out flankers to the right and left, and skirmishers and sharpshooters well to the front, under the command of Captain [John] Thrailkill, of the First Missouri Cavalry, First Brigade, and near the bridge just destroyed, we patiently awaited the approach of the enemy, determined to win a victory upon the grounds so recently deserted by the criminal outlaw and tory leader, General McNeil. Thus we remained until late in the evening, when a body of the enemy's advance cavalry, reconnoitering, received a well-directed fire from our sharpshooters, emptying several saddles and sending off their horses riderless. A recall from their bugles relieved our lines from further annoyance during the night. My command lay in line of battle and upon their arms during the night, and until 10 o'clock the next day, when, the enemy studiously avoiding any further demonstration, and in obedience to orders, I directed my brigade to mount their horses, and once more took up the line of march. After withdrawing my skirmishers and sharpshooters, the enemy furiously shelled the woods recently occupied by them, but made no further demonstrations until the morning of May 2, when a courier brought the intelligence that the enemy was annoying the rear guard of the army. Coming to a broken section of country, it was determined once more to offer them battle, but before the line of battle was completed it was determined to move on to a more eligible position, as being nearer and more convenient to the crossing of the Saint Francis River. My command having moved out, and just as the rear of Colonel Gordon's regiment was passing into the road, a body of the enemy's cavalry dashed into Colonel Carter's command, driving his rear guard before them and firing recklessly as they came. This created some confusion, which was soon allayed, and the enemy, with considerable loss, driven back by Carter's command. Halting the three rear companies of Colonel Gordon's regiment, commanded, respectively, by Captains [W. S.] Bullard and [W. R.] Edwards, and Lieutenant Bledsoe, I formed and held them as a reserve until the entire army had passed, when the enemy again advanced, and after exchanging a heavy fire the enemy fell back; nor did they attempt the experiment again. My loss here was 3 wounded, 2 severely.

Continuing our march to within 3 miles of the river, I again received orders to form my command in line of battle, which was promptly done, they being dismounted and the horses sent to the river by the unarmed men, to be crossed over, the ordnance and baggage wagons having gone on in front of the army. Placing out skirmishers and sharpshooters, we again awaited their coming. Noon passed and the evening wore on to near its wane, when a few random shots in the distance told of their cautious approach. Soon, however, the firing increased in the advance of my center, and as it advanced became more constant and determined, until within about 300 yards of my lines, when it became severe and obstinate. Masking Captain Collins' battery behind a small body of cavalry formed across the road, I anxiously awaited a dash of their cavalry; but finding the enemy more tender-footed than in the morning, gave up the hope of a charge by them. Here Captain Collins opened a scathing fire upon their heavy body of skirmishers and sharpshooters, completely routing and scattering them. They now opened upon us with a few pieces of artillery, but none of my command being in the tree-tops no damage was done. Captain Collins sending a few whistling shots from his rifled guns and shells from his iron and brass 6s in close proximity to their battery, they withdrew, it is supposed, in supreme disgust, as nothing further was heard from them during the night. With nothing to eat since early morning, we remained in line of battle until night, when the stillness became almost oppressive. About midnight the guns from our battery, one by one, silently withdrew; then regiment after regiment followed so silently the drowsy ear of night was scarcely disturbed. Upon arriving at the river, my command marched over upon a floating raft or pontoon which had been improvised for the occasion, and by 3 a. m. my entire command was safely over.

At about 10 o'clock, our battery firing them a farewell shot, my command moved off, leaving them alone in their glory. They did not pursue us with the spirit and determination of brave men fighting in a just cause, but prowled in the rear of our army like a band of wolves and jackals.

Nothing further of importance occurred until the morning of the 6th, when my command entered the almost impenetrable swamps through which the Cache River winds its devious, sluggish, sickly way. Day after day, in mud and water, with artillery, baggage, and ammunition wagons mired down, and horses and mules floundering in exhaustion, did my men and animals toil and struggle, when, after three days of untold trials and hardships, the entire command emerged from this wilderness of mud and disease-generating miasma more like an army of denizens of a semi-amphibio subterranean world than one of men and animals.

As nothing further of importance occurred on our march to the present encampment, and this report having assumed a frightful length, I will close it by respectfully referring you to the inclosed reports from the several commands composing my brigade for a more detailed account of the parts taken by them.

It affords me great pleasure to bear testimony to the noble, self-sacrificing, and chivalrous conduct of the officers and men of this command, and, with a few exceptions of wanton cowardice, which you will find reported in the inclosed reports, no body of men ever acted more gallantly.

All of which is respectfully submitted.

I have the honor to be, very respectfully, your obedient servant,

G. W. THOMPSON,
Colonel, Commanding Brigade.

Capt. [W. J.] McARTHUR,
Assistant Adjutant-General.

No. 15.

Report of Capt. John M. Muse, First Missouri Infantry (Confederate).

HEADQUARTERS MARMADUKE'S DIVISION,
Jacksonport, Ark., May 14, 1863.

CAPTAIN: According to orders received from headquarters Shelby's brigade, I left Fredericktown, Mo., on the night of April 21, with a detachment of 90 men of your command, and also 3 commissioned officers, viz, Captain [W. T.] Lineback, Burbridge's regiment, Lieutenant [Josiah L.] Bledsoe, Gordon's regiment, and Lieutenant [J. M.] Wills, Thompson's regiment, for the purpose of destroying some portion of the

Saint Louis and Iron Mountain Railroad. We left Fredericktown at 12 o'clock at night, and proceeded toward Farmington. At 5 o'clock in the morning, we stopped, fed our horses, and rested for two hours, and proceeded in direction of Farmington. We traveled through the woods and by-roads until we got in the vicinity of Farmington, when, through a fault of my guide, we entered a public place called Valley Forge, on the Ironton and Saint Genevieve plank road. This was the first place we were seen, being discovered by the enemy. We found some few enrolled militia, some of whom escaped; the balance we captured and turned loose on parole of honor, not having time to retain them as prisoners, knowing that our men had been discovered. It being important that we should travel as rapidly as possible, we went night and day, avoiding all public roads, impressing our pilots as we went, until we got within 1 mile of the Big River Bridge, which we had anticipated attacking, but when arriving within a short distance of said bridge I found that it was strongly guarded by 250 infantry and a section of artillery. Knowing that there would be an improbability of our success at that point, I thought it best to make an attack on some other portion of the road, so we proceeded south 3 miles to what is known as Mill Creek Bridges, which consists of three bridges of 100 to 150 feet in length, and all being within 300 yards of each other. When we got within half a mile of the bridges, we halted the command in an obscure hollow between two mountains, and Captain Lineback and myself went to the summit of the mountain on the east side of the road, which overlooked those bridges, to ascertain the strength and position of the enemy guarding those bridges. When we arrived at our place of reconnaissance, we found that the bridges were situated as follows: Mill Creek runs due north and south at this point and empties into Big River 3 miles north of the aforesaid bridges. When we got to the point overlooking those bridges, we saw that there were about 250 guarding the north bridge, 50 guarding the south bridge, and about 50 guarding the middle bridge. We saw they were not expecting an attack at that time, although they had not expected it the night previous (this was on the evening of April 24). I saw there was no chance to dismount my men and make an attack without being discovered, and if so, I knew it would be a failure, as there were two block-houses—one at the north and one at the south bridge—so I knew that our only success would be to surprise them and keep them stampeded until we could fire one bridge and cut the telegraph wire. There was one cut in the mountain which entered the creek valley about 60 yards from and opposite the center bridge, which was the only place we could make a charge on them mounted, so we quietly moved down the ravine until within 100 yards of the bridge, when we heard the whistle of a train coming from Ironton going in the direction of Saint Louis. We took advantage of that, and just as this train had passed the middle bridge, while their attention was drawn to that, we made a charge on the bridge guards and succeeded in stampeding them from and through the bridges. When we charged on the middle bridge, we captured 16 privates and 2 lieutenants of the Twenty-fourth Missouri Infantry. As soon as we had taken the bridge, I ordered the bridge fired and the telegraph cut, which was done with dispatch. At the same time I was so much interested about the destruction of the bridge and the telegraph that I forgot to send the prisoners to the rear.

In about half an hour after we had taken possession of the bridge those guards from the upper and lower bridges got around on the west side of the mountains overlooking those bridges on the west side of the road, and formed, marched up in line of battle, and obtained a position overlooking us, being a perpendicular height of 300 feet, giving us a very severe fire. Seeing there was no chance to get at them, and that it was everlasting destruction to us, I ordered my men to retreat, but not until I had 2 men killed and 6 wounded (4 severely), 12 horses killed and disabled. I carried off all my wounded and some of the small-arms, such as guns, pistols, and one officer's sword, but had to abandon the prisoners we had previously taken. I then learned that there had been a force of 2,000 cavalry sent out from Ironton to capture me and my party, and it was their intention to intercept me in the vicinity of Farmington. I would say, however, when we left the bridge it was well fired, and some hundred yards of the telegraph wire cut to pieces. I am well satisfied, and so is every man that was in my command, that the bridge was destroyed. When we started back, we traveled night and day, only stopping to feed about once every twenty-four hours. We suffered much from want of sleep and fatigue. On our return we traveled through the woods and by-roads all the way. When we got within about 5 miles of Farmington (east), we came on a party of about 300 Federals. We formed in line of battle, but before they got within range I concluded it would not be prudent to fight them, as they had other forces which would soon concentrate and destroy us; so just as the enemy were making preparations to charge us, I ordered my little band to scatter and concentrate some miles south of that. This was on the eve of the 26th.

On the morning of the 27th, by 10 o'clock, we had all got together, except two, who had stopped at their homes. This brought us within about 12 miles of where we had last heard of your command. We then felt as though we were out of the lion's den, but such proved not to be the case, for when we got within 2 miles of Patton, I learned your command had left the evening before in the direction of Cape Girardeau. At that time we could distinctly hear firing in that direction, and also learned that the enemy was again in my front, passing through Patton, following up your command, which force I learned to be about 3,000 strong. I halted in a secreted place, and waited until they had all passed; then I crossed the road immediately in their rear and made in direction of Dallas. When I reached Dallas I learned your pickets had been on the Dallas and Jackson road the day before; so I got an old, reliable citizen to carry a dispatch for me, and ordered him to report by 12 o'clock that night; but he did not return, so I took it for granted you were farther south; so I made in direction of Bloomfield. About 2 o'clock the same evening I came to the Bloomfield and Cape Girardeau road, and ascertained your rear guard had been gone about two hours previous; so we rode rapidly and overtook you when you were crossing the Castor River, near Bloomfield.

I can say with pleasure that both officers and men under my command acted most gallantly. Captain Lineback, of Burbridge's regiment, gallantly led the charge when we attacked the bridge. Private Robert N. Hagood, Company C, Gordon's regiment, and some men besides, whose names I am unable to record, made a great display of bravery and daring. The reason I cannot give their names, I was not furnished with a list with the details. I hope to be able to do so soon.

Respectfully submitted.

JNO. M. MUSE,
Captain, Commanding Detachment.

Captain [W. J.] MCARTHUR,
Assistant Adjutant-General.

No. 16.

Report of Col. John Q. Burbridge, Fourth Missouri Cavalry (Confederate), commanding brigade.

BRIGADE HEADQUARTERS,
Camp at Burden's Mill, 16 *miles from Jacksonport, May* 12, 1863.

MAJOR: Inclosed I send you a detailed statement of the part my brigade bore in the expedition into Missouri. It is a plain statement of facts, and can be hardly considered as an official report. I send a list of killed, wounded, and missing.*

I have sent Captain Reves' company west of Black River, with instructions to camp in the vicinity of Powhatan. He will scout in the direction of Pitman's Ferry and Thomasville, Mo. He is also instructed to thoroughly picket the country, to guard against any surprise of the enemy. My pickets are placed between Black River and Cache Swamp. I will send scouts east of the river. As yet I have received no information from Colonel [S. G.] Kitchen concerning the movements of the enemy in that direction. I will write him, in accordance with your instructions, and get all the information he possesses. But Colonel Kitchen informed me that he was ordered to report directly to Brigadier-General Marmaduke, and, of course, any information he will give me will be voluntarily given.

If Colonel Kitchen was ordered to report to me, I could then keep Colonel Shelby perfectly advised of the movements of the enemy. I have established my headquarters at Burden's Mill, 16 miles from Jacksonport. I suppose I can get forage to keep us between two and three weeks, by hauling 6 or 7 miles.

I have no paroled prisoners; all the prisoners captured by my command were turned over to Colonel Shelby's brigade.

I am, major, very respectfully, your obedient servant,

JNO. Q. BURBRIDGE,
Colonel, Commanding.

Maj. HENRY EWING,
Asst. Adjt. Gen., Marmaduke's Division, Jacksonport.

[Inclosure.]

BRIGADE HEADQUARTERS,
Camp at Burden's Mill, May 11, 1863.

MAJOR: In obedience to General Orders, No. ——, division headquarters, I herewith submit the following report of the part my brigade bore in the late expedition into Missouri:

On April 14, orders were received to immediately prepare my command for active service. I obeyed this order by sending train, baggage, &c., to the rear, and providing each of my companies, in addition to the regimental train allowed, with one pack mule, for the purpose of conveying such cooking utensils as could be conveniently transported.

On Friday morning, the 17th, I moved, marching 25 miles in a northerly direction, and camping on a small creek in Oregon County, Missouri.

The next morning I resumed the march, expecting to form a junction with Colonel [Joseph O.] Shelby, to whom I had been ordered to report, at Williams' Creek. Owing, however, to the scarcity of forage, Colonel Shelby had already started, leaving me to march in his rear through a country known as the Wilderness. After marching 28 miles, I was compelled to halt and encamp without obtaining a particle of forage for my horses.

---

* See revised statement, p. 288.

The next day I crossed Current River at Van Buren, camping 22 miles south of Patterson, which place I reached the next evening, learning, however, that the garrison occupying the place had retreated, burning their quartermaster's and commissary stores. Lieutenant-Colonel [William J.] Preston, with three companies of my regiment, was here ordered to report to Colonel [George W.] Carter, commanding Texas brigade of cavalry, he having been sent to attack Brigadier-General [John] McNeil's forces at Bloomfield, Mo. This part of my command did not report to me again until our forces fell back from Cape Girardeau.

I again resumed the march from Patterson, moving in the direction of Fredericktown, and encamped within 12 miles of that place, and entered the town next day at 12 o'clock, but found no enemy.

On the evening of the 25th, I received orders to move on the Cape Girardeau road, which I obeyed, passing through Jackson about daylight. At 10 o'clock we reached the city and made preparations to attack it. By Colonel Shelby's order I formed my brigade in line of battle upon his right, occupying a position that completely protected my men from the artillery of the enemy, and at the same time placing me in supporting distance from his battery. An artillery duel of an hour and a half duration was here kept up on either side, the enemy showering their shot and shell upon us, but doing little execution on account of our protected position. My loss here was only 7 wounded, 2 dangerously. Lieut. G. R. Gilmore, of Company D, and acting adjutant of Lieutenant-Colonel Preston's regiment, was slightly wounded in the ankle.

About 12 o'clock I received an order from Colonel Shelby to withdraw my force, it being Brigadier-General Marmaduke's intention to make only a demonstration, and not to assault the place. I then moved my command upon the Jackson road, and encamped about dark 4 miles beyond that place, upon the road leading to Dallas. Before I could post my pickets, and, in fact, before I had fairly encamped, a company belonging to Colonel [R. C.] Newton's regiment, which had unaccountably encamped some 300 yards from the regiment, was attacked by the enemy and scattered. This company lost 6 men killed, wounded, and missing, and almost the whole of their horses. I immediately formed the brigade on foot, and awaited the approach of the enemy, whom I rightly conjectured to be in force, sending the train to Jackson. Colonel Preston was here ordered to dislodge a small force of the enemy posted on the road between my camp and Jackson, which was done without loss. Not being sufficiently acquainted with the country to attempt an advance upon the enemy, whose strength and locality I was totally ignorant of, I ordered Colonel Newton to retire with his regiment toward Jackson, and form his line 1 mile west of town, and Colonel Preston was ordered to form his line of battle near the junction of the Dallas and Fredericktown roads, and to resist any movement of the enemy from that quarter.

At 3 o'clock the next morning an order was received from Brigadier-General Marmaduke to withdraw my command to Jackson. I immediately did so, leaving, however, a picket force to cover my rear, which an hour after I had left was attacked and driven into town.

The march southward from Jackson for several days, as far as my command is concerned, presents nothing worthy of consideration. The enemy, however, were pressing our rear, and frequent skirmishes were engaged in, which, owing to the position the brigade occupied, were more frequently heard than engaged in. Once, however, the rear guard gave way and was forced back upon the command without giving sufficient warning of the approach of the enemy. This for a time threw my brigade into disorder, but the men were promptly rallied by their officers, and formed in line ready to resist the approach of the enemy. The enemy was, however, gallantly repulsed by the Texans, under command of Colonel Carter.

After my brigade had passed Bloomfield, I received orders to march back to the town and form upon the right of Colonel Shelby, and to resist the farther advance of the enemy. A heavy skirmishing was soon begun in front, and kept up till dark. No firing was heard during the night, though my scouts reported to me continually that the enemy was making a flank movement upon my right, which would have given him possession of a hill that commanded our whole position.

I was ordered next morning to move in the direction of Chalk Bluff. When within 2 miles of that point, I received orders to dismount my men, and to send horses and train across the river, and to march the infantry thus dismounted back a short distance to a position that had been selected for fighting. The position assigned me was on the left of Colonel Shelby's brigade, my left resting on an open field. Not willing to expose the men any more than necessary, I ordered temporary breastworks to be made, which would have effectually protected them from the musketry of the enemy. The enemy soon commenced a vigorous shelling, remarkable for its accuracy, the shells passing directly over my lines, within 2 feet of the ground.

At 2 o'clock at night I received orders to withdraw my forces with the utmost secrecy and dispatch, and to leave my skirmishers in front to resist any night advance of the enemy. The brigade was safely crossed to the south side of the Saint Francis River, and occupied a position above the bluff on the bank of the river, which completely commanded the road leading to the bridge. I here received orders to march the brigade upon the Gainesville road and encamp until further orders, leaving, however, my sharpshooters upon the river, subject to Brigadier-General Marmaduke's order.

Subsequent events would be but a detailed list of short rations, hard marches through swamps, &c., in no way worthy of mention, save for the cheerfulness with which the men under me endured those hardships.

In conclusion, major, I would return my sincere thanks to both officers and men of this command for the bravery which, with but few exceptions, they have displayed upon the battle-field, and for the unflinching fortitude with which they endured every hardship.

I would take this occasion to acknowledge my obligations to Colonels Newton and Preston for the co-operation and assistance they gave me in carrying out all orders received.

I am, major, very respectfully, your obedient servant,

JNO. Q. BURBRIDGE,
Colonel, Commanding, &c.

Maj. HENRY EWING,
Assistant Adjutant-General, Jacksonport, Ark.

No. 17.

Report of Lieut. Col. S. G. Kitchen, Missouri Cavalry Battalion (Confederate.)

CAMP SUGAR CREEK, ARK., *May* 7, 1863.

I have the honor to submit a report of the operations of my battalion since its organization on April 9, 1863, in Greene County, Arkansas, by the election of a lieutenant-colonel and major, eight companies participating in said election.

I immediately assumed command, and on the 10th marched northward toward Chalk Bluff, with the intention of co-operating with Lieut. Col. W. J. Preston, who was on duty with several hundred men from your command at that time in this portion of the State. Having formed a junction with Colonel Preston, to resist a force of the enemy which was reported crossing the Saint Francis River for the purpose of making a raid into Arkansas, and Colonel Preston suddenly and unexpectedly retreating, I was compelled to retire with the force then at my disposal (about 100 men) before a superior force of the enemy, consisting of some 400 cavalry and two pieces of artillery.

My battalion then encamped 7 miles from Gainesville, where it remained until the morning of the 20th, when it marched to Chalk Bluff. I had learned, from my scouts, of an encampment of about 60 Federals at or near the Bluff, and determined to surprise and capture it, if possible. Arriving at the Bluff after dark, I left my horses on the south bank of the river, and, crossing my men over in a canoe, attacked the enemy at daylight with 100 men, and succeeded in completely surprising and routing the camp, a majority of the enemy escaping so rapidly and hurriedly they stampeded from their tents. The fruits of our victory consisted of 18 tents, 60 horses, 10 mules, 2 wagons, blankets, clothing, cooking utensils, &c., and 23 prisoners, including in the number Capt. Richard M. Hulse, of McNeil's regiment, Gamble militia. The enemy lost 3 or 4 killed and about the same number wounded. Our loss was 2 killed and 2 wounded.

On the same day (21st) I recrossed the Saint Francis and marched to my old camp near Gainesville, and from which place I sent the prisoners to Little Rock under a guard of 20 men.

Having learned of your movements in a letter to Brig. Gen. M. Jeff. Thompson, I marched my command to Chalk Bluff and reported for duty. A portion of my force was detailed to assist in building the bridge, another in scouting and picketing on each side of the Saint Francis, and the remainder of my available troops were ordered to blockade Taylor's Slough, which they accomplished on the morning of May 2. The battalion moved from Chalk Bluff with your column, and is now on duty guarding the northern frontier and performing other duties under your late orders.

S. G. KITCHEN,

Lieutenant-Colonel, Commanding Battalion Missouri Volunteers.

Brig. Gen. J. S. MARMADUKE.

No. 18.

Reports of Col. George W. Carter, Twenty-first Texas Cavalry, commanding brigade.

HDQRS. SECOND COLUMN, MARMADUKE'S DIVISION,

April 22, 1863—8 a. m.

MAJOR: I am now, with my brigade and Preston's detachment and Reves' company, on the road between Greenville and Bloomfield, 8 miles from the Mingo Swamp and 30 miles from Bloomfield. The Saint Francis was flooded, the boats gone, and great difficulty was found in crossing the trains. Greene's brigade could not get farther than Greenville, owing to the river, and was ordered to cross early this morning. I have ordered up his cavalry and artillery, with all possible speed, to this point. Have sent back to him 32 of my best mules, to enable him to make dispatch. The enemy have a picket of 200 at Mingo Ford, and Mingo is swimming and the boats gone. I am pressing teams, and shall find some difficulty in crossing the stream. I propose to leave the train well guarded at a point on this side, leaving also my unarmed men, and then, pushing on to the point directed in your orders, taking all, except the guard, with me. I believe I can capture the pickets and surprise the enemy by crossing a few miles above. The animals have suffered greatly by the forced marches and lack of forage. I have found forage at this point. If the train is left, it will be directed to move to a point and by a route of little danger to rejoin me. I do not propose to leave my ammunition. I am hopeful that my column will give a good account of itself. I will report to you again to-morrow. A dispatch will find me between Bloomfield and Mingo Swamp.

I am, major, very respectfully, your obedient servant,

G. W. CARTER,
Colonel, Commanding.

Major [HENRY] EWING,
Assistant Adjutant-General.

HEADQUARTERS CARTER'S BRIGADE,
In the Field, Arkansas, May 5, 1863.

MAJOR: By Special Orders, No. —, I was assigned command of the second column, Marmaduke's division, composed of Carter's and Greene's brigades, with instructions to move with all dispatch via Doniphan to Patterson, so as to make a junction with the first column, under Colonel [Joseph O.] Shelby, at the latter place. I collected the brigade and assumed command at Doniphan, moving toward Patterson on the morning of April 18, on the State road to Ironton.

I arrived with the column in 30 miles of Patterson on the 19th. A detachment, consisting of the Twenty-first Texas Cavalry, one section Pratt's battery, and Captain [Timothy] Reves' Partisan company, under command of Lieutenant-Colonel [D. C.] Giddings, made a forced march to Patterson, starting at 11 o'clock on the night of the 19th, moving by the lower road, and the rest of the column, under Colonel [Colton] Greene and Lieutenant-Colonel [Benjamin W.] Watson, moved at daybreak by the upper road toward the same point.

The detachment under Colonel Giddings surprised and captured the enemy's picket, 12 miles from Patterson, on the morning of the 20th; picket consisted of 1 commissioned officer, 2 sergeants, and 22 privates. Colonel Giddings then proceeded, reaching Patterson at 1 o'clock, meeting the enemy (supposed to be between 800 and 1,000 strong) 3 miles south of Patterson, routing them and driving them toward Ironton.

The larger portion of the public property in the hands of the enemy was burned by them before retreating; nevertheless, a large amount of quartermaster's and commissary stores were secured and turned over.

In the several engagements, Lieut. P. W. Connell, Company F, Twenty-first Texas, was severely wounded in the shoulder; 3 privates slightly wounded; none killed or missing. The loss of the enemy, from the best information at hand, was 100 killed, 19 wounded, and 38 prisoners, including 1 major, 1 captain, and 2 lieutenants.

On the morning of the 21st, I received orders to proceed with my column and attack the enemy in the vicinity of Bloomfield. High water in the Saint Francis and Mingo retarded my march, so that I did not reach Bloomfield with the entire command until the evening of the 23d.

In the meanwhile Lieutenant-Colonel [W. J.] Preston, of Burbridge's command, moved on Bloomfield, capturing a considerable amount of commissary stores and corn.

The enemy, under General [John] McNeil, had left Bloomfield and gone toward Jackson on the evening of the 21st, leaving a strong picket with block-house fortification at White Water Bridge, on the Cape Girardeau road.

At 12 o'clock on the night of the 23d, the column was moved toward Cape Girardeau. I moved, with my escort, 10 miles in advance of the column, intending to surprise the picket, distant some 35 miles from Bloomfield. When within 3 miles of the bridge, a detachment, consisting of Reves' company (under Lieutenant [B. A.] Johnson) and Texas brigade (under Captain [John S.] Carrington, assistant adjutant-general of Carter's brigade), was ordered to proceed by Williams' Ferry to intercept the retreat of the enemy and attack them in the rear. The enemy's force consisted of Company G (Captain [S. V.] Shipman), First Wisconsin Cavalry. They fought bravely; were 57 strong. Of this number 40 were destroyed, either killed, captured, or wounded. Among the number wounded and captured was Captain Shipman. We captured also the train, tents, and 25 horses. My loss was 4 wounded, including Lieutenant [H. C.] Sloan, of Reves' company.

The column reached White Water Bridge at 4 o'clock. McNeil was reported at Jackson, 10 miles from Cape Girardeau. Hoping to cut off his retreat from Jackson and force an engagement, Colonel Greene was ordered to move his brigade on the morning of the 24th, at 3 o'clock, toward Cape Girardeau. From some cause the order was not promptly obeyed, and my column did not reach the point contemplated until 4 o'clock on the 25th.

In the mean time the enemy had retreated from Jackson and taken refuge behind his fortifications at Cape Girardeau.

On the morning of the 26th, the first column, under Colonel Shelby, formed a junction with me near Cape Girardeau and attacked the fortification, when I was ordered to take position in his rear as support and to prevent a flank movement by the enemy. My command was not brought into action during the day, except for a few moments when a section of Pratt's battery engaged the Federal skirmishers. At 4 o'clock, by order of the general commanding, I was relieved of the command of the column and assumed command of my brigade, moving toward Jackson.

The marching, in view of the difficulty of forage and subsistence and the condition of the roads and teams, was creditable. The officers and men bore their privations with honorable cheerfulness.

I would here particularly commend Sergeant [Henry M.] Leary, of Captain [John B.] Williams' company, Nineteenth Texas Cavalry, for his gallantry at White Water Bridge.

I am, major, very respectfully,

G. W. CARTER,
Colonel, Commanding Second Column, Marmaduke's Division.

Major [HENRY] EWING,
Assistant Adjutant-General.

HEADQUARTERS CARTER'S BRIGADE,
In the Field, May 5, 1863.

MAJOR: By orders from division headquarters of 27th ultimo, my brigade constituted the rear guard, the division moving from Jackson to Bloomfield. I took up the line of march in rear of the column on the morning of April 27, throwing out skirmishers in rear and flankers on the right and left. At different points in the day, the Nineteenth Texas, Twenty-first Texas, and Morgan's squadron, in conjunction with a section of Pratt's battery, were successively placed in the rear of my command. The enemy made his appearance on the Fredericktown road about 8 a. m.; commenced shelling my rear regiment a few moments after the command had been given to move. The shelling was kept up at intervals until 4 o'clock without any loss to us. I did not deem it expedient to return their artillery fire. About 4 p. m. their advance engaged my rear skirmishers within 3 miles of White Water Bridge. Soon an entire Federal regiment was brought into action. They were at different points near the bridge successively charged by the Twenty-first, Nineteenth, and Morgan's squadron, with heavy loss.

My loss, 1 killed and 1 wounded in the Nineteenth Texas, 1 slightly wounded in the Twenty-first, and 1 killed in Morgan's squadron. I am not able to report the number of enemy killed. We captured 18 prisoners, including 1 captain.

Both men and officers acted with great coolness and courage.

At 5 o'clock, I crossed successfully over White Water Bridge, destroying the bridge and encamping my command 8 miles beyond.

On the 28th, I moved my command into camp within 3 miles of Bloomfield.

On the 29th, I placed my brigade in line of battle on the heights near Bloomfield, and remained there until the 30th, when I moved toward Chalk Bluff.

On May 2, my brigade again constituted the rear guard, throwing out skirmishers and flankers. At 10 a. m. I was informed that a cavalry brigade of the enemy were approaching, when I placed one section of Pratt's battery in position masked, directing my skirmishers to draw the enemy on. When within 400 yards, the artillery opened a very destructive fire with grape, driving them back in confusion. A charge was then made by two of their cavalry regiments, which was received by the First Squadron, Nineteenth Texas, under Captain [John B.] Williams, in the most gallant style. The enemy were charged in turn by Company K, Twenty-first, Captain [Martin M.] Kenney, with detachments from Nineteenth and Morgan, driving them with great confusion and heavy loss. My rear guard, under Major [C. L.] Morgan, made two other successful charges during the day.

My loss, 1 killed in Morgan's squadron; Nineteenth, 1 killed, 10 wounded, 8 missing. We captured a number of prisoners, including 1 captain. The enemy's dead strewed the road for half a mile. The officer leading the enemy's charge, supposed to be a lieutenant-colonel, was killed. A moderate estimate must make their killed during the day 150. I speak confidently on this subject, because this fighting took place under my own eye, within a few feet of the position I held.

At 5 o'clock, by order of the commanding general, I took position in rear of the line of battle selected subsequently; a squadron was held in reserve in the rear of the center, while the Twenty-first was sent as reserve on the extreme left, and the Nineteenth to the extreme right, Pratt's battery being withdrawn across the river. I then assumed command of the extreme left wing. The enemy opened on our lines spiritedly with shot and shell, but made no demonstrations with small-arms. Between midnight and daybreak my command was quietly withdrawn across the Saint Francis.

It is difficult to specify individual instances of merit when all have been so prompt. I will, however, say that all my staff have been faithful and efficient, and that Lieutenant-Colonels [B. W.] Watson and [D. C.] Giddings, Major Morgan, and Captain [J. H.] Pratt are deserving of special notice for gallantry and energy.

I am, major, very respectfully,

G. W. CARTER,
Colonel, Commanding Brigade.

Major [HENRY] EWING,
Assistant Adjutant-General, Marmaduke's Division.

No. 19.

Report of Col. Colton Greene, Third Missouri Cavalry (Confederate), commanding brigade.

HDQRS. GREENE'S BRIGADE, MARMADUKE'S DIVISION,
In the Field, near Pineville, Ark., May 15, 1863.

MAJOR: I would respectfully submit the following report of the part taken by my command in the late expedition into Missouri:

In compliance with your orders, I marched from Jackson, Ark., on April 17; crossed Eleven Points [River] on the same day; crossed Current River on the 19th instant [ultimo], and reported to Colonel [George W.] Carter, commanding Texas brigade.

I resumed the march, after a halt of two hours, in rear of Carter's brigade, which position in column I occupied on the 19th, 20th, 21st, 22d, and 23d instant [ultimo], arriving at Patterson some hours after its capture on the 21st, moving on toward Greenville, crossing Saint Francis River at that place, crossing Mingo Swamp and River near its mouth, and reaching Bloomfield at midnight on the 22d instant [ultimo], to learn that the enemy had retreated northward two days before.

After a halt of two hours, I again took up the line of march, reaching the main bridge on White Water River on the 23d, which was picketed by the enemy and captured by Colonel Carter's advance.

On the 24th instant [ultimo], I was informed that we were in presence of the enemy in force, commanded by Brigadier-General [John] McNeil, and was ordered to the front, taking a circuitous route until I struck the main road 4 miles from Cape Girardeau. Here I was ordered to halt and went into position, remaining in line during the night.

On the morning of the 25th, heavy firing being heard on the left, I was ordered by Brigadier-General Marmaduke to throw forward Colonel [M. L.] Young's battalion, and follow with the command to the support of the left. Colonel Young formed twenty minutes before my arrival, and had 1 man wounded while in long range of the enemy. Arriving on the Jackson road, 2 or 3 miles from Cape Girardeau, I was ordered into line, and covered Colonel [Joseph O.] Shelby's retiring column. After changing position several times, I was ordered into position 2 miles to the rear, which I left half an hour afterward to take up the line of march to Jackson.

About 4 o'clock of the following morning I was ordered to mount and proceed back to the bridge on White Water, and hold it. This was effected by 11 o'clock, and I occupied the position until the rear guard came up, when I resumed the march, reaching Bloomfield in the evening of the 27th instant [ultimo].

On the 28th instant [ultimo], I took position across the Cape Girardeau and Kitchen's Mill road; lay on my arms all night, and was ordered to fall back early next morning 20 miles. Arriving to the rear of Four Mile, I was ordered to dismount my men, to swim the horses across the Saint Francis River, and to go into line. At 2 o'clock at night I was ordered to cross the Saint Francis in rear of the whole column, which was accomplished without loss. Arriving on the south side of the river, the campaign may be said to have ended.

It is impossible to state at this time the exact number of my men who fell into the enemy's hands. Some were cut off, but are daily reporting. Not exceeding 5 have been reported captured.

I cannot avoid mentioning the good order and endurance of my command during these arduous marches. No case of cowardly straggling came under my observation, and the rigor of discipline and hardships of the field were alike borne with uncomplaining fortitude.

I am, major, very respectfully, your obedient servant,

COLTON GREENE,
Colonel, Commanding Brigade.

Maj. HENRY EWING, *Assistant Adjutant-General.*

No. 20.

Report of Asst. Surg. S. S. Harris, Jeffers' Missouri Regiment (Confederate).

JEFFERS' REGIMENT,
Camp near Wittsburg, Ark., May 27, 1863.

SIR: By your order, I was left with Drs. [John F.] Yancey and [J. F.] Brookheart in charge of our wounded after the withdrawal of our forces from Cape Girardeau.

Inclosed is a report of our wounded.

I asked permission of the Federal authorities to establish our hospital in or near Cape Girardeau. The request was not granted, and our wounded were removed to their post hospital. We were furnished with an escort to Bloomfield, to be sent through to our lines from there. We reached Bloomfield with the Federal forces, and were ordered to remain there until the excitement in front was over. We remained there until General McNeil's return from Chalk Bluff, when, instead of sending us to our command, he took us back with him to Cape Girardeau. After detaining us there for some four or five days, he started us to Little Rock, by way of Memphis and Helena. General McNeil alleged as a reason for his conduct toward us that the demand for the surrender of Cape Girardeau had been made by Colonel Carter, in the name of General Price, and that, therefore, he must consider us as belonging to General Price's command, and, from the best information he had, General Price's lines were at Little Rock; therefore, he should send us there. I asked for and received a copy of Colonel Carter's demand for surrender, which you will find inclosed. This subject, I know, is of but little consequence, and deserving, perhaps, of no further notice, but I thought it my duty to inform you of the facts.

On reaching Helena, General Prentiss permitted us, under a flag of truce, to come direct to our command. We reached our lines on the 20th instant.

Respectfully submitted.

S. S. HARRIS,
Assistant Surgeon, Jeffers' Regiment Missouri Cavalry.

Dr. C. PEYTON, *Medical Director Marmaduke's Division.*

[Inclosures.]

Report of wounded in the fight before Cape Girardeau.

Major	1
Lieutenant	1
Captain	1
Privates	18

I was not permitted to visit the battle-field; but, from the best information I could obtain, there were only 3 killed on the field. I could not learn their names or command. They were buried by our friends.

Of the five nurses that remained, two only were permitted to stay with our wounded, and the others were sent to Saint Louis as prisoners of war.

When I left Cape Girardeau our wounded were well cared for, and had everything requisite to make them comfortable.

Respectfully, yours, &c.,

S. S. HARRIS,
Assistant Surgeon, Provisional Army of the Confederate States.

HEADQUARTERS FOURTH DIVISION,
Near Cape Girardeau, Mo., April 25, 1863.

Officer Commanding U. S. Forces in and around Cape Girardeau:

SIR: By order of Maj. Gen. Sterling Price, commanding, I formally demand of you the immediate surrender, unconditionally, of the troops in Cape Girardeau and the adjoining forts, together with all the ammunition, stores, and other property belonging to the United States in the same. If the surrender is made, I pledge myself to treat the troops as prisoners of war, and to parole and exchange them as soon as practicable. I shall scrupulously protect private property. No difference will be made in this particular between parties, whether Union or Southern sentiment. One-half hour is allowed for your decision.

Colonel Watson, commanding Second Texas Cavalry Brigade, who bears the flag of truce, will present this demand and wait for your reply.

I am, sir, very respectfully, your obedient servant,

G. W. CARTER,
Comdg. Fourth Div., First Army Corps, Trans-Mississippi Dept.

APRIL 18, 1863.—Action at Fayetteville, Ark.

REPORTS.

No. 1.—Col. M. La Rue Harrison, First Arkansas Cavalry (Union), with congratulatory orders, &c.

No. 2.—Brig. Gen. W. L. Cabell, C. S. Army.

No. 1.

Reports of Col. M. La Rue Harrison, First Arkansas Cavalry (Union), with congratulatory orders, &c.

APRIL 18, 1863.

Arkansas is triumphant. The rebels, 2,000 strong, with two 6-pounder guns, attacked Fayetteville at daylight this morning, and, after four hours' desperate fighting, they were completely routed, and retreated in disorder toward Ozark. General Cabell commanded in person, assisted by Colonel Scott, of the Virginia Black Horse Cavalry, Colonel Monroe, Lieutenant-Colonel Thomson, Major Dorsey, and others. Their artillery was silenced at 9 p. m. by two companies of the First Arkansas Cavalry, and a brilliant cavalry charge under Colonel Monroe was repulsed in the center of the town by our cavalry and infantry. Our stores are all safe; not a thing burned or taken from us.

Our loss is 5 killed, about 17 wounded, and a few stragglers and pickets taken prisoners. The enemy's loss is estimated at 20 killed and 50 wounded, which does not include those taken off on their retreat. Every officer and man in my command was a hero; no one flinched.

M. LA RUE HARRISON,
Colonel, Commanding Fayetteville.

Maj. Gen. SAMUEL R. CURTIS.

HEADQUARTERS POST,
Fayetteville, Ark., April 19, 1863.

GENERAL: The following report of the battle of yesterday at Fayetteville is respectfully submitted, in addition to the telegraphic dispatches of last evening:

On Friday, 17th instant, a scout under command of Lieutenant [Joseph S.] Robb, First Arkansas Cavalry, returned from the direction of Ozark, and reported no apparent preparations of the enemy to move in this direction. Having no fresh horses, I ordered Lieutenant Robb to take his command to quarters, expecting to be able to send out a small scout again on the next day. On Saturday morning, 18th instant, at a few minutes after sunrise, the enemy having made a forced march from the Boston Mountains during the night, surprised and captured our dismounted picket on the Frog Bayou road, and approached the town with wild and deafening shouts. Their cavalry charged up a deep ravine on the east side of the city, and attacked my headquarters (the Colonel Tibbetts place). The firing of the picket had alarmed the command, and by the time the enemy had reached the town, the First Arkansas Infantry had formed on their parade ground, under command of Lieut. Col. E. J. Searle, assisted by Maj. E. D. Ham, and slowly retired, by my orders, toward the cavalry, then formed, dismounted, at their camp. Fearing that, not being uniformed, they might be mistaken for the enemy, and be fired upon by the cavalry, I ordered Lieutenant-Colonel Searle to post seven companies as a reserve in a sheltered position in our rear, two of which were afterward ordered to support the left wing. The remaining three companies of the First Infantry, together with four companies of the First Cavalry, formed the center of our line under my own immediate command. The right wing was composed of the Third Battalion First Cavalry, under command of Maj. Ezra Fitch; and the left wing, Second Battalion First Arkansas Cavalry, was commanded by Lieut. Col. A. W. Bishop, assisted by Maj. T. J. Hunt. Headquarters was made the "bone of contention," and was repeatedly charged by the rebels, but they were gallantly repulsed by our men. In less than thirty minutes after the first attack, the enemy planted two pieces of artillery, one a 12-pounder and one 6-pounder, upon the hillside east of town, near Colonel Gunter's place, and opened a sharp fire of canister and shells upon the camp of the First Arkansas Cavalry, doing some damage to tents and horses, but killing no men. At 8

a. m. our center had advanced and occupied the house, yard, outbuildings, and hedges at my headquarters; the right wing had advanced to the arsenal, and the left occupied the open field on the northeast of town, while the enemy had possession of the whole hill-side east, the Davis place, opposite to, and the grove south of, headquarters. This grove was formerly occupied by the buildings of the Arkansas College. At about 9 a. m., or a little before, Colonel Monroe led a gallant and desperate cavalry charge upon our right wing, which was met by a galling cross-fire from our right and center, piling rebel men and horses in heaps in front of our ordnance office, and causing the enemy to retreat in disorder to the woods. During this charge, Captains [William C.] Parker and [George W. R.] Smith, of the First Infantry, while bravely cheering their men, were both wounded in the head, though not dangerously. At about the same time, by my order, two companies of the First Cavalry, led by the gallant Lieutenant Robb, advanced within rifle-range of the enemy's artillery, and guided by the blaze of its discharges, fired several volleys into the midst of the artillerists, which effectually silenced their battery and caused its precipitate withdrawal from the field. The enemy's center, occupying the Davis place, made a desperate resistance for nearly an hour after both wings had partially given way, and skirmishing continued at intervals for some time with pickets, reconnoitering parties, and stragglers. At 12 m. their whole force was in full retreat for Ozark. Having only a very few horses, and they already on duty with picketing and reconnoitering parties, I was utterly unable to pursue them. During the whole action the enemy occupied ground covered with timber and brush, while my command was in the streets and open fields.

Since the battle I have ascertained the following particulars: General Cabell and staff, with about 2,000 men and two pieces of artillery, left Ozark on Friday morning with three days' rations and a full supply of ammunition. They halted at the crossing of the mountains at a little past noon and rested until nearly sunset, afterward marching rapidly toward Fayetteville. They were delayed by the darkness of the night and the incumbrance of their artillery, so that they did not commence the attack as early by nearly two hours as they had intended. Colonel Monroe recommended a cavalry attack, to be supported by the artillery, but was overruled by Cabell, and a halt was made until the artillery could come up. Their force was made up as follows: Brig. Gen. W. L. Cabell commanding, accompanied by staff and escort; Carroll's First Arkansas Cavalry Regiment, Colonel Scott, of Virginia, commanding, assisted by Lieutenant-Colonel Thomson; Monroe's Second [First] Arkansas Cavalry, Colonel Monroe commanding in person; First Battalion Parsons' (Texas) cavalry, Lieutenant-Colonel [S. M.] Noble commanding; one section of artillery, commanding officer not known, and four companies bushwhackers, commanded by Mankins, Palmer, Brown, and others. The enemy left all their dead and wounded, which they could not take away on their retreat, in our hands, leaving Surgeon Russell and Assistant Surgeon Holderness [?] to take charge of them. To-day Captain Alexander arrived at our picket with a flag of truce, bringing a communication from General Cabell, a copy of which I inclose. The flag was immediately ordered back with my reply, a copy of which is also inclosed. The following is a list of casualties on our side:*

* * * * * * *

*Nominal list reports 4 men killed, 3 officers (Capts. William S. Johnson, William C. Parker, and Randall Smith) and 23 men wounded, 16 men captured, and 35 men missing.

Ran away disgracefully to Cassville, Mo., First Lieut. C. C. Wells, regimental quartermaster First Arkansas Infantry.* Missing, 35, mostly stampeded toward Cassville during the engagement. Prisoners, 1 lieutenant and 8 men, First Arkansas Cavalry, taken while absent without leave at a dance, 9 miles from town; also 1 private First Arkansas Infantry, and 6 privates from other commands, taken in town.

The enemy's loss is not accurately known. At and about this post are not less than 20 killed and 50 wounded. Citizens report 1 colonel and several men as having died on the retreat; also a large number of wounded still moving on with the command. We captured, during the engagement, Major Wilson, General Cabell's commissary, wounded, and Captain Jefferson, of Carroll's regiment, wounded; also 4 sergeants, 3 corporals, and 46 privates, a part of them wounded; also not less than 50 horses and 100 stand of arms, mostly shot-guns. Among their killed are Captain Hubbard, of Carroll's regiment, and a captain of bushwhackers. The enemy admit the loss of over 200 horses, killed, taken, and stampeded.

Inclosed please find a rough sketch of the position of forces at 9 a. m., when the battle culminated.†

Every field and line officer and nearly every enlisted man fought bravely, and I would not wish to be considered as disparaging any one when I can mention only a few of the many heroic men who sustained so nobly the honor of our flag. Lieutenant-Colonel Searle and Major Ham, in command of the reserve, did good service in keeping their men in position and preventing them from being terrified by the artillery. Lieutenant-Colonel Bishop and Majors Fitch and Hunt, of the First Cavalry, led their men coolly up in the face of the enemy's fire, and drove them from their position. Capt. William S. Johnson, company M, First Arkansas Cavalry, had his right arm shattered while leading his men forward under a galling fire. Lieutenant [James] Roseman, post adjutant, and Lieut. Frank Strong, acting adjutant First Cavalry, deserve much praise.

I remain, general, your most obedient servant,

M. LA RUE HARRISON,
Colonel First Arkansas Cavalry, Commanding.

Maj. Gen. SAMUEL R. CURTIS,
Commanding Department of the Missouri.

P. S.—We had actively engaged during the battle between 300 and 400 men only. I should not neglect also to mention that S. D. Carpenter, assistant surgeon of volunteers, assisted by Assistant Surgeons Caffee, Drake, and Tefft, were actively engaged during the contest in carrying the wounded from the field and attending to their wants.

[Inclosures.]

HEADQUARTERS NORTHWESTERN ARKANSAS,
April 19, 1863.

Col. M. LA RUE HARRISON,
Commanding Post of Fayetteville:

SIR: The bearer of this letter, Captain [William A.] Alexander, visits your post under a flag of truce, to bury any of my command that may be left dead from the engagement of yesterday. I respectfully request

* Dismissed July 31, 1863.

† Omitted as unimportant.

that you will suffer him to get up the dead and wounded, and that you will extend to him such assistance as may be necessary to enable him to carry out his instructions.

I am, sir, very respectfully, your obedient servant,

W. L. CABELL,
Brigadier-General, Commanding Northwestern Arkansas.

HEADQUARTERS POST,
Fayetteville, Ark., April 19, 1863.

Brig. Gen. W. L. CABELL, *Commanding:*

GENERAL: In reply to dispatches from you by hand of Captain Alexander, bearing flag of truce, I would respectfully state that the dead of your command have all been decently buried in coffins. The wounded are in charge of Surgeons Russell and Holden [?], having been removed to our general hospital by my order. They are receiving every attention that men can receive—abundance of medicines, surgical instruments, and subsistence stores having been placed under the control of your surgeons. Rest assured, general, that your wounded shall receive the best of care, such as we would hope to have from you were we placed in a like situation. Under the circumstances I consider it unnecessary to retain your flag, and therefore return it. Your prisoners shall be paroled, and as fast as the men whose names are mentioned in your list report to our lines, the exchange will be made.

I am, general, very truly, yours,

M. LA RUE HARRISON,
Colonel, Commanding.

HEADQUARTERS ARMY OF THE FRONTIER,
April 19, 1863.

Col. M. LA RUE HARRISON,
Commanding at Fayetteville:

I must congratulate you on the success of yesterday. It augurs well for the future of Arkansas when her loyal troops have beaten the enemy in their first encounter. Such success should encourage us, and I hope soon to see 10,000 loyal men of Arkansas arrayed on the side of the Union. You have nobly sustained yourselves, and deserve a country's gratitude.

F. J. HERRON,
Major-General.

GENERAL ORDERS, No. 16. } HEADQUARTERS POST,
Fayetteville, Ark., April 19, 1863.

COMRADES IN ARMS: Let April 18, 1863, be ever remembered. The battle of Fayetteville has been fought and won. To-day the brave and victorious sons of Arkansas stand proudly upon the soil which their blood and their bravery have rendered sacred to every true-hearted American, but doubly sacred to them. In the light of this holy Sabbath sun we are permitted, through God's mercy, to gather together in His name and in the name of our common country, to offer up our heartfelt thanks to the "Giver of every good and perfect gift," for the triumphs of our arms and for the blessings which we this day enjoy.

When yesterday's sun rose upon us the hostile hordes of a bitter and unprincipled foe were pouring their deadly fire among our ranks; the booming of his artillery was re-echoing from mountain to mountain, and the clattering hoofs of his cavalry were trampling in our streets.

At meridian, General Cabell, with his shattered and panic-stricken cohorts, was retreating precipitately through the passes of the Boston Mountains toward the Arkansas River, leaving his dead and wounded in our hands.

Fellow-soldiers, it is to your honor and credit I say it, he could not have left them in better hands. Not one act of barbarity, or even unkindness, stains the laurels you so proudly wear. Such may your conduct ever be, brave and unflinching in battle, kind and generous to the vanquished. Abstain from all cruelty and excess; respect the immunities of private property; never insult or injure women or children, the aged, the sick, or a fallen foe. Let us show to our enemies that the Federal soldiers of Arkansas are as generous as they are brave and patriotic; let us prove to them the justice of our cause and the purity of our purposes, so that soon we may gather together under the broad folds of our time-honored and victorious banner every true-hearted son of Arkansas.

Fellow-soldiers, I congratulate you all upon the glorious victory you have won, by your cool and determined bravery, for that Union which our revolutionary sires established by their valor and sealed with their blood. More than all do I congratulate you that this battle was fought upon Arkansas soil, and this victory won by Arkansians alone, thereby testifying to our patriotic brethren in arms from other States that we are not only willing but anxious to second their efforts in rescuing our State from the dominion of traitors; but in all our rejoicing let us not neglect to shed the tear of regret over the graves of those heroic men who fell beside us fighting bravely for the nation's honor.

Green be their mossy graves;
Immortal be their name;
Above, their banner proudly waves,
While heaven records their fame!

A just cause is ours. The Stars and Stripes float gallantly over us. God is on our side. Who can be against us?

By order of Col. M. La Rue Harrison, commanding post:

JAMES ROSEMAN,
Lieutenant, Post Adjutant.

[DEPARTMENT OF THE MISSOURI],
April 20, 1863.

Colonel HARRISON, *Fayetteville, Ark.:*

Dispatch of yesterday received. Tender my thanks to the soldiers of your command for their gallant conduct in the battle of Fayetteville. You have done nobly. Arkansas vindicates her own honor by repulsing the rebel flag with her own brave sons. Send minute reports, naming the most deserving officers and men.

SAML. R. CURTIS,
Major-General.

No. 2.

Report of Brig. Gen. W. L. Cabell, C. S. Army.

HEADQUARTERS NORTHWESTERN ARKANSAS,
Ozark, April 25, 1863.

COLONEL: I have the honor to inform you that, having received what I supposed, and had every reason to believe, to be reliable information that the enemy at Fayetteville were making preparations to move from that place, and to re-enforce General Phillips in the Indian country, I took all the effective mounted men of my command, except three companies of Colonel [J. F.] Hill's battalion (that are badly armed and with horses unshod), with two pieces of artillery, the whole amounting to 900 men, and left here at 3 o'clock on the 16th, going by what is called the Mulberry and Frog Bayou road to Fayetteville, and attacked the enemy there at 5 a. m. on the 18th. I found the enemy about 2,000 strong, well armed with Springfield and Whitney rifles, no artillery, and nearly every hill dotted with rifle-pits. After a furious fight of three hours and ten minutes, I withdrew my command in good order. I found it impossible, with the arms I had, after my artillery ammunition was exhausted, to dislodge them from the houses and rifle-pits with the kind of arms my command had without losing all my horses and a large number of my men, as it was impossible to get near enough to them to make our aim effective without a great sacrifice of life, much greater than would have been justifiable under the circumstances.

The troops, with few exceptions, all fought well, and are now in fine spirits, ready and willing to try the enemy again. The enemy all (both infantry and cavalry) fought well, equally as well as any Federal troops I have ever seen. Although it was thought by a great many that, composed as they are of disloyal citizens and deserters from our army, they would make but a feeble stand, the reverse, however, was the case, as they resisted every attack made on them, and, as fast as driven out of one house, would occupy another and deliver their fire. Whenever, however, my troops could get to them they drove them before them every time. Colonel [J. C.] Monroe made two splendid charges with his command, one on foot and the other mounted. Colonel [Lee L.] Thomson, with his regiment, and [Caleb] Dorsey, with his squadron, under Colonel Scott, made a dashing charge and drove the enemy to their pits and to the houses, where they rallied and poured in a dreadful fire with their long-range guns. The artillery, managed by Captain [W. M.] Hughey, under my immediate command, did frightful execution in the enemy's camp, driving them out and completely scattering their cavalry for awhile. Captain Hughey was wounded in the arm by a sharpshooter at the commencement of the action, but continued in charge of his pieces, under a heavy fire from the enemy's sharpshooters, during the whole fight. His men were all taken a little over a month ago from the camp of instruction at Dardanelle, and, with one or two exceptions, did well.

Two horses were killed and 2 wounded in the battery; 1 man killed and several wounded.

Captain Hughey deserves especial mention for his bravery, skill, and energy in the management of his two pieces of artillery.

The loss is not positively known, but it will not exceed 20 killed, 30 wounded, and 20 missing. The enemy's loss in killed is fully equal to our total killed and wounded; the wounded were very great. We captured and paroled 26 prisoners, 1 lieutenant, 1 non-commissioned officer, and 24 privates; also destroyed a train of 10 or 15 wagons. I could have burned a large part of the town, but every house was filled with women and children, a great number of whom were the families of officers and soldiers in our service, and I did not deem it advisable to distress them any further, as their sufferings now are very grievous under the Federal rule.

The enemy's force consisted (notwithstanding all previous reports from persons living in Fayetteville to the contrary) of one cavalry regiment, twelve companies, 800; one infantry regiment, ten companies, 600; one battalion, seven companies, 300; artillery, one company, 150, making their total force 1,850. Besides this, they had a re-enforcement of four squadrons of cavalry, which had evidently escorted a train of wagons from Springfield, loaded principally with new uniform clothing. They were from the Second and Eleventh Kansas, Twenty-seventh Wisconsin, and Thirty-seventh Illinois, as will be seen from the inclosed list of prisoners captured and paroled.

Although I did not capture Fayetteville and drive the enemy out from it, yet my expedition will prove to be a beneficial one, as it will in future curb the lawlessness of the troops there; will cause them to send all their regular troops east, and it will keep the place in that condition in reference to numbers that will enable me, with a small increase of my force and with a few hundred long-range guns, to take the place. Besides this, I have obtained information that cannot be obtained from any other source, as it is impossible to get correct information from people living there. Our friends are all too anxious to rid the country of their presence to state things as they really are. I find this to be true in every respect but in reference to artillery. Our enemies (Union men) will give no information at all, either in reference to the enemy or country. The whole country north of the mountains is almost devastated, and but few people are to be seen, a great majority of them having abandoned their homes and gone north. A train of at least 100 wagons left Fayetteville a few days ago filled with Union families. A few Southern families live on the road, but they are stripped of everything; all their horses, cattle, and hogs taken from them; their wheat crops destroyed, and nothing to indicate preparation for another crop. When I got into the neighborhood of Fayetteville, I found houses where they were farming, and where cattle and horses could be seen.

Knowing that our good citizens had burdens imposed on them by the Federal troops too grievous to be borne much longer; that it was necessary for me to visit that section of the country, and having been appealed to by citizens, both male and female, to give them assistance, I determined that I would strike there the very first time that I saw the least hope, whether I succeeded in taking the place or not. As soon, therefore, as I learned that Phillips was moving around with his Indian brigade to flank General Steele, and, having consulted with General Steele, who agreed with me (and desired that a dash should be made at Fayetteville, if nothing more) that it was necessary, and, having heard that they were getting their wagons ready (which proved to be false) to re-enforce Phillips, besides being without forage (nothing to feed my horses), I determined to make a bold dash at that den of thieves, and, if possible, to take it. Although I did not take it, I will be ready in a few days with more troops and to strike a heavier blow again.

I regret to say that I lost a good many horses. The enemy's sharpshooters killed a good many with their long-range guns, and a few men left in charge of the horses evidently deserted them. Besides this, I had too many inefficient officers and not enough long-range guns. Had I had 500 long-range guns, with good cartridges, I could have taken the place in an hour. As it was, I could not advance my battery, as I had nothing to cover them with, as the enemy's guns were equal in range to the artillery. The Arkadelphia rifles, with the cartridges sent for them, are no better than shot-guns. I must, therefore, again appeal to the lieutenant-general commanding for a regiment of infantry and a number of rifled guns, as this section of the country should be protected.

The officers and men, with a few exceptions, acted well. Colonel

Monroe and his whole regiment deserve particular mention. Colonels Scott, [S. M.] Noble, Thomson, and Major Dorsey acted with great gallantry. Captain [J. Fen.] Rieff, Lieutenant [J. A.] Ferguson, Captain [T. P.] Jefferson, and Private [W. C.] Sublett, of Rieff's company, deserve to be particularly mentioned. My staff officers, Lieutenant [B. J.] Field, Surgeon [J. H.] Carroll, Major [H. G.] Wilson (commissary), Captain [J.] Crawford (quartermaster), and Lieut. Roberts, acted with great gallantry, and rendered every possible assistance. Major Wilson was, I am sorry to say, badly wounded.

I sent an officer back with a flag of truce to have the wounded properly cared for, and left surgeons to attend to them.

I withdrew with the hope that they would follow me, and fell back slowly, hoping that I could get them out of the houses and rifle-pits, as I could have whipped them badly. They did not follow, nor evince any desire to do so. I came leisurely back to this place, in good order, to feed my horses, that had had but one day's forage since the morning of the 16th, and also to have them shod and allow them a few days' rest, the distance marched, over mountains, rocks, &c., being nearly 150 miles.

I am, sir, very respectfully, your obedient servant,

W. L. CABELL,

Brigadier-General, Commanding Northwestern Arkansas.

Col. S. S. ANDERSON,

Adjutant-General, District of Arkansas.

APRIL 18–21, 1863.—Scout from Salem to Sinking Creek, Current River, and Big Creek, Mo.

Report of Capt. Peter Ostermayer, Fifth Missouri State Militia Cavalry.

HDQRS. DETACHMENT FIFTH MO. STATE MILITIA CAV.,

Salem, Mo., April 22, 1863.

GENERAL: I herewith beg leave to remit the following report of a scout through Shannon County, on Current River, and Big Creek:

Lieutenant [Augustus] Benz, of Company C, with 40 men of his company, went out last Friday, the 18th instant, to Sinking Creek, Current River, and Big Creek, as far as about 10 miles on the other side of Eminence. He found five of their general camping places; chased some of the guerrillas; killed 1, captured 2.

On returning last Monday, captured, on Current River, after a hard chase, Private Charles Burch, of Captain Magoffin's company (B), Steen's regiment, Fourth Brigade, Hindman's division, who was on recruiting service, in possession of a recruiting commission issued by General M. M. Parsons; also Augustus Dow, from Saint Louis, formerly in the same regiment, but since resigned, now carrier of secesh mails, and found in possession of a splendid secesh flag and a lot of letters. The rebel mail, as well as the flag, will be handed to you by Lieut. Charles Koch, who will give you also full particulars. I hold the prisoners in jail in compliance with Special Orders, No. 15, from your headquarters, dated March 31, 1863, awaiting the appointment of a military commission.

I remain, general, very respectfully, your obedient servant,

PETER OSTERMAYER,

Captain, Commanding at Salem.

Brigadier-General DAVIES,

Commanding Rolla District, Rolla, Mo

APRIL 19-20, 1863.—Scout near Neosho, Mo.

Report of Capt. Ozias Ruark, Eighth Missouri State Militia Cavalry.

POST NEOSHO, MO., *April* 21, 1863.

CAPTAIN: I have the honor to report that, in obedience to your orders, on the 19th of the present month, I took command of a detachment of 30 men from Companies L and M, Eighth Missouri State Militia Cavalry, with Lieut. John R. Kelso, and proceeded in the direction of Seneca Mills, in search of certain notorious bushwhackers in that region of country. Traveling till about 2 p. m., and finding no one, I detailed Lieutenant Kelso, with 5 men, all properly uniformed, and sent them forward for the purpose of obtaining reliable information, while I, with the remainder of the command, proceeded to Scott's Mill and encamped. Lieutenant Kelso returned to me about midnight, and informed me that he had found a kennel of bushwhackers, two of whom had fought till they died. He also had found in Cowskin Prairie a pasture containing a number of cattle jayhawked by the bushwhackers, who intended, in a short time, to drive them to the Southern army. We saddled our horses immediately, and returned to the place indicated, surrounded several houses, and found two more desperate bushwhackers, who fought till they died. We then went to a pasture, and found 40 head of cattle, jayhawked by these thieves to sell to the Southern army; all of which, with one two-horse wagon and one horse, I have brought to this post.

Too much praise cannot be bestowed upon Lieutenant Kelso for the daring and cunning he displayed. With five men in citizens' dress, and well armed, he succeeded in convincing the bushwhackers that he was a dispatch-bearer from General Marmaduke. They freely boasted to Lieutenant Kelso of having driven all the Union people out of the country. They bragged of having killed a number of Federal soldiers, of jayhawking the property of Union men, and said if they got any of the Neosho militia they would have them at the stake. One of these thieves stated that he had been a prisoner at Fort Scott; that he took the oath, put it in his pocket, and then stole two United States mules and a wagon, and returned to his home in McDonald County, Missouri, under protection of the oath. After conversing a short time with the bushwhackers, Lieutenant Kelso made an agreement with them that he and they would jayhawk and collect 100 head of cattle and drive them to the Southern army and sell them, and he and they went out and actually gathered in a few before he reported himself to me at midnight.

The scout was out about thirty hours, and traveled 60 miles, without loss or accident of any kind.

OZIAS RUARK,
Captain Company L, Eighth Missouri State Militia Cavalry.

Capt. MILTON BURCH,
Commanding Post Neosho, Mo.

APRIL 25, 1863.—Skirmish at Webber's Falls, Ind. T.

Reports of Col. William A. Phillips, Commanding Indian Brigade.

FORT GIBSON, C. N.,
April 26, 1863. (Received May 6.)

SIR: Crossed the Arkansas River on the night of the 24th, and marched 30 miles in the night, and at daylight struck the rebels of

Stand Watie's command near Webber's Falls; routed and broke them up, killing a number and taking prisoners; took the equipage, &c., that they had. Lost 2 killed.

Regret to announce the death of Dr. Gillpatrick, who was basely slain by a small force of the dispersed rebels that came out of the cane. Dr. Gillpatrick had gone to dress the wounds of a rebel soldier.

By a proclamation issued, the rebel Cherokee Legislature was to meet on the 25th, at Webber's Falls. Prevented, and dispersed with the rebel forces.

General Cooper has sent his adjutant, under flag of truce, to negotiate for exchange of prisoners.

Sent a heavy scout, with howitzers, under Major Foreman, to scout the Lee's Creek road and up toward Fayetteville, to watch toward Van Buren, and to prevent any force moving up east of this until Colonel Harrison moves.

Respectfully,

WM. A. PHILLIPS.

Maj. Gen. SAMUEL R. CURTIS,
Saint Louis, Mo.

(Received May 9, 1863.)

GENERAL: Ascertained that the rebel loss at Webber's Falls was much heavier than first reported. Two rebel captains killed. Crossed the Arkansas River 30 miles below Gibson, after the fight, and marched toward Evansville, where the rebel force was said to be. Rebels had precipitately retreated to Fort Smith on the news of Webber's Falls affair. Got dispatches. Learned of the evacuation of Fayetteville. Under your orders, demolished the works at Hildebrand's Mill, and have concentrated the force at Gibson. Here I have a strong work which cannot be taken by any force or artillery the enemy can bring to bear on it. It is on a commanding hill, with rear bluffs, on Grand River; water from river within lines; incloses 15 acres; defensible now, but needs much more work—a line of works, with angles and facings, over 1 mile in length, built by Indian soldiers. My rear is up Grand River Valley. The enemy has not transportation, and cannot subsist here so as to give a long siege. If hard pressed, I can retreat northwest, carrying a pursuing foe through a desolate country, where he might be taken in the flank.

I do not think the enemy can menace me with a heavy force for two or three weeks yet. It would be ruinous to the Government cause, as well as to these people, to abandon the country. As my orders permit me to remain, I shall maintain my ground at all hazards. I can send out heavy scouts of mounted men to strike the enemy in front and guard my rear from cavalry scouts, and hold the work with the remainder.

I shall strike wherever I can, as the best defense. The enemy was a good deal dispirited and demoralized by Webber's Falls, and if I can strike them again, I can keep them south of the Arkansas River until the army moves.

WM. A. PHILLIPS,
Colonel.

Major-General CURTIS.

HEADQUARTERS,
Fort Gibson, Ind. T., May 9, 1863.

SIR: For fear of accident to my last dispatches, I recapitulate briefly.

On the 25th ultimo we marched across the river and routed the enemy at Webber's Falls after a 30 miles' night march, besides fording the river.

After the fight was over, Dr. Gillpatrick, I regret to say, was killed (assassinated) while going to dress the wounds of a rebel soldier. His loss is a heavy one, as I trusted much in his judgment and fearless activity.

I sent 800 men and three guns into Arkansas, under Colonel [Frederick W.] Schaurte and Major Foreman. Those of the enemy on this side had fled over the river after the affair at Webber's Falls. They burned up the boats from here to Van Buren.

Colonel [R. P.] Crump, of Texas, with a command of Texans, arrived at Fort Smith last Friday.

Cooper and Steele are doing all they can to organize the Indian rebel forces.

I recrossed the river at Webber's Falls while it was deep fording, and rising rapidly; since then past all fording. Good boating stage at this point.

Have heard nothing of Colonel Harrison since he left Fayetteville. My army is suffering for bread. I have been able to issue none to the people since the last train came. The agent has done nothing for them. He consumed the stock in hand I had accumulated from Arkansas before I moved in, making me depend on the trains. It seems impossible to get supplies promptly from Fort Scott, or in sufficient quantities.

A very fine fortification (earthwork) has been thrown up on the hill just above and close to Fort Gibson. The lines of works are about $1\frac{1}{4}$ miles long.

The Indian soldiers have worked splendidly. I had about every man on duty, either working or scouting.

The fort could not be taken by 20,000 men, garrisoned by this command. It rests on the bluff close to Grand River, affording ample water, and I have four ferry-boats under its lee.

Very respectfully, your obedient servant,

WM. A. PHILLIPS,
Colonel, Commanding

Major-General BLUNT.

MAY 1, 1863.—Skirmish at La Grange, Ark.

Report of Capt. J. Q. A. De Huff, Third Iowa Cavalry.

HELENA, ARK., *May* 2, 1863.

SIR: I have the honor to report to you that yesterday morning, in pursuance of the orders of my commanding officer, I reported with 160 men of this regiment to General Gorman for instructions, and by him was directed to proceed to the neighborhood of La Grange and endeavor to learn the movements, if any, of the enemy. General Gorman himself accompanied my command beyond the pickets of the new Saint Francis road, as far as Mrs. Turner's plantation. I left him at about 9.30 a. m., and proceeded toward La Grange, keeping my advance guard in view, and with flanking parties on either hand. In this manner I had approached within a mile of the town of La Grange, along the main road, when my advance guard came upon the enemy, posted, on foot, in the woods on either side of the road, to the number, as I soon learned, of at least 300. I deployed my columns in squadrons to the right and left, and commenced a vigorous attack upon the enemy. My men behaved with great coolness, and their fire soon caused their lines in our front to waver. The fire on my front had been in successive volleys, but was now perceptibly slacking.

At this juncture, and at the moment I was about to charge in line, another force of at least 300 of the enemy, mounted, fell upon my rear and right flank, the enemy charging and delivering their fire by platoons.

This movement threw my force, now so greatly outnumbered, into some confusion, and the enemy rallied again on my front. My force had expended their revolvers, and most of their carbine fire, and it became evident that I must retire or be completely overwhelmed. I got my men into column, and directed them to the left, falling back through the timber a distance of some 3 miles.

The enemy pursued with vigor, but were kept in fear of too near approach by the firing of the reloaded carbines of my rear guard. Some of my men were also able to reload their revolvers and discharge them at the enemy.

Making a circuit, I again came to the La Grange road, to the rear of the place of attack about 4 miles. My men had become somewhat scattered, and on coming into the La Grange road I retired toward Helena, until re-enforced by the remainder of the regiment and the Fifth Kansas Cavalry. We then advanced to the place of conflict, and found that the enemy had fled, taking with them their dead and wounded.

The loss on our side was 3 killed, 8 wounded, and 30 missing, probably taken prisoners; total, 41.

Among the wounded are Regimental Adjt. Glenn Lowe and Second Lieut. Cornelius A. Stanton, Company I. A list of the names of the officers and men killed, wounded, and missing accompanies this report.

My advance guard, 29 men of Company D, under command of Lieutenant [William C.] Niblack, deserve particular notice for the manly stand they made against the enemy, whose hottest fire they withstood with the most determined bravery. Lieutenant Stanton was at the head of the column, and fearlessly assailed the enemy with his command, Company I. He was wounded in his left arm, very severely, early in the engagement, and from the loss of blood was compelled to retire from the field. Adjt. Glenn Lowe was also at the head of the column, and, throughout this uneven contest, displayed a heroism of unusual character. His horse was shot from under him as soon as he came up with the enemy. He at once mounted another, and as the attack in the rear commenced, he drew his saber and encouraged our men with his voice. At this time he was shot through the ankle and afterward fell into the hands of the enemy, who treated him with kindness, and left him at a neighboring house without paroling him.

Sergeant Breeding, Company A, and Corporal Birdsall, Company B, attacked a party of the enemy who had 5 prisoners, and, killing 2 of them, released our men, who thus escaped.

Many minor skirmishes took place during our retreat, in all of which a continual resistance was made with fatal effect to the enemy. I do not desire to give particular praise when all did as well as men could do against such odds, and I have only to regret my force was not greater. With the valor of my men I am satisfied. The loss inflicted upon the enemy was not less than 40 men killed and wounded. Many of their dead were seen upon the field.

J. Q. A. DE HUFF,
Captain Company B, Commanding.

Col. CYRUS BUSSEY,
Comdg. Second Cavalry Division, Army of the Tennessee.

MAY 3-11, 1863.—Scout in Cass and Bates Counties, Mo.

Report of Col. Edward Lynde, Ninth Kansas Cavalry.

PAOLA, *May* 11, 1863.

SIR: I have the honor to report that, on the 3d instant, I left camp with small detachments from Companies A, D, E, F, and K, of this regiment, for a scout in Cass and Bates Counties, Missouri. I scoured Cass County and found no enemy; then turned into Bates County, and when about 10 miles north of Butler received your letter of instructions, dated Fort Leavenworth, ——— —, 1863; also your letter dated Fort Leavenworth, May 5, directing Company D, Captain [Charles F.] Coleman, to move his company from Rockville to Butler, Mo., which was immediately complied with. I moved on to the Osage, intending to cross to Hog Island, but found the river too high, and did not cross; then turned east, and on the morning of the 8th, on Double Branches, found a gang of bushwhackers, under Jackman and Marchbanks, Quantrill having left on the night of the 6th instant for Henry County, Missouri, with 40 men. We found Jackman and Marchbanks with about 20 men, who fled by ones and twos, and then escaped, except 7, who were reported killed by my soldiers. I found county rapidly filling up by bushwhackers' families, who are returning from the South under the impression that Price is coming up, and had again taken possession, with their stock. This stream, called the Double Branches, is their rendezvous, and has been since the outbreak of this rebellion; but four loyal families live on it, and they are doubtful. About fifty or sixty families inhabit that country bordering on that stream. I notified them to leave and go south of the Arkansas River. A great part of them positively refused. I burned eleven houses, inhabited by bushwhackers' families, and drove off all the stock except that belonging to the reported loyal persons. We broke up four camps of bushwhackers and pursued them to the eastern side of Bates County. I think for the present no danger need be apprehended from that quarter. I will keep a close watch, for I am satisfied they intend to organize a force somewhere in that country; I think in Henry County.

The stock we took consists of a few yoke of oxen, mares and colts, young horses one and two years old, cows and calves, and young cattle; in all about 350 head; also about 300 sheep. I believe it all to be property of bushwhackers and rebel sympathizers. In view of the fact that pasture is scarce at Kansas City and plenty here, and the stock the kind our Kansas farmers would like to buy, and some of it may be proved away, I most respectfully ask for an order that will authorize the sale of it at this place.

Permit me to ask the question, How am I to send the rebel sympathizers and female rebels, who are plentiful where I have been for the last ten days, south of the Arkansas River, particularly those who have no way to go and those who refuse to go? I can see no way except to gather them all up and send them in a Government train, and reimburse the Government by selling their stock.

Company C, Captain [John E.] Stewart, has not yet reported at Olathe. Scouting parties are constantly moving from the different counties. Can I have your consent to go into the counties of Henry and Saline on our next scout, if I find no enemy in the border counties, or if they run into those counties?

I am, sir, respectfully, your obedient servant,

E. LYNDE,
Colonel, Commanding.

Capt. H. G. LORING,
Acting Assistant Adjutant-General.

MAY 4, 1863.—Operations about Lexington, Mo.

Report of Lieut. Col. Walter King, Fourth Missouri State Militia Cavalry.

HEADQUARTERS, *Lexington, May* 5, 1863.

GENERAL: I have the honor to report that Captain Morris returned last evening from the Wellington neighborhood, bringing 27 prisoners, and having in other respects carried out orders (copy sent you yesterday). Another officer goes into that section to-day with similar orders. On last night the same four thieves visited Wellington, and robbed the post-office and cut the telegraph wire.

As I finished the foregoing sentence, your letter of the 3d was handed me.

I have no information or belief that the party in Wellington exceeded 4 or 6. I do not think that there were any guerrillas outside the town. The 4 or 5 who were at the boat would have robbed it, but were restrained by the earnest representations of one Chancellor, a resident, who told them what certain fate would overtake the people of that place if they did harm to that boat. They accordingly desisted by sending one man up the stairway for a can of whisky and some cigars, &c., which I expect was in the way of a treat for their desisting. "Fifty or sixty" are liable to come there at any time from Quantrill's old grounds, on the Blue; but there are no reasons to believe other than I have now stated. I have talked with 4 or 5 men who saw the party that night, and some as late as an hour after sunrise next day. There were 4 of them. They went into the Upper Missouri Bottom that night; were seen with cigars and lemons about daybreak at Totetes, above Wellington, and an hour by sun they were seen on the Lone Jack road, going south. I have sent farther out to arrest other parties.

The result of my order yesterday, closing out all men in the city who are not friendly to the Government, and the subsequent meeting, I look to as the inception of a genuine reformation in this county. After the publication of the order, about 80 residents rushed to Ryland's office to sign the resolutions. But in the meeting they were excluded from participation in the meeting, and they are under arrest and their business closed, as yet. I stated in the meeting that in each case of those signing yesterday there would be special inquiry as to the motives of their signing so late. The meeting went off in fine spirit, and I assure you of my belief that much good will come of the movement. The resolutions were adopted by acclamation before the house crowded throughout.

An hour has elapsed since penning the foregoing paragraph, spent in interview with "John De Courcy," my most trusted spy, who reached here, and I gather the following: Quantrill is here; he came from Price to conscript; he came with 40 men; he has joined Reid's, Jarrett's, Todd's, Younger's, and Clifton's gangs to his own, which give him from 125 to 150 men; he disbanded his force on Sunday night, with orders to rendezvous on Thursday night on the Big Sni, precise place not definitely learned; has orders from Price to stop bushwhacking and horse stealing. Price is to invade Southeast Missouri, and Quantrill is to annoy Kansas and Western Missouri; intends to conscript all of military age; has secret notice among Southern men to come to his camp and get property taken by mistake; came here to stay, and not to take away any recruits; seems to be rather elevated in his purposes by his six or eight months' experience with the regular forces; proposes that he will not assail McF.'s men unless assaulted, but that he neither will give or expect quarter of K.'s or P.'s men.

I shall send a man into Quantrill's camp.

"De Courcy" informs me that one of the men (Wise) I have here, taken yesterday at Wellington, is an arrant guerrilla. I put him in irons to-day. Mail hour is past some minutes. I'll write to-morrow.

Very respectfully, your obedient servant,

WALTER KING,
Lieutenant-Colonel.

MAY 5-9, 1863.—Scout from Fort Scott, Kans., to Sherwood, Mo., and skirmishes.

Report of Maj. Charles W. Blair, Second Kansas Cavalry.

HEADQUARTERS, *Fort Scott, Kans., May* 9, 1863.

GENERAL: I have the honor to inform you that on Tuesday last, having heard that a rebel camp was established on Centre Creek, Mo., near the town of Sherwood, about 60 miles distant from this post, I dispatched Adjt. M. M. Ehle with a detachment of about 60 men to attack and disperse them, and bring back the stolen and contraband stock which I was informed they had gathered there in a very considerable amount.

By forced marches he got to the south of them, and, learning from his scouts that they numbered from 200 to 300, he applied to Colonel [J. M.] Williams, First Kansas (colored) Volunteers, for assistance, who promptly re-enforced him with two companies and one gun, of Blair's battery, under Lieutenant [Daniel C.] Knowles. With this added force, he attacked the enemy at daybreak, carrying the camp in gallant style and dispersing the rebels in every direction. He subsequently attacked and took another camp nearer the town and dispersed its occupants. Some few prisoners were taken, and about 50 head of young horses and mules, part of which, with the prisoners, were delivered over to Colonel Williams, and the residue, being the greater part thereof, were turned over to Capt. M. H. Insley, assistant quartermaster, at this post, upon their arrival here to-day.

This has been a most successful scout, and a very profitable capture to the Government. Great credit is due to the sagacity, persistence, and judgment manifested by Adjutant Ehle in the management of the whole affair. He conducted the whole scout himself, and is entitled to all the credit. It was well planned, maturely considered, and executed with rapidity, precision, and skill. I do not know that I can find a better opportunity of calling your attention to a brave and deserving officer. Since he has been associated with me I have found him able, capable, faithful, industrious, and energetic, and always at his post. In the execution of his duty he is one of the most promising and efficient young officers of the district, and well worthy of a higher rank and a broader field for the exercise of his capabilities.

I have the honor to be, general, very respectfully, your obedient servant,

CHAS. W. BLAIR,
Major Second Kansas Volunteers, Commanding Post.

Maj. Gen. JAMES G. BLUNT,
Commanding District of Kansas.

MAY 6-19, 1863.—Scout from Creek Agency, Ind. T., to Jasper County, Mo., including skirmishes at Martin's House, Centre Creek, and near Sherwood, and destruction of Sherwood.

REPORTS.*

No. 1.—Maj. T. R. Livingston, C. S. Army.

No. 2.—Lieut. Edward A. Smith, Second Kansas Battery, of skirmish near Sherwood, and affair (June 8) near Fort Scott.

No. 1.

Report of Maj. T. R. Livingston, C. S. Army.

DIAMOND GROVE, JASPER COUNTY, MO.,
May 28, 1863.

GENERAL: I left the Creek Agency on the 6th of May, *en route* for Missouri; crossed the Verdigris River at Sandtown; camped one day at the Union Saline Works, and from thence up the Texas road. At the house of Captain Martin, on Cabin Creek, met a scout of the enemy from Fort Scott. I immediately engaged him, killing 1 and wounding 1. He then took shelter in and around the houses. I endeavored to draw them out, but without success. He was soon re-enforced by a company of cavalry from Fort Gibson. I then retired to Cary's Gap and camped for the night. My loss was 3 men slightly wounded.

The following morning [9th?] I took up the line of march for Southwest Missouri, and arrived in Jasper County without any incidents worthy of note.

On the 15th of May, as I was crossing the timber of Centre Creek, about 10 miles southwest of Carthage, I encountered a scout of the enemy, consisting of 125 Newtonia militia. I immediately got my men in position to receive an assault from him, whom I vigorously repulsed. I charged upon him, Captain Estes commanding the left, Captain McCullough the center, and Captain Rusk a flanking party on the right. A sharp firing ensued; the enemy were soon flying before us, being completely put to rout. I pursued him about 3 miles. The enemy lost in

* See also May 13-18, 1863.—Scout from Newtonia to French Point and Centre Creek, Mo., &c., p. 328.

killed, 13; mortally wounded, 4; prisoners, 4. My loss, killed, none; wounded, Captain Estes, slightly in the arm; Captain McCullough, slightly stunned from the fall of his horse that was shot under him. I then retired to Twin Groves, about 3 miles distant.

The next day [16th] the enemy re-enforced to about 400. I moved on Spring River, but was not pursued.

On the 18th, my scouts reported 60 negroes and white men, belonging to Colonel [J. M.] Williams' negro regiment, with five six-mule teams, foraging on Centre Creek Prairie. I ordered out 67 of my best mounted men. I came upon them at Mrs. Rador's, pillaging her premises. I afterward learned that they were ordered not to take more plunder than they could take with them. I charged them at the house, flanking them on the right, routed them, and pursued them about 8 miles, to the crossing of Spring River.

The enemy's loss in killed was, negroes, 23, and 7 white men; wounded, unknown; and — prisoners; also captured 30 mules and 5 wagons; a box containing 1,400 cartridges and caps; a good many guns, pistols, &c. The prisoners I have subsequently exchanged for Confederate soldiers. I sustained no loss. The following day (19th) they returned with 300 infantry and two companies of cavalry and burned the town of Sherwood and eleven farm-houses in the vicinity. They put 10 of their dead (negroes) that had been left on the battle-ground the day preceding, and, together with the body of Mr. John Bishop, a citizen prisoner, whom they had murdered, into the house of Mrs. Rador, and burned the premises. They then returned to their camp at Baxter Springs.

With great respect, I am, your obedient servant,

T. R. LIVINGSTON,
Major, Commanding Confederate Forces.

Maj. Gen. STERLING PRICE, *C. S. Army.*

P. S.—Captain Estes and I were both slightly wounded in the last fight.

No. 2.

Report of Lieut. Edward A. Smith, Second Kansas Battery, of skirmish near Sherwood, and affair (June 8) near Fort Scott.

FORT SCOTT, KANS., *June* 30, 1863.

SIR: In accordance with Paragraph I, General Orders, No. 169, of 1862, Adjutant-General's Office, I have the honor to report as follows:

On the 18th day of May, 1863, a foraging party from the camp of Colonel [James M.] Williams, First Colored Volunteers, Baxter Springs, Kans., consisting in part of men belonging to my battery, was attacked in the vicinity of Sherwood, Mo., by a party of rebel guerrillas, and Corpl. Van Rensler Hancock, Private Joseph Endecott, and Private Cameron Garrett were killed. On the 8th day of June, 1863, the same rebel guerrillas attacked the herd grazing, and Private Arthur W. Gaines was killed, and Corpl. Thomas Larkin, and Private James Martin were taken prisoners.

Very respectfully, &c.,

E. A. SMITH,
First Lieutenant, Commanding Second Kansas Battery.

Maj. H. Z. CURTIS,
Assistant Adjutant-General, District of the Frontier.

MAY 9, 1863.—Skirmish in Stone County, Mo.

Report of Col. William F. Cloud.

SPRINGFIELD, *May* 16, 1863.

GENERAL: Captain Moore, of the Second Provisional Regiment Enrolled Missouri Militia, reports that on last Saturday a scout of 9 men of his company came upon a party of bushwhackers in Stone County, reported to be 50 in number, who were going south with stock that they had stolen from farmers in this district, and, after a brisk fight, in which 2 of the bushwhackers were killed, 3 severely wounded and left upon the field, and 4 captured, the chivalry decamped, leaving 31 head of horses and mules, blankets, overcoats, and other property, which fell into the hands of the Enrolled Missouri Militia, to be returned to the proper owners.

W. F. CLOUD,
Colonel, Commanding District of Southwestern Missouri.

Major-General CURTIS, *Saint Louis, Mo.*

MAY 11, 1863.—Skirmish at Taylor's Creek, or Crowley's Ridge, Ark.

REPORTS.

No. 1.—Abstract from "Record of Events," Second Cavalry Brigade, Thirteenth Army Corps.
No. 2.—Brig. Gen. John S. Marmaduke, C. S. Army.
No. 3.—Col. George W. Carter, Twenty-first Texas Cavalry.

No. 1.

*Abstract from "Record of Events," Second Cavalry Brigade, Thirteenth Army Corps.**

May 6, a scout of 1,200 cavalry of this command scoured the country between White and Saint Francis Rivers, being absent ten days. During that time, having divided, they fell in with Marmaduke's forces on L'Anguille River at two points, and, after a severe fight, retreated, losing 1 killed and 4 wounded of the First Indiana Cavalry. Among the wounded are Lieuts. W. C. Wilhelm and Charles Denaman. Enemy estimated at 6,000.

No. 2.

Report of Brig. Gen. John S. Marmaduke, C. S. Army.

HEADQUARTERS MARMADUKE'S DIVISION,
Jacksonport, Ark., May 24, 1863.

MAJOR: I have the honor to submit herewith a report of the skirmish with the Federal forces on Crowley's Ridge.

On April [May] 9, I received from Colonel [George W.] Carter information that a Federal force of 1,500 or 2,000 men (infantry, cavalry,

---

* From return for month of May, 1863.

and artillery) were marching from Helena toward Cotton Plant, either to capture [Arch. S.] Dobbin's regiment or destroy supplies at Cotton Plant. I supposed the enemy's movements were really intended to attack Dobbin's troops in the field or destroy his trains, which were on the east side of L'Anguille. I immediately dispatched a courier to Colonel Carter, commanding cavalry on Crowley's Ridge, not to cross the L'Anguille, but let the enemy cross the L'Anguille to him, and attack them as far as possible from Helena, and on the east side of the L'Anguille.

At 2 p. m. on the 10th, with Captain [Thomas C.] Newton and a guide, I started for Carter's headquarters, and joined him near Mr. Croper's, on Crowley's Ridge, 7 miles from Wittsburg, on the Batesville and Memphis road.

This was about 3 p. m. on the 11th. Carter's forces were then on the march toward Seaburn's Bridge. He informed me that his information from Dobbin was that the enemy (infantry, cavalry, and artillery) was about 1,800 men, with six pieces of artillery; that they had encamped at Sweitzer's on the night of the 10th, and were marching to cross the L'Anguille at Seaburn's Bridge. Carter had sent a scout to the bridge, who at sunset reported the enemy as having crossed Seaburn's Bridge in force, and had encamped at Taylor's Creek, 4 miles east of the bridge. I advised Carter to dispatch immediately to Dobbin (who was near Hughs' Ferry, on the L'Anguille, and 25 miles below Seaburn's Bridge) to move his command with all possible dispatch up the L'Anguille on west side to Seaburn's Bridge; attack the enemy in rear; cross the bridge if the enemy had passed; destroy the bridge, and fall upon the enemy's rear. At the same time Carter would attack them in front. This order was written by Colonel Carter and sent to Dobbin by a staff officer. Colonel Carter reported to me that his strength was as follows: Of his brigade, about 900 cavalry and Pratt's battery (four pieces); [Colton] Greene's brigade, 500 mounted men, and two mountain pieces of artillery. I advised Carter also to order up immediately from the several camps (where his wagons were) all his armed men, mounted and dismounted, also Lieutenant-Colonel Chrisman (who was at Dobbin's wagon camp), with all of Dobbin's armed men. Dobbin reported to Carter that his force in the field was 500 or 600 men. From the best information I could get, I presumed the Federal force was not less than 1,500, and not exceeding 2,000, with four to six pieces of artillery. This information was based upon Dobbin's positive reports to Carter. Carter's column encamped on the night of the 10th 4 miles from Taylor's Creek, a little town. This camp I reached about midnight.

A little after sun-up, the column moved against the enemy, and, between 9 and 10 o'clock on the 12th, Carter's advance (about half a mile ahead of the main column) engaged the enemy at Taylor's Creek, and were driven back by them. I was between the advance and the main column. The officer in the advance dispatched that he had engaged the enemy (cavalry, infantry, and artillery). I presumed that their whole force was there, and had every reason to believe so. I moved upon the enemy at the hour I did, that Dobbin might have further time to get into position, be ready for a simultaneous attack, destroy the bridge, and insure the enemy's capture. As soon as the advance was engaged, two pieces of artillery were ordered forward to support it and resist the enemy, who were advancing. At the same time I ordered all the other troops, except [D. C.] Giddings' Texas regiment, to dismount and form for battle. The whole was done with dispatch. The indications then were that the enemy knew of the forced movement, and were moving upon me. As soon as my troops were dismounted and formed in line of battle, I pushed forward cavalry to feel them and bring on the engagement. A brisk fight ensued between the advance. On both sides the troops fought mounted and dismounted, and with artillery. The enemy's force engaged returned in the direction of Seaburn's Bridge. Lieutenant-Colonel [M. L.] Young's battalion pursued and engaged them near and at this point, which they reached about 10 a. m.

During this time I learned that a large body of cavalry, variously estimated from 600 to 1,200, had moved to my left on the Madison road, which was down the L'Anguille, and had not participated in the fight, having moved out one [hour] before it, and was perhaps some 5 miles distant. I presumed the artillery firing would be heard by them, and they would make an attempt to return. I therefore ordered Carter's brigade to move to my left and thwart this movement by taking up a position on the Madison road, some 3 miles distant. I now had the enemy separated; one force moving down the L'Anguille on the Madison road—no outlet except to swim the L'Anguille or Saint Francis, or by a by-road to slip up the L'Anguille to Seaburn's Bridge—the other had retreated to the bridge, or rather to within half a mile of the bridge, where he was engaged by Young with his brave little battalion and two pieces of Greene's artillery. I immediately ordered Carter, with 700 men and two pieces of Pratt's battery, to pursue the force moving down the L'Anguille on Madison road. The rest of his brigade, with Greene's, I ordered to move down to Taylor's Creek. About the time the troops had reached Taylor's Creek, I received a dispatch from Colonel Young, who had been fighting the enemy, both using their men mounted and dismounted, and also their artillery, reporting that the enemy were in strong force, and were advancing upon him. I now presumed I had to fight the heaviest column, composed of infantry, artillery, and cavalry.

As yet I had heard not a word from Dobbin. Again, as Dobbin had made no attack in rear, had not answered my attack in front, and had not communicated with me, I feared that he had not received Carter's orders, or had been prevented by superior force from executing the orders given. At the same time I presumed, as the enemy made every demonstration of battle at the bridge, they deemed the force strong enough to give battle. I was impressed with this belief by a dispatch from Colonel Young, saying that the force which Carter was ordered to pursue had come in by a path up the L'Anguille. Upon this information from Young, I dispatched to Carter that the force he was pursuing had reached Seaburn's Bridge, and to return immediately. Carter obeyed the order, and had returned about 1 mile, when he was positively informed that my information was incorrect; that the force he was pursuing was 5 miles below him, burning and pillaging. He immediately (and very properly) turned, and again continued his pursuit.

After putting all the forces I had (about 500 men) in position to fight the enemy, should they come against me, I went in person to the advance, where Young was, and satisfied myself that the force which Carter was pursuing had not come in; dispatched Carter to that effect, ordering him to continue the pursuit, and, after a careful reconnaissance, was convinced that the enemy's position was such that 500 men could not dislodge them without great loss, if at all; and even then they would have the bridge to retreat on. To have thrown my command upon the enemy, they holding an admirable position in a miry swamp of dense undergrowth and heavy timber, approached for three-quarters of a mile only by a causeway, which the enemy had torn up in places, and which they commanded with their artillery, would have been criminal, without a prompt and vigorous co-operation from Dobbin in rear. Two or more demonstrations had been made upon them, and no answer of co-operation from the rear was given. As yet their force was not known; it was supposed to be even stronger in numbers than my own.

At 3.30 p. m. I received a dispatch from Colonel Dobbin saying he was near the bridge. I immediately dispatched back to burn the bridge, if possible, and, at all hazards, to prevent the enemy from retreating, and advising him to come and see me, if he could leave his command in good hands for that time (two and a half hours). He reported to me at a little after sunset, and immediately started on his return.

After Dobbin had communicated, and the actual strength of the enemy was known, and before a prompt co-operation from Dobbin could begin, there was not sufficient time before dark to make the attack. I therefore determined to attack at daylight. The enemy had but two ways to make his escape—across the bridge and toward Helena, in the face of Dobbin's force, or in the direction of my force. Colonel Dobbin informed me that his strength was 450 armed men. I put about one-half of my command on guard to watch the enemy to prevent his escape. The rest slept on their arms, ready at a moment's call.

The enemy, about dark, crossed the bridge and passed on the road which Dobbin's command was specially ordered to guard, and had retreated at least 16 miles before Colonel Dobbin's command informed me of their retreat. No resistance was made to them, and, indeed, the courier who brought me the intelligence reported that nothing was known of their retreat till the enemy had passed upon the road some 8 miles, and that they were going rapidly. This sentinel had to return 8 miles to bring me this intelligence. Had proper spirit and proper vigilance been displayed by Dobbin's command, the whole force would, undoubtedly, have been captured. The enemy, having fresh and far superior horses, with at least 16 miles' advantage, rendered pursuit useless.

Carter pursued the enemy, and, about sunset, encountered them. After a few desperate charges upon them (a part of them ambuscaded), in which he killed a number and lost himself some valuable officers and men killed and wounded, drove them from their position. Night coming on, and by the advice of his senior officers, who reported both men and horses exhausted, he halted his column for a few hours to feed and rest. During this time the enemy moved rapidly to Hughs' Ferry and crossed.

A more detailed report of Colonel Carter's operations will be found in his accompanying report.

The force (cavalry) which Carter pursued was about 900; no artillery. The force at Seaburn's Bridge was about 350 and two pieces of artillery. Had Dobbin's command fallen upon the rear of the enemy, or even destroyed the bridge, the 350 cavalry and two pieces of artillery would certainly have been captured, and that whole force could have been turned against the other column, which also should have been destroyed or captured. The failure deserves investigation and the punishment of the incompetent party.

Very respectfully,

J. S. MARMADUKE,
Brigadier-General, Commanding.

Maj. W. B. BLAIR,
Acting Assistant Adjutant-General, District of Arkansas.

No. 3.

Report of Col. George W. Carter, Twenty-first Texas Cavalry.

COLONEL GRAHAM'S,
May 15, 1863—6 p. m.

GENERAL: Have received reports from all my pickets and scouts. The enemy went direct to Helena, and has made no movement in any direction. The scouts report only 3,000 men there, all told. I have ordered Dobbin to rendezvous near the Saint Francis, on the Military road (2 miles from Saint Francis). There are 2,000 bushels of corn there and plenty of water. I have ordered Greene to keep his headquarters near Colonel Cross', and to consume all the forage in that vicinity. I have ordered Carter's brigade into camp, between Military road and Colonel Graham's place. Have ordered Young's battalion to picket and guard Seaburn's Bridge; I am afraid to trust Dobbin there; besides, Dobbin still has some cases of small-pox, and I want to separate him from the other commands. I furnish from Carter's command the pickets for Saint Francis and L'Anguille; from Greene, pickets above Harrisburg, and two lines of couriers, and at bridge. Have sent a select scout of my own men to Helena; will get report to-morrow. The couriers to Newport will bring papers to-morrow night, I hope. Lieutenant [D. A. T.] Walton reports that Dobbin reached the bridge time enough to have destroyed it, and subsequently reached Hughs' Ferry before the enemy had crossed, but would not fight at either point. I shall order a report on these points, and forward them to you. I will forward to-morrow my report of the movements of my command on the day of the fight. Lieutenant [William B.] McGehee and Private Benton have died of their wounds. Lieutenant Anderson is sinking rapidly; also Lieutenant [Wellington] Triplett. The other wounded, including Captains [M. M.] Kenney and Hosbrook, are doing well, and have some prospect of recovering. Have put all the shops to work shoeing horses; have sent detail to [work] upon road and repair bridge. Have ordered [S. G.] Kitchen to establish line of couriers to Greene's camp. Have taken all precautions to prevent spread of small-pox. Shall start to-morrow to visit my whole line of pickets. Will now give you the news:

Lee's report or dispatch to President Davis of the battle of Fredericksburg has been received. He reports a glorious victory, stating that our loss was comparatively small, and the enemy's was 30,000 or 35,000 killed and wounded. This does not embrace Stoneman's command, which is believed to have been captured. The Memphis papers also state that on the 9th and 10th Johnston had attacked Rosecrans' re-enforcements from Kentucky, near Shelbyville, and had destroyed them, and then attacked and routed Rosecrans, who retreated in great confusion to Nashville. This item comes by way of both Helena and Memphis, and is brought by Mr. Harris, of Louisiana, a friend of mine, who took the paper to Little Rock yesterday. A fight also at Vicksburg. There are two versions of the Vicksburg fight—one from Memphis and the other from Helena. The first states that the enemy had gotten in the rear of Vicksburg, and that we had been largely re-enforced from Mobile and Port Gibson, and were confident of whipping him, and that he was then striving to get back to the river. The second report is that three or four of our batteries were taken, and 700 men captured, but when the boats and transports moved upon the others we received them, killing and wounding 14,000, and taking a great many prisoners. The reports of Fredericksburg and Murfreesborough are true, I believe, but I don't know about the last. I will send you papers as soon as they come.

The number of my sick is on the increase; they are greatly damaged by our late expedition, but, I hope, will be rested and well again.

I am, general, very truly,

G. W. CARTER,
Colonel, Commanding Cavalry, Marmaduke's Division.

Brigadier-General MARMADUKE.

MAY 13-18, 1863.—Scout from Newtonia to French Point and Centre Creek, Mo., and skirmishes.

REPORTS.*

No. 1.—Lieut. Col. Thomas T. Crittenden, Eighth Missouri State Militia Cavalry.
No. 2.—Maj. Edward B. Eno, Eighth Missouri State Militia Cavalry.

No. 1.

Reports of Lieut. Col. Thomas T. Crittenden, Eighth Missouri State Militia Cavalry.

NEWTONIA, *May* 18, 1863.

COLONEL: Major Eno came in this evening, after a scout of five days. Divided his force, of 200 men, into three divisions, under himself, Captain Ballew, of Company I, Seventh Missouri State Militia Cavalry, and Captain Henslee, of Company L, Seventh Missouri State Militia Cavalry. The latter, in conjunction with Captain Cassairt, of Company I, Eighth Missouri State Militia Cavalry, with 60 men in all, moved down Centre Creek; found Livingston near the Centre Creek lead mines, strongly posted behind densely thick brush and an old shop, with 100 splendidly armed guerrillas. Attacked them vigorously; drove them from the bush; killed 7; wounded many others badly. One captain, 1 lieutenant, and Colonel Harrison are believed to have been killed. I lost 4 killed and 2 wounded, slightly.

After the fight, Major Eno, Captains Henslee and Cassairt joined their forces, and entirely scattered the rebels, by active chasing.

Ballew, in consequence of misunderstanding, became entirely separated—was not engaged. Colonel, the officers and soldiers behaved very gallantly in this fight. Major Eno is a vigorous, energetic officer. Livingston had 200 men under him, in Jasper County, a few days ago. His force is increasing rapidly. A large force, under Coffee & Co., are gathering in Jasper County, to attack this post, as currently believed by friend and foe. I will fight them. Will send tri-monthly report.

T. T. CRITTENDEN,
Lieutenant-Colonel, Commanding Post.

Col. WILLIAM F. CLOUD,
Commanding District of Southwest Missouri.

---

* See also May 6-19, 1863, p. 321.

NEWTONIA, MO., *May* 20, 1863.

SIR: Since I made my report to Colonel Cloud of the result of the fight between Captain Henslee, of Company L, of the Seventh Missouri State Militia Cavalry, and Captain [Jacob] Cassairt, of Company F, of the Eighth Missouri State Militia Cavalry, with about 70 men, and Livingston, rebel guerrilla, with 100 men, near Centre Creek lead mines, a day or so ago, I have the most positive evidence that there were 15 killed upon Livingston's side, and several mortally wounded. I was informed by several ladies of his own stripe that Livingston buried 12 of his men in one grave—were present at the burial. It was a desperate bushwhacking fight; both sides were hand-to-hand in the brush for awhile. Captain Henslee's horse became very much frightened, and charged immediately through the rebel crew; it is supposed fifty guns were fired alone at him in his passage; escaped unhurt. He fired as he went through; killed 1; charged back again in order to save himself and killed another. All through the country much excitement prevails in regard to the fight. Major Eno is preparing an official account of the scout; will forward it. It was eminently successful, of which fact I am more and more convinced daily.

On yesterday I saw a private note that Tom. [R.] Livingston had written to a lady friend in Granby, in which he stated he would start in a few days for Franklin, on the Pacific road, in this State, and would deliver any letters she would write. Did not state whether going alone or going down on a raid. Well enough to watch his movements. There is but little doubt in my mind of Colonel Harrison's (of C. S. Army) death. If your order in regard to Major Eno's remaining here, and co-operating with you, had not come, I would have started before this the same scout after Livingston.

A quick succession of vigorous scouts will destroy and disperse them. Kill Livingston, and there is no one else to mass and congregate these bands. Is a man of much influence.

Have you had a scout toward Pineville?

Yours, very respectfully,

T. T. CRITTENDEN,
Lieutenant-Colonel, Commanding Post.

Lieut. J. C. FRENCH,
Acting Assistant Adjutant-General.

P. S.—Lieut. Anson A. McElhoney, of Company M, Missouri State Militia Cavalry, was detailed a few months since to take charge of the stragglers' (now convalescent) camp, which order I hope you will rescind, as he is very much needed in his company. James C. Anderson, of same company and regiment, is with him as clerk; send him also, if possible, as that company needs him. I am very solicitous about the return of these men.

No. 2.

Report of Maj. Edward B. Eno, Eighth Missouri State Militia Cavalry.

HDQRS. 1ST BATTALION, 8TH MO. STATE MILITIA CAV.,
Greenfield, Mo., May 29, 1863.

COLONEL: I have the honor herewith to submit report of operations of a scout under my command against Livingston's guerrillas.

On the morning of the 13th instant, I marched from Newtonia, by order of Lieutenant-Colonel [Thomas T.] Crittenden, commanding post, in command of 84 men of the Seventh Missouri State Militia Cavalry, and 100 of my own battalion. After proceeding 9 miles, Capt. Squire Ballew, Seventh Cavalry, with 50 men, was detached, with orders to proceed down Shoal Creek about 15 miles; thence pass over on to Turkey Creek, avoiding roads as much as possible, and driving the brush thoroughly, and to encamp that night in vicinity of Turkey Creek Mines; thence he was directed to pass down the creek to a point 3 miles below Sherwood; thence to move up Centre, while, with the remainder, I moved down from a point above, and to meet me at French Point some time next day, 14th instant, with the additional caution that I probably would not arrive until late in the afternoon. I moved with the balance of the command through the brush on to Jones' and Jenkins' Creeks, and divided the scout again so as to scour them both. No sign was discovered, and the command encamped that night on Centre Creek, 5 miles from Carthage. Captain Ballew encamped as directed.

On the morning of the 14th instant, I again divided the portion of the command with me, sending Captain Cassairt, of the Eighth Cavalry, with 40 men, down the south side of the creek; Captain [M. C.] Henslee, Seventh Cavalry, with 35 on the north side, while, with the remainder, I passed down the Centre. By this disposition I hoped, as the result proved, either to engage and surround the guerrillas with the three subdivisions of my own immediate command, or to drive them to French Point, where Captain Ballew should have been ready to engage them, while I advanced on their rear and either flank, in which event the capture or destruction of the entire gang was inevitable. About 3 p. m., Captain Henslee drove in their pickets on the north, and Captain Cassairt on the south, side of the creek. Captain Henslee followed the trail hotly, crossed the creek, and joined Captain Cassairt on the other side; thence both pushed on, found the guerrillas, about 100 strong, commanded by Livingston, strongly posted under cover of a log-house and dense brush. A severe fight ensued of some fifteen minutes' duration, when our men were obliged to fall back. This, I am confident, would not have occurred had not Captain Henslee been cut off from his command. At the first fire his horse became unmanageable and dashed clean through the rebel lines, leaving his men without a commander. Many of the guerrillas were dressed in Federal uniforms. Captain Cassairt's detachment mistook them for our men, and before discovering their mistake were right among them, had received a galling fire, and were fighting hand-to-hand.

Captain Henslee, who had been carried far beyond the ground, as soon as his horse could be checked, dashed back, and with the greatest coolness and daring approached within close pistol-shot of the rebels, fired, and killed 1 before wheeling to make his escape. Captain Cassairt exerted himself to the utmost to rally his men, and finally succeeded in gaining the front on the edge of the prairie; threatened to shoot the first man who dared to move another step in retreat; immediately formed, and commenced firing upon the enemy, who, in turn, retreated, carrying off his dead and wounded. When the firing commenced, the detachment with me was 2 miles distant up the creek. I immediately started at a gallop in the direction, but was not able to reach the ground until all was over. This was 4½ miles east of Sherwood and 1½ miles from French Point.

I pushed on immediately in pursuit, pressing them so hard as to compel them to leave their prisoners, whom I recaptured, and expecting every moment to hear Captain Ballew's guns attacking the enemy in his front as he approached French Point, which place he was obliged to pass in his retreat. The trail, as I anticipated, led directly through French Point, and the bank was still wet with the water carried out in Livingston's crossing, but Captain Ballew was not there. I regret to have to report that he had arrived, was waiting for me, his advance had fired upon Livingston's advance as the latter approached, when an escaped prisoner, frightened and bewildered, reported to him the fight a short time previous, and that the rebels were not far off, and Captain Ballew disobeyed my orders, retreated with his 50 men without waiting to see the enemy or engage him, never halting until night, thus leaving the path open for Livingston's retreat. Had Captain Ballew obeyed orders and stood his ground, there can be no question but Livingston and his fiendish gang would have been completely annihilated.

The command bivouacked the night of the 14th instant 3 miles above Sherwood. Captain Ballew encamped 12 miles from French Point, near Grove Creek.

On the morning of the 15th, his rear was fired on by a squad of bushwhackers, when he retreated back on to Centre Creek, passed round by Bower's Mills, 25 miles out of his way, and arrived at Newtonia at 9 o'clock the same night, having lost 2 men prisoners, who fell into the hands of the men that fired on him, and who report that the bushwhackers numbered 8.

On the morning of the 15th, I sent Captain Cassairt, with 30 men, to bury the dead and convey the wounded to Newtonia. With the remainder of the command I passed over on to Spring River, following Livingston's trail over the prairie, but, at a distance of 2 miles, the trail divided, and finally diverged in every direction, not more than 4 men having gone together. I passed down Spring River 5 miles, thence across again on to Centre Creek, when, for the next ten days, the command was kept moving slowly through the brush and over by-roads, crossing and recrossing the creek, and from the time of the first skirmish, on the 14th, until leaving the creek, on the 18th instant, we were almost continually fighting them, starting up scattered squads of from 4 to 10, chasing and firing on them, when they invariably dashed into the brush and concealed themselves, rendering it impossible—except in two instances, when men were overtaken and shot down—to ascertain whether they were hurt or not.

Our total loss on the scout is 4 killed and 2 wounded. The enemy's loss, reported by parties present at the burial, is 15 killed, a captain wounded, and 15 or 20 wounded, 1 mortally, at different points on the creek.

The following is a correct list of the killed and wounded of both battalions: Killed—Charles Crude, sergeant Company M, Seventh Missouri State Militia Cavalry, shot and stripped naked after having surrendered; Winster C. Donely, corporal Company M, Seventh Missouri State Militia Cavalry; Henry C. Maxey, sergeant Company L; and Horace Palmer, private Company F, Eighth Missouri State Militia Cavalry, killed after being taken. Wounded—John T. Anderson, corporal Company L, Seventh Missouri State Militia Cavalry; Samuel Beach, private Company F, Eighth Missouri State Militia Cavalry.

In justice to the memory of Private Palmer, I cannot forbear mentioning that when the retreat from the first skirmish commenced he exclaimed, "I didn't volunteer to run; right here I'll die;" dismounted, deliberately tied his horse to a tree, and fired eighteen shots before he could be taken.

The guerrillas in that region were scattered in every direction and completely disheartened.

The scout was successful, but I cannot express my regret that it was not the complete success I had planned and hoped for in the total annihilation of the gang, which must have been the result had my orders been obeyed. The men behaved with steadiness and bravery with the one exception mentioned. I have to thank the officers with me for the assistance rendered by their cool, judicious conduct through the scout.

I have the honor to be, very respectfully, your obedient servant,

E. B. ENO,
Major Eighth Missouri State Militia Cavalry.

Col. WILLIAM F. CLOUD,
Commanding Southwestern District of Missouri.

MAY 15, 1863.—Skirmish at Big Creek, near Pleasant Hill, Mo.

Report of Maj. Wyllis C. Ransom, Sixth Kansas Cavalry.

HDQRS. FIRST BATTALION SIXTH KANSAS VOL. CAV.,
Westport, Mo., May 24, 1863.

CAPTAIN: I have the honor respectfully to report that on the 14th instant, learning that a considerable band of guerrillas were prowling near this place, with the evident intention of committing depredations along the Kansas line, I immediately started in pursuit with 60 men of Company B, Sixth Kansas Cavalry. I came in contact with the so-styled Colonel Parker and his gang the same evening; routed him, killing 2 of his men and capturing 3 of his horses. As I feared would be the case, a larger party of guerrillas passed to my rear during the night, notwithstanding that I used every precaution that the force at my command would allow to prevent such a movement. The enemy in my rear burned three houses, and the same night recrossed the Little Blue and retreated east as fast as his horses would carry him.

Upon learning of his movements during the night, I gave hot pursuit, and came up with a party of his force at Big Creek, near Pleasant Hill, Cass County, Missouri. We surprised his camp, killing 6 of his men, capturing 7 of his horses with equipments complete, his camp equipage, arms, provisions, &c.

The next day we routed him again, killing 2 of his men, wounding others, that escaped in the brush, and captured 3 more of his horses. Having driven them from that locality, I pursued them toward the Sni, where I again came up to them, they having joined the main body of guerrillas, at least 150 strong, under command of Quantrill and Parker, encamped among the thickly wooded hills of the Sni, in a very strong position. While feeling for the enemy, we encountered one of his forage parties taking flour to camp. We dispersed it, killing 1 and capturing and destroying the flour, their arms, and 2 more horses.

Judging that, with my men as poorly armed as they were, I could not attack the enemy successfully, I determined to await re-enforcements. I accordingly retired about 2 miles to a point where I could open communication with Major [William] Drumhiller, at Blue Springs. Major Drumhiller joined me that evening with 100 men, Fifth Missouri State Militia Cavalry, and we immediately moved upon the enemy in the midst of a terrible storm, which continued most of the night and the next day. We found that the enemy had moved their camp, but a reconnoitering party soon started a picket of 10 men, 1 of whom was killed and 3 of their horses captured. A close pursuit of several miles followed, but failed to discern the enemy's camp. The storm continuing with unabated violence, the streams rapidly rising, and our stock being nearly given out, and fearing that the enemy would again pass to the rear, together with the fact that our rations were exhausted, induced me to return to this place.

During the scout we have marched an aggregate of several hundred miles, and nearly the whole distance through the densest of brush, lying in ambuscade in detached parties night after night. I am confirmed in the opinion that the guerrillas in this and the adjacent counties can be concentrated within a few hours on any one point. They number several hundred, and great watchfulness will be required to prevent serious disaster. The enemy invariably fought us with desperation. My casualties are 1 man killed.

I feel it my duty to mention the name of Sergt. George W. Farnsworth, of Company B, Sixth Kansas Volunteer Cavalry, for the eminent valor he displayed and the untiring zeal with which he executed my orders in the field.

Very respectfully, your obedient servant,

W. C. RANSOM,
Major Sixth Kansas Cavalry, Commanding Detachment.

Capt. H. G. LORING,
Acting Assistant Adjutant-General.

MAY 18, 1863.—Affair at Hog Island, Bates County, Mo.

REPORTS.

No. 1.—Col. Edward Lynde, Ninth Kansas Cavalry.
No. 2.—Maj. Alexander W. Mullins, First Missouri State Militia Cavalry.

No. 1.

Report of Col. Edward Lynde, Ninth Kansas Cavalry.

PAOLA, KANS., *May* 26, 1863.

SIR: I have the honor to report that Captain [C. F.] Coleman, with a small detachment from Companies E and K, made a descent on Hog Island, in the southern part of Bates County, Missouri, last week, and found about 300 rebels, who had erected light breastworks, and were preparing for defense. They were attacked by Captain Coleman's detachment and routed, leaving 3 killed and 5 wounded, but no prisoners. Coleman had 1 man killed. The detachment also destroyed about 2,000 pounds of bacon, and a quantity of corn the rebels had gathered on the island. The rebels scattered and fled to Henry County. I have adopted the plan of hiding a few men in the bushes to watch for the Butternuts that infest our border, and have sent two small detachments back into the country to watch the route they seem to travel in going west. I hope in a few days to be able to give you an account of a good haul, but I have not enough troops at these headquarters to do as well as I might, if another company was here.

Captain [John E.] Stewart, of Company C, has not reported yet, and I have no knowledge of any troops at Olathe. If it would meet your approbation, I would change some of the companies, and station them a little different from what they are. I think they would be more effective; but I shall not do so without your consent. Would it not be possible to send two companies of infantry down here, and let them be divided between these stations, and they can hold the place and take care of the Government stores, and then all the mounted troops can be in motion? It would help very much.

I am, captain, respectfully, your obedient servant,

E. LYNDE,
Colonel, Commanding.

Capt. H. G. LORING,
Acting Assistant Adjutant-General.

No. 2.

Report of Maj. Alexander W. Mullins, First Missouri State Militia Cavalry.

GERMANTOWN, MO., *May* 20, 1863.

MAJOR: I have just returned from an extensive scout over the Osage River, in the southern part of Bates County.

On the night of the 17th, I received a message from Captain [Charles F.] Coleman, of the Ninth Kansas Cavalry, stationed at Butler, that he had found a large body of rebels about 8 or 10 miles south of Butler, and over the main branch of the Osage River, who were in a very strong position, and asked my assistance with all the available force I had at hand to co-operate with his force, and on the morning of the 18th, at sunrise, he would make the attack. By this time I had reached Papinsville, as arranged between Captain Coleman and myself, and from thence proceeded up the river and in the neighborhood of the rebel encampment. I found the most of Captain Coleman's command (the captain with a few men were out hunting my command). Captain Coleman had about 115 men of the Ninth Kansas Cavalry, but from some maneuvering of some rebel pickets he concluded they were too strong to attack. I took command, and proceeded to the rebel encampment, but found, on arriving there, that the large force supposed to be there numbered just 2, who were killed, and their arms, horses, &c., taken by the Kansas troops.

This place seems to have been used by the bushwhackers for a great while. They must have used it the greater part of last winter from appearances. The bushwhackers repulsed 60 of the Kansas troops and Enrolled Missouri Militia there a few days ago. From the appearances, and all the information I could gather, at least 100 bushwhackers have been for some time making that encampment their place of rendezvous. They claim to belong to one Colonel Parker's command. Parker keeps his headquarters in Jackson County, and I am inclined to think he is organizing a force all along the border.

Very respectfully, your obedient servant,

ALEX. W. MULLINS,
Major First Missouri State Militia Cavalry.

Maj. JAMES RAINSFORD,
Assistant Adjutant-General.

MAY 19, 1863.—Skirmish near Richfield, Clay County, Mo.

Report of Capt. Joseph Schmitz, Twenty-fifth Missouri Infantry.

U. S. ARSENAL, CLAY COUNTY, MO., *May* 22, 1863.

SIR: I received your letter of instruction, duly, from Richmond, Mo., of the 16th instant, in regard to the scouring out of Fishing River Bottom. I accordingly made every disposition of the forces under my command to secure success in the matter, but, unluckily, as you are already aware, the movement commenced about one hour and a half too late. The following special programme was laid down to be pursued: Lieutenant [George W.] Shinn, with his command, was to leave Camden at 9 p. m. on Tuesday, the 19th instant; Lieutenant Fleming, of the Provisional Missouri Militia, was to join Lieutenant [Louis] Grafenstein at Richfield, Mo., before 9 o'clock on Tuesday evening, at which hour they were to start to their different destinations; Lieutenant Fleming to the mouth of Fishing River, where he was to meet Lieutenant Shinn, with whom he wants to act in concert in scouring the country on each side of the river up to the lower bridge. Lieutenant Grafenstein, whom I had previously stationed at Richfield, with 16 men, and who were not mounted, were to start at the same time to the lower bridge, where they were directed to lie hidden and guard the roads on both sides of the river.

In accordance with this arrangement, Lieutenant Fleming left here at 6 p. m. for Richfield. When arriving near that place, he met two messengers with the intelligence of the bloody work; and shortly after, while hurrying up his men, he met Sergeant Clymo and the balance of Lieutenant Grafenstein's command (13 men) on the retreat to this post, having been assured by citizens of the place that the bushwhackers numbered from 60 to 100. * * * The whole command [being] but 36, all told, they concluded it best to return to this place (particularly because the reported force to oppose was too large to attack in the night without knowing definitely the situation of affairs in the place), which they did immediately. After making every preparation possible for an early pursuit next morning, we anxiously awaited daylight.

At dawn, Captains Garth and Tracey, of the Provisional Reserve Missouri Militia, with 40 men from Liberty, were here and ready to start in pursuit. With them I sent Lieutenant [H. C.] Carlile (and Dr. [J. Q.] Egelston volunteering) with 35 men. I concluded to give our party under Dr. Egelston's supervision. After nearly reaching Richfield, they first learned the true condition of affairs, and the sad result of the decoy and ambush of Lieutenant Grafenstein and Captain Sessions and squad.

The facts are simply as follows, to wit: Sixteen bushwhackers made their appearance 2 miles east of the town of Richfield, in the afternoon of Tuesday; two of them went to a house in the neighborhood, acting as if drunk, swearing they were Quantrill's men, &c. The men at whose house they were, started immediately after they left, and reported to Lieutenant Grafenstein, as above, when Lieutenant Grafenstein and Captain Sessions and 3 men started out to look into the matter. After getting out of the place 1½ miles, they were fired upon from the thick brush. Captain Sessions and Private Rapp fell the first fire; Lieutenant Grafenstein was hit soon after, and had to stop; the three were then rushed upon by the party of murderers. Rapp was robbed and left for dead. Captain Sessions was shot again two or three times through the head, and Lieutenant Grafenstein, after surrendering himself a prisoner, was coolly shot twice through the head also (a woman at the same time, near by, begging for his life). They both were stripped and plundered also. The gang then pursued the two remaining number of the squad in a direction not directly toward Richfield, but reached that place in about twenty minutes after the first firing, the two boys beating them in and escaping from them. In the mean time, some one passing near where Rapp was, brought him in to town, and was having his wounds dressed. After the devils entering the town, and learning that Rapp was not killed, one of them went directly to him and shot him three times more, and left him for dead the second time. (He yet will probably recover.) They then commenced to pillage the Union citizens particularly, but really made but little distinction between the loyal and disloyal; and after doing this pretty effectually, and destroying the Union flag, cutting the pole, &c., they left the place, on the same road they entered, about 9 or 10 o'clock the same night.

After my command reached Richfield, on Wednesday morning, and finding the true condition of things, the detachment of the Twenty-fifth, not being mounted, returned here, with the exception of the doctor and one man of my company as a guide, who paraded with the Provisional Reserve Missouri Militia to the mouth of the Fishing River. After arriving there, they found out that Lieutenant Story left there an hour in advance of them. They scoured the west side of the river, and returned to Liberty without finding anything except a camp where the bushwhackers camped a few days before.

The citizens around that country are all sympathizers, with very few exceptions, and it is hard to get information from them.

On yesterday I sent Lieutenant Cornell, with a detachment of 30 men, to Richfield, and Lieutenant Carlile, with 20 men, to the island below, to prevent the bushwhackers from crossing, and to arrest every one in that region that might be suspected of complicity in the affair of Tuesday evening. I also sent Captain Tourney, of the Provisional Reserve Missouri Militia, with his company, from Plattsburg to a place 12 miles north of Liberty, where the scoundrels were reported to have been all day Wednesday, and where he was to take their trail and follow them to their end, if possible to do so by that means, and, otherwise, to proceed from that point to Smithville, and from there to Centreville (both in this county), where he would meet and act in conjunction with the provost-marshal of Richmond, who has taken the field in person, with some of Ray County Militia, and Sergeant Lyle, with 10 men of my command.

From the best information that I can obtain, there were but 16 or 18 men of the bushwhackers, and were under command of one Ferdinand Scott, who was recognized by persons who know him well; so also were the following-named: Frank Turner, L. Easton, Frank James, Louis Vandever, Louis Gregg, and Churchill, and Moses McCoy, the husband of Mrs. McCoy, now on parole at your place. Joe Hart was not with the gang at Richfield on Tuesday evening, but was reported to have met them at the place before mentioned, 12 miles north of Liberty, on Wednesday (by the men at the house they stopped). Hart said then that he came from Saint Joe (direct) and visited Mrs. McCoy.

I have all the old arms of the militia boxed up, and will send them to Saint Joe by the first boat. I wish the arms, also tents for which requisitions are sent in, would be forwarded to this post; also stationery and blank reports.

I am, very respectfully, your obedient servant,

JOSEPH SCHMITZ,
Captain Twenty-fifth Missouri Infantry.

Col. CHESTER HARDING, Jr.

MAY 20, 1863.—Action near Fort Gibson, Ind. T.

Report of Col. William A. Phillips, Third Indian Home Guard.

HDQRS. INDIAN TERRITORY AND WESTERN ARKANSAS,
Fort Blunt, C. N., May 22, 1863.

SIR: I have the honor to report to you a somewhat severe engagement with the enemy on the 20th instant.

I had 800 mounted men guarding my supply line to cover approaching trains, when the enemy in the night crossed the Arkansas River with five regiments, going on a mountain road. A scout I had sent, failing to do his duty, left that road unwatched, and they approached within 5 miles of me, getting me on the left flank. They were, however, afraid to attack me in the works, and, taking a strong position on the mountains on the south, 5 miles distant and close to the Arkansas River, tried to cut off the stock. As all had been reported quiet for 20 miles in all directions this side of the river, the stock was, therefore, being sent out to graze, when the enemy pounced upon it. Sending all the mounted men I could raise, the larger part of the stock was taken from them. The Creek regiment refused to charge, or it could all have been saved. I sent forward Majors [J. A.] Foreman, Wright, and Pomeroy, with all the present available force, and as rapidly as possible moved everything within the works. The enemy, being strongly posted 5 miles distant, drove back Major Foreman and the others for some distance, although the ground was hotly contested. Captain [N. B.] Lucas, of the Sixth Kansas, was nearly surrounded, as was Captain [Henry S.] Anderson, of the Third Indian, but they gallantly cut their way through.

Leaving Colonel [George] Dole with a strong command, and most of my artillery, behind the works, I moved rapidly forward with two battalions of Indian infantry and a section of Hopkins' battery, under Lieutenant [B. S.] Bassett. Leaving one battalion as reserve, I supported the forces already in front, and soon drove the enemy into the woods. Here they contested the ground for a short time, but they were pushed over the mountain and rapidly driven in complete rout to Webber's Falls, where they crossed the Arkansas River. As we were following the enemy up the mountain, I learned that the enemy, with two 6-pounder field-pieces and one 12-pounder howitzer, were trying to cross Arkansas River 2 miles from Gibson. Leaving the mounted men to follow the retreating enemy, I took my infantry and two guns down to the river, and found that the enemy, although in considerable numbers on the opposite bank, were only making a feint. Desiring to dismount their artillery, I immediately opened on them, but they rapidly withdrew their guns and fell back.

The battle was a very severe one while it lasted, as I could only bring a portion of my forces to bear. My loss in killed is upward of 20—probably 25 or 26, as some are missing—and about half that number wounded. I understand that the enemy's loss is much more severe. We lost no officers. The rebels had 1 major killed. On the field there were Colonel [J. T.] Coffee (with Missouri and Arkansas troops), Major Bryan, Colonels D. N. and Chilly McIntosh, each with a regiment; Colonel Adair's regiment, and a Choctaw regiment.

Only one battalion of Texans came over, as the remainder (infantry) staid with the artillery across the river, with the design of crossing the short way if we were pressed back.

Yesterday the enemy kept up a heavy cannonade until dark over the river at my picket stations. This morning at daylight it had been renewed.

Lieutenant-Colonel [Frederick W.] Schaurte got in yesterday with the first part of the train and the paymaster. The refugee train, which I re-enforced 60 miles off, is also in safety.

The enemy have left Van Buren, and taken all but a handful of men from Fort Smith. They are massed south of the river in front of me, and give their forces at 11,000. Their real force is between 4,000 and 5,000 men. They are determined that I shall not recruit in the country south of the river, and tell the Indians that the United States forces are whipped in Virginia and will be obliged to evacuate the Indian country, and that their only safety is with the Confederacy. Three of my Indian picket stations behaved very badly, having deserted their posts without giving me notice, and allowed the enemy to get on my flank in the morning.

I feel it due to the majority of the men and officers to compliment their gallantry and heroism, by which we, without risking our position, achieved a decided victory over greatly superior numbers.

I am, respectfully, your obedient servant,

WM. A. PHILLIPS,
Colonel Third Indian Home Guard, Kansas Infantry, Comdg.

Maj. Gen. JAMES G. BLUNT.

MAY 21-30, 1863.—Scout from Cassville, through Northwestern Arkansas, into Newton and Jasper Counties, Mo., including skirmishes (22d) at Bentonville and (26th) near Carthage.

Report of Col. William F. Cloud, Second Kansas Cavalry, commanding District of Southwestern Missouri.

SPRINGFIELD, MO., *May* 30, 1863.

GENERAL: I have the honor to inform you that I have just returned from a movement to the south and west of this place.

I left Cassville on the 21st, and on the morning of the 22d surprised the rebel force at Bentonville, taking 2 commissioned officers, 1 first sergeant, and 11 privates prisoners, and killing 1. I also recaptured 3 prisoners in the hands of the enemy.

Learning that Coffee and Hunter were at Pineville, I immediately moved in that direction, and, taking their trail, followed them from Pineville, via Rutledge; then west of Neosho to Diamond Grove, and west of Carthage about 10 miles, where I overtook a part of their force, under Coffee, about 100 strong, and attacked them with about equal force at daylight of Tuesday, May 26, and as they would not stand and fight, but took to the woods and brush, I was obliged to be content with scouring the same, and dispersing them. Hunter had gone north to Cedar County with about 100 men, and Livingston was not to be found. After disposing of my command so as to annoy and capture as many of those roving bands as possible, I returned to my headquarters.

Lieutenant-Colonel Crittenden, Seventh Missouri State Militia, has been quite successful lately in damaging a part of Livingston's band, and a party of 16 men, under command of a so-called Colonel Harrison, were attacked and killed by Indians upon the Verdigris River, west of Missouri, while on their way to the west to plunder upon the road to

Pike's Peak. These bands are quite numerous and active in running about through the country, but are not doing much active harm.

I have a post at Cassville, at Newtonia, and at Neosho upon my south line, and with the force now at this place will endeavor to maintain the peace and quiet of the district.

From a flag of truce just in from Fayetteville, where they had gone after the sick and wounded left there upon the retreat of Colonel Harrison, I learn that the enemy have only about 400 or 500 men in all Northern Arkansas, who are scattered about through several counties.

Cabell is at Fort Smith, and, as far as I can learn from my scouts and travelers, I do not think that there are other forces this side the Arkansas, except those who may be with Price in the eastern part of the State.

The forces in the district are not sufficient in numbers, or well enough supplied with horses, to enable me to patrol to any great extent in Arkansas, nor east of Forsyth. If it is expected of me to scout down the White River, I wish to be informed of the same; also of the fact if Price is threatening Missouri.

The enemy here are basing their hopes upon Price's coming, which, in turn, depends upon the abandonment of the siege of Vicksburg by our forces.

Permit me, after congratulating you upon your appointment to the command of the department, to state that I shall take great pleasure in the performance of any duty to which I may be ordered.

I am, general, very respectfully, your obedient servant,

W. F. CLOUD,
Colonel, Commanding.

Major-General SCHOFIELD,
Commanding Department of the Missouri.

MAY 23-26, 1863.—Expedition from Helena to near Napoleon, Ark., and skirmish near Island No. 65, Mississippi River.

Report of Maj. Gen. Benjamin M. Prentiss, U. S. Army.

HEADQUARTERS DISTRICT OF EASTERN ARKANSAS,
Helena, Ark., May 27, 1863.

GENERAL: I have the honor to report that on the 23d instant I sent the steamboat Pike down the river for the purpose of obtaining recruits for the Second Regiment Arkansas Volunteers, of African descent, under command of Lieut. Col. George W. De Costa, of that regiment, with detachments of the First Indiana Cavalry and Thirty-sixth Iowa Infantry, and 25 men of the Second Arkansas Regiment, with one howitzer.

The expedition proceeded down the river, on the Arkansas side, to a point 1 mile from Napoleon, and returned on the Mississippi side, making frequent raids into the country, in some instances to a distance of 6 or 7 miles. The conduct of both white and colored soldiers is represented by Lieutenant-Colonel De Costa as being of the most creditable character. Near Island No. 65 the Pike was fired into by a party of about 150 rebels. Brisk firing was kept up for some time, the enemy having two pieces of artillery, one of which was silenced by the howitzer on the Pike. Captain Waters, of the Second Arkansas Regiment, was severely wounded in the leg, and 2 contrabands were mortally wounded. The enemy are thought to have lost from 10 to 15 killed and wounded.

The conduct of the colored soldiers was highly creditable; they fought with a hearty will, and did good service. The amount of property captured is as follows: 75 mules, 8 horses, and subsistence for the whole force. The blacks hailed with joy the appearance of the colored soldiers. In addition to the above, 125 recruits were obtained. The regiment is rapidly filling up, and in a few days it is hoped it will be full.

I am, general, very respectfully, your obedient servant,

B. M. PRENTISS,
Major-General.

Maj. Gen. JOHN A. MCCLERNAND,
Commanding Thirteenth Army Corps.

MAY 25, 1863.—Skirmish at Polk's Plantation, near Helena, Ark.

Report of Lieut. Samuel J. McKee, Third Iowa Cavalry.

CAMP THIRD IOWA CAVALRY,
Helena, Ark., May 25, 1863.

MAJOR: Pursuant to order, with 50 men of Companies A and B, I this morning reported to Major [Samuel] Walker, of the Fifth Kansas Cavalry. We were placed in advance of the column, Company A being thrown forward as advance guard, and in this position were marched out upon the road known as the Little Rock road, for about 6 miles, when the flankers of the advance guard encountered the enemy's pickets, and, in the exchange of shots, one of our men was wounded. We proceeded cautiously forward for a mile, when, acting upon some information received from a negro, Major Walker ordered me forward with Company B to the end of the line, and there, turning to the right, to make a circuit of the open field in that direction. I did as directed, and skirmished carefully through the woods till I encountered the rear company of the Fifth Kansas, sent out from the rear of the column, to act in conjunction with me. I then countermarched, and proceeded a short distance upon my return, when I became aware, by the heavy firing, the column was warmly engaged. Fearful of placing myself in a wrong position if I returned through the woods, I turned short to the left, and proceeded at full speed to the front, on reaching which I found that the enemy had broken the ranks of the Fifth Kansas and Company A, Third Iowa Cavalry, and were driving them back in considerable disorder. I formed my men and succeeded in checking the enemy for a few moments, and only left the ground when ordered to by Major Walker, who, finding he could not hold the position, resolved to fall back to a bridge over a deep ravine, a mile in our rear. I and my men occupied the position of rear guard, and engaged the enemy in a sort of running fight the entire distance. At one time the action was very severe, and 2 of the enemy were killed in a hand-to-hand fight, in which we had 2 men severely wounded. On reaching the bridge, my company rallied promptly; not one man had straggled. We formed our line and awaited the enemy's attack, but he, finding our position strong, drew off his forces, and we remained in position until ordered by Major Walker to accompany a flag of truce the enemy had sent us, and to search the ground of the conflict as carefully as possible, that the wounded might be relieved and the dead searched out.

I have to report that my entire command behaved in a manner entirely satisfactory to me. I was separated from Company A before the fight began, but from all the information I can gather I am satisfied that the honor of the Third Iowa Cavalry did not suffer in their hands, and for my own immediate company, I challenge the record of any conflict to show greater coolness and courage. We formed a line in face of a galling fire, and, when ordered to fall back, disputed the ground for a mile. Finally, when we were ordered to again rally for a determined stand, we presented every man in his place who has not since been proved to have been incapacitated through wounds or loss of his horse.

We have suffered a loss of 5 men wounded, and 2 missing.*

Very respectfully, your obedient servant,

SAMUEL J. McKEE,
First Lieut. Company B, Comdg. Detachment Third Iowa Cavalry.

[Indorsement.]

Maj. O. H. P. SCOTT,
Commanding Third Iowa Cavalry:

I heartily indorse every line of the above report. Lieutenant McKee, of the Third Iowa Cavalry, and the men under his command acted with distinguished gallantry during the whole engagement. The advance guard of the Third Iowa were commanded by Sergeant Wishard and numbered but about 10 men. In my former report I did not know the name of the lieutenant commanding the Third Iowa.

The troops composing my command all deserve the credit of having performed their duty, and I observed no distinction between the men of the two regiments engaged with me.

SAMUEL WALKER,
Major Fifth Kansas Cavalry, Commanding Expedition.

MAY 28, 1863.—Skirmish near Fort Gibson, Ind. T.

Report of Maj. Gen. James G. Blunt, U. S. Army, commanding District of Kansas.

FORT LEAVENWORTH, *June* 8, 1863.

GENERAL: Advices from Colonel [William A.] Phillips to the 30th of May represent that he is hard pressed, and much needs re-enforcements. The enemy are continually massing troops in his front, and frequently crossing the river below and harassing his flank and rear, and annoying his trains on the line of communication with Fort Scott. The last train down was attacked on the morning of the 28th, when near Fort Gibson. Colonel Phillips, anticipating that an attack would be made on it, had sent a force to meet it. The attack was repulsed, with a loss of 5 killed and several wounded on our side; 35 of the rebels killed were picked up and buried by our men.

---

* Nominal list omitted.

The rebels fled across the Arkansas River, hotly pursued by our forces. The train got in all safe, unloaded, and returned to Fort Scott, arriving there (at the latter place) on the 6th instant. I have ordered the First Kansas Colored Regiment, Colonel [J. M.] Williams, to re-enforce Phillips without delay, and shall send six companies of the Second Colorado and one section of the Second Kansas Battery with the next train, which will leave about the 15th; and, with the new cavalry companies I am getting ready for the field, I will be able to give him some additional mounted force. With this additional force, I am in hopes he will be able to maintain his position, unless some of the rebel forces with Price are moved against him. In that case, he will be compelled to fall back, unless other re-enforcements can be had. This will be disastrous to the Indian country, and greatly demoralize the Indian troops. They are making superhuman efforts to hold the country to the Arkansas River, and their endurance of hardships and privations, as well as their display of patriotism and gallantry, entitle them to be promptly supported. Coffee has joined Livingston, making a force of 800 or 1,000, who are operating in the rear of Phillips, on his line of communication for supplies, requiring a large force for escort duty with trains.

Please inform me if there has been any change in the lines of this district, taking therefrom the border counties of Missouri, and if provisions have been made to send troops into the border counties of that State. If so, it will enable me to send more mounted men below.

Major Weed having just arrived from Colonel Phillips' command, I have directed Colonel [William R.] Penick's regiment to proceed to Saint Joseph immediately, to be mustered out, in accordance with your order.

Very respectfully, your obedient servant,

JAS. G. BLUNT,
Major-General.

Major-General SCHOFIELD,
Commanding Department of the Missouri.

MAY —, 1863.—Affair near Patterson, Mo.

Report of Capt. Timothy Reves.

CAMP, *Kelley's Mill, May* 31, 1863.

MAJOR: We went on our trip near Patterson, and found a scout had started in the direction of Doniphan. We routed the enemy by killing 1 man, 6 horses, how many wounded we do not know; the horses killed were shot all over; the men with them were undoubtedly wounded. We captured about 22 horses and saddles, blankets, &c. We fell back on Current River, 15 miles above Doniphan, for the purpose of resting our horses and watching the enemy for two or three days, when we expect to return to camp.

Please forward a copy of the dispatch to Colonel [J. Q.] Burbridge forthwith.

Very respectfully,

T. REVES,
Captain.

Maj. LEE CRANDALL, *C. S. Cavalry.*

JUNE 1, 1863.—Skirmishes near Rocheport, Mo.

REPORTS.

No. 1.—Brig. Gen. Thomas J. Bartholow, Enrolled Missouri Militia.
No. 2.—Lieut. Col. John F. Williams, Ninth Missouri State Militia Cavalry.

No. 1.

Report of Brig. Gen. Thomas J. Bartholow, Enrolled Missouri Militia.

HDQRS. EIGHTH MILITARY DISTRICT OF MISSOURI,
ENROLLED MISSOURI MILITIA,
Macon City, Mo., June 2, 1863.

GENERAL: I received the following dispatch from Col. Clark H. Green, commanding post at Glasgow, at 10 o'clock last night:

GLASGOW, MO., *June 1, 1863.*

Captain Steinmetz, with 15 men, ran into a camp of bushwhackers 3 miles north of Rocheport at sunrise this morning. The rebels fired upon them, and a short skirmish ensued, our men getting scattered, and were driven within 3 miles of Fayette. Four of our men are missing. John Vance was captured. William Hensley is supposed to have been killed. Captain Steinmetz came to Fayette, got help, and has gone back. Jackman, Pulliam, Todd, and Rucker were with the rebels, having about 60 men.

C. H. GREEN,
Colonel.

I immediately telegraphed to Mexico and Sturgeon, ordering a force from each place to move forthwith in the direction of Rocheport, directing the officers to act in conjunction with the troops moving from Fayette, and not to return until this band of marauders was broken up or as long as they could learn of an armed rebel in that section. I also had a messenger dispatched to General Guitar, at Columbia, requesting him to send a force from Columbia. I ordered Colonel Green to arrest Jackman's family and hold them for the safety of Sergeant Vance, reported captured by this band. I also sent an order by the early train this morning to Captain Skinner, at Renick, who has a company stationed there, to march immediately in the direction above indicated with all the available force he could spare. Thus, by moving detachments from five different points, I hope by to-night to have the section infested by these rebels so surrounded that their escape will be cut off and the band effectually broken up. This band is the same which, under Pulliam, lately committed the depredations in Pike and Lincoln Counties. A few have doubtless joined them since they came into Howard. I have just received information that the forces from Mexico and Sturgeon are on the march.

Captain Steinmetz, at the head of 15 men, had moved from Glasgow on Saturday night, with the view of endeavoring to effect the capture of Jackman, who was known to be in the neighborhood of Rocheport, he not knowing that Pulliam had got into the vicinity with the men who were bushwhacking under him in Pike and Lincoln. I will keep you advised regarding this affair.

I am, general, very respectfully, your obedient servant,

TH. J. BARTHOLOW,
Brigadier-General.

Maj. Gen. JOHN M. SCHOFIELD,
Commanding Department of the Missouri, Saint Louis.

No. 2.

Report of Lieut. Col. J hn F. Williams, Ninth Missouri State Militia Cavalry.

HEADQUARTERS,
Fayette, Mo., June 1, 1863.

SIR: Learning this morning that the rebel leaders, Jackman, Rucker, Pulliam, and company, were in force in the vicinity of Rocheport, I sent out 50 men from Companies A and G, under Captain [Reeves] Leonard, to look after them, leaving here at 11 a. m. The captain found them about 2 p. m. posted in a pasture upon the farm and near the house of John L. Jones, about 3 miles northeast of Rocheport, and, throwing out flankers, made an attack on them at once, and in twenty minutes routed and drove them flying before him, with a loss of 2 men killed and several horses; number of wounded not known. The captain captured two horses and guns, one keg of powder, powder-flasks, canteens, caps, hats, &c. Casualties on our side, 5 wounded slightly, all buck-shot flesh wounds, the captain among the number being wounded in the leg and head. Captain [Henry N.] Cook came up from Columbia with 50 men, and, reaching the scene a few moments after the fight was over, went in pursuit of the flying rebels, assisted by Lieutenants [Marshall H.] Harris, [William B.] Kemper, [Charles] Albrecht, and [Tobe] Williams. Jackman's number is about 50. The detachment of Company A was under Lieutenants [Joseph M.] Street and Williams; of Company G, under Lieutenant Albrecht. Both officers and men fought gallantly. The fine gray gelding stolen from Willis Grims some two weeks ago was captured in the fight from Jackman.

In haste, yours,

JOHN F. WILLIAMS,
Lieutenant-Colonel, Commanding Post.

Brigadier-General GUITAR,
Commanding District of Northeastern Missouri.

JUNE 1, 1863.—Skirmish near Doniphan, Mo.

Reports of Maj. Lothar Lippert, Thirteenth Illinois Cavalry.

POST HEADQUARTERS,
Patterson, Mo., June 1, [2,] 1863.

SIR: I have the honor to transmit to you the following report of the skirmish yesterday morning:

Information had been received that Reves and Porter were encamped at Porter's Mill, 44 miles south of this place, on the Pocahontas road.

Saturday morning, May 30, 1863, I started two expeditions, one under command of Captain Erskine, of about 60 men of the Thirteenth Illinois Cavalry, and the other of 73 men—40 of the Third Missouri State Militia and 33 of the Thirteenth Illinois Cavalry. I took command myself.

Captain Erskine was to attack the enemy in front at 3 o'clock to-day, while I, by going a southwestern route, would be on hand to attack them in the rear at the same hour.

I marched from this camp to Carter's Mill, on the Van Buren road, 20 miles, and could not learn anything of the enemy at that place, the citizens telling me that they had not seen or heard of a rebel in that vicinity. I then marched back from Carter's Mill about 3 miles, and took the Doniphan road; kept it 10 miles; there left it, and camped at a small farm about 1½ miles off from the road. My object in doing this was to obtain forage. The militia were camped in a barn and yard, their horses being all inside the yard. The detachment of the Thirteenth was about 10 rods distant from the barn, in the woods. At about 3.45 o'clock the next morning, the enemy, who had come inside my pickets and gained a position behind the fence, along the edge of the woods, without being discovered, opened a heavy fire on the militia, who immediately ran for the woods, and were lost in the brush. I tried to get them to hold the barn and fence, but they could not stand the fire. After I had lost them, I went over to the company of the Thirteenth, who were in line, returning the enemy's fire lightly, and ordered them up on the hill, to a better position, where I halted and waited for stragglers from the militia to come up. The enemy in the mean time had ceased firing, and could not be seen. I then marched back to this camp.

The enemy was commanded by Reves and Porter, and numbered about 300 men. The attack was a complete surprise, and not expected at all by me. If my horses had not been saddled and bridled, I might have lost them all. On our way back, I learned that the enemy had followed me the day before for 12 miles, remaining about two hours behind.

The loss in my regiment is nothing, only myself wounded. The militia lost about 23 horses. All the men are in but 2. There are 3 wounded.

I have sent word for Captain Erskine to return, and he will probably be in to-night.

Most respectfully, your obedient servant,

L. LIPPERT,
Major Thirteenth Illinois Cavalry.

Colonel CLARK,
Commanding Sub-district, Pilot Knob, Mo.

HDQRS. THIRTEENTH REGT. ILLINOIS CAV. VOLS.,
Arcadia, Mo., June 27, 1863.

SIR: I have the honor to submit to you the following report:

In compliance with orders received from headquarters sub-district and post, Pilot Knob, Mo., I proceeded, on the morning of the 29th of May, 1863, with 5 commissioned officers and 110 non-commissioned officers and privates, to Patterson County, with instructions to reconnoiter the country south and west of that place. At Patterson I found 69 men of the Third Missouri State Militia, under command of Lieutenant [Samuel R.] Kelly, same regiment.

In the afternoon of the 30th of May, I received reliable information that the guerrilla chief Reves, with a force variously estimated at from 400 to 600 men, was encamped at or near Ponter's Mill, Mo. From this information I concluded to attack him in his camp.

Below Ponter's Mill there is a junction of three roads, one leading to Doniphan, one to Pitman's Ferry, and one out to the so-called Glass Settlement. To prevent Reves escaping without giving a fight, I organized two expeditions, one of 75 men, under command of Captain Erskine, with instructions to move, by the way of Greenville and Poplar Bluff, to the north side of Ponter's Mill, and to arrive there on the 2d of May [June], at 3 p. m., and, if the enemy was to be found, to attack him at once.

I, myself, took command of 49 men of the Third Missouri State Militia, under Lieutenant Kelly, and 32 men from the Thirteenth Illinois Cavalry, under command of Captain [G. Allen] May. I intended to march in a western direction to Carter's Mill, on Black River; from there to Doniphan, and arrive on the 2d of June, at 3 p. m., at the junction of the different roads south of Reves' camp, and act in conjunction with Captain Erskine.

I arrived at Carter's Mill at 12 m., and, as I had received information that a small rebel band was in the vicinity, I scouted the country around thoroughly, without finding any signs of an enemy. From this place I proceeded, the same afternoon, 14 miles farther on the Doniphan road. At 6 p. m. I left the main road, and went to a farm about 1½ miles in an eastern direction, for the purpose of obtaining forage. This farm consisted of about 16 acres of cleared ground, making a regular square, with a creek, lined on each side by small brushes, running from east to west through the center of the clearing. The field was surrounded by very steep hills on all sides, covered with heavy timber and thick underbrush. On the west side of the field was a large log barn, with a small fenced yard surrounding three sides. At arriving at the place, I ordered Lieutenant Kelly to camp his command in and around this barn-yard. I also ordered Captain May to camp his command on the north side of the creek, behind the undergrowth on its bank.

After the pickets had been stationed on the hills around the camp, the horses were fed and the men prepared their supper. When this was done, I ordered the whole command to saddle and bridle again, and sleep on their arms, close to their horses. Captain May received instructions from me to remain, in case of an attack, at the place on which he was encamped, as a reserve, and await my orders. Lieutenant Kelly was instructed, in case of an attack, to take half of his command and form a line of skirmishers behind the fence on the south side of the field, and the other half of his command was ordered to hold the barn-yard, and, in case the enemy came in overwhelming numbers, the whole of his command should fall back to the barn and hold it.

On the morning of June 1, at about 3.45 o'clock, I heard two shots fired in the direction of the picket on the east side of my camp. I immediately ordered the troops to the positions before designated. I told Captain May to hold his command in readiness, either to charge on the enemy, if he should attempt to come into the field, or to be prepared to fall in his rear, with dismounted men, but, under all circumstances, to await my orders. After this I went back to the Third Missouri State Militia, and saw Lieutenant Kelly leaving his place behind the fence, already, in double-quick. I asked him his reasons for such doings, and received an answer that the enemy could be heard coming through the woods. I then ordered him back behind the fence, but before he arrived there a tremendous fire was opened from the woods opposite the fence. This was sufficient to frighten his men so completely that all efforts on my part were insufficient to make them stand either in the field or in the barn. I further noticed that these men ran away without taking their saddled horses along, which, in order to save, I gave the men orders to mount at four different times, which was obeyed by but 7 or 8 men who remained on the ground. After this I proceeded to Captain May, and found him with his men in line of battle, awaiting my orders. In the mean time the enemy had crossed the fence and taken possession of the barn and surrounding yard, and secured the horses of the Third Missouri State Militia. The same moment I also saw a mounted force of the enemy going in the direction of the main road, and fearing that they might cut off my way of retreat, I ordered Captain May to bring his command, and trotted through the woods toward the main road; when there, a half mile back, I selected a good position, dismounted the men, and formed a line of skirmishers, and waited about three-quarters of an hour, in order that stragglers from the Third Missouri State Militia might come up. Afterward we started back toward Patterson, arriving at that place at 3 p. m. When arrived at Patterson, there were missing from the Third Missouri State Militia 27 men, horses, and equipments; among them the two officers who accompanied the expedition. All these men came in that night on foot. Three of the Third Missouri State Militia received slight wounds, and, after defending nobly the position in which they were stationed, left the field with me. During my efforts to make the Third Missouri State Militia hold their position, I received eight balls in different parts of my body.

On arriving at Patterson, I immediately sent word to Captain Erskine, recalling him, and he arrived safe in camp at Patterson June 2.

On the way back to Patterson I received from citizens the following information: Reves, with from 500 to 600 men, mounted, left his camp, near Ponter's Mill, on the 30th of May, marching, by way of Doniphan, toward Patterson, on a more western road than the one which I was coming, with the intention to attack Patterson on the morning of the 1st of June. Arriving at Carter's Mill about one hour after I had left, he changed his course and followed my tracks, remaining in my rear at a distance of 3 or 4 miles, and concealed himself, after having obtained information of the locality at which I camped.

I am, sir, very respectfully,

L. LIPPERT,
Major, Commanding Regiment.

Capt. H. C. FILLEBROWN, *Assistant Adjutant-General.*

[Indorsement.]

HEADQUARTERS CAVALRY DIVISION,
Arcadia, June 28, 1863.

I beg leave to file this report at department headquarters, as I am going out of the district.

Some inquiry may occur as to why I arrested 2 officers and 27 men of the Third Missouri State Militia, especially as Colonel [Richard G.] Woodson seems inclined to take the part of the men of his regiment, who have a second time misbehaved before the enemy. I have not had time to try the case, but I beg it be noticed, and this report filed, to show my ground of action.

J. W. DAVIDSON,
Brigadier-General, Commanding.

JUNE 1, 1863.—Affair at Waverly, Mo.

Report of Maj. George W. Kelly, Fourth Missouri State Militia Cavalry.

MARSHALL, SALINE COUNTY, *June* 2, 1863.

COLONEL: I drop you a line to inform you that my dismounted scout arrived last night. They ran on to a party of 4 guerrillas in the brush above Waverly, Mo.; killed 1, mortally wounded another, and captured their horses and equipments; 4 horses, 1 Sharps' carbine, 1 shot-gun, and their bedding. The brush was very thick, almost impenetrable, or my men would have killed the whole 4. Sergeants Sapp, Beeks, and Yarnell, of Company C, with 30 privates of Companies C and B, composed the dismounted scout. The sergeants report several small bands of guerrillas between Waverly and Dover, in La Fayette County, Missouri. My scout was armed with revolvers and double-barreled shotguns.

Yours, respectfully,

G. W. KELLY,
Major Fourth Regiment Missouri State Militia Cavalry, Comdg.

Col. GEORGE H. HALL,
Fourth Missouri State Militia Cavalry.

JUNE 6-20, 1863.—Operations about Fort Gibson, Ind. T., including skirmish (16th) on Greenleaf Prairie.

REPORTS.

No. 1.—Col. William A. Phillips, Third Indian Home Guards, commanding Indian Brigade.

No. 2.—Col. Stephen H. Wattles, First Indian Home Guards, of skirmish on Greenleaf Prairie.

No. 1.

Report of Col. William A. Phillips, Third Indian Home Guards, commanding Indian Brigade.

HEADQUARTERS INDIAN BRIGADE,
Fort Blunt, C. N., June 20, 1863.

SIR: I have to report military operations here up to date.

Two weeks ago (of which fact I advised you, and also Colonel Willams, supposed then to be at Baxter Springs), Col. Stand Watie, Colonel Bell, and other rebel commanders made a cavalry dash over the river, in considerable force, crossing Arkansas River 28 miles below this, and moving rapidly, on by-roads, through the mountains that border the Illinois River. Knowing the exhausted condition of my stock, I permitted no pursuit until I discovered definitely where they were going.

I learned that the enemy crossed the Illinois River, and that part of their force recrossed and went to Park Hill and Tahlequah, and then moved northeast. I at once concluded that their design was to cooperate with Livingston and others, and strike the negro regiment at Baxter Springs. I sent three separate messengers to notify Colonel Williams of his danger, and sent all the cavalry force I could then mount, with one howitzer, to follow the rebels; to strike them, if it could be done safely, and, if the enemy were re-enforced so as to be too heavy, to strike them in the rear when they struck at the negro regiment.

Major [J. A.] Foreman moved with his command some 80 miles northeast, and prepared to attack them near Maysville, when the rebels swung round on the Grand River, near the mouth of Spavina Creek.

Grand River was up. Captain [Hugh] Tinnin, and, I suspect, Livingston, with several hundred men, were on the west side of Grand River. Watie and Bell attempted to cross, but failed, drowning 2 of their men and some horses in the attempt.

The rebels retreated down the river to Grand Saline, where they again attempted to cross, but failed. Here Major Foreman overtook their rear, and in the attack 3 rebels were killed and some of their provisions taken.

The rebels retreated rapidly southeast, toward Tahlequah, pursued by Major Foreman. I had scouts in Tahlequah (20 miles from Fort Blunt), and learned that Watie had gone through Tahlequah about 2 or 3 o'clock on Monday [15th]. I got the news two hours afterward. I immediately sent orders to Foreman to press the enemy hard, so as to harass him; and I raised immediately a force of 400 men, half infantry, half cavalry, and one howitzer, and sent it with Colonel [Stephen H.] Wattles and a number of good captains, Indian and white, to assist him, and to cut off the retreat of the enemy. I directed him to proceed on the road parallel to the river, down the river, and sent orders to have Foreman's party post him as to the movements of the enemy, and watched the enemy myself.

Learning of the harassed condition of Watie and Bell, the rebels moved down some Texans and Choctaws, under Cols. Tandy Walker and Bass, and undertook to cross a force in the night. At the same time, the main rebel army, camped over the river, 4 miles from Fort Blunt, made a demonstration on my right to hold me in check.

Colonel Wattles in the night passed close to where the rebels were crossing the river without discovering them; but two scouts, who were watching Greenleaf Prairie, notified him at daylight that the rebels were forming in his rear. His force returned 6 miles, and engaged the enemy on Greenleaf Prairie, 18 miles distant from the fort. The rebels were first repulsed, but owing to pushing the retreating enemy with a ragged [force], the rebels turned on the pursuers and drove them back until they reached the infantry and the battery, which latter they attempted to take, but were repulsed and again driven toward the river, our force still being south of the rebels.

Unfortunately the stock under the command of Major Foreman was completely exhausted, and instead of pursuing the enemy, as I expected, so as to crush him with both commands, he abandoned the pursuit at Tahlequah and returned to Fort Blunt. Learning of his approach, and seeing that such co-operation would fail, I mounted everything, on mules, horses, &c., and sent out Colonel Schaurte with 500 men and one piece of artillery (part of his force with the gun was infantry), and pushed him forward to aid Colonel Wattles. I ordered the latter to stay and hold his position. He, although his command had repulsed and driven the enemy, deemed it advisable to fall back as soon as he learned that Foreman would not re-enforce him. He therefore made a march up, leaving the enemy on his left flank in the timber toward the river (defeated and beaten, but not destroyed). Learning that he was still falling back to Fort Blunt, I relieved him of command, and ordered Colonel Schaurte to pursue and destroy the enemy.

Meantime the rebels over the river opened their artillery on me, directly in front, and made a feint as if they were going to attack me in force directly at Fort Blunt. This they did in very lively style, sending their men into the river at different fords, as if they were crossing. Keeping everything in good style, I still sent out everything I could move rapidly to the Greenleaf Prairie.

Colonel Wattles, before being relieved, had unfortunately fallen back to the mountain, 6 miles from Fort Blunt. A rebel force, 300 or 400 strong, was watching his rear, but before the commands I sent could reach the field, the rebels had retreated down the river, and in the night and during next day succeeded in crossing the Arkansas at Webber's Falls, Vine and Sallison [Creeks]. Having once permitted them to escape, the condition of my stock rendered it utterly impossible to follow them.

The engagement on Greenleaf Prairie on the 16th was spirited and sharp, lasting several hours, and once or twice was sharply contested.

Our losses are: First Indian Regiment, 3 killed; Third Indian Regiment, 3 killed; Fourth Indian Regiment, 1 killed; and Second Indian Regiment, Lieutenant Palmer slightly wounded. Eight are reported wounded, but all slightly.

Of the Sixth Kansas, 5 are missing, supposed to be prisoners. They are from Company D. A detachment of 30 men, under Sergt. John N. Ewing, got in advance of our force, owing to the retreat of the command under Wattles; and this small detachment having taken a wrong road, they were surrounded by several hundred rebels. Sergeant Ewing gallantly fought his way out with most of his men; but 5 were taken, or are missing.*

* * * * * * *

While regretting that the inability to obey orders prevented the total destruction of the enemy's force on this side of the river, I must state that the fight was in the main a gallant one, and the enemy were driven several miles from the field.

Some Choctaw prisoners, taken by Captain Gritts and Lieutenant Thompson, stated that the rebels had crossed ten companies of Choctaws and ten companies of Texans to cover the retreat of Colonel Watie, but I do not believe they had so large a force over.

Amongst the officers exhibiting gallantry worthy of note are Captain [Budd] Gritts and Lieutenant [J. C.] Palmer, of the Second; Captains Smith Christy, [Solomon] Kaufman, and Lieutenant [John E.] Blunt, of the Third; Captain Kinter, of the Fourth; Captain Cox, of the Fifth, and Lieutenants [Robert T.] Thompson and [Fred.] Crafts, of the First; also Sergeant Ewing, of the Sixth Kansas.

The loss of the rebels, although heavier than ours, has been variously stated; but I decline a statement in the absence of positive knowledge.

WM. A. PHILLIPS,
Colonel, Commanding.

Major-General BLUNT.

No. 2.

Report of Col. Stephen H. Wattles, First Indian Home Guards, of skirmish on Greenleaf Prairie.

HDQRS. FIRST REGIMENT OF THE INDIAN BRIGADE,
In the Field, Fort Blunt, June —, 1863.

COLONEL: In obedience to your orders detailing me to take charge of a scout to intercept the retreat of Stand Watie, I marched from Fort Blunt at 10 o'clock on the evening of the 15th of June, 1863. When

---

* Nominal list omitted.

we arrived at the bayou, I ordered a halt, counted the men, and found but 316; proceeded on the march, halted at the top of the mountain, and rested the forces about one hour. The occasion of the halt was caused by one balky horse attached to the howitzer, rendering it necessary for the infantry supporters to pull the piece up the mountain. We then resumed march, with an advance guard and flankers right and left, and reached Greenleaf Prairie about an hour before daylight. We proceeded on across the prairie, and, when we entered the timber on the opposite side, left 2 men to watch the prairie. After crossing Greenleaf Creek some 2 miles, I was notified by one of the men left that the enemy was in my rear. Immediately dispatched Lieutenant ———, of the Second Indian Regiment, with 25 men, to learn the number of the enemy; halted for a report. At the same time I sent 2 men forward to Webber's Falls, 2 men to the Tahlequah road, and 2 men to Hildebrand's Ford, to ascertain the whereabouts of Major [J. A.] Foreman. In about three-quarters of an hour a messenger returned with the information that the lieutenant was attacked, and the men fighting a force of between 200 and 300. I countermarched, and sent 100 men forward, with Lieutenant [Robert T.] Thompson, to ascertain the strength of the enemy and their whereabouts, with instructions to report immediately, and to hold the enemy in check until I arrived with the rest of the forces. In a short time, the lieutenant reported the enemy in line of battle in the edge of the timber, about 1 mile in advance. I immediately dispatched Captain Bowlegs, with 75 men, to flank them on the left, and ordered the forces to advance. Upon arriving at a point near where the enemy were reported, I formed a line for the purpose of a charge, and gave the command, and moved forward with my cavalry, leaving the infantry to support the howitzer. We repulsed the enemy in the first charge, they falling back about three-quarters of a mile.

They formed again with re-enforcements, and forced us back a short distance. I again formed the men, and sent my adjutant, Lieutenant [Eli C.] Lowe, back for the howitzer. The enemy again made a charge and were repulsed. In the mean time the howitzer arrived. The enemy by this time had advanced in front, upon charge, flanking us on both sides, and within 30 yards of my force and howitzer, my men keeping up a constant fire. The howitzer then opened, and upon the first report checked the enemy. I then ordered a charge. The enemy retreated, and we followed, not giving them time to rally again. We pursued them through the timber, Captain [Solomon] Kaufman occasionally giving them a shell, or canister, until we reached the prairie; the enemy falling back toward the river. Upon arriving at the prairie, I formed and rested the men. While there, I discovered a small number of the enemy forming on my left, while farther behind them I saw a force, and a heavy cloud of dust, moving on toward the entrance of the timber, apparently to cut off my communication with you, while upon my right I discovered 4 or 5 men on a high point. I then sent Lieutenant Thompson forward, with 6 men, to learn who they were. He soon returned with 2 of the men as prisoners, and reported a rebel force forming on our right. I then ordered an investigation into the number of rounds of ammunition my men had, and found upon report that some were out of caps, others powder, and some bullets; and in that condition, and from the movements of the enemy, I deemed it necessary to move into the timber, so as to keep up my communication with you—to go into camp until I heard from Major Foreman.

While in camp I received your dispatch directing me not to regulate my movements by those of Major Foreman, and ordering me to proceed to the mouth of Vine and Sallison Creeks and destroy the two ferry-boats. I then counseled [with] the officers in charge of the cavalry, and found from them that the horses were, comparatively, given out, and the men almost exhausted by marching and fighting. Upon this report, and knowing myself the condition of the men and stock, after resting two hours, I proceeded on my return to Fort Blunt. When I reached the bayou, I received an order directing me to turn my command over to Lieutenant-Colonel [Fred. W.] Schaurte, and to report to you, which I accordingly did.

We lost, in the battle of Greenleaf Prairie, 4 killed and 8 wounded; none dangerously. That of the enemy was 7 killed; none found wounded; the latter supposed to be carried off the field by ambulances, as two were seen going to the battle-ground.

In closing my report, colonel, I cannot omit to mention the bravery and daring of the following officers, who rendered me good services in the battle: Captain [Smith] Christy, of the Third Indian; Captain Kaufman, of the Third Indian (commanding howitzer); Lieutenant [John E.] Blunt, of the Third Indian; Captain [Budd] Gritts, of the Second Indian; Lieutenant [J. C.] Palmer, of the Second Indian, who was wounded while leading his men of the Second; Captain Kinter, of the Fourth Indian; Captain Cox, of the Fifth Indian, and Adjutant Lowe, Lieutenant [Robert T.] Thompson, and Lieutenant [Fred.] Crafts, of the First Indian.

Respectfully submitted.

S. H. WATTLES,
Colonel, Commanding Detachment.

Col. WILLIAM A. PHILLIPS,
Comdg. Eighth and Ninth Districts, Dept. of the Missouri.

JUNE 16-SEPTEMBER 13, 1863.—The Sioux Expedition, Dakota.

SUMMARY OF THE PRINCIPAL EVENTS.

July 24, 1863.—Action at the Big Mound.
26, 1863.—Action at Dead Buffalo Lake.
28, 1863.—Action at Stony Lake.
29-30, 1863.—Skirmishes at the Missouri River.

REPORTS.

No. 1.—Brig. Gen. Henry H. Sibley, U. S. Army, commanding expedition.
No. 2.—Col. Samuel McPhaill, First Minnesota Mounted Rangers.
No. 3.—Col. William Crooks, Sixth Minnesota Infantry.
No. 4.—Lieut. Col. William R. Marshall, Seventh Minnesota Infantry.
No. 5.—Col. James H. Baker, Tenth Minnesota Infantry.

No. 1.

*Report of Brig. Gen. Henry H. Sibley, U. S. Army, commanding expedition.**

HEADQUARTERS DISTRICT OF MINNESOTA,
Camp Carter, Bank of James River, August 7, 1863.

MAJOR: My last dispatch was dated 21st ultimo, from Camp Olin, in which I had the honor to inform Major-General Pope that I had left

* See also Appendix, pp. 907-913.

one-third of my force in an intrenched position at Camp Atchison, and was then one day's march in advance, with 1,400 infantry and 500 cavalry, in the direction where the main body of the Indians were supposed to be.

During the three following days I pursued a course somewhat west of south, making 50 miles, having crossed the James River and the Great Coteau of the Missouri. On the 24th, about 1 p. m., being considerably in advance of the main column, with some of the officers of my staff, engaged in looking out for a suitable camping ground, the command having marched steadily from 5 a. m., some of my scouts came to me at full speed, and reported that a large camp of Indians had just before passed, and great numbers of warriors could be seen upon the prairie, 2 or 3 miles distant. I immediately corraled my train upon the shore of a salt lake near by, and established my camp, which was rapidly intrenched by Colonel Crooks, to whom was intrusted that duty, for the security of the transportation in case of attack, a precaution I had taken whenever we encamped for many days previously. While the earthworks were being pushed forward, parties of Indians, more or less numerous, appeared upon the hills around us, and one of my half-breed scouts, a relative of Red Plume, a Sisseton chief, hitherto opposed to the war, approached sufficiently near to converse with him. Red Plume told him to warn me that the plan was formed to invite me to a council, with some of my superior officers, to shoot us without ceremony, and then attack my command in great force, trusting to destroy the whole of it. The Indians ventured near the spot where a portion of my scouts had taken position, 300 or 400 yards from our camp, and conversed with them in an apparently friendly manner, some of them professing a desire for peace. Surg. Josiah S. Weiser, of the First Regiment Minnesota Mounted Rangers, incautiously joined the group of scouts, when a young savage, doubtless supposing from his uniform and horse equipments that he was an officer of rank, pretended great friendship and delight at seeing him, but when within a few feet treacherously shot him through the heart. The scouts discharged their pieces at the murderer, but he escaped, leaving his horse behind. The body of Dr. Weiser was immediately brought into camp, unmutilated, save by the ball that killed him. He was universally esteemed, being skillful in his profession and a courteous gentleman. This outrage precipitated an immediate engagement. The savages, in great numbers, concealed by the ridges, had encircled those portions of the camp not flanked by the lake referred to, and commenced an attack. Colonel [Samuel] McPhaill, with two companies, subsequently re-enforced by others, as they could be spared from other points, was directed to drive the enemy from the vicinity of the hill where Dr. Weiser was shot, while those companies of the Seventh Regiment, under Lieutenant-Colonel [W. R.] Marshall and Major [George] Bradley, and one company of the Tenth Regiment, under Captain [Alonzo J.] Edgerton, were dispatched to support them. Taking with me a 6-pounder, under the command of Lieutenant [John C.] Whipple, I ascended a hill toward the Big Mound, on the opposite side of the ravine, and opened fire with spherical-case shot upon the Indians, who had obtained possession of the upper part of the large ravine, and of smaller ones tributary to it, under the protection of which they could annoy the infantry and cavalry without exposure on their part. This flank and raking fire of artillery drove them from their hiding places into the broken prairie, where they were successively dislodged from the ridges, being utterly unable to resist the steady advance of the Seventh Regiment and the Rangers, but fled before them in confusion.

While these events were occurring on the right, the left of the camp was also threatened by a formidable body of warriors. Colonel [William] Crooks, whose regiment (the Sixth) was posted on that side, was ordered to deploy part of his command as skirmishers, and to dislodge the enemy. This was gallantly done, the colonel directing in person the movements of one part of his detached force, and Lieutenant-Colonel [John T.] Averill of the other, Major [Robert N.] McLaren remaining in command of that portion of the regiment required as part of the camp ground.

The savages were steadily driven from one strong position after another, under a severe fire, until, feeling their utter inability to contend longer with our soldiers in the open field, they joined their brethren in one common flight. Upon moving forward with my staff to a commanding point which overlooked the field, I discovered the whole body of Indians, numbering from 1,000 to 1,500, retiring in confusion from the combat, while a dark line of moving objects on the distant hills indicated the locality of their families. I immediately dispatched orders to Colonel McPhaill, who had now received an accession of force from the other companies of his mounted regiment, to press on with all expedition and fall upon the rear of the enemy, but not to continue the pursuit after nightfall, and Lieutenant-Colonel Marshall was directed to follow and support him with the company of the Seventh, and Captain Edgerton's company of the Tenth, accompanied by one 6-pounder and one section of mountain howitzers, under Captain Jones. At the same time all of the companies of the Sixth and Tenth Regiments, except two from each, which were left as a camp guard, were ordered to rendezvous and to proceed in the same direction, but they had so far to march from their respective points before arriving at the spot occupied by myself and staff, that I felt convinced of the uselessness of their proceeding farther, the other portions of the pursuing force being some miles in the advance, and I accordingly ordered their return to camp. The cavalry gallantly followed the Indians, and kept up a running fight until nearly dark, killing and wounding many of their warriors, the infantry, under Lieutenant-Colonel Marshall, being kept at a double-quick in the rear. The order to Colonel McPhaill, was improperly delivered, as requiring him to return to camp, instead of bivouacking on the prairie. Consequently he retraced his way with his weary men and horses, followed by the still more wearied infantry, and arrived at camp early the next morning, as I was about to move forward with the main column. Thus ended the battle of the "Big Mound." The severity of the labors of the entire command may be appreciated when it is considered that the engagement only commenced after the day's march was nearly completed, and that the Indians were chased at least 12 miles, making altogether full 40 miles performed without rest.

The march of the cavalry of the Seventh Regiment and of Company B, of the Tenth Regiment, in returning to camp after the tremendous efforts of the day, is almost unparalleled, and it told so fearfully upon men and animals that a forward movement could not take place until the 26th, when I marched at an early hour. Colonel [J. H.] Baker had been left in command of the camp (named by the officers Camp Sibley) during the engagement of the previous day, and all the arrangements for its security were actively and judiciously made, aided as he was by that excellent officer, Lieutenant-Colonel [Samuel P.] Jennison, of the same regiment. Upon arriving at the camp from which the Indians had been driven in such hot haste, vast quantities of dried meat, tallow, and buffalo robes, cooking utensils, and other indispensable articles were found concealed in the long reeds around the lake, all of which were by my directions collected and burned. For miles along the route the prairie was strewn with like evidences of a hasty flight. Colonel McPhaill had previously informed me that beyond Dead Buffalo Lake, as far as his pursuit of the Indians had continued, I would find neither wood nor water. I consequently established my camp on the border of that lake, and very soon afterward parties of Indians made their appearance, threatening an attack. I directed Captain [John] Jones to repair with his section of 6-pounders, supported by Captain [Jonathan] Chase, with his company of pioneers, to a commanding point about 600 yards in advance, and I proceeded in person to the same point. I there found Colonel Crooks, who had taken position with two companies of his regiment, commanded by Captain [Grant] and Lieutenant Grant, to check the advance of the Indians in that quarter. An engagement ensued at long range, the Indians being too wary to attempt to close, although greatly superior in numbers. The spherical case from the 6-pounders soon caused a hasty retreat from that locality, but, perceiving it to be their intention to make a flank movement on the left of the camp in force, Captain [Oscar] Taylor, with his company of mounted rangers, was dispatched to retard their progress in that quarter. He was attacked by the enemy in large numbers, but manfully held his ground until recalled and ordered to support Lieutenant-Colonel Averill, who, with two companies of the Sixth Regiment, deployed as skirmishers, had been ordered to hold the savages in check. The whole affair was ably conducted by these officers, but the increasing numbers of the Indians, who were well mounted, enabled them by a circuitous route to dash toward the extreme left of the camp, evidently with a view to stampede the mules herded on the shore of the lake. This daring attempt was frustrated by the rapid motions of the companies of mounted rangers, commanded by Captains [Eugene M.] Wilson and [Peter B.] Davy, who met the enemy and repulsed them with loss, while Major McLaren, with equal promptitude, threw out, along an extended line, the six companies of the Sixth Regiment under his immediate command, thus entirely securing that flank of the camp from further attacks. The savages, again foiled in their design, fled with precipitation, leaving a number of their dead upon the prairie, and the battle of "Dead Buffalo Lake" was ended.

On the 27th, I resumed the march, following the trail of the retreating Indians, until I reached Stony Lake, where the exhaustion of the animals required me to encamp, although grass was very scarce.

The next day, the 28th, there took place the greatest conflict between our troops and the Indians, so far as the numbers were concerned, which I have named the battle of "Stony Lake." Regularly alternating each day, the Tenth Regiment, under Colonel Baker, was in the advance and leading the column, as the train toiled up the long hill. As I passed Colonel Baker, I directed him to deploy two companies of the Tenth as skirmishers. Part of the wagons were still in the camp, under the guard of the Seventh Regiment, when I perceived a large force of mounted Indians moving rapidly upon us. I immediately sent orders to the several commands promptly to assume their positions, in accordance with the programme of the line of march; but this was done, and the whole long train completely guarded at every point by the vigilant and able commanders of regiments and corps, before the orders reached them. The Tenth gallantly checked the advance of the enemy in front; the Sixth and cavalry on the right, and the Seventh and cavalry on the left, while the 6-pounders and two sections of mountain howitzers, under the efficient direction of their respective chiefs, poured a rapid and destructive fire from as many different points. The vast number of the Indians enabled them to form two-thirds of a circle, 5 or 6 miles in extent, along the whole line of which they were seeking for some weak point upon which to precipitate themselves. The firing was incessant and rapid from each side; but as soon as I had completed the details of the designated order of march, and closed up the train, the column issued in line of battle upon the prairie, in the face of the immense force opposed to it, and I resumed my march without any delay. This proof of confidence in our own strength completely destroyed the hopes of the savages, and completed their discomfiture. With yells of disappointment and rage, they fired a few parting volleys, and then retreated with all expedition. It was not possible, with our jaded horses, to overtake their fleet and comparatively fresh ponies.

This engagement was the last desperate effort of the combined Dakota bands to prevent a farther advance on our part toward their families. It would be difficult to estimate the number of warriors, but no cool and dispassionate observer would probably have placed it at a less figure than from 2,200 to 2,500. No such concentration of force has, so far as my information extends, ever been made by the savages of the American continent. It is rendered certain, from information received from various sources, including that obtained from the savages themselves, in their conversations with our half-breed scouts, that the remnant of the bands who escaped with Little Crow had successively joined the Sissetons, the Cut-heads, and finally the Chank-ton-ais, the most powerful single band of the Dakotas, and, together with all these, had formed an enormous camp of nearly, or quite, 10,000 souls.

To assert that the courage and discipline displayed by officers and men in the successive engagements with this formidable and hitherto untried enemy were signally displayed would but ill express the admiration I feel for their perfect steadiness, and the alacrity with which they courted an encounter with the savage foe. No one for a moment seemed to doubt the result, however great the preponderance against us in numerical force. These wild warriors of the plains had never been met in battle by American troops, and they have ever boasted that no hostile army, however numerous, would dare to set foot upon the soil of which they claimed to be the undisputed masters. Now that they have been thus met, and their utmost force defied, resisted, and utterly broken and routed, the lesson will be a valuable one, not only in its effect upon these particular bands, but upon all the tribes of the Northwest.

When we went into camp on the banks of Apple River a few mounted Indians could alone be seen. Early the next morning I dispatched Colonel McPhaill, with the companies of the Mounted Rangers and the two 6-pounders, to harass and retard the retreat of the Indians across the Missouri River, and followed with the main column as rapidly as possible. We reached the woods on the border of that stream shortly after noon on the 29th, but the Indians had crossed their families during the preceding night, and it took but a short time for the men to follow them on their ponies. The hills on the opposite side were covered with the men, and they had probably formed the determination to oppose our passage of the river, both sides of which were here covered with a dense growth of underbrush and timber for a space of more than a mile. I dispatched Colonel Crooks with his regiment, which was in the advance, to clear the woods to the river of Indians, which he successfully accomplished without loss, although fired upon fiercely from the opposite side. He reported to me that a large quantity of transportation, including carts, wagons, and other vehicles, had been left behind in the woods. I transmitted, through Mr. Beaver, a volunteer aide on my staff, an order to Colonel Crooks to return to the main column with his regiment, the object I had in view in detaching him being fully attained. The order was received, and Mr. Beaver was intrusted with a message in return, containing information desired by me, when, on his way to headquarters, he unfortunately took the wrong trail, and was the next day found where he had been set upon and killed by an outlying party of the enemy. His death occasioned much regret to the command, for he was esteemed by all for his devotion to duty and for his modest and gentlemanly deportment. A private of the Sixth Regiment, who had taken the same trail, was also shot to death with arrows, probably by the same party.

There being no water to be found on the prairie, I proceeded down the Missouri to the nearest point on Apple River, opposite Burnt Boat Island, and made my camp. The following day Colonel Crooks, with a strong detachment of eleven companies of infantry and dismounted cavalry, and three guns, under the command of Captain Jones, was dispatched to destroy the property left in the woods, which was thoroughly performed, with the aid of Lieutenant Jones and a portion of the pioneer corps. From 120 to 150 wagons and carts were thus disposed of. During this time the savages lay concealed in the grass on the opposite side of the river, exchanging occasional volleys with our men. Some execution was done upon them by the long-range arms of the infantry and cavalry, without injury to any one of my command.

I waited two days in camp, hoping to open communication with General Sully, who, with his comparatively fresh mounted force, could easily have followed up and destroyed the enemy we had so persistently hunted. The long and rapid marches had very much debilitated the infantry, and as for the horses of the cavalry and the mules employed in the transportation, they were utterly exhausted. Under all the circumstances, I felt that this column had done everything possible within the limits of human and animal endurance, and that a farther pursuit would not only be useless, as the Indians could cross and recross the river in much less time than could my command, and thus evade me, but would necessarily be attended with the loss of many valuable lives. For three successive evenings I caused the cannon to be fired and signal rockets sent up, but all these elicited no reply from General Sully, and I am apprehensive he has been detained by insurmountable obstacles. The point struck by me on the Missouri is about 40 miles by land below Fort Clarke, in latitude 46° 12′, longitude 100° 35′.

The military results of the expedition have been highly satisfactory. A march of nearly 600 miles from Saint Paul has been made, in a season of fierce heats and unprecedented drought, when even the most experienced voyagers predicted the impossibility of such a movement. A vigilant and powerful, as well as confident, enemy was found, successively routed in three different engagements, with a loss of at least 150 killed and wounded of his best and bravest warriors, and his beaten forces driven in confusion and dismay, with the sacrifice of vast quantities of subsistence, clothing, and means of transportation, across the Missouri River, many, perhaps most of them, to perish miserably in their utter destitution during the coming fall and winter. These fierce warriors of the prairie have been taught by dear-bought experience that the long arm of the Government can reach them in their most distant haunts, and punish them for their misdeeds; that they are utterly powerless to resist the attacks of a disciplined force, and that but for the interposition of a mighty stream between us and them, the utter destruction of a great camp containing all their strength was certain.

It would have been gratifying to us all if the murdering remnant of the Minday, Wakomton, and Wakpaton bands could have been extirpated, root and branch; but as it is, the bodies of many of the most guilty have been left unburied on the prairies, to be devoured by wolves and foxes.

I am gratified to be able to state that the loss sustained by my column in actual combat was very small. Three men of the cavalry were killed and 4 wounded, 1, I fear, fatally. One private of the same regiment was killed by lightning during the first engagement, and Lieutenant [Ambrose] Freeman, of Company D, also of the Mounted Rangers, a valuable officer, was pierced to death with arrows on the same day by a party of hostile Indians, while, without my knowledge, he was engaged in hunting at a distance from the main column. The bodies of the dead were interred with funeral honors, and the graves secured from desecration by making them in the semblance of ordinary rifle-pits.

It would give me pleasure to designate by name all those of the splendid regiments and corps of my command who have signalized themselves by their gallant conduct, but as that would really embrace officers and men, I must content myself by bringing to the notice of the major-general commanding such as came immediately under my own observation.

I cannot speak too highly of Colonels Crooks and Baker and Lieutenant-Colonel Marshall, commanding, respectively, the Sixth, Tenth, and Seventh Regiments of Minnesota Volunteers, and Lieutenant-Colonels Averill and Jennison and Majors McLaren and Bradley, and of the line officers and men of these regiments. They have deserved well of their country and of their State. They were ever on hand to assist me in my labors, and active, zealous, and brave in the performance of duty. Of Colonel McPhaill, commanding the Mounted Rangers, and of Majors [John H.] Parker and [Orrin T.] Hayes, and the company officers and men generally, I have the honor to state that, as the cavalry was necessarily more exposed and nearer the enemy than the other portions of the command, so they alike distinguished themselves by unwavering courage and splendid fighting qualities. The great destruction dealt out to the Indians is mostly attributable to this branch of the service, although many were killed and disabled by the artillery and infantry. Captain Jones and his officers and men of the battery were ever at their posts, and their pieces were served with much skill and effect. To Captain [Jonathan] Chase, of the pioneers, and his invaluable company, the expedition has been greatly indebted for service in the peculiar line for which they are detailed.

Captain [William R.] Baxter's company (H) of the Ninth Regiment, having been attached to the Tenth Regiment, as a part of its organization, temporarily, upheld its high reputation for efficiency, being the equal in that regard of any other company.

The surgical department of the expedition was placed by me in the charge of Surgeon [Alfred] Wharton, as medical director, who has devoted himself zealously and efficiently to his duties. In his official report to these headquarters he accords due credit to the surgeons and assistants of the several regiments present with him.

Of the members of my own staff, I can affirm that they have been equal to the discharge of the arduous duties imposed on them. Captain [Rollin C.] Olin, my assistant adjutant-general, has afforded me great assistance; and for their equal gallantry and zeal may be mentioned

Captains Pope and Atchison, Lieutenants Pratt and Hawthorne, and Captain Cox, temporarily attached to my staff, his company having been left at Camp Atchison.

The quartermaster of the expedition, Captain Corning, and Captain Kimball, assistant quartermaster, in charge of the pioneer train, have discharged their laborious duties faithfully and satisfactorily; and for Captain Forbes, commissary of subsistence, I can bear witness that but for his activity, attention, and business capacity, the interests of the Government would have suffered much more than they did, by the miserable state in which many of the packages containing subsistence stores were found.

Chief guides, Maj. J. R. Brown and Pierre Bottineau, have been of the greatest service, by their experience and knowledge of the country; and the interpreter, Rev. Mr. Riggs, has also rendered much assistance in the management of the Indian scouts. The scouts, generally, including the chiefs, McLeod and Duley, have made themselves very useful to the expedition, and have proved themselves faithful, intrepid, and intelligent.

I have the honor to transmit herewith the reports of Colonels Crooks, Baker, and Lieutenant-Colonel Marshall, commanding, respectively, the Sixth, Tenth, and Seventh Regiments of Minnesota Volunteers, and of Colonel McPhaill, commanding First Regiment Mounted Rangers.

I am, major, very respectfully, your obedient servant,

H. H. SIBLEY,
Brigadier-General, Commanding.

Maj. J. F. MELINE,
Assistant Adjutant-General, Department of the Northwest.

No. 2.

Report of Col. Samuel McPhaill, First Minnesota Mounted Rangers.

IN CAMP ON THE PLAINS, *August* 5, 1863.

GENERAL: On the 24th of July, 1863, pursuant to your order to recover the body of Dr. J. S. Weiser, surgeon First Minnesota Mounted Rangers, murdered by the Indians, I proceeded to the hills in rear of Camp Sibley with Companies A and D, of my regiment. When some 500 yards from camp, we were fired upon by the Indians occupying the summit of the hill. I immediately ordered Company A, under Capt. E. M. Wilson, to advance and fire upon the enemy, which was done in good style. The ground being rocky and broken, Companies A, D, and E were ordered to dismount and skirmish the hills, Companies B and F, under Major [O. T.] Hayes, and Company L, under Captain [P. B.] Davy, to support them. The First Battalion, under Major [J. H.] Parker, cleared the hills and drove the Indians some 2 miles, followed by Companies B and F, mounted. Here I met Lieut. Col. W. R. Marshall, Seventh Minnesota Volunteers, and requested him to protect my right flank, which he did in gallant style. Major Parker was then ordered to rally the companies of his battalion and prepare to engage the enemy, mounted. I then moved forward of the skirmishers with Companies B and F, and ordered a charge upon the enemy posted on the highest peak of the range known as the "Big Hills." This order was promptly obeyed, and the Indians dislodged from their position and driven toward the plains west of the hills. While descending the hills, I ordered another charge by Company B, under Captain [Horace] Austin. While in the act of carrying out this order, 1 man was instantly killed by lightning and another seriously injured. This occasioned a momentary confusion; order, however, was soon restored, and we pushed the enemy from their positions on the hills and in the ravines in our front to the plains below. I then ordered a rally. Companies A, B, F, and L assembled, and we pushed forward upon the Indians, who had taken refuge behind a few rude and hastily constructed intrenchments in their encampments, from which they were quickly dislodged, and a running fight commenced. At this juncture, Lieut. J.[C.] Whipple, Third Minnesota Battery, reached us with one 6-pounder, his horses entirely given out, in consequence of which he could only give the fleeing enemy two shots, which apparently threw them in still greater confusion. I then again ordered the charge, which was kept up until we had reached at least 15 miles from the first point of attack, and during which we drove them from their concealment in the rushes and wild rice of Dead Buffalo Lake by a well-directed volley from the deadly carbines, ran into their lines five times, continuing the fight till nearly dark, when Companies H, D, and G arrived, and I received your order to return to Camp Sibley, at the Big Hills; and some time having been consumed in collecting our wounded and providing transportation for them, we attempted to return, and only succeeded in reaching camp at 5 a. m. on the morning of the 25th, having in the darkness been unable to preserve our course, and having been in the saddle twenty-four hours without guide, provisions, or water. The number of Indians engaged could not have been less than 1,000, and would doubtless reach 1,500 warriors. The losses of my regiment, including a skirmish on Sunday evening, the 26th, at Dead Buffalo Lake, are as follows:*

Dr. J. S. Weiser, surgeon, and Lieut. A. Freeman, Company D, were murdered by the Indians.

The number of Indians known to have been killed by the Mounted Rangers is 31, all found with the peculiar mark of cavalry upon them. Doubtless many more were killed by the Rangers, as the wounded concealed themselves in the marshes, where it was impossible to follow them with cavalry.

In this report I esteem it a duty, and it affords me great pleasure, to say of the officers and men under my command who were engaged in this series of fights and hand-to-hand encounters, that, without exception, the utmost coolness and bravery was displayed, the only difficulty I encountered being that of restraining the wild enthusiasm of the troops during the succession of cavalry charges, and I can only say of them further that they have won for themselves a reputation of which veteran troops might well be proud.

It is also a duty and gratification to mention favorably the name of First Lieut. E. A. Goodell, acting adjutant, whose aid in the hottest of the fight rendered me great service; also the name of John Martin, of Company F, who bore dispatches with certainty, celerity, and security.

I am, general, very respectfully, your obedient servant,

SAM. McPHAILL,

Colonel, Commanding Mounted Rangers.

Brig. Gen. H. H. SIBLEY,

Commanding Expeditionary Force.

---

* Nominal list shows 3 men killed and 4 wounded.

No. 3.

Report of Col. William Crooks, Sixth Minnesota Infantry.

CAMP WILLISTON, DAK., *August* 5, 1863.

SIR: Pursuant to order of Brig. Gen. H. H. Sibley, this regiment reported at Camp Pope, Minn., for service in the expedition directed against the Sioux Indians. The march was taken up early on the morning of the 16th, and on the 26th day of June the forces encamped at the foot of Lake Traverse, a distance of 119 miles from Camp Pope. From this point a train was dispatched to Fort Abercrombie for supplies, the guard consisting of three companies of infantry, including Company H, of the Sixth Regiment, Captain [W. K.] Tattersall, one battalion of cavalry, Major [J. H.] Parker commanding, and one section of artillery, the whole under command of Lieutenant-Colonel [J. T.] Averill, of this regiment. The brigade left Lake Traverse on the 30th of June, and reached the first crossing of the Cheyenne River on the evening of the 4th of July, distant from the foot of Lake Traverse 74 miles. At this point, called Camp Hayes, the command laid over six days, awaiting the arrival of the supply train from Fort Abercrombie. The train arrived on the 9th of July, and the expedition resumed the line of march on the morning of the 11th. From this point to the second crossing of the Cheyenne, where we arrived on the 17th, the distance was 83 miles.

On the morning of the 18th, we resumed the march, and made Camp Atchison, on Lake Emily, the day's march being 12 miles. At this point I was directed to lay out an intrenched camp, and a force was selected from the several regiments to hold the same, with a view to disembarrassing the active force of all men unable to march, and of all supplies not actually necessary in a more rapid pursuit of the enemy. Companies G and C, of my regiment, were designated by me as part of the garrison, together with invalids from all other companies.

Having put the command in light marching order, on the morning of the 20th of July, with twenty-five days' rations, the command again commenced, with renewed energy, the pursuit of the Sioux; and at noon on the 24th, at a distance of 78 miles from Camp Atchison, a shout from the advance told that our pursuit had not been in vain. The savages lined the crests of the surrounding hills, covering their camp some 5 miles to the southwest. By direction of the general, the Sixth Regiment, together with Company M, of the Mounted Rangers, under command of Lieutenant [D. B.] Johnson, and a section of artillery, under command of Lieutenant [H. H.] Western, occupied the east front, and threw up earthworks, supporting the guns. About this time Surgeon Weiser, of the Mounted Rangers, in company with others, rode up the heights and engaged in conversation with the Indians, who, true to their proverbial treachery, pierced his manly heart at the moment he offered them bread. Observing this act, I at once deployed Companies E, I, and K well to the front, and with Company E, under command of Captain [Rudolph] Schoeneman, together with Captain [Jonathan] Chase's company (A), of the Ninth Regiment, on Schoeneman's left, supported by Captains [T. S.] Slaughter and [W. W.] Braden, drove the savages for 3 miles, and prevented their turning our left.

Lieutenant-Colonel Averill was directed by me to advance three companies to support the extreme left, where a strong demonstration was being made, Major McLaren remaining in command of the reserve and camp.

The movements were well and regularly made, the officers and men displaying those traits of most consequence to soldiers. My advance was checked by an order to draw in my lines to the lines of the skirmishers of the other regiments to my right, and to report in person to the brigadier-general commanding. Having turned the command over to Lieutenant-Colonel Averill, with instructions to draw in his men, I reported to General Sibley, and, in conformity with his orders, I dispatched a messenger to Major McLaren to come forward, with all haste, with five companies, to the support of the Mounted Rangers, who were driving the Indians on toward their camp, at the moment supported by the Seventh Infantry and Capt. A. J. Edgerton's company of the Tenth. The major came forward at a double-quick with Companies A, B, D, I, and K, and reported to me some 4 miles in the advance, where General Sibley was awaiting the advance of re-enforcements. I immediately reported to the general the arrival of my men, and soon thereafter was ordered to return to camp.

The next day the camp was moved some 4 miles, in order to recruit the animals, and the command rested until Sunday morning, the 26th of July, when the march was resumed, and, having marched 14 miles, the Sixth Regiment leading, the Indians again assembled for battle. The regiment at once deployed skirmishers, and advanced steadily, driving the Indians, Lieutenant-Colonel Averill, with marked coolness and judgment, commanding the extended line of skirmishers, while the reserve, under McLaren, was but too eager to engage. At 2 p. m., General Sibley coming to the extreme front, and observing the state of affairs, pushed cavalry to our right, with a view to massing the Indians in front; also ordering Captain [John] Jones forward with the field pieces. Major McLaren was now ordered to take the reserve to camp, 1½ miles to the rear, the front being held by three companies of the Sixth and Company A, of the Ninth, the whole supporting Lieutenant [J. C.] Whipple with his section of the battery.

The Indians observing McLaren's movement, having made a feint to the left, made a desperate attack upon the north front, with a view to destroying our transportation; but the major had his men well in hand, and, throwing them rapidly on the enemy, completely foiled this their last move, and the savages, giving a parting volley, typical of their rage and disappointment, left a field where heavy loss and defeat but retold their doom.

Too much praise cannot be awarded Capt. Oscar Taylor, of the Mounted Rangers, who chafed for an order to advance, and who bore his part nobly when that order was finally given. His horses being exhausted, this officer dismounted his men, and, as skirmishers, added their strength to that of Company A, Sixth Regiment, where, under the immediate eye of Colonel Averill, they did splendid service. Lieutenant Whipple, in direct charge of the guns, was, as usual, cool and efficient; and Captain Jones had but another opportunity of congratulating himself upon the efficiency of his battery.

The march was resumed on the morning of the 27th, and in the afternoon we camped on Stony Lake, having marched 18 miles. No demonstrations were made by the Indians during the night; but as the column was forming on the morning of the 28th, and the transportation was somewhat scattered, the wily foe saw his opportunity, and, to the number of 2,000 mounted men, at least, made a most daring charge upon us. The Sixth Regiment holding the center of the column, and being upon the north side of the lake, Lieutenant-Colonel Averill commenced deploying the right wing, and having deployed strongly from my left, so as to hold the lake, the advance was ordered. The men went boldly forward and worked splendidly, Lieutenant-Colonel Averill displaying much judgment in an oblique formation to cover a threatened movement on my right by the Indians in great force, who, whooping and yelling, charged our lines. The consequences must have proven destructive in the extreme had the lake and flanks not been stiffly held. The savages were driven back, reeling under their repulse, and the general commanding coolly and determinedly formed his column of march in face of the attack, the object of which was manifold: First, to destroy our transportation, and, second, to delay our advance, allowing their families more time to escape.

No time was lost; the column moved on, and by 9 a. m. our advance saw the masses of the retreating foe. The pursuit was continued until late, when we camped on Apple River. Men and horses were not in a condition to pursue that night, but early on the morning of the 29th, with the regiment in the advance, pursuit was commenced, and, after marching 6 miles and overcoming a rise of ground, our eyes first beheld the timber on the Missouri River, distant 9 miles.

General Sibley had, with much forethought, early that morning dispatched Colonel McPhaill and his regiment, with Captain Jones and his field pieces, to the front, with the view of intercepting the savages ere they crossed the river. Rapidly McPhaill pushed forward, but the Indians' rear was covered by a dense forest and a tangle of prickly ash and thorn bushes, almost impenetrable. Our advance was soon up, and by order of the general, the Sixth Regiment was ordered to scour the woods to the river, and ascertain the exact position of the enemy. I deployed Companies D, I, and K, commanded by Captains [J.C.] Whitney, Slaughter, and Braden, as skirmishers, under the command of Major McLaren, while the five other companies, under Colonel Averill, were held as a reserve. Captain Jones accompanied me, with Whipple's and Western's sections of his battery. We advanced slowly but surely, shelling the woods in my advance, and we reached the river to find the enemy just crossed, after abandoning all their transportation, and losing many of their women and children, drowned in their hasty flight. Lieutenant-Colonel Averill, with the reserve, received the fire of an enemy in large numbers, concealed in the tall rushes across the river, and returned it with spirit; but an order having reached me to return, a retrograde movement was made.

Just prior to the fire of Colonel Averill's reserve, Lieut. F. J. H. Beaver, an English gentleman, of qualities worthy of the best, a fellow of Oxford University, and a volunteer aide to the general, rode up alone and delivered the order to return. I wrote a short dispatch, and directed him to return at once, as my communication might prove of much value to the general. All being accomplished that was desired, the regiment returned, and joined the camp near the mouth of Apple River, with the loss of N. Miller, of Company K. On my return to camp, I learned that Beaver had never reported, and we had just grounds to believe him lost. Guns were fired and rockets sent up, but our friend did not return.

At noon on the 30th of July, a detachment, consisting of Companies A, I, and K, of the Sixth Regiment, commanded by Captains [Hiram P.] Grant, Slaughter, and Braden; A, B, and H, of the Seventh, commanded by Captains [J. K.] Arnold, [James] Gilfillan, and [A. H.] Stevens, and B, F, and K, of the Tenth Infantry, commanded by Captains [A. J.] Edgerton, [G. T.] White, and [M. J.] O'Connor, and Companies L and M of the cavalry, commanded by Captain [P. B.] Davy and Lieutenant [D. B.] Johnson, Lieutenants Whipple's and Dwelle's sections of the battery, together with a detachment of Company A, Ninth Regiment of Infantry, as pioneers, under Lieutenant [Harrison] Jones, the whole under my command, was ordered to proceed to the place where I had been the day before, with directions to destroy the transportation left by the Indians, and to find the body of Lieutenant Beaver, and that of Private Miller, if dead, and engage the savages, if the opportunity presented. Lieutenant-Colonel [S. P.] Jennison, of the Tenth Infantry, Major [R. N.] McLaren, of the Sixth, and Major [George] Bradley, of the Seventh, commanded the detachments of the respective regiments. All the objects contemplated were fully accomplished.

It was apparent that Lieutenant Beaver, on his way back with my dispatch, became embarrassed by the many trails left by an alarmed and conquered enemy, lost his way, and, after bravely confronting a large party of savages and dealing death into their ranks, had fallen, pierced with arrows and bullets, his favorite horse lying dead near him. He was buried in the trenches with the honor due his rank, and every heart beat in sympathy with the family of this brave stranger, as we retraced our steps toward the boundary of our own State.

I take pleasure in mentioning the services of Surgeon and Acting Medical Director [Alfred] Wharton, and of Assistant Surgeons Daniels and Potter, for duties performed whenever they were needed in and out of the regiment; also to Lieutenants Carver and [F. E.] Snow for assistance fearlessly rendered in the field. Lieutenant-Colonel Averill and Major McLaren have proven themselves worthy of the regiment.

For the officers of the line and men, I proudly say that they did all that they were ordered to do with an alacrity and a spirit which promises well for the future.

I make the distance from Fort Snelling to the Missouri, by our line of march, 585 miles.

I have the honor to remain, captain, very respectfully, your obedient servant,

WM. CROOKS,
Colonel, Commanding Sixth Minnesota Infantry.

Capt. R. C. OLIN,
Assistant Adjutant-General.

No. 4.

Reports of Lieut. Col. William R. Marshall, Seventh Minnesota Infantry.

HDQRS. SEVENTH REGIMENT MINNESOTA VOLUNTEERS,
Camp Sibley, on Missouri Coteau, July 25, 1863.

CAPTAIN: I respectfully submit the following report of the part taken by the Seventh Regiment (eight companies) in the engagement with the Indians yesterday:

Immediately after news was received of the presence of Indians, the regiment was formed in order of battle on the line designated by you for the protection of the corral—subsequently the camp—then being formed. A detail of 10 men from each company was set to digging trenches in front of our line, which fronted a little south of east, the Big Mound being directly east. The men remained upon the color line until the firing commenced on the foot-hill directly in front, where

Dr. Weiser was killed. I was then ordered to deploy Captain [Rolla] Banks' company, armed with Colt's rifles, along the foot-hill to the left of the ravine that opened toward the Big Mound. This done, Major Bradley was ordered with two companies, Captains Gilfillan and Stevens, to the support of the first battalion of cavalry, then out on the right of the ravine, where Dr. Weiser was shot. Major Bradley's detachment became engaged along with the cavalry. As soon as he reached the top of the first range of hills, I asked to advance to their support with the other five companies, and received your order to do so. With Captains Kennedy's, Williston's, Hall's, Carter's, and Arnold's companies, leaving Captain Carter in charge of the detail to finish the trenches and protect camp, I advanced at double-quick up the ravine toward the Big Mound. When opposite the 6-pounder on the left of the ravine, where the general then was, I deployed the five companies at 3 paces intervals, without any reserve. The line extended from hill to hill, across the ravine, which was here irregular or closed. Advancing as rapidly as possible, the line first came under fire when it reached the crest of the first range of hills, below the summit peaks. The Indians then occupied the summit range, giving way from the highest peak or Big Mound, driven by the fire of the 6-pounder, but in great numbers along the ridge southward. Capt. Eugene Wilson's company of cavalry, dismounted, passed to my left, and occupied the Big Mound, while I charged across the little valley, and up to the summit south of the mound. We advanced, firing, the Indians giving way as we advanced. I crossed the ridge and pursued the Indians out on the comparatively open ground east of the peaks. Their main body, however, was to our right, ready to dispute possession of the rocky ridges and ravines into which the summit range is broken in its continuation southward. I had flanked them, turning their right, and now gradually wheeled my line to the right until it was perpendicular to the range, my left being well out on the open ground, over which the enemy's extreme right was retreating. I thus swept southward, and, as the open ground was cleared—the Indians in that direction making to the hills 2 miles southeast, just beyond which was their camp, as we afterward discovered—I wheeled still more to the right, directing my attention to the summit range again, where the Indians were the thickest. Advancing rapidly and firing, they soon broke, and as I reached and recrossed the ridge they were flying precipitately and in great numbers from the ravines, which partly covered them, down toward the great plain, at the southern termination of the range of hills.

Colonel McPhaill, who, with a part of the cavalry, had crossed to the east side of the range, and kept in line in my rear, ready to charge upon the Indians when they should be dislodged from the broken ground, now passed my line and pursued the enemy out on the open plain. After I recrossed the range, I met Major Bradley, and united the seven companies. He, in conjunction with Captains Taylor's and Anderson's companies of the cavalry, dismounted, had performed much the same service on the west slope of the range of hills that I had done on the east and summit, driving the enemy from hill to hill southward, a distance of 4 or 5 miles from camp to the termination of the range.

Happily no casualties happened in my command. Indeed, the Indians from the first encounter gave way, seeming to realize the superior range of our guns, yielding ridge after ridge and ravine after ravine, as we occupied successive ridges from which our fire reached them. The hat of one soldier and the musket stock of another gave proof of shots received, and other like evidences and their balls occasionally kicking the dust up about us, and more rarely whistling past us, were the most sensible evidences of our being under fire.

The Indians were in far greater numbers than I had seen them before, certainly three times the number encountered at the relief of Birch Coolie, afterward ascertained to be 350, and more than double the number seen at Wood Lake. I judged there were from 1,000 to 1,500. Their numbers were more apparent after we had combed them out of the hills into the plain below.

After uniting the battalion at the southern termination of the great hills, I received orders to follow on, in support of the cavalry and artillery. The men were suffering greatly for water, and I marched them to a lake on the right, which proved to be salty. I then followed on after the cavalry. We passed one or more lakes that were alkaline. It was the experience of the ancient mariner:

Water, water everywhere,
Nor any drop to drink.

We continued the march until 9 o'clock at night, reaching a point 12 or 15 miles from camp. The men had been on their feet since 4 o'clock in the morning; had doubled-quicked it 5 miles during the engagement; had been without food since morning, and without water since noon. They were completely exhausted, and I ordered a bivouac.

The trail was strewed with buffalo skins, dried meat, and other effects abandoned by the Indians in their wild flight. The men gathered meat and ate it for supper, and the skins for beds and covering. At this point, Captain Edgerton's company, of the Tenth Regiment, joined us, and shared the night's hardships. We had posted guard and lain an hour, when Colonel McPhaill returned from pursuing the Indians. He urged that I should return with him to camp.

The men were somewhat rested, and their thirst stimulated them to the effort. We joined him, and started to return to camp. About midnight we got a little dirty water from the marshy lake where the Indians had been encamped. We reached camp at daylight, having marched nearly twenty-four hours, and over a distance estimated at from 40 to 45 miles.

My thanks are due to Major Bradley and the line officers for steady coolness and the faithful discharge of every duty, and to every man of the rank and file for good conduct throughout. The patient endurance of the long privation of water, and the fatigue of the weary night march, in returning to camp, after such a day, abundantly prove them to be such stuff as true soldiers are made of.

Very respectfully, your obedient servant,

WM. R. MARSHALL,
Lieutenant-Colonel, Comdg. Seventh Regiment Minnesota Vols.

Capt. R. C. OLIN,
Assistant Adjutant-General.

HDQRS. SEVENTH REGIMENT MINNESOTA VOLUNTEERS,
Camp Williston, on Missouri Coteau, August 5, 1863.

CAPTAIN: I respectfully submit the following report of the part taken by the Seventh Regiment in the pursuit of, and engagements with, the Indians subsequent to the battle of the Big Mound, on the 24th ultimo:

In my report of the 25th of July, I detailed the movements of this regiment in that engagement. On Sunday, the 26th of July, when the column was halted at the Dead Buffalo Lake, and the Indians made a demonstration in front, I was with the right wing of my regiment, on the right flank of the train; Major [George] Bradley was with the left wing, on the left, the regiment being in the middle of the column in the order of march. Leaving Major Bradley to protect the left flank, I deployed Company B, Captain [A. H.] Stevens, obliquely forward to the right. He advanced farther than I intended, and did not halt until on the right of, and even with, the line of skirmishers of the Sixth Regiment, then in the extreme advance. Thinking it better not to recall him, I advanced the three other companies of the right wing (Captains [James] Gilfillan's, [John] Kennedy's, and [T. G.] Carter's) near enough to support Company B, and at the same time protect the right of the train, which was then well closed up on the site of our camp. I remained in this position, without the Indians approaching within range, until orders were given to go into camp. I had but just dismissed the battalion from the color line to pitch tents, when the bold attack of the mounted Indians was made on the teams and animals, in the meadow on the north side of the camp. My line was on the south side of the camp. I assembled and reformed the line, awaiting an attack from the south; but the Indians that appeared on that side quickly withdrew, after they saw the repulse on the north side, not coming within gun-shot range.

I cannot withhold an expression of my admiration of the gallant style in which the companies of cavalry (I believe Captains Wilson's and Davy's, the latter under Lieutenant [L. S.] Kidder) dashed out to meet the audacious devils, that were very nearly successful in gobbling up the teams and loose animals, that being their object. The Rangers, putting their horses upon the run, were but a few seconds in reaching the Indians, whose quick right-about did not save them from the carbine and pistol shots and saber strokes, that told so well. I also saw and admired the promptitude with which Major McLaren, with a part of the Sixth Regiment, moved from his color line on that side of camp to the support of the cavalry.

On the morning of the 28th of July, at Stony Lake, the Seventh Regiment, in the order of march, was in the rear. The rear of the wagon train was just filing out of camp, going around the south end of the lake, a part still within the camp ground, which extended almost to the end of the lake, my regiment being in line, waiting for the train to get out, when the alarm was given. Quickly the Indians appeared south of the lake, and circled around to the rear. I promptly advanced the right wing on the flank of the train, south of the lake, deploying Captains Gilfillan's and Stevens' companies as skirmishers. With these, and Captains Kennedy's and Carter's companies in reserve, I immediately occupied the broken, rocky ground south of the lake; but not any too soon, for the Indians had entered it at the outer edge, not over 500 yards from the train. Lieutenant [H. H.] Western, of the battery, was in the rear, and promptly reported to me. I placed his section of the battery (two mountain howitzers) on the first elevation of the broken ground, outside the train. The fire of my line of skirmishers, then somewhat advanced on the right of the howitzers, and a few well-directed shots from Lieutenant Western's guns, discouraged the Indians from attempting to avail themselves of the cover of the small hills near us, dislodged the few that had got in, and drove the whole of them in that quarter to a very respectful distance, quite out of range. One shot from the Indians struck the ground near my feet, while I was locating the howitzers.

While I was thus occupied, Major Bradley, with the left wing (Captains Banks', Williston's, Hall's, and Arnold's companies), advanced out upon my left so as to cover the portion of the train still in camp from the threatened attack from the rear. There was a battalion of cavalry also protecting the rear to the left of Major Bradley. We thus formed a line from the left flank of the train around to the rear that effectually protected it. The Indians galloped back and forth just outside the range of the howitzers and our rifles of almost equal range, until the order came to close up the train and continue the march. As the rear of the train passed the lake, I took the right wing to the right flank of the train, near the rear, marched left in front, and so deployed as to well cover that portion of the train. Major Bradley, with the left wing, did similarly on the left flank. As the column moved forward the Indians withdrew out of sight.

On the 29th instant, when the column arrived at the Missouri River, the Seventh Regiment was the second in order of march, and was held on the flanks of the train, while the Sixth Regiment, which was in the advance, penetrated the woods to the river. By order of the general, Companies B and H were advanced as skirmishers, obliquely to the right of the head of train, to explore for water. They had entered the woods but a little way when recalled by an aide of the general.

On the 30th instant, Companies A, B, and H, Captains Arnold, Stevens, and Gilfillan, were detailed, under Major Bradley, to form part of the force under command of Colonel Crooks to again penetrate to the river, to destroy the wagons and other property of the Indians on the bank, and to search for the bodies of Lieutenant Beaver and Private Miller, of the Sixth Regiment. (I prepared to accompany the detachments, but the general objected to both the field officers of the regiment leaving camp at the same time.) Major Bradley, with the companies named, participated in the successful execution of the duty assigned Colonel Crooks.

On the night of the 31st of July, at our camp on the Missouri, I was at expedition headquarters, when the general was advised of hostile Indians having been heard signaling to one another around the camp. I returned to my regiment, and had two companies placed in the trenches. Subsequently, while I was lying down, Major Bradley received instructions to place the entire regiment along the front and flank of our part of the camp. This was done. Major Bradley remained up the entire night. I slept a part of the night; I was up, however, about 2 o'clock, when the Indians fired the volley into the north side of the camp—that occupied by the Tenth Regiment. The volley was evidently aimed too high for effect in the tents or on the men in the trenches. That side of the corral was open for passing the animals in and out, and some of the shots must have struck the cattle, in addition to the horses and mule killed. The cattle dashed out of the corral utterly wild with fright, and making the ground tremble. They were turned back and to the right by part of the line of the Tenth Regiment. They then came plunging toward the left companies of my regiment. These rose up and succeeded in turning them back into the corral. It was providential that the camp was so encircled by the lines of the several regiments. But for the living wall that confronted them, the animals would have escaped or stampeded the mules and horses, with great destruction of life in the camp. I think it was the only time I have felt alarmed or startled. The prompt return of the fire of the Indians by the companies of the Tenth, on my left, discouraged any further attempt on the camp.

The next morning we resumed the march homeward. Since then no Indians have appeared, and nothing relating to this regiment occurred to add to the above.

In concluding this report, supplementary to that made on the 25th ultimo, I beg to add a few things of a more general nature, relating to the regiment I have the honor to command.

The health of the regiment during the long march from Camp Pope, has been remarkably good. There have been but two cases of severe illness, both convalescent. Surgeon [L. B.] Smith and Assistant Surgeon [A. A.] Ames have been assiduous and skillful in their attention to the medical wants and the general sanitary condition of the regiment. My highest acknowledgments are due and tendered to them. Adjutant [E. A.] Trader and Quartermaster [Ammi] Cutler have been laborious and efficient. During the first three weeks of the march, Lieut. F. H. Pratt was acting quartermaster, and gave the highest satisfaction in the discharge of his duties. Chaplain [O. P.] Light, who remained at Camp Atchison, has been faithful in his ministrations. The non-commissioned staff has been every way efficient. The good order and discipline of the regiment have been perfect; but two or three arrests have been made, and those for trivial offenses.

I feel it due to Major Bradley to again refer to him in acknowledgment of the assistance he has constantly rendered me. Soon after the march began, I became so afflicted with irritation of the throat from dust that the surgeon forbade my giving commands to the battalion. Major Bradley has relieved me almost entirely in this respect, and has otherwise shared with me fully the responsibilities of the command.

Grateful to the Divine Providence that has guided and protected us, I am, captain, very respectfully, your obedient servant,

WM. R. MARSHALL,
Lieutenant-Colonel, Comdg. Seventh Regt. Minnesota Infantry.

Capt. R. C. OLIN,
Assistant Adjutant General.

No. 5.

Report of Col. James H. Baker, Tenth Minnesota Infantry.

HDQRS. TENTH REGIMENT MINNESOTA INFANTRY,
Camp Williston, August 5, 1863.

CAPTAIN: I have the honor herewith to submit a report of such part as was borne by my regiment, or any portion of it, in the several actions from July 24, at Big Mound, to the Missouri River.

About 3.30 o'clock on Friday, the 24th of July, while on the march, doing escort duty in the center, I received information from the general commanding that a large force of Indians was immediately in our front, accompanied by an order communicated by Lieutenant Beaver to prepare my regiment for action, which order was immediately executed. Meantime the train was being corraled on the side of the lake; after which I received orders to form my regiment on the color line indicated for it, immediately in front of the corral, and fronting outward from the lake, and to throw up intrenchments along the line, which was speedily done. The action of this day began on my right, more immediately in front of the Seventh (which regiment, being in advance during the day's march, was entitled to the forward position), by the artillery under Captain Jones, when, at 4.30 p. m., I received an order by Captain Olin to deploy a company to support this battery. I immediately deployed Company B, Captain Edgerton, and that company, though fatigued already with an ordinary day's march, continued with the battery (marching for many miles on the double-quick) during the entire pursuit of the enemy, for 15 miles, and throughout the night till sunrise next morning, when they returned from the pursuit to camp, having made during the day and night the almost unparalleled march of quite 50 miles.

At about 5 o'clock I received an order by Captain Pope to send Lieutenant-Colonel Jennison with four companies, to be deployed and to follow in the direction of the retreating enemy, as a support for the cavalry and artillery. Colonel Jennison moved forward, with Companies A, F, C, and K, 5 miles, more than half of it on the double-quick, and reported his command to the general commanding, at that time in the front. After resting about one hour, by the order of the general commanding, Colonel Jennison was directed to return to camp with his force, and arrived at a little after 9 p. m. At the same time that the first order above alluded to was given, I was directed to assume command of the camp, and make the proper dispositions for its defense, which I did by completing all the intrenchments and organizing and posting such forces as were yet left in camp, not anticipating the return of our forces that night.

The action of the 26th of July took place on the side of the camp opposite from my regiment, and, consequently, we did not participate in it. We were, however, constantly under arms, ready at any moment for orders or an opportunity.

On Tuesday, the 28th of July, my regiment being in the advance for the day's march, we started out of Camp Ambler at 5 o'clock in the morning. The general commanding, some of the scouts, and a few of the headquarters wagons had preceded my regiment out of camp, and were ascending the long sloping hill which gradually rose from Stony Lake. I had just received, directly from the general commanding, orders for the disposition of my regiment during the day's march, when the scouts came from over the hill on the full run, shouting, "They are coming! they are coming!" Immediately a very large body of mounted Indians began to make their appearance over the brow of the hill, and directly in front of my advancing column. I instantly gave the necessary orders for the deployment of the regiment to the right and left, which, with the assistance of Lieutenant-Colonel Jennison and the great alacrity of commandants of companies, were executed with the utmost rapidity, though a portion of my line was thrown into momentary confusion by the hasty passage through it of the returning scouts and advance wagons. At this moment an Indian on the brow of the hill shouted, "We are too late; they are ready for us." Another one replied, "But remember our children and families; we must not let them get them." Immediately the Indians, all well mounted, filed off right and left along the hill in my front with the utmost rapidity. My whole regiment was deployed, but the Indians covered my entire front, and soon far outflanked on both sides, appearing in numbers that seemed almost incredible, and most seriously threatening the train to the right and left of my widely extended line. The position of the train was at this moment eminently critical. It had begun to pass out of the corral around both ends of the small lake, to mass itself in the rear of my regiment, in the usual order of march. The other regiments were not yet in position, as the time to take their respective places in the order of march had not arrived. Fortunately, however, Captain Jones had early moved out of camp with one section of artillery, and was in the center of my left wing, and Lieutenant Whipple, with another, near to the center of my right, which was acting under Colonel Jennison.

Simultaneously with the deployment of the regiment, we began a steady advance of the whole line up the hill upon the foe, trusting to the speedy deployment of the other infantry regiments and the cavalry for the protection of the train, so threatened on either flank at the ends of the lake. My whole line was advancing splendidly up the hill, directly upon the enemy, the artillery doing fine work, and the musketry beginning to do execution, when I received a peremptory order to halt the entire line, as a farther advance would imperil the train. So ardent were both officers and men for the advance, that it was with some considerable difficulty that I could effect a halt. Believing fully that the great engagement of the expedition was now begun, and seeing in my front and reaching far beyond either flank more than double the number of Indians that had hitherto made their appearance, I took advantage of the halt to make every preparation for a prolonged and determined action. Meantime long-range firing continued throughout the entire line, and frequently the balls of the enemy would reach to, and even pass over, my men, though it was evident that the range of the Indian guns bore no comparison to ours. About this time I twice received the order to cause the firing to cease, which order I found very difficult to execute, owing to the wide extent of my line and intense eagerness of the men. I then received orders that, as the train was closed up, I should form my regiment in order of battle, deploy as skirmishers, holding two companies in reserve, and that, thus advancing, our order of march would be resumed in the face of the enemy. In a few minutes, the dispositions being made, all was ready, and, in the order of battle indicated, we passed the hill, and found that the enemy had fled. We saw them but once again for a moment, on a distant hill, in great numbers, when they entirely disappeared. My regiment marched in deployed order of battle *en échelon* at the head of the column for 18 miles, expecting and ready to meet the enemy at any moment.

The number of Indians so suddenly charging upon us was estimated at not less than from 1,500 to 2,000. They were well mounted, and moved about with the utmost rapidity and with their characteristic hideous yells. The artillery, under Captain Jones and Lieutenant Whipple, did great execution, as I could well observe, and the fire of my men did effective service, and enabled us to hold the enemy at bay till the train was closed up and the regular dispositions for its defense made. At least 3 of the enemy were seen to fall by the fire from my line, their bodies being thrown on ponies and rapidly carried away. The artillery must have killed and wounded a considerable number. Nothing could exceed the eagerness, firmness, and gallant bearing of all the officers and men of my command during this unexpected and by far, numerically, the greatest effort the Indians had yet made upon the forces of the expedition. In their courage and earnest desire to clear the enemy from the hill by a double-quick charge, my officers and men were a unit. Nothing but the immediate peril of the train could induce them to cease the advance they had so gallantly begun.

On the 30th of July, while at Camp Slaughter, on the Missouri, I received an order to send three companies of my regiment, under Lieutenant-Colonel Jennison, to join an expedition under Colonel Crooks, the object of which was to skirmish through the timber and heavy underbrush to the river, and destroy the property of the Indians, known to be upon its banks. This most laborious task was assigned to Companies B, F, and K, and a portion of Company C. A report of their operations will, of course, be given you by the officer commanding the expedition.

I desire, captain, to avail myself of this opportunity to express my sincere gratification at the good order, faithful devotion to every duty, most determined perseverance in the long and weary marches, uncomplaining in the severe guard and trenching labors, submitting unmurmuringly to every fatigue, which has characterized the officers and men of my regiment during the tedious and arduous march we have made to the distant shores of the Missouri River. It is with justifiable pride that I here note how nobly they have performed all that has been required at their hands.

I have the honor to be, captain, very respectfully, your obedient servant,

J. H. BAKER,
Colonel Tenth Regiment Minnesota Infantry.

Capt. R. C. OLIN,
Assistant Adjutant-General, District of Minnesota.

JUNE 17, 1863.—Skirmish near Westport, Mo.

REPORTS.

No. 1.—Capt. Henry Flesher, Ninth Kansas Cavalry.
No. 2.—Capt. George W. Ashby, Twelfth Kansas Infantry.

No. 1.

Report of Capt. Henry Flesher, Ninth Kansas Cavalry.

OLATHE, *June* 18, 1863.

MAJOR: Just before sundown last night, my advance was fired on by from 200 to 300 rebels at the edge of the timber this side of Westport. They were strongly posted behind a stone wall. I was compelled to retreat through a long lane. They followed so closely that I could not form my command until we got to the end of it. By this time our loss was 25 men. We formed by a house, and drove them back a short distance. Night came on, and we retreated slowly toward Olathe. The rain came on, and we have come to this place for breakfast. We scouted so hard in Missouri that our men and horses are all given out. We heard that Westport was in the hands of the rebels, and thought that we could not reach you last night. Send orders by this messenger. We will either meet him on the road, or he will find us here. Lieutenant Haughout had 21 men. His loss is 7; mine is almost one-half.

In great haste, major, I am, yours, respectfully,

HENRY FLESHER,
Captain Company E, Ninth Kansas Volunteer Cavalry.

Maj. LINN K. THACHER,
Ninth Kansas Cavalry.

COMMANDING OFFICER AT KANSAS CITY:

If Major Thacher, Ninth Kansas Volunteer Cavalry, has left there, inform me where he has gone with his command.

HENRY FLESHER,
Captain Company E, Ninth Kansas Volunteer Cavalry.

No. 2.

Report of Capt. George W. Ashby, Twelfth Kansas Infantry.

HEADQUARTERS,
Westport, Mo., June 18, 1863.

GENERAL: The detachment sent out to bring in the dead have just returned, bringing 5 more dead, making 14 Union and 1 rebel. Two wounded were brought in; in all, 4 wounded. I have no information from our men that are out.

I am, your obedient servant,

G. W. ASHBY,
Captain, Commanding Post.

General EWING, *Kansas City.*

JUNE 17, 1863.—Affair near Wellington, Mo.

Report of Lieut. Col. Bazel F. Lazear, First Missouri State Militia Cavalry.

HEADQUARTERS,
Lexington, June 18, 1863.

SIR: I have the honor to report that at 1 o'clock yesterday morning Lieutenant [John H.] Smith, Company I, First Missouri State Militia Cavalry, with 50 men of the different companies here, fired upon a party of 4 bushwhackers, killing 3. This was near Wellington, where they had just left after robbing a store.

I sent this party out to watch the roads, and it is the only way we can get at the scoundrels, and I shall continue to pursue this course, unless disapproved by you, and for that reason would rather that no troops be sent into this county without my being advised of it.

Very respectfully,

B. F. LAZEAR,
Lieutenant-Colonel, Comdg. First Missouri State Militia Cavalry.

Brigadier-General EWING,
Commanding District of the Border.

JUNE 18, 1863.—Skirmish near Rocheport, Mo.

Report of Col. Odon Guitar, Ninth Missouri State Militia Cavalry.

STURGEON, MO., *June* 18, 1863.

GENERAL: Forty men of Companies A and B, my regiment, encountered Jackman, Rucker, and company, with 100, on the river, 1½ miles above Rocheport, at 9 a. m. this morning. A sharp skirmish ensued. There were several lost, killed and wounded, on each side. I leave in ten minutes for scene, and will be with them before midnight. I will endeavor to organize district when I get back.

O. GUITAR,
Colonel, Commanding.

Major-General SCHOFIELD.

JUNE 20-23, 1863.—Scouts from Waynesville, Mo.

Report of Capt. Josiah C. Smith, Fifth Missouri State Militia Cavalry.

WAYNESVILLE, MO., *June* 28, 1863.

MAJOR: Of the two late scouts made by your orders, I have the honor to report that on Saturday evening, the 19th [20th], when about 6 miles out of camp, I came across a gang of 26 bushwhackers. With my squad of 8, I pitched into them, and scattered them in all directions. It was in a short time a general running free fight, in which one of the men was taken prisoner, his horse and equipments taken, and he turned loose, on parole of a man signing himself S. S. Tucker, but whose real name is Benson Woods. The parole is, of course, not valid. Night coming on, we returned to camp, bringing only one pair of saddle-bags filled with provisions (as trophies).

Leaving camp again on the morning of the 20th, we scouted the country between Robideaux and Gasconade to near the line of Laclede County. On the 21st, discovered signs of a band. On the 22d, struck their trail; but previous to this I had joined Lieutenant [C. C.] Twyford, of my company, with a squad of men, now making our number up to 27. About noon we came across the band grazing their horses; but they discovered us about the same time we did them, but we were on to them so quick that only 2 of them succeeded in mounting, 1 of whom we caught, after a chase of nearly 2 miles; also 4 loose horses. Of those that we left afoot, 2 escaped, but their leader, a noted stage robber by the name of Casey, was killed. And here allow me to mention the noteworthy conduct of William Wilson, a citizen of this place, who evinced true courage and determination in chasing up and capturing these outlaws, having his horse shot under him, but never faltering as long as anything was to be done. On the 23d, we struck the trail of the two who had escaped on foot. After trailing them about 25 miles, we came upon them as they ran from their old den, which is in Wright County, 10 miles southwest of Mountain Store, and am sorry to say that circumstances were such that we were forced to take these two villains prisoners. We had now four out of the five first routed.

We then proceeded to their camp, near by, which the Lebanon troops said had been entered by them; but in this they were mistaken, although they had found several camps, and been within 200 yards of their last hiding place, and, no doubt, had caused them to evacuate in a hurry, as we found left in camp one Austrian rifle, one shot-gun, curry-comb, brushes, shoeing tools, &c. We could find nothing of their trail, owing to the heavy fall of rain. We now turned our heads toward camp, and scouted over many miles of country, visiting portions of your counties, and stirring the secesh up in general.

We captured in all 3 bushwhackers, killed 1, captured 7 head of horses, 1 Government mule, 4 saddles, 1 Austrian rifle, 2 revolvers, 1 musketoon, and a quantity of clothing and boots and shoes, which they said they had taken from the store of Mr. Stith, near Lebanon.

Allow me to say that during all the scouts and the two little skirmishes the men under me behaved nobly, and though a great many shots were fired at them, no one was hurt. I will also state that I have ascertained the whereabouts of a camp of 64 men near the Arkansas line, and entirely unsupported; this I had from Casey just before he died; also from the prisoners we now have. One of this gang, by the name of Frick, killed a man on the Gasconade last week, by the name of Sherwood, which information I also got from Casey as he was dying.

I close by saying that if we had the men here to work with, we could effectually break up this bushwhacking business, as we now know the country nearly as well as they.

I am, major, very respectfully, your obedient servant,

J. C. SMITH,
Captain Company H, Fifth Missouri State Militia Cavalry.

Major FISCHER,
Commanding Waynesville, Mo.

JUNE 23, 1863.—Skirmish at, and destruction of, Sibley, Mo.

REPORTS.

No. 1.—Brig. Gen. Thomas Ewing, jr., U. S. Army, commanding District of the Border.

No. 2.—Capt. Samuel A. Flagg, Fourth Missouri State Militia Cavalry.

No. 1.

Report of Brig. Gen. Thomas Ewing, jr., U. S. Army, commanding District of the Border.

KANSAS CITY, MO., *June* 30, 1863.

COLONEL: On the 20th instant, Captain [Samuel A.] Flagg, commanding detachments of four companies of the Fourth Missouri, reported to me that on his route here from Lexington, and especially in the neighborhood of Sibley and Napoleon, he encountered many bands of guerrillas, numbering in the aggregate several hundred men, of whom he killed 4 and wounded 6. On the night of the 22d instant I sent him in command of his detachments, numbering about 125 effective men, and of two companies of infantry from Independence to the Napoleon Bottoms, some 14 miles from Independence, being the district he reported as specially infested. He started the infantry, as ordered, at 10 o'clock at night, and it reached the neighborhood of the guerrilla camp before day. He himself, however, did not catch up with the infantry until after sunrise, and the guerrillas, having abundant notice, fell back to Sibley, he with the cavalry pursuing them. The captain reports to me:

I ordered Lieutenant [Richard C.] Anderson, with one squadron of cavalry, in the advance, to go into Sibley. As soon as they made the edge of the town, they were fired upon, and returned the fire with great vigor. I then ordered Lieutenant [James H.] Brown and Lieutenant [Reuben P.] Mooney forward to support the first squadron, when the bushwhackers made a hasty retreat, leaving 2 of their number dead and 4 wounded. It being a general place of resort for the bushwhackers, and where they concentrated to fire on all the boats that passed, for the purpose of plundering them, and as they used the houses as shelter to fire on my men, the town was burned, with the exception of one or two houses that were left, reported as Union property.

I think it probable that it was for the good of the service that the town was burned, for the reasons named by Captain Flagg; but, not feeling entirely satisfied, I will take care to ascertain the character of the people, and their conduct, as also the circumstances under which the town was burned.

It is reported the town of Butler, Bates County, or a large part, was burned by guerrillas on the 21st instant. Company D, Ninth Kansas, Captain [Charles F.] Coleman, was stationed there, but I was compelled to order it to West Point (on the line), to guard a considerable extent of the border, from which I had withdrawn two companies to fill the place of Penick's regiment, just taken from the upper border. Captain Coleman reports to me that nearly all the Union families in the town left there some days before he was ordered away with a militia company which went to Germantown, Henry County, and the rest of the Union families came with him to Kansas. He says there are no Union families in the county, and all the secessionists known to have been in the Southern army from that county are again at home or in the brush. He reports, on authority which he regards as reliable, that on the 24th instant about 200 rebel infantry passed northward near by Johnstown, Bates County, and that within the past three months parties have gone north, numbering in the aggregate, with this infantry, not less than 1,000. The captain is an entirely careful and reliable officer, and I have considerable confidence in his information and opinion. I am inclined to think, however, that, if so many as that have come north, a large part of them have done so to get home and quit fighting.

I am, colonel, very respectfully,

THOMAS EWING, JR.,
Brigadier-General, Commanding.

Lieut. Col. C. W. MARSH,
Assistant Adjutant-General, Department of the Missouri.

No. 2.

Report of Capt. Samuel A. Flagg, Fourth Missouri State Militia Cavalry.

KANSAS CITY, MO., *June* 28, 1863.

SIR: I have the honor to report, for the information of the commanding general, the scout commanded by me in the vicinity of Sibley and Napoleon Bottoms.

The infantry started at 10 o'clock Monday night, the 22d of June, with instructions to move near Sibley, and conceal themselves until I came up with the cavalry, so that we could act in concert. I formed a junction with them about 6 o'clock in the morning, when I moved on to Sibley. I ordered Lieutenant [R. C.] Anderson, with one squadron of cavalry, in the advance, to go into Sibley. As soon as they made the edge of the town, they were fired upon by a party of bushwhackers. They returned the fire with great vigor. I then ordered the infantry to skirmish the woods and get to the rear of the town, but the brush was so thick they could not make it. There was sharp shooting in my front while the infantry was in the brush. I then ordered Lieutenant [J. H.] Brown and Lieutenant [R. P.] Mooney forward to support the first squadron, when the bushwhackers made a hasty retreat, leaving 2 of their number dead and 4 wounded. It being a general place of resort for the bushwhackers, and where they concentrated to fire into all the boats that pass for the purpose of plundering them, and as they used the houses for shelter to fire on my men, the town was burned, except one or two houses that were left, reported as Union property.

From information I received at different times through the day that parties had left the evening before and gone toward the south, and as the force was light at Independence, I returned to that place. On my return, a party of my cavalry ran some bushwhackers from Mr. Roberson's house, where I had run them from the house three times before, and told them to be careful and not have them run from there again. They paid no attention to it, and their house was burned. I arrived at Independence with my command at 7 o'clock, on the 23d of June, 1863, with 6 horses captured; 4 of them were turned over to Captain [J.] Huntoon and 2 turned over to the owners by myself.

I have the honor to be, major, respectfully, your obedient servant,

S. A. FLAGG,
Captain, Comdg. Detachment Fourth Missouri State Militia.

Maj. P. B. PLUMB,
Assistant Adjutant-General.

JUNE 23, 1863.—Skirmish near Papinsville, Mo.

Report of Lieut. Col. Bazel F. Lazear, First Missouri State Militia Cavalry.

LEXINGTON, *June* 28, 1863.

SIR: I have the honor to report that, on the morning of the 23d instant, Major [Alexander W.] Mullins, in command of a detachment of the First Missouri State Militia Cavalry, from Germantown, followed a band of rebels, about 50 in number, to the Osage River, near Papinsville, Bates County, where they crossed the river, going south. Pursuit was kept up for some 12 miles south of the river, when the party were overtaken by Major Mullins' advance. A skirmish ensued, resulting in the killing of 1 rebel and wounding 1, and capture of 1 Enfield rifle, with 40 rounds of cartridges, 1 horse, and 1 mule. It was now night, and the rebels fled and were lost sight of. Major Mullins had 1 man badly, if not mortally, wounded.

Very respectfully,

B. F. LAZEAR,
Lieutenant-Colonel, Comdg. First Missouri State Militia Cavalry.

Brigadier-General EWING,
Commanding District of the Border.

JUNE 23, 1863.—Attack on Pawnee Agency, Nebr.

Report of Capt. Henry L. Edwards, Second Nebraska Cavalry.

PAWNEE RESERVATION,
June 23, [24,] 1863.

SIR: I have the honor to report that the Sioux (supposed to be Brules) attacked the agency yesterday, killing several Pawnees and wounding myself. I ordered First Lieut. Henry Gray to follow them with 35 men, and, if practicable, to attack them. After pursuing about 50 of them for about 15 miles, he came upon about 400 or 500 drawn up in line ready to receive him, and upon being assured that the Pawnees, who were with him, 300 or 400 strong, would fight with him, he threw out some skirmishers, when the Sioux opened upon them with rifles, killing Sergt. Joseph Dyson, and mortally wounding Private George Osborn; also killing their horses. At the first fire the Pawnees ran, leaving our men alone. Lieutenant Gray fought them about an hour, when they retreated. Four or five Sioux were killed and several horses. I had started to his assistance with 20 men and one howitzer, which I was compelled to send back, owing to the roughness of the country. When I reached Lieutenant Gray, the Sioux were still in force about 6 miles distant; but it being nearly night, I determined not to attack them, and fell back to my camp.

To better protect the whites living at the agency, I have crossed the Beaver and established camp near the agency, where I shall remain until I receive further orders.*

Very respectfully,

HENRY L. EDWARDS,
Captain Company D, Second Nebraska Cavalry.

Brigadier-General MCKEAN, *Omaha, Nebr.*

JULY 1-2, 1863.—Engagement at Cabin Creek, Ind. T.

REPORTS.

No. 1.—Col. William A. Phillips, Third Indian Home Guards, commanding at Fort Gibson.
No. 2.—Col. James M. Williams, First Kansas Colored Infantry.
No. 3.—Maj. John A. Foreman, Third Indian Home Guards.

No. 1.

Report of Col. William A. Phillips, Third Indian Home Guards, commanding at Fort Gibson.

HEADQUARTERS UNITED STATES FORCES,
Fort Blunt, July 7, 1863.

SIR: I have sent the reports of Colonel [J. M.] Williams and Major [John A.] Foreman, of the late engagement at Cabin Creek.

I sent Foreman with a howitzer and 600 men, all I could mount, to

---

* Return of casualties reports 1 man killed and 2 wounded.

Baxter Springs, to meet the train. Several delays occurred with the train, which I regret, as my command was in a suffering condition. I sent scouts to watch for Cabell, who was threatening to effect a junction from the east. Infantry [was sent] up to re-enforce them; but Grand River and Spring River were up very high, and I knew he could not cross.

The engagement at Cabin Creek was spirited, but I regret that there had not been a greater effort to push the broken enemy. A desire to lend everything to the safety of the train restrained it.

Colonel Watie, with 2 men, fled from his forces when they broke, and reported to General Cooper, in dismay, that he was defeated and broken, he having swam both Arkansas and Grand Rivers. Colonel McIntosh also fled; but [J. W.] Wells, Cooper's adjutant, who did the work, I expect, remained and held the force of the enemy as long as possible.

The plan of the enemy was undoubtedly to hold the strong natural position at Cabin Creek until Cabell re-enforced them. These the condition of Grand River prevented, and their judgment was unwise. I have reason to believe that Wells was killed or badly wounded.

By the scouts I sent on the east side of the river, I learn that Cabell came in from Arkansas with (said to be 2,000 men), I think, about 1,200 and three pieces of artillery. He passed close to Hildebrand's Mill, and through Long Prairie to Grand Saline. From Grand Saline he returned eastward last Saturday. My scouts followed him to within 5 miles of Hildebrand's Mill, when Cabell took the left-hand road to Fort Wayne. They returned. A few men are following, watching his movements, and will report to me.

I sent back the force directed with the train, and a heavy additional force, with one howitzer, under Colonel [George] Dole. Fearing from my last dispatches that Cabell might swing round from Maysville, I am sending after the train 500 more infantry and a section of Hopkins' battery.

I regret the wound of Major Foreman in the late affair, but hope he will recover. I learn that the other troops behaved very well. The Ninth Kansas made a gallant charge, sustaining some loss, and the negro regiment fought well and managed their two guns well. All the troops behaved gallantly, as I am informed.

Part of the enemy's men and horses got drowned trying to escape by fording Grand River. The dead men and horses floated past Fort Blunt.

Respectfully,

WM. A. PHILLIPS,
Colonel, Commanding.

Major-General BLUNT.

No. 2.

Report of Col. James M. Williams, First Kansas Colored Infantry.

FORT BLUNT, C. N., *July* —, 1863.

COLONEL: I have the honor to report to you the following account of incidents occurring upon the march of my command from Baxter Springs, Kans., to Fort Blunt, C. N.:

I left Baxter Springs on the 26th ultimo, and overtook the supply train the same day. I concluded to accompany this train on the route, with the view of offering assistance in case of an attack by the enemy, which was expected, as it was known that a large force of the enemy had been concentrated with this view.

Nothing unusual occurred until about noon of the 1st instant, when we came upon the enemy, strongly posted upon Cabin Creek, completely commanding the ford. Major Foreman, of the Third Indian Home Guards, skirmished with their pickets, killing 3 and capturing 3, when they retired across Cabin Creek, to their main body. I ordered up one of the 12-pounder howitzers attached to my command, which, with the mountain howitzers of Major Foreman, opened a brisk fire of shell and canister, under the fire of which the soundings of the creek were taken, and, finding it too high to cross the train, the forces were ordered into camp to await the falling of the stream, usually quite small, but now much swollen by the recent rains. That evening I held a consultation with Lieutenant-Colonel [Theodore H.] Dodd, commanding escort to the train, and Major Foreman, and it was determined to unite the different forces, as many as could be spared from the immediate defense of the train, which had been corraled upon the prairie, about 2 miles from the ford. Accordingly, Colonel Dodd ordered to my support three companies of the Second Colorado Infantry [Cavalry], under command of Major [J. Nelson] Smith, and Company B, Third Wisconsin Cavalry, Company C, Ninth Kansas Cavalry, and Company B, Fourteenth Kansas Cavalry, under the command of Captain [John E.] Stewart, Company C, Ninth Kansas Cavalry, and the Indian Battalion commanded by Major Foreman, with one section of Second Kansas Battery, commanded by Lieutenant [Aristarchus] Wilson. After making a careful reconnaissance on the evening of the 1st in company with Colonel Dodd and Major Foreman, I laid the plan of attack as follows, viz: To place the two 6-pounders under command of Lieutenant Wilson on a point to the extreme left; one 12-pounder howitzer and one mountain howitzer in the center, directly in front of and not more than 200 yards from the position held by the enemy, and one 12-pounder howitzer on the right, and to attempt to cross the stream under the fire of these pieces. Accordingly I formed a column of attack in the following order:

1st. One company Indian Home Guards, led by Major Foreman in person.

2d. First Regiment Kansas Colored Volunteers, commanded by Lieutenant-Colonel [John] Bowles.

3d. Battalion of Second Colorado Infantry.

4th. Battalion of three companies of cavalry, the balance of the Indian Battalion being detached guarding the river above and below.

This disposition being completed, at 8 a. m. of 2d instant I opened a brisk cannonade, with shell and canister, upon the enemy's position, which was continued for forty minutes without interruption, when the firing ceased, the enemy having apparently retired from his position, and I ordered the column forward, it having previously been ascertained that the creek had fallen sufficiently to allow a passage. As the advance, led by Major Foreman, had nearly reached the opposite shore, they were met by a violent fire of musketry from the enemy, who had concealed themselves behind logs in the thick brush which lined the opposite shore. Major Foreman was twice shot by musket-balls, his horse receiving five shots. Seeing their gallant leader fall, this advance company retired somewhat confusedly to the position formerly occupied by them. At this time the advance of the infantry had nearly reached the water's edge, and I ordered a halt, filed the three leading companies to the right, and opened upon the enemy a fire of musketry, and again opened the artillery upon their position, which was continued for twenty minutes, when I ordered the two pieces on my left to cease firing, and brought Company C, Ninth Kansas Cavalry, under command of Lieut. R. C. Philbrick, to replace the Indian company, who were directed to follow the column across. This disposition being made, I ordered the advance at the double-quick, still keeping up the fire from the three companies of infantry, formed as before stated, and the howitzers. The enemy again opened fire, but did not succeed in checking our advance, and, with the loss of but 3 or 4 wounded, I succeeded in crossing my column, the infantry wading to the arm-pits in water, and, driving the enemy from the brush, formed a line of battle directly in front of the enemy, who now formed in battle array about 400 yards in advance upon the edge of the prairie. I ordered two companies of cavalry, under Captain Stewart, to take position on my right, to prevent any flank movement that might be attempted by the enemy in that direction, and ordered the company commanded by Lieutenant Philbrick to charge the advance line of the enemy, penetrate it, and, if possible, ascertain his strength and position, which was gallantly executed by the lieutenant, who charged directly upon the center of the enemy's line, broke it, and put him to flight. Seeing this, I ordered forward all the cavalry in pursuit of the now fleeing enemy, who were pursued for 5 miles, killing many and dispersing them in all directions.

My whole loss in this engagement was 1 killed and about 20 wounded, among the latter Major Foreman, seriously, and Captain [Ethan] Earl, of the First Regiment Kansas Colored Volunteers, slightly.

The loss of the enemy is not definitely known, but, from the best I am able to obtain, I think it will not fall short of 50 killed, as many more wounded, and 9 prisoners.

The strength of the enemy, as near as can be ascertained from the prisoners, was from 1,600 to 1,800, consisting of Cols. Stand Watie's and McIntosh's Cherokee [and Creek] regiments, with detachment of 600 men from the Twenty-seventh [Fifth Texas Partisan Rangers*] and Twenty-ninth Texas [Cavalry] Regiments. My column of attack, which crossed the stream, was less than 900 men, all told.

I cannot close this communication without referring to the chivalrous and soldierly conduct of the entire command during the engagement; the whole command crossing this difficult ford, and forming in the face of the enemy, with as much ease and little confusion as if upon parade. Had there been no train to guard, so that the whole force could have been employed against the enemy, I don't know but I should have been able to capture the whole force. But as the prime object was to conduct the supply train to your command, it was not deemed proper to cause any delay in pursuing the enemy; consequently I directed that portion of my command which had been sent me from the escort to report back to Lieutenant-Colonel Dodd, and immediately on the evening of the same day resumed the march, arriving at Fort Blunt on the 5th instant without any further interruption.

I have the honor, colonel, to be, and remain, your obedient servant,

J. M. WILLIAMS,

Colonel First Regiment Kansas Colored Volunteers, Commanding.

Col. WILLIAM A. PHILLIPS.

---

* The Twenty-seventh Texas was in Mississippi at this time.

No. 3.

Report of Maj. John A. Foreman, Third Indian Home Guards.

FORT BLUNT, *July* 5, 1863.

SIR: In compliance with your instructions, I joined your supply train from Fort Scott, at Baxter Springs, on the 24th of June, instant [ultimo]. On the 25th, began the march with the train for this place. Arrived at Hudson's Ford, on the Neosho River, the 26th instant [ultimo], where we were obliged to remain until the 29th by high water, when we succeeded in crossing the train. On the 30th, we discovered a trail. I immediately detached Lieutenant [Luke F.] Parsons, of the Third Indian Regiment, with 20 Cherokees, to ascertain what had made the trail, as it was fresh. Parsons followed the trail about 4 miles, when he found 30 of the enemy, who proved to be Stand Watie's advanced picket. He gallantly attacked and defeated them, taking 3 prisoners and killing 4. On the 1st of July we arrived at Cabin Creek, where we found the enemy in force, concealed in a thicket on the south bank of the creek. I immediately deployed my command on the right and left of the ford. Lieutenants [David A.] Painter, of the Second, and Parsons, of the Third Indian Regiments, on the right; Lieutenant [Fred.] Crafts, of the First Indian, and Lieutenant [Benjamin H.] Whitlow, of the Third, on the left, Captain Armstrong, with one section of his battery, and Lieutenant [Jule C.] Cayot, of the Third Indian Regiment, with a mountain howitzer, coming promptly into position in the center. We opened a brisk fire upon the enemy in the thicket on the opposite bank, which we continued for half an hour. By this time the enemy's fire had nearly ceased, so we moved forward into the stream, which proved too deep to ford, and we were obliged to fall back.

On the morning of the 2d, one section of Blair's battery took position on an eminence about 900 yards to the left of the ford; one section of Armstrong's battery obtained a commanding position on the right; the main column, consisting of the Indians and five companies of the First Negro Regiment, were stationed in the center. After obtaining this position, we opened fire. The firing was continued about twenty minutes, when I received notice from the lookouts that the enemy were in disorder (not being able to see their movements from the creek, I had stationed a lookout or picket in some trees near Armstrong's battery). I ordered the firing to cease, and the main column to move forward. When nearly across the creek, I was wounded, and obliged to go to the rear. The column pushed on, under Colonel Williams, of the First Colored Regiment, and drove the enemy from their position. They were hotly pursued by Captain Stewart and his company, of the Ninth Kansas Cavalry. Our loss is 3 killed and 30 wounded. The enemy's loss is 9 prisoners. The number of their killed and wounded is unknown, but must be heavy.

As discrimination is impossible where all are brave, I return my heartfelt thanks to the officers and men of that command for their gallantry, energy, and perseverance on that trying occasion.

Very respectfully, your obedient servant,

JOHN A. FOREMAN,
Major Third Indian Regiment.

Col. WILLIAM A. PHILLIPS,
Commanding Forces in the Field.

JULY 3, 1863.—Scout from Salem, Mo., and skirmish.

Report of Lieut. William C. Bangs, Fifth Missouri State Militia Cavalry.

SALEM, MO., *July 3, 1863.*

CAPTAIN: I have the honor to report to you of the scout that I had command of this day.

I left this place this morning with 18 men of Company D, Fifth Regiment Missouri State Militia Cavalry, and marched 4 miles southeast, where I came upon a trail where horsemen had lately been. I followed it in a northerly direction about 12 miles through the brush, when I came upon 14 bushwhackers grazing their horses. I ordered an attack. The men charged in splendid style, leaving 10 of the enemy dead on the ground and capturing 10 horses, without any loss on our side.

I learned from one of the dying men that they were a part of Colonel Freeman's command, under Captain Lamb, and that they were going after salt to Captain Lamb's father, who lived on the Maramec River, and that the salt was brought from Rolla by the women of the neighborhood. He also stated that Colonel Freeman was on the other side of Jack's Ford, of Current River, with 300 men, but could not cross on account of high water; that Captain Lamb's men had swam the river.

I am, very respectfully, &c.,

WM. C. BANGS,
First Lieut., Comdg. Company D, Fifth Regt. M. S. M. Cav.

Capt. SAMUEL B. RICHARDSON,
Commanding Salem, Mo.

JULY 4, 1863.—Attack on Helena, Ark.

REPORTS.

No. 1.

Report of Maj. Gen. Stephen A. Hurlbut, U. S. Army, commanding Sixteenth Army Corps.

MEMPHIS, TENN., *July* 5, 1863—noon.

Prentiss was attacked in force by rebels under Holmes and Price at Helena yesterday. He estimates the force at 15,000. I think 9,000 will cover their strength. Prentiss sustained their attack until 3 p. m. from daylight, when the rebels were repulsed at all points, leaving 1,200 prisoners. Their loss in killed and wounded is about 500 to 600. Prentiss lost about 60. He has already sent me 860 prisoners, which I send to Alton to-day on the Silver Moon. He has asked re-enforcements. I have sent him the One hundred and seventeenth Illinois. I cannot spare any more. The enemy is picketing everything south of my line, and seems strong. I have no fear of my position, unless Joe Johnston turns north; but am unable to spare men from Memphis, which I hold with an effective force, not 4,000 strong. Ten days will determine all questions as to Vicksburg, and with its fall will come comparative quiet on my line. There are some 1,500, and all is irregular cavalry north of this, whom I will look after as soon as I get time. They are reported to have captured a detachment, perhaps 150, of Asboth's cavalry.

S. A. HURLBUT,
Major-General, Commanding.

Maj. Gen. H. W. HALLECK,
General-in-Chief.

ADDENDA.

HEADQUARTERS DISTRICT OF EASTERN ARKANSAS,
Helena, Ark., July 6, 1863.

Maj. Gen. STEPHEN A. HURLBUT,
Commanding Sixteenth Army Corps:

GENERAL: I feel under obligations to you for the re-enforcements you so kindly sent me yesterday. I am already receiving valuable aid from them, although the attack has not been renewed. I am satisfied the enemy is retiring. His cavalry made a demonstration yesterday afternoon, but I am of opinion it was merely a feint to cover a general retreat. I am this morning sending out a reconnaissance in force. I learn that the forces which attacked me consisted of the entire available forces of the enemy in Arkansas.

I have the honor to be, general, your obedient servant,

B. M. PRENTISS,
Major-General.

No. 2.

Reports of Maj. Gen. Benjamin M. Prentiss, U. S. Army, commanding District of Eastern Arkansas.

HEADQUARTERS DISTRICT OF EASTERN ARKANSAS,
Helena, July 4, 1863—10.30 a. m.

GENERAL: We have been hard pressed since daylight by the combined forces of Price, Holmes, Marmaduke, Parsons, Carter, Dobbin, and company. Thus far we have held our own, and have captured several hundred prisoners, whom I send to you by Major [Edward] Wright, of the Twenty-fourth Iowa, on board the steamer Tycoon. The enemy are now evidently preparing for a renewed attack in force. I wish you, by all means, to send me re-enforcements. The enemy is in superior force, but I shall do my best to hold them in check till re-enforcements arrive. Send also another gunboat, if possible. The Tyler has done good service to-day, but I need more. I trust I may have help from you at once, so that we may punish the rebel forces in Arkansas in earnest.

In great haste, your obedient servant,

B. M. PRENTISS,
Major-General.

Maj. Gen. STEPHEN A. HURLBUT,
Commanding Sixteenth Army Corps.

P. S.—Please send also ordnance stores as per inclosed memorandum, or as much of them as possible. Send the shell in particular.

HEADQUARTERS DISTRICT OF EASTERN ARKANSAS,
Helena, July 4, 1863—3 p. m.

GENERAL: We have repulsed the enemy at every point, and our soldiers are now collecting their wounded. We have taken in all 1,200 prisoners, and their loss in killed and wounded will reach 500 or 600. But, although the rebels are badly whipped, there is no doubt whatever that they will renew the attack at an early moment, and that they are now massing their troops for that purpose. My force is inferior to the rebels, and is much weakened by the action. I trust, therefore, that the re-enforcements I wrote you for this morning may be promptly forwarded, and that the ammunition also may reach me in due season. With the aid I expect from you and the gunboats, the rebel army may be severely beaten. The Tyler has been to-day a valuable auxiliary, and I depend much on the assistance of another gunboat.

I remain, general, your obedient servant,

B. M. PRENTISS,
Major-General.

Maj. Gen. STEPHEN A. HURLBUT,
Commanding Sixteenth Army Corps.

HEADQUARTERS DISTRICT OF EASTERN ARKANSAS,
Helena, July 4, 1863—7.30 p. m.

GENERAL: The enemy have not yet renewed the attack of this morning. Their loss is much greater than represented in my previous dispatches. Their dead and wounded strewed the bluffs in every direction after the action. Our loss is, as near as can be ascertained, 40 killed and from 100 to 125 wounded.* We are ready for a renewed attack, should the enemy see fit to make it, and we shall do our best to hold him at bay in that event. Our men have done nobly to-day, and can be depended upon to the full extent of our abilities.

The gunboat Covington is here. With a few more troops we can hold the place against any force they may bring.

I am, general, very truly, yours,

B. M. PRENTISS,
Major-General.

Maj. Gen. STEPHEN A. HURLBUT,
Commanding Sixteenth Army Corps.

HELENA, ARK., *July 5, 1863.*
Via Cairo, Ill., July 10.

We encountered the enemy, 15,000 strong, under Generals Holmes, Price, Marmaduke, and others, on the morning of July 4, and whipped them handsomely. We have captured 1,000 prisoners, 1,200 stand of arms, and 2 colors. Our total loss will not exceed 250.* The enemy's loss is very heavy, not less than 2,500 in killed, wounded, and prisoners.

B. M. PRENTISS,
Major-General.

H. W. HALLECK,
General-in-Chief.

HEADQUARTERS DISTRICT OF EASTERN ARKANSAS,
Helena, Ark., July 5, 1863.

GENERAL: I have the honor to report that the enemy's forces, estimated at from 15,000 to 18,000 strong, under Lieutenant-General Holmes and Generals Price, Marmaduke, and others, attacked our lines heavily at 3 a. m. of July 4. The engagement lasted till 10.30 a. m., when the enemy retreated, having been repulsed at every point with severe loss, and leaving hundreds of his killed and wounded on the battle-field. Occasional skirmishing continued till 1 or 2 p. m., but the attack in force has not been renewed.

We have taken 1,000 prisoners, about 1,200 stand of arms, and 2 colors. Our loss in killed and wounded is about 250.* The loss of the enemy in killed, wounded, and prisoners, as near as we can ascertain, is about 2,500.

The soldiers of my command, numbering about 4,000 effective men, are entitled to all credit for their determined and successful defense of this post. Their bravery and gallantry have not, I think, been surpassed in this war.

The gunboat Tyler rendered valuable assistance in this action. The Covington has since arrived, and I have applied to General Hurlbut for re-enforcements, as the enemy is still in superior force, and is still in the vicinity, supposed to be massing his troops for a renewed attack.

---

* But see revised statement, pp. 390, 391.

I will forward a more detailed report as soon as particulars can be received from the various parts of the command. You can rely upon my sparing no exertions or precautions to hold this point.

I am, general, your most obedient servant,

B. M. PRENTISS,
Major-General.

Maj. Gen. U. S. GRANT,
Commanding Department of the Tennessee.

HEADQUARTERS DISTRICT OF EASTERN ARKANSAS,
Helena, Ark., July 6, 1863—8 p. m.

GENERAL: I had the honor to forward yesterday a preliminary report of the result of the attack on this place by the enemy's force, under command of Lieutenant-General Holmes, assisted by Generals Price, Marmaduke, Parsons, and others.

I have the honor to report now that the enemy has not renewed the attack, and that our victory is complete and final. Our list of prisoners already exceeds 1,100, and among them are several field and line officers.

The enemy succeeded in taking away some of his killed and wounded, but we have already buried nearly 300 of his killed, and have captured more than that number of his severely wounded.

Our own loss in killed, wounded, and missing will not exceed 250.

I sent out a small reconnoitering party to-day, which came up with a small party of the enemy's rear guard some 6 miles out. This party reports the enemy as admitting to the inhabitants along the line of his retreat that he had met with a severe repulse. His wounded are found in whatever direction we search. The party to-day paroled over 100 at one place. The enemy is evidently very much demoralized, and I much regret that the number and condition of my small force will not warrant a pursuit.

I will forward a detailed report as soon as reports are received from subordinate commanders.

I have the honor to be, general, very respectfully, your obedient servant,

B. M. PRENTISS,
Major-General.

Maj. Gen. U. S. GRANT,
Commanding Department of Tennessee.

HEADQUARTERS DISTRICT OF EASTERN ARKANSAS,
Helena, Ark., July 9, 1863.

COLONEL: I have the honor to forward the following detailed report of the battle of Helena:

In addition to the vague rumors that have been floating in the public press for several weeks past, I had been informed by trusty scouts that the enemy was collecting his forces with the evident intention of making a demonstration at some point on this side of the river. Conceiving that Helena might be attacked sooner or later, I omitted no precaution and spared no labor to add to and strengthen its defenses. To this end I caused rifle-pits to be dug, substantial breastworks to be thrown up, and four outlying batteries to be erected in commanding positions on the bluffs west of the town, and designated respectively from right to left (north and south) by the letters A, B, C, and D.

For ten days previous to the battle, indications of a premeditated attack on this place began to multiply; citizens from the country were not permitted to come to our lines; disaffected residents were unusually reserved, and the enemy's pickets were pushed forward and strengthened. Advised of the character of one of the principal generals said to be in this vicinity, I expected the attack, if one was to be made, would be sudden, and at an early hour in the morning. It was, therefore, ordered, a week previous to the battle, that the entire garrison should be up and under arms at 2.30 o'clock each morning. Wednesday night I learned definitely that the enemy had collected a large force at Spring Creek, distant some 15 miles from Helena, and that an attack would not be long delayed. Arrangements had been made by my patriotic regimental commanders for celebrating in a fit and becoming manner the approaching anniversary of our National Independence. In view of the length of line to be defended by so small a number of troops, it was deemed imprudent to permit the garrison to be assembled *en masse*, and on Friday, therefore, orders were issued prohibiting a general celebration on the following day. Events justified these precautions.

On Saturday morning, July 4, at 3 o'clock, my pickets were attacked by the enemy's skirmishers. They made an obstinate resistance, holding the enemy well in check until 4 o'clock, when they reached over rifle-pits and breastworks, and joined their respective regiments, which before this time had assumed their designated positions in the intrenchments. The attack was now commenced in earnest, in front and on the right flank; but the enemy, although assured by his overwhelming numbers of a speedy victory, were driven back again and again. For four hours the battle raged furiously, the enemy gaining little, if any, advantage. Now, however, the attack in front became more furious; the enemy covered every hill-top, swarmed in every ravine, but seemed to be massing his force more particularly against Battery C. I now signaled the gunboat Tyler, the only one at hand, Lieutenant Commander Pritchett commanding, to open fire in that direction. The enemy (Parsons' and McRae's brigades), nothing daunted by the concentrated fire from Fort Curtis, Batteries B, C, and D, the Tyler, and all the infantry I could bring to their support, and led, as I since learn, by Lieutenant-General Holmes and Major-General Price in person, charged upon Battery C. Twice they were repulsed, but the third time, exhibiting a courage and desperation rarely equaled, they succeeded in driving my small force at the point of the bayonet and capturing the battery. Dividing his forces, and sending a part, as a feint, to menace Fort Curtis, the enemy then assaulted Battery D, to reach which they must pass through a deep ravine and encounter a heavy cross-fire. The enemy faltered, seeing which the men in Battery D, and those behind the breastworks, and in the rifle-pits supporting it, sallied forth, and, surrounding more than three times their number, brought them off prisoners. Not to be outdone by their comrades, the men who had been supporting Battery C, assisted by a detachment (dismounted) from the First Indiana Cavalry, under command of Lieutenant-Colonel [T. N.] Pace, gallantly charged upon the enemy in Battery C, retaking it, and capturing as well a large number of prisoners. This was about 10 o'clock. I immediately dispatched two of my aides to carry this information to Colonels [S. A.] Rice and [Powell] Clayton, who, with the remnants of two small brigades, were holding the enemy in check on the right flank, where the attack was only less severe and successful than it had been in front. At 10.30 it became evident that the enemy was withdrawing his forces; but, unaware how severely he had been punished, and learning somewhat of the strength of his forces from prisoners, I could but believe it was for the purpose of massing and attacking my left flank, which I considered the weakest point. The attack was not resumed, however, and, summing up the enemy's loss in killed, wounded, and prisoners, I am no longer surprised. Skirmishing to cover a retreat was kept up until 2 p. m., at which hour all firing ceased.

In the order published to his troops on the 23d of June ultimo, General Holmes says, "The invaders have been driven from every point in Arkansas save one—Helena. We go to retake it." I am happy to be able to say that the attempt to haul down the Stars and Stripes, on the 4th of July, was an ignominious failure. In short, sir, my whole command not only succeeded in repulsing the enemy's attack, and thus holding Helena, which, if I mistake not, is all that was expected of it, but, in addition, administered to the enemy as severe punishment as he ever received west of the Mississippi, and this, too, with a loss to itself so small as to seem almost miraculous, as will sufficiently appear from the following statistics:

My whole force numbered—

Infantry:	
Commissioned officers	162
Enlisted men	2,966
Cavalry:	
Commissioned officers	47
Enlisted men	784
Artillery:	
Commissioned officers	4
Enlisted men	166
Total	4,129

The enemy's force, from the best information I can obtain from prisoners and deserters, consisted of eight brigades, formed out of thirty-seven regiments, and numbered, at a low estimate, in aggregate 15,000 men, and was commanded by one lieutenant-general (Holmes), one major-general (Price), and seven brigadier-generals.

My troops lost in—

Killed:	
Commissioned officers	3
Enlisted men	54
Wounded:	
Commissioned officers	4
Enlisted men	123
Missing:	
Enlisted men	36
Total *	220

We have buried of the enemy's killed, at least	400
Of wounded and since dead	27
Paroled of his wounded	108
Sent North wounded	212
Remaining at Helena wounded	7
Sent North as prisoners, in addition to wounded	727
Remaining in Helena	47

The enemy's surgeons admit a loss in wounded ranging from 1,200 to 1,500. His total loss, therefore, in killed, wounded, and prisoners,

*But see revised statement, pp. 391, 392.

cannot be less than 2,500. We have also captured 2 colors and nearly 2,000 stand of arms. My thanks, as well as those of the nation at large, are due Brig. Gen. F. Salomon, who commanded the Thirteenth Division, Thirteenth Army Corps, in the temporary absence of Brigadier-General Ross, and to whom had been assigned the special supervision of the defenses of Helena; to Col. William E. McLean, Forty-third Indiana Infantry, commanding First Brigade, who held the left flank, and rendered very efficient service on the left wing of the center, about Batteries C and D; to Colonels [S. A.] Rice, Thirty-third Iowa Infantry, commanding Second Brigade, and [Powell] Clayton, Fifth Kansas Cavalry, commanding cavalry brigade, who held the right flank; to one and all the officers and men composing the garrison of Helena, and to Lieutenant-Commander Pritchett and the men under his command for very timely and efficient co-operation. The guns in Fort Curtis and Batteries A, B, C, and D, were handled with great precision and success by the Thirty-third Missouri Infantry.

The members of my personal staff were efficient and tireless in the discharge of their duties. The result shows that all did well, and are entitled to honorable mention.

My command consisted of the following regiments and batteries: Forty-third Indiana Infantry, Twenty-eighth Wisconsin Infantry, Thirty-third Iowa Infantry, Twenty-ninth Iowa Infantry, Thirty-fifth Missouri Infantry, Thirty-third Missouri Infantry, Thirty-sixth Iowa Infantry, Third Iowa, Battery K, First Missouri Light Artillery, constituting the Thirteenth Division, Thirteenth Army Corps; Fifth Kansas Cavalry and First Indiana Cavalry, constituting the cavalry brigade; and the Second Regiment of Arkansas Volunteers of African descent.

I have the honor to be, sir, very respectfully, your obedient servant,

B. M. PRENTISS,
Major-General.

Lieut. Col. JOHN A. RAWLINS,
Assistant Adjutant-General, Department of the Tennessee.

Return of Casualties in the Union forces, commanded by Maj. Gen. Benjamin M. Prentiss, in the attack on Helena, Ark., July 4, 1863.

[Compiled from nominal list of casualties, returns, &c.]

Command.	Killed.		Wounded.		Captured or missing.		
	Officers.	Enlisted men.	Officers.	Enlisted men.	Officers.	Enlisted men.	Aggregate.
THIRTEENTH ARMY CORPS.							
THIRTEENTH DIVISION.							
Brig. Gen. FREDERICK SALOMON.							
First Brigade.							
Col. WILLIAM E. MCLEAN.							
43d Indiana	......	3	......	6	......	......	9
28th Wisconsin	......	2	......	4	......	5	11
35th Missouri	1	3	......	18	......	......	22
Total First Brigade	1	8	......	28	......	5	42

Return of Casualties in the Union forces, &c.—Continued.

Command.	Killed.		Wounded.		Captured or missing.		
	Officers.	Enlisted men.	Officers.	Enlisted men.	Officers.	Enlisted men.	Aggregate.
Second Brigade.							
Col. SAMUEL A. RICE.							
29th Iowa	......	7	......	24	......	......	31
33d Iowa	......	19	......	50	......	16	85
36th Iowa	......	1	......	......	......	5	6
33d Missouri	2	14	2	23	......	9	50
Total Second Brigade	2	41	2	97	......	30	172
Cavalry Brigade.							
Col. POWELL CLAYTON.							
1st Indiana Cavalry	......	2	......	8	......	1	11
5th Kansas Cavalry	......	3	2	8	......	......	13
Total Cavalry Brigade	......	5	2	16	......	1	24
Light Artillery.							
3d Iowa Battery*	......	......	......	......	......	......	......
1st Missouri, Battery K	......	......	......	1	......	......	1
Grand total	3	54	4	142	......	36	239

OFFICERS KILLED.—Lieuts. Joseph W. Brooks and Adam B. Smith, Thirty-third Missouri, and Lieut. Daniel N. Onions, Thirty-fifth Missouri.

—

HEADQUARTERS DISTRICT OF EASTERN ARKANSAS,
Helena, Ark., July 9, 1863.

Rear-Admiral DAVID D. PORTER,
Commanding Mississippi Squadron:

ADMIRAL: I take pleasure in transmitting to you my testimony concerning the valuable assistance rendered me during the battle at this place on the 4th instant by Lieut. Commander James M. Pritchett, of the gunboat Tyler. I assure you, sir, that he not only acquitted himself with honor and distinction during the engagement proper, but with a zeal and patience as rare as they are commendable. When informed of the probabilities of an attack on this place, he lost no time and spared no labor to make himself thoroughly acquainted with the topography of the surrounding country, and I attribute not a little of our success in the late battle to his full knowledge of the situation and his skill in adapting the means within his command to the end to be obtained. Nor can I refrain from mentioning that, after the engagement, and while we were expecting a renewal of the attack, Commander Pritchett, commanding a division of your fleet, was unusually efficient in procuring timely re-enforcements. Permit me to add, sir, that I can conceive of no case wherein promotion would be more worthily bestowed than in the case of Commander Pritchett, and it will afford me much pleasure

* No loss reported.

to learn that his services have received a proper reward. I write this communication, sir, quite unsolicited, and without the knowledge of Commander Pritchett.

I have the honor to be, sir, with much respect, your obedient servant,

B. M. PRENTISS,
Major-General.

No. 3.

Reports of Brig. Gen. Frederick Salomon, U. S. Army, commanding Thirteenth Division, Thirteenth Army Corps.

HEADQUARTERS UNITED STATES FORCES,
Helena, Ark., July 4, 1863.

GENERAL: I have the honor to report that the enemy attacked our lines at 3 a. m. to-day, in force, under command of Lieutenant-General Holmes and General Price, 18,000 strong, and was repulsed everywhere with heavy loss. The engagement lasted until 10.30 a. m., when the enemy retreated, leaving his killed and wounded on the battle-field. We have taken 800 prisoners, about 1,000 stand of arms, and 2 colors. Our loss in killed and wounded is 143. The loss of the enemy, as far as ascertained, in killed, wounded, and prisoners, is 2,000.

The bravery and valor displayed by officers and men of my gallant little command stands unparalleled.

My detailed report will be forwarded as soon as the reports of brigade and battery commanders can be obtained.

Very respectfully, your obedient servant,

F. SALOMON,
Brigadier-General, Commanding.

Major-General PRENTISS,
Commanding District of Eastern Arkansas.

HDQRS. THIRTEENTH DIV., THIRTEENTH ARMY CORPS,
Helena, July 6, 1863.

GENERAL: I have the honor to submit the following report:

Anticipating an attack by a superior force, I ordered the whole command to be under arms and on their designated places before daybreak every morning several days before the 4th.

At 3 a. m. on the 4th of July, our whole lines were attacked, simultaneously, by the enemy, 18,000 to 20,000 strong, and under command of Lieutenant-General Holmes, General Price, Generals Marmaduke, McRae, and others. The attack was repulsed, but again and again came their legions ringing the air with their wild yells.

At about 5 a. m. a heavy fog came on, so thick that I could not see the batteries from the fort. Under cover of this fog, the enemy massed his troops in front of Batteries C and D. I immediately re-enforced these points by a portion of the Forty-third Indiana and the First Indiana Cavalry (dismounted), and ordered two companies of the Twenty-eighth Wisconsin in the valley west of Fort Curtis.

Battery D was attacked four times, and the enemy repulsed every time with great slaughter. Battery C was taken on the third assault. Expecting the enemy to attack Fort Curtis now, I ordered one piece of

Hayden's battery in front of the ravine, near the nunnery, together with five companies of the Thirty-fifth Missouri Infantry, while I opened upon them from Fort Curtis. The enemy, checked in their advance and subjected to a murderous fire from the fort and the gunboat Tyler, were either killed or taken prisoners. Soon afterward, Battery C was retaken, together with the guns. General Holmes commanded here in person.

On the left of our line, Colonel McLean commanding, the enemy was prevented from holding their battery in position by our Parrott guns on the levee, and the enemy refused to charge in face of our guns and gunboat. The right of our line, commanded by Colonel [S. A.] Rice, and the extreme right, commanded by Colonel [Powell] Clayton, held their ground, against heavy forces and artillery, without losing an inch.

At 10.30 a. m., after a continuous and desperate fight of seven and a half hours, the enemy fell back to come no more, leaving their dead and wounded on the battle-field.

We have taken 800 prisoners, amongst whom are many field and line officers, besides about 500 wounded; but the houses near the line of the retreating enemy are reported to be filled with them. The number dead and buried on the battle-field will be near 400. I estimate their loss at 3,000 in killed, wounded, and prisoners. We have taken two colors and a large quantity of arms. Our loss will appear on the schedule attached.*

Where every one fought so nobly and well, it would be injustice to mention some for meritorious conduct. The accompanying reports of the brigade, regimental, and battery commanders, to which I respectfully refer, will show whose good fortune it was to be in a position where they could do more service than others. I further attach a map, showing our first position and fortifications.†

Very respectfully, your obedient servant,

F. SALOMON,
Brigadier-General, Commanding.

Maj. Gen. B. M. PRENTISS,
Commanding District of Eastern Arkansas.

---

* Embodied in statement on pp. 390, 391.

† See p. 394.

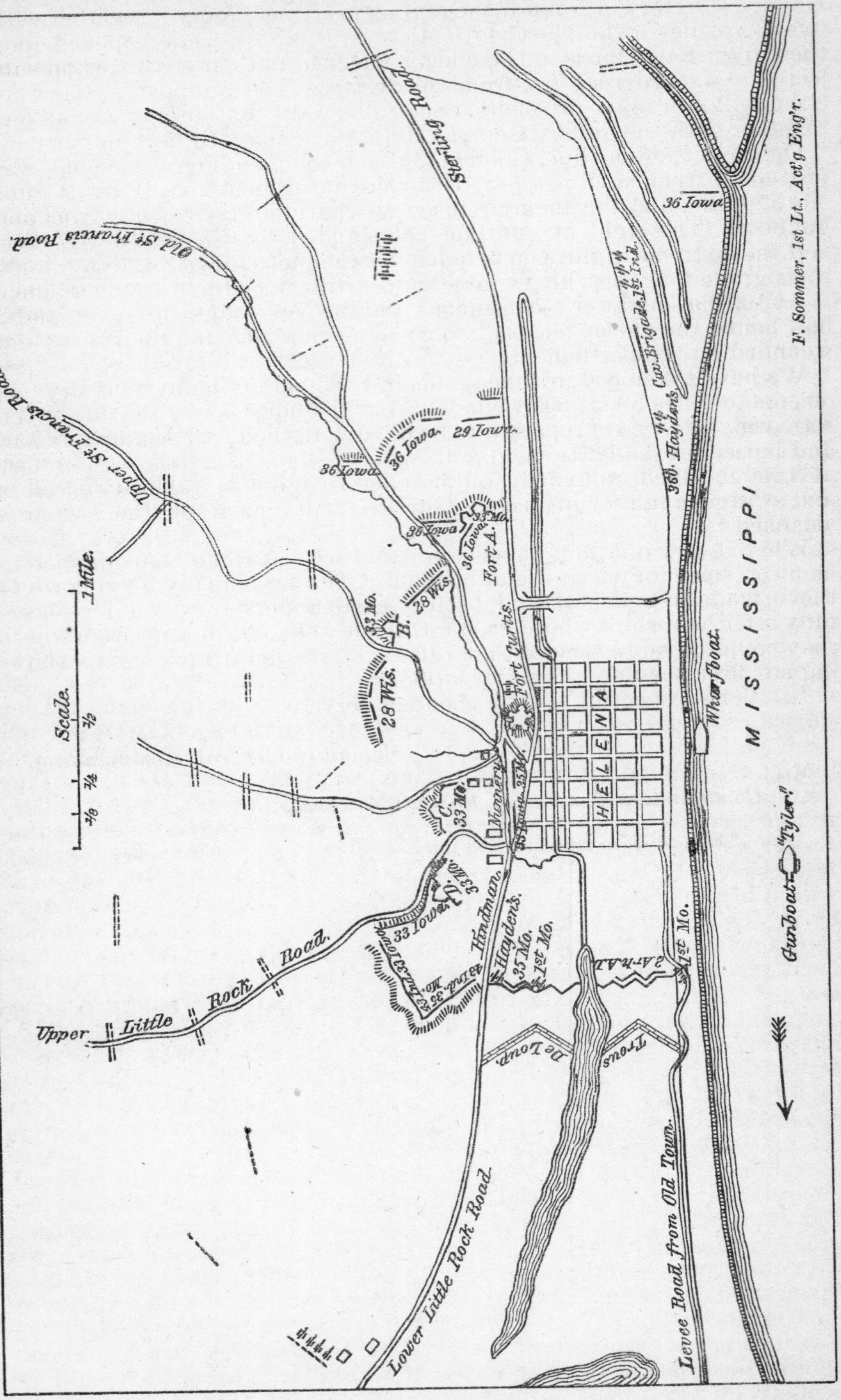
Sterling Road.
Old St. Francis Road.
Upper St. Francis Road.
Upper Little Rock Road.
Lower Little Rock Road.
Levee Road from Old Town.
MISSISSIPPI
HELENA
Fort Curtis.
Fort A.
Wharfboat.
Gunboat "Tyler"
36 Iowa
29 Iowa
28 Wis.
33 Mo.
35 Mo.
1st Mo.
Hindman.
Haydens.
Cav. Brigade 1st Ind.
De Loup.
Scale.
1 Mile.
F. Sommer, 1st Lt., Act'g Eng'r.

No. 4.

Report of Col. Samuel A. Rice, Thirty-third Iowa Infantry, commanding Second Brigade.

HDQRS. SECOND BRIGADE, THIRTEENTH DIVISION,
THIRTEENTH ARMY CORPS, DEPT. OF TENNESSEE,
Helena, Ark., July 7, 1863.

CAPTAIN: I have the honor to submit the following report of the part taken by the Second Brigade in the action of the 4th instant:

The Thirty-third Missouri Infantry were stationed at Fort Curtis and at Batteries A, B, C, and D, which covered your entire line of defense. At all of these points they manned the artillery, and also had a reserve who acted as sharpshooters. The Thirty-third Iowa Infantry was ordered to report to Fort Curtis, opposite the center of your line, at daybreak, so that, in case of an attack, they might readily be thrown to the support of either wing or the center of your line. At 4 a. m. the enemy, in heavy force, drove in our pickets, and opened the engagement on Batteries A, C, and D. The Thirty-third Iowa was promptly, in compliance with your orders, moved into the rifle-pits in front and flanking Batteries C and D, with a small portion acting as a reserve, who were posted so as to command the ravine between these batteries. Three companies of the Thirty-sixth Iowa were sent at once to support Battery A, and took possession of the rifle-pits, flanking it. The Twenty-ninth Iowa, with a reserve from the Thirty-sixth, was ordered to take possession of the sides of the bluffs, on the east side, and a short distance in front of Battery A, extending down to the Sterling road, and drive the enemy from the crests of the hills which they already had occupied. On Batteries C and D the main assault of the enemy was made. They hurled regiment after regiment in close column against the works, but were gallantly repulsed at Battery D, and only after a severe and bloody conflict took Battery C, driving our forces before them, but they promptly rallied and formed at the bottom of the hill. The artillery from Batteries A, B, and D, together with Fort Curtis, commanding Battery C, was opened upon the enemy, and after a severe cannonading, assisted by a galling fire from our infantry, they were driven back with a heavy loss, and the battery retaken. The heavy loss sustained by the Thirty-third Missouri and the Thirty-third Iowa on this portion of the field fully attests their undoubted courage. While the engagement was thus progressing in the center, the enemy were also concentrating a heavy fire on the right wing, which had been assigned to my command. They had planted a battery within 400 yards of Battery A, but protected from its fire by a point of the hill. From the concentrated fire of the First Indiana Battery (light artillery), and a section of the Third Iowa Battery, under Lieutenant Wright, assisted by our sharpshooters and a severe fire along the entire line, the enemy were compelled to withdraw their guns with a severe loss. On this portion of our line the enemy had, besides their artillery, a brigade of four regiments of infantry and a brigade of cavalry, under General Marmaduke, and at all points outnumbered us at least four to one, according to their own estimates. The officers and soldiers of the Twenty-ninth Iowa acted with the utmost coolness and bravery, and steadily gained ground from the first onset. The Thirty-sixth Iowa behaved in a manner worthy of all commendation. They were promptly moved to the relief of the Twenty-ninth Iowa, and drove by their well-directed fire the enemy before them, occupying the crests of the hills. The enemy could repeatedly be heard trying to rally their columns for the purpose of charging on our line, and were only prevented by the continuous fire of our line, assisted by a heavy and well-directed cross-fire from our artillery and the rifle-pits. The Thirty-third Missouri, manning the guns in the various batteries along the entire line, was at all points exposed to the hottest fire of the enemy, and deserve the highest praise for their bravery and efficiency.

The heavy loss sustained by the enemy fully attests the bravery, the discipline, and the efficiency of your entire command. There was taken by my command several hundred prisoners. We have buried 156 of the enemy. There were also taken three stand of colors and several hundred stand of arms. The rout of the enemy was complete at all points. The loss in my command was 45 killed, 96 wounded, and 30 missing.* A full report of the above from each regiment I append hereto. As a portion of my brigade, the Thirty-third Iowa and part of the Thirty-third Missouri, were in another part of the field from that assigned to my command, and acted more immediately under your own observation, I trust, in case I have not been able to present fully the part they took in the action, that you will supply the deficiency in your official report.

A detailed account of the part taken by the various regiments of the brigade would involve not only what was done by them, but by other brigades, who bore an equally honorable part in the entire engagement, and especially that of Colonel [P.] Clayton, of the Fifth Kansas, who, with the First Indiana Battery and his cavalry, bore an important part in the engagement on the right of the line. Where all did so well, invidious distinction would be out of place. If some bore more conspicuous parts than others, it was because the position of their own commands placed them in a more important position.

I take especial pleasure in referring to Colonel [Thomas H.] Benton, [jr.,] of the Twenty-ninth Iowa; Colonel [C. W.] Kittredge, of the Thirty-sixth Iowa; Lieutenant-Colonel [W. H.] Heath, commanding Thirty-third Missouri; Lieutenant-Colonel [C. H.] Mackey, commanding Thirty-third Iowa; Lieutenant-Colonel [R. F.] Patterson, Twenty-ninth Iowa; Majors [H. D.] Gibson, [G. W.] Van Beek, and [C. B.] Shoemaker, who, from their coolness, efficiency, and daring, are worthy of especial mention. They were at all times at the post of danger, cheering their men. Lieutenant [J. F.] Lacy, my acting assistant adjutant-general, acted as my aide during the engagement, and rode to whatever part of the field required his presence, and afforded me assistance of the most valuable character, and I take especial pleasure in referring to him.

I am, captain, very respectfully, your obedient servant,

SAMUEL A. RICE,

Colonel Thirty-third Iowa Infantry, Comdg. Second Brigade.

Capt. A. BLOCKI, *Assistant Adjutant-General.*

No. 5.

Report of Col. Thomas H. Benton, jr., Twenty-ninth Iowa Infantry.

HELENA, ARK., *July* 6, 1863.

COLONEL: I have the honor to make the following report of the part taken in the engagement of the 4th instant by my regiment:

My men were drawn up in line of battle at daylight, and at 4.30 a. m.,

* But see revised statement, p. 391.

in pursuance of orders from Col. Samuel A. Rice, commanding Second Brigade, we marched across the bottom at double-quick to a position on the Sterling road. Upon reaching the point designated, I found that the enemy occupied the crest of the hills with their skirmishers, north of Battery A, commanding my position. I immediately sent forward two companies of skirmishers to dislodge and drive them back; but finding them too strongly posted, I continued to re-enforce the line until eight companies were deployed. In the mean time the enemy had placed a battery of two guns in position, with which they opened a brisk fire, and moved rapidly upon us, cheering and exulting as they advanced, being partially shielded from view by a fog, which covered the hills at that moment. Our skirmishers met them with a galling and incessant fire, under which they gradually fell back, resolutely contesting every inch of ground as they retired. Our skirmishers advanced steadily and cautiously, and, having gained the crest of the hills previously occupied by the enemy, compelled him to abandon his guns, which, after several ineffectual attempts, he subsequently recovered, and withdrew, leaving one caisson on the field. My men were under a severe fire for more than five hours, and it affords me the greatest pleasure to speak of both officers and men in terms of the highest commendation for their coolness and bravery during the entire action. I saw no flinching or wavering during the day.

It is proper to add that several of my officers and quite a number of my men, who were excused from duty in consequence of physical debility, left their quarters and joined their respective companies when the signal gun was fired.

Any invidious distinctions among the members of my command would not be admissible in this report, but I would not do justice to an accomplished officer should I fail to acknowledge the efficient services of Lieut. Col. R. F. Patterson during the action, and the special obligations I am under for the thorough instruction previously given by him to both officers and men in the responsible duties and obligations of the soldier, the importance of which was so forcibly illustrated on the 4th instant.

My regiment was promptly supported by the Thirty-sixth Iowa Infantry, commanded by Colonel [C. W.] Kittredge, and was relieved by him a short time before the enemy left the field.

The enemy's force in front of our line, so far as I have been able to ascertain from the most reliable information within my reach, was one brigade of five regiments of infantry, one battery, and two regiments of cavalry in reserve, under command of Colonel [General] McRae.

I regret to have to report that during the engagement the loss in my regiment was 7 killed and 24 wounded, some of them mortally (2 of whom have since died), and many of them severely wounded, among the number some of my best and bravest men. The enemy's loss it is not possible to state definitely, as he succeeded in removing many of them from the field. We buried 14 of his dead, and found the graves of 17 more buried by himself, and brought 1 of his wounded from the field.

I have the honor to be, very respectfully, your obedient servant,

THOMAS H. BENTON, JR.,
Colonel Twenty-ninth Iowa Infantry.

Col. SAMUEL A. RICE,
Comdg. Second Brig., Thirteenth Division, Thirteenth Corps.

No. 6.

Report of Lieut. Col. Cyrus H. Mackey, Thirty-third Iowa Infantry.

HELENA, ARK., *July* 6, 1863.

COLONEL: I have the honor to make the following report of the part taken by the Thirty-third Regiment Iowa Infantry in the battle at this post on the 4th instant:

On the morning of the 4th of July, in compliance with orders issued from brigade headquarters, I formed the regiment in line and marched them to Fort Curtis, arriving there at 2.30 a. m. Shortly after 3 o'clock firing commenced on the part of the picket line occupied by my regiment, it being to the right and left of the Little Rock road. At 4 a. m. I received orders from Brigadier-General Salomon to move my regiment to the foot of the hill on the said road, and from that place to re-enforce Batteries C and D when attacked. I had no sooner arrived at this point with my regiment, when the enemy, in strong force, attacked Battery D. I immediately detached Companies B and G, under command of Maj. H. D. Gibson, to the assistance of this battery. Discovering at the same time that the enemy were making preparations to assault Battery C, I sent forward Companies A and F to the support of this battery. Finding that the force I had sent to Battery D was not sufficient to cope with the enemy, I ordered Companies H, E, I, and K forward, and occupied the rifle-pits on the Little Rock road; at the same time ordered Company D into the rifle-pits on the left of Battery C. I then occupied the ravine between the batteries with Company C. The assault on Battery D lasted about thirty minutes, when the enemy was repulsed and driven back in confusion. By this time the position of the enemy was concealed by a heavy fog, which did not rise until 8 a. m. During this time the enemy sent forward heavy bodies of skirmishers and sharpshooters, and once attempted to charge the battery, but did not succeed in bringing their forces forward.

At 8 a. m. they charged Batteries D and C, bringing forward Generals Fagan's and Parsons' brigades. They succeeded in carrying Battery C, but not until they had many of their men and officers killed and wounded; but their superiority in numbers was so great that they completely overpowered our force at the battery. The three companies from my own regiment and two from the Thirty-third Missouri constituted the entire force at this battery. The men retired from the battery in the direction of Fort Curtis, about 250 yards. By this time we had completely routed the enemy in front of Battery D. They succeeded here only sufficiently to get possession of the extreme left of the rifle-pits. Our force at this battery consisted of six companies of my own regiment, six of the Thirty-third Missouri, and two of the Forty-third Indiana. I now withdrew Companies I and K, and formed a new line with them, and Companies A, F, D, and C, to the rear of Battery C 250 yards, which succeeded completely in stopping any further progress of the enemy. Finding themselves repulsed at all points, they commenced to fall back to the timber. Things at this battery remained in this condition for some time. Many of them, instead of falling back to the timber, took refuge in the woods around the battery, and kept up a desultory fire therefrom. Finding that the enemy was not going to attempt anything more in this direction, I withdrew the two companies I had brought here, and returned to the Little Rock road, in front of Battery D; arriving there I ordered the whole force to charge forward on this road. The entire force advanced with a will that carried everything before them, and in ten minutes I had complete possession of the entire battle-ground on this road, and obtained several hundred prisoners and two stand of colors. As soon as I had completed this movement, I ordered a flank movement from this road on the enemy who were in front of Battery C. I selected Companies B and K for this purpose, and ordered them forward. I then ordered my right wing to attack the enemy in front, in conjunction with a part of the First Indiana Cavalry, dismounted, under the command of Lieutenant-Colonel [T. N.] Pace. This movement only partially succeeded, caused, as I suppose, by misapprehension by Colonel Pace of an order of General Prentiss. We succeeded so far, however, as to capture about 100 prisoners. This last movement terminated the battle. It was now 10 a. m. The men were very much exhausted, having been constantly engaged for six hours. From 80 to 100 rounds of ammunition had been expended to the man. The loss of my own regiment was—killed on the field, 17; wounded, 52; taken prisoners, 17.* (Three men were taken at Battery C.) Eight of the wounded have since died from their wounds. I went into the engagement with 500 men. The officers and men of the entire command behaved themselves splendidly. The force we had to contend with was at least five to one, and I feel perfectly safe in saying that the regiment took as many prisoners as we had men in action. They all did so well that it is a difficult matter for me to attempt to particularize who did best. I take particular pleasure in mentioning the names of Maj. H. D. Gibson, Capt. John P. Yerger, Capt. John Lofland, Lieut. Cheney Prouty, and Capt. L. W. Whipple. The manner in which these officers conducted themselves is deserving of the highest praise. I would also call your attention to the good conduct of Second Lieutenant [C. H.] Sharman, of Company G, who had command of the picket guard. He succeeded in holding the enemy in check until we were fully prepared to receive them, brought his guard all off (except a number that were killed and wounded) in good order, and joined the regiment. He was wounded in the head very severely, but I think not dangerously.

The foregoing report, hastily written, and not so complete as I should have wished, is most respectfully submitted.

CYRUS H. MACKEY,
Lieutenant-Colonel, Commanding Thirty-third Iowa.

Col. SAMUEL A. RICE, *Commanding Second Brigade.*

No. 7.

Report of Col. Charles W. Kittredge, Thirty-sixth Iowa Infantry.

HELENA, ARK., *July* 5, 1863.

SIR: Yesterday morning this regiment was in line at 3.30 a. m.; at 4 a. m. the engagement commenced, and I have much gratification in saying that every officer and enlisted man did his duty faithfully and well. We remained upon the field under arms until 11 o'clock to-day, when we returned, by your order, to camp. I am under obligations to the chaplain, Rev. M. H. Hare, and to Regimental Quartermaster Stevens W. Morrill for their valuable services, they being the only field and staff officers present, the others being absent on sick leave of absence.

The casualties of the regiment are 1 killed and 4 missing.*

Very respectfully,

C. W. KITTREDGE,
Colonel Thirty-sixth Regiment Iowa Infantry.

Col. SAMUEL A. RICE, *Comdg. Second Brig., Thirteenth Div.*

---

* But see revised statement, p. 391.

No. 8.

Report of Lieut. Col. William H. Heath, Thirty-third Missouri Infantry.

HELENA, ARK., *July* 6, 1863.

COLONEL: I have the honor to submit the following report of the part taken by the Thirty-third Missouri Volunteers in the action of the 4th instant:

Companies D and F manned the heavy guns in Fort Curtis; Company A the guns in Battery A; Company C the guns in Battery B; Company E the guns in Battery C, supported by Company H, acting as sharpshooters; Company B the guns in Battery D, supported by Companies G, I, and K, acting as sharpshooters.

The first assault of the enemy in force was made at 4 a. m. upon Batteries A, C, and D simultaneously. In front of Batteries A and D, they were handsomely checked before any advantage had been gained; but the entire Missouri brigade of Parsons (said to have been personally directed by Maj. Gen. Sterling Price), charging furiously upon Battery C, drove the infantry support (four companies of the Thirty-third Iowa) out of the rifle-pits in great confusion, and, after killing, wounding, and capturing 30 men of the two companies on duty at the guns, succeeded in driving them from the battery, but not before they had spiked one of the guns and brought away all the friction primers and priming wires, thus rendering the pieces useless to the enemy. The companies in Fort Curtis, with the siege guns, supported by the remnants of Companies E and H, with numerous stragglers from other commands, acting as sharpshooters, succeeded in checking the enemy's farther advance, and finally drove his main force back from Battery C, compelling him, by their steady and increasing fire, to leave the guns of the battery uninjured and beat a hasty and disastrous retreat, leaving over 350 prisoners, with their officers and colors, and his dead and wounded, in our hands. The prisoners were mainly of the Seventh and Tenth Missouri Regiments, and had taken refuge from the fire of our artillery in a deep ravine opening toward the river, but protected by a ridge from the direct fire of Fort Curtis. Immediately the Thirty-fifth Missouri was drawn up across the mouth of this ravine, part of the Thirty-third Iowa moving to attack the enemy's flank, and the siege guns playing shell, grape, and canister upon the ridge above them, preventing a retreat. They were surrendered by hoisting a white flag, their own sharpshooters upon the ridge at their rear firing from cover upon and cursing them as they marched out prisoners of war.

About 9 a. m. a second attack was made upon Battery D by Fagan's brigade of Arkansas troops, three regiments strong, and said by prisoners to have acted under the personal direction of Lieutenant-General Holmes. The battery was bravely supported by detachments from the Forty-third Indiana, under Major [W. W.] Norris, and the Thirty-third Iowa, under Major [H. D.] Gibson. In spite, however, of the most determined resistance, Bell's regiment, with small portions of Hawthorn's and Brooks', succeeded in penetrating our outer line of rifle-pits, and securing a position in a deep ravine to the left of the battery and below the range of its guns. The remainder of the brigade was broken and scattered by the terrific fire of our artillery in the works, and compelled to seek shelter in the woods out of range.

Immediately upon their retreating, our riflemen from all three regiments in the pits closed in upon those of the enemy who were in the ravine, from all sides cutting off retreat. The reserve of the Forty-third Indiana formed across the mouth of the ravine, and two Parrott guns of the First Missouri Battery, under Lieutenant [J.] O'Connell, were also brought to rake the enemy's position. Capt. John G. Hudson, of the Thirty-third Missouri, commanding Battery D, then demanded the surrender of the entire force. The men at once threw down their arms, and Lieutenant-Colonel Johnson, of Bell's regiment, made a formal surrender of his command, mustering 21 officers and between 300 and 400 men, with all their arms and one stand of colors. At about 10.30 a. m. the main body of the enemy had entirely drawn off from in front of our batteries and the firing ceased.

Companies E and H returned to Battery C, capturing some 50 of the enemy, and finding both guns of the battery turned upon Fort Curtis and loaded with shell, but not discharged, for want of friction primers. The rout of the enemy was materially assisted by flank fires from Batteries A, B, and D, and 10-inch shell from the gunboat Tyler.

Upward of 300 killed and wounded were left by the enemy in the vicinity of this battery, 70 of these being killed outright, and a great number so wounded that they cannot survive. Nearly the same number were found in front and on the left flank of Battery D. The immense power of the batteries supporting each other, and with the guns of the fort affording the most perfect concentration upon any given point, entirely demoralized the enemy, who broke at the first few rounds, and could only be coaxed and forced forward after that in a shapeless and disorganized mob. Considering that the gunners in Fort Curtis had had no target practice, the firing from the fort, as well as the batteries, was, in the main, remarkably good, and our riflemen and the infantry supports sent to the batteries behaved with rare courage and steadiness, being in position from 2 a. m. until 11 a. m., without food, and fighting steadily for six and a half hours of that time.

I desire especially to mention Majors Norris and Gibson, Captains [E. S.] Schenck and [G. H.] Tracy, and Lieutenant [M.] Reed for gallantry in leading their men, upon the suggestion of Captain Hudson, against Bell's regiment. Of the men of the Thirty-third Missouri, who distinguished themselves by coolness, activity, and determination, may be mentioned Maj. George W. Van Beek, superintending Batteries A and B; Capts. William J. McKee, commanding Fort Curtis; Daniel D. Carr, three siege guns; William M. Blake, Battery A; Alexander J. Campbell, Battery B; Thomas M. Gibson, Battery C; John S. Hudson, Battery G; Stuart Carkner, Company G (wounded); George H. Tracy, Company I; Elias S. Schenck, Company K; Lieuts. Henry Cochran, commanding Company H; Stephen J. Burnett (wounded), Adam B. Smith (killed at his post), Luther P. Eldridge, Isaac S. Coe, Charles L. Draper, F. E. Lombar, Joseph W. Brooks (killed while gallantly leading a charge), Moses Reed, R. M. Reed, Edgar L. Allen, Henry H. Knowlton, and James M. Conner; and gunners, Sergt. E. Bates, J. W. Wells, L. D. Alden, Company F; Sergt. Henry S. Carroll, Corpl. James K. Frier, Private J. S. Martin, Company D; Private John Driscoll, Kansas Cavalry, all in Fort Curtis. Battery A, Sergts. D. R. McClammer and George B. Maher; Battery B, Corpl. George W. Coleman; Battery C, Sergt. James M. Freeman, Privates Thomas W. Wheeler and Joseph W. Phillips; Battery D, Corpl. Robert McPhate (Dubuque Battery) and Luke P. Maxen. Nathaniel Leavitt, commissary sergeant, killed at his post; Color Sergt. Patrick Collins, a regular soldier of twenty-six years' standing, wounded in the face while bravely fighting over the parapet of Battery D. There were others who did as well as those named, but whose names have not been handed me. The entire regiment, officers and men, behaved with steadiness and judgment.

Very respectfully,

WM. H. HEATH,
Lieutenant-Colonel, Commanding Regiment

Col. SAMUEL A. RICE,
Comdg. Second Brig., Third Div., Thirteenth Army Corps.

No. 9.

Report of Capt. John G. Hudson, Thirty-third Missouri Infantry.

HEADQUARTERS BATTERY D,
Helena, Ark., July 4, 1863.

SIR: I have the pleasure of submitting the names of the following officers of the Confederate Army who were taken prisoner in the attempt to charge on my battery, with near 400 soldiers:*

* * * * * * *

I have received a few straggling prisoners after the engagement was over. I will give you the full account at any time you wish. I fired my first gun at 4.25 a. m., and ceased at 10 a. m. My men behaved finely. I was supported by a battalion of the Forty-third Indiana Volunteers and two companies of the Thirty-third Iowa Volunteers.

I am, respectfully, yours, &c.,

JOHN G. HUDSON,
Captain, Commanding Battery.

Maj. JAMES O. PIERCE, *Assistant Adjutant-General.*

No. 10.

Report of Lieut. Col. Thomas N. Pace, First Indiana Cavalry, Clayton's brigade.

HELENA, *July* 6, 1863.

SIR: In obedience to orders, I herewith transmit a list of killed and wounded of my command, First Indiana Cavalry, together with a statement of the part the regiment took in the attack on Helena, on the 4th of July, 1863.

A little before 4 o'clock, on the morning of the 4th of July, two messengers came in from the picket post on the Little Rock road, bringing word that the enemy were advancing, driving in the pickets before them. I immediately ordered the bugle to sound to horse, and, forming the regiment, moved up the levee near town, and awaited orders. Soon received orders from you, through your adjutant, to move tents and baggage within the line of fortifications as rapidly as possible, leaving part of the command to guard the train, and with the rest to form line of battle behind the Fifth Kansas, which was already drawn up in the open flats just above town. I immediately ordered Major [J. D.] Owen to take two companies, with one piece of our small rifled guns, and cover the rear of the train, and with the balance of my command I took positions as ordered. General [B. M.] Prentiss then ordered our guns some distance in front, up the levee, and Companies M and L were dismounted and sent forward as a support. Our battery was com-

---

* Nominal list reports 1 field officer, 6 captains, and 14 lieutenants.

manded by Lieutenant Leflar, of Company B. For the bravery shown and the terrible execution done by them, you are best able to judge, they having been under your immediate command. By this time Major Owen came up with his detachment, and fell in line with the regiment. Captain [W. V.] Weathers, aide to General Salomon, now came up with word that the enemy had captured a battery on the heights in the rear of General Salomon's headquarters, driving our infantry from their rifle-pits, and were rapidly advancing into town, and I was ordered to take my regiment under the walls of Fort Curtis, dismount them, and check their farther advance. I did so, taking the regiment on the top of the hill, to the left of General Salomon's headquarters. On the crest of the hill opposite was the battery the enemy had just captured, and over the breastworks from which our infantry had been driven they were pouring one dark, continuous stream. The boys wheeled into line, and with loud yells, commenced firing, pouring in such a storm of bullets that they soon retreated, with the exception of their sharpshooters, who, to the number of several hundred, took possession of a ravine running up the side of the hill, which was filled with fallen timber and stumps, from behind which they poured a continuous and deadly fire. Soon ten or twelve daring spirits now rushed down the hillside and up the steep ascent in front, getting a position on the enemy's left flank, just above them, occupying ground from which we had driven them. They held their position for some time, doing terrible execution, but were finally compelled to fall back, bringing with them quite a number of splendid English rifles which they had captured from the enemy's sharpshooters. Another detachment of our men soon went over, accompanied by some infantry, a company of which had come up on the hill where my regiment was stationed. (It may be proper to state here that several companies of infantry were at the foot of the hill to our right, around General Salomon's headquarters, who did good service, acting in concert with us.) The enemy, finding himself flanked, and having no chance of escape, as every one attempting to run up the hill-side was sure to fall, raised the white flag, and about 100 surrendered. Quite a number still held out, seemingly determined to die before they would become prisoners. Here more than half the regiment threw away their carbines, many of them being unserviceable, having been condemned by a United States inspecting officer some time since, and supplied themselves with Enfield rifles captured from the enemy. General Salomon now sent orders for us to charge and retake the battery. Two more hills had to be crossed before reaching it, the sides of which were covered with logs and brush. The hills were several hundred feet steep, almost perpendicular; but at the word "forward" they were accompanied by two companies of infantry, and where it was too steep to walk the boys would crawl on their hands and knees. The enemy did not wait to receive us, but left their works. I was now compelled to beat a hasty retreat in consequence of the shells from the gunboat Tyler dropping in all around us, and we fell back and resumed our former position. The men were now much exhausted from charging over the hills and back. The sun was shining out intensely hot, and I ordered the regiment to the foot of the hill, under the trees around head-quarters (the fighting was now over with the exception of some occasional shots), after being engaged for five hours under a continued and severe fire. My killed, wounded, and missing number as follows: Killed, 2; wounded, 8; missing, 1.

The officers and men all conducted themselves so as to meet my highest approbation. Such being the case, I find it impossible to name particular ones as deserving of notice for their bravery without doing injustice to the rest. To Major Owen, however, I am particularly indebted for the valuable aid and assistance he rendered me in carrying out the different orders I received, and for his coolness and bravery. Lieutenant [S. J.] Kelso, commissary, deserves notice for his timely aid in furnishing food and water to the men while they were engaged. Lieutenant [J. M.] Craig, quartermaster, also did his whole duty in his department, and B. J. Kilpatrick, ordnance sergeant, was always on hand with ammunition for the regiment and battery. Many of the men fired over 100 rounds.

Yours, &c.,

THOMAS N. PACE,
Lieutenant-Colonel, Commanding First Indiana Cavalry.

Lieut. M. W. BENJAMIN,
Acting Assistant Adjutant-General.

No. 11.

Report of Lieut. Melvil C. Wright, Third Iowa Battery.

HELENA, ARK., *July* 5, 1863.

CAPTAIN: In obedience to the order of the general commanding, I have the honor herewith to submit the following report of the part taken by the Third Iowa Battery in the engagement of yesterday:

In accordance with previous instructions, at 3.30 a. m. I ordered one section of the battery, under command of Second Lieut. O. H. Lyon, to a point near Battery D, on the left of our line.

The second section, under command of Sergt. L. S. House, which has for some time been in park on the right of the line, immediately upon the commencement of the battle pushed forward a few hundred yards to our extreme right, and took position, supported by a portion of the Second Infantry Brigade, Colonel [S. A.] Rice commanding, and the cavalry brigade, Colonel [Powell] Clayton commanding. Immediately after getting into position, this section was joined by a battery of steel guns, attached to the First Indiana Cavalry, and Colonel Clayton then assumed command of the whole. This officer then changed the position of his guns to a point on the east side of the levee, on our right, where he remained during the whole engagement. At 6 a. m. the 12-pounder howitzer, in charge of Sergt. L. S. House, was disabled by the breaking of the understraps which fasten the cheeks to the axle-tree, the accident being caused by a recoil of the gun. It was immediately taken to park for repairs, but could not be finished in time to take further part in the engagement.

At 6.30 a. m. the third section, which until then remained in camp, was dispatched, in charge of Orderly Sergt. J. J. Dengl, to re-enforce the right wing. On taking position, it immediately opened, and kept up a constant and effective fire against the guns of the enemy, posted on the hills on the extreme right, until recalled by order from the general commanding to Fort Curtis, where it was again effectively employed against the enemy in their last charge on our works.

The section under Lieutenant Lyon was first engaged about 7 a. m., and was after that constantly in action until the close of the battle, and for a considerable length of time very hotly pressed. During the charge on Battery C Lieutenant Lyon changed the position of his 6-pounder gun to command the ravine running from the Catholic Church westward, and, by his fire, contributed very materially in repulsing the enemy. Separated as the battery was during the whole engagement, it is impossible to give as complete an account of the part taken in it by the different sections, and to notice particularly the conduct of my officers and men, as I could wish. While my entire command did their duty nobly, justice to them compels me to report particularly with regard to the following officers: Lieutenant Lyon was during the entire engagement with his section, directing the fire of his guns and encouraging his men by his example to deeds of valor, which, I am confident, the general commanding will appreciate. The lieutenant had his horse wounded twice, severely though not fatally.

From Colonel Clayton I learn that Sergeant House, in charge of section, behaved finely, displaying a great deal of courage and energy, as did also the other non-commissioned officers in his command.

Of Orderly Sergt. J. J. Dengl, having charge of third section, I can speak from personal observation. He was on hand, ready and active; with a thorough appreciation of the situation, he showed himself to be emphatically an artillery officer.

Lieutenant Lyon speaks very highly of the conduct, under the most trying circumstances, of the non-commissioned officers of his command, particularly of Corpl. Daniel Folsom, gunner. The loss of the battery is very light, having lost 1 horse killed and 7 horses wounded.

All of which is respectfully submitted.

I am, your most obedient servant,

M. C. WRIGHT,
First Lieutenant Third Iowa Battery, Commanding.

Capt. A. BLOCKI,
Assistant Adjutant-General, U. S. Forces, Helena, Ark.

No. 12.

Report of Lieut. John O'Connell, Battery K, First Missouri Light Artillery.

HELENA, ARK., *July* 22, 1863.

SIR: I take pleasure in sending you a copy of a report of the part taken by Battery K, First Missouri Light Artillery, in the engagement of July 4, 1863, at this place.

Yours, respectfully,

JNO. O'CONNELL,
First Lieutenant First Missouri Light Artillery.

Lieut. GEORGE W. CUTLER,
Adjutant First Missouri Light Artillery.

[Inclosure.]

HDQRS. BATTERY K, FIRST MISSOURI LIGHT ARTILLERY,
Helena, Ark., July 5, 1863.

SIR: In compliance with your instructions, I have the honor to submit the following report of the part taken by Battery K, First Missouri Light Artillery, in the engagement of yesterday, July 4:

Soon after the alarm gun was fired, I received an order from the adjutant-general to send a section of the battery into the earthworks on the levee, and I immediately ordered the second section, under command of Lieut. Thomas D. Witt, to occupy the position indicated. The first section, under my immediate command, had been placed in position the night before, at the rifle works, a short distance south and east of the hospital, at about 6 o'clock, when the enemy made the charge upon the fort in rear of General Salomon's headquarters. The second section opened fire on the charging column, but soon after received orders from the adjutant-general to cease firing; that our shells were endangering the lives of our own men. But having so fair a view of the enemy, and being in good range, Colonel McLean, commanding brigade, took the responsibility of ordering the lieutenant in command of the second section to open fire again, which order was obeyed with alacrity, and apparently to the great annoyance of the enemy. Soon after this, about 6.30 or 7 o'clock, a second column of the enemy made a charge down the ravine to the left of the fort above the hospital. I opened fire with the entire battery upon the advancing column, and continued the fire until the enemy were repulsed. From the peculiarity of the position, the second section had either to hold its fire or else to fire over the entire length of rifle works which ran from the river to the bluff, and which was occupied by our own troops. The latter course was adopted; and, owing to the premature explosion of a defective shell, a brave soldier, of the Forty-third Indiana, I am informed, was killed. Sadness and regret will not, unfortunately, repair the damage. About 8 o'clock the enemy brought a battery in position upon the ridge next south of the white house occupied by Widow Clements. My entire battery opened fire on their position, and soon had the satisfaction of silencing their guns. During the forenoon the enemy again undertook to plant a battery in the same position, but we had such perfect range upon it that they could not hold long enough to fire over three shots, and I am informed that one of their guns was disabled. During the afternoon I fired occasionally a few shots at small bodies of the enemy, which were once in a while visible. I have no occasion to make special mention of any man of the battery for a display of coolness and courage; they all deserve it. I take pleasure, however, in remarking the splendid shooting made by Sergeant Matthias and Corporals Miller and Geen. I am happy to inform you that the list of casualties is very small, constituting, viz: Corporal Greenbeck, slightly wounded, and 1 horse killed. The battery fired during the day 456 rounds of ammunition.

I have the honor to be, your obedient servant,

JNO. O'CONNELL,
First Lieut. First Missouri Light Artillery, Comdg. Battery K.

Capt. A. BLOCKI,
Assistant Adjutant-General.

No. 13.

Reports of Lieut. Gen. E. Kirby Smith, C. S. Army, commanding Trans-Mississippi Department.

HEADQUARTERS TRANS-MISSISSIPPI DEPARTMENT,
Shreveport, La., July 10, 1863.

GENERAL: The inclosed dispatches show the action upon the suggestion of the Secretary of War in regard to Helena. It is with deep pain that I have to announce the result.

Very respectfully, your obedient servant,

E. KIRBY SMITH,
Lieutenant-General.

General S. COOPER,
Adjutant and Inspector General, Richmond.

[Inclosure No. 1.]

WAR DEPARTMENT,
Richmond, Va., May 25, [23,] 1863.

General JOSEPH E. JOHNSTON,
Commanding, &c.:

DEAR SIR: * * * * * *

[I venture with diffidence only one suggestion, and that not strictly applicable to your own field of operations.*] It is, that should opportunity to communicate with Generals Holmes or Price occur, it might be well to urge they should make diversions for you, or, in the case of the fall of Vicksburg, secure a great future advantage to the Confederacy by the attack on, and seizure of, Helena, while all the available forces of the enemy are being pushed to Grant's aid. Had I command of communications, this suggestion would be directly addressed and pressed by the Department. Its policy is so apparent that it is hoped it will be voluntarily embraced and executed.

[With best wishes, most cordially, yours,]

J. A. SEDDON.

[Indorsement.]

HEADQUARTERS TRANS-MISSISSIPPI DEPARTMENT,
Shreveport, La., June 13, 1863.

Respectfully forwarded to Lieutenant-General Holmes. It is impossible for Lieutenant-General Smith, at this distance, and without any knowledge of the strength of the force at Helena (which is continually varying), to give any orders in the case. It is, therefore, submitted to Lieutenant-General Holmes to act as circumstances may justify.

By order of Lieut. Gen. E. Kirby Smith:

S. S. ANDERSON,
Assistant Adjutant-General.

[Inclosure No. 2.]

LITTLE ROCK, *June* 15, 1863.
(Received June 16.)

Lieut. Gen. E. KIRBY SMITH:

I believe we can take Helena. Please let me attack it.

TH. H. HOLMES,
Lieutenant-General.

[Inclosure No. 3.]

SHREVEPORT, LA., *June* 16, 1863.

Lieut. Gen. T. H. HOLMES:

Most certainly do it.

E. KIRBY SMITH,
Lieutenant-General, Commanding.

---

* Parts in brackets not in extract forwarded by General Smith. The entire letter appears in operations January 20–July 31, 1863, Vicksburg campaign, &c., Series I, Vol. XXIV, Part I, p. 219

[Inclosure No. 4.]

LITTLE ROCK, ARK., *July* 7, 1863.
(Received July 8.)

Lieut. Gen. E. KIRBY SMITH, *Shreveport:*

General Holmes reports that he attacked Helena at daylight on the 4th instant, and was repulsed with a heavy loss.

W. B. BLAIR,
Assistant Adjutant-General.

HEADQUARTERS TRANS-MISSISSIPPI DEPARTMENT,
Shreveport, La., November 14, 1863.

GENERAL: Inclosed herewith I have the honor to forward, for the information of the War Department, reports of the battle of Helena, together with a map of the town and vicinity.*

I am, general, respectfully, your obedient servant,

E. KIRBY SMITH,
Lieutenant-General, Commanding.

General S. COOPER,
Adjutant and Inspector General, Richmond, Va.

[Indorsement.]

DECEMBER 19, 1863.

Respectfully submitted to the President. The attack on Helena, in my opinion, formed from these reports, should have been successful, but failed, not through want of gallantry in the men, but from defective discipline after success, and bad handling by some of the general officers. I fear, too, the report indicates some want of confidence and good understanding between some of the superior officers.

J. A. SEDDON,
Secretary of War.

No. 14.

Report of Lieut. Gen. Theophilus H. Holmes, C. S. Army, commanding District of Arkansas.

LITTLE ROCK, ARK., *August* 14, 1863.

GENERAL: I have the honor to submit to the lieutenant-general commanding the following report of the attack made by me upon Helena on July 4, 1863:

In the month of June, 1862, the Federal forces under General Curtis, from the attempted invasion of Arkansas, betook themselves to the city of Helena and there fortified. Since that time it has been constantly and heavily garrisoned by Federal troops. The possession of this place has been of immense advantage to the enemy. From it they have threatened at all times an invasion of Arkansas, thereby rendering it necessary that troops should be held in position to repel such invasion. From it they have controlled the trade and sentiments of a large and important

---

* Map omitted, in view of that on p. 394.

scope of country. It has been to them a most important depot for troops in their operations against Vicksburg. In view of these great advantages to them, of the great embarrassment to my movements elsewhere, arising from the proximity of a large and threatening army, and of the deleterious effect on that portion of the State cursed by their presence, it was deemed of very great importance that they should be driven from this their only stronghold in Arkansas. As a means of raising the siege of Vicksburg, and of keeping the Mississippi River closed, in the event of the surrender of that city, the policy of the move was perfectly apparent. Moreover, from information considered reliable in my possession, the capture of Helena by the forces at my disposal seemed perfectly practicable.

On June 14, 1863, I telegraphed to Lieutenant-General Smith that I believed I could take the place, and asked his permission to attack it. Two days after, I started to Jacksonport, there to consult with Generals Price and Marmaduke and to make the necessary preliminary arrangements. The result of this interview was the following orders: Price's command, consisting of General McRae's Arkansas and General Parsons' Missouri brigades of infantry, constituting Price's division, and Colonels [Colton] Greene's and [Joseph O.] Shelby's brigades of Missouri cavalry, Marmaduke's division, to rendezvous at Cotton Plant, and Brigadier-General Fagan's Arkansas brigade of infantry at Clarendon, on June 26 (Friday), whence, by converging roads, the two columns would move in the direction of Helena. I also informed General [L. M.] Walker, commanding brigade of cavalry in the vicinity of Helena, of my intention, and directed him to allow no ingress to the place.

Upon my return to Little Rock, I found that General Smith had fully sanctioned my proposed attack, and that the Secretary of War had written a strong letter suggesting, advising, and urging it. Thus encouraged, on June 26 I proceeded to Clarendon and assumed command of the expedition. From unavoidable necessity, consequent on rain, high water, and wretched roads, General Price's command did not reach its rendezvous for four days after the date fixed, thus giving the enemy abundant notice of my approach. General Fagan arrived at his place of rendezvous (Clarendon) on the 26th. As soon as the troops were in position, I proceeded toward Helena by converging roads, and reached Allen Polk's house, 5 miles from Helena, on the morning of July 3.

Having received full, accurate, and reliable information of the forces and fortifications of the enemy in Helena, and the topography of the surrounding country, I here made the final dispositions for the attack. That information disclosed that the place was very much more difficult of access, and the fortifications very much stronger, than I had supposed before undertaking the expedition, the features of the country being peculiarly adapted to defense, and all that the art of engineering could do having been brought to bear to strengthen it. The fortifications consisted of one regular work heavily armed with siege guns, and four strong redoubts mounted with field pieces and protected by rifle-pits, on suburban hills (see the map).

The disposition for the attack was as per following order:

The attack on Helena will be made to-morrow morning at daylight, and as follows:

1st. Major-General Price, in command of McRae's and Parsons' brigades, will proceed by the best route, assume position, assault and take Graveyard Hill at daylight.

2d. Brigadier-General Walker, with his cavalry brigade, will, in like manner, proceed to the Sterling road, where he will hold himself in position to resist any troops that may approach Rightor Hill; and when that position is captured, he will enter the town and act against the enemy as circumstances may justify.

3d. Brigadier-General Fagan will proceed by the best route, assume position, and take the battery on Hindman Hill at daylight.

4th. Brigadier-General Marmaduke will proceed with his command by the best route, assume position, and take Rightor Hill at daylight.

* * * * * * *

This plan of attack was fully concurred in by all my general officers, and the part assigned to each accepted with alacrity.

Between 11 and 12 o'clock at night, the troops began to move to their respective positions, whence to assault in the morning. General Fagan detached a regiment from his brigade and sent it forward to the right on the lower Little Rock road, to occupy the attention of the enemy in the rifle-pits below the city, and to protect his flank in case of an attack from that quarter. Three detached companies of cavalry, under Captain [W. B.] Denson, were ordered to act as vedettes in the plain south of the city, and to transmit to General Fagan rapid information of any attempt to flank him. His artillery was also sent forward on this the only practicable road, with the hope that it might assist in creating a diversion and thereby aid the general movement. I took position a little after daylight on the graveyard ridge, one-half mile from the fortifications (a central point), there to await the development of the attack.

Soon after daylight, Brigadier-General Marmaduke drove in the pickets of the enemy in his front and assaulted Rightor Fort. It is believed that a strong, vigorous, and sudden attack on this fort would have been successful, but some delay occurring, a heavy force of the enemy appeared on his left flank and rear, and held him perfectly in check during the whole day. It was the peculiar duty of Brigadier-General Walker to have prevented this movement on the part of the enemy, and, as represented by General Marmaduke, the same could have been easily accomplished. No satisfactory reason has been given by General Walker why this service was not rendered. This attack, being most remote, was not under my personal supervision, and was too distant for me to give specific orders.

The assault on the first line of rifle-pits in front of Hindman Hill was made at a few minutes after daylight. General Fagan, at the head of his brigade, charged gallantly over four lines under a deadly fire from the rifle-pits and guns on his front, and a most disastrous enfilading fire from Graveyard Hill, on the left, previous to the attack by General Price. Having driven the enemy from and carried the fifth and last line of rifle-pits, the brave men who had followed him thus far, overcome by sheer exhaustion, resulting from the inordinate exertion of their difficult charge and the intense heat of the day, were unable to proceed farther. A charge upon the fort was, nevertheless, attempted, and failed. The brigade thereupon took shelter behind the inner line of breastworks, anxiously awaiting assistance. This assistance never arrived. Major-General Price did not make his attack till after sunrise, and more than an hour after the time named in the order. As an explanation of this delay, his report states that, finding when he had gotten within 1½ miles of the position he had been ordered to take, his division would arrive upon the ground prematurely, he ordered a halt, and resumed his march at dawn of day. His troops, when brought into position and ordered forward, behaved magnificently, charging rifle-pits and breastworks without a falter, and taking the hill without a halt.

As soon as the works were carried, I rode rapidly into them. Finding the guns in the fort had been rendered useless by the enemy before being abandoned, I at once dispatched one of my staff to the rear to bring up some artillery. Owing to the impracticability of the roads, this could not be effected in time.

Perceiving the position of the gallant Fagan and his command, I ordered Brigadier-General Parsons, the only general officer present, to proceed at once to attack the Hindman fort in the rear. Everything was in confusion, regiments and brigades mixed up indiscriminately, and the order was not attended to. Immediately afterward I sent an order to General Price to the same effect, and then returned to my headquarters. Two or three hundred yards in the rear I passed Brigadier-General McRae, who had not joined his brigade since the assault. I ordered him at once to the fort. It seems that General McRae was the officer designated by General Price to go to General Fagan's assistance. After much delay he proceeded on this duty, but utterly failed to render the slightest aid, making no attempt to assault the hill. Not having been advised of this order for General McRae, and being impatient of the delay, I proceeded again to the fort on Graveyard Hill, where I found General Parsons with only 300 or 400 men of his brigade. He informed me that General McRae had been ordered to the relief of General Fagan. That officer was nowhere to be seen, while General Fagan, with greatly reduced force, was being assaulted and driven back by the enemy, largely re-enforced. Under these circumstances, at 10.30 a. m. I ordered the troops to be withdrawn. My retreat from Helena was effected in the most perfect order and without the slightest demoralization of any kind.

My whole force engaged in this expedition amounted to 7,646. My loss, as near as is ascertained, is 173 killed, 687 wounded, 776 missing; total, 1,636. See reports of division and brigade commanders, forwarded herewith.

I write this report with a deep pain. I commanded brave, gallant, and willing troops, and should have succeeded in the capture of Helena, for though the difficulties were very great, they were not insurmountable, and the misfortune of a failure was in a very great measure consequent on the men not being well in hand after success. Most of my loss in prisoners resulted from not restraining the men after the capture of Graveyard Hill from advancing into the town, where they were taken mainly without resistance. If instead of this the regiments and brigades had been reformed instantly, the capture of Hindman Hill and consequently of the town would have been of easy occurrence.

I cannot close this report without expressing my obligations to His Excellency Harris Flanagin, Governor of Arkansas, who accompanied me and had my confidence during the whole campaign. I owe to his cool, discriminating judgment many valuable suggestions. His presence, confidence, and zeal had no little influence on the spirit and energy of the Arkansas troops. He and Col. Gordon N. Peay, adjutant-general of the State, acted as volunteer aides-de-camp on my staff during the battle.

As the expedition failed, which should have succeeded, I refrain from all expressions of commendation, believing that the brave officers and men who distinguished themselves will willingly forego the applause due to them in consideration that our beloved country reaped no benefit from their exploits.

I have the honor to be, general, very respectfully, your obedient servant,

TH. H. HOLMES,
Lieutenant-General.

Brig. Gen. W. R. BOGGS,
Chief of Staff, Trans-Mississippi Dept., Shreveport, La.

ADDENDA.

Return of Casualties in the Confederate forces in the attack on Helena.

[Compiled from nominal lists and returns.]

Command.	Killed.		Wounded.		Missing.		Aggregate.	Officers killed.
	Officers.	Enlisted men.	Officers.	Enlisted men.	Officers.	Enlisted men.		
PRICE'S DIVISION.								
McRae's Brigade.								
32d Arkansas	5	12	7	39	1	25	89	Capt. J. R. Morris, and Lieuts. R. B. Camp, Thos. A. Eppes, R. F. McKinney, and W. T. Tompkins.
36th Arkansas	2	19	7	63	4	64	159	Capt. J. C. Garland and Lieut. J. R. Harlan.
39th Arkansas	1	7	8	38	5	34	93	Lieut. W. F. Rector.
Marshall's battery	....	......	1	5	....	......	6	
Total	8	38	23	145	10	123	347	
Parsons' Brigade.								
7th Missouri	2	14	15	109	2	51	193	Capts. B. N. Cocke and G. W. Perry.
8th Missouri	1	13	11	67	5	61	158	Capt. W. J. Lillard.
9th Missouri	3	9	4	23	....	15	54	Maj. T. B. Sandford, Capt. D. T. Lanius, and Lieut. R. Spencer.
10th Missouri	....	10	3	38	16	204	271	
Pindall's battalion	....	9	4	22	....	8	43	
Tilden's battery	....	1	......	8	....	3	12	
Total	6	56	37	267	23	342	731	
Fagan's Brigade.								
Brooks' regiment	....	......	......	1	....	......	1	
Hawthorn's regiment	2	15	3	50	6	61	137	See Hawthorn's report.
Bell's regiment	....	14	1	16	24	167	222	
King's regiment	....	16	6	38	....	15	75	
Total	2	45	10	105	30	243	435	
WALKER'S DIVISION.								
5th Arkansas Cavalry *	....	......	......	......	....	......	......	
Dobbin's regiment	....	4	......	8	....	......	12	
Total	....	4	......	8	....	......	12	
MARMADUKE'S DIVISION.								
Division staff	1	......	......	......	....	......	1	Maj. R H. Smith, quartermaster.
Greene's Brigade.								
3d Missouri Cavalry	....	3	......	6	....	......	9	
8th Missouri Cavalry	1	......	......	......	....	......	1	Lieut. G R. Norment.
Young's battalion	....	1	......	1	....	......	2	
Total	1	4	......	7	....	......	12	
Shelby's Brigade.								
5th Missouri Cavalry	....	3	3	8	....	......	14	
6th Missouri Cavalry	....	1	1	16	....	1	19	
Jeans' regiment	....	3	3	6	....	......	12	
Bledsoe's battery	....	1	......	6	....	......	7	
Total	....	8	7	36	....	1	52	
Grand total	18	155	77	568	63	709	1,590	

*Report of casualties not found.

No. 15.

Report of Maj. Gen. Sterling Price, C. S. Army, commanding division

HEADQUARTERS PRICE'S DIVISION,
Camp on Jones' Lake, July 13, 1863.

CAPTAIN: I have the honor to submit to the lieutenant-general commanding the following report of the part taken by this division in the attack made upon Helena on the 4th instant:

I left Jacksonport, in obedience to his orders, on June 22, with this division and Marmaduke's division of cavalry. My march was greatly impeded by the extraordinary rains, which, beginning on the evening of June 24 and falling almost without intermission for four days, made the river, bayous, and creeks over which my route lay, and the bottoms and swamps through which it ran, almost impassable to troops unprovided, as mine were, with the means of repairing roads and constructing bridges or rafts. I was, however, enabled, by the skill and energy of my officers, and by the willing endurance and laborious industry of my men, to surmount these unlooked-for obstacles, and to reach, on the morning of the 3d instant, a point within 5 miles of Helena. At this point Lieutenant-General Holmes, having assumed the immediate command of all the troops before Helena, detached Marmaduke's division from my command, leaving me two brigades—the one of Arkansians, under Brig. Gen. Dandridge McRae, consisting of three regiments of infantry and a field battery, with 1,227 men present for duty; the other, of Missourians, under Brig. Gen. M. Monroe Parsons, consisting of four regiments of infantry, a battalion of sharpshooters, and a field battery, having in all 1,868 men present for duty. These two brigades constituted this division.

The order of attack directed that I, "in command of McRae's and Parsons' brigades, should proceed by the best route, assume position, assault, and take the Graveyard Hill at daylight." I made my dispositions accordingly, and moved at midnight with Parsons' brigade in front. As my route lay for the greater part of the way across abrupt hills and deep ravines, over which it was utterly impracticable to move my artillery during the darkness, I ordered the pieces to be left behind until daybreak, and armed details from each battery to accompany the infantry, in order to man the guns which I expected to capture. Finding when I had gotten within 1½ miles of the position which I had been ordered to take, that my division would arrive upon the ground prematurely, I ordered a halt, during which the lieutenant-general commanding came to and remained with the division until the dawn of day, when the line of march was resumed. Then pushing forward rapidly, until my skirmishers had become engaged with those of the enemy, and within half a mile of his works, the troops were formed into two columns of divisions, Parsons' brigade occupying the right and moving in front. The enemy's fire becoming somewhat sharp about this time, the guides who were conducting the columns took occasion to leave unperceived. Some confusion and consequent delay ensued; but another guide having been obtained, the head of the column soon occupied the position from which the assault was to be made. A brief halt was here ordered, to give the troops time to recover somewhat from the exhausting fatigue consequent upon their rapid march over a succession of almost precipitous and heavily wooded hills. The order for the assault (as explained to the general officers and regimental commanders of the division the evening before) directed that General Parsons, moving in front, should halt the head of his column at the point from which he was to make the assault until the head of General McRae's column should reach its position on the left, when both columns should advance simultaneously to the assault.

During the brief halt just alluded to, and just as I had ordered General McRae forward, the lieutenant-general commanding rode up and asked why the assault had not been made. I explained the facts to him, and thinking that time enough had elapsed for General McRae to get into position, I dispatched one of my staff to General Parsons to ascertain why he was not advancing. He replied that he was waiting for General McRae to get into position.

Meanwhile General McRae had moved his brigade into its position, but (owing to the difficulties and necessities of the ground) farther to the left than had been originally ordered and explained to General Parsons, and with a high ridge interposing between it and Parsons' brigade, so that the latter officer could not see that it had gotten into position. I immediately directed one of my staff officers to communicate these facts to General Parsons, and to order him to make the assault without any further delay, as General McRae (to whom I had sent orders to that effect) would be advancing before he (General Parsons) could receive my order.

Both brigades moved forward on the instant, rapidly, steadily, unflinchingly, and in perfect order, under a storm of Minie balls, grape, and canister, which were poured upon them not only from the Graveyard Hill in their front but from the fortified hills upon the right and the left, both of which were in easy range. The enemy gave way before the impetuous assault of the attacking columns, which, entering the works almost simultaneously, planted the Confederate flag upon the summit of the Graveyard Hill.

Each brigade had done its allotted duty with equal zeal, devotion, and gallantry, and each is entitled to an equal share of the honor which justly attaches to those who discharge their duty as these men did, fearlessly, well, and successfully.

Being in possession of the hill, and finding that the captured guns had been shot-wedged, I directed my chief of artillery to bring forward the pieces which I had left behind. This he did as promptly as the difficulties of the ground would permit, but not until it was too late for them to be used in the action.

Meanwhile a heavy fire was concentrated upon the hill from the four fortified positions, which the enemy still continued to hold, and from the hill-sides and ravines, under cover of which their sharpshooters delivered a well-directed and very effective fire, while the gunboat which lay in front of the town kept up an unintermitting discharge of its heavy guns. Perceiving at once that the surest way to relieve my men from the disastrous effects of this galling fire was to aid General Fagan to take the enemy's works upon my right, and receiving information at the same time that that gallant officer had been repulsed in every attempt to assault those works, I sent to General Parsons an order directing him to move his brigade forthwith to the re-enforcement of General Fagan. He replied to the officer by whom I sent the order that General McRae (who was by his side at the time) would, with my permission, go to the assistance of General Fagan, while his (Parsons') brigade, being the stronger of the two, would hold the Graveyard Hill. Before this reply was brought back to me, I sent another of my staff, by direction of the lieutenant-general commanding, to deliver to General Parsons an order similar to the one already sent. General Parsons' reply having been meanwhile received, another order was sent, directing him to hold the hill and General McRae to re-enforce General Fagan as speedily as possible with his brigade.

It soon became obvious, however, that both brigades had been so much weakened by their heavy losses in killed and wounded, and particularly in prisoners (the most of the latter having been captured in the immediate vicinity of the town, whither they had gone without orders from me), and by the straggling of those whom thirst and the intense heat of the day overcame, or who had become disheartened by the failure of the other assaulting columns, that I could not send any effective aid to General Fagan without too greatly endangering my own position. It was equally obvious that, unless such aid could be promptly sent to General Fagan, the general attack upon Helena must fail. It was under these circumstances that I received an order from the lieutenant-general commanding to withdraw my division. In compliance with this order, my troops were withdrawn to a point about 4 miles from Helena, where they rested for the night, and resumed the march hither on the morning of the 5th.

The lieutenant-general commanding was himself a witness of the conduct of my division. He saw the alacrity with which they advanced to the positions to which they had been assigned. He knows the steadiness and unfaltering courage with which they moved, in the midst of a deadly fire, over deep ravines and precipitous hills obstructed with felled timber, to, into, and over the works which they had been ordered to take, driving everything before them. He was himself a witness of the undaunted bravery and enduring constancy with which, animated by his own inspiring example and gallant bearing, they stood, unshaken, in the very center of that unceasing fire which was hurled against them from gunboat, from forts, and from rifle-pits. I am sure that he will pay them that tribute of praise to which their courage and endurance entitle them.

The accompanying reports of Brigadier-Generals McRae and Parsons will explain in detail the part taken by their respective brigades, and point out to the lieutenant-general commanding such of their officers and men as are particularly deserving of mention.

I have not been able to obtain perfectly accurate reports of the casualties in this division, but these may be stated approximately as follows:

Command.	Killed.	Wounded.	Missing.	Total.
McRae's brigade	46	168	133	347
Parsons' brigade	59	336	369	764
Total	105	504	502	1,111

I will forward detailed reports of these casualties as soon as the lists can be carefully revised. The separation of the command will necessarily entail some delay in the revision of them.

The admirable conduct of Brigadier-General Parsons not only upon the field but upon the march, merits my earnest commendation, while his skill and gallantry, as well as his long and uninterrupted active service as brigadier-general (first in the Missouri State Guard and more recently in the Provisional Army of the Confederate States), are, in my opinion, worthy of recognition on the part of the Government.

I must also commend the excellent discipline which General McRae maintains at all times in his brigade; the marked good sense and energy with which he conducted its march to Helena; the promptitude with which he has always obeyed my commands, and the earnest efforts which he made to re-enforce General Fagan toward the close of the attack.

I have not in any former report mentioned the officers of my staff, though most of them have been eminently deserving of praise for gallant and meritorious conduct upon more than one hard-fought field. Justice requires that I should not permit the present occasion to pass without placing upon record my sense and appreciation of the merits and worth of those of them, at least, who participated in the present movement.

Maj. Thomas L. Snead, senior assistant adjutant-general of my command, to whom I have been often indebted for vigorous support in hours of perilous trial (apart from the intelligent and faithful performance of the responsible and onerous duties of his office), surpassed himself this day in the intrepid manner with which he bore himself throughout the conflict, rallying the troops again and again, and urging them forward to the scene of action. In this work, under the hottest fire of the enemy, and until we had swept their intrenchments and carried the hill, he was faithfully, fearlessly, and gallantly assisted by Maj. L. A. Maclean, assistant adjutant-general.

My thanks are due to my aides-de-camp—Lieut. Richard T. Morrison and Lieut. Celsus Price—for their willing assistance promptly rendered upon this as upon other hotly contested fields.

I commend all of these officers to the lieutenant-general commanding, and through him to the President, for promotion on account of gallant and meritorious conduct on the field.

Acting Engineers John Mhoon, of Alabama, and D. C. Cage, of Mississippi, not only deserve honorable mention for their gallantry upon the field, but for the skill and energy with which they overcame the difficulties that obstructed my road from Cache River to Helena. I have repeatedly recommended Mr. Mhoon for appointment in the Engineer Corps, and again respectfully urge the President to recognize the worth of so excellent an officer. Mr. Cage's services demand a similar recognition.

Nor should the less conspicuous but equally useful services of Maj. Isaac Brinker and Maj. John Reid be passed over in silence. To the practical good sense and untiring and well directed energy of the former, as chief quartermaster of my division, I am greatly indebted for the accomplishment of the march to Helena and back to this point; while the latter, as chief commissary of subsistence, has, in spite of many difficulties, continued to subsist the troops both regularly and well.

Lieut. Col. Clay Taylor, chief of artillery and acting chief of ordnance, discharged the onerous duties of both these offices with laborious fidelity and to my entire satisfaction.

To my chief surgeon, Thomas D. Wooten; to Surg. William M. McPheeters, and to Assistant Field Purveyor R. M. Slaughter, my constant thanks and commendation are due for the sedulous manner in which they have at all times devoted themselves to the sick and wounded, but never more humanely or more conspicuously than upon this occasion. These gentlemen tell me that they owe their grateful acknowledgments to the Rev. Mr. Marvin for the very important services which he rendered at their hospitals, not only offering the consolations of his holy office to the dying, but ministering assiduously to the wants of the wounded.

Maj. John Tyler, jr., C. S. Army, acting, for want of an appropriate command, as volunteer aide-de-camp, remained by my side in view of special contingencies which might fittingly task his valuable accomplishments.

Mr. Charles T. Perrie, volunteer aide-de-camp, is also entitled to my thanks for the activity which he displayed at the opening of the attack.

I would refer particularly to the gallant conduct and bearing of Mr. Gustavus A. Dyes, clerk in the office of the assistant adjutant-general, and of Orderly Daniel M. Kavanaugh, both of whom have, by their conduct on this field, merited commissions in the army, and both of whom have borne themselves equally well on more important battle-fields.

Maj. Henry M. Clark, assistant inspector-general, was detained from the field by serious illness; Maj. E. C. Cabell, paymaster, by duties elsewhere.

I am, captain, very respectfully, your obedient servant,

STERLING PRICE,
Major-General.

Capt. JOHN W. HINSDALE,
Assistant Adjutant-General.

No. 16.

Report of Brig. Gen. Dandridge McRae, C. S. Army, commanding brigade.

HEADQUARTERS MCRAE'S BRIGADE,
July 14, 1863.

MAJOR: I submit the following report of the action of my brigade in the assault upon the town of Helena upon the 4th instant:

On the 3d, orders were issued from district headquarters for General Parsons' and my brigades to assault and take the fort upon the Graveyard Hill at daylight upon the morning of the 4th. By agreement, General Parsons' brigade was to move in front until he got into position, so as to enable him to rush past the fortification by way of the ravine south of the Graveyard Hill, and then charge the fort in reverse. As soon as General Parsons was in position, my brigade was to move to the left and charge the works in front simultaneously with the assault to be made by General Parsons. The evening before the assault, General Parsons and myself had been furnished with five guides. We took up the line of march at 12 o'clock at night. Three of these guides went with General Parsons. I also sent to his front one company of sharpshooters, under command of Captain [C. N.] Biscoe, of [R. A.] Hart's regiment, Captain Biscoe being familiar with the country. Before daylight our column was halted to wait until the other attacking columns were in position. After forming into columns of divisions, we again moved on. As soon as the enemy's fire opened, General Parsons sent back for another guide, those sent with him having deserted him. I sent one, and the one that remained with me shortly after left me. At this time we were upon the ridges, three in number, each having a fort upon it and firing, and in appearance were exactly alike. Here I halted for a short time in doubt as to the route. Finding the correct route, we pushed on upon the crest of the hill to where the timber was cleared away, in front of the rifle-pits, and then crossed to the north side of the ridge, and moved up to a position that I thought near enough to make a charge; but between my position and the work that was to be carried there was a deep ravine just in front of the fort. As soon as the command was massed in position, a general rush was made into the fort and the works were carried. This assault was made from the north. The enemy were driven from the works and pursued into the verge of the town. About this time General Parsons' brigade entered into the fort, he having charged about the same time as my brigade, thus rendering the capture of the position certain, for, had our assault failed, he would have been so close that we could not have failed.

Here I would state that, while moving along the north side of Graveyard Hill, my command was exposed not only to the fire of the fort and rifle-pits in front, but also to the fort north of Graveyard Hill, which fort was not attacked, and to whose fire my command was exposed.

While moving along, I discovered a battery of field pieces was being moved to the rear, so as to completely enfilade my command, and being in point-blank range for canister. Before marching I had armed Captain [John G.] Marshall's company of artillery with muskets and moved it along in rear of my column, so that in the event we captured the fort I would be prepared to work the guns. I now was compelled to use this company as sharpshooters, and deployed them, ordering them to approach as close as possible to the battery and prevent it getting into position, which they accomplished in a very gallant manner.

As soon as the works were carried, I at once returned to where I had deployed Marshall's company, and ordered Captain Marshall to call in his men and take charge of the guns and work them.

While giving these orders, Lieutenant-General Holmes rode up and ordered me at once to the assistance of General Fagan, who was attacking the fort upon the south of Graveyard Hill. I at once went to the fort and ordered my officers to assemble their men; but before they were able to do so, General Holmes again, in a peremptory manner, ordered me to the assistance of General Fagan. I had not more than 200 men with me. With them I charged down the hill, aiming to assault the north front of the fort; but when I arrived at the foot of the hill the fire of the enemy was so withering that with the force I had it was madness to attempt to scale the hill, the hollow being raked by artillery situated opposite its mouth, and completely enfiladed with rifle-pits in point-blank range. I therefore deployed my men and commenced firing upon the rifle-pits and works, which were being attacked by General Fagan, aiming to make as great a diversion as possible.

I remained here until I was informed that the enemy had retaken the works on Graveyard Hill, when I sent Captain [P. M.] Cobbs, of Hart's regiment, with his company, to General Fagan, and to inform him that I was unable to attack the works in front, being now exposed to fire in rear as well as flank. I crossed over the narrow ridge in front of the fort attacked by General Fagan, and the fire was so great and severe that the men were compelled to cross this ridge singly. When I reached the crest of the hill, I discovered General Fagan's men in a rifle-pit in front of the main works, and they seemed too few, even re-enforced with what men I had, to accomplish anything, and within a short time I saw them rush out of the rifle-pits into a deep gorge immediately in their rear. Discovering the enemy moving around the crest of the hill, and fearing that I would be surrounded, I retreated into the ravine between the two forts attacked, and reorganized what command I had with me, and then moved to the rear, forcing every straggler that I found to fall into the ranks. The first field officer that I met was Colonel [A. T.] Hawthorn, at some huts where some of General Fagan's wounded were, and in a short time General Fagan came up. After moving a short distance from here, I met General Holmes.

I must here call your attention to the fact that the information concerning the localities, strength of the enemy, &c., was very erroneous. The ground over which we moved was almost entirely impracticable; the crest of the hill so narrow that it would have been murder to have attempted to have assaulted along it; the sides of the hill, full of gulches, with almost perpendicular sides, and that covered with fallen timber, so placed as to most impede an approach; the day one of the hottest; our column not only exposed to a storm of shell, but for a long way (say 600 yards) to a fire of canister and grape, front and flank, as well as from sharpshooters from rifle-pits, which were placed by the enemy to protect every possible approach. Under all this I am proud to say that my little brigade of less than three regiments, and these small, moved steadily, without faltering, upon the foe, protected by fortifications and artillery, and the hill up which the final rush was made was so steep and slippery that it was almost impracticable. For all that, with a wild shout they rushed up it, drove the concealed enemy from his position, and seized his works. I am happy and proud to state that the officers and men in my brigade did their whole duty, and where all did so well a distinction is difficult.

As for my field officers, that they did their duty it needs but to state that of 9 that went into the battle 6 were wounded, 2 mortally.

Attention is called to the gallant conduct of Colonel [R. A.] Hart, who led his men to the assault, and when in the fort seized one of the enemy's guns and fired it against them.

Here also fell mortally wounded Lieut. W. F. Rector, adjutant of Hart's regiment, whose gallantry and undaunted bravery signally distinguished him in the assault.

Major [J. M.] Davie, gallantly leading his men, fell shot through the thigh in front of the fort.

Captain [W. C.] Robinson, acting major, fell mortally wounded in front of his men.

There also fell mortally wounded the brave, the zealous Major [J. C.] Martin, of Hart's regiment, as also Major [A. F.] Stephenson, of Gause's regiment.

There also fell Captain [J. C.] Garland, of Glenn's regiment, Lieutenant [Thomas A.] Eppes, of Gause's regiment, than whom a better man or braver soldier has not offered up his life during the war.

Colonels [J. E.] Glenn and [L. C.] Gause, and Lieutenant-Colonels [J. W.] Rogan and [William] Hicks, deserve special mention for the cool and daring manner in which they led their men.

Lieutenant [J. W.] Crabtree, of Glenn's regiment, displayed the greatest intrepidity.

Sergeant [John H.] Champ, Company A, of Hart's regiment, deserves the greatest credit for gallantry, rushing in advance of his regiment in the charge.

Color-Sergeant Garland, of Glenn's regiment, also deserves special mention. He advanced his regimental colors to the front, and maintained his position through the assault, his colors being torn into ribbons.

My thanks are due my staff for efficient aid rendered me during the action; especially to Lieut. John W. McKay, my acting assistant inspector-general.

In conclusion, I will state that I left the field without orders. Having been ordered by General Holmes to the part of the field upon which General Fagan's brigade fought, I was unable to communicate with Major-General Price; but when I left, all effort upon our part had ceased.

My loss is as follows: Killed, 46; wounded, 168; missing, 133. Total, 347. For further particulars reference is made to list sent herewith, which is respectfully submitted.*

Respectfully,

D. McRAE,
Brigadier-General.

Maj. THOMAS L. SNEAD,
Assistant Adjutant-General, Price's Division.

No. 17.

Report of Brig. Gen. M. Monroe Parsons, C. S. Army, commanding brigade.

HEADQUARTERS FOURTH BRIGADE, PRICE'S DIVISION,
July 10, 1863.

MAJOR: I have the honor to report the following as the part taken by my brigade in the battle of Helena, on the 4th instant:

On the evening of July 3, the army bivouacked on the Little Rock and Helena road, and 6 miles from the latter place. It having been determined to attack the enemy at dawn next morning, the disposition of the troops for the various points of attack was immediately made by the lieutenant-general commanding the army and the major-general commanding this division. The assault and capture of the enemy's works on Graveyard Hill was assigned to the major-general commanding Brigadier-General McRae's brigade (Arkansas) and my brigade (Missouri Volunteers). This position was by the lieutenant-general commanding believed to be the strongest of all the enemy's works, and the key to all his defenses. He was particularly solicitous that it should be carried and held at all hazards. It was represented to contain six heavy pieces, protected by earthworks and a line of rifle-pits on its front, and extremely inaccessible on account of the numerous sharp ridges, steep ravines, and felled timber in its front and flank. These works were situated between Fort Hindman on the right and another fort on the left, both being within rifle range of the position to be assailed by my command, and supported in its rear by another fort between it and the town of Helena, and Fort Curtis, obliquely to the right and rear of the works to be assaulted. All these fortifications were situated upon high, steep hills, with deep ravines and felled timber between, rendering the rapid and orderly movement of troops very difficult.

At 12 o'clock on the night of the 3d the division was put in motion, my brigade in advance, which moved in the following order, viz: First, battalion of sharpshooters, Major [L. A.] Pindall commanding, in front; second, the Ninth Regiment, Colonel [J. D.] White; third, the Eighth Regiment, Colonel [S. P.] Burns commanding; fourth, the Seventh Regiment, Colonel [L. M.] Lewis commanding; fifth, the Tenth Regiment, Colonel [A. C.] Pickett commanding. After moving on the main road

---

* Embodied in statement on p. 412.

about 2 miles, the column diverged to the left along an obscure path for 2 miles farther, and then left this path to the left and followed up a rivulet until arriving within about 1½ miles of Graveyard Hill. Day having not yet dawned, a halt was ordered to await sufficient light, during which time my command was ordered to load. I had previously thrown out well to the front as skirmishers Major Pindall's battalion of sharpshooters, to which command was attached Captain [C. N.] Biscoe's company of sharpshooters from McRae's brigade. Taking advantage of this halt, I particularly instructed in person the commandants of regiments as to the plan of attack, and charged them that in the event any of their divisions should become disordered in carrying the works, that they should be promptly reformed, and, as the orders of my superiors extended only to the capture of Graveyard Hill, that no further movement should be made without orders. I deemed this precaution absolutely necessary, as it was impossible for either myself or staff to ride over the rough ground on which we moved, and consequently orders could not be transmitted with the usual rapidity.

At daylight the march was resumed, and in a short time we encountered the steep ridges and deep ravines, which rendered the movement very slow and fatiguing. At 5 a. m. Major Pindall encountered the enemy's pickets about half a mile from the fortifications. Sharp skirmishing ensued, and finally they were driven in. I ordered the column to form divisions at half distance and move steadily forward in that order. The enemy now commenced throwing shell and grape upon the column, killing and wounding about 20 men, but no signs of disorder or fear were apparent. They moved steadily and firmly forward. By this time Pindall's sharpshooters had arrived within musket range of the enemy's works, and from behind stumps and logs and the branches of felled trees were delivering an effective fire upon the gunners of the enemy's artillery.

Upon arriving within 300 yards of the line of rifle-pits, I again halted the column, to allow rest and to enable Brigadier-General McRae to move up on my left and take the position as previously agreed upon between that officer and myself, for the purpose of making a combined assault upon the works. So soon as it was announced to me that he was in position, I ordered the "forward" at double-quick, to which officers and men responded with alacrity. Just at this moment a heavy fire was opened on my right flank from a rifle-pit distant about 150 yards; also the shell and grape from Fort Hindman was showered down upon the column. This was the critical moment. I watched with an anxious eye to see whether my battalions would falter or break under this flank attack, but they moved gallantly on, unheeding the murderous missiles now being hurled on them both from front and flank. Turning my attention to the front, the head of the two columns (McRae's and mine) were beyond the rifle-pits, and in an instant White's battle-flag, waving over the works, announced that Graveyard Hill was won. Thirty men of [C. B.] Tilden's battery having been armed and sent forward with Colonel White's regiment, under command of Lieutenant [A. A.] Lesueur, for the purpose of working the enemy's guns upon their capture, this officer immediately took them in charge; but finding shot wedged in the bore, and the enemy having taken away the worms, he could not work them. He and his men resumed their muskets and fought as infantry throughout the battle. As previously ordered, the commandants of regiments proceeded to restore order in their commands wherever confusion had occurred. Just at this time the lieutenant-general commanding arrived upon the hill and gave orders directly to one of my colonels to attack and carry the fort in direction of the town, and he proceeding to execute the order, the other commandants understanding it to be a general movement toward the town, advanced in that direction, some portions of regiments rushing into the town and even to the river bank. All the way from Graveyard Hill to the town, and through it, those devoted troops were exposed to a fatal cross-fire from the enemy's artillery and musketry. It was here that my loss was the heaviest. Not more than half of those that went in that direction returned; the remainder were killed, wounded, and taken prisoners.

From time to time the enemy made repeated assaults on Graveyard Hill, but was always successfully repulsed. While General McRae and myself were thus holding it under the terrific storm of bullets hurled upon us, both from the right and from the left, he suggested that if I with my command would hold the position he would assault Fort Hindman in the rear, which General Fagan was then engaging in front. This arrangement having been agreed upon, he moved with what troops he had at his disposal to the assault; but being assailed by the guns from the fort, by the musketry from the rifle-pits, and in flank by the heavy artillery from the gunboat, he was compelled to withdraw his gallant command into the timber for shelter. During these operations against Fort Hindman the enemy was continually shelling my position from the fort upon my left, and repeatedly advanced against me, but was each time repulsed. General Fagan having retired from the assault upon Fort Hindman, no troops were now upon the field except my own. The enemy moved upon me in front and upon both flanks and opened a furious cross-fire of artillery from right and left. I still maintained my position, driving back the enemy's infantry wherever assaulted.

At 10.15 a. m. I received an order from the major-general commanding to retire. I immediately sent orders to commandants of regiments and Pindall's battalion to withdraw their commands in good order and fight the enemy as they retired. At 10.30 a. m. I withdrew my command from the field.

It gives me great pain to report the heavy losses in brave officers and men that my brigade sustained on that bloody field.

The following is a summary of my losses* in each regiment, battalion, and the artillery detachment:

Command.	Killed.	Wounded.	Missing.	Total.
7th Regiment	17	126	54	197
8th Regiment	14	82	67	163
9th Regiment	7	53	......	60
10th Regiment	11	41	237	289
Pindall's sharpshooters	9	26	8	43
Artillery detachment	1	8	3	12
Total	59	336	369	764

It will thus be seen that every regiment, battalion, and squad of my brigade was actively engaged with the enemy, and that each sustained its proportion of the heavy losses above reported, Captain Tilden's battery not having been taken into action, it being impracticable to do so on account of obstructions in the line of march.

While the country will long mourn the loss of the gallant officers and

* But see revised statement, p. 412.

men who fell as martyrs to our cause, the historians of this revolution will record them as "the bravest of the brave." For their gallant comrades who now lie disabled from their wounds, the officers and soldiers of this brigade feel the deepest solicitude, and cherish the hope that they will soon recover and return to their commands, to give the country more examples of unprecedented coolness and daring.

To mention the name of any particular officer or soldier as having distinguished himself for gallantry above his fellow would be to do injustice, for the brigade, as a whole, fully sustained its well-earned reputation, and gave additional evidence of the disinterested devotion of Missourians to the cause of their country, showing, as heretofore, that they are always among the first in the breach and the last to leave it.

I am indebted to my aides, Captain [James F.] Edwards and Lieutenant [P. E.] Chesnut, for the prompt and untiring energy with which they assisted me in the engagement. Major [T.] Monroe, my brigade quartermaster, and Major [John B.] Ruthven, my brigade commissary, deserve great praise for the activity [with] which they discharged the duties of their respective departments. Chief Surgeon [C. D.] Baer, with the regimental surgeons and their assistants, were on the field, and by their prompt professional attention to the wounded saved many valuable lives.

A report in detail of the killed, wounded, and missing will be forwarded at an early day to the proper department.

I have the honor to be, very respectfully,

M. M. PARSONS,
Brigadier-General, Commanding.

Maj. THOMAS L. SNEAD,
Assistant Adjutant-General.

Morning Report of Fourth Brigade, Missouri Volunteers, Brig. Gen. M. M. Parsons commanding, July 6, 1863.

Command.	Aggregate present.	Effective aggregate.
7th Missouri Infantry	433	325
8th Missouri Infantry	467	413
9th Missouri Infantry	168	161
10th Missouri Infantry	236	231
Sharpshooters	190	157
Tilden's battery	82	72
Total	1,576	1,359

M. M. PARSONS,
Brigadier-General.

No. 18.

Reports of Brig. Gen. J. F. Fagan, C. S. Army, commanding brigade.

HEADQUARTERS SECOND BRIGADE, &C.,
Camp at Searcy, Ark., July 21, 1863.

MAJOR: I have the honor to report as follows in regard to the part taken by my brigade in the attack on Helena upon the 4th instant:

On the evening of the 3d instant, at dark, I ordered Colonel [W. H.]

Brooks with his regiment, one section of [C. B.] Etter's battery of light artillery, commanded by Lieut. John C. Arnett, and three companies of cavalry, commanded by Captain [W. B.] Denson, to move to the front in support of the cavalry, then within 3 miles of the town of Helena.

About 11 o'clock at night with the three remaining regiments, commanded, respectively, by Colonels [J. P.] King, [A. T.] Hawthorn, and [S. S.] Bell, and Blocher's battery of light artillery, commanded by Capt. W. D. Blocher, I moved forward on the road toward Helena. On joining Colonel Brooks where the old hill road leaves the Little Rock road, I ordered him to advance at once with his command on the latter road, to attract and engage the attention of the enemy south of town, and hold his forces in the rifle-pits on the river. At the same time I ordered Colonel Hawthorn, whose regiment was in advance, to lead the brigade forward on the hill road. This was promptly complied with, and the brigade moved on without interruption until within 1 mile of the outer works of the enemy. At this point the road was completely filled with felled timber, the largest forest growth intermingling and overlapping its whole length, while on either side precipitous and impassable ravines were found running up even to the very intrenchments of the enemy. It was utterly impossible to move my artillery or ammunition train along this road. The obstacles were so great, indeed, that I was under the necessity of directing every officer of my command to dismount and proceed on foot—a dire necessity which subsequent events gave occasion seriously to deplore. After crawling through the interstices of the closely jutting limbs and boughs, and climbing over the thickly matted timber for 1 mile, my line of skirmishers, who had been ordered by me not to fire, came within sight of the enemy. I went to the front, and could plainly see that the enemy was on the alert, and evidently expecting and awaiting an attack. The order of the lieutenant-general commanding was to assault the fortifications with the several attacking columns precisely at daylight on the morning of the 4th. Not having been apprised of the obstructions in the road, I had made no arrangements to remove them. The limited time to daylight would not allow of an attempt even to take my artillery along. It was ordered to remain in the road where the obstructions were first met with. To conform to orders, it was necessary for me to move with the utmost celerity. Freeing myself of everything except my column of infantry, I pushed forward with all the haste in my power. At daylight I reached and attacked the enemy in his works. Colonel Hawthorn, being in advance, was hurried rapidly into line on the right of the road which led directly up to the fort on Hindman's Hill. He at once engaged the enemy, who occupied their extreme or outer line of rifle-pits. Bell's regiment emerged next from the confused mass of felled timber, and, coming up, was also double-quicked into line on the left of the road, engaging, as they came into position, the intrenched forces of the enemy over against them. King's regiment brought up the rear. He rapidly threw his men into position, and was ordered by me immediately to the support of Colonel Hawthorn. My entire force was now engaged. The assault upon the rifle-pits was made from both the right and left of the road. Never did men behave with greater steadiness and gallantry than did the troops of those three regiments. Over the heavy timber, the deep gorges, and the precipitous banks they moved. Over opposite to them ran the long line of fortifications, toward which they moved with eager, anxious steps. Cowering behind their strong works, the enemy beheld their advance with consternation. Still, on they moved, unhesitatingly, amid the leaden rain and iron hail. The gorge is passed, the ascent of the steep acclivity is nearly gained, and the red line of rifle-pits looms up clearly amid the uncertain light and haze of dawn. With a shout of triumph they rushed toward it, and the enemy are driven pell-mell from one row of the rifle-pits to another.

Up to this time there had been no attack at any other point. Daybreak had come and gone, and still the guns of my brigade, and those of the enemy, were the only ones that interrupted the stillness of the morning. Owing to this, my brigade was exposed to a constant and galling enfilading fire from the works on Graveyard Hill. This exposure, combined with the close and constant fire in our front, was most trying to the men. Their numbers were being rapidly decimated, not only by the fire of the enemy, but by extreme exhaustion, occasioned by their scaling the steepest of hills, made almost impassable by quantities of timber cut down, which was of itself an almost insurmountable barrier to our advance.

We reached and took possession of their fourth tier of rifle-pits. Now it was that the column commanded by Major-General Price (Parsons' and McRae's brigades) charged the works on Graveyard Hill, gallantly driving the enemy before them, and taking possession of their fortifications and artillery. There remained yet one row of intrenchments between my brigade and the fort on Hindman's Hill. I ordered a charge. My men, though thoroughly exhausted and worn, answered with a shout and sprang forward most gallantly. This being the inner and last line of works between us and the enemy, of course was defended with great stubbornness. It was of no avail. My men sprang forward bravely and defiantly, and after a severe contest succeeded in driving out the enemy, who fled, crowding back into the frowning fort and under cover of its heavy guns.

The fort yet remains to be taken. Of all the many obstacles and threatening fortifications that opposed our advance that morn, there only remained the fort. All other obstacles, natural and artificial, had been overcome. Rugged and almost impassable ravines, the steepest and most broken hill-sides, abatis, and line after line of breastworks, had been passed and left behind. Before us there only remained the fort and the plain on which it was built. Notwithstanding the reduced condition of my command and the exhaustion of those yet remaining, I ordered a charge upon the fort. My colonels (King, Hawthorn, and Bell) did all in their power to encourage the men to the attack. The effort was made, but the prostrate condition of my command prevented success, and, after losing in the attempt several gallant officers and many brave men, I formed again in rear of the inner line of rifle-pits, while the guns of the fort continued to pour forth a furious fire.

It was now verging on 11 o'clock in the day. More than three hours before, the guns on Graveyard Hill had been taken by our friends, and there seemed no obstacle in the way of their victorious march. Eagerly did we look to see their column coming to our aid, and at first with the most undoubting hope and confidence, but less confidently as hour after hour wore on and still they made not their appearance. Time wore on, the pleasant morning deepened into the sultriest and hottest of days. The thinned ranks of my regiments became thinner and thinner each moment. The guns of the enemy (not more than 100 or 150 yards distant) were telling sadly against us, while the heat, the want of water, and the toil were no mean auxiliaries. Still, the brave men left stood manfully up to the discharge of their duty.

At this time written orders were received from Lieutenant-General Holmes, directing that I withdraw my troops from the field and fall back to Allen Polk's, 6 miles in the rear. We retired from the field and fell back slowly to that point.

It was in the last assault upon the fort that Major [John B.] Cocke, of Hawthorn's regiment, received a severe wound in the shoulder. I would make special mention of this brave and accomplished officer. His daring was conspicuous throughout the engagement.

Here also the much-beloved Capt. Walton Watkins, while most gallantly leading his company over the enemy's works, fell. It has never been my lot to witness more gallantry and more determined courage than displayed by this young officer on that day. We mourn the loss of other brave and true officers who fell during the engagement.

Of the conduct of my colonels too much praise cannot be said. Brooks, King, Hawthorn, and Bell each and every one did his whole duty. Brooks' command, being on the lower road, was not immediately under my eye, but of the part taken by him I respectfully refer you to his report. He succeeded entirely in carrying out the orders he received to the letter. His report will show the number of prisoners captured by him, as well as the amount of property taken and brought from the field or destroyed. The position assigned to Colonel King threw him, perhaps, on that ground most difficult of all to get over. Had it not been for the determined character of this brave young colonel, his regiment, perhaps, would not have been advanced over all the difficulties he met with. Major [John J.] Dillard and Adjutant [W. T.] Bourne, of same regiment (King's), deserve much praise for the assistance they rendered Colonel King. Colonel Hawthorn was constantly to the front, cheering his men on from one success to another. When orders came from Lieutenant-General Holmes to abandon the field, Colonel Hawthorn remained with a small number of his men engaging the enemy until the last of the army had left the field and retired beyond the high hills which lay between them and danger. Colonel Bell and Lieutenant-Colonel [J. C.] Johnson, same regiment, with a large number of his officers and over 100 men, were captured by the enemy in an attempt to enter the fort from the south side. The loss of Colonel Bell is a serious one to us. It affords me pleasure to bear testimony to his distinguished gallantry and daring.

Major [T. H.] Blacknall (Bell's regiment) was intrusted by me with an important part on the field, and is entitled to my thanks for the successful manner in which he performed it.

Maj. B. T. Du Val, quartermaster on my staff, is entitled to my thanks for his constant attention to every duty on the march from Little Rock. He was with me on the field, and by his coolness and good judgment was enabled to render me important assistance up to the time of the withdrawal of my troops from the field.

Capt. Wyatt C. Thomas, assistant adjutant-general of the brigade, was, as usual, at his post. The conduct of this young officer has often before won for him honorable mention. On this field he was constantly with and cheering the troops forward. His bravery and gallantry justify especial mention.

My aide-de-camp, Capt. Albert Belding, always eager to discharge every duty, was sent by me at daylight with important orders to Colonel Brooks, some distance from me on my right. I was consequently deprived of the valuable assistance his quickness and daring so well qualify him to render on the field.

Capt. John B. Howell, my ordnance officer, was ordered to remain constantly with his ammunition train, which, as above stated, had to be left in the rear. This deprived me of the immediate services of this gallant officer.

The officers of my staff—Maj. B. F. Fall, brigade commissary; Mr. James H. Tucker, volunteer aid-de-camp, and Mr. J. W. Pauk, acting inspector-general—are all entitled to my thanks for the assistance rendered me during the engagement.

The aggregate force engaged against Fort Hindman and the defenses in front of it, 1,339.

I have, major, the honor to be, with much respect, your obedient servant,

JAS. F. FAGAN,
Brigadier-General.

Maj. W. B. BLAIR,
Actg. Asst. Adjt. Gen., Hdqrs. District of Arkansas, &c.

P. S.—A correct list of the casualties in the brigade will be rendered in three or four days.

HEADQUARTERS SECOND BRIGADE,
Camp near White River, July 15, 1863.

MAJOR: The following is a correct list of casualties of the different regiments in this brigade in the engagement at Helena on the 4th instant:

Command.	Killed.		Wounded.		Missing.		Aggregate.
	Officers.	Men.	Officers.	Men.	Officers.	Men.	
Brooks' regiment				1			1
Hawthorn's regiment	2	15	3	50	6	61	137
Bell's regiment		14	1	16	24	167	222
King's regiment		16	6	38		15	75
Total	2	45	10	105	30	243	435

The above is a correct list as reported by regimental commanders. It is respectfully submitted as a portion of the report of the part taken by this (Second) brigade in the engagement of the 4th instant, which report was forwarded to district headquarters a day or so ago.

I am, major, with much respect, &c.,

JAS. F. FAGAN,
Brigadier-General.

Maj. W. B. BLAIR,
Actg. Asst. Adjt. Gen., Hdqrs. District of Arkansas.

No. 19.

Report of Col. A. T. Hawthorn, Arkansas Infantry.

CAMP NEAR BAYOU DE VIEW, *July* 9, 1863.

SIR: In obedience to orders from brigade headquarters, I have the honor to submit the following report of the part my regiment took in the action at Helena on the 4th instant:

At 11 p. m. on the night of the 3d, we left our encampment, 6 miles from Helena, and marched to take up our position in front of the intrenchments, my regiment being in the advance. The road over which we passed (known as the Hill road, from Little Rock to Helena) was extremely rugged, and it was not without considerable difficulty and great fatigue to the men that we succeeded in getting within 1 mile of the enemy's intrenchments. At this point I found the road blockaded with fallen timber to such an extent that I halted the brigade of which I was temporarily in command, sent Captain Miller's company of cavalry, which had been in advance, to the rear, and sent forward Capt. P. G. Roper's company (A), deployed as skirmishers. General Fagan now arrived at the head of the column, and ordering all the field and staff to dismount, we moved forward as rapidly as possible toward the intrenchments, the skirmishers deployed on either side of the road keeping well in advance of the main body. At 4.05 a. m. my skirmishers reported the enemy in sight. By order of General Fagan, I moved my regiment in double-quick by the right flank along the crest of a ridge running at right angles with the road and parallel with the enemy's first line of intrenchments, and, without halting, so soon as my left had passed the road I moved by the left flank in line of battle toward the enemy. Without waiting for the other regiments of the brigade to form, I gave the order to charge, which was responded to by loud shouts along my entire line. The men dashed down the steep declivity amid a perfect storm of bullets, climbed step by step over vast piles of fallen timber up the rugged sides of almost perpendicular hills, and finally, after unheard-of toil and fatigue, scaled the opposing height and drove the enemy in consternation from their first line of defenses. Here I waited to recruit my men, whose strength was very much exhausted, and to give Colonel [S. S.] Bell time to form his regiment and move up on my left. As soon as Colonel Bell informed me that he was ready, our two regiments moved forward together, and, after encountering and overcoming obstacles similar to and even greater than those in front of the first line of rifle-pits, drove the enemy out and took possession of their second line. Colonel [J. P.] King had, by order of General Fagan, under a heavy and constant fire, and after almost superhuman exertions, placed his regiment 200 or 300 yards beyond my extreme right, partly in rear of the enemy's third line of intrenchments and nearly at right angles with the position occupied by Colonel Bell's regiment and mine. I sent a courier to communicate with him, who returned with the gratifying intelligence that his regiment was in position, and was ready and anxious to charge the enemy. The three regiments now moved forward with a shout, and notwithstanding the steep hill-sides covered with immense masses of fallen timber, up and over which we had to climb, and notwithstanding the perfect hail-storm of bullets that assailed us at every step, we soon drove the enemy out of his third line of defense. We soon rallied our exhausted troops, reformed our broken lines, and again charged the enemy, driving him from his fourth line of intrenchments. It was now about 7 a. m. My regiment had been hotly engaged for nearly three hours. The men were completely exhausted. Numbers had fainted from excessive heat and fatigue. Many had been killed and wounded, and a large majority in each of our three regiments were utterly unable to fight any longer. We began to be discouraged. From the very commencement of the action we had been listening for the guns of Generals Price, Marmaduke, and Walker, but thus far we had listened in vain. Every brigade, except ours, had failed to attack at daylight, as ordered. Even the very guns on Graveyard Hill were wheeled around and directed against our lines, which they swept again and again from one end to the other with grape and canister. Just at this moment the scene changed. Heavy and rapid volleys of musketry were heard on our left. General Fagan announced to us that our friends were storming Graveyard Hill, and ordered us to move forward at once. Our men responded with a shout, dashed down into the deep ravine, climbed the steep sides of the opposite hill, and just as the noble brigades of Parsons and McRae swept in triumph across the face of Graveyard Hill, drove the enemy from his fifth and last line of rifle-pits back to his forts and under cover of his siege guns. An attempt was now made by General Fagan to capture the fort on Hindman's Hill, which was immediately in our front, but our men were too much exhausted, and our numbers too few. The attack was unsuccessful, and resulted in the death and capture of many valuable officers and men.

It was here that Capt. Walton Watkins, commanding Company D, of my regiment, was killed while gallantly leading this last and most desperate charge. His conduct throughout the engagement had been chivalrous and manly; so much so as to attract universal attention and admiration.

Here also I lost the services of Maj. John B. Cocke, who was severely wounded and compelled to retire from the field. It affords me much pleasure to bear testimony to the coolness, courage, and efficiency of this gallant officer. His services throughout that desperate fight were invaluable, and his absence was most keenly and sensibly felt.

Lieuts. Richard J. Shaddock, [W. H.] Hinson, [L. R.] Kinniard, and [J. N.] Thompson* were killed while bravely fighting at their posts.

But to return to the fight. Graveyard Hill was evacuated soon after it was taken. The other positions to the left of that hill that were to have been taken at daylight had not even been attacked. The firing had ceased at all points, except the firing of our brigade and that of our enemies directed against us. This latter was now most terrific, and the whole force of the enemy seemed to be directed against our little band. Yet, notwithstanding their vast superiority in numbers and position, notwithstanding the terrible, withering fire that continued to thin our ranks, notwithstanding the repeated attempts of the enemy to flank our position, both on the right and on the left, we held our position firmly for three long hours.

At 10.30 a. m. I received an order from General Fagan to withdraw my regiment from the field. I had marched some 40 or 50 paces, in compliance with this order, when I received another, requiring me to leave a small guard to cover our retreat. I called for volunteers, but no one responding, I returned, myself, and with 9 men, who volunteered to accompany me, kept up a fire upon the enemy for twenty minutes longer. The ammunition was now expended, and I thought it prudent to retire. The enemy were close upon us and advancing from all points. Not a moment was to be lost. We retreated as rapidly as possible, but as we descended the first hill the enemy assailed us with a terrible volley of musketry. Three of our little party fell to rise no more. The remaining 6, myself, and a Yankee prisoner, whom we had kept with us all the time, succeeded in making our escape.

My officers and men, with but few exceptions, deported themselves with great gallantry.

My loss, so far as I have been able to ascertain, is as follows: Killed, 20; wounded, 70; missing, 43.†

Very respectfully, your obedient servant,

A. T. HAWTHORN,
Colonel, Commanding Regiment.

Capt. WYATT C. THOMAS, *Assistant Adjutant-General.*

---

* Reported by Captain Hudson as captured in charge on Battery D.
† But see revised statement, p. 412.

No. 20.

Report of Col. W. H. Brooks, Thirty-fourth Arkansas Infantry.

CAMP NEAR COTTON PLANT, *July* 10, 1863.

CAPTAIN: I have the honor to report the following as the part taken by my command in the engagement of the 4th instant at Helena:

At dusk on the 3d, in compliance with instructions from Brigadier-General Fagan, I moved forward with my regiment and one section of [C. B.] Etter's light artillery, Lieut. J. C. Arnett commanding, to the support of the cavalry, then within 3 miles of the enemy.

At 1.30 o'clock on the morning of the 4th, I received orders from Brigadier-General Fagan to advance on the Little Rock road with my regiment, Captains [W. B.] Denson's, Miller's, and ——— companies of cavalry, and the section of artillery; make a feint on the south of Helena; attract the attention of the enemy in that direction; hold the force in the rifle-pits south of the town, and operate otherwise as I could. Before reaching Beach Grove I withdrew the cavalry advance, and, deploying skirmishers, met the enemy's infantry and cavalry pickets at daybreak. A sharp skirmish ensued, in which 3 of the enemy were killed and 6 captured. Company of cavalry in position on the right of the line of skirmishers received a fire which killed 3 horses. Moving forward to the negro quarters, I found them abandoned, the occupants having fled to the town at the first alarm. Eight negroes were taken and sent to the rear. Shortly afterward I reached the hill at the Clements house, and, placing my command in position, advanced skirmishers well to the front and right, extending nearly to the river. The enemy soon opened with a rifled battery from the left of the rifle-pits next to the levee, but without doing any injury. Immediately the gunboat commenced firing, one shell exploding in Captain Denson's company, wounding 3 men and killing 3 horses.

Captain Blocher reported to me with his battery, but a position for it could not be obtained. I moved Etter's section to the hill, and upon gaining the summit it was found impracticable to use but one piece. This opened briskly, drawing a terrific fire from the battery and gunboat, and, after expending 13 rounds, Lieutenant Arnett was compelled to withdraw. About 11 o'clock I ordered Lieut. E. T. Deloney upon the hill with the gun. The range of the enemy's guns was so accurate and the fire so furious that he retired after firing 8 rounds. The force in front and on the right was fully three times as large as mine. An advance to attack the enemy in the rifle-pits would have subjected my small command to the heavy guns of Fort Curtis, a light battery in rear of the works, an enfilading fire from the rifled battery, and an attack in flank and rear from the levee. Under these circumstances I deemed it best to hold that force of the enemy in check, and prevent him from re-enforcing his most important points of defense, and by the use of a 6-pounder (not being able to bring more than one piece into position) divert as much as possible the fire of the battery and gunboat from the attacking columns. In this I was entirely successful.

At 12 m. I received orders from Brigadier-General Fagan to retire, and subsequently instructions from Lieutenant-General Holmes to halt at a designated position as the rear guard of the army.

By my direction, Captain Denson's company applied the torch to the negro quarters, which were consumed, together with 5,000 pounds of bacon, 1,500 bushels of corn, and a quantity of commissary stores and clothing.

During the entire morning the demonstrations of the enemy behind the levee were of a threatening character. Captain Denson, commanding cavalry detachment, rendered efficient service in counteracting his movements and protecting my right flank. ——— ———, of his company, distinguished himself in the capture of 3 prisoners.

I brought off 9 prisoners, 8 negroes, 5 mules, 1 horse and equipments, 1 ambulance and team, and a small lot of clothing and canteens.

Companies B and K (skirmishers), commanded, respectively, by Capts. F. R. Earle and Arkansas Wilson, deserve special mention for the steadiness with which they advanced, drove the enemy before them, and maintained their positions under a heavy artillery fire.

Lieutenant-Colonel [Thomas M.] Gunter and Major [J. R.] Pettigrew were constantly at their posts in the discharge of their duties.

The only casualty in my regiment was Private A. C. Peck, Company B, severely wounded in the chest.

I am, captain, very respectfully, your obedient servant,

W. H. BROOKS,
Colonel, Commanding.

Capt. WYATT C. THOMAS,
Assistant Adjutant-General, Second Brigade.

No. 21.

Report of Col. J. P. King, Thirty-fifth Arkansas Infantry.

CAMP AT SEARCY, *July* 22, 1863.

SIR: I have the honor to make the following report of the part taken by my regiment in the late battle fought at Helena on the 4th instant:

On the night of the 3d instant, I took up the line of march at 11 o'clock, taking the road leading to Helena, and when within about 10 miles of that place I, with Colonels [A. T.] Hawthorn and [S. S.] Bell, led by General Fagan, took the road leading into the town by the way of Hindman Hill. When arriving within about three-quarters of a mile of the hill, we found the roads so blockaded by fallen timber that it was impossible for anything but infantry to pass, and it was with great difficulty that the men could get through at all. By the time I got my regiment to the open road, skirmishing commenced by Colonel Hawthorn, who was moving in front. I immediately moved my regiment up at a double-quick, arriving at the scene of action about daylight. I was immediately ordered by General Fagan to take position on the right of Colonel Hawthorn, who had formed line of battle and was skirmishing with the enemy in the rifle-pits, which were immediately in front of us. I moved my regiment as ordered, taking position on the crest of a hill overlooking the town, where I was exposed to a galling fire from the enemy's rifle-pits or breastworks, which were about 150 yards in front of us. By the time I got my men well up and in line, I received an order from General Fagan to charge the works in front of me, which I did, but, as you yourself know, the ground was so very rough that it was impossible to move rapidly. After scrambling over and under fallen timber, across a ravine that I would at any other time or under any other circumstances have considered impossible to make my way through, and at last up the side of a hill that was so steep the men had to pull themselves up by the bushes, we reached the first line of breastworks and drove the enemy back. Here we were met with a terrific fire not only from the inner lines of works and an enfilading fire from our left, but from the fort on the hill in front of us near Hindman's house, which was about 200 yards distant from us, and also from the battery on what is known as Graveyard Hill. In this position we kept up a heavy fire, moving forward from one line of works to another until we reached the inner line, the enemy taking refuge in their forts. I then received an order from General Fagan to send a small force round to the right of my position to see that the enemy did not flank us; also to move my regiment to the left, where I found Colonel Hawthorn, with his regiment and a portion of Colonel Bell's, behind the last line of works, which was about 100 yards from the first line. Here we found that it was impossible for our men to go farther. Many of them had been left so exhausted that they could not go on. While in this situation, General Fagan ordered me to take the fort, but the men were so exhausted that most of them were unfit for further service. We remained behind the breastworks, keeping up a steady fire at the fort until about 11 a. m., at which time we were ordered off the field.

I cannot speak too highly of the most of my officers and men throughout the fight, particularly of the gallantry of Major [J. J.] Dillard and Adjutant [W. T.] Bourne, who were in every charge, and cheering the men on at all times.

My loss was as follows: 12 killed, 46 wounded, and 20 missing.*

I have the honor to be, your obedient servant,

J. P. KING,
Colonel, Commanding Regiment, &c.

Capt. WYATT C. THOMAS.

No. 22.

Report of Maj. T. H. Blacknall, Thirty-seventh Arkansas Infantry.

CAMP BAYOU DE VIEW, *July* 10, 1863.

CAPTAIN: I have the honor to make my report of the part taken by Bell's regiment in the engagement of the 4th instant at Helena.

We moved for half a mile at double-quick, passing through brush and logs with which the road was blockaded, and approached in view of Helena at 4.30 a. m., taking our position on Colonel [A. T.] Hawthorn's left, in line of battle, and commenced firing on the enemy in front. The enemy threatened to flank us on the left, when Captains [G. W.] Hurley's and [W. J.] Donaldson's companies were detached and thrown out to engage him, under my command, to protect our left flank. The regiment then advanced over the first hill. Here Captains [H. C.] Pleasants and [W. J.] Smith were wounded and many men killed and wounded. The ground at this point was almost impassable—an old road and deep ravine full of timber, which scattered our men—and it was impossible to keep in line; but we succeeded in getting through after remaining in the timber and hollows nearly two hours, under a heavy fire, and made a charge, when, the enemy giving way, we entered the rifle-pits. Here many of our men fell, perfectly exhausted from overheat.

At this point the firing ceased on our left, indicating that our forces had been called off. The enemy, seeing our condition, rushed upon and surrounded us, and compelled many of our officers and men to surrender.

The detachment under my command advanced over two ravines and up the hill fronting and nearest to the intrenchments and fort, about 300 paces distant, which position we held about two hours, keeping up a constant fire until the ammunition was exhausted.

About that time Colonel Hawthorn, on our right, ordered a charge on

---

* But see revised statement, p. 412.

the intrenchments. I called on my men to join in the charge, which, with the exception of Captain Donaldson and part of his company, followed, and in about twenty minutes we reached the intrenchments, where I remained awaiting ammunition which I had sent for, until I was ordered to fall back.

My men, with few exceptions, acted well. I will mention the names of Lieutenant [Joseph J.] Porter, of Company B; Lieutenant [J. D.] Thompson, Sergeant [P. W.] Lowery, and Private [J. T.] Dance, of Company A, as acting with marked bravery.

The loss of the detachment was 2 killed, 6 wounded, and 30 missing.

The regiment entered the fight with an aggregate of 432. The entire loss was 217.

I respectfully submit the above as my report of the part taken by Bell's regiment in the engagement of the 4th instant at Helena.

T. H. BLACKNALL,
Major, Commanding Bell's Regiment.

Captain [WYATT C.] THOMAS,
[*Assistant Adjutant-General.*]

No. 23.

Report of Brig. Gen. L. M. Walker, C. S. Army, commanding division.

HEADQUARTERS IN THE FIELD,
Camp near Lick Creek, July 7, 1863

MAJOR: I have the honor to submit the following report of the conduct of my cavalry brigade in the battle before Helena on the 4th instant:

In obedience to General Orders, No. 2, I moved my command toward Helena on Sterling road. Arriving at the blockade before daylight, I dismounted and sent forward three companies, attempting to capture the enemy's pickets in that direction. At daylight I sent forward three more companies, dismounted, and commenced the work of removing obstacles in the blockade for the passage of artillery. My advance soon became engaged with the enemy. Re-enforcing my advance, and forwarding and bringing into action my artillery, I was continually engaged until nearly 3 p. m. I effectually complied with the part assigned to me in the order of attack by preventing the enemy from throwing troops to Rightor Hill, which they were constantly trying to do, and made two strong efforts and were repulsed. I protected Brigadier-General Marmaduke's left flank. My command was engaged in front of his left.

At about 2 o'clock I was informed by General Marmaduke that he had already withdrawn his command. I had hard fighting to protect my left flank, and when my right became exposed I commenced to get loose from the enemy and retired.

I must speak in the highest terms of the officers and men of my command upon the occasion. No straggling in reaching the place assigned them, although accompanied by apparently insurmountable difficulties; resisted successfully the enemy, and drove him twice handsomely.

I send herewith reports of Colonels [Arch. S.] Dobbin and [Robert C.] Newton.

I am, major, very respectfully, your obedient servant,

L. M. WALKER,
Brigadier-General

No. 24.

Report of Col. Robert C. Newton, Fifth Arkansas Cavalry.

CAMP AT GIST'S, PHILLIPS COUNTY, ARK.,
July 8, 1863.

CAPTAIN: I have the honor, in obedience to your instructions of to-day, to submit the following report of the part taken by my regiment in the attack on Helena on the 4th instant:

I reached Mrs. Mooney's and halted there about 12 p. m. on 3d instant. About an hour before day on the morning of the 4th, in obedience to an order from the brigadier-general commanding, I resumed the march, taking the Sterling road toward Helena, moving in rear of Colonel [A. S.] Dobbin's regiment. Arriving at the spring about 1 mile from town, the brigade was halted by General Walker. We remained there until the firing commenced to our right, when I was ordered up to a point near the blockade of felled timber, there to await orders.

About 7 o'clock I received an order to send 30 sharpshooters to the support of those from Colonel Dobbin's regiment, who were deployed to our front beyond the blockade, and to the left of the skirmishers from General Marmaduke's command. I detailed the required number from the different companies, selecting men with long-range guns as far as practicable, placed them under command of Lieutenant [J. C.] Barnes, of Company A, and carried them forward to the left of Dobbin's skirmishers, and beyond the lagoon which, starting from near the base of the levee on the north side of Helena, runs eastward to Porter's Lake, where they were soon engaged with the enemy, and did good service.

At 7.30 [a. m.], by order of General Walker, I detached Companies B and G, under command of Captain [W. N.] Portis, of the former, and deployed them as skirmishers to support Barnes' sharpshooters, and resist a small force of Federal cavalry which was reported to be threatening our extreme left. About 8 o'clock Portis reported to me that the enemy had re-enforced in his front; that he was being pressed and needed two more companies. I immediately communicated the information to General Walker, and by his direction instructed Portis to observe the enemy closely, skirmish with him, and, if too heavily pressed, fall back slowly, advising me from time to time of what was transpiring.

About this time I received an order to send forward another company to support Dobbin's skirmishers, which I obeyed by sending Captain [P. J.] Rollow's company (E), under command of Lieutenant [W. W.] Garner.

Learning that the enemy had made several attempts to force Portis back and gain possession of the west bank of Porter's Lake—which would enable him, by means of his sharpshooters, to annoy the men at our battery posted on the hill in front of the blockade, and perhaps finally force us from the hill altogether—I went in person to where Portis was, to learn the true condition of affairs and ascertain what, if anything, could be done. I found that Portis with his small force had made a gallant resistance, and had thus far foiled the enemy in his several attempts to occupy the western or inner bank of Porter's Lake; but that he nevertheless had lost some ground and had but little more to lose. I deemed it important, therefore, not only to regain what had been lost, but to drive the enemy beyond the levee and into town, if possible, with my small force. There not being time left me to previously communicate with General Walker, I ordered up Companies C and F without first notifying him. The latter I deployed as skirmishers and advanced to the front. They were soon engaged. I moved Company C forward across the lagoon before mentioned, and, pushing the skirmishers to the front vigorously, ordered a charge. The enemy fled precipitately. We pursued him about 300 yards. Finding that he was rallying his men in his rifle-pits, which were situated to the left of the levee and near the river bank, I deployed my whole force then with me as skirmishers, posted them as best I could, and left them under command of Captain Portis, with instructions to hold the ground we had thus gained until he should receive other orders from me. I started to the headquarters of the brigadier-general commanding to get permission to use my whole regiment for the purpose of dislodging the enemy, or, failing in that, confining him to his rifle-pits and thus prevent him from annoying our left. Arriving there, I learned that our troops were withdrawing, and, by General Walker's direction, retired my command to the point where the mountain road, leading from the spring on the Sterling road to the Grant's Mill road, diverges from the Sterling road, and there disposed my force so as to cover the withdrawal of our troops. When the rear of Dobbin's regiment had passed, I moved back on the mountain road, as directed, and thence upon Grant's Mill road.

I inclose herewith a list of casualties.*

The officers and men engaged behaved in admirable style. Captains Portis and [L. D.] Bryant, commanding skirmishers, did their duty well. Lieutenant Barnes, who, with his 30 sharpshooters, was almost constantly engaged, here, as everywhere else that I have ever placed him, was prompt and faithful, and displayed great courage. Lieutenant [J. F.] Smith, adjutant of the regiment, brave to a fault, and seeking rather than avoiding danger, rendered much valuable service. And as were the officers, so were the private soldiers whom they led. Fearless of danger, each seemed intent solely on doing his duty well.

I am, captain, very respectfully, your obedient servant,

R. C. NEWTON,
Colonel, Commanding.

Capt. J. C. ALEXANDER, *Asst. Adjt. Gen., Walker's Division, &c.*

No. 25.

Report of Col. Archibald S. Dobbin, Arkansas Cavalry.

IN THE FIELD, *July* 5, 1863.

GENERAL: I respectfully submit the following report of the movement of my regiment on the 4th ultimo [instant]:

According to your order I moved my regiment and battery of four pieces on the evening of the 3d from the Bouie farm, on the Little Rock road, 4 miles west of Helena, to the old Porter farm east of Crowley's Ridge, on the road leading from Helena to Sterling, a distance of about 15 miles, and remained at that place until 2 o'clock on the morning of the 4th; then moved down the road to a point where the mill road intersects the Sterling road, 1½ miles north of Helena, where I dismounted 150 men, and sent them forward as skirmishers beyond the blockade to within three-quarters of a mile of Helena and a short distance above the levee leading out from the hills. I then dismounted 150 more men, and sent them forward to the same point, and extended the line of skirmishers from the hills to the Mississippi River. I then drew up the remainder

* Not found.

of the regiment in line of battle north of the blockade, about 400 yards in the rear of the line of skirmishers, and then awaited to learn the result of the attack made by General Marmaduke upon the battery and fortifications on Rightor Hill, and not learning anything definite, and discovering the enemy moving up between the levee and Mississippi River. I moved my battery forward, according to your order, and commenced firing on the enemy advancing, and also the enemy's batteries playing upon General Marmaduke's command and my front. I then advanced, causing the enemy to fall back, moving their battery some 600 yards farther down the levee. About two hours after, the enemy again advanced, with artillery, and much larger force than at first. I again opened fire on them with my battery and small-arms, and, with the assistance of a portion of Colonel [Robert C.] Newton's regiment, again caused them to fall back and move their battery still farther down the levee, after which skirmishing was kept up until some three hours after the firing had ceased along our entire line, at which time I received your order to fall back slowly on the Grant Mill road, which I succeeded in doing without losing any men after I left the battle-field.

The loss in my regiment, in the engagements, was 4 killed and 8 wounded—1 mortally, 2 seriously, and 5 slightly. For particulars, I refer you to report of Dr. Dunn, surgeon of my regiment, herewith inclosed.*

The officers and men of my regiment and battery deserve great credit for gallantry and courage displayed on that day.

Very respectfully, your obedient servant,

ARCH. S. DOBBIN,
Colonel, Commanding Regiment Cavalry.

Brigadier-General [L. M.] WALKER.

No. 26.

Report of ***Brig. Gen. J. S. Marmaduke, C. S. Army, commanding division.***

HDQRS. MARMADUKE'S DIV., *Jacksonport, Ark., July* 25, 1863.

MAJOR: I have the honor to report herewith the part taken by my command in the battle at Helena.

I was ordered, on the evening of July 3, to be in position, attack, and take the fort on Rightor's Hill at daylight on the morning of July 4. My command (mounted) consisted of [Joseph O.] Shelby's brigade, about 1,100 men, and [Colton] Greene's brigade, 650 men; total, 1,750.

At 10 p. m. July 3, I marched to get into position. When 3 miles from the fort, I dismounted my whole force, except one company, under Major [Benjamin] Elliott. I then moved forward. When within 2 miles of the fort, I found the road and country thoroughly obstructed, the enemy having chopped down the trees and rendered almost impassable that approach to the fort and town. The country was exceedingly rough. I was delayed some half hour or more by my guides, who lost their way, and reported that they were completely lost and unable to guide me farther, in consequence of which I did not get into position until a little after daylight, but before sun-up. The enemy's pickets and skirmishers were encountered some three-quarters of a mile from the fort, and driven to within 150 yards of the fort. In this the enemy lost several killed and

---

* But see revised statement, p. 412.

wounded, and 5 prisoners. Shelby's brigade was in the advance, and so narrow was the road, and so rough and rugged were the hills, that the troops could only march by the flank, and the artillery with great difficulty was brought up piece by piece, and by hand. By the time the advance had reached within 200 yards of the fort, and those in rear brought up and deployed along the ridges, the enemy had brought to my left and rear a body of infantry and several pieces of artillery, which, during the whole day's fight, poured upon me a deadly fire. I now had a heavy force in my front, infantry in rifle-pits and artillery in position, which it would have been difficult with my whole force to have carried. In addition, I had the force on my left (of infantry and artillery) thoroughly protected by the levee, which engaged a large part of my force, and, on every attempt to advance, enfiladed my line. It was from the sharpshooters and artillery on my left and rear that I suffered my greatest loss, and not until they were dislodged could I have advanced. I twice dispatched to Brigadier-General Walker to advance and assist me in dislodging them. It was not done.

From 4.30 a. m. till 11 a. m. I held my position, unable to advance, the enemy, with their infantry and artillery on my front and left flank, constantly engaging my forces. At 11 a. m. I received orders from General Holmes to retire.

My loss was 14 killed, 52 wounded, and 1 missing.* Among the killed were Maj. R. H. Smith, my division quartermaster, and Capt. J. C. Clark, of Company D, Shelby's regiment. Major Smith was a gallant and valuable officer. He was shot dead beside a piece of artillery, encouraging and assisting the cannoneers in their duties. Captain Clark was a most exemplary man and excellent officer. He was killed leading his men forward.

Among the wounded I regret to announce that Colonel Shelby, commanding brigade, who was ever in the thickest of the fight, received a painful and serious wound in the wrist.

For a more special report of the conduct of the several regiments and their officers, I respectfully refer you to the brigade commanders. As yet I have not received the report for Shelby's brigade; will forward it as soon as received; have delayed this report awaiting same. The conduct of every officer and soldier of my command, as far as I know, was excellent.

The attack upon Fort Rightor by my command was a failure. I have every reason to believe that my troops would have carried it had it not been for the force on my left and rear, which occupied that position after daylight, and which could and should have been prevented from taking that position, and, after they had gained the position, could have been driven from it by General Walker's brigade, which did not come to the support of my left till after 7 a. m.; and during the whole engagement his force was more than half a mile to my left and rear. I could see the force which engaged Walker's brigade, and at no time did it exceed 500. I think 300 a big estimate. Walker's brigade not only did not prevent re-enforcements from going to Fort Rightor, but the enemy after sunrise actually passed to my left and half a mile to my rear, and held that position during the day.

Very respectfully,

J. S. MARMADUKE,
Brigadier-General, Commanding.

Maj. W. B. BLAIR,
Acting Assistant Adjutant-General, District of Arkansas.

---

*But see revised statement, p. 438.

Return of Casualties in Marmaduke's division, July 4, 1863

[Compiled from nominal list.]

Command.	Killed.		Wounded.		Missing.		
	Officers.	Enlisted men.	Officers.	Enlisted men.	Officers.	Enlisted men.	Aggregate.
Division staff *			1				1
Greene's brigade:							
3d Missouri Cavalry		3		6			9
8th Missouri Cavalry †	1						1
Young's battalion		1		1			2
Total	1	4		7			12
Shelby's brigade:							
Staff			2				2
5th Missouri Cavalry		3	3	8			14
6th Missouri Cavalry		1	1	16		1	19
Jeans' regiment		3	3	6			12
Bledsoe's battery		1		6			7
Total		8	9	36		1	54
Grand total	1	12	10	43		1	67

No. 27.

Findings of Court of Inquiry in case of Brig. Gen. Dandridge McRae.

GENERAL ORDERS, No. 100. } HDQRS. TRANS-MISSISSIPPI DEPARTMENT, *Shreveport, La., December 29, 1864.*

I. At a Court of Inquiry convened at Camden, Ark., by virtue of Special Orders, No. 142, Paragraph IV, June 7, 1864, Department Headquarters, to examine into, report upon, and express their opinion as to the merits of a charge against Brig. Gen. Dandridge McRae, Provisional Army Confederate States, of misbehavior before the enemy at the attack upon Helena, Ark., July 4, 1863, the following conclusion was arrived at by the court:

FINDING AND OPINION OF THE COURT.

The testimony being before the court, with the statement of Brigadier-General McRae, and the court being cleared for deliberation, and having duly considered the testimony of all the witnesses, together with the papers and maps accompanying the record, are of opinion that General McRae's conduct at Helena on July 4, 1863, on the occasion of the attack on the enemy at that place, was obnoxious to no charge of misbehavior before the enemy.

II. The Court of Inquiry in the case of Brig. Gen. D. McRae is dissolved.

By command of General E. Kirby Smith:

S. S. ANDERSON,
Assistant Adjutant-General.

* Maj. R. H. Smith, quartermaster, killed.
† Lieut. G. R. Norment killed.

No. 28.

*Estimate of troops in Trans-Mississippi Department after battle at Helena.**

DISTRICT OF ARKANSAS.

Command.	Number of regiments, &c.	Troops.	Aggregate per reports of May 1.	Estimate for duty.
Price's division:				
Fagan's brigade	4 regiments	Arkansas Volunteers		
McRae's brigade	4 regiments	Arkansas Volunteers		
Tappan's brigade	3 regiments	Arkansas Volunteers	12,961	5,500
Parsons' brigade	4 regiments 1 battalion	Missouri Volunteers		
Marmaduke's division:				
Shelby's brigade	4 regiments	Missouri Volunteers		
Greene's brigade	3 regiments	Missouri Volunteers	6,370	3,000
Burbridge's brigade	2 regiments	Missouri Volunteers		
Kitchen's battalion		Missouri Volunteers		
Steele's division:				
Cooper's brigade	2 regiments 1 battalion 2 companies	Texas Volunteers	5,134	2,000
	5 regiments 4 battalions	Indians		
Cabell's brigade	2 regiments 2 battalions	Arkansas Volunteers	2,694	1,300
	1 regiment 1 battalion	Texas Volunteers		
Frost's brigade	5 regiments	Arkansas Volunteers	3,289	1,800
Dobbin's regiment		Arkansas Cavalry	914	605
Hill's battalion		Arkansas Artillery	422	251
Denson's company		Louisiana Cavalry	149	52
Total			31,933	14,508

DISTRICT OF WESTERN LOUISIANA.

Command.	Number of regiments, &c.	Troops.	Aggregate per reports of May 1.	Estimate for duty.
Carter's brigade†	2 regiments	Texas Cavalry	1,800	800
Parsons' regiment†		Texas Cavalry	800	300
Harrison's battalion†		Louisiana Cavalry	500	250
Fort Beauregard	1 battalion	Louisiana Volunteers	400	175
Walker's division (three brigades)	11 regiments 1 battalion	Texas Volunteers	9,000	3,500
Polignac's brigade	3 regiments	Texas Volunteers	1,712	1,255
Speight's brigade	2 regiments	Texas Volunteers	1,585	700
Major's brigade	4 regiments	Texas Volunteers	2,400	1,500
Green's brigade	3 regiments	Texas Volunteers		
	1 regiment	Louisiana Volunteers	5,400	3,000
Mouton's brigade	3 regiments	Louisiana Volunteers		
	3 battalions	Louisiana Volunteers		
Total			23,597	11,480

DISTRICT OF TEXAS, ETC.

Command.	Number of regiments, &c.	Troops.	Aggregate per reports of May 1.	Estimate for duty.
Eastern sub-district, Brigadier-General Scurry.	3 regiments	Texas Cavalry	1,977	1,500
	2 battalions	Texas Cavalry	790	400
	2 companies	Texas Cavalry	170	50
	3 regiments	Texas Infantry	2,486	1,400
	1 battalion	Texas Infantry	590	300
	12 companies	Texas Artillery	1,098	500
Western sub-district, Brigadier-General Bee.	1 regiment	Texas Infantry	1,305	600
	6 companies	Texas Infantry		
	5 battalions	Texas Cavalry	1,963	1,100
	7 companies	Texas Cavalry	567	290
	4 companies ‡	Light artillery	371	210
	4 companies §	Heavy artillery	400	245
Total			11,717	6,595

* NOTE ON ORIGINAL.- Does not allow for loss at Helena. No report.
† East of Monroe. ‡ Twenty-one guns. § Fourteen guns.

Estimate of troops in Trans-Mississippi Department after battle at Helena—Continued.

RECAPITULATION.

Districts.	Aggregate.	Estimate for duty.
Arkansas and Indian Territory	31,933	14,508
Western Louisiana	23,597	11,480
Texas	11,717	6,595

No. 29.

Reports of Surg. W. M. McPheeters, C. S. Army.

HOSPITAL AT MR. ALLEN POLK'S,
July 6, 1863.

SIR: A squad of Federal cavalry, under command of Colonel Clayton, took possession of this hospital about 1 p. m. to-day. General Ross, whose brigade was stationed near by, soon came up, when all the wounded remaining on hand were paroled, amounting to 72 in all. I had previously sent off on yesterday and to-day 63 of the more slightly wounded, including 5 nurses. Prior to the arrival of the troops, some five or six shot and shell were fired at the hospital, some of which came within a few feet of the main building, and one struck and fell inside of one of the cabins in which the wounded were lying. This induced me to address a communication to the Federal commander, informing him that this building was occupied as a hospital, and asking him to respect our wounded, but before it was sent Colonel Clayton came up, to whom it was delivered. He stated that he had not observed our yellow flag, but that as soon as he saw it he had sent back and ordered the artillery to cease firing. They remained about an hour. We had nothing to complain of in their treatment. Indeed, General Ross stated that, if we desired it, our wounded here might be sent into Helena, where they could have ice and other comforts; but as they are comfortable here, and as we will probably have an opportunity to send most of them forward to Trenton, where the others have gone, I think I shall not avail myself of his offer. Our wounded are almost all doing remarkably well. Only one death has yet occurred—Private [E.] Strickland, Company I, Gause's regiment, McRae's brigade. As yet I have had no means of ascertaining, with any certainty, the number of our killed and wounded remaining in possession of the enemy. The officers and men varied very much in their statements, some estimating the number at 400, others at 800, showing evidently that it was all guess-work with them. One officer stated to me that they had sent off 570 prisoners on one boat, on the evening of the 4th, including Colonel [L. M.] Lewis. Captain [J. R.] Morris, of Company H, Gause's regiment, who was reported killed, they say was taken prisoner. In the confusion of their occupation of the hospital, I was unable to learn as to the fate of others of our command.

[Federal] officers and men seemed to be in the finest possible spirits over the surrender of Vicksburg, which they assert took place on the 4th, unconditionally, and without a fight, with 22,700 prisoners. General

Grant, they say, first sent up a boat with the news of the surrender, and subsequently another giving the number of prisoners. He massed his forces, they say, and marched in unopposed. As marvelous as this is, the officers and men evidently believe it, and when Port Hudson is taken, they say they will have complete possession of the Mississippi River. I could get no definite information as to General Lee's army. One officer remarked that the news from Pennsylvania was "very much mixed." As soon as the wounded here are sent off, or in a condition to be left, I shall start to join your headquarters. Dr. Cunningham left yesterday evening for Trenton, thence for Little Rock, thinking that he could do more good in the latter place. Drs. [C. D.] Baer, [J. H.] Swindells, [A. N.] Kincannon, and Burckhart are still here. Mr. Polk is exceedingly kind, giving not only his house and everything in it, but his personal services to our wounded.

I have the honor to be, very respectfully, your obedient servant,

W. M. McPHEETERS,
Surgeon in Charge of Hospital.

Maj. Gen. STERLING PRICE.

P. S.—Since writing the above, Private John W. Haynes, Company A, Glenn's regiment, has died. Dr. McNair, of Bell's regiment, has also arrived from Helena, having been released, with his infirmary corps of 13 men, all of whom are *en route* for General Fagan's brigade. He states that all our wounded have been sent up to Memphis; Colonel [S. S.] Bell wounded, and a prisoner. The enemy estimate their loss at 200 killed and wounded. He heard the report of the capture of Vicksburg, but seems not to credit it himself. He was not permitted to bring out or to see a paper.

HOSPITAL AT MR. ALLEN POLK'S,
July 7, 1863.

GENERAL: I had the honor of writing you on yesterday, giving a report of the condition of our wounded here, of a visit from the Federals, and the current news, as far as I could get it, which letter I hope you will receive.

This morning the medical director, a corps of surgeons, and an ambulance train came out to take possession of our wounded, and, if desired by me, to take them into Helena. They brought out such medical and hospital stores as they supposed we needed—sugar, tea, coffee, potatoes, bandages, &c., and were, I must say, very polite and kind, indeed. I declined sending the wounded in, preferring to keep them here, where we will be able to make them comfortable; whereupon the medical director promised to send us out ice and such other articles as we stand in need of, a list of which I furnished him. I must repeat it again that they were exceedingly kind, and I wish to give them full credit for it. One of their ambulances, horses, and driver, sent out, as they say, to bring in our wounded, was captured, I understand, by General Fagan's command. This they complain of very much. I promised to report the fact to you, assuring them that if the facts were as stated you would certainly have it returned. All the surgeons who were left in Helena, and have since returned, speak in high terms of their attention to our wounded, and, as they claim that it was sent out for the benefit of our men, I am satisfied that we would consult our interest by having it promptly returned.

Colonel [R. A.] Hart was wounded in the left leg, not dangerously; has gone to Memphis. Adjutant [Edward] Warburg lost his leg. Lieutenant [W. F.] Rector was killed, or rather died; lived six hours. These are the only additional particulars that I have received since my last. Our wounded here are doing as well as could be expected. I am doing all that I possibly can to make them comfortable. Up to this time three deaths only have occurred. I write in great haste, as the messenger is anxious to get off. I will report from time to time.

Very respectfully, your obedient servant,

W. M. McPHEETERS.

Maj. Gen. STERLING PRICE.

P. S.—No additional news from Vicksburg.

JULY 4, 1863.—Affair in the Black Fork Hills, Mo.

Report of Brig. Gen. Odon Guitar, Missouri Enrolled Militia.

MEXICO, MO., *July* 7, 1863.

GENERAL: A party of the Ninth Cavalry, under Major Draper, on the 4th instant came on a band of rebels, under Pulliam, in the Black Fork Hills, routed them, taking a notorious character by the name of Palmer, and capturing 20 others and equipments. They are yet in pursuit.

O. GUITAR,
Brigadier-General, Commanding.

Major-General SCHOFIELD.

JULY 7, 1863.—Skirmish near Drywood, Mo.

Report of Maj. Elias A. Calkins, Third Wisconsin Cavalry.

CAMP ON DRYWOOD, MO., *July* 11, 1863.

MAJOR: In compliance with orders received by your hands, on the 7th instant, I detailed, under the command of Capt. [Alexander] M. Pratt, Company E, the following companies, of this regiment, for an attack upon the guerrillas, whose rendezvous was supposed to be near the junction of the Marmiton and Osage Rivers, some 28 miles north of this camp: Company D, Lieutenant [John] Crites; Company E, Lieutenant [William] Culbertson, and Company K, Lieutenant [John P.] McDowell.

The command left this camp at 10 p. m. of that day, and, by a circuitous march of about 40 miles, reached their destination at 10 a. m. the following day, where the advance came upon the pickets of the enemy, who were followed into the principal guerrilla camp, a high piece of ground, surrounded by swamps and stagnant water. Our force boldly dashed through the marsh and a thick growth of underbrush, where a sharp engagement ensued, lasting about an hour and a half. The enemy were well protected by the timber, but were at length obliged to give way, and fled in all directions. They were closely pursued by the three columns into which Captain Pratt divided his command, the pursuit lasting until near dark. Five of the enemy are supposed to be killed and 3 severely wounded. Among the wounded was the noted guerrilla Pony Hill. Captain Taylor is also reported wounded. Our loss was 1 killed—John H. Robinson, Company E. His body was stripped of the clothing worth carrying away, and his pockets were rifled by the enemy. Their camp was totally broken up and the guerrillas scattered in all directions. The intended raid into Kansas was thereby prevented, at least for the present.

The command returned to this camp at 3 p. m. yesterday, greatly fatigued, but in good health and spirits. The citizen guides who accompanied the expedition, I am sorry to say, knew nothing of the roads or country; led the command a roundabout, unnecessary, and fatiguing march; refused to communicate with the commanding officer, and are totally untrustworthy.

Great credit is due Captain [Alexander M.] Pratt for the energy and daring which characterized his action, and also to Lieutenant McDowell, Lieutenant Culbertson, and Lieutenant Crites, with the gallant men of their respective commands.

Inclosed please see invoice of contraband property taken and delivered to Capt. J. G. Haskell, assistant quartermaster.

Very respectfully,

E. A. CALKINS,
Major, Commanding Third Wisconsin Cavalry.

Maj. H. Z. CURTIS,
Assistant Adjutant-General.

JULY 7, 1863.—Skirmish with Indians at Grand Pass, Idaho.

REPORTS.

No. 1.—Col. John M. Chivington, First Colorado Cavalry, commanding District of Colorado.

No. 2.—Capt. Asaph Allen, Ninth Kansas Cavalry.

No. 1.

Report of Col. John M. Chivington, First Colorado Cavalry, commanding District of Colorado.

HEADQUARTERS DISTRICT OF COLORADO,
Denver City, Colo., August 7, 1863.

SIR: I have the honor herewith to send you the "official" report of Captain Allen, commanding Fort Halleck, of the recent skirmish with the Ute Indians near that post. On the receipt of a similar unofficial report from Captain Allen, and before I had received notice that the troops in that part of Idaho Territory were attached to this district, I ordered Maj. E. W. Wynkoop, First Cavalry of Colorado, to proceed with four companies of cavalry to that country, and recover, if possible, the stock they stole from the Overland Stage Line and others, and to chastise them if they refused to give them up. Major Wynkoop with his command proceeded, with forage and subsistence train, to a point about 100 miles southwest of Fort Halleck. I started on the 17th, and overtook the command on the 24th of July, and on the 27th saw them, with 56 mules packed and fifteen days' rations, taking 150 men, with instructions to penetrate the country to the headwaters of Bear, White, and Snake Rivers, and deeming the state of affairs on the Arkansas and other points in the district such as to require my attention, I returned to this place. Will in due time give a full report of the expedition.

Very respectfully, your obedient servant,

J. M. CHIVINGTON,
Colonel First Colorado Cavalry, Commanding District.

ASSISTANT ADJUTANT-GENERAL,
Saint Louis, Mo.

No. 2.

Report of Capt. Asaph Allen, Ninth Kansas Cavalry.

FORT HALLECK, IDAHO, *July* 7, 1863.

SIR: At 1 o'clock on the morning of the 7th instant, I started Lieutenants [Henry] Brandley and [Hugh W.] Williams, with nearly my entire command, save 3 men at the post, in pursuit of the Ute Indians, who had stolen 22 head of stock from the mail company, plundered their stations, and committed many other depredations. They overtook the Indians, posted in a pass of the mountains, about 30 miles from this post, shortly after sunrise. The Indians opened fire on the troops from the timber and thick underbrush, in which they were concealed. The troops engaged them, dismounting and charging up the steep hill-side, through the timber and brush, drove the Indians, 250 in number, steadily up and over the brow of the hill, when the Indians fled scattering through the mountains. The stock could not be recovered, neither has anything been seen of the Indians since. Sergt. S. N. Waugh was killed in the charge made on the Indians; was shot through the body; lived but a few hours. Six other men of my company were badly wounded, but are doing well.

There were 70 troops engaged. The Indians own to a loss of over 60 killed and wounded; over 20 killed on the field. They were better mounted and armed than the troops, having Hawkins' rifles, revolvers, bows and arrows, and spears, and would have killed a great many more of the troops, but in firing down the steep hill-side they invariably fired too high. It was a perfect hail-storm of lead over the heads of the troops. The battle lasted two hours. The troops deserve much praise for their coolness, steadiness, and courage while under fire; no men could have done better. I stopped all emigrants, enrolled and armed them for the protection of the post, as I had only 3 enlisted men left. These were permitted to resume their journey as soon as the necessity for their detention ceased. There is supposed to be about 600 to 1,000 of these Utes in this vicinity or in vicinity of Middle Park. Colonel Chivington, Colorado District, is sending troops over into the "Park" to look after them.

Very respectfully, your obedient servant,

A. ALLEN,
Captain Ninth Kansas Cavalry Volunteers, Commanding Post.

Capt. FRANK ENO,
Assistant Adjutant-General.

P. S.—I have kept a scouting party out in the mountains ever since the fight, *watching the devils.*

JULY 11, 1863.—Skirmish at Stockton, Mo.

Report of Maj. Charles Sheppard, Assistant Adjutant-General, Enrolled Missouri Militia.

HDQRS. FOURTH MIL. DIST., ENROLLED MISSOURI MILITIA,
Springfield, July 15, 1863.

COLONEL: I have the honor to report the following engagement with the enemy by the enrolled militia at Stockton, on Saturday, July 11, 1863:

Livingston, the chief of bushwhackers in this district, with 100 men, surprised and attacked the militia at Stockton at 1 p.m. that day. Lieut. W. A. McMinn, commanding detachment of Twenty-sixth Regiment Enrolled Missouri Militia, garrisoning the town, had his headquarters and arms at the court-house, and immediately commenced fighting. The fight was short, resulting in the killing of Livingston and 3 others (left dead on the field), and 15 men wounded, and left by the enemy at Whitehair, 10 miles southwest from Stockton. How many men were killed and wounded is unknown. Our loss is as follows: Lieutenant McMinn and 3 others mortally wounded, and 2 slightly.

Very respectfully, your obedient servant,

CHAS. SHEPPARD,
Assistant Adjutant-General.

Col. WILLIAM F. CLOUD,
Comdg. District of Southwestern Missouri, Springfield.

JULY —, 1863.—Skirmish near Cross Hollow, Ark.

Report of Maj. James J. Johnson, First Arkansas Cavalry.

CASSVILLE, MO., *July* 12, 1863.

COLONEL: My scout, under command of Captain [Joseph S.] Robb, has just arrived; went as far as Cross Hollow. The woods are full of Confederates. Two batteries of artillery at Fayetteville; the whole force said to be about 5,000 strong. They also claim that Marmaduke is to be their leader. They have their old Black Battery at Camp Ragan, 6 miles from Fayetteville, on the Huntsville road. Cabell is at Bentonville. Steele has gone in the direction of Phillips' command. The cannonading I heard was at Fayetteville Thursday, celebrating the victory of Helena. This they claim. My scout had a skirmish with one of Cabell's, in which Captain Maghan, of Cabell's command, was killed; also 6 privates, and captured 6 head of horses. Our loss was 1 horse killed. I have 100 of the Second Kansas out now on a scout.

Respectfully,

J. J. JOHNSON,
Major First Arkansas Cavalry, Commanding.

Colonel CLOUD, *Springfield.*

JULY 12, 1863.—Skirmish near Switzler's Mill, Chariton County, Mo.

Report of Capt. Henry S. Glaze, Ninth Missouri State Militia Cavalry.

BRUNSWICK, *July* 13, 1863.

LIEUTENANT: Sergeant Zimmerman with 20 men were attacked at the house of John Watson, some 3 miles east of Switzler's Mill, Chariton County, yesterday morning.

On the night previous they took Mr. Watson's son a prisoner, and during the night he made his escape. They then made every preparation for an attack, knowing he would bring them [the rebels?], if there were any in the country. About 6 o'clock, just as they were all ready to mount horses, and had withdrawn pickets, they observed, about 75 yards distant, in a corn-field, some rebels. Our boys got the first shot. The rebels sent their buckshot and balls very thick for some twenty minutes, or long enough [so] that one of the men loaded and shot nine times. They then made maneuvers as though they were going to surround the house, and having heard by one of the negroes, and his own observation convincing him, that there was between 60 and 100, he started a messenger to Glasgow for re-enforcements, calculating to take position in the house and out-buildings, but the rebels did not make any further attempt, leaving in a northwestern direction, going, I understand, up the east side of Chariton. Soon Colonel Denny arrived and started in pursuit, with 60 men. I also sent Lieutenant [George I.] Smith, with 38 men, to try and head them, if possible, near Keytesville; if not, to assist in pursuit. We had 1 man badly wounded, and 4 slightly. The boys say they saw several rebels fall when they fired, but they only found 1 man with his leg broken; will probably die. I did not send the sergeant out as an attacking party, but to try and locate them, and send for re-enforcements. The sergeant counted 72 men as they were marching off over the prairie. I had to call in the citizens to guard the camp, as I sent out every available man.

There is a party of rebels up on Grand River, but I have had no men to send after them. When they are chased out of the Persia and Monitor Hills, they come up here; and with one company to do camp duty, and pretend to cope with them, is rather hazardous. They are not going in small squads; they generally travel from 60 to 100. Had I the arms, I could get citizens to assist me, but I am short of them.

I shall need ammunition soon, and if I remain here I will get you to send me some, either by rail to Laclede or by river to this place.

If I stay here, I will need more provisions. Please send me word whether to get them or not. I have some of those old scoundrels that were feeding those rebels, but the evidence is only from negroes and circumstances. What shall I do with them? I also have very good evidence on several others feeding them.

This is the first time since I have been in the service that I was unable to go on a scout when needed.

The rebels were under the command of Holtsclaw, of Howard County, recently from Price's army.

No news from Lieutenant Smith and Colonel Denny, more than firing was heard in the direction of Beckelheimer's Mill about 9 or 10 p. m. yesterday.

I am, very respectfully, your obedient servant,

H. S. GLAZE,

Captain Company H, Ninth Missouri State Militia.

Lieut. LUTHER T. HAYMAN,

Actg. Asst. Adjt. Gen., Northeastern District of Missouri.

JULY 17, 1863.—Engagement at Elk Creek, near Honey Springs, Ind. T.

REPORTS.

No. 1.

Report of Maj. Gen. James G. Blunt, U. S. Army, commanding District of the Frontier.

HEADQUARTERS DISTRICT OF THE FRONTIER,
In the Field, Fort Blunt, C. N., July 26, 1863.

GENERAL: I have the honor to report that, on my arrival here on the 11th instant, I found the Arkansas River swollen, and at once commenced the construction of boats to cross my troops.

The rebels, under General Cooper (6,000), were posted on Elk Creek, 25 miles south of the Arkansas, on the Texas road, with strong outposts guarding every crossing of the river from behind rifle-pits. General Cabell, with 3,000 men, was expected to join him on the 17th, when they proposed attacking this place. I could not muster 3,000 effective men for a fight, but determined, if I could effect a crossing, to give them battle on the other side of the river.

At midnight of the 15th, I took 250 cavalry and four pieces of light artillery, and marched up the Arkansas about 13 miles, drove their pickets from the opposite bank, and forded the river, taking the ammunition chests over in a flat-boat. I then passed down on the south side, expecting to get in the rear of their pickets at the mouth of Grand River, opposite this post, and capture them, but they had learned of my approach and had fled. I immediately commenced crossing my forces at the mouth of Grand River in boats, and, by 10 p. m. of the 16th, commenced moving south, with less than 3,000 men, mostly Indians and negroes, and twelve pieces of artillery. At daylight I came upon the enemy's advance about 5 miles from Elk Creek, and with my cavalry drove them in rapidly upon their main force, which was formed on the south side of the timber of Elk Creek, their line extending 1½ miles, the main road running through their center.

While the column was closing up, I went forward with a small party to examine the enemy's position, and discovered that they were concealed under cover of the brush awaiting my attack. I could not discover the location of their artillery, as it was masked in the brush. While engaged in this reconnaissance, one of my escort was shot.

As my men came up wearied and exhausted, I directed them halted behind a little ridge, about one-half mile from the enemy's line, to rest and eat a lunch from their haversacks. After two hours' rest, and at about 10 a. m., I formed them in two columns, one on the right of the road, under Colonel [William R.] Judson, the other on the left, under Colonel [William A.] Phillips. The infantry was in column by companies, the cavalry by platoons and artillery by sections, and all closed in mass so as to deceive the enemy in regard to the strength of my force. In this order I moved up rapidly to within one-fourth of a mile of their line, when both columns were suddenly deployed to the right and left, and in less than five minutes my whole force was in line of battle, covering the enemy's entire front. Without halting, I moved them forward in line of battle, throwing out skirmishers in advance, and soon drew their fire, which revealed the location of their artillery. The cavalry, which was on the two flanks, was dismounted, and fought on foot with their carbines. In a few moments the entire force was engaged. My men steadily advanced into the edge of the timber, and the fighting was unremitting and terrific for two hours, when the center of the rebel lines, where they had massed their heaviest force, became broken, and they commenced a retreat. In their rout I pushed them vigorously, they making several determined stands, especially at the bridge over Elk Creek, but were each time repulsed. In their retreat they set fire to their commissary buildings, which were 2 miles south of where the battle commenced, destroying all their supplies. I pursued them about 3 miles to the prairie south of Elk Creek, where my artillery horses could draw the guns no farther, and the cavalry horses and infantry were completely exhausted from fatigue. The enemy's cavalry still hovered in my front, and about 4 p. m. General Cabell came in sight with 3,000 re-enforcements. My ammunition was nearly exhausted, yet I determined to bivouac on the field, and risk a battle in the morning if they desired it, but the morning revealed the fact that during the night they had retreated south of the Canadian River.

The enemy's loss was as follows: Killed upon the field and buried by my men, 150; wounded, 400; and 77 prisoners taken, 1 piece of artillery, 1 stand of colors, 200 stand of arms, and 15 wagons, which I burned. My loss is 17 killed, 60 wounded, most of them slightly.*

My forces engaged were the First, Second, and Third Indian, First Kansas (colored), detachments of the Second Colorado, Sixth Kansas, and Third Wisconsin Cavalry, Hopkins' battery of four guns, two sections of Second Kansas Battery, under Capt. E. A. Smith, and four howitzers attached to the cavalry.

Much credit is due to all of them for their gallantry. The First Kansas (colored) particularly distinguished itself; they fought like veterans, and preserved their line unbroken throughout the engagement. Their coolness and bravery I have never seen surpassed; they were in the hottest of the fight, and opposed to Texas troops twice their number, whom they completely routed. One Texas regiment (the Twentieth Cavalry) that fought against them went into the fight with 300 men and came out with only 60. It would be invidious to make particular mention of any one where all did their duty so well.

I am indebted to Col. Thomas Moonlight, chief of staff; Capt. H. G. Loring, acting assistant adjutant-general, and Captains Cox and Kinter, of the Fourth and Fifth Indian Regiments, acting aides-de-camp, for valuable aid rendered during the engagement.

Very respectfully, your obedient servant,

JAS. G. BLUNT,
Major-General.

Maj. Gen. JOHN M. SCHOFIELD,
Commanding Department of the Missouri.

P. S.—I have designated this engagement as the "Battle of Honey Springs," that being the headquarters of General Cooper, on Elk Creek, in the immediate vicinity of the battle-field.

---

* But see revised statement, p. 449.

Return of Casualties in the Union forces in the engagement at Elk Creek, near Honey Springs, Ind. T., July 17, 1863.

[Compiled from nominal list of casualties, returns, &c.]

Command.	Enlisted men killed.	Wounded.		
		Officers.	Enlisted men.	Aggregate.
2d Colorado	5	......	14	19
1st Indian Home Guards	2	......	6	8
2d Indian Home Guards	*3	......	3	6
3d Indian Home Guards	......	......	2	2
1st Kansas (colored)	2	1	29	32
2d Kansas Battery	......	......	1	1
Hopkins' Kansas Battery	1	......	1	2
6th Kansas Cavalry	......	......	5	5
3d Wisconsin Cavalry †	......	......	......	......
Total	13	1	61	75

No. 2.

Report of Lieut. Col. John Bowles, First Kansas Colored Infantry, Judson's brigade.

FORT BLUNT, C. N., *July* 20, 1863.

COLONEL: I have the honor to submit the following report of the First Regiment Kansas Colored Volunteers at the battle of Honey Springs, July 17, 1863:

Previous to forming a line of battle, Colonel [James M.] Williams was informed that his regiment would occupy the right and support Captain Smith's battery. Colonel Williams then called "attention," and said to the men, "I want you all to keep cool, and not fire until you receive the command; in all cases aim deliberately and below the waist. I want every man to do his whole duty, and obey strictly the orders of his officers." We then moved in column, by company, to the position assigned us, and formed in line of battle, when the engagement was opened by the battery. After the lapse of ten minutes, during which time the fire from the battery was incessant, General Blunt came in person to Colonel Williams, and said, "I wish you to move your regiment to the front and support this battery (which was already in motion); I wish you to keep an eye to those guns of the enemy, and take them at the point of the bayonet, if an opportunity offers." Colonel Williams then made some remarks to the men, intimating that we had work to do, and ordered them to "fix bayonet." We then moved to the front and center, forming to the right of a section of Smith's battery, consisting of two 12-pounder field pieces, that had already taken position within 300 yards of the enemy's lines, which was only apparent by the smoke from the frequent firing of their battery, so completely were they concealed by the brush in their position. Quite a number of rounds of shell and canister had been fired from our guns, when our gallant colonel gave the command "forward," and every man stepped promptly and firmly in

* Drowned while crossing the Arkansas River, *en route* to field of battle.
† No loss reported.

his place, advancing in good order until within 40 paces of the concealed foe, when we halted on the right of the Second Colorado. Colonel Williams then gave the command, "Ready, aim, fire," and immediately there went forth two long lines of smoke and flame, the one from the enemy putting forth at the same instant, as if mistaking the command as intended for themselves, or as a demonstration of their willingness to meet us promptly.

At this juncture Colonel Williams fell, he and his horse at the same instant; Colonel Williams badly wounded in the right breast, face, and hands. Being on the right, and partly shut out from view of the left by the thick brush, I was, therefore, ignorant of the fact that Colonel Williams had fallen, and could not inform myself until it was too late to give the command "charge bayonet," for which every man seemed so anxiously awaiting. In the mean time the firing was incessant along the line, except on the extreme right, where some of our Indians had ridden in the brush between us and the enemy. I immediately ordered them to fall back, and to the right. The enemy, which has since proven to have been the Twenty-ninth Texas Regiment, commanded by Colonel De Morse in person, who was badly wounded in the right arm, supposed from the command that we were giving way in front, and, like true soldiers, commenced to press, as they supposed, a retreating foe. They advanced to within 25 paces, when they were met by a volley of musketry that sent them back in great confusion and disorder. Their color-bearer fell, but the colors were immediately raised, and again promptly shot down. A second time they were raised, and again I caused a volley to be fired upon them, when they were left by the enemy as a trophy to our well-directed musketry.

As soon as I learned of Colonel Williams having been severely wounded and having left the field, I assumed command, our right pressing the enemy back to a corn-field, where he broke and fled in confusion. Further pursuit being impossible on account of the nature of the ground, I ordered the right back to our original line of battle. At this time Lieutenant-Colonel [F. W.] Schaurte, of the Second Indian, sent an orderly informing me of the near approach of his command, and that he wished to pass to the front, and I would please inform my command of the fact, to prevent accident. Some of his command passed to our front and carried off the colors we had three times shot down and driven the enemy from in defeat and loss. Some of my officers and men shouted out in remonstrance, and asked permission to break ranks and get them. I refused permission, and told them the matter could be righted hereafter.

Lieutenant-Colonel Moonlight, chief of staff, ordered us to the front. We advanced in line for a distance of 3 miles, skirmishing occasionally with the enemy from the high bluffs in front and to the left. The enemy being completely routed and defeated, we were ordered to fall back to the Springs, rest the men, and cook supper.

At 7 p. m. we were ordered to take position on the battle-field, near the ford, on Elk Creek, and bivouac for the night.

Our total on entering the battle was 500 men, including the commissioned officers. Our total in killed and wounded was 2 killed and 30 wounded.*

* * * * * * *

In conclusion, I feel it but justice and my duty to state that the officers and men throughout the entire regiment behaved nobly, and with the

---

* But see revised statement, p. 449.

coolness of veterans. Each seemed to vie with the other in the performance of his duty, and it was with the greatest gratification that I witnessed their gallant and determined resistance under the most galling fire. Where all performed their duty so well it would be hard to particularize.

J. BOWLES,
Lieut. Col., Comdg. First Regiment Kansas Colored Vols.

Col. WILLIAM R. JUDSON,
Commanding First Brigade, Army of the Frontier.

No. 3.

Report of Lieut. Col. Frederick W. Schaurte, Second Indian Home Guards.

FORT BLUNT, C. N., *July* 20, 1863.

SIR: I have the honor to forward to you the following report of the battle on Elk Creek, Creek Nation, July 17, 1863, in which my regiment was engaged:

I was ordered to get all my available force in readiness to march on Thursday, July 16, 1863. My command consisted of field and staff officers, Major [M. B. C.] Wright, Surg. A. J. Ritchie, Adjutant [Ezra W.] Robinson, Chaplain J. B. Jones, and Sergt. Maj. Ed. Baldrige; of line officers, 4 captains, 9 first lieutenants, and 5 second lieutenants; of enlisted men, 345, 10 of whom were mounted. Total, 368.

My command crossed the Arkansas River, below the mouth of Grand River, at 11 p. m. on the 16th instant. Three privates of Company F, Second Regiment Indian Brigade, were drowned while attempting to swim the river—Privates Huston Mayfield, Key Dougherty, and To-cah-le-ges-kie. We moved forward on the Texas road (course west of south), and arrived at camp, to the north of and near Elk Creek timber, at 8.45 o'clock, July 17, 1863. About an hour afterward I received orders to get my command in readiness, and take position in close column of companies in rear of the First Kansas Colored Regiment. The First Brigade, of which my regiment formed a part, moved forward in close column of companies, on the right of the Texas road, and formed in line of battle near and in front of Elk Creek timber. About 10.20 a. m. Blair's battery, consisting of four pieces, commanded by Capt. E. A. Smith, commenced firing. Soon afterward the right section changed position from the right to the left of the brigade, supported by the First Kansas Colored Regiment. As soon as the artillery ceased firing I was ordered to deploy my command as skirmishers, and enter the timber. My command continued to act as skirmishers during the entire engagement, which lasted about four hours. The enemy were repulsed from the field, and pursued till pursuing became useless, they being well mounted and our men worn down with fatigue. A little after 2 o'clock my command was ordered back to camp on Elk Creek, where it remained until 5 p. m., July 18, 1863, when we were ordered to march for Fort Blunt, on the same route pursued in going to the scene of action. We camped about 12 p. m., on the prairie 2 miles south of the Arkansas River. My command left camp soon after sunrise, and arrived at Fort Blunt at 11 a. m., July 19, 1863.

A stand of colors was captured by my men; also a quantity of arms; the number I could not ascertain, as the men threw them in a pile whenever they found them.

The casualties in my command are as follows: Private Huston Mayfield, Company F, drowned in the Arkansas; Private Key Dougherty, Company F, drowned in the Arkansas; Private Tocah-le-ges-kie, Company F, drowned in the Arkansas; Private Grass, Company B, wounded in left side, severely; Private Backwater, Company A, right thigh broken, wound mortal; Private Leach Rice, Company I, right hand wounded slightly.

I feel it my duty to state that the officers and men of my command behaved nobly and gallantly. They were the first who charged through Elk Creek and took position in the farther edge of the timber, opposite to where the enemy had massed their forces for the time.

I am, sir, very respectfully, your obedient servant,

FRED. W. SCHAURTE,

Lieut. Col. Second Regiment Indian Brigade, Comdg. Regiment.

ACTING ASSISTANT ADJUTANT-GENERAL,

First Brigade, Army of the Frontier.

No. 4.

Report of Lieut. Col. William T. Campbell, Sixth Kansas Cavalry.

CAMP NEAR FORT BLUNT, C. N.,
July 19, 1863.

SIR: I have the honor to report the part taken by my command, consisting of Companies A, C, F, and H, commanded, respectively, by Lieutenant [Thomas J.] Darling, Lieutenant [Richard L.] Phillips, Captain [William] Gordon, and Captain [David] Mefford; also section of mountain howitzers, under Lieutenant [John P.] Grassberger, in action on the 17th instant, at Honey Springs, Creek Nation.

My command left camp at 4 o'clock on the morning of the 16th instant, with a section of Second Kansas Battery, crossing the Verdigris and Arkansas Rivers without loss. After a halt of a few hours, I, with my command, was ordered to take the advance, Company F, Captain Gordon, being advance guard. About daybreak the advance came up with the enemy in considerable force, posted on a rise of ground, and near the timber. The captain immediately formed his men and opened a brisk fire on the enemy, but was compelled by superior numbers to fall back. I brought the rest of my command forward at a gallop to the support of the advance, and, after a sharp skirmish, drove the enemy from his position, with a loss of 1 killed and 3 wounded. Private Banks, of Company C, and Allingham, of Company F, were slightly wounded; also had 1 horse killed. I then advanced and came up with the enemy, posted in force under cover of timber at Elk Creek. Here I came to a halt, and sent a company forward to reconnoiter; found the enemy strongly posted in the woods, their line extending on the right and left of the road. I kept up a brisk fire on them; they, however, kept under cover. Private White was here shot through the shoulder. At 7 o'clock I was transferred from the command of Colonel Judson to that of Colonel Phillips (Colonel Judson retaining the section of howitzers), and assigned to the extreme left of our line of battle. Shortly after the general engagement commenced, I discovered the enemy endeavoring to flank us, under cover of timber. I immediately dismounted Companies C, F, and H, and sent them into the woods as skirmishers, and after sharp work of about an hour and a half succeeded in driving the enemy back, and turning his right flank, with slight loss. During this time Colonel [S. H.] Wattles, First Indian Regiment, made a gallant charge, driving the enemy from his position, which relieved my flank. I immediately recalled my men, and, after obtaining a supply of ammunition, mounted and started in pursuit. Shortly after crossing the creek, I charged into a large body of rebels, whom I took to be Stand Watie's Indians and Texans. They retreated to the woods, where they made a stand. My men dismounted and opened a vigorous fire, which, together with a section of Hopkins' battery and the mountain howitzers, soon put them to flight. I followed on until ordered to cease pursuit, the enemy retreating in great disorder. Hospital Steward Holdeman was badly wounded while on the field.

I state with great pleasure that the officers and men under my command behaved, without exception, coolly and bravely.

I have the honor to be, very respectfully, your obedient servant,

W. T. CAMPBELL,
Lieutenant-Colonel, Commanding Regiment.

Col. WILLIAM R. JUDSON,
Commanding Troops in the Field, &c.

No. 5.

Report of Capt. Edward R. Stevens, Third Wisconsin Cavalry.

CAMP NEAR FORT BLUNT,
July 19, 1863.

SIR: I have the honor to make the following report of the part taken by the battalion of the Third Cavalry Wisconsin Volunteers in the action at Honey Springs, on the 17th instant:

My command was formed in battle order on the right about 10 a. m., in accordance with your orders, and moved forward toward the enemy, posted in the edge of the timber. A portion of my battalion was sent farther on to the right, for the purpose of flanking the enemy. The howitzers, which we were supporting at this point, opened upon the enemy, posted behind a rail fence, in the edge of a corn-field. These two movements forced the enemy to fall back upon their center. Dismounting a portion of my command, I skirmished the woods, capturing 8 prisoners, with their arms, and, following the enemy through the timber, I encamped on the prairie beyond.

I am highly gratified to speak in terms of praise of the conduct of officers and men under my command, and of their bravery and promptness in obeying orders. The able manner in which our force was handled in other parts of the field drew the attention of the enemy in such a manner that they inflicted no loss upon my command.

Very respectfully, your obedient servant,

E. R. STEVENS,
Capt. Third Wisconsin Volunteer Cavalry, Comdg. Battalion.

Col. WILLIAM R. JUDSON,
Commanding Brigade.

No. 6.

Report of Capt. Edward A. Smith, Second Kansas Battery.

CAMP NEAR FORT BLUNT, C. N., *July* 19, 1863.

SIR: I have the honor to make the following report of the part taken by the Second Kansas Battery in the battle of Honey Springs, on the 17th instant:

My command consisted of two 12-pounder brass guns and two 6-pounder iron guns, manned by 77 officers and men. At 3 a. m. of the 16th instant, my two 6-pounder guns, under Lieutenant [Aristarchus] Wilson, were ordered out to assist the Sixth Kansas Volunteers in forcing a passage at the upper ford of the Arkansas. This was effected without opposition, and that portion of the command proceeded to the ford at the mouth of Grand River, where I rejoined it at 5 p. m. of the same day with the 12-pounder guns. The march was continued during the night in the direction of Honey Springs, Creek Nation, and at 8 a. m. of the 17th we came in sight of the enemy's line on Elk Creek. After a rest of two hours, I was ordered forward, preceded by the Third Wisconsin Cavalry, and supported by the First Regiment Kansas Colored Volunteers and the Second Regiment Indian Home Guards. Changing direction to the right of the road, I continued in that direction about 600 yards, when I wheeled the battery into line, and moved down upon the left of the enemy's line, which could be faintly discerned through the timber and brush. At this moment the rebel batteries on their right opened upon Captain Hopkins' battery, in Colonel Phillips' brigade. By direction of General Blunt, I came forward at a trot, and went into battery facing the rebel guns on my left. A single shot from one of their rifled guns flew over my head as I went into position. I opened with spherical-case shot, shell, and solid shot on the rebel batteries, which were soon silenced, as rebel prisoners report, by my 12-pounder guns. The commanding general then ordered me to move my 12-pounder guns to the left, near the road, go up within 300 yards of the rebel line, and open with canister. I did so, passing through and 100 yards in front of the line of the Second Colorado Regiment, and, going into battery almost at the edge of the brush, I fired 3 or 4 rounds of canister and 10 or 12 of shell at the rebel position on the hill, when we could see them retreating in the direction of a small corn-field in my immediate front. Before I had time to open on this position I was ordered to cease firing, and the infantry charged the timber. I limbered up and moved forward, in rear of the infantry, which was soon hotly engaged with the enemy. For a few moments the firing was terrific, and I was compelled to dismount my drivers, and, our own men being directly in front of me, was compelled to remain a silent spectator of the contest, which, fortunately, was soon ended by the rout of the foe. Our infantry lines had now disappeared in the timber, across which the rebels were being driven rapidly and with severe loss, and I was ordered to follow. This order was countermanded soon after I reached the timber, and I moved back and encamped on the prairie, north of the creek.

My officers and men behaved throughout with great coolness and courage, a fact worthy of notice, as it was the first time they had ever been under fire.

My losses were as follows: Private William C. Caskey, wounded severely in the thigh; 3 horses slightly wounded.

All of which is respectfully submitted, by your obedient servant,

E. A. SMITH,

Captain, Commanding Second Kansas Battery.

Col. WILLIAM R. JUDSON.

No. 7.

Report of Maj. J. Nelson Smith, Second Colorado Infantry, Phillips' brigade.

FORT BLUNT, *July* 19, 1863.

COLONEL: I have the honor to transmit the following report of the part taken by the battalion of the Second Regiment Colorado Volunteers at the battle of Honey Springs, after having been put in command by Colonel [Theodore H.] Dodd, he going to the rear with prisoners:

I was ordered by General Blunt to rally two companies of my command to support Hopkins' battery, which was to cross the creek in pursuit of the enemy. After rallying my companies, we crossed the stream, and discovered the enemy on a hill, or rise of ground in the advance. Here Hopkins' battery, supported by my infantry, opened upon the enemy, who fled in confusion after the second fire. I was here ordered by Colonel [William A.] Phillips, commanding brigade, to have the rest of my command brought forward, which order was promptly obeyed, I at the same time moving my two companies forward in support of the battery, until we occupied the enemy's former position. Here the remainder of my command came up. After halting a short time we were ordered into camp.

Killed or wounded, none.*

I have no one to censure or praise, as every officer and soldier tried to do his duty.

Very respectfully, your obedient servant,

J. NELSON SMITH,
Major Second Regiment Colorado Volunteers.

Col. WILLIAM A. PHILLIPS,
Third Indian Volunteers, Commanding.

No. 8.

Report of Col. Stephen H. Wattles, First Indian Home Guards.

HDQRS. FIRST REGIMENT OF INDIAN HOME GUARDS,
Fort Blunt, C. N., July 18, 1863.

COLONEL: On the morning of the 17th of July, 1863, we came upon the enemy at Elk Creek. My command was ordered to the left, in support of Hopkins' battery, and then ordered to charge the enemy out of the timber. I advanced, under a destructive fire from the enemy, after hard fighting, gained a position in the timber, and finally drove them across the stream, on the left of the bridge, the enemy forming several times, and desperately contesting every foot of ground.

Too much praise cannot be awarded to both officers and men for their gallant conduct in the battle. Among the former who did efficient service were Lieut. Col. George Dole, who had command of the left wing, and was the first to cross the stream, which he accomplished, under a most galling fire from the enemy, who were formed on the opposite side; Actg. Adjt. E. C. Lowe, Captains No-ko-so-lo-chee and So-nuk-mik-ko,

---

* But see p. 449 for casualties in remainder of regiment.

and Lieuts. R. T. Thompson, Fred. Crafts, Ferd. R. Jacobs, and Charles N. Rix. Of the latter who deserve honorable mention are O. P. Willetts, A. Flanders, and Thompson Overton.

My loss was: Killed, 2; wounded, 6; missing, none. Number of guns captured, 24.

I am, colonel, very respectfully, &c.,

STEPHEN H. WATTLES,
Colonel, Commanding First Indian Regiment.

Col. WILLIAM A. PHILLIPS,
Commanding Fort Blunt

No. 9.

Report of Capt. Henry Hopkins, Kansas Battery.

FORT BLUNT, C. N., *July* 21, 1863.

COLONEL: I would submit the following as a report of the part taken by Hopkins' battery in the engagement of July 17, 1863, at Honey Springs, Ind. T., between the forces under Major-General Blunt and the rebels under Cooper:

Receiving orders to be in readiness to march at 6 a. m. on the 16th instant, with six days' rations, at 12 m. of the same day orders were received to cross the Arkansas, at the mouth of Grand River. Effecting a crossing at dark, marching 2 miles south, and resting for three hours, we again took up line of march in a southwest direction, coming upon the enemy's outposts at daylight. Line of battle was formed, but, discovering the enemy had fled, we were again ordered forward. Moving forward 6 miles, the enemy, under command of Cooper, was discovered in force, occupying a strong position, in a thickly wooded ravine. Moving up in line of battle to within 300 yards of the enemy's position, we were ordered by yourself to commence firing and shell the woods in the immediate front, which continued for one hour and a quarter. Immediately after our fire opened, the enemy's battery was discovered occupying a position to our right and front, which opened fire upon us with shot, shell, and canister, wounding 1 sergeant, mortally (left leg shot off above the knee), killing 1 private, killing 4 horses, and wounding 4 others, totally unfitting them for service.

Discovering one of their guns occupying an open space in the woods, an order was given to direct the fire of two guns upon it, and, if possible, dismount it, which was soon effected. By the explosion of one of our shells, the cannoneers belonging to that piece and all their horses were killed or wounded. Orders were given to cease firing, limber up, and move forward to the edge of the woods, the position the enemy's battery first occupied, and halt until one section of Captain Smith's Second Kansas Battery should pass and cross the ravine.

One of the teams being disabled, I ordered Lieutenant [John F.] Aduddell forward, with three pieces, and as quickly as the disabled horses were replaced I followed with the other piece, and rejoined the other three. The section of Captain Smith's battery not passing, orders were received to move forward on double-quick, and occupy a position on the prairie beyond the ravine. Lieutenant Aduddell moving to the left of the road with one section, opened upon the enemy's cavalry, upon a hill beyond, causing them to fall back quite precipitately, the shell bursting in their immediate vicinity. Again moving forward one-quarter of a mile, a line of the enemy's cavalry was discovered and driven back after the firing of a few rounds of shell. At this point the sections were divided and ordered to move forward to the right and left of the road, the right section under command of First Lieut. John F. Aduddell and the left under Sergeant [C. M.] Greve. Firing now almost entirely ceasing, excepting a few rounds from the left section, and moving forward about 1½ miles, we were ordered to halt, as the enemy had retreated, and our stock was too much exhausted to follow them farther. Immediately after fighting had ceased, and we were selecting a camp-ground, we discovered at the edge of the woods, in their old camp, nearly the entire camp-equipage of one regiment, cooking utensils, tents, &c., which we destroyed.

Casualties: One killed and one mortally wounded, since died.

The sections and pieces were commanded as follows: Right section by Lieut. J. F. Aduddell; left section by Sergeant Greve, acting first sergeant; first piece, Sergeant [J. G.] Pettigrew; second piece, Sergeant [Daniel] Sayre, mortally wounded; third piece, Corporal [J. R.] Rice; fourth piece, Sergeant [O. F.] Fahnestock. Sergeant [J. F.] McKibben, on detached service, recruiting, not being assigned to any duty, assisted, and much credit is due him for his services rendered during the action. Great credit is due Lieutenant Aduddell for his coolness and bravery during the entire action, moving to any part of the battery when necessary, and directing the fire of the pieces with good effect; also Sergeants Greve, Fahnestock, Pettigrew, Corporals Rice, [J. S.] Payne, [T.] McClain, and Farrier [Joseph] Ibbatson, acting gunner to second piece. The fire of the enemy's artillery being directed at us, and taking considerable effect among both men and horses, great praise is due the men for their coolness and courage during the entire fight, and [they] proved themselves worthy of promotion.

I have the honor to be, colonel, very respectfully, your obedient servant,

H. HOPKINS,
Captain, Commanding Hopkins' Battery.

Col. WILLIAM A. PHILLIPS,
Commanding Brigade.

No. 10.

Report of Brig. Gen. Douglas H. Cooper, C. S. Army, commanding Confederate forces.

HEADQUARTERS FIRST BRIGADE, INDIAN TROOPS,
Imochiah Creek, near Canadian, August 12, 1863.

GENERAL: My official report of the affair at Elk Creek, on the 17th ultimo, has been delayed in consequence of the movements of the troops under your command and the difficulty of getting correct reports from subordinate officers of the killed and wounded. Referring to my notes of the 18th ultimo, I now have the honor to submit the following:

On July 15, reports were sent to me from the officer in charge of the pickets on Arkansas River that it had become fordable above mouth of Verdigris; that Federal officers were seen examining the fords; that the two spies, Clark and Lane, formerly employed in the quartermaster's department at Forts Arbuckle and Cobb, who imposed themselves upon you, and thereby obtained permission to enlist in this brigade, had reached Gibson; that they had been at the agency examining that ford, &c. Believing there was a probability that the attack might be made upon me before General Cabell arrived, whose movements were known to these spies, or at all events that a heavy scout might be sent across to capture the pickets on the Arkansas, I directed their concentration on Coody's Creek, with instructions to send vedettes to the different fords.

Early on the 16th ultimo, information reached me that the Federals were crossing in force at the Creek Agency. Col. Tandy Walker, commanding First Cherokee and Choctaw Regiment, and Captain [L. E.] Gillett, commanding squadron Texas cavalry, with their commands, accompanied by Lieutenant [T. B.] Heiston, aide-de-camp and acting assistant adjutant-general, were ordered out in the direction of the Chimney Mountain, where the roads to Creek Agency and to Gibson intersect, with orders to send out small parties of observation on both roads and to withdraw the pickets from Coody's Creek. Up to this time I had been unable to determine whether the force which crossed at the Creek Agency was merely a heavy scout or the advance of the main body of the enemy. About 200 or 300 had been reported moving from the Creek Agency down the river toward Nevins' and Rabbit Fords, near Frozen Rock, to capture or drive off our pickets, who were supposed, no doubt, still to be there.

About daylight on the morning of the 17th, the advance of the enemy came in sight of the position occupied by the Choctaws and Texans; commenced a brisk fire upon them, which was returned and followed by a charge, which drove the enemy back upon the main column. Lieutenant Heiston reported the morning cloudy and damp, many of the guns failing to fire in consequence of the very inferior quality of the powder, the cartridges becoming worthless even upon exposure to damp atmosphere. Soon after the Federals had been driven back, it commenced raining heavily, which rendered their arms wholly useless. These troops then fell back slowly and in good order to camp, for the purpose of obtaining a fresh supply of ammunition and preparing for the impending fight. A few remained with Lieutenant Heiston at Prairie Mountain, about 3 miles north of camp on the Gibson road, and were so disposed as to create the impression on the enemy that a large force was there awaiting them. Accordingly, their advance halted until the main body came up and formed in line of battle, thus affording my aide opportunity to form an estimate of their strength. He reported their force to be probably 4,000, which I found nearly correct, though some 500 under the mark. After ascertaining that the enemy were advancing in force, orders were issued to the officers commanding corps to prepare for immediate action and take their positions, all which had been, in anticipation of an attack, previously defined by General Orders, No. 25, to copy of which, marked A, herewith, reference is made. Captain [R. W.] Lee's light battery had been moved up on the Gibson road the evening previous, intending it to go with the scout under Colonel Walker, but, owing to some misunderstanding or neglect in delivering the order, the scout left without it. Colonel [T. C.] Bass, with his regiment, was ordered forward to support Lee's battery. [John] Scanland's squadron and Gillett's squadron were directed to support the creeks at the upper crossing of Elk Creek, and Colonel Walker to hold his regiment in reserve at their camp near Honey Springs, sending pickets out on the road across the mountain in the direction of Prairie Springs. Having made these arrangements, I rode forward to the position north of Elk Creek, where Captain Lee's light howitzer battery had been posted, and found it supported by Colonel Bass' regiment (Twentieth Texas dismounted cavalry), by a portion of the Second Cherokee Regiment, and a body of skirmishers on the right, under command of Capt. Hugh Tinnin, of the First Cherokee Regiment, the remainder of the Cherokee regiments being near the creek.

A movement on my right was discovered, and Captain Tinnin reported that the skirmishers would soon be engaged. One-half of Colonel Bass' regiment, under Captain [J. R.] Johnson, was then ordered to the right to support Captain Tinnin, and I rode over to their position and found, by movements of officers, that there was a body of troops on my extreme right. A part of Second Cherokee Regiment, just returned from a scout to Prairie Springs, who were getting breakfast at camp, were then ordered up and conducted by myself to the right, and a messenger sent for half of the Choctaw regiment, which soon arrived and were placed also on the right along the edge of the prairie. Upon reconnoitering the enemy from the high prairie, where I had a full view of them, then advancing upon the Gibson road, I found their force larger than reported by Lieutenant Heiston, and larger than I supposed they would bring from Gibson; and, seeing a heavy force wheeling off to their right and taking the road up the creek to the second crossing above the bridge—our weakest point, and from which the road continues up to the third crossing, where the Creeks were posted—I rode back to the main road, sent orders to the Creeks to move down and support Colonels [Charles] De Morse and [L. M.] Martin, who were directed to support Colonel Bass, and, if possible, flank the enemy on our left. I then rode to where I expected to find the Choctaws, in order to bring them to the support of Colonel Bass' command and the battery, which was engaged with that of the enemy. Colonel Walker, mistaking the order, had moved off on the mountain several miles with his whole force, instead of sending a picket. Messengers were sent after him and he returned promptly, but too late for the defense of the bridge. Riding back near the creek, I discovered our men in small parties giving way. These increased until the retreat became general. Colonel Bass' regiment and Captain Lee's battery, after a most gallant defense of their positions, were compelled to fall back; Colonel De Morse's regiment and Colonel Martin's, on the left, also retiring, except a few who were cut off from the main body.

We have to mourn the loss of many brave officers and men who fell here, sacrificing their lives in opposition to an overwhelming force to save our little battery, all of which was brought off, except one howitzer, dismounted by the heavy ordnance of the enemy.

Colonel Martin, who retired in good order across the creek when the line along the prairie near the battery gave way, was directed to hold the ford above the bridge; but seeing the whole right wing falling back from the bridge and below it, Colonel Martin was withdrawn and ordered to fall back to Honey Springs. Our forces were now in full retreat and the enemy pressing them closely. The Texans, under Scanland's and Gillett's command, were ordered to join me at Honey Springs, and the Creeks to withdraw from the extreme left and also concentrate at the same place. Colonel Bass' and Colonel De Morse's regiments, a part of which (under Major [J. A.] Carroll) had reached their horses, were directed also to rally at the same place. The remainder of this regiment, under Lieutenant-Colonel [O. G.] Welch, who bravely maintained his position on the north side of the creek too long to rejoin his [regiment], were cut off and compelled to make a circuit via North Fork to this camp. Captain Gillett's squadron, arriving promptly, was formed on the road, and for a short time held the advance of the enemy in check. The Choctaws, under Colonel Walker, opportunely arrived at this time, and under my personal direction charged the enemy, who had now planted a battery upon the timbered ridge about 1,000 yards north of Honey Springs. With their usual intrepidity the Choctaws went at them, giving the war-whoop, and succeeded in checking the advance of the enemy until their force could be concentrated and all brought up. The Choctaws, discouraged on account of the worthless ammunition, then gave way, and were ordered to fall back with the others in rear of the train, which had moved off in an easterly direction, covered by our troops, who remained formed for hours in full view of the enemy, thus giving the train time to gain some 6 or 8 miles on the road to Briartown, which had been indicated by yourself as the route by which re-enforcements would be sent.

Too much praise cannot be awarded the troops for the accomplishment of the most difficult of all military movements—an orderly and successful retreat, with little loss of life or property, in the face of superior numbers, flushed with victory. The retreat of the forces under my command eastward instead of south completely deceived the enemy, and created, as I anticipated, the impression that re-enforcements from Fort Smith were close at hand, and that by a detour in rear of the mountain east of Honey Springs our forces might march upon Gibson and destroy it while General Blunt was away with almost the whole Federal force. Under the influence of this reasonable fear, General Blunt withdrew his forces and commenced a hurried march for Gibson. North Fork, where we had a large amount of commissary stores, was then saved, as well as the whole of the train, except one ambulance purposely thrown in the way of the enemy by the driver. A quantity of flour, some salt, and sugar were necessarily burned at Honey Springs, there being no transportation for it.

Our loss was 134 killed and wounded and 47 taken prisoners, while that of the enemy exceeded 200, as I learned from one of our surgeons who was at Gibson when General Blunt's forces returned.

I feel confident we could have made good the defense of the position at Elk Creek but for the worthlessness of our ammunition. The Choctaws, who had skirmished with the enemy on the morning of the 17th, returned wet and disheartened by finding their guns almost useless, and there was a general feeling among the troops that with such ammunition it was useless to contend with a foe doubly superior in numbers, arms, and munitions, with artillery ten times superior to ours, weight of metal considered. Notwithstanding all these untoward circumstances, the men of Colonel Bass' regiment stood calmly and fearlessly to their posts in support of Lee's battery until the conflict became a hand-to-hand one, even clubbing their muskets and never giving way until the battery had been withdrawn; and, even when defeated and in full retreat, the officers and men of different commands readily obeyed orders, formed, falling back and reforming at several different positions, as ordered, deliberately and coolly. Their steady conduct under these circumstances evidently intimidated the foe, and alone enabled us to save the train and many valuable lives. The Creeks, under Col. D. N. McIntosh, at this juncture behaved admirably, moving off in good order slowly and steadily across the North Fork road in full view of the enemy. They contributed greatly to the safe retreat of the train and brigade.

Among the officers who were distinguished for gallantry and good conduct, Col. T. C. Bass and Captain Lee were particularly conspicuous.

Colonel De Morse's conduct, though suffering under a severe wound, has been represented to me as all that should characterize a brave man. Colonel Martin, for his coolness and good management of his command, deceiving the enemy as to his real strength, and preventing our left from being turned, deserves great credit. Captain Gillett behaved with his usual gallantry. Major Carroll was active and prompt in bringing his men into line to cover the retreat. Colonel Walker and his Choctaws behaved bravely, as they always do. Captain [F. M.] Hanks, of Bass' regiment, was also distinguished for his gallantry, being dangerously wounded while carrying orders which I had sent to Colonel Bass to draw the right wing to his support. And the lamented [H. H.] Molloy, of the same regiment, fell, mortally wounded, soon after having delivered my order to his colonel to move De Morse's and Martin's regiments up on the right flank of the enemy, who were advancing upon the battery at the center.

Captain Johnson, who commanded a detachment from Colonel Bass' regiment, came under my immediate notice. His conduct was, at the most trying time, cool and collected—that of a brave man and good officer. The nature of the ground precluded the possibility of personally observing all the movements of our troops and the conduct of the men and officers. Among those who were mentioned with praise by their immediate commanding officers are Capts. Hugh Tinnin, James L. Butler, and James Stewart, First Cherokee Regiment; Adjt. L. C. De Morse, Twenty-ninth Texas Cavalry; Lieut. Henry Forrester and Sergt. J. Riley Baker, Lee's light battery; Lieut. A. G. Ballenger, Second Cherokee Regiment (killed), and Acting Sergt. Maj. J. H. Reierson, of Bass' regiment, and Sergt. Henry Campbell, of same regiment, were particularly distinguished, &c.

Mr. P. N. Blackstone was particularly distinguished for his courage on the field. After being severely wounded, he succeeded in repulsing three of the enemy who attacked him, killing one of them and taking his gun, which he brought off with him, together with his own, closely pursued by the enemy, after the greater portion of our troops had left the field.

Of my personal staff, Lieut. T. B. Heiston, aide-de-camp and acting assistant adjutant-general, all speak in the highest terms. He was on this, as on all former occasions, wherever duty called him, conspicuous for his gallant bearing.

My son, Douglas H. Cooper, jr., additional aide-de-camp, is mentioned favorably by Colonel Bass in his report for his good conduct while conveying my orders amid the thickest of the fray.

I am also indebted to Mr. S. A. Robinson for valuable assistance in conveying orders.

Referring to accompanying reports for further details, and to list of killed and wounded, I am, general, respectfully,

DOUGLAS H. COOPER,
Brigadier-General.

Brig. Gen. WILLIAM STEELE,
Commanding Department of Indian Territory.

[Inclosure A.]

GENERAL ORDERS, No. 25. } HDQRS. FIRST BRIG., INDIAN TROOPS,
Elk Creek, July 14, 1863.

I. The First and Second Cherokee Regiments will constitute the right wing of the brigade, Col. Stand Watie, senior colonel, commanding.

II. The left wing will be composed of First and Second Creek Regiments, Col. D. N. McIntosh commanding.

III. The center will consist of Twentieth Texas dismounted cavalry, Twenty-ninth Texas Cavalry, Fifth Texas Partisan Rangers, and Lee's light battery, Col. Thomas C. Bass, senior colonel, commanding.

IV. Scanland's squadron, [L. E.] Gillett's squadron, and First Choctaw and Chickasaw Regiment, Col. Tandy Walker commanding, will be attached to headquarters and constitute the reserve, to which such other troops belonging to this brigade as may report will be added until further orders. Captain [John] Scanland will fall back to a position which will be assigned him near headquarters, Honey Springs.

The right wing will encamp convenient to the two lower crossings on Elk Creek; the center near or at such places as may be convenient to the middle ford, and the left wing at or near the upper ford; the reserve near headquarters, Honey Springs Depot. Commandants of each wing will see that necessary ways are opened along the front and near Elk Creek to enable the troops to move with facility from point to point, and also that proper roads from the camps perpendicular to the way along the bank of the creek are opened. Each regiment will occupy a front at least equal to the number of files, minus one-fifth. For example: If the total of a regiment be 1,000 men, or 500 files, the front will be 400 yards. The proper intervals between squadrons and regiments will be observed, and kept free from obstruction, to allow the passage of the troops. These intervals may be increased where the ground is obstructed, and in timbered places the line may be extended. In case of attack there should be an advance party thrown out to and along the skirt of the prairie in front (north side of the creek), with adequate supports formed near the creek. The enemy must, if possible, be prevented from gaining the cover of the timber on the north side. Commandants will examine the ground in front of them, and especially creeks, bayous, or wooded ways leading from the prairie north and west of camp down southward and connecting with the main bottom of Elk Creek. These smaller creeks will be used in case of attack by the enemy to penetrate to Elk Creek, and thus flank the different positions near the fords. These can be used by our troops to advantage in gaining a position in advance of the general line of the prairie to flank the columns of the enemy while advancing on the roads leading to the fords. It is necessary that commanding officers should examine and understand the ground in front of their own positions, and also those occupied by other corps.

By order of Brig. Gen. D. H. Cooper:

THORNTON B. HEISTON,
Lieutenant and Acting Assistant Adjutant-General.

JULY 18-26, 1863.—Scout from Cassville, Mo., to Huntsville, Ark., etc.

Report of Col. James W. Johnson, Twenty-sixth Enrolled Missouri Militia.

HEADQUARTERS POST,
Cassville, Mo., July 26, 1863.

GENERAL. A scout under Captain Galloway has just returned from an eight days' scout, in the direction and vicinity of Huntsville, Ark., and to Berryville, killing 6 rebels and capturing 3, chasing pretty much all the guerrillas out of the country for 50 or 60 miles southeast. No force of enemy this side the mountain in that direction. All the small parties seemed to be concentrating in the direction of Ozark, Ark. Nothing of a reliable character as to forces at Fayetteville. I will send in that direction to-morrow.

JAMES W. JOHNSON,
Colonel, Commanding Post.

Brigadier-General McNEIL.

JULY 24, 1863.—Skirmish in Dade County, Mo.

Report of Maj. Charles Sheppard, Assistant Adjutant-General, Enrolled Missouri Militia.

SPRINGFIELD, MO., *July* 29, 1863.

CAPTAIN: I have the honor to report the following engagement between a scout, commanded by Capt. E. J. Morris, Company E, Seventh Provisional Regiment Enrolled Missouri Militia, and a band of bushwhackers, on Friday, July 24, 1863, in Dade County:

The guerrillas had just taken 15 negroes, and had them on horses to carry off, when the captain attacked them, with the following results: Killed 1, severely wounded 3, released the negroes, and captured 10 horses, 5 saddles, and 2 Colt's navy revolvers. Private William Stockton, Company A, Eighth Missouri State Militia, who was in company with Captain Morris, was severely wounded.

Very respectfully, your obedient servant,

CHAS. SHEPPARD,
Assistant Adjutant-General.

Capt. C. G. LAURANT,
Assistant Adjutant-General.

JULY 27, 1863.—Affair near Cassville, Mo.

Report of Col. James W. Johnson, Twenty-sixth Enrolled Missouri Militia.

HEADQUARTERS POST,
Cassville, Mo., July 28, 1863.

GENERAL: A scout of Second Infantry, headed by one Caleb Baker, on the 27th, encountered about 20 rebels, some 25 miles southeast of this place, killing 1 captain, 3 men, and wounding 4. Our loss is 3 missing. Some arms were captured also.

JAMES W. JOHNSON,
Colonel, Commanding Post.

Brigadier-General McNEIL.

JULY —, 1863.—Expedition from Greensborough to Helena, Ark.

Congratulatory orders.

GENERAL ORDERS, No. 28. } HDQRS. DAVIDSON'S CAV. DIV., DEPT. MO., *Camp at Wittsburg, Ark., July* 29, 1863.

The commanding general of the division desires to thank, in General Orders, Capt. James D. Jenks, of the First Iowa Cavalry, and the 50 brave men of that regiment under his command.

Starting from a point 100 miles from Helena, they marched through a country held by the enemy and infested by guerrillas; dashing upon his outposts wherever he found them; crossing the L'Anguille River under fire of the enemy's pickets; taking 6 prisoners on his road; wounding 1 officer and 1 private, who fell into our hands; destroying his dispatches and communicating their contents to the commander at Helena, without losing an item, his whole conduct presents an example of brilliant cavalry daring worthy of the study and imitation of every officer in this command.

By order of Brigadier-General Davidson:

AUGUSTUS S. MONTGOMERY,
Lieutenant and Acting Assistant Adjutant-General.

JULY 30, 1863.—Skirmishes near Elm Springs, Ark.

Report of Lieut. John E. Phelps, Third U. S. Cavalry.

AUGUST 7, 1863.

GENERAL: On the 28th of July, with 28 men of the Second Arkansas Cavalry, I left Cassville, with a scout, under the command of Major [T. J.] Hunt, First Arkansas Cavalry. We marched with that command to Mudtown, Ark. There we left it, and went to Elm Springs. Learning that Captain Arrington, of the rebel army, was near that place with a small force of rebels, we fell in his rear at 12 o'clock at night on the 29th. My men and horses being tired, we stopped. Early next morning we started in the direction of Fayetteville, and came on the enemy's rear guard 6 miles from Elm Springs, and had a skirmish. One rebel was killed and 4 wounded, and 1 horse captured. We joined Major Hunt's command at Fayetteville, and all returned to Elm Springs that night and camped. The next morning, the 31st, we left Major Hunt's command, and took the road to Maysville. About 8 miles from Elm Springs we came upon the enemy, 25 strong, and had another skirmish, killing 4 and wounding 5, and capturing 3 horses. We then proceeded to Maysville. There I learned that Colonel Coffee was encamped within 10 miles of that place, on Butler's Creek, with 500 men. Not having a force sufficient to attack Coffee, we returned to Springfield, by Neosho, Newtonia, Jollification, Morrisville, and Little York, without meeting any more of the enemy.

My men behaved bravely. The only casualty to my men was 1 injured by the fall of his horse. We captured in all 16 horses.

JOHN E. PHELPS,
Lieut. Third U. S. Cav., Recruiting Officer Second Ark. Cav.

Brigadier-General MCNEIL

JULY 30, 1863.—Skirmish near Lexington, Mo.

Report of Col. James McFerran, First Missouri State Militia Cavalry.

LEXINGTON, MO., *August* 3, 1863.

GENERAL: I have the honor to report that, on the 29th instant, Captain [H. F.] Peery, Company K, of the First Missouri State Militia Cavalry, with a detachment of 27, of Companies K, C, and I, of said regiment, together with 15 men of Enrolled Missouri Militia, left this post as an escort for the paymaster (Major Smith) *en route* for Marshall, in Saline County, distant about 40 miles. The Enrolled Missouri Militia having arms under escort for Freedom Township, in this county, left Captain Peery about 20 miles below here, and the paymaster's escort continued their march for about 5 miles, and put up for the night. The next morning, Captain Peery's command was attacked by about 100 guerrillas, under Blunt and Graves, and, after a sharp conflict, were repulsed, with the loss of 2 horses and 3 men mortally wounded. Captain Peery lost 1 man mortally wounded and 7 horses. The paymaster reached his destination in safety.

All of which is most respectfully reported by order of—

JAMES McFERRAN,
Colonel, Commanding First Missouri State Militia Cavalry.

General EWING,
Commanding District of the Border.

AUGUST 1, 1863.—Skirmish at Taylor's Farm, on the Little Blue, Mo.

Report of Capt. Charles F. Coleman, Ninth Kansas Cavalry.

CAMP NEAR LITTLE SANTA FÉ,
August 2, 1863.

DEAR SIR: On Friday, July 31, I received information that a band of guerrillas intended to rob a train which was encamped in the vicinity of Westport. I immediately sent word to the commanding officer at Westport, by Lieutenant Brown, that the train would be robbed that night, unless prevented, and that if he came out, to come on the north side, next to the timber, and that I would watch the train on this side. I arrived in the vicinity of the train about 9.30 p. m., and took a position close enough to see any party that might approach; but having received no answer from the commanding officer at Westport, I had no idea that he was coming. I had been there about thirty minutes when I saw a body of men approach the train from the east, and, from their action, I was certain at that time that they were guerrillas, and immediately ordered an attack, they retreating and we pursuing. I did not discover the mistake until we overtook some of their men, and found that they were Federal soldiers. I called off my command and ordered a halt until daylight, and, while waiting there, the party that had robbed the train came in sight of us. I started in pursuit of them, and about 1 p. m. the next day run on them at Mrs. Taylor's, on Little Blue. We gave them one volley, which they returned, but when we fired the second time they ran, leaving 4 dead on the ground. I had my men dismounted, and by the time we got in the saddle again, and owing to the timber being so thick, I did not succeed in capturing the guerrillas. They numbered about 40 men, and were well mounted. I think there were several wounded. None of my men were hurt.

Yours, respectfully,

C. F. COLEMAN,
Captain Company D, Ninth Kansas Volunteer Cavalry.

General EWING.

AUGUST 1, 1863.—Affair at Round Ponds, near Castor River, Mo.

REPORTS.

No. 1.—Brig. Gen. Clinton B. Fisk, U. S. Army, commanding District of Southeast Missouri.

No. 2.—Col. John B. Rogers, Second Missouri State Militia Cavalry.

No. 3.—Lieut. Col. J. Ellison, Tenth Missouri Cavalry (Confederate).

No. 1.

Report of Brig. Gen. Clinton B. Fisk, U. S. Army, commanding District of Southeast Missouri.

PILOT KNOB, MO., *August* 3, 1863.

GENERAL: One of General Davidson's trains, of 30 wagons, was attacked on Saturday night, near Castor River, and destroyed. Ten of our men were killed outright; others mortally wounded. The mules have been recovered; the horses were lost; train burned. The entire country along the border is swarming with guerrillas. Burbridge is near Greenville with his own regiment, and is being re-enforced by Reves and Freeman. I have sent every mounted man I have to Patterson this morning. It requires more than half of the force in the district to guard General Davidson's line of communication and garrison the posts of Bloomfield and Chalk Bluff.

CLINTON B. FISK,
Brigadier-General, Commanding.

Maj. Gen. JOHN M. SCHOFIELD,
Commanding Department of the Missouri.

No. 2.

Reports of Col. John B. Rogers, Second Missouri State Militia Cavalry.

CAPE GIRARDEAU, MO., *August* 2, 1863.

GENERAL: The attack on the train last night was serious. Ten men were killed, 2 mortally wounded, and 2 slightly; all the train was burned but 3 wagons; all the mules are recovered; the horses are lost. The party was surprised by the Bolands and murdered. There were but 12 of the attacking party. There must have been inexcusable negligence; but in those swamps the party can approach very near before being seen.

J. B. ROGERS,
Colonel, Commanding.

Brigadier-General FISK.

CAPE GIRARDEAU, MO., *August* 3, 1863.

GENERAL: The guard was stronger than the attacking party, but the surprise was complete; they were shot in sleep. It is difficult to guard against such surprises, as the swamp is close to the road and very dense. General Davidson sent his train up without any guard, camping on the same ground. He came through in person with but 12; I did the same with 5. One train had just passed; another was but 10 miles behind, with 140 men. The bridge guard was but 3 miles distant. I thought the middle train secure with a small guard. They had about 20 men, besides 40 drivers, armed mostly.

J. B. ROGERS,
Colonel, Commanding.

General FISK.

CAPE GIRARDEAU, MO., *August* 3, 1863.

GENERAL: The sergeant in charge of captured train just in. He reports that the attack was made from the swamps, but his sentinels on that side were killed instantly and the guerrillas rushed on to the half-awakened men and killed them before resistance could be made. Camping too close to the swamp was the fatal error. It happens the sentinels were posted properly, but the cover was so dense that they were killed before the alarm was given. The teamsters fled to the swamps. Their guard paid for their fault with their lives.

J. B. ROGERS,
Colonel, Commanding.

Brigadier-General FISK,
Commanding District.

No. 3.

Report of Lieut. Col. J. Ellison, Tenth Missouri Cavalry (Confederate).

CAMP BROWN, *August* 16, 1863.

GENERAL: Capt. John McWherter, who has been out scouting on Crowley's Ridge, has just arrived. Lieutenant [John P.] Taylor and Lieutenant [John R.] Miller are on their way to camp. Captain [Timothy] Reves has not yet arrived at Batesville. Report says he (Captain Reves) has gone into Missouri. Capt. John McWherter and 8 other men had an engagement with the enemy at Round Ponds, on the road between Cape Girardeau and Bloomfield, Mo. Captain J. [John McWherter] and the others all belong to this command. An account of the fight is as follows: The above little party, finding that a train of wagons belonging to the enemy were on the road, followed, and when the guard, numbering 16, also the drivers, were all asleep they rushed in on the camp and succeeded in killing and wounding 30. Destroyed the entire train of 65 wagons by fire. They captured 19 horses and 7 pistols, and could have taken any number of horses if they had had men to lead them away, as there were at least 400 head of horses and mules at the camp.

I have had all the boats above and below sunk, as per your order. The boat at Jacksonport has not been sunk, although I had given the orders to sink it; but finding that the enemy had not advanced as I supposed they would when I gave the order, therefore I countermanded it.

The enemy was reported at Augusta, but I learn from my scouts that they are all gone back. My scouts learn that the citizens at Augusta brought in all the produce they possibly could and traded to the enemy, principally cotton. There is but a small force at Bloomfield, Mo. Colonel [S. G.] Kitchen's health is improving slowly.

I am, respectfully,

J. ELLISON,

Lieutenant-Colonel, Commanding Tenth Missouri Cavalry.

Brig. Gen. J. S. MARMADUKE.

P. S.—When the balance of the scout get to camp I will write all the particulars of the above-mentioned engagement, day and date.

[R. D.] KATHREN,

Adjutant.

AUGUST 1–SEPTEMBER 14, 1863.—Advance of the Union forces upon Little Rock, Ark., etc.

SUMMARY OF THE PRINCIPAL EVENTS.

Aug. 1– 8, 1863.—Davidson's cavalry division moves from Wittsburg to Clarendon.
10, 1863.—Steele's column advances from Helena.
13–16, 1863.—Expedition up the White and Little Red Rivers, including engagement (14th) at West Point and skirmish (16th) at Harrison's Landing.
17, 1863.—Skirmish at Grand Prairie.
25, 1863.—Skirmish at Brownsville.
26, 1863.—Skirmish near Bayou Meto.
27, 1863.—Action at Bayou Meto, or Reed's Bridge.
30, 1863.—Skirmish at Shallow Ford, Bayou Meto.
Sept. 2, 1863.—Skirmish near Shallow Ford.
7, 1863.—Skirmish at Ashley's Mills, or Ferry Landing.
10, 1863.—Engagement at Bayou Fourche, and capture of Little Rock.
10–14, 1863.—Price's army retreats to Rockport and Arkadelphia.
12, 1863.—Skirmish near Brownsville.

REPORTS.*

No. 1.—Maj. Gen. John M. Schofield, U. S. Army, commanding Department of the Missouri.

No. 2.—Roster of the "Arkansas expedition," August 31.

No. 3.—Maj. Gen. Frederick Steele, U. S. Army, commanding expedition.

No. 4.—Return of Casualties in the Union forces.

No. 5.—Brig. Gen. John W. Davidson, U. S. Army, commanding Cavalry Division, with congratulatory orders.

No. 6.—Capt. Julius L. Hadley, Twenty-fifth Ohio Battery, Chief of Artillery, of engagement at Bayou Fourche.

No. 7.—Col. Washington F. Geiger, Eighth Missouri Cavalry, commanding First Brigade, of skirmish at Brownsville.

No. 8.—Col. Lewis Merrill, Second Missouri Cavalry, commanding First Brigade, of engagement at Bayou Fourche, and pursuit of the Confederates.

No. 9.—Lieut. Col. John L. Chandler, Seventh Missouri Cavalry, of engagement at Bayou Fourche, and pursuit of the Confederates.

---

*For report of Lieut. George M. Bache, U. S. Navy, of expedition up the White and Little Red Rivers, see Annual Report of the Secretary of the Navy, December 7, 1863.

No. 1.

Report of Maj. Gen. John M. Schofield, U. S. Army, commanding Department of the Missouri.

HEADQUARTERS DEPARTMENT OF THE MISSOURI,
Saint Louis, Mo., September 27, 1863.

COLONEL: I forward herewith official copy of the report of Major-General Steele, commanding the "Arkansas expedition,"* including also the report of Brigadier-General Davidson, commanding the cavalry division.

* That of September 12, p. 474 *et seq.*

This report is a general summary of the operations of General Steele's command, commencing with the organization of the expeditionary force at Helena, and ending with the capture of Little Rock. As soon as General Steele's more detailed report shall be received, I will forward it, with such recommendations as individual merit and services shall seem to have justified.

General Steele's operations have been conducted with marked skill and good judgment, and the importance of his success can hardly be overestimated.

My troops at Fort Smith have already opened communication with Little Rock. All Arkansas and the Indian country west of it are virtually in our possession. Our troops are cordially welcomed by a large proportion of the Arkansas people.

I am, colonel, very respectfully, your obedient servant,

J. M. SCHOFIELD,
Major-General.

Col. E. D. TOWNSEND,
Assistant Adjutant-General, Washington, D. C.

No. 2.

Roster of the "Arkansas Expedition," August 31.

ESCORT.

3d Illinois Cavalry, Company D, Lieut. James K. McLean.
Kane County (Illinois) Cavalry, Lieut. Eben C. Litherland.

FIRST (CAVALRY) DIVISION.

Brig. Gen. JOHN W. DAVIDSON.

First Brigade.

Col. WASHINGTON F. GEIGER.*

2d Missouri, Maj. Garrison Harker.
7th Missouri, Lieut. Col. John L. Chandler.
8th Missouri, Maj. William J. Teed.

Second Brigade.

Col. JOHN M. GLOVER.

10th Illinois, Col. Dudley Wickersham.
1st Iowa, Lieut. Col. Daniel Anderson.
3d Missouri, Maj. Albert D. Glover.

Reserve Brigade.

Col. JOHN F. RITTER.

13th Illinois, Maj. Lothar Lippert.
3d Iowa, Maj. John W. Noble.
32d Iowa Infantry, Maj. Edward H. Mix.
1st Missouri, Col. John F. Ritter.

Artillery.

Capt. JULIUS L. HADLEY.

2d Missouri Light Artillery, Battery K, Lieut. T. S. Clarkson.
2d Missouri Light Artillery, Battery M, Capt. Gustave Stange.
25th Ohio Battery, Capt. Julius L. Hadley.

---

*Succeeded by Col. Lewis Merrill.

SECOND DIVISION.

Col. WILLIAM E. MCLEAN.*

First Brigade.

Col. WILLIAM H. GRAVES.

18th Illinois, Col Daniel H. Brush.
43d Illinois,† Maj. Charles Stephani.
54th Illinois, Col. Greenville M. Mitchell.
61st Illinois, Lieut. Col. Simon P. Ohr.
106th Illinois, Lieut. Col. Henry Yates.
12th Michigan, Lieut. Col. Dwight May.

Second Brigade.

Col. OLIVER WOOD.

126th Illinois, Lieut. Col. Ezra M. Beardsley.
40th Iowa, Lieut. Col. Samuel F. Cooper.
3d Minnesota,† Col. Christopher C. Andrews.
22d Ohio, Lieut. Col. Homer Thrall.
27th Wisconsin, Col. Conrad Krez.

THIRD DIVISION.‡

Brig. Gen. SAMUEL A. RICE.

First Brigade.

Col. CHARLES W. KITTREDGE.

43d Indiana, Lieut. Col. John C. Major.
36th Iowa, Lieut. Col. Francis M. Drake.
77th Ohio, Col. William B. Mason.

Second Brigade.

Col. THOMAS H. BENTON, jr.

29th Iowa, Lieut. Col. Robert F. Patterson.
33d Iowa, Lieut. Col. Cyrus H. Mackey.
28th Wisconsin, Maj. Calvert C. White.

UNATTACHED.

Cavalry Brigade.

Col. POWELL CLAYTON.

1st Indiana, Lieut. Col. Thomas N. Pace.
5th Kansas, Lieut. Col. Wilton A. Jenkins.

Artillery.

Capt. MORTIMER M. HAYDEN.

3d Iowa Battery, Lieut. Melvil C. Wright.
1st Missouri Light Artillery, Battery K, Capt. Stillman O. Fish.
5th Ohio Battery, Lieut. John D. Burner.
11th Ohio Battery, Capt. Frank C. Sands.

True's Brigade. §

Col. JAMES M. TRUE.

49th Illinois, Col. Phineas Pease.
62d Illinois, Lieut. Col. Stephen M. Meeker.
50th Indiana, Lieut. Col. Samuel T. Wells.
27th Iowa, Col. James I. Gilbert.
Vaughn's (Illinois) battery, Capt. Thomas F. Vaughn.

---

* Relieved by Col. Adolph Engelmann, September 6.
† Transferred September 18.
‡ Organized for this expedition from the Thirteenth Division, Sixteenth Army Corps.
§ Third Brigade, Third Division, Sixteenth Army Corps, *en route* from Helena, and not accounted for on the original returns till September 10. On September 13 it was assigned to Kimball's (Second) division, and on the 18th it was designated as the First Brigade of that division.

No. 3.

Reports of Maj. Gen. Frederick Steele, U. S. Army, commanding expedition.

DEVALL'S BLUFF, ARK., *August* 23, 1863.

GENERAL: Having reconnoitered the different routes, I have decided to commence my line of operations at this point, and have moved the depot and hospital here to-day. The site chosen is a plateau (oak opening), high bluff on the river, and sloping on both sides, on one side a deep ravine. The two gunboats which are to remain here can defend the flanks, and an intrenchment can be thrown up in rear which will make the place tolerably secure against any force that will be likely to annoy us while we are pushing the enemy to the front. The buildings here do not amount to much, but there is considerable lumber, and, by sending to Clarendon for more, we can erect tolerable shelter for the sick and the supplies. The sick list is frightful, including many officers. One brigade is commanded by a lieutenant-colonel, two colonels having given up in the last three days. If you do not send re-enforcements I shall very likely meet with a disaster. This is the poorest command that I have ever seen, except the cavalry. More than 1,000 here present are reported unfit for duty, and about one-half of the command proper are absent. Davidson is at Deadman's Lake, about 15 miles this side of Brownsville; he was to reconnoiter the latter place in front to-day. Deserters report that one brigade of Kirby Smith's troops, under Frost, were at Bayou Meto. Everything indicates that the rebels will make a determined resistance at this point. We need four gunboats on this river—one at Saint Charles, two at this point, and one as a convoy. Of those I have now, one is unfit for service and the other three out of repair. White River is at present a better one for the purpose of navigation than the Mississippi; it is falling now, but will rise again next month, and can be depended upon all the time for over 4 feet of water to this point. No matter what steamboatmen say, this is a fact. I refer you to Commander Bache, U. S. Navy, in regard to the facts in the case. No pilot is required. All that is necessary is to keep a boat from running into the banks. With such a base as this, it will be a very easy matter to carry on operations against Little Rock, if proper means be supplied. We hear nothing of General Blunt. Prisoners say General Cooper has fallen back to Little Rock. A Frenchman, from New Orleans, who was at Des Arc, confirms the accounts which I have received from other sources in regard to the strength and intentions of the enemy. He says Marmaduke was peremptorily dismissed the service for allowing our gunboats to capture the two steamers up Little Red.

I have the honor to be, general, very respectfully, your obedient servant,

FRED'K STEELE,
Major-General.

Maj. Gen. STEPHEN A. HURLBUT,
Commanding Sixteenth Army Corps, Memphis, Tenn.

P. S.—I have received notice from Helena that there is a supply train from this command waiting there for an escort. Part of this train was sent from Cape Girardeau, and belongs to Davidson's division. I cannot send an escort. The rebels have destroyed the bridge we built over Big Creek. This train would probably be sufficient transportation for another brigade. I think this command has enough already to keep it supplied from this place.

HEADQUARTERS ARKANSAS EXPEDITION,
Devall's Bluff, Ark., August 26, 1863.

GENERAL: Our advance, under Davidson, has driven Marmaduke's cavalry, about 3,000, out of Brownsville, capturing Colonel Burbridge and some privates. At date of dispatch from Davidson, [J. M.] Glover's brigade was pushing the enemy toward Bayou Meto. Marmaduke has not been dismissed; he was in command.

There is no running water between here and Bayou Meto; there are wells at Brownsville, which will be headquarters of the cavalry division, until the enemy's position can be thoroughly reconnoitered, and an approximate estimate made of his strength.

I was informed by a respectable citizen of Brownsville that their principal fortifications were between Bayou Meto and Little Rock. He (Dr. Wright) also informed me that there was a road which crossed the bayou, west of the one occupied by the enemy, which might, perhaps, be rendered passable for us by some repairs. Until I get a report from the front, giving me the result of the reconnaissance, I shall continue to strengthen this camp, build shelters, and cut the timber, so that the gunboats can have a clear sweep along the ravines on our flanks.

This is a healthy locality; high plateaus, no swamps in the vicinity, and the current in the river rapid. The health of the command has improved perceptibly since our arrival here.

There is a grist-mill and a saw-mill, about 2 miles distant by a good road and 4 by water, which can be put in order by supplying a few deficiencies. This can be done by sending to Des Arc, and breaking up an establishment which has been patronized by the rebel army.

Our lumber has been obtained thus far principally by taking down vacant buildings, including one large church, where secession doctrines have been extensively promulgated.

There are some large crops of corn within a few miles of this, owned by rebels, and we hear of considerable old corn not very far off. There is also considerable beef.

I recommend that some rolling stock be sent for the railroad, which we know to be in good order as far as, and beyond, Brownsville. The telegraph is also nearly complete.

I hope the re-enforcements will come up soon. If the reports which we get continually in regard to the enemy's strength and animus should be confirmed by the reconnaissance, I shall wait for them. I should like very much to have the famous Memphis Brigade, if it should be necessary to send more than a brigade you have already ordered. As I wrote you before, there will be no difficulty in getting supplies up this river. I have been told that there is only one locomotive and but few cars on the railroad, but the wagon road is said to be good. Fort Smith was formerly supplied by this route. I regard the plan of building the road from here to Memphis as impracticable, on account of the difficulty of raising it above the overflow. My opinion is based entirely upon information derived from people who have seen the route at all seasons. If ever the rebels should be routed by us, our cavalry would annihilate them.

I send back all the steamers that brought up supplies except the Hamilton Belle, which is required for getting forage, lumber, &c., and the Sallie List, which is at present needed for the storage of commissary stores.

Very respectfully, general, your obedient servant,

FRED'K STEELE,
Major-General, Commanding.

HEADQUARTERS ARKANSAS EXPEDITION,
Devall's Bluff, Ark., August 31, 1863.

The rebel troops, including Marmaduke's, are positively west of Bayou Meto. They are fortifying 3 miles this side of Little Rock, Price in command, and intend to hold us in check until Kirby Smith collects his forces at Little Rock. I advance to-day.

Very respectfully,

FRED'K STEELE,
Major-General.

Major-General HALLECK,
General-in-Chief.

DEVALL'S BLUFF, ARK., *September* 1, 1863.

DEAR SCHOFIELD: General Hurlbut writes me that he understands my command is in your department. I have received no orders to that effect.

General Grant directed me to report to headquarters Sixteenth Army Corps. Yesterday I sent you a dispatch in reply to the one about Marmaduke. I don't believe there are 100 Confederate soldiers north of White River, in Arkansas. They have collected everything in front of Little Rock. There is good reason to believe that Kirby Smith is collecting all the troops in the Trans-Mississippi Department at Little Rock. He has been heard to say frequently that if he could not hold Little Rock he could not hold Texas.

Davidson with his cavalry drove Walker and Marmaduke from Brownsville across Bayou Meto. Marmaduke was superseded by Walker in command of the cavalry division, for allowing our gunboats to take the two steamers up Little Red River.

Marmaduke is reported wounded at Bayou Meto. My troops are on the march, and I expect to be at Brownsville with my entire force tomorrow. True's brigade crossed at Clarendon yesterday, and will be at Deadman's Lake to-day. There is more water on this route than I had anticipated, such as it is.

Price is intrenched 3 miles this side of Little Rock, and is supposed to have about 14,000 men; his position is covered in front by swamps heavily timbered. As soon as I have reconnoitered his position, I will write you.

My entire force for duty will fall considerably short of 12,000. Many of our men have been taken down with fevers, and chills and fever, lately.

Very truly, yours, in haste,

FRED'K STEELE,
Major-General.

HEADQUARTERS ARKANSAS EXPEDITION,
Little Rock, Ark., September 12, 1863.

GENERAL: I have the honor to submit the following as a summary of the operations which led to the occupation of the capital by the expeditionary army under my command:

On the 31st day of July, I arrived at Helena, and, pursuant to instructions from Major-General Grant, reported by letter to the commander of the Sixteenth Army Corps for instructions relative to the fitting out of an expedition against Little Rock. General Hurlbut placed under my command all the troops at Helena, and the cavalry division under Brigadier-General Davidson, then operating in Arkansas. The garrison at Helena had been re-enforced by two brigades of Kimball's division, which had just arrived from Snyder's Bluff, and were suffering severely from the malarious influences of the Yazoo country. The proportion of sick among the Helena troops was also very large. Three regiments were designated to remain at Helena, and these, with the sick and convalescents of the whole command, were to constitute the garrison of that place. The troops at Helena designated for the expedition amounted to about 6,000 of all arms. There were three six-gun and one four-gun batteries, including six 10-pounder Parrotts. The cavalry (First Indiana and Fifth Kansas), amounted to less than 500 for duty. The First Indiana had three small rifled guns. Davidson reported something less than 6,000 present for duty in his cavalry division, and eighteen pieces of artillery—showing an aggregate of about 12,000 for duty. Brigadier-Generals Kimball and Salomon obtained leave of absence, and the resignation of General Ross was accepted, which left me with but one general officer (Davidson).

The resignation of my assistant adjutant-general was accepted just at this time, and there were no officers of the quartermaster's or subsistence department at Helena, except Captain Allen, assistant commissary of subsistence, and Captain Noble, assistant quartermaster, who were in charge of the stores in the depot. I ordered the establishment of camps for the sick and convalescents, and organized the command in the best manner possible. Davidson pushed on to Clarendon and established a ferry for crossing the troops, corduroying 2 miles of bottom, and laying down the pontoon bridges across the Rock Rae Bayou. On the 10th of August, the Helena troops, organized into a division, under Col. (now Brig. Gen.) S. A. Rice, marched toward Clarendon, with orders to reconstruct the bridges which had been destroyed by the rebels, and to make all necessary repairs on the road, which was in bad condition. Kimball's division, under Colonel McLean, followed next day. The whole command was at Clarendon, and commenced crossing the river on the 17th of August. Before the crossing was effected, I found my operations encumbered by over 1,000 sick. To have established a hospital and depot at this point would have involved the necessity of occupying both sides of the river. Devall's Bluff was a more healthy location, and the route from there to Little Rock possessed many advantages over the other as a line of operations. I therefore ordered all the stores and sick to be sent to Devall's Bluff by water. The enemy had constructed rifle-pits in a commanding position fronting the crossing on Rock Rae Bayou, but, on the approach of Davidson's division, had fallen back, leaving only a picket. This position could easily have been turned by the road leading up from Harris' Ferry.

On the 22d, Davidson was directed to move with his division to Deadman's Lake, and reconnoiter the enemy's position at Brownsville. On the 23d, the rest of the command moved to Devall's Bluff, the transports carrying the sick and stores under convoy of the gunboats. An advantageous site was selected on the bluff for a hospital and depot, and details immediately ordered to throw up intrenchments, cut away the timber on the flanks, to give the gunboats clear range, and to erect sheds, &c.

On the 24th, Davidson advanced to Two Prairie Bayou, and on the 25th continued the march, skirmishing with Marmaduke's cavalry up to

Brownsville, dislodging him at that place, and driving him into his intrenchments at Bayou Meto on the 26th. The attack was renewed on the 27th, and the enemy driven from his works on the bayou, and fired the bridge as he retreated. Davidson was unable to save the bridge, everything having been prepared for its destruction beforehand. The bayou was deep and miry, and the pursuit of the rebels being thus checked, Davidson withdrew to his camp at Brownsville, leaving pickets at the crossings on the bayou. I received information that True's brigade from Memphis would arrive at Clarendon on the 29th, and immediately sent a party to construct a bridge across Rock Rae Bayou, and a ferry-boat to cross the troops over the White River. True crossed on the 30th of August, and on the 1st of September moved up to Deadman's Lake. The advance from Devall's Bluff also commenced on the 1st, the place having been put in such a state of defense that the convalescents and a small detail left there were deemed sufficient to hold it against any force the enemy would be likely to send against it. On the 2d instant, all my available force was concentrated at Brownsville. It had been ascertained that the military road on the south side of Bayou Meto passed through a section impracticable for any military operations—swamp, timber, and entanglements of vines and undergrowth—and was commanded by the enemy's works. I therefore directed Davidson to make a reconnaissance in force around to the enemy's left by way of Austin, and, if practicable, to penetrate his lines and ascertain both his strength and position. Rice's division was ordered forward, to make a diversion in Davidson's favor on Bayou Meto. Rice drove in the enemy's pickets, shelled the woods on the south side of the bayou for several hours, and encamped for the night. In the mean time Davidson pushed his reconnaissance until the numerous roads on his flanks and rear rendered it dangerous for him to proceed any farther. The great length to which it would increase our line of communication with our base rendered it impracticable for us to attack the enemy on his left flank. This reconnaissance occupied two days.

By this time I had collected information in regard to the road leading by Shallow Ford and Ashley's Mills to the Arkansas, and the right of the enemy's works, which determined me to take that route. The march to the front was resumed on the 6th. Here we found ourselves again encumbered with a large number of sick—near 700. True's brigade and Ritter's brigade of cavalry were left to guard the supply train and the sick. On the 7th, we reached the Arkansas, near Ashley's Mills. At this point Davidson's cavalry, in advance, had a sharp skirmish with the enemy. The 8th and 9th were employed in reconnaissance, repairing the road back to Bayou Meto, and in bringing up the sick and the supply train, with the two brigades left at Brownsville.

I had now definitely determined upon a plan of attack. Davidson was directed to lay the pontoon bridge at an eligible point, throw his division across the Arkansas River and move directly on Little Rock, threatening the enemy's right flank and rear, while I moved with the rest of the force on the north bank and assailed the right of his works. During the night of the 9th, Davidson made his dispositions for crossing the Arkansas, and on the morning of the 10th had the pontoon bridge laid. The Second Division was ordered to report to him at daylight, to assist in covering his crossing. The bridge was placed in a bend of the river, and the ground on the south side was so completely swept by Davidson's artillery that the enemy could not plant a battery in any position from which he could interrupt the crossing.

Two regiments of infantry passed over the river to drive the enemy's skirmishers out of the woods, and the cavalry division passed on without serious interruption until they reached Bayou Fourche, where the enemy were drawn up in line to receive them. The rebels held their position obstinately, until our artillery on the opposite side of the river was opened upon their flank and rear, when they gave way and were steadily pushed back by Davidson, the artillery constantly playing upon them from the other side of the river. Our two columns marched nearly abreast on either side of the Arkansas. Volumes of smoke in the direction of Little Rock indicated to us that the rebels had evacuated their works on the north side of the river, and were burning their pontoon bridges. Heavy clouds of dust moving down toward Davidson, on the other side of the river, made me apprehensive that the enemy contemplated falling upon him with his entire force. He was instructed, in such event, to form on the beach, where his flanks could be protected by our artillery on the other side, and where aid might be sent him by a ford. But they were in full retreat. Marmaduke's cavalry only were disputing Davidson's entry of the city. The rebels had fired three pontoon bridges laid across the Arkansas at the city, and several railroad cars. Two locomotives were also on fire, but were saved by us; part of the pontoons were also saved. Six steamboats were entirely destroyed by fire, and we are informed that Price intended to have blown up the arsenal, but was pressed so close that he failed in this.

Our cavalry was too much exhausted to pursue the enemy's retreating columns far on the evening of the 10th. Next morning, Merrill's and Clayton's brigades renewed the chase and followed them 20 miles, taking a number of prisoners and causing the enemy to destroy a part of his train. Little Rock was formally surrendered by the municipal authorities on the evening of the 10th. Price had undoubtedly intended to give us battle in his intrenchments, but was entirely surprised by our movement across the Arkansas, and did not suspect it until after the pontoon bridge was laid. When it was reported to him that our infantry were crossing, he took it for granted that our whole force was moving to cut off his retreat to Arkadelphia. I have been assured by citizens that General Cabell, with about 4,000 troops from Fort Smith, had joined Price on his retreat, he having failed to reach here in time to assist in the defense of the place. I marched from Ashley's Mills on the morning of the 10th, with not more than 7,000 troops, having parked the trains and left a strong guard to defend them and the sick.

The operations of this army from the time that I commenced organizing it, at Helena, has occupied exactly forty days.

Our entire loss, in killed, wounded, and prisoners, will not exceed 100.* The enemy's is much greater, especially in prisoners; at least 1,000.

I shall reserve the list of casualties and my special recommendations for a future communication. However, I will say that Davidson and his cavalry division deserve the highest commendation.

I inclose Brigadier-General Davidson's report.

Very respectfully, your obedient servant,

FRED'K STEELE,
Major-General, Commanding.

Major-General SCHOFIELD,
Commanding Department of the Missouri.

---

* But see revised statement, p. 482.

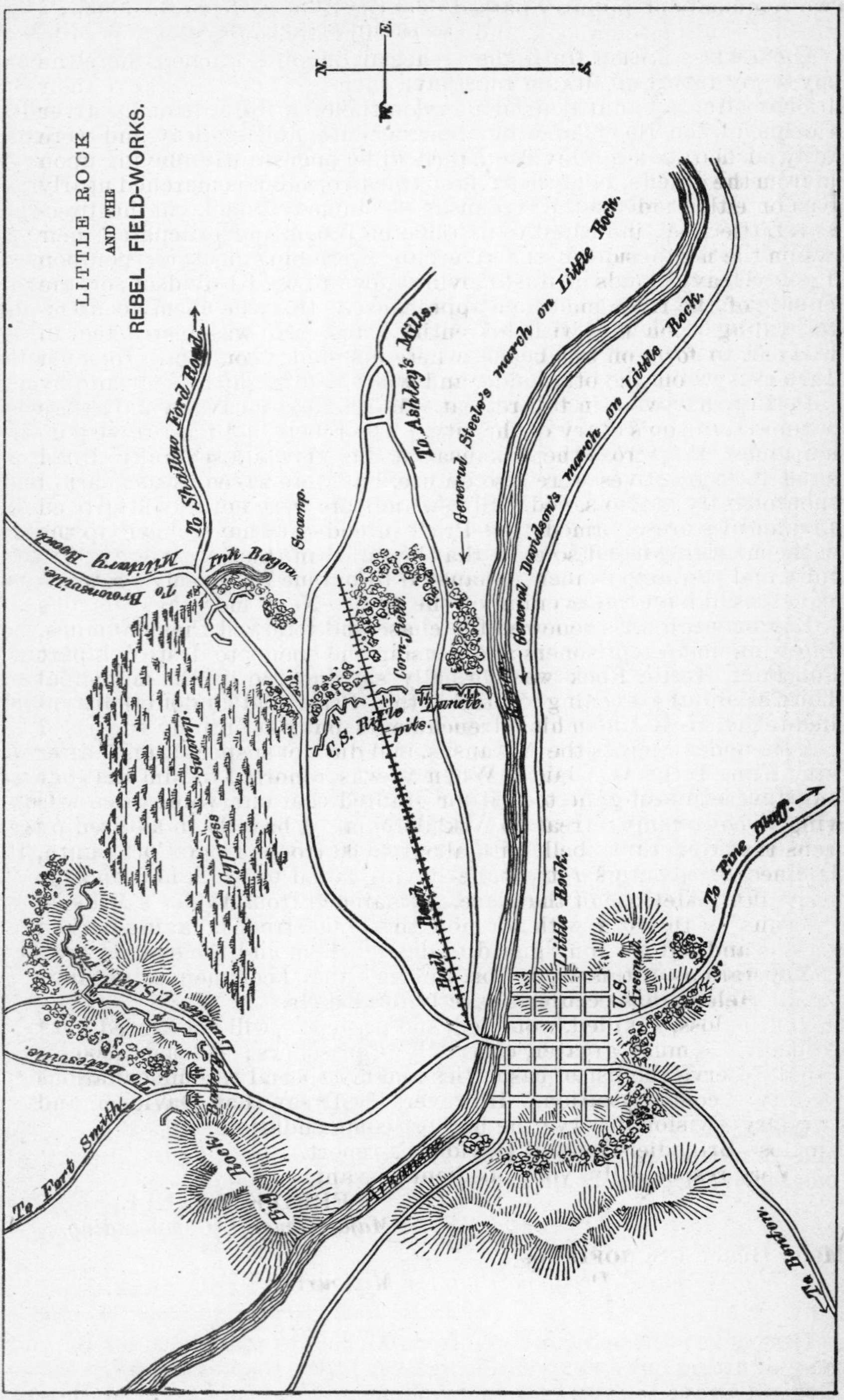
LITTLE ROCK
AND THE
REBEL FIELD-WORKS.
N.
E.
S.
W.
To Shallow Ford Road.
To Ashley's Mills
General Steele's march on Little Rock.
General Davidson's march on Little Rock.
To Brownsville, Military Road
Ink Bayou
Swamp.
Corn-field
C.S. Rifle pits.
Lunette.
Cypress Swamp.
Rail Road
Little Rock
U.S. Arsenal
To Pine Bluff.
To Batesville.
C.S. Rifle pits
Big Rock
Arkansas
To Fort Smith
To Benton

HEADQUARTERS ARMY OF ARKANSAS,
Little Rock, Ark., September 22, 1863.

GENERAL: I have the honor to submit the following, as supplementary to my report of the 12th instant:

Soon after my arrival at Helena, I received a letter from Commander Phelps, of the Navy, offering the gunboats, under Lieutenant Bache, lying at the mouth of White River, to co-operate with me. I wrote to Lieutenant Bache, requesting him to make a reconnaissance up White River. He met General Davidson at Clarendon, and, having received a part of [G. A.] Eberhart's battalion on board, proceeded up the river, entered Little Red, and, in the face of Marmaduke's cavalry, destroyed a pontoon bridge and captured two steamers, the Kaskaskia and Sugg. Subsequently, he made an expedition from Devall's Bluff to Augusta, and captured Colonel Matlock, C. S. Army, and broke up a recruiting party at that point. Commander Phelps and Lieutenant Bache have done everything in their power to further the object of the expedition.

It is reported that the rebel force at the fight on Bayou Fourche was composed of the brigades of Tappan and Fagan and the cavalry division under Marmaduke. At the city the rebels abandoned five iron guns, including two siege pieces disabled by us at Arkansas Post, and subsequently patched up by them. At the arsenal we found a small amount of stores. There were about 3,000 pounds of powder (assorted) in the magazine in good condition. Merrill destroyed a portion of Price's train and captured some prisoners, but the pursuit was not as vigorous as it should have been.

I recommend for the favorable consideration of the Government the following-named officers: Brig. Gen. J. W. Davidson, U. S. Volunteers; Col. F. H. Manter, Thirty-second Missouri Infantry; Col. J. M. Glover, Third Missouri Cavalry; Col. J. F. Ritter, First Missouri Cavalry, and Lieut. Col. H. C. Caldwell, Third Iowa Cavalry.

I am under obligations to the following officers for valuable services, viz: First Lieut. G. O. Sokalski, Second Cavalry, U. S. Army, acting assistant adjutant-general; Capt. Charles Scammon, Ninth Illinois Cavalry, aide-de camp; Capt. A. H. Ryan, Seventeenth Illinois Infantry, aide-de-camp; First Lieut. F. Summers, acting engineer, and Capt. B. O. Carr, assistant quartermaster.

Very respectfully, general, your obedient servant,

FRED'K STEELE,
Major-General.

Maj. Gen. JOHN M. SCHOFIELD,
Commanding Department of the Missouri.

[Indorsement.]

HEADQUARTERS DEPARTMENT OF THE MISSOURI,
Saint Louis, November 3, 1863.

Respectfully forwarded to the Adjutant-General of the Army. The officers named by Major-General Steele have done gallant and meritorious service. I concur in General Steele's recommendation.

J. M. SCHOFIELD,
Major-General.

HEADQUARTERS,
Little Rock, Ark., September 23, 1863.

GENERAL: On being ordered from Vicksburg to Helena, for the purpose of fitting out an expedition against Little Rock, I was directed by General Grant to report for instructions to the commander of the Sixteenth Army Corps. General Hurlbut designated the troops which were to constitute my command, and gave me general directions in regard to the expedition. Before I left Devall's Bluff, he wrote me that I was under command of General Schofield, whom I had regarded as my junior. I immediately wrote to Schofield on this subject, and informed him that I had received no orders placing me under his command, and that General Grant had directed me to report to Hurlbut. Subsequently, I received orders from Hurlbut to report to Schofield. My report of the operations of the campaign which terminated with the capture of Little Rock, was addressed to Schofield. I sent you a dispatch immediately on entering the city.

After we had occupied the place for nine days, I received a letter from Schofield proposing a plan for the campaign. This was the first advice I had received from him on the subject. It was announced in the newspapers that he had gone to Kansas, and it was therefore evident that he could not communicate with me for some time to come. I thought it important you should be informed immediately in regard to the status of affairs in Arkansas, and some things were required here at once. I have, therefore, addressed several communications to General Hurlbut, who is in telegraphic communication with you, and within supporting distance of me. In fact, I have kept him constantly advised in regard to my movements and the wants of my command, and he has manifested a disposition to render every assistance in his power. I am also greatly indebted to General [J. W.] Davidson for the energy, perseverance, intelligence, and gallantry with which he has executed my orders. Col. F. H. Manter, Thirty-second Missouri Infantry, also deserves especial mention as acting chief of my staff. The enemy's defenses, covering the city on the north bank of the river, were very formidable. I will send a drawing delineating them.* Price seems not to have considered the possibility of our crossing the Arkansas and getting in his rear until our arrangements for the movement were completed, or nearly so. On being informed that his flank was turned, he replied that the Yankees were not going to entrap him like they did Pemberton, and immediately gave the order to retreat. Fagan's and Tappan's brigades and Marmaduke's cavalry division were sent to hold us in check until they could get their train well on the road. This is the force Davidson's cavalry division encountered on Fourche Bayou, and which our artillery played upon from the other side of the river. A clerk at Price's headquarters informs me that the rebel force amounted to over 20,000 on paper, and that they had about 12,000 fit for duty on the 10th instant, the day we entered the city. This clerk was a tutor in the family of Mr. Bertrand, the first man in this place, and a Crittenden Union man; and I regard his statement as perfectly reliable. The pontoon bridges were broken and burning, and I could not get the infantry across the river in time to pursue the retreating rebels. The pursuit by the cavalry, under Merrill, on the 11th, I regret to say, was not as vigorous as I expected it would be. If I could have followed Price with my whole force, I have no doubt but that his army could have been dispersed in two days. As it was, his troops were greatly demoralized, and deserted almost by regiments. It is represented to me by citizens that they are scattered over the country in every direction. Many have come in and voluntarily taken the oath of allegiance, and gone to their homes. Some have enlisted in our service and others have joined companies of Union men who have banded together for self-protection. Organizations of this sort are daily presenting themselves at my headquarters and beg-

---

* See p. 478.

ging for arms and ammunition. Marmaduke's men have been going about the country south of this, disguised as Federal soldiers, hanging Union men, and committing depredations upon their property. I have in some instances issued captured arms and ammunition to the Union men on their producing the most undoubted proof in regard to their character. It is my opinion that several regiments of good troops could be raised in Arkansas within a short time, for the purpose of putting down guerrillas and operating against the rebel army, if it should be required of them. Near Batesville the Union men have organized, and are sending out scouts to disarm the deserters from Price's army. Mr. Padgett, a member of the Legislature, who has been a fugitive for over a year, is about to return to his home in Independence County, and wishes authority to raise a regiment. There are about 50 of his people here now. Raising regiments, of course, involves the necessity of arming and equipping them. The people in this State have been driven to desperation, and thousands who have been in the rebel army are now represented as being anxious to take up arms in favor of the Federal Government. I have been informed that there were many thousand captured arms at Memphis. There was a large amount of powder captured in the arsenal here. Price intended to have blown it up, but did not have time. The penitentiary escaped for the same reason. I have disposed of my cavalry force in such a manner as to keep the rebels at some distance south of the Arkansas. Very seldom that any of Marmaduke's cavalry, who stick to their cause with more tenacity than any of the rest of Price's army, are seen north of Saline River. Two regiments are posted at Pine Bluff, two at Benton, and two at Brownsville. Of the latter, three battalions are required to guard the railroad bridges on Bayou Meto, and one is posted at Austin. This disposition prevents a deal of scouting, and gives the horses a chance to recuperate, which is very necessary, as they were nearly broken down. In fact, most of our cavalry ought to be remounted. I have ordered one regiment to reconnoiter as close as possible to Arkadelphia, where Price's army is supposed to be. Part of Marmaduke's cavalry is reported at Rockport, 22 miles from Benton. The people who have committed themselves in favor of the Federal Government here are quite alarmed at a report that Kirby Smith and Price have united their forces and are coming back on us. Stevenson and Crocker withdrew their divisions from Ouachita and Red Rivers at the very time they were most needed to make a demonstration. It was known at Little Rock that they had retired several days before I reached here. McPherson sent me a division under supposition that I was very much in need of re-enforcements. About the time they reached Helena, Hurlbut heard of the fall of Little Rock, and stopped them there, subject to my orders. I presume it is not expected that I will order this division forward, except in a case of emergency. I do not know whether it is intended that I shall follow up Price now, or whether it is expected that I will only hold the line of the Arkansas for the present. I shall soon have supplies enough here to enable me to make a forward movement. The railroad is now in operation to Devall's Bluff, and there is an abundance of corn in the valley of the Arkansas. There are three good grist-mills in operation at this place, and several more in the vicinity. It has been reported to me that there is considerable wheat in the country, and beef enough for some time to come. There is, from all accounts, a vast amount of cotton on Ouachita, Red, and Arkansas Rivers. A delegation of citizens from Pine Bluff waited on me and expressed a great desire that trade should be opened soon, that they might save their cotton from the burners that are dashing in upon them occasionally. The Union people all appear anxious to have a provisional government established at once. Colonel Cloud, of Blunt's command, has been here. His command is at Dardanelle. He says the people in the high lands are all loyal to the United States. He wishes to get supplies from here. With 6,000 more infantry, I think I could drive Smith and Price into Mexico.

Very respectfully, general, your obedient servant,

FRED'K STEELE,
Major-General.

Major-General HALLECK,
Commander-in-Chief, U. S. Armies.

No. 4.

Return of Casualties in the Union forces.

[Compiled from nominal list of casualties, returns, &c.]

Event and command.	Killed.		Wounded.		Captured or missing.		
	Officers.	Enlisted men.	Officers.	Enlisted men.	Officers.	Enlisted men.	Aggregate.
Skirmish near Searcy, August 14:							
32d Iowa		2	1	5			8
Skirmish at Grand Prairie, August 17:							
10th Illinois Cavalry				1			1
Skirmish near Bayou Meto, August 26:							
2d Missouri Cavalry (Lovejoy's howitzer battery)		1					1
Action at Bayou Meto, August 27:							
10th Illinois Cavalry	*1	1		6			8
1st Iowa Cavalry		2	1	25			28
3d Iowa Cavalry (Clarkson's Missouri battery)				2			2
32d Iowa Infantry		1		2			3
3d Missouri Cavalry		2		2			4
Total action at Bayou Meto	1	6	1	37			45
Skirmish at Shallow Ford, Bayou Meto, August 30:							
1st Missouri Cavalry			1	4			5
Skirmish at Ashley's Mills (Bear-Skin Lake), or Ferry Landing, September 7:							
2d Missouri Cavalry		1		3			4
Engagement at Bayou Fourche, September 10:							
10th Illinois Cavalry		1	3	31			35
1st Iowa Cavalry		1	1	3			5
2d Missouri Cavalry (Lovejoy's howitzer battery)		3	1	7		1	12
3d Missouri Cavalry	†1	1		1			3
8th Missouri Cavalry				14			14
Illinois Light Artillery, Vaughn's battery				2			2
2d Missouri Light Artillery, Battery K				1			1
Total engagement at Bayou Fourche	1	6	5	59		1	72
Skirmish near Little Rock, September 11:							
7th Missouri Cavalry				1			1
Grand total	2	16	8	110		1	137

* Lieut. John P. Kavanaugh.

† Lieut. Herbert Reed.

No. 5.

Reports of Brig. Gen. John W. Davidson, U. S. Army, commanding Cavalry Division, with congratulatory orders.

HDQRS. CAVALRY DIVISION, DEPT. OF THE MISSOURI,
Clarendon, Ark., August 15, 1863.

GENERAL: I have the honor to report to you that the expedition which I sent up the river, consisting of two gunboats, under Captain Bache, U. S. Navy, and a battalion of the Thirty-second Iowa Infantry, under Maj. G. A. Eberhart, and of which I advised you by letter of the 11th instant, has returned completely successful. The gunboats captured in the Little Red the two rebel steamers, Kaskaskia and Tom Sugg, in complete running order, and destroyed the bridge of flats, or pontoon bridge, over which the ubiquitous Marmaduke had crossed the greater part of his cavalry to the south side of Little Red. This was near Searcy. Major Eberhart lost 2 men killed and 5 wounded, and one of the naval officers was wounded slightly. This infantry was attached to my division as the guard to my batteries.

The information brought by the expedition is of a very positive character. Kirby Smith is at Little Rock, and the rebels are concentrating and throwing up rifle-pits at Bayou Meto, 12 miles this side of Little Rock, their left resting upon Brownsville. Marmaduke, who keeps Missouri in a fright, is positively on the south side of Little Red, where I believed him to be, and on his way, with part of his cavalry dismounted, to join Price.

I think, my dear general, every hour is precious to us now, and that you should have another brigade, at least, of infantry. We are rich in artillery. I am endeavoring to gain all needful information for you. I would be obliged to you to inform Schofield of our success, so that he may not be apprehensive of a raid into Missouri.

We must have water-kegs sent out; one for each ambulance and wagon, if possible.

Very truly, your obedient servant,

J. W. DAVIDSON,
Brigadier-General, Commanding.

Major-General STEELE,
Commanding Army of Arkansas.

[Indorsement.]

HEADQUARTERS ARKANSAS EXPEDITION,
Camp on Big Cypress, August 16, 1863.

Respectfully forwarded to Headquarters Department of the Tennessee. The original was forwarded to General Hurlbut. I agree with Davidson that we ought to have at least another brigade. The rebels know exactly what force I have, and if they make a stand, they will be well prepared for it. I shall be at Camden to-morrow morning.

FRED'K STEELE,
Major-General.

HDQRS. CAVALRY DIVISION, DEPT. OF THE MISSOURI,
Camp near Bayou Meto, Ark., September 1, 1863.

COLONEL: I have the honor to recount to you the operations of this division from August 1, 1863, up to the present date.

On the date above mentioned, August 1, the cavalry division left

Wittsburg *en route* for Clarendon, Ark.; arrived at the L'Anguille River on the 3d. On the 4th, the supply train was sent from that point to Helena for the purpose of procuring supplies, while the command continued its march. On the 6th, the Tenth Illinois and Third Missouri Cavalry were detached, under command of Colonel [Dudley] Wickersham, of the Tenth Illinois Cavalry, and sent to Cotton Plant to cut up Walker's brigade, which was reported at that place. It was found this brigade had crossed White River. On the 8th of August, the division arrived at Clarendon. The next day the gunboats, sent for by me from Wittsburg, came up White River to Clarendon, under command of Captain Bache, U. S. Navy.

On the 13th, an expedition, consisting of three gunboats, under Captain Bache, having Major [G. A.] Eberhart's battalion, of the Thirty-second Iowa Infantry, on board, went up the Little Red to Searcy. This expedition returned on the 15th, having captured two rebel steamers, in good running order (the Kaskaskia and Tom Sugg), and having destroyed the bridge of flats over which Marmaduke crossed his command, and within 3 miles of his (then) headquarters. Subsequently information has been received that, among others, Colonel Gilkey, C. S. Army, was killed by the troops of this expedition.

On the 17th, General Steele arrived at Clarendon and assumed command of the Arkansas expedition, of which the cavalry division now forms a part. The cavalry division crossed White River, August 18, having been detached to the front by Major-General Steele, to ascertain the position and intention of the enemy.

On the 23d, the reserve brigade, Colonel [J. F.] Ritter commanding, was detached to hunt up Walker, said to be camped in observation from 7 to 10 miles on our right front. Walker had fallen back on Ritter's approach. The whole division marched on the 25th (the baggage train being left in charge of Lieutenant-Colonel [James] Stuart, with his regiment, the Tenth Illinois Cavalry, at Bayou Two Prairies), and encountered Marmaduke's and Walker's troops posted at Brownsville, with two pieces of artillery. The enemy were driven out after a short action by the First Brigade, under Colonel [W. F.] Geiger, and Hadley's battery, and pursued 9 miles, when, night coming on, the brigade returned to Brownsville. Among the prisoners captured this day was Colonel Burbridge, C. S. Army, commanding a brigade. Major Rogers, Merrill's Horse, commanding line of skirmishers, deserves special mention.

The next morning a reconnaissance, consisting of the First Iowa and Third Missouri Cavalry, of the Second Brigade, and Clarkson's battery, was pushed out toward Bayou Meto, on the main Little Rock road. The enemy were found posted in force at a position about 9 miles beyond Brownsville, estimated by Colonel [J. M.] Glover, commanding, at 6,000 strong, who, after examining their position, returned. On this day the baggage train, under Lieutenant-Colonel Stuart, moved up to the command.

The whole division marched again on the 27th, leaving the baggage parked in depot camp at Brownsville, under charge of Lieutenant-Colonel [J. L.] Chandler, with his regiment (Seventh Missouri Cavalry) and Lovejoy's battery. The enemy was found posted in the position of the day before. The ground not admitting of the display of more troops, the Second Brigade was brought into action, under Colonel Glover, commanding, in the following order: Line of skirmishers—one battalion Tenth Illinois Cavalry, under Lieutenant-Colonel Stuart; Major Eberhart's battalion, Thirty-second Iowa Infantry, on the left; the Third Missouri Cavalry (dismounted), armed with carbines and rifles, on the right; Clarkson's four-gun battery and a section of Hadley's in the center, supported by two dismounted squadrons of the First Iowa Cavalry, the balance of the First Iowa and the remaining battalion of the Tenth Illinois forming the second line. The Reserve and First Brigades were directed to hold themselves in readiness to move up to the support of the other troops in case an opportunity should occur for employing them. The enemy were driven from this position and a second one, until finally they were met in their intrenched camp, three-quarters of a mile this side of the bridge, over the Bayou Meto. After a sharp action they were driven out of their rifle-pits and across the Bayou Meto. A dash of the First Iowa Cavalry, under my orders, gallantly led by Lieutenant-Colonel [D.] Anderson, commanding, under fire of the enemy's battery and sharpshooters lining the opposite bank, failed to save the bridge, which had been set on fire by the enemy, everything having been prepared beforehand for that purpose. Our batteries engaged those of the enemy, and the skirmishers on both sides were busy for about an hour and a half, when, finding no further good could be accomplished (the bridge over the bayou being destroyed and the ground improper for cavalry), the division returned to the camp of its baggage. Our loss in this action was 7 killed and 35 wounded;* that of the enemy is variously reported, and is not at this date known. Among their wounded were Brigadier-General Marmaduke, commanding a division, and Captain Anderson and two other members of Major General Walker's staff.

On the 29th, another reconnaissance was made, on a different road, to the left, consisting of a battalion of Merrill's Horse, and one battalion of the Eighth Missouri Cavalry, and a section of Lovejoy's battery, under Colonel Geiger, commanding First Brigade, accompanied by Lieutenant-Colonel [H. C.] Caldwell, chief of staff, 12 miles beyond Brownsville, without discovering any force of the enemy.

On the 30th, Ritter's brigade was ordered to follow up this reconnaissance, on the same road, having with it Stange's battery of mountain howitzers. The enemy were encountered in some force beyond the Bayou Meto, 8 miles from Brownsville, evidently making a reconnaissance. They were driven, with sharp skirmishing, by Colonel Ritter, 8 miles, and until the ground became totally unsuitable for the action of cavalry; the enemy leaving 9 of their killed upon the field. Ritter's loss was 1 captain and 4 men wounded.

Information obtained from a wounded prisoner shows the enemy to be intrenched about 3 miles this side of Little Rock, with a force of 11,000 infantry and 4,500 cavalry, the infantry consisting of the brigades of Frost, Fagan, Parsons, McRae, and Tappan, and the cavalry of the divisions of Marmaduke and Walker. Their artillery is variously estimated from thirty to fifty guns. All subsequent information from captured citizens, spies, and deserters confirms this statement in a greater or less degree.

On the 1st of September, the infantry began to arrive, preparatory to the whole army taking up its line of march. The railroad and the three bridges over the Bayou Meto are preserved uninjured. The brigade commanders, Colonels Glover, Ritter, and Geiger (Merrill being sick), especially deserve commendation throughout these operations. All my staff—Lieutenant-Colonel [H. C.] Caldwell, Third Iowa Cavalry, acting chief of staff; Major [William] Thompson, First Iowa Cavalry, division inspector; Captain [W. W.] Cantine, subsistence department; Lieut.

*But see revised statement, p. 482.

A. S. Montgomery, Seventh Missouri Cavalry, acting assistant adjutant-general, and Lieutenants [J. M.] Sprague, [G. K.] McGunnegle, and [J. R.] Gray, aides-de-camps, and Capt. Anton Gerster, chief engineer (Captain [B. O.] Carr, chief quartermaster, was transferred to the staff of Major-General Steele, August 18, and merited my warmest approval while with me)—have efficiently aided me, especially Lieutenant-Colonel Caldwell, Third Iowa Cavalry, whose accomplishments and gallantry as a soldier deserve acknowledgment.

Recapitulation of the actions of Brownsville, Bayou Meto, and Shallow Ford, August 25, 27, and 30.

Officers killed	1
Officers wounded	2
Enlisted men killed	8
Enlisted men wounded	49
Total	60

I am, sir, your most obedient servant,

J. W. DAVIDSON,
Brigadier-General, Commanding.

Col. F. H. MANTER,
Chief of Staff, Arkansas Expedition.

(Same to assistant adjutant-general, Department of the Missouri.)

P. S.—The battalion (Thirty-second Iowa Infantry), four companies strong, Major Eberhart commanding, deserves the greatest praise for having marched 400 miles with this division, sharing in all its labors and actions. I have to especially thank Colonel Wickersham, Tenth Illinois Cavalry, who left his sick bed, although too unwell to take command of his regiment, and accompanied it during the action of the 27th.

—

HDQRS. CAVALRY DIV., DEPT. OF THE MISSOURI,
Little Rock, Ark., September 12, 1863.

COLONEL: I have the honor to report the operations of my division on the 10th instant, the day of the capture of Little Rock.

The plan agreed upon by General Steele the preceding day was that he, with the whole infantry force, should move up the north bank of the Arkansas, directly upon the enemy's works, while my cavalry division should force the passage of the river, move up the south bank, and assail the city in the rear. All necessary arrangements were made that night. Lieutenant-Colonel Caldwell, Captains [J. L.] Hadley and [Anton] Gerster, of my staff, worked all night at the cutting of the steep bank of the river, the location of the batteries, and the laying of the bridge. A division of infantry, under Colonel Engelmann, was placed temporarily at my disposition, and was in position above the crossing at daylight. So also were Hadley's and Stange's batteries and the Fifth and Eleventh Ohio. Merrill's and Glover's brigades were massed out of sight, behind the crossing, at 8 a. m., and the laying of the pontoon bridge was completed at that hour. Ritter's brigade, with Clarkson's battery, was ordered to make a demonstration 4 miles below, at Buck's Ford, then held by the enemy. The passage was effected by 11 a. m., all three brigades crossing at the same point, the opposition of the enemy not lasting fifteen minutes under the concentrated fire of our batteries.

No further opposition was met with by my division until we reached Fourche Bayou, 5 miles from Little Rock. Here we found the enemy, consisting of Marmaduke's cavalry, dismounted, and Tappan's brigade of infantry, with two batteries, strongly posted.

A sharp fight of Glover's brigade on one road and Merrill's on another, leading into the main one, during which the Second Brigade lost two howitzers, drove the enemy from this position toward the city. Every advantageous foot of ground from this point onward was warmly contested by them, my cavalry dismounting and taking it afoot in the timber and corn-fields. I had previously sent an officer of my escort, Lieutenant Armstrong, with a guidon, to follow along the bank of the river to mark the progress of my column to General Steele. The fire of his batteries from the opposite bank, progressively, was of infinite service to us.

My advance was here somewhat slow, from the fact that the enemy, finding themselves threatened in rear, evacuated their works in front of General Steele, and I did not know at what moment their whole force might be thrown upon me. I received a message from General Steele in such event to withdraw my horses under the bluff bank of the river on the bar, and his batteries would protect my flanks. Finding, however, that the opposition of the enemy was not stubborn enough to warrant the belief that they were all in front of me, I ordered a vigorous advance of Glover's brigade, and when they became exhausted within 2 miles of the city, threw Ritter's brigade and Stange's howitzers, supported by two squadrons of the First Iowa Cavalry, under the gallant Captain Jenks, into the city and on the heels of the enemy, saber in hand. At 7 p. m. the capital of Arkansas was formally surrendered by the acting civil authorities, and the United States arsenal, uninjured, with what stores remained in it, was repossessed.

Later in the evening, General Steele, whose forces had entered the works on the opposite side of the river, came over, the enemy not being able to entirely destroy their bridge of boats.

A column was organized under Colonels Merrill and Clayton to pursue vigorously the next morning.

My loss does not exceed, as far as known, 60 killed and wounded. That of the enemy is not known. Among their killed is Colonel [S.] Corley, of Dobbin's former regiment.

My whole staff—Lieutenant-Colonel Caldwell, Captains Hadley and Gerster, Lieutenants Montgomery and McGunnegle, Gray and Sprague, and Surgeon Smith, Quartermaster Johnston, and Captain Thompson, commissary of subsistence—served me faithfully throughout the day. The brigade commanders, especially Colonel Glover, Second Brigade, deserve honorable mention. Colonel Glover deserves his promotion as a general officer. Lieutenant-Colonel Caldwell, whose untiring devotion and energy never flag during the night nor day, deserves, for his gallantry and varied accomplishments as a cavalry officer, promotion to the rank of a general officer. Beyond these, I must refer to the reports of brigade commanders, herewith inclosed, for the many cases of individual good judgment and gallantry displayed.

I am, sir, your obedient servant,

J. W. DAVIDSON,
Brigadier-General.

Col. F. H. MANTER, *Chief of Staff.*

GENERAL ORDERS, No. 62. } HDQRS. CAV. DIV., DEPT. OF THE MISSOURI, *Little Rock, Ark., September* 13, 1863.

Soldiers of the cavalry division! I congratulate you that your long, weary march is at length terminated by victory. Little Rock, the capital of the State of Arkansas, the key of the Trans-Mississippi Department, is in our hands. The United States arsenal, uninjured, is repossessed. The feet of the rebel army, who, but a day ago, filed with downcast heads through the streets of this city, will tread the sands of the Arkansas no more.

But, comrades, you have gained two victories on the same day. Though flushed with success, though entering this city when the darkness of night would have covered up misdeeds, though your passions were stirred that our soldiers were shot from their saddles within the suburbs of the city, no outrage upon its defenseless inhabitants has stained your hands. I thank you from the bottom of my heart. Your conduct has more than repaid me for many an anxious day and sleepless night. For you, may there be continuous success wherever it may be our lot to go. For me, I have no higher aim and ask no greater honor than to lead such men.

J. W. DAVIDSON,
Brigadier-General, Commanding.

No. 6.

Report of Capt. Julius L. Hadley, Twenty-fifth Ohio Battery, Chief of Artillery, of engagement at Bayou Fourche.

LITTLE ROCK, ARK., *November* 19, 1863.

COLONEL: I have the honor to forward the report of the chief of artillery of my division, of the operations of the batteries of the division on the 10th of September. This report has been delayed until now, because Captain Hadley was absent on special business at Saint Louis. I beg it may be forwarded, to accompany my own report of the operations of that day, as it shows the conduct of a gallant officer (Lieutenant Lovejoy) in a proper light.

I am, colonel, your most obedient servant,

J. W. DAVIDSON,
Brigadier-General, Commanding.

Col. F. H. MANTER, *Chief of Staff.*

[Inclosure.]

OFFICE OF CHIEF OF ARTILLERY, CAVALRY DIVISION,
DEPARTMENT OF THE MISSOURI,
Little Rock, Ark., September 16, 1863.

GENERAL: I have the honor to submit the following report of the operations of the batteries of the division in the action of the 10th of September, resulting in the capture of the city of Little Rock:

In obedience to your verbal orders, I proceeded, on the night of the 9th of September, to arrange the artillery at my disposal to protect the construction of the pontoon bridge across the Arkansas River at the point selected for crossing, and to cover the crossing of the cavalry division to the south side of the river. The Twenty-fifth Ohio Battery, Stange's and Lovejoy's howitzers, and Sands' Eleventh Ohio Battery were posted on each side of the bridge, around the semi-circular bend of the river at that point, in such a manner as to concentrate the fire of twenty guns on any point from which the bridge or crossing could be assailed by the enemy.

Clarkson's battery was sent to cover the feigned crossing of Colonel Ritter's brigade, at the ford 3 miles below the point selected for the bridge. This ford was defended by a rebel battery of four guns, posted behind a breastwork of cotton bales, and supported by a large force of cavalry dismounted.

The action at the ford commenced shortly after daylight, and continued about two hours, resulting in the retreat of the rebels from their position at this point; Lieutenant Clarkson having, with his four guns, posted in plain open ground, at a distance of less than 900 yards, nearly destroyed their cotton defenses, and compelled their battery to abandon its position with considerable loss.

About 8 a. m. the enemy moved a battery of four guns into position in the woods, about 800 yards from the bridge, and opened fire on the bridge with solid shot, hoping to destroy it. Before the smoke of the first discharge of their guns had scarcely reached the tops of the trees, which concealed their movements, twenty guns belched forth from their concealment on the north side of the river a stream of shell into the midst of their battery, compelling it to retire disabled, after firing only three shots, entirely harmless to us. This ended the opposition to our crossing. Immediately after the crossing of the infantry, for the purpose of taking possession of the woods on the opposite shore, Captain Stange, with his command of eight howitzers, including Lovejoy's, was ordered to cross and report to the commanding officer of the infantry on the south side of the river, until the arrival of Colonel Glover, commanding Second Brigade, cavalry division, when he would report with his command to Colonel Glover. This order was disobeyed, and Captain Stange moved forward toward Little Rock with his command, without any support, exposing his entire command to capture, and was stopped by Lieutenant-Colonel [H. C.] Caldwell, chief of staff, who overtook him over 1 mile ahead of the command, and peremptorily ordered him back with his command, to move with the Second Brigade. The Twenty-fifth Ohio Battery moved forward toward Little Rock at the head of the First Brigade. Clarkson's battery moved up from the ford with Colonel Ritter's brigade, and crossed at the bridge. Fearing some disaster might occur to the howitzers, in the advance, and knowing from past experience that, where artillery was plenty, too much was expected of it, with your permission I sent an order to Captain Stange to fall back to the rear of the Second Brigade with six of his pieces, and leave Lieutenant Lovejoy in the advance guard with two pieces. This order either failed to reach its destination or was disobeyed. Hearing heavy firing in the advance some time after, I hurried forward with the Twenty-fifth Ohio Battery, and found our advance checked at Fourche Bayou by two rebel batteries, strongly posted, covering the roads leading to the city across the bayou, and supported by a large force of infantry and cavalry.

I found on my arrival at this point that the howitzers under Captain Stange, supported by the Tenth Illinois Cavalry, had advanced along the woods next to the Arkansas River, past the mouth of Fourche Bayou, and taken a position within a short distance of an ambushed force of the enemy, about 500 strong, who opened on them from their concealment a severe fire of musketry, driving their support back in confusion, and killing and wounding all of the horses of the section of howitzers nearest the woods. These two pieces, though gallantly defended by Lieutenant Lovejoy and his men, fell into the hands of the enemy. Lieutenant Lovejoy succeeded in escaping with a severe wound from a Minie ball in his leg. These guns could only have been saved by a sacrifice of life, of far more value than the guns, or the moral effect of their recapture, as they were in the power of a concealed force of the enemy, at least 500 strong, covered by a naturally strong position.

I succeeded in stopping the remaining six howitzers, which were retreating in confusion, and placed them in battery about 400 yards from the scene of the disaster. I had previous to this ordered Lieutenant Doolittle, with four pieces of the Twenty-fifth Ohio Battery, to take a position a little to the rear, and on the right of where the howitzers were stopped. As soon as our front was clear of our own men, I opened fire on the enemy in their position, and soon drove them back.

I had also ordered Lieutenant [E. B.] Hubbard, with two rifle guns from the Twenty-fifth Ohio Battery, to assist the First Brigade, occupying the left of our line, and opposed by two guns of a rebel battery, covering the upper crossing of Fourche Bayou. These two guns of Lieutenant Hubbard's, being badly posted and supported, did but little good. I found them afterward posted in a corn-field at least a quarter of a mile from any support, and ordered Lieutenant Hubbard, after firing a few rounds from another position selected by myself, to move to the mouth of Fourche Bayou, and there await orders from me, with his whole battery. I then went forward with the howitzers to the front of the Second Brigade, occupying the right of our line, and found that the rapid advance of the Second Brigade had compelled the rebel battery and its support, posted at the upper crossing of the bayou, to retire, one of the caissons of the battery falling into our hands, and the remainder barely escaping. I am of the firm conviction that had the advance of the left of our line been as vigorous as that of the right, this battery and a large portion of its support could not have escaped capture.

On returning to the mouth of the bayou, to order the artillery forward, I found an order from Colonel Merrill, commanding First Brigade, for the Twenty-fifth Ohio Battery to join his brigade. This order I refused to sanction, knowing that the enemy had at that time retired from his front. I immediately moved forward with the artillery, and entered the city without firing another shot from the artillery, except from the howitzers in the advance.

The conduct of Lieutenant Lovejoy, commanding the howitzer battery, from Merrill's Horse, is deserving of the highest praise. He remained by his guns until every man and horse of the section was killed or wounded, and was himself badly wounded while attempting to fire upon the enemy. His men are also deserving of great credit.

Lieutenant Hubbard, commanding Twenty-fifth Ohio Battery, and Lieutenant Clarkson, commanding Battery K, Second Missouri Artillery, are both deserving of praise for the efficient manner in which their batteries were handled during the day.

Respectfully, your obedient servant,

JULIUS L. HADLEY,

Capt. 25th Ohio Batt., and Chief of Art., Cav. Div., Dept. of the Mo.

Brig. Gen. J. W. DAVIDSON,

Commanding Cavalry Division, Dept. of the Missouri.

No. 7.

Report of Col. Washington F. Geiger, Eighth Missouri Cavalry, commanding First Brigade, of skirmish at Brownsville.

BROWNSVILLE, ARK., *August* 29, 1863.

SIR: I have the honor to report that on the morning of the 25th instant, in compliance with orders from division headquarters, I moved from Two Mile Prairie Bayou with my brigade, in the direction of Brownsville, on the military road. One battalion of the Merrill Horse was ordered forward as advance guard and skirmishers, under command of Major Rogers, who, after marching a distance of some 6 miles, came upon the enemy's outposts, driving them back into a dense underbrush bordering on the prairie. The Merrill Horse and Seventh Missouri Volunteer Cavalry were immediately formed in order of battle and moved forward.

The Eighth Cavalry Missouri Volunteers, under command of Lieutenant-Colonel [J. W.] Lisenby, forming the left wing of the brigade, was pushed forward to the timber to flank the enemy, if possible, while a battery was brought forward and commenced a brisk fire upon the enemy. In the mean time, a detachment of the Merrill Horse made a brilliant saber charge upon him, forcing him to fall back upon the town, but being closely pursued by my command, was forced to beat a precipitate retreat in the direction of Bayou Meto, keeping up a running fire for a distance of some 7 miles; but night coming on put a stop to farther pursuit, when my command fell back near Brownsville, and bivouacked for the night.

I am, very respectfully, yours, &c.,

W. F. GEIGER,
Colonel, Commanding Brigade.

Lieut. A. S. MONTGOMERY,
Acting Assistant Adjutant-General.

No. 8.

Reports of Col. Lewis Merrill, Second Missouri Cavalry, commanding First Brigade, of engagement at Bayou Fourche, and pursuit of the Confederates.

LITTLE ROCK, ARK., *September* 15, 1863.

SIR: In compliance with the order of the general commanding the cavalry division, I have the honor to make the following report of the part taken by the First Brigade, under my command, in the engagement with the enemy on the 10th, resulting in the capture of Little Rock:

During the evening of the 9th, in a personal interview with the general commanding the cavalry division, he explained the general features of the plan of attack, and gave me my orders for the succeeding day, as far as was then possible to do. These were, to move with my brigade so as to reach by 8 o'clock of the following morning a point near the pontoon bridge, but masked from the view of the enemy; to take position upon arriving there upon the left of the Second Brigade, and be prepared to cross immediately behind it; that, after crossing the river, my brigade would march in the rear of everything and be held in reserve, except that it was charged with the protection of the left and rear of the main column.

My brigade was promptly on the ground indicated, and, after some delay for the completion of the bridge, I requested and received permission of the general to ford the river above the bridge. This was accomplished without difficulty, the ford being entirely practicable for anything. During the succeeding march up the right bank of the Arkansas toward the town (some 8 miles distant), the Second Brigade, in my front, became sharply engaged with the enemy at the crossing of the Fourche Bayou. Here I was directed to halt my column and send a regiment to support four pieces of Hadley's battery, then in position on the sand-bar, and engaged. For this purpose I sent the Seventh Missouri, under Lieutenant-Colonel [J. L.] Chandler, my leading regiment. From some misconception of orders, the regiment was left in my rear after being relieved from this duty, and I did not again have a report from them until late in the engagement, after it was too late to bring them into action. I had meanwhile moved up the rest of my column on the road near to where I found two of Hadley's pieces in position, and held it there awaiting orders. In the course of half an hour I received, through Lieutenant-Colonel [H. C.] Caldwell, chief of staff, an order to take the left-hand or main road across Fourche Bayou, and, making my own dispositions against the enemy, to push up the road.

I immediately dismounted the Eighth Missouri, under Colonel [W. F.] Geiger, and ordered him forward on the left-hand road, directing him to push forward a line of skirmishers in the corn-fields, between which the road ran, and feel the position of the enemy, believed to be upon that road. I followed him immediately with the section of Hadley's battery, then ordered to report to me, supported by Merrill's Horse, under Major [G.] Harker, my last remaining regiment. Just as I was starting, I was informed by the general's chief of staff that he had just that moment learned that the First Iowa was on the road ahead of me, and directed to be careful and not mistake them. The information was conveyed to the Eighth at once, and Colonel Geiger immediately deployed his line, pushing forward to the support of the two squadrons of the First Iowa, then skirmishing with the enemy in front. The remainder of the First Iowa I found drawn up in line of battle in the corn-field, on the right of the road. One of their guidons was incautiously exposed near the road, and a hot fire of shells and spherical case was drawn upon them from the enemy's battery, posted at the dam across the bayou. I ordered them to move back into the field farther and conceal their guidons, which was done. Shortly afterward, upon sending for them to support a battery, I was informed that they had been ordered out and had moved to the rear, by whose orders I could not learn, as the order was not given through me. Just at this time a heavy fire of artillery opened from the left of the road, and near my line of skirmishers, somewhat alarming me at first, from thinking that the enemy had opened a battery on my left rear. I found immediately, however, upon riding toward where the battery was posted, that it was a section of Stange's howitzers, of whose presence on my line of attack I now learned for the first time. The ground, as will be seen by the accompanying sketch,* was very difficult to reconnoiter. It was impossible to see anything in the corn-fields or beyond them except on the road where the enemy's battery was posted, and only the smoke and flash of their guns could be seen there, as they were behind the levee, across the bayou. My line of skirmishers was so weak from the smallness of my force that I could not push it to connect with Glover's left, which I wished to do. This left me in great doubt as to his position. I

* See p. 493.

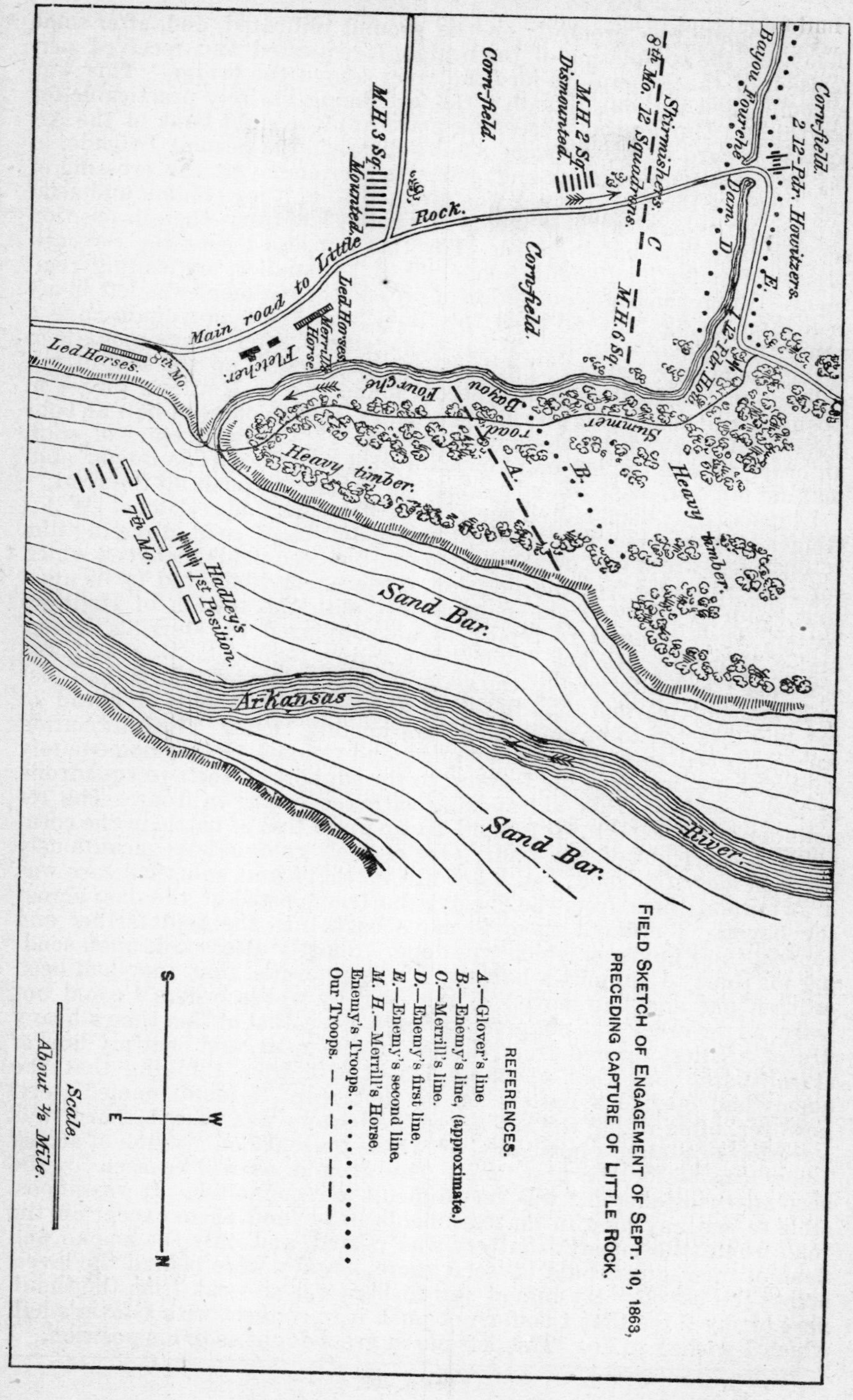

FIELD SKETCH OF ENGAGEMENT OF SEPT. 10, 1863, PRECEDING CAPTURE OF LITTLE ROCK.

had found that in my front, commanding the road, and very well served, was a battery of two 12-pounder howitzers, well sheltered behind the levee, across the bayou, on my right front, and where I afterward learned the bayou makes a sharp curve to the east was a single 12-pounder howitzer. These guns were supported by a strong line of skirmishers on the west side of the bayou, and a weak line in the same corn-field in which my line was advancing. On my right was the Bayou Fourche, between [J. M.] Glover and myself, as it proved afterward, entirely impracticable, though all the guides with whom I conversed stated that it was entirely dry and passable anywhere below the dam. I supposed at first that Glover's line extended to the bayou, and that it was moving up *pari passu* with mine and on its prolongation. It proved afterward that at first his left did not extend to the bayou, and that the direction of his line formed a sharp angle with mine, bending more to the front, and lying in my right rear. Simultaneous with the movement of Geiger's line of skirmishers, Hadley's section, notified of the position in front, was ordered to move to the left of the road, supported by two squadrons of Merrill's Horse, into the corn-field, and move forward parallel with the road, and, when the enemy's skirmishers were driven from the corn-field, to push to the front until the enemy's battery could be seen, and open on it. This order, for some reason not as yet satisfactorily explained to me, was not obeyed; and when the battery was about midway of the corn-field it was withdrawn by Captain Hadley, the general's chief of artillery, and taken, under his direction, to the road leading to the left of the main road, and afterward to the right of the main road, where he received my reluctant permission to fire at the enemy's battery at a long range. No apparent effect was produced by his fire, except to explode one shell among our own skirmishers, and I ordered his firing to cease and his section to be taken to the rear out of any possible danger, and where I could use it in case what seemed to be an effort to turn my right flank should prove successful.

Being under the impression that the bayou below the dam was perfectly dry and practicable at every point, my inability to connect with Glover's left gave me some apprehensions as to my right, which I feared might be turned, as I knew, from the character of Glover's first attack, that the enemy occupied the woods beyond the bayou on my right in force. All that I could spare of Merrill's Horse were dismounted and sent in on the right, in the endeavor to find out where Glover's left extended. Just as they got into position, and still not reaching to the bayou, the whole line of skirmishers being then advanced to the position marked in the accompanying sketch,* I heard a heavy infantry fire on my right rear, and, riding toward the right to observe, if possible, what it was, was met by a message from Major [J. B.] Rogers, commanding the right of the line of skirmishers, to the effect that he was flanked by the enemy on the right, and that they were pouring in a heavy discharge of grape and canister from the gun on his right front and of musketry from his right rear. At the same time Colonel Geiger, commanding the center of the line, informed me that the two guns on the road had gotten the range of his line of skirmishers, and had them under a heavy fire of grape and canister. Major Harker, with the remaining three squadrons of Merrill's Horse, was now disposed behind the right of the line to foil any attempt to turn it. Already a staff officer and then an orderly, having no staff left, had been sent to find where the left of Glover's line was, and, hearing nothing from them, I gave Colonel Geiger orders to hold everything as it was, and went myself to examine the

---

* See p. 493.

bayou on the other side, and find, if possible, what Glover's position was with reference to mine. On reaching the bayou, I found to my surprise that it was full of water, except just at the mouth, and apparently impassable. Riding a little farther, I found that the left of Glover's line of skirmishers was very considerably in rear of my right, and was overshooting the enemy into my line. I immediately sent an order to the whole of my line to move forward and drive the enemy from his position, informing Major Rogers that his right was protected by the bayou. Shortly after, on my way back, I was overtaken by the general, and informed him of the state of the case, and asked to have the left of Glover's line notified. The line moved forward as directed, driving the enemy from the corn-field and across the bayou; at the same time Glover had upon his side, as I was informed by the general, pushed back the right of their line, and they at once limbered up their guns and retired their whole line together. I pushed up to and over the bayou, and reconnoitered the corn-field in front, without finding anything.

The road here makes a sharp turn to the right, and runs along the bayou until, reaching the turn of the bayou, it intersects the right-hand road, upon which Glover was marching. While reconnoitering the ground in my front and right, I received a message from the general, saying that Glover passed the intersection of the two roads, and directing me to bring up my brigade in column in rear of Glover's (Second) brigade and Ritter's (Third) brigade, protecting the rear and left flank. I had meanwhile informed the general of the disposition I had made of my force—the Eighth behind the bayou, with Stange's section of howitzers, to prevent any attempt of the enemy to recross the bayou, and Merrill's Horse, on Glover's left flank, protecting his left. This latter movement was not well executed, from ignorance of the topography of the country and the direction of the main road. The Eighth was now withdrawn, and the brigade reformed and marched in column in the place indicated by the order, with occasional exceptions, rendered necessary to secure the left flank of the main column. In this place it was marched, without being again engaged, into Little Rock.

The misfortune of having only a vague idea of the topography of the battle-ground prevented me from using my position in the right rear of the line of the enemy opposed to Glover to greater advantage in giving them a flank fire, and the weakness of my force prevented me from learning earlier in the action that the bayou was impracticable below as well as above the dam, a knowledge that would have freed me from apprehension in regard to the heavy firing on my right rear, and left me free to push the right of the line boldly instead of with the caution with which it was advanced. The negro guide whom I had with me disappeared with the first shell that exploded near me, and was not to be found again during the action. It is due to Colonel Glover's line of skirmishers to say that they could not see my line of skirmishers, and that it was their overshooting of the enemy which made the fire fall among my men.

The loss in my brigade was 12 wounded (1 mortally, and since dead), all belonging to the Eighth Missouri. I have understood, unofficially, that the part of the First Iowa on my line lost several men, though I have no authenticated report.

Of the conduct of the Eighth and Merrill's Horse during the whole action, I cannot speak too highly. They moved forward through the corn-field under a heavy cross-fire of grape, canister, and spherical case from the guns in front and right front, and at one time a sharp fire from

Glover's left upon their right rear, steadily driving the enemy's skirmishers before them, until they drove them across the bayou.

Colonel Geiger, of the Eighth Missouri, deserves especial mention for the ability with which he handled his part of the line; and the coolness and courage with which the field officers of both the Eighth and Merrill's Horse held their men steady, and pushed forward under a galling fire, is worthy of praise.

The officers of my staff—Lieutenant [H. A.] Gleim, Second Missouri Artillery, and Lieutenants [D. O.] Crane and [A. S.] Phelps, Merrill's Horse—bore themselves throughout like soldiers; especially at one time while I was changing horses, and happened to be in range of the two-gun battery of the enemy while it was shelling Stange's section (the first time under fire for two of them), they brought and carried their messages and orders with as much coolness as veterans of many battles.

This report has been delayed from the fact that the 11th and 12th were occupied in the pursuit of the enemy, and the report of the different regimental commanders could not be made out in time to have made up this report any sooner.

Congratulating the general and his command upon the brilliant finale of our long and tedious march, I have the honor to remain, your obedient servant,

LEWIS MERRILL,
Colonel, Commanding First Brigade.

Lieutenant [A. S.] MONTGOMERY,
Acting Assistant Adjutant-General.

HDQRS. FIRST BRIG., CAV. DIV., DEPT. OF THE MO.,
Little Rock, Ark., September 16, 1863.

SIR: I have the honor to submit the following report of the operations of the troops under my command in the pursuit of the rebel forces under General Price on the 11th of September succeeding the capture of Little Rock on the 10th:

By orders of Brigadier-General Davidson, given me in a personal interview during the night of the 10th, I assumed command of a division of cavalry and artillery, made up for the occasion, consisting of the following troops:

First Brigade.—Col. W. F. Geiger, Eighth Missouri, commanding; Merrill's Horse, Major [G.] Harker commanding; Seventh Missouri Cavalry, Lieutenant-Colonel [J. L.] Chandler commanding; Eighth Missouri Cavalry, Lieutenant-Colonel [J. W.] Lisenby commanding.

Second Brigade.—Col. Powell Clayton, Fifth Kansas, commanding; Tenth Illinois Cavalry, Lieutenant-Colonel [J.] Stuart commanding; First Indiana Cavalry, Lieutenant-Colonel [T. N.] Pace commanding; Thirteenth Illinois Cavalry, Major [L.] Lippert commanding; the First Indiana having only six squadrons present, and the Thirteenth Illinois only three.

Artillery.—Capt. G. Stange, Second Missouri Artillery, commanding; six 12-pounder mountain howitzers of Stange's Second Missouri and Lovejoy's Merrill Horse Batteries; two 6-pounder rifled steel guns, prairie carriages, attached to the First Indiana; Clarkson's battery, Second Missouri Artillery, two 3-inch rifle and two 12-pounder (heavy) howitzers.

The general directed me, with this force, to pursue the retreating column of the enemy, and exercise my own discretion both as to the character and extent of the pursuit.

The fatigue of the troops from the previous day's fighting, and the darkness of the night, together with the scattered camps of the different troops, prevented my getting off at daylight, as the general desired. By 6 o'clock, however, the division was on the march, the First Brigade (with the Eighth Missouri leading) having the advance, and a part of Stange's battery, under his own supervision, following the leading regiment.

The enemy had retreated by the Arkadelphia road, and we had scarcely left the suburbs of the town before we began to find the *débris* of a retreating and demoralized army—broken wagons, arms and equipments, partly destroyed, ammunition upset into small streams and mud-holes, and deserters and fagged-out soldiers in numbers continually brought in by our advance and flankers.

The road itself, as far as we followed the enemy, was, at this season of the year, good; being a wide road, through a broken and hilly country, but evidently a bad road during wet weather, as the numerous corduroys indicated.

The country, however, through which the road ran was of such a character as to render successful pursuit exceedingly difficult, affording numerous strong defensive positions, compelling a cautious pursuit, and, from the entire absence of side roads, affording no opportunities for attempts at annoying the enemy's flanks, or cutting off his rear guard. On both sides of the road the country was thickly covered with a heavy growth of pine and oak, generally with thick undergrowth, and at rare intervals a small clearing, with a settler's cabin in it. Small streams and ravines putting into the Fourche Bayou, afforded, at short distances, places where a few men could make a stand, which would for some time delay a pursuing column.

Some 4 miles out the advance stirred up the enemy's outer pickets, and for several miles they were rapidly driven by mounted skirmishers. At about 6 miles from Little Rock a small stream crosses the road, and here it became evident, from the obstinacy of the stand made by the pickets, that their support was close behind them. Colonel Geiger, having charge of the advance, now dismounted the Eighth Missouri and deployed them as skirmishers. A brisk engagement with their extreme rear guard soon drove them upon their main guard, posted upon the crest of a steep hill, about a half a mile from the stream. They were gallantly and promptly followed by the Eighth, whose rapid and accurate fire soon drove the main guard to take to their horses and seek a new position in their rear. The Eighth followed them up as fast as the ground would permit them, occasionally exchanging shots with their skirmishers, posted to retard us, and compel a cautious advance. Their main guard had by this time retired to another position, where we soon found they had posted two pieces of artillery, commanding the road. Merrill's Horse was now dismounted and ordered to the support of the Eighth (and shortly after relieved the latter as skirmishers), together with a section of Stange's howitzers. A sharp engagement followed. The enemy opened with their battery, well and rapidly replied to by Stange, soon resulting in driving them from their position and compelling them to retreat.

I had learned, from a refugee, who had been warned from his house near the crossing of the Fourche Bayou, that the enemy had told him that their determined stand would be made at that point. This confirmed the impression I previously had, as it was a strong position for defense, and we were evidently, from the character of their resistance, and the signs of recent bivouacs of an infantry column, pushing their rear guard close upon their main body. My guide (a very poor one, but the only one I could get) now mistook Henry's Bayou (a tributary) for the crossing of the main Fourche, and my advance was pushed cautiously in order to reconnoiter the ground in expectation of a stout resistance. This mistake delayed us nearly an hour. When we approached the bayou we found a very strong position, but the enemy had not chosen to occupy it, fearing probably the open ground in the vicinity. Finding my mistake, and that the advanced regiment was becoming very weary, I ordered up first the Seventh Missouri and then the Tenth Illinois, as skirmishers and supports. While this was doing, Clarkson, one of whose rifled pieces had been previously ordered to the front, received permission to open fire at long range at what seemed to be the dust of their column on the road, about 1½ miles ahead.

The new disposition now being complete, and the Thirteenth Illinois being thrown out as flankers, we moved on toward Fourche Bayou, and, to my great astonishment, found this strong position evacuated, and no enemy in sight. This fact was accounted for by some negroes at the house, near the bayou, who stated that Marmaduke had formed his whole force, with four pieces of artillery, at this point, and was, with his staff, seated in the house at dinner, when one of Clarkson's shells exploded over the house; another immediately followed, falling near his line of battle, and two others in quick succession exploded so near them that the whole line precipitately turned and fled, led by Marmaduke himself. The evidence of a hasty evacuation of their position confirmed the negroes' story.

The day was now well worn away, and my troops, weary from the previous day, were worn out with 16 miles of skirmishing through thickets and heavy timber. I ordered the main column to halt, and directed Colonel Clayton, with the First Indiana (which, having fresh horses and poor fire-arms, had been held in reserve to act as cavalry, should the opportunity offer), with their two rifled guns and two light howitzers, to move on to the front, mounted, and to move on rapidly, but with proper caution, until he should again overtake the enemy, informing him that I would immediately follow him with the Eighth and Merrill's Horse and one of Clarkson's rifles. Clayton moved promptly forward, and before the two supporting regiments had come up from the rear I heard his skirmishers engaged with the enemy about 2 miles to the front. Sending orders to hurry up the support, I rode rapidly to the front, where I found the enemy strongly posted on the crest of a hill, with another higher hill behind them, just beyond the intersection of the Hot Springs road, while Clayton had posted his guns on a hill opposite, with his skirmishers well up to their line. A few rounds from the Indiana section drove the two guns from the first hill, and a single well-directed shot striking in their battery while unlimbering on the second hill, started them on again without firing a shot from the second position. It was now after sunset, and the troops and horses were jaded and worn out, and with a few parting shells from Clarkson's rifled gun, hastening their retreat, the pursuit was abandoned for that day; and, for convenience of water and forage, the command was brought back to Fourche Bayou to camp.

Early next morning, Clayton, with his brigade, and the small rifles and four howitzers under Stange, was directed to pursue again, and, if possible, stir up their rear guard. He found that after leaving their last position of the day previous, they had not halted again until after dark, when they had taken a position behind Hurricane Creek, from which they again retreated at 2 o'clock at night, and that farther pursuit was useless with his force, as they had by this time crossed the Saline, and were within short support of their main column, which had camped behind Saline River, 7 miles from Hurricane Creek. He had been ordered to return when he found pursuit useless, and accordingly returned about 12 o'clock.

The character of the country, and utter weariness of the men and horses, especially of the artillery, some of which had been in harness forty-eight hours, rendered rapid pursuit impossible on the second day, and nothing less than a rapid movement would overtake them. This determined me to return, deeming the probability of accomplishing anything further so small as not to be worth the sacrifice of the horses it would cost, the more especially as it was entirely evident that nothing could add to the haste of their flight. I accordingly returned to Little Rock, reaching there about sunset of the 12th.

Everything along the road indicated hasty flight of their whole army, and the numbers and stories of the prisoners captured showed a great demoralization of their forces, all agreeing in the statement that the army was greatly dissatisfied and demoralized by the evacuation of their works near Little Rock without firing a shot.

My loss was 1 private, of the Seventh Missouri, wounded. The enemy lost 4 killed, whose bodies were found on the field, and, from the accounts given by the people along the road, must have carried off a number of killed and wounded.

A large number of prisoners were captured at various times during the day, many of them deserters; others, men who had been worn out by the rapidity of the march. I did not have time to take any account of the prisoners, and sent them all directly to the town, ordering them to be reported to the provost-marshal. I should think, however, that the number captured was about 250 to 300. The wagons and arms found scattered everywhere along the road had been, in every case which I observed, rendered useless or entirely burned up, and were not worth the effort to collect them, and were accordingly left where they were found.

The conduct of all the troops was such as might have been expected from men who have always fought as well as they have, and it would be unjust to mention specially any particular regiment.

Colonel Geiger, who, during the first part of the day, and Colonel Clayton, who afterward had charge of the advance and the line of skirmishers, handled their commands with courage and good judgment, steadily pushing the enemy through the whole day.

Captain Stange, who was in the front with two pieces of his battery, at every stand made by the enemy, except the last, managed them admirably, showing excellent judgment in sheltering his pieces from the enemy, while he had their range so accurately that his little pieces soon silenced the heavier guns of the enemy, and compelled them to limber up and retire.

Lieut. T. S. Clarkson, commanding battery, of Second Missouri Artillery, and Lieutenant ——* (the name of this officer I have unfortunately forgotten), commanding battery, attached to First Indiana Cavalry, handled their guns with accuracy and ability while in action. The force of the enemy opposed to me was about 2,200, cavalry and mounted infantry, under Marmaduke, having also four guns, two 10-

* Samuel Leflar.

pounder Parrotts and two 12-pounder howitzers. Probably a thousand of their force, with two guns, were engaged with me at any one time, the rest retiring to seek a new position, and so alternating throughout the day. In no instance were more than 500 of my men engaged at any one time, or more than two guns, this being all that was found necessary to drive them whenever they made a stand.

For gallant and meritorious services in the engagement at Fourche Bayou, September 10, and in the pursuit of the enemy on the 11th, I have the honor to recommend Col. W. F. Geiger for the brevet appointment of brigadier-general (*vide* also previous report).

For gallant and meritorious service and able handling of his command at the affair near Ashley's Mills, September 7, in the engagement at Fourche Bayou, September 10, and during the pursuit of the enemy, September 11, I have the honor to recommend Maj. Garrison Harker, Merrill's Horse, for the brevet appointment of lieutenant-colonel.

I have the honor to be, sir, very respectfully, your obedient servant,

LEWIS MERRILL,
Colonel, Commanding First Brigade, First Division Cavalry.

Lieut. A. S. MONTGOMERY,
Acting Assistant Adjutant-General, Cavalry Division.

No. 9.

Report of Lieut. Col. John L. Chandler, Seventh Missouri Cavalry, of engagement at Bayou Fourche, and pursuit of the Confederates.

LITTLE ROCK, ARK., *September* 13, 1863.

SIR: In compliance with orders, I have the honor to report the following as the part taken by the Seventh Cavalry Missouri Volunteers in the assault and capture of this city and subsequent pursuit of the enemy:

On the morning of the 10th of September, the regiment, being the advance of the brigade, forded the Arkansas River without opposition from the enemy. Upon reaching a point of timber near the Bayou Fourche, the regiment was ordered to deploy to the right of the road, in support of Hadley's battery, where it remained during the engagement at that point. Hadley's battery being withdrawn, the regiment marched into the city, with the remainder of the brigade, without further opposition. No loss was suffered by the regiment during the day. At about 8 o'clock on the morning of the 11th, the regiment was ordered, with the remainder of the brigade, forward on the Arkadelphia road, in pursuit of the retreating army of the enemy. When about 10 miles on the road, the regiment was dismounted and ordered to deploy on the first line of skirmishers, relieving Merrill's Horse Regiment. After about two hours' skirmishing, the men were remounted, and proceeded to a point about 2 miles in advance, where they bivouacked for the night, and on the afternoon of the next day returned to this city.

The regiment sustained a loss of 1 private, wounded during the skirmish of the 11th of September.

I have the honor to be, very respectfully, your obedient servant,

J. L. CHANDLER,
Lieutenant-Colonel, Commanding Seventh Missouri Cavalry.

Lieut. H. A. GLEIM,
First Brigade, Cavalry Division.

No. 10.

Reports of Col. John M. Glover, Third Missouri Cavalry, commanding Second Brigade, of skirmish and action at Bayou Meto, and engagement at Bayou Fourche.

HEADQUARTERS SECOND BRIGADE, CAVALRY DIVISION,
Camp near Brownsville, Ark., August 28, 1863.

LIEUTENANT: I have the honor to report that, on the 26th of August, 1863, two regiments of my brigade (the First Iowa and the Third Missouri Cavalry Volunteers) and one section each of [G. F.] Lovejoy's and [T. S.] Clarkson's batteries were ordered on a reconnaissance, and to push the enemy as far as possible toward the Bayou Meto without bringing on a general engagement. The First Iowa Cavalry being in advance, a heavy line of skirmishers, in command of Captain [J. D.] Jenks, was thrown to the front, some 6 miles from Brownsville; struck his pickets and drove them about 4 miles back to their main body, some 2 miles east of the bayou, killing 1 rebel captain (Powell, of Platte City, Mo.), 2 privates, and capturing 1 prisoner. Here the enemy opened artillery upon us, to which ours soon replied. After a considerable artillery duel, I ordered Lieutenant Lovejoy to advance his section, in the doing of which he had one cannoneer pierced through with a solid shot and killed instantly, so well did the enemy have the range of the road. I then advanced in person, reconnoitered hastily the enemy's position, and determined to feel him further, and so ordered up Lovejoy's section, well supported with cavalry. In this position we stood face to face. After a more thorough review of the enemy's position and my own, perceiving his great advantage in this respect, and knowing his great superiority in numerical strength, and being satisfied a further offensive demonstration would result in a general engagement, in which all the advantages were against me, I deployed quite an amount of cavalry in front of my artillery, masking the same, while it was rapidly taken from the field, and retired with my command to a safe distance. This done, I called off the force covering my rear, and withdrew the whole in good order, and without further loss, to my former encampment near Brownsville.

On the morning of the 27th, at sunrise, the division moved out upon the road leading to the Bayou Meto Bridge, my brigade taking the advance, protected by a battalion of the Tenth Illinois, deployed as skirmishers, supported by two other squadrons, all under the immediate command of Lieutenant-Colonel Stuart. At some 5 miles from the bridge, our advance skirmishers met those of the enemy. A brisk fire ensued, the enemy falling back. At some 3 miles from the bayou he made another stand, where he was again sharply encountered by the Tenth Illinois. At this place Lieutenant [J. P.] Kavanaugh was killed. Here the commanding general ordered my whole brigade formed for action, in obedience to which I made the following dispositions, viz: Placed two battalions Third Missouri Cavalry Volunteers (dismounted) to fight on foot on the right of the road in order of battle; on the left of the road, placed in order of battle one battalion of the Thirty-second Iowa Infantry, as it was ordered to report to me during the day; on the left of this, placed the Third Battalion of the Third Missouri (dismounted), the artillery being in the center. As a reserve, the First Iowa Cavalry and four squadrons of the Tenth Illinois Cavalry (mounted) were formed in the rear, and six squadrons of the Tenth Illinois were placed on the right flank. In this order, with a heavy line of skirmishers covering my whole front, the brigade moved forward. It soon met opposition from the enemy's small-arms and artillery, but he was steadily driven from ridge to ridge through the thick brush on either side of the road by the firm and resolute advance of my brigade, assisted by the timely use of the artillery, back to a very strong and elevated position, covered by extended rifle-pits on the left, where he made a more obstinate stand, holding my command in check for a brief period, when the Third Missouri Cavalry, on the right, charged and drove back the enemy in their front, thus flanking his rifle-pits, and compelling him to abandon them under a simultaneous charge upon the left of the line, when the whole force of the enemy gave way, and fled in the greatest disorder and confusion toward the Bayou Meto. The artillery was now ordered up, and poured a terrible bombardment on their fleeing columns for twenty-five or thirty minutes, when the bridge was seen to be on fire. The general commanding then directed that the First Iowa Cavalry should charge and save the bridge, if possible. Lieutenant-Colonel [Daniel] Anderson, at the head of his regiment, led a gallant charge in the face of a terrible fire of artillery and small-arms, having his own horse shot under him, his command suffering considerably. From the intensity of the fire in the direction of the First Iowa Cavalry, it was evident they needed support. I suggested that a new position be selected for our batteries to cover and relieve the First Iowa Cavalry, now dismounted, and sharply engaged with the enemy. Receiving permission, I hastened to the front amidst a heavy fire of the enemy's artillery, reconnoitered, and selected an excellent position overlooking and commanding his. Our artillery was instantly ordered up, with supports, and placed in position under a continued fire from that of the enemy. Our batteries, in position, opened a tremendous fire, soon silencing the enemy's guns and driving them from their position. The Third Missouri Cavalry and Thirty-second Iowa Infantry had now boldly enforced their way to the bank of the bayou on the left, pushing the enemy across it, it now being evident that there was a strong force of the enemy on this side the bayou, on the right of our line. After taking proper precaution for the safety of my right flank, I ordered Lieutenant-Colonel Stuart, of the Tenth Illinois, with a portion of his regiment, to drive them back, which this excellent officer promptly executed, putting them across the bayou, after a very hot contest. The purpose of the commanding general now having been consummated, and the evening far advanced, I was ordered to retire with my brigade to my former camp, near Brownsville, as there were no comforts for man or beast short of that point.

I now desire to speak in the highest terms of Lieutenant-Colonel [T. G.] Black, of the Third Missouri, Stuart, of the Tenth Illinois, and Anderson, of the First Iowa, my regimental commanders, for coolness, daring, and good judgment, cheerful and prompt in obedience to orders. The efficiency of our dismounted cavalry was to-day thoroughly tested. Of the Third Missouri and Tenth Illinois I must say they fought with the confidence of veteran infantry. I desire to bear testimony to the universal good conduct of officers and men. It is due to Major [G. A.] Eberhart and his battalion, of the Thirty-second Iowa Infantry, to say they gave a hearty and efficient co-operation.

Although the artillery was not formally under my command, yet circumstances sometimes placed it there. I am gratified to acknowledge the cheerful obedience to orders and the fearless conduct of the officers in charge, especially in the case of Lieutenant Clarkson, whose battery was in the advance during the day. The earnest but honorable competition between the three regiments of my brigade resulted, as it is likely to do in the future, in the complete rout and defeat of the foe.

I must express my admiration for the coolness, bravery, and efficiency of my staff officers. Captains Freeman and Snelling and Lieutenants Haines and Johnson, who were exposed to the hottest of the fire and thickest of the danger, have my sincere thanks for their cordial support.

Casualties, 43 killed and wounded in my brigade proper.

I have the honor to be, respectfully, your obedient servant,

J. M. GLOVER,
Colonel, Commanding Second Brigade, Cavalry Division.

Lieut. A S. MONTGOMERY,
Actg. Asst. Adjt. Gen., Cavalry Division.

—

HDQRS. SECOND BRIG., CAV. DIV., DEPT. OF THE MISSOURI,
Timm's House, near Little Rock, Ark., September 14, 1863.

LIEUTENANT: I have the honor to make the following report of the operations of the troops under my command on the 10th instant, by which Little Rock fell into our hands:

Late in the evening of the 9th instant, I was summoned to the headquarters of General Davidson, at Ashley's Mills, with other brigade commanders of our division. There it was announced by him that early the next morning the whole available force of the army would move; the infantry, under General Steele, to assault the enemy's strong works on the north side of the river, while our cavalry division was to cross the Arkansas River 8 miles below, and move to the capture of Little Rock. He stated that no ordinary obstacle was to be allowed to defeat the purpose of the division; that we were to make a dash upon the city and capture it, and either hold or destroy the enemy's bridges, though it cost us one of our regiments. I was pleased with the announcement that it was my turn to lead the division in this honorable but hazardous enterprise, unless Colonel [J. F.] Ritter, who was to effect a crossing with his cavalry force below, should reach a certain point on the main road before I did, which he did not do.*

At 6.30 a. m. on the 10th instant, my brigade moved up the river some 3 miles, Colonel Merrill's following, and was masked in a thick woods adjacent to the pontoon bridge then being thrown across the river. As soon as the bridge was done, General Davidson ordered over a brigade of infantry to take possession of a levee in the opposite woods, to cover and protect my brigade while crossing and forming, as the enemy had opened artillery upon us. At about 9 a. m. my brigade began to cross the river. When two squadrons of the First Iowa Cavalry were over, they were ordered to the woods in front, where I found the infantry. I requested the officer commanding infantry brigade, as per his orders, to move out and cover my front until my troops were over. This he refused to do,† when I promptly ordered up two squadrons of the First Iowa (to cover and protect his front, deeming he felt in need of it) to move forward, take, and hold the levee, which was done at the word. As soon as my command was fairly over, it moved out to the

* Colonel Ritter was ordered away from Buck's Ford by me, and directed to cross in rear of the other two brigades at the pontoon bridge.—J. W. DAVIDSON, *General of Division.*

† This officer had my orders to advance only to the edge of the woods.—J W. DAVIDSON, *General of Division.*

road running up the river to Little Rock in the following order of march: The First Iowa Cavalry leading, with a line of skirmishers of three squadrons (A, L, and M), in command of the intrepid Captain [J. D.] Jenks; an advance guard of same regiment, followed by one section of Stange's battery, Second Missouri Artillery. In rear of the First Iowa came the remainder of said battery; then the Tenth Illinois Cavalry, and in rear of the Tenth came the Third Cavalry Missouri Volunteers. In this order my brigade had not moved more than 1½ miles on the river road, when the enemy opened a heavy volley of musketry, soon repeated, accompanied with artillery. The firing commenced precisely at 12 m.

In obedience to the orders of the commanding general of the division (and a habit of the Second Brigade), we forced our way rapidly to the mouth of one branch of the Fourche Bayou, which empties into the Arkansas River at this point, some 6 miles below the city. Here the road forks, the right-hand road running up the river through a dense forest of heavy standing and fallen timber. The left-hand road turns, at a right angle, to the left of the Fourche Bayou. Corn-fields on both sides for the distance of nearly a mile, where it again forks, the right prong turning across the Fourche and what is called the levee, and in 600 or 800 yards again intersects the river road. Having been previously informed of the character of the country and the direction of these roads, and having discovered from the head of my column dense lines of dust rising on the levee road, and having received information from negroes to the same effect, I at once concluded that the heavier forces of the enemy had gone on that road. In view of these things, and the further reason that my left flank was entirely open, with no natural defenses, and the supporting brigade not being at hand, and fearing if I should move with my whole brigade on the direct right-hand road, having the impassable Fourche on my left and the Arkansas River on my right, the enemy would rush between me and Colonel Merrill, dividing our forces—in view of these facts and surroundings, I made the following disposition of my forces: Sent the First Iowa Cavalry on the levee road, with one section of howitzers, and a caution about our left flank; the Tenth Illinois on the direct road to the right of the bayou, with Lovejoy's section of howitzers, intending to support the First Iowa with the Third Missouri Cavalry. Lieutenant-Colonel [J.] Stuart, commanding Tenth Illinois Cavalry, had not moved but a short distance into the dense woods when he met the enemy's mounted skirmishers. He at once assailed and drove them back with the two advance squadrons of his regiment (Companies B and H), to a point where a deadly fire was poured in upon him from an overwhelming force of the enemy, dismounted and in ambush. This caused these squadrons to fall back upon the balance of the regiment advancing to his support, which necessarily fell into some disorder; the enemy pursuing and pouring in a terrible fire. When the enemy first opened on the Tenth, I ordered Lovejoy's section to take position and operate against him by the right flank of the two squadrons engaged in the woods, while the balance of the Tenth was moving up to give sure support to the artillery, as I thought, for at this time I did not suppose the enemy was strong there. I soon discovered, however, that he was in force, and that the cavalry of the Tenth alone could not successfully resist him, as they were necessarily becoming more confused where the leaden hail filled the air. Seeing the howitzers would soon be in danger, I repeatedly ordered them back, and, by the assistance of Lieutenant-Colonel Stuart, who here received a severe contusion on the top of the head by a bullet, held the cavalry as long as possible to save the section, but in vain, as no one at the howitzers would obey orders. I then ordered Captain Stange to put another section of his that had arrived in battery, and open upon the enemy, which, had he done, the other section of howitzers could have been saved; but, instead of obeying orders, he fell back, and even failed to fire from where he was, which was an excellent range for grape and canister. I can assure the commanding general the loss of these two guns is attributable to the officers in charge, and the unavoidable confusion in the cavalry, having to contend with a dismounted enemy, covered by a thick forest. I believe the commanding general will do me the justice to say, as he was himself on the field and saw part of my efforts, that I exhausted every means in my power, save that of life, to rescue these guns. I remained on the ground until my horse was shot three times under me, and then retired only to bring up my own regiment. These demonstrations proved that the enemy had massed his heavy forces between the Bayou Fourche and the Arkansas River. I now determined to fight him in his own way, and brought up the Tenth Illinois and Third Missouri, and dismounted them to fight on foot, in three lines. The first, a line of skirmishers; the second, the line of battle; the third, a reserve; my right resting on the beach of the Arkansas River; my left on the Bayou Fourche. It now became necessary to combine all my forces to vanquish a vaunting and defiant foe. I therefore ordered the First Iowa Cavalry to countermarch and follow, mounted, at a supporting distance, our dismounted lines. Before withdrawing the First Iowa, I explained to Colonel Merrill the nature and connections of the roads, and suggested to him to send up his brigade as a substitute, and fall on the rear of the enemy by way of the levee, and I would drive back and capture his whole force. This result seemed to me inevitable, if this movement on the left should be made. I now returned to my command, gave the order to advance, and in a few moments a terrific and deadly fire prevailed along the whole line from friend and foe. Inch by inch did the Tenth Illinois, Lieutenant-Colonel Stuart commanding, and the Third Missouri, Capt. J. [H.] Reed commanding, drive back the stubborn and sullen enemy. When, by the advance of my lines upon the lost ground of the enemy, and by the divergence of the Fourche to the left, the front became so expanded that our scanty troops could not occupy the ground, I ordered portions of the First Iowa to both flanks and center, where they did heroic service, giving a general impetus to our whole line. When our advance had reached that point at which the two roads intersect on our left, and not finding Colonel Merrill's brigade co-operating, as I expected, I immediately ordered Major Caldwell to move to the left, in a corn-field, two or three squadrons, who at once unmasked the front of Colonel Merrill's brigade by driving the enemy in disorder, and capturing a caisson filled with ammunition, and 6 mules. We failed of any co-operation from Colonel Merrill's brigade on the north side of the bayou. With small-arms alone did we contend with an enemy four times our number, supported and encouraged by a battery of artillery, which sent a steady hail of solid shot, grape, and canister among our ranks. Such was the determination and impetuosity of the officers and men of the Second Brigade, that the enemy had no time or place to rest until he had been driven 3 miles, through the woods into the open fields, where they broke and fled in the utmost disorder and confusion in the direction of Little Rock.

The Second Brigade, without any relief, having fought on foot some three hours, and traveled some 3 miles, being perfectly exhausted, and their horses being behind, ceased the pursuit in 2 miles of Little Rock, while other portions of the division rode into the city.

The enemy left many of their dead upon the field, some of whom were devoured by hogs before we could inter them.

If the commanding general will pardon the suggestion, I would say he was risking too much in riding in front of and leading our lines during the battle.

It is with deep melancholy that I mention the death of First Lieut. Herbert Reed, of Company E, Third Missouri Cavalry Volunteers. He was one of the noblest men of our army. He fell on the left of our line by a solid shot from the enemy's battery, while he was dislodging it with small-arms. I regret there is not time and space to mention by name all those that merit the highest commendation. I cannot omit to mention the names of the following regimental and battalion commanders, to wit: Major Caldwell, Major [L.] Chase, and Captain Jenks, of the First Iowa Cavalry; Major [E. P.] Shaw, Captains [S. N.] Hitt and [W. A.] Chapin, of the Tenth Illinois Cavalry; Captain [J. H.] Reed, commanding Third Missouri Cavalry, and his battalion commanders, Captains [J. A.] Lennon and [J. D.] Crabtree, all for coolness, daring, and good judgment. It is due especially to speak of the general good conduct and gallantry of the men and officers of the Second Brigade. On this as on all other occasions they are strangers to defeat.

I now desire to speak in the most especial manner in commendation of Lieutenant-Colonel Stuart, commanding Tenth Illinois Cavalry, as one of the most accomplished, brave, and self-sacrificing officers in the cavalry service. I do not overrate his merits when I say to-day he should wear a star for his long, able, and faithful services to his country. My staff officers, Captains Freeman and Snelling and Lieutenants White and Haines, are worthy the most honorable mention for their devotion, daring, and energy, going wherever my orders directed them, regardless of every danger.

Accompanying, I submit a list of killed and wounded, which is very light, considering the length of time and the obstinacy of the contest. It is to be attributed only to my injunctions that the men should shelter themselves as much as possible.

I have the honor to be, sir, your obedient servant,

J. M. GLOVER,

Colonel, Commanding Second Brigade, Cavalry Division.

Lieut. A. S. MONTGOMERY,

Acting Assistant Adjutant-General, Cavalry Division.

No. 11.

Report of Lieut. Col. James Stuart, Tenth Illinois Cavalry, of engagement at Bayou Fourche.

LITTLE ROCK, ARK., *September* 14, 1863.

COLONEL: I have the honor to make the following report of the operations of the Tenth Illinois Volunteers, under my command, during the engagement near Little Rock, Ark., September 10, 1863:

I was ordered by you to move my regiment to the front, at the point of woods, and to deploy one squadron as skirmishers in front, with a support. I immediately deployed B squadron as skirmishers, and placed H squadron as a support for it. I then ordered Major [E. P.] Shaw, whom I left in command of the balance of the regiment, to march it in column of platoons close along the bank of the river. My motive for directing the latter movement was to guard against a repulse of B and H squadrons, which I then ordered to advance and attack the enemy, believing at the time that the enemy's skirmishers was all I had to cope with at that point; and being informed by you that the First Iowa Cavalry would move on the left-hand road along the bayou, and attack the enemy on the center, while the First Brigade would move on the extreme left flank, and attack them there, I moved my command up rapidly and opened the attack, the enemy keeping up a sharp fire from their mounted skirmishers, whom we drove into a line of dismounted men in ambush, who opened with such a murderous fire on my two squadrons as to cause them to fall back, and, through some error, the balance of the regiment was deployed right front into line instead of left into line, as I directed, and which would have brought them under the shelter of the river bank, and enabled me to protect the other two companies in falling back. The consequence was that they were exposed to a severe fire from the enemy, and fell into some confusion. At that time I ordered Captain Stange to withdraw his howitzers. He said he could not move them without orders from you. He then galloped to the rear, leaving them. I then ordered the men to run them out by hand, but they all got under the gun carriages and did not obey. I then rallied and brought up Companies B and H to their support, and while in the act of bringing up Company E, I received a slight contusion by a rifle ball on the head, and before I recovered from the effect of it, the enemy had possession of the two howitzers. I then reformed my regiment, and dismounted them by your order; formed them into line of battle, and again attacked the enemy, driving them several miles, and completely routing them.

I would likewise beg to state that, being left entirely without support, and the attack on the left not having been made, as you gave me to understand would be, simultaneous with mine, the enemy was enabled to concentrate all his forces against me; consequently the disorder in my ranks and the loss of the howitzers. Had Captain Stange moved the two howitzers to the rear when I directed it, or had the howitzers in the rear been placed in position to command the river bank between the woods and the howitzers in advance, which could have been done without any danger to them, and fired a few charges of canister, the enemy could not have taken the guns; but instead of that, they galloped off the field, until I brought them up with a cocked pistol at the drivers' heads, to compel them to bring their pieces to the front, but too late to save the other howitzers.*

I am, sir, very respectfully, your obedient servant,

JAMES STUART,
Lieutenant-Colonel, Commanding Regiment.

No. 12.

Report of Lieut. Col. Daniel Anderson, First Iowa Cavalry, of skirmish and action at Bayou Meto.

CAMP NEAR BROWNSVILLE, ARK., *August* 28, 1863.

GENERAL: I have the honor to make the following report of the part taken by the First Regiment Cavalry Iowa Volunteers in the operations of the 26th and 27th instant:

On the evening of the 25th, I received an order from Colonel Glover, commanding Second Brigade, cavalry division, to report at daylight on the morning of the 26th, with my entire effective force, to General

* Nominal list of casualties omitted. See p. 482.

Davidson, commanding cavalry division. At daylight on the morning of the 26th, I reported with my regiment, and was assigned the advance on the road leading from Brownsville to Bayou Meto.

Squadrons D, E, F, and G, under the immediate command of Captain [J. D.] Jenks, were sent forward as advance line of skirmishers, and came upon the enemy's pickets soon after passing our own outposts, to which place they had been driven on the evening of the 25th.

The regiment, supported by the Third Missouri Cavalry and a section of artillery, advanced steadily, driving the enemy back toward their rifle-pits, a distance of 6 miles. No casualties occurred during the day. The enemy's loss is not known. Captain [B. S.] Powell, of Marmaduke's regiment [division], was left mortally wounded on the field.

In the afternoon we returned and bivouacked for the night on the road, 3 miles from Brownsville.

On the morning of the 27th, the regiment moved forward in rear of the Third Missouri Cavalry. Squadron E, having the advance, was deployed as skirmishers. Squadrons D and F were sent to reconnoiter on the left of the main road leading to Bayou Meto. Squadrons G and H supported the advance battery. When our advance had driven the enemy out of his camp and rifle-pits, and he was retreating across the bayou at the bridge, the bridge was discovered on fire, and the regiment was ordered by General Davidson, commanding division, to charge with drawn sabers, and save the bridge, if possible. In making this charge, the regiment was exposed to a terrible fire from the enemy's artillery and sharpshooters. We reached the bridge, but not in time to save it; it was already enveloped in flames. The enemy were strongly posted in rifle-pits beyond, and their batteries, having good range, were well directed. I then dismounted the command and went forward on foot. Never have I seen greater coolness or courage displayed. Not a man flinched from performing his whole duty as a brave and loyal soldier. When I had ascertained the position of the enemy by severe skirmishing half an hour, I withdrew under cover of the hill and out of range of their guns. In the charge my own horse was shot five times, and many of my men were dismounted.

The following is a correct list of the killed, wounded, and missing of the regiment: Squadron A, killed, 1; wounded, 3. Squadron B, wounded, 5. Squadron C, wounded and missing, 1; wounded 6. Squadron E, wounded, 5. Squadron K, wounded and missing, 1; wounded 3. Squadron L, wounded, 1. Squadron M, wounded, since dead, 1; wounded, 1.

Respectfully submitted.

DANIEL ANDERSON,
Lieutenant-Colonel First Iowa Cavalry, Commanding.

E. D. TOWNSEND,
Assistant Adjutant-General, Washington, D. C.

No. 13.

Report of Maj. Joseph W. Caldwell, First Iowa Cavalry, of engagement at Bayou Fourche.

LITTLE ROCK, ARK., *September* 13, 1863.

GENERAL: I have the honor to make the following report of the action of the First Cavalry Iowa Volunteers in the battle of the 10th instant:

On the evening of the 9th instant, I received orders to be in readiness to move early on the morning of the 10th, with the effective force of the regiment, the transportation to remain behind, under the direction of the regimental quartermaster.

On the morning of the 10th, the regiment marched from camp, at Ashley's Mills, at 6 o'clock, and crossed the Arkansas River on a pontoon bridge, 8 miles below Little Rock. We were at once assigned the advance, with orders to attack and drive the enemy, who was well posted on the direct road to Little Rock. Squadrons A, L, and M, under the immediate command of Capt. [J. D.] Jenks, were deployed as skirmishers. In this manner we moved forward 2 miles, through corn-fields and timber, successfully driving the enemy from every position, exposed most of the time to a heavy fire of artillery and musketry. At this point, the Tenth Illinois, which followed in supporting distance, became engaged on the right, and lost two small howitzers. The First Iowa was then withdrawn from their position on the left, and moved to the right. The regiment was here dismounted and moved forward. In a corn-field to the left of the road we captured 6 mules and a caisson filled with ammunition. When we had driven the enemy, in vastly superior numbers, beyond the house now occupied by Colonel Glover as his headquarters, having fought on foot 3 miles, facing a tempest of lead and iron hail unflinchingly, almost exhausted, and the enemy routed, we were relieved by the Third Brigade. After resting a short time, we were again ordered forward, and moved into Little Rock. We bivouacked for the night in a grove in the south part of the city.

I cannot speak too well of the officers and men of the regiment. Their conduct was unexceptionable, and characteristic of the First Iowa Cavalry.

The following is a correct list of casualties: Nominal list reports 1 man killed and 1 officer and 3 men wounded. We captured a few prisoners and lost some horses.

Respectfully submitted.

J. W. CALDWELL,
Major, Commanding First Regiment Cavalry Iowa Volunteers.

General E. D. TOWNSEND, *Assistant Adjutant-General.*

No. 14.

Reports of Col. John F. Ritter, First Missouri Cavalry, commanding Reserve Brigade, of action at Bayou Meto and engagement at Bayou Fourche.

HDQRS. RESERVE BRIGADE, CAVALRY DIVISION,
Camp near Brownsville, Ark., August 29, 1863.

ADJUTANT: In compliance with request from division headquarters, dated August 28, 1863, I have the honor to submit the following report of the Reserve Brigade in the action of August 27, 1863, at Bayou Meto, Ark:

On the advance upon the enemy at Bayou Meto, Ark., on the 27th August, 1863, the Reserve Brigade was ordered to support the First Brigade. In the evening, after the First and Second Brigades had gone back toward Brownsville, the Reserve Brigade started back, leaving at 7.45 p. m., and arriving at camp, near Brownsville, at 11.15 p. m., not having been engaged.

By order of Colonel Ritter:

W. S. HAMILTON,
Lieutenant and Acting Assistant Adjutant-General.

Lieut. A. S. MONTGOMERY, *Actg. Asst. Adjt. Gen.*

HDQRS. RESERVE BRIGADE, CAVALRY DIVISION,
Little Rock, Ark., September 17, 1863.

SIR: In compliance with your request of September 12, I have the honor to submit the following report of the operations of this brigade during the engagement of the 10th instant:

On the arrival of my brigade at Ashley's Mills, on the evening of the 9th, I was informed by General Davidson that this brigade would attempt the crossing of the Arkansas at Buck's Ford. About sunset I made a personal examination of the ford, and found the enemy posted on the opposite side, apparently in force. Early next morning, by General Davidson's order, I marched toward the ford with my cavalry, and sent Clarkson's battery into a corn-field to a position which would cover the crossing. It was found that the enemy had thrown up a considerable fortification of cotton bales, two deep, so as to have a raking fire on the ford. Not knowing where their batteries might be posted, or whether this fort was manned by infantry, I sent Captain [I. W.] Fuller's company (E), First Missouri Cavalry, to draw the fire, which he succeeded in doing, with a loss of 3 wounded horses. Clarkson's battery then opened upon the fort, and, after a sharp fire, he succeeded in setting the cotton on fire and driving the enemy from the place. In the mean time orders were received from General Davidson to proceed on that side of the river and cross at the pontoon bridge, 2½ miles above, which was effected at about 1 p. m., the cavalry fording above the bridge. The men of Clarkson's battery were exposed to a broiling sun, and 4 or 5, also Lieutenant Clarkson himself, were attacked with sun-stroke. One man wounded and 2 horses killed.

A short time after joining General Davidson, the brigade was ordered forward to relieve the First and Second Brigades, which was done within a few miles of Little Rock. After proceeding some distance without any particular skirmishing, the Third Iowa Cavalry and Thirteenth Illinois Cavalry, Majors [G.] Duffield and [L.] Lippert commanding, were ordered to charge into the city, which they did, driving the enemy before them, the First Missouri Cavalry following. After this there was no firing until the First Missouri Cavalry reached the upper end of town, near the arsenal, when a sharp fire was opened from the enemy's batteries in the timber, doing no damage, however, except the killing of 1 horse. The brigade then went into camp, pushing forward pickets on the Pine Bluff and Arkadelphia roads. This brigade was the first to enter the city, under the orders of General Davidson, and occupied the west end of the city during the night.

In conclusion, I wish to state that the conduct of officers and men throughout the entire day was such as to elicit the highest praise, and I cannot forbear mentioning the following officers by name as worthy of the highest encomiums: Capt. J. M. Adams, First Missouri Cavalry, brigade inspector; First Lieut. W. T. Hamilton, acting assistant adjutant-general; Capt. I. W. Fuller, First Missouri Cavalry; Maj. L. Lippert, Thirteenth Illinois Cavalry; Maj. George Duffield, Third Iowa Cavalry, and First Lieut. T. S. Clarkson, battery. The battery was particularly exposed, and was well handled.

I am, sir, very respectfully,

JNO. F. RITTER,
Colonel First Missouri Cavalry, Commanding Reserve Brigade.

Lieut. A. S. MONTGOMERY,
Acting Assistant Adjutant-General, Cavalry Division.

No. 15.

Reports of Maj. Gustavus A. Eberhart, Thirty-second Iowa Infantry, of operations August 1–27, including expedition up the White and Little Red Rivers, and action at Bayou Meto.

CAMP AT HARRISON'S LANDING,
Eight miles below Clarendon, August 18, 1863.

DEAR COLONEL: I wrote you last at Wittsburg, about the 30th ultimo.

On the 1st instant, received orders to march. Started at noon; reached the L'Anguille River at noon on the 3d, 33 miles from Wittsburg. Captain [T.] De Tar informed you of the number shipped under Lieutenant [A.] Greer to Helena. With great difficulty they rode on the boat; that hardly any one was well enough to bear the motion of the boat, although the day previous nothing appeared to be the matter with them.

Left the L'Anguille on the 5th. Reached Clarendon, after a march of 53 miles, on the 8th.

On the 9th, gunboats 2, 3, 6, and 10 came up. While we were there our detachment was kept busy going out with forage trains.

On the 12th, received orders to take the detachment on board gunboats Cricket (6) and Marmora (2). Embarked at dark Companies A and D, under Captain De Tar, on board the Cricket; Companies F and G, myself in command, on the Marmora.

At 3 a. m., 13th instant, we moved up the river, accompanied by the gunboat Lexington. Captain Bache was in command of the fleet. At Des Arc we took some citizens, and burned a large warehouse containing a quantity of Confederate States Army property. While there, by request of Captain Bache, I went on board the Lexington during the rest of the trip. Anchored at the mouth of Little Red that night.

Next morning the Cricket went up Little Red River in search of two Confederate steamers. We continued up White River until 12 m., at which time we arrived at Augusta. Threw out skirmishers around the town, but found no soldiers. After remaining there about half an hour, we started on our return down the river; came to the mouth of Little Red about 3 p. m., when, seeing nothing of the Cricket, the Lexington started up in search of her. (Marmora anchored until we returned.) When up the river about 20 miles, we met her, with the two boats she went after. Shortly after she left us in the morning, the captain ascertained, from some negroes on shore, that one of them was about an hour and a half ahead of him, she having laid near us in the river during the night.

The Cricket continued up the river about 40 miles, when, turning a bend, came in sight of the town of Searcy, the two boats, and a good pontoon bridge across the river. Took possession of the boats without trouble. Company D was thrown out around the town. Company A, under Lieutenant [M.] Ackerman, piled up the bridge and burned it, leaving part of Marmaduke's force yet on the east side of the river. A crew was placed on the prize steamers (Tom Sugg and Kaskaskia), and Company D placed on the two boats, Company A remaining on the Cricket, Lieutenant [W. D.] Templin on the Kaskaskia, and Lieutenant [R. J.] Shannon on the Tom Sugg. When 10 miles below Searcy, on their return, they were fired into by about 500 of Marmaduke's men. The fight lasted about twenty minutes, along the bank, our boys pitching into them in fine style. The pilot of the Kaskaskia was wounded in the arm and head. The boat swung around, but the rebels were driven away before she could go ashore, and the Cricket took her in tow. It was very warm work, the firing being at a distance of about 30 yards. Company D had 6 wounded (1 mortally—George Fox—died that night). The rebels had a great many more hurt, for they were seen to fall in a peculiar manner. Ten miles below the scene of the fight we met them, turned around, and accompanied them down. We had not made more than 5 miles when we were again attacked by a number of them. Our boys again fed them pretty well. No one hurt with us The Cricket opened with her howitzers; the old Lexington with her 8-inch guns, which must have given them such a scare as they never had before, for they left very suddenly. We received quite a number of shots on the Lexington, but no one was hurt. Anchored for the night at the mouth of the river. Next day (15th) returned to Clarendon, firing occasional shots at rebel pickets seen on shore.

Captain Bache and myself waited on the general (Davidson) to make our reports. He (the general) was tickled wonderfully at the unexpected success of the expedition, as we did not think of getting the boats, which we supposed would be up some bayou, where we could not run. The general now thinks a great deal of the detachment, but gives us, in consequence, plenty to do, for, on the 16th, received orders to report, with the command and baggage train, at the transports After loading with part of the Thirteenth Illinois Cavalry and our detachment, we ran to this place, landed about dark, and threw the troops out, who were fired into by the pickets of the rebels.

At 2 a. m. yesterday, Major [L.] Lippert, with the Thirteenth Illinois Cavalry, started out on the Little Rock road, met some of the enemy 2 miles out, had a running fight about 5 miles, and sent in for re-enforcements. I went out, with parts of three companies, about 3 miles, the place designated for me to stay until further orders; remained there until about 3.30 p. m., when they returned, and we came in.

This morning Lieutenants [J.] Devine and [W. L.] Carpenter, John Courtney, a man from Company F, and two contrabands, went out to get some things for the officers' mess. They traveled outside the pickets, and ran into 9 rebel pickets; had to run for it; succeeded in getting to our lines. Courtney has just completed his report of the fun. He came in ahead. The others have not yet arrived. It will probably be a good thing for them. I only consented to their going out where we were yesterday, because Major L. [Lippert] stated that his pickets were at that place.

* * * * * * *

Yours, most truly,

G. A. EBERHART,
Lieutenant-Colonel Thirty-second Iowa Infantry.

Col. JOHN SCOTT,
Thirty-second Iowa, Columbus, Ky.

HDQRS. DETACHMENT THIRTY-SECOND IOWA INFANTRY,
Camp near Brownsville, Ark., August 29, 1863.

COLONEL: On the 27th instant, when the advance was made to feel the strength of the enemy, my detachment was ordered forward with the battery in the advance brigade.

The enemy was found within about 3 miles of Bayou Meto, when we were ordered to form on the left of the main road. Three squadrons of the Third Missouri Cavalry, under command of Major ———, were then dismounted and attached to my command, and formed on my left. After throwing out Company D, Thirty-second Iowa, and a platoon of the Third Missouri Cavalry as skirmishers, we advanced, driving the enemy before us until we were in possession of his rifle-pits, within a half mile of the bayou. My command was then thrown forward to the bayou, where we remained about three hours, getting an occasional shot at the enemy concealed on the other side. At 5 p.m. we were ordered back to support the batteries then in position. The detachment of the Third Missouri Cavalry was then ordered to rejoin the regiment.

My detachment remained until the battery was withdrawn, when we received orders from you to retire from the field. Officers and men in both detachments under my command conducted themselves in a creditable manner during the day. Casualties in the Thirty-second Iowa were as follows: Killed, Private Robert Atkinson, Company D; wounded, John W. Kearby, private, Company D, severely in thigh, and Samuel B. Williams, private, Company D, severely in breast.

The detachment of the Third Missouri Cavalry lost 2 or 3 killed and wounded, whose names will probably appear in the report of that regiment.

I am, colonel, your most obedient servant,

G. A. EBERHART,
Major, Commanding Detachment.

Colonel RITTER,
Commanding Reserve Brigade.

No. 16.

Report of Col. Adolph Engelmann, Forty-third Illinois Infantry, commanding Second Division, of engagement at Bayou Fourche.

HDQRS. SECOND DIVISION, ARKANSAS EXPEDITION,
Near Little Rock, Ark., September 15, 1863.

LIEUTENANT: I beg leave to report that, in compliance with instructions received from the major-general commanding, on the morning of the 10th instant, at 3.30 o'clock, I left the camp at Ink Bayou with the Third Minnesota Infantry and Eleventh Ohio Battery, and proceeded to a point on the Arkansas River 7 miles below Little Rock, where, during the night, General Davidson had been making preparations to construct a pontoon bridge. The battery had its position assigned it by Colonel Caldwell, chief of staff to General Davidson, the Third Minnesota being posted on its right as its support. I then proceeded to make a reconnaissance of the position. The other troops of the division now arriving, were placed in position; the Second Brigade, Col. O. Wood commanding, to cover the construction of the bridge; the First Brigade, Colonel [W. H.] Graves commanding, to guard the approach from Little Rock.

I beg leave to exhibit herewith a plat* showing the positions of the regiments and batteries of my command. The construction of the bridge was well advanced, when a battery of the enemy, concealed in the woods on the opposite side of the river, opened fire. It was speedily silenced

---

* See p. 515.

by our batteries. The bridge being completed, at the request of General Davidson, the Fortieth Iowa and Twenty-seventh Wisconsin Regiments were ordered across, to take possession of the woods in which the enemy's battery had been concealed. Immediately preceding the crossing of the regiments, I ordered the whole of the Eleventh Ohio Battery and the two rifled pieces of the Fifth Ohio Battery to throw shell into the woods to be occupied. The two regiments advanced with alacrity across the half mile of sand, and without opposition took possession of the woods beyond.

Large bodies of the enemy were now to be seen moving at a great distance beyond. Both batteries were, by the suggestion of General Davidson, ordered to keep up a brisk fire with their rifled pieces. Their practice at this great distance, being at least 2 miles, was very commendable, many of the shells dropping in the midst of the enemy. At this time the skirmishers thrown out on the right flank of the Eighteenth Illinois Volunteers were fired upon by a small party of the enemy. The fire being returned, the latter retired.

General Davidson's command having crossed the river, the two infantry regiments were called back; and, in compliance with instructions received, the Fortieth Iowa Volunteer Infantry was left as a guard at the bridge, whilst the division advanced with the column, under the immediate command of General Steele, on the road to Little Rock.

It affords me pleasure to record the efficient manner in which I was assisted by Colonels Graves and Wood, commanding brigades, and by the officers composing my staff. D. H. Brush, late colonel of the Eighteenth Illinois Volunteers, rendered me valuable service as volunteer aide-de-camp. To Col. William H. Graves I am indebted for the excellent position held by his brigade on the road to Little Rock.

I have the honor to be, with high regard, yours,

ADOLPH ENGELMANN,

Colonel Forty-third Regiment Illinois Vols., Comdg. Division.

GEORGE O. SOKALSKI,

First Lieutenant Second Cavalry, and Actg. Asst. Adjt. Gen.

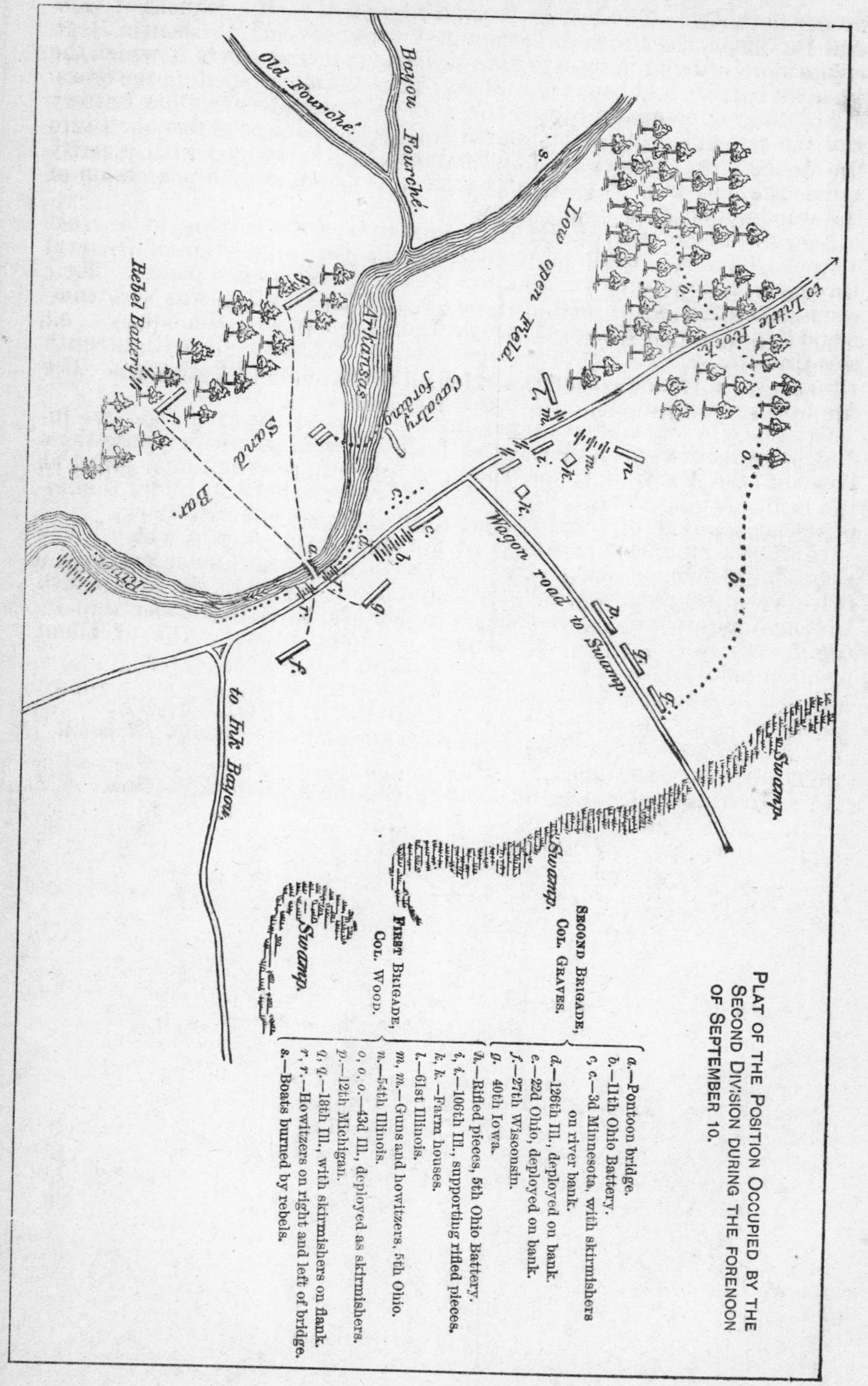

PLAT OF THE POSITION OCCUPIED BY THE SECOND DIVISION DURING THE FORENOON OF SEPTEMBER 10.

No. 17.

*Itinerary of the First Brigade, Second Division, Col. William H. Graves commanding, August 1–September 11.**

August 1.—The last of this brigade, then consisting of the Forty-third, Sixty-first, and One hundred and sixth Illinois, and Twelfth Michigan Regiments of Infantry, arrived at Helena, Ark. [from Snyder's Bluff], and encamped on the banks of the Mississippi, 2 miles below the town.

August 6.—The Eighteenth and Fifty-fourth Illinois Regiments assigned to the brigade.

August 8.—The Fifth Ohio Battery assigned. During the expedition men were detailed from the infantry to make the battery effective for field service.

August 13–17.—Marched from Helena to Clarendon. The men suffered from heat, and from the want of water and medicines.

August 22.—Crossed White River.

August 24.—Arrived at Devall's Bluff.

September 1.—Brigade left Devall's Bluff, and marched 20 miles toward Brownsville.

September 2.—Arrived at Brownsville and encamped.

September 6.—Marched from Brownsville to Bayou Meto.

September 7.—Marched to Ink Bayou, about 3 miles from Arkansas River and 12 miles from Little Rock.

September 10.—Broke camp at 4 a. m., and moved to a point on Arkansas River about 12 miles below Little Rock, where a pontoon bridge was being constructed, and a considerable body of cavalry and some artillery occupied the opposite shore; but no enemy made his appearance on the north side of the river. The rebel battery opened on one of the regiments as it was marching past the bridge to take up a position, but was soon silenced by the artillery of this and other brigades. No casualties occurred. In the afternoon the brigade moved to a point on the north side of the Arkansas River, 1½ miles below Little Rock, and on the 11th went into camp.

No. 18.

Itinerary of the Second Brigade, Second Division, Col. Oliver Wood commanding, August 13–September 10.†

August 13–31.—The brigade has marched from Helena to Clarendon, 54 miles, and thence to Devall's Bluff, 22 miles.

September 1–2.—Marched from Devall's Bluff to Brownsville.

September 7.—Marched from Brownsville to Ink Bayou.

September 10.—Marched from Ink Bayou to Little Rock, occupying that place on the same evening. No casualties during the engagements.

---

*From "Record of Events" on returns of First Brigade, Second Division, Arkansas expedition, for August, and of Third Brigade, Kimball's division, Army of Arkansas, for September, 1863. Kimball's division was organized September 13, 1863, True's brigade becoming the First, Engelmann's (formerly Wood's) the Second, and Graves' the Third.

†From "Record of Events" on the brigade returns for August and September, 1863.

No. 19.

Report of Col. Christopher C. Andrews, Third Minnesota Infantry, Second Brigade, of engagement at Bayou Fourche.

CAPITOL, *Little Rock, Ark., September* 11, 1863.

GENERAL: I embrace the first opportunity to report, for your information, the part taken by the Third Regiment in the operations of yesterday, resulting in the complete rout of the rebel army and the capture of Little Rock.

During the 8th and 9th instant, our forces were in camp 9 miles below Little Rock, and 2½ miles from the Arkansas River.

At 8 o'clock on the evening of the 9th, I was notified that a general movement against the enemy would be made the next day; that the Second Division, commanded by Colonel [A.] Engelmann, of the Forty-third Illinois, would be in the advance, and that my regiment would be the advance of the division. I was ordered to be ready to march at 3 o'clock in the morning. Accordingly, at 3 o'clock yesterday morning, we moved out from camp, followed immediately by the Eleventh Ohio Battery, and proceeded to a point on the Arkansas River about 7 miles below Little Rock, which had been selected for a pontoon bridge. It was beginning to be daylight when we arrived. We found the grading of the high bank of the river nearly finished, preparatory to laying the bridge, and could just discern mounted scouts of the enemy on the opposite shore, in the edge of the woods, 800 yards distant. In obedience to orders, we moved up a short distance above the proposed crossing, taking position in the edge of a corn-field, on the right of the road and behind a low levee, which answered the purpose of a breastwork. Immediately caused some of the best sharpshooters from each company to get position in front under cover, and well secluded from the enemy. This arrangement met the cordial approval of the division commander. The Eleventh Ohio Battery of six pieces took position on our immediate left, and extended to where the pontoon was about to be laid. We did not then know the force of the enemy on the opposite bank, as he had the advantage of woods, but have since learned that he had two batteries of artillery, supported by infantry. We had orders not to fire until he commenced. Supposing it to be his purpose to obstruct the laying of the bridge, we had every reason to apprehend his opening fire almost any minute, and we remained watching his movements. The place selected for the bridge was where the river is unusually narrow. It there winds close to the bank on which we were posted, forming an extensive bend, and leaving at its present low stage a sand-bar about 600 yards in width between the channel and the opposite bank, on which the enemy was concealed. The line of battle for our forces was, therefore, much in the form of a crescent. About half an hour after the Third Regiment had taken position, the rest of our forces continued to move up. Two batteries were also posted, one about half a mile on the left and the other half a mile on the right of the Eleventh Ohio, which was in the center.

I have described our line of battle with some particularity, that it may appear more plainly how effective was the cross-fire of our artillery.

Where the pontoon was being constructed the river was between 100 and 200 yards wide, and when the bridge was little more than half done the enemy opened on us with his artillery. Our batteries responded, and, soon getting good range, made it quite too uncomfortable for the enemy.

There was but little firing of small-arms on either side, and none by the Third Regiment, except the sharpshooters in advance.

The enemy's fire was chiefly directed at the bridge and the Eleventh Ohio Battery, and we being close to the latter, many of his shells and solid shots came in sufficiently close proximity to us. It appeared, however, to be only too welcome sport for our boys to dodge them.

The artillery firing continued with few intermissions for about an hour, during which time the Third was under the enemy's fire, but fortunately suffered no casualties whatever. The behavior of officers and men alike was all that could be desired.

The bridge was completed and the crossing commenced at about 10 o'clock. Two infantry regiments, the Twenty-seventh Wisconsin and Fortieth Iowa, first crossed in excellent order, and were followed by General Davidson's cavalry division on the bridge, a part also fording.

It would be digressing from the object of this report to relate matters as to the crossing, and I will only say that, after the cavalry division had crossed, the infantry regiments returned. This successful feint, devised by Major-General Steele, of crossing all our forces at that point, surprised the enemy, who hastily abandoned his fortifications on the opposite bank of the river from Little Rock, and retreated through the city and toward the southwest. His rear guard opposed some resistance to our columns, which pushed forward at noon on each bank of the river, and there were frequent halts and skirmishes during the afternoon march. It was not until about 8 in the evening that the Third Regiment, having been upon the alert nineteen successive hours in the heat and dust, was allowed to halt and bivouac, 1½ miles below the town.

The next morning, at 7, our division commander in person notified me to march into Little Rock, and report to General Davidson. We therefore immediately proceeded into town, crossing on the pontoon bridge erected by the enemy, and which he had unsuccessfully attempted to burn.

Immediately on entering the town, the major-general commanding informed me that he had selected the Third Minnesota Regiment as one of two infantry regiments to come into the city on duty, because of its efficiency and good discipline. We then proceeded in column by company to the capitol, where we are comfortably quartered, thankful that, after a summer of hardship, and, we may hope, honorable toils, fortune does not desert us.

Very respectfully, your obedient servant,

C. C. ANDREWS,
Colonel, Commanding Third Minnesota Volunteers.

General OSCAR MALMROS, *Adjutant-General, Minnesota.*

No. 20.

Itinerary of brigade commanded by Col. James M. True, September 1–10.*

September 1.—Left Clarendon, Ark.

September 2.—Reached Brownsville, Ark. (38 miles), joining the forces under Major-General Steele.

September 8.—Marched toward Little Rock.

September 9.—Remained in camp at Ashley's Mills.

September 10.—Took the advance of the force on the north bank of the river, moving on Little Rock. During the afternoon, Battery A, Third

---

*From "Remarks and Record of Events," return of First Brigade, Kimball's division, Army of Arkansas, for September 30, 1863.

Illinois Light Artillery [Vaughn's], afforded material aid to our force on the opposite bank, who were constantly opposed by the enemy. Several hundred rounds were fired, mostly at long range, but with marked good effect. The brigade was in range and exposed to the fire of the enemy's artillery for some time, but sustained no loss therefrom. Two men of Battery A were dangerously wounded by a premature explosion of a howitzer shell from a battery in action near by. The brigade arrived opposite Little Rock at sunset.

No. 21.

Report of Capt. Thomas F. Vaughn, Independent Battery, Illinois Light Artillery, of engagement at Bayou Fourche.

HDQRS. BATT. A, THIRD REGT. ILLINOIS LIGHT ARTY.,
Camp opposite Little Rock, Ark., September 14, 1863.

DEAR SIR: In compliance with the suggestions of Colonel Chetlain, I respectfully make the following statement in regard to the part Battery A took in the battle at Little Rock, Thursday, 10th instant:

The battery left Ashley's Mills at 10 a. m., with the brigade to which it is attached, the Forty-ninth Regiment Illinois Infantry being in advance. We moved up the right bank of the river for about 4 miles. Soon after 2 o'clock, I received an order to move forward the right section to shell the woods and a point of land which made out into the river, which I judged to be about 1½ miles distant, and elevated the piece accordingly 7½ degrees. Finding it fell short, I elevated another degree. This shell did reach. I then turned the elevating screw way down, which is 9½ degrees, the full elevation without sinking the trail; the shell fell short. I was deceived in estimating the distance, but could have placed a shell there had I been allowed to sink the trail, to bring the piece to the proper elevation. We continued moving up by sections to the front, advancing from 500 to 1,000 yards at a time, as the nature of the ground would admit, the left section advancing as the right got into action. The last 2 miles we moved up with great rapidity, and I have reason to believe rendered good service to General Davidson's division (who was engaging the enemy on the left bank of the river), completely breaking up the enemy's line of battle twice, producing disorder, and the tallest kind of skedaddling.

Five commanding officers, 14 non-commissioned officers, and 100 privates were in the engagement; all of whom did their duty most nobly, working their guns with great rapidity and precision. We were about three hours in action, and fired 8 canister, 292 shell, 14 shot; total 314 rounds.

Privates Joseph Vliet and Charles F. Mentemeyer were dangerously wounded by the explosion of a shell fired from a mountain howitzer by a detachment of cavalry, which was placed too near No. 1 gun. Mentemeyer died yesterday morning, 13th instant. Vliet still lingers, but there is not the slightest chance for him to recover. This is the first battle in which the battery has been engaged. We were with General Brayman last December in the chase after Forrest, and shelled the rebs at Bolivar, December 25, 1862.

All of which is respectfully submitted.

T. F. VAUGHN,
Captain, Commanding.

Colonel TRUE, *Commanding Third Brigade.*

No. 22.

Report of Maj. Gen. Sterling Price, C. S. Army, commanding District of Arkansas, including operations July 24–September 25.

HEADQUARTERS PRICE'S DIVISION,
Camp Bragg, November 20, 1863.

COLONEL: I have the honor to submit the following report of the military operations which terminated on September 10 in the evacuation of Little Rock by the forces then under my command:

Having been notified on July 23 that Lieutenant-General Holmes desired to relinquish his command to me during the continuance of his severe illness, I left Des Arc, the then headquarters of my division, the same day, and having reached Little Rock the next, assumed command of the District of Arkansas. Being satisfied that the enemy was about to advance in heavy force upon Little Rock, I sent orders the same day to Brigadier-General Frost, commanding the defenses of the Lower Arkansas, near Pine Bluff, to move at once with his infantry and artillery to Little Rock. Orders were also sent on that day to Brigadier-General Fagan, upon whom the command of my division (Fagan's, Parsons', and McRae's brigades of infantry) had devolved, directing him to withdraw his forces from Searcy and Des Arc, and to take position upon Bayou Meto, about 12 miles northeast of Little Rock.

On the next day I ordered Brigadier-General Marmaduke, commanding a division of cavalry, to establish his headquarters near Jacksonport, and to dispose his troops so as to observe and retard the movements of the column of Federal cavalry which was then advancing into Northeastern Arkansas from Missouri. Brigadier-General Walker, commanding a brigade of cavalry, was on the same day ordered to remain with his command in the vicinity of Helena, for the purpose of watching the enemy in that direction, and checking his advance from that point. These were the only troops at my disposal for the defense of Little Rock, except a very weak regiment, a small battalion, and a few unattached companies of cavalry, which I kept on the south side of the Arkansas, picketing the country from Little Rock to Napoleon, and thence to the boundary of Louisiana. Brigadier-General Steele, commanding in the Indian Territory, was already hard pressed by the enemy, and on the defensive, and could not spare a man.

I wrote to the lieutenant-general commanding the department on July 27, communicating these facts to him, and stating that while I should attempt to defend Little Rock, as the capital of the State and the key to the important valley of the Arkansas, I did not believe it would be possible for me to hold it with the force then under my command. About this time I commenced the construction of a line of rifle-pits and other defensive works on the north side of the Arkansas, and about 2½ miles in front of Little Rock, and pushed them forward to completion as rapidly as I could.

The continued advance of Davidson's column of Federal cavalry making it hazardous to retain Walker's brigade any longer on the eastern side of White River, I ordered him, on August 2, to move it to the western side of that stream. As soon as this was done, the enemy unveiled his intention to cross White River at Clarendon, and I consequently moved Walker's brigade and Marmaduke's division of cavalry, both under command of Brig. Gen. L. M. Walker, to that vicinity. Tappan's brigade, which had been detached from my division several months before, and which had been ordered back to Arkansas by Lieutenant-General Smith, having reached Little Rock, whither I had ordered it to move by rapid marches, I directed Brigadier-General Frost to move his brigade to the northern side of the river, and to assume command of my division, which comprised all the infantry near Little Rock, except Tappan's brigade, which I held in reserve on the south side of the river. Seeing that the position on Bayou Meto could be easily turned, and that it was otherwise untenable, I ordered General Frost at the same time to withdraw his entire command within the line of defenses to which I have before referred, and upon which I continued to labor both day and night. The enemy continued to advance meanwhile, my cavalry, under Generals [L.] Marsh Walker and Marmaduke, falling back before him, but contesting stubbornly every mile, until I ordered General Walker, on August 25, to take position on Bayou Meto with the whole of his and Marmaduke's cavalry, and to hold it as long as possible.

About midday on August 27, he was attacked in this position by the enemy in greatly superior force and with considerable spirit. The engagement lasted until dark. My troops, which were under the immedate command of Brigadier-General Marmaduke, behaved admirably, and the enemy was repulsed with heavy loss. General Walker, fearing from the indications given that the enemy was about to flank his position, withdrew his troops after dark. The enemy also retired from the field, leaving his dead unburied.

Knowing that if I delayed the removal of the public stores from Little Rock until the eve of its evacuation, the greater part of them would be lost, in consequence of the insufficiency of transportation, I had, very soon after assuming command of the district, ordered the chiefs of the several staff departments to send their stores to Arkadelphia as speedily as possible, removing first such as were least likely to be required by the army. These officers were zealously executing this order when intelligence reached me, on August 29, that the enemy was occupying Monroe, La., in force, and thereby not only endangering the valuable stores at Camden, but menacing my line of retreat. A few days later I received a communication from Brigadier-General Cabell informing me that Brigadier-General Steele, commanding the Confederate forces in the Indian Territory, was falling back toward Texas before a superior force, and that he had, himself, been driven by the enemy from Fort Smith, and was then retreating in the direction of Caddo Gap. These facts necessitated still greater activity in the removal of the public stores from both Camden and Little Rock, and orders to that effect were consequently given. I continued meanwhile to strengthen the defenses on the north side of the river and to perfect the means of communication between the two banks of the Arkansas, so as to be able to throw my forces readily from the one side to the other, and particularly to secure the safe withdrawal of my army from the northern side of the river in the event of defeat. My troops were at this time in excellent condition, full of enthusiasm, and eager to meet the enemy; but I had barely 8,000 men of all arms, while the enemy had brought against me nearly or quite 20,000. My only chance of meeting him successfully lay in the possibility that he would attack me in my intrenchments. I would have given him battle confidently had he done this. But I had little hope that he would do it, as it was comparatively easy for him to turn my position by crossing the Arkansas below Little Rock. That river was at that time fordable in a great many places, and I could not guard it effectually without weakening my force within the trenches to a dangerous extent. I communicated these facts at the time to the lieutenant-general commanding.

There was, during the last days of August and the first days of September, constant skirmishing between the cavalry advance of the two armies, without any marked change, however, in their relative positions, except that the enemy began to develop more plainly his intention to cross the Arkansas below Little Rock. I therefore ordered General [L.] Marsh Walker, on August 31, to move his headquarters to some point on the south side of the river, within 12 or 15 miles of the city, and to assume command of and concentrate in that vicinity (in addition to his own brigade) all the cavalry which was south of the Arkansas and east of Little Rock. I also gave orders, on September 9, for the construction of a line of defenses on that side of the river, and the work was immediately begun.

Early on the morning of the 10th, the enemy appeared in heavy force on the north bank of the river, about 8 miles below Little Rock. Col. A. S. Dobbin, upon whom the command of Walker's division had been devolved by the unfortunate death of that lamented officer, immediately concentrated his whole disposable force (about 1,200 men) to dispute his passage. He was, however, embarrassed, not only by the fact that the river was fordable in twelve different places within 12 miles of Little Rock (at one of which the enemy actually made a strong feint of crossing), but by the additional fact that the place at which the enemy did finally force the passage was selected with excellent judgment, it being the upper point of a horseshoe-like bend, upon the three sides of which he planted five batteries. These, after two hours' heavy cannonading, silenced the guns which Colonel Dobbin had opposed to the enemy's passage, and drove them and the supporting cavalry from the peninsula. I ordered Tappan's brigade to the relief of Dobbin as soon as I learned that the enemy was seriously threatening to cross the river, and immediately thereafter ordered General Marmaduke to move his division to the south side, to assume command of all the cavalry, to hold the enemy in check until I could withdraw my infantry and artillery from the north side of the river, and, when this had been accomplished, to cover the retreat, the orders for which were at once given. The infantry began to leave the intrenchments at 11 o'clock in the morning. The city was finally evacuated about 5 o'clock in the afternoon. The trains had been sent to the rear early in the forenoon. The cavalry, under Brigadier-General Marmaduke, constituted the rear guard. It was skillfully handled, and behaved admirably.

My infantry, and most of my artillery, reached Arkadelphia on September 14, without any unusual loss of either men or material, and were encamped in that vicinity. I disposed my cavalry so as to completely cover my front, General Marmaduke occupying the center, having his headquarters at Rockport; Colonel Dobbin, in command of the right, having his at Tulip, and Colonel [J. C.] Monroe, in command of the left, having his at Caddo Gap.

I respectfully refer to the reports of Brigadier-General Marmaduke and Col. A. S. Dobbin for a detailed statement of the operations of their respective commands. They will be forwarded as soon as they shall have been received.

Lieutenant-General Holmes resumed command of the District of Arkansas, at Arkadelphia, on September 25.

I am, colonel, very respectfully, your obedient servant,

STERLING PRICE,
Major-General.

Lieut. Col. J. F. BELTON,
Assistant Adjutant-General, District of Arkansas.

ADDENDA.

Return of Casualties in the Confederate forces during the advance of the Union forces upon Little Rock, Ark.

[Compiled from nominal lists, and incomplete.]

Command.	Killed.		Wounded.		Captured or missing.		Aggregate.	Remarks.
	Officers.	Enlisted men.	Officers.	Enlisted men.	Officers.	Enlisted men.		
Shelby's brigade:								
Gordon's regiment		1				4	5	August 25.
Do	1			2			3	August 27. Lieut. John S. Percival killed.
Do		2					2	September 10.
Thompson's regiment				1			1	August 27.
Do		1		2			3	September 10.
Bledsoe's battery				3			3	August 27.
Do						2	2	September 10.
Total	1	4		8		6	19	
Marmaduke's brigade:								
Jeffers' regiment			1	2			3	August 27. Lieut. J. F. Caldwell wounded.
Do		1	1	2			4	September 10. Lieut. R. M. Snider wounded.
Greene's regiment				4			4	September 10.
Young's battalion	1			1			2	August 26. Capt. B. S. Powell killed.
Do				1			1	August 27.
Bell's battery		1	1				2	August 27. Lieutenant [C. O.] Bell mortally wounded.
Total	1	2	3	10			16	
Newton's brigade:								
Dobbin's regiment				1	1		2	August 27. Lieut. C. M. Richards captured.
Do	2		2	4		4	12	September 10. Maj. S. Corley and Lieut. W. H. Bowers killed. Capt W. H. Crawford and Lieut. David Morgan wounded.
Newton's regiment		2		2			4	August 30.
Do				4		7	11	September 10.
Denson's squadron								No report.
Pratt's battery								Do.
Total	2	2	2	11	1	11	29	
Grand total	4	8	5	29	1	17	64	

No. 23.

Report of Col. Archibald S. Dobbin, Arkansas Cavalry, commanding Walker's division, of skirmish at Ashley's Mills, and engagement at Bayou Fourche.

CAMP BRAGG, *November* 19, 1863.

In obedience to your request, I have the honor herewith to submit a report of the military operations of my command in front of Little Rock from the time I assumed command of the division formerly commanded by Brigadier-General Walker, on September 6, until the 10th of same month. I must here, however, state that this report will necessarily be general in its terms, omitting details, as I am now, and have been for the last six weeks, separated from my command, and I have now no access to the papers requisite to make a full report.

On the evening of September 6, by order of Major-General Price, I assumed command of Brigadier-General Walker's division, consisting of Dobbin's brigade Arkansas cavalry and [George W.] Carter's brigade Texas cavalry, to which was also attached [Alf.] Johnson's spy company and [W. B.] Denson's company. At that time one regiment of Dobbin's brigade was encamped on north side Arkansas River, at Ashley's Mills. The remainder was on south side river, near Buck's Ford. Carter's brigade, except about 100 men and one section of [J. H.] Pratt's battery, were engaged in picketing from Buck's Ford, on Arkansas River, to Gaines' Landing, on Mississippi River.

On the morning of the 7th, the enemy advanced on the regiment encamped at Ashley's Mills, driving the same back to the river. Colonel [Robert C.] Newton, then commanding the brigade, was present in command. The regiment lost 1 killed, 3 wounded, and 2 captured, including Captain [Edward H.] Cowley, adjutant of the brigade. The enemy advanced in greatly superior force, and Colonel Newton crossed the river about 8 miles below Little Rock with that portion of his command, fording the same. This was about 10 o'clock in the morning. That night the enemy encamped at Ashley's Mills and Terry's Ferry. From that time until the evening of the 9th, there was continual skirmishing between my scouts and the enemy, and also constant firing across the river, with no loss in my command and with some damage to the enemy, they reporting to have had 3 killed at Terry's Ferry.

On the evening of the 9th, the enemy moved down in considerable force of cavalry and artillery to Buck's Ford, [and] built up camp-fires within sight of the ford. About 10 o'clock on that night, Colonel Newton reported to me that the enemy were moving their artillery to Terry's Ferry, and were throwing out lumber as if they intended building a bridge at that place. I had previously, as soon as I discovered them at Buck's Ford, moved to that point about 200 bales of cotton, and planted my artillery so as to resist their crossing. I at the same time reported to Major-General Price, commanding the District of Arkansas, that the enemy were in front of me in heavy force of infantry, cavalry, and artillery, reported by a citizen named Calvin Pemberton, who had that day seen Generals Steele and Davidson, to be 30,000 strong, and that I would be unable to prevent their crossing, my command being very much scattered, and there being twelve fords between Little Rock and Buck's Ford, a distance of 12 miles.

On the morning of the 10th, about 3 o'clock, I left my camp near Buck's Ford and rode up the bank of the river to ascertain, if possible, what movement the enemy was making, the reports from scouts having been very unsatisfactory and conflicting. When about 4 miles above Buck's Ford, and about 2 miles above Terry's Ferry, I discovered the enemy digging down the bank and making preparations to cross the river. This was just at daylight. The river here made a bend in the shape of a horseshoe, the enemy being about the center of the bend. I immediately ordered a section of [C. B.] Etter's battery, which had previously been attached to my command, to occupy the point opposite to where the enemy were engaged in cutting down the bank, and to open fire on them, which it did. The enemy immediately opened on Etter's battery from five batteries placed on the opposite bank, and from the nature of the bend and the position of the batteries, being planted on each side of the horseshoe, swept the entire point on which Etter's battery was placed. At the same time the section of [J. H.] Pratt's battery was also hotly engaged with the enemy at Buck's Ford, they having made a demonstration of crossing there. Finding that Etter's battery was unable to prevent the enemy from throwing a bridge across the river, I ordered one piece of Pratt's battery to his assistance. It came up and opened on the enemy, but the fire from the enemy's batteries was so terrific that they were unable to hold their position, and, after being engaged about two hours, were compelled to retire, leaving one piece of Etter's battery, which I had brought off afterward by the cavalry. Very soon after the artillery was removed the enemy crossed the river—I think at about 10 o'clock in the morning. They crossed first one regiment of cavalry, followed immediately by the infantry, artillery, and cavalry in heavy force. I fell back to Bayou Fourche, a distance of about 5 miles, fighting all the time. When within about 1 mile of the bayou, I ordered Colonel Newton, with a portion of the brigade commanded by him (about 500 men), to go back to the bayou and form on the bank, while I remained and held the enemy in check. This he did. I had, as soon as I found the enemy would cross, ordered all the force from Buck's Ford to join me, and had the entire force with me (not exceeding 1,200 men) at the time the enemy crossed the river.

When I reached Bayou Fourche, about 2 p. m., Colonel Newton had his command formed ready to receive the enemy. There I met Brigadier-General Marmaduke, with orders to assume command of all the cavalry, and I immediately turned over the command to him.

I sent Major-General Price, from time to time, all the information I could obtain in regard to the movements of the enemy, and kept him constantly informed of all their movements.

I lost in the entire action and skirmishing about 65 men in killed, wounded, and missing, including 1 major (Maj. S. Corley) killed and 1 lieutenant (W. H. Bowers) killed, 1 captain wounded, and 1 captain captured. The loss I give from memory alone, and cannot now say how many privates were killed and how many wounded.

I have the honor to be, yours, with high respect,

ARCH. S. DOBBIN,
Colonel, &c.

Maj. THOMAS L. SNEAD,
Assistant Adjutant-General.

ADDENDA.

CAMP BRAGG, ARK., *November* 25, 1863.

COLONEL: I cheerfully make the following statement of the circumstances of your arrest on September 10 for disobedience of orders, and of my subsequent preferment of charges against you:

Having been informed toward midnight of September 5, that a duel was pending between Brig. Gens. L. M. Walker and Marmaduke, I sent to each of them an order to remain closely at his headquarters for twenty-four hours. This order did not reach General Walker, but did reach General Marmaduke. The duel took place, nevertheless, the next morning, and General Walker was mortally wounded. I immediately ordered General Marmaduke and the seconds of both parties in arrest. Feeling, however, the great inconvenience and danger of an entire change of cavalry commanders in the very presence of the enemy, and when a general engagement was imminent, I yielded to the urgent and almost unanimous request of the officers of General Marmaduke's division and his own appeal, and suspended his arrest, and ordered him to resume his command during the pending operations. I did this in spite of the apprehension that such leniency toward General Marmaduke might intensify the bitter feelings which had been already aroused in General Walker's division by the result of the duel.

When the enemy had forced the passage of the Arkansas on September 10, and you were falling back before their overwhelming numbers (the command of Walker's division having devolved upon you by his death), I sent General Marmaduke with his division to re-enforce you, ordering him, of course, to assume command as senior officer of all the cavalry. You reported to me a few hours later, in arrest, as you informed me, by order of Brigadier General Marmaduke, for disobedience of orders. I at once suspended your arrest for reasons similar to those governing in General Marmaduke's case, and ordered you to resume your command during the pending operations. When about a fortnight later I turned over the command of the district to Lieutenant-General Holmes, I communicated the above facts to him. He at once released General Marmaduke, who was present, from arrest, and at the same time ordered me to prefer charges against you. I insisted that if charges were to be preferred against you, General Marmaduke, and not I, should make them, as it was he who had placed you in arrest, and for an alleged disobedience of his orders. General Holmes, nevertheless, required me to prefer the charges. General Holmes informed me the next day that he had released General Marmaduke's second from arrest. In reply to my suggestion that, having released the living principal and his second from arrest, he ought to release the other second from arrest, he replied that he would not release him, but I might do so if I chose. I released him. A few days later General Holmes again ordered me to prefer the charges against you, and told me I must do it that very day. He afterward gave me till the next day, and on the next day I preferred them.

The above is a plain statement of the facts attending your arrest and my preferment of charges against you, so far as they are known to me. Justice requires me to add that during the eighteen months that I have known you in Mississippi and Arkansas, your conduct as an officer and a gentleman, except upon this single occasion, has not only met my approval, but incited my very sincere admiration.

And I am, colonel, very truly, your obedient servant and friend,

STERLING PRICE,
Major-General.

Col. ARCHIBALD S. DOBBIN.

No. 24.

Report of Brig. Gen. John S. Marmaduke, C. S. Army, commanding division, of operations August 17–28.

HEADQUARTERS MARMADUKE'S DIVISION,
December —, 1863.

COLONEL: I have the honor to submit the following brief report:

My division for some months consisted of Shelby's Missouri brigade, commanded by Col. J. O. Shelby, and Marmaduke's Missouri brigade, commanded by Col. Colton Greene.

On my arrival at Des Arc, August 17, to which place I was ordered by General Price, I received orders dated Headquarters District of Arkansas, August 16, 1863, detaching Shelby's brigade, and ordering them to report to Brigadier-General Walker, who was at Brownsville, Ark.

August 23, I received orders from Major-General Price to march my brigade to Brownsville and report to Brigadier-General Walker.

On the morning of August 24, I reported to General Walker, who ordered Shelby's brigade to report to me, and ordered me to hold my force in the vicinity of Brownsville, to guard the main approach (Wire road) to Little Rock.

The next morning, at sunrise, the enemy were reported advancing in force. I moved my two brigades (Shelby's, about 700 effective, and Marmaduke's, about 600 effective, with two pieces of artillery) forward to engage the enemy, Shelby's brigade in the advance. At this time Walker's brigade, commanded by Colonel [Archibald S.] Dobbin, was encamped some 10 miles southward of Brownsville, guarding another important approach from Clarendon to Little Rock. A sharp engagement ensued between the Federal force and my division. The Federals were under command of General [J. W.] Davidson, and consisted of about 6,000 cavalry and sixteen pieces of artillery. Being unable to meet the enemy's forces in a general engagement, I withdrew my command, retiring slowly through Brownsville toward Little Rock. The Yankees were exceedingly cautious in their pursuit. My rear guard, under Major [Benjamin] Elliott, a most excellent and brave officer, seized every opportunity to check the enemy's advance. After retiring some 4 miles, my division was ordered into position by Brigadier-General Walker, commanding the cavalry. At this time I was with my rear guard.

Upon my arrival at my new line of battle, I made all necessary preparations to check the enemy's advance. This was an important point, and absolutely necessary to hold, as Walker's brigade, troops and trains, would come into the main (Wire) road at this place, and they had not yet reached the junction. The enemy came upon me and were handsomely repulsed. They then commenced pushing their forces on my right and left, which forced me to retire. No farther pursuit was made. I received orders to encamp my division on and in the vicinity of Bayou Meto. The next day I withdrew my whole force, except scouts and pickets, to the south side of Bayou Meto.

On the morning of August 27, I advanced a light force, engaged the enemy's advance, and after brisk skirmishing my troops fell back to the main force.

My troops were disposed as follows: Shelby's brigade, commanded by Lieutenant-Colonel [B. Frank] Gordon, in line of battle above the bridge; Marmaduke's brigade, commanded by Colonel [William L.] Jeffers, (except [J. Q.] Burbridge's regiment, commanded by Lieutenant-Colonel [W. J.] Preston, which was held in reserve some half mile to the rear), below the bridge; [Joseph] Bledsoe's battery, on the main road, commanding the bridge, and [C. O.] Bell's section of artillery near the main road below the bridge, commanding the bridge and road leading to it. I should also add that immediately below the bridge and between my two brigades was formed Dobbin's regiment. The whole force, except Preston's regiment, was dismounted.

Davidson (commanding Federal forces) advanced his troops—cavalry and artillery, a part mounted, part dismounted—and came dashing down toward the bridge (which Lieutenant [John] Mhoon, of the engineer troops, had prepared for, and was now handsomely burning) and bayou. Suddenly artillery and small-arms opened upon them with deadly effect and caused a precipitate retreat. Soon the enemy formed their lines, brought up their artillery, and the fight continued until sunset, when the enemy, failing to occupy the river, retired after a heavy loss, leaving a number of their dead on the ground.

I was ordered to retire at dark to within 5 miles of Little Rock. My troops, until after the evacuation of Little Rock by our forces, were engaged in scouting and picketing.

All the officers and soldiers of my command behaved with marked coolness and bravery. My escort and the command of Captain [D. R.] Stallard behaved most handsomely. My staff, for their gallantry and promptness in executing my orders, deserve my thanks.

Maj. C. C. Rainwater, volunteer aide-de-camp, received a severe wound in the head from a shell.

My loss is as follows:* Killed, —; wounded, —; missing, —.

See accompanying reports for more detailed accounts.

Very respectfully,

J. S. MARMADUKE,
Brigadier-General, Commanding.

Lieutenant-Colonel [J. F.] BELTON,
Assistant Adjutant-General.

No. 25.

Reports of Col. G. W. Thompson, Sixth Missouri Cavalry (Confederate), commanding Shelby's brigade, of engagement at West Point, and operations September 10–14.

HEADQUARTERS SHELBY'S BRIGADE,
In Camp, half mile below West Point, August 14, 1863—9 p. m.

MAJOR: When Major [M. W.] Smith got here with the scout sent out this morning, the boats had just passed up. He took position on the river just above town and awaited the return of the boats. Colonel [C. A.] Gilkey arrived in time to take position just above him, and when the boats came down opposite them they gave them a broadside fire for several minutes, but had to fall back. We then tried to head them again 4 miles below town, but only got there in time to fire into them as they passed.

We had 7 or 8 men wounded, Colonel Gilkey and Major [David] Shanks among the number. I fear Colonel Gilkey's wound is mortal; Major Shanks slightly.

We were not able to get our battery up in either stand. If we had good horses in our battery we would have captured them easily.

Respectfully,

G. W. THOMPSON,
Colonel, Commanding Brigade.

Major [HENRY] EWING,
Assistant Adjutant-General, Searcy, Ark.

HEADQUARTERS SHELBY'S BRIGADE,
Camp on Ouachita River, September 15, 1863.

MAJOR: In obedience to orders, I have the honor to submit the following report of facts gathered from the records of the past:

On the morning of September 10, while encamped at the gap at the junction of the Van Buren and Batesville roads, a heavy cannonading down the river admonished us of the approach of the enemy in force. Hour after hour passed away without any tidings as to the nature of

---

*Blank in the original, and no list of casualties found therewith.

the contest, when at length a courier arrived with orders from General Price to withdraw and cross the Arkansas River on the upper pontoon bridge as rapidly as possible. A few moments after, Captain [John C.] Moore, of General Marmaduke's staff, arrived with similar orders, stating we were three hours behind time, owing entirely to the couriers having taken the wrong road in transmitting his message. Moving across and down the river as rapidly as possible, at 1 p. m. we arrived at a point 3 miles below the city, and formed in line of battle across a large open field; but the enemy, running up their batteries on the opposite side of the river, opened an enfilading fire, which swept up and through our lines in a most unsatisfactory manner, compelling us to change our positions every few moments, and without being able to return the fire with any effect. At one time Captain [Joseph] Bledsoe opened fire with one of his rifled guns upon a body of cavalry moving upon the opposite side of the river, which sent them scampering out of sight. A large force coming up on either bank of the river compelled us to fall back, and, when near the city, the battalion under Major [Benjamin] Elliott formed on the extreme left, awaited their approach, and, delivering a well-directed fire into the advance of their elated masses, for a time checked up their mad career, and not until the sun went down did they take possession of the city. The nature of the ground and the distribution of their forces and numbers rendered any attempt on our part to keep them back, futile and vain.*

After night drew her sable curtain down we moved back to a point some 8 miles, where the infantry was encamped, and rested for the night without food or forage or further annoyance.

On the following morning, after the command had moved out, the enemy's cavalry pressed our rear guard till reaching a point some 3 miles from the camp of the night previous, where this brigade, after having fed their horses, formed, and awaited their coming, which was not long—in their usual precautionary manner, *i. e.*, in line of battle, with their sharpshooters well to the front. Captain [T. H.] Lea, of my regiment, in ambush with his company, delivered them a deadly fire, which was taken up by my regiment and [B. G.] Jeans' regiment in one deafening volley, after which they filed out of the way and range of Captain [S. T.] Ruffner's splendid battery of four guns, which occupied a position immediately commanding the road. This was the signal for Captain Ruffner, who in quick succession sent shot, shell, and grape roaring and whizzing through the woods in such a demoralizing manner as to drive the enemy out of sight and hearing for the time, with (as we learned subsequently) many killed and wounded. Moving out and again forming, [B. Frank] Gordon's regiment and Elliott's battalion tendered them another reception, after which we were no further annoyed or molested by them during the march.

In these skirmishes we lost none, either killed or wounded. Since that time and up to the present we have moved at our leisure, keeping pickets far in front to warn us of any approaching danger.

In all of these skirmishes, &c., the men under my command proved themselves worthy of their positions and the name of soldier.

I am, major, very truly, your obedient servant,

G. W. THOMPSON,
Colonel, Commanding Brigade.

Maj. HENRY EWING,
Assistant Adjutant-General.

---

*Nominal list of casualties, here omitted, is embodied in statement on p. 523.

No. 26.

Report of Lieut. Col. B. Frank Gordon, Missouri Cavalry (Confederate), commanding Shelby's brigade, of operations August 24–September 6.

HEADQUARTERS SHELBY'S BRIGADE,
Camp in front of Little Rock, September 6, 1863.

MAJOR: In obedience to orders, I have the honor to submit the following report of the actions, marches, and detours participated in by this brigade from August 24 to the present time:

While encamped at Brownsville, Ark., and acting under orders from General Walker, I received orders through him from General Price to report this brigade back to General Marmaduke for duty, which order was greeted by both officers and men with entire satisfaction.

On the morning of the 25th, and ere the men had partaken of their scanty meal, I received orders to saddle up and fall in line, which was hastily obeyed, and the command moved rapidly to the prairie beyond and east of town, and there formed in line of battle, with one section of [Joseph] Bledsoe's battery in and commanding the road upon which the enemy were approaching, while Major [Benjamin] Elliott, with his battalion, moved out into the prairie (distant 1½ miles), forming the advance and acting as skirmishers. The enemy's lines, extending across the prairie, could be plainly seen advancing, supported by a large body of cavalry with artillery, and when within about 200 yards of our lines Major Elliott, from his entire line, opened fire upon them, which was immediately returned, and the charge sounded by the bugles of the enemy brought their columns sweeping across the prairie and down upon our retiring column like a whirlwind. As soon as our men had approached sufficiently near to distinguish them from the enemy, Captain Bledsoe let slip with shell and shot, completely checking up their furious onslaught and driving them out of range as rapidly as they had come.

In this skirmish we lost 1 killed and 4 captured.* The occasion of the capture of these men was by their horses and mules falling with them.

Move out was ordered, and, slowly falling back through the town and to a position across a small prairie some 6 miles west, we again formed in line of battle, in the same order as before, save Major Elliott's being to the front, commanding the road. Some time was spent by the enemy in shelling our first position, and the woods through which the road passed to the prairie, across which we now awaited their coming. "Here they come!" is again passed up the lines, and, as one column filed right and another left, in the most perfect order, with their banners gaily streaming in the wind, we could but admire their perfect discipline and soldierly bearing. Again forming, they advanced as before, and, when about midway across this 2-mile prairie, Captain [C. O.] Bell, with his little battery mischievously ambushed, opened upon the squadrons of white horse, which was the signal for Captain Bledsoe, who sent crushing through their lines shell after shell, throwing them in the most beautiful confusion; but running out two batteries into position, they threw a shower of shells into our lines, which, however, fell harmless. As nothing advantageous could be gained by longer holding this position, we again received orders to, and moved out, without further annoyance, and, crossing the Bayou Meto, encamped for the night.

*Nominal list omitted.

August 26.—Formed in line of battle in the following order, viz: Bledsoe's battery occupying a position commanding the road and bridge which spanned the bayou, while my regiment, commanded by Capt. George [P.] Gordon, took position to the left of the bridge, with his right resting near it, with [B. G.] Jeans' regiment, commanded by Captain [R. H.] Adams, resting upon his left, and [G. W.] Thompson's regiment, commanded by Lieutenant-Colonel [J. C.] Hooper, resting upon his left, and Major Elliott's battalion occupying the extreme left. Thus we remained to-day, with only slight skirmishing, with our pickets well to the front.

August 27.—Early this morning a detail of 125 men, dismounted, was ordered to report to General Marmaduke as skirmishers and sharpshooters, who in person accompanied them to a position some 2 miles in front (with other details from the division), where they were deployed as skirmishers. But a short time elapsed ere the enemy's advance, though cautiously approaching, received a spirited fire from the "little teaser" (Bell's battery) and our advanced line of sharpshooters. Dismounting a body of men, with one battery and a body of cavalry on their right as flankers, they pushed forward their columns impetuously until, coming upon the main body of our skirmishers, a roar of musketry sent death crippling through their ranks, completely breaking up their lines for the time, in dismay and confusion. Taking advantage of this, our lines fell back, and again awaited their approach; but finding the enemy were attempting a flank movement, we continued to fall back until across the bayou, where the detail joined their respective commands, then in line of battle near the banks and up the bayou.

After the command was safely over, the bridge was tarred and fired. The enemy, from the crest of the hill some half mile beyond, and down the broad, sandy road, saw the dense column of smoke rising from the burning structure, and, perhaps, thinking the "frightened rebels in terror fled," charged down the road in splendid style, as if to save the bridge; but it were better had many of them never been born. The dense cloud of smoke from the crackling, burning bridge, like sorrow's veil, hung between them and Bledsoe's battery, and when the head of their long lines had nearly reached the bridge, these noble old guns sent shell and shot, winged with fury, screaming and hissing up their lines, scattering the mangled fragments of men and horses like chaff before the wind. In great confusion they wheeled to the left and sought the woods for safety; but not before my regiment, on the left of the bridge, and Colonel [William L.] Jeffers' brigade, on the right, swept many from their saddles and sent off their horses riderless. The enemy now brought two batteries into position in an open field immediately fronting this brigade, with which they attempted to silence the fiery tongues of Bledsoe's rifled guns. Their shell and shot ripped and roared through the forest, tearing the trees around the battery into fragments, and plowing up the earth in the most approved demoniac style; but all without avail. The two long, rakish-looking pirate rifles seemed to shout in proud defiance, as with great precision they sent tearing through their ranks their iron missiles, driving them from position to position, while our sharpshooters kept up the death-rattle along the entire line.

Late in the evening they concentrated a heavy body on my left, fronting Thompson's regiment and Elliott's battalion, the latter mounted, with which they attempted to gain possession of the bayou; but my men, standing firm, dealt them such stunning blows their lines reeled, staggered, and fell back cowed and disheartened. At every point the enemy had now been driven back. Gathering up their scattered masses, they hastily left the field, Bledsoe firing them the last shot as they went over the hill and out of sight. The sun went down smoke-begrimed, red-faced, and furious.

In this day's action we lost Lieutenant [John S.] Percival, of Gordon's regiment (an excellent officer and accomplished gentleman), with the following wounded:*

The sharpshooters from Thompson's regiment brought in 1 prisoner, mortally wounded. The loss of the enemy not known, but, undoubtedly, very heavy.

August 28, moved to a position at the Robertson place, where we remained until the 31st, when Thompson's regiment was ordered down on the Shallow Ford road to the support of Colonel [Robert C.] Newton.

September 2, under orders, moved down on Shallow Ford road and relieved Colonel Newton. Some slight skirmishing with the enemy at the crossing of the bayou.

September 3, countermarched and took up position at the forks of military and Shallow Ford roads.

September 4, moved the command to the gap and at the forks of the Van Buren and Batesville roads, where we still remain.

I take great pleasure in commending the conduct of the troops while under my command for their untiring energy and courage upon the field.

I am, major, with great respect, your very obedient servant,

B. FRANK GORDON,

Lieutenant-Colonel, Commanding Shelby's Brigade.

Maj. HENRY EWING,

Assistant Adjutant-General.

No. 27.

Reports of Col. William L. Jeffers, Eighth Missouri Cavalry (Confederate), commanding Marmaduke's brigade, of operations August 25–September 14.

DECEMBER 3, 1863.

MAJOR: In accordance with the order from division headquarters, requiring a statement of marches, camps, actions, &c., of Marmaduke's brigade during the time occupied between the fight at Brownsville and its arrival at Little Rock, I have the honor to forward the following report:

On the morning of August 25, having received information that the enemy had made their appearance on the prairie east of Brownsville, I ordered the brigade, consisting of [J. Q.] Burbridge's and [William L.] Jeffers' regiments, [M. L.] Young's battalion, and Lieutenant [C. O.] Bell's battery, to take a position on the edge of town fronting the enemy, Bell's battery on the right. A few shots from the artillery drove the enemy's advance back, when, by order of General Marmaduke, the brigade fell back some 5 miles west of Brownsville, on the Little Rock road, where the enemy, who had slowly followed, were again repulsed. Slight skirmishing occurred with the enemy from this time until nightfall, when the brigade encamped at the springs, about 1½ miles east of Bayou Meto.

---

* Nominal list omitted. See p. 523.

On the morning of the 26th, Lieutenant-Colonel Young's battalion, supported by General Marmaduke's escort, Captain [J. W.] Porter's company, of Burbridge's regiment, and Lieutenant Bell's battery, were ordered to reconnoiter and feel the enemy while the brigade moved across the bayou, along the bank of which Jeffers' regiment was dismounted and drawn up in line of battle. Burbridge's regiment was ordered half mile in the rear to act as reserve. Lieutenant-Colonel Young firmly contested in many skirmishes the advance of the enemy, and encamped that night on the east bank of Bayou Meto.

On the morning of the 27th, Jeffers' regiment was thrown forward beyond the camp of the night before, engaged the enemy with sharpshooters, and, thus fighting, fell slowly back across the bayou. Young's battalion was placed on the extreme right of the brigade; Jeffers' regiment and four companies under Major [D.] Smith, from Burbridge' regiment, in the center, and Bell's battery on the left in the road, commanding the bridge. The enemy attempting to cross at Shallow Ford, were met and driven back by Young's battalion. They then advanced with their whole force in line directly in front of the brigade, and, when arrived at the bayou, were met with a terrific fire that drove them, crippled and disordered, back. Bell's battery engaged the enemy's artillery with great success, driving it from every position by well-aimed shots, during which engagement the gallant Lieutenant Bell was mortally wounded by a shell. The fight raged more or less intense during the day, and ended in great loss and discomfiture to the enemy. As near as could be ascertained, the enemy's force exceeded 4,000.

On the morning of the 28th, I was relieved of the command of the brigade and ordered to proceed with my regiment to a point across and 8 miles down the Arkansas River from Little Rock. As I was not possessed of a brigade book, in which to note down movements, actions, &c., of the brigade, I have been forced to rely chiefly upon reports of commanders of regiments and battalions, all incomplete and frequently conflicting, which makes it impossible to furnish the facts in detail or make the report as complete as you desire. Believing, however, that the most important facts are properly set forth, I beg leave to submit them.*

I have the honor to be, very respectfully, your obedient servant,

WM. L. JEFFERS,
Colonel, Commanding.

Maj. HENRY EWING,
Asst. Adjt. Gen., Marmaduke's Div., Missouri Vol. Cav.

DECEMBER 3, 1863.

MAJOR: In obedience to the order from division headquarters, requiring a report of marches, camps, actions, &c., of Marmaduke's brigade during the time occupied between the fight at Bayou Fourche and the arrival of the troops at Rockport, I beg leave to make the following report:

For several days prior to September 10, this brigade was engaged in picketing the different roads leading to the fortifications at Little Rock. At sunrise on the morning of the 10th, the brigade, with the exception of Colonel [S. G.] Kitchen's regiment, which was directed to remain on the north side of the Arkansas River, was ordered to leave the forks of the Brownsville and Shallow Ford roads (at which point we had

*For casualties, see p. 523.

bivouacked the night previous), cross at the lower pontoon, and move down the river at a double-quick to meet the enemy, who had early in the morning effected a crossing at Terry's Ferry. Arriving at Bayou Fourche (4 miles south of Little Rock), the enemy were discovered drawn up in battle line, their right resting on the river, and their left extending parallel to our front. According to orders, I dismounted the men, and made the following disposition of the forces under my command: Colonel [Colton] Greene's regiment, commanded by Major [L. A.] Campbell, on the right; my regiment, commanded by Lieutenant-Colonel [S. J.] Ward, and Lieutenant-Colonel [W. J.] Preston, commanding Colonel [J. Q.] Burbridge's regiment, in the center, and Lieutenant-Colonel [M. L.] Young's battalion on the left. Two companies of Lieutenant-Colonel Ward's regiment were deployed as skirmishers. After some slight skirmishing, the enemy, with a body of cavalry and a section of howitzers, attempted to flank us on the left from the river bank. Here a severe engagement took place, which lasted nearly half an hour, and we succeeded in driving the enemy from his position, completely routing him, and forcing him to leave his artillery (two 12-pounder mountain howitzers), which we captured, on the field. I was then ordered to withdraw the brigade (leaving Lieutenant-Colonel Ward with his regiment, supported by General Marmaduke's escort, to cover our retreat), and form about one-half mile from the bayou, in an open field, as the enemy was making a flank movement on our right. Lieutenant-Colonel Ward remained in position about two hours, skirmishing heavily with the enemy, when, finding that there was imminent danger of being surrounded on both flanks, he was compelled to withdraw from the bayou, and retreat to the main body. As the enemy, with vastly superior force, attempted to flank us on the right, and kept up an incessant and harassing fire from their batteries planted on the river bank, I, according to orders, fell back slowly, in line of battle, to Little Rock, skirmishing all the while.* Here Colonel Kitchen, who had been ordered to burn the pontoon bridges and protect the removal of the public stores from the fort, joined the brigade, and I was ordered to march 10 miles on the Benton road, where I bivouacked for the night.

On the morning of the 11th, I was ordered to continue the march, Major Campbell's regiment acting as rear guard. At 10 a.m. the enemy drove in his vedettes. Retiring slowly by company, making successive formations, Major Campbell fought the enemy for 7 miles, drew them into an ambuscade, and completely checked them for the time. At noon the brigade halted, fed, and [Major] Colonel Campbell was relieved by Lieutenant-Colonel Preston, who skirmished with the enemy until late in the evening, when they ceased their pursuit.

I encamped that night 6 miles west of the Saline. Left camp at 12 m. the next day, traveled 7 miles, and encamped for the night.

At 8 o'clock the following morning moved forward, and reached Rockport on the evening of the same day.

During the engagement at Bayou Fourche and the subsequent skirmishes the officers and soldiers of this brigade all fought with the coolness and intrepidity of veterans, and did their duty nobly. Lieutenant [T. J.] Williams, commanding the prairie gun battery, did special execution on the retreat, and deserves honorable mention.

Respectfully submitted.

WM. L. JEFFERS,
Colonel, Commanding Brigade.

---

* For casualties, see p. 523.

No. 28.

Report of Col. Robert C. Newton, Fifth Arkansas Cavalry, commanding brigade, of operations August 25–September 14.

HEADQUARTERS CAVALRY BRIGADE,
Camp near Washington, Ark., December 3, 1863.

MAJOR: I have the honor, in obedience to orders, to submit the following report of the operations, camps, marches, &c., of my command from the day of the battle at Brownsville to the time of the arrival of General Marmaduke's division at Rockport:

The engagement at Brownsville occurred on August 25. Colonel [A. S.] Dobbin's brigade (composed of Dobbin's and [Robert C.] Newton's regiments) was encamped at Legate's Bridge, on Bayou Meto. About 7 a. m. scouts reported the enemy moving upon Brownsville and near the town. By Colonel Dobbin's order I moved my regiment, in rear of his, out into the prairie about a mile from Legate's, the brigade trains being sent on the prairie road to get upon the main military road at Baker's. About 9 a. m. scouts sent by Colonel Dobbin toward Brownsville reported that the enemy was in town, and General Marmaduke retiring on military (or Wire) road toward Little Rock. We accordingly retired on the prairie road to the Wire road at Baker's, where General Marmaduke's command was formed, and thence down Wire road to Long's Prairie, where we formed to cover retirement of General Marmaduke's forces. Remained there an hour or so, and then, by order of Brigadier-General Walker, (commanding the cavalry at that time), we moved on to Bayou Meto at Reed's Bridge, where line of battle was formed on the west bank of the bayou. My regiment was immediately to the right of the bridge. We remained there all night.

The next morning (August 26) my regiment was detached by General Walker and ordered to Shallow Ford, to cover that crossing of Bayou Meto. I moved from Reed's Bridge about 9 a. m., and reached Shallow Ford at 3.30 p. m. Learning from citizens that a party of Federals had been there the day before, I immediately upon my arrival there, and after posting my pickets so as to guard against surprise, sent out small scouts upon all the roads on the east side of the bayou leading to the ford. Lieutenant [J. C.] Barnes, of Company A, whom I sent with 8 men upon the road leading from Shallow Ford to Long's stage stand, on the Wire road, encountered a party of 10 or 12 Federals about 2 miles beyond the bayou, who fled precipitately at his approach. He pursued them some distance, but was unable to overtake them. Being satisfied, from the result of the reconnaissance of the different roads, that no force of the enemy was in the neighborhood of the ford, I encamped on the bayou, near Mrs. Ewell's, and about a mile above the ford, picketing carefully toward Brownsville and other points from which an attack was possible. Here I remained all night.

Early the next morning (August 27) heavy cannonading commenced at Reed's Bridge, indicating an engagement there. The firing in that direction increasing, I pushed out small scouts upon all the roads leading from the ford toward the Wire road, and satisfying myself that the enemy were making no demonstration toward me, I left Major [J. P.] Bull with the bulk of my force to hold the crossing at Shallow Ford and keep up communication with General Walker at Reed's Bridge, and with about 80 men I crossed the bayou and moved toward the Wire road. Reaching Baker's place, on that road, about 4 or 5 miles from Shallow Ford, I there encountered a small Federal picket, which my advance, under Lieutenant Barnes, attacked and scattered, some of them going in the direction of Brownsville and the others toward Reed's Bridge. Pushing on down the Wire road toward Little Rock, I ran off about one company of Federals picketing at Long's stage stand. They left in great confusion without firing upon me. I pressed on in pursuit some 2 or 3 miles beyond Long's, whence I returned to that place, and from there by the direct road made my way back to Shallow Ford. Soon afterward the firing ceased at Reed's Bridge.

About 8 p. m. got a note from General Walker's assistant adjutant-general informing me that he was withdrawing from Reed's Bridge, and directing me to retire on the direct road leading from Shallow Ford toward Little Rock to the point where that road intersects the Wire road, about 4 miles from the river, opposite Little Rock, and to move at once, sending a few trusty scouts across the bayou to get upon the Wire road in rear of [J. W.] Davidson, and report to me in the morning what should transpire during the night.

I withdrew my pickets and commenced the retrograde movement in obedience to General Walker's order. Reached the point designated in the order about 12 p. m., and immediately dispatched a courier, reporting to General Walker my arrival there, according to order. Bivouacked there for the remainder of the night.

About 8.30 a. m. the next day (August 28) received an order from General Walker to move to English's, on the Shallow Ford road, about 2½ miles from its intersection with Wire road, camp there, and picket 6 or 8 miles in advance of me. Obeyed the order at once; remained in camp there that night; sent Captain [L. D.] Bryant with his company (G) to Shallow Ford to ascertain if there was any news there of the enemy.

The next morning (August 29), about 8 o'clock, Bryant returned; no news of enemy toward Shallow Ford. At 3 p. m., by General Walker's direction, I moved from camp at English's toward Shallow Ford for the purpose of taking position near that place; camped for the night at Hicks' plantation, 5 miles from English's; sent Captain [John H.] Dyer with his company (D) to Legate's Bridge, on lower road, scouting.

The next morning (August 30) moved from Hicks' at sunrise, in direction of Shallow Ford. Just beyond Greenwood's met a small party of Federals; advanced Major Bull, with 15 men, to ascertain enemy's strength; Federals fled at his approach. He pursued them rapidly to Mrs. Ewell's, where he learned a considerable body of the enemy had been in the morning. Arriving there, I placed 40 men under command of Major Bull, and sent him forward to ascertain enemy's whereabouts and strength. About a half mile beyond we found some little force of enemy. It retired to the railroad, where a heavy force of dismounted cavalry was lying concealed behind the railroad embankment. In a short time, being re-enforced from Shallow Ford by cavalry and artillery, the enemy commenced advancing from his position behind the railroad. Bull resisted his advance almost at every step, his men behaving with admirable courage and steadiness. I immediately ordered forward all the men with long-range guns in the command, and made my preparations to retire before the vastly superior force of the enemy, determining, however, to fight him as I fell back. He now commenced using his artillery upon me very freely, and, although I had none to reply with, I continued the fight with my small-arms at every available point, dispatching a courier to General Walker with information of the enemy's movement, and suggesting that more force be sent upon the Shallow Ford road. The fighting, which commenced a little before 9 o'clock, had now continued with but short intermissions until 2 o'clock, when, being forced back to Martin's place, I took pos tion there for the purpose of delaying the enemy as long as possible and give the re-enforcements, if any should be sent, time to come up, inasmuch as Ashley's Mills and the crossing of the Arkansas River at Terry's Ferry would be left entirely exposed should I be forced back a mile farther. About 3 o'clock the enemy advanced to the attack. I had concealed Companies B and E, the two under command of Captain [P. J.] Rollow, of the latter company, in the edge of Hicks' field, in front of which was an open clearing of 30 or 40 paces, and cautioned my men to let the enemy get well into this clearing before they fired, and then to rake them with their shot-guns. Displaying a few scouts in front on the road, the enemy in line pushed rapidly on, and Companies B and E, having obeyed the injunctions given them, delivered a volley into their forces when they were not expecting any resistance whatever. Recovering from his confusion, the enemy, not being willing to run onto the ambuscade a second time, although my men had then been withdrawn from there, commenced sending heavy bodies of dismounted cavalry to my right and left. The nature of the country permitting this double flank movement, and my force being wholly inadequate to prevent it (as I had but 180 fighting men), I retired slowly to Hicks', three-quarters of a mile distant, leaving a rear guard of 40 men to observe the enemy and resist any farther advance should he attempt it. Arriving at Hicks', I put my little force into position to meet him again, but he advanced upon me no farther. About sundown Lieutenant-Colonel Hooper, with [G. W.] Thompson's regiment Missouri cavalry and one section of Collins' battery from General Marmaduke's command, with orders to report to me, arrived at Hicks'. I disposed the whole force for battle, and pushed forward my scouts to ascertain what the enemy was doing.

About dark he moved back toward Shallow Ford, crossing Bayou Meto at that place, and leaving a strong picket there. I accordingly encamped for the night at Hicks', and remained there the next day (August 31), skirmishing continuing between my advance and their pickets at Mrs. Ewell's nearly all the morning, and some considerable skirmishing during the night.

This state of things continued also during the following day (September 1). About 11 p. m. of that day received an order from General Walker to move with my regiment to Ashley's Mills at once, and encamp on road leading from the mill to Terry's Ferry.

Moved at 11.20 p. m., and reached the point designated about 2.30 a. m. September 2, and encamped as directed, leaving Lieutenant-Colonel [J. C.] Hooper, with his regiment and the section of [R. A.] Collins' battery, at Hicks'.

Remained in the camp near Ashley's Mills, on road from there to Terry's Ferry, during September 3 and 4.

On morning of September 5, by direction of General Walker (through Colonel Dobbin, commanding brigade), moved onto the road which leads directly from Eagle's Bridge (over Bayou Meto) toward Little Rock, on north side of river, and encamped on that road a half mile from Ashley's Bayou and about a mile from Ashley's Mills.

Remained in that camp on September 6. Scouted to Shallow Ford and Legate's Bridge, driving the enemy's pickets to the bayou at the former place, and finding no Federals at the latter. About dark received an order from General Price's headquarters (through intermediate commanders, &c.), directing Colonel Dobbin to assume command of

Walker's division and for me to assume command of Dobbin's brigade. Dobbin's regiment (which with my regiment composed that brigade) was encamped on south bank of river, at Buck's Ford, some 4 or 5 miles distant from where my own regiment was. Brigade headquarters had been established by Colonel Dobbin at Terry's house, intermediate between the two regiments.

The next morning (September 7) went to the brigade headquarters, leaving Major Bull in command of my regiment. About 8.30 a. m. Major Bull reported the enemy rapidly advancing upon him from Shallow Ford, and that skirmishing was going on at Ashley's Bayou, in front of his camp. I immediately sent him an order to resist his advance with all possible obstinacy, and retire, when forced, on the Little Rock road to the Arkansas River at Mrs. Adamson's plantation, and there cross by the ford at that place; but only to retire as he was driven, and contest every inch of ground. I at the same time sent directions to Major [S.] Corley, commanding Dobbin's regiment, to have his command well in hand to resist the enemy should he (by moving directly from Ashley's Mills to Terry's Ferry, as he could do, and thence to Buck's) attempt to force a crossing at that place. I then went by a cross-path to the road upon which Bull was engaging the enemy, and found him, in obedience to the orders sent him, making a most gallant resistance against overwhelming odds, and causing the enemy to pay dearly for every inch of ground he gained upon him. Detaching Lieutenant [J. T.] Lawler with Company L from Major Bull, I ordered him to move rapidly to the road which leads directly from Ashley's Mills to Terry's Ferry, and move up it as far as possible, to ascertain if the enemy were moving there, and, in case he should be forced back, to retire down the river and cross at Buck's. Returning to Terry's, I learned that the enemy were driving Lawler before them, and would soon be at the ferry as well as upon the river at Adamson's, toward which point they were forcing Bull, notwithstanding his stubborn resistance. Repeating the instructions to Lawler as to his point for crossing the river, I forded the stream just below Terry's, and ordering Major Corley to be in readiness to move to Bull's assistance should the enemy attempt to follow him across, I went up the river to the point where Bull was to cross, and found him effecting the crossing in safety and without molestation from the enemy, who ceased the pursuit as soon as they reached the river just below Adamson's. By direction of Colonel Dobbin, commanding division, I encamped Bull's regiment just below Temple's, on the Arkansas River, opposite Adamson's, to guard the ford there, leaving Corley with his regiment at the ford at Badgett's, just above Buck's Ford, and between there and Terry's Ferry, keeping a strong picket at Terry's Ferry.

On next day (September 8) matters remained in about same condition, considerable firing going on all day between enemy's pickets and mine at Terry's Ferry; but as they were firing across the river, no damage of consequence was done. Etter's Arkansas battery was put in position at ford at Bull's camp and placed under my orders. All quiet during that night.

On the next day (September 9) considerable activity observable among the enemy. Bodies of cavalry moved up the river and returned. About dark my pickets reported that enemy was hauling lumber to near the ford in the point of the bend, half mile above Terry's Ferry, and putting batteries in position. Heavy knocking heard during the night; enemy evidently preparing to construct bridge across the river. Reported all this information, sent me by my pickets, to division headquarters.

A little before daylight (September 10), by direction of Colonel Dobbin, commanding division, moved section of [C. B.] Etter's battery into the bend opposite to where the bridge was being constructed. At daylight could see workmen engaged in constructing the bridge, which was one-fourth of the way across the river. Sent Major Bull with a party of sharpshooters to support Etter. A little after daylight Etter opened upon the bridge. His second shot took effect, clearing the bridge of workmen. Immediately the enemy opened with three batteries, so posted as to pour a murderous cross-fire in upon Etter, which soon silenced him and drove him out. The sharpshooters kept up a desultory fire, but without much, if any, effect. About 10 a. m. the enemy, having completed his bridge, threw forward two regiments of infantry, and crossed them over onto the bar on this side, his batteries keeping up a continuous and well-directed fire upon the road leading up the river on the south side, and upon the woods in front of his bridge and above it. I withdrew Major Corley to a point above the bridge on the river, and sent Etter on up the river with instructions to halt at Fourche, whither I also sent Corley with his regiment in a few minutes. The enemy now commenced pouring their troops across the bridge in large numbers. By Colonel Dobbin's directions, I left Bull with his regiment to resist the enemy's advance and retard him as much as possible, and went in person to put the other troops in position at Fourche. Brigadier-General Marmaduke arrived with orders to assume command of all the cavalry. Colonel Dobbin being placed in arrest by General Marmaduke's directions, I assumed command of all of Dobbin's force, which included my own brigade, [W. B.] Denson's Louisiana cavalry company, [C. L.] Morgan's Texas squadron, and Pratt's and Etter's batteries. Major Corley's regiment being dismounted, was sent to where the road leading to the mouth of old Fourche and the road leading across the dam diverge, at the corner of Vaughan's field, and Etter's battery was likewise put in position there. Pratt's battery was placed in position in Vaughan's field, opposite the dam across Fourche, and Bull's regiment, Denson's company, and Morgan's squadron disposed along the bayou on the right and left of the battery in such manner as to support it, and at the same time to be used to our right should the enemy attempt to cross the bayou above us. The battle opened on our left. The enemy in small parties came up in my front so as to be distinctly visible between my position and Fletcher's house, but I directed Pratt to reserve his fire until they advanced in some force and came within easy range, when he was to ply them vigorously with grape and canister. It was not until after their repulse by Jeffers' brigade, on our left, that they advanced upon me, when Pratt opened with his two guns and quickly drove them back. Moving to our right, they attempted to force a crossing of the bayou, but were met and handsomely driven back by Bull's command, assisted by Pratt's trusty guns, which continued to rake them with canister and grape until Fletcher's field, which was immediately in my front, was entirely cleared of them.

I respectfully call attention to Captain [J. H.] Pratt's report, herewith forwarded, and earnestly commend him for the skill and bravery displayed here, as he has displayed them on every field where I have had occasion to observe him.

The enemy being driven from my front, I reported the fact by a staff officer to the brigadier-general commanding. The firing in the mean time grew hotter on our left, and indicated that we were retiring there. In a short time I received an order to withdraw through Vaughan's field, and get upon the river road near Keatt's, which I did. I received an order to report to Colonel Dobbin, and by his directions moved through Little Rock and upon the southern road to Ayliff's, where the command encamped for the night.

Next day (September 11) moved to Saline River, just beyond Benton, and encamped on south bank of the river.

On the morning of the 12th, by order of General Price, I was detached, temporarily, from Colonel Dobbin's command, and ordered to report, with my regiment, to General Marmaduke. Moved back to Benton and reported to General Marmaduke. He immediately formed a brigade, composed of my regiment, Morgan's Texas squadron, [J. J.] Miller's Arkansas cavalry company, and Blocher's Arkansas battery, and, placing me in command, ordered me to take position at Benton as rear guard. Moved there accordingly. The enemy ascertained to be on the Wire road, 6 miles east of Benton, and scouting on Hot Springs road. Enemy retired about 12 m., and about 5 p. m., by direction of General Marmaduke, I moved down the Wire road and joined balance of division at Saline River, and, retiring still farther, we encamped for the night at the Wills place, 2 miles from the river.

On September 13, moved 7 miles on Rockport road, and encamped for the night at Cash's.

On September 14, moved to Rockport, and encamped 1½ miles south of town.

This embraces a full history of my command during the time embraced in your order.

I forward herewith lists of the killed, wounded, and missing during that time.*

I cannot too strongly commend the bravery and dash of Maj. John P. Bull, Newton's regiment, and take great pleasure in here making honorable mention of Lieut. J. C. Barnes, Company A, same regiment, who, in every action in which my command was engaged, rendered valuable service, and was distinguished for his coolness and bravery. To Captain [W. N.] Portis, same regiment, I am indebted for valuable services during the time mentioned.

In the engagement at Fourche the brave Maj. Samuel Corley, commanding Dobbin's regiment, was killed while fighting in gallant style. To that command it was an irreparable loss, and in his death the country was deprived of the services of one of its bravest and most devoted officers. To an unflinching courage was added a sincere piety, and in him was furnished as noble a specimen of the Christian soldier as any our cause can boast. As that regiment was not immediately under my observation at Fourche, I cannot here speak of the conduct of those who most distinguished themselves, but refer you to the report of killed and wounded for evidence as to how well the regiment did its duty. It was under the immediate command of Colonel Dobbin himself, engaged in the fight at Reed's Bridge, but, of course, its part in that affair is not included in the foregoing report.

I have also to tender my acknowledgments to Major Morgan, commanding Texas squadron, for his promptness and zeal at Fourche, and during the whole time that he was under my command.

Captain Pratt has already been mentioned, and attention called to his services.

While I have here mentioned the names of some who were under my command during that period, I must ask that it be not taken as any dis-

*See revised statement, p. 523.

paragement of others. Officers and men, without any known exception, did their duty well, and all deserve the thanks of the country.

I am, major, very respectfully,

R. C. NEWTON,
Colonel, Commanding.

Maj. HENRY EWING,
Assistant Adjutant-General, Marmaduke's Division, &c.

ADDENDA.

Officers and men of Newton's regiment "particularly distinguished" in the engagement at Bayou Fourche.

Lieuts. J. C. Barnes and John Bradley; Sergts. C. D. England and B. F. Rodgers; Corpl. John Hinkle, and Privates A. Bradley, S. H. Bradley, John Griggs, C. C. Rodgers, and James Woddel.

No. 29.

Report of Capt. M. M. Bateman, Dobbin's regiment, of operations August 25–September 11.

NOVEMBER 21, 1863.

COLONEL: On August 25 last, immediately after the engagement with the enemy at Brownsville, Ark., the command, under orders from General L. M. Walker, commanding, took up the line of march to Bayou Meto, where we arrived the evening of the same day. We encamped there for the night and two succeeding days, or part thereof, when we were attacked by the enemy about 9 p. m. of the same date. At the above engagement the regiment was commanded by Col. Archibald S. Dobbin, who evinced the energy, skill, and daring of an intrepid leader, always foremost, encouraging the men to firmness, resolution, and precision. It occupied a position near the center of our lines, and received, in connection with the remainder, the repeated charges of the enemy, forcing them to retire discomfited and with heavy loss. At 6 o'clock the enemy withdrew from the engagement. Casualties will be found in the annexed report.*

Some three hours after the above engagement we were ordered to march, which we did, to a position some 5 or 6 miles east of Little Rock, where we encamped till the evening of August 31; from which place, under command of Maj. S. Corley, we marched to Terry's Ferry, on the north and east side of Arkansas River, where we remained till September 6, when the regiment was ordered to the south and west side of the river, at which point it remained, picketing it, until the morning of the 10th. At this place our pickets exchanged repeated shots with the enemy.

On the 9th, while occupying the latter position, we were repeatedly shelled through the day, though with no effect.

On the following morning (the 10th), they opened their batteries on our troops occupying the point at Terry's Ferry, and also upon those at Badgett's Ferry (or ford). The regiment at this time was divided—one squadron ordered to the support of our troops and battery at the first named, and the other to those of the latter place, and from thence

---

* See revised statement, p. 523.

covered the retreat of the battery to Bayou Fourche without any casualties during the engagement.

The command arrived at Bayou Fourche about 10 o'clock on the morning of the same day, and were formed in order of battle on the north side of the bayou (dismounted), where they so remained for a short time, then in front of the enemy's left wing. From this point they were ordered up the bayou to the angle of the road, and there remounted in front of the enemy's center, at which point they confronted the enemy till compelled to retire before an overwhelming force, together with the want of ammunition, having exhausted the few rounds in resisting the enemy's approach. From this position the command retired in good order, and only when surrounded on three sides by the enemy.

In this engagement we lost our gallant commander, Maj. S. Corley, and Lieut. W. H. Bowers, of Company A, together with other casualties to be found in the annexed report.*

The above account may be incorrect in many particulars. Two companies in the regiment (and in the engagement at Bayou Meto) are now absent from the command; consequently, no report of the casualties in them, if any. Besides, the regimental books were captured, together with the adjutant (Capt. [Edward H.] Cowley), at Terry's Ferry, of whom I omitted making mention in the above report, he having been captured before the engagement commenced.

Respectfully submitted.

M. M. BATEMAN,
Captain, Commanding Regiment.

[Col.] W. O. PEPPER, *Assistant Adjutant-General.*

No. 30.

Report of Capt. J. H. Pratt, Texas Battery, of engagement at Bayou Fourche.

HEADQUARTERS ARTILLERY BATTALION,
November 20, 1863.

COLONEL: I have the honor to forward the following as a report of the part my battery took in the action before Little Rock, September 10:

On the morning of September 9, I was ordered to move my battery to Badgett's Ford, on the Arkansas River, to prevent, if possible, the enemy's advance in that direction, and resist the passage of the river should they attempt a crossing. During the night of the 9th, I constructed a cotton fort by hauling the bales from a farm near by and placing them upon the bank of the river in such a manner that I thought would resist the enemy's shot and protect my men.

On the morning of the 10th, the enemy's cavalry moved up in my front, some 600 or 700 strong. When they had arrived within range, I ordered my battery to fire upon them, which was promptly done, driving the enemy from the bank of the river behind the levee for shelter. The enemy's loss during this time was 6 killed and 8 wounded. They moved up and placed in position behind the levee two six-gun batteries and opened fire upon my fort. I returned the fire after they had fired the second round, which proved very destructive, killing all the cannoneers of two pieces of the enemy's guns, causing them to have their guns carried off by the cavalry. My cannonading was so destructive that it

* Embodied in statement on p. 523.

caused them to change position up the river some 200 yards. They did not succeed in getting my range until one of my shells, which failed to explode, fell in the vicinity of their battery, when it was examined and their fuses cut in accordance with it. After this their shelling was very accurate. General [J. W.] Davidson reported this to Surgeon [A.] Dunlop, C. S. Army, left at hospital in Little Rock. I could have held the fort any length of time but for the enemy's effecting a crossing some miles above me, which caused me to evacuate the fort and move up the river to Bayou Fourche, where I was ordered to take position on the west side of the stream. The enemy threw forward their sharpshooters, engaging my battery, when I ordered my battery to open upon them with canister, which was done, driving the enemy from us in perfect confusion and causing considerable loss. A four-gun battery was placed in position by the enemy immediately in my front, and while it was going into battery I poured canister into it so rapidly that they could only fire two rounds, and were driven off the field. After this the sharpshooters moved up on our right, opening a hot fire upon Col. R. C. Newton's command, but they were driven off by the colonel, notwithstanding their repeated efforts to advance. At this time a six-gun battery of the enemy was run forward and placed in battery, and fought for some half hour very gallantly, but I succeeded in silencing it, and driving it from the field. This last battle was supported by infantry. Everything having been withdrawn from my front, I was ordered to retire, marching through Little Rock and on the Arkadelphia road. We moved out some 15 miles south of Little Rock, and encamped for the night.

The next morning the march was resumed, and we encamped that evening on the Saline River, 2 miles south of Benton, on military road.

On the 12th, we marched to Rockport, on Ouachita River, and remained there until September 21, when I was ordered to report to General Price, at Arkadelphia, and was ordered by him to Convalescent Camp, 16 miles south of that place, on Washington road.

My loss was: None killed and none wounded.

Officers and men conducted themselves very gallantly during the whole of the day.

Too much praise cannot be given Corporal [M.] Gorman for his gallant conduct on the field, and for his skill as a gunner and an artillerist.

I am, colonel, very respectfully, your obedient servant,

J. H. PRATT,
Captain, Commanding Battery.

Col. R. C. NEWTON, *Commanding Brigade.*

No. 31.

Report of Brig. Gen. D. M. Frost, C. S. Army, commanding division, of operations August 23.

HEADQUARTERS PRICE'S DIVISION,
August 23, 1863.

MAJOR: I propose to move Clark's brigade to Redoubt No. 1, because the position he now occupies is covered by the troops in front at Bayou Meto, while the road by Shoal Ford is entirely unguarded, unless our cavalry now occupy it in sufficient force, of which I have received no notice. While the fords and crossings of the river below are unguarded, I do not feel at liberty to recommend Tappan's brigade to this side of the river. I have ordered the advance brigades to fall back to the rifle-pits (which in their incomplete condition are hardly worthy of the name), and have directed Colonel Clark to move to Redoubt No. 1. and if General Tappan should be ordered over, Clark can very readily be advanced to Mount Gallant or Redoubt No. 3.

I am, major, very respectfully, your obedient servant,

D. M. FROST,
Brigadier-General, Commanding Division.

Maj. THOMAS L. SNEAD, *Assistant Adjutant-General.*

[Indorsement.]

HEADQUARTERS DISTRICT OF ARKANSAS,
Little Rock, August 23, 1863.

Respectfully returned to Brigadier-General Frost, who will make such disposition of the troops as he may think best.

By order of Major-General Price:

THOS. L. SNEAD,
Major and Assistant Adjutant-General.

AUGUST 2, 1863.—Skirmish at Stumptown, Mo.

Report of Maj. Alexander W. Mullins, First Missouri State Militia Cavalry.

HDQRS. DETACHMENT 1ST MISSOURI STATE MILITIA CAV.,
Germantown, Mo., August 6, 1863.

COLONEL: I returned to camp yesterday evening, having been out on a scout four days with 100 men of Companies F, G, and H, under my command at this station. On Sunday evening (the first day out) we had a skirmish with a squad of bushwhackers at Stumptown, on the Double Branches, Bates County, in which Private John S. Luyster, of Company F, First Missouri State Militia Cavalry, was killed. We routed the bushwhackers in short order, but did not succeed in killing a single one. I ascertained afterward that two or three of them were wounded. The next day we drove some twenty or more across the Marais-des-Cygnes, or Big Osage, very precipitately, causing them to swim the stream at a very uninviting place. The next day we followed in pursuit as far as the Marmiton (southwest branch of the Osage); but, in consequence of high water, we did not go farther. Yesterday, in returning to camp, we had several chases after straggling bushwhackers, but did not succeed in accomplishing anything. We captured during the trip 4 horses, which the bushwhackers were forced to leave. One of the horses belonged to a loyal citizen of Bates County, and was stolen about one month ago, which I have restored to his owner. Marchbanks and Handcock, with their bands, have retired south of the Osage and of Bates County, and between the Osage and Grand Rivers. There are now comparatively few of them around, but bands of from 200 to 500 men are passing very frequently, I will safely say every night. Owing to great fatigue, caused by hard riding and excessive hot weather, I am scarcely able to write this morning.

Very respectfully, your obedient servant,

ALEX. W. MULLINS,
Major First Missouri State Militia Cavalry.

Col. JAMES MCFERRAN,
First Missouri State Militia Cavalry.

AUGUST —, 1863.—Scout from Pocahontas, Ark., to Patterson Mo.

Report of Lieut. Col. William J. Preston, Fourth Missouri Cavalry (Confederate).

HEADQUARTERS BURBRIDGE'S REGIMENT,
Near Pocahontas, August 6, 1863.

MAJOR: I have just returned from a scout into Missouri. I visited Greenville with the intention of destroying 30 wagons of commissaries deposited at Widow McMinn's, near Hog-Eye, in Bollinger County. Upon arriving at Greenville, I was reliably informed that they had some days before destroyed their goods and left in haste. I then proceeded to Patterson, where I caught a sutler's wagon with a load of goods, a Federal captain, paroled by Colonel Greene, 3 privates of Leeper's company, and the deputy provost-marshal and enrolling officer. There were two squadrons of cavalry at Stony Battery, apprised of my whereabouts and lying in ambush. My force being small, I concluded not to attack them, but endeavored to draw them out. After staying in Patterson for four or five hours, I moved slowly in the direction of Van Buren, with the intention of attacking a company at Barnesville, who, however, withdrew toward Ironton. I succeeded in interrupting their Congressional election and enrollment. I have advanced my individual scouts as far as Lebanon, in Laclede County, with the intention of visiting that section and the tributaries of the Osage River, and mounting this regiment should General Marmaduke permit me. It is perfectly feasible, and would diversify the forces of the enemy.

At present there are three companies of cavalry at Big Creek Bridge, just beyond Stony Battery, 300 infantry at Rolla, and one company of militia at Lebanon. Pursuing scout by-ways, I would meet with no opposition. I sincerely petition for permission to make the trip.

Captain Reves would engage the attention of the enemy near Patterson, and Captain Lineback on the ridge. Major Smith (now on the ridge) would be recalled to make the trip.

I forward under guard two privates of Leeper's company and the provost-marshal, who was enrolling negroes. I inclose his documents.* I hope and respectfully request that none of the three be released from guard for awhile. Should the general conclude to release Whybark, send him through my lines, giving me due notice of the same.

Respectfully,

WM. J. PRESTON,
Lieutenant-Colonel, Commanding Regiment.

Maj. HENRY EWING,
Assistant Adjutant-General, Marmaduke's Division.

P. S.—Don't forget my trip to Missouri. I move to-day to the intersection of the Thomasville road and Eleven Points for forage, leaving a lieutenant and 12 men here to guard the ferry and sustain the line of communication.

---

*Not found.

AUGUST 6-9, 1863.—Scout from Greenfield to Golden Grove and Carthage Mo.

Report of Capt. Jacob Cassairt, Eighth Missouri State Militia Cavalry.

GREENFIELD, MO., *August* 10, 1863.

GENERAL: I herewith transmit to you the report of a scout that left here on the 6th of August, 1863, under the command of Captain [J. J.] Akard, Company A, First Battalion Eighth Missouri State Militia Cavalry.

Scouting the brush of Horse Creek, and crossing from Horse Creek to Golden Grove, over muddy [roads], about 3 o'clock the same day, surprising a band of guerrillas, 6 in number, killing 5; but 1 escaped. Among the killed are Captain Osburn and 1 recruiting officer by the name of Bebee. No other names known. Captured 6 horses and saddles and arms. Captain Akard, with his command, marched from said Grove to Carthage, and learned from Captain [M.] Burch that Coffee is supposed to be at or in the vicinity of Maysville, Ark. Captain Burch informed Captain Akard that there were but few guerrillas in the surrounding country of Carthage. Captain Akard returned on the 9th of August, 1863.

Very respectfully, your most obedient servant,

JACOB CASSAIRT,

Captain Eighth Missouri State Militia Cavalry, Comdg. Post.

Brigadier-General MCNEIL,

Commanding Southwestern District of Missouri.

AUGUST 6-9, 1863.—Scout from Lexington to vicinity of Hopewell, Mo.

Report of Col. James McFerran, First Missouri State Militia Cavalry.

LEXINGTON, MO., *August* 10, 1863.

GENERAL: I have the honor to state that, pursuant to your directions by telegraph of the 6th instant, I left this post at 10 p. m. on the night of the 6th instant, with all the available force at this post, being 150 men and three pieces of light artillery, to make the point suggested. We took up the line of march for Wellington. The night was very dark, and the rain descended in torrents. We continued our march, and were delayed in crossing the Big Sni, east of Wellington. We, however, passed through Wellington before daylight, and continued our march to Texas Prairie. About 11 o'clock we reached Eagin's Point, and there saw a small band of bushwhackers, who fled at our approach. While reconnoitering, to ascertain the point described in your telegram, another band of about 30 came in sight, going in the direction of Eagin's Point. As soon as they saw our force, they fled in an easterly direction. I sent out scouting parties, with a view of ascertaining the position of the enemy, and ascertained that there were but few in the immediate vicinity of Eagin's Point, which is about 3 miles northeast of Lick Skillet. I was unable to find the Seacock place, where Kogin lives. I could find no person who knew where the place was. Night coming on, we encamped at Colonel Elliot's place. The next morning we took up the line of march in the direction of Round Prairie. The rains enabled us to track any force that might be in the vicinity. We, however, failed to see any sign of a camp, and, after going nearly to Round Prairie, we turned east to Chapel Hill, then to Hopewell. Here we ascertained that the guerrillas were not concentrated, but were on Davis Creek, on the waters of the Sni, and in Greenton Valley. One of our reconnoitering parties killed 2 of the guerrillas, and, night coming on, we encamped in the vicinity of Hopewell.

The next morning I divided our force into three parties. Sent one down the Sni, one down Davis Creek, and came, with the artillery, through Greenton Valley, reaching here on the evening of the 9th. The expedition determined clearly to my mind that the guerrillas had not concentrated. I am very much inclined to think that our appearance in Texas Prairie on the 7th, and the heavy rain-storm of the night of the 6th, prevented their concentration.

At 10 o'clock of the 7th, as we came east, we found that the guerrillas had gone east. On the night of the 7th, our men chased numerous small bands on the Sni and Davis Creek, but were unable to overtake them. I directed some seven families of the most influential rebels, who have been feeding and harboring guerrillas, to report at Lexington, within ten days, with their families and effects, prepared to leave the country. The women gave more aid and comfort than the men to the guerrillas. I learned that the guerrillas had notified some Union families to leave, and I did not know of a better plan than to retaliate, to afford protection to the loyal men. I hope this move will meet your approval, because it will be impossible to rid the country and protect the loyal people while these notorious and influential families remain to feed and comfort them.

The two companies that came from the south, as it is said, to escort Quantrill out, commanded by Blunt and Graves, were on the Sni, west of Hopewell, on the night of the 7th, and, from the best information I could get, I supposed they had gone east from there. Diligent search failed to find them on the Sni on the 8th and 9th. Graves was killed on the evening of the 7th, west of Hopewell, on the Sni, by his own men.

I will keep up constant scouting, and if I can learn anything in relation to concentration, advise you at once by telegraph.

While absent, the post being in charge of a few men, mostly Provisional Militia, 2 prisoners, named Carlisle and Porter, made their escape.

I have the honor to be, general, your humble servant,

JAMES McFERRAN,
Colonel First Missouri State Militia Cavalry, Commanding Post.

Brigadier-General EWING, *Kansas City.*

AUGUST 6-11, 1863.—Scout from Houston to Spring River Mills, Mo., and skirmishes.

Report of Capt. Richard Murphy, Fifth Missouri State Militia Cavalry.

ROLLA, MO., *August* 16, 1863.

GENERAL: I have the honor to make the following report of a scout made by me, in accordance with special orders from your headquarters:

On the 6th instant, I started from Houston, Mo., with detachments from Companies B, C, F, and G, of the Fifth Missouri State Militia Cavalry, with two pieces of artillery from Captain Backof's battery, under command of Lieutenant [C.] Stierlin, the whole force amounting to 270 men. On the night of the 6th, I reached Hutton Valley without meeting with anything of importance.

On the 7th, about 15 miles south of Hutton Valley, the advance, under command of Lieutenant Benz, came upon a band of rebels, numbering about 20. Our men fired on the rebels, when they fled, and a running fight ensued, in which 2 of the rebels were killed. I encamped that night about 15 miles southeast of West Plains.

On the morning of the 8th, when I had advanced about 8 miles from my last camp in a southeasterly direction, the advance guard, under Lieutenant [A.] Muntzel, was fired on by a party of guerrillas, numbering from 25 to 30, and posted on an eminence. Lieutenant Muntzel charged on the rebels, when they fled precipitately, pursued by him. In this skirmish there were 3 rebels killed by the men under Lieutenant Muntzel, and 5 more by the scouts and flankers. On this same day I proceeded 2 miles farther to Gouge's Mill, at which place I found a notice posted up, calling on the citizens to enlist in the Confederate army. I surrounded this mill and took the inmates by surprise. There were 5 Confederate soldiers, 2 of whom belonged to Burbridge and the remaining 3 to Freeman's command. This mill I found to be a rendezvous for the guerrillas and horse thieves which infest this vicinity. I also found a gunsmith shop at this place, where these lawless bands get their arms repaired. Both of these buildings I had burned. I then proceeded in the direction of Spring River Mills, but when only 3 miles on the way, the advance was again fired on by the rebels, who were concealed in a corn-field on the rise of a hill. A slight skirmish then took place, when 5 of the rebels (as near as I can learn), and a fine horse, supposed to belong to the notorious Nick Yates, were killed. I then proceeded through a rough country to Spring River Mills. My scouts being in the advance, saw 3 men running with guns on their shoulders. The scouts gave chase, and succeeded in killing them all. I still kept on, and reached the mill about 4 o'clock in the evening. At this place I found no rebels, but arrested one man on suspicion, who, I think, will yet prove to be a Confederate soldier. This mill, although I found no rebels there, is nevertheless a great rendezvous for these guerrillas. Colonel Freeman encamped the greater part of the summer at this place. Part of his camp I found still standing. He had vacated it about two weeks before, and is now supposed to be about 35 miles south of this, with a very small force. This mill, on account of its reputed bad name and my own knowledge of it heretofore, I had burned, with a quantity of flour and corn, which was in it. After feeding, and resting about two hours, I started back in a northerly course to a good camping place, about 4 miles from the mill. My scouts, at this place, went out and found 5 rebels, all armed and on foot, running to the woods. The scouts succeeded in killing 2 of these. The house at which I was now camped I found to be a notorious den. I found one Minie and several small bird rifles; also some unserviceable United States horse equipments. The house I burned. The bird rifles and horse equipments I also destroyed.

The next morning, having fulfilled my orders, and my horses being very much broken down, I started back, and, after marching a few miles, I sent Lieutenant Muntzel, with 30 men, about 5 miles in advance. They reached the vicinity of Thomasville, when they were fired on by a party of rebels hid in the woods, and a corporal of Lieutenant Muntzel's command slightly wounded in the left arm. That night I encamped 4 miles north of Thomasville.

The next day I marched to Jack's Fork, over a very rough country, and on the 11th I reached Houston, after an absence of six days, marching a distance of 250 miles, killing at least 20 rebels; destroying at least all their principal places of rendezvous; capturing a great many prisoners, 11 of whom I brought to Houston, the others I released, not having sufficient evidence against them; also 20 horses, 5 of which, being without shoes and very poor, I was forced to leave on the road, and 5 more I gave back to citizens on my return to Houston, they proving their loyalty and lawful ownership. The remaining 10 I still have, awaiting your disposal. Also one Minie and three bird rifles, they being all I found worth bringing with me. The others I had destroyed, so as to be entirely useless.

Hoping, general, this will meet with your approval, and anxious for authority from you to make another such trip as soon as consistent, I have the honor to remain, very respectfully, your obedient servant,

RICHARD MURPHY,
Captain, Commanding.

Brig. Gen. THOMAS A. DAVIES,
Commanding Rolla District, Rolla, Mo.

AUGUST 8, 1863.—Affair on Clear Creek, near Ball Town, Mo.

Report of Capt. Robert Carpenter, Third Wisconsin Cavalry.

BALL TOWN, MO., *August* 12, 1863.

MAJOR: After my compliments, I have the honor of reporting my proceedings relative to your order. I had designed, and it was agreed upon, that Company D, of the Third Wisconsin Cavalry, commanded by Lieutenant [J.] Crites, of same company, should start from Fort Scott on the 6th of August, at noon, and proceed as far as Moore's Mill, on the Marmiton, scouting the country thoroughly as they proceeded; Lieutenant [H.] Pond to start from Dry Wood, to arrive at Nevada early on the morning of the 7th of August, scouting the country also as he came. Colonel Brag was to proceed from Lamar, coming down Little Dry Wood, to meet Lieutenant Pond at Nevada on the morning of the 7th, whence all were to proceed toward Ball Town, Mo., until they met me, with my force divided in two parts. My ground of operation was from Timbered Hill, at the junction of the Little Osage and the Marmiton, scouting both sides of the Marmiton, all parties closing in until we all met. The parties performed their respective portions of the labor allotted them with promptness and dispatch, with the exception of Colonel Brag, who failed to report as per arrangement. We all worked hard all day, and found out the enemy had left in the direction of Horse Creek, whereupon we determined to pursue him, thinking we might intercept him in some of the recesses of Clear Creek.

We all started on the morning of the 8th from Ball Town, Mo., and proceeded in a little east of south course toward the head of Clear Creek. When we proceeded down the creek a short distance, our scouts reported fresh trail. We had gone but about 100 rods, when, turning an angle in the road, we came upon 5 of the enemy. The scouts being on the advance, immediately fired upon them. Three of them, being mounted, escaped, after a race of about 2 miles (it being nearly dark); the other two we shot, capturing their horses and arms. Thence we proceeded 1 mile down the creek. Rode up to a house. A man running from the house, the boys fired on him, but it being dark he escaped in the brush and weeds, an abundant growth of which every house is surrounded with. We went into camp for the night.

Next morning early we determined to divide our command and institute a thorough search from that point up both sides of the creek, clear to its very head. I took the north and Lieutenant Pond the south side. I proceeded to the head of the creek without discovering any signs of the enemy; but not so with Lieutenant Pond. He had not proceeded more than a mile when he discovered an old camp where they had staid the night previous. He immediately sent me word of what he had found, viz, 5 horses secreted in their camp, accompanied with a request that he might be allowed to remain in their camp that night, with a view of capturing them on their return. I acceded, and moved my force within supporting distance, and remained on our arms the remainder of the night; but they did not return, and it appeared they had gone farther south. Whereupon I despaired of even a possibility of finding more than one man in a place, and thinking I could do no more at present, I returned, scouting the brush and woods thoroughly to the head of Clear Creek; thence down Little Dry Wood, where we found out the fact of their having camped on Dry Wood on the night of the 7th, and directly on the route the militia were to take to come to our place of meeting of said day; thus proving to us plainly that had Colonel Brag performed his part of the contract, the guerrillas, in all probability, would have been, if not quite, very nearly annihilated; and, major, I was greatly chagrined to think of the colonel's failure to do his part. Thence I returned to Ball Town, scouting the country thoroughly for signs, but found none.

I remain, very respectfully, your most obedient servant,

R. CARPENTER,
Commanding Detachment.

Major BLAIR,
Commanding Post at Fort Scott.

AUGUST 9, 1863.—Skirmish at Garden Hollow, near Pineville, Mo.

Report of Capt. Charles B. McAfee, Sixth Missouri State Militia Cavalry.

NEWTONIA, MO., *August* 10, 1863.

GENERAL: Lieutenant [R. B.] Riggs, at Neosho, reports to me this evening that he on yesterday, with a small party, marched to within 3 miles of Coffee's camp, at Garden Hollow, near Pineville. There he came in contact with a small party of Coffee's men, and succeeded in killing 3 and wounding 2, and took 2 prisoners. He reports Coffee to be at Garden Hollow, near Pineville, with from 300 to 500 men; his intentions unknown.

I have the honor to be, very respectfully, yours, &c.,

C. B. McAFEE,
Captain Third Battalion, Sixth Missouri State Militia Cavalry.

Brigadier-General McNEIL,
Commanding Southwestern District of Missouri.

AUGUST 9-18, 1863.—Scout from Cape Girardeau to the Ash Hills and Poplar Bluff, Mo., and skirmish (13th) at the Ash Hills.

Report of Maj. Frederick R. Poole, Second Missouri State Militia Cavalry.

HDQRS. 1ST BATT. 2D MO. STATE MILITIA CAV.,
Cape Girardeau, August 20, 1863.

SIR: In compliance with your instructions of the 9th instant, I marched with my battalion and one company of the Second Arkansas Cavalry, under command of Lieutenant [W. F.] Orr, at 9.30 p. m. same evening, to re-enforce Major Montgomery, commanding Post Bloomfield, whom you had informed me you supposed to be in imminent danger. I marched all night, though with some difficulty, having in several instances, owing to the darkness and the thickly wooded glades, to light the port-fires (belonging to the mountain howitzer which I brought with me) to enable the drivers to keep the road, and arrived next day at Bloomfield.

I telegraphed you from Bloomfield that, from all information and indications, I thought that Major Montgomery need have no fears of an attack; and on the 12th received orders from you to move my command through the Ash Hills, in the direction of Pocahontas, to obtain all the information possible touching rebel forces in the southern tier of counties; and, should I find no body of rebels, was to proceed no farther south than the Ash Hills, and return via Greenville, or in that direction, to the Cape.

In obedience to the above instructions, I moved in the direction indicated the same evening. Marched all night, to avoid the intense heat, resting a few hours at Camp Poole, near Saint Francisville, to rest and feed. Then, moving forward, we crossed the Saint Francis River at Indian Ford, and proceeded down the Ash Hill road 10 miles, along the west bank of the Saint Francis, and entered the Ash Hills country about 5 p. m. on the evening of the 13th. At this point, hearing of no enemy, and my men and animals being very much fatigued, I took Captain [P. D.] McClanahan and two men in advance to select and lay out our camp, when, coming to a short angle of the road, we met, face to face, about 80 armed guerrillas. The column being about 200 yards in rear, we charged them with saber and pistol, killing 6 on the spot, wounded several, and captured several horses; also a large lot of ammunition and arms, when they broke like sheep to the swamp. In the *mêlée*, I received a shot through the right leg, which proved very painful. Having no doctor nor ambulance, I had to ride on horseback five days after being wounded. I also had my horse shot nearly at the same instant that I was wounded myself, and he fell heavily upon me, injuring me considerably.

The casualty occurring to myself and horse was the only one received by my command during the entire scout. About 2 miles from the scene of the skirmish we went into Camp McClanahan, and rested for the night; distant from Bloomfield about 40 miles.

On the morning of the 14th, continued our course through Ash Hills until we arrived at their base, striking Black River; then moved north on the east bank of the river, and arrived and encamped at Poplar Bluff, 25 miles from Camp McClanahan. Came up with 3 more guerrillas during the day, who were all killed.

On the morning of the 15th, we marched up 6 miles on the west side of Black River, crossed the ford, and proceeded in the direction of Greenville, encamping at Camp Law, on Otter Creek, 25 miles from Poplar Bluff.

On the 16th, broke up camp at daybreak, passed through Greenville, and went into Camp Rogers, 18 miles from Dallas and 25 from Camp Law.

[August] 17, reveille at 3 a. m. Left Camp Rogers at 4 a. m., and marched to Camp Thomson, within 23 miles of the Cape.

[August] 18, left Camp Thomson at 4 a. m., and arrived safely in camp at Cape Girardeau about 3 o'clock the same day.

From Bloomfield to Saint Francisville the road leads across a high and rolling country, but from Saint Francisville to Ash Hill there is little or nothing but glades and swamps, which, at any other season of the year, would be utterly impracticable for artillery. The roads through Ash Hills are indistinct and wretchedly bad, and again, upon striking the river, there are about 10 miles of glades to pass through before reaching Poplar Bluff. The little howitzer that I had with me was the first thing in the shape of artillery that ever passed over that road. I think the distance from Bloomfield to Poplar Bluff, via Ash Hills, is about 50 miles. Forage out of the question, the men in that country preferring bushwhacking to honest labor. The roads from Poplar Bluff to Dallas mostly pass through rolling, barren, and uninhabited sections, but are good, and must be at all times practicable for the heaviest artillery. I found great difficulty in procuring forage enough for my command between Poplar Bluff and Dallas, Marmaduke's and General Davidson's commands having consumed everything within reach. New hay is plenty between Dallas and the Cape, and the farmers at those points are assiduously at work raising good crops of corn.

From all the information that I could collect, I have good reason to believe that there are no considerable armed bodies of rebels in the State, as I had good information that they were all ordered south toward the line of Texas, and those that now remain are merely mutineers or guerrillas, who have refused to obey the orders, taking it as a subterfuge that they belong to the old State Guard and cannot be taken out of the State. I should have no hesitancy to take one squadron and move in any direction through this portion of the State.

To the officers and men under my command I tender my sincere thanks for their good conduct and cheerfulness throughout the trip. During the march of 200 miles I never heard a murmur, although we frequently marched twenty-four hours without eating. I especially recommend to your notice Captain McClanahan and Buglers [E. Z.] Shannon and [W. C.] Thatcher for their unflinching courage and bravery in following me where none but the brave and true could have fought and lived. To them I owe my life and a never-ending debt of gratitude.

I am, colonel, very respectfully, your obedient servant,

FRED. R. POOLE,
Major, Comdg. First Batt. Second Missouri State Militia Cav.

Col. J. B. ROGERS,
Commanding Second Missouri State Militia Cavalry.

AUGUST 10, 1863.—Skirmish at Dayton, Mo.

Report of Maj. Alexander W. Mullins, First Missouri State Militia Cavalry.

HEADQUARTERS,
Harrisonville, Mo., August 12, 1863.

COLONEL: In compliance with orders from Headquarters District of the Border, I arrived at this place yesterday, and am now stationed here with my command. Company B, First Missouri State Militia Cavalry, and Company I, Sixth Kansas Volunteer Cavalry, are also stationed here. One company of the Eleventh Kansas Cavalry Volunteers and two companies of the Fourth Missouri State Militia Cavalry have just started from here to Napoleon, and one company of the Fourth Missouri State Militia Cavalry to Trading Post, 40 miles southwest from here.

While on the march from Germantown, day before yesterday evening, Company H, my advance, came in collision with a squad of bushwhackers at Dayton, 15 miles south of Harrisonville, and a brisk skirmish ensued, in which 2 bushwhackers were killed and 1 severely wounded. Our boys came through unscathed, although they charged upon a barn where the rebels took shelter, and drove the rebels from it. The horse of Sergeant [W. L.] Meek, Company H, received three wounds, and one other of our horses was slightly wounded. We captured 3 horses, 4 pistols, 2 miniature rebel flags, &c.

Pleasant Hill was a few days since evacuated by the Federal troops, and has been partially burned by the bushwhackers. I do not suppose that it was contemplated that we should remain at this place longer than the present (assumed) emergency. However, it may be different, and the removal of other troops from this station looks as though we might possibly remain here some considerable time. I am inclined to think the force of bushwhackers in this part of the country has been, and now is, by most officers, greatly overestimated. But I may, myself, be mistaken. They are scattered all over the country. The forage guard had a skirmish to-day a few miles from town.

Very respectfully,

ALEX. W. MULLINS,
Major First Missouri State Militia Cavalry.

Col. JAMES MCFERRAN,
Commanding, Lexington, Mo.

AUGUST 13, 1863.—Skirmish at Pineville, Mo.

Report of Col. Edwin C. Catherwood, Sixth Missouri State Militia Cavalry.

HEADQUARTERS,
Springfield, Mo., September 19, 1863.

GENERAL: Pursuant to Special Orders, No. 154, from your headquarters, I left Springfield, August 9, 1863, with detachments of Sixth Missouri State Militia Cavalry, First Arkansas Cavalry, and section of howitzers, in pursuit of Coffee. After three days and nights' marches, I met the enemy at Pineville, in McDonald County, Missouri. He was completely routed, with loss of between 60 and 70 killed, wounded, and prisoners, principally killed; all his train, stores, &c. The rout was so complete that no remnant of his command could be found together.

At White Rock Prairie I was re-enforced by a battalion of the Eighth Missouri State Militia Cavalry, with orders to march to Bentonville, Ark, and report to Colonel [W. F.] Cloud. Arriving at Bentonville, found Cloud had moved, leaving instructions for me to move in southwest direction toward Fort Gibson, in Indian Nation. At Fort Gibson received instructions to march to Honey Springs, on the Canadian. Here joined Major-General Blunt's command, and moved with him throughout his entire raid into Arkansas and Indian Nation, participating in all the engagements of the expedition. At the battle of Back Bone Mountain I lost 2 men killed and 2 wounded. Returned to Fort Smith, which place we occupied September 1, 1863. We remained at Fort Smith one week, continually scouting in direction of the enemy, giving aid to thousands of oppressed loyal men, who had been forced into the rebel ranks by the brutality and despotism of the Confederate rulers, to come into our lines, which they did, with horses and arms, and, in almost every instance, enlisted in the United States service. It was clearly demonstrated that three-fourths of the rebel army of Arkansas and Texas were Union men, and could not be forced to fight the armies of the Federal Government. Throughout the entire raid the people rejoiced at the change; their only fear was that the country would not be held by our troops. We remained at Fort Smith until re-enforcements had arrived sufficient to make the post secure, when, upon representation of the condition of my command, being destitute of stores, I was relieved by order from General Blunt, and allowed to return. On the return march I destroyed two large tanneries, one distillery, and a large lot of leather, hides, &c.

We were out six weeks, without tents or a change of clothing, and a great portion of the time on very short rations; marched over 700 miles. The sanitary condition of the command could not have been better. I did not leave a sick man on the trip.

I am, sir, very respectfully, your obedient servant,

E. C. CATHERWOOD,
Colonel, Commanding Expedition.

Brig. Gen. JNO. MCNEIL,
Commanding District of Southwestern Missouri.

ADDENDA.

HDQRS. DISTRICT OF SOUTHWESTERN MISSOURI,
Springfield, Mo., August 15, 1863.

Col. E. C. CATHERWOOD,
Commanding Expedition against Coffee:

COLONEL: Your dispatch from the field* near Pineville, announcing your defeat of Coffee and his band, has been received. I heartily congratulate you on this distinguished success. You will tender to the brave officers and men of your command, including the command of Captain Burch, my cordial and sincere thanks for their bravery, endurance, and devotion to duty, testified on this expedition. The rout of Coffee seems to have been signal and complete, and the southwestern counties of our State are thus relieved of the terrors of a ruthless marauder and thief. I hope the pursuit may continue to be conducted with the

* Not found.

same energy and determination that has marked your progress thus far. Southwest Missouri, by a few such examples, will be relieved of the presence of those lawless bandits and marauders that have so long crimsoned her hearths and desolated her fields.

I have the honor to be, your obedient servant,

[JOHN McNEIL,]
Brigadier-General, Commanding.

AUGUST 13-SEPTEMBER 11, 1863.—Expedition against Indians in Dakota.

SUMMARY OF THE PRINCIPAL EVENTS.

Sept. 3, 1863.—Action near White Stone Hill, Dak.
5, 1863.—Skirmish near White Stone Hill, Dak.

REPORTS.

No. 1.—Brig. Gen. Alfred Sully, U. S. Army, commanding expedition.
No. 2.—Col. David S. Wilson, Sixth Iowa Cavalry.
No. 3.—Maj. Albert E. House, Sixth Iowa Cavalry.
No. 4.—Col. Robert W. Furnas, Second Nebraska Cavalry.

No. 1.

Report of Brig. Gen. Alfred Sully, U. S. Army, commanding expedition.

HEADQUARTERS NORTHWESTERN EXPEDITION,
Camp at mouth of Little Cheyenne River, September 11, 1863.

MAJOR: The last report I had the honor to send you was from the mouth of this Little Cheyenne River, bearing date August 16, 1863; since which time my movements have been too rapid, and the danger of sending any communication such that it has been impossible for me to do so. I therefore have the honor to report my movements from last report up to date.

On the morning of the 19th, the steamer I was waiting for, with supplies, finally arrived. She was immediately unloaded, and all the baggage of the officers and men of the command was sent down by her to the depot at Fort Pierre, together with every man who was in the least sick or not well mounted. By this I reduced my force considerably, and was enabled to transport, with the wretched mules that had been furnished me, about twenty-three days' rations, and forage enough to keep these transportation animals alive, depending on grass I might find to feed the cavalry and artillery horses. Luckily for me, I found the grazing north in much better condition than I had dared to hope for.

On the 20th, we were visited by one of the most terrific rain and hail storms I have seen. This stampeded some of my animals, and a few were lost—they swam across the Missouri—and it also destroyed a quantity of my rations in the wagons, thereby causing me some delay in the march; but I succeeded in getting off on the afternoon of the 21st, and marched up the Little Cheyenne about 11 miles, the road being very heavy. The next day we marched only 7 miles, camping at a slough on the prairie without wood. The next day we marched in a northwesterly direction to the outlet of Swan Lake.

On the 24th, we marched due north 18 miles, and encamped on a small creek called Bois Cache. Here we came into the buffalo country, and I formed a hunting party for the command, which I had soon to disband, as they disabled more horses than buffaloes. We continued our march north about 22 miles, and reached a small stream called Bird Ache Creek. This day the hunters succeeded in killing many buffaloes, and reported that they saw Indians near the Missouri.

Early on the morning of the 26th, I sent out a small scouting party, who captured two squaws and some children, and brought them in to me. These Indians reported that General Sibley had had a fight near the head of Long Lake, and that they were on their way to the agency at Crow Creek, but were lost, and were alone; but the scouts found tracks of lodges going up the Missouri. I therefore immediately detailed Companies F and K, of the Second Nebraska Cavalry, under command of Captain [D.] La Boo, ordering them to go to the Missouri and follow up the trail, with orders to capture some Indians if possible, and bring them in, so that I might get information; if they could not do that, to kill them and destroy their camps. I continued the march with the rest of the command that day, passing through large herds of buffaloes, and was obliged to make a march of 35 miles before I could reach water. The weather was very hot, and it was night before we reached camp on the Beaver River.

On the 27th, I started late, having had some difficulty in crossing the river, making a march of 5 miles, still in a northerly direction, and encamped on another branch of the same river. Company K, of the Second Nebraska, joined me this day, having been separated from the other company. The next day we had to make some deviations to the west on account of hills and sloughs, and made the outlet of Long Lake, a march of about 20 miles. On the way we saw numerous signs of Indians in large numbers having been recently there, and found an old lame Indian concealed in the bushes, who was well known by many of the men of the command as having for some years resided near Sioux City. He had the reputation of being what is called a "good Indian." He stated that his horse had been taken away from him, and that he had been left there. He looked almost starved to death. He gave me the following details, which have since mostly turned out to be correct: He stated that General Sibley had fought the Indians at the head of Long Lake, 50 miles northeast from me, some weeks ago; that he followed them down to the mouth of Apple Creek; that the Indians attacked him on the way, and that there was some skirmishing. At Apple Creek Sibley had another fight, and that in all the fights about 58 Indians were killed; that General Sibley fortified his camp at Apple Creek, and after a while returned to James River; that a few days after General Sibley left, the Indians, who had their scouts out watching, recrossed the Missouri, and while doing so discovered a Mackinaw boat on its way down. They attacked the boat, fought the entire day until sundown, sunk her, and killed all on board—21 men, 3 women, and some children; that before she was sunk, the fire from the boat killed 91 Indians and wounded many more; that a small war party followed Sibley some days; returned with the report that he had crossed the James River; then some of the Indians went north; the larger portion, however, went toward the head of Long Lake, and that he thought a portion of them were encamped on the Missouri River west of me.

This report was so much in keeping with the Indian mode of warfare that, though it came from an Indian, I was led to give it some consideration, particularly the part that stated the Indians, after watching

Sibley's return, recrossed when all danger was over, and went back to their old hunting grounds. Besides, the guides who were acquainted with the country stated that "a large body of Indians could not live on the other side long without going a great distance west; that always at this season of the year the Indians camped on the Coteau, near the tributaries of the James, where the numerous lakes or springs kept the grass fresh; here the buffalo were plenty, and the lakes and streams full of fish; and that here they prepared their meat for the winter, moving to the Missouri, where the fuel was plenty, to winter." I therefore determined to change my course toward the east, to move rapidly, and go as far as my rations would allow.

I felt serious alarm for the safety of Captain La Boo, who had about 50 men with him, and who had already been out over two days without rations. I encamped here for the next day, and sent out four companies of the Second Nebraska and one of the Sixth Iowa, under command of Major [J. W.] Pearman, Second Nebraska, to hunt him up, and see if there were any Indians on the Missouri. The next day, however, Captain La Boo's company returned, having made a march of 187 miles, living upon what buffalo and game they could kill, scouring the country to my left, overtaking the camp of ten lodges he was sent after, destroying them, but seeing no Indians. This same day (29th) I sent two companies of the Sixth Iowa to the mouth of Apple Creek. They reported on their return that they found the fortified camp of General Sibley, his trail, and his return trail toward the east; that they could see no signs of there having been any fight there, nor could they see the Mackinaw boat reported by this old Indian. This detachment was under command of Captain [D. W. C.] Cram, Sixth Iowa Cavalry. The battalion of Major Pearman joined me before starting, having seen nothing, and, after a march of above 90 miles through a country with no wood whatever, but with good grass and plenty of lakes of the most abominable water, on the 3d of September we reached a lake, where, on the plains near by, were the remains of a very large number of buffaloes killed, some quite recently. Here I encamped to wait the reports of the commands I had out during the march, who every day discovered fresh signs of Indians, their lodge trails spread over the country, but all moving toward a point known to be a favorite haunt of the Indians. I had this day detailed one battalion of the Sixth Iowa, Major [A. E.] House commanding, and Mr. Frank La Framboise as guide, to keep ahead of me 5 miles, and, in case they saw a small band of Indians, to attack them, or take them prisoners. If they should find a large band, too large to successfully cope with, to watch the camp at a distance, and send word back to me, my intention being to leave my train under charge of a heavy guard, move up in the night time so as to surround them, and attack them at daybreak. But, for some reason satisfactory to the guide, he bore off much to my left, and came upon the Indians in an encampment of over 400 lodges, some say 600, in ravines, where they felt perfectly secure, being fully persuaded that I was still on my way up the Missouri. This is what the Indian prisoners say. They also state that a war party followed me on my way up, in hope of stampeding me; but this they could not do. I marched with great care, with an advanced guard and flankers; the train in two lines, 60 paces apart, the troops on each side; in front and center, myself with one company and the battery; all loose stock was kept between the lines of wagons. In this way I lost no animals on the campaign except some few, about a dozen, that got out of camp at night; nor did the Indians, during all the trip, ever attack me or try to stampede me.

Major House, according to my instructions, endeavored to surround and keep in the Indians until word could be sent me; but this was an impossibility with his 300 men, as the encampment was very large, mustering at least 1,200 warriors. This is what the Indians say they had, but I, as well as everybody in the command, say over 1,500. These Indians were partly Santees, from Minnesota; Cut-heads, from the Coteau; Yanktonais, and some Blackfeet who belong on the other side of the Missouri, and, as I have since learned, Uncapa-pas, the same party who fought General Sibley and destroyed the Mackinaw boat. Of this I have unmistakable proof from letters and papers found in the camp and on the persons of some of the Indians, besides relics of the late Minnesota massacre; also from the fact that they told Mr. La Framboise, the guide, when he was surrounded by about 200 of them, that "they had fought General Sibley, and they could not see why the whites wanted to come to fight them, unless they were tired of living and wanted to die." Mr. La Framboise succeeded in getting away from them after some difficulty, and ran his horse a distance of more than 10 miles to give me information, Major House, with his command, still remaining there. He reached me a little after 4 o'clock. I immediately turned out my command. The horses at the time were out grazing. At the sound of the bugle, the men rushed with a cheer, and in a very few minutes saddled up and were in line. I left four companies, and all the men who were poorly mounted, in the camp, with orders to strike the tents and corral all the wagons, and, starting off, with the Second Nebraska on the right, the Sixth Iowa on the left, one company of the Seventh Iowa and the battery in the center, at a full gallop, we made this distance of over 10 miles in much less than an hour.

On reaching near the ground I found that the enemy were leaving and carrying off what plunder they could. Many lodges, however, were still standing. I ordered Colonel [R. W.] Furnas, Second Nebraska, to push his horses to the utmost, so as to reach the camp and assist Major House in keeping the Indians corralled. This order was obeyed with great alacrity, the regiment going over the plains at a full run. I was close upon the rear of the regiment with the Sixth Iowa. The Nebraska took to the right of the camp, and was soon lost in a cloud of dust over the hills. I ordered Colonel [D. S.] Wilson, Sixth Iowa, to take to the left, while I, with the battery, one company of the Seventh Iowa, Captain [A. J.] Millard, and two companies of the Sixth Iowa, Major Ten Broeck commanding, charged through the center of the encampment. I here found an Indian chief by the name of Little Soldier, with some few of his people. This Indian has always had the reputation of being a "good Indian" and friendly. I placed them under guard and moved on. Shortly after I met with the notorious chief Big-head, and some of his men. They were dressed for a fight, but my men cut them off. These Indians, together with some of their warriors, mustering about 30, together with squaws, children, ponies, and dogs, gave themselves up, numbering over 120 human beings. About the same time firing began about a half mile from me, ahead, and was kept up, becoming more and more brisk, until it was quite a respectable engagement. A report was brought to me (which proved to be false) that the Indians were driving back some of my command. I immediately took possession of the hillocks near by, forming line, and placing the battery in the center on a higher knoll. At this time night had about set in, but still the engagement was briskly kept up, and in the *mêlée* it was hard to distinguish my line from that of the enemy. The Indians made a very desperate resistance, but finally broke and fled, pursued in every direction by bodies of my troops. I would here state that the troops, though mounted, were armed with rifles, and, according to my orders, most of them dismounted and fought afoot until the enemy broke, when they remounted and went in pursuit. It is to be regretted that I could not have had an hour or two more of daylight, for I feel sure, if I had, I could have annihilated the enemy. As it was, I believe I can safely say I gave them one of the most severe punishments that the Indians have ever received. After night set in, the engagement was of such a promiscuous nature that it was hard to tell what results would happen; I therefore ordered all the buglers to sound the "rally," and, building large fires, remained under arms during the night, collecting together my troops.

The next morning early (the 4th) I established my camp on the battle-field, the wagon train, under charge of Major Pearman, Second Nebraska, having in the night been ordered to join me, and sent out strong scouting parties in different directions to scour the country to overtake what Indians they could; but in this they were not very successful, though some of them had some little skirmishes. They found the dead and wounded in all directions of them, some miles from the battle-field; also immense quantities of provisions, baggage, &c., where they had apparently cut loose their ponies from "travois" and got off on them; also large numbers of ponies and dogs, harnessed to "travois," running all over the prairie. One party that I sent out went near to the James River, and found there 11 dead Indians. The deserted camp of the Indians, together with the country all around, was covered with their plunder. I devoted this day, together with the following (the 5th), to destroying all this property, still scouring the country. I do not think I exaggerate in the least when I say that I burned up over 400,000 to 500,000 pounds of dried buffalo meat as one item, besides 300 lodges, and a very large quantity of property of great value to the Indians. A very large number of ponies were found dead and wounded on the field; besides, a large number was captured. The prisoners (some 130) I take with me below, and shall report to you more specially in regard to them.

The surgeon of the Second Nebraska Regiment, Dr. Bowen, who has shown great energy and desire to attend to his duties during the campaign, started out during the night of the engagement with a party of 15 men, to go back to the old camp to procure ambulances. But as they did not return on the morning of the second day, I knew that he was either lost or captured. (He returned about noon of the second day.) I therefore sent out small scouting parties in every direction to hunt them up. One of these fell into an ambuscade, by which 4 of the party were killed and the rest driven in. I immediately sent out five companies of the Nebraska regiment, Colonel Furnas in command, who, after a long march, found the Indians had fled. They succeeded, however, in overtaking three concealed in some tall grass, whom they killed. The fight has been so scattered, the dead Indians have been found in so many different places, that it is impossible for me to give an accurate report of the number killed of the enemy. I, however, think I am safe in reporting it at 100. (I report those that were left on the field and that my scouting parties found.)

During the engagement, for some time, the Second Nebraska, afoot and armed with rifles (and there are among them probably some of the best shots in the world), were engaged with the enemy at a distance not over 60 paces, pouring on them a murderous fire in the ravine where the enemy were posted. The slaughter, therefore, must have been immense. My officers and the guides I have with me think 150 will not cover their loss. The Indian reports make it over 200. That the general may know the exact locality of the battle-field, I would state that it was, as near as I could judge, about 15 miles west of James River, and about half-way between the latitudes of Bone Bute and headwaters of Elm River, as laid down on the Government map. The fight took place near a hill called by the Indians White Stone Hill.

In conclusion, I would state that the troops of my command conducted themselves well; and though it was the first fight that nearly all of them had ever been in, they showed that they are of the right material, and that in time, with discipline, they will make worthy soldiers. It is to be regretted we lost so many valuable lives as we did, but this could not be helped; the Indians had formed line of battle with good judgment, from which they could be dislodged only by a charge. I could not use my artillery without greatly endangering the lives of my own men; if I could, I could have slaughtered them.

I send you, accompanying, the reports of Colonel Wilson, Sixth Iowa, and Colonel Furnas, Second Nebraska, also official reports of killed and wounded, and take this occasion to thank both those officers for the good conduct and cheerfulness with which they obeyed my orders on the occasion. Both of them had their horses shot in the action. I would also request permission to state that the several members of my staff rendered me every possible assistance.

On the morning of the 6th, I took up my line of march for Fort Pierre. If I could have remained in that section of country some two or three weeks I might have accomplished more; but I was satisfied by the reports of my scouts that the Indians had scattered in all directions—some toward the James River; some, probably the Blackfeet, to recross the Missouri; and a part of them went north, where the Indians say they have friends among the half-breeds of the north. My rations were barely sufficient with rapid marches to enable me to reach Fort Pierre. The animals, not only the teams I have already reported to you as worthless, but also the cavalry horses, showed the effect of rapid marching and being entirely without grain.

I brought with me all the prisoners I had, and tried to question them to gain some information. The men refused to say much, except that they are all "good Indians," and the other bad ones joined their camp without their will.

The squaws, however, corroborate the report I have already given you in regard to the destruction of the people on board the Mackinaw boat and the fights with General Sibley, in which these Indians had a part. They also state that the Indians, after recrossing to this side of the Missouri, sent a party to follow Sibley until he went to the James River, then returned to their camp near Long Lake to procure a large quantity of provisions and other articles they had "cached" there, and then came to the camp where I met them.

After marching about 130 miles we reached the mouth of the Little Cheyenne on the 11th, where I found the steamboat I had ordered to be there on the 8th instant. It was lucky she was there, for without the grain she brought up I could not have brought my empty wagons back, for some miles north of Cheyenne and to Pierre the grass now is about all gone. I placed my wounded on the boat, and as many empty wagons as she could carry. I am afraid the loss of horses and mules will be considered very great, but it could not be helped. When I found it impossible for the rear guard to get an animal along, I had it killed, to prevent its falling into the hands of the enemy.

Very respectfully, major, your obedient servant,

ALF. SULLY,
Brigadier-General, Commanding.

Maj. J. F. MELINE,
Actg. Asst. Adjt. Gen., Department of the Northwest.

P. S.—By actual count the number of my prisoners is 156—men 32, women and children 124. I would also beg leave to say that in the action I had of my command between 600 and 700 men actually engaged. My killed number, as far as ascertained, 20; wounded, 38.

Return of Casualties in the United States forces engaged with Indians near White Stone Hill, Dakota, September 3 and 5, 1863.

[Compiled from nominal list of casualties, returns, &c.]

Command.	Killed.		Wounded.		
	Officers.	Enlisted men.	Officers.	Enlisted men.	Aggregate.
September 3:					
6th Iowa Cavalry	......	9	1	21	31
2d Nebraska Cavalry	......	2	1	12	15
September 5:					
6th Iowa Cavalry	......	2	......	......	2
2d Nebraska Cavalry	......	4	......	1	5
Total	......	17	2	34	53

NOTE.—Lieut. Thomas J. Leavitt, Sixth Iowa Cavalry, mortally wounded September 3.

No. 2.

Report of Col. David S. Wilson, Sixth Iowa Cavalry.

IN BATTLE-FIELD OF WHITE STONE HILL,
September 3, 1863.

SIR: I have the honor to submit to you an account of the participation of the Sixth Iowa Cavalry in the battle of White Stone Hill on the 3d of September, 1863.

As you are aware, the command left the mouth of the Big Cheyenne on the 21st day of August last. Nothing occurred to vary the monotony of the usual hard marches until the date above. On the morning of that day I received an order from you to detail from my command one battalion. It being the turn of the Third Battalion to scout, an order was issued directing Maj. A. E. House to report to your headquarters for instructions, which was promptly done. Company M, commanded by Capt. V. J. Williams, of said battalion, having their horses used up by constant scouting, it was unable to proceed with the detail, its place being supplied by Company H, of the Second Battalion. The detail for the scout was Company C, L. L. Ainsworth, captain; Company I, L. R. Wolfe, captain; Company F, S. Shattuck, captain; and Company H, of Second Battalion, C. J. Marsh, captain. In speaking of the Third Battalion, I always include Company H in this battle. They left the command at an early hour. After its departure the brigade took up its line of march to a point 10 miles east of this place, where we arrived about 2 p. m. In the space of two hours the messenger dispatched by Major House rode swiftly into camp with the information that there was a very large body of Indians near him, and that he was in process of negotiation with them until we could arrive. It was but the work of a few minutes for the whole command to be upon its way to the battle-field. The 10 miles distance was passed quickly. When we neared the battle-field I received an order from you directing me to take one of my battalions, in addition to the Third. The First was taken by me, and the Second Battalion was left with brigade headquarters. I then proceeded to carry out your orders to surround the Indians and drive them in. On every side of the battle-field were straggling Indians, endeavoring to escape. Immediately joining the flank of the First upon the Second Battalion, and marching both in line, we succeeded in driving a large portion of the Indians toward your headquarters, down into a ravine. By the shifting and dressing of the line as it marched, I became detached from the First and was thrown into the Third Battalion. The Indians, after having been quietly driven quite a distance into a common center, availed themselves of the darkness that was coming by suddenly firing upon us, which fire, though entirely unexpected, was immediately returned by us with terrible effect. We then commenced making preparations to fight on foot, when the darkness became so impenetrable that it was impossible to proceed farther. It was at this fire of the enemy, when riding some little distance in advance of the battalion, that my horse was shot with a slug, fatally wounding him. He lived long enough to carry me about 30 rods. After the darkness set in we went into camp immediately upon the battle-field; corralled our horses and threw out pickets, while the command slept upon its arms. The night was excessively dark and cold, but the picket guard killed 2 Indians that were found straggling near our camp. At length the day appeared, when we found that the enemy, availing themselves of the darkness, had suddenly decamped, but leaving the country strewed for miles around with their dried meats, provisions, packs, robes, tepees, goods, and ponies.

We lost in this engagement 1 commissioned officer, 10 privates, and had 11 wounded, 1 of them since dying; some of the rest being wounded badly, and some very slightly.

I take pleasure in bearing testimony to the cheerfulness with which the First Battalion, commanded by that veteran, Acting Major [J.] Galligan, obeyed every order during the time they were under my command.

Company G, of the First Battalion, and Captain [A. B.] Moreland, Lieutenant [W. A.] Heath, and Sergeant [R.] Aubrey, I understand, deserve the highest praise for intrepidity in action. Company K, and Captain [J.] Logan and Lieutenant [S. M.] Parker, behaved very bravely, and deserve most favorable notice for their bravery.

Company D, Captain [T. W.] Burdick and lieutenants, although temporarily detached by my orders, are entitled to the highest praise.

The Second Battalion did not participate immediately in the fight, as stated; but from the zeal with which they entered on the march to the battle-field, and the cheerfulness with which they obeyed all orders, I have no doubt but the highest desire would have been that of active participants in the battle, under the command of their gallant major.

I wish to call your particular attention to every one of the field and line officers of the regiment, without enumerating them by name. From the highest to the lowest they deserve the most favorable consideration, and the same may be said of almost the entire command engaged. Being their first battle, this was their baptism of fire and steel, and most nobly did they behave. The high valor earned by the noble action of the Iowa troops upon the bloody field of battle has not been tarnished by the gallant Iowa Sixth at White Stone Hill.

I have spoken more minutely of the action of the Third Battalion, because it was my destiny to be thrown with them in this battle. I cannot close my report without again calling your attention to the noble part borne by them on this day under their brave Major House. They treated and talked with that large force of Indians until we arrived to their aid, and then the part they bore in the fight deserves the highest praise that can be paid to brave, heroic men.

I desire to state that Dr. [J. H.] Camburn, by his personal presence in my camp on the battle-field, rendered the wounded most invaluable service through that long night. The same meed of praise can also, I understand, be awarded to Assistant Surgeon [S. C.] Haynes, with the First Battalion. Assistant Surgeon [T. S.] Bardwell, being left with the sick at camp, was not present at the fight, but rendered such assistance as he was able the next morning. Chaplain D. U. Mitchell was present on the field of battle, and afterward rendered all the assistance and consolation he could to the wounded, spiritual and bodily.

The commissioned officer mentioned as being lost was Lieut. T. J. Leavitt, second lieutenant of Company B, and acting as regimental adjutant for some time. He had performed the duties of said office with great fidelity and ability. Possessed of great natural ability, with heroic courage and gallant bearing, the entire regiment mourns his loss unceasingly.

Lieut. George E. Dayton, of Company C, and Sergt. Maj. Charles W. Fogg, deserve favorable notice for bravery during the night of the battle, and also in going out in charge of a detail searching for wounded men upon the battle-field.

Permit me, sir, to congratulate you upon the magnitude of your victory and the great results that will follow from it. By skillful management you completely surrounded hundreds of Indians, whom you signally routed, camping on the battle-field, killing and wounding over 100 of them, besides destroying immense supplies of provisions and tepees, and taking several hundred prisoners. They have never before received such a terrible blow, and it will certainly be the means of securing a permanent peace with these heretofore troublesome Indians. When we take into consideration the immense obstacles with which your expedition had to contend at every step, and to see them so signally overcome, must astonish every one.

Whilst I thus congratulate you upon your brilliant victory, I must not neglect to pay a passing tribute to the gallant dead of my regiment. They were numbered among the very best men in the command, and most gallantly did they fight and fall. To their bereaved families and relatives I tender my most heartfelt sympathies.

I inclose herewith a couple of letters* that were found upon an Indian by some of my regiment. Inclosed in one were two gold dollars and

---

* Not found.

some gold dust. They seem to corroborate the story that the Indians in July last surrounded a Mackinaw boat descending the Missouri River from the gold mine, and, after fighting with the crew all day, succeeded in killing the entire number.

I have the honor to be, very respectfully, your obedient servant,

D. S. WILSON,
Colonel Sixth Iowa Cavalry.

Capt. JOHN H. PELL,
Assistant Adjutant-General.

No. 3.

Report of Maj. Albert E. House, Sixth Iowa Cavalry.

IN CAMP ON BATTLE-FIELD OF WHITE STONE HILL.
[*September* —, 1863.]

SIR: On the 3d day of September, 1863, in obedience to your orders and under instructions from Brigadier-General Sully, I took the line of march from our camp of the previous night (which was about 30 miles from White Stone Hill) at 5.30 a. m., having under my command Companies C, I, F, and H, of the Sixth Iowa Cavalry, and proceeded in a southerly direction, halting every hour, dismounting the men and allowing the horses to graze ten minutes at a time. At about 3 p. m. our guide informed me that a camp of Indians was about 3 miles distant. I ordered the men to load their carbines and pistols, and started on a gallop for the Indian camp. When within a mile of the camp, we halted and formed in line of battle, with I in line, H and F as flankers, and C as a reserve. In this order we proceeded and took position behind a ridge about 50 rods from the enemy, where we had then an easy range, and where we were protected from their fire. Captain [C. J.] Marsh, of Company H, and Lieutenant [G. E.] Dayton, of Company C, were then sent forward to reconnoiter. They returned, and reported that there were 400 lodges of the enemy. Upon gaining this information, our guide, with two picked men from Company C, were started back to your camp to give you information of our whereabouts, and that re-enforcements might be sent if they were necessary. As the ground was very uneven, and it was difficult to ascertain what defenses the enemy had, it was determined to make a reconnaissance in force. For this purpose Company C was sent to the left, in command of Captain [L. L.] Ainsworth, who, with great personal bravery, pushed forward with vigor and rapidity in the face of the enemy, outnumbering his force ten to one. Captain Marsh, with Company H, also pushed forward in the same direction, with a courage which would have done honor to a veteran of a hundred battles. As soon as these companies had returned and reported, Captain [S.] Shattuck, with Company F, was sent out to the right, to ascertain the position of the enemy in that direction. While these things were being done, the chiefs came in under a flag of truce and attempted a negotiation. They offered to surrender some of their chiefs; but as the commandant did not know who was entitled to speak by authority, he demanded the unconditional surrender of all. This the Indians refused to do, and, having sent away their squaws and papooses, together with their stock of provisions, they placed themselves in battle array. Our command moved forward, and the enemy retreated precipitately, abandoning everything except their ponies.

While we were thus following and scattering the enemy, the Second Nebraska Regiment appeared on the hill, under the command of Colonel

Furnas, who immediately informed the commander of the forces of the Sixth Iowa that he would take the right of the flying enemy and drive them in. Whereupon we formed our forces in column and took the left, first upon a trot, then a gallop, and finally at a full charge. The enemy, having abandoned everything in their flight, and finding that we were fast gaining upon them, collected together in a ravine and prepared for battle. We again formed in line of battle, and were advancing upon the enemy when we discovered the Second Nebraska upon our left flank; they were dismounting and preparing to fight on foot. At the same time we saw that part of the Sixth Iowa, which had been left behind, formed in line parallel to the Nebraska Second. We at once advanced our lines within 20 rods of the enemy, and were fired upon by them. We returned the fire from our whole line with terrible effect, covering the ground with dead men and horses. The horses then became so restive as to be unmanageable under the fire even of our own men from their backs. The command was then taken back 25 rods in the rear, and were preparing to fight on foot, when, darkness setting in, the command was formed in a hollow square, the men in front of their horses, and slept on their arms. We placed a picket guard around our camp, under the charge of Sergeant-Major Fogg and Lieutenant Dayton, who promptly performed the duties assigned them; they went to the battlefield after dark, to look after wounded, and for this I recommend them to your favorable consideration. I also recommend Dr. J. H. Camburn, who came promptly to the relief of the wounded, and did all he could in the darkness. Among those who distinguished themselves for personal bravery, I wish to mention Capt. L. R. Wolfe, who stood in front of his company and killed an Indian every shot he made. The whole command did well, and I must not mention individual instances for fear of making this report too long. About 100 of the enemy were killed. We took a large number of prisoners, and destroyed all the winter stores of the enemy, among which was 400 tons of dried meat.

I am, respectfully, yours,

A. E. HOUSE,
Major, Commanding Detachment Sixth Iowa.

Col. D. S. WILSON.

No. 4.

Report of Col. Robert W. Furnas, Second Nebraska Cavalry.

HDQRS. SECOND NEBRASKA CAVALRY, CAMP NO. 35,
Dakota Territory, September 6, 1863.

SIR: On the 22d of August, 1863, I left the mouth of Little Cheyenne River, Dakota Territory, under command of Brigadier-General Sully, in company with the remainder of the troops of the general's expedition, arriving at the foot of Long Lake, Dakota Territory, on the 28th of same month, where it was hoped we might encounter the hostile Indians. Scouting parties sent out in various directions returned and reported no Indians to be found; but the trail of General Sibley's command, on Apple Creek, was discovered, and an old Indian, captured some days before, reported that General Sibley had been through that country a short time previous, and had had two fights, and that many of the Indians had crossed the Missouri River after the fight, but had recrossed to this side of same recently, and were to be found somewhere in the direction of Elm River, Dakota Territory. On the march from this camp additional scouting parties were sent out by the general, but without success; and our rations beginning to run short, the expedition took a circuitous route for Fort Pierre, by way of James River. It was with feelings of despondency at what appeared to be the inevitable ill-success of the expedition under General Sully, from causes that could not be avoided by any human power, that I realized that it must probably return without accomplishing that for which it was designed.

On Thursday, September 3, 1863, about 4 p. m., and soon after going into camp, the scouts of the expedition reported 600 Indian lodges 10 miles distant, and, in compliance with General Sully's orders, I immediately proceeded with the eight companies (viz, E, F, G, H, I, K, L, and M) of the Second Nebraska Cavalry, numbering in all present 350 in rank and file, under my command, from Camp No. 33, to assist Major House, commanding the Third Battalion of the Sixth Iowa Cavalry, in surrounding the hostile Indians. On approaching the Indian encampment I found House's battalion drawn up in order of battle on the north side, and on reconnoitering the enemy's position perceived that the Indians were leaving as fast as possible. I immediately ordered Major House to pursue on the left flank of the enemy, while I, with the Second Nebraska, moved on their right flank. Arriving opposite that position, I perceived the Indians at a halt, formed in line of battle, apparently awaiting our attack. I immediately formed my men in line of battle. As the enemy was then situated and my men formed, I intended to have advanced the Second Battalion (Companies F, G, L, and M), commanded by Captain La Boo (Major Pearman, being field officer of the day, was, by order of Brigadier-General Sully, left in command of the camp; the command therefore devolved upon Captain La Boo, lieutenant captain), with the First Battalion, commanded by Major [J.] Taffe (Companies E, H, I, and K), as a reserve, and await further orders from the general commanding. As it was then nearly dark, I felt that time was precious, and if anything was to be done that night it must be done speedily, and made up my mind to attack the enemy immediately. I therefore changed my plan of operations. I ordered Major Taffe, with his battalion, to proceed to the head of the ravine in which the Indians were posted, to cut off their retreat in that direction, which order was promptly executed, and his command formed in line awaiting further orders. I then ordered the Second Battalion to advance directly upon the enemy, which it did. Major Taffe then, by my order, came forward, the line of the two battalions forming an obtuse angle. When within 400 yards, I ordered my men to dismount, and after advancing 100 yards nearer, ordered the Second Battalion to open the battle by a volley from their Enfields, which they did with precision and effect, creating quite a confusion in the enemy's ranks. At this time I perceived what I supposed to be House's battalion, about 1½ miles distant, advancing upon the enemy's rear. In the order in which my line was now formed, I advanced upon the enemy, pouring in upon him as I advanced a fire from my whole line, which was immediately and vigorously returned by the Indians. When within 30 yards of the enemy's lines, I ordered a halt in rear of a slight elevation of ground, in front of which was a ravine in which the Indians were posted. The fight now became general, and my whole line was hotly engaged. At this juncture, what I supposed to be House's battalion (as it was now quite dark) advanced, and commenced an attack upon the enemy's left. As they were now formed, and fearing that the Indians would attempt to escape by way of a ravine a short distance beyond the left of my line, or get in my rear by the same way, I ordered Major Taffe to extend the left wing of my line. in order to cover this supposed outlet for the Indians with my guns. The battle now raged with great fury for some time on both sides. The enemy successively, by a desperate charge, attempted to turn my right and left flanks, but they were repulsed with slaughter. They fell in every direction in front of my line by the unerring aim of my brave soldiers, who, both officers and men, fought with the courage and coolness of veterans, exposed as they were to a galling fire from the enemy during the whole time. At this juncture I became convinced that House's battalion, mistaking my command in the darkness for Indians, were firing into it. I therefore ordered my men to fall back out of range of House's guns and mount their horses, as the Indians were now in a rout and were fleeing out of range of my guns up a ravine some distance to the front. The horses becoming alarmed, and to a considerable extent unmanageable for a short time, created a slight confusion as the men were in the act of mounting, but it was only momentary, as my squadrons were in a few moments again formed in line on the crest of a hill 200 yards in the rear of my last line of battle, mounted and ready to follow up the victory, as the enemy were fleeing, leaving everything behind them. But it being very dark, and in view of the position of the Sixth Iowa, I deemed it imprudent to attempt a pursuit before morning, as it was then 8.30 or 9 p. m. Having no means of communicating that night with the general commanding, I ordered my men to dismount and lay on their arms, holding their horses, until early dawn, when I marched from the battle-ground of the previous evening, and went into camp about 1 mile from it and at the upper end of the Indian encampment. On passing over the ground of the recent encampment of the Indians and of the battle, I found that the enemy had abandoned all their tents, clothing, cooking utensils, valuables, supplies, and, in fact, everything they possessed was strewn over the ground of their retreat for miles. Their flight had been so precipitate that they had abandoned everything but their dead, whom they carried away as fast as they fell. Their rout was so complete and their flight so sudden that many of their children were left behind on account, as I suppose, of their being an incumbrance to their flight. From the best information derived from guides, the enemy's strength was not less than 1,000 warriors. Their loss in killed will not fall short of 150, as scouts sent out next day after the battle report their dead as scattered over the country for miles on the line of their retreat, and their wounded is twice that number.

The casualties in the Second Nebraska Cavalry are 2 killed, 13 wounded, and 10 missing men. There were 5 horses killed, 9 wounded, and 9 missing. I found among the effects of the Indians Minie rifles and rifle cartridges; also several boxes of army revolvers and rifle cartridges were found, and various other articles, some of which were undoubtedly taken from the whites in the late Minnesota massacre. The enemy was composed of Santees, Brulé, Yanktonais, and Blackfeet Sioux, and Cuthead Indians, and were evidently the same Indians with whom General Sibley recently had an engagement on Apple Creek. The Indians are now destitute of supplies, clothing, and almost everything else, they having abandoned all except their ponies and arms. Many of the former were, however, killed or captured during the battle. I would have pursued the enemy the following morning after the battle had it not been for the exhausted condition of my men and horses.

The officers and men under my command are not only entitled to my thanks, but the confidence of their country, for their bravery, efficiency, and promptness on this occasion. Not a man in any capacity flinched a particle. My special thanks are due to Adjt. Henry M. Atkinson, Regimental Quartermaster J. S. McCormick, and Commissary Lieut. J. Q. Goss, for valuable services rendered me immediately preceding and during the engagement.

All of which is respectfully submitted.

R. W. FURNAS,
Colonel Second Nebraska Cavalry.

Capt. JOHN H. PELL,
Assistant Adjutant-General, Indian Expedition.

AUGUST 14, 1863.—Skirmish near Wellington, Mo.

Report of Col. James McFerran, First Missouri State Militia Cavalry.

HDQRS. FIRST MISSOURI STATE MILITIA CAVALRY,
Lexington, Mo., August 16, 1863.

GENERAL: I have the honor to report that Lieutenant [N.T.] Rogers' company (L) of the First Missouri State Militia Cavalry, with 65 men from this post, left here on the morning of the 14th instant on a scout, and passed up Davis Creek to near Hopewell, and thence down the Sni to Wellington. Lieutenant Rogers reports that they saw numerous small bands of bushwhackers on their march, who fled. He is satisfied that one of the bushwhackers was wounded by his men near Hopewell; he made his escape, however. Near Wellington he reports coming upon a band of 4, of whom he killed 1, wounded 2 others, and captured 3 horses. After which he returned to this post, without sustaining any loss on his part.

All of which is most respectfully submitted.

I have the honor to be, your obedient servant,

JAMES McFERRAN,
Colonel First Missouri State Militia Cavalry, Commanding Post.

General EWING.

P. S.—Lieutenant Rogers returned to this post on Friday evening the 14th instant.

AUGUST 14, 1863.—Skirmish near Jack's Fork, Mo.

Report of Capt. Richard Murphy, Fifth Missouri State Militia Cavalry.

HEADQUARTERS POST AT HOUSTON,
Houston, Mo., August 22, 1863.

GENERAL: I have the honor to make the following report to you of a scout made by a detachment from this command:

On the 12th instant I learned that a Union man named Hackwerth, living at present at Salem, Mo., but who had gone to Casto Valley, and, with the assistance of a man named Johnson, and another whose name I am unable to learn, were engaged in collecting this Hackwith's cattle, when they were taken prisoners by a band of 5 rebels. On learning this, I sent Sergeant McDowell with 26 men in pursuit, who proceeded to Spring Valley, 25 miles southeast from this post, where they struck the trail of the rebels. This they followed for two days, and at last succeeded in overtaking and killing 2 of the rebels and capturing 1 horse.

The rebels then scattered in the woods on Jack's Fork, where all traces of them were lost, as also the whereabouts of the three Union men they had as prisoners. In the country through which the scout passed, Sergeant [T. J.] McDowell notified the citizens that they would be held responsible for the safe return of these three Union men, and upon this startling intelligence a number of citizens started to try to effect the release of the prisoners.

Sergeant McDowell now finding further pursuit to be useless, returned to this post, where he arrived on the 16th of August, with horses very much fatigued from the heat of the sun, want of forage, and traveling a distance of 130 miles.

Hoping, general, the means we use for preserving the peace and upholding our national flag in this vicinity will meet with your approval, I have the honor to remain, very respectfully, your obedient servant,

RICHARD MURPHY,
Captain, Commanding Detachment.

Brig. Gen. THOMAS A. DAVIES,
Commanding Rolla District, Rolla, Mo.

[Indorsement.]

Write a letter commending the energy, &c., displayed by Captain Murphy, Sergeant McDowell, and the latter's party in protecting Union men and preserving law and order, and direct them to persevere in their duties.

JAS. TOTTEN,
Brigadier-General.

AUGUST 17-26, 1863.—Expeditions from Cape Girardeau and Pilot Knob, Mo., to Pocahontas, Ark.

REPORTS.

No. 1.—Col. Richard G. Woodson, Third Missouri State Militia Cavalry.
No. 2.—Capt. Henry C. Gentry, Second Missouri State Militia Cavalry.

No. 1.

Report of Col. Richard G. Woodson, Third Missouri State Militia Cavalry.

PILOT KNOB, MO., *August* 27, 1863.

SIR: In obedience to orders from Colonel Livingston, of the 17th instant (he then commanding the post of Pilot Knob), I moved with a detachment of my regiment from this point on the 18th instant for Greenville, to form a junction with a battalion from Cape Girardeau. I arrived at Greenville at noon on the 20th, and had to remain there till the evening of the 21st for the troops from the Cape, when they joined me on the morning of Thursday, the 22d. I moved with the whole force, about 600 strong, for Pocahontas, by as rapid marches as the extreme heat of the weather and the condition of my stock would permit, and arrived at Pocahontas, Ark., on Saturday evening, the 24th instant. When I was within 4 miles of Pocahontas, I ascertained that Brig. Gen. Jeff. Thompson was there with little or no force. My column was then scattered over several miles, from the extreme rapidity of my march. Being very desirous to capture him, and knowing that I had to act with promptness or fail in that object, I ordered Captain [H. C.] Gentry, of the Second Missouri State Militia Cavalry, to move forward with all possible dispatch, with the advance, and surprise and capture the general, and that I would support him as soon as I could get the column up.

So thoroughly and efficiently did Captain Gentry obey this order that General Thompson, sitting quietly in his office, and having a map of Southeastern Missouri, as he thought, in absolute security, had no idea of any Federal force within 100 miles of him, until Captain Gentry, having occupied all the passes out of town, rode up to the window of the office and demanded General Thompson.

Captain Gentry deserves the highest credit for this capture, it depending mainly, if not entirely, upon his promptness and efficiency in obeying my order to move forward of the column and surprise him. I remained in Pocahontas about six hours, and being a good deal encumbered with prisoners, and fearful of their escape, camping in the brush, I determined to move back to this point with all possible dispatch, and arrived here on the evening of the 26th instant, having sent the battalion from Cape Girardeau back there by Greenville. In ten days I have marched about 250 miles, and laid still one day and a half of the time. I had no fight, but fired on several parties of guerrillas, and killed 4 of them and wounded 3 that I know of. I captured and brought in Brig. Gen. Jeff. Thompson, his adjutant-general (Captain Kay), his medical director (Dr. Frame), a captain of artillery, a lieutenant of cavalry, and a captain of ordnance, and about 50 other prisoners, mostly deserters, discharged soldiers, and stragglers from the Confederate army; also about 30 horses, the most of them taken to Cape Girardeau by the other battalion.

I regret exceedingly to have to report several cases of highway robbery, plunder, and theft by the detachment of the First Missouri Volunteers. I am satisfied that some of that detachment stole horses, watches, money, anything they could lay their hands on, from citizens and prisoners.

I am, sir, respectfully, your obedient servant,

R. G. WOODSON,

Col. Third M. S. M. Cav., Comdg. late Expedition to Pocahontas.

General C. B. FISK,

Commanding District of Southeastern Missouri.

No. 2.

Report of Capt. Henry C. Gentry, Second Missouri State Militia Cavalry.

CAPE GIRARDEAU, MO., *August* 27, 1863.

COLONEL: In compliance with orders from Col. J. B. Rogers, Second Missouri State Militia Cavalry, I marched from this post with the following commands: Of the First Missouri Cavalry, 100 men, under command of Captain [Valentine] Preuitt; of the Second Missouri State Militia Cavalry, 125 men, under command of Capt. Lewis Sells; of the Eighth Missouri Provisional Enrolled Militia, 50 men, commanded by Capt. Philip Schriner; and of the Second Arkansas Cavalry, 25 men; in all, 300 men. Left on the morning of the 17th instant, marching by the way of Jackson and Dallas to Greenfield, Mo., where we arrived on the morning of the 19th, and reported to Colonel [R. G.] Woodson, of the

Third Missouri State Militia Cavalry; from thence the whole command marched south in the direction of Pocahontas, Ark., on the morning of the 20th; continuing our march, without molestation, until the morning of the 22d, when we were informed of a protracted meeting being in progress some 20 miles north of Pocahontas, when I received orders to send forward 25 men to capture any of the enemy that might be there. I therefore ordered Lieutenant [J. H.] Burnett, of the First Missouri Volunteers, forward with the requisite number of his command, who surprised the meeting. In attempting to escape, 6 were killed and 1 was wounded, many of them having their arms with them, some of which were captured.

Continuing our march, being in the advance, were informed by a contraband, at a mill 4 miles north of Pocahontas, that General Thompson and staff were at that time in the town, and a number of rebel soldiers were strolling about the place with their guns. I immediately informed the colonel of the fact, when I was ordered forward and "to catch him if I could." The advance, consisting of 60 men of the First Missouri Volunteers, and not liking to delay for the others to come up, moved forward rapidly, finding horsemen on the road, who fled in the direction of Pocahontas; but owing to the superiority of our horses, they deemed it prudent "to hunt their holes" in the brush. When within a mile of the town, we halted a short time to blow our horses, with a hope that we might be re-enforced, not knowing the number of the rebels; but as there is danger in delay, and the command anxious to "go in and win," we pushed rapidly into the town, picketing all the approaches. On entering the suburbs of the town, a lady, seeing our guidons, swung her handkerchief and shouted, "Glory, glory, glory!" when the boys raised a shout that would have done credit to the Chickasaws, and made the straggling rebels shiver in their shoes (those that had any), and brought the general himself to the window of a lower room at the Saint Charles, and, being in front of the house, inquired for General Thompson, and he informed me that he was the man. I informed him that he was my prisoner; he replied, "Certainly, certainly." When I dismounted and entered the room, he pointed to his saber setting in the corner of the room. He then introduced me to his adjutant-general, and I told him that I was glad to see him; he said he "did not doubt it." An ordnance officer, a captain, not knowing that the Feds. were in possession of the town, entered the general's room, by permission of the guard, and saluted the general, who inquired where he was from; he said from Major Crandall's camp, and, on seeing me, remarked, "You have a Federal prisoner, I see." "Yes," says the general, "you are a prisoner yourself." I then ordered him to hand over his dispatches, when he moved toward the door. The guard brought his "sharp" to bear on him; the general told him to fork over—it was no joke—when he handsomely came down with the papers, and seemed to realize his situation. We also had captured some 15 rebel soldiers. In the mean time Colonel Woodson arrived, when the prisoners were turned over. We remained in the town until midnight, when we resumed our march northward, having accomplished our mission, and arrived here on this afternoon at 5 o'clock, without loss or accident.

All of which is respectfully submitted.

I have the honor to be, your obedient servant,

H. C. GENTRY,
Captain, Commanding.

Col. H. M. HILLER,
Commanding Second Missouri State Militia Cavalry.

AUGUST 20-28, 1863.—Quantrill's raid into Kansas, and pursuit by Union forces.

SUMMARY OF THE PRINCIPAL EVENTS.

Aug. 21, 1863.—Massacre at Lawrence, Kans.
Skirmish near Brooklyn, Kans.
Skirmish near Paola, Kans.
22, 1863.—Skirmish on Big Creek, near Pleasant Hill, Mo.
25-26, 1863.—Skirmishes near Hopewell, Mo.

REPORTS.

No. 1.—Maj. Gen. John M. Schofield, U. S. Army, commanding Department of the Missouri.*
No. 2.—Brig. Gen. Thomas Ewing, jr., U. S. Army, commanding District of the Border.
No. 3.—Lieut. Col. Charles S. Clark, Ninth Kansas Cavalry.
No. 4.—Lieut. Col. Bazel F. Lazear, First Missouri State Militia Cavalry.
No. 5.—Maj. Linn K. Thacher, Ninth Kansas Cavalry.
No. 6.—Capt. Charles F. Coleman, Ninth Kansas Cavalry.
No. 7.—Capt. John Ballinger, First Missouri State Militia Cavalry.
No. 8.—Lieut. Cyrus Leland, jr., Tenth Kansas Infantry.
No. 9.—Lieut. Col. Walter King, Fourth Missouri State Militia Cavalry.

No. 1.

Report of Maj. Gen. John M. Schofield, U. S. Army, commanding Department of the Missouri.

HEADQUARTERS DEPARTMENT OF THE MISSOURI,
Saint Louis, Mo., September 14, 1863.

COLONEL: I have the honor to forward herewith, for the information of the General-in-Chief, Brigadier-General Ewing's report of the burning of Lawrence, Kans., and massacre of its inhabitants, and of the operations of his troops in the pursuit and punishment of the rebels and assassins who committed the atrocious deed.

Immediately after his return from the pursuit of Quantrill, on the 25th of August, General Ewing issued an order depopulating certain counties, and destroying all forage and subsistence therein. The reasons which led him to adopt this severe measure are given in his report.

The people of Kansas were, very naturally, intensely excited over the destruction of one of their fairest towns, and the murder of a large number of its unarmed citizens, and many of them called loudly for vengeance, not only upon the perpetrators of the horrible crime, but also upon all the people residing in the western counties of Missouri, and who were assumed to be more or less guilty of aiding the criminals. It would be greatly unjust to the people of Kansas, in general, to say that they shared in this desire for indiscriminate vengeance; but there were not wanting unprincipled leaders to fan the flame of popular excitement and goad the people to madness, in the hope of thereby accomplishing their own selfish ends.

---

* See also General Schofield's general report, p. 12.

On the 26th of August, a mass meeting was held in the city of Leavenworth, at which it was resolved that the people should meet at Paola, on the 8th of September, armed and supplied for a campaign of fifteen days, for the purpose of entering Missouri to search for their stolen property and retaliate upon the people of Missouri for the outrages committed in Kansas. This meeting was addressed by some of the leading men of Kansas in the most violent and inflammatory manner, and the temper of these leaders and of their followers was such that there seemed to be great danger of an indiscriminate slaughter of the people in Western Missouri, or of a collision with the troops, under General Ewing, in their efforts to prevent it. Under these circumstances, I determined to visit Kansas and Western Missouri, for the purpose of settling the difficulty, if possible, and also for the purpose of gaining more accurate information of the condition of the border counties of Missouri, and thus making myself able to judge of the wisdom and necessity of the severe measures which had been adopted by General Ewing.

I arrived at Leavenworth City on the 2d of September, and obtained an interview with the Governor of the State and other prominent citizens. I found the Governor and his supporters opposed to all unauthorized movement on the part of the people of Kansas, and willing to co-operate with me in restoring quiet, and in providing for future security. I then sought and obtained an interview with the Hon. J. H. Lane, United States Senator, who was the recognized leader of those engaged in the Paola movement. Mr. Lane explained to me his views of the necessity, as he believed, of making a large portion of Western Missouri a desert waste, in order that Kansas might be secure against future invasion. He proposed to tender to the district commander the services of all the armed citizens of Kansas to aid in executing this policy. This, I informed him, was impossible; that whatever measures of this kind it might be necessary to adopt must be executed by United States troops; that irresponsible citizens could not be intrusted with the discharge of such duties. He then insisted that the people who might assemble at Paola should be permitted to enter Missouri "in search of their stolen property," and desired to place them under my command, he (General Lane) pledging himself that they should strictly confine themselves to such search, abstaining entirely from all unlawful acts. General Lane professed entire confidence in his ability to control, absolutely, the enraged citizens who might volunteer in such enterprise. I assured Mr. Lane that nothing would afford me greater pleasure than to do all in my power to assist the outraged and despoiled people to recover their property, as well as to punish their despoilers: but that the search proposed would be fruitless, because all the valuable property which had not already been recovered from those of the robbers who had been slain had been carried by the others far beyond the border counties, and that I had not the slightest faith in his ability to control a mass of people who might choose to assemble under a call which promised the finest possible opportunity for plunder. General Lane desired me to consider the matter fully, and inform him, as soon as possible, of my decision, saying if I decided not to allow the people the "right" which they claimed, he would appeal to the President. It was not difficult to discover that so absurd a proposition as that of Mr. Lane could not have been made in good faith, nor had I much difficulty in detecting the true object which was proposed to be accomplished; which was to obtain, if possible, my consent to accept the services of all who might meet at Paola, and take them into Missouri under my command, when I, of course, would be held responsible for the murder and robbery which must necessarily ensue.

I soon became satisfied that, notwithstanding Mr. Lane's assertion to the contrary, he had no thought of trying to carry out his scheme in opposition to my orders, and that the vast majority of the people of Kansas were entirely opposed to any such movement. On the 4th of September I published an order, a copy of which is inclosed, prohibiting armed men, not in the military service, from passing from one State into the other, and sent a sufficient force along the State line to enforce the order against any who might be disposed to disobey it. The people quietly acquiesced. The Paola meeting, which had promised to be of gigantic proportions, dwindled down to a few hundred people, who spent a rainy day in listening to speeches and passing resolutions relative to the Senator from Kansas and the commander of the Department of the Missouri.

I inclose copies of correspondence with Governor Carney, showing the measures which have been adopted to place the State in a condition to protect itself against such raids as that made against Lawrence. These measures, together with those which are being carried out in Western Missouri, will, I believe, place beyond possibility any such disaster in future.

Not the least of the objects of my visit to the border was to see for myself the condition of the border counties, and determine what modifition, if any, ought to be made in the policy which General Ewing had adopted. I spent several days in visiting various points in the counties affected by General Ewing's order, and in conversing with the people of all shades of politics who are most deeply affected by the measures adopted, I became fully satisfied that the order depopulating certain counties, with the exception of specified districts, was wise and necessary. That portion of the order which directed the destruction of property I did not approve, and it was modified accordingly.

The evil which exists upon the border of Kansas and Missouri is somewhat different in kind and far greater in degree than in other parts of Missouri. It is the old border hatred intensified by the rebellion and by the murders, robberies, and arson which have characterized the irregular warfare carried on during the early periods of the rebellion, not only by the rebels, but by our own troops and people. The effect of this has been to render it impossible for any man who openly avowed and maintained his loyalty to the Government to live in the border counties of Missouri outside of military posts. A large majority of the people remaining were open rebels, while the remainder were compelled to abstain from any word or acts in opposition to the rebellion at the peril of their lives. All were practically enemies of the Government and friends of the rebel guerrillas. The latter found no difficulty in supplying their commissariat wherever they went, and, what was of vastly greater importance to them, they obtained prompt and accurate information of every movement of our troops, while no citizen was so bold as to give us information in regard to the guerrillas. In a country remarkably well adapted by nature for guerrilla warfare, with all the inhabitants practically the friends of the guerrillas, it has been found impossible to rid the country of such enemies. At no time during the war have these counties been free from them. No remedy short of destroying the source of their great advantage over our troops could cure the evil.

I did not approve of the destruction of property, at first contemplated by General Ewing, for two reasons, viz: I believe the end can be accomplished without it, and it cannot be done in a reasonable time so effectually as to very much embarrass the guerrillas.

The country is full of hogs and cattle, running in the woods, and of potatoes in the ground and corn in the field, which cannot be destroyed or moved in a reasonable time.

I hope the time is not far distant when the loyal people can return in safety to their homes, and when those vacated by rebels will be purchased and settled by people who are willing to live in peace with their neighbors on both sides of the line.

The measure which has been adopted seems a very harsh one; but, after the fullest examination and consideration of which I am capable, I am satisfied it is wise and humane. It was not adopted hastily, as a consequence of the Lawrence massacre. The subject had long been discussed between General Ewing and myself, and its necessity recognized as at least probable. I had determined to adopt the milder policy of removing all families known to be connected with or in sympathy with the guerrillas, and had commenced its execution before the raid upon Lawrence. The utter impossibility of deciding who were guilty and who innocent, and the great danger of retaliation by the guerrillas upon those who should remain, were the chief reasons for adopting the present policy. In executing it, a liberal test of loyalty is adopted. Persons who come to the military posts and claim protection as loyal citizens are not turned away without perfectly satisfactory evidence of disloyalty. It is the first opportunity which those people have had since the war began of openly proclaiming their attachment to the Union, without fear of rebel vengeance.

It is possible that General Ewing might have done more than he did do to guard against such a calamity as that at Lawrence; but I believe he is entitled to great credit for the energy, wisdom, and zeal displayed while in command of that district. The force at his command was larger, it is true, than in other portions of the department, yet it was small for the service required—necessarily so, as will be readily understood when it is considered how much my troops have been reduced by re-enforcements sent to Generals Grant, Rosecrans, Steele, and Blunt, and how much the territory to be occupied has been increased by our advance into Arkansas and the Indian country.

I am, colonel, very respectfully, your obedient servant,

J. M. SCHOFIELD,
Major-General.

Col. E. D. TOWNSEND,
Assistant Adjutant-General, Washington, D. C.

[Inclosure No. 1.]

GENERAL ORDERS, No. 92. } HDQRS. DEPARTMENT OF THE MISSOURI,
Saint Louis, Mo., September 4, 1863.

The militia of Kansas and Missouri, not in the service of the United States, will be used only for the defense of their respective States. They will not be permitted to pass from one State into the other, without express orders from the district commander. No armed bodies of men, not belonging to the United States troops, or to those portions of Kansas and Missouri which have been placed under the orders of the department commander by the Governors of the respective States, will be permitted, under any pretext whatever, to pass from one State to the other.

By command of Major-General Schofield:

C. W. MARSH,
Assistant Adjutant-General.

[Inclosure No. 2.]

LEAVENWORTH, KANS., *August* 24, 1863.

Major General SCHOFIELD,
Saint Louis, Mo.:

SIR: Disaster has again fallen on our State. Lawrence is in ashes. Millions of property have been destroyed, and, worse yet, nearly 200 lives of our best citizens have been sacrificed. No fiends in human shape could have acted with more savage barbarity than did Quantrill and his band in their last successful raid. I must hold Missouri responsible for this fearful, fiendish raid. No body of men large as that commanded by Quantrill could have been gathered together without the people residing in Western Missouri knowing everything about it. Such people cannot be considered loyal, and should not be treated as loyal citizens; for while they conceal the movements of desperadoes like Quantrill and his followers, they are, in the worst sense of the word, their aiders and abettors, and should be held equally guilty. There is no way of reaching these armed ruffians while the civilian is permitted to cloak him.

There can be no peace in Missouri, there will be utter desolation in Kansas, unless both are made to feel promptly the rigor of military law. The peace of both States and the safety of the republic demand alike this resolute course of action. I urge upon you, therefore, the adoption of this policy, as the only policy which can save both Western Missouri and Kansas; for if this policy be not immediately adopted, the people themselves, acting upon the common principle of self-defense, will take the matter in their own hands and avenge their own wrongs. You will not misunderstand me. I do not use, or intend to use, any threats. I tell you only what our people almost to a man feel. The excitement over the success of Quantrill is intense—intense all over the State—and I do not see how I can hesitate to demand, or how you can refuse to grant, a court of inquiry by which the cause of that fatal success may be fully investigated, and all the facts laid before the public. I go even further. I demand that this court of inquiry shall have power to investigate all matter touching military wrong-doings in Kansas, and I do this most earnestly, to guarantee alike our present and future safety.

As regards arms, we are destitute. There are none at the fort, and none in the State. I telegraphed the Secretary of War this fact, asking him to turn over to me here arms in sufficient quantity to meet our wants. He ordered it done, and replied, further, that anything the Government could do to aid Kansas should be done. This being so, will you not express to me arms for cavalry and infantry sufficient to arm three regiments?

I inclose the copy of the dispatch of the Secretary of War to me, that you may see its purport and understand its spirit.

Very respectfully, your obedient servant,

THOS. CARNEY,
Governor.

[Inclosure No. 3.]

WASHINGTON, *August* 24, 1863.

Governor CARNEY:

The order for arms and ammunition requested in your telegram of this morning has been given. They will be turned over on your requisition. Any other aid you require will be given if in the power of the Government.

EDWIN M. STANTON,
Secretary of War.

[Inclosure No. 4.]

HEADQUARTERS DEPARTMENT OF THE MISSOURI,
Saint Louis, August 29, 1863.

His Excellency THOMAS CARNEY,
Governor of Kansas:

GOVERNOR: I have forwarded a copy of your letter of the 24th to the War Department, and requested the President to appoint a court of inquiry, with full powers to investigate all matters touching military affairs in Kansas, and have urged it strongly. I have no doubt the court will be appointed, and that the responsibility of the sad calamity which has befallen Lawrence will be placed where it properly belongs.

Be assured that nothing in my power shall be omitted to visit just vengeance upon all who are in any way guilty of the horrible crime, and to secure Kansas against anything of the kind in future; meanwhile let me urge upon you the importance of mollifying the just anger of your people, or rather of reconciling them to the necessity and propriety of leaving it to the United States troops to execute the vengeance which they so justly demand.

It needs no argument to convince you of the necessity of this course. Without it there would be no end of retaliation on either side, and utter desolation on both sides of the border would be the result.

Anything you may require in the way of arms for your militia, and complete outfit for your new regiments of volunteers, shall be furnished at once. Immediately upon the receipt of your letter, I ordered 3,000 stand of arms to be shipped to you at once, and to-day have ordered some horses for the Fifteenth Regiment. The arms are not of the best class, but are the very best I have, and are perfectly serviceable.

Permit me to suggest that your militia should be thoroughly organized throughout the State, and that every town should have arms in store, under a small guard, sufficient to arm the militia of the town. The arms can be easily supplied by the General Government. Without such organization, no town in Missouri or Kansas near the border is safe, unless it be occupied by United States troops, and to occupy them all, you will perceive, is utterly impossible with the force under my command.

To entirely prevent the assemblage of such bands of desperate outlaws as that under Quantrill in the summer season is simply impossible without five times my present force. In a State like Kansas, where everybody is loyal, such a state of things could not exist; but when half or more of the people are disloyal of all shades, as in Western Missouri, and consequently cannot be permitted to carry arms, whether willingly or unwillingly, they are the servants of these brigands, and are entirely at their mercy. If they resist their demands or inform upon them, it is at the peril of their lives. I do not wish to extenuate in any degree the crimes of those who are responsible for these inhuman acts; they shall suffer the fullest penalty; but I simply state what, at a moment's reflection, will convince you are facts, to show the necessity for full preparation on your part to assist me in preventing the recurrence of any calamity like that which befell Lawrence.

I am informed that a meeting was held in Leavenworth a few days ago, in which it was resolved that the people should meet at Paola, on the 8th of September, for the purpose of entering Missouri to recover their stolen property. If this were the only result of such expedition, or if their vengeance could be limited to those who are actually guilty, there would be no objection to it; but it is a simple matter of course that the action of such an irresponsible organization of enraged citizens would be indiscriminate retaliation upon innocent and guilty alike. You cannot expect me to permit anything of this sort. My present duty requires me to prevent it at all hazards, and by all the means in my power. But I hope a few days of reflection will show the popular leaders in Kansas the folly and wickedness of such retaliation, and cause them to be abandoned.

I shall confidently rely upon your powerful influence to prevent any such action on the part of the people of Kansas as will force me into the painful position of having to oppose them in any degree, particularly by force.

Be assured, Governor, of my earnest desire to do all in my power to promote the peace and security of Kansas. I shall be glad at all times to know your views and wishes touching your State.

Very respectfully, your obedient servant,

J. M. SCHOFIELD,
Major-General.

[Inclosure No. 5.]

LEAVENWORTH, KANS., *September* 3, 1863.

Maj. Gen. JOHN M. SCHOFIELD,
Commanding Department of the Missouri:

SIR: The brutal outrages committed upon the unoffending and unarmed citizens of Lawrence by Quantrill and his band have not only aroused every man in the State, but shocked the whole country. The wish of both is that the doers of these bloody deeds—their aiders and abettors—shall be steadily pursued and surely punished, for there can be no safety in the present or the future while these miscreants are permitted to live.

The 9th day of this month, by order of your district commander, is the day fixed upon to begin this summary punishment. That this punishment may be swift and sure, I offer you any forces at my command. You have promptly sent me a sufficient quantity of arms to meet the wants of the State. With these arms in their hands, and organized, our citizens can repel any raid which brutal marauders like Quantrill and his band may attempt, or punish, instantly and severely, those who shall aid or abet them. I have confidence only in organized action, and, satisfied both of your ability to lead our forces and your resolve to punish the guilty, I shall be happy to place the military of the State at your disposal.

I am, very respectfully, your obedient servant,

THOS. CARNEY,
Governor.

[Inclosure No. 6.]

KANSAS CITY, MO., *September* 3, 1863.

His Excellency THOMAS CARNEY,
Governor of Kansas:

GOVERNOR: I am in receipt of your letter of this morning. I fully sympathize with your feeling of anxiety to give security to the Kansas border, and to avenge on the rebels in Missouri the unparalleled atrocities of the Lawrence massacre. My forces in Missouri and Kansas having been greatly reduced by re-enforcements sent to Generals Grant, Steele, and Blunt, I am glad to avail myself of your offer of a part of the Kansas militia to aid the United States forces in this district.

With the chief towns on the eastern border of Kansas garrisoned by the militia of the State, and with two regiments of volunteers, which I have lately ordered to re-enforce the troops already in the district, the military authorities will be able not only to execute the orders for the expulsion of disloyal persons, but also to pursue and destroy the guerrilla bands which have so long ravaged the border.

For the purpose named, I will accept the services of so many companies of militia as may be deemed necessary by you and the district commander to protect the towns referred to.

I have the honor to be, very respectfully, your obedient servant,

J. M. SCHOFIELD,
Major-General.

No. 2.

Report of Brig. Gen. Thomas Ewing, jr., U. S. Army, commanding District of the Border.

HEADQUARTERS DISTRICT OF THE BORDER,
Kansas City, Mo., August 31, 1863.

SIR: Some commanders of detachments engaged in the pursuit of Quantrill are still out after his scattered forces. In advance of their return, I submit a report of the raid, which, in some respects, may be deficient, for want of official information from them.

Three or four times this summer the guerrillas have assembled, to the number of several hundred, within 20 or 30 miles of the Kansas border. They have threatened, alternately, Lexington, Independence, Warrensburg, and Harrisonville, and frequent reports have reached me from scouts and spies that they meant to sack and destroy Shawnee, Olathe, Paola, Mound City, and other towns in Kansas near the eastern border. I placed garrisons in all these Kansas towns, and issued arms and rations to volunteer militia companies there. From reliable sources I learned, toward the last of July, that they were threatening a raid on Lawrence, and soon after they commenced assembling on the Snibar, in the western part of La Fayette County. I at once ordered a company of infantry, which was then coming down from Fort Riley, to stop at Lawrence, which they did for more than a week, and until after the guerrilla force had been dispersed by a force I sent against them.

From this time, though constantly receiving information as to their movements and plans, I could learn nothing of a purpose to make a raid into Kansas. Their forces were again scattered in small predatory bands, and I had all available forces in like manner scattered throughout the Missouri portion of this district, and especially the border counties, besetting their haunts and paths.

Quantrill's whole force was about 300 men, composed of selected bands from this part of Missouri. About 250 were assembled on Blackwater, near the eastern border of this district, at least 50 miles from the Kansas line, on the 17th and 18th instant, and I am informed by Major [J. T.] Ross, Missouri State Militia, who has been scouting in the southwest part of Saline County, that the rendezvous was there.

Lieutenant-Colonel [B. F.] Lazear, commanding two companies of the

First Missouri, at Warrensburg, heard, on the morning of the 20th, that this force had passed the day before 12 miles north of him, going west, and moved promptly after them, sending orders to Major [A. W.] Mullins, commanding two companies of the same regiment, at Pleasant Hill, to move on them from that point.

On the night of the 19th, however, Quantrill passed through Chapel Hill to the head of the Middle Fork of Grand River, 8 miles northwest of Harrisonville, and 15 miles southeast of Aubrey, the nearest station in Kansas. There he was joined, on the morning of the 20th, by about 50 men from Grand River and the Osage, and at noon set out for Kansas, passing 5 miles south of Aubrey at 6 p. m., going west. Aubrey is 35 miles south of Kansas City, and about 45 miles southeast of Lawrence. Kansas City is somewhat farther from Lawrence.

Captain [J. A.] Pike, commanding two companies at Aubrey, received information of the presence of Quantrill on Grand River at 5.30 p. m. of the 20th. He promptly forwarded the information up and down the line and to my headquarters, and called in his scouting parties to march upon them. One hour and a half later he received information that Quantrill had just passed into Kansas. Unhappily, however, instead of setting out at once in pursuit, he remained at the station, and merely sent information of Quantrill's movement to my headquarters, and to Captain Coleman, commanding two companies at Little Santa Fé, 12 miles north of the line. Captain [C. F.] Coleman, with near 100 men, marched at once to Aubrey, and the available force of the two stations, numbering about 200 men, set out at midnight in pursuit. But Quantrill's path was over the open prairie, and difficult to follow at night, so that our forces gained but little on him. By Captain Pike's error of judgment in failing to follow promptly and closely, the surest means of arresting the terrible blow was thrown away, for Quantrill would never have gone as far as Lawrence, or attacked it, with 100 men close on his rear.

The first dispatch of Captain Pike reached here at 11.30 p. m.; the second an hour later. Before 1 o'clock Major [P. B.] Plumb, my chief of staff, at the head of about 50 men (which was all that could be got here and at Westport), started southward, and at daylight heard at Olathe, 25 miles from here, that the enemy had passed at midnight through Gardner, 18 miles from Lawrence, going toward that town. Pushing on, Major Plumb overtook Captains Coleman and Pike, 6 miles southeast of Lawrence, at 10.30 o'clock Friday, the 21st instant, and by the light of the blazing farm houses saw that the enemy had got 6 miles south of Lawrence, on their way out of the State. The enemy were overtaken near Palmyra by Major Plumb's command, to which were there added from 50 to 100 citizens, who had been hastily assembled and led in pursuit by General Lane. By this time the horses of our detachments were almost exhausted. Nearly all were young horses, just issued to the companies, and had marched more than 65 miles without rest, and without food from the morning of the 20th. Quantrill had his men mounted on the best horses of the border, and had collected fresh ones going to and at Lawrence, almost enough to remount his command. He skillfully kept over 100 of his best mounted and best trained men in the rear, and often formed line of battle, to delay pursuit and give time and rest to the most wearied of his forces. By the time our scattered soldiers and citizens could get up and form line, the guerrillas' rear guard would, after a volley, break into column, and move off at a speed that defied pursuit. Thus the chase dragged through the afternoon, over the prairie, generally following no roads or paths, until night, when Quantrill's rear guard formed line of battle 3 miles north of Paola and 20 miles from where they entered the State. A skirmish ensued, the guerrillas breaking and scattering, so that our forces, in the darkness, lost the trail, and went into Paola for food and rest, while search was being made for it. Lieutenant-Colonel [C. S.] Clark, Ninth Kansas Volunteers, with headquarters at Coldwater Grove, was in command of the troops on the border south of Little Santa Fé, including the stations at Aubrey, Coldwater Grove (13 miles south of Aubrey), Rockville (13 miles south of Coldwater Grove), Choteau's Trading Post (15 miles south of Rockville), and Harrisonville. There were two companies at each station, but the force out patrolling rarely left 50 men in camp at each post. He received Captain Pike's message as to the gathering of Quantrill's forces on Grand River on the night of the 20th, and at once sent for the spare troops at Rockville and Trading Post to march up to Coldwater Grove. At 3 o'clock on the morning of the 21st, he received a dispatch from Captain Coleman, at Aubrey, saying that Quantrill had crossed into Kansas, and he set out with 30 men, following Quantrill's trail nearly to Gardner, and thence going south to Paola, reaching there at 5 p. m. With this command, and a force of perhaps 50 citizens, and a part of Captain [N. L.] Benter's company of the Twelfth Kansas Infantry, which had been garrisoning Paola, he prepared to attack Quantrill at the ford of Bull Creek, 3 miles south of Paola, toward which he was then retreating. But Quantrill, on coming within 4 or 5 miles of that crossing, soon after dark, formed line of battle, as I stated above, broke trail, turned sharp to the north, and dodged and bewildered the force in waiting for him as well as that in pursuit.

These troops at the ford returned to Paola about the time the command which had followed Quantrill reached there. One of the parties in search of the trail found it 5 miles north of Paola, and reported the fact to Lieutenant-Colonel Clark, who was the ranking officer there, at between 1 and 2 o'clock. He was slow in ordering pursuit, which was not renewed until daybreak. He, at that time, sent Captain Coleman forward, with 30 men of the Ninth Kansas, which he himself had brought to Paola, and 40 of the same regiment, which had got there from the Trading Post at about 2 o'clock that morning, and about 70 militia, chiefly of Linn County. He marched soon after himself with the troops which had followed Quantrill the day before.

Half an hour before Major Plumb started from Kansas City on the night of the 21st, Captain Palmer, Eleventh Kansas, was sent by him from Westport with 50 men of his company down the line to near Aubrey, where he met a messenger from Captain Coleman, directing reenforcements to Spring Hill, at which point he struck Quantrill's trail, and followed it to within 7 miles of Lawrence. Thence, learning that Quantrill had gone south, he turned southeast; and at Lanesfield (Uniontown) was joined by a force about 80 strong, under Major Phillips, composed of detachments of Captain Smith's company, Enrolled Missouri Militia, Captain [T. P.] Killen's Ninth Kansas, and a squad of the Fifth Kansas. This latter force had been collected by Major [L. K.] Thacher, at Westport, and dispatched from there at noon on Friday, the 21st, via Lexington, Kans. The command of Major Phillips, thus increased to 130, pushed southeast from Lanesfield, and struck Quantrill's trail about sunrise, 5 miles north of Paola, and but a little behind the commands of Coleman and Clark.

Major Thacher, commanding at Westport when news arrived that Quantrill was returning by way of the Osage Valley, took the rest of the mounted troops on the upper border (Company A, Ninth, and Company E, Eleventh Kansas, numbering 120 men) and moved down the line. He struck Quantrill's trail below Aubrey, immediately in the rear of Lieutenant-Colonel Clark's command.

Quantrill, when, after dark, he had baffled his pursuers, stopped to rest 5 miles northeast of Paola, and there, after midnight, a squad of Linn County militia, under Captain Pardee, in search of the trail, alarmed the camp. He at once moved on, and between that point and the Kansas line his column came within gunshot of the advance of about 150 of the Fourth Missouri State Militia, under Lieutenant-Colonel [W.] King, which had been ordered from the country of the Little Blue, in Jackson County, down the line, to intercept him. The advance apprised Lieutenant-Colonel King of the approach of another force. Skirmishers were thrown out, but Quantrill, aided by the darkness and broken character of the prairie, eluded the force, and passed on. Lieutenant-Colonel King was unable to find his trail that night.

The pursuing forces thus thrown behind, Quantrill passed out of Kansas and got to the timber of the Middle Fork of Grand River in Missouri, near his last rendezvous before starting, about noon of the 22d, an hour in advance of the head of the pursuing column. There his force scattered, many dismounted, or, worn out through fatigue or wounds, sought concealment and safety in the fastnesses of that region. About 100 moved down Grand River, while the chief part of the force passed northeast toward Chapel Hill. Our forces divided in like manner at that point, Major Plumb and Major Thacher following the main body.

On the 20th of August, I went to Leavenworth on official business. The dispatches of Captain Pike were not sent to Leavenworth until 8 a. m. on the morning of the 21st, because the telegraph offices at Leavenworth City and Fort Leavenworth close at 11 p. m. for want of relief of operators. I received those dispatches, and the one announcing that Quantrill had passed through Gardner going toward Lawrence, not until 10.45 a. m. on the 21st. There was no cavalry stationed at Fort Leavenworth, though five companies of the Eleventh Ohio were there outfitting for Fort Laramie, but without arms. There was one company at Leavenworth City, just receiving horse equipments. Arms and horse equipments were issued at once, and at 1 p. m. I started from Fort Leavenworth with near 300 men of these companies. News reaching me at Leavenworth City of the burning of Lawrence, and of the avowed purpose of the rebels to go thence to Topeka, I thought it best to go to De Soto, and thence, after an unavoidable delay of five hours in crossing the Kansas River, to Lanesfield. Finding there, at daybreak, that Quantrill had passed east, I left the command to follow as rapidly as possible, and pushed on, reaching, soon after dark, the point on Grand River where Quantrill's force had scattered.

Lieutenant-Colonel Lazear, with the detachments of the First Missouri, from Warrensburg and Pleasant Hill, numbering about 200 men, after failing to find Quantrill on Blackwater on the 20th, encountered him at noon of the 21st on Big Creek, broke up his force, and has since had five very successful engagements with different parties of his band. The pursuit of Quantrill, after our forces had caught up with him at Brooklyn, was so close that he was unable to commit any further damage to property on his route, but was compelled to abandon almost all his horses and much of the plunder from the Lawrence stores; and since he reached Missouri a large part of his men have abandoned their horses and taken to the brush afoot. The number of equipments so far captured exceeds one hundred, and the number of participants in the massacre already killed is fully as great. The most unremitting efforts are being made to hunt down the remainder of the band before they recover from the pursuit

Familiar as many of Quantrill's men were with our prairies—unobstructed as to course by any roads or fords, with a rolling country to traverse, as open as the sea—to head off his well-mounted, compact, and well-disciplined force was extremely difficult. The troops which followed and overtook him south of Lawrence, without a co-operating force to stop him, were, practically, useless from exhaustion; and the forces which did not follow, but undertook to head him, failed, though they nearly all exerted themselves to the utmost to accomplish it. There were few of the troops which did not travel a hundred miles in the first twenty-four hours of the pursuit. Many horses were killed. Four men of the Eleventh Ohio were sun-stricken, among them Lieutenant Dick, who accompanied me, and who fell dead on dismounting to rest. The citizens engaged in pursuit. Though they were able, generally, to keep close upon the enemy between Brooklyn and Paola, killing and wounding many stragglers and men in the rear guard, they were without the requisite arms, organization, or numbers to successfully encounter the enemy.

Although Quantrill was nearly eleven hours in Kansas before reaching Lawrence, no information of his approach was conveyed to the people of that town. Captain Pike, at Aubrey, sent no messenger either to Paola, Olathe, or Lawrence, one or the other of which towns, it was plain, was to be attacked. Captain Coleman, on getting the news at Little Santa Fé, at once dispatched a messenger to Olathe, asking the commanding officer there to speed it westward. That officer, not knowing in what direction the guerrillas were moving, sent a messenger out the Santa Fé road, who, when nearly at Gardner, hearing that Quantrill had just passed through there, returned to Olathe.

With one exception, citizens along the route who could well have given the alarm did not even attempt it. One man excused himself for his neglect on the plea that his horses had been working hard the day before. A boy living 10 or 12 miles from Lawrence begged his father to let him mount his pony, and, going a by-road, alarm the town, but he was not allowed to go. Mr. J. Reed, living in the Hesper neighborhood, near Eudora, started ahead of Quantrill from that place to carry the warning to Lawrence, but, while riding at full speed, his horse fell and was killed, and he himself so injured that he died next day.

Thus surprised, the people of Lawrence were powerless. They had never, except on the occasion I referred to above, thought an attack probable, and, feeling strong in their own preparations, never, even then, asked for troops to garrison the town. They had an abundance of arms in their city arsenal, and could have met Quantrill, on half an hour's notice, with 500 men. The guerrillas, reaching the town at sunrise, caught most of the inhabitants asleep, and scattered to the various houses so promptly as to prevent the concentration of any considerable number of men. They robbed most of the stores and banks, and burned one hundred and eighty-five buildings, including one-fourth of the private residences and nearly all of the business houses of the town, and, with circumstances of the most fiendish atrocity, murdered 140 unarmed men, among them 14 recruits of the Fourteenth Regiment and 20 of the Second Kansas Colored Volunteers. About 24 persons were wounded.

Since the fall of Vicksburg, and the breaking up of large parts of Price's and Marmaduke's armies, great numbers of rebel soldiers, whose families live in Western Missouri, have returned, and being unable or unwilling to live at home, have joined the bands of guerrillas infesting the border. Companies which before this summer mustered but 20 or 30 have now grown to 50 or 100. All the people of the country, through fear or favor, feed them, and rarely any give information as to their movements. Having all the inhabitants, by good will or compulsion, thus practically their friends, and being familiar with the fastnesses of a country wonderfully adapted by nature to guerrilla warfare, they have been generally able to elude the most energetic pursuit. When assembled in a body of several hundred, they scatter before an inferior force; and when our troops scatter in pursuit, they reassemble to fall on an exposed squad, or a weakened post, or a defenseless strip of the border. I have had seven stations on the line from which patrols have each night and each day traversed every foot of the border for 90 miles. The troops you have been able to spare me out of the small forces withheld by you from the armies of Generals Grant, Steele, and Blunt, numbering less than 3,000 officers and men for duty, and having over twenty-five separate stations or fields of operations throughout the district, have worked hard and (until this raid) successfully in hunting down the guerrillas and protecting the stations and the border. They have killed more than 100 of them in petty skirmishes and engagements between the 18th of June and the 20th instant.

On the 25th instant I issued an order* requiring all residents of the counties of Jackson, Cass, Bates, and that part of Vernon included in this district, except those within 1 mile of the limits of the military stations and the garrisoned towns, and those north of Brush Creek and west of Big Blue, to remove from their present places of residence within fifteen days from that date; those who prove their loyalty to be allowed to move out of the district or to any military station in it, or to any part of Kansas west of the border counties; all others to move out of the district. When the war broke out, the district to which this order applies was peopled by a community three-fourths of whom were intensely disloyal. The avowed loyalists have been driven from their farms long since, and their houses and improvements generally destroyed. They are living in Kansas, and at military stations in Missouri, unable to return to their homes. None remain on their farms but rebels and neutral families; and practically the condition of their tenure is that they shall feed, clothe, and shelter the guerrillas, furnish them information, and deceive or withhold information from us. The exceptions are few, perhaps twenty families in those parts of the counties to which the order applies. Two-thirds of those who left their families on the border and went to the rebel armies have returned. They dare not stay at home, and no matter what terms of amnesty may be granted, they can never live in the country except as brigands; and so long as their families and associates remain, they will stay until the last man is killed, to ravage every neighborhood of the border. With your approval, I was about adopting, before this raid, measures for the removal of the families of the guerrillas and of known rebels, under which two-thirds of the families affected by this order would have been compelled to go. That order would have been most difficult of execution, and not half so effectual as this. Though this measure may seem too severe, I believe it will prove not inhuman, but merciful, to the non-combatants affected by it. Those who prove their loyalty will find houses enough at the stations, and will not be allowed to suffer for want of food. Among them there are but few dissatisfied with the order, not-

* See Ewing to Schofield, August 25, 1863, Part II, pp. 472, 473

withstanding the present hardship it imposes. Among the Union refugees it is regarded as the best assurance they have ever had of a return to their homes and permanent peace there. To obtain the full military advantages of this removal of the people, I have ordered the destruction of all grain and hay, in shed or in the field, not near enough to military stations for removal there. I have also ordered from the towns occupied as military stations a large number of persons, either openly or secretly disloyal, to prevent the guerrillas getting information of the townspeople, which they will no longer be able to get of the farmers. The execution of these orders will possibly lead to a still fiercer and more active struggle, requiring the best use of the additional troops the general commanding has sent me, but will soon result, though with much unmerited loss and suffering, in putting an end to this savage border war.

I am, colonel, very respectfully, your obedient servant,

THOMAS EWING, JR.,
Brigadier-General.

Col. C. W. MARSH,
Asst. Adjt. Gen., Dept. of the Missouri, Saint Louis, Mo.

[Inclosure.]

LAWRENCE, *August* 21, 1863—5 p. m.

GENERAL: I have, with regret, to report that Quantrill, alias Charley Hart [?], reached this town at about 4.30 o'clock this morning; burned the town; slaughtered in cold blood about 60 citizens; then left by Blanton Bridge, and by way of the town of Brooklyn. As near as I can estimate, he had about 200 men, armed principally with revolvers. It is said that Lane, with a few men, held him at bay in Brooklyn, and has sent back for help. Quantrill left about 10 o'clock.

Respectfully,

A. R. BANKS.

No. 3.

Report of Lieut. Col. Charles S. Clark, Ninth Kansas Cavalry.

HEADQUARTERS TROOPS ON THE BORDER,
Coldwater Grove, August 30, 1863.

GENERAL: In compliance with Special Orders, No. 51, Headquarters District of the Border, I have the honor to submit the following brief report of the part my command took in the chase after Quantrill's murderers in their raid on Lawrence:

In the evening of the 20th of August, 1863, I received a dispatch from Captain [J. A.] Pike, commanding at Aubrey, that reliable information had been received that Quantrill, with a large command, was camped on Grand River, 10 miles from the Kansas line. I immediately sent orders to Captain [B. F.] Goss, commanding Trading Post, also to Rockville for the troops to march forthwith to Coldwater Grove; also that Captain Pike should watch the movement of the enemy and report. I also sent scouting parties to see if any troops had crossed the lines.

At 3 a. m. 21st, I received a dispatch from Captain [C. F.] Coleman that Quantrill had crossed into Kansas, and he was in pursuit with 180 men. I learned from other sources that the enemy was moving in direction of Paola. Having with me a part of Captain Flesher's company (30 men), I started in direction of Paola; but finding, after traveling

12 miles, that Quantrill had turned north, I changed my direction, and soon found the trail of the enemy. I followed to within 4 miles of Gardner; there I learned that Quantrill had gone through Gardner at 11 o'clock the night before. Being about twelve hours behind, and learning that a force was in pursuit, and believing that Quantrill could not pass back [by] the same route he entered into the State, I turned my detachment of 30 men in the direction of Paola; called out the people of Marysville as I passed through; instructed them to send scouts out on the road leading from Paola to Lawrence, and report to me at Paola. At 5 o'clock reached Paola, having marched 55 miles; found the citizens in arms; sent men to Osawatomie and Stanton to raise the citizens, and to communicate any and every movement of the enemy. The scout sent to Stanton met Quantrill on his retreat, 5 miles out, and returned to report. This was the first information I had of Quantrill's whereabouts after leaving Coldwater Grove. He was then on the road leading into Paola. I made arrangements to attack him at the ford on Bull Creek. It was now dark, and as the enemy did not make his appearance, as I had hoped and expected, I sent Lieutenant [J. E.] Parsons to feel the enemy and learn his destination. Lieutenant Parsons found Major [P. B.] Plumb, with the entire command which had been in pursuit, together with General Lane, in command of the militia, all eager to find the marauders, but none knew what had become of them. Various opinions as to direction were now discussed, and out of the diversity of opinions it was thought advisable to rest the command until the direction was ascertained by scouts from the less jaded troops.

At 2 o'clock the following morning, having received satisfactory information as to the direction of the enemy, I got the command together and gave chase at daylight, and followed the murderers to Grand River, where they commenced breaking up in small bands. Finding my command, both men and horses, very much exhausted, and feeling farther pursuit that day useless, I halted and spent the time picking up scattering ones that had stopped in the brush on Grand River. At this time I was out of cartridges, both pistol and carbine.

The 24th, 25th, and 26th were spent in thoroughly scouring the country about Pleasant Hill and the tributaries of Grand River. Quantrill made his escape into Johnson County on the 28th. His forces were completely scattered and disbanded. We had information of Younger on the waters of Big Blue, and, having divided my forces, I sent a portion on to the headwaters of Grand River and the rest in the direction of the Blue.

The detachment sent on Grand, under command of Captain [H.] Flesher, has not been heard from. The detachment up the Blue, under Captain [C. F.] Coleman, up to last night, were doing a good work.

I am happy to say that the officers and men under my command deserve much credit for their promptness in carrying out orders, and for their fortitude in bearing up under the trials of a severe march.

The result, so far as heard from, of our scouting since entering Missouri is the capturing and killing of 21 of the devils, with presumptive evidence that 14 others have gone the way of all the world.

In conclusion, general, I am happy to be able to give my testimony in defense of all and every accusation that may be brought against the troops under your command, making them responsible for the raid upon Lawrence. Taking into consideration the position of the country, the number of troops at your disposal, and the manifest treachery and duplicity of the citizens on the immediate border of Missouri, nothing was to prevent Quantrill from doing just what he executed. Had the citizens of Missouri, those [from] whom we had reason to expect something given the information they possessed, the raid might have been arrested and the marauders routed.

While we mourn over the massacre at Lawrence, we have reason to rejoice that many of the murderers have paid the penalty of their hellish deeds, and many more will repent the day they entered a loyal State to murder and plunder an innocent people.

I am, general, your obedient servant,

C. S. CLARK,

Lieut. Col. Ninth Kansas Vol. Cavalry, Comdg. Troops on Border.

Brigadier-General EWING,

Commanding District of the Border, Kansas City, Mo.

No. 4.

Report of Lieut. Col. Bazel F. Lazear, First Missouri State Militia Cavalry.

LEXINGTON, MO., *August* 27, 1863.

GENERAL: I have the honor to report that at 10 o'clock, August 20, I received information, at Warrensburg, that Quantrill, with 250 men, had passed 12 miles north of that place on the 19th, going west. I immediately dispatched messengers to Lexington and Harrisonville, asking for all the force that could be sent from those stations to meet me at Chapel Hill at daylight next morning.

I left Warrensburg at 10 o'clock a. m. with 100 men of Companies C, I, and K. We formed a junction near Chapel Hill with Major Mullins, with 130 men of Companies B, F, G, and H, all of First Missouri State Militia Cavalry. Delayed here until late in the evening waiting on detachment from Lexington, when Colonel Neill, with 50 men of Fifth Provisional Regiment Enrolled Missouri Militia, came up; pushed on that night as far as Lone Jack. Started early on the morning of the 22d on Quantrill's trail as far as Big Creek, 5 miles northwest of Pleasant Hill, where we stopped to feed, and as soon as the advance came out of the brush west of Big Creek they discovered a body of men some half mile in their front. The whole command was immediately ordered up and parties sent out to discover who they were, when they replied that they were Federal troops, but would not say whose command they belonged to. Fearing they were Federal troops, I rode forward and satisfied myself they were bushwhackers, and were forming line of battle behind a fence; and as they were on top of a ridge, and were still coming up, I thought it prudent to dismount a company to take the advance. While engaged in this, they commenced retreating from their right. After going some three-quarters of a mile, they changed their course to their left, and formed just over a ridge, where we came up with them and exchanged several rounds, when they broke for the brush. Five were killed. Have heard since several were wounded; several horses killed and some captured. Some goods were picked up, but mostly left. The ground they passed over was strewed with goods of every description. As soon as I found they had scattered, the force was divided, and Capt. H. F. Peery, in command of one of the detachments, came up with them late in the evening, and fought them in the brush a considerable time, when they again scattered in every direction. Five more were killed in this engagement. Our casualties were none, so far. I attempted to guard the passes that night to keep them from passing east, but the most of them passed over, several parties of them being fired upon, and 1 rebel killed. From two prisoners we learned this party was commanded by Quantrill, and that there were 200 men.

August 23, the brush of Big Creek was scoured, but none found.

[August] 24, marched from Pleasant Hill to Lone Jack, and from there to the head of Texas Prairie. Saw some trails, but no rebels. One of the prisoners took us to one of their camps, but found nothing but about a keg of powder and some corn, which was destroyed.

[August] 25, divided the command (except Colonel Neill's force, who left the 24th) into small parties, and scoured the country from the head of Texas Prairie north of Big Sni, and some 10 miles south of the prairie, sending Captain Jackson as far south as Kingsville, where I learned the party passed the day before. I have not heard from him yet, although he was to report to me at Hopewell. We had a number of skirmishes this day, killing 3 (no doubt wounding several) and capturing a number of horses, and some prisoners, who were unarmed, and a female, by the name of Miss Hutchins, of this place, who was standing picket while 2 bushwhackers were eating their dinner, and since their capture by giving them timely notice of the approach of troops. Our casualties to-day were 1 killed and 1 wounded, viz: Killed, Robert C. Key, private Company K, and wounded, Joshua Stevens, Company I.

[August] 26, a picket skirmish this morning near Hopewell, and a long chase after a party of 30, but they scattered in the brush. Learned 1 was wounded in the skirmish this morning. From here scoured the country to Greenton, and, finding no fresh traces, I concluded best to come to this place and get our horses shod, some supplies, and learn something of the movements of other troops, so that I could co-operate with them.

I cannot close this report without calling your attention to the fact that if we had been armed so that we could have made a charge, we could have captured Quantrill's entire command; but cavalry armed with long guns, and these empty, are not in a very good condition to make a charge on an enemy.

Officers and men behaved well, and I take pleasure in mentioning the names of Captains Peery, W. Meredith, M. Burris, and Lieutenants [B. F.] Johnson, J. D. Mullins, D. Groomer, and P. S. Kenney. The latter is our quartermaster, and is certainly one of the bravest and coolest men I have met with during an engagement, and is well worthy of promotion. I must also call your attention to Corpl. Andrew J. Fuller, of Company I, who seized a bushwhacker, after they had emptied their revolvers, and beat his brains out with his pistol. This is the same man who a short time since attacked 3 bushwhackers, killing 2 and running the third. His bravery is certainly worthy of reward.

In closing this report, I would recommend that every citizen, man, woman, and child, in Texas Prairie, and near it, be sent out of the country, and troops sent there to use up the forage, or that it be destroyed. There are large quantities of it there, and every farmer there, with one or two exceptions, favors and feeds the bushwhackers, and the quickest way to destroy them is to destroy their subsistence and remove their friends.

The whole number killed during the scout was 16; brought in 8 male and 2 female prisoners; ordered a number of females to report to the provost-marshal; 25 horses, several guns and pistols.

I am, general, very respectfully,

B. F. LAZEAR,

Lieutenant-Colonel First Missouri State Militia Cavalry.

Brigadier-General EWING,

Comdg. Border District, Dept. of the Missouri, Kansas City, Mo.

No. 5.

Report of Maj. Linn K. Thacher, Ninth Kansas Cavalry.

HEADQUARTERS, *Westport, Mo., August* 27, 1863.

SIR: I have the honor to submit the following report of my chase after Quantrill, on the evening of the 20th instant, by the order of the general commanding:

I marched with all the available forces I could collect. I had, in all, with me about 120 men. At Olathe, I learned that Quantrill was, when last heard from, aiming for Paola, Kans. I pressed on in that direction, and, a little after daylight, struck the trail of the enemy about 5 miles north of Paola, leading eastward. I followed this for 10 miles, and then halted long enough to feed the horses, after which I pressed on until I reached Grand River. There the enemy separated, a part going into the Grand River bottom, and the other steering for Lone Jack and the Sni Hills. I pursued the latter, Colonel [C. S.] Clark being in pursuit of the former. On Big Creek, a half hour before dark, a small party of guerrillas showed themselves as I approached. I charged them, and they fled to the woods, and thus baffled pursuit. There I awaited until daylight, and then followed. They moved direct to the Sni Hills. I scoured the intermediate country and woods, and scouted for three days the Sni country, dividing my command into small parties, and at night secreting my men in squads along the paths and roads I supposed they would pass. For two days I also searched the guerrilla haunts on the Little Blue, running into a party of two of them near Fristoe's place, capturing a revolver and horse of one of them, but, to my chagrin, killed neither of them. I returned to-day, after having been out six days and nights, having traveled over many a long and difficult mile, and having failed to accomplish what I hoped to.

I am, your obedient servant,

L. K. THACHER,
Major Ninth Kansas Volunteers, Commanding Post.

Lieut. H. HANNAHS,
Acting Assistant Adjutant-General, District of the Border.

No. 6.

Report of Capt. Charles F. Coleman, Ninth Kansas Cavalry.

LITTLE SANTA FÉ, MO., *August* 30, 1863.

SIR: On the night of the 20th, at 8 p. m., I received a dispatch from Captain [J. A.] Pike, commanding at Aubrey, stating that he had just received reliable information that Quantrill with 700 men was in camp on the head of Grand River, 8 miles east of that place. I immediately sent a messenger to Westport and Kansas City with a dispatch stating the facts as I received them. In about fifteen minutes afterward, I received the second dispatch from Captain Pike, stating that Quantrill had passed into Kansas 5 miles south of Aubrey, with 800 men. The second messenger was immediately sent to Westport and Kansas City with the above news, also one to Olathe, with the request that the word be carried on west.

At 9 o'clock I started with all my available force, consisting of a detachment of Company M, Fifth Kansas Volunteer Cavalry, and a part of my own company, in all about 80 men. At Aubrey I was joined by Captain Pike, Company K, Ninth Kansas Volunteer Cavalry, and Company D, Eleventh Kansas Volunteer Cavalry. My force then consisted of about 180 men. From Aubrey I sent a dispatch to Lieutenant-Colonel [C. S.] Clark, commanding at Coldwater, that at 11 o'clock I would start after them. I struck their trail 5 miles south of Aubrey, followed it some 3 miles, when we lost it, they having scattered and divided their force to prevent pursuit in the night (in again finding it, I lost near two hours).

At Gardner I learned that they had passed through six hours before. From Gardner I sent runners south and west to notify the inhabitants that Quantrill had gone north with a large force. I soon could see the smoke from the burning of Lawrence, and pressed on as fast as our jaded horses would permit. When about 6 miles south of Lawrence, I was relieved from command by the arrival of Major [P. B.] Plumb, Eleventh Kansas Volunteer Cavalry, with about 30 men. From there we turned south for Baldwin City, and, when near there, saw them burning Brooklyn. We halted there a short time to hear from our scouts which way they were moving, who reported that they were on the Fort Scott road, moving south. From Baldwin City we struck southwest, and intercepted them on the Fort Scott road, and engaged their rear with what men we could get up, we having made a charge for the last 3 miles, and the most of our horses being totally given out, having traveled them upward of 30 miles without feed, water, or rest. After a few rounds their rear gave way and joined their main command. We then divided our command and attempted to cut them off from the crossing of Ottawa Creek, but failed on account of the jaded condition of our horses. We then got together about 40 soldiers and the same number of citizens (all the rest of the horses having given out), and again attacked them in the rear, and kept up a running fight for the next 18 miles, and till we drove them into the Bull Creek timber west of Paola. Night coming on, we abandoned the chase, having been in our saddles twenty-four hours without food or water for man or horse, and having traveled over 100 miles. The enemy here took around Paola on the north. From the best information received during the day, we killed and wounded about 30 of them. We rested at Paola during the night, and in the morning Lieutenant-Colonel Clark took command and resumed the chase.

Respectfully, your obedient servant,

C. F. COLEMAN,
Captain Ninth Kansas Volunteer Cavalry.

Brigadier-General EWING,
Commanding District of the Border, Kansas City, Mo.

No. 7.

Report of Capt. John Ballinger, First Missouri State Militia Cavalry.

KANSAS CITY, MO., *August* 27, 1863.

GENERAL: In compliance with your order, you will find a brief statement of such facts as I have been able to obtain relative to the Quantrill raid.

On the night of the 20th of August, Lieut. Col. B. F. Lazear informed

Major [A. W.] Mullins that a large body of guerrillas were reported to be in the neighborhood of Chapel Hill, and ordered him to move without delay with the effective portion of his command in that direction. Accordingly, Major Mullins moved, with 126 men; formed a junction in the vicinity of Lone Jack, or Chapel Hill, with Lieutenant-Colonel Lazear; ascertained that the guerrillas had gone toward Kansas. The whole force, about 300 strong, met Quantrill and his band of murderers and thieves 5 miles west of Pleasant Hill about 2 o'clock Saturday, when, after a short parley, which was thought necessary in order to ascertain who they were. As soon as this was done our gallant lieutenant-colonel ordered the boys of the First Cavalry, and a portion of the Fifth Provisional Regiment, under Colonel Neill, to open fire on them, which was done with a will. The bushwhackers fled in great confusion, hotly pursued by our soldiers. I am credibly informed that there were 5 of the enemy killed in this engagement, and 10 wounded. Several horses were killed, some captured, and plunder, from a horse to a finger ring, all of which was turned over, by order of Lieutenant-Colonel Lazear, to the quartermaster First Missouri State Militia Cavalry.

After this the lieutenant-colonel divided his forces and began to scour the brush in the neighborhood of Pleasant Hill. A detachment of his force, G and K, under command of Capt. [H. F.] Peery, had an engagement with some stragglers and succeeded in killing 5. Next day 2 prisoners were captured, from whom some valuable information was obtained. This band of bushwhackers, whom it is supposed was commanded by Quantrill, passed through or near Lone Jack on the night of the 19th of August, came within 1½ or 2 miles of Pleasant Hill, and then turned abruptly north for a distance of 5 miles, then west toward the headwaters of Grand River.

The above is a rough statement of such facts as I have been able to obtain.

I am, general, your obedient servant,

JOHN BALLINGER,
Capt., Comdg. Detachment First Missouri State Militia Cavalry.

General EWING.

P. S.—Some papers were captured that had been intrusted to care of Captain Quantrill, &c.

No. 8.

Report of Lieut. Cyrus Leland, jr., Tenth Kansas Infantry.

KANSAS CITY, MO., *August* 31, 1863.

GENERAL: I have the honor to report the part taken by myself, and what I know of the late Quantrill raid.

I joined Major [P. B.] Plumb, at Olathe, Kans., about sunrise on the morning of the 21st instant. He had about 50 men. We started out on the road to Gardner, but soon learned that Quantrill had passed through Gardner the evening previous, in the direction of Lawrence. We then struck across the country direct for Lawrence. When nearly 3 miles north of Gardner, we found Quantrill's trail, and learned that Captain

[C. F.] Coleman, of the Ninth Kansas, was but 4 or 5 miles ahead of us. Major Plumb knew before this that Captain Coleman was ahead of us, and that he was on the trail. We overtook Captain Coleman about 4 miles southeast of Franklin about 9 a. m. Long before this we could see the smoke over the city of Lawrence. Here we moved in a southwesterly direction. We had gone but a short distance when we could see the smoke and dust on the Lawrence and Fort Scott road. Then we knew about where the enemy were. As we moved along we could see the dust and fresh smoke, and could see by this which way they were moving. Along here I asked Major Plumb to give me charge of the militia (the citizens that had and would join us). He did so. Near Brooklyn we made a halt of a few minutes; I suppose it was to find out where the enemy were. While here, a good many of the citizens joined us, and I formed them into companies. I assigned about 50 to a company; had enough to form three companies. Near here we had a skirmish with the enemy; this was about 11 a. m.; the cavalry doing about all of it. Just before this skirmish, General Lane joined us with about 30 men. After this skirmish, Major Plumb ordered me to take the advance with all the militia that I could get. At the first skirmish all the militia, with the exception of one company, broke ranks, some to go farther in the advance, while others would keep away in the rear. I took the advance with the militia; had from 50 to 200 men, but they were strung out in squads away back to our cavalry. There were from 20 to 50 of the militia that would fight very well. Whenever we would press up pretty close and commence firing on the enemy, they would halt and form line of battle, and fight us until our cavalry would come in sight, or come pretty near their range, when they would commence their retreat again. Our cavalry horses were very much worn out, and could not catch up with the advance militia. During the day after the first skirmish, our cavalry, with the exception of one company of the Ninth Kansas, was from 1 to 3 miles in our rear. This company of the Ninth succeeded near sundown in getting near enough to give the enemy a few shots. Along in the afternoon, Major Plumb came up in the advance. He told me that the cavalry horses were completely tired out. The rest of the day Major Plumb was in the advance with the militia, or with this company of the Ninth Kansas, which was then from a quarter to a half of a mile in rear of the advance militia. Just about dark I was in advance with about 40 of the militia. We had just driven the rear guard of the enemy over the brow of a hill when we heard yelling just over this hill. Soon we saw the enemy come up on the hill. They were in line, I think, about 200 strong. They came charging down upon us. We fell back to this company of cavalry. They formed in line as they saw us coming back. We formed on their right. The enemy came up near enough to fire a few shots, when they commenced to retreat again. This was within 2 or 3 miles of Paola, right west of it. It was soon so dark that we lost them. We went into Paola. Reached Paola about 8 o'clock. Found Colonel [C. S.] Clark there. He soon sent out scouts to find Quantrill's trail. Some time during the night they found the trail. Colonel Clark said that he would start out at 3 o'clock in the morning with all the force that he could get. I staid with Major Plumb Friday night at Paola. Saturday morning we started on the trail with a few citizens. Near the line we fell in with Majors [W. C.] Ransom and [L. K.] Thacher; they had three companies of cavalry. At Williams' place, some 12 miles in Missouri, we found Colonel Clark. We stopped and fed here. Before we left Williams', Major Phillips came in with a command. Here the command separated. Majors Plumb, Ransom, and Thacher, with their companies, started out in a northeast direction; I kept with them. They scouted the country as they moved.

Sunday we scouted country in toward Lone Jack. Twice we fell in with some Missouri troops. They were scouting the country in every direction. Sunday night we reached Lone Jack, and sent out detachments to guard all the crossings. We could see by the enemy's trail that they had disbanded, nearly all of them leaving the direct trail. Monday we scouted the Sni Bottom. Tuesday morning I left Majors Plumb and Thacher near Blue Springs, and came into Independence with Major Ransom, with one company of cavalry. I came into Kansas City in the afternoon with 6 or 8 scouts.

Through the whole of the expedition I do not know of any of our command being killed or wounded. In the chase from Brooklyn to Paola we killed 4 of Quantrill's gang. They were left where they were killed. During the chase in Missouri we killed several men, but I do not know just what number.

I am, general, very respectfully, your obedient servant,

CYRUS LELAND, JR.,
First Lieutenant Tenth Kansas Volunteers

Brigadier-General EWING,
Commanding District of the Border.

No. 9.

Report of Lieut. Col. Walter King, Fourth Missouri State Militia Cavalry.

WHITE OAK CAMP, *August* 23, 1863.

GENERAL: I have the honor to report my return to this camp at 10 o'clock last night.

Upon approaching Paola at daybreak yesterday I found that our forces, under Colonel Clark, Captain Coleman, and others, had arrived and had not overtaken or intercepted Quantrill. Upon searching for the trail after day, it appears that Quantrill crossed Bull Creek, about 4 miles north of Paola; but, instead of passing out of Kansas by that route, he turned north and passed out of Kansas at nearly the same point at which he entered, going east. Thinking he designed returning to the Blue Hills to scatter out, I marched as rapidly as possible to the position that would enable me to cut him off from either of the Blues and keep him in the open country, and held that position at sunset yesterday. But I learned that Quantrill continued his course due east, as if for the waters of Grand River. Troops are in other directions to intercept, and others were on the trail; I know not with what success.

When departing on the scout, I ordered my baggage and train to a camp 2 miles from Independence for safety. I order the same to return to this camp to-day.

I have the honor to be, very respectfully, your obedient servant,

WALTER KING,
Lieutenant-Colonel.

Brigadier-General EWING.

AUGUST 23, 1863.—Scout on Bennett's Bayou, Mo., and skirmishes.

Report of Maj. Charles Sheppard, Assistant Adjutant-General, Enrolled Missouri Militia.

HDQRS. FOURTH MIL. DIST., ENROLLED MISSOURI MILITIA,
Springfield, Mo., August 28, 1863.

CAPTAIN: I have the honor to report that Colonel Sheppard, with a portion of the Sixth Provisional Regiment, Enrolled Missouri Militia, made a scout from the head of Bennett's Bayou to its mouth, sending a detachment, under Lieutenant Faught, Company H, Sixth Regiment, to meet him at the mouth of the bayou. In going down he captured 8 rebels, killed 5, wounded 2, and took a lot of horses. Lieutenant [I. W.] Faught's scout killed a rebel lieutenant named Biffles about sunset of the 23d instant. The pickets captured Capt. Henderson Green, a member of the Legislature of 1860-'61 from Christian County. Becoming satisfied that the rebel force which had been on the bayou had moved south, Colonel Sheppard moved toward Big North Fork. On the way came upon Captain Vanzoot's band. The advance attacked them, killing 2, and capturing their outfit. We had 2 men wounded and 2 horses shot.

Very respectfully, your obedient servant,

CHAS. SHEPPARD,
Assistant Adjutant-General.

Capt. C. G. LAURANT,
Assistant Adjutant-General.

AUGUST 23, 1863.—Skirmish at Fayetteville, Ark.

Report of Lieut. Edgar A. Barker, Second Kansas Cavalry.

SPRINGFIELD, MO., *September* 14, 1863.

GENERAL: I have the honor to submit herewith the following report for your examination:

I started from this post to join my company and regiment on the 14th day of August last, accompanied by a detachment of 20 men from the Second Kansas Cavalry, under my command, having just returned to the post, having been an escort to a forage train, and during my absence the regiment marched south.

I arrived at Cassville, Mo., on the 16th day of August; remained there until the 19th; then started for Bentonville, Ark., being joined by detachments from the First Arkansas Infantry and Second Arkansas Cavalry, expecting to find my regiment, or some portion of it, there. Upon arriving there, I did not find any troops. I then started for Fayetteville, supposing that Colonel [W. F.] Cloud was there with his command, having received information to that effect from, as I thought, reliable sources. I arrived at Fayetteville on the 22d instant, but did not find any troops there. I was told by parties living in Fayetteville and vicinity that Colonel Cloud was at Cane Hill, and was expected to arrive there (Fayetteville) daily, which caused me to have no apprehensions of any attack from the enemy, although I at the same time used all necessary precautions, having pickets properly posted to prevent surprise.

On Sunday morning, the 23d, we were re-enforced by about 150 Mountain Federals, under the command of [Capt. J. R.] Vanderpool and others. They had been in town but about five minutes, when we were attacked by about 150 rebels, commanded by Captain Brown. On their approach the Mountain Federals fled in utter confusion. In the mean time, I made efforts to get my men together; ran into the stable to get my horse, and while there was captured by the rebels. They remained in town but a short time, and left at their leisure. Five men—Corpl. George Heidel, and Privates [P.] Cleary, [J. N.] Skelton, and [E.] Benson, of Company C, Second Kansas Cavalry, and Private [J.] Sligher, of Company E, Second Kansas Cavalry—were captured during the skirmish, which lasted about fifteen or twenty minutes. Owing to having been captured at the commencement of the fight, I am unable to give any further particulars. Myself and the other prisoners were taken to Fort Smith, where we gave our paroles on the 28th day of August. We were then escorted to Cassville, Mo., under a flag of truce, arriving there on the 8th instant, and reported to Captain Gilstrap, commanding. I received no orders from him, but was told by the post adjutant that an order had been received from district headquarters to the effect that I should take charge of the paroled prisoners and take them to Springfield. I asked to see the order, but it could not be found. I was afterward told that the prisoners would not be sent, and an order shown me, stating that all enlisted men taken by the rebels in the vicinity of Fayetteville on late scout should be returned to their commands, as paroles would not be recognized. I immediately started for Springfield, and reached there on Sunday the 13th instant, and reported to district headquarters on this date.

I have the honor to remain, general, very respectfully, your obedient servant,

ED. A. BARKER,
First Lieutenant Company C, Second Kansas Volunteers.

General McNEIL.

[Indorsement.]

HDQRS. DISTRICT OF SOUTHWESTERN MISSOURI,
Springfield, September 16, 1863.

Respectfully referred to Maj. Gen. J. M. Schofield, commanding Department of the Missouri.

JOHN McNEIL,
Brigadier-General, Commanding.

AUGUST 25, 1863.—Skirmish near Waynesville, Mo.

Report of Maj. Waldemar Fischer, Fifth Missouri State Militia Cavalry.

WAYNESVILLE, MO., *August* 25, 1863.

An escort of 14 men, coming back from Lebanon, was attacked 4 miles from here by 25 rebels. They killed 1 of our men and wounded 1; both are here. I have sent 35 men, under Captain [G.] Muller, in the direction of the California House, and 14 men in another direction. Mr. McCain brought in the wounded man and the killed.

W. FISCHER,
Major, Commanding.

Brigadier-General DAVIES.

AUGUST 25, 1863.—Skirmish near Independence, Mo.

Report of Lieut. John G. Lindsay, Eleventh Kansas Cavalry.

INDEPENDENCE, MO., *August* 26, 1863.

GENERAL: I had a fight yesterday at sunrise; killed 1, wounded 2; had 1 of my men wounded. Am now about to start for Rockville. I know all the roads on the Sni and Sibley bottom. For God's sake let me stay and scout there. I can do good work there. Major [W. C.] Ransom will tell you same.

J. G. LINDSAY,
Lieutenant.

General EWING.

AUGUST 25-28, 1863.—Scout from Sedalia, and skirmish (26th) at Clear Fork, Mo.

Report of Col. John F. Philips, Seventh Missouri State Militia Cavalry.

HDQRS. THIRD SUB-DIST., CENTRAL DIST. OF MISSOURI,
Sedalia, August 28, 1863.

GENERAL: I have the honor to report that the scout sent to Johnson County on the 25th instant, under command of Captain [R. L.] Ferguson, Company B, Seventh Missouri State Militia Cavalry, returned last night, having traveled 120 miles.

Captain Ferguson reports that, on the evening of the 26th, he came upon a body of 30 rebels at the head of Clear Fork, in Johnson County, and attacked them immediately, killing 3 and wounding several severely. The rebels fled precipitately, and were pursued by Lieut. G. W. McGuire, of same company, with a small detachment, some 5 or 6 miles. The conduct of this officer deserves the highest commendation. He pressed closely upon the rear of the enemy, and having 22 shots, fired them all, killing 3 of the enemy and wounding 2 or 3, including the leader of the band. He was often far ahead of his soldiers, and, though receiving two shots from pistols and one from a shot-gun in his coat, he pressed on, and fired so rapidly and accurately as to stampede the enemy every time he halted for fight.

We captured 7 or 8 horses, 6 or 7 guns, some blankets, &c., without any loss to our side.

The scout sent to La Fayette has also returned, being unable to discover any trace of the enemy. After the 31st (day of muster) I will again move on the enemy.

Very respectfully, your obedient servant,

JNO. F. PHILIPS,
Colonel Seventh Missouri State Militia Cavalry.

General E. B. BROWN,
Comdg. Central District of Missouri, Jefferson City, Mo.

AUGUST 26, 1863.—Skirmish at Perryville, Ind. T.

REPORTS.*

No. 1.—Maj. Gen. James G. Blunt, U. S. Army, including operations from August 22.
No. 2.—Col. William F. Cloud, Second Kansas Cavalry.
No. 3.—Brig. Gen. William Steele, C. S. Army.

No. 1.

Report of Maj. Gen. James G. Blunt, U. S. Army, including operations from August 22.

HEADQUARTERS ARMY OF THE FRONTIER,
Perryville, Choctaw Nation, August 27, 1863.

GENERAL: On the evening of the 22d instant, I crossed the Arkansas River with a force of near 4,500, for the purpose of attacking Steele, who had concentrated all the forces of Cabell, Cooper, and Stand Watie, numbering about 9,000, on the south side of the Canadian, 60 miles from Fort Blunt. After a march of 60 miles in forty-eight hours, I came to the point where they had been encamped, and learned that they had divided their forces and commenced to retreat twenty-four hours before my arrival, Cabell, with 3,000 men, going to Fort Smith, McIntosh, with the Creeks, going west, on the headwaters of the Canadian, and Steele, Cooper, and Stand Watie to Red River.

At 3 o'clock on the morning of the 25th, I learned from my scouts that the latter force, of about 5,000, was encamped 20 miles south, on the Texas road, and immediately moved in pursuit, with all the cavalry and light artillery in advance. About 10 o'clock the advance guard met (in the timber) a company of Choctaws, who had been sent out to watch our movements. Four of their men were killed and their captain taken prisoner. From him I learned that he belonged to a new regiment of Choctaws, who had arrived from Red River the day previous (800 strong). During the after part of the day the advance several times came upon the enemy's rear guard. About 8 p. m. the advance guard came upon the town of Perryville, which is closely surrounded with timber, when they were fired upon from two howitzers charged with canister, and 4 of them wounded.

I now dismounted the Sixth Kansas and deployed them to the right and left of the road, and advanced through the timber to within 300 yards of the barricades erected by the enemy, when a dozen shells from our howitzers made them leave in haste. The main portion of the enemy, with their transportation, were several miles in advance, with their stock in good order and comparatively fresh, while we had made a march of 40 miles with stock in bad condition and completely exhausted. I therefore considered farther pursuit through a rough and timbered country in the night entirely futile.

On entering the town I learned the force there was a strong rear guard, with two howitzers, who were endeavoring to remove and destroy their commissary stores, which they had not time to accomplish. This was a regular military post and an important depot, being the only point between Boggy Depot and North Fork Town. As nearly every building contained Government stores, I directed the burning of the

* See also General Schofield's report, p. 12.

whole place. Quite a large amount of clothing was captured and destroyed at their depot at North Fork Town, on the Canadian.

I shall send a part of my force up the Canadian in pursuit of McIntosh, and with the remainder proceed to Fort Smith in pursuit of Cabell.

I remain, very respectfully, your obedient servant,

JAS. G. BLUNT,
Major-General.

Maj. Gen. JOHN M. SCHOFIELD,
Commanding Department of the Missouri, Saint Louis.

No. 2.

Reports of Col. William F. Cloud, Second Kansas Cavalry.

HEADQUARTERS,
Gaines' Creek, Choctaw Nation, August 27, 1863.

GENERAL: I have the honor to report that we attacked and drove the rear of the enemy at Perryville, Choctaw Nation, last night by moonlight, having followed them all day, about 40 miles. We left the pursuit this morning, 52 miles from Boggy Depot and 82 miles from Red River. During the day we killed 4, and captured 12 to 20. In the night we had 4 wounded, slightly.

The enemy go to Texas, and we are now *en route* to Fort Smith. Cabell is at that post with an uncertain command. Steele and Cooper go south to Red River. I will report at the next favorable opportunity. [E. C.] Catherwood and [E. B.] Eno are with me and go to Fort Smith, from which place they will probably return to Southwest Missouri.

Respectfully,

W. F. CLOUD,
Colonel, Commanding.

Brigadier-General MCNEIL,
Commanding Southwestern District of Missouri.

HEADQUARTERS,
Fort Smith, September 8, 1863.

GENERAL: I have the honor to inform you that, in obedience to instructions from General McNeil, and the request of General Blunt, I joined the force of the Southwestern District of Missouri, under my command, to those of General Blunt, and reported to him, co-operating in the march against Cooper and the taking of Perryville, Choctaw Nation.

After dispersing Cooper's forces, we turned upon Cabell. General Blunt took with him only my brigade, disposing of his own troops at Fort Gibson and Webber's Falls. Cabell retreated in haste, and the general gave me about 600 cavalry and two sections of Rabb's battery to pursue and operate against the enemy, while he came into this place, from which the enemy had withdrawn in the retreat. I overtook the enemy at Devil's Back Bone, a ridge of the Poteau Mountains, 16 miles southeast of Fort Smith, and attacked him. After three hours of skirmishing and use of artillery, the enemy quickly made his way down the southern slope of the mountains, leaving his dead and wounded, in number 15 to 20, in our hands; also several wagon loads of baggage, arms, &c. I pursued across the mountain; but as the enemy's trains were many miles to the rear, and my horses and men were completely tired down, having marched 450 miles of rapid marches within sixteen days, I was obliged to halt and feed and care for my own dead, 2 in number, and wounded, 12. I lost 2 and took 30 prisoners.

Upon arriving at this post, General Blunt, who was and still is quite sick, ordered me to assume command, and work up the case of the country.

My office has been constantly thronged by Mountain "Feds," deserters from the rebel army, who deliver themselves up, and citizens from the country, to the distance of 80 miles, who come in with joyful countenances and cheering words, to assume the relation of citizens of the United States. Cabell has retreated to Red River, leaving behind a few guerrilla parties, and losing fully one-third of his army by desertion. This I know to be true. I believe that several regiments of soldiers can be raised on the south side of the river, especially if they are to be retained as a species of militia, as the Missouri State Militia.

I start in the morning to Dardanelle, to cut off a force there, and to operate with the Union men in organizing for home defense. If arms, &c., could be furnished to these men, they could hold this part of the State themselves.

My duty here, in view of these facts, has proved most pleasant, and permit me respectfully to present the importance of creating a District of Southwestern Arkansas.

There are here my regiment (Second Kansas), the First Arkansas Infantry, a part of the Second Colorado, and two sections of Rabb's battery. These, with the armed mountaineers, are enough to hold to Red River.

I would also inform you that the Choctaws, having been abandoned by Cooper, are much disgusted, and are disposed to lay down their arms. I have had friendly members of the Nation at work, and have strong hopes that they will cease to fight, and return to treaty relations.

I trust that you will pardon this liberty, especially under the circumstances.

Most respectfully, your obedient servant,

W. F. CLOUD,

Colonel Second Kansas Volunteers, Commanding Fort Smith.

Major-General SCHOFIELD.

No. 3.

Report of Brig. Gen. William Steele, C. S. Army.

HEADQUARTERS INDIAN TERRITORY,
Camp on Little Boggy, C. N., August 28, 1863.

MAJOR: I have the honor to report that I arrived at this place yesterday, having been obliged to fall back before superior numbers. We were closely pursued until we left Perryville, since which time we have not been molested. On the 26th, shots were exchanged frequently between their advance and my rear, and in the evening it was necessary to use my whole force to hold them in check until my train could get away. The advance of General Bankhead's command is now within a few miles, in consequence of orders sent direct to the regimental commanders. I retired on this road to meet the troops that I expected, and to enable me to concentrate. The Creeks, who were encamped above North Fork Town, were ordered to join at Perryville, which they had ample time to do, but failed to do so. I have not heard from them. A Choctaw regiment joined, but about half of its numbers were unarmed. Col. Stand Watie, who was on a scout to Webber's Falls, where the enemy were reported crossing, has not joined. Many of the Cherokees have left to look after their families. Of the two regiments, there are probably not more than 100 in camp. General Cabell's brigade had been ordered to the vicinity of Fort Smith to resist a threatened movement from Cassville, and in the hope that the movement in that direction would arrest the desertions in the Arkansas troops. My communications by way of Fort Smith have been rendered very uncertain by recent movements.

Very respectfully,

WM. STEELE,
Brigadier-General.

Maj. THOMAS L. SNEAD,
Assistant Adjutant-General, Little Rock.

AUGUST 29, 1863.—Skirmish at Texas Prairie, Mo.

Report of Capt. Lyman D. Rouell, Second Colorado Infantry.

HEADQUARTERS,
Hickman's Mill, Mo., August 30, 1863.

GENERAL: I have the honor to report that I left this station yesterday morning, with verbal orders from Lieutenant-Colonel Hayes to go to Texas Prairie on a scout. After marching 15 miles, I met Lieutenant-Colonel [C. S.] Clark, of the Ninth Kansas Cavalry, who ordered me to join Captain [C. F.] Coleman's command and scout the Blue timber. I accordingly turned my command, consisting of 75 men of Company F, Second Regiment Colorado Volunteers, and reported to Captain Coleman. He ordered me to cross the Blue and scout the north side of it to this station. I started to do so, but soon after discovered a trail of a single horseman on a by-path, and followed it for about 8 miles, when I came upon a gang of 8 bushwhackers at a house in the timber. They immediately broke for the brush, and I went after them. We crowded them so close that they had not time to mount their horses, which were already saddled and bridled about 300 yards from the house. We captured them, and I immediately ordered Lieutenant [W.] Wise, with the first and second platoons, to deploy and follow them through the brush. I also ordered Lieutenant [J.] Parsons, with the third platoon, to proceed up the road to the prairie and cut off their retreat. Lieutenant Wise performed his duty, and Lieutenant Parsons proceeded with his detachment, as ordered, and came upon a picket of 4 of them mounted. He at once attacked them, and killed 2 of them and 1 horse, capturing another horse; the other 2 escaped. The result of our scout is 2 bushwhackers killed, 1 horse killed, and 9 horses captured. No casualties on our side. We took them so completely by surprise that they did not fire a shot. I ascertained that the house where I found them was a regular boarding place for them, and I thought it ought to be destroyed.

I accordingly ordered it burned, together with a crib of corn, containing about 100 bushels, which they had been feeding from.

I cannot say too much of the zeal and efficiency of Lieutenants [W.] Wise and [J] Parsons; they were ready and prompt in the execution of all orders. I must also say a word for my men. This was the first time I had ever seen them under fire, but they went to their work like old hands, and obeyed every order as readily as though on parade.

Very respectfully, your obedient servant,

L. D. ROUELL,

Captain Company F, Second Regt. Colorado Vols., Comdg. Station.

Brigadier-General EWING,

Commanding District of the Border.

SEPTEMBER 1, 1863.—Action at Devil's Backbone, or Backbone Mountain, Ark.

REPORTS.*

No. 1.

Report of Maj. Gen. James G. Blunt, U. S. Army.

HEADQUARTERS ARMY OF THE FRONTIER,

Fort Smith, September 3, 1863.

GENERAL: I have the honor to report that, in pursuance of my plans, announced to you in my dispatch dated at Perryville, Choctaw Nation, the 27th ultimo,† I returned from the pursuit of Steele and Cooper, and marched with Colonel Cloud's brigade in the direction of this place.

On the 31st ultimo, I encamped 3 miles west of the ford of the Poteau, 12 miles from its mouth. I there learned that Cabell was strongly posted near the ford, on the right bank of the creek, and had obstructed with fallen trees all the other roads leading this way. His force consisted of six regiments of infantry and cavalry and four pieces of artillery, in all numbering about 2,500 effective men.

At daylight the following morning, I advanced to attack his position, but found that he had retreated during the night a short distance toward Fort Smith, and that from that point his force had divided, proceeding by various routes southward. I then detached Colonel Cloud, with the Second Kansas and Sixth Missouri Cavalry and two sections of Rabb's battery, in pursuit of the fleeing enemy. He followed them closely 16 miles, when he engaged their rear, killing and wounding from 20 to 30, and capturing 40 prisoners. His advance guard, Capt. Edward Lines' company, of the Second Kansas, unfortunately fell into an ambush prepared by the enemy, and suffered a loss of 8 wounded, 2 of them mortally. One of the latter was Captain Lines, a brave and skill-

---

* See Schofield's report, p. 12. † See p. 597.

ful officer, whose loss is sincerely deplored. After detaching Colonel Cloud, I marched with my staff and body guard and the First Arkansas Infantry to this place, and possessed the fort and city without opposition.

Colonel [W. R.] Judson reports that he has returned with his brigade from their march toward the upper waters of the Canadian River. All the members of the two Creek rebel regiments, except about 150 men, have deserted from McIntosh, and are secreted near their homes in the Creek Nation. Numbers are coming into our lines, some to volunteer in the United States service, others pledging their allegiance and asking protection.

I have the honor to be, general, your obedient servant,

JAS. G. BLUNT,
Major-General.

Maj. Gen. JOHN M. SCHOFIELD,
Commanding Department of the Missouri.

No. 2.

Report of Col. William F. Cloud, Second Kansas Cavalry, including skirmish (September 12) at Dardanelle, Ark.

HEADQUARTERS IN THE FIELD,
Camp opposite Little Rock, September 20, 1863.

GENERAL: I have the honor to inform you that, after receiving your order to co-operate with General Blunt, and his request for assistance, I joined him on the 21st ultimo, and on the 22d crossed the Arkansas River. We immediately started in pursuit of Generals Steele and Cooper, and, after a march of 100 miles, came up to their rear guard on the night of the 26th, and, after a slight skirmish, drove them from their position. They continued their retreat during the night, and in the morning, abandoning the pursuit, our army turned toward the forces of General Cabell, who was reported at the crossing of the Poteau near Fort Smith, with from 3,000 to 4,000 troops. General Blunt disposed of his troops by sending them to Fort Blunt and Webber's Falls, upon the Arkansas and took only the troops of your district and his personal escort.

On the evening of the 31st, we camped within 3 miles of the enemy, and at dark I took a small party to reconnoiter the enemy's position. We approached to one-fourth of a mile of his artillery, driving in his outpost, which had been strongly re-enforced, and took a prisoner, receiving a volley of artillery, as well as musketry.

In the morning, moving my brigade to the attack, the enemy were found to have retreated, at 12 o'clock in the night, in the direction of Fort Smith; but, upon following in his trail, it was determined that he had turned in the direction of Arkadelphia, entering that road at a town named Jenny Lind.

At my request, General Blunt consented that I should take the efficient cavalry and the two sections of Rabb's Second Indiana Battery and two mountain howitzers and push the retreating enemy, hoping to capture baggage, &c. At 12 o'clock we came to their rear guard in ambush, whose deadly fire cut down Captain Lines and 10 or 12 of his command.*

* The casualties were Capt. E. C. D. Lines and 1 man killed, and 9 men wounded.

I found a line of dismounted cavalry and howitzers, and steadily drove their rear from their position, and up the mountain side, to within one-fourth of a mile of their line of battle, skillfully formed upon the summit of Backbone Mountain, of the Poteau range. I here brought my whole force into action, and for three hours the battle raged with variable violence. During a suspense of my fire, the enemy suddenly withdrew, leaving his dead and wounded, together with arms, baggage, &c., in our possession. I immediately occupied the field, and extended my pickets beyond, taking prisoners and receiving deserters, who came flocking in.

Our entire loss was 14. The enemy's, in killed and wounded, was from 15 to 20.

In the morning I returned to Fort Smith and assumed command, where I remained until the 9th, receiving several hundred deserters, to whom I extended the lenient policy directed in General Schofield's letter upon that subject. I also learned of the capture of Captain Gardner, and the destruction of your dispatches to myself. A movement of the command of Colonel [E. C.] Catherwood was ordered, with a view to serve their interests and to punish guerrillas.

On the 9th, I took 200 of the Second Kansas, Captain [J. M.] Mentzer commanding, and one section of artillery, Lieutenant Haines commanding, and started toward Little Rock, via Dardanelle, at which place I attacked a brigade of the enemy, under Colonel Stirman, about 1,000 strong, with four pieces of artillery. After from two to three hours fighting, the enemy retreated in confusion down the river and across the same. Many were killed or drowned in the passage, probably 10 to 15, and I took a captain and about 20 privates prisoners. Also captured 200 head of Confederate cattle, several hundred bushels of wheat, much flour, and other commissary stores, upon which I subsisted my command, having no rations with me, and obliged to depend upon the country.

One gratifying feature of much interest and importance to the cause presented itself in our march, *i. e.*, we were joined by six companies of Union men, about 300 all told, with the Stars and Stripes flying, and cheers for the Union. These men assembled at one day's notice and accompanied me in the attack upon the town, and justly share the victory. I remained at that place three days, and received assurances that hundreds of men, on both sides of the river, stand ready to take arms for the Union.

Hearing of the occupation of Little Rock by General Steele, I took an escort of 100 of the Second and started to explore the river, and open communications with our forces. On the way down I took possession of two steamboats, which I obligated to report at this place when the river rises, and, meeting with no obstacle, arrived here on the 18th, all safe and well, and am camped at the extreme southeast point of your district. I am convinced that thousands of men stand ready to take arms as soon as they can be furnished, and this is the case also with Northern Texas. The people come to me by hundreds, and beg of me to stand by them and keep them from being taken by the conscript officers or from being taken back to the rebel army, from which they have deserted, and to show their earnestness they came in with their old guns and joined us.

In the attack upon Dardanelle I was assisted by three officers and about 100 men, who had fought me at Backbone, under Cabell, and it was a novel sight to see men with the regular gray uniform and Confederate State belt-plate fighting side by side with the blue of the army, and this novelty was intensified by knowing that they were fighting their old command. I have them now at work hunting guerrillas, and hope to make good soldiers out of many of them. I return in the morning to Dardanelle and Fort Smith.

General Steele, under his instructions, is attending to Price, who is at Arkadelphia, and cannot at this time send troops up the river. He tells me to organize the Union men and use them until something new is developed.

It is true that my chief operations are below the river, and consequently out of your district, but it merely happens that the points I occupy are on the south side. The results to the cause and the benefit to your district are the same, and as the people are accidentally placed in the position to call upon me for assistance, I cannot find it in my heart to desert them. I trust that you will justify this, and in your future orders take this in consideration. When these men are organized, they can keep their own locality clear, and I can then move with more certainty to clean out Washington and Benton Counties. The forage and subsistence are abundant.

I shall continue to report to your headquarters, and take the orders which I may receive from Blunt and Steele, as advisory, looking to you for those which I am to follow.

Should I arrive safely at Fort Smith, I will communicate again.

Most respectfully, your obedient servant,

W. F. CLOUD,
Colonel, Commanding.

Brigadier-General MCNEIL,
Commanding Southwestern District of Missouri.

No. 3.

Report of Brig. Gen. W. L. Cabell, C. S. Army, including operations July 17–September 14 (skirmishes between the San Bois and Scullyville and at Jenny Lind, &c.).

HEADQUARTERS CABELL'S BRIGADE,
December 7, 1863.

CAPTAIN: I have the honor to submit the following report in reference to the evacuation of Fort Smith by the troops of my command. The command I had, which was called a brigade, consisted of [J. C.] Monroe's, [Lee L.] Thomson's, and [J. F.] Hill's regiments of cavalry, [J. L.] Witherspoon's, [W. A.] Crawford's, and Woosley's battalions of cavalry, [A. S.] Morgan's infantry regiment, four iron 6-pounder battery, also several little independent companies of Partisan Rangers. (Hill's regiment, and Woosley's and Crawford's battalions were raised from deserters and jayhawkers who had been lying out in the mountains, and forced into service.) The aggregate of the whole amounted to over 3,000, yet, notwithstanding, I could never get into the field at any one time over 1,600 men, and never more than 1,200 of them for duty. During the month of July, after having made a big scout into Northwest Arkansas and Southwest Missouri, I was ordered to join General Cooper's command in the Indian country, which I did a few days after General Cooper's fight with Blunt.

I joined him on the east side of the Canadian at Camp Pike. Remained there, under command of General Steele, for a few days, when we moved to Prairie Springs, within 20 miles of Fort Gibson. From there we went to Honey Springs; remained a short time, and fell back to Soda Springs. Remained there a few days, when I was ordered to move to the east side of the Canadian, at old Camp Pike. The next day, it having been reported that the enemy were crossing the Arkansas in large force, General Steele, with General Cooper's command, joined me on the march to Camp Pike. I remained there a few days, and on the 12th of August I left and took a position, by General Steele's direction, on the San Bois, where the Beale road crosses that stream, about 15 miles distant. Up to this date nearly all of Hill's regiment, a large number of Thomson's regiment, and nearly all of Crawford's battalion have deserted. Morgan's regiment was garrisoning Fort Smith, and, although a part of my brigade had always been kept detached by General Steele, and was never, up to that time, in the field with me while at the San Bois, after remaining about a week at the San Bois, I received an order from General Steele to move to Scullyville, and to concentrate, as far as possible, my brigade there, to resist the enemy should he advance on me, and, if compelled to fall back, to take the road leading to Riddle's Station, where there was a commissary depot. I obeyed these orders strictly; moved to Scullyville, and encamped within 3 miles of it, as there was neither water nor grass nearer than that distance.

On the 21st [of August] I received an order from General Steele directing me to assume the direction of affairs in my (your) vicinity, and ascertain, if possible, the strength of the enemy in Northwestern Arkansas. As it was impossible to get a position, on account of the scarcity of water and grass, near Scullyville, I concentrated all my troops at McLean's Crossing of the Poteau, 9 miles southwest of Fort Smith, and about 8 miles from Scullyville, on the middle road. I there made preparations to hold that place. After sending a command to Northwestern Arkansas, as ordered, I blocked up the fords and roads above my position, and also the bottom road leading to Fort Smith. Leaving one regiment on picket in advance of Scullyville (as water could not be had sufficient for any greater number), to picket the roads leading to Fort Smith, I went to Fort Smith and found all the public property there. I also learned that there was a train of wagons loaded with ammunition for General Steele's ordnance officer at Dardanelle. I immediately sent an escort for it, and ordered it to Waldron, Scott County.

On the morning of the 22d, I received a note from General Steele stating that the enemy was advancing on him in heavy force. I notified General Steele of the position I had taken on the Poteau, and after receiving his approval of the same, I made preparations to protect and send off the public property of every description at Fort Smith. I had all the ordnance of every description, all the tools and materials of every description, all the quartermaster's and commissary property of every description that I could find or hear of loaded up and placed in a position of safety. My attention was also directed to gathering up my men as much as possible and scouting in the rear of the enemy, as directed.

On the evening of the 28th of August, I received a letter from Capt. J. H. Hunter, acting commissary of subsistence, inclosing a letter from General Steele, dated 16th (evidently intended for the 26th of August), and was no doubt written from Gaines' Creek, stating that the enemy was following him, and that I must keep out scouts on both sides of the river. This I did as directed. Kept out heavy scouts on both sides of the river, and sent scouts daily 25 miles in advance of Scullyville, beyond the San Bois. The enemy, after having followed General Steele to Perryville, returned to Camp Pike with the greater portion of their command.

On the 30th, my scouts encountered the advance guard of General Blunt, 2 miles west of the San Bois, and skirmished with them until within 12 miles of Scullyville (and 20 miles of my camp), where they encamped, within 4 miles of my pickets.

About 2 a. m. on the 31st, General Blunt's advance, under Colonel Cloud, attacked my pickets, and, after a brisk engagement (in which I lost 1 man killed and several wounded), drove them back to the main body, under Colonel Thomson, near Scullyville. Colonel Thomson skirmished with them and held them in check at times until 4 p. m., until they reached the field near the Poteau Bottom, within 3 miles of my command, where they stopped farther pursuit with their cavalry, and awaited the arrival of their infantry and artillery. My command had been reduced at that time, by desertion, to about 1,250 men in all. After their infantry and artillery came up, they attacked my skirmishers and penetrated nearly to the river. After a brisk fire on both sides for about an hour, the enemy fell back, with several killed and wounded (the number could not be ascertained, as it was some time after dark). Knowing positively that the enemy had at least 2,300 effective men and eight pieces of artillery, and knowing that I could rely on but little more than one-half of the small number of men I had to fight, I determined to fall back, and to reach, if possible, a range of mountains in my rear, and to get all the trains and public property of every description across these mountains, with the hope that I might possibly save them. It was impossible for me to fall back to the road that General Steele had designated, for two reasons: First, the enemy had possession of the road; second, had I moved in that direction, my men would have deserted, and not left men enough to protect the public property or my battery, as every regimental and battalion commander reported to me.

About 9 p. m. on the 31st, I determined to fall back, if possible, to Waldron, in Scott County. The baggage trains were all ordered to a little place called Jenny Lind, 10 miles on that road, early in the day. As soon as I commenced falling back, taking the Jenny Lind road, I sent and started the train. The ordnance train, which was an ox train, I had previously sent to Waldron.

General Blunt, finding out that I had abandoned the position I had on the Poteau, sent Colonel Cloud, with 1,500 cavalry, six pieces of artillery, and 40 wagons, loaded with infantry, in pursuit of me. They followed, and attacked the picket I left at Jenny Lind about 9 o'clock on the 1st day of September. The picket skirmished with their advance until they reached the foot of Backbone Mountain, about 16 miles from Fort Smith, where I had formed my command for battle. I placed Monroe's regiment in ambush at the foot of the mountain, and placed all the different regiments *en échelon* along the sides of the mountain, near the road; the battery being placed so as to command the whole field of operations. The enemy came dashing up, yelling and shouting, confident of success, their cavalry in advance. When they came within gunshot, Monroe's regiment opened fire on them, and dismounted every man except two in the front companies. The action soon became general, and, after a heavy fire of nearly three hours and a half, especially of artillery, the enemy were repulsed, with a loss of about 30 killed and from 100 to 150 wounded. My loss was 5 killed and 12 wounded. The number of missing I cannot state, as eight companies of Morgan's infantry regiment, Hill's and Thomson's regiments, and Woosley's battalion of cavalry ran in the most shameful manner. Hill's regiment, in running, ran through the provost guard, where I had 80 prisoners under sentence for treason and desertion. These men in running carried all the prisoners off with them. Thomson's and Hill's regiments acted in the most disgraceful manner. The eight companies of Morgan's regiment acted but little better. There was nothing to make these regiments run, except the sound of the cannon. Had they fought as troops fighting for liberty should, I would have captured the whole of the enemy's command, and gone back to Fort Smith, and driven the remainder of the enemy's force off, and retaken the place. As it was, I was forced, on account of the smallness of my force, to content myself with repulsing the enemy and protecting the public property. Leaving a party to bury the dead and take off the wounded, I, after posting a heavy picket on the battle-field, withdrew in good order, and marched to Waldron, Scott County, arriving there on the 2d of September.

After reaching that place, resting my command, and hearing nothing from General Steele, knowing nothing of any re-enforcements that were coming, and also hearing that the enemy were investing Little Rock with a heavy force, I concluded that I could do nothing more than look to the protection of the public property under my charge, and take the most direct route on which supplies could be had, and join General Steele as soon as possible with all the men I could.

After reaching Waldron, and remaining one day for the stragglers to come in, I could not raise more than 900 men, and from that number deserters were continually leaving. I therefore moved from Waldron, taking the Caddo Gap road to Centre Point, in Sevier County, intending to go from there to Doaksville, in the Choctaw Nation, and thence join General Steele at Boggy Depot, where I supposed I would meet him. I had previously sent stores to Lewis' old store, on the Fort Towson road, intending to take that road and then to cross over to Riddle's Station; but I found, as I have already stated, that I was compelled to take roads that would keep my men from deserting, and not to take roads that I knew I should take to carry out my instructions, and would have been proper under the circumstances. Nothing could prevent the men from deserting; the officers had no control over them, and both officers and men were impressed with the idea that the proper way to defend the country was for each man to go home and defend his own home. When the general commanding will consider the kind of troops I had, the kind of men which composed my command, men a larger part of whom were either deserters from other regiments or conscripts and jayhawkers forced into the service, he will see at once the difficulties I labored under, and how unreliable troops composed of such men are, and how worthless as troops to defend a country they are.

By comparing my military operations in Northwestern Arkansas (with this bad material) with that performed by other commanders in the District of Arkansas, I feel confident that it will be found that I have done as much toward the defense of the country as any other commander.

After reaching Centre Point, while *en route* to General Steele, on the 10th, I received an order from General Price, commanding District of Arkansas, to move as rapidly as possible with my whole command to Little Rock. I obeyed this order, and met the army falling back from Little Rock at Arkadelphia.

I must mention the gallantry of Captain [W. M.] Hughey, commanding the battery, and his two lieutenants, [W. A.] Miller and Henley, as well as all his men. Captain Hughey and Lieutenant Miller particularly distinguished themselves with their old iron battery. Monroe's regiment, under Lieutenant-Colonel [J. M.] O'Neil and Major [A. V.] Reiff (Colonel Monroe being sick), Captain [W. T.] Barry, with his company of Missouri Cavalry, Major [F. P.] Yell, of [A. S.] Morgan's regiment, with Captains [W. L.] Sims' and [Iverson L.] Brooks' companies, commanded respectively by those officers, and Captain [J. O.] Sadler and his company deserve especial mention. Colonel Morgan and Lieutenant-Colonel [J. C.] Wright also acted with gallantry.

I cannot close without bringing to notice the gallant conduct of Maj. Robert J. Duffy, inspector-general, and Lieutenant [B. J.] Field, ordnance officer, Lieutenant [D. A.] Corder, acting aide-de-camp, and Surgeon [J. H.] Carroll, of my staff. I am particularly indebted to them, as well as to Lieutenant [E. H.] McDaniel, of Monroe's regiment, Lieutenant [L. T.] Kretschmar, of Barry's company, and Lieutenant [W. J.] Tyus, acting assistant adjutant-general, all of whom acted with the greatest coolness in endeavoring to rally the men who were running, and also in carrying orders.

Maj. John Crawford, brigade quartermaster, and Captain Smith, acting commissary of subsistence, were zealous and untiring in the discharge of their duties. Under the direction and good management of these two officers, all the public property was saved except a few commissary stores abandoned at Lewis' old store, on the Fort Towson road. These stores were afterward saved by General Bankhead's command.

A lot of beef cattle, I understand, was lost which had been under the direction of Capt. A. H. Cline, acting commissary of subsistence, and turned over to Capt. J. H. Hunter, acting commissary of subsistence. No information was given me by Captain Cline of the whereabouts of this herd of cattle. I knew nothing about them until I reached Waldron, Scott County, late on the 2d of September, when, informed by Captain Hunter, acting commissary of subsistence, that there was a large herd of cattle in the neighborhood of Hodges' prairie, I immediately sent to look for them, and, when found, they were moving rapidly in the wrong direction. I have not heard whether or not they have all been taken to General Steele's command. Captain Cline's neglect to give me the proper information was the cause of any loss, and if any loss has taken place, he deserves to be censured for his neglect in not taking proper care of these cattle, and giving me such information as would have enabled me to have taken precautionary measures for their safety.

The loss of the brigade in the two days' fighting was 6 killed and 14 wounded; number missing not known.

I am, sir, very respectfully, your obedient servant,

W. L. CABELL,
Brigadier-General, Commanding Brigade.

Capt. B. G. DUVAL,
Assistant Adjutant-General, Indian Territory.

P. S.—The courier from General Bankhead, informing me that he was on the way to re-enforce me, did not reach me until the morning of the 10th, nine days after the fight at Backbone. I was then at Centre Point, making preparations to leave for Little Rock. The order of the 10th, from General Steele's headquarters, dated at camp on Middle Boggy, was not received by me until the 16th. His letter of September 1 was received on the 9th. This letter approves of the position I had at the Poteau. The letter of Adjutant-General Duval, of the 2d of September, was also received on the 9th. I communicated with General Steele by express and by special courier on the 20th, 21st, 22d, 24th, 26th, 27th, 28th, and 29th of August. I communicated with General Price's headquarters, as directed by General Steele, on the 24th, 26th, and 30th of August, and on the 5th and 6th of September. I communicated also with General Steele on the 7th and 10th of September. The dates of General Bankhead's communications were the 2d and 7th of September. Sickness prevented me from sending this report at the proper time.

[Indorsement.]

DOAKSVILLE, *December* 28, [1863.]

The written report just received is respectfully forwarded. That the enemy had the main road to Riddle's Station would only require that another should be taken, which is little, if any, farther, viz, the one via Lewis' store. Had that road been taken, Bankhead's brigade would have been met by the 4th of September, and the enemy's forces, scattered from Scullyville to Dardanelle, would have been an easy conquest. The *morale* of his command presents a better reason. The movement, as reported from Soda Springs to the east side of the Canadian, and again to San Bois, and finally to the vicinity of Fort Smith, was for the purpose of trying to prevent desertions, which were diminishing our strength at a rapid rate. A strict obedience to orders would have resulted better if only one regiment had remained.

WM. STEELE,
Brigadier-General.

SEPTEMBER 4, 1863.—Affair at Quincy, Mo.

REPORTS.

No. 1.—Col. John F. Philips, Seventh Missouri State Militia Cavalry.
No. 2.—Lieut. Thomas A. Wakefield, Eighth Missouri State Militia Cavalry.

No. 1.

Report of Col. John F. Philips, Seventh Missouri State Militia Cavalry.

HDQRS. THIRD SUB-DISTRICT, CENTRAL DISTRICT,
Sedalia, Mo., September 7, 1863.

GENERAL: I beg leave to report that, on the 4th instant, a band of guerrillas, under the lead of the notorious Rafter, dashed into Quincy, at once firing into a squad of citizens sitting in front of a store, killing 1, a Mr. Thomas, and wounding a soldier of the Eighth Missouri State Militia, who chanced to be in town. The stage had just come in, having for passengers 3 or 4 soldiers of the Eighteenth Iowa. These, it seems, took refuge up stairs in a house. Rafter went in person after them. As he entered the door, one of these soldiers shot him twice, killing him instantly. The Iowa soldiers were taken prisoners and carried off. It is quite probable that they have been killed, as nothing has been heard of them since. I have stationed a small force there, and wish I had a company of Enrolled Missouri Militia to send there.

My scouts in Saline, La Fayette, and Johnson have started no bushwhackers recently. Everything is as quiet as the grave, except in the vicinity of Knobnoster. There is an independent company, under the leadership of one Mattox, who are terrifying, robbing, and running quiet, peaceable citizens of Johnson County. General Ewing should be advised of it, and order them to disperse.

Very respectfully, your obedient servant,

JNO. F. PHILIPS,
Colonel Seventh Missouri State Militia Cavalry.

Brig. Gen. E. B. BROWN,
Comdg. Central District of Missouri, Jefferson City, Mo.

No. 2.

Report of Lieut. Thomas A. Wakefield, Eighth Missouri State Militia Cavalry.

SPRINGFIELD, MO., *September* 8, 1863.

GENERAL: I have the honor to inform you that, on my return from Sedalia, with arms for Major Eno's battalion, on the 4th instant, I came upon a band of rebels at Quincy, commanded by Captain Rafter. They had robbed the town and shot some Union citizens and taken 4 soldiers, purporting to belong to the Eighteenth Iowa Volunteers. They were in the act of firing the town. I made a dash in town, scattering them, and killing their leader, Captain Rafter. We also captured a great many of the goods that had been taken. One of my men was mortally wounded. I learned the next morning that they had killed the Iowa boys. I sent out about 6 miles, and found 1 dead and 1 mortally wounded.

I am, general, with much respect, your obedient servant,

THOS. A. WAKEFIELD,

First Lieut. Company A, Eighth M. S. M. Cav., Comdg. Escort.

General MCNEIL.

SEPTEMBER 4-7, 1863.—Scout from Cold Water Grove to Pleasant Hill and Big Creek, Mo., and skirmishes.

Report of Lieut. Col. Charles S. Clark, Ninth Kansas Cavalry.

HEADQUARTERS TROOPS ON THE BORDER,
Cold Water Grove, September 8, 1863.

GENERAL: On the morning of the 4th of September, 1863, I ordered a scout of 40 men from Companies E and G, of the Ninth Kansas, to accompany me to Pleasant Hill, where I had previously instructed Captain [C. F.] Coleman to march and join the scout from this station, with Companies D, of the Ninth Kansas, and M, of the Fifth Kansas, which he did on the 5th instant. The same night we marched 15 miles east, concealed our men in the brush, dismounted, and sent out four parties, of 12 men each, under Captains Coleman and [H.] Flesher. Killed 6 bushwhackers, remounted, marched 4 miles south; divided the command; the scout from this station to scour Big Creek, in the direction of Pleasant Hill; Captain Coleman, with his command, was to take in those run off Big Creek, and scour the brush east.

The scout on Big Creek, under Captain Flesher, and myself included, surprised a party at a house; killed 4, captured 8 horses, saddles, and bridles, and some Lawrence goods, and wounded, as I think, 4 others. Our loss, 2 men slightly wounded, viz, Corpl. John Walters, Company E, and Private S. Pentico, Company G, and returned to this station the 7th instant.

Captain Coleman was to remain in the vicinity of Pleasant Hill two or three days, to watch Quantrill's movements. I found a trail of about 100 men 5 miles east of Harrisonville, who had passed the night of the 3d, twelve hours in advance of my scout, the trail taking a northeast direction.

I am, general, your obedient servant,

C. S. CLARK,

Lieutenant-Colonel Ninth Kansas Volunteer Cavalry, Comdg.

Brigadier-General EWING.

SEPTEMBER 5, 1863.—Skirmish with Indians near White Stone Hill, Dak

Report of Lieut. Charles W. Hall, Second Nebraska Cavalry.

HDQRS. COMPANY F, SECOND NEBRASKA CAVALRY,
Camp No. 41, Dakota Territory, September —, 1863.

CAPTAIN: In compliance with orders from Brigadier-General Sully, commanding Indian expedition, I proceeded, on the morning of September 5, 1863, with 12 men of the Second Nebraska Cavalry and 15 men from the Sixth Iowa Cavalry under my command, on a scout in search of Surgeon Bowen, Sergeant Newcomb, and 8 others missing from the Second Nebraska Cavalry, after the battle of White Stone Hill, on the 3d instant. I proceeded in a northeasterly direction from the battle-field, and, when 15 miles distant therefrom, I was attacked by a party of some 300 Indians, and, seeing that I could not successfully resist their attack, I retreated slowly, returning the enemy's fire until my command was so closely pressed by the enemy that the men increased the rapidity of their retreat, without orders. I attempted to halt them several times, but unsuccessfully. The enemy all the time pressed closely on my rear, and also endeavored to cut off my retreat to camp, from which I had started in the morning, and at which I had arrived with what remained of my command about 12 m. that day, the enemy pursuing to within 4 miles of the camp. The casualties on this scout were 6 men and 4 horses killed. Sergeant Blair, Company K, Second Nebraska Cavalry, Sergeant Rogers, Sergt. S. N. Smith, and Sergt. Isaac L. Winget, of the Sixth Iowa Cavalry, assisted me in my efforts to control the men and check their hasty retreat.

The following is a list of the killed under my command:*

I discovered no trace of the missing, of whom I was in search, who, however, returned to camp a short time after my return and on the same day.

The men under my command succeeded while retreating in killing 6 Indians and 4 ponies, and wounding many others, the number not known.

All of which is respectfully submitted.

CHARLES W. HALL,
First Lieut. Co. F, Second Nebraska Cav., Comdg. Detachment.

Capt. JOHN H. PELL,
Assistant Adjutant-General.

SEPTEMBER 5, 1863.—Skirmish near Maysville, Ark.

Report of Capt. John Gardner, Second Kansas Cavalry.

SPRINGFIELD, MO., *September* 14, 1863.

CAPTAIN: I have the honor to report, through you, to the commanding general, that I left Springfield, according to orders, on the 31st day of August, 1863, and arrived at Cassville, Mo., at 11 a. m. on the 1st of September, and immediately reported to Captain [J. M.] Gilstrap, First Arkansas Cavalry, commanding post, and requested an escort, in order

*Nominal list, omitted, shows 6 killed.

to proceed forward at once. He did not furnish me with an escort until the morning of the 3d. The escort consisted of 75 men, under command of Capt. J. [I.] Worthington, First Arkansas Cavalry Volunteers. One-third of the escort were drunk, whooping and hallooing when we left Cassville. We camped, on the night of the 3d, 18 miles from Cassville. About daylight on the morning of the 4th, we broke camp, and moved in the direction of Bentonville. When within a half mile of Bentonville (about 9 a. m.) we ran in the rebel pickets. We charged the town, and took 1 prisoner, whom Captain Worthington paroled. We went the same night to the headwaters of Flint Creek, and camped, where we took 2 prisoners, who said they belonged to Marmaduke's army. We took them along with us. On the morning of the 5th, we moved at daylight, and, being informed by one of our prisoners that a party of 65 men, formerly of Livingston's band, were waiting to meet us, we prepared to receive them in case they should attack us. We met them about 2 miles from our camp. We attacked them; killed 1 horse and took 1 prisoner. Soon after we arrived at a house, and the occupant (a woman), supposing that we were a part of Quantrill's band, informed me that there was a party of 65 rebels half an hour ahead of us. Not wishing to engage them, we took the left-hand road, after seeing by their tracks that they had taken the right. We traveled about 4 miles on this road in the direction of Flint Creek. We were here attacked by the party. We drew them from their position. They divided, part getting in our front and part in our rear, and we had a running fight for about 10 miles without any disaster on our side. We then struck the State Line road, about 12 miles south of Maysville, when they left. We marched about 8 miles, and stopped to feed. We put out pickets about one-half of a mile in our rear. The advance of the enemy came up. Our pickets fired on them and came in. Immediately after, an attack was made on us by about 300 men. About 50 of our men broke and ran. While Captain Worthington was trying to rally them, I took command of those that remained (about 25), and held the enemy in check until, being flanked on right and left, I fell back one-half mile to a place called Hog-Eye, and formed. They flanked me again. I then fell back to Round Prairie, where I was again attacked. I formed my men on the prairie; the enemy were in the timber. After a fight of about twenty minutes, in which I lost 1 killed and 2 wounded, and my horse being shot under me, I gave the order to my men to retreat, knowing that they could not compete with the numbers against them. Captain Worthington not having succeeded in rallying his men, I had no support. As soon as my horse was shot, knowing that I could not escape, I destroyed the dispatches of which I was the bearer. I was then taken prisoner by Captain Brown, C. S. Army, together with 22 men of the First Arkansas Cavalry Volunteers. We were marched about 25 miles that night, to Captain Brown's camp, where we arrived at 2 a. m. of the 6th. On the morning of the 6th, the enlisted men were paroled, by order of General Cabell; after which I was offered my choice, either to go to Little Rock, Ark., or accept a parole. I accepted the latter. In the morning we left their camp under a flag of truce. I hired a wagon to convey the sick and wounded to Cassville, where we arrived at about 12 m. on the 9th instant.

Respectfully submitted.

JOHN GARDNER,
Captain Company E, Second Kansas Cavalry.

Capt. C. G. LAURANT,
Asst. Adjt. Gen., Dist. Southwestern Missouri, Springfield, Mo.

[Indorsement.]

HEADQUARTERS DEPARTMENT OF THE MISSOURI,
Saint Louis, September 21, 1863.

General McNeil is respectfully referred to General Orders, No. 207, War Department, Adjutant-General's Office, Washington, July 3, 1863. Captain Gardner has accepted parole for himself and men in violation of the cartel and the above-named order, and General McNeil will have the spirit of said order carried out. The men will be ordered back to duty with their companies.

By order of Major-General Schofield:

LUCIEN J. BARNES,
Assistant Adjutant-General.

SEPTEMBER 6, 1863.—Attack on train between Fort Scott, Kans., and Carthage, Mo.

Report of Capt. Milton Burch, Eighth Missouri State Militia Cavalry.

CARTHAGE, MO., *September* 9, 1863.

GENERAL: I have the honor of informing [you] for the information of the commanding general [that] on the 2d day of September I sent 2 men from Company L and 2 men from Company M, Eighth Missouri State Militia Cavalry, to form an escort for Joel P. Hood to Fort Scott on official business. They transacted their business and started back to this post, and overtook 4 wagons loaded with dry goods and groceries, bound for this post. They traveled together till within 8 miles of this place. On the 6th day of September they were attacked by a largely superior force of the enemy, who succeeded in capturing 2 wagons and killing 1 man belonging to Company A, Eighth Missouri State Militia Cavalry, under the command of Major [Edward B.] Eno. He had been home on furlough, and was on his return to his command; his name was Ross. They captured 3 prisoners, 1 a soldier from Company M, the other 2 citizens. They tried to take the other two wagons, but could not succeed. News was sent to camp for re-enforcements, which arrived in the quickest of time, and gave them chase, coming up with them about one-half hour before sundown. We recaptured the 2 wagons and 2 of the prisoners, and killed 3 of the rebels and wounded some more. Our loss in the retaking of the wagons ———. I never saw troops display such courage and determination as the men under my command; both officers and men seemed striving to excel each other in deeds of daring. Mr. Joel P. Hood killed the rebel captain, Turk, and wounded several others. They still retain 1 of my men prisoner, and we have 1 of theirs. We aim to exchange with them for the man they retain of ours. Half belonged to Colonel Coffee, and the others are deserters. They are more numerous at this time than any time I have been here. They made an attempt to capture our wagon train yesterday, but were driven off into their favorite cover—the brush. Their loss is not known. I have no further reliable news from Captain Rusk regarding his surrender. The party that attacked the train last Sunday was under the command of Meadows. I had forgotten to state I had 1 of my men wounded in their onset on the wagons, and he has since died.

So no more, but remain, your obedient servant,

MILTON BURCH,
Captain, Commanding Post at Carthage.

C. G. LAURANT, *Assistant Adjutant-General.*

SEPTEMBER 7-19, 1863.—Expedition from Springfield, Mo., into Arkansas and Indian Territory, and skirmish (15th) near Enterprise, Mo.

Report of Col. M. La Rue Harrison, First Arkansas Cavalry.

HEADQUARTERS ARKANSAS VOLUNTEERS,
Near Elkhorn, Ark., September 19, 1863.

GENERAL: I have the honor to submit the following report of the late expedition in Southwest Missouri, Indian Territory, and Arkansas:

I left Springfield, with my command, in obedience to your orders, on the 7th day of September, 1863, *en route* for Carroll County, Arkansas; but receiving dispatches from you on the same evening, changing the direction of my march, I turned toward Cassville, Mo., where I arrived on the 10th instant, at noon. There I was detained two days in foraging and procuring information of the enemy's movements. My first intention was to divide my command, sending 100 men, under Capt. Charles Galloway, across White River, into Carroll County, and thence west to attack Hunter in the rear, at the mountains, 14 miles north of Fayetteville, Ark., and at the same time take 250 men, and the first section of Stark's battery, by way of Pineville, to Sulphur Springs, near Bentonville, Ark., where Brown was encamped, and drive him from his position, meeting Captain Galloway near Cross Hollows, and returning by the Telegraph road. By this movement I expected to rid the country on each side of the road of bushwhackers, and render our line of communication south comparatively safe. Just before leaving Cassville, I learned that Hunter had left the mountain, and probably had joined Brown, near Bentonville, who was reported as moving north with a force of not less than 400 men, estimated by some as high as 800. This information led me to abandon the plan of sending a detachment on the east side of the Telegraph road, and to consolidate my force.

At 12.30 a. m. Sunday, 13th instant, I left Cassville, taking the direction of Pineville, with the following troops, viz:

	Men.
Detachment of First Arkansas Cavalry, Maj. J. J. Johnson commanding	265
Detachment of First Arkansas Light Artillery (Stark's), Lieutenant Thomson commanding	25
Eighteenth Iowa Infantry, Lieutenant [J. H.] Looby commanding	20
Total	310

Taking, in addition, 3 ambulances, in charge of Asst. Surg. J. E. Tefft, First Arkansas Cavalry, and 4 wagons loaded with ammunition and subsistence stores.

I arrived at Pineville, Mo., on Sunday evening [13th], where I encamped for twenty-four hours, in order to ascertain the enemy's position, having learned that he had left Bentonville. Before night on Monday, I became apprised that rebel troops had been moving north to Elk Mills, Mo., to re-enforce Coffee, who was reported as stationed there, with about 300 men. On Monday night, I moved toward Elk Mills, and crossed Cowskin Prairie on Tuesday morning [15th]. On the prairie, I learned from a Union woman that Coffee had been strongly re-enforced on Sunday, and had moved to Enterprise, 4 miles beyond Elk Mills; that his command numbered about 1,000 men (the report of his numbers I believe to have been exaggerated). Moving forward rapidly, I drove in the enemy's pickets near Elk Mills (killing 1 man), and attacked his skirmishers at 10 a. m., whom I found in line 1 mile west of Enterprise, in a dense thicket. I immediately dismounted a portion of my command as skirmishers, and at the same time commenced shelling the town, where his reserve was stationed. After the engagement had continued about one hour, my right and rear were attacked by a strong force, said to be Brown's, which was repulsed and scattered in a short time. The enemy ceased to reply to our fire at 12 m., and retreated through the thicket in great disorder. I could not at first ascertain the direction of his retreat, and my men and horses being completely exhausted by the last night's march and the severe duties of the morning, I went into camp.

The enemy is known to have lost in the engagement 1 captain (said to be M. R. Johnston, of Partisan Rangers) and 4 men. His loss is presumed to be much greater, as the ground in the woods and a cornfield, where our shells burst, was discovered to be tracked in blood in many places, but owing to the denseness of the thicket it was impossible to ascertain the facts definitely. I lost no men, either in killed, wounded, or missing.

On the morning of the 16th instant, following the line of the Indian Territory southward, I pursued several small parties for some miles, but they eluded capture by taking to the thicket. The prairies and paths were filled with the tracks of their horses, all moving southward. At Maysville I encamped on Wednesday night. Here I sent in pursuit of a party of about 30 of the enemy, whom I saw on the south side of the prairie, drawn up in line; but they were well mounted, and made good their escape to the Spavinaw Hills. On Thursday I passed the Double Spring and Round Prairie, near where Capt. J. I. Worthington's escort was routed on the 4th instant. There I learned that Brown had passed the day before with 40 men, going toward Rhea's Mills. At noon the rear of my command was fired into by a small party of guerrillas, but no one was injured. On Wednesday night I encamped 10 miles southwest of Bentonville, and reached this place yesterday evening, where I intend staying until the commissary trains and telegraph corps come up. I am most advantageously located for sweeping the bushwhackers from the valleys of the two Sugar Creeks, and my men are busily engaged in the enterprise. During the last day's march several were captured and 3 killed. My command is in excellent condition and spirits. I have lost no men, and only one or two horses. I herewith submit the report of Assistant Surgeon [Jonathan E.] Tefft,* to whom much praise is due for his strict attention to the sanitary condition of the command, as well as to Majors Johnson and Fitch, Captains Galloway and Mass, commanding battalions, Lieutenant Thomson, commanding section of First Arkansas Light Artillery, and Lieutenant Looby, of the Eighteenth Iowa Infantry, for their promptness in executing my orders, and their strict attention to the discipline of their men. In the engagement of the 15th, the artillery lost none of its well-deserved reputation. The accuracy of its firing was remarkable.

Very respectfully, your obedient servant,

M. LA RUE HARRISON,

Colonel First Arkansas Cavalry, Commanding Troops in Field.

Brig. Gen. JOHN MCNEIL,

Commanding Southwestern District of Missouri.

---

* Omitted, as of no present importance.

SEPTEMBER 7-30, 1863.—Expedition to Big Lake, Mississippi County, Ark.

Report of Maj. Frederick R. Poole, Second Missouri State Militia Cavalry.

HEADQUARTERS,
Camp Lowry, October 1, 1863.

COLONEL: I have the honor to report that, in accordance with your orders of the 7th ultimo, I left Camp Lowry in command of 200 men and one gun, and proceeded as far as Big Lake, Mississippi County, Arkansas, returning through Pemiscot County, as per instructions. At New Madrid I received orders from you to make a junction with re-enforcements sent me from Cape Girardeau and Bloomfield, comprising 50 men from the Second Missouri State Militia, 100 from the Sixth Missouri, and 50 from the Eighth Provisional Enrolled Missouri Militia, with one gun sent from the Cape, which juncture was effected on the evening of the 17th. I then proceeded again toward the point indicated, scouring the country as I advanced. At Osceola, I met the re-enforcements from Col. Chester Harding, Twenty-fifth Missouri Infantry, commanding at New Madrid, who had been directed to co-operate with me. I must confess that we were all rather disappointed in not meeting the rebel force said to be in that vicinity, and, in obedience to certain instructions, returned as directed. During the expedition I killed 13 noted guerrillas, nearly all of whom were armed and fought with desperation. I captured some 26 or 30 others, receipts for whom are herein inclosed; captured a number of horses, mules, guns, &c. The people of Arkansas I found to be much more loyal than those residing in Missouri, and it is my firm and decided belief that the people residing in the neighborhood of the river, in that State, only require a show of protection to establish their loyalty and fidelity to our Government. My command, on arriving at this camp on yesterday, exhibited more health than could be expected from a march of 700 miles without tents or blankets. Our only casualties on the entire trip were 4 men wounded, none dangerously. I would especially recommend Captain [A. P.] Wright, commanding Company L, for his untiring attention to duty and zeal in the interest of our cause and Government.

I am, colonel, very respectfully, your obedient servant,

FRED. R. POOLE,
Major, Commanding Expedition.

Colonel [J. B.] ROGERS,
Commanding Cape Girardeau, Mo.

SEPTEMBER 12, 1863.—Affair near Houston, Texas County, Mo.

Report of Capt. Richard Murphy, Fifth Missouri State Militia Cavalry.

HEADQUARTERS POST OF HOUSTON,
Houston, Mo., September 14, 1863.

CAPTAIN: I have the honor to make the following report to you, for the information of the general commanding:

At midnight, September 11, information was brought to me that 6 guerrillas, with 5 horses, had just passed a house 10 miles south of me. I immediately sent Captain [S. B.] Richardson, with 10 men of Company B and 10 of Company D, in pursuit, who, on arriving at the place where the rebels were seen, found that they had got supper and gone south. Captain Richardson followed them for 57 miles without stopping, and ascertained that one of the rebels (Martin Dodds), had left the party and gone to Thomasville, and another had lost the way the night before, but that the remaining four were in the woods farther on. Captain Richardson finding farther pursuit impossible at this time, as he had traveled 67 miles without feeding, now rested in the woods until morning, when he pushed forward, and found the rebels asleep in the woods, who, on their approach, awoke and ran. Three, in the attempt to escape, were killed on the spot. Their names are William Lingo, of Waynesville; Lieut. Obe Moss, of Pulaski County, and Jacob Bottom. The remaining man (Oscar D. Blount), of Saint Louis, was shot through both thighs, and is now in the hospital at this post. With these men were captured 11 horses, 2 of which were stage horses, and 3 taken from a wagon on the road near Rolla; 7 citizens' saddles and 3 bridles, 1 of them belonging to the stage company; 32 pairs of men's shoes, 17 pairs of women's shoes, 2 bolts of domestic, 3 sacks of coffee, 1 United States newspaper bag, and 1 set of stage lines. This is the most important capture made in this country, and too much credit cannot be awarded Captain Richardson and these men for their perseverance in the pursuit of these outlaws.

I inclose a letter found on the body of Lieutenant Moss, and written by Col. Brodie Hull to his wife in Arkansas. This letter was given Moss for delivery.*

I have gained some valuable information from the wounded man Blount. He gave me the names of those that harbor and feed them. Among these are Andy Hall, living close to Judge Yorks, and Purcell, close to Licking. I also found that William Lingo had 13 horses and a great variety of other stolen property at the house of John King, close to the Arkansas line; and Lee Tilly, son of Tilly near Waynesville, has also a number of horses and other articles secreted in that vicinity. If I could get permission to make a scout down there, I think it would be profitable; but my horses are completely worn out from the amount of duty to perform, and with 25 of Company G taken away for the two howitzers, and 8 more of the same company under arrest at Rolla for mutiny, my available force is very much reduced; and if the general should approve of this anticipated scout, I would request that he send me about 50 men, with fresh horses; and these, with what I can mount here, would make a force amply sufficient for this enterprise.

The horses and other property taken in this scout I will send to Rolla by next train, and by mail I will send you a complete statement of the wounded man Blount.

Believing this will receive your careful attention, I have the honor to remain, very respectfully, your obedient servant,

RICHARD MURPHY,
Captain, Commanding Post.

J. LOVELL,
Assistant Adjutant-General, District of Rolla.

---

* Omitted.

SEPTEMBER 13, 1863.—Attack on, and skirmish near, Salem, Mo.

Reports of Capt. Levi E. Whybark, Fifth Missouri State Militia Cavalry.

SALEM, MO., *September* 13, 1863—8 p. m.

COLONEL: After the dispersion of Colonel Freeman and his band of thieves, [they] attempted to attack this post last night at 3 o'clock; were routed and driven off, with loss of 1 man killed and — mortally wounded, and the loss of some 10 guns and hats, boots, &c., which they left on the ground. Our loss none. Lieut. Charles Koch just returned and made the following report:

In compliance with orders received from headquarters detachment Fifth Missouri State Militia Cavalry, I started, together with Lieutenant [M. S.] Eddleman and 80 men of Companies C and M, Fifth Missouri State Militia Cavalry, at about 6 a. m., in pursuit of the rebel force which attempted to attack our camp last night. We followed their trail with the utmost possible speed, and ascertained of the inhabitants of houses which we passed that their force was from 200 to 300 strong. They did not keep any road, but went right through the woods and over the mountains, so that we were several times obliged to dismount to get our horses down the cliffs. After three hours' hard ride, making about 20 miles in that time, we had the satisfaction to see the force right before us, on a hill, ready for a fight. While myself, with the men of Company C, attacked in the front, Lieutenant Eddleman, with the men of Company M, made a flank movement on the right flank, charging on the enemy at the same time, as well as my command from the front. The rebels could not stand this combined charge, and, after about twenty minutes' resistance, fled in every direction. Rebel loss, 14 killed, and wounded a good many more, as we found in the pursuit many signs of blood. We captured in all about 24 guns, 5 horses, and 2 mules. Among the killed was Captain Post, whose recruiting commission I herewith inclose. No others were recognized. The rebels were commanded by Colonel Freeman, and had in their company William Orchard and a certain Duckworth, from this place. Our loss was 3 men wounded of Company M, one of them severely in the knee; also one citizen, Mr. Copeland, who voluntarily joined Company C, and was shot in the thigh. We had 1 horse killed and 5 wounded, among them the horse of your reporter. We also have to report the supposed capture of a private of Company M, who got wounded, and, being unable to follow any farther, started homeward with other wounded, and supposed is captured, as they were followed by a part of the rebels, and his horse gave out, and nothing has been heard from him since, while the others have arrived in camp.

Closing this my respectful report, I must express my entire satisfaction with the behavior of all men under my command, who charged on the enemy, far superior in numbers, with such great gallantry; and if it had not been for the thick underbrush, which was almost impassable, we would have been more successful.

Transmitting to you the written report, I assure you that I have all necessary steps taken to secure the safety of the camp, and to ascertain all rebel movements going on in this section of the country, as far as my small command is capable. I must say that Lieuts. Charles Koch and Eddleman and men deserve the greatest of praise for their coolness and promptness in pursuing the rebels.

Please refer this report to the general commanding the district.

L. E. WHYBARK,
Captain, Comdg. Detachment Fifth Missouri State Militia Cavalry.

Lieut. Col. JOSEPH P. EPPSTEIN,
Commanding Fifth Missouri State Militia Cavalry.

HDQRS. DETACHMENT FIFTH MISSOURI S. M. CAVALRY,
Salem, Mo., September 14, 1863—6 a. m.

COLONEL: All quiet. No rebels around. We have driven them out of the country with our small force. We apprehend no danger at present. I am able to hold this camp and country with my force. I will inform you of all movements of rebels, so you may rest assured all is right. The officers and men deserve the greatest praise for their gallant conduct, especially Lieut. Charles Koch, for his promptness and strictness to orders, and killing rebels.

Your most obedient servant,

L. E. WHYBARK,
Captain, Commanding Detachment.

P. S.—The bearer of dispatches yesterday was mistaken. Our force did not fall back, but drove the rebels away entirely. From best reliable information I can obtain, Freeman and Woods have some 600 or 700 men, but did not have near them 300; had the remainder on Sinking and Spring Rivers. Captain Lovell just arrived. All quiet now. I apprehend no danger for the present.

SEPTEMBER 15, 1863.—Skirmish in Jackson County, Mo.

Report of Col. William Weer, Tenth Kansas Infantry.

PLEASANT HILL, MO., *September* 15, 1863.

SIR: After a week spent in bushwhacking, in search of Quantrill's guerrillas, I became convinced that his band continued to secrete themselves upon the waters of the Snibar and Blue Creek, in Jackson County, Missouri. This morning I made another night march, with a view to surprise him, if possible. I crossed the intervening prairie, and entered the timber of the Snibar without being observed. At daylight, the command being divided into four detachments, we commenced a thorough scouring of the Snibar Hills. The country is very rugged, and filled with almost impenetrable thickets. Half of the different detachments were dismounted, and penetrated the woods deployed as skirmishers, the horses being led in the rear. By three of the detachments nothing particular was discovered, except evidences that the guerrillas inhabited these woods.

Captain [C. F.] Coleman, of the Ninth Kansas, who commanded on the extreme left, in the course of the day fell upon a trail, by following which he soon came upon Quantrill's own camp. He promptly attacked it, killed 2 of the guerrillas, captured some 40 horses, destroyed all their subsistence stores, including some flour recently stolen from a citizen, all their bedding, clothing, ammunition, and some arms. The enemy fired but one volley, and at once disappeared in the thick underwood, where pursuit was impossible.

Too much credit cannot be given to Captain Coleman for the ingenuity, courage, and energy with which he conducted this as well as other attacks upon guerrillas, or to the zeal and bravery of the men of his command, in seconding the labors of their chief. The effect of this surprise and capture is most damaging to the designs of Quantrill in making another raid upon Kansas. The loss of horses and clothing is to him worse than the loss of men, as the country is denuded of both.

The expedition demonstrates the fact that Quantrill's band is still secreting itself in Jackson County, though evidently preparing for another raid.

The bushwhackers have within a day or two burned the splendid flouring mill at Lone Jack.

To-morrow morning I shall start an expedition to endeavor the capture of another camp of the guerrillas.

Respectfully, your obedient servant,

WM. WEER,
Colonel, Commanding.

Brigadier-General EWING, *Commanding District of the Border.*

SEPTEMBER 15-18, 1863.—Scout from Greenfield, Mo.

Report of Maj. Wick Morgan, Seventh Provisional Enrolled Missouri Militia.

GREENFIELD, MO., *September* 18, 1863.

GENERAL: On the 11th instant I sent Captain [E. J.] Morris out to the head of Cedar, to assist a Union man to move out, when a band of rebels run on to him, and caught Private Samuel Downing and murdered him. He had thirty-two bullets shot into him and was beaten up with his musket.

I started out on the 15th instant, with a detachment of 70 men, and returned yesterday evening; traveled 90 miles; killed 1 rebel; ordered all rebels south of the Federal lines; I burned everything from a pigpen to a mansion on Cedar and Horse Creeks.

The band that killed Downing has gone out south. They started last Monday morning. There were about 100 rebs, negroes, women, and children. They went out between Horse Creek and Lamar.

I understand there are some bushwhackers collecting on Big Jack. I have sent a scout to ascertain their whereabouts and their strength. I think as soon as I get shut of the rebel women in these parts we will have peace.

There were 2 men some 7 miles east of town, calling themselves soldiers, stealing horses. They stole a horse from a Mr. Gilmore, as loyal a man as there is in Missouri. One of the men was William Rowan, the other Ragsdale. They claim to belong to the Second Kansas. They also took a horse from Samuel Harris. Please send the horses down by Captain Morris, and oblige, yours, respectfully,

WICK MORGAN,
Major, Commanding.

Brig. Gen. JOHN MCNEIL,
Commanding District of Southwestern Missouri.

SEPTEMBER 22-25, 1863.—Scout in La Fayette County, Mo., and skirmishes.

Report of Lieut. Col. Bazel F. Lazear, First Missouri State Militia Cavalry.

HDQRS. FIRST MISSOURI STATE MILITIA CAVALRY,
Lexington, September 27, 1863.

GENERAL: I have the honor to report that, on the morning of the 22d instant, I left this place, with 140 men of Companies B, H, L, and M, First Missouri State Militia Cavalry, for a scout in the eastern part of this county. At the same time I ordered 100 men of Companies C, I, and K, from Warrensburg to the headwaters of Blackwater and Davis Creek. I have no official report from them yet, but learn they are doing good work. I returned to this place on the 25th, having had a severe skirmish in the brush on the Tabo on the 22d, which resulted in the killing of 1, wounding 2 (since dead), capturing 8 horses, 5 revolvers, 1 carbine, 1 double-barrel shot-gun. Our casualty was 1 killed, a Mr. Sullivan, who was acting as guide. In another skirmish, on the 24th, we killed another; captured his horse and equipments and revolver. We brought in 6 prisoners, 3 of whom have everything necessary to prove them bushwhackers, except we could not find their arms.

The result of the scout was 4 killed, 6 prisoners, 17 horses and 1 mule, 13 horse equipments, 6 revolvers, 2 guns, and 1 carbine. The body of the guerrillas seem to be west of us. Captain [M.] Morris, Company A, First Missouri State Militia Cavalry, reports that on the 22d he surprised Marchbanks on the Double Branches, in Bates County, capturing 18 horses and equipments, 18 guns, their camp equipage, and Marchbanks' private papers. Thinks none were killed.

Very respectfully,

B. F. LAZEAR,
Lieutenant-Colonel First Missouri State Militia Cavalry.

General BROWN, *Comdg. Dist. of Central Mo., Jefferson City.*

SEPTEMBER 22-OCTOBER 26, 1863.—Shelby's Raid in Arkansas and Missouri.

SUMMARY OF THE PRINCIPAL EVENTS.

Sept. 22, 1863.—Shelby's command sets out from Arkadelphia, Ark.
27, 1863.—Skirmish at Moffat's Station, Franklin County, Ark.
Oct. 4, 1863.—Action at Neosho, Mo.
Skirmish at Oregon, or Bowers' Mill, Mo.
5, 1863.—Skirmish at Greenfield, Mo.
Skirmish at Stockton, Mo.
6, 1863.—Affair at Humansville, Mo.
7, 1863.—Skirmish near Warsaw, Mo.
9, 1863.—Skirmish near Cole Camp, Mo.
10, 1863.—Affair at Tipton, Mo.
Skirmish at Syracuse, Mo.
Affair at La Mine Bridge, Mo.
11-12, 1863.—Skirmishes at Boonville, Mo.
12, 1863.—Skirmishes at Merrill's Crossing and Dug Ford, near Jonesborough, Mo.
13, 1863.—Action at Marshall, Mo.
14, 1863.—Skirmish at Scott's Ford, Mo.
15, 1863.—Skirmish at Cross Timbers, Mo.
16, 1863.—Skirmish at Johnstown, Mo.
Skirmish on Deer Creek, Mo.
Skirmishes near and at Humansville, Mo.
17, 1863.—Skirmish in Cedar County, Mo.
18, 1863.—Skirmish at Carthage, Mo.
24, 1863.—Skirmish near Harrisonville, Mo.
Skirmish at Buffalo Mountains, Ark.
26, 1863.—Skirmish in Johnson County, Ark.

REPORTS.*

No. 1.—Brig. Gen. Egbert B. Brown, U. S. Army, commanding District of Central Missouri, of operations October 6-26.

---

* See also Schofield's report, p. 12, and "Correspondence, etc.," Part II.

No. 1.

Reports of Brig. Gen. Egbert B. Brown, U. S. Army, commanding District of Central Missouri, of operations October 6-26.

HEADQUARTERS IN THE FIELD,
Sedalia, Mo., October 10, 1863—3 p. m.

GENERAL: I moved with eleven companies of Missouri State Militia and two pieces First Missouri State Militia battery from Osceola to this place yesterday. Lieutenant-Colonel Lazear, with 700 men and three pieces of light artillery, of the Missouri State Militia, is following the enemy from Cole Camp. I sent Major Kelly, with 300 men, at daylight this morning down the railroad, with orders to act against the enemy, in conjunction with Colonel Lazear, or toward Brownsville, if he found the enemy had crossed the railroad. He has reported that a force of 200 men passed through Otterville, toward Syracuse, burning the bridge and block-houses at the La Mine. The guard abandoned it without firing a gun. They could have protected the bridge and defended themselves if they had made the effort.

I have just received dispatches from the west. Colonel Weer was at Clinton yesterday with 500 men. There were about 400 there before. General Ewing will be at Warrensburg to-day with 500 men. I have dispatched to them the situation of the enemy.

There appears, from the information I have, a breaking up of the enemy's forces. They are in small bodies to the southeast of this point.

I have sent small scouting parties out to obtain information of the movements of the rebels. I have failed in getting a telegram to you by Kansas City.

I am, very truly, your obedient servant,

E. B. BROWN,
Brigadier-General of Volunteers, Commanding.

Maj. Gen. JOHN M. SCHOFIELD,
Commanding Department of the Missouri.

MARSHALL, MO., *October* 13, 1863—3 p. m.

GENERAL: I have the honor to report that the troops under my command attacked the enemy's forces, commanded by Brig. Gen. Joseph Shelby, at this place this morning, and, after five hours' hard fighting, defeated him, capturing his artillery and a large number of small-arms and part of his train. The list of casualties is large on the part of the enemy. Ours quite severe. The enemy is being pursued in every direction. They may concentrate again.

I am, very truly, yours,

E. B. BROWN,
Brigadier-General.

Major-General SCHOFIELD.

HEADQUARTERS IN THE FIELD,
Marshall, Mo., October 13, 1863—6 p. m.

GENERAL: I have the honor to report that, after following the enemy through Cole Camp, Syracuse, and Boonville, skirmishing with his rear all the distance, he was forced to make a stand at Merrill's Crossing of the Salt Fork River, a point 8 miles southwest of Arrow Rock and about the same distance from Marshall, and commenced a skirmishing fight at 6 o'clock on the evening of the 12th, in the midst of a cold, driving rain. We fought him as long as we could see, and lay down on our arms in the rain during the night. At 3 o'clock this morning, I detached Lieutenant-Colonel Lazear, with about 900 men, with orders to move to the south, avoiding the route of the enemy, and intercept him, if possible, at Marshall, and bring on an engagement, while I followed him (the enemy) with the balance of my command. The result was as I had hoped. Lieutenant-Colonel Lazear moved on in advance of the enemy, and an engagement commenced at 8 a. m.

The enemy had possession of the ford on my arrival, and checked my advance for a few moments, but, by making a detour to the left, I found another crossing, and gained a position in their rear on the bank of the creek, along which they were formed. They soon gave way, and broke through the dense timber and brush which for a mile and a half fringed the borders of the creek. By throwing a force through their center, their forces were divided, part being driven east toward Arrow Rock, and part, under Shelby, to the northwest, both bodies pursued by our victorious troops.

I was misinformed when I reported to you by telegraph to-day that the enemy's artillery had been captured. We got his best gun, an iron 10-pounder (Parrott pattern), originally in Bledsoe's battery, but he succeeded in getting away with one piece (since captured), a brass 6-pounder, that was captured from me at Springfield on the 8th of January. I am unable to give a correct account of the killed and wounded. Ours, including all our losses from Cole Camp to this place and the fight of to-day, will not exceed 30. Of the enemy, I am officially advised that 53 dead have been found in the brush, and 98 seriously wounded, who have been left at the hospitals here and at the houses on the road in the vicinity. They lost a considerable number in the different attacks we made on the march. At Merrill's we found 16 dead in the morning after the skirmish. At Larnier's Crossing they lost 9 killed. We have taken a number of prisoners, and they are coming in hourly. A portion of their train was captured. I think they are effectually broken up, and I shall not give them time to rally or concentrate. The pursuit and fighting has been done by the Missouri State Militia and Enrolled Missouri Militia. I can only point to the result of their efforts as the best commentary on their gallantry and endurance. For the past three days they have followed and engaged the enemy night and day, in the rain, without subsistence, except that gathered by the wayside, or protection from the storm.

I hope, general, that the department will recognize the value of the services of the Missouri State Militia by furnishing them with good arms. Nearly one-half of my command was armed only with navy revolvers, purchased by themselves. This came very near causing a most disastrous defeat. It has forced me to move with less rapidity and great caution. The enemy were completely armed, and numbered nearly 2,000 men. My own force was about 1,600. At an early day I will make a more full report.

I am, very truly, your obedient servant,

E. B. BROWN,

Brigadier-General of Volunteers, Commanding.

Maj. Gen. JOHN M. SCHOFIELD,

Commanding Department of Missouri, Saint Louis.

SEDALIA, MO., *October* 15, 1863—4 p. m.

GENERAL: After the defeat of the enemy at Marshall, which divided their forces, a part of my command, under Colonel Philips, followed the larger body, about 600 men, under Shelby, which moved to the west with a portion of their train. About 300, under Colonel Hunter, with one piece of artillery, which they managed to get off the field, moved southeast and crossed the Pacific Railroad between Syracuse and Otterville last night, pursued by Major Houts, of the Seventh Missouri State

Militia. This force will probably cross the Osage in the vicinity of Warsaw. The portion pursued by Colonel Philips passed south between this and Warrensburg last night. Colonels Weer and Lazear, who moved west immediately after the battle of Marshall, managed to get in ahead of Colonel Philips, and took up the pursuit, having fresh horses, Colonel Philips abandoning the pursuit. I have just learned that Hunter was 10 miles east of Cole Camp at 11 this morning, closely pursued by our troops. I arrived here at 3 o'clock this morning, and have ordered all the fresh troops under Colonel Hall in pursuit. I am informed that Jackman, Marchbanks, and Quantrill are in the border counties, and will endeavor to form a junction at some point south of the Osage. Colonel Philips dispatches that the enemy is running like wild hogs, and that [he] has captured all their train and ambulances, and two wagon loads of ammunition.

E. B. BROWN,
Brigadier-General.

Major-General SCHOFIELD.

SEDALIA, MO., *October* 16, 1863.

GENERAL: Major Houts was with me in all my rapid marches pursuing the enemy from Marshall, after his defeat, as long as was necessary, as I had sent a fresh force from here, under Colonel Hall, who has taken up the pursuit. The stragglers and convalescents are not required. Commanding officers of sub-districts are ordered to relieve them.

The operator at Saint Joseph, in the first instance, refused to receive my dispatch to you yesterday morning, and did not forward it last night.

The enemy was 9 miles east of Cole Camp at 11 a. m. yesterday, and Colonel Hall was about two hours behind him. I will be able to relieve General Totten by Sunday.

E. B. BROWN,
Brigadier-General.

Major-General SCHOFIELD.

SEDALIA, MO., *October* 16, 1863.

GENERAL: Shelby reports on the route of his retreat his losses in killed and wounded in the different fights at over 400 men. This agrees with my advices from other sources. Our loss will not exceed 30.

E. B. BROWN,
Brigadier-General.

Major-General SCHOFIELD.

HEADQUARTERS DISTRICT OF CENTRAL MISSOURI,
Jefferson City, Mo., October 27, 1863.

MAJOR: I have the honor to report that on the 16th instant Lieutenant Devinney, Fifth Provisional Enrolled Missouri Militia, attacked a small band of Shelby's scattered raiders in Clinton County; killed 4, and captured their arms and 3 horses.

On the 17th, Major Pugh attacked another band of the same force in Cedar County, killing 5, wounding 2, and capturing 3 prisoners, with a number of horses, arms, equipments, &c. Thirteen of the same command have surrendered to the commanding officer of the post at Lexington.

I am, very truly, your obedient servant,

E. B. BROWN,
Brigadier-General of Volunteers, Commanding.

Maj. OLIVER D. GREENE,
Assistant Adjutant-General, Saint Louis, Mo.

HEADQUARTERS DISTRICT OF CENTRAL MISSOURI,
Jefferson City, Mo., October 28, 1863.

MAJOR: I have the honor to report that, on the 6th instant, while at Clinton, Henry County, I received a dispatch from the major-general commanding, advising me that a rebel force, 1,400 strong, under Shelby, had entered the southwest corner of the State, and was moving north, and that it might become necessary to concentrate the troops in this district, and that co-operation with the commands of Brigadier-General Ewing might be required. Acting upon this information, I ordered all the available force in the district to concentrate at Sedalia, Warrensburg, Clinton, and Warsaw, and that 2,000 Enrolled Missouri Militia be called into active service.

Upon receiving information, deemed reliable, that the enemy had advanced as far north as Stockton, and was moving west from that point, and that a rebel force under Quantrill was in the border counties, for the purpose of uniting with Shelby, I marched with about 600 men to Osceola, while Colonel Weer was at Butler with 500, and General Ewing at Harrisonville with about an equal force, prepared to meet the enemy in front.

Soon after arriving at Osceola, on the evening of the 8th instant, I learned that my information was incorrect, and that the enemy had passed Warsaw, and was moving toward the Pacific Railroad. I ordered Lieutenant-Colonel Lazear, who had arrived at Clinton with the First Missouri State Militia, to move to the east in search of the enemy, and, as soon as my horses were rested, I marched rapidly to Sedalia, a distance of nearly 70 miles, making this march on the day and night of the 9th instant.

At daylight of the 10th, I ordered Major Kelly, Fourth Missouri State Militia, and Major Gentry, Fifth Provisional Enrolled Missouri Militia, with all their available force, to march to the east along the Pacific Railroad and harass the enemy, and prevent his advance, and form a junction with Lieutenant-Colonel Lazear, who was following him from Cole Camp toward Syracuse. In the night of the 10th, I learned that a detachment from the enemy had burned La Mine Bridge, having captured Captain Berry with 30 men (who were left to guard it), without firing a gun, and that he was moving toward Boonville, closely followed by the united forces of Lazear, Kelly, Gentry, and a small detachment of the Ninth Provisional Enrolled Missouri Militia, commanded by Capt. W. D. Wear, making in all about 1,000 men. Major Foster, Seventh Missouri State Militia, who had been sent with about 100 men from Osceola to Warsaw, returned to Sedalia, reporting that near Warsaw he encountered a gang of rebel stragglers, killing 5 of them, and that he had fought small parties of the enemy nearly all the way to Cole Camp.

At daylight of the 11th, I marched with ten companies of the Seventh

Missouri State Militia and Thurber's First Missouri State Militia Battery, to Otterville, and thence to a point 8 miles from Boonville, on the Boonville and Georgetown road (McGruder's), where I arrived at dark. My scouts reported before daylight next morning, "No signs of the enemy west of Boonville." Believing that he had heard of my approach, and had turned to the east, I moved at daylight 5 miles east, to a point 8 miles south of Boonville, with a view to be able to support Lieutenant-Colonel Lazear, if necessary, or intercept the enemy should he turn east. At the same time I dispatched a small force, under Lieutenant Houts, Seventh Missouri State Militia, toward Boonville, with orders to drive in the advance of the enemy if he should be moving southwest, and give me the earliest information of the direction in which he was moving. Lieutenant Houts met and attacked the enemy's advance, killing 1 and mortally wounding the commanding officer and 2 others. Learning that the enemy had moved southwest from Boonville, followed by Colonel Lazear's command, I marched back to the point I started from, advising Colonel Lazear that I would move on a line parallel with and 2 miles south from his column. The country here was very broken and hilly, with narrow gorges covered with dense brush. To prevent the enemy holding us in check with a small force, I ordered my command rapidly forward, crossing the La Mine at Salt Spring, above the mouth of the Blackwater, turning north, crossing that stream, and attacked his rear guard, forcing the enemy to make a stand, where a sharp fight commenced. I pursued the enemy closely, Lazear now following in my rear to Jonesborough, a point 9 miles southwest of Arrow Rock and about the same distance from Marshall, on Salt Fork of the La Mine. Here the enemy made a stand, and opened with musketry and artillery. We fought him until dark, in the midst of a drenching rain. The men were ordered to rest on their arms, occupying the original battle-field during the night. The enemy lost 16 killed and a number wounded, one man of Thurber's battery, killed, being the only casualty on our side. Here I was joined by Lieutenant-Colonel Lazear's command, my united forces consisting of the Seventh Missouri State Militia, Col. J. F. Philips; detachment of the First Missouri State Militia, Lieut. Col. B. F. Lazear; Fourth Missouri State Militia, Maj. George W. Kelly; Fifth Provisional Enrolled Missouri Militia, Maj. William Gentry; Ninth Provisional Enrolled Missouri Militia, Capt. W. D. Wear, and four small guns of Thurber's First Missouri State Militia Battery, numbering about 1,600 men.

At 3 a. m. of the 13th, I ordered Lieutenant-Colonel Lazear to march with his command, by a road to the left, direct to Marshall. At daybreak I marched in the enemy's trail toward the Arrow Rock and Marshall road, and thence toward Marshall. The enemy attacked Lieutenant-Colonel Lazear at 8 a. m. near Marshall, the latter occupying the town. I arrived on the field about 9.30 o'clock. Finding the bridge and ford across Salt Fork disputed by about a regiment of the enemy, Majors Suess and Houts, Seventh Missouri State Militia, with three companies and two pieces of Thurber's battery, engaged them, and covered the crossing of the main force about three-fourths of a mile below, attacking the enemy on his left flank, while Major Suess, after crossing the bridge, attacked them in rear. The enemy soon gave way, and, on being hard pressed, broke in every direction, losing his best piece of artillery, a 10-pounder, the main body retreating toward Miami, Colonel Philips taking up the pursuit, fighting him to a point 6 miles south of Miami and 10 miles from Marshall. Here Colonel Philips bivouacked during the night, following the enemy to the Missouri River, and thence south through Waverly next day, capturing all of his transportation, ambulances, 5 wagon loads of fixed ammunition, 500 pounds rifle powder, and a number of mules and horses. Part of the rebel force, about 300, under Hunter, was heard from moving east, and I dispatched Major Houts, with two companies of the Seventh Missouri State Militia and two companies of the Forty-third Enrolled Missouri Militia, commanded by Captain Hart, in pursuit. Major Kelly, with battalion Fourth Missouri State Militia, and Gentry's battalion, Fifth Provisional Enrolled Missouri Militia, marched toward Sedalia, arriving there on the night of the 14th. Lieutenant-Colonel Lazear, with the First Missouri State Militia, marched toward Lexington, pushing forward rapidly, and got ahead of Colonel Philips, who gave up the pursuit (his horses being nearly worn out) to Lieutenant-Colonel Lazear.

Colonel Weer, of General Ewing's forces, who had moved north through Clinton, and on the night of the 13th had arrived at a point 10 miles south of Marshall, and on the morning of the 14th marched west, with the expectation of being able to intercept the enemy south of Lexington, shortly after relieved Lazear's troops, the former having fresh horses, and pursued the enemy west of Warrensburg.

I returned to Sedalia on the night of the 14th, leaving two companies of the Seventh Missouri State Militia to scout the country east and west of Marshall as far as the Missouri River, for stragglers from the shattered rebel forces.

On arrival at Sedalia, I dispatched Colonel Hall, Fourth Missouri State Militia, with fresh troops, in pursuit of that part of the enemy which had gone east, and had crossed the Pacific Railroad, near Otterville, relieving Major Houts' command. Colonel Hall followed this part of the forces of the enemy across the Osage, and gave up the pursuit when he found General McNeil's troops had obtained the advance with fresh horses.

As soon as I became satisfied that the enemy were broken up into small bodies, scouting parties were ordered to move through all parts of this district and attack straggling bands, and secure as much abandoned property as possible. This has been successfully done.

The enemy entered this district at Warsaw on the 8th, with 1,600 well-armed men, soon increased to about 1,800 by two bands that joined him from the east. Within twenty-four hours afterward he was attacked, and for four days a running fight was kept up, until he was forced to make a stand at Marshall, with the result as stated.

When the raid began, the troops of the district were stationed over a tract of country 120 miles square, occupying thirty-seven posts. In seven days they were concentrated, and marched 280 miles (some of the commands over 300), without trains, and but a scanty subsistence, three days and nights in rain, and have killed and wounded a large number of the enemy, capturing about 100 prisoners, with a part of his artillery and arms, and all of his trains, ambulances, and ammunition wagons. As the skirmishing and fighting extended over 100 miles of thickly wooded country, no reliable report of the exact loss of the enemy can be made.

The loss on our side was 5 killed, 26 wounded, and 11 missing and captured, making a total of 42. We had 17 horses killed, 34 wounded, and 61 broken down and abandoned on the march. Total loss of horses, 112. The enemy captured from us at Warsaw 2 wagons and camp and garrison equipage for one company (which they destroyed), and 12 mules.

The accompanying reports of Colonel Philips, Colonel Hall, Lieutenant-Colonel Lazear, and Major Kelly will explain the movements of their respective commands.

The troops of this district deserve the special consideration of the major-general commanding for their courage, endurance, and the cheerful manner they have done their duty. Without being invidious, I may be permitted to express my obligations to Col. George H. Hall, Col. John F. Philips, Lieut. Col. B. F. Lazear; Majors Foster, Houts, Suess, Kelly, Williams, and Gentry, and Captain Thurber for their active co-operation, and to the members of my staff, Lieut. Col. T. A. Switzler, Dr. R. P. Richardson, and Lieut. R. G. Leaming, for their assistance.

It is with peculiar pleasure that I refer to the orderly conduct of the troops, in the respect paid to the rights of the citizens, notwithstanding their privations and exposure on their fatiguing marches.

To the citizens of Sedalia and the country generally, and to the Enrolled Missouri Militia, who readily obeyed the call "to arms," the State is in part indebted for the unsuccessful issue of the raid.

I am, very truly, your obedient servant,

E. B. BROWN,
Brigadier-General Volunteers, Commanding.

Maj. OLIVER D. GREENE,
Assistant Adjutant-General, Saint Louis, Mo.

No. 2.

Reports of Lieut. Col. Bazel F. Lazear, First Missouri State Militia Cavalry, of operations October 7-19.

HDQRS. FIRST MISSOURI STATE MILITIA CAVALRY,
Warrensburg, October 19, 1863.

GENERAL: I have the honor to report that at 11 p. m., 7th instant, Companies B, C, D, E, F, G, H, I, K, and L, First Missouri State Militia Cavalry (Companies B, F, G, H, and L having just come in from Lexington and Wellington), left Warrensburg for Clinton, where we arrived at 11 a. m. 8th instant; marched that evening and night to Calhoun; 9th, marched from Calhoun to Cole Camp, where we struck the trail of Shelby, who was some four hours ahead of us. Shelby's men murdered two citizens at this place and robbed the town of everything in it.

Early on the morning of the 10th, started on Shelby's trail, pressing forward as rapidly as possible, passing on through Florence to Tipton, on Pacific Railroad.

The enemy plundered the country as they passed along of everything they could make use of. Learned that Shelby's force consisted of five regiments, of 300 men each, one battalion of 100 men, and two pieces of artillery, one brass 6-pounder and one iron Parrott 9-pounder gun, and that their force was picked from twenty-three regiments for the raid.

As we came near Tipton, I learned we would have to cross a prairie some 4 miles, and, having only 600 men of the First Missouri State Militia Cavalry and 70 men of the Seventh Missouri State Militia, under Captain Darst and Lieutenant Becker, who fell in with us at Calhoun, I deemed it best not to expose our whole force to view on the prairie. We halted at the edge of the brush, selected a very favorable position, and formed line of battle, and sent forward two companies to reconnoiter. When we arrived at Tipton, we found a few stragglers left in town; killed 2 while in the act of knocking down and robbing citizens, and took 1 prisoner. After the main column moved up, we learned that the enemy were drawn up in line of battle some 3 miles up the railroad, where we had heard some cannon shots, but supposed it was some of our own troops, as we expected every hour that some party would certainly head them. We determined to go up and give them battle, leaving two squadrons to protect our train, but found they had left, and returned just in time to find our pickets skirmishing with a body of men advancing from the east. I felt certain they were Federal troops, and sent an order to Major Mullins, who was in the advance with Companies E and H (and going at a dash, as he had seen the advancing party fire on two of our guidons that had been sent out), to halt. At the same time a line of battle was formed, and another attempt made to ascertain who the party was, when they proved to be a party of the Enrolled Missouri Militia from California. The officer in charge of their advance acted very badly in swearing he did not care a damn for our flags nor who we were, and fired on two men who went forward with the guidons to learn who the advancing party was. Our loss in this skirmish was one horse wounded. It being now dark and raining, the troops were bivouacked in line of battle for the night. Lieutenant Dailey, Company D, was ordered, with 50 men, to follow the trail of the enemy to his pickets, and annoy them all night, to prevent their getting any rest; but, unfortunately, being entirely incompetent, he only went out 4 miles and returned, and did not report until 6 o'clock next morning. During the night we were joined by Major Kelly and 200 men of the Fourth Missouri State Militia Cavalry, and Major Gentry and 200 men of the Fifth Provisional Regiment Enrolled Missouri Militia. Just as the command was moving on the morning of the 11th, we received what was deemed reliable information that the enemy was at Otterville and fighting. We left their trail, and pushed on up the railroad as far as Syracuse, where we learned the report was false, and the enemy were on the road to Boonville. Here I ordered all our train, except two ammunition wagons, to remain, under charge of Captain Folmsbee, with his company (B). We pushed on rapidly to Boonville, coming on to strong picket of the enemy just at dark, 4 miles out from Boonville. Their pickets were driven from their positions, when we again bivouacked in line of battle, without fires and nothing to eat. Night very dark and rainy. Were joined this evening at camp by Captain Ware [Wear?] and 120 men of the Ninth Provisional Enrolled Missouri Militia.

Started on the morning of the 12th, at 5 o'clock. Pushed on rapidly through Boonville (as we expected the enemy would be stopped by a force supposed to be in their front), when the advance, composed of Captain Darst's company and a detachment under Lieutenant Becker, of the Seventh Missouri State Militia Cavalry, and Companies D and E, First Missouri State Militia Cavalry, under Major Mullins, came in sight of the rear guard of the enemy as they left their camp. Skirmishing was soon commenced, and kept up almost continuously, lasting, in one place, half an hour, until we reached Dug Ford, on La Mine. Here the enemy left a force of some 200 or 300 men to defend the ford. They were charged on by Captain Little and his brave Company E, who dashed across the river, receiving a most terrible fire from the enemy, only a few yards distant, which resembled a loud crash of thunder more than a report of fire-arms; but they were routed, and fled, 5 or 6 of their men being mortally and badly wounded, one of whom was a lieutenant-colonel of Hunter's regiment (wounded in the arm), and 1 prisoner. Company E's loss in this charge was 2 killed on the spot, 1 mortally, 2 severely, and 2 slightly wounded. One of the latter, Lieutenant Hardesty, had three balls through his clothes, one of which was in the center of the body, but was turned off by a breast-plate. His and Captain Little's horses were wounded, and Lieutenant Madden's killed. Besides our loss here, we had previously lost 2 killed and 2 slightly wounded of the Seventh Missouri State Militia. Up to this time the enemy's loss was 8 killed, 4 prisoners, and, no doubt, a large number wounded.

Major Mullins deserves great praise for the manner in which he conducted the advance up to this time. Shortly after crossing the La Mine, the command fell in your rear, when our work for the day ceased, except moving up to your command, where you had the skirmish near Jonesborough. The detachment of the Seventh Missouri State Militia joined their regiment this evening, leaving under my command 500 of the First Missouri State Militia Cavalry; 200 of the Fourth Missouri State Militia Cavalry, Major Kelly; 200 of the Fifth Provisional Regiment Enrolled Missouri Militia, Major Gentry, and 120 men of the Ninth Provisional Regiment Enrolled Missouri Militia, under Captain Ware [Wear ?], making an aggregate of 1,020 men. At 11 p. m. we bivouacked in line of battle. At 5 a. m. on the 13th, moved for Marshall, reaching that place at 7 o'clock, placing pickets on the different roads, and fed. In a short time the pickets on the road east of town reported the enemy in sight, advancing on the town. "To horse!" was sounded, and Major McGhee, in command of Second Battalion, and Captain Ware [Wear ?], Enrolled Missouri Militia, were ordered to take position on a hill southeast of town, and hold the hill at all hazards. Major Mullins, with the First Battalion, except Company F, was ordered to dismount and take the center; Company L on the left of the battalion, in the town, and Major Gentry and his command on the left, and Major Kelly and his command and Company F held as reserve in rear of our two small pieces of artillery.

The enemy opened with his artillery on Major McGhee's column before he got his position, killing 1 horse in Company C the second round. By the time Major McGhee's battalion were dismounted and got in position, a large body of the enemy were advancing to take the hill he (McGhee) was ordered to hold. They were repulsed by Major McGhee's riflemen in gallant style, and he continued to hold the hill until the enemy gave way. The second point of attack by the enemy was on the center, Major Mullins, where the gallant boys of the First Battalion resisted and drove back three separate charges of the enemy, with heavy loss to them. At the same time our two small pieces opened on the enemy, but could not reach them, as we had no ammunition but canister. Took a new position with our artillery within 250 yards of the enemy's guns, when a most desperate charge was attempted on our pieces. The support on the left of the pieces (Major Gentry's command) fell back in confusion without firing a gun. Four gunners at one gun wounded, and all support gone, the pieces were ordered to fall back to the edge of the town, where the whole force was rallied and placed in good position, and gallantly held their position against several charges until the enemy began to fall back, when our whole lines were advanced after the enemy. As soon as the left of the line was made secure, Major Kelly's battalion was ordered north and to our left, to watch and prevent any attempt the enemy might make to outflank us on our left. We were in this position when you arrived upon the ground. The battle had been going on some two or three hours. Up to this time, and for the first hour and a half, it was very severe. It was after your arrival, and after the enemy was in full retreat, with the loss of his Parrott gun, which was disabled and abandoned, that Major Kelly and his battalion of the Fourth Missouri State Militia Cavalry made his gallant charge, cutting the enemy's lines in two and scattering his forces. Our casualties were very light, owing to our advantageous position and to the fact that our men fought most of the time lying down on the ground. Killed, none; wounded, 2 dangerously, 3 seriously, and 2 slightly. Two horses killed; my own wounded badly twice, and several slightly. With the exception of one or two cases, officers and men acted bravely, and did their work coolly, calmly, and with a will. Allow me here to thank Major Kelly, Fourth Missouri State Militia Cavalry, for the voluntary aid he rendered me, his command being held in reserve. He spent the most of his time with me during the engagement, and too much praise cannot be bestowed upon him for the services rendered me.

As soon as the battle ended, I was ordered by you with the First Missouri State Militia Cavalry to Lexington, to take care of that place and the Sixth Sub-District. Owing to some of the command taking the wrong road, it was late when we started for Lexington; lost the way several times in the night, and the men so worn out with hunger and the want of sleep that they were falling from their horses while marching, and I thought it best to halt half-way between Marshall and Lexington, near a road leading directly south from Waverly. In about three hours a scout I had sent out reported the enemy crossing the road 9 miles farther west, and going in the direction of Sedalia. Started immediately, and when we struck the trail found it was some 500 to 700 of Shelby's men, and Shelby with them, retreating south by the way of Warrensburg. They had no train, and were moving rapidly. This was a hard day's march on us, as the rebels kept bearing in the direction of Warrensburg. We rode at a trot and gallop most of the afternoon, reaching Davis Creek at the crossing of the Lexington and Warrensburg road a little before sundown. Shelby went up the creek, struck the Columbus road, but in a short distance left that road and bore in the direction of Warrensburg. We left his trail at Davis and took the road direct to Warrensburg, where we arrived at 9 o'clock, having been for the last four days without rations, and little or nothing to get to eat on the road.

[October] 15, moved out near Rose Hill. Learned that Shelby had passed Holden at 2 a. m., and General Ewing having started out south, I knew it was useless to follow any longer. As our horses had been under the saddle for eight days and nights, and the men four days without rations, we were broken down, and returned to camp. During the whole march, officers and men stood up to their work like soldiers, and never made a complaint.

The following is a list of casualties at Dug Ford, on La Mine River, October 12, 1863:*

In addition to the above, 2 men of the Seventh Missouri State Militia were killed, and 2 slightly wounded same day, names not known. One horse killed and 5 wounded.

Casualties, October 13, 1863, at the battle of Marshall, 2 officers and 5 men wounded; 2 horses killed and 1 wounded.

This comprises all our casualties. We captured but little property, as we were in pursuit all the time; did not stop to pick up property; saw large numbers of horses and mules abandoned and left in the enemy's camp and on the road.

---

*Nominal list shows 2 men killed, 1 man mortally wounded, and 1 officer and 2 men wounded.

Leaving all the detachments under my command, except the First Missouri State Militia Cavalry, at Marshall, I have no report of their casualties at Marshall.

I am, general, very respectfully,

B. F. LAZEAR,
Lieutenant-Colonel First Missouri State Militia Cavalry, Commanding Detachment in the Field.

Brigadier-General BROWN,
Commanding District of Central Missouri.

HDQRS. FIRST MISSOURI STATE MILITIA CAVALRY,
Warrensburg, October 31, 1863.

CAPTAIN: In my official report to the commanding general of Central District of Missouri of the expedition against Shelby, I omitted to mention the very valuable services rendered me by the two detachments of the Seventh Missouri State Militia, and particularly the detachment commanded by Lieutenant Becker. He and his men, being acquainted with the country, were in the advance the most of the time, and, with the exception of the engagement at Dug Ford, participated in all the skirmishes of October 13, and, as I am informed by Major Mullins, who was in command of the advance, acted their part bravely, losing 2 men killed and 2 slightly wounded. I make this amendment to my report, as I wish to do full justice to all officers and men, particularly so to detachments of other regiments who were under my command.

I am, captain, very respectfully,

B. F. LAZEAR,
Lieutenant-Colonel First Missouri State Militia Cavalry, Commanding Detachment in the Field.

Capt. JAMES H. STEGER,
Assistant Adjutant-General, District of Central Missouri.

No. 3.

Report of Col. George H. Hall, Fourth Missouri State Militia Cavalry, of operations October 7–20.

HDQRS. FOURTH MISSOURI STATE MILITIA CAVALRY,
Marshall, Mo., October 23, 1863.

MAJOR: In obedience to circular order from Headquarters Central District of Missouri, Jefferson City, October 19, 1863, I have to report that, on the morning of the 7th instant, I received orders to march with the troops under my command to Sedalia, Mo., and there await further orders. With three squadrons of the Fourth Missouri State Militia Cavalry and a section of Thurber's Missouri State Militia battery, under command of Lieutenant Newgent, I arrived at Sedalia, Mo., on the evening of the 7th instant; distance, 35 miles. Company A, Fourth Missouri State Militia Cavalry, being on a scout near Waverly, reached Sedalia on the evening of the 8th instant.

About 12 m. of the 8th instant, I received information that Shelby, with his rebel force, estimated at 2,000 men, had captured Warsaw and dispersed the Federal troops stationed at that post (which was 40 miles south of Sedalia), and that the enemy were advancing toward Sedalia. I immediately sent a detachment toward Warsaw and other detachments on the several roads leading southeast and southwest from Sedalia, to ascertain the movements of the enemy. I also ordered the quartermaster and commissary at Sedalia to ship by railroad the public stores in their possession to Jefferson City. I also had breastworks made of railroad ties and bales of hay, and barricaded the streets, and had the citizens called out. The constant scouting necessary to watch the enemy at so great a distance was very laborious. Maj. William Gentry, with about 60 men of the Fifth Provisional Regiment of Enrolled Missouri Militia, was very active, and did all that his small force could do.

At noon of the 9th instant, I ascertained that the enemy were on the march and going toward Cole Camp from Warsaw. At 1 p. m. I learned that the enemy had passed Cole Camp, on the road leading to Syracuse, at noon, and at 3 p. m. I learned from my scouts that the enemy were, at 1 p. m., 5 miles beyond Cole Camp, on the road to Syracuse. All the commanding officers of co-operating forces were kept advised of the movements of the enemy by telegrams and by messengers, so far as I could learn their positions. At 5 p. m. Major Foster, with about 80 men, came to Sedalia from General Brown's forces, bringing 4 prisoners captured by him, and confirming the news already sent off by me. The forces were kept in readiness to march on the enemy at a moment's warning.

On the morning of the 10th instant, at daybreak (General Brown having arrived at Sedalia), Major Kelly, with four squadrons Fourth Missouri State Militia Cavalry, with Major Gentry and the men of the Fifth Provisional Regiment Enrolled Missouri Militia, heretofore mentioned, marched east after the enemy. At about 3 p. m. Major Kelly struck the enemy. His report is herewith filed as a part of my own.

On the morning of the 11th instant, I was again left in command of the post of Sedalia.

On the morning of the 15th instant, I received orders to take what men were at Sedalia on the 14th instant that were mounted, and ascertain where a portion of the enemy were that had gone in a southeast direction from Marshall on the 13th instant. I marched first to Cole Camp. Not hearing anything definite, I continued east from Cole Camp till nightfall.

On the morning of the 16th instant, I struck the trail of the enemy near Buffalo Mills. The enemy were going toward Duroc, and were twenty-four hours ahead of me. I continued on their trail, and, after traveling on the road from Duroc to Linn Creek about 5 miles, their trail gave out. I ascertained that about 40 Federal soldiers had met their advance at that point, had had a skirmish with the enemy, and that the enemy had then left the road in a westerly direction. It was near night before I could find their trail. I would have to wait till morning before I could follow it, which would give the enemy thirty-six hours the start of me. The Federal forces south of the Osage River had come in contact with the enemy. The enemy were traveling rapidly, and using every effort to get south. I therefore abandoned farther pursuit, and returned to Sedalia, thence to Marshall, Mo.

All of which is respectfully submitted.

GEORGE H. HALL,
Colonel Fourth Missouri State Militia Cavalry.

Maj. HENRY SUESS,
Chief of Cavalry, Central District of Missouri, Jefferson City, Mo.

No. 4.

Report of Maj. George W. Kelly, Fourth Missouri State Militia Cavalry, of action at Marshall, Mo.

HDQRS. FOURTH MISSOURI STATE MILITIA CAVALRY,
Marshall, Mo., October 22, 1863.

COLONEL: I have the honor to report that, by the order of Brig. Gen. E. B. Brown, commanding Central District of Missouri, I marched, on the morning of the 10th instant, with Companies A, B, E, and F, of the Fourth Missouri State Militia Cavalry, and some 60 men of the Fifth Provisional Regiment Enrolled Missouri Militia, under Maj. William Gentry and Captain Brown, down the Pacific Railroad, to find the whereabouts of General Jo. Shelby and his raiders, and to annoy him if found, and form a junction with Lieutenant-Colonel Lazear, of the First Missouri State Militia Cavalry. I struck Shelby's pickets at the town of Syracuse; skirmished some 4 miles east of Syracuse, and struck the entire force of the enemy, some 1,600 or 2,000, with two pieces of artillery; forced the enemy to a stand; opened on me with his artillery. My force being too small, I retired, without loss or injury, to Syracuse. I then took a circuitous route, and formed a junction with Lieutenant-Colonel Lazear, same evening at 11 p. m., at Tipton, Mo. Distance traveled, 55 miles.

On the morning of the 11th, left Tipton with Lieutenant-Colonel Lazear, and marched to Syracuse; from there in the direction of Boonville, Mo. Struck the enemy's picket about 4 miles south of Boonville at dark. Animals and men being tired, and the night very dark, we lay upon our arms in line. Distance traveled, 30 miles.

On the morning of the 12th, marched at daylight for Boonville; found the enemy had encamped 5 miles west, on the Georgetown road; pushed on; came up to the enemy's rear guard, skirmishing all day, killing several and capturing some prisoners; joined General Brown's command at 9 p. m.; lay on arms in line; traveled 30 miles to-day.

On the morning of the 13th, received orders to march at 4 a. m. direct to Marshall, Mo.; marched pursuant to orders; arrived at Marshall about 7 a. m.; found no enemy; ordered men to feed horses; picketed different roads. At 8 o'clock pickets on the road east of Marshall, leading to Arrow Rock, gave the alarm of the approach of the enemy. Lieutenant-Colonel Lazear ordered me to hold the enemy with my command until he could get his line formed. I ordered Capt. Joe Parke, with Company E, Fourth Missouri State Militia Cavalry, down to skirmish with the enemy, which he did in good style. I then moved my other squadrons, A, B, and F, to his support. The enemy soon made his appearance in force. Lieutenant-Colonel Lazear opened on the enemy with two small guns of Johnson's battery, Company L, First Missouri State Militia Cavalry, on my right, doing no execution. About this time the roar of musketry told that the battle had begun. The enemy made a desperate effort to force his way into town on the road from the east, but was repulsed.

We fought some three hours, when the roar of a different gun was heard in their rear, which told that General Brown was there. In a very short time the enemy had begun his retreat, General Shelby, with about two-thirds of the command, going north and northwest, and Colonel Hunter, who was cut off from main force, going east some 8 miles, and then south with the balance of command, leaving one piece of artillery and other arms.

Officers and soldiers of my command behaved well. Casualties in four squadrons of Fourth Missouri State Militia Cavalry, under my command, are as follows: Company A, Privates William Frund and Ellis Edwards, shot in the neck; Company B, Second Lieut. William McClelland, shot in the thigh, Private George Fitzwaters, shot in the knee; Company E, Privates A. J. Bradley, shot in the thigh, George H. Baughn, in the hand. I had 6 horses killed and 14 wounded in the command. I followed up the retreat of the enemy from Marshall to Vansuet's, 12 miles northwest, same day, killing 1 and wounding several; encamped for the night.

October 14, received orders to march my command back to Marshall. Arrived at Marshall at 10 o'clock; received orders to march; left at 11 a. m.; marched to Sedalia; distance traveled, total, 180 miles.

G. W. KELLY,
Major Fourth Missouri State Militia, Commanding Detachment.

Col. GEORGE H. HALL,
Fourth Missouri State Militia Cavalry.

No. 5.

Report of Maj. William Gentry, Fifth Provisional Regiment Enrolled Missouri Militia, of operations October 7–17.

HDQRS. FIRST BATTALION FIFTH PROV. REGT. E. M. M.,
Georgetown, Mo., October 31, 1863.

In accordance with an order issued by Col. John F. Philips, commanding Third Sub-District, Central District of Missouri, of which the the following is a copy, to wit:

SPECIAL ORDERS, No. —. } HDQRS. THIRD SUB-DIST., CENTRAL DIST. OF MISSOURI,
Sedalia, October 6, 1863.

I. Maj. William Gentry, Fifth Provisional Regiment Enrolled Missouri Militia, will assume command of the post of Sedalia until further orders.

* * * * * * *

III. Major Gentry will so dispose of his forces as to cover Sedalia, Dresden, and the bridge on the Pacific Railroad in Pettis County.

JOHN F. PHILIPS,
Colonel Seventh Missouri State Militia Cavalry, Commanding Sub-District.

I took command of the post at Sedalia on the 7th instant, and ordered Captain Brown, of Company E, to that place with 30 men, and proceeded to organize about 100 citizens, and fortified the place as best we could with railroad ties and bales of hay, leaving the balance of Captain Brown's company at Dresden, under Lieutenant Funk; Lieutenant Satterwhite, of Company D, at the railroad bridge across Big Muddy, with 30 men, as a guard, and Sergt. J. E. Rigg, with 15 men, at Georgetown, to guard the records of the county, &c., with an order on the officers at the different posts to be on the alert, and, if we should be attacked, to proceed at once to Sedalia with their several commands. In this position we remained until the morning of the 10th, when I ordered all the different squads of my command to be at Sedalia by 7 o'clock of that morning, which order was promptly obeyed, and at about 7.30 o'clock we started in the direction of Tipton, in search of the enemy. Our command consisted of four companies of the Fourth Missouri State Militia, under Major Kelly, and parts of Companies D and E, of my battalion, about 100 men, and 25 men, under Captain Freund, of the Sixtieth Regiment Enrolled Missouri Militia. As Major Kelly was the ranking officer, we were placed under his command. We proceeded to Smithton, where the rebels had been the night previous about 9 o'clock, and sacked the town, tore down the telegraph line, &c.

The next point was Otterville. There we met some of our captured men who were taken at the bridge the night previous. The rebels did no damage nor made any stay at Otterville. They procured a guide, went hurriedly to the bridge, where we had Captain Berry, of Company D, with 28 men, stationed. They captured and swore or paroled the captain and 17 of his men; the rest of the men made their escape. The enemy burned the bridge, block-house, all the tents, wagons, commissaries, &c., and took their horses, a lot of clothing, &c. They left the bridge about midnight, in the direction of Syracuse. We made no halt at any of these places, but pushed on at a brisk gait until we came near Syracuse. There we came on the enemy's pickets and drove them in; run them out of town. Found their force to be about 120 men. We pursued them to a point of timber north of Tipton; there we exchanged quite a number of shots with the enemy; captured 2 horses and some goods that were taken the night previous at Smithton. Here we drove out their whole force, and, after they shot at us several times with their cannon, we retired out of their reach in the direction of Otterville. They did not follow us far. We then made a detour around Syracuse, and formed a junction with Colonel Lazear, First Missouri State Militia, at Tipton at 11 o'clock that night. We all set out on their trail next morning, and came upon their pickets, about 5 miles from Boonville, at sundown, and drove them in. We pursued them on the following morning by the way of Boonville, Choteau Springs, Dug Ford, on the La Mine, Dick Marshall's, on Blackwater, Salt Fork, near Jonesborough, skirmishing at intervals all day long. We encamped near Jonesborough for the night. We were posted on picket that night without fire, it raining during the whole night. Just at the dawn of day we set out with the commands of Colonel Lazear, Major Kelly, and my own, by a circuitous route, to try, if possible, to head the enemy at Marshall, which we did.

We arrived at Marshall about 7 o'clock in the morning, and were ordered to get breakfast and horse-feed wherever we could, which order was promptly obeyed, as we had eaten nothing since we left Tipton, except just as we could catch it. We made apples and cabbage suffer along the roadside. We scarcely had time to get breakfast for ourselves and horses when our pickets were driven in by the enemy. Captain Parke, with about 30 men, was ordered to hold the enemy in check, whilst I was ordered to support him, which order was promptly obeyed on the part of my command. I heard the rebel officer give command to his command for every fourth man to hold horses, whereupon I followed his example. My men fought well; did as good service as any troops engaged. When the enemy ran, we pursued them to Tete Saw Plains, to Van Meter's, where we encamped for the night.

We were ordered on the following morning, and [moved] from there in the direction of Sedalia, to see if any portion of the enemy had crossed in a southwest direction, but we found no traces of them. We arrived at Sedalia about 9 o'clock that night.

We were ordered on the following morning, under the command of Col. G. H. Hall, of the Fourth Missouri State Militia, to intercept, if possible, about 500 or 600 rebels, under command of Colonel Hunter, who were bearing southeast of Sedalia. We proceeded by the way of

Cole Camp and Buffalo Mills to Duroc, 15 miles below Warsaw. Upon arriving at the latter place, we found they had crossed the river and were too far ahead of us to be overtaken. We then returned to Sedalia on the evening of the 17th. During the whole time we were upon forced marches without rations, and my men obeyed every order without a murmur, and acted upon the battle-field and elsewhere as veteran soldiers.

The casualties are as follows: *

Hoping the above details of our campaign will be satisfactory, I remain, general, very respectfully, your obedient servant,

WM. GENTRY,
Major, Commanding Battalion.

Brig. Gen. E. B. BROWN,
Jefferson City, Mo.

No. 6.

Report of Col. John F. Philips, Seventh Missouri State Militia Cavalry, of operations October 6–18.

HDQRS. SEVENTH MISSOURI STATE MILITIA CAVALRY,
Sedalia, Mo., October 19, 1863.

GENERAL: I have the honor to report that, in obedience to your order of the 6th instant, received at 5 p. m., to move to Clinton to assist in repelling the raid of the rebel general Shelby, I left camp at Sedalia at 7 p. m., with three companies of my regiment and Company L, of the Fourth Missouri State Militia Cavalry. Marching all night, I reached your headquarters at Clinton at 11 a. m., 7th instant. (I omitted to state that I also had one section First Missouri State Militia Light Artillery, commanded by Captain Thurber.) On the night of the 7th instant, I was joined by seven companies of my regiment and Maj. T. W. Houts.

On the 8th instant, we marched to Osceola, 30 miles, and bivouacked on the south side of the Osage River. Learning through the night that the enemy had appeared at Warsaw and possessed that place, Major Foster, of my regiment, was detached, with 200 men, to go to Warsaw that night and follow up the enemy and observe his movements. At daylight next morning, we marched toward Sedalia, apprehending that the enemy designed making a descent upon that place. That day and night we marched 65 miles, reaching Sedalia at 5 a. m. Company E, of my regiment, was at Warsaw, occupying that station, when the enemy attacked the town. This company formed on the river bank and fought very determinedly, holding the enemy in check for half an hour on the south side of the river, until it was discovered that he had crossed a part of his force at the Hackberry Ford, 6 miles below town, and already occupied a commanding position in rear of the company. Thus virtually surrounded and largely outnumbered, nothing was left them but to seek safety in fleeing, which they did, passing out northeast, soon finding shelter in the brush. They wounded several of the enemy, but lost their transportation, consisting of 2 Government wagons and 12 mules. Assistant Surgeon Edwards, in charge of hospital, narrowly escaped with the ambulance. The hospital stores fell into the enemy's hands, with the surgeon's case of surgical instruments, new and com-

* Nominal list, omitted, shows 5 men wounded.

plete. Five men of Company I fell into the enemy's hands, and were paroled, and also 3 of Company E. This company retreated to Calhoun, where it joined the forces under Lieutenant-Colonel Lazear, of the First Missouri State Militia.

On the 11th instant, at 6 a. m., I moved with eleven companies of my regiment and four pieces of Thurber's First Missouri State Militia Light Artillery in direction of Otterville; from Otterville, via Lebanon, toward Boonville, camping that night at McGruder's, 10 miles southwest of Boonville. At dawn next morning, in obedience to your orders, I moved eastward to the south of Boonville 8 miles, where we learned the enemy had passed through Boonville, going west. Here we countermarched, and 4 miles west of our last camping ground struck the enemy's left flank, and 6 miles farther, near Dug Ford, on Blackwater, passed in advance of Colonel Lazear's command, and came up with the enemy's rear, rapidly moving to the west. Our advance, under Major Suess, soon began skirmishing with them, killing 1, capturing horse, equipments, &c. Here the advance, composed of Companies A, C, D, and F, was given in charge of Major Foster, who pressed forward with so much energy as to bring the enemy to a stand at Salt Fork. He crossed the creek, leaving a line of skirmishers on the south side, and throwing forward, in line, a whole regiment, dismounted and strongly posted behind a fence and in thick brush, completely covering the ford, which was a narrow defile, with abrupt banks. The major threw forward his entire force, stretching along the summit of a high woodland, most favorably situated, when a most fierce fire of musketry ensued. Two pieces of Thurber's artillery were ordered forward into action. A sharp cannonading between our and the rebel guns took place. The infantry pressing hard on the ford, the enemy fell back in haste. We had several horses wounded here, and 2 or 3 men struck with musket balls and 1 with a piece of shell. One man belonging to the battery was killed with a cannon ball. We killed 1 of the enemy and wounded a number.

The evening was cloudy, dark, and rainy, and night approaching with such intense darkness, we halted, the men lying all night in line on their arms, impatiently awaiting the morning to renew the struggle or the chase. Here I was joined by Captain Darst, Company E, of my regiment, with about 45 men of his command. This company had been through the day the advanced guard of Lieutenant-Colonel Lazear's force, and had several brilliant encounters with the enemy, killing —— of them, and capturing several horses and much personal property from them. Two men of Company E were killed through the day, one with musketry and the other supposed to have fallen from his horse in the charge, as there was no evidence on his person of gunshot wounds.

As soon as it was light enough to discover our way on the morning of the 13th instant, we moved out the advance under Major Foster, quickly followed by the column, Colonel Lazear's force having been sent by your order direct to Marshall, to head off the enemy. At 8 a. m. Major Houts was sent forward with Companies H, I, and K, to relieve Major Foster and take the advance. This the major did with characteristic promptness and eagerness for the fray. Near Marshall, he came up with the enemy's rear and attacked him vigorously. It was soon ascertained that Colonel Lazear had reached Marshall in advance of the enemy and had engaged him there. Between us and town and the enemy was a creek difficult to cross, the enemy occupying on his side high ground completely overlooking the crossing, which was spanned by a mean bridge, already partly torn up by the enemy. Under your direction, I dispatched Captain Foster with his company to occupy a ford one-half mile above, and soon followed him with the balance of my command, and one section of the artillery, the other section having been sent to Major Houts, who was now struggling hard to pass over the bridge, which, despite the resistance, he crossed, and for one hour fought the enemy in force, compelling him to retire toward the west, where the main force was contending for the mastery of the town. In the mean time I had succeeded, with indescribable difficulty, through dense underbrush, over ravines and rugged hills, in gaining position on the enemy's left flank. No sooner than he discovered me, did he open on us a most furious cannonading, throwing round shot and shell into our ranks, with more of terror than of danger. The distance was yet too great to make rifles effective, and the intermediate ground being so broken and brushy as to render the movement of cavalry in that direction impracticable, I at once dismounted the men and moved them in line directly toward the enemy. He took fright at this movement, and at once put his force in motion, evidently endeavoring to escape to the north. I therefore mounted the men and conducted them at the gallop three-quarters of a mile to the northwest of town, and in rear of the enemy's right, giving the battery a position. I left squadrons to support it, and, dismounting the others, threw them rapidly into action on the left of the battalions of the Fourth Missouri State Militia and the Fifth Provisional Enrolled Missouri Militia, commanded, respectively, by Majors Kelly and Gentry. Here the fighting was severe for nearly an hour, when the enemy's center was broken by a charge from the battalion just named, and the enemy's right being closely pressed and seriously punished by my command, gave way, and precipitately retreated to the northwest, under the lead of General Shelby. I at once mounted the men, and with nine companies of my regiment (the other three yet being with Major Houts in the enemy's rear), also the battalions of Majors Kelly and Gentry, making about 750 men, and the section of Thurber's battery, I pursued the enemy hotly in the direction of Waverly. He made an attempt to tear up the bridge across Salt Fork, but was so closely pursued by the advance that he failed. We then had a chase at the gallop, and a running fight for 10 miles, over prairie land. At 5 p. m. his rear was so vigorously assailed as to bring his entire column to a halt and into line of battle. I pressed forward with the artillery and cavalry, and opened on him with the guns at half-mile range, with considerable effect. The cavalry charged; the enemy fell back at a run, losing 1 man killed and several wounded. At this point, he struck the road to Miami, and turned the head of his column directly north, running at right angles with my command. Anticipating our designs on his transportation, he took the precaution to place it far to the front. As soon as I discovered his movements to the north, I determined to cut him off or perish in the attempt. Accordingly, I led off three squadrons across the prairie to engage the head of his column, while Majors Foster and Kelly should charge his rear and center, if possible. At one-half mile, I discovered myself mired in a wretched swamp, almost beyond extrication. I was here detained five minutes in recovering my horse, and found that I had to describe a semi-circle in passing this swamp, which threw me so far back as to completely thwart my plans. The enemy, likewise, discovering my object, abandoned the Miami road, and turned abruptly westward, through Van Meter's farm, on a dim and unfrequented path. He was going at full run, and, while we shouted and shot at him, he used his hats on his jaded horses, throwing overboard every weight (not the arms) that beset him and retarded his movements. It was quite evident that he was fearfully demoralized, and sought safety alone in flight. It was now growing dark. The horses and men were exhausted. Having left camp that morning before breakfast, we had not eaten that day. Our transportation was left at Marshall. We were then without rations, and found rest on a soldier's bed. In obedience to your orders, the commands of Majors Kelly and Gentry and the battery were sent back to Marshall.

At 4 a. m. on the 14th instant, I renewed the pursuit, being joined by 200 men of the Ninth Provisional Regiment Enrolled Militia, under Lieutenant-Colonel Brutsche. The enemy's trail bore evidence of panic. It was strewn with hats, clothes, plunder, &c. He made no halt for the night, and, having to pass through a dense forest, his transportation greatly retarded his progress. Information received from citizens, with whom Shelby and others conversed, showed that he had 600 men with him; that his force was cut in twain at Marshall; he supposed they were captured; that he believed I was pursuing him through the night, and 5 miles east of Marshall he became so greatly alarmed at the report of our approach that he abandoned his transportation, viz, 2 ambulances, 5 army wagons, and 40 head of team mules. The wagons were precipitated over a steep bank into the Missouri River. Three of them were laden with ammunition—pistol, rifle, and artillery ammunition, fixed. The ambulances I brought along. The ammunition, &c., I hurled into the river. The wagons could not be drawn out, and were left. The mules were running at large on the commons. A scout sent in there might secure this property. I lost as little time as possible, and pressed forward at a trot. The enemy passed through Waverly at 3 a. m. Two miles beyond there he turned south from the Lexington road. I followed up 12 miles out. Colonel Weer, of the Ninth Kansas Cavalry, passed in front of me and took up the trail, and a few miles farther Colonel Lazear, who had gone direct from Marshall, *en route* for Lexington, passed in front of Colonel Weer, and took up the pursuit. The enemy had traveled with such unremitting energy, and so much celerity, as to outstrip all efforts to head him off. I continued the chase to where he crossed the Georgetown and Lexington road, 14 miles from Lexington. Night was now approaching; a larger force than that of the enemy was in advance of me several miles; my horses were worn down, and men suffering with hunger. I therefore abandoned the chase; dropped down the road to the east 6 miles, intending to look after that portion of the enemy cut off at Marshall, entertaining the idea that he might attempt to escape up Blackwater and through the timbers of Davis. This day I had marched 45 miles without stopping to feed. At 9 p. m. we fed the horses, but the men were unfed, except with bacon.

The next day I moved down Blackwater 25 miles, and remained that night on the creek, at an intermediate point between Sedalia and Marshall. Supplies sent me from Sedalia did not reach us until the morning of the 16th, when I was moving out of camp. The men had fared so sumptuously and so long on bacon and fresh beef, that we would not then halt to eat crackers, coffee, &c., but returned, in obedience to your orders, direct to Sedalia, having first sent two companies to scout Saline County for rebel stragglers. When I reached Sedalia, I had been on the march nine days, two nights and parts of seven, having marched in all a distance of 310 miles.

The number of the enemy killed and wounded by my command is difficult to state; 29 or 30 are known to have been killed outright in the several skirmishes; how many in the main engagement at Marshall is not known. We took no prisoners.

My casualties, so far as I can ascertain, are as follows: In Company A, 2 men slightly wounded; horses broken down and abandoned on march, 5. Company B, 1 horse broken down and abandoned on march. Company C, 2 men wounded slightly; 5 horses broken down and abandoned on march. Company D, 2 men wounded; 5 horses shot and 6 abandoned on march. Company E, 2 men killed, 1 wounded slightly, and 3 taken prisoners and paroled at Warsaw; 3 horses killed, 4 wounded, and 4 abandoned on march; 2 army wagons and 12 mules, 1,500 rounds of ammunition, camp and garrison equipage, &c., captured at Warsaw, and a number of guns. Company F, 2 slightly wounded; 10 horses broken down and abandoned on march. Company G, 6 horses abandoned on march. Company H, 3 horses abandoned on march. Company I, 5 men taken prisoners and paroled at Warsaw; 1 man missing; 10 horses captured; 2 horses abandoned on march. Company K, 2 men captured and paroled at Warsaw; 2 horses abandoned on march. Company L, 1 man wounded slightly; 7 horses broken down and abandoned on march. Company M, 2 men wounded slightly.

We captured quite a number of horses and mules and small-arms from the enemy.

It is a matter of sincere gratulation that, in view of the many fierce engagements and dashes of this campaign, so few of my men were hurt. They behaved well in action and on the march; in their valor and discipline the nation will ever find a sure palladium to guard its property against the inroads of such plunderers as Shelby and his traitor confederates. I likewise commend to your good opinion the gallantry and conduct of my line officers. They acted well their part. The service has not in it a nobler trio than my three majors.

Congratulating you, general, upon your brilliant success, and hoping that you may be as useful to the country in the future as you have been in the past, I am, with much respect, your obedient servant,

JNO. F. PHILIPS,
Colonel Seventh Missouri State Militia Cavalry.

Brigadier-General BROWN,
Commanding District of Central Missouri.

No. 7.

Reports of Lieut. Col. Thomas T. Crittenden, Seventh Missouri State Militia Cavalry.

BOONVILLE, *October* 12, 1863—12 m.

MAJOR: Instant arrived. Found about 1,000 rebels, with two pieces of artillery, in possession of the town. Could not cross. Major Leonard, of the Ninth Missouri State Militia, with 200 soldiers, was attempting to cross the river just as the enemy came in town; was driven back, so we remained on the opposite side of the river. I concealed the boat behind an island. Have 300 men with me. Will move out immediately to join our pursuing forces. I know nothing of General Guitar. Rebels took all the clothing, boots, shoes, arms, and horses that could be found in town; robbed the county treasury of $6,000 or $8,000; robbed the sheriff; killed no citizens; moved out on Georgetown road. Shelby said he was going to Waverly and Lexington.

T. T. CRITTENDEN,
Lieutenant-Colonel Seventh Missouri State Militia Cavalry.

Maj. LUCIEN J. BARNES, *Assistant Adjutant-General.*

JEFFERSON CITY, *October* 14, 1863.
(Received at Boonville, 4.35 p. m.)

Lieutenant-Colonel CRITTENDEN:

General Schofield directs that you scour the country, especially along the river, and pick up the scattered rebels who may come that way. News of General Brown's victory yesterday received. Watch the La Mine country.

LUCIEN J. BARNES,
Assistant Adjutant-General.

HEADQUARTERS SECOND SUB-MILITARY DISTRICT,
Tipton, October 26, 1863.

GENERAL: Learning that a large number of guerrillas, under Jackman, were crossing from the north to the south side of the Missouri River, near the La Mine, in Cooper County, on or about the 5th of the present month, I moved to Boonville in person, in order that I could more effectually use the troops stationed at that place to check the movements of the enemy. I am prompted to believe that this was done to a certain extent, and would have been entirely so had I possessed at the time a few more troops to have placed between Boonville and the Rocheport Landing, upon the south side of the river. During my absence from this place, an order came to myself, or the commanding officer at Tipton, to move, with celerity, with Company M, Seventh Missouri State Militia Cavalry, under Captain Queen, stationed at Tipton; Company L, Seventh Missouri State Militia Cavalry, under Captain Henslee, stationed at Versailles, and Company H, Seventh Missouri State Militia Cavalry, under Captain Box, stationed at Syracuse, to Clinton, Henry County, Missouri, and there report to Col. John F. Philips, commanding Seventh Missouri State Militia Cavalry. Captains Box and Henslee were notified by Captain Queen, commanding at Tipton during my absence. And here permit me to say, general, that those companies moved with creditable promptitude; were in line, with transportation moving, in one hour from the time that the bugle sounded the assembly. I have made this digression that the companies of the Seventh Missouri State Militia Cavalry within my sub-district should be properly commended to your notice for their alacrity and eagerness for the fray. As soon as I was notified, I moved from Boonville to Tipton, for the purpose of proceeding to Sedalia; thence to the field, in order to join my command. The enemy, under Colonel Shelby, was approaching the Pacific Railroad so rapidly that it was deemed imprudent to proceed farther than Syracuse with the cars on the evening of the 8th instant. Finding myself, in company with several other officers of the Fourth and Seventh Missouri State Militia Cavalry, cut off from our commands, I determined to return to Tipton, organize the disbanded militia, and render as much obstruction as possible to the movements of the enemy, who, I learned from scouts and other sources, were moving upon or toward the railroad. I commenced immediately communication with General Totten, who had temporarily assumed command in your stead at Jefferson City. Kept him advised of the movements, courses, and actions of the enemy. I will here say that, to his foresight in forwarding a large train of freight cars, the merchants and tradesmen of this town and county can congratulate themselves, and feel obligated to him upon saving $75,000 worth of valuable property from the eager grasp of unscrupulous men.

On Saturday morning, October 10, between daylight and sunrise, in company with Captain Turley, Company D, Seventh Missouri State Militia Cavalry, and several citizens, proceeded up the railroad west cautiously upon a locomotive, with the design of ascertaining whether the La Mine Bridge had been burned on the night previous by the enemy. I had not gone more than 2 miles from Tipton before I came upon a squadron of the enemy drawn up in line upon the left, and within 20 yards of the road, under the command of Major Hayden, who had taken the precaution to blockade the road in front of his position. He immediately rode out in front and to the right of his command, and demanded a surrender of the locomotive, at the same time ordering his men to "close around the machine," using his language. I ordered the engineer to reverse the locomotive and go backward with all possible speed, which was done with commendable coolness, under a furious volley of musketry by the enemy, whose balls pelted vigorously the locomotive and tender, but fell as harmless as snowflakes, as we were iron-clad. Captain Turley, with his usual dauntlessness and skill even amidst the heavy fire of the enemy at short range, took deliberate aim with his faithful Sharps' rifle, before which many guerrillas have fallen, at one assuming secondary command under Major Hayden, and as we receded I saw him fall a lifeless corpse from his horse. I returned to Tipton; ordered Captain Turley and Lieutenant Argo, assistant provost-marshal for the Second Sub-Military District, to gather the few soldiers of the Seventh Missouri State Militia Cavalry then remaining in town, and as many of the Enrolled Missouri Militia as could be secured, and proceed up the Syracuse road, and ascertain where the main body of the enemy was, promising them at the same time that I would go up the road again on the locomotive, to ascertain, if possible, the damage the enemy had done to the track, and to discover whether they were approaching the town through some corn-fields adjoining the road. Accomplishing my purpose, I returned to Tipton, and was soon notified by Captain Turley that they had driven the squadron under Major Hayden, with only 20 men, from the road into the brush south of town, assisted by F. L. Parker, of Sedalia, formerly captain of a company of Home Guards at the battle of Lexington, and Charles Leonard, of Cooper County, formerly captain of a company of the Enrolled Missouri Militia, in Colonel Pope's regiment, to whom I must favorably call your attention, as they exhibited the true bravery of their nature by at once using every exertion to repel the common enemy. Captain Turley also informed me that the brush south of town was full of rebels; that they were proceeding down the railroad rapidly, and unless I moved east immediately on the locomotive, I would lose it and be captured. I ordered Captain Turley to retreat toward California, in command of the soldiers in Tipton, and it would have been utter folly and a foolish sacrifice of life to have attempted longer to resist the numerous foe.

I had not gone more than a mile down the road before I discovered a large body of cavalry a mile or more ahead of me, on the road running east and parallel with the railroad, moving with great rapidity toward Clark's Station. I at once conceived that their effort was to intercept the locomotive at that point. My supposition was confirmed by the desperate exertion made by them to reach the desired goal before I could; but steam and iron were tireless, were too fleet and enduring for horse flesh. I passed the station just as they reached the mouth of the lane leading to it, about 300 yards distant, and, without other incidents of moment, I passed on to Jefferson City, in compliance with a telegram from General Totten. Upon my arrival at Jefferson City, I reported to General Totten for further orders. He soon notified me by a circular order, dated Jefferson City, Mo., October 10, 1863 (a copy of which I herewith transmit), that I should assume command of the following detachments of troops: Detachment of First Provisional Regiment Enrolled Missouri Militia, 44 men and 2 officers, and detachment of Ninth Missouri State Militia Cavalry, 36 men and 1 officer; embark without delay on steamboat Isabella, and proceed rapidly to Boonville; organize the citizens, and make all possible preparations for the defense of the town and Government property; remain there until the arrival of General Guitar; then report to headquarters at Jefferson City for further orders. The Isabella was unladed as rapidly as possible by the joint labor of the hands and convicts from the penitentiary. I embarked with the designated command about sundown, and would have proceeded up the river forthwith had not a dark night, occasioned by wind and rain, set in, and rendered navigation impossible.

At daylight Sunday morning, October 11, the boat moved out, and progressed with unusual speed, considering the condition of the river. When within 3 miles of Boonville, about 3 o'clock that evening, the boat was hailed by a squad of soldiers from the north side of the river, of the Ninth Missouri State Militia Cavalry, sent from the ferry landing, immediately opposite Boonville, by Maj. Reeves Leonard, of the same regiment, and by them I was notified that the enemy, variously estimated at from 1,000 to 2,000 strong, had possession of the town, and had a section of artillery planted in a position to command the river. I also learned from some fugitive citizens that I took on board from the south side of the river, that Shelby, in anticipation of the approach of steamers from below, had given orders, soon after his arrival in town, to one of his captains, to take a company and guard the river against all such surprises. I ordered the captain of the boat to land her on the north side of the river, behind an island, heavily timbered, formed in the middle of the river, as a protection against the artillery of the enemy. In person I proceeded to the landing opposite Boonville; held a conference with Major Leonard; attended to the promiscuous and irregular firing that was done by the enemy and the Federal troops at each other across the river. The enemy used his Parrott gun upon us; accomplished but little, only killing 1 horse. I was informed that several of the enemy had been wounded by the small-arms of the Federal troops. I will state before I proceed further, that Major Leonard had under him at the time I assumed command about 200 soldiers of the Ninth Missouri State Militia Cavalry, which, added to the detachments above mentioned, gave me a force of 300 soldiers.

Immediately after his arrival upon the bank of the river, Major Leonard, with about 50 soldiers and horses, embarked upon the ferry to cross over to Boonville. The rebels entered the south side of the town about the same time, and, learning from some loyal man what was going on at the river, passed rapidly with a piece of artillery to the ferry landing, and opened fire furiously with his artillery and small-arms upon that brave band, then near the south shore, who returned the compliment with small-arms, with apparently no conception or fear of the three-fold danger they were in of steam, water, and lead. The boat was struck several times by the cannon shots, one penetrating her hull and another passing immediately between her tiller ropes, the cutting of either of which would have placed the boat unavoidably at the mercy of those reckless men. Strange, indeed, no lives were lost, no men or horses wounded. Major Leonard perceiving at that critical crisis that the pilot, fearfully alarmed, had forsaken the wheel, with unsurpassed coolness and bravery placed himself at that dangerous post, and safely landed the boat upon the north side of the river, amidst the applause of his gladdened soldiery and admiring comrades. We bivouacked in the brush that night, supperless and bedless, save the warm welcome of mother earth. At daylight next morning their strong lines of pickets were discovered at their usual places. From the hurrying to and fro of those soldiers in sight, I conceived that the main body of the enemy had left the town, which proved to be true. I gave orders for the boats to prepare immediately to cross us. Soon the waving of handkerchiefs by several ladies in Boonville (the purest of all patriots, when loyal) notified me that the enemy was gone, and the Stars and Stripes once more, in more than wonted beauty "full high advanced," borne by gallant men, were waving over that town in which treason received its first mortal wound by him whose name and memory are canonized in the American heart. I crossed over as rapidly as possible with my command, and moved out in pursuit of the enemy on the Georgetown road, as soon as the soldiers were fed from baskets by the generosity of the citizens of that town. I learned from various passing citizens of the county and town that Colonel Lazear, in command of the First Missouri State Militia Cavalry, had engaged the enemy near Choteau Springs, in Cooper County; and being apprised of the fact that the enemy greatly outnumbered him—that his men and horses were exceedingly fatigued—I moved in a trot for 10 miles, fully hoping to render that service to the Government at an hour of need, which the brave troops of the dauntless Guitar was capable of performing. Before reaching the Springs, I overtook Colonels Cole and Brutsche, in command of some provisional troops and one piece of artillery. We soon learned that the rumored battle was only heavy skirmishing between the rear guard of the enemy and the advance guard of the Federal troops.

We moved on over a rugged road until 11 o'clock that night in the trail of Colonel Lazear and the enemy, crossing the La Mine at Dug Ford. It became so densely dark that we encamped at Fisher's, near the Prairie Ridge post-office. Supper and breakfast we made off Irish potatoes. At daylight next morning we moved west toward Blackwater, crossing it near old Dick Marshall's, where we learned you had fed the previous evening. Knowing the number of hours I was behind you, the uncertainty of your whereabouts, and learning at Marshall's that the enemy had divided at or near that place, part passing in toward Jonesborough and some 300 passing on toward Arrow Rock, upon consultation with Colonel Cole, I determined to move with my command after those. Before reaching Arrow Rock, I learned that the enemy had been to that place, plundered it, and left. I then concluded, after having so far transcended my order in what I deemed a good cause, to return to Boonville. Crossed the La Mine at Turley's Ferry, and reached Boonville on Wednesday evening, from which place I immediately reported by telegraph to headquarters at Jefferson City for further orders, a copy of which I herewith transmit you, marked B.

I complied strictly with the above order of General Schofield. I had no casualties of interest in my command. I cheerfully commend the activity of the troops, and the unusual capacity of the officers placed temporarily under my command, to your consideration. I look upon them as an honor to the power that called them into existence and a credit to the gallant leader that molded them into soldiers. Hoping, general, that the chastisement, as unexpected to the enemy as it was creditable to yourself and the maligned militia of the State, will hereafter deter other outlaws from violating the quiet and the dignity of the commonwealth, I subscribe myself, your obedient servant,

T. T. CRITTENDEN,

Lieutenant-Colonel Seventh Missouri State Militia Cavalry.

No. 8.

Report of Maj. Emory S. Foster, Seventh Missouri State Militia Cavalry, of skirmish near Cole Camp.

ON THE MARCH,
Twenty miles from Sedalia, on the Warsaw Road,
October 9, 1863—1.30 p. m.

GENERAL: I left Warsaw this morning at 7.45. Moved out on the Sedalia road to the Cole Camp road, to within 4 miles of that place, encountering and driving in heavy pickets on these roads. Afterward, in a skirmish with a scouting party, we wounded 2, one supposed to be Shelby's adjutant, and captured 3 prisoners. I did not shoot them, because the enemy have possession of several of our men. These prisoners say there are over 1,500 Confederate troops, armed and equipped as themselves, which is excellent, with two small guns. For the last three hours I have been in sight of Cole Camp; could see the dust their pickets made going in, and for the last hour a heavy dust has been lengthening out north of Cole Camp. The prisoners say it is the command marching on Sedalia or Boonville. I go on immediately to Sedalia.

I am, respectfully,

EMORY S. FOSTER,
Major Seventh Missouri State Militia Cavalry.

General E. B. BROWN.

No. 9.

Report of Capt. H. A. Yarnell, Ninth Provisional Regiment Enrolled Missouri Militia, of action at Marshall, Mo.

HDQRS. COMPANY C, NINTH PROVISIONAL REGIMENT,
California, Mo., October 27, 1863.

SIR: I have the honor to report to you the operations of this company from the 9th of October, 1863, to the 22d, inclusive.

Friday morning, October 9, received orders to march to Sedalia. A portion of the company being on a scout, rendered it impossible to obey the order forthwith, and delaying us until 6 p. m., when we started, intending to go by the way of Otterville; reached a point 3 miles distant from Otterville at 4 o'clock in the morning, when we learned that the rebels had burned the La Mine Bridge, and were still there, 300 of them. Colonel Weer then ordered us back 6 miles, to the Georgetown road. Taking this, we arrived at Sedalia at 2 p. m. We then received orders to march to Otterville; distance, 15 miles; camped there that night.

Sunday morning, October 11, by order of Colonel Weer, moved east, to try and effect a junction with Colonel Lazear, reported to be at Tipton; came up with his command, 4 miles south of Boonville, at sunset, having traveled something near 60 miles to-day. Fed our horses and camped on the ground, having no fires.

Next morning, October 12, we were placed in the rear, with the ambulances and ammunition. Marched into Boonville at sunrise, and out, without halting, on the Georgetown road. We remained in the rear all day; camped at 9 p. m.

October 13, moved at daybreak; halted at Marshall, Saline County,

9.30 a. m. The battle commenced at 10 o'clock, by the enemy driving our pickets into town. We were then ordered out on the prairie, the enemy being in the brush north of us. When opposite their batteries, they commenced shelling us, the third one striking in McGhee's battalion, which occupied our right. Then, dismounting, we advanced down the hill and into the brush about 50 paces. Held this position some thirty minutes; then were ordered back to the edge of the prairie. While in the brush we received a heavy fire of musketry, to which we replied all along our line of skirmishers. Held our last position until the enemy began to fall back, when we were ordered to charge, when we advanced some 3 miles, they contesting the ground about 2 miles. They were pushed so close as to be compelled to leave one piece of artillery, having dismounted it. Fortunately we lost no men. Returned to Marshall and quartered for the night.

October 14, was ordered over the battle-field in the morning; then in the evening ordered to Sedalia as a prison guard.

October 15, reported at Sedalia at 6 o'clock this morning; remained in camp.

October 16, marched to Syracuse as a prisoners' guard.

October 17, a portion of the command were detailed to guard the prisoners to Jefferson City, on the Pacific Railroad morning train; the remainder were ordered to report to Colonel Crittenden, at Tipton.

October 18, at Tipton; nothing of interest on hand.

October 19, at Tipton; Colonel Crittenden not having arrived.

October 20 and 21, still in camp at Tipton.

October 22, ordered to California.

H. A. YARNELL,
Capt., Comdg. Company C, Ninth Provisional Regt. E. M. M.

No. 10.

Reports of Brig. Gen. John McNeil, U. S. Army, of operations October 9–27.

BUFFALO, MO., *October* 14, 1863.

GENERAL: From intelligence received from General Brown, I shall move west to-morrow morning, as soon as I can concentrate my forces. My object for this movement is, that if the enemy is defeated by General Brown, they will scatter in small bands, and retreat through Jackson County and make for Taberville Ford.

JOHN McNEIL,
Brigadier-General.

Major-General SCHOFIELD,
Saint Louis, Mo.

BUFFALO, MO., *October* 14, 1863.

GENERAL: Colonel Bishop received this morning a telegram from Major Hunt, commanding at Fayetteville, to the effect that at 11 o'clock, October 12, flag of truce was sent in signed by Colonel Brooks, commanding Confederate forces, demanding surrender of the post in thirty minutes, stating that the place was surrounded. The flag was returned with the information that the place could not be taken without a fight. The Confederates ———.

Here the line gave out west, probably cut again by bushwhackers. Colonel Harrison was ordered back to Fayetteville on the 12th, and ought to be at Bentonville to-night.

JOHN McNEIL,
Brigadier-General, Commanding.

Major-General SCHOFIELD.

—

GREENFIELD, MO., *October* 18, 1863.

GENERAL: On leaving Buffalo I proceeded to Bolivar, and then to Ricker's Mills, where I learned that the enemy had passed through Humansville on the 16th instant. I then made a night march to Stockton, where I arrived in the morning, and learned that the enemy had passed 10 miles east of that place at 1 o'clock this morning. I left Stockton this a. m., and arrived here at 4 p. m. I shall leave in the morning in pursuit of the rebels, estimated at from 500 to 1,000. Major King had a running fight with them as far as Humansville, and captured one piece of artillery and 40 rounds of ammunition. The rebels crossed the Sauk at Subert's Mill, and are pursuing the course of the Linn Creek, with the intention of going out by Mount Vernon.

JOHN McNEIL,
Brigadier-General.

Major-General SCHOFIELD.

—

SARCOXIE, MO., *October* 18, 1863—5 p. m.

GENERAL: I have just arrived at this place, and received a dispatch from General Holland, now at Mount Vernon, informing me that Major Hart, commanding scouts in direction of Marionville, came up and fired on a force of the enemy, camped at John Dunkle's, on Rock Prairie, about 12 miles from Greenfield. Major Hart estimates the force at 1,500 and more. General Holland says he has reliable information that Shelby and Coffee passed Lamar yesterday at 1 o'clock, traveling in the direction of Carthage and Neosho, with a force estimated at 600. With the force that General Holland has, he can defeat the enemy, if he meets them. I think the number of the enemy greatly exaggerated. Major King has joined me. I shall leave in pursuit in the morning, in the direction of Neosho.

JOHN McNEIL,
Brigadier-General.

Major-General SCHOFIELD.

—

CASSVILLE, MO., *October* 19, 1863—7 p. m.

GENERAL: Just came in from Gadfly. My column is moving to Keytesville. Shelby crossed the Wire road at Cross Timbers at 2 this p. m. Hunter and Coffee crossed the Springfield road, 21 miles above here, yesterday. Brooks has moved to Huntsville, and I suppose these three bands will concentrate at that place. I shall take all the available force I can march, and try to anticipate their concentration. Edwards will be here to-morrow evening. I will order him after me with his force. I can beat them combined, or drive them toward the Arkansas River, and upon any force you may order out of Little Rock or Fort

Smith. I can get subsistence stores from here, and shall trust mainly to living on the country. General Ewing was at Carthage yesterday, and captured a major and 30 men of the enemy. I expect to hear from him during the night.

JOHN McNEIL,
Brigadier-General.

Major-General SCHOFIELD.

MADISON COUNTY, ARK.,
Fifteen miles south of Hartville, October 23, 1863.

GENERAL: I have the honor to acknowledge receipt of telegram assigning me to command at Fort Smith, and directing that I proceed to that place so soon as I have attended to the enemy in my front. I am in close pursuit, but have been terribly impeded to-day and yesterday in this mountainous country by my transportation, breaking wagons, caissons, and gun-carriages. I could only make 15 miles to-day. I have received a message from General Ewing, and expect him to join me to-morrow. If he does, I can cut loose from all wheeled impediments, and lay aboard of the enemy when I overtake him. We have some 20 prisoners, and have released some who were conscripts. We are to-night within 14 miles of the camp of the combined forces of Shelby, Brooks, and Hunter. I hope to catch them this side of the Arkansas River, and have no doubt of the result. When I arrive at Fort Smith, I will furnish you a detailed account of the expedition.

An order of the War Department prohibits the removal of assistant adjutant-generals without consent of department commanders. Will you please to order Captain [C. G.] Laurant to report to me at Fort Smith? I regard him as almost indispensable to me, and shall be much obliged to you to telegraph the order to Springfield, where I send him to-morrow to turn over matters to my successor. I would also be glad to have Capt. J. W. Rabb ordered into my new district; he will be of great advantage to me.

I have the honor to be, your obedient servant,

JOHN McNEIL,
Brigadier-General of Volunteers.

Major-General SCHOFIELD.

HEADQUARTERS FRONTIER DISTRICT,
Fort Smith, November 1, 1863.

GENERAL: I have the honor to report the following facts as the result of the expedition, to the command of which I was verbally ordered at Saint Louis on the 9th of October:

I arrived at Lebanon on the 12th, and finding that Lieut. Col. Quin Morton had marched to Linn Creek with a detachment of the Twenty-Third Missouri Infantry Volunteers, and another of the Second Wisconsin Cavalry, and that he expected to be joined by a detachment of the Sixth and Eighth Missouri State Militia Cavalry, I ordered Major Eno, in command, to fall back on Lebanon, and proceeded to Buffalo, where I found Col. John Edwards, Eighteenth Iowa Volunteers, in command, with a few cavalry and some Enrolled Militia. I at once addressed myself to the work of concentrating force enough for pursuit when the enemy should cross the Osage on his retreat south. With about 260 men and a section of Rabb's battery, I marched to Bolivar, where General Holland was in camp with parts of two regiments Enrolled Militia, and a demi-battery, under Lieutenant Stover. Leaving the general directions to observe and pursue Coffee and Hunter, if they should cross the Osage at Warsaw, I marched in the direction of Lamar, via Humansville and Stockton, to cut off Shelby, who was reported as in full flight south of Snibar, with General Ewing in pursuit. At Stockton I was joined by Major [A. A.] King, [jr.,] Sixth Missouri State Militia Cavalry, with 375 men of the Sixth and Eighth Regiments Missouri State Militia. This force had entered Humansville from the north, in pursuit of Hunter and Coffee, four hours after I had passed through it toward the west. Major King attacked and drove this force through Humansville, capturing their last cannon.

Finding that Shelby had passed through Stockton in advance of me, I marched to Greenfield and Sarcoxie, via Bowers' Mill, and on the night of the 19th camped at Keytesville, when I learned of scouts of Colonel [J. S.] Phelps, commanding at Cassville, that the enemy had crossed the Telegraph road at Cross Timbers that day at about noon. I kept up a rapid pursuit, following the trail of our flying foe, via Sugar Creek and Easley's Ferry, to Huntsville. Our advance party entering Huntsville with a dash, took quite a number of soldiers of Brooks' rebel command, with their horses and arms. I was there joined by Colonel Edwards, Eighteenth Iowa Infantry, with 300 men of his regiment, and Major [T. J.] Hunt, First Arkansas Volunteer Cavalry, 175 men and two mountain howitzers. This gave me an effective force of 600 cavalry and 300 infantry, with four guns, two of these being 12-pounder mountain howitzers. These last would have been a much greater acquisition to me than they proved had they been properly supplied with ammunition. They were sent from Fayetteville with only 67 rounds for the two howitzers, and, of course, could not be relied upon for any length of time. We had here information that Shelby and Brooks had united their forces on War Eagle Creek, and that Hunter and Coffee were also there, the combined force amounting to 2,500 men. We marched toward this camp to attack, but found that the enemy had gone.

On the 24th, we marched across a tremendous mountain called Buffalo Mountain, and finding the enemy in camp in a snug little valley on the other side, attacked and drove him at sundown, dropping a few shells into his camp. The mountain on the other side was too steep and the passes too narrow for a night pursuit, and we had to content ourselves by waiting for the light of morning. At nearly dawn we struck again into the mountains. Our advance, under Major Hunt, First Arkansas Cavalry, was skirmishing with the enemy all day, driving them before us.

On the 26th, while engaged in an attack on the enemy's rear guard, who were posted in a narrow pass, Lieutenant [J. G.] Robinson, of the First Arkansas Cavalry, was mortally wounded. He was brought into camp and died that night at 10 o'clock.

On the 27th, we marched into Clarksville, and learned that Shelby had made good his escape and crossed the river, and that Brooks had gone down into the valley of the Big Piney with about 400 men, with instructions to pick up stragglers from the rebel army, and to cut off any train that might be coming to me from Fayetteville. My cavalry and artillery horses were too badly used up to permit of pursuit across the river, so I turned my course toward Fort Smith. At a point 4 miles north of Ozark, I sent Colonel Catherwood with the men of the Sixth and Eighth Regiments of Missouri State Militia, and Major Hunt with the men and howitzers of the First Arkansas Volunteer Cavalry, to Springfield and Fayetteville. I arrived at Fort Smith on the evening of the 30th.

Although I have been disappointed in my earnest hope to attack and destroy the force under Shelby, I feel confident of having done all that men could do under the circumstances. We have driven the enemy so that he had to stick to the road, and thus prevented a widely extended pillage both in Arkansas and Missouri.

We have taken 44 prisoners, besides discharging as many more who were conscripts. We have killed and wounded many of his men, and driven numbers to the mountains, where he will not easily get them again. The captures in horses were also large.

My officers and men bore the fatigue and exposure of this campaign without tents and on small rations in a manner to excite my admiration. Colonels Edwards and Catherwood were earnest in their co-operation in duty, and Majors King, Eno, and Hunt were always ready for any duty assigned them. Major King deserves especial mention for his gallant attack on the enemy at Humansville on the 15th, in which he captured the last cannon the enemy brought into Missouri with him, a 6-pounder brass gun. Major Hunt, with his battalion of Arkansians, were, on account of their knowledge of the country, pushed forward in the advance from Huntsville to Clarksville. This duty was promptly and cheerfully performed by the major and his gallant command, who drove the enemy from every position, killing and wounding many and taking prisoners at every charge.

To Captain Rabb, chief of artillery, and Lieutenants Whicher, Rabb's battery, and Johnson, section of howitzers, I am under obligations for services which mark them as true soldiers.

Lieutenant [A. T.] Baubie, quartermaster of the Sixth Missouri State Militia Cavalry, acted as chief quartermaster of the expedition, and gave unqualified satisfaction. Lieutenant [F. W.] Selle, commissary of the same regiment, acted as chief commissary, acquitting himself with great credit.

Captain [D. C.] Hopkins, First Arkansas Cavalry, joined me at Clarksville with 34 men. I had sent him from Buffalo on the 13th toward Duroc, to observe the enemy and report his motions. While on this duty he ran on to the enemy in force, killing 6 and losing but 2 of his own men. The day after he rejoined me, he attacked a party belonging to Brooks, of 150 strong, and drove them back upon a detachment of the Third Wisconsin Cavalry, that had been sent from Van Buren in pursuit of this same party, taking several horses, and killing and wounding 6 of the enemy. The captain is a most active and efficient scout, and a brave soldier.

The health of the command has been uniformly good. We had but 3 sick men on all the trip.

I have the honor to be, general, your obedient servant,

JOHN McNEIL,
Brigadier-General of Volunteers.

Major-General SCHOFIELD.

No. 11.

Reports of Col. John Edwards, Eighteenth Iowa Infantry, of operations October 6–12.

SAC RIVER,
Fifteen [miles] East of Greenfield October 7, 1863—6 a. m.

GENERAL: I arrived here last night with 150 men and three pieces of artillery. Shelby and Coffee left Greenfield yesterday at 12 m. for

Melville, stating that they were going to Stockton. It is possible that they intend going to Osceola or cross the Osage at Warsaw. I will follow up, and, if I can get within striking distance, they may swing on my right flank and endeavor to get out by the way of Lebanon. They are reported to be from 1,500 to 2,500 strong, with three pieces of artillery. They burned the court-house at Greenfield and gobbled up the horses, arms, and commissary stores of the company of Captain Morris, of the Seventh Provisional Enrolled Missouri Militia, stationed at that post. I am expecting General Holland and Major Eno to come up with me to-day. Colonel Harrison, First Arkansas Cavalry Volunteers, was at Pineville yesterday, and is ordered to follow up as rapidly as possible.

JNO. EDWARDS,
Colonel, Commanding.

Major-General SCHOFIELD, *Saint Louis, Mo.*

—

HUMANSVILLE, MO., *October* 8, 1863—1 p. m.

I have just arrived here. My command has been increased by re-enforcements to 1,200 men and three pieces of artillery. Shelby and Coffee passed through here at 5 p. m. last night. They burned the court-house at Stockton yesterday morning. Their present destination is undoubtedly Sedalia. They were at Quincy last night. I am pursuing them as rapidly as possible.

JNO. EDWARDS,
Colonel, Commanding.

Major-General SCHOFIELD.

—

QUINCY, MO., *October* 9, 1863—9 p. m.

A dispatch just received from my scout at Warsaw states that the enemy, after going on the Sedalia road 7 miles, took the road to Versailles. As it will be impossible for him to go north, I shall act on the assumption that he will endeavor to get out by way of Linn Creek and Lebanon, and move my command, via Bolivar and Buffalo, toward Lebanon, leaving in the morning at 4 o'clock.

JNO. EDWARDS,
Colonel, Commanding.

Major-General SCHOFIELD.

—

BUFFALO, MO., *October* 10, 1863—6 p. m.

I have just arrived here. A band of rebels, 45 in number, passed here last night, going south. They were doubtless of Shelby's command, and became detached before the command reached Warsaw. To-morrow I shall dispose of the force in this vicinity in such a manner as to render them most efficient to meet the divided and scattered bands of Shelby's command. I am inclined to believe they will pass east of Lebanon. I changed intended course by Bolivar, and came through by Hermitage. The country is full of guerrillas. To-day I threw out heavy scouting parties south of the Osage River. My messengers will wait at Lebanon for an answer.

JNO. EDWARDS,
Colonel, Commanding.

Major-General SCHOFIELD.

BUFFALO, MO., *October* 10, 1863—6 p. m.

Captain [G. W.] Murphy, of the Sixth Missouri State Militia, in command of my advance guard, has just arrived. He left Warsaw this morning at 1 a. m.; had skirmish last evening near Warsaw with the enemy's rear guard. Lieutenant [R. B.] Riggs, of this command, was wounded. He killed 2 rebels and took 1 prisoner. Captain Murphy reports a suspicious train of 40 wagons and a large amount of stock, which has been following Shelby's command, and there are several families with the train claiming to be loyal. The supposition is that the large number of wagons and stock plundered by the rebels have been turned over to this train. It was making its way to Sedalia. Captain Murphy detained it several hours, but, being under orders, had to leave it.

JNO. EDWARDS,
Colonel, Commanding.

Major-General SCHOFIELD.

HEADQUARTERS ARMY IN THE FIELD,
Buffalo, October 12, 1863—10 p. m.

GENERAL: A dispatch just received from Captain Laurant, informing me of your expected arrival in Springfield, to resume command of the district, I avail myself of the earliest opportunity to report to you the present distribution of the troops in the field and of my operations since I have been in command.

On assuming command, it was reported to me that the enemy, under Shelby and Coffee, were in force at Huntsville, Ark. I was ordered by the department commander to concentrate the troops as rapidly as possible. I ordered Major Eno, Eighth Missouri State Militia, with his command, to Cassville, and Major King, Sixth Missouri State Militia, to concentrate all the troops on the western border, at Newtonia. The messenger carrying the dispatch to Major King was captured, and consequently the concentration was delayed. The enemy passed through Bentonville, *en route* for Neosho. I ordered Major Eno to endeavor to intercept him. The enemy were too far in the advance for him to be able to accomplish this, and passed rapidly through to Greenfield, Stockton, Quincy, and Warsaw. I ordered the two 12-pounder howitzers and 6-pounder to be equipped and fitted for active operations with them, and about 150 men started to intercept the enemy at Greenfield. I arrived there twenty-four hours after the enemy had passed, with a force variously estimated from 2,000 to 4,000. From prisoners I learned that he had 2,600, and subsequent events lead me to believe that this was correct. At Greenfield I was re-enforced by Majors Eno and King with about 500 men, and by General Holland with 600 Enrolled Missouri Militia. We pursued the enemy as far as Quincy, where I received a dispatch from General Schofield ordering me to keep south of the enemy, and he would undoubtedly be driven back; and also to keep my men and horses in good condition. I directed General Holland to Osceola, to watch the enemy in that direction. I remained at Quincy from the morning of the 9th until the morning of the 10th, as it was uncertain whether the enemy would turn to the east or west of Sedalia. My scouts having brought me information, late on the night of the 9th, that the enemy had turned eastward, I moved my command east to within 7 miles of this place. On the morning of the 11th, I received a dispatch from Colonel [J. J.] Gravely that the enemy were crossing a large amount of stock at Linn Creek. I ordered Major Eno, with 500 cavalry and one 12-pounder, to intercept at that point. I had strong scouts out all the roads leading from fords of the Osage.

On arriving here, I found Lieut. Col. Quin Morton, with a force of 400 infantry and about 300 cavalry, encamped on the Little Niangua. He reported to me, and then, without my knowledge and in disregard of my request, moved his whole force to Linn Creek, as I had ordered him to move his infantry to Lebanon, to garrison the post and relieve the cavalry there, which could move more rapidly and effectively than infantry.

I received a dispatch from department headquarters to the effect that the enemy had crossed the Pacific Railroad, going north. I have ordered Lieutenant-Colonel Morton to move his command immediately to Lebanon, and Major Eno to return to this place with all his command, when the troops can be so distributed as to intercept them should the enemy break up into small squads, and yet be concentrated at short notice should they attempt to return in force.

All the force on my base line of operations, from Lebanon to Osceola, will amount to, in round numbers, 2,500 men and three pieces of artillery, not including Colonel Harrison's command, which I have ordered to Fayetteville. I did not, in my hurried movements, forget the importance of a proper defense of Springfield. After drawing away so many of the troops at that point, I have everywhere endeavored to arouse the loyal citizens to organize and assist in expelling or capturing the enemy.

General, I have done all in my power commensurate with the means at my disposal to meet the enemy.

Hoping what I have done may meet your generous approval, I have the honor to be, very respectfully, your obedient servant,

JNO. EDWARDS,
Colonel, Commanding.

General JOHN MCNEIL,
Commanding District of Southwestern Missouri.

No. 12.

Reports of Maj. Austin A. King, jr., Sixth Missouri State Militia Cavalry, of skirmishes near and at Humansville, Mo.

HUMANSVILLE, MO.,
October 17, 1863—5 a. m.

GENERAL: I chased the rebels all day yesterday; overtook their rear 15 miles from Quincy a half hour before sunset; had a running fight to this place, where we captured their artillery (6 or 9 pounder brass) and 40 rounds of ammunition. I then pursued to near Stockton, by which time it was too dark to do anything; besides, my cavalry having given completely out. I left Warsaw at 10 o'clock. I send artillery and company back to Warsaw, as per order; also one company to Lebanon. I will report to you wherever I can find you with the remaining command immediately.

My horses are much worn.

Very respectfully, your obedient servant,

AUSTIN A. KING, JR.,
Major, Commanding.

Brig. Gen. JOHN MCNEIL,
Commanding District in the Field.

STOCKTON, MO., *October* 17, 1863.

GENERAL: I have just arrived. Learn from scouts that Shelby's command crossed the Osage at Menifee's Mill yesterday at 3 o'clock, and camped in the northwest corner of this county last night. General Ewing is three hours behind him. Shelby is reported 1,500 strong; no artillery. I sent you dispatch this morning, supposing you near Richey's Mills. I will join you as soon as possible. My cavalry has almost given out. I pursued the rebels yesterday; attacked their rear near Humansville; captured their artillery and 40 rounds of ammunition. Killed 3; lost no men. I followed with my cavalry 12 miles, when it became too dark to follow the road with success. I broke their rear guard line three times without any loss.

I am, very respectfully, your obedient servant,

AUSTIN. A. KING, JR.,
Major, Commanding.

Brig. Gen. JOHN MCNEIL,
Commanding District in the Field.

No. 13.

Report of Capt. Charles B. McAfee, Sixth Missouri State Militia Cavalry, of action at Neosho, Mo.

SPRINGFIELD, MO., *October* 10, 1863.

COLONEL: I have the honor to report that, in obedience to Special Orders, No. 197, from Headquarters Southwestern District of Missouri, dated October 2, 1863, I moved from Newtonia at 8 a. m., October 4; arrived at Neosho at 11 o'clock, on my way to join Major [A. A.] King in the field (supposed to be in the neighborhood of Pineville). Not learning anything of the whereabouts of Major King, I immediately started in a southwest direction, on the Buffalo road, in search of him, and when I had marched about 2 miles from Neosho, I met Coffee's band of guerrillas, about 300 strong. They formed line, but immediately fell back, and started through the woods in direction of Neosho. I sent messengers back by the road to apprise the guard (left with stores and baggage at that place) of their approach, and moved my column by small circuit back to Neosho, and entered the town on one side at the same time that the rebels entered it on the other. We opened a brisk fire upon them, driving them back. They recovered in a few moments, and again moved upon the town, and at the same time I discovered three or four different bodies of rebel cavalry approaching from different directions. I saw that it was impossible to cut our way through their lines. We therefore immediately occupied the brick court-house, and again drove them out of the town. We remained in the court-house about one and a half hours, and fought them, and until they had shot four cannon balls through it. At this time a white flag appeared, the object of which was to demand an immediate and unconditional surrender, which I refused, but offered to surrender provided we were treated as prisoners of war, the men to retain their clothing, money, &c., the Enrolled Missouri Militia to receive the same treatment, and the Union citizens to be unmolested, to which General Shelby at first objected, refusing to treat Enrolled Missouri Militia as prisoners of war. I replied that we would all share the same fate, and would not surrender unless all would be treated as prisoners of war. General Shelby replied that he would accept my conditions, provided I would agree to have my whole command paroled on the ground. I positively refused to agree to the paroling of my command in this way. General Shelby refused to parley any further, and said he would shell the town in four minutes if we did not agree to the above conditions. I therefore surrendered my command, consisting of 123 men and 5 officers of Third Battalion Sixth Missouri State Militia Cavalry, and 34 men and 1 officer of Captain Stall's detachment of Sixth Missouri State Militia Cavalry, a few Enrolled Missouri Militia and citizens, making in all about 180 men; were paroled by companies, the officers in writing. The men's names were taken by Shelby, and they were sworn not to take up arms against the Confederate States of America until duly exchanged. No written parole was given them.

We lost our entire train and baggage, which had been moved to Neosho on that morning. The loss on our side was 2 killed and 2 wounded, and 2 Enrolled Missouri Militia (one a lieutenant) killed by Coffee's men after they had been paroled. The rebels had 5 killed and 9 wounded that I have learned of. I believe their loss was greater. Our men fought bravely, and we could not have been taken if the enemy had had no artillery.

General Shelby was in command of the rebel forces, which I estimated at 1,500; they claimed to be 2,200 strong. They had three pieces of artillery, one of them a good gun, the other two indifferent. I understood that one of the indifferent ones got bursted or otherwise damaged at Neosho.

I have the honor to be, very respectfully, your obedient servant,

C. B. McAFEE,

Captain Third Battalion, Sixth Mo. State Mil. Cav.

Col. J. EDWARDS,

Comdg. Southwestern District of Missouri, Springfield.

No. 14.

Reports of Capt. Henry V. Stall, Sixth Missouri State Militia Cavalry, of action at Neosho, Mo.

NEWTONIA, MO., *October* 4, 1863.

GENERAL: I have the honor to report that, in pursuance of your orders, I moved my command from Neosho to this place (court having adjourned at that place). About 1 mile from Neosho, the train of Captain McAfee was attacked and mostly captured. My train had just passed that of Captain McAfee, but I succeeded in bringing it out, with the loss of 2 men wounded. I had left 30 of my men at Neosho, to receive Captain McAfee's baggage, &c., when it should arrive there. This force of the rebels is evidently strong. They have some artillery, which I heard some distance off, engaging, as I supposed, Captain McAfee's command.

From the best information I can obtain, I am confident that the forces of Coffee or Shelby are in this vicinity. I shall send my train to Mount Vernon to-night, and take what force I can raise here and go and reconnoiter in the direction of Neosho.

I am, sir, respectfully, your obedient servant,

HENRY V. STALL,

Captain, Commanding Detachment.

Brigadier-General McNEIL,

Commanding Southwestern District of Missouri.

NEWTONIA, MO., *October* 4, 1863—10.30 p. m.

GENERAL: I have just received reliable information that Captain McAfee, commanding detachment of three companies (I, K, and M) of the Sixth Missouri State Militia Cavalry, was captured at Neosho this afternoon by a rebel force, under command of Coffee, and about 1,200 or 1,500 strong, with three pieces of artillery. The rebels are reported to have burned Neosho, and then moved in the direction of Pineville.

I am, sir, respectfully, your obedient servant,

HENRY V. STALL,
Captain, Commanding.

Brig. Gen. JOHN MCNEIL,
Commanding Southwestern District of Missouri.

No. 15.

Report of Maj. Edward B. Eno, Eighth Missouri State Militia Cavalry, of action at Neosho, Mo.

NEWTONIA, *October* 5, 1863—11 a. m.

COLONEL: Reached here with force from Cassville at 4 a. m. Shelby attacked Captain McAfee at Neosho yesterday, capturing him and his whole force, 165 men, with a train of 6 wagons loaded with subsistence. Captain McAfee fought them as long as he could, but they knocked the court-house down with their artillery (three pieces). Their force is 1,200 or 1,500 strong. They left Neosho for Carthage about 4 o'clock last evening. About 200 prisoners paroled have arrived. I suggest that you order the artillery, with the balance of the cavalry, to join us here, when we could push on and be further re-enforced at Greenfield. Shelby will march night and day to reach Jackson County. If we start after him, subsistence must be sent after us. We have five days' rations. Will arrive to-day.

E. B. ENO,
Major [Eighth] Missouri State Militia [Cavalry].

Col. J. EDWARDS, *Springfield.*

No. 16.

Reports of Col. John D. Allen, Seventh Provisional Enrolled Missouri Militia, of action at Neosho, Mo.

NEWTONIA, *October* 5, 1863.

COLONEL: General Shelby, with a force estimated at from 1,000 to 1,500, stated by them as 2,200, attacked Captain McAfee at Neosho yesterday at 1.30 p. m. Enemy have three pieces of artillery. Captain [C. B.] McAfee, after a short fight, surrendered, having 7 or 8 killed and wounded. His force was 185 men. Prisoners were paroled yesterday evening, and have arrived. The enemy left Neosho yesterday evening about 4 o'clock, in direction of Carthage. We reached here about 4 a. m. Major [A. A.] King has just arrived. Our total force is 550. Coffee is with the enemy, and probably will visit Greenfield.

Shelby will probably attempt to go to Jackson County. Can you re-enforce us, and with artillery? No commissary stores here. Our commissary stores from Cassville not yet arrived. Will arrive by night.

JOHN D. ALLEN,
Colonel, Commanding.

Col. J. EDWARDS, *Springfield, Mo.*

NEWTONIA, *October* 5, [1863]—6.30 p. m.

COLONEL: A soldier just in, who was released by the enemy 4 miles this side of Carthage at 9 o'clock this morning, states that he heard their guns firing at Carthage; that part would go by Greenfield; all were destined for Jackson County, and were taking away all the wagons they could find. They are going to take their plunder out. We will move rapidly, via Brownsville, to-night, to Greenfield. Our subsistence should meet us on the 7th or night of 6th. You can send the artillery, via Mount Vernon, to Greenfield, which do rapidly, if possible.

JOHN D. ALLEN,
Colonel, Commanding.

Col. J. EDWARDS, *Springfield, Mo.*

No. 17.

Report of Maj. Wick Morgan, Seventh Provisional Enrolled Missouri Militia, of skirmish at Greenfield, Mo.

HEADQUARTERS,
Melville, Mo., October 6, 1863—11 a. m.

GENERAL: Stockton was taken last night. What damage done not known. Greenfield was taken this morning just at daylight. It is supposed to be Shelby's command there. Is supposed to be 4,000 strong (cavalry). I had one company at Greenfield; had 30 men out on patrol scout; some sick; several on detached service. I managed to get my men in the brush all safe. They are coming in here. My patrols have not come in yet. I have sent out for them, and sent men to watch the enemy.

Yours, respectfully,

WICK MORGAN,
Major, Commanding.

General JOHN MCNEIL.

(Please send this to General Holland.)

HDQRS. FOURTH MIL. DIST., ENROLLED MISSOURI MILITIA,
Springfield, October 6, 1863.

COLONEL: The bearer, Mr. Morgan, brings a verbal dispatch from his son, Major [Wick] Morgan, commanding at Greenfield. The enemy, about daylight this morning, surrounded Greenfield. Major Morgan succeeded in drawing off his men (one company) before they had completed investing it, and did not lose any of his men.

Very respectfully, your obedient servant,

CHAS. SHEPPARD,
Assistant Adjutant-General.

Col. J. EDWARDS,
Commanding District of Southwestern Missouri.

OCTOBER 6, 1863—2 p. m.

This dispatch has just been brought in from Greenfield.

A. W. BISHOP,
Lieutenant-Colonel, &c., Commanding Post.

[Indorsement.]

Captain LAURANT:

Order Colonel Campbell, at Cassville, to send back immediately Lieutenant Espey, with his battery, and Lieutenants [C.] Finley and Phelps, to Springfield. Telegraph him for Colonel Campbell not to send the ammunition over to Colonel Harrison, at Newtonia; for Colonel Campbell to hold Cassville with his infantry and Lieutenant George's command. Order them to hurry up. Telegraph General Schofield the enemy were in Greenfield this morning, 2,000 strong, going northeast. I am after them.

JNO. EDWARDS,
Colonel, Commanding.

No. 18.

Reports of Col. M. La Rue Harrison, First Arkansas Cavalry (Union), of operations October 15–21.

HEADQUARTERS,
Cross Timbers, via Cassville, October 15, 1863.

GENERAL: Brooks and Brown attacked our train this morning at sunrise with a large force, claimed by rebels to be 1,000 men, but estimated by citizens to be 600. They were gallantly repulsed by Major [E.] Fitch, commanding escort. He was supported by Captain [J.] Ray, with his company of Eighteenth Iowa Infantry, and Lieutenant [William] Mayes, with one section of Stark's battery, all of whom behaved nobly. I had already started for Fayetteville, with two battalions of the First Arkansas Cavalry, Captain [D. D.] Stark, and one section of his battery, and the First Arkansas Howitzers. After having marched 7 miles, on hearing the firing, I returned rapidly, but arrived about fifteen minutes after the enemy had retreated. Our loss, 1 sergeant and 1 private killed, 1 private mortally wounded, and 1 taken prisoner. Enemy's loss not known. I shall retain my whole command as escort to the train, and move as rapidly as possible to Fayetteville.

M. LA RUE HARRISON,
Colonel, Commanding Arkansas Volunteers.

Brigadier-General MCNEIL, *Commanding.*

HEADQUARTERS,
Fayetteville, Ark., October 21, 1863—6 p. m.

GENERAL: After the attack by Brooks and Brown, on the 15th instant, at Cross Timbers (in which the enemy lost 15 killed and quite a number wounded), I remained with the whole command, escorting the train to this place, where it arrived on the 18th instant. Learning on that day that Brooks and Brown had passed Elm Springs early in the morning, with about 1,000 men, and that they would probably camp at Brown's Mill, 5 miles northwest of Elm Spring, I immediately ordered out 300 dismounted men, 280 mounted men, and four pieces of artillery, and started in pursuit at 1 a. m. of the 19th, expecting to strike the enemy at daybreak. I reached Brown's Mill (17 miles) at sunrise, and found that the enemy had moved toward Maysville by a neighborhood road at noon of the day previous. So many men being dismounted, and both men and horses being completely exhausted by the eleven days' Missouri expedition, I was forced to abandon the pursuit until I should be able to renew it with mounted men on fresh horses. I learn since that the enemy left the Maysville road on our return and went toward Huntsville, by way of Black's Mill. They are well mounted. I have tried in vain to force them to an engagement. They will not fight, and never intend to.

My horses must have a little rest before doing much duty. I have nearly 100 men unfit for duty from the effects of the 34-miles march of Sunday last.

I hardly know which way you wish my men to move to-morrow. You will please send a messenger to them at Black's Mill to-morrow noon with orders. You will probably find Brooks (if he does not run) in camp, 4 miles east of Huntsville.

I remain, general, your obedient servant,

M. LA RUE HARRISON,
Colonel, Commanding Arkansas Volunteers.

Brigadier-General McNEIL.

No. 19.

Report of Capt. DeWitt C. Hopkins, First Arkansas Cavalry (Union), of skirmish on Deer Creek.

NORTH PRAIRIE, *October* 16, 1863.

SIR: On my arriving within one-half mile of Duroc, I met the enemy, about 150 or 200. It was on Deer Creek. I formed my men and sent out skirmishers. They moved around and had me in a half circle. They charged us with a yell; we repulsed them the first time, then they charged again. I lost 5 of my men, and it was impossible to hold out longer. I took the woods, and brought my men off in good order, disputing every inch of the ground. I killed a number of them. I came to this place, 12 miles from that place, and will watch the road and find out as much as possible. I have men out on the scout to try and learn their number. There are a number of land fires on the other side of the river; think they are the enemy's.

I am, sir, your obedient servant,

D. C. HOPKINS,
Commanding Scout.

General McNEIL.

No. 20.

Reports of Brig. Gen. Thomas Ewing, jr., U. S. Army, commanding District of the Border, of operations October 12-21.

SEDALIA, *October* 12, 1863—7 p. m.

COLONEL: I got here at 11 a. m. from Knobnoster, and Colonel Weer from same point, four hours behind me. I have waited all day for dispatches from General Brown, but have not a word since 11 a. m. yesterday. The failure can only be accounted for on the supposition that bushwhackers or stragglers or scouting parties cut off the messengers. A party of 4, sent by Colonel [G. H.] Hall in the night, have returned this evening, being driven back, not getting through.

I sent a strong party through this afternoon, and move all my command to-night toward Boonville. I cannot get there before noon to-morrow, as it is dark and raining violently. I can now whip Shelby with my command, and will catch up with him if he keeps his command together, unless he changes all his horses.

My convictions are that if Shelby gets out of Boonville, he will try to get out west or southwest. Hence I would go up the west side of La Mine until I could hear from General Brown, but for the fact that the road is very rough and hard to travel, and the rumors of fighting at Boonville are so frequent and persistent that I cannot fail to move toward it to-night.

I am, very respectfully, your obedient servant,

THOMAS EWING, JR.,
Brigadier-General.

Lieut. Col. C. W. MARSH,
Assistant Adjutant-General, &c.

FOUR MILES SOUTHWEST OF CHILHOWEE, MO.,
October 14, 1863—10.30 a. m.

GENERAL: I failed to co-operate with General Brown because I had to delay for information and make wrong moves on rumors, getting no word from him of any avail to me, and, from the separation of nearly all my cavalry from the rest of my command, being unable to scout the country thoroughly for information as to the enemy's movements. Some of General Brown's messages are known to have miscarried. I started at 1 a. m. from Knobnoster, and came by Warrensburg, and reached Shelby's trail three hours behind the column. This is 10 miles southwest of Warrensburg. I can't overtake them before they reach Clinton, as my stock has had no feed or rest since 1 a. m; but I can probably harass them, so as to keep them out of Clinton. Colonel Weer is 3 miles behind. Lazear was to leave Warrensburg at 8 this morning, going northwest, on a venture as to the enemy's whereabouts. Colonel Neill was at Warrensburg this morning, and going down to Clinton to-day. The Seventh Missouri camped last night 17 miles southeast of Lexington. I suppose a part of General Brown's command is following about half Shelby's force, which passed down Boonville and Warsaw road. I have advised commanding officers at Warrensburg, Cole Camp, and Fort Scott, and also Colonel Lazear. I will follow as long as the enemy keep together. They number 400 to 600.

THOMAS EWING, JR.,
Brigadier-General.

Maj. Gen. JOHN M. SCHOFIELD, *Saint Louis, Mo.*

CROOKED CREEK,
Fifteen Miles East of Butler, October 14, 1863—7 p. m.

GENERAL: I overtook enemy's rear guard in timber here at sundown, and had some skirmishing, killing 1 and capturing several. I am compelled to halt half the night for food and rest. Hope to have fresh troops from Clinton, Fort Scott, and border stations by to-morrow night. Enemy turned from Clinton road, and now moves toward Papinsville. Weer can't catch up, I fear.

THOMAS EWING, JR.,
Brigadier-General.

Maj. Gen. JOHN M. SCHOFIELD,
Saint Louis, Mo.

CARTHAGE, MO., *October* 18, 1863—8 a. m.

GENERAL: After a march of 76 miles in twenty-four hours, I reached here at daylight, expecting to encounter Shelby's whole command. He passed through here, however, last night for Neosho, leaving a small command of about 30 to run the mill and collect stragglers. These I captured, with their horses, arms, and equipments. Among the prisoners are Maj. J. F. Pickler and other officers and men belonging to seven different Missouri regiments. Throughout the pursuit, and especially for the last 50 miles, the trail has been lined with Shelby's horses, broken down in the chase. His men have been leading large numbers of horses, stolen in La Fayette County, to supply the place of those abandoned. He has no transportation nor artillery, keeps no roads, and is hard to follow rapidly by night. I think, if not re-enforced from below, he will push on to the Arkansas, without unnecessary halt, though his command is suffering intensely for want of rest.

THOMAS EWING, JR.,
Brigadier-General.

Major-General SCHOFIELD.

CARTHAGE, *October* 18, 1863—9 a. m.

GENERAL: Having heard that General McNeil will be in Sarcoxie to-night, I write him, offering co-operation. I had intended a march to-morrow night on Newtonia, where I expect Shelby to concentrate and remain a day or two to get flour, unless pursued at once. I hear reports from scouts and otherwise that Marmaduke is advancing from Fayetteville to re-enforce Shelby, and will not withdraw any considerable number of troops until I ascertain what foundation there is for the report.

THOMAS EWING, JR.,
Brigadier-General.

Maj. Gen. JOHN M. SCHOFIELD,
Saint Louis, Mo.

DIAMOND SPRING, MO.,
October 21, 1863—1 p. m.

GENERAL: Yesterday at daybreak General McNeil wrote from Sarcoxie, in reply to my proffer of assistance, that he was strong enough without me. I had before sent a strong scouting party, via Neosho and

Pineville, which has reported that Shelby's force, which we pursued, passed west of Pineville Sunday night, going south.

I this morning received a letter from the commanding officer at Cassville, saying General McNeil will be at Elkhorn to-night, and wants me to march there. I go at once; infantry afoot, horses going back to Fort Scott, and escorting trains for rations and clothing. My force, 350 infantry, 500 to 600 cavalry, two small rifled steel guns, and two mountain howitzers.

THOMAS EWING, JR.,
Brigadier-General.

Major-General SCHOFIELD.

No. 21.

Reports of Maj. Richard H. Brown, Twelfth Missouri Cavalry, District of Saint Louis, of operations October 9-19.

LA MINE BRIDGE, *October* 15, 1863—7 p. m.

Brigadier-General TOTTEN:

Major [T. W.] Houts, commanding detachment of Seventh Regiment Missouri State Militia, has just returned from pursuing the rebels, and reports that 500 of them camped 16 miles south of this place and near Florence; also that they are making for the Osage, between Cole Camp and Versailles. They have one piece of artillery. General Brown was at Sedalia this morning. I started 10 wagon loads of rations to him. The force of rebels that crossed west of this place will probably form a junction near the Osage. Lieutenant-Colonel Cole will probably give you the particulars of the fight at Marshall. I received your dispatch at 4 p. m. to-day. Several scouts that I sent to Generals Brown and Ewing were captured yesterday. I have got some horses from the rebels, and shall mount scouts for my use.

R. H. BROWN,
Major, Commanding.

N. B.—This dispatch is dated 13th. Operator at Tipton says it is so dated in his copy, but that it should have been 15th. Don't know how he knows.

HANFORD,
Telegraph Operator.

HEADQUARTERS SAINT LOUIS DISTRICT,
October 25, 1863.

COLONEL: I have the honor to report that, in pursuance of Special Orders, No. 93, dated Headquarters Saint Louis District, October 9, 1863, I gathered together on that date all the effective men at Benton Barracks, Soldiers' Home, and Schofield Barracks, No. 1, amounting, in all, to 250 men. For 200 of these I drew arms and equipments from Major [F. D.] Callender, commanding Saint Louis Arsenal, and divided the detachments into four companies, placing them, respectively, under the charge of the following-named commissioned officers, properly belonging to the First Regiment Nebraska Volunteer Infantry: Company A, Captain [S. M.] Curran; Company B, Lieut. Morgan A. Hance; Company C, Lieut. Theodore Lubbes, and Company D, Lieut. Lewis Lowry. To each of these officers I issued 50 Springfield rifle-muskets, caliber .69, model 1842, and the necessary accouterments, with 40 rounds of ammunition to each man, and had the detachment ready to move at 8 p. m. of the 9th instant. At 10 p. m., in compliance with verbal orders received from you, I marched the detachment to the Fourteenth street depot of the Pacific Railroad, with the exception of a few men who were too sick to travel; these I left at Schofield Barracks. On arriving at the Pacific Railroad depot, my detachment was put on board the cars, with two companies of the Second Regiment Missouri Artillery, Lieutenant-Colonel [N.] Cole, of that regiment, assuming command of the entire force, and we left for Jefferson City at 11.30 p. m., arriving at 7 a. m. of the 10th instant. After staying at Jefferson City about four hours, and drawing a supply of rations and necessary cooking utensils, also getting a detail of one assistant surgeon to take care of the sick and a lieutenant to assist in commanding the detachment of convalescents, Lieutenant-Colonel Cole was ordered to proceed, with his command and one piece of the First Kansas Battery, to California, Moniteau County, Missouri, and assume command of that post, taking arms for the Thirty-fifth Regiment Enrolled Missouri Militia, Colonel Hickox commanding. The entire command remained at California until the afternoon of the 11th instant, at which time Lieutenant-Colonel Cole was ordered to make a reconnaissance with the locomotive and necessary cars to Tipton, which he did, taking with him one piece of artillery, with men sufficient to man the gun, and 25 picked men from Captain Curran's company, to act as sharpshooters on the train; also 85 mounted men from Lieutenant-Colonel [J. D.] Brutsche's command of provisional troops, to act as flankers along the railroad. Whilst he was absent I received a large supply of commissary stores from Jefferson City; also dispatches from Lieutenant-Colonel Lazear, then in pursuit of the enemy from Tipton toward Boonville, with 1,100 men. These dispatches I forwarded, by telegraph, to Brigadier-General Totten, at Jefferson City, and in reply received an order to get all the cavalry together that I could, and furnish them with ammunition and five days' rations of bread and meat, ordering them to report, without delay, to Lieutenant-Colonel Cole, at Tipton. This I did, sending the balance of Lieutenant-Colonel Brutsche's command, amounting to 175 men, and 75 men from the Thirty-fifth Regiment Enrolled Missouri Militia, under the command of Colonel Hickox, making an aggregate of 375 mounted men and one piece of artillery. With this force, Lieutenant-Colonel Cole, of the Second Missouri Artillery, started from Tipton on the night of the 11th, in pursuit of the enemy, toward Boonville, with instructions to join Lieutenant-Colonel Lazear's command, if possible.

On the 12th instant, I received an order from Brig. Gen. James Totten to hold my command in readiness to move, and to get 100 of the Thirty-fifth Regiment Enrolled Missouri Militia ready to move to Tipton, to relieve a company of the Second Regiment Missouri Artillery that I had sent to that place in pursuance of orders received from him on the morning of the 12th. On the same day I received an order from the general commanding to assume command of four companies of the First Missouri State Militia, on their arrival at California with 60,000 rations for the army of Generals Brown and Ewing, and to proceed with my entire command to La Mine Bridge, and report by messenger to commanding officers of troops in that vicinity, and supply them with subsistence. In compliance with special order issued to Captain [J.] Dietrich, then in command of a battalion of First Missouri State Militia, guarding subsistence stores from Jefferson City to California, at 5 p. m. of the 12th instant, on the arrival of the train, I put my entire command on the cars, composed as follows: One company of the Second Regiment Missouri Artillery, four companies of convalescents, and four companies of the First Regiment Missouri State Militia, as well as a detachment of 100 men belonging to the Thirty-fifth Regiment Enrolled Missouri Militia, with whom I relieved a company of the Second Regiment Missouri Artillery at Tipton, and, taking 12 mounted men to act as scouts, I proceeded to La Mine Bridge, with an aggregate of 550 men, 12 horses, and 70,000 rations. At Syracuse I found one company of the First Missouri State Militia Cavalry, guarding a train of wagons belonging to the force under Lieutenant-Colonel Lazear, then supposed to be in pursuit of the enemy near Boonville. Ten of these men I had detailed for the purpose of carrying a message to the commanding officer at Sedalia, in accordance with instructions received from Brigadier-General Totten. On arriving at La Mine Bridge at 12 p. m. of the 12th, I started parties of mounted men out in all directions to obtain information of the movements of the rebels, and to carry information to the commanding officers of our forces in the field of my arrival at La Mine Bridge with 60,000 rations, under the charge of Captain [E.] Harding, commissary of subsistence.

At 10 a. m. of the next day, 10 six-horse wagons arrived from Sedalia, under the charge of Captain [J. E.] Howard, commissary of subsistence at that post. These wagons I had loaded and ready to move toward Sedalia by 4.10 p. m., but just as they were going to start, a report was brought into camp that the rebels were at Lebanon, 1,000 strong, and one piece of artillery, robbing the citizens of horses and all property that they could carry off. I immediately sent out a party of 10 mounted men, belonging to Captain Howard's escort, to watch the movement of the rebels, and see as to the truth of the citizen's statement, sending him along as a guide. I also sent a message to Tipton by the locomotive, under the charge of Captain Curran, of the First Regiment Nebraska Volunteers, to be forwarded by telegraph to Brigadier-General Totten, at Jefferson City, informing him of the position of the enemy. I also placed my men in what I considered the best position for successfully defending the large amount of public property in my charge. My encampment was on a piece of cleared land, nearly the shape of a horseshoe; this was caused by the La Mine River running in a crescent-like shape in my rear. In my front was an almost perpendicular bluff, with two ravines, by which infantry could gain the top, immediately under the bluff and sheltered from all fire. In front was the train of railroad cars, with 60,000 rations aboard; in the rear of the railroad, and completely hid from the sight of the enemy, yet covered and under the protection of my own men, was Captain Howard's train of 10 wagons and 10,000 rations. I immediately detailed one company, to be divided into squads, and placed so as to command all approaches to the camp; and as a report came into camp that the enemy was approaching, I ordered one company of the First Missouri State Militia to deploy as skirmishers in the timber on the east side of my camp, and one on the west side. I also ordered three companies of convalescents to deploy as skirmishers on the top of the bluff, and one company to be held as a reserve; one company I placed behind the railroad track, so as to defend the railroad train and Captain Howard's wagon train; two companies of the Second Regiment Missouri Artillery I kept in line, to move anywhere they might be needed, and the camp guard watching the river in my rear.

At 4.20 p. m., a company of the First Missouri State Militia Cavalry came with a train of 30 wagons, driving furiously toward my camp.

The wagons I ordered to be parked in the open space of ground in the rear of the railroad, and under the cover of my men on the bluff, with each driver holding the team well in hand. I then took the company of cavalry and divided it into two squads, and sent them out on the main roads leading toward Lebanon, to watch the approach of the rebels. At 4.30 o'clock, a squad of cavalry brought me intelligence that the enemy was crossing the railroad 2 miles east of my camp; but as the locomotive was then absent with dispatches to Tipton, I could not send infantry to hold them in check, and I had but about 30 mounted men at hand; these I sent after them to pick up stragglers and harass their rear. I also sent one entire company of infantry on foot to watch the crossing of the railroad, and another to stay in ambush for any small squad of rebels that might be following the main body. I also sent as soon as possible 10 mounted men with a dispatch to Brigadier-General Brown (whom I naturally supposed would be on the heels of the rebels), informing him at what point the rebels crossed the railroad, and that I could furnish him with a wagon train ready loaded with provisions, so that there need be no delay in the pursuit of the enemy. I also telegraphed General Totten, at Jefferson City, the direction the rebels had taken, so that a force might get between them and Warsaw on the way to the Osage River, and it would be well, perhaps, to state that there was a rumor among the people around Otterville that General Price was expected to come through the country with 3,000 men and some artillery. What gave tone to this rumor was the fact that a number of men from that section of country known to belong to General Price's body guard was with Shelby, and I do believe that Shelby's raid was merely a feeler to find out what kind of a reception a larger force would receive. This belief is strengthened by the fact that the rebels tried to conciliate as much as possible the people in the country through which they passed.

In reviewing the conduct of the commissioned officers and enlisted men during the expected attack of the enemy, it is but justice to them to state that, with a few exceptions, they behaved admirably; the enlisted men going as steadily to their positions as if it was an every day occurrence; especially was this the case with the four companies of stragglers, although some of them had barely sufficient clothing to cover their nakedness—without a murmur, they bivouacked all night without fire, some of them not having a blanket or covering of any kind—and I would also respectfully state that I consider the enlisted men of the detachment of the First Missouri State Militia well calculated to do good service in the field if placed under the charge of commissioned officers who will fearlessly enforce their orders.

The detachment of the Second Regiment Missouri Artillery were well behaved, and I had no trouble with them during the time they were under my command, and to Lieut. Henry Troll, of that regiment, I am under great obligations for the efficient manner in which he did his duty as officer of the day, enforcing my orders and keeping the camp in good order; also to Capt. Edward Harding, commissary of subsistence, for providing for the wants of the men during our stay at La Mine Bridge. It would be well, perhaps, to state that when the four companies of the First Regiment Missouri State Militia joined my command there was considerable disorder among the enlisted men of that regiment and a continuous hurrahing for Jim Lane and cursing of General Totten; also a considerable disposition shown among the men to appropriate other people's property in the shape of sheep, chickens, &c., to their own use, thereby setting a pernicious example to the balance of the command, and, as some of the commissioned officers did not appear to interest themselves in the suppression of these irregularities, I felt it my duty to issue an order calling the attention of the entire command to the fact that a strict compliance with revised Army Regulations and existing orders would be required of both commissioned officers and enlisted men, and that no enlisted man should be allowed to take his gun outside of the camp line unless on duty. By this means, and the assistance of some of the commissioned officers, I stopped to a great extent the propensity to rob the people of their property, and had my camp in good order during my stay at La Mine Bridge.

On the 19th instant, I was ordered by Brigadier-General Brown to prepare to move to Saint Louis with my entire command, and at 11 o'clock the next day, on the arrival of two companies of the Ninth Regiment Minnesota Volunteers, I left La Mine Bridge with my command, taking 13 captured horses, to turn over to the post quartermaster at Jefferson City.

On the 20th, I had a camp and picket guard detailed as usual, and instructed Morgan A. Hance, first lieutenant of Company G, First Regiment Nebraska Volunteer Infantry, who was detailed as officer of the day, to have 10 good men picked from the number detailed for guard, and whenever the railroad train stopped betwixt La Mine Bridge and Saint Louis to have these guards placed so as to stop the men from straggling from the cars and getting whisky or stealing people's property. The latter part of this order, I am sorry to say, he did not obey, and when the train stopped near Pacific City, between 100 and 200 men entered the orchard of a citizen and stole a large quantity of fruit, and when I ordered Lieutenant Hance to have his guard keep the men on the cars, he simply went out of the passenger car and returned in a minute stating that he could not find the guard; this whilst the officer of the guard was standing by his side. Indeed, the conduct of this officer has been such during the entire trip that I would not recommend him to take charge of a corporal's squad, and I felt it to be my duty to place him under arrest for neglect of duty, reporting his case to you, and awaiting further instructions as to whether I should prefer charges against him or not.

I would also respectfully state that, on my arrival at Saint Louis, my entire command was disposed of in accordance with your instructions.

I have the honor to be, very respectfully, your obedient servant,

R. H. BROWN,
Major Twelfth Regiment Missouri Volunteer Cavalry.

R. R. LIVINGSTON,
Colonel First Regiment Nebraska Volunteer Infantry,
Commanding District of Saint Louis, Saint Louis, Mo.

No. 22.

Report of Lieut. Col. Quin Morton, Twenty-third Missouri Infantry, District of Rolla, of operations October 7–22.

HEADQUARTERS POST,
Rolla, Mo., October 23, 1863.

GENERAL: In obedience to your order of October 7, 1863, I assumed command of three companies of Twenty-third Missouri Volunteers, and marched from this place at 5 p. m. for Lebanon. I was joined by three companies of Second Wisconsin Cavalry Volunteers before reaching

Waynesville. We reached Lebanon on the 8th, at 4 p. m.; reported to Colonel Gravely. Left Lebanon at 2 p. m. on the 9th, in command of 600 men, consisting of four companies of Eighth Missouri State Militia, two companies Fifth Missouri State Militia, under Major [W.] Fischer; three companies of Second Wisconsin Cavalry Volunteers, and three companies of Twenty-third Missouri Volunteer Infantry. Marched slowly, in obedience to Major-General Schofield's order, for two days, awaiting three companies of Eleventh Missouri Cavalry Volunteers, under command of Captain Kauffman. Arrived on the Little Niangua on the 10th; communicated with Colonel Edwards, commanding Southwest District; found that the enemy had left Warsaw. Colonel Edwards was falling back south, although the enemy were going north, scouts informed, and General Schofield telegraphed me that the enemy would probably cross the river at Linn Creek. I marched for that place on the 11th, arriving in the evening; received order, dated 12th, from Colonel Edwards, to fall back to Lebanon, which order I declined to obey. On the 12th, was joined by Captain Kauffman and three companies of Eleventh Missouri Volunteers. I sent four companies of cavalry to Tuscumbia, to hold the fords from Brockman's to 15 miles below Tuscumbia. One company of Fifth Missouri State Militia held the fords from Brockman's to Linn Creek. One company of Fifth Missouri State Militia held Cabell's Ford, 10 miles above Linn Creek. On the 15th, I received information from General Totten that Colonel Edwards was holding the fords from Warsaw down the river with 1,500 men. On the 16th, received order from General Totten to hold fords as far west as Warsaw. Sent Major Fischer at daylight on the 17th with five companies of cavalry, in obedience to order. He reached Rainy Creek Ford that evening, but the enemy had crossed on the night of the 15th, about 200 strong, Colonel Edwards having drawn his forces off. On the evening of the 18th, a message from Colonel Gravely informed me that the enemy were threatening Lebanon. I ordered all the available force to march immediately. They left at 12 p. m.; reached Lebanon at 9 o'clock on the 19th. On the evening of the 19th, I arrived at that place with four companies of cavalry and one of infantry. On arriving, I received orders from Major-General Schofield to march my infantry to this place; reached here on 22d, noon.

I am, respectfully, your obedient servant,

QUIN MORTON,
Lieutenant-Colonel, Commanding Post.

Brig. Gen. THOMAS A. DAVIES,
Commanding District of Rolla.

No. 23.

Report of Brig. Gen. Colly B. Holland, Enrolled Missouri Militia.

HEADQUARTERS,
Mount Vernon, October 18, 1863.

COLONEL: I arrived this morning at 3 o'clock, traveling all night and night before. Men and horses pretty well worn out. Got in enemy's advance before they got to Greenfield. They passed around Greenfield, traveling through the woods part of the time. By my orders, Captains Holden and Maiss followed, with instructions to give me information from time to time of their whereabouts, and also Major Hart to advance on them, it being impossible to follow them in main force, on account of our artillery and wagons. Major Hart engaged them 8 miles east of here, and sent for re-enforcements. I sent immediately Colonel Jones with all his available men to Marionville, to intercept them, having previously sent Captain Roberts with fresh horses and men and part of Colonel Boyd's men, in charge of Lieutenant Robertson, to move forward, leaving all their wagons, &c. I hope to announce capture and rout of the enemy. Colonels McMahon and King, I suppose, are following another party west; have not heard from them since their success at Humansville, taking one piece of artillery. The party going out this way is from 1,200 to 1,500 men, many bareheaded. We have pursued them closely; they have had no time to plunder since we got near them at Quincy. General McNeil has moved toward Sarcoxie, ready for emergencies; is in pursuit of Shelby and Coffee, they having about 600 men.

Your obedient servant,

C. B. HOLLAND,
Brigadier-General, Commanding.

Lieut. Col. A. W. BISHOP,
Commanding at Springfield, Mo.

No. 24.

Reports of Col. Joseph O. Shelby, Fifth Missouri Cavalry (Confederate), commanding expedition, of operations September 22–November 3.

CAMP PRICE,
Two miles west of Washington, Hempstead Co., Ark., Nov. 4, 1863.

GENERAL: I have arrived safely with my entire command, increased about 600. I have fought five battles; had daily skirmishes; traveled 1,500 miles; captured and paroled 500 prisoners; destroyed 6 railroad bridges; torn up 30 miles of track; entered Boonville; marched to Marshall; met Generals Brown and Ewing there with 8,000 men; fought them six hours; lost 125 men; expended all my ammunition, and retreated in splendid order. The trail of the rifled gun broke short off, and I was forced to leave it. The wagons I carried off 20 miles and sunk in the river at Waverly. The brass gun I brought to Humansville, where General [John] McNeil pressed my rear so closely that I was forced to leave it after the horses were completely exhausted. My men and horses are worn out, and must rest here for a week or two. I would be pleased if you would send me all my wagons and the rest of my men now with you, so I can organize and get them in condition again. I will communicate more fully in the course of five or six days.

Very respectfully,

JO. O. SHELBY,
Colonel, Commanding Expedition.

General J. S. MARMADUKE,
Commanding Cavalry Forces.

HEADQUARTERS SHELBY'S BRIGADE,
Camp Price, November 16, 1863.

MAJOR: I have the honor to make to you the following detailed report of my operations in Arkansas and Missouri:

On September 21, I received General Price's final orders, and on the next day (the 22d) started on the march for 1,500 miles. My command consisted of detachments from the three regiments composing my brigade, [Benjamin] Elliott's battalion of scouts, and a section of two pieces of artillery, under Lieutenant [David] Harris, of [Joseph] Bledsoe's battery, the entire force numbering about 600 men, rank and file. The weather was propitious, and the glorious skies of a southern autumn flashed cheerily down upon waving banners and glittering steel as we marched proudly by the white-haired chieftain, General Price, and his hearty benediction was solemnly prophetic of my entire success.

From the 23d to the 27th I traveled hard, determining to force the line of the Arkansas River before notice could possibly be given of my advances, and then, if necessary, rest in the Boston Mountains, whose fast and eternal precipices could bear no fatal dispatch ahead.

My advance on the 27th, always led by the daring and dashing [W. W.] Thorp, skirmished for miles with these Federal outlaws and jayhawkers, always killing or scattering them, when suddenly he ran directly upon some 200 of the First Arkansas Infantry; charged them furiously, but they, gaining the cover of heavy timber, forced Thorp back from range. I immediately ordered two regiments to dismount, who skirmished with them until [G. P.] Gordon and [David] Shanks got on either flank, when a simultaneous charge scattered them like chaff, and our rough riders rode them down like stubble to the lava tide. The enemy's loss was about 10 killed, 20 wounded, and 50 prisoners. This fight occurred 12 miles from the Arkansas River, so I determined to push rapidly for it, cross, and pass north of Ozark before morning. The fording was shallow, but treacherous and dangerous from the shifting sands, yet no accident marred the spirits of the men, and the last beams of the golden sun went down upon 600 veterans with bright eyes looking far away northward, and the stern purpose in their hearts to conquer or die. After halting two hours, feeding both men and horses, distributing captured property (which consisted of three wagons loaded with quartermasters' and commissary supplies), and scouting well toward Clarksville and Dardanelle, I commenced march again at 10 o'clock, and by daylight passed through Ozark, and continued over the Boston Mountains to Mulberry Creek, where the tired and jaded horses had rest. For the next three days I made slow and easy marches, gathering up the utmost strength of my command, for soon it would be stretched to its utmost tension, and the gleam of its banners, yet warm with southern breezes, would sparkle with the frosty diamonds of a northern latitude.

On the 29th, I passed through Huntsville, and encamped for the night at Bentonville, destroying, as I crossed, the telegraph wire, on the Fayetteville road, for miles.

On the 31st, I moved out to McKissick's Springs, and waited until Colonel [D. C.] Hunter joined me with 200 men, which he had been recruiting for some time in Missouri and Arkansas.

October 2, I marched from McKissick's Springs to Pineville, where Missouri breezes blew and Missouri skies looked down upon us. Here Colonel [J. T.] Coffee joined me with 400 men. I had determined to march upon Neosho the night of the 2d, but Colonel Coffee's forces coming in only by squads and companies, I resolved to remain in camp at Pineville until the next morning, in the mean time guarding and picketing every highway and by-way leading in a northerly direction.

At daylight on the morning of the 3d [4th], I started for Neosho, where there were 300 Federal cavalry stationed—a terror to the country, the insulters of unprotected women, and the murderers of old and infirm men. I made my dispositions as follows: Coffee was to make a detour and gain the rear of the town; Gordon to take position on the right flank and extend his line to Coffee, as was Shanks on the left, while I, with [J. C.] Hooper and Hunter, the artillery and the battalion, made the attack and drove them in their fortifications. The plan was well and skillfully carried out, and the doomed enemy were encompassed by a cordon of steel before they knew of a foeman near. Thorp, with his usual dash, drove their pickets into town, where they, with the main body, took refuge in a strong brick court-house, pierced and loop-holed for musketry, where they kept up a hot fire upon our advancing columns. Without artillery this position could only be taken at a heavy sacrifice, and the Federals were already beginning to laugh at the fire of my skirmishers, when I ordered my cannon into position and sent two balls crashing through the walls. This was followed by an immediate demand for unconditional surrender, which, after some little parley, they agreed to, and all their horses, arms, stores, and everything they possessed fell into my hands. The men I paroled and left at liberty, thinking it best not to weaken my command by detaching from it the guards it would have been necessary to furnish to send them to our lines.

Halting in Neosho only long enough to distribute the arms and ammunition, I pushed on rapidly for Sarcoxie, resting on Jones Creek some five hours, and fed my command.

October 4, passed through the blackened and desolated town of Sarcoxie, whose bare and fire-scarred chimneys point with skeleton fingers to heaven for vengeance; then to the town of Oregon, or Bowers' Mill, a notorious pest spot for the militia, which was sacked and then swept from the face of the earth, to pollute it no more forever, and halted within 18 miles of Greenfield.

By daylight of the 5th the town was surrounded. The nest was there, and warm, but the birds had flown. Our advance had a brief, short fight with their rear, killing some and capturing some. Here I appropriated the contents of several stores, captured a quantity of arms, and destroyed a strong fort, and rested for the night 10 miles north of Stockton, after burning a fort there and driving out a few militia.

All along this road the inhabitants had their household furniture taken from their houses, and waiting in silence and in sorrow for us to apply the torch, it having been represented to them that my command was laying the country waste, as though God had sent the whirlwind and the storm to drive back the laws of nature and desolate the land with fire, pestilence, and famine. On this route every house belonging to a Southern family has been burned, and the family as effectually destroyed as if the waves of the Dead Sea had rolled over them with their dread monotony.

October 6, passed through Humansville and encamped within 10 miles of Warsaw, capturing on the road some 30 Government wagons, and picking up many prisoners. This day's march was fruitful of good horses, and many changed hands in a few hours. At Humansville a force of militia attempted to dispute the march of my victorious army, but they were charged and scattered, and driven like sheep to the thick undergrowth and timber that skirts the town.

On the morning of the 7th, I reached Warsaw, and found the Federals drawn up in line of battle to dispute the crossing of the river. Before reaching the town, however, I had sent Gordon's regiment to cut them off from the road toward Osceola and the battalion on the east. Dismounting Hooper's regiment, I formed them in line of battle and sent them straight for the ford, which was about 2 feet deep. The men, impatient for the fray, dashed across the river, deployed as skirmishers, and, supported by Shanks and Hunter, drove all opposition away, and soon the banner of the bars flung its proud folds on the breeze, emblem of a pure and high nationality. Vast quantities of all kinds of stores were captured here, with some arms and prisoners, and a strong and well provisioned fort. Thus far I had traveled ahead of all information, but now the telegraph flashed out its view-halloo, and the railroads groaned under the dire preparations to meet me, and the thunderer of Saint Louis threatened vengeance as dark as death and terrible as the grave.

Upon the 8th and 9th, I leisurely marched through Cole Camp, the cradle of most of liberty in Missouri, and the fount of glory to the gallant [W. S.] O'Kane, and Florence, another beautiful little town in this most beautiful section. Vast herds of horses covered the prairies, a sight most refreshing to my grim old dragoons, and during the two days quantities of good Union steeds were changed into rebel chargers, and their reckless riders went spurring away for the Missouri River.

At daylight on the 10th, Tipton was surrounded and taken, after driving out a detachment of militia, together with its large depot, stores, and quantities of all kinds of supplies, just missing a party of Federal officers coming down from Sedalia on a kind of reconnaissance with an unattached locomotive. The night before, I picked 100 men of my command, and sent them, under Capt. James Wood, with instructions to attack and destroy the La Mine Bridge at all hazards. Slowly and surely, in the dark and murky night, this gallant officer approached the block-house in which 40 Federals were keeping watch and ward over their precious charge, and before the sentinel on post could give the alarm, he was shot down by Captain Wood, who then, with a wild yell, charged headlong upon the fort. Bloody and brief the fight. The surprise was a panic; the panic a defeat; the defeat almost annihilation. In five minutes not an armed enemy was near, and in five minutes more this magnificent structure, reared at the cost of $400,000, stood tenable against the midnight sky, one mass of hissing, seething, liquid fire. Captain Wood encamped upon the ground and saw the last blackened timber plunge into the gulf below. He then, after paroling the remaining Federals, gathered up their horses, revolvers, guns, and overcoats, and rejoined me the next morning without the loss of a man.

While at Tipton I sent out a cloud of scouts, ordering them to do their worst upon both telegraph and railroad. For 30 miles either way rails were torn up, ties burned, bridges destroyed, wire carried off, and cattle-stops and water-tanks obliterated. Syracuse was also entered, stormed, and some prisoners taken, and by 4 o'clock I was off for Boonville.

Just on the outskirts of Tipton I met Colonel [T. T.] Crittenden drawn up in splendid line with about 1,000 men, ready and willing to dispute my farther advance. I determined to crush him at a blow. Organizing my whole column by eights and closing them well up, I charged with both cavalry and artillery. The enemy, totally unprepared for such close work, wheeled to the rear and retreated in dire confusion. My artillery sent a few balls after them by way of compliment, and leaving a large scout to follow them, I pursued my way. This scout followed them for

10 miles, killing and wounding a great many, for few prisoners were taken.

I had almost forgotten to mention that, during my occupation of Humansville, Lieut. Thomas J. Keithley, of Gordon's regiment, with but 10 men, charged into Osceola, engaged a Federal force of 53, drove them from town, burned a large and strong fort, and returned without losing a man.

On the night of the 10th, a very hard rain-storm came up, and my command were thoroughly drenched, but a genial sun soon drove away the damp air, and Sunday morning came with its golden glow and breath of ripened grain. While yet 10 miles from Boonville, the front axle of my rifled gun broke short off, and I was delayed three hours in its repair. While at work upon it, a flag of truce came out from Boonville, praying mercy and protection, with the offer of unconditional submission.

By 11 o'clock the gun was repaired, and the lofty domes and spires of the city rose towering to view. Again the flag came out, and again was mercy solicited. They knew their evil course, and they feared its consequences. The night before our arrival all the citizens had been armed and resistance determined on, but daylight brought sober reason, and the trembling mayor was only too glad to take the oath of allegiance. Now the broad bosom of the grand old Missouri lay unvailed before us in the red beams of an autumn [sun], and the men, forgetting all their privations and dangers, broke out in one long, loud, proud hurrah, which sounded above the roar of the cannon and the rattle of musketry, for drawn up on the other side in line of battle was Colonel [Odon] Guitar's regiment, having the ferry-boat in their possession. A few well-directed volleys from my artillery scattered them in every direction, and I saw them no more. In a short time a steamboat came in sight, which was loaded with troops. She was evidently suspicious, and I could [not] possibly by any stratagem decoy her within range of my artillery, and very soon she left in a hurry for Jefferson. Here my gun again broke, and I immediately [set] to work on its repair.

Meanwhile a great storm was gathering. General Brown, with 4,000 men, came up like a black cloud from Jefferson City, where he had been hurriedly concentrating, expecting us to attack him there under the shadow of [Hamilton R.] Gamble's usurped dynasty, and was thundering in my rear with disappointed hate and malice. My pickets were driven in on the main body pell-mell, and the sounds of conflict came nearer and nearer. I resolved to mend my rifled gun if I had to fight to do it, so I ordered Hooper to dismount and hold the enemy in check. Gallantly he obeyed, and soon the far-away sound of battle told that his fierce charge had driven them back for some distance. Skirmishing, with now and then a hot fight, was kept up until 10 o'clock at night, when I had removed to camp, 4 miles from town, with all the stores I needed and the damaged gun thoroughly repaired. Hooper was then quietly withdrawn, and the men enjoyed a good night's repose, which the heavy rain the night before made them stand very much in need of.

At daylight the next morning (the 12th) my pickets were again driven in and the camp aroused. Forming line of battle immediately and choosing a good position, I waited an hour for General [E. B.] Brown, intending to give him battle then, but he not accepting the proffered wager, I moved out slowly on the main Marshall and Boonville road. I captured in Boonville one iron 4-pounder, which, not having any ammunition of sufficient size, was destroyed, with many stand of arms and colors. After traveling perhaps for two hours uninterruptedly, General

Brown again charged my rear furiously, and I saw he must be checked then and there. At the crossing of the La Mine the banks on either side are rugged and precipitous; so stationing Major [G. P.] Gordon with his regiment on the western side, I had him to dismount and ambush them, leaving two companies on the eastern side to fire and then retreat in apparent confusion. The bait took completely, and the yelling, shouting Federals dashed into the stream and up the farther side to within 10 feet of the ambushed Confederates. A hot, close, deadly fire from rifles and revolvers left 50 dead on the spot, many wounded, and the rest routed and demoralized. Among those killed was a Federal colonel, supposed to be Col. Thomas [T.] Crittenden. This modified General Brown's desires somewhat from a vigorous pursuit, but toward night he came on again with a heavy force of cavalry and artillery. Near Jonesborough, at the crossing of Blackwater, I took up my position and waited for developments. Very soon the enemy made a furious attack. In twenty minutes I silenced their batteries, charged and drove them 3 miles, they leaving the ground covered with their killed and wounded. After this my rear was left unmolested, and I halted for the night within 6 miles of Marshall, sending a scout to Arrow Rock, which returned about 10 o'clock, reporting all quiet there.

On the morning of October 13, I broke camp early and started for Marshall. When within a mile of the town my advance sent word that a heavy body of Federals were formed in my front, too strong to be attacked by them. I immediately galloped to the advance, and found, sure enough, General Ewing drawn up with 4,000 Federals, of all arms, ready to receive me. The force in the rear would be on me in an hour, I knew; so I determined, if possible, to defeat Ewing before Brown came up. Dismounting Major Shanks' regiment, and forming it at the bridge over which we had just crossed, I ordered him to destroy it and hold Brown in check to the last extremity. In the attack upon Ewing, Hooper held the left, Hunter and Coffee the right, the artillery and the battalion, with Gordon, in the center, the cavalry all dismounted. Ewing had admirably chosen his position, which was a high ridge, with a deep ravine in his front between his lines and mine. The men were eager for the fight, and when the order was given to advance, went at the Federals right gallantly. For two hours the fight raged evenly along the entire line, and the sun came out and looked down upon the dying and the dead, and the green fields of Missouri drank the blood of her best and bravest. On the left, Hooper held his ground against overwhelming numbers, and Gordon and the rest fought manfully. I ordered a charge along the whole line. Hunter and Coffee doubled Ewing's left wing back upon his right, and gained the town of Marshall, my artillery sweeping the crowded streets with fearful slaughter. Just as their rout was inevitable, the roar of artillery in the rear warned me that Brown was hurling his strong columns upon the heroic and devoted Shanks, and must bear him back. For two mortal hours Shanks, with his 200 men, held Brown's 4,000 in check, although he brought to bear upon him the whole weight of his six pieces of artillery. The fight had now continued four hours furiously, and my ammunition was getting low.

In the mean time General Brown, unable to drive Shanks from his position, had crossed the creek above and below him, and was coming up on either flank rapidly. Shanks, true to his trust, fell back a short distance, and formed again to dispute his passage. Brown soon formed a junction, however, with Ewing, and their combined forces, outnumbering us eight to one, looked absolutely fearful. While forming a line for a final, crushing charge, I determined to retreat, knowing it was madness to continue the unequal contest.

My rifled gun had again become useless. The trail, which was shivered by a cannon shot at Helena, broke short off and left it unmanageable. I determined to save it, if possible, and had it fixed up, under a hot fire, with poles; but in crossing a deep ravine it hopelessly gave way, in which condition it was well spiked and left.

Withdrawing my forces by regiments, and forming them as if to charge, got my entire command mounted in splendid order, with the ordnance wagons in the center, at the same time keeping up a furious fire of grape and canister wlth the remaining piece of artillery. The enemy's twelve pieces of artillery were playing upon my ranks, but the men stood the fire without flinching.

As soon as my command were mounted and straightened out, I saw the Federals were almost entirely around me, and only on the right was there a way open for escape, and this every minute getting narrower and narrower. The undergrowth here was thick and matted, almost impassable for cavalry; besides, directly in my way was a deep, wide ravine or ditch. This, however, I had bridged two hours before. Now gathering my command well in hand, I dashed furiously at the enemy's left, knowing that it was his weakest point, and, besides, if I succeeded in forcing this line before he swung his right around, I could change my front and have the entire force behind me. Hard blows were given and received. The Federals gave way in terror before the momentary shock, and Gordon, Coffee, the battalion, and the wagons passed safely through, but the head of Hunter's regiment, being entangled in the thick brush, did not keep well closed up, and the Federals, rallying, dashed in between him and the rear of Gordon, thus dividing them. Hunter, seeing it impossible to join me without a great sacrifice, turned squarely to the right, and by a quick gallop placed the whole enemy's force in the rear. My object was thus far safely attained. True, the command was divided, but each division had escaped the Federals and were in a condition to retreat with safety. After waiting an hour for the separated forces to come together, and they not appearing, I continued my retreat toward Waverly. For 8 miles they pressed me sorely; but forming by a two-squadron front, and taking position [advantage] of every natural position, I invariably drove the enemy back. At Germantown they made a desperate onslaught, but, meeting them with promptness and firmness, they fell back, as usual, in confusion.

At 3 o'clock the next morning I passed through Waverly, and then turned directly southward. At Hawkins' Mill, finding my wagons troublesome, and having no ammunition left except what the men could carry, I sunk them in the Missouri River, where they were safe from all capture.

The 14th, 15th, and 16th were spent in constant travel, halting only long enough to feed and take a few hours' repose. At Warrensburg there were about 2,000 Federals waiting for us, but they were passed without alarm, and at Johnstown, Johnson County, they attacked us, but were repulsed; so thus, upon the evening of the 16th, I encamped within 8 miles of the Osage River, making through from river to river in two days.

On the 17th, 18th, and 19th I traveled hard, fighting once at Carthage; crossed the Springfield road 3 miles east of Keytesville, all the time followed by a large force, and on the 20th was rejoined on the banks of the Little Osage, in Arkansas, by Hunter, Hooper, and Shanks, with their entire commands in fine spirit. This party, after having been separated from me, also started southward, but pursued only a mile by the enemy. They had with them the brass 6-pounder, with some 50 rounds of cartridges in the limber. They traveled rapidly; crossed the railroad 4 miles from Tipton, which entire road was now guarded by Federal infantry; charged a herd of 400 mules and captured them within 8 miles of Syracuse; took about 50 prisoners on the trip; destroyed 20 wagons; tore up the newly laid track; again damaged the repaired road considerably; fought and defeated the Federals at Florence, Humansville, and Greenfield; crossed the Osage at Duroc; charged and destroyed a detachment of the First Arkansas Cavalry 2 miles south of the river; fought McNeil's advance of 2,000 men at Humansville, and held him in check until the rear of the column passed safely through. It was here the brass 6-pounder was abandoned. Owing to the almost unparalleled rapidity of the retreat, rendered necessary by the vast number of Federals after us and before us, and all around us, it was impossible to keep the gun up, and more than impossible to follow with it the devious and zigzag march of the cavalry; therefore, when the eight large horses attached to it fell in their traces at Humansville, and General McNeil was coming at us fast and furious, the gun was left, after being spiked, the harness destroyed, and the wheels and axles chopped into kindling wood. After uniting my command and seeing the forlorn and jaded condition of the horses, I determined to march by easy stages to the Arkansas River. For three days I was left unmolested by the beaten and baffled enemy; but Colonel [William F.] Cloud, then at Fayetteville, hearing of my successful escape from Missouri, came hard after me with 3,000 men. A scout I sent from my camp to Huntsville, distant 14 miles, brought me the first intelligence of their advance. I retired slowly before them, and they as slowly followed, never urgent in their pressure until we arrived at the foot of the Buffalo Mountains, where they made a weak charge, easily repulsed. They followed us to Clarksville, where I crossed the Arkansas River.

On the 26th, and from thence to Washington, which I reached on November 3, I took plenty of time in marching, encountering a very severe rain and snow storm.

In speaking of the conduct and services of the various officers under my command, it would seem invidious to make any distinction; but the course of some, marked by every attribute of daring and desperate courage; noble, chivalrous gallantry; patience under privations; cheerfulness and resignation amid reverses and dangers, leaves no alternative but to mention them by name. Major Shanks deserves special mention for the heroic hardihood with which he held his position at Marshall against fearful odds, and his continual services upon the long retreat. Colonels Hunter, Coffee, Hooper, and Captain [George P.] Gordon, commanding his brother's regiment, handled their commands with great skill, and were ever where the fire was hottest and heaviest—a host in themselves. Captain [W. W.] Thorp, of the battalion; Captain [W. R.] Edwards, of Gordon's regiment; Captains [M. M.] Langhorne and [J. W.] Franklin, of Shanks' regiment; Adjutant [D. A.] Williams, Captain [T. H.] Lea, Lieutenant [J. M.] Wills, of Hooper's regiment, and Lieutenants [W. H.] Ferrell and [W. M.] Moorman, of Gordon's regiment, deserve the thanks of the entire command for their conspicuous bravery. Captain [Joseph] Kelly and Lieutenant Harris, of the battery, were always ready and willing, and handled their pieces with remarkable effect. To the members of my volunteer and regular staff I return my thanks for their services. Capt. James Wood, the hero of the La Mine, deserves a high position for his cool daring.

The fight at Marshall lasted about five hours, and was hot and desperate. The loss of the Federals I have no exact means of knowing; but from the statements of prisoners and citizens, coupled with the fact of their weak pursuit, it must have been very severe. I fought there 8,000 men, aided by twelve pieces of artillery, in their own chosen position, with troops from Kansas, Iowa, Illinois, Nebraska, Minnesota, and Missouri; was surrounded; cut my way out without losing a wagon; beat them back in every charge they made upon my rear, and I finally eluded them altogether.

I have traveled 1,500 miles, and found the people of Missouri, as a mass, true to the South and her institutions, yet needing the strong presence of a Confederate army to make them volunteer. The southern, southwestern, and some of the middle counties of Missouri are completely desolated. In many places for 40 miles not a single habitation is to be found, for on the road we met delicate females fleeing southward, driving ox teams, barefooted, ragged, and suffering for even bread.

Here, before closing my report, I will recapitulate the chief events of the raid:

Number of Federals killed and wounded	600
Number of Federals captured and paroled	500
Number of forts captured and destroyed, 10; at an aggregate cost of	$120,000
Amount of railroad property destroyed, consisting of rails, ties, tanks, cattle-stops, telegraph wire and poles, bridges and piers	$800,000
Number of guns captured	600
Number of stand of colors taken	40
Number of revolvers	600
Number of wagons captured and destroyed	300
Number of horses and mules captured	6,000
Amount of supplies used and destroyed	$1,000,000
Pieces of artillery taken	1
Number of recruits gained	800
Amount of ordnance captured and destroyed (reduced to cost)	$50,000

My entire number of killed and wounded on the trip will not exceed 150. Besides the damage thus inflicted, I kept [from] re-enforcing Rosecrans (then terribly defeated by General Bragg) at least 10,000 men, which were on the eve of being sent to him, and held them in Missouri for two weeks. The raid lasted forty-one days, and in traveling the 1,500 miles I averaged over 36 miles per day.

Hoping this report may prove satisfactory, I remain, major, very respectfully, your obedient servant,

JO. O. SHELBY,
Colonel, Commanding Expedition.

Maj. L. A. MACLEAN,
Assistant Adjutant-General, Price's Division.

[For map, showing the route pursued by Shelby in his raid, see p. 679.]

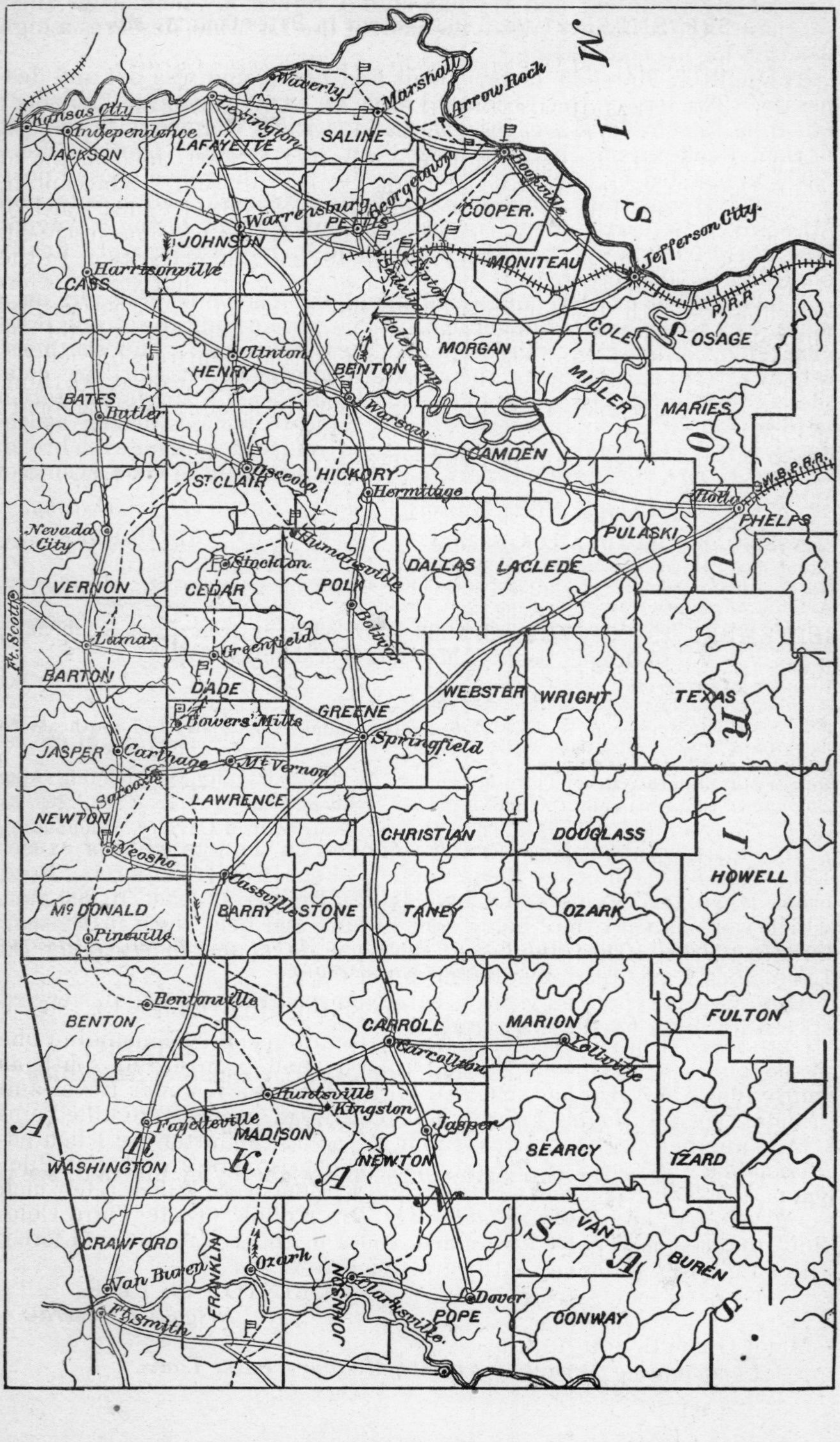
M I S S O U R I
A R K A N S A S
Kansas City
Independence
Lexington
Waverly
Marshall
Arrow Rock
Boonville
Jefferson City
P.R.R.
JACKSON
LAFAYETTE
SALINE
COOPER
Warrensburg
Georgetown
JOHNSON
PETTIS
MONITEAU
Harrisonville
CASS
COLE
OSAGE
Clinton
HENRY
BENTON
MORGAN
MILLER
MARIES
BATES
Butler
Warsaw
CAMDEN
St CLAIR
Osceola
HICKORY
Hermitage
Rolla
S.W.B.P.R.R.
PHELPS
PULASKI
Nevada City
Stockton
Humansville
DALLAS
LACLEDE
VERNON
CEDAR
POLK
Ft. Scott
Bolivar
Lamar
Greenfield
BARTON
DADE
WEBSTER
WRIGHT
TEXAS
Bowers' Mills
GREENE
Springfield
JASPER
Carthage
Mt Vernon
Sarcoxie
LAWRENCE
NEWTON
CHRISTIAN
DOUGLASS
Neosho
HOWELL
Cassville
McDONALD
BARRY
STONE
TANEY
OZARK
Pineville
Bentonville
BENTON
CARROLL
MARION
FULTON
Carrollton
Yellville
Huntsville
Kingston
Fayetteville
MADISON
Jasper
SEARCY
WASHINGTON
NEWTON
IZARD
CRAWFORD
FRANKLIN
Ozark
JOHNSON
VAN BUREN
Van Buren
Clarksville
Dover
Ft. Smith
POPE
CONWAY

SEPTEMBER 27-28, 1863.—Scout in Bates County, Mo.

Report of Col. Edward Lynde, Ninth Kansas Cavalry.

HEADQUARTERS TROOPS ON THE BORDER,
Trading Post, Kans., September 28, 1863—11 p. m.

SIR: A dispatch is just in from Captain [G. F.] Earl, in command of scouts that left yesterday to scour Bates County, Missouri. The captain says he met a small party at the crossing of Marais des Cygnes, south of Butler; killed 4 of them, and had 2 men wounded; the colonel escaped. He afterward found the trail of about 40, and followed it on to the Miami, and there learned, by some women living on that stream, that Marchbanks, with 40 men, passed up on to Grand River yesterday. The captain also writes that quite a number of families still inhabit the houses in the timber, and that the town of Butler is entirely burned. I shall take measures to have all the families removed at once. I think by the last of the week I can give you a definite account of all this part of your district.

Respectfully, your obedient servant,

E. LYNDE,
Colonel Ninth Kansas Volunteer Cavalry, Commanding.

ASSISTANT ADJUTANT-GENERAL, DISTRICT OF THE BORDER.

SEPTEMBER 29-OCTOBER 26, 1863.—Expeditions from Pilot Knob, Mo., to Oregon County, Mo., and Pocahontas, Ark.

REPORTS.

No. 1.—Brig. Gen. Clinton B. Fisk, U. S. Army, commanding District of Southeastern Missouri.

No. 2.—Maj. James Wilson, Third Missouri State Militia Cavalry, commanding expedition to Oregon County.

No. 3.—Capt. William T. Leeper, Third Missouri State Militia Cavalry, commanding expedition to Pocahontas.

No. 1.

Reports of Brig. Gen. Clinton B. Fisk, U. S. Army, commanding District of Southeastern Missouri.

PILOT KNOB, MO., *October* 13, 1863.

GENERAL: I have dispatches from Captain Leeper, commanding one of the border expeditions, stating that he had been as far south as Smithville, Ark. He had met and fought the enemy, under Reves and Crandall, near Pitman's Ferry. Thirteen of the rebels were killed and a large number of prisoners captured. Among the latter are 1 lieutenant-colonel, 1 major, and 2 captains. The prisoners are now at Pilot Knob. Casualties on our part were light; none were killed, a few men were wounded, and a few are missing. Dr. Pollok, of the Third Colorado Infantry, is reported wounded and a prisoner. Additional force, with supplies, will move southward to-morrow.

CLINTON B. FISK,
Brigadier-General.

Major-General SCHOFIELD,
Commanding Department of the Missouri, Saint Louis.

PILOT KNOB, MO., *October* 13, 1863—5.30 p. m.

GENERAL: Major [J.] Wilson, Third Missouri State Militia Cavalry, in command of one of the detachments I ordered to the State line to resist the threatened approach of the enemy from Arkansas, sends me dispatches from Alton, Oregon County, under date of the 10th instant. He had made a rapid march to Evening Shade, Ark., 60 miles south of Alton, where, on the 7th instant, he surprised the enemy in their camp and attacked him. He captured 1 captain, 3 lieutenants, and 56 privates, with their horses and arms, and afterward destroyed their camp, pursuing the fleeing rebels toward White River; returned to Alton. The prisoners have arrived at Pilot Knob, and will be forwarded to Saint Louis.

The citizens of Lawrence County, Arkansas, are organizing to resist the rebel conscription, and are stretching out their hand to the old flag for protection. The rebel general [colonel] Waldo P. Johnson, Missouri State Guard, who succeeded M. Jeff. Thompson, with authority to organize a force in Southern Missouri, which, "from friendly trees," might shoot Union soldiers and citizens, is said to have abandoned the enterprise, and would be very glad again to represent Missouri in the service of the Union.

CLINTON B. FISK,
Brigadier-General.

Major-General SCHOFIELD.

HEADQUARTERS DISTRICT OF SOUTHEASTERN MISSOURI,
Pilot Knob, Mo., November 4, 1863.

MAJOR: I have the honor to report that, on 28th day of September, 1863, I issued the following letter of instructions to Col. R. G. Woodson, commanding post and forces at Pilot Knob:

HEADQUARTERS DISTRICT OF SOUTHEASTERN MISSOURI,
Pilot Knob, Mo., September 28, 1863.

Col. R. G. WOODSON,
Commanding Post, Pilot Knob:

COLONEL: On Tuesday morning, 29th instant, at 6 o'clock, you will move from this post two detachments of cavalry, commanded, respectively, by Major [J.] Wilson, Third Misssouri State Militia Cavalry, and Capt. William T. Leeper, Third Missouri State Militia Cavalry. Major Wilson's detachment will consist of 200 men; that of Captain Leeper 150 men. Captain Leeper will move to Wayne, Butler, and Ripley Counties, and as far south as Pocahontas, Ark., if he thinks best. Major Wilson will move, via Centreville, Eminence, and Van Buren, to Oregon County, and into Arkansas, if he thinks best.

The mission of each detachment will be the extermination of bushwhackers, guerrillas, thieves, and murderers, and the restoration of good order and quiet in the regions through which they operate. Straggling, plundering, pillaging, and burning must be prohibited. Let swift and summary punishment be inflicted upon offenders against this order. Let the people among whom these detachments move be made to understand that the United States troops are sent among them to put down disorder, and not to create it.

Each expedition will remain along the border for such time as may by them be deemed best. Much will be expected from them. Vigilance, determination, and perseverance will put an end to the reign of terror, jayhawking, and murder which has been supreme in the border counties.

Commanders will be directed to keep you advised of their movements by frequent dispatches.

Subsistence, ammunition, &c., will be made ready to-day. The detachments will move promptly, with instructions to march rapidly and surprise the gathering clans of insurgents.

I am, colonel, very respectfully, your obedient servant,

CLINTON B. FISK
Brigadier-General.

In obedience to orders, the respective detachments were moved promptly at the designated hour. The results of the expeditions are fully set forth in the following reports of the commanding officers of the detachments, to which attention is respectfully directed.

I am, major, very respectfully, your obedient servant,

CLINTON B. FISK,
Brigadier-General.

Maj. OLIVER D. GREENE,
Assistant Adjutant-General, Department of the Missouri.

No. 2.

Report of Maj. James Wilson, Third Missouri State Militia Cavalry, commanding expedition to Oregon County.

HDQRS. THIRD MISSOURI STATE MILITIA CAVALRY,
Pilot Knob, Mo., October 28, 1863.

COLONEL: In compliance with your instructions of the 28th of September, I placed my command in order, and moved out on the following morning with 200 men of the Third Missouri State Militia Cavalry; encamped at night near Centreville, Mo.

On the 30th ultimo, I detached Captain [G. L.] Herring, with 70 men, directing him to move via Eminence, and to rejoin me at Alton as soon as practicable. Commanding the main force myself, we followed the Van Buren road, encamping at night near what is known as Henpeck Creek.

October 1, I ordered another detachment of 60 men, under command of Captain [H. B.] Milks, to take a lower route, cross Eleven Point River at Boyce's Mill, and to proceed to Alton. The main force on this date crossed Current River; encamped at the head of Pike Creek, and on the morning following in the direction of Alton. Upon arriving at Falling Springs, I detached Captain [J. W.] McFaden, with 30 men, with orders to go by way of Boyce's Ford and meet us at Alton, and with the remainder of the force I crossed the river, about 8 miles east, at a place known as Simpkins' Mill, and also arrived at Alton that p. m.

Captain McFaden's command encountered a party of guerrillas, under one Lieutenant Duckworth, whom they routed, as well as capturing several horses, saddles, &c. My immediate command captured 4 guerrillas, with their horses, arms, and equipments.

From Alton, on the 3d of October, I sent out three scouts, respectively, to Boyce's Mill, Simpkins' Mill, and Boyce's Ford, with instructions to scour the country for guerrillas. Captain [C. W.] Rush, commanding one of these detachments, fell in with the command of Duckworth, whom he succeeded in routing again, besides capturing several horses, camp equipage, &c.

All of the several detachments having reported to me at Alton, on the 5th of October I started for Arkansas with 140 men (leaving Captain McFaden with 60 men), proceeding in a southeasterly direction to Jaynes' Creek, Arkansas; thence west to Spring River; thence southeast to Strawberry River and to Evening Shade, on Piney Creek. At Evening Shade we captured 35 prisoners, including 1 captain and 3 lieutenants, as well as all their horses, arms, and equipments.

On the morning of October 7, we moved east, on the Smithville road, 15 miles; thence north, crossing Strawberry River, near its mouth, to

Mill Creek; thence northeast to Jaynes' Creek, returning to Alton on the 9th instant. Captain McFaden, with an escort, was then sent with what prisoners we had taken, to report to you at Pilot Knob. I remained at Alton, sending scouts into the surrounding country frequently, and wherever I could hear of any guerrillas, until the 18th instant, when, my provisions being nearly exhausted, we started to return to Pilot Knob, but met Captain McFaden on the 20th, with re-enforcements, provisions, &c., for us.

In pursuance of your further orders, we returned to Alton, and remained there until the 21st instant, when, with 120 men (sending the remainder of my force, under command of Captain [G. L.] Herring, to Pilot Knob, in charge of prisoners, and to escort a train of refugees from Oregon County), I moved west to Thomasville, scouring the country thoroughly *en route*.

Learning that Alton had been burned since our departure, we hoped to intercept the rascals by traversing the northeastern portion of Oregon County, but in this we were unsuccessful. We then returned, via Delaware Creek and Jack's Fork, arriving at Pilot Knob October 26, after an absence of twenty-eight days.

As the result of our expedition, we have killed 1 captain, 4 men, and wounded 2 others. Captured 1 captain, 3 lieutenants, and 76 men, as well as about 70 horses, a lot of arms of various kinds, horse equipments, &c. This list does not include men who had been previously in the rebel army, and who voluntarily surrendered to me. I ordered all such to report to the nearest provost-marshal, and to comply with the law concerning their cases. We lost 1 man captured and paroled (Joseph Shram, Company G, Third Missouri State Militia Cavalry), and had another wounded in the left arm (Martin D. Gray, Third Missouri State Militia Cavalry).

I have to speak in the highest terms of all the officers and men under my command, and to report that I have conformed to the requirements of Circular No. 1, District of Southeastern Missouri.

I have the honor to be, colonel, very respectfully, your obedient servant,

JAMES WILSON,
Major, Commanding Expedition.

Col. R. G. WOODSON,
Commanding Post of Pilot Knob, Mo.

No. 3.

Reports of Capt. William T. Leeper, Third Missouri State Militia Cavalry, commanding expedition to Pocahontas.

BRUSH CREEK,
Twenty-five Miles South of Patterson, October 11, 1863.

GENERAL: I am on my way to Patterson. I will be there on the night of the 12th. I have gone where I pleased. I could not let you know where I was. There has been a band of guerrillas on my rear. They were organized after I went down, about 100 or 125 strong. I have them scattered, but I am so bothered with my train and other incumbrances that I must get clear of some of it.

I do not wish to go back to Pilot Knob. Let me move the balance of our companies to Patterson. I want to go back in a few days. I have made a very bold dash into Arkansas, and I think I have done some good. I was bushwhacked on yesterday, and had 2 of my men wounded; none killed. We killed 2 of the rebels, and scattered them so in the thickets that we could not follow them.

My men are all in good condition, and in good fighting order. Dr. Pollock and Sergeant Gillespie are missing. I think they are safe. I am sure they are not killed, and I do not think they are captured. I hope they are all right. I think the doctor is at Patterson before now. I will give you all the particulars when I get there.

W. T. LEEPER,
Captain, Commanding Expedition.

General FISK.

PATTERSON, MO., *October* 12, 1863.

COLONEL: In obedience to your orders, I left Pilot Knob September 28, 1863, with Companies D, M, and L, Third Missouri State Militia Cavalry, numbering 150 men, with instructions to go to Pocahontas, Ark., or any other point in that vicinity that seemed to demand attention. We reached Doniphan on the 30th ultimo. Company L having been sent by another road (somewhat to the right), killed 2 men *en route*. Also, on the 1st of October, Captain [R.] McElroy, with 30 men, was ordered forward, via "Buck Scull," where he found 6 men, who ran, and were fired upon by the party. Four of the men were killed and another wounded. Captain [W. T.] Hunter, with a detachment, went via Current River, where he captured 2 soldiers and some Government property.

The several detachments arrived at Pocahontas on the 2d of October, and remained until the 6th instant (a squad captured 2 notorious jayhawkers in the mean time), when we moved to Smithville, Ark., and on the 7th instant opposite to Powhatan, on the east side of Black River. On the next day we followed Black River until opposite to Pocahontas, where we captured and killed one Francis Taylor, a guerrilla and thief of the worst sort. We then crossed Black River, above the mouth of Current River, and followed up between the two streams until, on the morning of the 10th instant, we discovered indications of a rebel force, which we encountered at about 9 a. m. They were about 100 strong, remaining in ambush, so that our first indication of their presence was a volley fired at our advance guard, which fell back to the main column. We forwarded to receive the enemy, and, after waiting some time to ascertain his intentions, followed him into the swamp and brush, but were unsuccessful in finding any of them. We had 1 soldier wounded; also a citizen who was with us. Dr. Pollok, surgeon Third Colorado Infantry (medical officer of the expedition), is missing; also a sergeant, [J.] Gillespie, of Company L, but I think both were captured and not killed. At the time of the attack we killed 2 men. We proceeded to Doniphan; thence to Patterson, Mo. (an outpost), where we arrived on the 12th instant. Our captures consisted of 15 prisoners (Confederate soldiers and guerrillas), 36 guns in fair condition, about 100 other guns nearly worthless, and 20 horses and mules. On the west side of Black River the inhabitants were friendly; but upon the east side they are decidedly hostile. All civil men were treated with consideration and respect; the guerrillas fared but middling. I learned beyond a doubt that that portion of Arkansas on the north side of Arkansas River is formed into a sub-district for the purpose of carrying on a border warfare, which will be of a guerrilla character.

I must speak in highest praise of both officers and men under my command, who have behaved nobly, and did their duty well. We did not lack for subsistence or forage.

I have the honor to be, colonel, very respectfully, your obedient servant,

W. T. LEEPER,
Captain, Commanding Expedition.

Colonel WOODSON,
Commanding Pilot Knob, Mo.

OCTOBER 4, 1863.—Skirmish near Widow Wheeler's, southwest of Neosho, Mo.

Report of Capt. Milton Burch, Eighth Missouri State Militia Cavalry.

HEADQUARTERS,
Carthage, Mo., October 6, 1863.

GENERAL: I have the honor of informing you of a scout I made on the 3d instant, with 40 men from Companies L and M, Eighth Cavalry Missouri State Militia. I marched down on Turkey Creek, some 8 miles west of this place, to escort some Union families out, and try to waylay and destroy a party of guerrillas that infest that portion of country. On the night of the 3d instant I received information that 40 armed rebels had passed 1 mile above where I was camped, traveling south. I moved up the creek. I found that they had some four hours' start of me, but I was determined to try and overtake them, if possible; so at 9 p. m. I started in pursuit with my little band, now numbering 29 men, 11 of my men going back to Carthage to escort the moving wagons.

I started on the trail and followed them within 1 mile of Shoal Creek, 15 miles from where I started. They then left the road they were traveling, and took to the woods. I still followed on. I went to Shoal Creek to feed and rest, as our horses were becoming jaded. This was 5 miles south of Baxter Springs. I did not remain long, as I was anxious to again get on the trail; so I started on their trail again. I followed them about 30 miles, when about 2 o'clock in the evening of the 4th instant I overtook them at the Widow Wheeler's, 15 miles southwest of Neosho. I expected to find them there, as that was the only place where feed could be procured. I sent Joel P. Hood, my Government scout, and one other man dressed in butternut, to ascertain where their pickets were stationed. They succeeded in capturing the only man that was on picket, and returned to my command. From him I learned that they were camped at the back of the farm, in the brush, with 30 armed men.

I started immediately, but they had started, and we gave chase. They started down an open prairie hollow. We chased them about 4 miles, killing 10 of them and wounding a good many more, and took 2 prisoners, one of them by the name of Miller, a regular secesh pilot, and about 25 head of horses, mostly young stock. I started then for this place, aiming to go by Neosho. When I got within 1½ miles from Neosho, I stopped my command and sent 2 men to ascertain if all was right. They went to Mr. Wade's, and found his house in flames, and there learned that the town was full of rebels. At the same time they learned that they intended to go to Carthage; so I started on quick time, aiming to beat them there, if possible. I had to leave the young stock I had captured, as it was hard to drive, and take the nearest route to Carthage, traveling without a road.

I reached Carthage about day on the morning of the 5th instant, and immediately commenced preparing to give them a warm reception. About 8 o'clock it was reported that 15 men were advancing south of this place. I sent 3 men to ascertain who it was. They passed on, not seeing any person till they had turned to come back to camp, when they met 15 men, advancing from the direction of town, dressed in Federal uniform. The boys halted them, and sent one man to ascertain who they were. When he got close to them they fired and killed him; his name was John Wells, a private of Company L, Eighth Missouri State Militia. The other boys succeeded, after a hard chase, in escaping.

Major [A. A.] King, of the Sixth Missouri State Militia Cavalry, started with all of the effective force to Newtonia, to ascertain what was going on in that direction. He sent orders to me to have my baggage moved to Mount Vernon, and for me, with all the effective force I could muster, to follow on the trail taken by the enemy. The train and baggage is under command of Sergt. John Bentley, Company L, Eighth Missouri State Militia Cavalry.

I remain, respectfully, your obedient servant,

MILTON BURCH,

Captain, Commanding Detachment at Carthage, Mo.

C. G. LAURANT,

Assistant Adjutant-General.

OCTOBER 5, 1863.—Skirmish near Syracuse, Mo.

REPORTS.

No. 1.—Lieut. Col. Thomas T. Crittenden, Seventh Missouri State Militia Cavalry.

No. 2.—Capt. Richard M. Box, Seventh Missouri State Militia Cavalry.

No. 1.

Report of Lieut. Col. Thomas T. Crittenden, Seventh Missouri State Militia Cavalry.

HEADQUARTERS,

Tipton, October 9, 1863.

SIR: On Monday morning last a detachment of Company H, Seventh Missouri State Militia Cavalry, of 30 men, under Captain [R. M.] Box, trailed about 60 guerrillas into a thick, brushy hollow, near Syracuse, Mo.; vigorously attacked them, regardless of the disparity in numbers, and soon put them to flight. Twelve guerrillas were killed and 4 wounded—generally mortal shots; 7 or 8 horses, fully equipped, were captured; also a large lot of old and new clothing, and several pieces of unmanufactured cloth. These were a part of Jackman's men, from Howard; supposed to have been under him. It is currently reported that a Colonel Eades, from Cooper County, Missouri, was one of the killed. These guerrillas were evidently on their way to join Jo. Shelby in his present raid into this State. Many of them were in Federal uniform, and finely armed, having a double-barreled shot-gun and from two to five Colt's navy revolvers.

Captain Box and his fearless men deserve credit for the brave and manly manner they attacked and defeated this rebel chief and gang, who have so often boasted that Federals were afraid of them. As General Brown is absent in the field, I will make this report directly to your headquarters.

Yours, very truly,

T. T. CRITTENDEN,
Lieut. Col. 7th M. S. M. Cav., Comdg. 2d Sub-Military Dist.

Col. C. W. MARSH,
Assistant Adjutant-General.

No. 2.

Report of Capt. Richard M. Box, Seventh Missouri State Militia Cavalry.

HDQRS. CO. H, SEVENTH MISSOURI STATE MILITIA CAV.,
Syracuse, Mo., November 1, 1863.

COLONEL: I have the honor of submitting to you the following report of a fight which took place between a portion of my command and a company of rebel bushwhackers, under Lieutenant-Colonel Willhite, on Monday, the 5th of October last, about 10 miles from this place:

On the morning of the 5th ultimo, I learned that a company of rebels had passed near Syracuse about daylight. I at once ordered out 30 men, and started in pursuit; discovered their trail about 1½ miles from town; followed it some distance, when we found that their track scattered through the woods. I then ordered half of my men to dismount, at the same time dismounting myself, and followed the scattering tracks through the thick brush for about 10 miles, keeping the cavalry about 100 yards in our rear. Came up with them about 2 p. m., when we surprised them with a volley from our rifles. I then ordered a charge, which was done in splendid style by my men, killing several of the rebels. They (the rebels) then fell back, in confusion, some 60 or 80 yards. I then ordered the horses forward, but seeing the rebels forming their line very rapidly, I made another charge, on foot, within 5 paces of their line, pouring a hot and deadly fire into their ranks from our revolvers. I again ordered the horses forward mounted and into line on the double-quick. During this time the rebels had crossed a small ravine, and had again formed in line. I ordered the third charge, which was successfully made by breaking their line. They then fell back in confusion, and continued firing while retreating. Chased them through the woods, scattering them in every direction. I kept all my men in line until I saw the rebels were so scattered that it was impossible for them to make another stand. I then deployed them, and searched the woods till night came on and the darkness prevented further action. Camped out that night about half a mile from where we had the fight. Two of my men were slightly wounded. The rebel loss was 12 killed; several were also wounded, but managed to make their escape. A number of horses were killed and wounded on both sides. My horse was shot in the head and shoulder, and my saddle was struck with some buck-shot.

Among the trophies of our victory was a large rebel flag (the same I sent you, and by you taken to General Brown); four horses; a number of shot-guns and revolvers; a quantity of new boots, clothing, and other articles, as well as some Confederate uniforms.

Among the killed on the rebel side were Lieutenant-Colonel Willhite and a captain, whose name I did not learn. They belonged to Jackman's band of outlaws and guerrillas, and numbered 61.

On the following morning (Tuesday) I ordered the citizens to bury the dead, which was promptly done.

I still have with me the black boy formerly belonging to Lieutenant-Colonel Wilwhite. He appears to be a smart lad.

My men fought bravely, and great credit is due them for the gallantry and courage displayed on that occasion. I feel proud of my command, and commend them, colonel, to your good graces.

With much respect, I remain, your obedient servant,

R. M. BOX,
Captain Company H, Seventh Missouri State Militia Cavalry.

Lieut. Col. T. T. CRITTENDEN,
Commanding Second Sub-District, Tipton, Mo.

OCTOBER 6, 1863.—Action at Baxter Springs, Kans.

REPORTS.

No. 1.

Report of Maj. Gen. James G. Blunt, U. S. Army.

HEADQUARTERS DISTRICT OF THE FRONTIER,
Fort Scott, Kans., October 19, 1863.

COLONEL: I have the honor to report, for the information of the general commanding, the following facts:

On the 4th instant, upon the receipt of dispatches from Fort Smith, informing me that the command there was threatened with a superior force of the enemy, I immediately left for that post, accompanied by a part of my staff, and taking with me the records, papers, and property belonging to the headquarters of the district. My escort consisted of Company I, Third Wisconsin Cavalry, and Company A, Fourteenth Kansas, about 100 men (all the available mounted men that could be spared from this post). I arrived near Baxter Springs about 12 m. of the 6th, and being in advance of the escort and wagons, I halted near the camp at the Springs, commanded by Lieutenant [James B.] Pond, of the Third Wisconsin Cavalry. This camp, being in low ground under the hill, was not visible from the point where I halted, although not more than 400 yards distant. After the escort had closed up, and while waiting a few moments for the wagons, my attention was called to a body of men in line (about 100) advancing from the timber of Spring River, which was some 500 yards on our left. When within 300 yards, they halted; and they being all dressed in Federal uniform, I supposed them at first to be Lieutenant Pond's cavalry (of which he had two companies) on drill; and my first suspicion of their being an enemy was aroused by seeing several men, supposed to be officers, riding hurriedly up and down their line, and apparent confusion among the men I directed the escort to be brought into line facing them, while I advanced toward their line to satisfy myself as to the character of the force. I had proceeded but 50 or 75 yards when they commenced an irregular firing, and at the same time I heard a brisk firing of musketry in Lieutenant Pond's camp, under the hill. Being no longer in doubt that they were rebels, I turned toward my escort to give the command to fire, when I discovered the line broken, and all of them in full gallop over the prairie, completely panic-stricken. Seeing the disorderly and disgraceful retreat of the escort, the enemy made a charge, using their revolvers, followed by another force of about 200, who were formed in the edge of the timber, and, being better mounted than the escort, they soon closed in on them. In vain I endeavored, with the assistance of Major [H. Z.] Curtis, my assistant adjutant-general, to halt and rally the escort, and succeeded only in rallying 15 men, after following them 1½ miles. When turning upon them with this small force, they retreated back over the ground which they came, and formed in line upon the main road. After sending Lieutenant [J. E.] Tappan, of my staff, with 6 men to Fort Scott for troops, with the remaining 9 men I kept close to them, watching their movements closely, which, doubtless, impressed them with the belief that I had a larger force coming up, as they burned all the wagons, and moved hurriedly off south, on the Fort Gibson road.

On looking over the ground for the wounded, I soon discovered that every man who had fallen, except 3, who escaped by feigning death, had been murdered, all shot through the head. The brigade band, teamsters, and all headquarters' clerks who were first captured were murdered in the same way. On reaching Lieutenant Pond's camp, I found the command all safe. A part of the force, carrying a Federal flag, had attacked his camp in the rear, which was in close proximity to the timber, while a force of 300 advanced through the timber on the left of his camp, and were forming on the edge of the prairie, for the purpose of surrounding him. The unexpected meeting of my escort diverted their further plans, and enabled Lieutenant Pond to successfully resist the force that attacked his camp. And in this connection I desire to compliment Lieutenant Pond and his command, consisting of two companies of the Third Wisconsin Cavalry and one company of the Second Kansas Colored Volunteers, for their gallantry in repulsing the enemy.

Having ascertained that the rebel force, 600 strong, was under the command of Quantrill, and that they designed moving directly south, I immediately sent messengers to Fort Gibson and Fort Smith, directing the commands at those forts to intercept them, if possible, at the Arkansas River, while at the same time I kept scouting parties on their trail to watch their movements until I could procure troops to pursue them. After leaving the ground, they moved south on the Fort Gibson road until they had crossed Cabin Creek, when they made a detour to the right across the Verdigris, and crossed the Arkansas River, 18 miles west of Fort Gibson, on the morning of the 10th. At this point they captured a scout of 12 men, belonging to the First Indian Home Guards (Creeks), and murdered them all. On the night of the 11th, they camped on the North Fork of the Canadian River, 45 miles south of the Arkansas; since which I have no reliable information concerning them. From information obtained from a colored boy who escaped from Quantrill's command at Cabin Creek, I learned that they came direct from La Fayette County, Missouri, by rapid marches, seeing no Federal troops on the route, and that their destination was to join the rebel forces south of the Arkansas. They evidently had no knowledge of my being *en route* south, and their design was to capture the force at Baxter Springs, which they supposed to consist only of one company of colored troops and a part of a company of cavalry, but which had been re-enforced the previous night by an additional company of cavalry and a 12-pounder mountain howitzer. Had the escort stood their ground and fought instead of running, I have no doubt that I could have driven them in a few minutes, and, with the addition of Lieutenant Pond's cavalry, pursued and captured many of them.

Inclosed is a list of the casualties.*

Very respectfully, your obedient servant,

JAS. G. BLUNT,
Major-General.

Colonel MARSH, *Chief of Staff.*

No. 2.

Report of Lieut. Col. Charles W. Blair, Fourteenth Kansas Cavalry.

HEADQUARTERS,
Fort Scott, Kans., October 15, 1863.

SIR: I have the honor to report to you, for the information of the major-general commanding, the following particulars, as far as they came to my knowledge or under my observation, of the late disaster at Baxter Springs:

On the 4th instant, Major-General Blunt, his staff, consisting of Maj. B. S. Henning, Third Wisconsin Cavalry, provost-marshal; Maj. H. Z. Curtis, assistant adjutant-general; Lieut. J. E. Tappan, Second Colorado Cavalry, aide-de-camp, and Lieut. A. W. Farr, Third Wisconsin Cavalry, judge-advocate, his clerks and orderlies, brigade band, and parts of two companies of cavalry, respectively under the command of Lieut. Robert [H.] Pierce, Fourteenth Kansas Cavalry, and Lieut. Josiah G. Cavert, Third Wisconsin Cavalry, left this place for Fort Blunt, Cherokee Nation. About 4 o'clock on the morning of the 7th instant, Lieutenant Tappan returned, informing me that about 1 o'clock the day previous General Blunt had been attacked within a few hundred yards of Lieutenant Pond's camp, at Baxter Springs, and the entire command, except the general himself and about 10 men, either killed or taken prisoners, and the baggage and transportation captured and destroyed. He also informed me that the general could not be persuaded to come away, but remained with his few men hanging near the enemy to watch their movements and succor any of the wounded who might be left alive, while he dispatched him (the lieutenant) to me to inform me of the circumstances. The lieutenant further stated that the enemy came over the brow of the hill, just from the direction of Pond's camp. It seemed, without a doubt, that his little force had been captured and destroyed also. He was further under the impression that Majors Curtis and Henning and Lieutenant Farr were prisoners.

Within an hour I was *en route* to the general's relief with three companies of the Twelfth Kansas Infantry and two companies of the Second Kansas Colored Infantry and about 100 cavalry, under Lieutenants [B.

---

*Nominal list, omitted, shows 79 killed, 8 wounded, and 5 missing.

F.] Josling and [W. B.] Clark. Twenty miles out I met a dispatch from General Blunt that he was safe with Lieutenant Pond, who had been fortunate enough to repulse the enemy in their attack on his camp. I pushed on, however, without relaxation, and arrived at the Springs, a distance of 70 miles, in the afternoon of the second day, although it was the first heavy marching the infantry had ever attempted. On my arrival I found that the general had sent off every mounted man he could find, either as scout or messenger, and had notified the officers in command on the line of the Arkansas River of the disaster at the Springs, the direction in which the enemy was heading, and where he would probably cross the river.

The graves were being dug and the dead being carried in for burial as I arrived. It was a fearful sight; some 85 bodies, nearly all shot through the head, most of them shot from five to seven times each, horribly mangled, charred and blackened by fire. The wounded, who numbered 6 or 7, were all shot at least six times, and it is a remarkable fact that, with the exception of Bennet, of the Third Wisconsin Cavalry, all who were alive when they were brought in are in a fair way of final recovery.

The circumstances of this double conflict, as well as I can gather them on the spot, are about these: Quantrill, with a force variously estimated at from 600 to 1,000, was passing south on the border line of counties in Missouri, and made a detour, to attack the camp at Baxter Springs, which up to that time had been defended by one company of colored men, under Lieutenant [R. E.] Cook, and a fragment of a company of the Third Wisconsin Cavalry only. Fortunately, however, the day before I had sent Lieut. James B. Pond with part of another company of the Third Wisconsin Cavalry and a mountain howitzer. The cavalry was, however, all absent with a forage train at the time the camp was attacked; but the blacks, the dismounted men of the cavalry, the howitzer, and Lieutenant Pond were still left. The first attack of the enemy, at 12 m. of the 6th instant, was so sudden and impetuous that he was inside the rude breastworks, and firing pistol shots into the tents, before our forces recovered from the surprise into which they were thrown by the onset. They rallied, however, promptly and gallantly, under the direction of the lieutenant, and, after a severe struggle, repulsed the enemy, and drove him outside the fortifications. He then concentrated his force for a more careful attack, formed in line of battle, but before the word could be given to charge, Lieutenant Pond opened upon them with the little howitzer, getting outside his breastworks to operate it, which again threw them into confusion, and drove them over the brow of the hill. At this point, it seems, they first perceived General Blunt's little column, which had halted for the wagons and band to close up, and immediately formed in line to attack it. They formed in two lines, one on the prairie and the other under the cover of the timber, and commenced the advance. Coming in the direction they did, the general, of course, supposed it was Lieutenant Pond's cavalry, either on drill or coming out to receive them. For safety, however, he formed his little force in line of battle, and sent the wagons, with the band, clerks, orderlies, cooks, and other non-combatants, to the rear, and then rode about 50 paces to the front, accompanied by his staff, to reconnoiter and endeavor to ascertain to a certainty what the approaching force was. Whatever doubts he may have entertained were soon dispelled, for the front line, firing a volley and raising the guerrilla yell, charged forward at full speed. The general, turning in his saddle to order his body guard to advance and fire, saw, with shame and humiliation, the whole of it in disgraceful flight over the prairie. There was nothing left for him then but to follow, and attempt to rally them. He accordingly turned with his staff officers, all except Major Henning, to endeavor to overtake the fugitives. By this time the enemy were upon and all around them, and their escape with life seemed almost a miracle. At this time, too, it seems to have struck Major Henning that the enemy approached from an angle which might miss Lieutenant Pond's camp, and that, consequently, he might be safe. With these thoughts, he determined to strike for the camp, and endeavor to bring Pond's force to the assistance of the general. Accordingly he charged straight forward at full speed, passing through a shower of bullets, and through the enemy's line. Deflecting a little to the right, he was over the brow of the hill before the enemy could recover from his astonishment at the daring feat. About half-way from the brow of the hill to the camp, he saw a party of five guerrillas, who had taken 3 of Lieutenant Pond's men prisoners, and were hurrying them off. As they were directly in his way, and a much larger force behind him, he was cool enough to reflect that temerity was here discretion, and instantaneously charged them. He shot 2 of them, killing 1 and frightening the others so badly that they abandoned the prisoners and took to flight. He then approached the camp at full speed, swinging his cap around his head to announce that he was a friend, and, after narrowly escaping being shot by our own men, at length arrived there in safety. He here learned of the attack on the camp, and that not a cavalryman was left, all being absent with a forage train. The distant sounds of the battle showed already that infantry was useless, and he again turned his horse's head in the direction of the field, and, solitary and alone, forced his way through the scattered bands of the enemy back to the side of his chief and his little band of supporters. History should not fail to record such deeds of gallantry and devotion. General Blunt, in his endeavor to rally his men as fast as he could catch up with any of them, was frequently thrown behind, and several times almost surrounded, although mounted in a superior manner. He finally rallied some 15 men, and, charging his foremost pursuers, compelled them in turn to retire. He then started Lieutenant Tappan with 4 men to me, and determined with the balance to watch the enemy. They killed our men as fast as they caught them, sparing none. The members of the band were shot as they sat in the band-wagon, and it was then set on fire. They rifled all the trunks, boxes, &c., in the different wagons, and then set them on fire, with the bodies of the teamsters in them, and all others who happened to be in them when taken. The non-combatants were slaughtered as ruthlessly as the soldiers. Lieutenant Farr was killed early in the struggle. Major Curtis came very near escaping, although his full uniform and showy horse made him a conspicuous mark. He was some distance in advance of his pursuers, when, just as his horse was gathering himself to spring over a deep ravine, he was struck on the hip with a ball, which so stung or frightened him that he missed his leap, and, falling short, threw the major over his head. The horse gathered himself almost instantly, and galloped wildly over the prairie. The major was first taken prisoner and then brutally murdered. Thus died as gallant a soldier and as true a gentleman as ever drew a sword in defense of his country. It may well be said of him, as of Chevalier Bayard of old, "He was without fear and without reproach." The enemy seeing that General Blunt persistently kept them in view, keeping away if pursued, and returning as soon as the pursuit slackened, were no doubt forced to believe that a large force was approaching, of which he was only the advance. His persistent following them up doubtless riveted this conclusion in their minds, as they hurried through their wholesale work of slaughter, and then moved off slowly to the south. General Blunt hovered near them until near night, and then returned to the melancholy work of caring for the wounded and collecting the dead. But few were left alive, as their evident intention was to kill all. The bodies of Major Curtis and Lieutenant Farr were not found until the next day.

Lieutenant Pond is entitled to great credit for his gallant defense of his camp, and Lieutenant Pierce also, who strove hard to rally the flying soldiers. But the men seemed struck by a sudden and uncontrollable panic, and I met many of them within 10 miles of Fort Scott as I moved out with my force. The enemy left between 20 and 30 dead on the field, and as their wounded were taken away with some ambulances and buggies they captured, it is impossible to state the number.

Disastrous as this engagement has been, it would undoubtedly have been as bad, if not worse, if General Blunt and his little force had not been near. In that event, a more careful and combined attack would have been made on Pond's camp, which, with the force around it, must have finally succumbed, and every person there would undoubtedly have been put to death.

The names and number (accurately) of our killed and wounded will be forwarded in a subsequent report.

I have the honor to be, very respectfully, your obedient servant,

CHAS. W. BLAIR,
Lieutenant-Colonel, Commanding.

Col. OLIVER D. GREENE,
Assistant Adjutant-General, Department of the Missouri.

No. 3.

Report of Maj. Benjamin S. Henning, Third Wisconsin Cavalry.

BAXTER SPRINGS, CHEROKEE NATION,
October 7, 1863.

COLONEL: I have the honor to report the following facts in regard to the fight at Baxter Springs, Cherokee Nation, October 6, 1863:

On Sunday, the 4th, General Blunt, with the following members of his staff, viz: Maj. H. Z. Curtis, assistant adjutant-general; Maj. B. S. Henning, provost-marshal of district; Lieutenant Tappan, Second Colorado Volunteers, aide-de-camp; Lieut. Asa W. Farr, judge-advocate, together with the brigade band, and all clerks in the different departments of district headquarters, and also an escort consisting of 40 men of Company I, Third Wisconsin Cavalry, under Lieut. H. D. Banister; 45 men of Company A, Fourteenth Kansas Cavalry, under Lieutenant [R. H.] Pierce, and the whole escort under the command of Lieut. J. G. Cavert, Third Wisconsin Cavalry, and a train of 8 wagons, transporting the effects of district headquarters, company effects, &c., left Fort Scott for Fort Smith, Ark., and on that day marched 6 miles, and camped. On the succeeding day marched 34 miles, and camped on Cow Creek; and on Tuesday, the 6th instant, marched from Cow Creek to within a distance of 80 rods of a camp at Baxter Springs, Cherokee Nation, and halted at 12 m. for the train to close up, as it had become somewhat scattered. The halt continued about fifteen minutes, and the command had just been given for the column to move, when horsemen were seen coming out of the woods, a distance of about 80 rods to the left, and forming in line. As we were so near Baxter Springs (although not in sight of it by reason of an intervening ridge), many supposed them to be our own troops, drilling or returning from a scout. The general immediately ordered the two companies into line of battle, and the train to close up in rear of the line, which was done under the immediate direction of Major Curtis, assistant adjutant-general; and at the same time a reconnoiter was made by Mr. Tough, a scout of the general, who reported that the force were enemies, and that an engagement was going on at the Springs. I had ridden forward myself and discovered that the force was large, and reported the same to the general, who then rode forward to reconnoiter for himself. At this time I discovered that the enemy were being re-enforced from the southwest, on a line between us and the camp at Baxter Springs, the main body of the enemy being east of us; and, wishing to ascertain the condition of things in that quarter, I rode forward to the crest of the hill, where I saw that the camp was nearly surrounded by the enemy, and the fighting very brisk. While there, stragglers of the enemy continued to pass from the southwest to their main body. Although within range of the camp and receiving a straggling fire therefrom, I immediately commenced to fire upon these stragglers, and received their fire in return, and was seconded by Mr. Tough and Stephen Wheeler, of Company F, Third Wisconsin Cavalry, both of whom acted with great bravery, and was just on the point of returning to our line, when I saw 5 mounted rebels with 3 Federal soldiers as prisoners, trying to pass as the others had done. I immediately recognized one of the prisoners as a private of Company C, Third Wisconsin Cavalry, one of the companies stationed at the Springs (and belonging to my own regiment). I determined to rescue them, and called to Tough and Wheeler to advance with me, but the former had just shot one rebel, and was in close pursuit of another in a direction taking him away from me. Wheeler advanced with me, and by pressing hard on the rebels and firing fast, we drove them, killing 1, wounding another, and rescuing the prisoners, who all belonged to Company C, Third Wisconsin Cavalry. As the rebels escaped they attempted to shoot the prisoners, and wounded one in the shoulder. As this was right under the fire of the camp, two of the prisoners made for the camp without stopping to say, "Thank you." The other, and the one personally known to me, named Heaton, seemed to be so bewildered that I had to ride up to him and force him to start in the right direction. All this had taken me over the brow of the hill, so that when I turned to go back, our forces were partially out of sight; but a few jumps of my horse brought them in sight again, and I saw them still in line of battle, while the enemy, to the number of about 450, were advancing upon them in line of battle, and firing very rapidly. I will here state that of the 85 men of our escort, 20 men acted as rear guard to the train, and did not form in line at all, leaving only 65 men in line, of which 40 men were of Company A, Fourteenth Kansas Cavalry, on the right, and 25 of Company I, Third Wisconsin Cavalry on the left. At this time the distance between the two lines was not 200 yards, and the enemy advancing at a walk, firing. I had just time to notice these facts, when I saw 2 men in the center of Company A, Fourteenth Kansas, turn to run, but before they could fairly turn round, Major Curtis and the officers of the company forced them back, and I concluded the fight would be desperate, and was hopeful, but before the officers could get their places the same 2 men and about 8 more turned and ignominiously fled, which the enemy perceiving, the charge was ordered, and the whole line advanced with a shout, at which the remainder of Company A broke, and despite the efforts of General Blunt, Major Curtis, Lieutenants Tappan and Pierce, could not be rallied. At this time a full volley was fired by Company I, Third Wisconsin Cavalry, which so staggered the right of the enemy that I began to have hopes again; but as their left continued to advance their right rallied, but were checked so much that their line, as seen by me, was crooked, their right being behind. The firing then became indiscriminate, and I saw that Company I stood firing their revolvers until the enemy were within 20 feet, and then turned, but before any distance could be made the enemy were in their midst, and out of 40 of the company 23 were killed and 6 wounded and left for dead upon the field. At this time my attention was attracted to my own danger, the enemy having advanced so fast as to cut me off from the rest, and, after trying a couple of dodges, I succeeded in getting into camp at Baxter Springs, all the while closely pursued, and found Lieutenant Pond, who was in command, busily engaged in firing a mounted howitzer outside of his breastworks. The garrison at Baxter Springs consisted of parts of two companies of Third Wisconsin Cavalry and one company of the Second Kansas Colored Regiment,* the whole under the command of Lieut. J. B. Pond, Company C, Third Wisconsin Cavalry. The camp had only been established a few days, and in that time the lieutenant caused to be built a breastwork like a log fence on three sides of a square, in which were his tents and quarters. The attack on the camp had been a partial surprise, but the troops acted splendidly, and Lieutenant Pond, taking the exposed position outside the breastworks, loaded and fired the howitzer three times without any assistance, and the engagement was so close that during this time some of the rebels had entered the breastworks, and at the time I entered the defenses and got where Lieutenant Pond was the bullets were pelting against the logs near by and all around him. As the fight with the force of General Blunt was out of sight of the camp, Lieutenant Pond had been unable to tell what it meant, and was very much surprised to see me, and in answer to my order for his cavalry (with which I hoped to be of some use to our scattered troops), told me that he had that morning started out a forage train of 8 wagons and an escort of 60 men, who had gone in the direction from which the enemy had come, and he supposed they were gobbled up, and in response to his order only 7 men reported to me. With these I returned to the brow of the hill in the direction of the first attack, and plainly saw the enemy engaged in sacking the wagons, and while there saw the band brutally murdered. At the time of the attack the band-wagon, containing 14 members of the brigade band, James O'Neal, special artist for Frank Leslie's pictorial newspaper, one young lad twelve years old (servant of the leader of the band), Henry Pellage, of Madison, Wis., and the driver, had undertaken to escape in a direction a little to the south of west, and made about half a mile. when one of the wheels of the wagon ran off, and the wagon stopped on the brow of the hill in plain sight of where I stood. As the direction of the wagon was different from that in which most of the troops fled, it had not attracted such speedy attention, and the enemy had just got to it as I returned, giving me an opportunity to see every member of the band, Mr. O'Neal, the boy, and the driver shot, and their bodies thrown in or under the wagon and it fired, so that when

* Known after December 13, 1864, as the Eighty-third U. S. Colored Infantry.

we went to them, all were more or less burned and [the wagon] almost entirely consumed. The drummer-boy, a very interesting and intelligent lad, was shot and thrown under the wagon, and when the fire reached his clothes it must have brought returned consciousness, as he had crawled a distance of 30 yards, marking the course by bits of burning clothes and scorched grass, and was found dead with all his clothes burned off except the portion between his back and the ground as he lay upon his back. A number of the bodies were brutally mutilated and indecently treated. Being satisfied that Lieutenant Pond could hold the camp against their force, I took two of the men and started out on the prairie in search of General Blunt, Major Curtis, or any others I could find, and in about an hour after succeeded in hearing of the general's safety, and learned also that Major Curtis was supposed to be a prisoner, as his horse had been shot from under him. I learned this from a wounded soldier that had concealed himself in the grass while the enemy had passed by him; and just then observing a deserted buggy and horse, I placed him in it with a man to take care of him, and they reached the camp in safety. The enemy were still in plain sight, and remained on the prairie till about 4 o'clock, when they marched south in a body. General Blunt and Major Curtis had tried to stop the flight of our troops from the start, and had several very narrow escapes in doing so, as the enemy were close upon them, and finally the general succeeded in collecting about 10 men, and with these he worried the enemy, attacking them in small parties, and, when pursued by too large a force, falling back until they turned, and then in turn following them, so that at no time was he out of sight of the enemy, and most of the time close enough to worry and harass them. As they withdrew from the field, he searched for and took care of the wounded, and remained upon the ground till they were all taken in and cared for, and then went into camp.

The ground on which the fight took place is rolling prairie, extending west a long distance, covered with grass, and intersected with deep ravines and gulleys, on the banks of which grow willow bushes, sufficient to conceal any difficulty in crossing, but not sufficient to protect from observation; and in retreating, many of our men were overtaken at these ravines, and killed while endeavoring to cross. Major Curtis had become separated from the general, and while riding by the side of Lieutenant Pierce his horse was shot and fell. All supposed he was taken prisoner by the enemy, being close upon them, and Lieutenant Pierce saw him alive in their hands. The next day his body was found where his horse had fallen, and he was, without doubt, killed after having surrendered. Thus fell one of the noblest of all the patriots who have offered up their lives for the cause of their country. Maj. H. Z. Curtis was a son of Major-General Curtis, and served with his father during his memorable campaign through Arkansas, and was present with him at the battle of Pea Ridge, where he did good service as aide to his father. When General Curtis took command of the Department of the Missouri, the major remained with him as assistant adjutant-general on his staff, and when General Curtis was relieved of that command, the major sought for and obtained an order to report to General Blunt, as assistant adjutant-general, and in that position had done much toward regulating and systematizing the business of district headquarters of Kansas and the frontier; and on General Blunt's determining to take the field, Major Curtis accompanied him with alacrity, parting with his young and affectionate wife at Fort Scott, on the 4th of October, and met his horrible fate at Baxter Springs, on Tuesday, October 7. All who knew Major Curtis acknowledge his superior ability, and in his particular duties he had no equal. Beloved by the general and all his staff, his loss has cast a heavy gloom over us, "whose business is to die," unusual and heartfelt. In looking over the field, the body of Lieut. [A. W.] Farr was found next to where the first attack was made, with marks of wounds by buckshot and bullets. The lieutenant was unarmed at the time of the attack, and had been riding in a carriage, but had evidently jumped therefrom and attempted to escape on foot. Lieutenant Farr was a prominent young lawyer from Geneva, Wis., and had been a partner of General B. F. Butler, at Worcester, Mass. At the time of the breaking out of the rebellion he took a patriotic view of the difficulty, and, although a strong Democrat, like General Butler, had accepted a position where he thought he could be of service to his country, and has fallen in the good cause. Well does the writer of this remember the night before his death, while we were lying on the ground with our blankets over us. The lieutenant said it was not ambition nor gain that prompted him to enter the army, but only that he might do his mite towards crushing the rebellion; that he did not seek promotion, but was willing to serve where he could do the most good. Truly a patriot was lost when Lieutenant Farr was killed. Other dead, many of them brave and true men, were scattered and strewn over the ground for over a mile or two, most with balls through their heads, showing that they were killed after having surrendered, which the testimony of the wounded corroborates. They were told, in every instance, that if they would surrender and deliver up their arms they should be treated as prisoners of war, and upon doing so were immediately shot down. Sergt. Jack Splane, Company I, Third Wisconsin Cavalry, was treated in this way, and the fiend that shot him, after taking his arms, said, "Tell old God that the last man you saw on earth was Quantrill." Sergeant Splane is now alive, although he received five balls, one in his head, one through his chest, one through his bowels, and the others in his leg and arm. Private Jesse Smith was shot nearly as bad and under the same circumstances, but he did not lose his consciousness, and says that the rebel who shot him, and as he lay upon his face, jumped upon his back and essayed to dance, uttering the most vile imprecations. Some unarmed citizens that were with us were killed, and their bodies stripped of clothing. Take it all in all, there perhaps has not a more horrible affair (except the massacre at Lawrence, in Kansas) happened during the war, and brands the perpetrators as cowards and brutes. I will here also state that a woman and a child were shot at the camp; both will recover. It was done premeditately, and not by random shots, and the brute who shot the child was killed by a shot from the revolver of Sergeant McKenzie, Company C, Third Wisconsin Cavalry.

I respectfully call your attention to the facts set forth in this report, in hopes the Government will see fit to retaliate for the actions of this band of desperadoes, who are recognized and acknowledged by the Confederate authorities, and whose report of this affair stated that the brutality of the beast was exultingly published by the Confederate papers, and approved by the Confederate officials. Capt. A. H. Campbell, Fourteenth Kansas Volunteers, while a prisoner in the hands of the enemy at Fort Smith, Ark., was in presence of this person, Quantrill, and heard him say that he never did, and never would, take any prisoners, and was boasting of the number of captured soldiers he had caused to be shot, stating particulars, &c. These facts should be published to the civilized world, that all may know the character of the people against whom we are contending. I would also respectfully call the attention of the general commanding to the fact that passes in and out of the posts of Sedalia, Springfield, and Kansas City, signed by commanders of the posts, and also permits to carry arms, were found on the bodies of a number of the rebels killed in the fight; and from them and other papers, there is no doubt but that a portion of Quantrill's force was made up of persons belonging to the Missouri militia.

I desire to take special notice of the bravery and coolness of Lieut. James B. Pond, Company C, Third Wisconsin Cavalry, commanding the camp; Sergeant McKenzie, of Company C, Third Wisconsin Cavalry, and the first sergeant, R. W. Smith, of said company.

The number of the killed is as follows:

Maj. H. Z. Curtis, Lieut. A. W. Farr, Lieutenant [Ralph E.] Cook	3
Members of brigade band	14
Clerks and orderlies	6
Company A, Fourteenth Kansas	18
Company I, Third Wisconsin	23
Company C, Third Wisconsin (in camp)	6
Citizens	10
	80
Wounded	18
Total	98

The loss of the enemy, as far as known, is between 20 and 30.

Very respectfully, your obedient servant,

B. S. HENNING,
Major Third Wisconsin Cavalry.

Col. OLIVER D. GREENE,
Asst. Adjt. Gen., Department of the Missouri, Saint Louis.

No. 4.

Report of Lieut. James B. Pond, Third Wisconsin Cavalry.

BAXTER SPRINGS, CHEROKEE NATION,
October 7, 1863.

COLONEL: I was attacked to-day by Quantrill with about 650 men, and, after one hour's hard fighting, I am able to report to you that I still hold the post, and the old flag floats over us as proudly as ever.

The attack was made from the woods east of the camp. It was unexpected, as I had sent my cavalry out not more than an hour previous to reconnoiter on the same road the enemy came in on. My men were at dinner when the attack was made, and most of them were obliged to break through the enemy's lines in order to get their arms, which were in camp. In doing this, 4 of my men were shot down. I was in my tent about 200 yards west of the camp when I heard the first firing. The reason for my camp being here was, that I had just arrived with re-enforcements, and the camp was not large enough to accommodate the whole of my command, and I had just had the men at work extending the defense up to my quarters. When I looked out, I saw the camp surrounded on all sides by mounted men two ranks deep. I called what men were near to me to get inside the camps if possible. At the same time I ran through the enemy's ranks myself, and got safely inside, where I found the enemy's men as numerous as my own. In a moment every man was rallied, and we soon succeeded in getting the enemy outside the camp. This done, I called for men to get the howitzer, which stood just over the intrenchment, on the north side. Whether the men heard me or not I am unable to say, as the volleys of musketry and the yells of the enemy nearly drowned every other noise; but no one came to my assistance. I got the howitzer at work myself, and, after three shots into their ranks, succeeded in repulsing the main force, which retreated in good order over the hill north of camp, where I heard firing, and supposed they had attacked my cavalry, which was then out; but upon looking round, I discovered Major Henning, of our regiment, who had gallantly cut his way through the enemy, and rescued 3 of my men, who had been taken prisoners, and brought them safely to camp. The major informed me that General Blunt was close by, and that the enemy were driving him, and called for cavalry to go to the general's relief. This I could not furnish him, as every effective man had been sent out in the morning, and all I had was about 25 of my own company (C) and 20 of Company D, Third Wisconsin Cavalry (none of which had serviceable horses), and 50 negroes. The major thought that, under the circumstances, I could do no better than hold my camp, while he went out in hopes to meet General Blunt, and inform him that my camp was still in our possession; and shortly afterward I discovered that General Blunt's escort and band had been massacred, their wagons burned, and the bodies burned and stripped of clothing, and left upon the ground, and the enemy had formed in line of battle on the prairie. At 2 o'clock a flag of truce approached. The bearer, George Todd, demanded the surrender of the camp, which, being refused, he stated that he demanded in the name of Colonel Quantrill, of the First Regiment, First Brigade, Army of the South, an exchange of prisoners. I answered that I had taken no prisoners; that I had wounded several of his men, whom I had seen fall from their horses, and would see that they were cared for, provided he would do the same by our men. He said he had 12 privates and the adjutant-general (Major Curtis) prisoners, and that I had killed about 50 of his men, and if I would promise to take care of his wounded, and see that they were paroled after they were able to leave, he would promise me that no harm should befall Major Curtis or our men. This, I think, was intended for a blind to find out what I had done, as they had already murdered Major Curtis and all the prisoners. This evening General Blunt came, accompanied by Tough, who, with 6 or 8 men, have been following Quantrill on his retreat, and report that he crossed the Neosho at the Fort Gibson road, and had gone south. Is there a braver man living than the general?

My losses are, 6 killed and 10 wounded, of Company C, Third Wisconsin Cavalry. Lieutenant [R. E.] Cook, of the Second [Kansas] Colored, and John Fry, the express rider, and 1 negro were killed. As near as I can learn, the casualties of General Blunt are about 80 killed and 6 or 7 wounded. Most of the killed are shot through the head, showing that they were taken prisoners and murdered. Lieutenant Farr, judge-advocate, is among the murdered; also Henry Pellage, and the entire brigade band.

Here allow me to make mention of some of the noble acts of some of the men of my command. Sergeant [W. L.] McKenzie, of my company, exchanged eleven shots with a rebel officer, and succeeded in killing his horse. The man then dismounted, and took to the timber, followed by McKenzie, who, with only one shot in his revolver, killed his man, while his adversary was firing at him. Sergeant [R. W.] Smith, I think, was the coolest man on the ground, and did not fail to see that every order was executed to the letter. Sergeant [R.] Chestnut, of Company D, Third Wisconsin Cavalry, commanded the men of his company, and did nobly. The darkies fought like devils. Thirteen of them were wounded the first round, and not one but what fought the thing through.

The number of the enemy killed, as far as heard from, are 11, and I know that we wounded more than twice that number, which they carried off the field.

There are several other interesting items, of which I will give a full detail in future.

Respectfully, your obedient servant,

JAMES B. POND,

First Lieut. Co. C, Third Wis. Cav., Comdg. Post, Fort Blair.

Lieut. Col. C. W. BLAIR,

Commanding Post, Fort Scott.

No. 5.

Report of Col. W. C. Quantrill, Confederate service.

IN CAMP ON CANADIAN,
October 13, 1863.

I have the honor to make the following report of my march from the Missouri River to the Canadian, a distance of 450 miles:

I started on the morning of October 2, at daybreak, and had an uninterrupted march until night, and encamped on Grand River for three hours; then marched to the Osage. We continued the march from day to day, taking a due southwest course, leaving Carthage 12 miles east, crossing Shoal Creek at the falls, then going due west into the Seneca Nation.

On October 6, about 2 p. m., the advance reported a train ahead. I ordered the advance to press on and ascertain the nature of it. Captain Brinker being in command of the advance, he soon discovered an encampment, which he supposed to be the camp of the train; in this we were mistaken. It proved to be the camp belonging to Fort Baxter, recently built and garrisoned with negroes, 45 miles south of Fort Scott, Kans. When the advance came near the camp they saw that they were not discovered, and they fell back a short distance to wait for the command to come up. I now ordered the column to close in and to form by fours and charge, and leading the head of the column myself with Captains Brinker and Pool, took about one-half of the column to the encampment which they had discovered, still being ignorant of the fort. This they charged, driving everything before them, and in two minutes were in possession of the fort. The negroes took shelter behind their quarters. Having no support, my men were compelled to fall back. Not knowing myself where the fort was, I moved with three companies—Captains Todd, Estes, and Garrett, in all 150 men—out on the prairie north of the camp, and discovered a train with 125 men as an escort, which proved to be Major-General [J. G.] Blunt and staff with body guard and headquarters train, moving headquarters from Fort Scott, Kans., to Fort Smith, Ark. I immediately drew up in line of battle, and at this time I heard heavy firing on my left, and on riding out discovered, for the first time, the fort, with at least half of my men engaged there. I ordered them to join me immediately, which they did, on the double-quick. General Blunt formed his escort, still in doubt as to who we were. I now formed 250 men of all the companies and ordered a charge. Up to this time not a shot had been fired, nor until we were within 60 yards of them, when they gave us a volley too high to hurt any one, and then fled in the wildest confusion on the prairie. We soon closed up on them, making fearful havoc on every side. We continued the chase about 4 miles, when I called the men off, only leaving about 40 of them alive. On returning, we found they had left us 9 six-mule wagons, well loaded; 1 buggy (General Blunt's); 1 fine ambulance; 1 fine brass band and wagon, fully rigged.

Among the killed were General Blunt, Majors Curtis, Sinclair, and [B. S.] Henning, Captain Tufft [Tough], and 3 lieutenants of the staff, and about 80 privates of the escort. My loss here was 1 man killed (William Bledsoe) and 1 severely wounded (John Coger). In the charge on the fort, my loss was 2 men killed (Robert Ward and William Lotspeach); wounded, Lieutenant Toothman and Private Thomas Hill. Federal loss at the fort, 1 lieutenant and 15 privates killed; number wounded, not known.

We have as trophies two stand of colors, General Blunt's sword, his commission (brigadier-general and major-general), all his official papers, &c., belonging to headquarters. After taking what we wanted from the train; we destroyed it, fearing we could not carry it away in the face of so large a force. We then sent a flag of truce to the fort to see if we had any wounded there. There was none.

I did not think it prudent to attack the fort again, and, as we had wounded men already to carry, and it was so far to bring them, [I concluded] that I would leave the fort. So at 5 p. m. I took up the line of march due south on the old Texas road. We marched 15 miles, and encamped for the night. From this place to the Canadian River we caught about 150 Federal Indians and negroes in the Nation gathering ponies. We brought none of them through.

We arrived at General [D. H.] Cooper's camp on the 12th in good health and condition.

At some future day I will send you a complete report of my summer's campaign on the Missouri River.

Your obedient servant,

W. C. QUANTRILL,
Colonel, Commanding, &c.

Major-General PRICE.

P. S.—In this report I neglected to say that Colonels Holt and Roberson and Captain Tucker, who have been in Missouri on business for the army, were with me, and took an active part in leading the men on the enemy.

OCTOBER 11-14, 1863.—Demonstration against Fayetteville, Ark.

Reports of Maj. Thomas J. Hunt, First Arkansas Cavalry (Union).

HEADQUARTERS POST,
Fayetteville, Ark., October 13, 1863.

GENERAL: Colonel Brooks with a force of from 1,000 to 1,200 men, is now camped on White River, within 10 miles of this post. He made a formal demand for the surrender of the post on Sunday, the 11th, at 11 a. m. I have been ready to fight them ever since, and expecting they would attack. I have sent scouts to their camp each day since driving in their pickets, and at one time going close to their headquarters, into which they fired with revolvers.

According to the best information I can get, Brooks is being re-enforced daily, and will attack us when his force is, in his opinion, equal to the emergency. He has now about 1,000 men, and probably knows our force and position. I cannot oppose him with half so many men, and am becoming quite concerned in regard to the safety of some of the stores now in my charge. The camp and garrison equipage of the First Arkansas Cavalry and of the First Arkansas Battery is all here, and can hardly be defended by the force now here without risk of loss; besides this, there is the telegraph train and supplies, post and quartermaster stores to a considerable extent. I have no one to look to for re-enforcements excepting you. I sent to Cincinnati, Ark., where Major Foreman was said to be with a battalion of Indians; but, from the length of time the messengers have been gone, have given up hope.

I desire re-enforcements immediately, and also ammunition, rifle and pistol, especially rifle, caliber .54. It is said a supply for our regiment has been at Cassville; we have none here. The commissary will be unable to issue full rations for the five days succeeding the 15th, from the supply on hand here. I am now making the best arrangements of the force here, in view of defending the place to the last.

T. J. HUNT,
Major First Arkansas Cavalry Volunteers, Comdg. Post.

Brigadier-General McNEIL.

HEADQUARTERS POST,
Fayetteville, Ark,, October 16, 1863.

SIR: After receiving your dispatch from near Carthage, Mo., advising me to keep a lookout for Brooks, I made use of all the opportunities that offered to find out his whereabouts. I did not hear anything more definite than a report, brought by Major Stephenson from Fort Smith, that Brooks with his force had crossed the Arkansas River, until Saturday night, October 10, the provost-marshal reported movements among sympathizers, from which he inferred that an enemy was near. I kept patrols on all roads from which danger was expected, with instructions to be vigilant.

On Sunday, October 11, about 11.30 a. m., a flag of truce was brought to the picket on the Old Missouri road, by Captain [S.] Smithson, of Brooks' regiment, Confederate Army, and the following demand sent in, viz:

HEADQUARTERS DISTRICT OF NORTHWESTERN ARKANSAS,
Near Fayetteville, October 11, 1863.

To the Commander of the Federal Troops at Fayetteville:

SIR: Having the town of Fayetteville surrounded by a superior force, and to prevent the effusion of blood, I demand the immediate surrender of the place and the troops within the same. Thirty minutes will be given for a reply.

Very respectfully,

W. H. BROOKS,
Colonel, Commanding.

A reply was sent to the effect that no surrender would be made without a fight. The pickets were re-enforced, and patrols sent out to feel the enemy on the several roads leading in his direction without delay.

Lieutenant [J. G.] Robertson and 12 men came onto a company of 30 or 40 rebels, under Tuck Smith. He immediately charged the party, who were in Walker's house, on the Huntsville road, on the West Fork of White River. They retreated a half mile through a lane, and then formed in line of battle in the brush, when our party withdrew, having captured 1 horse and equipments, and, it is supposed, seriously wounding 1 man, if not more.

The most reliable reports placed the rebel force at 600 armed and 200 unarmed men.

My main force during this time was drawn up in line of battle on the public square, where they remained until after dark, when they moved to camp, and spent the night on their arms. The quartermaster's train and all wagons available were drawn around the square for breastworks, and orders given to fall back to them if an attack commenced. About 8 p. m., Vougham and 20 men of his independent company came in from near Huntsville, confirming the reports in regard to Brooks, his force, and his intention of attacking the place. All the patrols reported promptly and favorably, excepting Lieutenant [J.] Vougham, of Company I, who was sent on a very important road—the Old Missouri—and came in drunk, not reporting.

The main command was formed in line of battle on the public square at the first intimation of danger. They remained in this position until after dark, when they were moved to quarters, and ordered to lie on their arms during the night. All were wakened at 3 a. m. of the 12th, and preparations made to meet the enemy if an attack was made at daylight.

In the morning the sergeant who patroled the upper Huntsville road reported that Brooks' command had crossed the Middle Fork of White River at dusk of the evening before, and had gone on to Green McGuire's to camp. As soon as this was known, Captain [R. B.] Mack and Lieutenant [M. J.] Patton and 40 men were sent to find the camp, and ascertain if possible the number of men. They reported on return at 1 p. m. to have found the camp at McGuire's, and that there were 500 or 600 men there. Lieutenant Patton and 5 men drove the pickets in on a run, and charged a small church, where Brooks had headquarters, shooting into it with their revolvers. They were immediately followed by Brooks' whole command, and were once surrounded on the road, but took a by-path and came in safe. Shortly after, a lady came in who was a prisoner, and being examined by Brooks at the time of the charge, corroborating their statements in regard to numbers and the confusion of the charge, &c.

At night all the wagons that could be found, including quartermaster's train and sutlers' and citizens' wagons, were drawn around the public square, and the men slept in line of battle on the square. The usual patrols were sent out, and men sent to find if Brooks had moved camp. They reported he had gone to Widow Hannah's, 4 miles farther up on White River. Meantime rumors came in of scouts of men passing round and through the country; one of 100 men on the Wire road to Cassville, one of 60 men on the Elm Springs road, &c.; also of re-enforcements coming to Brooks. Rumors reached camp that Major Foreman and 400 loyal Indians were in camp near Cincinnati, and a dispatch was sent to find him. Dispatches were sent to Cassville explaining our condition on the 12th.

At 2 p. m. of Tuesday, the 13th, a council of officers was held to consult on the feasibility of defending the place and stores and protecting all. It was decided unanimously to move all property to the public square, and erect breastworks and await re-enforcements. This order was being carried out when our patrol on the Old Missouri road was driven in, sharp firing having taken place. The whole command were in line of battle without loss of time, and all expected a fight. No enemy appeared, and the work of moving to the public square was again commenced. During the night a formidable breastwork was built around the square from the materials found in the ruins of the town. Dispatches were sent to General McNeil at night, via Cassville.

At 9 p. m. a well-known citizen came in from Brooks' command, and reported that it had been Brooks' intention to attack the place; but he thought that there would be no attack made.

During the day of the 14th work was continued on the wall around the square. At night Captain Freeburn, with 150 men, came in from Cassville, reporting Brooks as having been at Black's Mill, near Cross Hollows, but that he had gone. With this re-enforcement, I considered all danger from that quarter over, but kept out the same patrols, and exerted the same vigilance as before, until relieved of my command by your arrival.

My thanks are due to the officers and men for their hearty assistance at all times. They seemed anxious to have an opportunity of proving themselves in a fight, and I have no doubt would have sustained themselves nobly against Brooks and his superior forces.

T. J. HUNT,

Major First Arkansas Cavalry, Commanding Post.

Col. M. LA RUE HARRISON,
Commanding Arkansas Volunteers in the Field.

OCTOBER 12-16, 1863.—Scout from Fort Garland, Colo., and killing of outlaw Espanoza.

Report of Lieut. Horace W. Baldwin, McLain's Colorado Battery.

FORT GARLAND, COLO., *October* 16, 1863.

SIR: I have the honor to report that, in compliance with Special Orders, No. —, dated Fort Garland, October —, 1863, I left Fort Garland at 11 o'clock a. m. on the 12th day of October, 1863, and proceeded up the road toward the Sangre de Cristo Pass, to a spot in the road where a man, supposed to be Espanoza, had committed certain outrages a day or two previous. Camped near this spot the first night. Next morning we discovered the trail of the party or parties who were supposed to have committed such outrages as were known to have been committed, from the fact that two mules had been shot and one carriage burned, the remains of which were then lying in the first-mentioned spot in the road, about 18 miles from Fort Garland, Colo., on the Sangre de Cristo Creek. We followed this trail until it led us into the main traveled road, when and where we were obliged to leave it. Going again to the ruins in the road, we took a new direction, directly opposite to the one we had taken the day before. We followed along the mountains on the north side of the road until we struck the range of the Sierra Madre Mountains. Finding no signs of importance, we followed along this range in a southern direction, entering the Great Cañon at its mouth, near the main road. Here we discovered a moccasin track, which we followed a number of miles, but left it, as signs indicated that it was old and of no importance to us. Upon leaving this cañon, about 5 miles from its mouth, the trail of two men (or man and boy) was found. From signs it was evident that these persons had either led or driven two cattle along that spot not to exceed two days before. Following this trail through an almost impassable fall of dead timber a distance of about 5 miles, a number of crows were seen flying over a spot on the side of, and near the top of, a lofty mountain, indicating a camp or carrion near; two magpies were also seen flying about near this spot. Being convinced that a camp was near, I sent a few men with the horses which were being led (several men being dismounted and in advance) to the rear and behind a hill, that they might not be seen, or their heavy tramp over dead timber might not be heard, in case the object of our search should be near at hand. Thomas Tobin (guide) and 4 soldiers were in advance. The horses were scarcely out of sight, behind the hill, when a shot was fired from Tobin's rifle, he having approached the camp and discovered a man (Mexican) sitting on a log at the spot indicated by crows, &c., and fired, wounding the man. A boy was at this time seen to run from a spot near where the man was sitting. He was instantly shot The man, Espanoza, had dodged behind a log or logs, which had been thrown up as a sort of defense. While lying in this position behind the logs he was fired at several times by advancing party (soldiers). From this sort of defense Espanoza fired two shots at soldiers, but without effect. He then raised his body enough to be visible, when he was pierced by many balls, killing him instantly. The heads of the two dead persons were severed from the bodies and taken to our first night's camp, on Sangre de Cristo Creek, about 18 miles from Fort Garland.

Started before daylight from this camp on morning of the 16th of October, 1863, for Fort Garland, arriving at the latter place at 9 a. m. same date. We delivered to you the heads of the two persons as soon as we arrived.

While furnishing you this imperfect and hurried report, I have the honor to remain, your obedient serant,

H. W. BALDWIN,
Lieutenant, Commanding Expedition.

Lieut. COL. SAMUEL F. TAPPAN.

OCTOBER 14, 1863.—Skirmish near Man's Creek, Shannon County, Mo.

Report of Lieut. Michael S. Eddleman, Fifth Missouri State Militia Cavalry.

HEADQUARTERS CO. M, FIFTH M. S. M. CAVALRY,
Camp Glover, Mo., October 18, 1863.

CAPTAIN: In compliance with orders from you, received on the morning of the 14th instant, I took command of the squad of men, numbering 40, detailed to escort the enrolling officer of Shannon County, Missouri. I proceeded to the southeast part of the county, on Jack's Fork of Current River; from there I went to Man's Creek, some 8 miles. The road from Jack's Fork to Man's Creek had the appearance of being traveled daily by considerable quantities of troops; in some places the roads were beaten down quite smooth by horses. After crossing the creek, and gaining the tops of the hills, the roads were strewn with particles of forage, and here seemed to be regular picket posts. I had gone but a short distance when I came upon a party of between 20 and 30 men. Quite a skirmish occurred between them and about 15 of my men, being the advance of the party under my immediate command. The fighting lasted about ten minutes. We emptied four saddles, killing 2 and badly wounding 2 others. The enemy then fled in all directions. I captured four horses and saddles. None of my men were hurt, but several were shot through their clothes. The fight occurred at about 5 p. m. I halted on the ground, and fed my horses on the rebel forage that lay on the ground. I remained here until near 10 o'clock, when I mounted and returned to Salem.

I am of the opinion that there is a considerable rebel force in the neighborhood of where I met what I supposed to be their pickets.

Respectfully, sir, your obedient servant,

M. S. EDDLEMAN,

First Lieut. Co. M, Fifth Missouri State Militia Cavalry.

Capt. LEVI E. WHYBARK,

Comdg. Detachment Fifth Missouri State Militia Cavalry.

OCTOBER 19, 1863.—Affair on Honey Creek, Mo.

Report of Col. Henry Neill, Fifth Provisional Regiment Enrolled Missouri Militia.

HEADQUARTERS SUB-MILITARY DISTRICT,

Clinton, Mo., October 20, 1863.

GENERAL: I have the honor to report to you that Lieutenant Devinney, of Company K, Fifth Provisional Regiment, was sent out Sunday night, with 9 men and three days' rations, to watch the roads in what is called the Honey Creek neighborhood, and to kill some bushwhackers and house robbers who have been for months a terror to the people in that part of the country. Yesterday, while passing quietly up the creek, he came suddenly upon 4 men, who had just finished a nice dinner, which had been furnished them. The lieutenant charged them and killed them all. They were by name Thomas Burks, Joseph Gibson, Riddle, and Hogle. They had only 3 horses, one of them having lost his horse in the raid with Shelby. They were each supplied with small amount of Southern money, and intended to leave for the South as soon as Burks could steal a good horse, so their friends said.

Maj. A. J. Pugh, stationed at Osceola, killed a captain, T. Alexander, formerly of Warsaw, and captured 3 others, a few days ago.

I am using every exertion to keep my district clear. I will protect peaceable, law-abiding citizens, but will show no quarter to armed marauders.

I have the honor, sir, to be, your friend and servant,

HENRY NEILL,

Col., Comdg. Fifth Provisional Regt Enrolled Missouri Militia.

General E. B. BROWN.

OCTOBER 21, 1863.—Affair in Greenton Valley, near Hopewell, Mo.

Report of Lieut. Col. Bazel F. Lazear, First Missouri State Militia Cavalry.

HEADQUARTERS SIXTH SUB-DISTRICT,
Warrensburg, November 1, 1863.

CAPTAIN: Captain [W. H.] Folmsbee, Company B, First Missouri State Militia Cavalry, stationed at Hopewell, reported that, on October 21, Lieutenant [J.] Rhoades and a detachment of same company came upon a party of 4 bushwhackers in Greenton Valley, killing 2 and badly wounding another.

I also have the honor to report that the Sixth Sub-District is remarkably quiet at this time. Only occasionally can hear of a bushwhacker. I have my command distributed in the district, so that I think this state of affairs will continue, and I risk nothing in saying that there is a better state of affairs existing now in Johnson and La Fayette Counties than has since the beginning of the war.

Very respectfully,

B. F. LAZEAR,
Lieutenant-Colonel, Comdg. First Missouri State Militia Cavalry.

Capt. JAMES H. STEGER, *Asst. Adjt. Gen., Dist. Central Missouri.*

OCTOBER 22, 1863.—Mutiny at Bloomfield, Mo.

REPORTS, ETC.

No. 1.—Col. John B. Rogers, Second Missouri State Militia Cavalry, commanding at Cape Girardeau.
No. 2.—Maj. Samuel Montgomery, Sixth Missouri Cavalry, commanding at Bloomfield.
No. 3.—Lieut. Herman J. Huiskamp, Sixth Missouri Cavalry.
No. 4.—Findings and sentences of general court-martial, &c.

No. 1.

Report of Col. John B. Rogers, Second Missouri State Militia Cavalry, commanding at Cape Girardeau.

CAPE GIRARDEAU, MO., *October* 23, 1863.

GENERAL: I received a message [following] by courier last night, signed by all the officers at Bloomfield excepting two, in which they say that they are true and loyal, and are willing and anxious to do right. They say that they are not in revolt against authority, but believing that they were commanded by a traitor, and that the post of Bloomfield, with all the stores, troops, arms, &c., was about to be betrayed and sold into the hands of the enemy, they thought it their imperative duty to seize the commander and commandant.

They, over the names of five commissioned officers, attest all this, and send to me a list of formidable charges, which, if sustained, will go far to justify apprehensions. I do not know of the truth of all this. I will say this: In my headquarters, on the 21st instant, the startling remark was made by an officer high in command, "Look out for disaster, Colonel; Bloomfield is sold, and in a short time will be in the hands of the enemy." I said, "What do you mean?" He replied, "It was sold once to a woman," and all the assertions of Major Montgomery led to similar conclusions. It will not be necessary to go to Bloomfield. Those officers lay the case before me, and express the earnest determination to obey all orders. They will come here if ordered, or do anything else.

I await orders. Answer immediately.

J. B. ROGERS,
Colonel, Commanding.

General FISK.

ADDENDA.

HEADQUARTERS POST, *Bloomfield, Mo., October* 22, 1863.

Col. J. B. ROGERS, *Commanding Post at Cape Girardeau:*

SIR: The extraordinary and flagitious conduct of the major commanding this post, as well as his management of the troops here, has of late created such a vast distrust and loss of confidence in the command, that it was and still is feared that his designs were to betray this whole command into the hands and control of rebels and rebel emissaries.

Among the majority of commissioned officers stationed here it was deemed necessary that a meeting for consultation should be held, which was accordingly done on the evening of the 21st instant, at which meeting, after mature deliberation, the following conclusions were arrived at, viz:

1st. That, under the command of Maj. Samuel Montgomery, the holding and continued possession of the place for any time longer was a matter fraught with serious doubts.

2d. That, judging from the recent conduct of the major commanding, he has wholly lent himself and completely gone over to those who are well known by himself to be and have been the leading traitors in and around this place ever since the commencement of the rebellion. His son, Capt. R. H. Montgomery, and Dr. T. W. Johnson are all in this connection acting with him.

3d. To save and hold in possession this place to the Government which we all represent, it was further agreed upon that the most imperative necessity clearly indicates that the major commanding must immediately be put under arrest, and the further exercise of his power be stayed until this fearful and disgracing condition of things can be reported to the proper authorities.

4th. That to save ourselves, as officers true and faithful in our allegiance to the Government, from the apparently impending disgrace and disaster, we proceed early by to-morrow's dawn to arrest Maj. Samuel Montgomery, commanding this post, and so hold him until our action can be reported, and further directions had thereon. The real causes leading and conducing to the proceedings had, as stated, are embodied in the accompanying charges and specifications against the said Maj. Samuel Montgomery, Sixth Missouri Cavalry Volunteers.

Very respectfully,

WILLIAM H. CROCKETT,
Capt. Company D, Comdg. Second Battalion Sixth Missouri Cav.

JOHN H. PAYNTER,
Captain Company A, Second Battalion Sixth Missouri Cavalry.

V. B. S. REBER,
Lieutenant, Comdg. Section Company K, Second Missouri Artillery.

LUTHER D. POTTER,
Second Lieutenant, Comdg. Company L, Sixth Missouri Cavalry.

E. J. BURROSS,
Second Lieutenant, Comdg. Company E, Sixth Missouri Cavalry.

CAPE GIRARDEAU, *October* 23, 1863.

GENERAL: I have sent Lieutenant-Colonel Hiller to take command at Bloomfield. I have ordered Major Montgomery here. I have ordered Hiller to arrest the leaders of the revolt. Would I better have them sent here or let them stay there? If you think best, they can come up with the guard that accompanies Hiller.

J. B. ROGERS,
Colonel.

General FISK.

CAPE GIRARDEAU, *October* 26, 1863.

General FISK:

The following just received from Bloomfield:

Col. J. B. ROGERS:

Having arrested the company officers, I placed the orderly sergeants in command of the companies. The men are quiet and orderly, and I can see no appearance of mutiny among them. Everything goes on well. I cannot hear of a single rebel squad in this country, and believe there is none. I can learn of nothing having been done that would justify the officers in the course they took. They acted very sillily.

H. M. HILLER,
Lieutenant-Colonel, Commanding.

J. B. ROGERS.

No. 2.

Report of Maj. Samuel Montgomery, Sixth Missouri Cavalry, commanding at Bloomfield.

CAPE GIRARDEAU, *October* 22, 1863.

GENERAL: The following just received, dated—

BLOOMFIELD, 22*d*—9 a. m.

Col. J. B. ROGERS:

I am sorry to inform you that the troops at this post are in open mutiny, headed by the officers who have had the invitations to resign, as well as others. The battery in command of Lieutenant Reber is planted in front of my headquarters, and the men of my battalion drawn up in line, supporting it; myself placed under arrest, and a guard placed over the telegraph operator and instruments. Captain Crockett is commanding the mutineers, although Lieutenant Reber is, to all appearances, the principal insurgent. I, of course, refused to recognize their arrest.

SAML. MONTGOMERY,
Major.

Send me orders.

J. B. ROGERS,
Colonel.

General FISK.

Bloomfield operator says the first intelligence he had of the affair was the whole battalion and battery drawn up in front of headquarters. The major went out and asked them why it was, and Captain Crockett said they had come to arrest him. The major said he would not recognize their arrest, and called them mutineers, and ordered them back to quarters. They then all came in my office to let Colonel Rogers know about it, and Crockett put a guard in my office, and drew carbines on me; said I could not send any message anywhere. The guard was relieved regularly till about 11, when the line went down. I expect some of them went out to cut it.

All quiet here now. The adjutant thinks there is no danger to-night.

HOFFS.

No. 3.

Report of Lieut. Herman J. Huiskamp, Sixth Missouri Cavalry.

BLOOMFIELD, MO., *October* 22, 1863—8.40 p. m.

COLONEL: This morning at 7 I was awakened by Captain Crockett, who told me Lieutenant Reber wished to see me at his headquarters at 8 o'clock. I arrived there at about 8, and found in Lieutenant Reber's office Captain Crockett, Captain Paynter, Lieutenant Burross, Lieutenant Reber, and Lieutenant Potter. They were armed, all of them but Captain Crockett, who only had his belt on. On entering the room I noticed that all battery horses were harnessed. I was requested to take a seat; after doing which, Lieutenant Reber got up and first read a paper signed by the above-named officers, in which they had come to the conclusion that this post was in the hands of a traitor, or words to that effect, and stating also that they intended immediately to arrest the major by force; after which a tremendously long list of charges were read, too voluminous to mention. After getting through this, I was informed that it was decided in a meeting previously that I should not be called in; but upon further deliberation I was called and asked to put my signature to their writings, which I flatly and emphatically refused to do, telling them I did not believe a single one of their charges, and, therefore, considered the thing hasty and wrong. The battery lieutenant then told me he would immediately move his battery in front of the major's headquarters. I told him he might move it there, and, if he pleased, let it off when he got there. After leaving their council, Captain Crockett walked a small distance toward headquarters with me. I told him he was pursuing a wrong and shameful course, and advised him to forward the charges, and the investigation would naturally follow. He said those were his counsels last night, but they were overruled, and it was too late now to back out. Immediately afterward the battery was planted in front of headquarters, and the cavalry, dismounted, supporting it. The major just then coming up, I told him what was the matter. We both then walked up toward them. Upon seeing us approach, Captain Paynter ordered a detail of 4 men from each company, who, seeing that the old major was about to be arrested, were very slow in coming; being, however, ordered by their commanding officer, could not disobey. Captain Potter then asked the major to surrender himself, saying that Captain Crockett would now assume command of the post. The major refused to recognize the arrest, as coming from an inferior officer. We then turned around and walked toward headquarters, closely followed by a guard of 16 men, headed by Captain Paynter. The major at first ordered the officers to dismiss these men, which order was flatly disobeyed. Upon entering the house the guard was instructed to let no man out. Three men were then sent inside, under command of Lieutenant Burross, to prevent the sending of dispatches, with orders to shoot the operator if he attempted to work his line. The guard standing with cocked pistols to prevent him, he told them to shoot, and be damned. In the mean time I left the major talking with Captain Crockett, who shortly afterward ordered the officers to march their men to their quarters. The guard over the telegraph was also released, and so the matter stands.

The main instigator, Lieutenant Reber, has been drunk ever since the occurrence. The men were not aware, as a general thing, what they were ordered out for, and a great many deserted the ranks upon finding out. The whole thing has thus far resulted in a grand fizzle.

H. J. HUISKAMP,
Adjutant.

Col. J. B. ROGERS,
Commanding at Cape Giardeau.

No. 4.

Findings and sentences of General Court-Martial, &c.

GENERAL ORDERS, No. 15. } HDQRS. DEPARTMENT OF THE MISSOURI,
Saint Louis, Mo., January 25, 1864.

I. At the general court-martial which convened at Saint Louis, Mo., pursuant to Special Orders, No. 145, series 1863, from Headquarters Saint Louis District, and of which Col. John F. Tyler, of the First Regiment Missouri State Militia Infantry, is president, were arraigned and tried, first:

Capt. John H. Paynter, Company A, Sixth Regiment Cavalry, Missouri Volunteers, on the following charges and specifications:

CHARGE 1ST.—Mutiny.

Specification.—In this, that he, Capt. John H. Paynter, Company A, Sixth Regiment Missouri Cavalry Volunteers, did begin, excite, cause, and join in a mutiny in the troops in the service of the United States at the post of Bloomfield, Mo., with divers other commissioned officers of said forces, said mutiny having for its object, and resulting in, the unlawful, unwarrantable, and wanton arrest and forcible dispossession from command and authority of the commanding officer of said post, Major Montgomery, of said Sixth Regiment; in said mutiny the accused was a chief actor and a leader. This at Bloomfield, Mo., on or about the 22d day of October, 1863.

CHARGE 2D.—Being present at a mutiny, and not using his utmost endeavors to suppress the same.

Specification.—In this; that he, Capt. John H. Paynter, Company A, Sixth Regiment Missouri Cavalry Volunteers, was present at a mutiny in the forces in the service of the United States at the post of Bloomfield, Mo.; did not use his utmost endeavors to suppress the same; said mutiny having for its object and its result the wanton and unlawful arrest of the commanding officer of said post, Major Montgomery, who was by the mutineers, in the presence and with the co-operation of the accused, so arrested and deposed from his command. This at Bloomfield, Mo., on or about the 22d of October, 1863.

CHARGE 3D.—Coming to the knowledge of an intended mutiny, and not giving information thereof, without delay, to his commanding officer.

Specification.—In this, that he, Capt. John H. Paynter, Company A, Sixth Regiment Missouri Cavalry Volunteers, did seasonably come to the knowledge of an intended mutiny in the forces of the United States service at Bloomfield, Mo., and did not, without delay, or at all, give, or attempt to give, information thereof to his commanding officer, Major Montgomery, of the same regiment, then commanding said post of Bloomfield, Mo., and against whom said mutiny was directed. This on or about the 22d day of October, 1863, at Bloomfield, Mo.

CHARGE 4TH.—Offering violence against his superior officer in the execution of his office.

Specification.—In this, that he, Capt. John H. Paynter, Company A, Sixth Regiment Missouri Cavalry Volunteers, did offer violence against his superior officer, Major Montgomery, of said regiment, then being in the execution of his office as commander of the post of Bloomfield, Mo., by marching his (the accused's) company menacingly under arms against the headquarters of said Montgomery, in which he then was, and, with other officers, forcibly, wantonly, and unlawfully seizing, arresting, and placing under guard the said Montgomery, and confining him in his headquarters. This at Bloomfield, Mo., on or about October 22, 1863.

CHARGE 5TH.—Conduct to the prejudice of good order and military discipline.

Specification.—In this, that he, Capt. John H. Paynter, Company A, Sixth Regiment Missouri Cavalry Volunteers, did, wantonly and forcibly, arrest Major Montgomery, commanding the post of Bloomfield, Mo., with the aid and co-operation of other officers, and then, in order to conceal and screen themselves, and prevent the transmission of intelligence of their conduct to higher military authorities, he and they did seize the United States military telegraph, and place a guard over it, with instructions to shoot the operator if he attempted to send any message. This at Bloomfield, Mo., on or about October 22, 1863.

CHARGE 6TH.—Disobedience of orders.

Specification.—In this, that he, Capt. John H. Paynter, Company A, Sixth Regiment Missouri Cavalry Volunteers, when lawfully ordered by his superior and commanding officer, Maj. Samuel Montgomery, of said regiment, then commanding the post of Bloomfield, Mo., to disperse and remove from headquarters of said post his company, then and there menacingly drawn up under arms without lawful orders, did disobey said order, and refused and neglected so to disperse and remove his said company. This at Bloomfield, Mo., on or about the 22d day of October, 1863.

To all of which charges and specifications the accused pleaded "Not guilty."

FINDING OF THE COURT.

The court having maturely considered the evidence adduced, finds the accused as follows:

Of the *specification*, 1ST CHARGE, "Guilty."
Of the 1ST CHARGE, "Guilty."
Of the *specification*, 2D CHARGE, "Guilty."
Of the 2D CHARGE, "Guilty."
Of the *specification*, 3D CHARGE, "Guilty."
Of the 3D CHARGE, "Guilty."
Of the *specification*, 4TH CHARGE, "Guilty."
Of the 4TH CHARGE, "Guilty."

Of the *specification*, 5TH CHARGE, "Guilty, except the words 'with instructions to shoot the operator if he attempted to send any messages.'"

Of the 5TH CHARGE, "Guilty."

Of the *specification*, 6TH CHARGE, "Guilty."

Of the 6TH CHARGE, "Guilty."

SENTENCE.

And the court does, therefore, sentence him, the said John H. Paynter, captain Company A, Sixth Regiment Missouri Cavalry Volunteers, "*to be dismissed the service of the United States.*"

II. Finding and sentence confirmed. Capt. John H. Paynter, of Company A, Sixth Regiment Missouri Cavalry Volunteers, ceases to be an officer in the service of the United States from this date.

III. 2d. Capt. William H. Crockett, Company D, Sixth Regiment of Cavalry, Missouri Volunteers, on the following charges and specifications:

CHARGE 1ST.—Mutiny.

Specification.—In this, that he, Capt. William H. Crockett, of Company D, Sixth Regiment Missouri Cavalry Volunteers, did begin, excite, cause, and join in a mutiny in the troops in the service of the United States at the post of Bloomfield, Mo., said mutiny having for its object, and resulting in, the unlawful and wanton arrest and forcible dispossession from his command of Maj. Samuel Montgomery, then the commanding officer of said post and troops. This on or about the 21st day of October, 1863.

CHARGE 2D.—Being present at a mutiny, and not using his utmost endeavors to suppress the same.

Specification.—In this, that he, Capt. William H. Crockett, Company D, Sixth Regiment Missouri Cavalry Volunteers, was present at a mutiny in the troops in the service of the United States at the post of Bloomfield, Mo., and did not use his utmost endeavors, or any efforts, to suppress the same, but, instead, aided and abetted the mutineers, officers in said troops, who were unlawfully and wantonly arresting and placing under guard Major Montgomery, their commanding officer. This on or about the 21st of October, 1863, at Bloomfield, Mo.

CHARGE 3D.—Coming to the knowledge of an intended mutiny, and not giving information thereof, without delay, to his commanding officer.

Specification.—In this, that he, Capt. William H. Crockett, Company D, Sixth Regiment Missouri Cavalry Volunteers, did come to and possess knowledge of an intended mutiny in the troops in the service of the United States at the post of Bloomfield, Mo., and did not, without delay, or at any time, give information thereof to his commanding officer, Maj. Samuel Montgomery, the commander of said post, and against whom said mutiny was especially intended and directed. This on or about the 21st day of October, 1863, at Bloomfield, Mo.

CHARGE 4TH.—Offering violence against his superior officer in the execution of his office.

Specification.—In this, that he, Capt. William H. Crockett, Company D, Sixth Regiment Missouri Cavalry Volunteers, did offer violence against his superior officer, Maj. Samuel Montgomery, Second Battalion

Sixth Regiment Missouri Cavalry Volunteers, then in the execution of his office of commander of the post of Bloomfield, Mo., by detailing, and causing to be detailed, a guard of 16 men (soldiers) unlawfully and wantonly to arrest and forcibly detain the said Major Montgomery, who was so arrested and detained by the soldiers of said guard, under the directions, instructions, and commands of said Crockett and others acting with him. This on or about the 21st day of October, 1863, at Bloomfield, Mo.

CHARGE 5TH.—Disobedience of orders.

Specification.—In this, that he, Capt. William H. Crockett, Company D, Sixth Regiment Missouri Cavalry Volunteers, when the officers and men of the troops in the service of the United States at the post of Bloomfield, Mo., were in a state of mutiny, and when lawfully ordered by his superior and commanding officer, Maj. Samuel Montgomery, the commander of said post, to disperse his men and return them and himself to duty, did flatly refuse and disobey the order, and declared that he had assumed command of that post, with other language of like import. This on or about the 21st day of October, 1863, at Bloomfield, Mo.

CHARGE 6TH.—Conduct to the prejudice of good order and military discipline.

Specification.—In this, that he, Capt. William H. Crockett, Company D, Sixth Regiment Missouri Cavalry Volunteers, at the post of Bloomfield, Mo., with divers other officers and soldiers, did unlawfully, wantonly, and maliciously seize, arrest, and depose Maj. Samuel Montgomery, the commanding officer of said post. and then, in order to prevent the transmission of intelligence of their said conduct to higher military authorities, and in order to screen himself and his coadjutors, he and they ordered and placed a guard over the United States military telegraph at said post, with instructions to shoot the operator in case he undertook to send any message by said telegraph. This at Bloomfield, Mo., on or about the 21st day of October, 1863.

To all of which charges and specifications the accused pleaded "Not guilty."

FINDING OF THE COURT.

The court having maturely considered the evidence adduced, finds the accused as follows:

Of the *specification*, 1ST CHARGE, "Guilty."
Of the 1ST CHARGE, "Guilty."
Of the *specification*, 2D CHARGE, "Guilty."
Of the 2D CHARGE, "Guilty."
Of the *specification*, 3D CHARGE, "Guilty."
Of the 3D CHARGE, "Guilty."
Of the *specification*, 4TH CHARGE, "Guilty."
Of the 4TH CHARGE, "Guilty."
Of the *specification*, 5TH CHARGE, "Guilty."
Of the 5TH CHARGE, "Guilty."
Of the *specification*, 6TH CHARGE, "Guilty, except words 'with instructions to shoot the operator in case he undertook to send any message by said telegraph.'"
Of the 6TH CHARGE, "Guilty."

SENTENCE.

And the court does, therefore, sentence him the said William H. Crockett, captain Company D, Sixth Regiment Missouri Cavalry Volunteers, "*to be dismissed the service of the United States.*"

IV. Finding and sentence confirmed. Capt. William H. Crockett, Company D, Sixth Regiment Missouri Cavalry Volunteers, ceases to be an officer in the United States service from this date.

V. 3d. Second Lieut. E. J. Burross, of Company E, Sixth Regiment Missouri Cavalry Volunteers, on the following charges and specifications:

CHARGE 1ST.—Mutiny.

Specification.—In this, that he, Second Lieut. E. J. Burross, of Company E, Sixth Regiment Missouri Cavalry Volunteers, did, without just cause or excuse, begin, excite, cause, and join in a mutiny, in the troops and companies in the service of the United States at the post of Bloomfield, Mo., said mutiny having for its object, and resulting in, the unlawful arrest and forcible dispossession from his command of Maj. Samuel Montgomery, then in command of that post. This at Bloomfield, Mo., on or about the 21st day of October, 1863.

CHARGE 2D.—Being present at a mutiny, and not using his utmost endeavors to suppress the same.

Specification.—In this, that he, Second Lieut. E. J. Burross, of Company E, Sixth Regiment Missouri Cavalry Volunteers, was present at a mutiny of the officers of the troops and forces stationed at Bloomfield, Mo., and did not use his utmost endeavors to suppress the same, but, instead, aided and abetted the mutineers, who unlawfully arrested and deprived from command and put under guard Maj. Samuel Montgomery, then commanding said post of Bloomfield. This at Bloomfield, Mo., on or about the 21st day of October, 1863.

CHARGE 3D —Coming to the knowledge of an intended mutiny, and not giving information thereof, without delay, to his commanding officer.

Specification.—In this, that he, Second Lieut. E. J. Burross, Sixth Regiment Missouri Cavalry Volunteers, did come to the knowledge of an intended mutiny in the troops stationed at Bloomfield, Mo., and did not, without delay, give information thereof to his commanding officer, Major Montgomery, against whom the mutiny was especially directed, but aided and abetted the same. This at Bloomfield, Mo., on or about the 21st day of October, 1863.

CHARGE 4TH.—Offering violence to his superior officer in the execution of his office.

Specification.—In this, that he, Second Lieut. E. J. Burross, of Company E, Sixth Regiment Missouri Cavalry Volunteers, did march his company menacingly in front of the headquarters of the post of Bloomfield, Mo., and did detail 4 men of his company to unlawfully arrest, and aid in arresting, by force and violence, Major Montgomery, of the Sixth Regiment Missouri Cavalry Volunteers, then commanding said post, and then being by said men arrested by violence while in the execution of his office.

CHARGE 5TH.—Conduct to the prejudice of good order and military discipline.

Specification.—In this, that he, Second Lieut. E. J. Burross, of Company E, Sixth Regiment Missouri Cavalry Volunteers, did unlawfully and forcibly arrest, and aid to arrest, Major Montgomery, then in command of the post of Bloomfield, Mo., and in order to prevent transmission of intelligence of his conduct to the higher military authorities, and in order to conceal and screen himself and his coadjutors, the accused did take command of the guard in charge of the telegraphic instruments, and order said guard to shoot the operator if he attempted to send any messages. This at Bloomfield, Mo., on or about the 21st day of October, 1863.

CHARGE 6TH.—Disobedience of orders.

Specification.—In this, that he, Second Lieut. E. J. Burross, of Company E, Sixth Regiment Missouri Cavalry Volunteers, having been lawfully commanded by his superior officer, Major Montgomery, to disperse his company, then menacingly drawn up before the headquarters of said major, who was in command of the post at that time, did disobey said order, and refuse utterly so to disperse his men. This at Bloomfield, Mo., on or about the 21st day of October, 1863.

To all of which charges and specifications the accused pleaded "Not guilty."

FINDING OF THE COURT.

The court having maturely considered the evidence adduced, finds the accused as follows:

Of the *specification*, 1st CHARGE, "Guilty."
Of the 1ST CHARGE, "Guilty."
Of the *specification*, 2D CHARGE, "Guilty."
Of the 2D CHARGE, "Guilty."
Of the *specification*, 3D CHARGE, "Guilty."
Of the 3D CHARGE, "Guilty."
Of the *specification*, 4TH CHARGE, "Guilty."
Of the 4TH CHARGE, "Guilty."
Of the *specification*, 5TH CHARGE, "Guilty, except words, 'and order said guard to shoot the operator if he attempted to send any messages.'"
Of the 5TH CHARGE, "Guilty."
Of the *specification*, 6TH CHARGE, "Not guilty."
Of the 6TH CHARGE, "Not guilty."

SENTENCE.

And the court does, therefore, sentence him, the said Second Lieut. E. J. Burross, Company E, Sixth Regiment Missouri Cavalry Volunteers, "*to be dismissed the service of the United States.*"

VI. Finding and sentence confirmed. Lieut. E. J. Burross, of Company E, Sixth Regiment Missouri Cavalry Volunteers, ceases to be an officer in the service of the United States from this date.

VII. 4th. Second Lieut. Luther D. Potter, of Company L, Sixth Regiment Missouri Cavalry Volunteers, on the following charges and specifications:

CHARGE 1ST.—Mutiny.

Specification.—In this, that he, Second Lieut. Luther D. Potter, of Company L, Sixth Regiment Missouri Cavalry Volunteers, did begin, excite, cause, and join in a mutiny in the troops of the United States stationed at the post of Bloomfield, Mo., in this wise: That he agreed with other officers there stationed that they should march their respective commands against the headquarters of Major Montgomery, of the Sixth Regiment Missouri Cavalry Volunteers, commanding said post, and forcibly seize and arrest their said commander, and deprive him of his command, and, in pursuance thereof, he did march his company, then being in command thereof, before the headquarters of said Montgomery, and did forcibly seize and arrest him, and deprive him of his command, and place a guard of soldiers over him, without just cause or excuse. This at Bloomfield, Mo., on or about the 21st day of October, 1863.

CHARGE 2D.—Being present at a mutiny, and not using his utmost endeavors to suppress the same.

Specification.—In this, that he, Second Lieut. Luther D. Potter, of Company L, Sixth Regiment Missouri Cavalry Volunteers, was present at a mutiny of the officers and soldiers of the troops of the United States at the post of Bloomfield, Mo., in which the commanding officer of said post, Maj. Samuel Montgomery, was forcibly seized, unlawfully arrested, placed in confinement, and deprived of his command; and he, the said Potter, did not use his utmost endeavor to suppress the same, but rather encouraged and incited it. This at Bloomfield, Mo., on or about the 21st day of October, 1863.

CHARGE 3D.—Coming to knowledge of an intended mutiny, and not giving information thereof, without delay, to his commanding officer.

Specification.—In this, that he, Second Lieut. Luther D. Potter, of Company L, Sixth Regiment Missouri Cavalry Volunteers, coming to the knowledge of an intended mutiny by the officers of the command and troops at the post of Bloomfield, Mo., did not, without delay, give information thereof to his commanding officer, but concealed from said officer such knowledge. This at Bloomfield, Mo., on or about the 21st day of October, 1863.

CHARGE 4TH.—Conduct unbecoming an officer and a gentleman.

Specification.—In this, that he, Second Lieut. Luther D. Potter, of Company L, Sixth Regiment Missouri Cavalry Volunteers, did, without orders, cause, provocation, or excuse, aid in forcibly arresting and detaining Maj. Samuel Montgomery, of the Sixth Regiment Missouri Cavalry Volunteers, and did, without order or authority, place, and assist to place, a guard over the said major, and keep and detain him in durance for a considerable time, to the scandal of the service. This at Bloomfield, Mo., on or about the 21st day of October, 1863.

CHARGE 5TH.—Offering violence to his superior officer, being in the execution of his office.

Specification.—In this, that he, Second Lieut. Luther D. Potter, of Company L, Sixth Regiment Missouri Cavalry Volunteers, did offer violence to his superior officer, Maj. Samuel Montgomery, Sixth Regiment Missouri Cavalry Volunteers, then commanding the post of Bloomfield, Mo., and being in the execution of his office, where said Potter was stationed, by marching his company, under arms, before the headquarters of said post, and ordering and causing 4 men of said company to arrest, forcibly and violently, and to aid in forcibly and violently arresting, said Major Montgomery, without just cause, provocation, or excuse. This at Bloomfield, Mo., on or about the 21st day of October, 1863.

CHARGE 6TH.—Disobedience of orders.

Specification.—In this, that he, Second Lieut. Luther D. Potter, of Company L, Sixth Regiment Missouri Cavalry Volunteers, having been lawfully commanded by his superior officer, Maj. Samuel Montgomery, of the Sixth Regiment Missouri Cavalry Volunteers, commanding the post of Bloomfield, Mo., to disperse his company, which he had unlawfully marched up before the headquarters of said post, did disobey said order, and did not disperse his company, and utterly refused to do so. This at Bloomfield, Mo., on or about the 21st day of October, 1863.

To all of which charges and specifications the accused pleaded "Not guilty."

FINDING OF THE COURT.

The court having maturely considered the evidence adduced, finds the accused as follows:

Of the *specification*, 1ST CHARGE, "Guilty."
Of the 1ST CHARGE, "Guilty."
Of the *specification*, 2D CHARGE, "Guilty."
Of the 2D CHARGE, "Guilty."
Of the *specification*, 3D CHARGE, "Guilty."
Of the 3D CHARGE, "Guilty."
Of the *specification*, 4TH CHARGE, "Guilty."
Of the 4TH CHARGE, "Not guilty."
Of the *specification*, 5TH CHARGE, "Guilty."
Of the 5TH CHARGE, "Guilty."
Of the *specification*, 6TH CHARGE, "Not guilty."
Of the 6TH CHARGE, "Not guilty."

SENTENCE.

And the court does, therefore, sentence him, the said Second Lieut. Luther D. Potter, Company L, Sixth Regiment Missouri Cavalry Volunteers, "*to be dismissed the service of the United States.*"

VIII. Finding and sentence confirmed. Second Lieut. Luther D. Potter, Company L, Sixth Regiment Missouri Cavalry Volunteers, ceases to be an officer in the service of the United States from this date.

* * * * * * *

By command of Major-General Schofield.

OLIVER D. GREENE,
Assistant Adjutant-General.

SPECIAL ORDERS, No. 564. } WAR DEPARTMENT, ADJT. GEN.'S OFFICE, *Washington, December* 21, 1863.

* * * * * * *

X. By direction of the President, Second Lieut. V. B. S. Reber, Second Missouri Artillery, is hereby dishonorably dismissed the service of the United States, with loss of all pay and allowances now due, or that may become due, him, for mutiny, disobedience of orders, neglect of duty, and desertion while under arrest.

* * * * * * *

By order of the Secretary of War:

E. D. TOWNSEND,
Assistant Adjutant-General.

OFFICE OF JUDGE-ADVOCATE-GENERAL,
April 15, 1864.

To the PRESIDENT:

Capt. John H. Paynter, of Company A; Second Lieut. E. J. Burross, of Company E, and Second Lieut. Luther D. Potter, of Company L, of Sixth Missouri Cavalry, were found guilty, by general court-martial convened at Saint Louis, Mo., the 9th of January, 1864, of mutiny; of being present at a mutiny, and not using their utmost endeavors to suppress the same; of coming to the knowledge of an intended mutiny, and not giving information thereof, without delay, to their commanding officer; of offering violence to their superior officer in the execution of his office; of conduct to the prejudice of good order and military discipline, and of disobedience of orders.

They were severally sentenced to be dismissed the service of the United States.

From the records of the trials of these officers, it appears that the Second Battalion Sixth Missouri Cavalry, to which they were attached, was, on the 22d October, 1863, stationed at Bloomfield, Mo., under the command of Maj. Samuel Montgomery, who commanded the post; and that, from rumors brought in from the adjacent country that the post was surrounded by the rebels and that a body of rebel troops, 500 strong, was advancing on the post to attack it, the commissioned officers of the battalion appear to have been impressed with the belief that the command was in great danger of betrayal and surrender to the enemy by Major Montgomery; and on the evening of 21st October, 1863, held a meeting for consultation with each other, at which they unanimously determined to place the major in arrest, and to report the state of facts to headquarters as speedily as possible.

On the next morning (22d October), Major Montgomery received notice from Capt. W. H. Crockett, of Company D, that he was under arrest, and, on going to the door of his quarters, found the troops drawn up in line. A guard of 4 men from each company was detailed and posted by Captain Paynter, with instructions to prevent the major from passing out from his quarters. A guard, too, was placed in the telegraph room of the headquarters, with orders to prevent the operator from sending any message without orders from Captain Crockett. While these circumstances were occurring, Major Montgomery was in conversation with Captain Crockett, in the course of which he said, "Captain, there is no use of this thing. If you will disperse your men, I will give you time about on the telegraph to inform Colonel Rogers of this matter, and await his orders." Colonel Rogers was then at Cape Girardeau, and in communication by telegraph. On reiterating this assurance, the major was told by Captain Crockett that it was satisfactory, and the troops were immediately dispersed to their quarters. It does not appear that any act of violence was committed or threatened, nor that Major Montgomery was really subjected to personal restraint, for at the moment when arrangements were made for such restraint the whole difficulty was accommodated, and the guard discharged.

The circumstances set forth in the testimony as tending to palliate the very grave offense of which these officers were found guilty are these:

1st. His allowing, indiscriminately, rebel deserters, large numbers of whom came into the post from day to day, to return to their homes, without requiring them to take any oath or give any bond for their future loyalty, saying, when remarks were made to him on the subject, that he was trying an experiment on his own account, and acknowledging that he had no authority or directions to do so.

2d. His habit of associating constantly while at Bloomfield with the most dangerous and notorious rebels, some of whom were known to have acted as spies; this after he had been specially warned against them by men of character and established loyalty.

3d. His habit of cursing and abusing many of the highest military and civil officers of the Government, including the President and Governor Gamble, in the most profane and bitter terms, in the presence of such associates as have been described, whilst he kept himself isolated from the officers of his command, thus, and by other acts, denouncing and depreciating them, as they thought, to propitiate rebel influence for some ulterior purpose.

4th. That in the sale of contraband goods he favored a notorious secessionist, who at a time "sported a secession badge in his hat."

5th. That he married one of the two most notorious rebel women in the country, who had carried dispatches and written ballads for the rebel army, and of whom it was so currently reported that Major Montgomery must have known it, that she boasted, at a time when the enemy was supposed to be marching on the post, that she ruled it, and that although the Sixth Missouri Cavalry were holding the place now, her Southern friends soon would hold it. That knowing, as he must, of these rumors, he neither said nor did anything to remove the impression made by them on the minds of soldiers and citizens.

It is perfectly clear from the testimony produced before the several courts-martial in this case that when these officers and others stationed at Bloomfield met for conference on the evening of October 21, each one of them was fully of the opinion that Major Montgomery was acting in the interest of the rebels, and would betray and surrender the post to them if the attack then supposed to be impending should be made.

The proceedings of that meeting, a copy of which is appended to each record, exhibit the depth of feeling and sense of responsibility under which these officers acted in the procedure which led to their dismissal. They well knew that it was perilous to themselves; but, after grave consultation, concluded it to be necessary for the safety of the post they were as much bound to defend against treachery and treason from within as against open rebellion from without. There is no evidence whatever that either of them was actuated by a mutinous, insubordinate spirit, or by any unworthy motive. Neither is it shown that their apprehensions of treachery were well founded, but the suspicious circumstances set forth in the testimony recited were well calculated in the dangerous and excited condition of affairs then prevailing in the country surrounding the post to produce such.

All the charges and specifications against these officers were founded on their procedure above described. Their general character and conduct is shown to have been good. It was testified of Captain Paynter, "that he was the most prompt officer in the battalion, gentlemanly, and obedient to orders;" of Lieutenant Potter, that "his conduct was unexceptionably good;" "paid strict attention to his duties, and was never away from his post;" and of Lieutenant Burross, "that his conduct was unexceptionably good."

The Hon. S. H. Boyd, of the House of Representatives, has presented to the President a petition from 35 members of the Legislature of Missouri, praying the restoration of these officers to their former rank and command in the Sixth Missouri Cavalry. These petitioners declare their disbelief that they were guilty of willful mutiny, or could possibly be, as they are true patriots, who have from the outbreak of the rebellion devoted themselves to the cause of their country; that when, in the spring of 1861, efforts were made by the rebels to force the State out of the Union, and the Home Guard sprang to arms, these officers were their leaders, and "that many a sanguinary field has since attested their patriotism and valor;" among them Lebanon, Wilson's Creek, Sugar Creek, Pea Ridge, and Prairie Grove.

The petitioners further declare that the term of service of the regiment to which these officers were attached expires on the 4th of July next, and that the men will not re-enlist as veterans unless with their influence.

The Hon. Messrs. Boyd, McClurg, and Scott concur in the prayer of the petitioners. Mr. Boyd, in presenting the petition, takes occasion to state that he knows these officers personally; that "they served under Lyon at Wilson's Creek, and are as good men as ever breathed."

It is recommended that the disability under which these officers labor, in consequence of their several sentences, be removed.

J. HOLT,
Judge-Advocate-General.

WAR DEPARTMENT, ADJUTANT-GENERAL'S OFFICE
May 17, 1864.

The GOVERNOR OF MISSOURI:

SIR: I have the honor to inform you that, by direction of the President of the United States, the disability resting upon J. H. Paynter, E. J. Burross, and Luther D. Potter,* formerly captain and second lieutenants, respectively, in the Sixth Missouri Cavalry, by reason of their dismissal from service under sentence of general court-martial, is hereby removed, and they may be recommissioned if Your Excellency so desires.

I am, sir, very respectfully, &c.,

THOMAS M. VINCENT,
Assistant Adjutant-General.

OCTOBER 25, 1863.—Action at Pine Bluff, Ark.

REPORTS.†

No. 1.—Maj. Gen. Frederick Steele, U. S. Army, commanding Army of Arkansas, with congratulatory order.
No. 2.—Col. Powell Clayton, Fifth Kansas Cavalry, commanding at Pine Bluff, Ark.
No. 3.—Lieut. Col. Thomas N. Pace, First Indiana Cavalry.
No. 4.—Maj. Thomas W. Scudder, Fifth Kansas Cavalry.
No. 5.—Lieut. Milton F. Clark, Fifth Kansas Cavalry.
No. 6.—Lieut. Col. Henry C. Caldwell, Third Iowa Cavalry, of the pursuit of Marmaduke.
No. 7.—Brig. Gen. John S. Marmaduke, C. S. Army, commanding expedition.
No. 8.—Col. Colton Greene, Third Missouri Cavalry (Confederate), commanding Marmaduke's brigade.

---

* The President's indorsement removed the disability in case of Capt. William H. Crockett also. It does not appear that any of these officers re-entered the service.

† See General Schofield's report, p. 12.

No. 9.—Col. Robert R. Lawther, Tenth Missouri Cavalry (Confederate), commanding brigade.
No. 10.—Col. G. W. Thompson, Sixth Missouri Cavalry (Confederate), commanding Shelby's brigade.
No. 11.—Col. J. C. Monroe, First Arkansas Cavalry, commanding Cabell's brigade.
No. 12.—Col. Robert C. Newton, Fifth Arkansas Cavalry, commanding division.
No. 13.—Maj. John P. Bull, Fifth Arkansas Cavalry, commanding Newton's brigade.
No. 14.—Capt. W. B. Denson, commanding squadron.
No. 15.—Maj. B. D. Chenoweth, Twenty-first Texas Cavalry, commanding Texas Cavalry Brigade.
No. 16.—Maj. R. C. Wood, Missouri Cavalry Battalion (Confederate).

No. 1.

*Report of Maj. Gen. Frederick Steele, U. S. Army, commanding Army of Arkansas, with congratulatory orders.**

LITTLE ROCK, ARK., *November* 3, 1863.

MAJOR: I have the honor to inclose Colonel Clayton's report of his gallant defense of Pine Bluff. Also Lieutenant-Colonel Caldwell's report of his pursuit of Marmaduke. Caldwell captured more property than fell into the possession of Marmaduke during his raid.

Very respectfully, major, your obedient servant,

FRED'K STEELE,
Major-General, Commanding.

Maj. OLIVER D. GREENE,
Assistant Adjutant-General.

GENERAL ORDERS, No. 41. } HEADQUARTERS ARMY OF ARKANSAS,
Little Rock, Ark., November 7, 1863.

It is fit that the conduct of troops on the battle-field, especially gallant and heroic, should be publicly approbated by the commanding officer, and officially published, for the emulation of the whole army. Therefore, the major-general commanding the Army of the Arkansas publishes to his command these facts: On the 25th day of October last the cavalry brigade consisting of the Fifth Kansas and First Indiana Cavalry, commanded by Col. Powell Clayton, and numbering less than 600 men, was attacked at Pine Bluff, Ark., by an army of rebels, 2,500 in number, with twelve pieces of artillery. Unawed by the overwhelming force, they fought them for five hours, and drove them, discomfited and with heavy loss, from the field. Retreat or surrender were words unknown to these brave men, and their determined heroism has inflicted a blow upon the rebel army not soon to be forgotten. The major-general commanding hereby tenders to Col. Powell Clayton and his brave command his sincere and earnest thanks for their gallant conduct in the defense of Pine Bluff, and they can rest well assured that their gallantry deserves, and will receive, the applause of their Government and the loyal people, the highest ambition of the true soldier.

By order of Maj. Gen. Frederick Steele:

[F. H. MANTER,]
Colonel and Chief of Staff.

---

*See also Steele to Schofield, October 28, 1863, in "Correspondence, etc.," Part II, p. 682.

No. 2.

Report of Col. Powell Clayton, Fifth Kansas Cavalry, commanding at Pine Bluff, Ark.

HEADQUARTERS POST,
Pine Bluff, October 27, 1863.

GENERAL: I respectfully submit to you the following report of the battle fought at this place October 25, between General Marmaduke's forces and the garrison of this post:

About 8 o'clock in the morning I sent Lieutenant [M. F.] Clark, Fifth Kansas Cavalry, with one company, out in the direction of Princeton. He did not go far before he met the enemy advancing in force. The enemy's skirmishers fired on him at once, but soon after, an armed party, bearing a flag of truce, came forward, and the officer in command of this party insisted that he should be allowed to pass in immediately. Lieutenant Clark told him it was no way to first fire on him, then insist on going in with a flag of truce; but he would give him half an hour for him (Clark) to send in to headquarters and get an answer. He rejected the proposition, and said he had dispatches from General Marmaduke to the commanding officer, he supposed, demanding a surrender of the place. The lieutenant replied, "Colonel Clayton never surrenders, but is always anxious for you to come and take him, and you must get back to your command immediately, or I will order my men to fire on you." He fell back, and they commenced skirmishing again. Meantime the whole command was ordered out, and skirmishers sent in every direction; also 300 negroes set to work rolling cotton-bales out of the ware-houses. In less than half an hour I had all the streets leading into court square completely and very formidably fortified with cotton-bales, and my artillery—six mountain howitzers and three small steel-rifled guns—planted so as to command every street leading into the square; my sharpshooters posted in all of the houses and other buildings on the square, so that the enemy could in no way approach the works only through the open spaces. I then had about 200 negroes commence carrying water from the river up to the square, and fill all the barrels they could find, so that, if necessary, I could hold out two days, even though cut off from the river. The enemy succeeded in driving in my skirmishers about 9 o'clock, and approached the works in three columns, as follows: On my right, center, and left, the main one being in the center, and opened on me with their artillery, twelve pieces, a part of which were 12-pounder rifle guns, throwing both the Hotchkiss and the James projectiles. The firing from both sides, from the artillery and sharpshooters, continued with great rapidity until 2 o'clock. Between 12 m. and 1 p. m., the enemy set fire to the buildings on my right, expecting thereby to rout me; but I put some 200 negroes to carrying water and throwing it on the buildings immediately joining the square, and thus prevented the fire from doing me any damage. The enemy, seeing that he failed in his efforts to drive me by fire, as well as by force, planted another battery on my center, and kept up a heavy cannonading for a short time, then retreated (about 2 p. m.), leaving a great portion of his wounded and dead on the field. I followed him for about 1 mile, then returned and stationed my pickets as usual. My loss was 11 killed, 27 wounded, and 1 missing. There were also 5 negroes killed and 12 wounded. The enemy's loss in killed and wounded, as far as ascertained, is about 130, and will probably reach 150. I have also 3 lieutenants and 30 men prisoners, 15 of whom are wounded. The buildings that were burned by the enemy were occupied by the Fifth Kansas Cavalry as quarters; consequently their camp and garrison equipage and their books and papers were all burned. The train was also corralled in sheds in rear of the buildings that were burned. When the fire was raging, the mules were cut loose to keep them from burning, and 62 of them are missing. The enemy also burned one warehouse, containing over 200 bales of cotton. In setting fire to these buildings, General Marmaduke committed the gross and barbarous deed of burning some of his own wounded. Several of his own men, who were wounded, were burned to death, and almost entirely consumed by the flames that he kindled. The court-house, General James', General Yell's, and John Bloom's houses were all nearly destroyed by the enemy's artillery. There is scarcely a house in town that does not show the effects of the battle. The enemy plundered every house he could get to, and stole every horse and mule from the citizens that he could lay his hands on. The prisoners that I captured reported General Marmaduke's force from 2,000 to 3,000 men, and twelve pieces of artillery. I think he had some 2,500 men and twelve pieces of artillery.

My force consisted of the Fifth Kansas Cavalry, commanded by Maj. Thomas W. Scudder, and the First Indiana Cavalry, commanded by Lieut. Col. Thomas N. Pace, and one company of State militia, commanded by Captain [R.] Murphy, amounting in all to some 550 men. Captain Murphy's company behaved like veterans. The officers and men both of the Fifth Kansas Cavalry and of the First Indiana Cavalry behaved most admirably. The fact that so small a force kept four times their number at bay for five hours, and finally drove them from the field, bespeaks for the whole command greater efficiency and gallantry than words can do. Every officer and soldier in the whole command seemed determined to fight them as long as there was a round of ammunition left. The negroes also did me excellent service (see Captain Talbot's report, which I fully indorse), and deserve much therefor.

I am, general, very respectfully, your obedient servant,

POWELL CLAYTON,
Colonel, Commanding.

Major-General STEELE,
Commanding Army of Arkansas.

[Inclosure.]

HEADQUARTERS FREEDMEN,
Pine Bluff, Ark., October 27, 1863.

Colonel CLAYTON,
Commanding Post of Pine Bluff:

SIR: The following report of the part taken by the negroes under my charge in the action of the 25th instant at this post is respectfully submitted:

When the skirmishing first commenced, I received orders from you to furnish as many men as possible to roll out cotton-bales and form breastworks. I had 300 immediately brought from camp, on double-quick, and from the short space of time in which every street and opening was blockaded you may judge of their efficiency in that respect, especially when you consider that much of the work was accomplished under a heavy fire from the enemy's skirmishers.

By the time the breastworks were completed the fight had become general, and calls for water were urgent to supply the soldiers and quench the fire that had caught to the cotton-bales from our artillery.

I immediately pressed every water-holding vessel within reach, and formed a chain of negroes with buckets from the top of the bank to the water's edge. At this time a galling fire that opened on them from the enemy killed 1, wounded 3, and for a moment threw them all into confusion, but they were soon rallied, and resumed their work with the most astonishing rapidity. About this time the danger was imminent of the enemy making a charge down the river under cover of the bank. Agreeably to your orders, a breastwork was immediately formed under the bank, and while engaged at this work another was wounded. Fifteen of them had arms, and were ordered to hold the point along the river, which they did throughout the action, some of them firing as many as 30 rounds, and one actually ventured out and captured a prisoner. None of them had ever before seen a battle, and the facility with which they labored and the manly efforts put forth to aid in holding the place excelled my highest expectations, and deserves the applause of their country and the gratitude of the soldiers. Their total loss is 5 killed and 12 wounded. All their clothing left in camp was burned, their cooking utensils carried off, and near 100 tents were either carried off or destroyed; also 2 negroes and 8 mules, belonging to the contraband camp taken.

Most respectfully, your obedient servant,

JAMES B. TALBOT,
Captain and Superintendent of Contrabands.

Return of Casualties in the Union forces engaged at Pine Bluff, Ark., October 25, 1863.

[Compiled from nominal list of casualties, returns, &c.]

Command.	Killed.		Wounded.		Captured or missing.		Aggregate.
	Officers.	Enlisted men.	Officers.	Enlisted men.	Officers.	Enlisted men.	
1st Indiana Cavalry	......	3	......	9	......	......	12
5th Kansas Cavalry	......	8	......	17	......	1	26
Murphy's company Missouri State Militia	......	......	......	1	......	......	1
Freedmen	......	5	......	12	......	......	17
Total	......	16	......	39	......	1	56

No. 3.

Report of Lieut. Col. Thomas N. Pace, First Indiana Cavalry.

HEADQUARTERS FIRST INDIANA CAVALRY,
Pine Bluff, Ark., October 27, 1863.

SIR: I would respectfully tender the following report of the part enacted by the First Regiment Indiana Cavalry in the engagement at this place on the 25th instant:

It was about 9 o'clock in the morning, whilst the regiment was undergoing inspection of arms, that a courier from the pickets gave the first intimation of the approach of the enemy. "Boots and saddles" was sounded without delay, and the horses were corralled inside the court-house lot. The regiment was then assembled in front of regimental headquarters. Shortly afterward, in compliance with orders received, I sent out Companies A and H, mounted, under Major [M.] McCauley, to feel the enemy and notice his movement, and two companies (D and F) in and on top of the court-house, as sharpshooters, and two companies (B and G), as skirmishers from the front, with orders, if pressed, to fall back and occupy the houses in front, and to hold them at all hazards. The detachment sent out under Major McCauley were subject to the same orders, but to occupy and hold the houses on the right. In the mean time, through the timely assistance of about 100 contrabands, excellent barricades of cotton were made across the streets leading from court square. I ordered the light battery of English steel rifle cannon into position behind these works. During this time the enemy slowly advanced. Our skirmishers were driven from place to place, until they were compelled to seek shelter in the houses. We were besieged on all sides. Their batteries opened fire on the court-house, compelling our men to vacate on the double-quick. After which, Companies D and F were held in reserve, to be brought forward should the enemy charge the works. The companies were soon needed. The enemy's repeated assaults were of no avail. We drove them back on all sides. The enemy next set fire to the buildings on the right, determined to do with fire what they could not accomplish by force; but our men arrested the flames before any material damage was done; and the enemy, finding that they were foiled in this also, retired for a time, but soon reopened a battery of large guns, which was planted in a very strong position in rear and to the right of the Methodist church, immediately in our front. I moved the battery forward to the left of General Yell's residence, and opened on them, and, after a hot contest of more than an hour in duration, succeeded in silencing them.

The regiment was engaged fully six hours, sustaining a loss of 3 killed and 9 wounded. We captured 12 prisoners during the day.

It would be to the disparagement of others who did their whole duty to mention any officer or enlisted man for meritorious conduct. I am gratified to say that one and all went into the work with a will, and nobly did their duty. Lieutenant [S.] Leflar deserves mention for his indefatigable efforts in the performance of the arduous duties imposed on him in the command of the battery of light artillery. So also Majors [J. D.] Owen and McCauley for their assistance in the many duties of the day.

I am, sir, very respectfully, your obedient servant,

THOMAS N. PACE,
Lieutenant-Colonel, Commanding First Indiana Cavalry.

Lieut. M. W. BENJAMIN,
Acting Assistant Adjutant-General.

No. 4.

Report of Maj. Thomas W. Scudder, Fifth Kansas Cavalry.

HEADQUARTERS FIFTH KANSAS CAVALRY,
Pine Bluff, Ark., October 26, 1863.

SIR: I have the honor to submit the following as an outline of the part taken by the Fifth Kansas Cavalry in the engagement at this place on the 25th instant:

As soon as informed of the rebel approach, the men formed (dismounted) in front of their quarters, by instructions received from you, colonel. I then ordered one-half of each squadron detailed to saddle their squadron horses and secure them within the court-house square. Company I, being on picket, was first engaged with the enemy. Companies B and D were moved out near our picket line, on the outskirts of town, and commenced skirmishing. They all fell back slowly until they reached our line of defense, on the square, then dismounted, and were assigned positions behind hastily constructed barricades of cotton-bales, as follows: Companies A and I at the northwest angle of the square, supporting section of Fifth Kansas Battery; Company K, southwest angle, supporting First Indiana Battery; Companies C and F, the battery directly south of the court-house, Companies B, D, and E on their left, by General Yell's house; Company H at the southeast angle, with two pieces of the Fifth Kansas Battery, and Company G, with one gun (same battery), at the northeast angle. All kept skirmishers as far in advance as practicable. Of the conduct of both officers and men during the day I can truly and proudly say they did their duty well. Stimulated by brave words from you, colonel, as you passed among us from time to time, they rent the air with cheers that inspired the whole line with courage and the resolve to conquer. Commencing at 8 a. m., the battle raged (with occasional intervals, when firing would almost cease) about seven hours, when the rebels commenced retreating. By your order, Companies A, F, E, and part of G mounted and started in pursuit, overtaking their rear in the outskirts of town. After some skirmishing, the enemy moved rapidly off, and our forces returned.

Thus ended the part taken by the Fifth Kansas Cavalry in the battle of Pine Bluff. During the height of the engagement the enemy fired the quarters and stable of my regiment, and nearly every article of public and private property, together with most of the company officers' records and papers, were destroyed. Accompanying this report is a statement* of regimental quartermaster of amount of public property belonging to his department lost and destroyed by the burning of the stables. The fire made such rapid progress the mules were turned loose to save them, and many of them were captured by the enemy or lost.

I am, colonel, yours most obediently,

T. W. SCUDDER,
Major, Commanding Fifth Kansas Cavalry.

Col. POWELL CLAYTON,
Commanding Cavalry Brigade.

No. 5.

Report of Lieut. Milton F. Clark, Fifth Kansas Cavalry.

PINE BLUFF, ARK., *October* 27, 1863.

SIR: I have the honor herewith of transmitting to you a list of the killed and wounded on the 25th instant.

The loss of the enemy is as follows: Two captains killed (one of whom, Captain Proctor, was buried); 2 lieutenants wounded (prisoners); 19 enlisted men killed (buried by us); 3, rank not known, killed (buried by themselves), and 15 enlisted men wounded.

I have also to state that, from all the information I can gather (from strictly reliable sources), I am led to believe the enemy carried off a great portion of their killed and wounded; in fact, I have found 3 men

* Omitted.

buried by themselves, and hear of others at some distance from our lines which I did not visit.

Our own loss in the engagement is as follows: Six enlisted men killed; 6 enlisted men have since died of wounds, and 18 enlisted men wounded.

The above comprises the entire loss of this brigade, 9 of whom are of the Fifth Kansas, killed, and 3 of the First Indiana Cavalry. The loss of the enemy has necessarily been much heavier than our own, from the fact that we were protected, while they were exposed to the fire of our sharpshooters all the time; and in this connection I will mention that among all the killed and wounded I found but 3 men who had been hit with cannon shot; the rest were rifle balls.

I am, sir, with great respect, your obedient servant,

M. F. CLARK,

Lieut. Fifth Kansas Cavalry, and Supt. of Burial Party.

Col. POWELL CLAYTON,
Commanding Cavalry Brigade.

No. 6.

Report of Lieut. Col. Henry C. Caldwell, Third Iowa Cavalry, of the pursuit of Marmaduke.

HEADQUARTERS RESERVE BRIGADE,
Benton, Ark., October 31, 1863.

LIEUTENANT: I have the honor to submit the following brief report of the cavalry expedition in pursuit of Marmaduke:

At 7 a. m. on the 26th instant, I received an order from Major-General Steele, stating that "Colonel Clayton was attacked at Pine Bluff," and directing me to "march in the direction of Pine Bluff with all the available cavalry at this post immediately." At 9 a. m. of the same day, I left Benton, with 500 cavalry and one section of the Twenty-fifth Ohio Battery, and marched in the direction of Pine Bluff. About 12 o'clock at night of the same day, and when 12 miles from Pine Bluff, I came upon the camp of part of [J. M.] Glover's brigade, which had left Little Rock, and there learned that Colonel Clayton had repulsed the enemy, and stood in no need of re-enforcements. My stock being very tired, I halted till morning, when I proceeded to Pine Bluff, and reported to Colonel Clayton. Colonel Clayton had just received an order from Major-General Steele to assume command of the forces ordered to his assistance from Benton, Little Rock, and Brownsville, and, with them and all the available force at Pine Bluff, pursue the enemy. The order further states that General [S. A.] Rice had been ordered to Benton with a brigade of infantry, and would be ordered to go on to Arkadelphia, and that when he (Colonel Clayton) joined General Rice, or came within communicating distance, he would act under orders from General Rice. Colonel Clayton being sick and unable to go, turned this order over to me, as the ranking officer present, and directed me to take charge of the expedition. The horses attached to the Twenty-fifth Ohio Battery were completely broken down, in consequence of which the section of that battery taken by me from Benton, as also the section taken by Lieutenant-Colonel Caldwell, of the First Iowa Cavalry, from Little Rock, were left at Pine Bluff, and Colonel Clayton's howitzers taken in lieu of them. Owing to the non-arrival of the forces from Brownsville, I did not leave Pine Bluff till 5 p. m. on the 27th instant; marched that night to Saline River, a distance of 30 miles; halted at 4 o'clock in the morning, fed my stock, and moved on to Tulip, arriving there at 3 p. m.; drove out the rebel pickets and captured one lieutenant. Halted to feed; got reliable information in the evening that Marmaduke was at Princeton on the morning of that day with all his cavalry, but no train, having sent that forward on the Camden road the day previous. Up to the time I got to Tulip all information was to the effect that Marmaduke was not at Princeton, but moving on toward Camden, the march of his train, captured stock, and negroes having been mistaken for the march of his whole column. As soon as I learned the enemy was at Princeton, I determined to attack him the next morning, for which purpose I moved early; but on arriving at Princeton, I learned he had left in haste the day previous, immediately after his pickets reported my arrival at Tulip, and that he went 12 miles out on the Camden road that night. Having no train to encumber him, I was satisfied farther pursuit would be fruitless of any satisfactory result, and at Princeton I took the road to Arkadelphia, at which point I arrived at 2 o'clock in the morning of the 29th instant. I succeeded in completely surrounding the town before my presence was known to a single inhabitant. Our coming was not known anywhere on the road between Princeton and Arkadelphia, and we captured a good many horses and mules on the road, and at Arkadelphia I captured 2 lieutenants, some $1,370 in Confederate money, belonging to the Confederate Government, being proceeds of sale of Government salt; 3 six-mule teams, belonging to the Confederate Government; a large mail, and 8 or 10 Confederate soldiers. Not finding General Rice there, as I was led to expect from the order which I had received at 10 a. m. on the 30th instant, I took up my line of march for Benton; halted for the night near Rockport, and marched into this place to-day.

All information from every source was to the effect that there were no rebel troops west of Ouachita County, but that all the rebel forces of any moment in that part of the State were in and south of that county.

I cannot conclude this report without again calling attention to this post. As it now stands, it is a very difficult place to defend successfully. One or two redans at proper points, and a small square redoubt on a high point in the rear of the town, will insure us against any attack from the rebels, or, if they do attack, will insure their defeat. If the mechanics' train is sent me I will construct these defenses; there are no tools here for the purpose. I will send a battalion to Pine Bluff in the morning to get the four guns of the Twenty-fifth Ohio Battery, left there. As soon as the guns arrive at this post I will send to Little Rock the section which left that place, unless the colonel commanding will permit it to remain here. I send herewith the captured Confederate money, and one or two letters taken from the captured mail. The prisoners will be sent forward to the provost-marshal as soon as possible. I will take care that all captured property is turned over to the brigade quartermaster and properly accounted for.

For the last three days I was out my command had no rations, and Marmaduke left little in the country behind him for us to live on; but officers and men endured the hardships of the march and subsisted on short rations cheerfully and without a murmur.

Very respectfully, your obedient servant,

H. C. CALDWELL,

Lieutenant-Colonel, Commanding Expedition.

Lieut. J. M. SPRAGUE,

Acting Assistant Adjutant-General, First Cavalry Division.

No. 7.

Report of Brig. Gen. John S. Marmaduke, C. S. Army, commanding expedition.

HEADQUARTERS MARMADUKE'S DIVISION,
Princeton, Ark., October 26, 1863.

COLONEL: I have just returned from Pine Bluff, which I attacked yesterday about 8 a. m. The post was garrisoned by two cavalry regiments (Fifth Kansas and First Indiana), effective force about 600 men, and seven pieces of artillery. I occupied the whole town except the court-house and yard, which was fortified by heavy and effective breastworks of cotton-bales. The Federals could only be captured by storming the works, which would have cost me the loss of at least 500 men. I did not think it would pay. I have captured about 250 mules and horses, about 300 negroes (men, women, and children). The women and children I could not bring away. Some 400 blankets and quilts destroyed (burning a considerable amount of quartermasters', commissary, and ordnance stores), also about 600 or 1,000 bales of cotton, which had been brought to Pine Bluff for sale.

My loss is about 40 men killed and wounded. Federal loss I do not know; do not think it is large.

My troops behaved well. The Federals fought like devils. No news. No sign of their moving southward nor eastward.

Very respectfully,

J. S. MARMADUKE,
Brigadier-General, Commanding, &c.

Lieut. Col. J. F. BELTON,
Assistant Adjutant-General, District of Arkansas.

No. 8.

Report of Col. Colton Greene, Third Missouri Cavalry (Confederate), commanding Marmaduke's brigade.

HEADQUARTERS MARMADUKE'S BRIGADE,
In the Field, October 28, 1863.

MAJOR: In compliance with orders from division headquarters, my command marched, at 1 p. m. on the 24th instant, in the direction of Pine Bluff, with an effective aggregate of 800, and reached that place at 9 o'clock on the morning of the 25th, having halted two hours *en route*. I dismounted my men on the southwest edge of Pine Bluff, and moved in column, Colonel [Robert R.] Lawther, commanding Greene's regiment and [M. L.] Young's battalion, in advance. Colonel [S. G.] Kitchen's regiment remained mounted. The enemy's pickets were driven in by the advance, and the column deployed into line and advanced, skirmishing with the enemy, several hundred yards. My command formed the center column, and Colonel Kitchen's regiment was thrown on the flanks, to communicate with the columns moving east and west. We advanced rapidly, driving in the enemy's skirmishers, and took the following position within 150 and 250 yards of the court-house, to which the enemy had retired and strongly fortified with cotton-bales: Colonel Lawther commanded the left wing, composed of Greene's regiment (on the extreme left), Young's battalion, and [D. B.] Griswold's light battery; the right consisting of [S. T.] Ruffner's battery (three guns), [W. L.] Jeffers' and [J. Q.] Burbridge's regiments (commanded by Lieutenant-Colonel [W. J.] Preston), in the order named. Burbridge's regiment was advanced, wading through a lagoon, until it rested on Newton's left. After reconnoitering the enemy's works, I placed Ruffner's battery in position near the Methodist church, which played upon the court-house and adjoining buildings with effect, while Griswold's battery opened farther to the left and drove the enemy's sharpshooters from their shelter. The enemy's works were defended in the direction in which my right lay by four howitzers and two heavier pieces on the left, all well protected by cotton bales. The action was maintained, chiefly by sharpshooters and artillery on both sides, for five hours. No serious effect was produced upon the enemy's works, and it became evident that they could only be carried by a *coup de main*. He was well covered, and could only be approached over many obstacles. At 3 o'clock I was ordered to retire my troops to the position occupied in the morning. The enemy observed the movement, and soon attacked my rear, consisting of Greene's regiment and Young's battalion, but were repulsed with loss. As the rear again withdrew, another demonstration was made, but upon the delivery of one fire from Colonel Kitchen (formed on the right and rear), the enemy hastily retreated. I again went into position one-half mile back, on the Princeton road, and formed once more 2 miles farther on, but the enemy did not pursue. I now took up the line of march, and reached Princeton at 7 p. m. on the 26th instant.

I would particularly commend the conduct of the troops under my command during the action. The batteries were well handled, and their officers and men bore themselves with coolness and spirit.

I regret deeply to record the death of Lieutenant [W. D.] Biser, adjutant of my own regiment, who fell at the close of the action. He was an efficient and useful officer and a gallant gentleman.

My loss during the engagement was 7 killed and 21 wounded, for the particulars of which I refer you to the accompanying document.*

I am, major, very respectfully, yours, &c.,

COLTON GREENE,
Colonel, Commanding Brigade.

Maj. HENRY EWING,
Assistant Adjutant-General.

No. 9.

Report of Col. Robert R. Lawther, Tenth Missouri Cavalry (Confederate), commanding brigade.

HEADQUARTERS POST OF CAMDEN,
October 29, 1863.

MAJOR: On the morning of October 25, while advancing on Pine Bluff, I was ordered, with my command, by Brigadier-General Marmaduke, to the front of the center column, commanded by Colonel [Colton] Greene. My command consisted of Colonel Greene's regiment, commanded by Major [L. A.] Campbell, and Colonel [M. L.] Young's battalion. By 8 o'clock in the morning we had arrived within $1\frac{1}{2}$ miles of

*Not found.

the city. I here ordered forward Major [G. W. C.] Bennett, with the companies of Captains [H. S.] Randall and [William T.] Barry, to reconnoiter the enemy's position. After advancing a short distance, Major Bennett met the enemy's skirmishers, and immediately charged and drove them in, killing 2 and wounding 4. About a mile from the court-house I dismounted my men and formed them to the left of the road in an open field, Colonel Young on the right and Major Campbell on the left. After some skirmishing with the enemy, we drove them into their fortifications in and near the court-house. My command was then formed in about 150 yards of the court-house, where it remained during the engagement, a portion of the command being deployed as skirmishers and doing good execution whenever the enemy dared to show themselves above their works. When it was determined to withdraw from the place, I was ordered, with my command, to cover the retreat of our army. After marching less than half a mile, we were attacked by some 500 of the enemy, who came out from their fortifications. After a severe engagement of about fifteen minutes, the enemy were repulsed with heavy loss, and did not molest us further.

I cannot speak too highly of both the officers and men under my command. Where all acted so well it is difficult and almost invidious to make a distinction between them.

Colonel Young, Major Bennett, and Captain Randall conducted themselves with conspicuous gallantry during the day.

Major Campbell had his horse killed under him, and acted with the greatest coolness and bravery during the day.

Our loss was 4 killed and 13 wounded. Among the former I regret to mention Lieutenant [W. D.] Biser, adjutant of Greene's regiment, who fell in the last charge of the enemy. He was a brave and efficient officer, and died while nobly discharging his duty as an officer and soldier.

I cannot close without acknowledging my indebtedness to Lieut. H. Ferrill, who was with me during the day, and acted with much coolness and bravery.

I am, major, respectfully, your obedient servant,

R. R. LAWTHER,
Colonel, &c.

Maj. HENRY EWING,
Assistant Adjutant-General.

No. 10.

Report of Col. G. W. Thompson, Sixth Missouri Cavalry (Confederate), commanding Shelby's brigade.

HEADQUARTERS SHELBY'S BRIGADE,
Camp on Ouachita River, October 30, 1863.

MAJOR: After a few weeks of comparative rest, I have the honor to report another wearisome march and another battle, with its results and consequences.

During the night of the 23d instant I received orders to have three days' rations cooked and 25 rounds of ammunition issued to each man, and the command ready to march at 9 a. m. the following day, which order was promptly obeyed. At the appointed hour I moved the command into Princeton, where it remained halted until about 12 m., when we moved out and on the road leading toward Pine Bluff, and after a rapid march of some six hours, halted near the waters of the Saline River and foraged our animals. After a short rest, the command was again in saddle and moving as rapidly as the shadows of night and rough roads would permit, until near midnight, when the intense coldness drove many of the thinly clad soldiers to building fires by the roadside whenever a halt in front admitted of the delay. Cold, weary, and sleepy, the march became tedious and irksome in the extreme. At length the bright burning morning star, blazing through a forest of wailing pines, admonished us of the morn's early coming. Soon the gray which precedes the dawn spread its mantle over the east, then rosy-fingered dawn brushed away each trembling star, and proclaimed the coming of the god of day and the world's bright, tranquil Sabbath morn.

"Close up and move up rapidly," was now echoed along the lines, and by 8 a. m. the command filed to the left, and, under Colonel [J. C.] Monroe, as commander of the division, took position up the river and above town. With my command remaining mounted, I placed one company, under Lieutenant [H. K.] Dollins, of my regiment, as flankers on the right of Colonel Monroe's brigade, which was dismounted, and the remainder took into position on his left, commanding all that portion of the grounds between him and the river. The enemy's cavalry, appearing in front, were hastily dislodged by our sharpshooters, and steadily driven behind their cotton-bale fortifications in and around the court-house. A large encampment was here taken possession of, containing tents, various articles of clothing, &c., with horses, mules, and wagons; also many negroes.

My command was now dismounted and marched to the front and formed in line of battle, resting my right on Colonel Monroe's left; but, being in the rear of a row of large buildings, we could effect nothing more than to keep up a running fire from our sharpshooters. In this position we remained until about noon, when we moved to the right, crossing one of the principal streets leading to and from the court-house, adown which the enemy continually rained a shower of balls from their long-range guns. Their artillery continued to play upon our positions, but without any effect. The town immediately in front of us and between our position and that of the enemy was fired, but by whom I know not. Families escaping from the burning buildings came to us, and were sent to the rear and out of danger. It now became evident from this standpoint of view that to capture the enemy would require a very great sacrifice and slaughter—far too great for sound judgment and discretion to sanction or justify.

At length we received orders to retire, which was done without any disorder or confusion, to the vicinity of the captured encampment, where every tent that could be taken on horseback was taken, besides a large amount of various kinds of clothing, and the remainder piled and burned. Gathering up the captured negroes, horses, and mules, we withdrew without further annoyance from the enemy, only having lost during the day John Beaty, private, Company A, [B. G.] Jeans' regiment, wounded in leg and brought off in safety.

With the exception of some straggling, my men gave another evidence of their devotion, energy, and courage.

With high esteem, major, I am, respectfully, your obedient servant,

G. W. THOMPSON,

Colonel, Commanding Shelby's Brigade.

Maj. HENRY EWING,

Assistant Adjutant-General, Marmaduke's Division.

No. 11.

Report of Col. J. C. Monroe, First Arkansas Cavalry, commanding Cabell's brigade.

HEADQUARTERS CABELL'S BRIGADE,
October 27, 1863.

MAJOR: In obedience to orders from division headquarters, I make the following report of the part taken by my brigade in the battle of Pine Bluff, on the 25th instant:

I arrived at the Little Rock road near town about 8 o'clock, dismounted my men, and formed on foot. Colonel [G. W.] Thompson's brigade remained mounted and extended from my left to the river. Colonel Thompson also sent some mounted men to my right to act as flankers. I then deployed one company of dismounted men as skirmishers. These dispositions being made, I awaited the signal for the attack. When the signal was given, I moved cautiously forward without any opposition until I arrived in the suburbs of town, when my skirmishers encountered the skirmishers of the enemy and drove them steadily back until within a short distance of their fortifications, when a destructive fire was poured into my ranks from the buildings and fortifications. Not being able to effect anything with small-arms, I immediately fell back and ordered up my artillery, and attempted to shell them out. My dismounted men were not engaged again during the day.

Each regiment and battalion under my command fought well and obeyed strictly the orders concerning pillaging. Nothing was taken until the retreat commenced.

I am, major, respectfully, your obedient servant,

J. C. MONROE,
Colonel, Commanding Brigade.

No. 12.

Reports of Col. Robert C. Newton, Fifth Arkansas Cavalry, commanding division.

HEADQUARTERS CAVALRY BRIGADE,
Near Washington, Ark., December 4, 1863.

MAJOR: I have the honor, in obedience to instructions, to submit the following report of the part taken by the troops under my command in the engagement at Pine Bluff, Ark., on October 25:

My brigade moved from Princeton on the morning of October 24, as the advance of the division. At Sparks' place that night the brigadier general commanding announced the plan of attack to the brigade commanders. The column which was placed under my command was composed of my own brigade (Maj. John P. Bull, Newton's regiment, commanding), the Texas Brigade, Major [B. D.] Chenoweth commanding, and Maj. Robert C. Wood's battalion, Missouri Cavalry.

We moved from Sparks,' on Mahony's Ferry road, toward Pine Bluff about 10.30 o'clock that night. We reached Cantrell's Springs a little after daylight on October 25. There, in accordance with instructions from General Marmaduke, my column left the main road, moving upon a right-hand country road a distance of about 2 miles to the Talladega road; thence down it to Womack's place, and from there by dim country roads to the Bayou Bartholomew road. Arriving at Clay's brick-yard, near the edge of the town of Pine Bluff, I dismounted the Texas brigade and Wood's battalion, and all of Bull's brigade except 100 men. My instructions were to place my troops in position and wait until the signal-gun should be fired on the road on which Colonel [Colton] Greene's column was moving, when I should press forward vigorously toward the court house in town. I accordingly sent Captain [W. B.] Anderson with the 100 men whom I had retained mounted, with instructions to attack the Federal picket at the edge of town on the Bayou Bartholomew road, and after driving it in to push a small party over toward the Arkansas River, to give me early information should the enemy attempt to leave the town. At the same time I ordered Wood to move onto the Bartholomew road and form there, and deploy a line of skirmishers in front of him. While this order was being executed, the signal-gun was fired, and I immediately moved Wood on up the Bartholomew road to the southeast corner of town, and advanced Chenoweth's brigade up onto his right, and at the same time advanced [J. H.] Pratt's battery to the front, and opened with it upon the court-house. The enemy's sharpshooters now commenced firing upon me from the different houses along the lower edge of town, and, ordering Pratt to turn his fire upon them, I advanced Wood's and Chenoweth's skirmishers, and soon drove the Federal sharpshooters out of the houses in which they had first concealed themselves. They fell back to the houses on the next street, and, being strengthened from toward the court-house, they kept up a brisk fire upon me. Finding that they would have me at disadvantage should I waste time in sharpshooting with them, I pushed forward my skirmishers and charged with Wood's and Chenoweth's commands, driving the enemy through the houses and inclosures in the town, until I reached the block upon which the residence of Anthony Rodgers stands, where I halted to give the men breathing time and to reform my line. I found that the enemy had constructed a cotton breastwork around the court-house square, and my line being within one block of it, I concluded, inasmuch as the firing had ceased in the direction of Greene and [J. C.] Monroe, to push my sharpshooters up as close to the enemy as could be done without too much exposure, and not charge, if at all, until I could rely upon being supported by at least Greene's column. Nevertheless, in order to extend my line to the river, I ordered up Bull's brigade (which had been withheld as a reserve up to this time), and directed him to take position on an extension of Chenoweth's line in the block of buildings upon the river street, and to push his skirmishers well up toward the enemy's works. Brisk skirmishing continued all the time between my sharpshooters and those of the enemy. I ordered up Pratt's battery, and put it in position at the southwest corner of Rodgers' inclosure, and opened with it upon the court-house and the adjoining buildings, in which the enemy's sharpshooters were posted. In a short time he had silenced such of them as were firing from the cupola of the court-house and those in Rodgers' store-house, but the shots seemed not to do other very great good. Pratt was, therefore, by General Marmaduke's direction, sent around the lake to where Colonel Greene's artillery was, near the Methodist church, and was not with me any more during the day.

I remained in the position above indicated, considerable skirmishing going on, as stated, almost continuously, until about 2.30 p. m., when, in obedience to General Marmaduke's order, I withdrew my command, bringing away with me a number of horses and mules captured in the enemy's stables, as also quite a number of negroes found in the contraband camp, all of which were taken possession of by the division quartermaster upon our arrival at Princeton. I brought off likewise the papers found in the office of Colonel [Powell] Clayton's adjutant-general. These have heretofore been forwarded to division headquarters.

I presume the reports of Major Wood, commanding battalion, and Major Chenoweth, commanding Texas brigade, were forwarded directly to division headquarters. They were never sent to me. I have the honor to forward herewith the report of Major Bull, commanding my own brigade on that day. I respectfully refer you to these reports for the names of those who deserve special mention, and also for lists of the killed and wounded. All did well, and had the order been given to charge the cotton-bales it would have been hailed with joy. I have never seen more determination evinced by any troops. Every one seemed anxious to do his whole duty, and a generous emulation inspired the whole command. Every order was obeyed with alacrity, and none shrank from responsibility or danger.

I have to acknowledge my obligations to Majors Wood, Chenoweth, and Bull for their activity and zeal. Pratt, as usual, did good work that day, and his men behaved with their accustomed bravery and steadiness.

To the gentlemen of the brigade staff who were with me, I am indebted for valuable assistance, as also to Capt. W. N. Portis, of Newton's regiment, and Lieutenant [J. F.] Pulliam, of [A. S.] Dobbin's regiment, who were with me as volunteer aides-de camp. Colonel [W. S.] O'Kane, of General Marmaduke's staff, likewise deserves my warmest thanks for valuable assistance rendered me during the entire day.

I am, major, very respectfully, &c.,

R. C. NEWTON,
Colonel, Commanding, &c.

Maj. HENRY EWING,
Assistant Adjutant-General, &c., Marmaduke's Division.

DECEMBER 19, 1863.

MAJOR: Your note calling my attention to your previous order for a report of my killed and wounded in the engagement at Pine Bluff is received. As I stated in my report of that engagement, the reports of Majors Wood and Chenoweth, who were under my command on that day, were never sent to me, but, as I supposed, were forwarded directly to division headquarters. In Denson's squadron there were 2 men wounded, and Denson's report, stating their names, &c., was forwarded to you. In Colonel Dobbin's regiment there were no killed and wounded. In my own regiment 1 man was killed (Private [John] Smith, Major Bull's orderly), and that fact was stated in Major Bull's report, also forwarded. If you desire a consolidated report, showing the three casualties in Denson's squadron and my own regiment, please return me Denson's report, and I will furnish the required report without further delay. I supposed that the report of the facts heretofore made was sufficient. The principal casualties were in Wood's and Chenoweth's commands.

I am, major, very respectfully,

R. C. NEWTON,
Colonel, Commanding.

Maj. HENRY EWING,
Assistant Adjutant-General, Marmaduke's Division.

No. 13.

Report of Maj. John P. Bull, Fifth Arkansas Cavalry, commanding Newton's brigade.

NEAR CAMDEN, *October* 31, 1863.

LIEUTENANT: I have the honor to submit the following report of the part taken in the late attack upon Pine Bluff by the brigade (composed of Newton's regiment, [A. S.] Dobbin's regiment, and Denson's squadron) commanded by myself:

When the division commanded by Colonel [Robert C.] Newton arrived within about one-half mile of town, I was ordered to send forward the regiment commanded by Captain [W. B.] Anderson and one company from Newton's regiment, to operate as cavalry. I did so, and for the part taken in the action by this portion of my command I refer you to the report of Captain Anderson, as they were entirely detached from me during the day. I then received orders to dismount the rest of my command and move them rapidly to the front, which order was promptly obeyed. I formed my men in the edge of the woods, and remained in line for about thirty minutes, when I was ordered forward to support Captain [J. H.] Pratt's battery, which was firing upon the court-house. In the course of one-half hour I received an order from Captain [William M.] Price, aide-de-camp of General Marmaduke's staff, that the enemy had left the court-house and were attempting to cross the river; to move forward to the river bank and intercept them. I ordered a charge, and moved forward at a double-quick. In crossing Main street the enemy opened on me with grape, and their sharpshooters poured a perfect shower of bullets into my ranks. I attained the river bank with the loss of but 1 man slightly wounded, of Captain [W. B.] Denson's squadron, for a report of which I refer you to Captain Denson's report. I remained in this position for about forty minutes, and the enemy keeping up a severe fire, I concluded I had better move my position to where my men would be protected from the enemy's fire, sending a courier to inform Colonel Newton of my position. I retired to a corn-field some 200 yards to the rear, forming my men and sending forward 40 sharpshooters to occupy my position on the river bank. About 1 o'clock Colonel Newton ordered me to retire my brigade, and mount them, and act as the rear guard of the division.

To the officers and men under my command I return my thanks for the prompt and energetic manner in which they obeyed every order given them. Their conduct was gallant in the extreme, and although not warmly engaged at any time, showed a willingness and desire to be led into action I have scarcely seen equaled. Captain Denson, of the squadron, deserves my warmest thanks for assistance rendered upon the field, as also Lieutenant [G. D.] Worley, of Company D, of my regiment, who was acting as my aide-de-camp. Should I particularize every instance of merit, hardly a man of my command but would receive some mention. It is impossible to do so, and I therefore mention a few who came particularly under my notice.

I am sorry to relate, under the head of casualties, the death of John Smith, my orderly, who was shot about 1 o'clock in the afternoon. He deserted some time since from the enemy and joined my regiment. Upon the 25th instant he won the esteem and respect of the whole brigade, and, indeed, every one with whom he came in contact, by the cool, brave, and gentlemanly manner in which he executed all of my orders.

Very respectfully submitted.

JOHN P. BULL,
Major, Commanding Brigade.

Lieut. H. CARLTON,
Acting Assistant Adjutant-General, Newton's Division.

No. 14.

Report of Capt. W. B. Denson, commanding squadron.

OCTOBER 27, 1863.

LIEUTENANT: In the late attack upon Pine Bluff (of the 25th instant), my squadron, forming a part of the brigade commanded by Major [John P.] Bull, after being dismounted, moved up to the east side of Pine Bluff, and for a short while acted as a support for [J. H.] Pratt's battery. The brigade was then ordered to advance, and we moved at a double-quick up into town and across Main street to the bank of the river (Arkansas). Main street was crossed under a shower of grape and shell, but fortunately only 1 man was wounded (Private W. W. Goolsby, Company B, Captain [D. A.] Nunn's). The wound was through the foot (not serious), and he was promptly taken from the field by the surgeons in charge. This was the only casualty of my command during the action. After halting some ten minutes on the bank of the river, about 300 yards from where the enemy was posted, I received an order to retire into the field on the east of the town. I retired down the bank of the Arkansas River, and took the position designated, where I remained until ordered to withdraw from the field.

Permit me to represent the conduct of the men under my charge as being admirable. Every man seemed eager for the fray, and though none but my sharpshooters had an opportunity of firing a gun, they begged to be led to the face of the enemy. Indeed, all the troops who came under my observation during the day behaved well.

Respectfully submitted.

W. B. DENSON,
Captain, Commanding Squadron.

Lieutenant [H.] CARLTON,
Acting Assistant Adjutant-General.

No. 15.

Report of Maj. B. D. Chenoweth, Twenty-first Texas Cavalry, commanding Texas Cavalry Brigade.

HEADQUARTERS TEXAS CAVALRY BRIGADE,
October 27, 1863.

GENERAL: I have the honor to submit the following report of the part taken by the Texas brigade in the action of the 25th instant:

The Texas brigade, composed of the Twenty-first Regiment Texas Cavalry, [J. H.] Pratt's battery, [B. D.] McKie's and [C. L.] Morgan's squadrons (dismounted), and under orders of Colonel [Robert C.] Newton, commanding division, approached the eastern part of the town and encountered an advance of the enemy in the suburbs, which was quickly repulsed by an effective fire of shell from Pratt's battery. This battery was then opened upon the location of the enemy's guns, but receiving no reply, I received orders from Colonel Newton to advance my line toward the court-house square. This order was as promptly executed as the many obstacles in the way would admit of, the men driving before them, from house to house, the enemy's sharpshooters, until orders were received to halt the line. Captain Pratt, with one rifled gun, followed the advance of the line until a position was obtained, when at short range he opened on the court-house square a destructive fire, which continued until the artillery was ordered into works on the opposite side of the town.

Of the conduct of officers and men I have nothing to say except that all, without exception, did their duty with zeal and promptness.

I am, general, respectfully, your obedient servant,

B. D. CHENOWETH,
Major, Commanding Texas Cavalry Brigade.

No. 16.

Report of Maj. R. C. Wood, Missouri Cavalry Battalion (Confederate).

CAMP MARMADUKE, ARK., *October* 27, 1863.

MAJOR: In obedience to the requirements of your circular of this morning, I have the honor to state that on the morning of the 25th instant, at about 9 o'clock, my command was halted in front of the column of the right wing of the division, commanded by Colonel [Robert C.] Newton, 1 mile southeast of Pine Bluff. The pickets of the enemy having been driven in, my command was ordered to be dismounted and line of battle formed, and marched to [in] the direction of the court-house. This was promptly done, with my skirmishers deployed in front, who drove the enemy's rapidly before them. When within 100 yards of the court-house, a brisk fire was opened upon the battalion. They were then ordered to lie down. Soon after, a cover from the enemy was made by blockading one of the streets with bales of cotton taken from a shed near by. I then ordered my sharpshooters to take possession of the houses near the court-house. This was speedily effected, making the enemy take shelter there. My sharpshooters remained at their posts until their ammunition was expended, then came to the command for a supply, and returned to their posts.

The only casualties were among them, as per accompanying list, which I respectfully submit.

My battalion remained under cover of the cotton-bales until the colonel commanding ordered me to withdraw, upon which I sent into the houses and collected my sharpshooters, who, with the battalion, left the field in good order.

Officers and men, without exception, obeyed all orders with alacrity.

I am, major, your most obedient servant,

R. C. WOOD,
Major, Commanding Battalion.

Maj. HENRY EWING,
Assistant Adjutant-General.

OCTOBER 26, 1863.—Skirmish at King's House, near Waynesville, Mo.

Report of Lieut. Charles C. Twyford, Fifth Missouri State Militia Cavalry.

WAYNESVILLE, MO., *November* 12, 1863.

MAJOR: I have the honor of submitting the following statement, agreeably to orders:

On the 25th day of October, 1863, I was ordered on a scout south from Waynesville, with 15 men, to gain all the information concerning Benjamin Moore, whether taken prisoner or killed, but supposed to be killed. After riding all day, gained no information. Staid all night 15 miles south of Waynesville. In the night, about 3 a. m., the guard woke me up; said there was some one around. Three of us ran out; the guard halted them, and they fired. Immediately upon firing several shots, they left in a hurry. The guard received a slight wound in the breast. In the morning he was sent into Waynesville with 7 men; the others proceeded farther south, to Hiram King's (distance, 10 miles). Saw no signs, trails, or fresh tracks, and heard nothing concerning any bushwhackers or rebels in the country. At Hiram King's we learned that Benjamin Moore was taken prisoner; afterward escaped, or was paroled, he did not know which. It was very near noon; concluded we had better have some dinner and horses fed, and make Waynesville that night. Could hear of no rebels (bushwhackers) in the country. While waiting for dinner, I saw 20 or 25 men come on a charge out of the brush toward the house. I ordered the men to fall in. The bushwhackers halted. It was too far off to give them a volley from revolvers. We went in the smaller log-house joining the main building, with 4 or 5 feet space between them, and prepared to give them a nice reception. Hiram King and family were in the house that we occupied; raised the floor; put all of them under; they appealed to us in every way possible to leave the house, but we made them remain under the floor. Thirty-six of the bushwhackers came charging on the house, mounted, firing several shots from revolvers well loaded. They found other quarters would be more comfortable, they meeting with considerable loss. None on our side. They tried all the ways possible to dislodge us, and found it a dangerous business. They sent word to Colonel Love, in command of 150 men from his and Major Freeman's command, to attack Waynesville. They made a charge on foot. Finding that two revolvers in the hands of men in the house were used to a good advantage, concluded to try other means not quite so dangerous. After trying every way possible, they set fire to the main building; then awaited the result. Knowing the house was on fire, we began to prepare ourselves for the worst. We burned all the papers that would give any of our names or identify us in any way; changed our names, company, and regiment, for the reason that the bushwhackers had often sworn and circulated the report in the country if Frank Mason, Michael Williams, and Lieutenant Twyford should fall into their hands, they would burn or shoot them full of holes; thought it best to assume fictitious names. The fire was coming through the roof; something was soon to be done. I thought of making a blacksmith shop 200 or 300 feet in the rear of the house, but concluded to ask for terms of surrender. Saw from the number it was useless to contend against them. A white flag was run out. Commander, called Captain Bristoe, acting adjutant for Colonel Love, came up, and I asked him on what terms we could surrender. He (captain) asked if the family were all right. I answered, "Yes." I wanted to know what were the conditions of surrender. Captain said we should be treated as prisoners of war; give you my word and honor he did. It was 3 p. m. when we gave up our arms. Some of the bushwhackers wanted to shoot us. They stripped us of clothing, but gave us some old clothes in return. Colonel Love would not allow any unbecoming language used to us. The command marched until dark, and encamped within 12 miles of Waynesville. Some questioned us very closely. At 1 a. m. broke up camp. The bushwhackers (75) left Colonel Love's command. Love marched until 3 p. m.; stopped for something to eat and horses fed. The colonel then told me he was going to parole us. We were paroled. Sent an escort with us outside of the lines, but sent for us to come back. The reason—three of Ben. Wood's men had followed the command all day, supposed to see if we were to be paroled. They (the bushwhackers) swore we should never see Waynesville. Colonel Love put them under guard, and sent escort with us out of the lines. It was after sundown. We started across hills and hollows; no road to follow, walking all night. In passing near two houses we heard men talking and riding; afterward learned they inquired for us. We succeeded in reaching Lebanon after dark on Wednesday, the 28th, completely worn out in feet, losing sleep, and nothing to eat. Colonel Love said we killed 5 men and wounded 4, killing and wounding 7 of their horses. Killed 1 and wounded 1 of our horses.

I am, very respectfully, your obedient servant,

C. C. TWYFORD,

2d Lieut. Co. H, 5th Missouri State Militia Cav., Comdg. Scout.

Maj. WALDEMAR FISCHER.

OCTOBER 26–NOVEMBER 12, 1863.—Scout from Cape Girardeau to Doniphan, Mo., and Pocahontas, Ark.

Report of Maj. Josephus Robbins, Second Missouri State Militia Cavalry.

CAMP LOWRY, *November* 14, 1863.

COLONEL: I have the honor to report, in conformity to orders, I marched on the morning of the 26th October with 250 men of the Second Missouri State Militia Cavalry in the direction of Doniphan, Mo. When near Greenville, Mo., I dispatched Captain [L.] Sells with 75 men to Poplar Bluff, to guard the polls and scout the country, which he successfully did. The remainder of my command marched to Doniphan, where Captain [W. T.] Leeper, of the Third Missouri State Militia Cavalry, joined me, with 70 men. I remained there some three days, until after the election, scouting the country in all directions. The next day after the election I dispatched Captain [J. W.] Edwards, with 40 men of the Second Regiment and 10 men of the Third Regiment, to Cape Girardeau, with prisoners and contraband horses. I then, with the remainder of my command (195 men), marched straight upon Pocahontas, hoping to come upon Captain Reves' rebel command, which was somewhere between Pocahontas and Powhatan, on the opposite side of Black River. Arriving at Pocahontas, I found the boats had been taken by Reves, and could not cross. I then marched in the direction of Davidsonville, hoping to find a boat there or at Powhatan, which would have enabled me to cross the river, fall upon Reves, and capture him or drive him into Cherokee Bay upon Captain Sells, who was stationed there, by my order, after having done his work at Poplar Bluff. Arriving near Davidsonville, I learned that the boats there, as well as at Powhatan, had been destroyed or taken off by Reves. I then marched to Seven Points, where we captured Captain Martin, of the Confederate Army, and learned from a prisoner that the boat at Pocahontas had been taken down Black River 2 or 3 miles and hauled out into the woods. I then dispatched Captain [R. M.] Hulse, with 30 men, at 4 o'clock next morning, to go and look after the boat and bring it up to Pocahontas, which he successfully accomplished. At 6 o'clock same morning, I marched the command to Pocahontas, and commenced crossing the river. By 2 o'clock the entire command had all passed over, and were on the track of Reves, down the river. The advance came up with him near night, and gave chase, pressing him so closely that he dropped his blankets, coats, and hats, and drove him to the swamps, his native resort. Next day I marched as far down the river as Powhatan, and learned that Reves and his men had scattered out into the swamps, each fellow on his own hook. I did not think it worth while to look further after him. Finding no regularly organized foe in the country, I turned the column toward the Cape, marched up, and crossed Black River at the Indian Ford, in the lower end of Cherokee Bay, where I found Captain Sells quartered, and where I camped for the night. Next day the entire command marched for their respective headquarters, scouting the country as they passed along. When near Poplar Bluff, Captain Leeper, of the Third Regiment Missouri State Militia Cavalry, left me to join his command, stationed at Patterson, Mo. To him and his command I tender my heartfelt thanks for the valuable information and efficient services rendered me during the expedition. To the officers and soldiers of my own regiment many thanks are due, all having done their duty with alacrity and precision. I arrived at the Cape on the evening of the 12th instant, having been out eighteen days, want of rations driving me in sooner than I would otherwise have come.

During the expedition we killed 1 rebel captain, captured 16 prisoners, 5 out of the 16 being commissioned officers, 3 of them captains and 2 of them lieutenants. Many other prisoners were taken and discharged, there being no evidence against them sufficient to warrant a further detention of them as prisoners of war. We also captured 47 head of horses and mules, a lot of shot guns and squirrel rifles, many of which were broken to pieces by the soldiers and left behind as worthless. No casualties to my command during the expedition. All returned in good health.

With great respect, I am, colonel, your obedient servant,

JOSEPHUS ROBBINS,

Maj. Second Battalion, Second M. S. M. Cav., Comdg. Expedition.

Col. J. B. ROGERS, *Commanding Cape Girardeau, Mo.*

OCTOBER 27-NOVEMBER 15, 1863.—Expedition from Cape Girardeau to Clarkton, Mo.

Report of Capt. Henry C. Gentry, Second Missouri State Militia Cavalry.

CAPE GIRARDEAU, MO., *November* 15, 1863.

COLONEL: In compliance with orders, I left this post on the 27th of October, 1863, and arrived the same evening 4 miles west of White

Water. On the next evening we arrived at Bloomfield. On the 29th, we encamped on West Prairie. On the 30th, we moved to Four Mile, in Dunklin County. I arrested Captain Whitaker and Lieutenant Walker, of the rebel service, and paroled them, to report to the commander of Post Bloomfield, Mo. On the 31st, I moved to Clarkton and encamped. I there sent out scouting parties, who returned and reported no guerrillas in the neighborhood. On the 1st of November, I moved to Kennett, and encamped in the vicinity of that place during the next day, and scouted the neighboring country. On the 3d, I moved to Clarkton, with the intention of protecting the polls and giving the people an opportunity of voting, which they declined to do. I remained at Clarkton until Thursday, the 5th, when I moved up the road, sending Lieutenant [L. E.] Irwin, with 15 men, into the swamp, some 10 miles northwest of Clarkton, where he found the two guerrillas, Smith and Lacy, whom he pursued, mortally wounding Lacy, Smith escaping, seemingly wounded. He also captured 2 horses. He then returned to camp, 6 miles north of Clarkton. On the next day I moved a short distance and encamped. Sent Lieutenant [J. A.] Rice to Brown's Ferry, with some 20 men. He came upon 2 guerrillas. He captured them, killing 1 horse. On the 7th, I moved a short distance. I sent the 2 prisoners to Bloomfield, where they were safely delivered to Captain [V.] Preuitt. On the next day I sent another scout, by Four Mile, to Brown's Ferry, back through Clarkton, seeing no enemy. On the 9th, I encamped near Bloomfield. On the 10th, I came to Bloomfield and passed through, and in the evening encamped near Sikeston. Hearing of guerrillas in the vicinity of Charleston, I moved to that place, where I arrived on the evening of the 11th. I remained there during the 12th and 13th, and, sending parties out in all directions, I scouted the country thoroughly. I moved to Benton on the 14th, and on the 15th of November I arrived safely at Cape Girardeau, Mo., in accordance with orders.

This I must respectfully offer as my report.

H. C. GENTRY,
Captain, Commanding Expedition.

Col. J. B. ROGERS,
Comdg. 2d Mo. State Mil. Cav., and Post Cape Girardeau, Mo.

OCTOBER 29, 1863.—Affair near Warsaw, Mo.

Report of Col. John F. Philips, Seventh Missouri State Militia Cavalry.

SEDALIA, MO., *October* 31, 1863.

GENERAL: I have the honor to report that, on the 29th instant, Captain Squire Ballew, Company I, Seventh Missouri State Militia Cavalry, commanding at Warsaw, received information of 15 or 18 rebels, stragglers from Shelby's force, 15 miles south of Warsaw. He sent out 25 men after them. About sundown they came up with the rebels, attacked them vigorously, killed 2 or 3, and captured 10 or 12 horses and a lot of stolen goods. Our casualties, none.

JNO. F. PHILIPS,
Colonel Seventh Missouri State Militia Cavalry.

Brig. Gen. E. B. BROWN.

OCTOBER 29-NOVEMBER 5, 1863.—Scout from Pilot Knob to Alton and Doniphan, Mo.

Report of Capt. Robert McElroy, Third Missouri State Militia Cavalry.

CAMP OF THE THIRD REGT. MO. STATE MILITIA,
Pilot Knob, Mo., November 9, 1863.

DEAR SIR: According to order, I left this post with the command assigned me on the 29th day of October, at 9 a. m., and camped that night on Little Black River, on Burford's farm.

On the morning of the 30th, we moved at daylight, although the day was very disagreeable, the command having to face the snow and rain. We camped that night on Henpeck Creek; from thence we moved on to Eleven Point River, and camped near the farm of the notorious Lieutenant Huttleson; thence to Simpson's, 4 miles from the town of Alton, in Oregon County; and on the morning of the 3d we moved into town, and remained until the election was over. The election passed off quietly, although Lieutenant Bricker was much mortified at the result thereof; but the thing was done and could not be helped. In the evening we moved in a southeast direction, and camped on the farm of Mr. Saunders.

November 4, we moved at daybreak through the hills in toward Doniphan, in Ripley County, and camped on the farm of Oliver (one of Reves' men). On the 5th, we came through Doniphan, and camped on the Little Black River; thence to Otter Creek; thence to Bailey Station; thence to Pilot Knob.

During our trip we killed 8 and captured 5 of the most notorious guerrillas and jayhawkers that have infested that part of the State. Among them was a man by the name of Farmer, who had taken the oath of allegiance at Saint Louis, and had a copy of the same in his pocket, dated the 14th of April, 1863; also was found in his pocket a certificate from Major Crandall, certifying that the said William W. Farmer had furnished a substitute in the person of Jesse Hollice, of Oregon County, Missouri; age fifteen years; 5 feet 7 inches in height; dark complexion; dark hair; hazel eyes, and by profession a farmer. The certificate was dated the 7th day of September, 1863, and signed Lee Crandall, major commanding. We also captured 10 horses and 1 mule, a number of which were branded C. S. There are no regularly organized bands in that part of the country; but any man that can creep on his belly into a camp of Federals and steal a horse is entitled to the name and rank of captain.

That portion of the State once cleaned of these marauders, jayhawkers, and thieves, and we will have peace throughout South Missouri.

I am of the opinion that the women in that region are even more daring and treacherous, and, in fact, worse than the men, as we found in their possession a number of newly made rebel uniforms, &c.

I have the honor, sir, to subscribe myself, your obedient servant,

ROBERT McELROY,
Captain, Commanding Expedition.

Maj. JAMES WILSON,
Commanding Third Missouri State Militia Cavalry.

NOVEMBER 4, 1863.—Skirmish near Lexington, Mo

Report of Brig. Gen. Egbert B. Brown, U. S. Army, commanding District of Central Missouri.

HEADQUARTERS DISTRICT CENTRAL MISSOURI,
Jefferson City, November 12, 1863.

MAJOR: I have the honor to report, for the information of the major-general commanding, that Lieut. David Groomer, commanding a detachment of Company G, First Missouri State Militia Cavalry, on the morning of the 4th instant, came up with a party of 8 bushwhackers (who had been passing themselves as Shelby's men) near the Sedalia road, 12 miles east of Lexington, killing 2, capturing 4 horses and equipments, 2 guns, and a lot of clothing. The balance scattered, and made their escape. Casualties on our side, 1 horse wounded.

Very respectfully, your obedient servant,

E. B. BROWN,
Brigadier-General of Volunteers, Commanding.

Maj. OLIVER D. GREENE,
Assistant Adjutant-General, Department of the Missouri.

NOVEMBER 4–6, 1863.—Skirmishes at and near Neosho, Mo.

Report of Capt. James J. Akard, Eighth Missouri State Militia Cavalry.

HDQRS. DETACHMENT EIGHTH MISSOURI STATE MILITIA,
Neosho, Mo., November 10, 1863.

I have the honor to inform you that I arrived here on the evening of the 4th. My advance had a skirmish with some bushwhackers in this place; my loss was 1 man killed. We wounded 1 of the rebels; he has since died. We routed them, and captured most of the plunder they had taken from town.

On the morning of the 6th, I made a scout down on Butler's Creek. I had with me 30 of my men and 40 of Captain Richey's company of the Rangers. We ran upon a squad of about 30 bushwhackers. We killed 8 of them upon the ground; the number wounded is not known. I then returned to camp, not leaving a very strong guard there. From the reports, I think there are about 200 in squads scattered over the country. My force is not strong enough to be effective; if I remain here, I would be glad to have more force. There is a portion of my men on foot, and a portion sick, which leaves but few for duty. There is forage sufficient for a battalion of cavalry here. I am too weak to do any scouting and leave a guard that would be safe. I would be glad to know if I have to stay here. My rations will be out the 15th of this month; if I stay, I will have to send soon to get them here in time. I don't think it safe for so small a force as I have to remain too long at this place.

I am, general, with much respect, your obedient servant,

JAMES J. AKARD,
Capt., Comdg. Detachment Eighth Missouri State Militia Cav

Brigadier-General SANBORN,
Commanding District of Southwestern Missouri.

NOVEMBER 4-9, 1863.—Scout from Houston to Jack's Fork, Mo.

Reports of Lieut. John W. Boyd, Sixth Provisional Regiment Enrolled Missouri Militia.

HOUSTON, MO., *November* —, 1863.

SIR: In compliance with Special Orders, No. 42, issued from your headquarters November 3, 1863, on the morning of the 4th instant, I started on scout with 15 men of my company, 5 men of Company B and 5 of Company G, Fifth Missouri State Militia, in the direction of Spring Valley. Marched that day 25 miles, without discovering anything worthy of note. Visited the residences of Benjamin Carter and Wilson Farrow, that were engaged in burning Houston; they were gone. Burned Carter's house. November 5, divided the scout. Sent 10 men, under Orderly Sergeant Basket, Company I, to march by way of Bay Creek to Jack's Fork. I proceeded with the balance of the command by way of Leatherwood or Wollsey's trail; found fresh trail of horses; followed them on Jack's Fork to the residence of Miles Stephens and brother, Jack Stephens, whom I was satisfied were bushwhackers. Burned the house. Heard that Fed Taylor had been at Stephens' last week with 25 men. Proceeded down Jack's Fork 10 miles, having marched 30 miles that day. Camped at Widow McCormick's. Had positive evidence that the widow had kept a general rendezvous for Freeman's and Coleman's guerrillas. On the morning of the 6th, burned the buildings. Learned from the widow's son, a young lad, that on the previous evening James Mahan had got him to give news of our approach. Sent back and took Mahan prisoner. Went down Jack's Fork to mouth of Mahan's Creek; turned up said creek on Thomasville road. Prisoner Mahan attempted to escape, and was shot by the guard. Camped at William Mahan's that night, [having] marched 24 miles. On the morning of the 9th, marched up Mahan's Creek. About 9 o'clock discovered about 20 of the enemy on the bluff above us; fired a few shots at them, when they fell back. I took 20 men up the hill and reconnoitered, expecting to find them in force to give us battle, but they had all fled into the rocky ravines and hills, where it was impossible to pursue to advantage, mounted; returned to the road, and had gone about 1 mile, and met 3 men, who started to escape on seeing us; killed 2 of them, whom I ascertained from papers found on their persons to be William Chandler, supposed to live in Dent County, and a man named Hackley, who had in his pocket a discharge as lieutenant from Company F, Mitchell's regiment, rebel army. He also had several packages of letters from persons in the rebel army and citizens in Arkansas, directed to persons in Dent and Phelps Counties, all of which are submitted for your disposal. Two miles farther on we captured William Story on a United States horse. He was recognized and well known as a notorious horse-thief and house-robber. He attempted to escape, and was killed. Camped that night at Morgan Dean's, on Birch Prairie. November 8, started in the direction of Houston; marched 5 miles, and captured William Hulsey, James Hulsey, William McCuan, and Samuel Jones at the house of James Harris, all well provided and packed, going to Freeman. One of them had a horse that was stolen some time since from one of our men; also goods of different kinds. The first three, viz, the Hulseys and McCuan, were killed. Jones, on account of his extreme youth and apparent innocence, I had brought in, prisoner. Five miles farther, at the house of John Nicholson, a known rebel and bushwhacker, we captured the said

John Nicholson, Robert B. Richards, alias Bruce Russell, and Jesse Story, all of whom were killed. We then marched by way of McCubbin's Mill to Spring Valley, and camped at Wiley Purcel's. November 9, started direct for this post, sending a few men by way of Upper Jack's Fork, and all arrived here in the evening, all in good health, having been out six days, marched 145 miles, killed 10 men, returned 1 prisoner, burned 23 houses, recaptured 9 horses that had been previously stolen, and took 6 contraband horses and mules. All of which is respectfully submitted.

JOHN W. BOYD,
First Lieut. Co. I, Sixth Prov. Regt. E. M. M., Comdg. Scout.

Captain MURPHY, *Commanding Post, Houston.*

[Indorsement.]

HEADQUARTERS DEPARTMENT OF THE MISSOURI,
Saint Louis, November 18, 1863.

Respectfully returned to Brig. Gen. Thomas Davies, commanding District of Rolla, for report as to whether the conduct of this officer in killing prisoners and burning houses was in accordance with his (General Davies') instructions. If not, General Davies will report what action he has taken in the matter.

By order of Major-General Schofield:

J. A. CAMPBELL,
Assistant Adjutant-General.

SPECIAL ORDERS, No. 43. } HDQRS. DETACHMENT 5TH MO. STATE MIL.,
Houston, November 3, 1863.

Lieutenant Boyd, Company I, Sixth Provisional Regiment Enrolled Missouri Militia, with 15 men of his company, 5 of Company B and 5 of Company G [Fifth Missouri State Militia Cavalry], provided with three days' rations, will start on a scout at 7 a. m. to-morrow, November 4, 1863, in the direction of Spring Valley. Lieutenant Boyd will report at these headquarters for special instructions before starting.

By order of R. Murphy, captain commanding post:

THOS. B. WRIGHT,
Adjutant.

Upon making report to Captain Murphy for "special instructions," he ordered me to "clean them out."

JOHN W. BOYD,
First Lieut. Co. I, Sixth Prov. Regt. Enrolled Missouri Militia.

SPECIAL ORDERS, No. 186. } HEADQUARTERS DISTRICT OF ROLLA,
Rolla, Mo., November 20, 1863.

* * * * * * *

II. Captain Lovell, assistant adjutant-general, will proceed to Houston with an escort of 5 men and 1 sergeant, and investigate the conduct of Lieutenant Boyd on a late scout to Jack's Fork, and ascertain by what authority twenty-three houses were burned; whether William Hulsey, William McCuan, John Nicholson, Robert B. Richards, alias Bruce Russell, and Jesse Story were killed while prisoners; and, if so, was it done by his order; if not done while prisoners, in what manner they were killed.

By order of Brig. Gen. Thomas A. Davies:

J. LOVELL,
Captain and Assistant Adjutant-General.

HEADQUARTERS DISTRICT OF ROLLA,
Rolla, Mo., November 25, 1863.

I have the honor to state that, in accordance with Special Orders, No. 186, Headquarters District of Rolla, I proceeded to Houston, November 20, 1863, and made a thorough investigation of the "conduct of Lieutenant Boyd on a late scout to Jack's Fork." It appears by Lieutenant Boyd's first report that William Hulsey, James Hulsey, William McCuan, John Nicholson, Robert B. Richards, alias Bruce Russell, and Jesse Story were killed after having been captured. Lieutenant Boyd failed in making his report clear. The facts I believe to be stated in Lieutenant Boyd's amended report (herewith inclosed), and are that they were captured by surrounding the houses; but, on their attempting to secure them, they all broke for the brush and in that manner were killed.

As regards burning the houses, the houses that were burned were well known to be the resort of bushwhackers, where they were fed and lodged, and where a portion of their stolen property was found secreted. In some three or four of the houses several barrels of salt were found, besides other goods belonging to sutlers who have been robbed. The presence of men whom we know to be bushwhackers in some of the houses confirms this. I am of the opinion that Lieutenant Boyd acted correctly, and for the good of the service.

On my investigation being completed, I returned to Rolla on the 24th day of November, 1863.

Very respectfully,

J. LOVELL,
Captain and Assistant Adjutant-General.

Brig. Gen. THOMAS A. DAVIES,
Commanding District of Rolla, Mo.

[Indorsement.]

HEADQUARTERS DISTRICT OF ROLLA,
Rollo, Mo., November 26, 1863.

Respectfully forwarded, for the information of the major-general commanding Department of the Missouri. The amended report of Lieutenant Boyd states the manner of killing the men referred to in his previous report, supposed to have been killed while prisoners. The burning of the houses is also explained. The explanation is satisfactory to me, and hope it will meet the approval of department commander.

THOS. A. DAVIES,
Brigadier-General, Commanding.

HEADQUARTERS,
Houston, Mo., November 23, 1863.

SIR: In regard to inquiries contained in Special Orders, No. 186, dated Rolla, November 20, 1863, in reference to killing William Hulsey, James Hulsey, William McCuan, John Nicholson, Robert B. Richards, alias Bruce Russell, and Jesse Story, while on a scout in Shannon and Oregon Counties, under Special Orders, No. 43, from Captain Murphy, commanding Post Houston, I respectfully beg leave to report further, or to explain the report I made at Houston, on my return, that William Hulsey, James Hulsey, William McCuan, and Samuel Jones were at the house of James Harris, eating breakfast, when we approached the house on a charge; but, owing to the location of the house, being inside of a lot or yard adjoining a corn-field on one side and thick brush on the other, we could not well surround it until the men named had discovered us and attempted to escape through the back yard, and, running some distance under fire, were finally shot, except the boy Jones, who, instead of attempting to get under cover of the brush as the others, took the main road, was pursued by 2 or 3 men, mounted, brought back to the house, and finally delivered up to the commander of the post here, as set forth in my former report.

In regard to John Nicholson, Bruce Russell, and Jesse Story, the circumstances were similar to the others. I knew the men were of notorious character as horse-thieves and house-robbers; I knew they were in the neighborhood, and I was looking carefully for them, when we came upon them at the house of Nicholson, which was a double log-house with three outside doors, through which they attempted to escape, and were shot, running. Nicholson had gone more than half a mile before we got him.

In regard to the burning of the houses, I beg leave to state that many of the buildings were vacant huts or cabins, used as camping places and quarters for the bushwhackers; many of them located in secret places in the hills and ravines of that broken country. The others, from the dying confessions of Roush, and positive evidence derived from other sources, were the houses and rendezvous of the men actually engaged in burning Houston and West Plains.

In conclusion, I take the liberty to say that these things were done by my sanction and order, and that I have acted throughout as I felt it my duty to do under the circumstances, being an officer of the United States, and knowing, as I do, that these men (with others) have murdered loyal citizens at their own homes, viz, Wilson Smith, of Spring Valley; that they captured N. P. Hackwith and Graham, while scouting for this post, carried them to Jack's Fork, and murdered them, where they are now buried; that they have stolen and burned Government property, and also that whilst I was endeavoring to live a peaceable citizen of the county, they have hunted me like a wild beast and tried to kill me for my principles, and that were I again placed in similar circumstances I would do as I have done.

Respectfully submitted.

JOHN W. BOYD,

First Lieut. Co. I, Sixth Prov. Regt. Enrolled Missouri Militia.

Captain LOVELL,

Assistant Adjutant-General.

NOVEMBER 7-13, 1863.—Expedition from Fayetteville to Frog Bayou Ark., and skirmishes (9th) near Huntsville and (10th) near Kingston.

Report of Col. M. La Rue Harrison, First Arkansas Cavalry (Union).

FAYETTEVILLE, ARK., *November* 13, 1863.

GENERAL: The following report of my late expedition in pursuit of the rebel Colonel Brooks is respectfully submitted:

On the morning of the 7th instant, I received an order from Brigadier-General McNeil, commanding District of the Frontier, a copy of which is herewith transmitted.

From the tenor of this letter I felt assured that General McNeil was not thoroughly informed as to the whereabouts of Brooks or his strength. I had ascertained from reliable sources that on the 4th instant Brooks was encamped near Yellville, Marion County, Arkansas, on Crooked Creek, with 1,200 men, about 700 of whom were either poorly armed or wholly unarmed, and were conscripts from Northwestern Arkansas, in whom no dependence could be placed. The remaining 500, constituting the commands of Colonel Stirman and Captain Brown (commanding a battalion), were well armed, well drilled, well clothed, and efficient troops. (This account is perfectly corroborated by prisoners since captured.)

In pursuance of this information, I moved the mounted men of my command, an aggregate of 412 men, with two 12-pounder mountain howitzers, on the afternoon of the 7th instant, in the direction of Crooked Creek. On the evening of the 8th, I encamped near Huntsville, where I detached Company A, First Arkansas Cavalry, to move north on War Eagle River, in search of some bushwhackers, reported to be in that direction. On the morning of the 9th, while crossing a mountain 9 miles east of Huntsville, while waiting for my rear guard to come up with the train, I learned from citizens that Brooks left Yellville on the 7th, with his whole command; that he was moving in the direction of Huntsville; that he encamped at Osage, 12 miles east of me on the previous evening, and that he was to cross the mountain at 12 m. It being 11.30 a. m., I immediately deployed my advance guard as skirmishers, dismounted my main column, and moved it forward with the howitzers, and sent messengers to hurry up the rear guard and train. Before these arrangements had been completed, my advance skirmishers were attacked by the enemy, and repulsed, though with a loss to the enemy of 1 killed, several wounded, and 1 lieutenant (William Mayes) captured (by Ensign Wilkes, Company L, First Arkansas Cavalry). Five rounds of spherical case from the howitzers and three rounds of Minie balls from our main line caused the enemy to retreat in great disorder across King's River, toward Carrollton. As soon as led horses and train could be brought up, I pursued. At dark he appeared to have divided his forces, and I was obliged to make camp. Before daybreak on the next morning, learning that his whole force had again concentrated in the direction of Kingston, I pursued, over a mountain road. At an hour after sunrise I found and attacked him in camp, 1 mile below Kingston, routing and driving him from his breakfast in twenty-five minutes. Here I used five shells from the howitzers. Six miles south of this, on the Clarksville road, he was so hard pressed that he made a stand at the ascent of the mountain, and disputed our passage. My advance engaged him until the howitzers came up, when he again retreated southward. I again came up with him, 14 miles farther south, after sunset, where he made a stand at the descent of the mountain. It being quite dark before my main column could arrive and be deployed, and the enemy having again divided, a portion going toward Clarksville and a portion in an easterly direction, I made camp, and sent out parties to obtain information. After midnight I learned that he had again concentrated, and moved toward Scullyville. At noon of the 11th, I halted to feed horses and issue rations, neither men nor horses having eaten a mouthful for thirty hours. Arriving at the Morgan Buck place, 22 miles south of Fayetteville, I found that the enemy had moved all night; had fed horses there (the only time in 67 miles' travel), and had turned to the left, crossing Frog Bayou Mountain, and at 1 p. m. were moving at a rapid pace down Frog Bayou River, toward Therikyl's Ferry, on the Arkansas.

On the morning of the 12th, I detached Capt. J. I. Worthington, with one howitzer and 136 men, composed of 53 of the Second Kansas Cavalry, and the remainder of the First Arkansas Cavalry, to pursue over the mountain to the river. All of my officers and men deserve praise for their gallant conduct and eagerness to engage the enemy. Capt. Joseph S. Robb, First Arkansas Cavalry, who led the advance; Lieutenant [P.] Cosgrove, Second Kansas Cavalry, who, with his brave boys, charged the enemy at the bluff south of Kingston; Chaplain [R.] North, who encouraged the men by his presence and cheering words; Majors Fitch and [T. J.] Hunt, who were always where danger was thickest; Sergeant [W. R.] Wilks, Company L, First Arkansas Cavalry, who advanced from his own line to within 20 paces of the enemy, and captured Lieutenant Mayes in the thickest of the fight, and Private Hugh Cook, Company L, First Arkansas Cavalry, who stood his ground at Kingston alone against 8 of the enemy until the column came to his assistance, all deserve especial mention. I met with no loss during the scout, either in killed, wounded, or prisoners. I captured from the enemy 2 lieutenants and 15 enlisted men. His loss in killed and wounded is not known, and is variously reported by citizens. The hurry of the pursuit prevented the ascertaining of the facts. Five out of 7 Federal prisoners in the hands of Brooks escaped during his retreat.

November 16, 1863.—Maj. Ezra Fitch, First Arkansas Cavalry, returned this morning from pursuing Brooks to the mouth of Frog Bayou River, where he crossed his men in great hurry and confusion on the morning of November 12, before daybreak. Lieutenant Inks, commanding a detachment of Brown's command, which has been stationed in the neighborhood of Cane Hill for some time, crossed on the morning of the 14th near the mouth of Frog Bayou. Prisoners returned report the rebels much frightened and demoralized, and short of provisions, not having had any flour or bread for seven days previous to crossing the river; no meat for two and a half days, and no salt for more than a month; that they made no camp, and halted only twice to feed from the time they were first attacked, on the morning of the 9th, to the morning of the 12th, when they crossed the river. No organized band of rebels is known to be now in Northwestern Arkansas.

I remain, general, your most obedient servant,

M. LA RUE HARRISON,
Colonel First Arkansas Cavalry Volunteers, Commanding.

Brigadier-General SANBORN,
Commanding District of Southwestern Missouri.

[P. S.]—Brooks' command represented four regiments, and the following officers were known to have crossed with him: Col. W. H. Brooks, commanding; Colonel Peel, Colonel Stirman, Lieutenant Colonel Reynolds, Captain Brown, commanding battalion, and the notorious J. M. Ingraham.

M. LA RUE HARRISON,
Colonel, Commanding.

[Inclosure.]

HEADQUARTERS DISTRICT OF THE FRONTIER,
Fort Smith, Ark., November 5, 1863.

Col. M. LA RUE HARRISON,
Commanding at Fayetteville, Ark.:

COLONEL: You will, on receipt of this, move squadrons of your regiment to make an aggregate of from 200 to 250 men and your howitzer section, with full supply of ammunition, say 107 rounds to the gun, in pursuit of Brooks, now north of the Arkansas River. About the same sized command will move from Van Buren to-morrow, and are instructed to drive him in your direction. I do not think he can have more than 400 men, and those very inferior and much demoralized. He must be found, attacked, and destroyed.

The force from Van Buren is directed to scour the country contiguous to Mulberry Creek and toward Ozark.

I am scouring the south side of the river, and this is part of my programme to redeem the State of Arkansas. I think I can rely on your active and zealous co-operation.

We shall have the wires at Van Buren to-morrow, I am told, and the first use I make of them will be to inform Major-General Schofield that I assume command of all the troops in this district, and that I have directed you to report to me.

I have the honor to be, &c.,

JOHN McNEIL,
Brigadier-General, Commanding.

NOVEMBER 10-18, 1863.—Expedition from Benton to Mount Ida, Ark., and skirmish (11th) at Caddo Gap.

Report of Lieut. Col. Henry C. Caldwell, Third Iowa Cavalry, commanding First Brigade, Cavalry Division.

HEADQUARTERS FIRST BRIGADE, CAVALRY DIVISION,
Benton, Ark., November 18, 1863.

LIEUTENANT: I have the honor to report the result of the recent cavalry expedition undertaken in pursuance of orders from Major-General Steele.

I left this post with my command on the morning of the 10th instant; halted that night near Hot Springs. The next day I marched by the way of Hot Springs, on the Murfreesborough road, through Clark County, to a point within 18 miles of Murfreesborough. At this point a prisoner was captured, who informed me that Major Witherspoon, of the rebel cavalry, with a detachment of his command, was encamped 12 miles from me, on the Fort Smith and Washington road.

Although I had already marched 40 miles, I determined to strike this force at once, lest they might get information of my presence in the country and escape me.

I accordingly selected 125 men, under command of Captain [J.] Baird, of the First Missouri Cavalry, accompanied by my adjutant, Lieutenant [W. T.] Hamilton, and sent them forward rapidly, guided by the prisoner whom we had taken, with orders to charge into the rebel camp and give them no time to form or make any resistance. My orders were obeyed; the rebel pickets were run down, and the first intimation the rebels had of the presence of my men was when they charged right into their camp, guided by the light of their camp-fires, and opened a volley on them. The rebels, wild with fright, fled into the woods, in some instances without other covering than their shirts. The underbrush and woods and the darkness of the night prevented any successful pursuit of the fugitives.

Major [J. L.] Witherspoon himself, 1 captain, 2 lieutenants, together with 10 privates, and all their horses, horse equipments, arms, camp equipage, and transportation, were captured. The transportation and camp equipage were burned. The firing in camp caused many horses to break loose, and in the darkness of the night they could not be found, but not a single rebel got away with his horse.

At this point I sent out all the loyal men of that region then with me to notify the loyal men who were in the mountains to meet me at Caddo Gap, which point I determined to take possession of and hold till these people would join me. Accordingly, on the 12th instant, I marched up to the gap, where I left part of my command to hold that position, and with the balance I hurried forward to Mount Ida, expecting to surprise and capture a small rebel force garrisoned at that place. When near the place, I learned that a Federal force from Waldron, being part of a column which had come from Fort Smith to Waldron, had on the day previous been in Mount Ida, and that the rebels, learning of their approach, had fled precipitately, abandoning their camp equipage and transportation, which, together with the house in which the rebels barracked, our forces from Waldron burned. I remained at Mount Ida until the evening of the 14th instant.

While at Mount Ida I caused the roads leading to Fort Smith, Waldron, Dardanelle, and Little Rock to be patrolled for a distance of 15 miles, and scoured the country in every direction for a like distance, and in this way picked up a good many straggling rebel soldiers, and succeeded in capturing several leading guerrillas of that country, who have been prominent and taken an active part in robbing, persecuting, imprisoning, and hanging Union men. I have caused the names of these guerrillas, with a statement of their crimes and the witnesses by whom the facts can be proved, to be forwarded to the provost-marshal-general; and on behalf of the loyal men of that country, and for the sake of justice and humanity, I beg that those men be not treated as prisoners of war and exchanged, but that they be turned over to a military commission, and tried, convicted, and executed for the many inhuman and horrid crimes they have committed.

On the evening of the 14th instant, that part of my command left at Caddo Gap reached me, together with nearly 300 loyal men, who had come from the surrounding mountains to join the Federal Army. It is true that in this number there are a few who did not come to enter the service, but they are old, gray-headed men, who are compelled to flee their homes to save themselves from being hanged by the rebels. These people who came out with me are hardy, vigorous, and resolute men; they represent every trade, pursuit, and profession of life, and in intelligence and appearance are equal to the same number of men in any country.

As soon as these loyal men reached my camp, they were furnished with arms, which had been taken along for that purpose, and put under the command of Colonel Arnold, a resident of that region, and whom I understand has been commissioned to raise a regiment from the loyal men of that county. Colonel Arnold and his men were on duty day and night. Every part of that county was visited by Colonel Arnold in person or by his scouts. While out one night gathering in the loyal men, Colonel Arnold, with 17 men, came upon 23 rebels in camp, charged on them, killed 4, captured 7, and drove the rest in confusion to the woods, capturing all their camp equipage and arms and 10 horses, and retook 8 Union men whom the rebels held as prisoners, and some of whom they were about to hang.

From Mount Ida I marched on the direct road to this place, halting one night at Cedar Glades and one night at Cunningham's, the point where the Hot Springs, Danville, and Perryville roads intersect the Mount Ida and Little Rock road. Ten miles east of Cedar Glades my advance guard came upon a rebel company, charged them, killed 2, wounded others, and captured 30 horses and horse equipments and 20 guns.

In a mountain pass, 1 mile east of Cunningham's, bushwhackers, concealed behind rocks in the mountains, fired on the head of my column, and then fled rapidly over the mountains and escaped.

My casualties on the expedition were 3 men of the First Missouri Volunteer Cavalry seriously wounded.

My line of march took me through the counties of Hot Spring, Clark, Pike, Polk, and Montgomery. My scouts, under the command and direction of Colonel Arnold, went into Hempstead and Sevier Counties.

The great majority of the inhabitants of the district of country through which I marched are soundly loyal. They occupy the mountainous districts in the counties named, and from the commencement of the rebellion they have never faltered in their devotion to the old flag.

Every conceivable means has been used to force these loyal men into the rebel service; they have been hung by scores; they have been hunted down with bloodhounds by the slaveholding rebels of Red River Valley; they have been robbed of their property, chained and imprisoned, yet amidst all this persecution and suffering these people stood out, and everywhere I went through their country they greeted my column with shouts of joy. There are several hundred more loyal men in the same region of country, but farther south, who are anxiously waiting for an opportunity to get out of the rebel lines and enlist in our service.

I cheerfully acknowledge my indebtedness to Colonel Arnold. His perfect knowledge of the country, intimate acquaintance with the people, energy and courage, enabled him, with the assistance of his men, to keep me constantly advised of the movements and position of the enemy.

My acting assistant adjutant-general, Lieutenant [W. T.] Hamilton, served me most ably and faithfully day and night, and officers and men, without a single exception, behaved admirably on the whole trip.

I subsisted my men, as far as practicable, on the country, and supplied myself liberally with forage, horses, and mules whenever wanted, but I was always careful to see that secessionists supplied me with these wants, and that they were taken in an orderly manner.

It is due to my command to say that not a single private house was entered by a soldier on the whole trip except for a legitimate purpose, under direction of a commissioned officer or upon invitation of the occupant, and not a cent's worth of property was taken which it was not legitimate or proper to take.

I am, lieutenant, very respectfully, your obedient servant,

H. C. CALDWELL,

Lieutenant-Colonel, Commanding First Brigade.

Lieut. A. S. MONTGOMERY,

Acting Assistant Adjutant-General, Cavalry Div., Little Rock.

NOVEMBER 10-18, 1863.—Expedition from Springfield, Mo., to Huntsville, Carrollton, and Berryville, Ark., and skirmishes.

Report of Maj. Austin A. King, Sixth Missouri State Militia Cavalry.

HDQRS. FIRST BATTALION SIXTH M. S. M. CAVALRY,
Springfield Mo., November 18, 1863.

GENERAL: In compliance with Special Orders, No. 231, Headquarters Southwestern District of Missouri, dated November 10, 1863, I left Springfield, in command of 200 men, Sixth Missouri State Militia Cavalry and Eleventh Missouri Volunteer Cavalry. Marched to Linden; thence southeast to Forsyth, where I left my train; thence south, across White River, to Carrollton, Ark., killing 1 guerrilla on the way and capturing 2 prisoners; thence I moved southwest to the vicinity of Huntsville, capturing 2 prisoners; thence north, in direction of Berryville, at which place I captured 2 prisoners; thence north to King's River. *En route* came upon a small band of guerrillas, killing 2, and wounding 1 citizen, who ran, and refused to stop when halted. Continued to march north across White River and up Roaring River. Detached one squadron, under Lieutenant [C.] Finley, Sixth Missouri State Militia Cavalry, to move northeast through the country in search of bands reported in that vicinity; he has not yet reported. With main command I moved up Flat Creek to its head; thence to this post.

From information obtained, I learned that Brooks had been on Rolling Prairie with about 600 men, but had crossed the mountains, and had likely gone south of the Arkansas River. The country is comparatively quiet; forage and subsistence very scarce. The disposition of all armed rebels appears to be to get south as fast as possible.

I had 1 man wounded (accidentally); sent him to Cassville. The prisoners I turned over to provost-marshal at this post, with descriptive rolls of same; horses I turned over to Lieut. A. T. Baubie, regimental quartermaster Sixth Missouri State Militia Cavalry, and obtained receipts for same. Marched eight days; distance, 200 miles.

Awaiting further orders, I am, sir, very respectfully, your obedient servant,

AUSTIN A. KING, JR.,
Major Sixth Missouri State Militia Cavalry, Commanding.

Brigadier-General SANBORN,
Commanding District of Southwestern Missouri.

NOVEMBER —, 1863.—Expedition into Arkansas, and skirmish.

Report of Brig. Gen. Colly B. Holland, Enrolled Missouri Militia.

HEADQUARTERS IN THE FIELD,
North Fork, November 16, 1863.

GENERAL: I have just arrived here from a scout into Arkansas, having received information that there was a camp of rebels below Salem, and determined to break them up. I started with 400 men, and arriving near them, I learned they had moved up this way, and Colonel Love was concentrating for a move into Missouri. We met with small parties, killed 14 and have 6 prisoners, routing the remainder, who, I think, fell back to Calico Rock.

I shall soon move south, crossing White River at Buffalo City, and will move in the direction of Crooked Creek, southeast of Yellville, unless circumstances make it necessary to change my course.

Am short of rations; have to employ part of the men to procure provisions. Will send wagons back.

I am, your obedient servant,

C. B. HOLLAND,
Brigadier-General, Commanding Enrolled Missouri Militia.

Brigadier-General SANBORN.

NOVEMBER 13, 1863.—Skirmish at Mount Ida, Ark.

Report of Brig. Gen. John McNeil, U. S. Army.

FORT SMITH, ARK., *November* 18, 1863.

GENERAL: Captains [J. R.] Vanderpool and [G. W. R.] Smith, of Colonel [J. M.] Johnson's command, stationed at Waldron, with 100 men attacked Bankhead's camp, at Mount Ida, on the 13th, killing and wounding several, and taking prisoners Major Moulton, of Clarkton, and 8 or 10 men. They captured 10,000 rounds of ammunition, 15,000 pounds of bacon, and a room full of flour, which they destroyed. This raid was a complete success, routing and driving an enemy of ten times their number 5 miles beyond Mount Ida, and scattering them through the country. Marmaduke is at Washington, having just returned from Pine Bluff. He has 4,000 men and seventeen pieces of artillery. Price is scattered from Washington to Camden, with about 10,000 infantry.

JOHN McNEIL,
Brigadier-General.

Major-General SCHOFIELD.

NOVEMBER 14–17, 1863.—Expedition from Helena, Ark.

Report of Maj. Eagleton Carmichael, Tenth Illinois Cavalry.

HELENA, ARK., *November* 17, 1863.

SIR: I have the honor to make the following report of an expedition under my command, November 14, 1863:

On Saturday, November 14, at 4.30 o'clock, I left Helena on board the steamer Hamilton Belle, and landed at Delta, Miss., at 6 o'clock the same day, arriving at Friar's Point at 7 o'clock, and found nothing of importance. The night being such that the boat commander thought it dangerous to run, we lay up for the night. On the next morning (November 15), I left at daylight. The boat landed at Island Sixty-three, putting some passengers off. From there we proceeded down to the foot of Island Sixty-five, where we disembarked, at Gillen's wood-yard; got a prisoner at Gillen's house, by the name of Dyer, belonging to the Third Arkansas Cavalry, Company F, and with him one horse and equipments, with some mail matter of no importance. On the shore near here I captured a commissary sergeant, of [Casteel's?] company, and a negro man, one having a mule and the other a horse; no arms. From here I went back 2 miles on the road from Simms' to McKee's (Casteel's old camping ground), and found nothing. I then returned to Gillen's wood-yard. I here sent for the negro to the boat, and by threats and persuasion induced him to guide me to their camps. I had to take a circuitous route through cane-brakes, &c., in order to reach their camp without their apprisal. I struck the road within 3 miles of their camp, and at the same time came upon 8 men, who were on their way to relieve a picket post. We then had a running skirmish with these, killing 3 of them, mortally wounding 1, and capturing 1, the other 3 making good their escape. We then came upon their camps, only a few of them being in camp, the balance being out foraging. We here captured 3 men, 1 of whom was wounded; killed 4, and think there were several others wounded. I found in their camp a lot of provisions, horse equipments, all their camp and garrison equipage, &c., all of which I had completely destroyed, with a lot of shotguns. I also captured in their camp a lot of horses and mules. I then sent a party about a half mile distant, to a house where I learned their ammunition was stored, with a lot of arms and forage that had been collected there for their use. They found about 4,000 rounds of cartridges, a number of shotguns, quite a quantity of forage, &c., all of which they destroyed. From their camp I then returned to the main road leading to the river. I found their pickets about 5 miles from their camp, on this line. About 8 miles below Gillen's, at the foot of Islands Sixty-seven and Sixty-eight, owing to my having to approach their pickets through an open field, they discovered us and fled, some up and some down the river. We killed one of their horses, captured another, and supposed that some were wounded. It being now nearly dark, they made their escape. The advance, upon approaching the residence of Dr. Monroe, discovered some men running from there, supposed to be soldiers. I found at Dr. Monroe's house Dr. Monroe, R. C. Flournoy, and T. B. Warfield. I released Flournoy and Warfield, and brought the doctor with me, appearances being that he was giving aid to the enemy. I then returned to Gillen's Landing without further discoveries. We here encamped for the night. On the following morning (November 16) we re-embarked on board the Hamilton Belle. After we had got under way, it was discovered that one of her boilers was leaking badly, and after a tedious run we reached the foot of Sixty-three. I there went on board the steamboat Cheek, and found that things looked suspicious on board, and found or thought that she was violating Orders, No. 57. I arrested the crew, and had them tow the Hamilton Belle up to Helena. I arrested a man on board named Miffleton, who is supposed to be an agent of Weaver (cotton speculator), supposed to be engaged in hunting negroes down with bloodhounds.

I brought back with me, and turned over to the post quartermaster, 16 horses, 8 mules, some harness, and a number of old saddles, blankets, and bridles. I also ordered to be turned over to the ordnance department 5 carbines and 3 shot-guns.

Too much praise cannot be given to Capt. T. C. Meatyard, for the efficient service he rendered during the expedition. While the skirmish was going on, he was in the hottest of the fight, firing over a dozen shots at the rebels, and, in my opinion, made them tell severely.

The above is respectfully submitted.

E. CARMICHAEL,
Major, Commanding Expedition.

Brig. Gen. N. B. BUFORD,
Commanding District of Eastern Arkansas.

NOVEMBER 19, 1863.—Skirmish at Dr. Green's farm, near Lawrenceville, Ark.

Report of Col. Jonathan Richmond, One hundred and twenty-sixth Illinois Infantry.

DEVALL'S BLUFF, ARK., *November* 20, 1863.

SIR: Major [W. J.] Teed, in command of Eighth Missouri Cavalry detachment, has just returned from a scout to Lawrenceville. He reports that he attacked Major Cocke's forces, 8 miles west of Lawrenceville, on the farm of Dr. Green, on yesterday morning, about 7 o'clock, killing 4 men, who were left on the field, and took 1 prisoner. Citizens report Major Cocke killed; also Lieutenant McBride, but the major cannot vouch for its being correct. He also brought in Lieutenant Sutton, of Captain Edmonson's company. One horse killed was the only loss we sustained. Captured and destroyed cooking utensils, provender, &c.

J. RICHMOND,
Colonel, Commanding Post.

Lieut. GEORGE O. SOKALSKI,
Acting Assistant Adjutant-General.

NOVEMBER 21, 1863.—Affair at Jacksonport, Ark.

REPORTS.

No. 1.—Lieut. Col. Thomas G. Black, Third Missouri Cavalry.
No. 2.—Maj. John A. Lennon, Third Missouri Cavalry.

No. 1.

Report of Lieut. Col. Thomas G. Black, Third Missouri Cavalry.

JACKSONPORT, ARK., *November* 26, 1863.

LIEUTENANT: I have the honor to report the arrival of my command at this point, on the 21st instant.

Upon my arrival at Austin, I found that Captain [C. E.] Berry, commanding a squad of Arkansians, had left with his command. I encamped 4 miles north of Austin. The next morning I sent forward an order to Captain Berry to halt until I came up; but he had started early, and was not overtaken until he had encountered the enemy some 6 miles in my advance. He was fired upon from an ambush, wounding 6 of his men and 1 citizen. Captain Berry retreated until he met my advance, which immediately charged the rebels, killing 3 and wounding several.

I moved on to Bayou Des Arc, where I found them posted in brush and high weeds, on the north side of the bridge (the only crossing). Up to this time I was unable to get any correct information of their numbers. I therefore threw a few shell into the brush, which started them from their ambush. I immediately crossed my men over and pursued them; they scattered through the brush in all directions, General McRae, with a squad, going through the woods in an easterly direction. I pursued them until dark, and went into camp near Searcy.

November 19, learning that McRae had crossed White River below the mouth of Red River, I resumed the march.

[November] 21, I sent a battalion forward, under Major Lennon, to secure the boat at this place. There were 100 rebels, under Shaver, encamped near here; some of them in town.

Upon the arrival of our men on the opposite bank, the rebels fired at them and made a rush for the ferry-boat, which was upon the Jacksonport side, but the fire of our men being too hot for them, they fell back under cover of the houses. Sergeant [J. J.] Hiles and Corporal [J. H.] Yeldell, of Company C, Third Missouri Volunteer Cavalry, volunteered to cross in a yawl and row the ferry-boat over, which they did, under the enemy's fire. The boat was immediately loaded with men and crossed, and the enemy driven out of town, wounding 3 of them, as I have since learned. One battalion was crossed that evening. Repairs being necessary to the ferry, I did not cross the remainder of the command until next day (22d).

Much credit is due Major [J. A.] Lennon for the energetic manner in which he conducted the crossing under the enemy's fire. Sergeant Hiles and Corporal Yeldell are entitled to the highest praise for their noble daring in crossing the river in the face of whizzing bullets.

There are a great many squads of rebels in the country, who have committed many depredations, to the annoyance of the citizens. I have not been able to learn anything of the whereabouts of McRae, except that he crossed to the east side of White River. In the skirmish with McRae we captured 6 of his men and 12 horses. I have also captured three caissons for 12-pounder guns (new), and am informed that the guns are secreted near here. A small stock of goods was also captured, mostly boots and shoes.

I have the honor to be, most respectfully, yours,

T. G. BLACK,

Lieutenant-Colonel Third Missouri Cavalry, Commanding Post.

Lieut. GEORGE O. SOKALSKI,
Acting Assistant Adjutant-General.

No. 2.

Report of Maj. John A. Lennon, Third Missouri Cavalry.

HDQRS. THIRD MISSOURI VOLUNTEER CAVALRY,
Jacksonport, Ark., November 26, 1863.

SIR: In obedience to orders received from you, 11 miles southwest of this place, on the 21st instant, I started for this place to prevent the destruction of the ferry by the rebels, with Squadrons C and E, Captain [J.] Kirkpatrick commanding, Company C being in the advance. When within three-quarters of a mile from the ferry, the advance took the trot, the rear keeping at its proper distance. When within about a quarter of a mile, we took the gallop. Captain Kirkpatrick, being in the advance, discovered a man under the opposite bank of the river in a canoe, which he promptly ordered to this side. I dismounted the men, and placed them in skirmishing order, when commenced a random firing with the enemy on the opposite bank. I then called for volunteers to man the canoe, to go to the opposite bank of the river and bring over the ferry. Sergeant Hiles, of Company C, stepped forward promptly and said he would go. When he started, I found that his companion in the canoe was Corporal Yeldell, of the same company. They performed their duty with coolness and a great deal of skill, for which I desire to tender them my thanks. As soon as the ferry touched our side of the river, Captain Kirkpatrick, with Company C and a small portion of Company E, jumped aboard and made for the opposite shore. Feeling that my rear was safe, the next load I sent Lieutenant [C. M.] Coan with the remainder of Company E, except a few to take care of the horses. The command was crossed just in the nick of time to prevent our passage across the river. As soon as they saw the array of blue-coats presented to their view, they skedaddled for very life. The officers and men all performed their duty nobly. For one, I believe that the Government has no better fighting material than the Third Missouri Volunteer Cavalry.

Hoping that the next time we find the enemy he will fight before he runs, I have the honor to be, your obedient servant,

JOHN A. LENNON,
Major, Commanding Regiment.

Lieut. Col. T. G. BLACK,
Third Missouri Cavalry, Commanding Post.

P. S.—If our men would just quit jayhawking, I believe that I could clean out the rebels of Arkansas with them.

NOVEMBER 23-29, 1863.—Scouts from Houston, Mo.

Report of Capt. Richard Murphy, Fifth Missouri State Militia Cavalry.

HDQRS. FIFTH MISSOURI STATE MILITIA CAVALRY,
Houston, Mo., November 30, 1863.

CAPTAIN: I have the honor to submit the following as my report, required by General Orders, No. 28, from Headquarters District of Rolla, for the week ending November 29, 1863:

On the 23d instant, I sent out a scout of 7 men, under command of Sergeant Basket, Company I, Sixth Enrolled Missouri Militia, to pursue some rebels who had the previous day captured 2 of my men (a report of which has been sent in). The scout pursued them some 30 miles in a southwest direction, but, finding they were far behind, they abandoned the chase and returned to camp, having been out two days.

On the 24th, while two of my men were riding about 4 miles from camp, they were met by what they supposed to be three Federal soldiers, as they were dressed in Federal uniform, and one of them wore an officer's uniform. When they were just in the act of passing, however, the three men drew their revolvers and ordered them to surrender, which, owing to the surprise and the disadvantage under which they labored, they were compelled to do. They were taken to the brush, deprived of their horses and equipments, arms, and clothing, with the exception of their under-clothing, after which they were sworn, and allowed to return to camp. Immediately upon learning of the circumstance, I sent out two scouts of 10 men each, under the respective commands of Lieutenant [William C.] Bangs, of Company D, and Sergeant [T. J.] McDowell, Company B, with instructions to scout the country in every direction for 20 miles around this post, and ascertain, if possible, the hiding-places of the bushwhackers.

The scout under Lieutenant Bangs returned yesterday, having traversed the country for 20 miles in a south-southeast and southwest direction, without having ascertained anything of their whereabouts or secret hiding-places.

The scout under Sergeant McDowell discovered, about 12 miles northeast from this place, a trail of six horses, and it appearing fresh they immediately commenced pursuit. After following it some 8 miles in the direction of Big Piney, they suddenly came upon three bushwhackers, at the house of one Blankenship. Upon discovering the approach of my men, two of the rebels succeeded in mounting their horses and making good their escape. The third (Blankenship) not having time to mount, took to the brush on foot, hotly pursued by two of the sergeant's party. Before reaching the brush he came within range of the pursuers, and two shots were fired at him, both of which took effect in the body. He succeeded, however, in reaching the wood, and, taking advantage of the trees, managed to protect himself for some time. While in this position he raised his rifle, which he had carried throughout, and, taking deliberate aim, fired, mortally wounding Henry J. Rennison, private of Company B. The next instant a volley was fired at him from the remainder of the sergeant's party, who had arrived, and Blankenship fell, pierced by at least twelve balls, either of which would have proved fatal. The wounded soldier was conveyed to the residence of Mr. Bradford, near Licking, and died the next day while being conveyed in the ambulance to this post, where he could receive medical treatment.

The scout is still out, and since then has not been heard from.

Lieut. S. A. Franklin returned yesterday from Rolla, whither he had gone on escort with 20 men of Company D, having been out seven days. Nothing of importance transpired during the trip.

I also sent out a scout of 8 men under command of Sergeant [H.] Heinze, Company G, on the 26th instant. They found, about 12 miles west from Houston, a trail of some seven horses, and, upon inquiry at a house, they were informed that the trail was made by three persons with four led horses and that they were about an hour behind them. They commenced pursuit, but their progress was very slow, owing to the mode of travel of the rebels. They followed to Mountain Store, where they lost the trail entirely, and, giving up the chase, returned to camp yesterday.

Very respectfully, your obedient servant,

RICHARD MURPHY,
Captain, Commanding.

Capt. J. LOVELL,
Assistant Adjutant-General.

NOVEMBER —, 1863.—Scout from Neosho to Shoal and Turkey Creeks, Mo.

Report of Capt. Milton Burch, Eighth Missouri State Militia Cavalry.

HEADQUARTERS,
Neosho, November 29, 1863.

SIR: For the information of the commanding general, I report the success of a scout taken by me with 20 men to Jasper County. Having learned, a few days previous to my starting out, of 10 or 15 bushwhackers harboring on Turkey Creek, in Jasper County, about 20 miles from this place (the weather being very cold), I thought it would be a good time to catch them, and I started.

I proceeded on my route about 9 miles, on to the waters of Shoal Creek, and discovered a light in the thick brush, and in the direction that I knew the light did not proceed from any house, and I knew it must be the camp-fire of guerrillas. I then dismounted my men, leaving a small force with the horses, and I with the remainder started on foot, proceeding very cautiously to within about 200 yards, and then halted. I then sent Lieut. John R. Kelso to reconnoiter and ascertain the force of the enemy and their situation. Lieutenant Kelso reported that they had a tent, and, from the best of his knowledge, there were only 3. I then, with Lieutenant Kelso and 3 men [*sic*]. Owing to the dense thicket we had to penetrate, we thought that we could slip up and surprise with a small force better than a large one, knowing if there were more rebels than we expected, the remaining portion of the men under my command were in easy striking distance. We arrived at the appointed place, the signal was given, and we fired, killing 2 of them, that being all there were there at that time. Their names were Martin Levacy, of Lawrence County, and Woods, given name not known. It was now about 10 o'clock of the night, and we pushed on for Turkey Creek, and arrived at one of the places. When within about a quarter of a mile of the house, we again dismounted, and moved stealthily onward toward the house, which we succeeded in surrounding before being discovered. I immediately hailed the inmates of the house, and demanded a surrender of all the men and arms there were in the house. After some little delay, occasioned, I suppose, in secreting one of their tribe under the floor of the house, after they had him put away decently, they concluded to surrender, and commenced handing their arms out of the window. The woman that handed out the arms stated that there was only one man in the house. We went in and arrested him, and started. I noticed a fine black overcoat hanging in the house, and mistrusted that there must be another somewhere. After I had got about 40 yards from the house, I turned back, and asked the lady if there was not another man somewhere about the house. She replied that if there was she could not help it. I then snatched up a fire-brand, and was going to dash it under the floor, and poor Secessia came crawling out, saying, "Here is my arms; I am your prisoner." I should have killed him then, but we were close to the rendezvous of another party, and I did not want to raise any alarm, although he justly deserves death, as there are a good many Union citizens in this portion of the State that are knowing to his jayhawking and shooting at good Union men; in fact, from the story of loyal citizens round this place, he is a perfect desperado; his name is Dempster Lindsay, formerly of Jasper County, of this State.

We then proceeded toward another house. Before getting to the place, we again dismounted and surrounded the house, as before, hailing in the same manner. After there was a light made in the house, they commenced handing out their arms. One of the rebels was up stairs, and was going to jump out of the window, but was deterred by two of my men shooting at him, which alarmed some others that were near, who made their escape. We captured 3 rebels at this place, and recaptured a Federal soldier, taken prisoner by the same party. He belongs, he says, to the Fourteenth Kansas Cavalry, Company I. He was left, sick, by a train passing down. We succeeded in capturing all his arms, excepting a revolver, together with his horse and equipments. The alarm being raised, and knowing that the hunt was broken up for that time, we started back to camp, with 5 rebel prisoners, 1 Federal soldier, and 6 horses, belonging to the prisoners we captured. The prisoners are all men of desperate character, being regular guerrillas, that have infested and been a terror to all the loyal citizens of the Southwest.

I subscribe myself, your obedient servant,

MILTON BURCH,

Capt., Com'dg Detachment Eighth Missouri State Militia Cavalry.

NOVEMBER 29-30, 1863.—Attack on Bloomfield, Mo., and pursuit of the Confederates to Brown's Ferry, Ark.

REPORTS.

No. 1.—Capt. Valentine Preuitt, First Missouri Cavalry.
No. 2.—Maj. Josephus Robbins, Second Missouri State Militia Cavalry.
No. 3.—Maj. Samuel Montgomery, Sixth Missouri Cavalry.

No. 1.

Report of Capt. Valentine Preuitt, First Missouri Cavalry.

HEADQUARTERS,
Bloomfield, Mo., December 2, 1863.

SIR: I received information, about the 25th of November, that a force was being concentrated some 50 miles south of here, for the purpose of co-operating with other forces being raised farther south, with a design of making a raid upon this place. About the 27th of November, I learned that a large force had been raised, and were on the west side of the Saint Francis.

In the mean time I received your dispatch, wanting me to be on the alert to defend myself. I immediately made preparations to defend the post until the last, and remained in readiness until the morning of the 29th, when I was surrounded by 500 rebels, about 7 a. m., and immediately opened the fight with two small howitzers, throwing shell into the ranks of the enemy, which soon made them disappear from the hills which surrounded the place, and take refuge in the hollows and sinks beyond. At 8 a. m. they sent in a flag of truce, demanding the surrender of the place, stating that they had us completely surrounded, my communications cut, and that we should be treated as prisoners of war, threatening to charge and take the place on a refusal to comply with the demand. I went over and met the flag myself. It was signed by one Lee Crandall, colonel, C. S. Army, commanding. I simply answered that "I was ready to fight, but not to surrender; if they wanted to fight, to open the ball."

I returned to the court-house and opened fire on them the second time. After firing several shots into them, they withdrew, threatening to return soon. I then sent Lieutenant [W. B.] Dorsey, under a flag of truce, proposing to fight them, which they declined, and intimated an intention to retain Dorsey as a prisoner. His ready wit saved him, and he was permitted to return, under an escort. On his return he made good use of his tongue, and succeeded in finding out that they expected re-enforcements from McRae, when they would return and take us in.

I then built as strong a barricade as I could with such materials as I could find about the post, encircling the whole court-house square; placed my men and horses and arms inside, waited patiently until night for their reappearance, but they failed to show themselves again. At night I caused my men to sleep on their arms, inside their barricade.

At about 11 p. m. I received a dispatch from Major [J.] Robbins, informing me that he was ordered to make inquiries concerning the condition of the post. I immediately informed both [S.] Montgomery and Robbins of what had transpired during the day, when they moved their columns into town. Major Montgomery tendered me the use of his battalion to assist me in pursuing them. I gladly accepted it, placed myself in the saddle, and began the pursuit. Overtaking them this side of Chalk Bluff, engaged them and dispersed them, following them in their flight to Brown's Ferry, below Chalk Bluff, where they became so scattered that I concluded to return, which I did, arriving here at 12 m. December 2, having marched a distance of over 100 miles in two days and a half.

I captured and brought into Bloomfield 5 dirty, hungry-looking scamps, who looked too poor to live, besides having killed several. I also captured 2 horses and returned them to the post. The only firing done by the rebels was upon the pickets.

I am satisfied that their only object was plunder. I also learned from old citizens who were taken and held by Crandall during his stay about the place, that all the notorious horse-thieves, cut-throats, and guerrillas who infest this country were with them.

I am, respectfully,

VALENTINE PREUITT,
Captain, Commanding Post.

Col. J. B. ROGERS,
Commanding Cape Girardeau, Mo.

No. 2.

Report of Maj. Josephus Robbins, Second Missouri State Militia Cavalry.

CAPE GIRARDEAU, MO., *December* 6, 1863.

COLONEL: In reply to your inquiry as to the causes which led to the total failure of the expedition sent against the marauders who recently came into the southeast portion of this State, I have the honor to report that, in my opinion, it was because not sufficient force was sent from Bloomfield in pursuit, and want of zeal and energy in the commander of the force which was sent; and for the causes for this opinion I beg leave to submit the following narrative of the whole transaction:

Upon the night of the 29th ultimo, after a hard day's march, I went into camp 13 miles from Bloomfield, not then having heard of any force being in the vicinity of Bloomfield, or of the attack upon that outpost; but, in obedience to the order of Brigadier-General Fisk, to learn if there was any enemy near that place, I sent Lieutenant [E. G.] Rathburn, with 24 men, in the night, to Bloomfield, to learn of affairs there.

Upon arriving at Bloomfield, he learned of the presence of the enemy, and he wished Captain Preuitt to send me dispatches, as his men and horses were fresh, while the guard of Lieutenant Rathburn had ridden all day and then ridden 13 miles with their jaded horses. This Captain Preuitt refused to do, and Lieutenant Rathburn was compelled to return to my camp in person, leaving at Bloomfield all but three of the tired guard. Upon the arrival of Lieutenant Rathburn with the news, at 2 o'clock on the morning of the 30th, I immediately moved, by a rapid march, to Bloomfield, and reported to Major [S.] Montgomery for orders before sunrise. He told me to feed and be ready to march at a moment's notice, which I did, telling him at the same time that I did not want more than an hour. The time passed until, becoming impatient at the long and seemingly fatal delay, I again went to Major Montgomery, and told him my men and horses were good ones and fresh, and I wanted to go in pursuit of the enemy. He again told me to hold my men in readiness to march. At 10.40 o'clock I found that Captain Preuitt, with a detachment of 250 men, were marching out in pursuit, and I was ordered by Major Montgomery to remain at Bloomfield, to hold the post and act as a reserve. After five or six hours of impatient waiting in idleness, I asked the adjutant if Colonel Rogers knew of the movements which were being made. He told me that he did not; that they reported over his head, direct to General Fisk. I then said, "I shall inform him," which I did by telegraph, saying that I had been left idle with 400 men and two cannon. Within five minutes I received orders from Colonel Rogers to march in pursuit of the rebels; to assume command of the whole force under Preuitt, and pursue until pursuit became useless. I marched with 300 men immediately; marched 16 miles that evening, rested until 2 o'clock a. m., 30th, and was again in the saddle. I soon met the force under Preuitt returning. I still pressed on, and came to the camp of the enemy at Taylor's Mill. It was then 11 o'clock.

The enemy had marched at daylight, and was then across the Saint Francis River. I found that Preuitt had come up with the stragglers, in the rear of the enemy's column; had captured 2, and camped within 3 miles of the enemy and west of him, and between him and the river. Why he did not attack or pursue I cannot explain. The fact is, Preuitt marched back and the enemy marched on at nearly the same hour. If the whole force had been sent out together, nothing could have prevented the capture of the whole force of the enemy, as the river, where he crossed by swimming, was difficult to cross, and the swamps on each side of the road would have prevented him escaping in any other way. My command, both officers and men, were eager to pursue, which I told Major Montgomery early in the morning, and if we had marched when Preuitt did, or, what would have been better, at 8 o'clock, which we were ready to do, we should have come up with the enemy and had engaged him, and the issue would not have been doubtful. My force alone was ample; the men and horses were in good condition. I assure you in this it was not want of energy or zeal upon the part of my command, as the disappointment in not being allowed to join in the pursuit was extreme. I did not report to you, because I deemed it my duty to report to the ranking officer present, which I did, and only reported to you when I found you did not know how affairs were being managed, and because I knew you would not approve of such inexcusable inactivity.

The event has proven that if the full force had been sent out at the proper time, the enemy would have been severely punished for his temerity.

I am, colonel, very respectfully, your obedient servant,

JOSEPHUS ROBBINS,

Major Second Battalion, Second Regt. M. S. M., Comdg. Expedition.

Col. J. B. ROGERS,

Comdg. Second Missouri S. M. Cav., and Post, Cape Girardeau, Mo.

No. 3.

Reports of Maj. Samuel Montgomery, Sixth Missouri Cavalry.

BLOOMFIELD, MO., *November* 30, 1863.

GENERAL: I arrived here at 5 a. m. The Confederates were 15 miles on the Chalk Bluff road last night. The information gained at Poplar Bluff was correct. I shall send Captain Preuitt with the First, Sixth, and Captain [A.] Johns' company of Missouri State Militia. Major Robbins is here with part of his command, and will remain unless you order otherwise.

SAML. MONTGOMERY,

Major, Commanding.

Brig. Gen. C. B. FISK.

BLOOMFIELD, MO., *November* 30, 1863.

GENERAL: I took the Poplar Bluff road, and did not go to Ash Hills. At Poplar Bluff I captured 1 prisoner, who belongs to Reves' company, who yesterday arrived at Poplar Bluff, from Arkadelphia. From him, and from other reliable sources, I got the information that General McRae, with 500 cavalry and one regiment of infantry, was 6 miles below Pocahontas. They were there last Thursday, and the supposition was that they would march toward Bloomfield. Reves has been around, killing some more Union men, and, I think, acts as a kind of advance. It was understood by several men at Poplar Bluff that a large body was coming. The infantry is dismounted cavalry.

SAML. MONTGOMERY,

Major, Commanding.

Brigadier-General FISK.

BLOOMFIELD, MO., *December* 2, 1863.

GENERAL: Captain Preuitt and command have just returned. They gave the enemy chase until they crossed the Saint Francis, where our horses could go no farther, they being literally worn out. The enemy are the most ragged and thieving rascals that ever invaded the State. Positive evidence shows that they came for nothing but plunder, in which they signally failed. Captain Preuitt met Major Robbins' command 6 miles this side of Chalk Bluff. Captain Preuitt captured 5 or 6 of the enemy, while giving them a galloping chase of 8 miles. The horses of my battalion are very much worn down, this being the eighth day out from the Knob.

SAML. MONTGOMERY,

Major.

Brig. Gen. C. B. FISK.

DECEMBER 1, 1863.—Skirmish near Benton, Ark.

REPORTS.

No. 1.—Col. Cyrus Bussey, Third Iowa Cavalry.
No. 2.—Capt. H. S. Randall, Third Missouri Cavalry (Confederate).

No. 1.

Report of Col. Cyrus Bussey, Third Iowa Cavalry.

DECEMBER 1, 1863.

SIR: I sent out a patrol of 40 men on the Hot Springs road at 3 o'clock this morning, under Lieutenant [A. D.] Mills, First Missouri Cavalry. He has just returned, having gone out 25 miles. When within 10 miles of Benton, on his return, he was attacked by a force of 400 rebels, and lost 3 men killed and 2 wounded, who got into camp. He came near being captured with his whole force. He thinks this force was there for the purpose of capturing our forage trains, which have been going out on that road. The train was hurried in yesterday by a reported force near Hot Springs. Two men of Lieutenant Mills' command had their horses shot, and took to the brush. They have come in on the road. The enemy did not advance. They have no doubt fallen back to the mountains.

CYRUS BUSSEY,
Colonel.

Brigadier-General DAVIDSON,
Commanding Cavalry Division, Little Rock, Ark.

No. 2.

Report of Capt. H. S. Randall, Third Missouri Cavalry (Confederate).

CAMP NEAR HOT SPRINGS, ARK.,
December 2, 1863.

GENERAL: After leaving camp, I proceeded in the direction of Benton. I learned that a forage train of 50 wagons was foraging in 14 miles of Hot Springs, but was too late to attack them.

On yesterday I attacked a Federal scout of about 50, in 8 miles of Benton, on the Hot Springs road, killing 2, wounding 4, and taking 1 prisoner, with their arms, with the loss of 1 horse. The strength of the Federals at Benton is believed to be about 1,200 men and five pieces of artillery. The Federals hear that you are hovering in their direction. They are moving their heaviest baggage to Little Rock, where the citizens say there are 10,000 or 12,000. I intend moving on the Arkansas River. You will hear from me soon.

Respectfully, yours,

H. S. RANDALL,
Captain Company F, Third Missouri Cavalry.

Brig. Gen. J. S. MARMADUKE,
Commanding Cavalry.

DECEMBER 1, 1863.—Skirmish near Devall's Bluff, Ark.

Report of Col. Jonathan Richmond, One hundred and twenty-sixth Illinois Infantry.

DEVALL'S BLUFF, *December* 2, 1863.

SIR: Major [William J.] Teed and Captain [L. J.] Matthews, Eighth Missouri Cavalry, were out drilling yesterday p. m. On their return the major found he had lost his pocket-book, and went back, with Captain Matthews, to find it. About 1 mile out from this post they were attacked by 8 guerrillas, dressed in Federal uniform, who demanded their surrender. They refused, and were fired on; the major received five shots, and succeeded in making his escape; the captain was brought in with three shots through him. I sent a party immediately after them, with orders to take no prisoners. They soon overtook them, and killed 3 and wounded 3. Am I justified in giving such orders when they are found with our uniforms on? One corporal of the Eighth Missouri was shot in the leg last night. The major and captain will both recover.

J. RICHMOND,
Colonel.

Lieut. GEORGE O. SOKALSKI,
Acting Assistant Adjutant-General, Little Rock, Ark.

DECEMBER 1, 1863.—Affair with Ponca Indians.

Report of Maj. Herman H. Heath, Seventh Iowa Cavalry.

DAKOTA CITY, *December* 20, 1863.

GENERAL: In compliance with your verbal instructions to inquire into and report upon the late unfortunate affair between a detachment of the command at this post and a small body of the Poncas, I have the honor to submit the following facts:

It seems that, on or about the first of the present month, a sergeant in command of a detachment of our troops discovered some 20 Indians, of the tribe mentioned, on the south side of the Missouri River. They appear to have been encamped there. He demanded to see their passes. Either they had none to exhibit, or, from perverseness, declined to produce them. The former is probably the fact, as their agent was not among the tribe at the agency when they left. The chief ordered the sergeant away, and the latter complied.

On the day of the 4th, it seems that these Indians fell in with a couple of citizens of Niobrara, and made some demonstrations not calculated to please them, and they fled from the Indians with haste. I understand that the Indians circled near the white men, and rode toward them, but did not fire nor appear to intend anything serious. The white men were, with wagons and oxen, some 2 miles from town. After thus frightening the whites, the Indians seem to have gone off in a direction away from the settlement. The white men came into the town, and reported the thing to the sergeant in command of the soldiers. The latter were at once ordered out, and the pursuit under the sergeant commenced. The Indians were overtaken and fired upon by our men. The Indians returned two shots, but continued retreating, followed by our men, whose fire was rapid and continuous, until 7 of the Indians were killed. None of our troops were injured. Subsequently the Indians demanded the bodies of their slain, which were accorded to them, and here the unfortunate affair closes for the present.

The facts given above I received from Captain [J.] Wilcox, which he may have already detailed to you. I make no comment upon them, further than to observe that it seems to me so unfortunate an affair as the killing of so many men at the time might, with prudent foresight, have been avoided; and, thinking thus, and seeing a strong probability that similar occurrences may transpire, I have recommended Captain Wilcox to keep one of his lieutenants at the important place of Niobrara, who it would seem would be likely to act with a greater degree of caution and a deeper sense of responsibility than an enlisted man seems likely to do. This course I believe the captain has determined to adopt.

I have the honor to remain, very respectfully, your obedient servant,

H. H. HEATH,
Major and Chief of Cavalry and District Inspector.

Brigadier-General MCKEAN, *Omaha, Nebr.*

DECEMBER 2-7, 1863.—Scout from Waldron to Mount Ida, Caddo Gap, and Dallas, Ark.

REPORTS.

No. 1.—Col. James M. Johnson, First Arkansas Infantry (Union).
No. 2.—Lieut. Col. Owen A. Bassett, Second Kansas Cavalry.
No. 3.—Maj. John M. Harrell, Brooks' Arkansas Cavalry.

No. 1.

Report of Col. James M. Johnson, First Arkansas Infantry (Union).

HEADQUARTERS FIRST ARKANSAS INFANTRY,
Waldron, Ark., December 7, 1863.

GENERAL: I have the honor to make the following report:

I started with my available force (mounted), consisting of the Second Kansas Cavalry, under Colonel [O. A.] Bassett, numbering 250 strong; one company (C), First Arkansas Infantry, under Captain [J. R.] Vanderpool, and two pieces of Rabb's battery, commanded by Sergt. George B. Sink. I took up the line of march at sunrise on the 2d instant, and proceeded in the direction of Mount Ida, stopping a few hours on the evening of the 2d to rest our stock. We kept on, making no halt of consequence until we reached Mount Ida. We brought up there on the morning of the 4th instant, at 7 o'clock. Charging into town with my advance, found nothing there, but ascertained there was a small body of rebels left there the evening before. I halted my command in Mount Ida, and sent out small scouts in different directions, but could hear of nothing within striking distance.

On the following morning I inspected the stock of the battery and cavalry, and found that the battery horses were so much fatigued that they would not make Arkadelphia, the point I started for. I took them and the worn-out horses of the cavalry and returned to Waldron.

The cavalry force I sent out, under Colonel Bassett, in the direction of Washington, Hempstead County, Arkansas. They went as far as the Caddo Narrows, leaving a force there, and scouting the country for 15 miles below, going within 6 miles of Murfreesborough, and east of there some 20 miles, scouting the country clean as they went.

I also sent a scout to Hot Springs (Buckskins), and their report amounts to the following, which I think is correct, as it is corroborated by citizens coming within our lines: They say that Marmaduke had a force of 600 men in there on the morning of the 4th instant, they reaching there in the evening. Part of them were State troops. The report there was, they were going to attack Benton, where a small force of ours is stationed. Shelby and the rest of Marmaduke's forces are together, stationed at Okolona, on the Ouachita River. Both commands, it is said, have 4,000 men. They are deserting fast; their transportation is very poor. Colonel Dorsey is in the mountains between Benton and Hot Springs, and has 400 men.

The following is a statement of a prisoner from Marmaduke: He left Marmaduke's command, Thomson's regiment, Cabell's brigade, one week ago to-day, at Okolona, on Ouachita River, and reports 8,000 men, the combined forces of the various guerrillas and larger forces from Missouri. Price is 20 miles west of Camden, at Woodlawn, and has 6,000 men (infantry), and is building cabins and hauling in large quantities of subsistence stores. Kirby Smith is near Monroe, on Red River, and not recruiting very fast. Marmaduke has twenty-eight pieces of artillery. Monroe commands Cabell's brigade, and has 800 men and four pieces of artillery. Cabell in person has gone to Texas.

I have the honor to remain, yours, truly,

JAMES M. JOHNSON,
Colonel, Commanding.

Brigadier-General MCNEIL,
Commanding District of the Frontier.

No. 2.

Report of Lieut. Col. Owen A. Bassett, Second Kansas Cavalry.

HEADQUARTERS SECOND KANSAS CAVALRY,
Waldron, Ark., December 8, 1863.

CAPTAIN: I have the honor to report that, in obedience to orders from Col. J. M. Johnson, First Arkansas Infantry, at that time commanding troops at this place, I left Waldron at 8 a. m. on the 2d instant, with 230 men from the Second Kansas Cavalry, and proceeded in the direction of Mount Ida. Seven miles from Waldron, I took the left-hand road, crossed the Fourche la Fave, and bivouacked at the foot of the Washita Mountains, 25 miles from Waldron. Started the next morning at 1 o'clock and crossed the Ouachita, and arrived at Mount Ida, the county seat of Montgomery County, Arkansas, situated on South Fork of Ouachita, at 9 a. m.; 25 miles. Halted at Mount Ida, and sent out scouting parties. Sent Captain [J.] Gardner with 25 men south, toward Caddo Gap, 12 miles; Lieutenant [B. B.] Mitchell with 10 men west, up South Fork 8 miles, and Lieutenant [D. E.] Ballard east, down South Fork, with 20 men, 10 miles, all of whom returned, reporting nothing worthy of note.

Left Mount Ida at 8 a. m. on the 4th instant, with 200 men (having sent Lieutenant Mitchell with 30 men back to Waldron), and proceeded to Caddo Gap, 20 miles, where I halted, and sent out Captain [A.] Gunther with 30 men 11 miles southeast, to the crossing of Caddo, on the Arkadelphia road; Lieutenant [W. P.] Phillips with 20 men 10 miles south by east on the Murfreesborough road, and Lieutenant [E. S.] Stover with 17 men 10 miles south on the Washington road, all of whom returned that night. Captain Gunther brought in 3 prisoners (Confederate soldiers). Lieutenant Phillips reported nothing worthy of note. Lieutenant Stover met with a party of 19 men, under Lieut. John Ranson; charged the party, killed 2, and took 4 prisoners (Confederate soldiers). While at Caddo Gap I took 2 prisoners, 1 Confederate soldier and 1 citizen. Left Caddo Gap at 5 a. m., 5th instant, and proceeded up the south side of Caddo to its head, crossed over the dividing ridge to the head of Big Fork, and followed down that creek to Ouachita, and bivouacked, having traveled 36 miles. Started next morning and proceeded, in northwesterly direction, to the Waldron and Dallas road (known as the Red River road), 10 miles from Dallas, from which point I sent Captain Gunther and Lieutenant Stover into Dallas with 63 men. I proceeded toward Waldron, on the Red River road, and, arriving at Fourche la Fave, bivouacked, having traveled 30 miles. Captain Gunther reported from his scout at 8 p. m., having been into and around the town of Dallas, at which place he captured 2 prisoners (Confederate soldiers). On the morning of the 7th started at 7 o'clock, and arrived at this place at 1 p. m., a distance of 20 miles. Whole distance traveled since leaving Waldron, 156 miles.

From prisoners taken, and from citizens, I learned that Marmaduke was encamped between Arkadelphia and Murfreesborough, his main camp being 12 miles from the former place. It was rumored that he was about to move up to within 6 miles of Arkadelphia. He had three pieces of artillery in Murfreesborough, and expected that place would be attacked by our forces. He had no large scout out very far northward. His forces were estimated generally at 6,000. The latest information I had direct from him was up to Wednesday morning, 2d instant. Major Wood was encamped with about 300 men near a cotton factory, 2 miles northwest from Murfreesborough, guarding the factory, and preparing to take out the machinery. The latest information I had from him was up to Wednesday evening, 2d instant.

Cabell's brigade was encamped south of Arkadelphia, under command of Colonel Monroe. Cabell had gone to Texas.

Price was in command between Washington and Camden. Parsons' brigade was 20 miles from Camden. It was rumored in his camp that Price was going to move across the river to Princeton, in Dallas County, toward Pine Bluff. The infantry, however, were building cabins, as if for winter quarters; whether by order from headquarters or not was unknown. The latest direct information from Price was up to the 30th instant. Shelby was south of Washington; I have no very definite information concerning him. Brooks was 7 miles south of Centre Point, expecting to go still farther south. The latest direct information from him was up to Wednesday, the 2d instant. Cooper was at Boggy Depot with a small force. His command, considerably scattered, intends moving across Red River, if pushed. Bankhead's command is at Shawneetown, 30 miles below Doaksville, and now commanded by Colonel Gano. Bankhead has gone to Texas (to the coast). Steele is at Doaksville, or in that vicinity. He has under his command thirteen pieces of artillery, three of which are mountain howitzers. My information from

Steele's command is definite, and dates up to the 30th of November. I received it from four men, who just arrived from Boggy Depot.

The country over which I traveled is for the most part mountainous and rocky; still, the roads are passable for artillery and army trains. Water is abundant, even in dry and hot weather. At least one-half of the farm houses are deserted, and a large portion of those now inhabited will (judging from the feelings of the people) be deserted before spring. Forage is not abundant north of the southern boundary of Montgomery County, although there is a sufficient quantity to subsist small scouting parties for some time to come. But I should consider it impracticable to forage an army between here and Caddo Gap or Centre Point for a longer period than would be required to march that distance.

The Little Missouri Mountains are the most difficult to pass, and I am informed that west of the road leading from Little Rock and Arkadelphia there are but three passes by which an army could be moved: First, on the road leading from Hot Springs to Washington, 12 miles east of Caddo Gap; second, Caddo Gap; and, third, on the road leading from Dallas to Centre Point. The last crosses over the mountain, and is very rough, running down a rocky creek bed on the southern slope. The Caddo Gap road runs along the bank of Caddo Creek, and passes the mountains without elevation.

Very respectfully, your obedient servant,

OWEN A. BASSETT,
Lieutenant-Colonel, Commanding.

Capt. C. G. LAURANT,
Assistant Adjutant-General, District of the Frontier.

No. 3.

Report of Maj. John M. Harrell, Brooks' Arkansas Cavalry.

HEADQUARTERS BROOKS' CAVALRY,
December 5, 1863.

MAJOR: On Thursday, the 2d instant, I started a scout of 25 men, which I did not refer to in my dispatch of yesterday, to Caddo Gap and Mount Ida. On Friday, 2 p. m., the scout met Lieutenant Hurt, of Head's company, consisting of 30 or 40 men directly from Mount Ida, 10 miles this side of Caddo Gap, who reported no Federals at Caddo Gap and none at Mount Ida, and no talk of any. Afterward the scout met 2 men who were just from the gap, and heard of no Federals. Proceeding on the march, with 6 unarmed men in front (who had been arrested from Hunt's company as deserters from the infantry, at the instance of Captain East, in compliance with orders from division headquarters, Captain East having accompanied the scout), about an hour by sun on Friday evening, within 5 miles of the gap, they were met by a party of Federals, who fired on and immediately routed them, with a loss of 7 missing. One of the men of the scout who was taken prisoner made his escape soon after his capture. He reports that, upon being disarmed, he was permitted to keep his horse (run down), and ordered to sit down at the foot of a tree, while the pursuing party, his captors, went on and left him. Of this party he counted 25. Upon seeing the front of another column of Federals following on, he took to the woods and escaped. The pursuers were all dressed in full Federal uniform, and addressed the leader of the party in advance as captain. This is all I have been able to learn. The fugitives have just arrived. I shall send 100 men in the same direction to-morrow.

Early this morning I started Lieutenant Jenks and 24 men on the direct road to Waldron.

I have the honor to be, most respectfully, your obedient servant,

JOHN M. HARRELL,
Major, Commanding Brooks' Cavalry.

Major [HENRY] EWING,
Assistant Adjutant-General, Marmaduke's Division.

DECEMBER 5–13, 1863.—Reconnaissance from Little Rock and skirmish (8th) at Princeton, Ark.

Reports of Col. Lewis Merrill, Second Missouri Cavalry.

DECEMBER 11, 1863.

GENERAL: We surprised a rebel camp 2 miles below Princeton on Tuesday—about 600 of them. Drove them within 16 miles of Camden, where they scattered so much that we could do nothing more. They were entirely routed, losing 8 killed, 6 of them killed with the saber; 18 wounded, and 3 commissioned officers and 25 privates captured, and 1 four-mule wagon, loaded with blankets, captured. The rest of their train was out foraging, and got warning, and escaped before we learned where they were.

There are no indications of an immediate advance that I could discover. Fagan and Parsons are at Camden. Price with the rest of his old army is at Woodlawn, 18 miles from Camden. Marmaduke is west of Arkadelphia, near Spoonville, with small outposts at Arkadelphia, and scouting as far as Rockport. Holmes is relieved from command, and ordered east of the Mississippi. Kirby Smith is said to be still at Shreveport; has been to Washington recently. Price's force is recuperated considerably, but does not exceed, including Marmaduke's, 14,000 or 15,000 effective men; many of these are conscripts, just taken in, and State troops. Will make detailed report upon my return.

Our loss, 1 man, wounded severely.

Yours, respectfully,

LEWIS MERRILL,
Colonel, Commanding.

Major-General STEELE,
Little Rock, Ark.

HEADQUARTERS SECOND BRIGADE, CAVALRY DIVISION,
Little Rock, Ark., December 17, 1863.

COLONEL: I have the honor to report below the result of the reconnaissance which I have just completed, in compliance with the orders of the major-general commanding the army:

On the 4th instant, I received from Brigadier-General Davidson, commanding cavalry division, orders to report in person to the major-general commanding, for further instructions, and to take command for the duty assigned me of the following troops: Seventh Missouri Cavalry, Major [M. H.] Brawner commanding, 400; two battalions of First Iowa

Cavalry, Captain [J. D.] Jenks commanding, 250; one battalion of Merrill's Horse, Captain [William H.] Higdon commanding, 125; and to be joined at Benton by detachment of First Missouri Cavalry, Major [A. P.] Peabody commanding, 200; detachment of Third Iowa Cavalry, Captain [B. S.] Jones commanding, 200; and four guns of Hadley's battery, Lieutenant [E. B.] Hubbard commanding, making an aggregate of little more than 1,000 men. Upon reporting to the major-general commanding for further instructions, he informed me that Parsons' brigade of rebel cavalry was camped near Princeton, with some artillery, and that he wished me to drive them away, and find out what I could of the strength, position, and intentions of the enemy; to exercise my own discretion as to when and how to advance, and also as to what was necessary to be done.

On the following morning I left this place with part of my command, and reached Benton that evening, being there joined by the artillery and the rest of my command. The next day I reached Rockport, on the Washita, and found that about 150 rebel cavalry, belonging to Cabell's brigade, had left there about two hours before my arrival. Here, as elsewhere throughout the entire march, I heard all sorts of reports of the enemy, from which reports I judged that Cabell's brigade was camped that night on Caddo Creek, 4 miles north of Arkadelphia, on the west side of the Washita; that some command was camped below Princeton, and that Price's whole army was advancing from Camden, probably toward Little Rock or Pine Bluff. The Washita is subject to very sudden rise, and the sky was threatening rain. This, with the importance of finding out the truth of Price's reported advance, determined me to make a feint toward Arkadelphia, while I moved upon the force near Princeton, and drove them far enough to determine Price's movements.

For several miles below Rockport the roads to Tulip and Arkadelphia are the same, and I accordingly moved my whole command toward Arkadelphia, as far as the dividing point, from which I sent the Third Iowa and First Missouri, under Major Peabody, to make a demonstration of movement toward Arkadelphia, while I marched the main body on the road to Tulip.

About 10 o'clock I received reliable information that the command near Princeton was an outpost from Camden, about 700 strong, under the command of Colonel Crawford, and that Parsons' brigade was not there. I pushed forward now with all possible haste, hoping to be able, by throwing a part of my troops in their rear, to cut them off and capture the whole body. About noon, however, a heavy rain began falling, and continued until daylight next morning. This made the roads so heavy that I could not keep the artillery up without entirely wearing it out, and entirely frustrating the plan proposed, as it would make the night too dark to move troops across the country with success. I accordingly went into camp at Tulip, which I reached just at dark.

At sunrise next morning I moved out, Major Peabody's command having joined me during the early night. I feared that the delay, caused by the rain, would have given the enemy time to hear of my movements and get out of my way.

About 4 miles from Princeton my advanced guard found a small picket of the enemy, which immediately retreated too rapidly to be caught. I now gave the immediate command of the advance guard, comprised of the First Iowa, to Major Brawner, Seventh Missouri, and added to his command the Seventh Missouri, with instructions to push on as rapidly as possible, and develop the force and position of the enemy. Driving their outposts rapidly before him, he came upon their main body about 2 miles below Princeton, posted behind a small stream, which was crossed behind a bridge. Here he dismounted the First Iowa and part of the Seventh Missouri, and quickly drove the enemy from their position through their camp and to the second position, which they had assumed behind the crest of a hill about half a mile from their camp. A similar disposition drove them from the hill in confusion, and only one more attempt was made to withstand our troops. This was by some 50 men, under a Captain McMurtee, who rallied in the road and attempted to stand. They were gallantly and vigorously charged by two squadrons of the Seventh Missouri, under Captain [L.] Bunner, who, when he reached them after some miles of hard riding, unhesitatingly dashed into them with only the 6 men who had succeeded in keeping up in the race. They stood for a moment only before Bunner's sabers, and then fled in the wildest disorder, still pursued by the Seventh Missouri. The vigor of the charge and courage and hardihood of Captain Bunner and his men are attested by the killed and wounded, nearly all of whom were killed or wounded with the saber. The rest of the chase was simply a trial of speed between their horses and ours, in which they proved themselves better mounted than we. For some 10 or 12 miles the chase was kept up, resulting, however, only in the capture of a few more prisoners, and the enemy, as chance offered, disappearing through the heavy woods and undergrowth through which the road ran.

The result of the attack was the complete rout of the enemy and disorderly flight toward Camden, and through the woods in every direction. Six of the enemy were reported killed with the saber, 2 by gunshot wounds, and 18 wounded, principally saber cuts; 3 commissioned officers and 25 privates captured, and 1 wagon of their train, loaded with 50 blankets, captured; the mules retained, and the wagon and harness (worthless) destroyed. Numerous arms were picked up along the track of their flight, and the road for miles was strewn with saddlebags, blankets, clothing, and arms. The horses belonging to the men captured were nearly all lost, as they dashed off down the road with the flying enemy as soon as their riders were unhorsed.

Major Brawner, of the Seventh Missouri, Captain Jenks, of the First Iowa, but more especially Captain Bunner, of the Seventh Missouri, deserve the highest praise for courage and good conduct. Captain Bunner's gallant charge turned a disorderly retreat into a disgraceful flight, in which, it is said, the commanding officer of the rebels led off, with his troops, completely panic-stricken, clattering along at his heels, "*sauve qui peut.*"

Directing Major Brawner, with part of the troops, to continue the pursuit as far as he deemed fruitful of results, I returned to Princeton with the artillery and Major Peabody's brigade, and sent a reconnaissance toward Arkadelphia, which returned in the course of the day, having seen no signs of the enemy in that direction. Satisfied that the objects sought to be accomplished by the reconnaissance had been obtained, as far as it was possible, I returned, by easy marches, to Little Rock, reaching this place on the eighth day, making an average of 30 miles marching a day, and with the horses improved by having had, during the expedition, plenty of long forage.

The information obtained from various sources is given below, such of it as in my estimation is of doubtful value being noted from the rest.

Kirby Smith is at Shreveport, having recently made a visit to Washington, with no great number of troops at that point. Holmes is said to have been ordered east of the Mississippi. Price is at Woodlawn, about 18 miles south of west of Camden; has with him, or in that vicinity, McRae's, Parsons', Frost's, and probably Tappan's brigades, with the same artillery that he had at Little Rock. Fagan and "Texas" [W. H.] Parsons are at Camden, with about 1,000 infantry, 800 cavalry, and several pieces of artillery. A number of conscripts, returned deserters, and State troops are under his command, but widely scattered through the country, on outpost and foraging service. "Texas" Parsons was at Mount Elba, on the Saline, a few days before I reached Princeton, but had returned with his command to Camden.

On the 4th, General Fagan came up to the camp below Princeton, and thence to Tulip, where he staid about half an hour. I could not discover the object of his visit. He returned next day to Camden.

The country is full of rumors of an advance in the direction of Benton and Little Rock, but I did not discover any signs of any serious intention to do so.

The enemy are engaged in building one or more pontoon bridges at Camden, but this is probably simply a precaution against the rise of the Washita.

Marmaduke's headquarters were said to be at Clear Spring, 17 miles west of Arkadelphia, and 6 miles south of the road from Arkadelphia to Washington. His command was reported to be at various points in that section of country; nothing, so far as I could learn reliably (except a small outpost on the Caddo and one at Arkadelphia), nearer than the body with him at headquarters.

The Washita was rising slowly and the sky threatening rain when I reached Rockport, on my return, and I feared, if I crossed, the stream would become impassable before I could get back.

The whole force of the enemy, from what I could gather, I take to be about 13,000 to 15,000 effective men, including Marmaduke's command, and all armed. Many of them are conscripts and raw State troops, which can hardly be called effective, and little likely to become so.

I have prepared a careful sketch of the road, from notes taken while on the march. This is taken without instruments, and with only such appliances and facilities as could be used on the march; but is, as far as may be under these drawbacks, accurate. The sketch will be forwarded, and a general description of the road and country, as soon as I can procure proper paper upon which to make it.

I have the honor to be, very respectfully, your obedient servant,

LEWIS MERRILL,
Colonel, Commanding Second Brigade, Cavalry Division.

Col. F. H. MANTER, *Chief of Staff.*

P. S.—List of killed and wounded: William McChesney, private Company D, First Iowa Cavalry, severely wounded in shoulder; arm amputated.

DECEMBER 9-19, 1863.—Scouts from Houston, Mo.

Report of Capt. Richard Murphy, Fifth Missouri State Militia Cavalry.

HDQRS. DETACHMENT FIFTH MISSOURI S. M. CAVALRY,
Houston, Mo., December 20, 1863.

CAPTAIN: I have the honor to submit the following as my report, required by General Orders, No. 23, from District Headquarters, dated November 24, 1863, for the week ending December 20, 1863:

December 9, 1863, Lieutenant Boyd, Company I, Sixth Provisional

Regiment Enrolled Missouri Militia, with a force of 20 men of Company I, Enrolled Missouri Militia, in the direction of the Mountain Store, after marching to Opossum Creek, a distance of 15 miles, struck a trail of several rebels, the same that had captured and stripped some of Company D the day previous. After following some distance, he discovered he was too far in the rear to accomplish much by following the trail. He marched for the Mountain Store. While in that vicinity he got close after a band of rebels that had just robbed some families. He pursued them for several miles, when they left the road and struck into the woods and scattered, still bearing south. Being there joined by 2 of our scouts and 2 men of our command, he concluded it would be best to march still farther south, and get beyond these bands that were bearing him in that direction. He accordingly took a course that brought him to the headwaters of the North Fork of White River, and followed it for 15 miles. Not finding any bushwhackers, he turned in the direction of West Plains, and thence to Indian Creek and Howell Valley; and having ascertained the men he was pursuing had passed twelve hours ahead of him, the men and horses being worn down for the want of feed, having marched one time thirty hours without forage, he thought it prudent to return to camp, which he did by the way of Jack's Fork. While passing the last-named place he came upon the notorious guerrilla Clark, who, in attemping to escape, was killed. Without getting any further information worthy of note, he returned to camp, being absent eight days, making a march of 200 miles.

Sergt. A. L. Thomas, Company F, Enrolled Missouri Militia, started on the morning of December 18, with 6 men, in the direction of Big Creek, scouting the country for 12 miles around without discovering anything worthy of note, and camped at the Widow Brown's. Next day, the 19th, returned again.

Corpl. John Gortscamp, of Company G, Fifth Missouri State Militia, started in the direction of Johnson's Mills, with 6 men, on the morning of December 19. He scouted all that day, and camped at the mills at night. He started at 6 o'clock on the following morning. During the course of the day he fell in with Sergeant McDowell, of Company B, Fifth Missouri State Militia Cavalry. He then changed his course. He fell in with Captain McKinney, of Company I, Enrolled Missouri Militia. Changing his course again, he scouted through that section of the country, and arrived on the 20th, at 7 p. m., without making any further discoveries worthy of note.

Captain McKinney started, with 12 men of our detachment, in the direction of Piney on the morning of December 16, in search of mail robbers. He traveled the country for 30 miles all around, and, not finding any trace of them, he returned to camp on December 20, having been absent four days and marched a distance of 100 miles. I have another scout out, which I have not heard from as yet. I have sent 4 men with dispatches to Rolla, and [they] have not returned.

I have the honor to be, very respectfully, your obedient servant,

RICHARD MURPHY,

Capt., Comdg. Detachment Fifth Missouri State Militia Cavalry.

Capt. J. LOVELL,

Assistant Adjutant-General, Rolla District, Rolla, Mo.

DECEMBER 14, 1863.—Skirmish at Caddo Mill, Ark.

Report of Lieut. Col. Owen A. Bassett, Second Kansas Cavalry.

HEADQUARTERS SECOND KANSAS CAVALRY,
Waldron, Ark., December 16, 1863.

CAPTAIN: I have the honor to report that, on the 13th instant, I sent Lieutenant [P.] Cosgrove, Company G, and Lieutenant [B. B.] Mitchell, Company K, with 40 men of the Second Kansas Cavalry, to Caddo Gap, and, having returned, Lieutenant Cosgrove reports:

That on Sunday morning, at 9 o'clock, he left Waldron, and proceeded south 7 miles out from this place, taking the right-hand road, and, having crossed Fourche la Fave, took the left-hand road (known as the Texas road), and bivouacked between Fourche la Fave and Ouachita, 30 miles from Waldron. Monday, crossed Ouachita and South Fork at McConnell's Mill, and there learned that there had been a force (detachment from Shelby) there the night before, and proceeded on to Farrar's Mill, on Caddo, reaching that place at sundown. There learned that a party of 15 men were half an hour ahead of him. He pushed on as rapidly as possible 7 miles, and came upon a camp in the woods half a mile from Caddo Mill; charged upon the camp, killed 2 and wounded 1 at least; captured 1 prisoner, 8 negroes, 3 wagons, 6 mules, 6 horses, and a number of worthless arms. It was dark, the woods thick and bushy, and most of the men made their escape. Made a bonfire of the plunder. Brought away 1 wagon, and returned to Farrar's Mill and fed, having traveled 42 miles. Started again about 2 a. m. Tuesday, and reached Mount Ida at daylight, and fed. Marched again at 8 a. m. on the road leading to Waldron, and bivouacked in Fourche la Fave Valley, 38 miles from Farrar's Mill. Started this morning at 8 o'clock, and arrived here at 4 p. m.; 20 miles. Total distance marched, 139 miles.

Lieutenant Cosgrove learned that on Friday (the day I left Caddo Gap) a scout came up the road as far as Farrar's Mill, and returned the same day, claiming to have 200 men, and he could not ascertain that there had been any other party up from the south since that day. He learned also that Lieutenant [E. S.] Stover, who had the skirmish as reported in my letter of the 8th instant, killed 3 men. One of the men killed by Lieutenant Cosgrove was Captain Daniels.

Lieutenants Cosgrove and Mitchell were sent without rations. I was unable to furnish even salt for their fresh meat, which latter article constituted their entire subsistence, and they state to me that they found only enough corn to feed their animals four times.

I consider them and their men entitled [to praise] for the manner in which they performed their duty.

Respectfully, your obedient servant,

OWEN A. BASSETT,
Lieutenant-Colonel, Commanding.

Captain LAURANT,
Assistant Adjutant-General, District of the Frontier.

DECEMBER 16, 1863.—Demonstration on Fort Gibson, Ind. T.

*Abstract from "Record of Events," District of the Frontier.**

December 16, the rebels, under Colonels Stand Watie, Adair, and Quantrill, moved to attack Fort Gibson, but fell back as troops moved out of the post. Federal loss, 2 men killed and 2 wounded. Rebel loss, killed and wounded, 5.

DECEMBER 16-31, 1863.—Scout from Fayetteville, Ark., including skirmishes (23d) at Stroud's Store and (25th) on Buffalo River.†

REPORTS.

No. 1.—Brig. Gen. John B. Sanborn, U. S. Army, commanding District of Southwestern Missouri.

No. 2.—Capt. John I. Worthington, First Arkansas Cavalry (Union).

No. 1.

Reports of Brig. Gen. John B. Sanborn, U. S. Army, commanding District of Southwestern Missouri.

SPRINGFIELD, MO., *January* 3, 1864.

MAJOR: The force of the First Arkansas that left Fayetteville on the 15th ultimo has returned, after marching through Carroll, Marion, Searcy, and Madison Counties. Captain Worthington, in command, reports that he had skirmishing nearly every day and hard fighting on the 23d, 24th, and 25th. On the two first days the enemy numbered about 200, and were routed in confusion. On the 25th they were re-enforced by 800 men, and fought in Searcy County, on Richland Creek, with great determination, charging his howitzers and losing 30 men killed, and the usual proportion of wounded. After these affairs the force came back to Fayetteville, bringing all material except 2 wagons, left on account of the roads. Our loss is 7 killed and 8 wounded; 1 officer wounded. I think this rebel force is Colonel Love's. I will endeavor to dispose of this force in a few days, if the weather is such that I can move troops. Our force at Neosho has had quite a success in destroying bands of rebels. Full report will be sent forward in due time.

JOHN B. SANBORN,
Brigadier-General.

Maj. OLIVER D. GREENE,
Assistant Adjutant-General.

HDQRS. DISTRICT OF SOUTHWESTERN MISSOURI,
Springfield, Mo., January 16, 1864.

MAJOR: A detachment of the Second Arkansas Cavalry, of 40 men, was in Searcy County on the 25th ultimo, and within 10 miles of Captain Worthington's command during its engagement on that day, but could not join him. On the following day this scout had an affair with the

* From return for month of December, 1863. † See also Appendix, p. 913.

rebels at the county seat (Barronsville), at which 6 rebels were killed, among them Captain Wright, and 4 wounded, and 16 taken prisoners, First Lieutenant Hensley being one of them.

Our loss in this affair none.

JOHN B. SANBORN,
Brigadier-General, Commanding.

Maj. OLIVER D. GREENE,
Assistant Adjutant-General.

No. 2.

Report of Capt. John I. Worthington, First Arkansas Cavalry (Union).

FAYETTEVILLE, ARK., *January* 8, 1864.

MAJOR: Acting under orders from Colonel Harrison, commanding troops in the field, I marched, on the 16th day of December, 1863, with 112 men of the First Arkansas Cavalry and one gun of the howitzer battery attached to the regiment. My orders required me to scout the counties of Carroll, Marion, and Searcy. I reached Carrollton (county seat of Carroll County) on the 19th, after skirmishing slightly with a few bushwhackers. On the 22d we marched to Stroud's Store, having dispersed and broken up all the small bands of the enemy that infested Carroll County, killing 11 men and losing 2, who were wounded; neither dangerously. On the 23d, at daybreak, we resumed our march in the direction of Yellville, and had not proceeded more than a quarter of a mile when our advance was fired upon, and we soon after encountered a rebel force of 200 or 300 men, under command of Captain Marshall. Dismounting 75 men, I attacked, routed, and pursued him through the brush about 5 miles, driving him from every position, and scattering his men in every direction. On the 24th, the enemy were constantly in sight, but kept out of range. On the 25th, while encamped on Buffalo River, in Searcy County, the enemy, having been re-enforced by Major Gunning with 200 men from Yellville, aided by Colonel Freeman with 500 men from Izard County, advanced again upon us, driving in two parties that I had out foraging and to gain information of the movements of the enemy. In this affair we lost 4 men killed and 4 wounded, making our total loss to this date 10 men killed and wounded. At 3 p. m. I received a flag of truce from the enemy, asking a suspension of hostilities until daylight next morning, for the purpose of burying the dead and taking care of the wounded and exchanging prisoners. My wounded men having fallen into the enemy's hands, this I refused; but granted a truce of one and a half hours, and then sent and brought the wounded into camp, and buried the dead. I learned from the enemy that they had lost during the day 9 killed and 5 wounded. Finding that Major Gunning, with his own force and Marshall's men, was encamped within a mile below my camp, while Colonel Freeman's command was about 2½ miles above, and intending to attack me at daybreak the next morning, I immediately determined to assume the offensive, and attacked Major Gunning about 8 o'clock at night, and, after fighting ten or fifteen minutes, routed him, with a loss of 14 killed and between 30 and 40 wounded. The whole rebel force, as I have since learned, fell back during that night and the next day to Clapper's Mill, in Carroll County. We then returned without any further interruption, by way of Newton County, Arkansas, to this place, which we reached on the 31st day of December,

1863, our whole loss while out being 4 killed and 6 wounded. After leaving King's River we found an abundance of forage. During the past season a large quantity of corn and wheat was raised in the counties of Carroll, Marion, and Searcy. In the vicinity of Marshall's Prairie, Marion County, in a circuit of 10 miles, there are corn and oats enough to supply a regiment of cavalry twelve months. Flouring mills, wheat, and pork are also obtainable to an extent sufficient for the same purpose. The same remark will apply to the country east of Carrollton and north of the mountains as far east as Fulton County. The country is filled with refugee Missourians, who are committing all kinds of mischief, plundering the families of the soldiers who are serving in our regiment and the First Arkansas Infantry.

There is no part of Arkansas where the loyal sentiment was stronger at the commencement of the war than in these counties. At the first call for volunteers, the men left their homes and joined the Federal Army, and their families are now a prey to the refugee rebels of Missouri. A post in the vicinity of Marshall Prairie would completely break up this rebel rendezvous, and do more, I respectfully submit, toward restoring peace to that section of Arkansas than anything else that could be done.

In conclusion, let me say that the men of my command behaved in a manner highly creditable to their coolness and courage.

I have the honor to remain, your obedient servant,

JOHN I. WORTHINGTON,
Captain Company H, First Arkansas Cavalry, Commanding.

Maj. T. J. HUNT,
Commanding Arkansas Volunteers.

DECEMBER 18, 1863.—Skirmish near Sheldon's Place, Barren Fork, Ind. T.

Report of Capt. Alexander C. Spilman, Third Indian Home Guards.

FORT GIBSON, CHEROKEE NATION,
December 23, 1863.

SIR: I have the honor to report that, in compliance with your instructions, I marched from Fort Gibson at 3.30 p. m., December 17, with a force of about 290 infantry, consisting of details from the First, Second, and Third Indian Regiments, and one howitzer. I took the Park Hill road, and, passing that place, went into camp at the crossing of the Illinois, at midnight. By inquiry at Park Hill, I learned that Col. S. Watie's force, variously estimated at from 500 to 800 men, after plundering Murrel's house and burning the negro cabins at Chief Ross' place, had moved during the afternoon toward the Illinois River, stating their intention to camp in the Illinois bottom that night. Morning came, and I was still ignorant of the exact whereabouts of the rebels, though satisfied that their camp was not far distant. I moved out of camp between 7 and 8 o'clock in the morning, taking the road leading up the Barren Fork. During the morning two small parties of rebels, one of 10 and another of 5 men, approached our column, mistaking us for their own men. They were fired upon, and 1 was killed; but not having mounted men to pursue them, the remainder escaped. I now became satisfied that we were in close proximity to the rebel force. The road lay first on one and then on the other side of Barren Fork, the valley of which was narrow, and covered with thick timber and underbrush, and walled in on either side by precipitous hills. About three-quarters of a mile beyond Sheldon's place the advance guard reported the enemy in force just ahead. I proceeded to the front, and discerned, through the thick undergrowth of brush, their line, formed in a heavily timbered ravine, of dismounted men, the right resting upon the road, and the left reaching up the ravine into the hill on the right of the road. I immediately brought forward the howitzer, supported by 95 men of the First Indian Regiment, under command of Captain Willets, placed it in position on the right of the road, and deployed the Cherokees, under command of Lieutenant [L. F.] Parsons, Third Indian Regiment, still farther to the right, between the gun and the foot of the hill.

These preparations were not completed when the enemy opened on us a heavy fire from small-arms. This was replied to by our men with promptness and spirit. As soon as the howitzer opened upon the rebels, their line was completely broken, and they retreated in some confusion up the ravine, to the top of the hill. The Cherokees, under command of Lieutenant Parsons, followed them, and drove them about a quarter of a mile beyond the crest of the hill, where they again formed, and were a second time routed by our men. The road being now clear in front, I ordered the men back, and moved on about a quarter of a mile to take a better position, where there was higher ground and several log buildings, for the protection of our infantry. We had no sooner taken this position than the rebels, rallying, renewed the attack. A few discharges of canister and shell from the howitzer drove them out of the valley, and they took possession of the adjoining hill, which was heavily timbered. Sheltering themselves here behind trees and rocks, the rebels opened a fire at long range upon our men, who replied from the cover of the log-houses. The fighting here lasted for more than two hours, without any decided advantage to either party. I saw that to drive the enemy from the crest of the hill by a charge would be difficult and hazardous. I also knew that if they came over the hill into the valley to fight, we had decidedly the advantage of them. Thinking to draw them out, I ordered the command forward on the road, as if to abandon the position. It had the desired effect. The enemy supposing, doubtless, that we were retreating, came over the hill, all dismounted, and in larger numbers than they had before shown themselves, and advanced toward the houses we were leaving. Our men were immediately rallied, and returned to their former position on the double-quick. The howitzer was quickly brought up, and opened fire upon the advancing enemy, who withstood the shock but one moment, and then turned and fled. Our men pursued them, driving them over the hill and beyond it nearly a mile. The rout of the rebels was now complete; they did not again make the least attempt to rally. Our casualties during the engagement were comparatively light. I regret that I must record the loss of Captain Willets, First Indian Regiment, who fell, mortally wounded, while gallantly leading his men in the early part of the engagement; Private Arch Benner, Company H, Third Indian Regiment, and ———, Company F, First Indian Regiment, received severe, but, it is thought, not fatal, wounds. Two of the howitzer horses were wounded, one so badly that it had to be abandoned on the road; also 2 mules, belonging to the six-mule team, were wounded, one of which had to be abandoned.

I am not prepared to state with accuracy the loss of the rebels. From their own admission, and the statement of parties who visited the field after the engagement, I should estimate their loss to be not less than 12 killed and 25 wounded, besides a large number of horses killed and disabled.

The conduct of our officers and men during the engagement was in the highest degree commendable. In particular I must be allowed to acknowledge the valuable services of Lieutenant Parsons, Company E, Third Indian Regiment, whose fearless demeanor and spirited conduct animated and encouraged our men, and tended greatly to secure our success. Lieutenant [William] Roberts, First Indian, upon whom the command of the First Indian devolved after Captain Willets was wounded; Captains [B.] Gritts and Ahleechar, Second Indian, and Lieutenant [I.] Turner, Third Indian, all did their duty bravely and well.

The gun detail, belonging to Company L, Third Indian, under command of Sergeant Hendricks, are also entitled to credit for the coolness and skill they displayed.

As my instructions were to proceed with all possible dispatch to reenforce Major Foreman, at Rhea's Mills, I resumed the march as soon as satisfied that the enemy had no intention of returning.

Surg. [A. J.] Ritchie, Second Indian Regiment, who was in attendance upon the wounded, deemed it advisable to leave them at Roach's house, 4 miles from the scene of the engagement, which was accordingly done. I went into camp at Duncan's place about sundown, having accomplished a march of about 18 miles. The next morning we were again in motion at daylight, and, without further hinderance or incident worthy of note, joined Major Foreman, at Rhea's Mills, that evening.

In conclusion, I must be allowed to compliment the soldiers of my command upon their constancy and endurance in accomplishing, without murmur or complaint, this difficult march, in weather at times bitterly cold, and all the while scantily supplied with food.

I am, colonel, very respectfully, your obedient servant,

A. C. SPILMAN,
Capt. Company B, Third Indian Regiment, Comdg. Detachment.

Col. WILLIAM A. PHILLIPS,
Commanding First Brigade, Army of the Frontier.

DECEMBER 23–25, 1863.—Attack on Centreville, Mo., and pursuit of the Confederates, including skirmish (25th) at Pulliam's.

REPORTS.

No. 1.—Maj. Oliver D. Greene, Assistant Adjutant-General, U. S. Army.
No. 2.—Maj. James Wilson, Third Missouri State Militia Cavalry.

No. 1.

Report of Maj. Oliver D. Greene, Assistant Adjutant-General, U. S. Army.

HEADQUARTERS DEPARTMENT OF THE MISSOURI,
Saint Louis, December 28, 1863.

GENERAL: An entire company of the Third Missouri State Militia was captured at Centreville, Reynolds County, by guerrillas, under Reves, on the 23d instant. Major Wilson, of the Third Missouri State Militia, followed the party, and, at 3 p. m. Christmas day, he overtook and attacked; killed and wounded 35, captured 150 prisoners (13 officers), all equipage and ammunition, and 125 horses; recaptured all prisoners. Our loss, 1 killed and 8 wounded.

OLIVER D. GREENE,
Assistant Adjutant-General.

Major-General SCHOFIELD,
West Point, N. Y.

No. 2.

Report of Maj. James Wilson, Third Missouri State Militia Cavalry.

HDQRS. THIRD MISSOURI STATE MILITIA CAVALRY,
Pilot Knob, Mo., December 30, 1863.

SIR: In compliance with your orders of the 23d instant, I left Pilot Knob, in command of 200 men, about 10 a. m. December 23, 1863, arriving at Patterson at 9 p. m. Left there at daylight on the 24th, and encamped at Long's at 9 p. m., having traveled 35 miles. Marched again at 3 a. m. 25th instant; passed through Doniphan, taking a southwesterly direction toward the Arkansas line. Eight miles from Doniphan, I captured 2 pickets; 2 miles farther I captured one other post, and still 2 miles farther on came upon a rolling picket or patrol, and run them off of the road, capturing 1 and compelling him to lead us to the camp of Reves.* Arriving at the camp, I divided my men into two columns, and charged upon them with my whole force. The enemy fired, turned, and threw down their arms and fled, with the exception of 30 or 35, and they were riddled with bullets or pierced through with the saber almost instantly. The enemy lost in killed about 30; wounded mortally, 3; slightly, 2; total killed and wounded, 35. Prisoners captured, 112; horses, besides those of Company C, 75; also all their arms, ammunition, and camp equipage. Not having means of transportation, I was compelled to destroy the bigger portion of the arms and all the tents and other camp equipage.

On the morning of the 26th, I started for Pilot Knob, arriving here about 4 p. m. on the 29th of December, 1863.

I cannot speak in too high terms of praise of the officers and men under my command. There was no loss on our side in killed or wounded.

JAMES WILSON,
Commanding Third Missouri State Militia Cavalry.

Col. R. G. WOODSON,
Commanding Post, Pilot Knob, Mo.

DECEMBER 24–29, 1863.—Scout from Cassville, Mo.

Report of Lieut. John E. Phelps, Third U. S. Cavalry.

HEADQUARTERS POST,
Cassville, Mo., January 4, 1864.

GENERAL: I forward report of two scouts, one under command of Lieutenant [A. A.] Irwin, the other in charge of Lieut. A. J. Garner, Second Arkansas Cavalry.

---

* At Pulliam's, 17 miles southwest of Doniphan.

On the 24th ultimo, I gave orders to Lieutenant Garner to proceed in the direction of and beyond Pineville and reconnoiter with 50 men, and ascertain, if possible, the movements of Stand Watie, who was said to be in that neighborhood with 500 or 600 men.

Lieutenant Garner arrived on Cowskin Creek; found that Stand Watie had been there, but left the day before. He followed his trail to the line; but the enemy being too far ahead, the pursuit was fruitless, and abandoned. At the headwaters of Butler's Creek, where he had turned out, Lieutenant Garner found and took possession of a cave, with a blacksmith's shop, and about 100 bushels of corn in it. He destroyed all. Ten miles below, on the same stream, in another cave, of 3 guerrillas found there, 1 was killed, 1 wounded, the other escaped. In this cave Lieutenant Garner found a small parcel of dry goods, about 2 pounds of gunpowder, 1 bushel salt, 1 shotgun, and 1 rifle. These, but the dry goods, he ordered destroyed. From a point 12 miles farther down stream, he scouted in various directions, and found himself in a section of country swarming with guerrillas. He burned four houses on Butler's Creek, and seized three yokes of oxen and as many wagons. On his return, the 29th ultimo, he turned over the captured property to the quartermaster at this post. He had marched, while scouting and reconnoitering, about 150 miles. In the mean time information was received that one of my men, under Lieutenant [J.] Brown, had been wounded by guerrillas near Cross Hollow. I dispatched Lieutenant Irwin to that vicinity with 26 men. There he joined Lieutenant Brown. With his party augmented by 4 of Lieutenant Brown's men, the balance of whom were ordered to return to Cassville to escort the wounded man, Lieutenant Irwin, hearing of the noted guerrilla Glover, of that neighborhood, proceeded to his house, and set fire to it. Glover was not there. From that place he advanced in a northeasterly direction, and, at a distance of about 1 mile from the burning house, made out 3 bushwhackers lurking in his front. He gave chase for about 2 miles, in vain; the guerrillas had taken refuge in the brush. At night (27th of December, 1863) Lieutenant Irwin camped at Black's Mill. Next morning his pickets were fired into; but the enemy fled on the approach of Irwin's party. From Black's Mill, Lieutenant Irwin descended in a southeasterly direction, on White River. At the ford saw, but failed to capture or kill, a mounted guerrilla. Crossed over to the northeast, among the hills bordering the river, and, in a ravine, at the residence of Coon Baker, the most notorious guerrilla of that region, surprised John Roller, another bandit. In attempting to escape, this Roller was shot dead, and his horse, arms, and accouterments captured. They were turned over to the quartermaster at the post. Lieutenant Irwin thence proceeded northwest toward Indian Creek. Here another guerrilla and robber (Hairbright) was shot. The hills known as Roller's Ridge were next searched. They are a well-known rendezvous for bandits, murderers, and highwaymen. Nothing was found, and Lieutenant Irwin, after four days of meandering march through a very rugged country, his horses tired, almost exhausted, returned to this post on the 30th ultimo without injury or loss. He marched about 125 miles.

I am, very respectfully, your obedient servant,

JOHN E. PHELPS,
Lieutenant Third U. S. Cavalry, Commanding Post.

Brig Gen. JOHN B. SANBORN,
Commanding District of Southwestern Missouri.

DECEMBER 26-28, 1863.—Scout from Salem, Mo.

Report of Capt. Levi E. Whybark, Fifth Missouri State Militia Cavalry.

SALEM, MO., *January* 3, 1863 [1864].

CAPTAIN: In compliance with orders received from Headquarters District of Rolla, I have the honor to transmit to you the following report of scouts and escorts:

On the 26th instant [ultimo], I sent Lieut. C. Ringer and 10 men of Company C, and 1 corporal and 10 men of Company M, Fifth Missouri State Militia Cavalry, on a scout on Current River. They proceeded down Gladden Valley, but gained no information of any bushwhackers. When they struck Current River they came across a small band of bushwhackers, 8 or 10 in number, firing on them, killing 3, and the remainder escaped. The men killed were Eli Louis, Sam. Louis, and Bill Boyce. Captured all their plunder and some 6 or 7 horses. These were the men who had robbed and shot old man Wasson a few days previous.

They then proceeded up the river to Big Creek, and scouted the country thoroughly; then returned to camp, on the 28th instant [ultimo], traveling a distance of 60 miles.

* * * * * * *

I am, very respectfully, your obedient servant,

L. E. WHYBARK,
Captain, Commanding Detachment, Salem, Mo.

Capt. J. LOVELL,
Assistant Adjutant-General.

DECEMBER 26, 1863—JANUARY 2, 1864.—Scout from Forsyth, Mo., to Batesville, Ark.

Report of Capt. James J. Akard, Eighth Missouri State Militia Cavalry.

SPRINGFIELD, MO., *January* 11, 1864.

SIR: I have the honor of submitting to you the following report of my trip from Forsyth, Mo., to Batesville, Ark., and back to Springfield, Mo.:

I left Forsyth, Mo., the 26th of December, 1863, for Batesville, Ark., with dispatch, with 93 men. I traveled north of White River. The first day and a half travel I found no forage, which was about 45 miles from Forsyth. After that I found plenty on down to Batesville. I captured 9 prisoners and 19 head of horses, which I turned over to the provost-marshal at Batesville; killed 2 going down. Arrived at Batesville on the 29th of December, 1863, and left on the 30th *en route* to Springfield, Mo., with Lieutenant-Colonel [William] Baumer, First Nebraska Cavalry, and 200 men. Remained and scouted with them until the morning of the 2d of January, 1864, when we separated. I marched for Springfield. On my way I captured 8 prisoners and killed 2. Turned over at Springfield, Mo., 8 prisoners and 4 horses. As I went down I traveled through Mountain Home, Ark., and passed near Calico Rock, Ark., where Colonel Freeman's headquarters were said to be at that time; from there down through Wild Haws. Came back through Salem,

Ark., and left West Plains to the right. Came through Bloomfield, Hazelwood, and Marshfield; found forage plenty on that route.

JAMES J. AKARD,
Capt. Company A, Eighth Mo. State Mil. Cav., Comdg. Scout.

Lieut. W. D. HUBBARD,
Actg. Asst. Adjt. Gen., District of Southwestern Missouri.

DECEMBER 29, 1863.—Attack on Waldron, Ark.

*Abstract from "Record of Events," District of the Frontier.**

December 29, outpost at Waldron, Ark., consisting of 35 men from the Second Kansas Cavalry, under command of Capt. John Gardner, attacked by 100 rebels, under Major Gibson. Rebels repulsed, with 8 men wounded and Major Gibson killed. Federal loss, 1 man killed and 6 wounded.

CORRESPONDENCE, ORDERS, AND RETURNS RELATING TO OPERATIONS IN MISSOURI, ARKANSAS, KANSAS, THE INDIAN TERRITORY, AND DEPARTMENT OF THE NORTH-WEST, FROM NOVEMBER 20, 1862, TO DECEMBER 31, 1862.†

UNION CORRESPONDENCE, ETC.

HEADQUARTERS POST OF ELKHORN TAVERN,
November 23, 1862.

Brig. Gen. F. J. HERRON,
Comdg. 2d and 3d Divs., Army of the Frontier, Camp Curtis:

Yellville is farther to the east than our scouts have penetrated. Companies G and K, First Arkansas Cavalry, are now in Carroll County. They have met with occasional detachments of Home Guards, but in no strength. They have lately been within 30 miles of Yellville, but did not think it prudent to try to enter the town. I am now about to recall them, as their horses are in bad shape.

General Blunt is still at Camp Babcock, where he was on the 15th instant, the date of an important dispatch to General Schofield. Camp Babcock is near Lindsey's Prairie, in Benton County. The enemy seem to have retired from before him, and from conscripts and escaping Missourians I learn that Hindman's main force is the other side of the Arkansas River. I received a dispatch from Blunt last night directing me to throw out scouting parties toward Huntsville and Fayetteville. I have done so, but apprehend no particular danger from those directions just at present. There is something mysterious, however, about the reports of forces at Huntsville that I have as yet been unable to fathom. A day may clear matters up.

A. W. BISHOP,
Lieut. Col. First Arkansas Cavalry, Comdg. at Elkhorn Tavern.

[NOVEMBER 23, 1862.—For Curtis to Halleck, in reference to troops at New Madrid, Mo., see Series I, Vol. XVII, Part II, p. 356.]

---

*From return for month of December, 1863.

†Correspondence, etc., January 1–December 31, 1863, appears in Part II.

DEPARTMENT OF THE MISSOURI,
November 23, 1862.

Rear-Admiral D. D. PORTER, *Cairo, Ill.*:

Dispatch from Elkhorn, Ark., reports Arkansas River bank full at Van Buren. I am also informed there is very little force on river bank. It would be a good time to run gunboats up Arkansas and take boats and Little Rock.

The only force at Arkansas Post has probably been routed by my forces, under General Hovey.

SAML. R. CURTIS,
Major-General.

GENERAL ORDERS, No. 19. } HDQRS. DEPARTMENT OF THE NORTHWEST, *Saint Paul., Minn., November* 23, 1862.

I. The Second, Third, and Fourth Military Districts of this department are consolidated into one, to be called the District of Minnesota, under the command of Brig. Gen. H. H. Sibley, with headquarters at Saint Paul.

II. The headquarters of this department are for the present transferred to Madison, Wis.

By command of Major-General Pope:

R. O. SELFRIDGE,
Assistant Adjutant-General.

HEADQUARTERS DEPARTMENT OF THE MISSOURI,
Saint Louis, Mo., November 24, 1862.

Maj. Gen. H. W. HALLECK,
General-in-Chief, Washington, D. C.:

GENERAL: Another month has transpired since my acceptance of your order placing me in this command. The enemy has again fallen back, and beyond the Boston Mountains, except about 6,000 near Cotton Plant and 1,500 near Yellville. In the valley of the Arkansas, as near as I can ascertain, there are about 50,000, distributed at different points near Little Rock and Van Buren.

The Secretary of War has ordered a regiment from Alton, and Blair's brigade (three regiments), and the Second Ohio Cavalry. All except this last regiment go down the river.

Under your order to send General Steele with all I could spare from Pilot Knob, I sent about 4,000. To meet pressing demands occasioned by these drafts from this vicinity, and to guard prisoners, who have greatly accumulated by the surrender of most of the bushwhackers of Missouri, I have detained the Thirty-second and Thirty-third Iowa Infantry.

I have authorized a short expedition from Helena on the Arkansas Post, via White River, which only requires a trip of one day up White River on boats and a 15-mile march. I deemed it very important to check the progress of fortifications the rebels had commenced at that place. This move from Helena is so short that it will not prevent the force falling into line just as readily for a down river movement, which I take for granted you are maturing.

In connection with this, being telegraphed from Elkhorn Tavern that the Arkansas was bank full at Van Buren, I suggested a move of the Navy on that river with a gunboat; but the rear-admiral replied that his boats were all otherwise engaged. The attack on the Old Post should have transpired before this time.

The Army of the Frontier has been divided, and General Schofield is here recruiting his impaired health. General Blunt is near Fayetteville, his outposts being in the Indian Territory and at Elkhorn Tavern. General Brown, with most of the Missouri troops, is in command of the District of Southwestern Missouri. General Herron commands the main force near Ozark, Mo., occupying and scouting the country south of that region. The rebels have recommenced the manufacture of saltpeter near Yellville, and I have directed a cavalry company to go and effectually destroy it and the surrounding buildings.

I halted the main force near Ozark because the enemy some days since moved toward General Blunt in formidable force; but he fell back, and I only wait to know how far back, in order to make further use of the force under General Herron.

General Davidson has command of forces in front of Pilot Knob, and is arranging bridges so as to make it convenient to unite with the forces of Herron, and, if occasion offers, strike down on to the waters of Black and White Rivers, so as to co-operate with movements from Helena.

Except some bands in Jackson and adjacent counties, the rebels seem to have gone south, surrendered, or returned to their homes, apparently tired of bushwhacking.

The elections in this State went off without a particle of strife between soldiers and citizens, except, if you please, in Saint Joseph, where the enrolled militia assailed enrolled sympathizers or rebels. My orders were that soldiers should only interpose in case of actual riot. The result of the election is also an important demonstration, showing the loyalty of the people and their hatred of rebellion. The most radical candidates, taking the boldest stand in favor of the Government, have been generally elected over men who only sought to run on conservative Union grounds. The folly of trying to make Missouri a rebel State is thus clearly exposed, and this result will also speak for other border States similarly situated, such as Arkansas, when we fairly get possession of the mouths of her great rivers, and hold them.

Other parts of my department are quiet, and I am only seeking to regulate their careful and economical administration. With further assurance of my increasing efforts to carry out the wishes and aims of my commanding general, I have the honor to be, your obedient servant,

SAML. R. CURTIS,
Major-General.

HDQRS. FIRST DIV., SOUTHWESTERN DIST. OF MISSOURI,
Springfield, November 24, 1862.

Maj. H. Z. CURTIS,
Assistant Adjutant-General, Saint Louis, Mo.:

A spy from south of Carrollton, Ark., reached here this morning, and reports that Price has superseded Holmes in command of the enemy's forces in Arkansas, and is massing his troops on Big Mulberry for a movement into Missouri. It is country rumor, but may be in part true. Numbers of small bodies of the guerrillas crossed Osage River above Taberville on Thursday, and have appeared in some force in Newton County. Colonel Philips, Seventh Regiment Missouri State Militia, commanding at Newtonia, reports that they become so strong that additional force is necessary to hold them in check.

E. B. BROWN,
Brigadier-General, Commanding.

SPRINGFIELD, *November* 24, 1862.

Brig. Gen. JOHN M. SCHOFIELD,
Saint Louis:

The time of service of the Enrolled Missouri Militia expired on the 20th. The county is overrun with guerrillas, and to disarm the people at present would leave them and their families at the mercy of these hordes of robbers. No order has yet been made from State headquarters to continue the service. I respectfully urge immediate action. Philips * has asked for re-enforcements. General Herron has sent him 500 men. The commanding officer at Bowers' Mills reports large bands in his vicinity, and fears he will be forced to abandon the position. From that and all portions of the western portion of the district the robbers have become very bold, shooting our soldiers and Union men, and driving their families from their homes.

E. B. BROWN,
Brigadier-General.

HDQRS. FIRST DIVISION, ARMY OF THE FRONTIER,
Camp Babcock, Ark., November 24, 1862.

Brig. Gen. JOHN M. SCHOFIELD,
Commanding Army of the Frontier:

GENERAL: I have the honor to report that Lieutenant-Colonel Jewell, with a detachment of 600 men, sent on reconnaissance in direction of Van Buren and Fort Smith, returned last night. He met the enemy's pickets 15 miles this side of Van Buren, who retreated at his approach. Learning that a large force was at Van Buren, he deemed it prudent to proceed no farther, and returned. Information obtained from various sources, which I deem quite reliable, is that Hindman's, Marmaduke's, Cooper's, and Stand Watie's forces are at Van Buren and Fort Smith. Their entire force is estimated as high as 30,000, but I am quite sure it does not exceed 15,000 effective men, and probably not over 12,000. If a small re-enforcement could be sent me, to enable me to leave a small force in the vicinity of Evansville, to protect my rear and line of communication from any flank movement that might be made by any small rebel force sent by some other route than the one upon which my column would move, I would not hesitate to attack them on the other side of the mountains, and do not doubt of my ability to occupy and hold Van Buren and Fort Smith, provided General Steele occupies the attention of General Holmes, so that re-enforcements cannot be sent from Little Rock.

Very respectfully, your obedient servant,

JAS. G. BLUNT,
Brigadier-General, Commanding.

SAINT PAUL, MINN.,
November 24, 1862—12.20 p. m.

His Excellency ABRAHAM LINCOLN,
President of the United States:

Official information has reached me from the officer in charge of the condemned Indians that organizations of inhabitants are being rapidly made with the purpose of massacring these Indians. He has been

---

* At Newtonia, Mo.

obliged in consequence to concentrate a considerable force for their protection, and during the cold weather it is impracticable to protect so large a body of troops and Indians from the weather. I trust that your decision and orders in the case will be transmitted as soon as practicable, as humanity to both the troops and Indians requires an immediate disposition of the case. I apprehend serious trouble with the people of this State, who are much exasperated against the criminal Indians.

JNO. POPE,
Major-General.

SAINT LOUIS, MO., *November* 25, 1862.

Maj. Gen. H. W. HALLECK,
General-in-Chief:

General Warren, commanding at Hartville, telegraphs that a train of 47 wagons was attacked by rebels and destroyed between Houston and Hartville, and 5 men killed. Have ordered cavalry pursuit. Expedition against Arkansas postponed. Low water in White River the cause of too much delay.

SAML. R. CURTIS,
Major-General, Commanding.

BRIGADE HEADQUARTERS,
Hartville, Mo., November 26, 1862.

Maj. Gen. SAMUEL R. CURTIS,
Saint Louis, Mo.:

Burbridge, Mitchell, and Greene are on the North Fork of White River, with 3,000 men, cavalry, infantry, and artillery (two pieces). They are 35 miles from here. I can take care of myself at Hartville and Houston, but cannot follow them; they are all after trains. Saved 22 wagons, losing only 25. Colonel Pile's arrival at Houston barely saved it from capture.

FITZ HENRY WARREN,
Brigadier-General, Commanding.

HEADQUARTERS POST OF ELKHORN TAVERN,
November 26, 1862.

Brig. Gen. F. J. HERRON,
Comdg. Second and Third Divisions, Army of the Frontier:

A scout just in, who left Cane Hill yesterday afternoon about 4 o'clock, reports at that point between 4,000 and 5,000 cavalry. He left Van Buren the night before, and while there had an interview with General Parsons Parsons told him that it was the intention of the army to go into Missouri immediately. He heard Parsons say that the infantry and artillery would cross to this side of the Arkansas River the next day, and when at Cane Hill he heard they were crossing. My informant, when at Van Buren, crossed the river and went into the artillery and infantry camps. He saw twenty pieces, iron and brass, none heavier than 12-pounders. The infantry were armed promiscuously with shotguns, rifles, and knives. He saw a large number of men parching corn and barreling it up, likewise baking bread, and understood that thirty days' rations were being prepared.

The river was navigable, and he saw steamboats arriving at Van Buren from below.

There is a telegraph in operation from Fort Smith to Little Rock.

A. W. BISHOP,
Lieut. Col. First Arkansas Cav., Comdg. at Elkhorn Tavern.

HDQRS. FIRST DIVISION, ARMY OF THE FRONTIER,
Camp Babcock, Ark., November 26, 1862.

Brig. Gen. JOHN M. SCHOFIELD,
Commanding Army of the Frontier:

GENERAL: I have the honor to report that General Marmaduke, with his entire command, followed about twenty-four hours in the rear of Lieutenant-Colonel Jewell on his return from reconnaissance in direction of Van Buren. He is now encamped at Cane Hill, 7,000 or 8,000 strong. A detachment sent from my command attacked a large reconnoitering party of the enemy yesterday and scattered them. Spies from their camp this morning informed me that General Hindman, with a large force of infantry, is expected to join them, when they will make an attempt to get north into Missouri. My supply train arrived this evening all right. I shall move on Marmaduke to-morrow morning, leaving my transportation at this point, with a small guard. Shall strike him next morning at daylight, unless he runs. Hope to destroy him before he can be re-enforced by Hindman. Distance to Cane Hill, 30 miles. Can you not send a cavalry force to Pineville or Neosho to protect my supply trains, as detachments of the enemy, in considerable force, are hanging in my rear, for the purpose of capturing or annoying them?

Respectfully, your obedient servant,

JAS. G. BLUNT,
Brigadier-General, Commanding.

GENERAL ORDERS, No. 17. } HDQRS. FIRST DIV., ARMY OF FRONTIER,
Camp Babcock, Ark., November 26, 1862.

In compliance with General Orders, No. 11, dated Headquarters Department of the Missouri, Saint Louis, Mo., November 2, 1862, the undersigned hereby assumes command of the District of Kansas, headquarters at Fort Leavenworth, Kans.

JAS. G. BLUNT,
Brigadier-General, Commanding.

HDQRS. SECOND DIVISION, ARMY OF THE FRONTIER,
McCullough's Spring, Mo., November 27, 1862.

Capt. WILLIAM HYDE CLARK,
Asst. Adjt. Gen., 2d and 3d Divs, Moody Spring, Mo.:

CAPTAIN: I have the honor to report, for the brigadier-general commanding Second and Third Divisions, that the troops sent under Captain Brawner, Seventh Missouri Cavalry, to re-enforce Colonel Philips' command at Newtonia, have returned to this division.

Captain Brawner reports that Quantrill came within about 8 miles of Newtonia, having then about 1,000 men, with whom he intended attacking Colonel Philips, but learning of the prospect of having a greater force to contend against, he disbanded his main force, with the understanding that they should meet again on Sauk Creek, whither he had gone with some 200 of his men. I send you a messenger from Berryville, Ark., with information of an engagement between Captains Mack and Youngblood, First Arkansas Cavalry, and some 300 Home Guards (rebels). He brings the rumor that Hindman's command was ordered to Texas, the rebels anticipating work in that quarter. If this be true, it explains previous reports of that force having crossed the Arkansas River at Van Buren.

I am, captain, very respectfully, your obedient servant,

CLARK WRIGHT,
Colonel, Commanding Second Division.

[NOVEMBER 27, 1862.—For Steele to Curtis, announcing departure of expedition from Helena, see Series I, Vol. XVII, Part I, p. 529.]

GENERAL ORDERS, No. 20. } HDQRS. DEPT. OF THE NORTHWEST,
Milwaukee, Wis., November 27, 1862.

Brig. Gen. W. L. Elliott, U. S. Volunteers, will repair to Madison, Wis., and assume command of the Department of the Northwest during the absence of the major-general commanding.

JNO. POPE,
Major-General, Commanding.

WASHINGTON, *November* 28, 1862.

Brig. Gen. JOHN M. SCHOFIELD,
Saint Louis:

MY DEAR GENERAL: Yours from Springfield of the 18th is just received.* I am as much dissatisfied and discouraged at the non-action of our troops in Arkansas. If the campaign had been carried out as I directed, there would have been no very serious trouble in Missouri; but it seems there were too many private axes to grind. I hope for a remedy, but when it will come is uncertain. If you could be here a few weeks you would see how difficult it is to resist political wire-pulling in military appointments. Every Governor, Senator, and Member of Congress has his pet generals to be provided with separate and independent commands. I am sick and tired of this political military life. The number of enemies which I have made because I would not yield my own convictions of right is already legion. If they would only follow the example of their ancestors, enter a herd of swine, run down some steep bank and drown themselves in the sea, there would be some hope of saving the country.

Rest assured, general, your services are appreciated, and will not be overlooked. I have already presented your name to the Department, and will again urge it on the first opportunity. There are, however,

---

* Not found.

only a few vacancies to fill, and hundreds of applications backed by thousands of recommendations. Under such circumstances results are always uncertain.

Yours, truly,

H. W. HALLECK,
General-in-Chief.

WAR DEPARTMENT,
Washington, November 29, 1862.

Major-General CURTIS, *Saint Louis, Mo.:*

Your communication of the 19th has been received* and submitted to the Secretary of War, who does not approve of your sending troops to Kansas, or your issuing arms or rations to Kansas militia. You were within telegraphic reach of the War Department, and should not have assumed authority which belongs alone to that Department when you could readily have consulted it. All available troops, both in Kansas and Nebraska, not absolutely required there, should be sent down the Mississippi River.

H. W. HALLECK,
General-in-Chief.

HDQRS. 2D AND 3D DIVISIONS, ARMY OF THE FRONTIER,
November 29, 1862.

Maj. Gen. SAMUEL R. CURTIS, *Saint Louis, Mo.:*

The cavalry expedition sent by me to Yellville returned last evening, having made the march of 250 miles in less than five days. It was a complete success, and not only were all the saltpeter works in that section and at Dubuque destroyed, but the arsenal and store-houses of the rebels were burned. Sixty of Burbridge's command were taken prisoners, about 500 shot-guns and rifles at the arsenal were destroyed, and over 100 good horses brought out. The rebels have a large hospital at that place, and the inmates were paroled. The force usually congregated there is now south of West Plains. Our troops have left the place in such shape that I do not think the rebels will again attempt to make it a depot. The expedition consisted of the First Iowa Cavalry, the Tenth Illinois Cavalry, and one battalion of the Second Wisconsin, all under command of Colonel Wickersham, Tenth Illinois. This movement, with Blunt's victory at Cane Hill, effectually clears the north side of the mountains of all troops, except guerillas.

F. J. HERRON,
Brigadier-General, Commanding.

GENERAL ORDERS, No. 21. } HDQRS. DEPARTMENT OF THE MISSOURI,
Saint Louis, Mo., November 29, 1862.

The commanding general is informed that because some of the United States Reserve Corps have been mustered out, other troops of other names suppose they should be. There is no reason for such a claim. Other troops, not United States Reserve Corps, cannot be mustered out.

The Second Missouri Artillery was first enrolled as Home Guards, but, with their own consent, they were afterward regularly mustered in as three years' volunteers, by Lieutenant Sanford, U. S. Army, and

*See Series I, Vol. XIII, p. 801.

the matter was fully explained in German and English. All officers, soldiers, and citizens should inculcate quiet obedience to duty, and any person or persons engaged in circulating petitions to be mustered out, or threats of mutiny, in the Second Artillery or any other troops not United States Reserve Corps, will be arrested and punished by a military commission.

By command of Major-General Curtis:

H. Z. CURTIS,
Assistant Adjutant-General.

HDQRS. FIRST DIVISION, ARMY OF THE FRONTIER,
Cane Hill, Ark., Nov. 30, 1862, *via Elkhorn, Dec.* 2, 1862.

Lieut. H. G. LORING,
Acting Assistant Adjutant-General:

General Marmaduke continued his flight all night after the battle of the 28th, and is now in Van Buren. General Hindman was expected to re-enforce him at this place on the evening of that day. Prisoners, of whom I captured 25, state that Marmaduke's force was 11,000. They were compelled to abandon two pieces of artillery, disabled by my batteries. A number of their officers were killed, among them a Lieutenant-Colonel Monroe, of a Texas [Arkansas] regiment, and a Captain Martin, of an Arkansas [Missouri] regiment. They will not advance this side of the mountains except with their combined forces, but I am prepared to meet them, and with my little army whip 25,000 of such chivalry. An officer who came inside of our lines under a flag of truce, after night terminated the fighting, acknowledged that they were badly whipped and worse chased. Lieutenant Johnson, Sixth Kansas, dangerously wounded, may possibly recover.

JAS. G. BLUNT,
Brigadier-General, Commanding.

Abstract from return of the Department of the Missouri, Maj. Gen. Samuel R. Curtis commanding, for the month of November,* 1862; *headquarters Saint Louis, Mo.

Command.	Present for duty.		Aggregate present.	Aggregate present and absent.	Pieces of artillery.		Aggregate present and absent last monthly return.
	Officers.	Men.			Heavy.	Field.	
District of Saint Louis, Mo	318	7,568	10,727	12,054	......	......	8,734
District of Rolla, Mo	184	3,921	5,575	6,999	4	2	6,149
Southwestern District of Missouri	153	2,522	3,913	4,761	......	......	4,721
Army of the Frontier:							
First Division	251	5,390	6,676	8,442	......	28	8,649
Second Division	128	3,043	3,767	5,008	......	8	5,008
Third Division	205	4,158	5,038	6,387	....	12	6,387
Central District of Missouri	105	2,051	2,834	3,718	......	......	4,009
Northeastern District of Missouri	132	2,821	3,385	4,045	......	4	4,431
District of Kansas	84	1,491	2,245	2,902	......	2	1,791
District of Colorado	10	230	407	495	......	2	754
District of Nebraska	26	357	705	807	......	......	803
Alton, Ill	22	325	493	545	......	......	560
District of Eastern Arkansas (Helena):							
Infantry	578	11,034	14,597	16,999	......	......	16,999
Cavalry	182	3,126	4,962	6,278	......	4	6,278
Artillery	17	502	615	806	......	38	806
Grand total	2,395	48,539	65,939	80,246	4	100	76,079

HEADQUARTERS,
Saint Louis, Mo., December 1, 1862—3.30 p. m.

Maj. Gen. H. W. HALLECK,
General-in-Chief:

The Secretary of War disapproving, no guns have been or will be issued to Kansas militia. I have ordered no troops to Kansas. I desire an Iowa regiment nearly full to move down from Council Bluffs to Leavenworth, but it has not moved. No surplus troops in Nebraska or Kansas.

SAML. R. CURTIS,
Major-General.

HEADQUARTERS,
Saint Louis, Mo., December 1, 1862.

Hon. E. M. STANTON,
Secretary of War:

General Halleck says you disapprove loan of refuse muskets to Kansas volunteers. I will not, therefore, loan them. I disclaim all idea of disrespect. I supposed a temporary loan of one thousand or fifteen hundred refuse arms a matter of military discretion within my responsibility.

SAML. R. CURTIS,
Major-General.

HEADQUARTERS SIXTH MILITARY DISTRICT, MISSOURI,
Lexington, December 1, 1862.

Col. WILLIAM D. WOOD,
Adjutant-General, &c., Saint Louis:

COLONEL: On the evening of the 25th of November, I received a message from Colonel Penick, commanding at Independence, informing me that a force of between 300 and 400 men from Kansas, consisting in part of negroes and Indians, had, in violation of his express orders, marched through his lines at Independence, and were then engaged in plundering the people of the lower end of Jackson and upper end of La Fayette Counties. I immediately telegraphed to General Curtis, at Saint Louis, and General Loan, at Jefferson City, asking if this force was in Missouri in compliance with any orders to that effect, and was promptly informed that they were here without orders.

So soon as this information was received, I dispatched to Colonel Penick, at Independence, to dispose such of his force as might be at that post, so as to prevent their retreat in case they might attempt to make their escape. I also ordered over the militia of Ray County, under Lieutenant-Colonel Black, and part of Colonel Neill's regiment of La Fayette militia, with the command of Colonel McFerran, of Missouri State Militia, stationed at this post, who promptly co-operated with me, and were immediately marched toward the southwest part of this county as far as Grimton, where the command, consisting of about 350 men, were quartered for the night.

Early in the morning of the 27th, the command proceeded in the direction of Pink Hill, in Jackson, and about 3 o'clock of that day came up with Colonel Penick's command of 110 men, in pursuit of the Kansas men, and about a mile beyond overtook that command drawn up in line of battle to receive us, with their artillery, of which they had one piece, planted so as to rake the lane through which the command had to pass.

This was at the house of Jeans. Colonel Penick's command, which was in advance, marched up in range of their guns, and the commands of Colonels McFerran, Neill, and Lieutenant-Colonel Black formed in the rear. An officer was then sent forward with a written demand of the person in command to know by what authority he was there, and requiring to see the orders under which he acted. The orders under which he claimed to be in Missouri, and under which he claimed the right to confiscate the property of rebels (citizens of Missouri), are herewith sent, marked A; after seeing which, I addressed to Colonel Adams the note marked B, to which his note, marked C, is the reply, to which I answered that my demand to have the negroes turned out of his camp must be complied with. This note is marked D, and received for answer his note marked E, desiring a personal interview, which was at once granted, at my headquarters, in the house of Mr. Jeans. In that conversation I explained to Colonel Adams the great irregularity and impropriety of his course in thus invading our State, not only, as I conceived, without authority, but in direct violation of his orders from General Blunt. I also endeavored to explain to him the peculiar situation of most of the counties of Missouri, in which large assessments had been made on the property of disloyal citizens, for the murder of loyal men, and for the support of the families of such militiamen as were in circumstances of destitution, and that these assessments could never be collected if whole regiments from Kansas were permitted to come in and plunder our country at pleasure. Before leaving my quarters, I arrested Colonel Adams, and required him to report at Saint Louis to General Curtis on the 15th of December. Night coming on, our several commands had been dispersed through the neighborhood for the purpose of procuring quarters, and I retired, supposing that, in accordance with the promise of Colonel Adams, the property would be promptly turned over in the morning; but, instead of doing so, at an early hour the command was on the march, taking with them all the property, except about 20 horses, which they had turned over.

So soon as it was apparent that they intended acting in bad faith, I commanded Colonel Penick to form his men (who had moved up the road to the west the night before) directly across the road, and plant his gun so as to prevent their passing him, and at the same time orders were given to Colonels McFerran, Neill, and Black to put their several commands in motion and pursue them. I at the same time sent forward an officer to communicate this determination to Lieutenant-Colonel Hayes, then in command, with orders at once to turn the negroes out of his lines, and to deliver over to Captain Little, of Colonel McFerran's regiment, all the horses and mules, oxen, wagons, &c., which he had taken from the citizens of Missouri. Seeing that our purpose was to enforce this order, he reluctantly complied with it. About 40 negroes, mostly children, were turned out; about 100 horses, 6 or 8 ox-teams and wagons, some 2-horse teams and wagons, all of which were loaded heavily with every imaginable variety of plunder—feather-beds, bedding, clothing of every description, household and kitchen furniture, cooking-stoves, pots, pans, saddles, and harness, and, in short, everything which could be picked up in a community of wealthy farmers. After the stock was turned in, I arrested Lieutenant-Colonel Hayes also; and as their major was already arrested, by command of the lieutenant-colonel, the command of the Twelfth Kansas devolved on the senior captain. I instructed Colonel Penick with his command to escort them beyond the limits of the State, and to report that fact and the manner in which it was done at these headquarters.

After marching the command with the captured property some 6 or 8 miles in the direction of Lexington, I appointed a committee of four responsible and respectable gentlemen of the neighborhood to take charge of the property, and, on satisfactory proof of ownership, to restore it to the various persons from whom it had been taken, and report to me in Lexington after it had been distributed. The march was then resumed, and the command reached this post at 8 p. m. on the 27th.

I cannot close this report without earnestly calling the attention of the Governor to the fact that if these raids from Kansas on the people of Missouri are to continue we shall work in vain for a return of peace and prosperity to our State. The bitterness and strife which are engendered thereby cannot fail to blaze out on every occasion which shall present itself, and to keep up a continual state of war—a war, too, of the most unrelenting and pitiless character.

All of which is most respectfully submitted.

Your obedient servant,

RICH'D C. VAUGHAN,

Brigadier-General, Sixth Military District of Missouri.

[Inclosure A.]

HEADQUARTERS DISTRICT OF KANSAS,

In the Field, October 9, 1862.

Col. C. W. ADAMS,

Commanding Twelfth Regiment Kansas Volunteers:

SIR: Immediately on receipt of this you are directed to dispose the force under your command so as to cover the eastern border of the State, from the Kansas to the Osage River. It is confidently believed that you can, by a system of patrols and signals, prevent the ingress of bands of Missouri guerrillas, who have heretofore been devastating that portion of the State, and by activity and courage drive them from their hiding places in the border counties of Missouri. You will carefully instruct your men that the persons, property, and rights of the people of Kansas and the loyal people of Missouri should be held sacred, and any infractions should be promptly and severely punished. Parties sent into Missouri should be placed under the command of active and prudent officers, with instructions to pursue bushwhackers to the death. After you have matured your plans and disposed your forces, you should issue a proclamation to the citizens of Johnson and other border counties of Kansas and Missouri who have fled their homes to return thereto, promising them safety and protection. To you and the troops under your command is intrusted the delicate and important duty of restoring peace to the border between the points named. You should communicate frequently with the military authorities at Fort Leavenworth and Fort Scott. Keep your troops well in hand, that they be not cut off in detail, and that they may be concentrated at any given point without delay or confusion.

Major Henning, Third Wisconsin Cavalry, provost-marshal for the District of Kansas north of Kansas River, will from time to time issue such orders to you as he may deem necessary in relation to the disposition of your forces, &c. You will immediately on the receipt of this order report by letter to Major Henning, stating your forces, station, &c.

By order of Brigadier-General Blunt:

THOS. MOONLIGHT,

Assistant Adjutant-General.

HEADQUARTERS FORT SCOTT,
October 24, 1862.

To Commanding Officer Twelfth Regiment Kansas Volunteers:

I have the honor to send you a copy of orders received from department headquarters this day.

Respectfully, &c.,

B. S. HENNING,
Major Wisconsin Cavalry, Commanding Post.

[Sub-inclosure.]

HEADQUARTERS,
Saint Louis, October 19, 1862.

Commanding Officer Fort Leavenworth:

The troops at or north of Fort Scott will remain on the line of communication, unless special orders arrive from General Blunt. I approve of general distribution suggested by General Lane. It will not be proper for officers to issue proclamations, and the troops must not be so divided as to invite attack. A strong force must be detained at the depot of public stores. Send this forward for the benefit of officers commanding posts or pickets along the line. Orders from Brigadier-General Blunt will be forwarded.

SAML. R. CURTIS,
Major-General.

[Inclosure B.]

NOVEMBER 27, 1862.

Colonel ADAMS:

SIR: As I can see nothing in the order of General Blunt authorizing the camp you have taken, and as my orders from the commander of this division are positive, I am bound to demand the surrender of all property taken from citizens of this State, and that the negroes taken from citizens of Jackson and La Fayette Counties be forthwith turned out of your lines; and, as there is no organized enemy either in Jackson or La Fayette County, that you at once march your force beyond the limits of this State. If this proposal is acceded to, I will send an officer to arrange the conditions. I retain the orders only to take a copy, after which they will be immediately returned.

I am, sir, &c.,

RICH'D C. VAUGHAN,
Brigadier-General, Commanding.

[Inclosure C.]

HEADQUARTERS TWELFTH KANSAS VOLUNTEERS,
In the Field, November 27, 1862.

Brig. Gen. R. C. VAUGHAN:

SIR: I am ready to comply with all your demands at the earliest possible time, except that pertaining to negroes. They are at liberty to do as they choose, as they came within my lines voluntarily.

Very respectfully, your obedient servant,

CHAS. W. ADAMS,
Colonel, Commanding Regiment Kansas Volunteers.

P. S.—I cannot agree with you in relation to the orders from Generals Curtis and Blunt.

[Inclosure D.]

Colonel ADAMS:

SIR: Your note is received. The demand relative to the negroes must be complied with. The matter of disagreement relating to your orders from General Blunt and General Curtis is a matter which can be more readily settled elsewhere than here.

I am, sir, your obedient servant,

RICH'D C. VAUGHAN,
Brigadier-General, Commanding.

P. S.—As it is already late, I must require that you permit no portion of the property and negroes above alluded to to leave your lines.

[Inclosure E.]

HDQRS. TWELFTH REGIMENT KANSAS VOLUNTEERS,
November 27, 1862.

Brigadier-General VAUGHAN:

SIR: My guards are out, and I shall follow your orders relative to keeping whatever is within my lines here. I am subject to arrest from you, and choose a trial by court-martial rather than turn the negroes out of my camp. I do not do this, believe me, General Vaughan, out of disrespect to you, but because I believe it to be contrary to a general order from the War Department to do so.

Very respectfully, your obedient servant,

CHAS. W. ADAMS,
Commanding Twelfth Regiment Kansas Volunteers.

DEAR GENERAL: If you will receive an informal visit from me, I will be glad to see you.

Yours, truly,

CHAS. W. ADAMS,
Twelfth Regiment Kansas Volunteers.

[Inclosure F.]

Order for arrest.

IN THE FIELD,
Jackson County, November 27, 1862.

Colonel ADAMS,
Commanding Twelfth Kansas Volunteers:

You are hereby arrested, and required to report at Saint Louis to General Curtis on the 15th December.

I am, sir, your obedient servant,

RICH'D C. VAUGHAN,
Brigadier-General, Commanding.

[Inclosure G.]

SPECIAL ORDER.] IN THE FIELD,
Jackson County, November 27, 1862.

To the officer in command of the Twelfth Kansas Regiment:

The bearer, Major Biggers, visits your camp for the purpose of delivering this order and conducting the property taken by your command from citizens of this State to my lines. You are hereby ordered to deliver the same without unnecessary delay. An officer will be ready to receive it.

I am, sir, your obedient servant,

RICH'D C. VAUGHAN,
Brigadier-General, Commanding.

[Inclosure H.]

SPECIAL ORDER.] IN THE FIELD,
Jackson County, November 27, 1862.

To the officer in command of the Twelfth Kansas Regiment:

SIR: You are hereby required to mount all the men that were mounted when you left Kansas (not exceeding 20), and immediately march your command, with such transportation and baggage as you brought with you into the State.

RICH'D C. VAUGHAN,
Brigadier-General, Commanding.

SAINT LOUIS, MO., *December* 1, 1862.

His Excellency Gov. H. R. GAMBLE:

GOVERNOR: The undersigned, your memorialist, who is now and always has been an unconditional Union man, and a hearty supporter of the Government, most respectfully represents that the assessment now in progress, to be levied upon secessionists and Southern sympathizers, is working evil in this community, and doing great harm to the Union cause. Among our citizens there are all shades of opinion, from what is called neutrality, which is little better than treason, through all the grades of lukewarmness, half-way measures, and hesitating zeal up to the unqualified loyalty, which your memorialist, in common with yourself, claims to possess. To assort and classify these, so as to indicate the dividing line of loyalty and disloyalty, and to establish the rates of payment by those falling below it, is a task of great difficulty. If it can be done at all, it must be by patient investigation, and after hearing evidence on both sides, giving each person the opportunity of self-defense. It would require not only a competent tribunal, sitting for a great length of time, and possessed of full authority to call and examine witnesses under oath, but also a kind and degree of scrutiny inconsistent with republican institutions. Such an investigation, so far as practicable, has been attempted in the present case; but although the character and standing of the members of the assessment board give assurance that the faithful endeavor to be impartial and just has been made, yet they have been compelled to admit hearsay evidence, rumors, and "general impressions," and have in no case required witnesses to testify under oath. The unavoidable consequence has been that many feel themselves deeply aggrieved, not having supposed themselves liable to the suspicion of disloyalty; many escape assessment who, if any, deserve it; and a general impression of inequality in the rule of assessment and its application prevails. This was to be expected, because no two tribunals could agree upon the details of such an assessment, either as to persons or amounts to be assessed, without more complete knowledge of facts than can be obtained from *ex parte* evidence and current reports. Nothing short of a thorough judicial investigation could lead to a satisfactory result.

Your memorialist also respectfully represents that nothing but clear evidence of disloyalty would justify assessment, and that where such evidence exists the party so proved guilty should not be permitted to remain in the community without coming under bonds, and in extreme cases should be required to go "beyond the lines." To keep such persons here, especially after they have been exasperated by fines and held up to public contempt, is dangerous to the public peace, and gives the most favorable opportunity for treasonable practice. The great object in view is to free the community from all who are determined to promote disorder, and to give every encouragement to those who remain to fulfill the duties of loyalty and good citizenship. The doubtful should be brought back, if possible; the wavering should be confirmed, and a door opened for the return of those who see the error of the past. The wise and energetic measures taken in this State the last six months, and since the assessment was ordered, have wrought a great change in these respects. The hope of disturbing the status of Missouri is well-nigh abandoned, and hundreds of those who until lately have scarcely known their own minds are now openly avowing themselves on the right side. Enlightened policy, as well as the liberality of justice, dictates that where such avowal is seemingly made in good faith, and where no overt act has been committed, the retribution of the past should be foregone. Social quiet, the peace of neighborhoods, and returning homogeneousness of feeling should be encouraged by all practicable means, and by such methods of action the cause of loyalty is best strengthened. The bitterness of feeling likely to be engendered by the progressing assessment will renew the personal hostilities which were beginning to disappear, and, thus fanned, the secession element will refuse to die. Your memorialist, therefore, respectfully petitions that you will use your influence, Governor Gamble, with the commanding general and with the authorities at Washington that the proceedings in assessment be stayed at least until other methods of obtaining the funds required by the State shall first have been tried. Perhaps, if the case were fully presented before Congress, the just demand of the State would be met, and the payment of our State militia in defense of the common cause would be made. If not, a special tax by the State Legislature would be a preferable plan to that now adopted; and if unavoidable, after failure of other methods, the assessment could then be enforced as a last resort. But it is the opinion of your memorialist that under anything but Congressional authority and judicial action such assessment would only amount to a forced loan, for which reclamation would eventually be made and sustained.

All of which is most respectfully submitted, Governor Gamble, to your favorable consideration by your obedient servant,

W. G. ELIOT.

[Indorsements.]

This communication of Rev. Dr. Eliot is sent to General Curtis, with a request that he will bestow upon it very careful consideration, as it is upon a subject now of deep interest to the community.

H. R. GAMBLE.

HEADQUARTERS DEPARTMENT OF THE MISSOURI,
Saint Louis, December 9, 1862.

I have carefully read this communication of the Rev. Dr. Eliot, and considered the grave questions involved.

An order was issued by General Schofield, commanding the District of Missouri, to levy half a million of dollars from the "secessionists and Southern sympathizers of Saint Louis County, for subsisting, clothing, and arming the enrolled militia while in active service, and in providing for the support of such families of militiamen and United States volunteers as may be left destitute." As the fund is only to apply to State troops and State paupers, I supposed the order was issued by General Schofield in his capacity of a State brigadier-general; but the indorsement to me by the Governor, and the communication of General Schofield of the 5th instant, directed to the board of commissioners, seem to invoke the responsibility of the United States as the sole author of this assessment. Before taking any step myself in this matter, I therefore submit certain legal questions which arise in my mind to the consideration of the commanding general-in-chief:

Can the United States levy and collect a special tax of this sort for a State purpose?

Are the enrolled militia in "active service" a State or United States charge?

Does not such direct tax by the United States conflict with the general direct tax levied by Congress?

Does it not conflict with the confiscation law?

Does it not conflict with the Constitution in the mode and object of taxation, and the right of the State to provide for its own militia?

The right to meet a military necessity by forced laws or forced assessments I claim as a military necessity, but I do not perceive that such a necessity is presented now where the order seems to apply.

I have, therefore, to refer the matter to Maj. Gen. H. W. Halleck, whose determination will be communicated to the reverend and very worthy author of this document, and to His Excellency the Governor.

Respectfully,

SAML. R. CURTIS,
Major-General.

GENERAL ORDERS, No. 23. } HDQRS. DEPARTMENT OF THE MISSOURI, *Saint Louis, Mo., December* 1, 1862.

I. The provost-marshal's department will be composed of one provost-marshal-general, district provost marshals, and assistant provost-marshals. District and assistant provost-marshals will be appointed by the provost-marshal-general, as he shall see fit, or upon the recommendation of commanders of districts. Assistant provost-marshals will report direct to district provost-marshals, and they direct to the provost-marshal-general, though in any important cases, when the delay would work injury to the public service or individuals, assistant provost-marshals will report direct to the provost-marshal-general. District and assistant provost-marshals will, however, be considered as staff officers of the commanding officer to whom they are assigned, as in the case of quartermasters, commissaries, &c.

II. The provost-marshal-general of the department will prescribe the necessary general rules and regulations for the guidance of district and assistant provost-marshals, and, until otherwise ordered, existing rules and regulations will remain in force. Commanders of troops and districts, as well as district and assistant provost-marshals, will see that such rules and regulations are sustained, and uniformity of action and proper accountability secured.

III. The provost-marshal-general of the department will, as he shall see fit, or upon the recommendation of district provost-marshals, fix the limits of the assistant provost-marshals, so as to include any number of counties or any region of country.

IV. To preserve a record of the current business of this branch of the service, assistant provost-marshals will report to district provost-marshals, and the latter, in full, to the provost-marshal-general, at least as often as twice a month, to wit, on the 15th and last days of each month, as near as may be.

V. At all posts where assistant provost-marshals are not regularly appointed, the commanding officer for the time will perform the duties, and report, as hereinbefore provided.

* * * * * * *

VII. Officers of the provost-marshal's department, during the existence of civil war, are especially intrusted with the peace and quiet of their respective districts, counties, and sections; and to this end may cause the arrest and confinement of disloyal persons, subject to the instructions and orders of the department. They will have charge of all prisoners taken from the enemy; the keeping of the records, as far as possible, of the prisoners taken by the enemy, that the proper data for an exchange may be at any time obtained; the arrest and return or imprisonment of deserters, and in general all duties relating to prisoners of war or state.

VIII. Before any assistant provost-marshal, or the commander of any troops or post, shall send any prisoners to the provost-marshal-general, at these headquarters, or to district provost-marshals, he shall make a list of such prisoners, stating when and where and by whom captured (and, if prisoners of war, the rank, regiment, and company to which they belong), and also the charge against each prisoner, with the substance of the evidence against each, which statement and evidence must be sent with the prisoners. And where persons arrested by assistant provost-marshals are sent to the provost-marshal-general, or to district provost-marshals, the witnesses against them must be first examined, their residence stated, and their testimony written down and sworn to, and sent along with the prisoners. Assistant provost-marshals and commanders should dispose of prisoners, not charged with serious offenses, without sending them to Saint Louis, and they must be careful not to send prisoners unless there is some evidence to warrant imprisonment.

IX. Prisoners of war are entitled to be exchanged as soon as practicable; and all officers holding or capturing such prisoners will send them forward at once to these headquarters, to the provost-marshal-general, to be exchanged or to be sent to the commissary-general of prisoners, as may be ordered.

X. All orders or parts of orders heretofore issued conflicting herewith are rescinded.

By command of Major-General Curtis:

H. Z. CURTIS,
Assistant Adjutant-General.

SAINT LOUIS, MO., *December* 2, 1862—3.30 p. m.

Maj. Gen. H. W. HALLECK,
General-in-Chief:

I informed you of my organization of forces to move on Grenada, and asked your approval. General Steele now writes me that the movement has been made by a request of General Grant.* I hope you will approve. My instructions were full of caution, and will be pursued. Further information from General Blunt informs me that Marmaduke retreated to Van Buren, where he joined Hindman, their joint force being about 20,000. Blunt took two pieces of disabled artillery. He remains at Cane Hill.

SAML. R. CURTIS,
Major-General, Commanding.

[DECEMBER 2-4, 1862.—For Halleck to Curtis, and reply in reference to proposed expedition down the Mississippi, see Series I, Vol. XVII, Part II, pp. 376, 383.]

HDQRS. FIRST DIVISION, ARMY OF THE FRONTIER,
Cane Hill, Ark., December 2, 1862—9 a. m.

Maj. Gen. SAMUEL R. CURTIS,
Commanding Department of the Missouri:

GENERAL: My scouts just arrived report Hindman and Marmaduke concentrating their forces, 25,000 strong, at Lee's Creek, 25 miles from this place on the route to Van Buren, and 15 miles from the latter place, and I expect an attack to-morrow morning, but shall not abandon my position without a fight. I have requested General Totten to re-enforce me by forced marches on the Fayetteville road, but I have no knowledge of his present locality, and have got to hunt him up.

Respectfully,

JAS. G. BLUNT,
Brigadier-General, Commanding.

HDQRS. FIRST DIVISION, ARMY OF THE FRONTIER,
Cane Hill, Ark., December 2, 1862—9 a. m.

Brig. Gen. JAMES TOTTEN,
Comdg. Second and Third Divisions, Army of the Frontier:

GENERAL: Hindman and Marmaduke are concentrating their whole force, 25,000 strong, at Lee's Creek, 25 miles from this place, on the route to Van Buren, and 15 miles from the latter place, and in my opinion intend advancing upon me here. I desire you to move as much of your force as possible, especially the infantry, to my support, as I do not intend to leave this position without a fight. You should move by forced marches via Fayetteville, and keep me constantly advised of your position and movements. Answer by telegraph to Elkhorn as soon as you receive this.

JAS. G. BLUNT,
Brigadier-General, Commanding.

SPECIAL ORDERS, } HDQRS. CENTRAL DISTRICT OF MISSOURI,
No. 58. } *Jefferson City, December* 2, 1862.

I. The sum of $10,000 is hereby levied upon the disloyal inhabitants of Cass County, whereof the sum of $2,500 will be applied to subsist

---

* See Series I, Vol. XVII, Part I, p. 529.

the enrolled militia whilst engaged in active service, and the remaining $7,500 is appropriated to the relief of the destitute families of the soldiers engaged in actual service, and to relieve temporarily destitute refugees who have been driven from their homes by rebels or guerrillas, and of citizens who have become destitute in consequence of the lawless acts of disloyalists.

II. Lieut. Col. P. A. Thompson, of Fifth Regiment Missouri State Militia Cavalry, commanding at Harrisonville, Mo., will provide by order for the assessment, levy, collection, and distribution of said sums of money so assessed upon the disloyal inhabitants by the appointment of commissioners, and directing the means of enforcing this order in detail.

BEN. LOAN,
Brigadier-General Missouri State Militia, Commanding District.

SPECIAL ORDERS, No. 60. } HDQRS. CENTRAL DISTRICT OF MISSOURI,
Jefferson City, December 2, 1862.

I. The sum of $10,000 is hereby levied upon the disloyal inhabitants of Johnson County, whereof the sum of $2,500 will be applied to subsist the enrolled militia whilst engaged in active service, and the remaining $7,500 is appropriated to the relief of the destitute families of the soldiers engaged in actual service, and to relieve temporarily destitute refugees who have been driven from their homes by rebels or guerrillas, and of citizens who have become destitute in consequence of the lawless acts of disloyalists.

II. Col. E. C. Catherwood, of the Sixth Regiment Missouri State Militia Cavalry, commanding at Warrensburg, Mo., will, by order, provide for the assessment, levy, collection, and distribution of said sum of money so assessed upon the disloyal inhabitants of Johnson County, by the appointment of commissioners, and directing the means of enforcing this order in detail.

BEN. LOAN,
Brigadier-General Missouri State Militia, Commanding District.

SAINT LOUIS, *December* 3, 1862.

General BLUNT, *Cane Hill:*

You are too far in advance of support and supplies. Had better fall back to meet Herron's re-enforcements that go at your request toward Fayetteville.

SAML. R. CURTIS,
Major-General.

SAINT LOUIS, *December* 3, 1862.

General HERRON, *in Field:*

Dispatch received. Have advised Blunt to fall back so as to join your advance. Push forward.

SAML. R. CURTIS,
Major-General.

SAINT LOUIS, *December* 3, 1862.

General BROWN, *Springfield* :

Do not abandon Newtonia. It would be better to strengthen it if necessary. Do what you can to help Blunt without danger to other places.

SAML. R. CURTIS,
Major-General.

HEADQUARTERS SECOND AND THIRD DIVISIONS,
Wilson Creek, December 3, 1862—8 a. m.

Brigadier-General BLUNT :

Your telegram just received.* Will move both divisions entire at noon to-day, and will make good time to your position. The Second Division is camped at Crane Creek, the Third at Wilson Creek. Will keep you well posted of my movements. The distance from here is so great that it may be necessary for you to fall back a short distance, but I will do my best to make that unnecessary.

F. J. HERRON,
Brigadier-General.

HEADQUARTERS DEPARTMENT OF THE MISSOURI,
Saint Louis, December 3, 1862.

Brig. Gen. BEN. LOAN,
Jefferson City, Mo.:

GENERAL : Provost-marshal-general, Colonel Dick, advises the general commanding that you complain to him (the provost-marshal) that permits for trade in conflict with your circular of September 14, 1862, have been issued from these headquarters. The general directs me to advise you that only in a few cases has he granted permits to trade in the interior of the State, and then only to persons of known or established loyalty, and connected with loyal dealers in this city. A copy of a letter from Major Mullins, provost-marshal at Sedalia, under date of November 28, has been submitted to the general's consideration. The major complains that Messrs. Newland and Courtney, residents near Sedalia, had been granted a permit to purchase hogs and cattle from farmers generally, and to ship the same to Saint Louis. He (the major) says he is informed that Messrs. Newland and Courtney were disloyal some time heretofore. Such might have been the case, but their loyalty at the present time was very satisfactorily established by reliable Union men, and if persons were formerly disloyal, and now give evidence of an honest espousal of loyalty, let such be encouraged by all means.

We are led to believe that there is a change of sentiment taking place throughout the State. Men are in a measure giving up their madness, and are inclined to return to reason and right. The conviction that they were wrong in their rebellion against the Government, or the conclusion that the rebellion so far as Missouri is concerned cannot in any event be of avail, is leading many individuals to do works meet for repentance. All such persons should be encouraged to continue in well-doing until their reformation shall become complete. Let blows and

---

* Of 2d instant, addressed to Totten. See p. 805.

restrictions fall thick and heavy upon the traitor; extend the hand of encouragement to the repentant.

Major Mullins writes that he infers that the policy of General Curtis is "to permit traders to purchase of all farmers, both rebel and loyal, without any restriction or distinction." Such is nearly the general's policy. He would permit loyal dealers to buy indiscriminately from the farmers or producers; he would not permit a disloyal dealer to buy from any one. The rebel or sympathizer who owns a few hogs may owe their value to a loyal merchant in the interior, and that merchant in turn may be indebted to a loyal merchant here or eastward. The refusal to allow the farmer to sell his hogs works a far greater injury than any possible good to our cause and friends. Let no disloyal trader be allowed to reap benefits from trade or commerce until he submits to the authority of the land, and gives good evidence of his sincerity. If your subordinates find that any party bearing permit from these headquarters is an actual rebel, such subordinates are hereby instructed to take up and cancel said permit, but they should be careful to closely scrutinize charges of disloyalty coming only from competitors in the same trade.

I am, general, very respectfully, your obedient servant,

CLINTON B. FISK,
Brigadier-General and Aide-de-Camp.

HDQRS. FIFTH MISSOURI STATE MILITIA CAVALRY,
Independence, Mo., December 3, 1862.

Brig. Gen. BEN. LOAN, *Jefferson City:*

GENERAL: Your telegram of the 26th, ordering me to disperse the Kansas troops, was received. After returning from the expedition, I took 110 men, by order of Brigadier-General Vaughan, and pursued the Twelfth Kansas for twenty-six hours. We were with them, or in sight of them, one-half of the time, but kept our business to ourselves until General Vaughan, Colonel McFerran, Colonel Neill, and other officials, with 370 men, arrived in sight. Knowing the size of my force, and supposing that my business was to take from them their stolen property, they formed a line of battle and placed their artillery in the road to receive me. I halted my men within 60 yards of their line, and formed a line of battle, by order of General Vaughan, and waited for his column to arrive. The correspondence between the general and Colonel Adams will be reported by the general.

The whole command scattered and camped in the neighborhood. On the morning of the 28th, the Kansas troops loaded their baggage train and marched one-half a mile with all their stolen property before the matter was discovered by the general. I was then ordered to arrest them, which I did, without my men and without difficulty. After Colonel McFerran took from them their stolen property, I was ordered to escort them out of the State.

Inclosed find Captain Vansant's report.*

I suppose General Vaughan will make you a full report.

Yours, respectfully,

W. R. PENICK,
Colonel Fifth Missouri State Militia Cavalry.

---

*

GENERAL ORDERS, No. 24. } HDQRS. DEPARTMENT OF THE MISSOURI, *Saint Louis, Mo., December* 3, 1862.

I. Brigadier-General Davidson, having been assigned to a command in the field, is relieved from the command of the Saint Louis District, to which Brigadier General Carr is assigned, dating from the 12th ultimo.

II. Brigadier-General Gorman is assigned to the command of the District of Eastern Arkansas.

III. Kansas, Western Arkansas, and the Indian Territory, known as the Eighth, Ninth, and Tenth Districts, will, until further orders, be commanded by Brig. Gen. J. G. Blunt.

By command of Major-General Curtis:

H. Z. CURTIS,
Assistant Adjutant-General.

SPRINGFIELD, *December* 4, 1862.

Maj. Gen. SAMUEL R. CURTIS, *Saint Louis*:

In assuming the command, I find the force in the Southwest District posted as follows: Springfield, 641; Ozark, 263; Newton, McDonald, and Jasper Counties, 635; Wright and Webster and for escort of trains between Lebanon and Springfield, 507; making a total of 2,046 enlisted men for duty.

Two guns at Fort No. 1, without men to work them, comprises the artillery.

The guerrillas are very active and numerous in all parts of the district, and demands for protection cannot be met. The large number of sick in hospital and other departments requires every man at Springfield to be detailed for guard and fatigue duty. Nearly every officer on detached service at this post has been ordered to join his regiment, and educated officers to fill their places are not in the command. The army moving west leaves the country from North Fork of the White River to Cassville open to the inroads of Burbridge and Greene, who are known to be near the mouth of North Fork with some force. Under these circumstances, I respectfully urge the necessity of an increase of the force of the district.

E. B. BROWN,
Brigadier-General.

SAINT LOUIS, *December* 5, 1862.

General F. J. HERRON:

Glad to see you are nearing Blunt. The danger is he will be attacked by greatly superior forces before you reach him. Be cautious. Hindman is shrewd and active. He will try hard to deceive you by drawing you into ambush.

SAML. R. CURTIS,
Major-General.

ELKHORN, ARK., *December* 5, 1862.

Brig. Gen. JAMES G. BLUNT:

GENERAL: I arrived here this evening, and have the Third Division at Sugar Creek, with the Second 6 miles back. To-morrow the Third will make Halcombe Springs, and probably Fayetteville. Should I hear anything stirring from below, I will push through to Fayetteville. I have brought the Third Division from Wilson's Creek and the Second from 8 miles the other side of Crane Creek, making 30 miles per day. It is impossible to make day and night marches on a trip of this length. I hope to God we will reach you before they get too close, and with our combined forces I do not fear the result. I am afraid when they hear of re-enforcements coming up they will back down. I think our plan beyond question under such circumstances is to make them fight, even if we have to follow to the other side of the river. Nothing new from the east.

Respectfully, your obedient servant,

F. J. HERRON,
Brigadier-General.

SAINT LOUIS, MO., *December* 5, 1862.

JAMES S. THOMAS, Esq.,
President Saint Louis County Board:

SIR: I have the honor to acknowledge the receipt of your communication of the 3d instant, in which you request me to answer, for the information of the county board, the following questions touching Special Orders, No. 91, issued by me, and under which your board is now acting:

1st. Is it ordered under the authority or approval of Hamilton R. Gamble as Governor of the State of Missouri?

2d. Is it an order of your own as commander of the State troops of Missouri, or as commander of the militia enrolled under the order of the Governor?

3d. Is it an order of your own as commander of the military district of Missouri; and, if so, is it recognized by the War Department?

These questions can doubtless be most satisfactorily answered by a brief reference to the military condition of Missouri at and about the time the order was issued, and to the position occupied by myself at that time. By appointment from the major-general commanding the Department of the Mississippi, I was commander of the military district of Missouri, and as such acted purely under the authority of the United States. I was placed here for a certain definite purpose, which may be briefly stated—to restore the authority of the United States throughout the State of Missouri and to restore and preserve the peace of the State. To enable me to accomplish this, there was placed at my disposal a certain military force, composed of United States volunteers and the State militia, raised for this special service, under an agreement between the Governor of Missouri and the President of the United States.

For a time this force seemed quite sufficient for the purpose, but soon military operations in Arkansas and Tennessee rendered necessary the withdrawal from Missouri of a large portion of the troops originally assigned to my command.

Soon after this, in pursuance of a plan of the rebel Government, large numbers of rebel troops from Missouri were sent back into the State, with commissions to recruit and organize troops for the Southern army. Some of these returned rebels succeeded in passing secretly through our lines, others were arrested, and others gave themselves up and took the required oath and parole, professing their desire to return to their allegiance. These emissaries from the rebel Government spread themselves over the State, and secretly enlisted, organized, and officered a very large number of men; places of rendezvous were designated, and all were ordered to hold themselves in readiness to assemble when the signal should be given. Their plan was to maintain their ground in Missouri, if possible, and, if not, to make the best of their way into Arkansas. They were promised, and to some extent received, co-operation from the enemy's forces in the latter State. So extensive was their organization that, notwithstanding the discovery and partial prostration of the scheme, not less than 10,000 guerrillas were at one time in arms in Missouri. Aware of the impending danger, I called upon the United States Government for more troops. The reply was that not a single regiment could be furnished. There was nothing left, then, but to call forth the latent power of the State to save her from the horrors of guerrilla war, and to preserve the authority of the United States within her borders. I therefore availed myself of my position as brigadier-general of the Missouri militia, and called upon the Government for authority to enroll and organize all the militia of the State, and to call into active service such force as I might deem necessary. This authority was readily granted, and the work immediately commenced. With the immense difficulties which lay in the way of its successful prosecution, arising from the apprehension and distrust excited in the minds of the people, both loyal and disloyal, and the doubts existing in the minds of many of the success of so great an experiment, tried for the first time in the country, your board are, perhaps, as familiar as myself. Its final triumph and happy results are known to every one in Missouri.

Not the least of the difficulties to be overcome was to provide the means for arming and subsisting this force. Some arms were furnished by the United States, but soon this source failed. Subsistence was entirely denied. I was, therefore, again thrown upon my own resources to provide the means for performing the duty assigned me by the Government, viz, "to take care of Missouri." Under these circumstances I determined that those who, by their open or secret aid and encouragement to the rebellion, had brought upon the State so great a calamity should bear the extraordinary expense necessary to bring back a state of peace and prosperity, and at the same time be made to realize that such crimes could not be committed with impunity. The mode of accomplishing this was a matter for careful consideration, particularly whether it should be done under State or Federal authority. The money was to be chiefly used for the support of a State force, for whose maintenance the United States were in no way responsible, and provided for by no law of Congress. The State was entirely without means to meet such expense, and I was so informed by the Governor. On the other hand, this force was called into existence solely to enable me to discharge the important and difficult duty assigned me by the United States Government, and to enable me and my predecessors to accomplish which we had been intrusted with all the powers of martial law. There was manifestly no other law, either State or Federal, under which the money required could be raised for the specific purpose, either by assessment of disloyal persons or otherwise, nor by which those guilty of aiding in bringing calamity upon the State could be made to feel the sting of just retribution before it should be too late to produce good results. It was, therefore, manifest that the order should spring from United States authority, the source of martial law. Hence the order was issued from "Headquarters District of Missouri," and possessed whatever of force I could give it in my capacity as representative of the military power of the United States in Missouri.

The above is substantially an answer to all your questions. I acted in this, as in all other matters, upon my own responsibility as an officer of the United States, and not under the orders of the Governor of Missouri. It was a matter with which the Governor had, officially, nothing to do, although he expressed unhesitatingly his approval of the measure, and proceeded at once to raise funds to meet the present necessities of the military service, pledging, as he was authorized by me to do, the money to be raised by assessment to meet the liabilities thus incurred.

Your first question may therefore be briefly answered thus: The order was issued not under the authority but with the approval of the Governor of Missouri.

Your second question is answered in the negative.

In order that your third question may be fully answered, it is proper for me to state that no intimation of either approval or disapproval of the measure has ever reached me from the War Department.

Very respectfully, your obedient servant,

J. M. SCHOFIELD,
Brigadier-General.

HEADQUARTERS,
Saint Louis, Mo., December 6, 1862—11.30 a. m.

Col. J. C. KELTON:

General Blunt, at Cane Hill, Ark., telegraphed on the 3d that Hindman and Marmaduke had concentrated about 20,000 to return upon him, and asked for re-enforcements. I ordered General Herron forward and advised Blunt to fall back. General Herron expects to reach Fayetteville to-day, and Blunt reports himself still at Cane Hill, the enemy within 15 miles. A conflict is probable.

SAML. R. CURTIS,
Major-General.

HDQRS. 2D AND 3D DIVISIONS, ARMY OF THE FRONTIER,
Elkhorn, December 6, 1862—3 a. m.

Brig. Gen. JAMES G. BLUNT:

Your dispatch is just received. My former note will explain to you the exact position of the divisions, &c. They are both moving at present, and the Third Division will reach Fayetteville at 10 or 11 to-night. The Second will reach the same place by daylight in the morning (7th). I send forward at once 2,000 cavalry, the best armed and mounted men of both divisions. My cavalry force was reduced by the withdrawal of all Missouri State troops for State purposes. I will make the best possible marching to you. In my opinion, if the enemy presses you in force, it would be advisable to fall back and meet the Second and Third Divisions, so we can make a good fight of it. Keep me advised of any change of location you make; also send me a guide from Fayetteville to Cane Hill.

Respectfully, &c.,

F. J. HERRON,
Brigadier-General.

HDQRS. FIRST DIVISION, ARMY OF THE FRONTIER,
Cane Hill, Ark., December 6, 1862.

Brigadier-General HERRON
Commanding Second and Third Divisions:

SIR: The enemy's advance, represented 10,000 strong, are now within 8 miles of my headquarters. They drove in my outposts 3 miles this morning. Nothing more than picket fighting has occurred during the day, but they are steadily advancing, and will, no doubt, attack in force at daybreak to-morrow morning. You will endeavor to get your command here by that time.

Respectfully, your obedient servant,

JAS. G. BLUNT,
Brigadier-General, Commanding.

HEADQUARTERS ARMY OF THE FRONTIER,
Cane Hill, Ark., December 6, 1862—7 p. m.

Maj. T. J. WEED,
Acting Assistant Adjutant-General, Fort Leavenworth:

The enemy, 25,000 strong, have attempted for three days to force my position here, which I have determined to hold at all hazards until re-enforcements can arrive. They attacked yesterday, and again this morning, but were driven back to the mountains. General Herron, with the Second and Third Divisions, is making a forced march to re-enforce me. His advance will arrive to-night. You will soon hear of one of the damnedest fights or foot races that has taken place lately. Lieutenant Johnson is doing well.

JAS. G. BLUNT,
Brigadier-General, Commanding.

ELKHORN, ARK.,
December 6, 1862—4 a. m.

Major-General CURTIS, *Saint Louis, Mo.:*

Messenger just in from Blunt. The enemy is within 15 miles of him, marching on to Cane Hill. I have advised him fully of my location each day, and have advised him to fall back and meet me, should the enemy press him in force. He will make a mistake if he undertakes to fight before we get up. I will have both divisions in Fayetteville during the night. The entire column has marched 30 miles per day since we started. I am doing my best to reach him. To-morrow will tell the story. May the God of battles be with us.

F. J. HERRON,
Brigadier-General.

FORT RILEY, KANS., *December* 6, 1862.

Brig. Gen. JAMES G. BLUNT, *Fort Leavenworth, Kans.:*

SIR: I thought it my duty to inform you of the condition of the people on the frontier northwest of this post, which I am able to do from the report of Captain Read, Company I, Ninth Regiment Kansas Volunteers, who has just visited that section, at the earnest solicitation of many of the sufferers. Captain Read left this post December 10, 1862, with 60 men, with ten days' provisions. He met with nothing remarkable until he arrived about 55 miles up the Republican. Here he found a number of families who had been driven in by the Indians. They were in a most destitute condition; scarcely a family escaped being plundered or outraged. The Indians came upon them in large numbers, in some instances compelling them to cook rations for them, which being devoured, they would load themselves with anything they wanted, taking principally breadstuff. When they found nothing that suited their purpose, they broke or burst everything before them. A gentleman by the name of Fox is the owner of the farm upon which these refugees have found an asylum. Here they have built a rude fort for protection, hoping some change may take place or some protection be afforded them; but if not, they must entirely abandon the country, as many, less courageous, have already done. There is no food for man or beast above Fox's, though a beautiful crop of corn and other things were raised. Captain Read went 100 miles up the Republican, and all along the route saw the ashes of burnt corn and houses and the fragments of broken and destroyed property. The principal object of these marauders appears to have been to drive out the settlers by plunder and outrage, and prevent pursuit by destroying everything they could not carry off. The thriving settlements around Lake Sibley and White Rock are entirely abandoned. Captain Read described the country over which he passed as very fertile as well as beautiful, and capable of sustaining a dense population. The timber on the numerous tributaries of this stream is very abundant, and, could the settlers remain there unmolested, it would soon vie with any portion of the State. There are two salt springs in successful operation near the residence of Mr. Fox, and a good article of salt is produced. I much regret the removal of Companies G and I, Ninth Regiment, from this post will prevent me from affording that protection to the people which they need and desire. But I assure you, major, I shall be untiring in my endeavors to shield them, though the small force I can spare without endangering the safety of this post will be entirely inadequate for the purpose.

Respectfully, your obedient servant,

JOHN E. STEWART,

Captain Company C, Ninth Kansas Volunteers, Commanding Post

HEADQUARTERS THIRTY-SECOND IOWA INFANTRY,
New Madrid, Mo., December 6, 1862.

Brig. Gen. E. A. CARR,
Saint Louis, Mo., Commanding Southeastern Missouri:

GENERAL: Under your orders, I left Saint Louis on the 25th ultimo with part of my regiment, and stopped over at Cape Girardeau from the evening of the 26th ultimo until the morning of the 1st instant, arranging the companies left there. Maj. G. A. Eberhart, of the Thirty-second Iowa, commands that post. Lieutenant Bannon is provost-marshal.

I found a state of affairs there that in some respects was unsatisfactory. The Germans as a class and some few others are fully loyal. The loyal citizens of that place and vicinity are much dissatisfied with the appointment of General Stockton over the Enrolled Missouri Militia of that district. I think they will never acquiesce, nor do I believe he will ever aid the Government or really sustain it. I had no intercourse with him, and am reliably informed that he has not usually called on parties commanding loyal troops. I look upon his appointment as very injudicious. What bad results may follow remains for the future to show.

I arrived at this point on the evening of the 3d instant. I have endeavored to inform myself respecting the state of affairs in this section. I have already learned that, with the exception of Captain Moore's company of Illinois Cavalry, the troops here have been and still are quite popular with the rebels. Matters at this post have gone at loose ends to a degree that rendered our troops quite a convenience to the rebels.

There has been quite a trade in contraband stores from this point to the country west of "the swamps," and much of it to Arkansas.

On the 4th instant I stopped several teams bound to Gainesville, Ark., and each carrying from two to four barrels of salt. I am informed that certain parties have made regular trips. This state of affairs could only have occurred through the connivance of the commander of the post, or at least through great negligence.

I have appointed First Lieut. A. Converse, of Thirty-second Iowa, provost-marshal for this place. I have no fears that contraband trade will be carried on under his eye.

I learn that the rebels are now preparing to carry off large numbers of fat hogs from the counties of Stoddard and Dunklin. If I had 100 mounted men, I could send an infantry force as a nucleus, and could gather in much of this stock, thus distressing our enemy and obtaining supplies for the Government. I will perhaps do so, or attempt it, as it is, at the earliest practicable moment.

It strikes me that an active force could occupy a central position near Chalk Bluff, on the Saint Francis, and save the counties of Stoddard, Scott, Mississippi, New Madrid, Cape Girardeau, and nearly all of Dunklin and Pemiscot from the ravages of the rebels. An important advantage would be that they would draw most of their subsistence from disloyal men.

It is said that Jeff. Thompson was at Four Mile, Dunklin County, eight days since, and made a speech to his followers. He is represented as being now without a command, and on a stealing expedition.

As far as I can learn, the settlers out through and beyond the swamp are more of them loyal than in this section.

This statement embodies the material facts in my possession. I might add that, only for the delay in removing the troops from this place to No. 10, the rebels would most likely have been in possession. I learn that they were counting on such a state of facts.

Very respectfully, your most obedient servant,

JOHN SCOTT,
Colonel Thirty-second Iowa Infantry, Commanding Post.

HEADQUARTERS DISTRICT OF MINNESOTA,
Madison, December 6, 1862.

Brigadier-General ELLIOTT,
Commanding Department:

About 11 o'clock on the night of the 4th instant, the guard around the Indian prisoners at Camp Lincoln were assaulted by nearly 200 men, who attempted to reach the prisoners, with the avowed intention of murdering the condemned prisoners. Colonel Miller, commanding, warned previously of the design, surrounded the assailants and took them prisoners, but subsequently released them. Colonel Miller informs me that large numbers of citizens are assembling, and he fears a serious collision. I have authorized him to declare martial law, if necessary, and call to his assistance all the troops within his reach. He thinks it will require 1,000 true men to protect the prisoners against all organized popular outbreak. He will have nearly or quite that number, but it is doubtful if they can be relied on in the last resort.

Please telegraph the facts to the President, and ask instructions. Any hour may witness a sad conflict, if it has not already occurred.

H. H. SIBLEY,
Brigadier-General, Commanding.

HEADQUARTERS DEPARTMENT OF THE NORTHWEST,
Madison, Wis., December 6, 1862.

Maj. Gen. H. W. HALLECK,
Washington, D. C.:

General Sibley reports that, on the 4th, the guard around the Indian prisoners at South Bend were assaulted by about 200 citizens, with intent to murder the Indians. The citizens were taken prisoners, but subsequently released; that a large number of citizens are assembling, and a serious collision is feared. I have ordered strong re-enforcements to the guard over the prisoners.

W. L. ELLIOTT,
Brigadier-General, Commanding.

DECEMBER 7, 1862.

Brigadier-General BLUNT,
Cane Hill, Ark.:

All my reports go to show there are about 20,000 troops about Little Rock, mostly at Austin. There is no special move on Little Rock. Everything looks down-river. Do not allow yourself to be drawn into ambush. Have been very anxious. Hope you have been re-enforced. Herron is a true man. Success to you.

SAML. R. CURTIS,
Major-General.

HEADQUARTERS TRANS-MISSISSIPPI DEPARTMENT,
Little Rock, Ark., December 7, 1862.

Maj. Gen. SAMUEL R. CURTIS,
Or Officer Comdg., &c., Dept. of Missouri, Saint Louis, Mo.:

GENERAL: Inclosed you will find a slip from the Memphis Daily Appeal, of the 3d ultimo, containing an account, purporting to be derived from the Palmyra (Missouri) Courier, of the murder of ten Confederate citizens of Missouri, by order of General McNeil, of the U. S. Army. This slip was transmitted to me by the President of the Confederate States, who instructs me to ascertain from you whether the facts are as stated.

In accordance with these instructions, I have respectfully to request that you will give me full information in regard to the circumstances related, and at the earliest practicable day.*

I am, general, very respectfully, your obedient servant,

TH. H. HOLMES,
Major-General, Commanding.

HORRIBLE FEDERAL OUTRAGE—TEN CONFEDERATES MURDERED—THE FULL PARTICULARS OF THE SCENE.

[From the Palmyra (Missouri) Courier.]

Saturday last, the 18th instant, witnessed the performance of a tragedy in this once quiet and beautiful city of Palmyra, which, in ordinary and peaceful times, would have created a profound sensation throughout the entire country, but which now scarcely produces a distinct ripple upon the surface of our turbulent social tide.

It will be remembered by our readers that on the occasion of Porter's descent upon Palmyra, he captured, among other persons, an old and highly respected resident of this city, by name Andrew Allsman. This person formerly belonged to the Third

---

* See Curtis to Holmes, December 27, 1862, p. 879; Smith to Curtis, June 3, 1863. Part II, p. 307.

Missouri Cavalry, though too old to endure all the hardships of very active duty. He was, therefore, detailed as a kind of special or extra provost-marshal's guard or cicerone, making himself generally useful in a variety of ways to the military of the place. Being an old resident, and widely acquainted with the people of the place and vicinity, he was frequently called upon for information touching the loyalty of men, which he always gave to the extent of his ability, though acting, we believe, in all such cases with great candor, and actuated solely by a conscientious desire to discharge his whole duty to his Government. His knowledge of the surrounding country was the reason of his being frequently called upon to act as a guide to scouting parties sent out to arrest disloyal persons. So efficiently and successfully did he act in these various capacities, that he won the bitter hatred of all the rebels in this city and vicinity, and they only waited the coming of a favorable opportunity to gratify their desire for revenge. The opportunity came at last, when Porter took Palmyra. That the villains, with Porter's assent, satiated their thirst for his blood by the deliberate and predetermined murder of their helpless victim no truly loyal man doubts. When they killed him, or how, or where, are items of the act not yet revealed to the public. Whether he was stabbed at midnight by the dagger of the assassin, or shot at midday by the rifle of the guerrilla; whether he was hung and his body hidden beneath the scanty soil of some oaken thicket, or left as food for hogs to fatten upon, or whether, like the ill-fated Wheat, his throat was severed from ear to ear, and his body sunk beneath the wave, we know not. But that he was foully, causelessly murdered it is useless to attempt to deny.

When General McNeil returned to Palmyra, after that event, and ascertained the circumstances under which Allsman had been abducted, he caused to be issued, after due deliberation, the following notice:

"PALMYRA, MO., *October* 8, 1862.

"JOSEPH C. PORTER:

"SIR: Andrew Allsman, an aged citizen of Palmyra, and a non-combatant, having been carried from his home by a band of persons unlawfully arrayed against the peace and good order of the State of Missouri, and which band was under your control, this is to notify you that unless said Andrew Allsman is returned, unharmed, to his family within ten days from date, ten men, who have belonged to your band, and unlawfully sworn by you to carry arms against the Government of the United States, and who are now in custody, will be shot as a meet reward for their crimes, among which is the illegal restraining of said Allsman of his liberty, and, if not returned, presumptively aiding in his murder.

"Your prompt attention to this will save much suffering.

"Yours, &c.,

"W. R. STRACHAN,
"*Provost-Marshal-General, District of Northeastern Missouri.*

"Per order of brigadier-general commanding McNeil's column."

A written duplicate of this notice he caused to be placed in the hands of the wife of Joseph C. Porter, at her residence in Lewis County, who it was well known was in frequent communication with her husband. The notice was published widely, and as Porter was in Northern Missouri during the whole of the ten days subsequent to the date of this notice, it is impossible that, with all his varied channels of information, he remained unapprised of General McNeil's determination in the premises.

Many rebels believed the whole thing was simply intended as a scare, declaring that McNeil did not dare [?] to carry out the threat.

The ten days elapsed, and no tidings came of the murdered Allsman. It is not our intention to dwell at length upon the details of this transaction. The tenth day expired with last Friday. On that day ten rebel prisoners, already in custody, were selected to pay with their lives the penalty demanded. The names of the men so selected were as follows: Willis Baker, Lewis County; Thomas Humston, Lewis County; Morgan Bixler, Lewis County; Herbert Hudson, Ralls County; John M. Wade, Ralls County; Marion Lair, Ralls County; Capt. Thomas A. Sidner, Monroe County; Eleazer Lake, Scotland County, and Hiram Smith, Knox County. These parties were informed on Friday evening that unless Mr. Allsman was returned to his family by 1 o'clock on the following day, they would all be shot at that hour. Most of them received the announcement with composure or indifference. The Rev. James S. Green, of this city, remained with them during that night, as their spiritual adviser, endeavoring to prepare them for their sudden entrance into the presence of their Maker. A little after 11 a. m. the next day, three Government wagons drove to the jail; one contained four and each of the others three rough board coffins. The condemned men were conducted from the prison and seated in the wagons, one upon each coffin. A sufficient guard of soldiers accompanied them, and the cavalcade started for the fatal grounds. Proceeding east to Main street, the cortege turned and moved slowly southward as far as Malone's livery stable; thence turning east, it entered the Hannibal road, pursuing it nearly to the residence of Col. James Culbertson; there, throwing down the fences, they turned northward, entering the fair grounds (half a mile east of the town), on the west side, and, driving within the circular amphitheatrical ring, paused for the final consummation of the scene.

The ten coffins were removed from the wagons and placed in a row 6 or 8 feet apart, forming a line north and south, about 15 paces east of the central pagoda or music stand, in the center of the ring. Each coffin was placed upon the ground, with its foot west and head east. Thirty soldiers of the Second Missouri State Militia were drawn up in a single line, extending north and south, facing the row of coffins. This line of executioners ran immediately at the east base of the pagoda, leaving a space between them and the coffins of 12 or 13 paces. Reserves were drawn up in line upon either bank [flank] of these executioners.

The arrangements completed, the doomed men knelt upon the grass between their coffins and the soldiers, while the Rev. R. M. Rhodes offered up a prayer. At the conclusion of this, each prisoner took his seat upon the foot of his coffin, facing the muskets which in a few moments were to launch them into eternity. They were nearly all firm and undaunted, two or three only showing signs of trepidation.

The most noted of the ten was Capt. Thomas A. Sidner, of Monroe County, whose capture at Shelbyville, in the disguise of a woman, we related several weeks since. He was now elegantly attired in a suit of black broadcloth, with a white vest. A luxurious growth of beautiful hair rolled down upon his shoulders, which, with his fine personal appearance, could not but bring to mind the handsome but vicious Absalom. There was nothing especially worthy of note in the appearance of the others. One of them, Willis Baker, of Lewis County, was proven to be the man who last year shot and killed Mr. Ezekiel Pratt, his Union neighbor, near Williamstown, in that county. All the others were rebels of lesser note, the particulars of whose crimes we are not familiar with.

A few minutes after 1 o'clock, Colonel Strachan, provost-marshal-general, and Reverend Rhodes shook hands with the prisoners, two of them accepting bandages for their eyes. All the rest refused. A hundred spectators had gathered around the amphitheater to witness the impressive scene. The stillness of death pervaded the place. The officer in command now stepped forward, and gave the word of command, "Ready, aim, fire." The discharges, however, were not made simultaneously, probably through want of a perfect previous understanding of the orders and of the time at which to fire. Two of the rebels fell backward upon their coffins and died instantly. Captain Sidner sprang forward and fell with his head toward the soldiers, his face upward, his hands clasped upon his breast and the left leg drawn half way up. He did not move again, but died immediately. He had requested the soldiers to aim at his heart, and they obeyed but too implicitly. The other seven were not killed outright, so the reserves were called in, who dispatched them with their revolvers.

It seems hard that ten men should die for one. Under ordinary circumstances it would hardly be justified; but severe diseases demand severe remedies. The safety of the people is the supreme law. It overrides all other considerations. The madness of rebellion has become so deep seated that ordinary methods of cure are inadequate. To take life for life would be little intimidation to men seeking the heart's blood of an obnoxious enemy. They could well afford to make even exchanges under many circumstances. It is only by striking the deepest terror in them, causing them to thoroughly respect the lives of loyal men, that they can be taught to observe the obligation of humanity and of law.

ADDENDA.

EXECUTIVE OFFICE,
Richmond, November 17, 1862.

Lieut. Gen. T. H. HOLMES,
Commanding Trans-Mississippi Department:

GENERAL: Inclosed you will find a slip from the Memphis Daily Appeal of the 3d instant, containing an account, purporting to be derived from the Palmyra (Missouri) Courier, a Federal journal, of the murder of ten Confederate citizens of Missouri, by order of General McNeil, of the U. S. Army.*

You will communicate, by flag of truce, with the Federal officer commanding that department, and ascertain if the facts are as stated. If

* See Holmes to Curtis, December 7, 1862, p. 816, and Curtis to Holmes, December 24, 1862, p. 860; also Smith to Curtis and to Cooper, June 3, 1863, Part II, pp. 307, 852.

they be so, you will demand the immediate surrender of General McNeil to the Confederate authorities, and if this demand is not complied with, you will inform said commanding officer that you are ordered to execute the first ten United States officers who may be captured and fall into your hands.

Very respectfully, yours,

JEFFERSON DAVIS.

[DECEMBER 8, 1862.—For Curtis to Halleck, in reference to expedition from Helena to Grenada, see Series I, Vol. XVII, Part I, p. 528.]

[DECEMBER 8, 1862.—For Grant to Steele, in reference to Sherman's expedition against Vicksburg, see Series I, Vol. XVII, Part II, p. 392.]

MADISON, *December* 8, 1862.

Brigadier-General ELLIOTT,
Commanding Department:

Dispatches and private letters just received indicate a fearful collision between the United States forces and the citizens. Combinations, embracing thousands of men in all parts of the State, are said to be forming, and in a few days our troops, with the Indian prisoners, will be literally besieged. I shall concentrate all the men I can at Mankato. But should the President pardon the condemned Indians, there will be a determined effort to get them in possession, which will be resented, and may cost the lives of thousands of our citizens. Ask the President to keep secret his decision, whatever it may be, until I have prepared myself as best I can. God knows how much the excitement is increasing and extending. Telegraph without delay to headquarters.

H. H. SIBLEY,
Brigadier-General, Commanding.

DECEMBER 8, 1862.

General CURTIS, *Saint Louis:*

I learn that General M. Jeff. Thompson is moving up to Black River, to gather the corn on it for Holmes' army. I shall gather it before him. I send a brigade to the crossing at Reeves' Station to-morrow morning, to gather all the corn between its position and Benton's. Look at the map; it will cover about 17 miles of the river. I shall move with all the cavalry in the evening, or next day, for the double purpose of making the bridge reconnaissance on Current River, which you indicated to me, and to get in Jeff.'s rear. He is said to have Preston's, White's, Jeffers', and Boone's regiments with him.

DAVIDSON,
Brigadier-General.

WAR DEPARTMENT,
Washington, December 9, 1862

Major-General CURTIS, *Saint Louis, Mo.:*

It is represented to the War Department by reliable authorities that two companies of cavalry and one of infantry are sufficient at Fort

Laramie and one company of cavalry at Fort Kearny, some artillery being used for defense of forts, and that all the remainder of General Craig's command is available for service in Mississippi or elsewhere.

H. W. HALLECK,
General-in-Chief.

SAINT LOUIS, MO.,
December 9, 1862—6.30 p. m.

Maj. Gen. H. W. HALLECK, *Commanding:*

Dispatch concerning Nebraska troops received. At present we have only 715 in the Territory, distributed from Fort Kearny to South Pass. The department's informant ignores all necessity of troops at Camp Collins, Fort Halleck, and the telegraph stations. There is also some trouble with Indians near Running Water, which I think worthy of notice. The volunteer regiment ordered by General Pope is full, ten companies, but not mustered, armed, or equipped. I have directed this force to be substituted as fast as possible for old troops, in order to draw away all we can as soon as we can.

SAML. R. CURTIS,
Major-General.

HEADQUARTERS DEPARTMENT OF THE MISSOURI,
Saint Louis, Mo., December 9, 1862.

Brigadier-General GORMAN, *Helena, Ark.:*

GENERAL: I am required to have most of the troops now at Helena ready for a down-river expedition. I am anxious to have Hovey's command back on the river bank, so there may be no delay. Do all you can to facilitate any orders I may receive from General Halleck in this regard. I am sorry to have to leave you with only force enough to hold Eastern Arkansas, but I have urged the necessity of an early return or the accommodation of the matter by the immediate supply of new forces. Blunt and Herron have fought a battle and won a victory at Fayetteville over Hindman.

Truly, yours,

SAML. R. CURTIS,
Major-General.

[DECEMBER 9, 1862.—For Curtis to Steele, in reference to operations down the Mississippi, &c., see Series I, Vol. XVII, Part II, p. 395.]

HDQRS. 2D AND 3D DIVISIONS, ARMY OF THE FRONTIER,
Camp Prairie Grove, December 9, 1862.

Brig. Gen. E. B. BROWN, *Springfield, Mo.:*

Send a messenger to Colonel Philips, at Newtonia, to move his regiment without delay to Elkhorn Tavern, and assume command of that post. Instruct him to be expeditious about the movement. General Blunt has sent a cavalry force in there to protect his line and keep clear that section. Colonel Philips will find full instructions awaiting him at Elkhorn. Order forward to join me Lieutenant-Colonel Baldwin and his detachment, instructing them to take charge of and guard through the commissary train now on the route here. Colonel Richardson and his command will be sent back to Cassville, as you request. Please inform the Springfield "secesh" that we have given Hindman & Co. a damned sound thrashing, and that they have indefinitely postponed their Missouri trip.

F. J. HERRON,
Brigadier-General, Commanding.

HDQRS. 6TH MIL. DIST., MO., *Lexington, December* 9, 1862.

Major-General CURTIS, *Commanding Department of the Missouri:*

GENERAL: I herewith inclose to you the charges and specifications against Col. Charles W. Adams and Lieutenant-Colonel [J. E.] Hayes, of the Twelfth Regiment of Kansas:*

AGAINST COLONEL ADAMS.

CHARGE 1st.—Violation of the thirty-third article of war.

Specification 1st.—In this, that Col. Charles W. Adams, commanding Twelfth Regiment of Kansas Volunteers, with a portion of said regiment, between the 20th and 27th of November, 1862, in the counties of Jackson and La Fayette, in the State of Missouri, did rob, plunder, and despoil the inhabitants of said counties of their horses, mules, oxen, wagons, beds, bedding, and household furniture.

Specification 2d.—In this, that Col. Charles W. Adams, commanding Twelfth Regiment of Kansas Volunteers, did, in the month of November, 1862, with a portion of said regiment, under the pretext of following guerrillas and bushwhackers, enter the above-named counties of Jackson and La Fayette, in the State of Missouri, and took from the loyal and disloyal inhabitants of said counties a vast amount of horses, over 100 in number, a large number of oxen, several wagons and carriages, and every species of household furniture, consisting of beds, bedding, bedsteads, chairs, cooking stoves and utensils, and that they also broke to pieces about 30 bee-hives at one farm-house.

CHARGE 2D.—Violation of orders.

Specification 1st.—In this, that Col. Charles W. Adams, commanding Twelfth Regiment Kansas Volunteers, in violation of the orders of General Blunt, which authorized him to enter the State of Missouri only in pursuit of guerrillas and bushwhackers, did enter the said State of Missouri not in pursuit of guerrillas and bushwhackers, but for the purpose of plundering, robbing, and despoiling the inhabitants of said State of their property.

Specification 2d.—In this, that said Col. Charles W. Adams, commanding Twelfth Regiment of Kansas Volunteers, did, in open violation of the orders of General Blunt, which expressly forbade him to interrupt the peaceful and quiet citizens in their rights and property, rob and plunder said citizens of every species of property.

RICH'D C. VAUGHAN,
Brigadier-General, Sixth Military District of Missouri.

AGAINST LIEUTENANT-COLONEL HAYES.

CHARGE 1ST.—Violation of orders.

Specification 1st.—In this, that Lieutenant-Colonel Hayes, Twelfth Regiment of Kansas Volunteers, after receiving from me orders for the delivery of the property illegally taken from citizens of the State of

---

* See Chipman to Blunt, January 15, 1863, Part II, p. 46.

Missouri, did wilfully disobey said orders by attempting to make his escape with said property into Kansas.

CHARGE 2D.—Disrespect to superior officers.

Specification 1st.—In this, that Lieutenant-Colonel Hayes, in command of a part of Twelfth Regiment Kansas Volunteers, being ordered by me to deliver over said property, did thereafter fail to do so, and endeavored, feloniously and contemptuously, to convey said property away.

CHARGE 3D.—Conduct unbecoming an officer and a gentleman.

Specification 1st.—In this, that Lieutenant-Colonel Hayes, of Twelfth Kansas Volunteers, after pledging his word as an officer and a gentleman to Maj. Thomas B. Biggers, Fifth Regiment Missouri State Militia, that all of said property should be delivered in accordance with my orders, did wholly fail to comply with the promise so given, and that he had the brand of the United States put upon said horses, thereby manifesting a design, fraudulently and feloniously, to deceive, and afterward attempted, in violation of his promise, to escape with said property.

RICH'D C. VAUGHAN,
Brigadier-General.

I submit the names of the following gentlemen, who, if necessary, can be had as witnesses: Col. James McFerran, Missouri State Militia; Colonel Penick, commanding at Independence, Missouri State Militia; Maj. Thomas B. Biggers, Missouri State Militia; Col. H. Neill, Enrolled Missouri Militia, La Fayette; Lieutenant-Colonel Black, Enrolled Missouri Militia, Ray County; Judge Jeans, Jackson County; Archibald Renick, Jackson County, and General Gray, Jackson County.

RICH'D C. VAUGHAN,
Brigadier-General.

[Inclosure No. 1.]

NOVEMBER 27, 1862.

Colonel ADAMS:

As I can see nothing in the orders of General Blunt authorizing the course you have taken, and as my orders from the commander of this division are positive, I am bound to demand the surrender of all property taken from citizens of this State, and that the negroes taken from citizens of Jackson and La Fayette be forthwith turned out of your lines; and as there is no organized enemy either in Jackson or La Fayette Counties, that you at once march your force beyond the limits of this State.

If this proposal is acceded to, I will send an officer to arrange the conditions. I retain the orders only to take a copy, after which they will be immediately returned.

I am, sir, yours, &c.,

RICH'D C. VAUGHAN,
Brigadier-General, Commanding.

[Inclosure No. 2.]

HDQRS. TWELFTH REGIMENT KANSAS VOLUNTEERS,
In the Field, November 27, 1862.

Brig. Gen. R. C. VAUGHAN:

SIR: I am ready to comply with your demands at the earliest possible time, except that pertaining to negroes. They are at liberty to do as they choose, as they came within our lines voluntarily.

Very respectfully, your obedient servant,

CHAS. W. ADAMS,
Colonel, Commanding.

P. S.—I cannot agree with you in relation to the orders from Generals Curtis and Blunt.

[Inclosure No. 3.]

Colonel ADAMS:

SIR: Your note is received. The demand relative to the negroes must be complied with. The matter of disagreement relating to your orders from General Blunt and General Curtis is a matter which can be more readily settled elsewhere than here.

I am, sir, your obedient servant,

RICH'D C. VAUGHAN,
Brigadier-General, Commanding.

[P. S.]—As it is already late, I must require that you permit no portion of the property and negroes, above alluded to, to leave your lines.

[Inclosure No. 4.]

HDQRS. TWELFTH REGIMENT KANSAS VOLUNTEERS,
November 27, 1862.

Brig. Gen. R. C. VAUGHAN:

SIR: My guards are out and I shall follow your order relative to keeping whatever is within my lines here. I am subject to arrest from you, and choose a trial by court-martial rather than turn the negroes out of my camp. I do not do this, believe me, General Vaughan, out of disrespect to you, but because I believe it to be contrary to a general order from the War Department so to do.

Very respectfully, &c.,

CHAS. W. ADAMS,
Colonel, Commanding Twelfth Regiment Kansas Volunteers.

DEAR GENERAL: If you will receive an informal visit from me, I will be glad to see you.

Yours, truly,

CHAS. W. ADAMS,
Colonel, Commanding.

[Inclosure No. 5.]

IN THE FIELD,
Jackson County, November 27, 1862.

Col. C. W. ADAMS,
Commanding Twelfth Kansas:

COLONEL: You are hereby arrested and required to report at Saint Louis to General Curtis on the 15th of December.

I am, sir, your obedient servant,

RICH'D C. VAUGHAN,
Brigadier-General, Commanding.

[Inclosure No. 6.]

SPECIAL ORDERS.] IN THE FIELD,
Jackson County, November 28, 1862.

Officer in Command of the Twelfth Kansas Regiment:

The bearer, Major Biggers, visits your camp for the purpose of delivering this order and returning the property taken by your command from citizens of this State. You are hereby ordered to deliver the same without unnecessary delay. An officer will be ready to receive it.

I am, sir, yours, &c.,

RICH'D C. VAUGHAN,
Brigadier-General, Commanding.

[Inclosure No. 7.]

SPECIAL ORDERS.]

IN THE FIELD,
Jackson County, November 27, 1862.

Commanding Officer of the Twelfth Kansas:

SIR: You are hereby required to mount all the men that were mounted when you left Kansas (not exceeding 20), and immediately march your command with such transportation and baggage as you brought with you into the State.

RICH'D C. VAUGHAN,
Brigadier-General, Commanding.

[Inclosure No. 8.]

SPECIAL ORDERS.]

IN THE FIELD,
Jackson County, November 28, 1862

Lieutenant-Colonel HAYES,
Commanding Twelfth Kansas Volunteers:

You are hereby arrested and required to report at Saint Louis, Mo., to Major General Curtis, on the 15th of December, 1862.

By order of Brig. Gen. R. C. Vaughan:

THOMAS B. BIGGERS,
Major and Acting Aide-de-Camp.

[Inclosure No. 9.]

INDEPENDENCE, *December* 2, 1862.

Col. W. R. PENICK:

DEAR SIR: In compliance with your orders of November 28, I left the line of march near Judge Jayne's, in Jackson County, Missouri, with 10 men of my company, to escort the Twelfth Regiment Kansas U. S. Volunteers, under command of Major Kennedy. On their line of march to the Kansas State line, after marching a short distance, Major Kennedy requested me to send a messenger to overtake your command and get permission to withdraw the escort, as a portion of his command objected very much to being marched out of the State. I declined complying with his request, as I knew the order came from General Vaughan, and you would not countermand it, of which fact I informed him.

We encamped the first night at Blue Springs. The night after the second day's march, encamped at Rock Ford. On the morning of the third day's march, when near Hickman Mills, their command separated, a portion, under command of a captain, marching by the way of Santa Fé to Olathe. The major with his command went by the way of Aubrey to Paola, the headquarters of the regiment. I remained with them until they crossed the Kansas State line, within about 2 miles of Aubrey, on the afternoon of November 30.

I have no reason to think they committed any depredations on the march, with the exception of taking one bee gum, which came to my knowledge after the act was committed.

I did hear they had stolen 2 horses, the owners' names not known, neither the persons who committed the act. When they crossed the line they had not as many negroes as report says they brought with them. I heard from several citizens that a portion of the same regiment took another route and returned with about 1,000 head of stock—horses, oxen, sheep, and hogs.

Yours, respectfully,

J. B. VANSANT,
Capt. Company F, Fifth Regt. Missouri State Militia Cavalry.

[Inclosure No. 10.]

HEADQUARTERS DISTRICT OF KANSAS,
In the Field, October 9, 1862.

Col. C. W. ADAMS,
Commanding Twelfth Regiment Kansas Volunteers:

SIR: Immediately on receipt of this, you are directed to dispose the forces under your command so as to cover the eastern border of the State from the Kansas to the Osage River. It is confidently believed that you can, by a system of patrols and signals, prevent the ingress of bands of Missouri guerrillas, who have heretofore been devastating that porti n of the State, and by activity and courage drive them from their hiding places in the border counties of Missouri. You will carefully instruct your men that the persons, property, and rights of the people of Kansas and the loyal portion of Missouri should be held sacred, and any infraction should be promptly and severely punished. Parties sent into Missouri should be placed under the command of active and prudent officers, with instructions to pursue bushwhackers to the death. After you have matured your plans and disposed your forces, you should issue a proclamation to the citizens of Johnson County and the other border counties of Kansas and Missouri who have fled their homes to return thereto, promising them safety and protection.

To you and the troops under your command is intrusted the delicate and important duty of restoring peace to the border between the points named. You should communicate frequently with the military authorities at Fort Leavenworth and Fort Scott.

Keep your troops well in hand, that they be not cut off in detail, and that they may be concentrated at any given point without delay or confusion. Major Henning, Third Wisconsin Cavalry, provost-marshal for the District of Kansas, south of Kansas River, will, from time to time, issue such orders to you as he may deem necessary in relation to the disposition of your forces.

You will immediately on receipt of this order report by letter to Major Henning, stating your forces, station, &c.

By order of Brigadier-General Blunt:

THOS. MOONLIGHT,
Assistant Adjutant-General.

[Inclosure No. 11.]

HEADQUARTERS,
Fort Scott, October 24, 1862.

Commanding Officer Twelfth Regiment Kansas Volunteers:

I have the honor to send you a copy of orders received from department headquarters this day.

Very respectfully,

B. S. HENNING,
Major Third Wisconsin Cavalry, Commanding Post.

[Sub-inclosure.]

HEADQUARTERS,
Saint Louis, October 19, 1862.

Commanding Officer:

The troops at or north of Fort Scott will remain on the line of communication, unless special orders arrive from General Blunt. I approve of general distribution suggested by General Lane. It will not be proper for officers to issue proclamations, and the troops must not be so divided as to invite attack. A strong force must be retained at the depots of public stores.

Send this forward, for the benefit of officers commanding posts or pickets along the line. Orders from Brigadier-General Blunt will be forwarded.

SAML. R. CURTIS,
Major-General.

HEADQUARTERS DEPARTMENT OF THE NORTHWEST,
Madison, Wis., December 9, 1862.

Maj. Gen. H. W. HALLECK,
Washington, D. C.:

General Sibley reports that combinations, embracing thousands in all parts of Minnesota, are forming to get the condemned Indians in their possession. I ask that the action of the President may be kept secret until we can concentrate the troops, to prevent a collision, if possible.

W. L. ELLIOTT,
Brigadier-General U. S. Volunteers, Commanding.

EXECUTIVE MANSION,
Washington, December 10, 1862.

Major-General CURTIS, *Saint Louis, Mo.:*

Please suspend, until further order, all proceedings on the order made by General Schofield, on the 28th day of August last, for assessing and collecting from secessionists and Southern sympathizers the sum of $500,000, &c., and in the mean time make out and send me a statement of facts pertinent to the question, together with your opinion upon it.

A. LINCOLN.

ADDENDA.

SPECIAL ORDERS, No. 91. } HEADQUARTERS DISTRICT OF MISSOURI,
Saint Louis, August 28, 1862.

* * * * * * *

III. The following-named gentlemen are hereby appointed a county board for Saint Louis County, viz: Messrs. Henry Moore, John Cavender, G. F. Filley, Charles Borg, and Ferdinand Meyer. This board will assess and collect, without unnecessary delay, the sum of $500,000 from the secessionists and Southern sympathizers in Saint Louis County. The money thus obtained will be used in subsisting, clothing, and arming the enrolled militia while in active service, and in providing for the support of such families of militiamen and U. S. volunteers as may be left destitute.

* * * * * * *

By order of Brigadier-General Schofield:

C. W. MARSH,
Assistant Adjutant-General.

HDQRS. 2D AND 3D DIVISIONS, ARMY OF THE FRONTIER,
Camp Prairie Grove, December 10, 1862.

Major-General CURTIS, *Saint Louis, Mo.:*

One of my spies, who came to the battle-field with Hindman's troops and retreated with them to Dripping Springs, has just come in. He reports the rebel loss at 2,500 killed and wounded, including a very large number of officers. Brigadier-General Steen, of Missouri, was killed, and some 6 or 7 field officers are in the hospitals within our lines. Two batteries were so much damaged by the firing from Foust's and Murphy's guns as to be entirely worthless, and several guns were hauled off in wagons. All of their artillery horses were left dead on the field, and the caissons taken away by mules in the night. Hindman's entire force was here, and from personal observation I can say they were well clothed and well armed.

My division took over 60 prisoners, including 2 commissioned officers, during the fight, and all refuse to be exchanged except 12. Over 150 have come in since the battle, and the report is that hundreds are coming back on the roads to give themselves up.

The large proportion of their dead have been left by them unburied, and were buried to-day by my order.

The advance has arrived at Van Buren, and the rumor was they were all going to Little Rock.

The loss in my divisions is heavy, and will almost reach 1,000 killed and wounded. For four hours the fighting was the most desperate I ever witnessed, and within a space of two acres 250 of our own and the enemy's dead were found. The victory is more complete and decisive than I had imagined. The Iowa regiments fought nobly, the Nineteenth particularly distinguishing itself. We mourn the loss of Lieutenant-Colonel [S.] McFarland and several other officers of that regiment, killed. The Twentieth Wisconsin, Twenty-sixth Indiana, and Thirty-seventh Illinois fought nobly. The battle-field is on the road from Fayetteville to Cove Creek, and just half way between the former place and Cane Hill.

General Blunt has moved to Rhea's Mills, while I occupy the battle-field. I am strengthening my line of communication with Springfield, and will have it safe to-morrow. Have established a hospital at Fayetteville, and removed all our sick and wounded to it. If Steele could take Little Rock, now is the best opportunity to open the Arkansas River. I hope you will let us do it.

F. J. HERRON,
Brigadier-General, Commanding Second and Third Divisions.

HEADQUARTERS DEPARTMENT OF THE MISSOURI,
Saint Louis, December 10, 1862.

GOV. HAMILTON R. GAMBLE, *Saint Louis, Mo.*:

[SIR:] Your note of the 1st instant, on the subject of assessment, saying that you inform gentlemen who come to you "that the assessment stands upon United States authority, and not upon State authority," was duly received and carefully considered. I have supposed it a State proceeding, and expressed my determination to support your officers in their efforts to execute your will, if found necessary. Since you and General Schofield regard it as an act of the United States, grave questions arise in my mind as to the harmony of my exercise of such powers in the face of the Constitution, the revenue laws, and the confiscation act. I have, therefore, referred the whole matter to headquarters, for the consideration of General Halleck, pending which the President has directed me to stay all further proceedings.

I have the honor to be, Governor, Your Excellency's obedient servant,

SAML. R. CURTIS,
Major-General, Commanding Department of the Missouri.

HEADQUARTERS DEPARTMENT OF THE MISSOURI,
Saint Louis, December 10, 1862.

Hon. JAMES W. GRIMES:

DEAR SIR: Yours of the — instant is received. Stanton is here, and will report, according to orders. In the matter of a down-river movement, Commodore Davis properly states the facts. The fleet came up to Helena soon after my arrival, leaving the mouths of the Arkansas rivers in the enemy's hands. My proper lines of operation in Arkansas require me to move across these rivers, and I was therefore anxious to have possession of them. But the clearing out of the Mississippi, so that the rebels could not come out of their hives and go prowling up and down the rivers, was obviously a necessary preliminary measure. Commodore Davis concurred with me, and we came together at Cairo to confer with our chiefs at Washington. The commodore was ill, and I conducted a telegraphic correspondence through General Halleck, which concluded by the general saying, in substance, that the taking of Vicksburg should not be attempted at that time. I showed my correspondence to the commodore, and went back to Helena, when we got up a joint movement on a small scale. Went down and took and destroyed a battery in the mouth of the Yazoo, within 10 or 15 miles of Vicksburg; took a steamer loaded with muskets; marched into Louisiana, opposite Vicksburg, and destroyed the railroad depot and telegraph station some 15 miles west of Vicksburg. I am since informed that our movement created a great stampede in Vicksburg.

I am thus careful to reply only simple facts to your letter, as I dislike to speak of what I have suggested to a superior officer, and should not now have done so, if you had not asked me concerning what Commodore Davis had informed you. I ask no credit for what I have not done, it having been my fate to find my hands always busy, as my heart is still earnest, in efforts to quell this infernal rebellion. Iowa has tarnished every battle-field in the West with the blood of her gallant sons, and it is enough for me to feel confident the country will award us our due share of commendation.

You will mourn with me the recent loss of Lieutenant-Colonel McFarland, the only field officer we lost in the battle near Fayetteville, Ark.

Please give my kindest regards to Mrs. Grimes, and believe me, very truly, your obedient servant,

SAML. R. CURTIS,
Major-General.

HEADQUARTERS ARMY OF THE FRONTIER,
In the Field, Rhea's Mills, Ark., December 12, 1862.

Maj. Gen. SAMUEL R. CURTIS,
Commanding Department of the Missouri:

GENERAL: The only movement of the rebel army of which I have any fear is, that Hindman may unite his forces with those at Austin, in which case I would not have sufficient force to risk a battle. Cannot a force be sent to menace Little Rock, and attract the attention of the rebels at Austin? Can you inform me of the locality of General Warren's command, and can he be brought in supporting distance if I am threatened with an overwhelming force?

Respectfully, &c.,

JAS. G. BLUNT,
Brigadier General, Commanding.

[DECEMBER 12, 1862.—For Sherman to Gorman, in reference to Vicksburg expedition, see Series I, Vol. XVII, Part II, p. 402.]

HEADQUARTERS DEPARTMENT OF THE MISSOURI,
Saint Louis, December 12, 1862.

Brig. Gen. FITZ HENRY WARREN, *Houston:*

GENERAL: Our movements in Southeast Missouri are still suspended to await other more important ones. The return of the rebels on General Blunt somewhat disconcerted my plans, but your position is the more important since the Army of the Frontier has moved so far away. The mutations now projected must influence my plans, and I cannot therefore determine anything for you or myself. The only way is to be always ready to move. I am procuring additional trains at Pilot Knob, which I expect to turn to your account as a supply train, for I still contemplate a junction below, perhaps at Mountain Store, as you suggested. Fredericksburg was taken yesterday, and we suppose fighting is going on to-day, but no dispatches are received when we most need them. I was glad to get the report from the Iowa deserter. I wish you had given dates of the times he was at different places. It corroborates reports of others. Send out cavalry to ascertain Burbridge's movements. Thompson is reported southeast from Pilot Knob, and Davidson, with cavalry, after him. Keep me informed of everything. I have ordered a change of regiments, so as to put an Iowa regiment in place of the Missouri troops. The down-river move is pretty well prepared to make a demonstration on Vicksburg. I hope Burnside is pressing "on to Richmond," but we have had so many miscarriages in that direction one dare not hardly hope for good news.

I am, general, very truly, yours,

SAML. R. CURTIS,
Major-General.

HDQRS. 2D AND 3D DIVISIONS, ARMY OF THE FRONTIER,
Camp Prairie Grove, December 13, 1862.

Maj. Gen. SAMUEL R. CURTIS,
Saint Louis, Mo.:

I do not think our wounded could be carried back with safety to themselves. They are very comfortably fixed at Fayetteville in good houses, but I want sanitary goods. I have established a post there, Colonel Wickersham commanding. I have telegraphed Colonel McFarland's friends to bring a coffin that he can be removed in. The weather is too mild here to permit its being done without a metallic coffin. All of our officers have been neatly buried at Fayetteville. In my opinion the telegraph should be put up at once to Fayetteville; the cost is trifling, even if for a few weeks' service. Our cavalry are now out on all the roads leading south. A portion of Hindman's force crossed the river at Van Buren, but he has a camp at Dripping Springs, 7 miles this side of Van Buren. One of my spies in last night states that he is expecting the Little Rock force to his assistance, and will give us another turn. The deserters coming in state that Hindman is terribly afraid of my command, and says I have forty Parrott guns. Hindman has been communicating with General Blunt daily since the fight, and pitches into me severely. I can hear nothing definite in regard to the Arkansas River, except that boats are running to Little Rock.

We have plenty of good forage at our present camp. There are large mills here and plenty of wheat. Quartermaster Allen must send more wagons to this route. Our line is very long, and without he furnishes more transportation at once there will be trouble. I must have on my line 100 wagons more. Will you please order them to Rolla?

F. J. HERRON,
Brigadier-General, Commanding Second and Third Divisions.

[DECEMBER 13, 1862.—For Steele to Grant, in reference to Vicksburg expedition, &c., see Series I, Vol. XVII, Part II, p. 410.]

[DECEMBER 13 and 19, 1862.—For Sherman to Curtis and Curtis' reply, in reference to Vicksburg expedition, see Series I, Vol. XVII, Part II, pp. 407, 433.]

HDQRS. 2D AND 3D DIVISIONS, ARMY OF THE FRONTIER,
Camp Prairie Grove, December 13, 1862.

Maj. Gen. SAMUEL R. CURTIS, *Saint Louis, Mo.:*

Your telegram in regard to the Little Rock force is received. Where is Steele, and does he propose to move on Little Rock? Without he does and prevents Holmes from forming a junction with Hindman, we may have to fall back and lose all the results that might be reached from this hard-fought battle. With a few more regiments of infantry, however, we can whip anything Hindman can get together. How is it about the Twenty-second Iowa at Rolla? Could they be ordered forward to me?

F. J. HERRON,
Brigadier-General.

WASHINGTON CITY, *December* 13, 1862.

Maj. Gen. H. W. HALLECK, *Washington, D. C.:*

DEAR GENERAL: I had no thought of my humble memorial ever leaving Governor Gamble's office, or it should have been written with more care. It contains, I think, an exact statement of facts, as far as it goes; but I do not mean to call in question General Schofield's action in ordering the assessment, which was probably the only available means of giving the needful credit to the Governor in obtaining money from the banks. It was, as I believe, suggested, advised, and approved by the Governor, and without it the enrollment of the military could not have been effected, for want of funds. But that enrollment and other efficient action have changed the whole state of things, and now the banks offer credit and do not want their money. The Governor will not take the money if collected. Besides this, the assessment upon "sympathizers" has been very arbitrary, and has been more or less by the accident of evidence offered, everything being under strict secrecy. If held in abeyance for awhile, it may be a good *in terrorem*, but, if enforced, should be thoroughly revised.

Pardon the liberty I now take. You know how deeply interested I am in the great cause.

I remain, truly, yours,

W. G. ELIOT.

SPECIAL ORDERS, } HDQRS. NORTHEASTERN DIST. OF MISSOURI,
No. 39. } *Warrenton, Mo., December* 13, 1862.

The following notice, left upon the premises of Mr. John H. Holdsworth, a loyal citizen of Monroe County, Missouri, has been brought to the notice of the general commanding:

MR. JOHN HOLDSWORTH:

SIR: You are hereby informed that the Monroe County Avengers have determined that you must quit this county before January 1, 1863, if you would save your property from the flames.

Your open approval of Lincoln's hell-born proclamation, and voting for those that were in favor of it, have determined us to make you quit the county. If but one of us is left, it will be carried out.

THE AVENGERS.

Such threats as this can only be executed by the connivance and with the consent of the disloyal of Monroe County. These disloyal persons are warned that if they again bring about insurrection, violence, and bloodshed in Monroe County, now quiet, that none of them will be spared. If they remain quietly attending to their legitimate business, they will be protected in their persons and property.

The time has passed when such acts as here threatened can be even palliated by disloyal sentiments, and any repetition of them will be punished with the utmost rigor of a severe code.

The following neighbors of John Holdsworth will be held in person and property responsible that no harm comes to him or his property: John Forsyth, David Wooldridge, John Vaughan, Gilmore, Gonell, Beauchamp, Hiram Powell, Jacob Cox, William Bridgeford, and Charles Browning.

If, therefore, these men desire to live in the peaceful and quiet enjoyment of their property, let them see to it that the said John H. Holdsworth is permitted to do the same.

By order of Brigadier-General Merrill:

GEO. M. HOUSTON,
Major and Aide-de-Camp.

Organization of troops in the District of Eastern Arkansas, Brig. Gen. Willis A. Gorman commanding, December 13, 1862.*

FIRST DIVISION.

Brig. Gen. FREDERICK STEELE.

First Brigade.	*Second Brigade.*
Brig. Gen. P. J. OSTERHAUS.	Brig. Gen. J. M. THAYER.
3d Missouri.	26th Iowa.
12th Missouri.	28th Iowa.
17th Missouri.	30th Iowa.
58th Ohio.	34th Iowa.
76th Ohio	

Third Brigade.

Col. ——— ———.

9th Iowa.
24th Iowa.
25th Iowa
31st Iowa.

---

* As announced in General Orders, Nos. 11 and 13, District Headquarters, December 12 and 13. The assignment of batteries not indicated by these orders.

SECOND DIVISION.

Brig. Gen. A. P. HOVEY.

First Brigade.

Brig. Gen. C. E. HOVEY.

43d Indiana.
46th Indiana.
47th Indiana.

Second Brigade.

Col. ——— ———.

13th Illinois.
4th Iowa.
56th Ohio.
29th Wisconsin.

Third Brigade.

Col. ——— ———.

11th Indiana.
24th Indiana.
34th Indiana.

THIRD (CAVALRY) DIVISION.

Brig. Gen. C. C. WASHBURN.

First Brigade.

3d Illinois.
5th Illinois.
10th Illinois.
Kane County Illinois.
1st Indiana.
1st Missouri.
6th Missouri.

Second Brigade.

2d Arkansas.
9th Illinois.
3d Iowa.
4th Iowa.
5th Kansas.
2d Wisconsin.

HEADQUARTERS ARMY OF THE FRONTIER,
Camp at Rhea's Mills, Ark., December 14, 1862.

Maj. Gen. SAMUEL R. CURTIS,
Commanding Department of the Missouri:

GENERAL: It is not advisable to remove the wounded from Fayetteville.

In about one week more I shall have eaten up all the forage west of the Telegraph road and north of the mountains for 50 miles. There is considerable forage east of the Wire road, in the valley of the White River. There is no forage between the mountains and the Arkansas River; neither is there any south of the river, within 50 miles of Van Buren. Hindman cannot remain long at Fort Smith, unless he obtains his supplies and forage by water up the river.

This army has accomplished all it can, except to hold the country north of the mountains, while we can obtain forage, until some movement is made upon Little Rock, and the Arkansas River opened and made the base of our operations.

Respectfully, your obedient servant,

JAS. G. BLUNT,
Brigadier-General, Commanding.

WASHINGTON, D. C., *December* 15, 1862.

Maj. Gen. SAMUEL R. CURTIS,
Saint Louis, Mo.:

GENERAL: I have received from the Rev. Dr. Eliot, of Saint Louis, the documents forwarded by you in relation to the assessment ordered by Brigadier-General Schofield on the city and county of Saint Louis, and have submitted them to the Secretary of War for his decision.

I am instructed to say in reply that, as there seems to be no present military necessity for the enforcement of this assessment, all proceedings under the order of General Schofield will be suspended.

Should new insurrections occur in Missouri, and the people of Saint Louis again afford aid and comfort to the enemy, they may expect to suffer the legitimate consequences of such acts of treason.

Very respectfully, your obedient servant,

H. W. HALLECK,
General-in-Chief.

HDQRS. 2D AND 3D DIVISIONS, ARMY OF THE FRONTIER,
December 15, 1862.

Major-General CURTIS, *Saint Louis, Mo.:*

All reports from spies and other sources go to show that Hindman has crossed the Arkansas River with his infantry and artillery, and that his cavalry, under Marmaduke, is still hovering around on this side. I will probably cross the mountains in a few days, with our united cavalry force, and give Marmaduke another turn. The trip can be made rapidly, and will carry out your idea of a few days since.

I still occupy the battle-field.

F. J. HERRON,
Brigadier-General.

HDQRS. NORTHEASTERN DISTRICT OF MISSOURI,
Warrenton, Mo., December 15, 1862.

Lieut. Col. F. A. DICK,
Provost-Marshal-General, Department of the Missouri:

COLONEL: Your letter of the 3d has had my serious attention. It is not necessary that I should again go over the ground, which was fully discussed between us while in Saint Louis. I apprehend that an examination of the status of the men who are pressing the matter will, in ninety-nine cases out of one hundred, show the following state of facts: First, that they are, and always have been, thoroughly disloyal, but from prudential motives have so trimmed their course as to have no very bad reputation as disloyal men; or, second, that they are Union men whose loyalty is extremely dubious and shaky, and who are now making that loyalty pay either pecuniarily, by directly asking fees for their services, or in courting favors with their secesh friends, by using their influence for this purpose, or weak enough to permit themselves to be used, through their correct and proper pity for a criminal, by the friends of those criminals, to secure their immunity from punishment; or, lastly, that they are men, like Judge Leonard, true and pure patriots, who have always been such pure patriots, who have always been such pure men themselves that they are willing always to believe the protestations of penitence, which these rascals never make until they have been caught and shut up, and which penitence the experience of eighteen months among them has thoroughly convinced me is always simulated, and never more than skin-deep. Among some 1,500 rebels whom I have arrested and released upon oath and bond in times past, and with whose after history I have had occasion to become familiar, I cannot point to one single instance in which they have faithfully kept their promises to behave in all respects as loyal citizens. A slight investigation of the causes which led to their original disloyalty will show the good reason for this.

The disloyal of Missouri are composed mainly of two classes: One the designing, unscrupulous, shrewd, and unprincipled leaders, and the other (by far the largest) of their poor deluded dupes—men who, but for the poisonous talk and influence of these men, would have remained, at worst, neutral, and who, under better influences, would have been thoroughly loyal. These leaders have, in almost every instance, confined themselves to the secret exertion of their influence and the spreading of mischievous lying reports, while their cat's-paws have done the work in which they were too cowardly and too shrewd to be implicated directly. Of this class are such men as Senator Jim Green; Anderson, of Palmyra; Stephens and Samuels, of Boone; Haden, of Howard; Miner, of Adair, and hundreds of others, with whose names I have become most disagreeably familiar in the discharge of my duties. Men of the second class commit crimes, are arrested, and, perhaps, really believe that they repent, and wish again to become good citizens; they are released, returned to their homes, and are once again brought under the very influences which originally led them astray. Is it surprising that these men should forget their promise? It is especially true of North Missouri that the people are more extensively influenced for good or bad than by any other fifty causes. Now, confining these poor dupes, while it takes out of the country the men who did the mischief, leaving these "haven't done nothing" class of leaders no good material to work upon, and yet, if one of these men is arrested, from a well-founded belief that his presence and influence are dangerous to the public safety, you will find that he has always influential friends enough to beg him off, and especially when only that general charge is made against him. I have endeavored to rectify this evil by summarily banishing a number of these men; but until I find that I am to be sustained, and that no influence, however strong, of personal friendship can recall the sentence of banishment, I am unwilling to carry the experiment any further, especially in view of the recent order from the War Department on the subject. So far, both the commanding general and yourself have heartily co-operated with me, and the result you see is the perfect quiet which now prevails in the northeast district—a quiet that I stake my life will not again be disturbed if this policy is continued, and which will just as surely be destroyed, and the old trouble back on our hands, if these very men, who have so often been forgiven and told to sin no more, are permitted to return to do the same thing over again. I think that the experience of more than a year in handling these people (and always successfully) should give my opinion some weight, and I tell you, colonel, that the policy of forgiving them and turning them loose will not do, while the very men who set them wrong at first are at home ready and willing to do it again. If I am permitted to send these men out of the State, and hang them if they come back without authority, then the men who have heretofore been thus instrumental in their villainy may be permitted to return without detriment to the public safety. If, however, this is not done, there will be the same work to do over again, and every time it is repeated it is going to cost us more blood of good men and more treasure than all the lives of the rebel herd are worth. Experience shows that the present policy is successful; it has had the hearty support and approbation of all true Union men in the district, and they will tell you that their lives will not be safe if it is changed. Why, then, change this because a few criminals (whom it is inconvenient to keep, it is true) show the same signs of repentance with which they have so often betrayed us before?

You must not go for the expression of opinion to the Union men of Saint Louis, who do not know what the needs of the interior are, nor yet such men as Judge Leonard, who is not capable of forming an accurate judgment, because ill-health has confined him to his bed, almost constantly to his house, during the whole war. Ask such men as Major Gates, of Adair; Colonel Eberman and Major Bean, of Macon; Colonel Hayward and Major Hunt, of Hannibal; W. Casper, of Schuyler; W. Yeisir, of Audrain; W. J. B. Douglass, of Boone; Messrs. Lewis, of Glasgow; W. Orrick, of Saint Charles; any Union men, in fact, who know of what they speak, and you will find that my opinion and policy is indorsed by every one of them as the only safety for the district. Such, then, being the case, the question is simply, Shall a few hundred undoubted rebels, who have honestly earned hanging, be turned loose, to harass away and drive from the country thousands of quiet Union men, whose only safety is in the punishment of these men? Which is of most value, the peace and quiet of half a State or the personal liberty of a few hundred criminals?

As to the promise that their obligations will be kept, and your belief that they will, I can only refer you to the experience of the past, and point you to the million dollars of forfeited bonds, and the broken oaths of thousands of these men, to show you that such a hope is idle.

I beg you will bring the whole matter to the serious attention of the general commanding, especially in view of the fact that I have at his urgent call reduced the number of troops in my district by four regiments within a week.

I am, sir, very respectfully,

LEWIS MERRILL,
Brigadier-General, Comdg. Northeastern District of Missouri.

HEADQUARTERS EASTERN ARKANSAS,
Helena, December 15, 1862.

Maj. H. Z. CURTIS,
Assistant Adjutant-General:

MAJOR: I have the honor to inform the general commanding the department that, in obedience to his note of the 9th instant, I have ordered General Steele with his division of three brigades of infantry, and two regiments of General Blair's brigade (the Thirtieth and Thirty-first Missouri), and two full batteries and 600 cavalry, to be fully ready to embark on transports on the 18th instant, the time fixed by General Sherman in his dispatch to me when he would be here. General Grant also sent a special dispatch 80 miles by a cavalry escort to me, asking for the forces of Hovey's expedition, and also sending me a copy of General Halleck's dispatch to that effect addressed to him. I replied to General Grant before receiving your dispatch, fully anticipating your order, and told him I would send the full force of the Hovey expedition, and more, to the points indicated by him, and have them ready when General Sherman should arrive.*

General Sherman is now in Memphis, preparing to start for a point near the mouth of the Yazoo River. He brought 7,000 men from Oxford, Miss., to Memphis with him, and found two divisions there, making in all about 21,000 men, and he asks 10,000 men from Helena. The forces I have ordered to be in readiness will amount to about 11,000 men, which will leave me with less than 3,000 effective infantry and 2,000 effective cavalry and four miserable batteries, with 1,500 sick on

*See Gorman to Grant, December 13, Series I, Vol. XVII, Part II, p. 406.

my hands; but the importance of General Grant's and General Sherman's movements is so great and seemingly pressing, I felt it my duty to let go every man I could possibly spare and pretend to hold this point. The enemy have an effective force of 5,000 men and strong earthworks at Post Arkansas, while McCulloch has 10,000, mostly Texans, part Arkansas conscripts, at Brownsville; and Holmes has about 1,200 only at Little Rock. Of the force of Hindman, Marmaduke, Rains, Hawes, &c., I have no reliable information, but think it perhaps not more than 12,000, mostly conscripts.

I received and forwarded to you dispatches from General Holmes, dated at Little Rock on the 8th instant, and learned certainly that he was then at Little Rock, and not yet gone to Vicksburg. But I have learned from spies, refugees, and deserters, within a day or two, that McCulloch's troops were under marching orders south, perhaps to Vicksburg. If Vicksburg falls, Arkansas must be abandoned by them very soon.

I trust it is your design to push Blunt, Herron, and Schofield down toward Little Rock at once, so as to compel them to abandon it, or create a diversion in favor of Grant and Sherman, and keep Holmes in Arkansas.

I most respectfully ask that General Davidson be ordered here at once, by the Ridge road, down the Saint Francis region. He will not meet an enemy, except a handful of guerrillas, as everybody here and the scouts and citizens and contrabands tell me. If he was here, we ought to move up the Arkansas River at once, as the rainy season of this country has fairly set in, and the Arkansas and White Rivers have ample water for gunboats and transports. This point can then, with this programme, be abandoned. It is not the point for our base of operation on Little Rock, but Napoleon.

No possible danger can be apprehended to Missouri with Blunt, Herron, and Schofield advancing or stationary, if General Davidson was here with 10,000 more troops, and join me in the advance, first to Napoleon, and then to Post Arkansas. While at Napoleon, I am 110 miles nearer Vicksburg, where we might be needed by Grant and Sherman, if Holmes crosses over to Vicksburg. Therefore every military reason and consideration combine to urge that you send General Davidson here at once.

I therefore respectfully submit this view for your consideration. I far prefer that General Davidson be sent than that new forces supply the place of those about to start with General Sherman.

The guerrillas are all around here in small detachments, and if they see proper to attack this place in force, while I am so weak, they might inflict upon us serious injury, but I have no fears of their taking it.

I am, major, very respectfully, your obedient servant,

W. A. GORMAN,
Brigadier-General, Commanding, &c.

EXECUTIVE MANSION,
Washington, December 16, 1862.

Major-General CURTIS, *Saint Louis, Mo.:*

N. W. Watkins, of Jackson, Mo. (who is half-brother to Henry Clay), writes me that a colonel of ours has driven him from his home at Jackson. Will you please look into the case and restore the old man to his home, if the public interest will admit?

A. LINCOLN.

EXECUTIVE MANSION,
Washington, December 16, 1862.

Brig. Gen. H. H. SIBLEY,
Saint Paul, Minn.:

As you suggest, let the execution fixed for Friday, the 19th instant, be postponed to, and be done on, Friday, the 26th instant.

A. LINCOLN.

OPERATOR.—Please send this very carefully and accurately.

HEADQUARTERS,
Fort Scott, December 16, 1862.

Brigadier-General BLUNT,
Commanding District of Kansas, in the Field:

GENERAL: I have the honor to report to you that since my last report everything at this post and vicinity has passed off quietly. The guerrillas of the South Osage have been effectually scattered, some of them having been killed by my scouts, 8 of them taken prisoners, and the balance gone off. Of those, one by the name of Hartman, an old offender, was shot while trying to escape, and one equally as bad, by the name of Cinnamon, died in prison. The whole tribe of guerrillas on the Little Osage and Marais-des-Cygnes have been driven off, and gone south, on Horse Creek and Spring River. For the last week I have had forage trains out, and have brought in about 2,000 bushels of corn, and am busy at it still. Most of the Osage Indians are off on their hunt, and those remaining behind are quiet, although I have had to send for their chiefs and threaten pretty strongly to keep them so. I shall send a competent officer and a few men over to Humboldt and the Mission, as per your order of December 2, with instructions similar to those given Captain Stanhope while on that duty. Quite a number of officers have appeared here upon orders of the regimental surgeon and medical director, ordering them to report to general hospital at Leavenworth or at this post. The authority is insufficient without your approval, and hereafter I shall send all back to their commands. Of those that came up, most of them left before I could get to stop them, and I suppose are in Leavenworth now. We expected that you would return so that you might be with us at Christmas and New Year, and hope still that it will be so, but suppose that it will be regulated by events there.

I have to report that the last train up, in charge of Major Purington, lost two wagons and teams by being taken by the enemy near Neosho, and that, as near as I can learn, it was by carelessness. I shall gather the testimony in regard to the matter, and forward to you for your action. As these are the first and only teams lost on the road, I feel mortified at it, as I was in hopes to get through without losing a single wagon. I have also to report that I have stationed Company C, Third Wisconsin Cavalry, at Morris' Mill, on Dry Wood, for the protection of the loyal citizens in that neighborhood; also to prevent guerrillas from destroying the hay put up in that neighborhood for the use of the Government. It has given great satisfaction and restored confidence in the people. The troops under my immediate command are strictly ordered not to interfere with forage on the property of Union people, but the detachments escorting trains belonging to other commands are not so particular, and considerable complaint has been made of such.

The state of the whole country south of the Kansas is quiet, and no complaint of jayhawking to any extent. I hear but little from the Twelfth Regiment, and suppose they are acting upon orders received from you. I am not now informed where they are stationed. I am of the opinion, however, that a couple of good companies of cavalry would be more efficient than the whole regiment in that particular duty.

B. S. HENNING,
Major Third Wisconsin Cavalry.

HEADQUARTERS CENTRAL DISTRICT OF MISSOURI,
Jefferson City, December 17, 1862.

General CLINTON B. FISK, *Saint Louis, Mo.:*

GENERAL: On my return from Saint Louis, I found the trade in the western part of my district and the transportation that could be furnished by the Pacific Railroad monopolized by disloyalists, and that there was great complaint of the want of transportation by our Union friends and traders. I was, and am, satisfied that great injury was being done to the country, our cause, and our friends by reason thereof, and I believed it to be my imperative duty to check the evil at once. To enable me to do so effectually, I do not propose to allow any stock to be shipped past this place without a special permit from these headquarters, so that I may as far as possible prevent permits being given to those who are not known to be loyal. Messrs. Newland and Courtney are notoriously disloyal. I have a remonstrance in my office remonstrating against any permits to trade or ship stock being issued to these men, signed by the prominent Union men of the county of Pettis. Among the names I notice that of Colonel Spedden, of the Enrolled Militia, and Samuel Lowe, clerk of the circuit court of Pettis County.

You will pardon me for saying that the tone of your dispatch is hardly as kind as I should have expected, in this, that it insinuates wrong on my part in prohibiting these men from shipping hogs. You say that "I have the certificate of your provost-marshal at Sedalia that they are loyal men, and upon such certificate they were permitted to purchase 3,000 hogs for Henry Ames & Co., of this city." The provost-marshal at Sedalia is not my provost-marshal, nor am I bound for any blunder or fraud he may commit, should he unfortunately be guilty of the one or the other. They (Newland and Courtney) ought to have known whether they were loyal or disloyal men, and it is only adding insult to injury for them or their friends to claim any advantages on account of their fraud in procuring said certificate from the provost-marshal at Sedalia. Your statement is not exactly accurate when you say it was "upon such certificate they were permitted to purchase 3,000 hogs for Henry Ames & Co." No certificate or permit was required to enable them to purchase these hogs. There never was, by my authority, any prohibition against purchasing property. The restriction is against shipping it without a permit; but even if they had purchased upon the certificate, that fact has nothing to do with the case. No one objects to the purchase, nor do I understand them to complain of the purchase. It is the prohibition to ship that I understand is the cause of complaint.

Of Messrs. Ames & Co. I know nothing; but, as at present advised, I am satisfied that it would be prejudicial to the interests of the district to permit these hogs to be shipped. If Messrs. Ames & Co. are loyal merchants, they should not have held any commerce with traitors for the sake of filthy lucre. Such things are forbidden, and their loss in this case is but a just punishment for their misdeeds, and it will prove a warning to all evil-doers to turn from their ways, and the punishment so promptly executed upon them "will fire the Union heart," and convince the loyal men that reward for treason "is about played out" in this district, and that honest men who, with an unwavering faith, have looked to the flag of their country for protection will hereafter reap the reward due their fidelity. If Messrs. Ames & Co. are disloyal, as a matter of course their property should not be shipped.

Very respectfully, your obedient servant,

BEN. LOAN,
Brigadier-General, Missouri State Militia.

EXECUTIVE MANSION,
Washington, D. C., December 17, 1862.

Major-General CURTIS, *Saint Louis, Mo.:*

Could the civil authority be introduced into Missouri in lieu of the military to any extent with advantage and safety?

A. LINCOLN.

SAINT LOUIS, MO.,
December 17, 1862—9.15 p. m. (Received December 18, 5.45 p. m.)

His Excellency ABRAHAM LINCOLN,
President of the United States:

Dispatch received. The peace of this State rests on military power. To relinquish this power would be dangerous. It would allow rebels to rule some sections and ruin the Union men who have joined the military power to put down the rebellion. The civil authority is gradually coming into use, but sneaking rebels are in office, anxious to encourage new raids, and secure revenge for past military surveillance. It requires a considerable military force to keep things quiet in Missouri.

SAML. R. CURTIS,
Major-General, Commanding.

[DECEMBER 17, 1862.—For Gorman to Curtis, in reference to co-operation with Sherman, see Series I, Vol. XVII, Part II, p. 421.]

EXECUTIVE MANSION,
Washington, December 18, 1862.

Governor GAMBLE, *Saint Louis, Mo.:*

It is represented to me that the enrolled militia alone would now maintain law and order in all the counties of your State north of the Missouri River. If so, all other forces there might be removed south of the river or out of the State. Please post yourself, and give me your opinion upon this subject.

A. LINCOLN.

JEFFERSON CITY, MO., *December* 18, 1862.

ABRAHAM LINCOLN, *President:*

I can maintain law and order north of the Missouri River with the enrolled militia alone if they can be certainly provided for with subsistence, clothing, and pay for time they may be in actual service. Many of them are very poor. Taking other troops would help rather than hinder me. I would keep the smallest number in service that could protect the country.

H. R. GAMBLE.

WAR DEPARTMENT,
Washington, December 18, 1862.

Major-General CURTIS, *Saint Louis, Mo.:*

It is the President's wish that the Mississippi expedition be made as effective as possible by re-enforcements from Helena; but it is not intended to weaken your forces there, so as to endanger any necessary operation in Arkansas. If the movement into Arkansas cannot wait for the result of the other, it must be made; but it is inexpedient to undertake too much at once, if it can be avoided. Please state how many troops you propose to retain in Arkansas.

H. W. HALLECK,
General-in-Chief.

HDQRS. THIRD DIVISION, ARMY OF THE FRONTIER,
Camp Prairie Grove, December 18, 1862.

Major-General CURTIS, *Saint Louis, Mo.:*

There is no doubt but that Hindman has moved all his infantry force over the Arkansas River. The citizens of Van Buren and Fort Smith are leaving and traveling south. Hindman's headquarters are at Van Buren, while Marmaduke, with a cavalry force, is also on this side. The Arkansas River is very high; now is the time for Steele. Colonel Orme left for Van Buren yesterday with a flag of truce.

F. J. HERRON,
Brigadier-General.

HDQRS. 2D AND 3D DIVISIONS, ARMY OF THE FRONTIER,
Prairie Grove, December 18, 1862.

Major-General CURTIS, *Saint Louis, Mo.:*

The location of the rebel forces is settled beyond the question of a doubt. They are camped half way between Van Buren and Fort Smith, on the south side of the river. Two regiments of cavalry are on this side of the river, on outpost duty, and one regiment of infantry, with three pieces of artillery, is in Van Buren. Hindman and Marmaduke are determined to keep their own persons safe, and are with the main body of infantry on the other side of the river. They have given up all hope of getting any farther north, and say they will be satisfied if they can hold the Arkansas River. They are living on corn alone. Among the rebel officers killed in the battle of Prairie Grove was Lieutenant-Colonel Chappel, from Saint Louis County. He was in Steen's regiment. Governor Claib. Jackson died about ten days ago at Little Rock, of cancer. This may be old news to you, but has just reached us.

Our wounded are getting on well.

F. J. HERRON,
Brigadier-General.

HEADQUARTERS DISTRICT OF KANSAS,
Fort Leavenworth, Kans., December 18, 1862.

Maj. H. Z. CURTIS,
Assistant Adjutant-General, Department of the Missouri:

MAJOR: I have the honor to transmit herewith an official report from Major Kennedy, Twelfth Regiment Kansas Volunteers (paper marked A); also a report from Lieutenant-Colonel Abernathy, Eighth Kansas Volunteers,* with copy of order on which it was made attached (paper B), as well as the statements of several officers, in relation to the expedition of a portion of the Twelfth Regiment Kansas Volunteers into the State of Missouri, marked, respectively, as indicated in report B.

I am, sir, very respectfully, your obedient servant,

T. J. WEED,
Major and Acting Assistant Adjutant-General.

A.

HDQRS. TWELFTH REGIMENT KANSAS VOLUNTEERS,
Camp Blunt, Paola, Kans., December 4, 1862.

Maj. T. J. WEED, *Acting Assistant Adjutant-General:*

SIR: Having received orders from Colonel Adams upon the evening of the 19th of November to march the next morning, we left these headquarters accordingly, with a force consisting of Company K and portions of Companies B, D, and E, amounting to 230 men. Marching to Olathe, Johnson County, Kansas, we left a portion of Company K, and were joined by Company I and a portion of Company H, augmenting our force to 260 men, rank and file. We then marched to Kansas City, Mo. The design was to secure transportation down the river as far as Lexington, Mo., but, failing in this, we proceeded on the road to Lexington. Arriving at Big Blue, we pitched camp and sent out our foraging parties, with orders not to molest Union people or those having enrollment papers, but to confiscate all that was of immediate use to the Government belonging to rebels. A number of horses were brought in and 1 bushwhacker killed by these parties. On the morning of the 26th, we struck tents and proceeded on our march. Hearing of a camp of rebels in a secluded position, a detachment of 100 men was made to take them by surprise, if possible. This detachment, leaving the main command at 1 a. m., advanced upon the position indicated, where at about daylight were found 19 horses and a wagon load of household goods. Soon after, in another direction, were found 5 horses and a deserted camp. Near the last-named position 3 prisoners were taken, who were brought before a drum-head court-martial, and released upon the presentation of certificates of enrollment from Colonel Penick, Missouri State Militia. In the mean time men, women, and children of the colored population had come into our camp to the number of 60 or 70. Proceeding to the Sni Hills, we again pitched our camp. Soon after, our scouts brought intelligence of an advancing force, consisting of cavalry and artillery. We were ordered to form in line of battle. Two lines were formed; one of reserve, under command of Major Kennedy. Lieutenant-Colonel Hayes and Adjutant Lovejoy then proceeded to ascertain the nature of the advancing force. Finding they bore the Stars and Stripes, and concluding they were Missouri State Militia (as a force upon request had passed through our camp the night previous), such intelligence was taken to

---

*See Chipman to Blunt, January 15, 1863, Part II, p. 46.

our commanding officer, Colonel Adams. An officer representing himself as belonging to the staff of Brigadier-General Vaughan then advanced and called for the commanding officer of our force. Colonel Adams advanced, and, after a short conversation, the above-named staff officer returned to his command. Soon after, the following order was received by Colonel Adams:

To the person in command of the forces in front of this position:

SIR: As the commander of this military district, I desire to know by what authority you have marched into it.

I am, sir, your obedient servant,

RICH'D C. VAUGHAN,
Brigadier-General, Sixth Military District of Missouri.

In reply thereto, Colonel Adams forwarded to General Vaughan orders received from General Blunt, dated October 9, 1862; also orders from General Curtis, dated October 19, 1862. General Vaughan then forwarded the following communication:

NOVEMBER 27, 1862.

Colonel ADAMS:

SIR: As I can see nothing in the orders of General Blunt authorizing the course you have taken, and as my orders are positive, I am bound to demand the surrender of all property taken from citizens of this State, and that the negroes taken from citizens of Jackson and La Fayette Counties be forthwith turned out of your lines, as there is no organized enemy either in Jackson or La Fayette. I further require that you at once march your force beyond the limits of this State. If this proposal is acceded to, I will send an officer to arrange the conditions. I retain the orders sent only to take a copy, after which they will be immediately returned.

I am, sir, obediently,

RICH'D C. VAUGHAN,
Brigadier-General, Commanding.

Colonel Adams immediately forwarded to General Vaughan the following reply:

HEADQUARTERS TWELFTH REGIMENT KANSAS VOLUNTEERS,
In the Field, November 27, 1862.

Brigadier-General VAUGHAN:

SIR: Your note is received. All the demands therein made will be complied with at the earliest opportunity, except that portion relating to negroes. As they came within my lines voluntarily, I do not see fit to order them out; they are, however, at liberty to do as they choose.

CHAS. W. ADAMS,
Colonel, Commanding Twelfth Regiment Kansas Volunteers.

In reply to this, Colonel Adams received the following from General Vaughan:

Colonel ADAMS:

SIR: Your note is received. The demand relative to the negroes must be complied with. The matter of disagreement relating to your orders from General Blunt and General Curtis is a matter which can be more readily settled elsewhere than here.

I am, sir, your obedient servant,

RICH'D C. VAUGHAN,
Brigadier-General, Commanding.

P. S.—As it is already late, I must require that you permit no portion of the property and negroes, above alluded to, to leave your lines.

Colonel Adams replied by the following note:

HEADQUARTERS TWELFTH REGIMENT KANSAS VOLUNTEERS,
In the Field, November 27, 1862.

Brig. Gen. R. C. VAUGHAN:

SIR: My guards are out, and I shall follow your orders relating to keeping whatever is within my lines here. I am subject to arrest from you, and choose a trial by court-martial rather than turn the negroes out of my camp. I do not do this, believe me, General Vaughan, out of disrespect to you, but because I believe it to be contrary to a general order from the War Department to do so.

Very respectfully, your obedient servant,

CHAS. W. ADAMS,
Colonel Twelfth Regiment Kansas Volunteers.

By request (through an orderly), Colonel Adams called upon General Vaughan at his headquarters, where he (Colonel Adams) was arrested and ordered to report to Saint Louis, Mo., on the 15th of December, 1862. Lieutenant-Colonel Hayes then assumed command. The demands previously made upon Colonel Adams were now made upon Lieutenant-Colonel Hayes.

On the morning of the 28th, Lieutenant-Colonel Hayes proceeded to comply with the above-named demands from General Vaughan, except that portion relative to the negroes. This being done, the order to march was given. Proceeding but a short distance, the column halted, and an altercation, to the following effect, took place between Lieutenant-Colonel Hayes and General Vaughan:

General VAUGHAN. If you will turn these slaves out of your lines, you will save time and trouble, for we are strong enough to take them.

Lieutenant-Colonel HAYES. No consideration of personal safety will ever induce me to turn a slave back to his rebel master.

General VAUGHAN. Do you dare to disobey your superior officer?

Colonel HAYES. I dare to do that very thing; if you take these negroes, you must take them by force.

General Vaughan's artillery was then brought in range of our column, his cavalry being stationed in our front and rear and on our right flank. A detachment advancing possessed themselves of the colored women and children, with their effects, the men making a flank movement "for the brush." This being done, Lieutenant-Colonel Hayes received notice of his arrest, with an order to report at Saint Louis on the 15th of December, 1862. I, being next in rank, then assumed command of the detachment, and with it marched *en route* for these headquarters, accompanied by 1 captain and 12 men of Colonel Penick's command, Missouri State Militia, acting as a rear guard. Notwithstanding former arrests, my scouts were ever vigilant and on the alert. Bushwhackers were, in accordance with orders from General Blunt, pursued to the death, 3 being killed near the head of the Blue River. Also near the same position was found a deserted camp, showing signs of a hasty retreat; several horses were secured—in all, 22. Several negroes, who had previously "taken to the brush," rejoined our command ere we reached the Kansas line.

THOMAS H. KENNEDY,
Major, Commanding Twelfth Regiment Kansas Volunteers.

B.

FORT LEAVENWORTH, *December* 17, 1862.

Brigadier-General BLUNT:

GENERAL: In pursuance to Special Orders, No. 160, from your headquarters, directing me to proceed to Westport and other places in Missouri and Kansas, for the purpose of investigating the late expedition of Colonel Adams, of the Twelfth Kansas Volunteers, I have the honor to report:

I first visited Independence, Mo., and took the statement of Colonel Penick, Fifth Missouri [State] Militia Cavalry (paper marked C). I next visited Paola, Kans., and there took the statement of Major Kennedy, Twelfth Regiment Kansas Volunteers (paper marked D); also statement of Lieutenant Town, Twelfth Regiment Kansas Volunteers (paper marked E); also statement of Captain Ashby (paper marked F). I next visited the town of Olathe, Kans., where I took the statement of Lieutenant-Colonel Hayes, Twelfth Regiment Kansas Volunteers (paper marked G). I found Colonel Adams at Fort Leavenworth upon my return, and submit his statement with the others (papers marked H and I).

I regret to report that I was unable to see Brigadier-General Vaughan, Enrolled Missouri Militia, he having left Independence before I reached there.

All the statements herewith submitted are as I received them from the respective parties.

I have the honor to remain, general, your obedient servant,

J. L. ABERNATHY,
Lieutenant-Colonel Eighth Kansas Volunteers.

SPECIAL ORDERS, No. 160. } HEADQUARTERS DISTRICT OF KANSAS, *Fort Leavenworth, Kans., December* 8, 1862.

* * * * * * *

III. Lieutenant-Colonel Abernathy, Eighth Kansas Volunteers, will, on receipt hereof, proceed to Westport, Independence, Paola, and such other places as may be necessary, and make a thorough investigation of the late expedition into the State of Missouri of a portion of the Twelfth Kansas Volunteers, under command of Col. Charles W. Adams. The statements of all the officers concerned, as well as those familiar with the facts, will be taken, and a full report of all the circumstances attending the expedition and the results of the same, accompanied by the evidence on which it is based, will be made to these headquarters as soon as practicable.

By order of Brigadier-General Blunt:

T. J. WEED,
Major and Acting Assistant Adjutant-General.

C.

Statement of Colonel [*W. R.*] *Penick.*

On the 22d November I received intelligence that there were some men coming into Missouri by way of Kansas City, and wishing to ascertain its character, I issued an order to Lieutenant Crandall to go to the camp of this force and ascertain under whose orders they were acting, and, if not acting under the orders of Generals Curtis or Loan, to order them to leave the State. Lieutenant Crandall reported to me, after visiting the camp on Blue, that the camp was commanded by Colonel Adams, Twelfth Kansas Volunteers, and that the force amounted to about 400 men, comprised of whites, negroes, and Indians. He told me that Colonel Adams said he was acting under the orders of General Blunt directly, and indirectly under the orders of General Curtis; stated further that he intended passing through Independence, and would call and see me. I felt satisfied that the Kansas troops were here on business, and that the colonel would call and see me, as he had promised. In this, however, I was mistaken. The colonel passed through without seeing me. In a few hours reports began to come in from Union and secesh men that the Kansas troops were taking property indiscriminately. I then sent for Captain Meader, Enrolled Missouri Militia, who is well acquainted all through the county, to ascertain if the persons bringing in these reports were reliable. He stated to me that they might be depended upon. I then telegraphed the facts to Governor Gamble, and asked him what I should do. He gave me no answer. Reports of depredations committed by the troops continued to come in the balance of the day. The next morning it was ascertained that they were taking the property of the Enrolled Missouri Militia. I permitted Captain Meader to send a number of his men home to try to protect their property. Being fully satisfied that the Government would not indorse acts of this kind, I telegraphed General Loan the facts, and asked him what I should do. In a short time I received a dispatch from General Vaughan, of Enrolled Missouri Militia, stating that he had been authorized by General Loan to disperse the Kansas troops, and asked my co-operation.

About 4 o'clock that evening I moved with all my available force, about 110 men, and overtook the Kansas troops near Hambright's, on the Lexington road. I kept in sight or near them until the next morning, when General Vaughan arrived with his force, about 370 men. Just before General Vaughan arrived, I came upon the Kansas troops, drawn up in line of battle across the road, their artillery toward me. As General Vaughan arrived, I dismounted my men and formed in line, facing them. General Vaughan came up and formed in line on my left, with two pieces of artillery. The Kansas troops then stacked their arms and went to their tents. The soldiers and negroes reported along the route that they intended to fight me when I came up with them. I had no disposition to fight the troops under Colonel Adams, because they were United States troops. I told my men this, and cautioned them to make no threats nor do anything imprudent. I did not read the correspondence between General Vaughan and Colonel Adams, but understood that Colonel Adams had agreed to give up all the property taken in the State except negroes. Next morning, however, Colonel Adams marched off with all the property. General Vaughan ordered me to take my men and stop them. As my men were about 2 miles away, I went alone, and prevailed upon the officer in command to halt his men. This was about 1 mile from the place they had encamped. General Vaughan then arrested Colonel Adams, and Lieutenant-Colonel Hayes assumed command. In a short time Colonel McFerran came up and stated that he was sent by General Vaughan to take all the property from the command that they had taken in the State. He also assured the officers of the Kansas troops that he understood the orders from the War Department on the subject of negroes, and that he was the last man that would return one to his master. They informed me that they would not resist. The property was then taken from the Kansas troops. I saw about 100 horses taken and several wagons. I have no doubt the horses had been taken from rebels; they belonged to citizens of La Fayette and Jackson Counties, and had been concealed in the brush for fear they would be confiscated. Many of them were branded U. S. when they were returned. I was then ordered by General Vaughan to escort the Kansas troops out of the State, and went with them 3 miles, when it was agreed that Captain Vansant and 10 men should go with them to the lines. The troops were under command of Major Kennedy, Lieutenant-Colonel Hayes having been placed in arrest by General Vaughan at the time the property and negroes were taken from the command. I then returned to Independence with the balance of my command. After reaching camp, I found an order there from General Sloan [Loan], ordering me to disperse the Kansas troops. The order came in my absence. I herewith submit the report of Captain Vansant,* who accompanied the troops to the State line.

D.

Statement of Maj. T. H. Kennedy.

I think that Colonel Adams received information on the 19th of November which led him to suppose that there were parties of guerrillas between Lexington and Independence. He also had some information of some artillery being concealed near Lexington. We marched from camp on the 20th and arrived at Kansas City on the 22d; failed to get transportation down the river, and started by way of Independence. On the night of the 23d, a man came into camp from Colonel Penick, then in command at Independence, Mo., and stated that he had heard that there was a band of 30 jayhawkers encamped on the Blue, and that it was the request of Colonel Penick that they leave the State at once. He showed no orders, and we had no official notice of his being an officer; he did not wear any uniform.

Next day we passed through Independence, and camped near Blue Mills. We learned that there were quite a number of rebels concealed a few miles from camp. Colonel Adams went out to try and capture them. He found their camp, and captured quite a number of horses and a quantity of camp equipage. Some horses were brought in that were afterward claimed by the Enrolled Missouri Militia. These were always returned upon presentation of their enrollment papers. We next moved to Pink Hill, where we encamped. Soon after, word was brought into camp that the Enrolled Missouri Militia were after us. Soon General Vaughan, Enrolled Missouri Militia, came up. General Vaughan demanded by what authority we were in Missouri.

The following is the correspondence that passed between General Vaughan and Colonel Adams:

To the person in command of the forces in front of this position:

SIR: As the commander of this military district, I desire to know by what authority you marched into it.

RICH'D C. VAUGHAN,
Brigadier-General, Sixth Military District of Missouri.

Colonel Adams replied by forwarding to General Vaughan the orders he had received from General Blunt and General Curtis. (Papers marked I.) The following is a copy of reply received:

NOVEMBER 27, 1862.

Colonel ADAMS:

SIR: As I can see nothing in the orders of General Blunt authorizing the course you have pursued, and as my orders from the commander of this district are positive, I am bound to demand the surrender of all property taken from citizens of this State, and that the negroes taken from the citizens of Jackson and La Fayette Counties be forthwith turned out of your lines. As there is no organized enemy in Jackson or La Fay-

---

* See p. 824.

ette Counties, I further require that you at once march your force beyond the limits of this State. If this proposal is acceded to, I will send an officer to arrange the conditions. I retain the order sent, only to take a copy, after which it will be immediately returned.

I am, sir, obediently,

RICH'D C. VAUGHAN,
Brigadier-General, Commanding.

Colonel Adams immediately forwarded to General Vaughan the following reply:

HEADQUARTERS TWELFTH KANSAS VOLUNTEERS,
In the Field, November 27, 1862.

Brigadier-General VAUGHAN:

SIR: Your note is received. All the demands therein made will be complied with at the earliest opportunity, except that portion relating to negroes. As they came voluntarily, I do not see fit to order them out; they are, however, at liberty to do as they choose.

CHAS. W. ADAMS,
Colonel, Commanding.

CHARLES J. LOVEJOY, *Adjutant.*

In reply to this, Colonel Adams received the following:

Colonel ADAMS:

SIR: Your note is received. The demand relative to negroes must be complied with. The matter of disagreement in relation to your orders from General Blunt and General Curtis is a matter which can be more readily settled elsewhere than here.

I am, sir, your obedient servant,

RICH'D C. VAUGHAN,
Brigadier-General, Commanding.

P. S.—As it is already late, I must require that you permit no portion of the property and negroes above alluded to to leave your lines.

Colonel Adams replied as follows:

HEADQUARTERS TWELFTH KANSAS VOLUNTEERS,
[*In the Field, November 27, 1862.*]

Brigadier-General VAUGHAN:

SIR: My guards are out, and I shall follow your order relating to keeping whatever is within my lines here. I am subject to arrest from you, and choose a trial by court-martial rather than turn the negroes out of my camp. I do not do this, believe me, General Vaughan, out of disrespect to you, but because I believe it to be contrary to a general order from the War Department.

Very respectfully, your obedient servant,

CHAS. W. ADAMS,
Colonel Twelfth Kansas Volunteers.

By request of General Vaughan, Colonel Adams then visited him at his headquarters, and was put in arrest by General Vaughan, and ordered to report to General Curtis, at Saint Louis, on the 15th of December, 1862.

The demands previously made upon Colonel Adams were now made upon Lieutenant Colonel Hayes, the next in command.

On the morning of the 28th, Lieutenant-Colonel Hayes proceeded to comply with the demand of General Vaughan, except that portion relating to negroes. This being done, the order to march was given. We proceeded but a short distance when the command was halted, and the following conversation took place between Lieutenant-Colonel Hayes and General Vaughan:

General VAUGHAN. If you will turn those slaves out of your lines, you will save time and trouble, for we are strong enough to take them.

Lieutenant-Colonel HAYES. No consideration of personal safety will ever induce me to turn a slave back to his rebel master.

General VAUGHAN. Do you dare to disobey your superior officer?

Lieutenant-Colonel HAYES. I dare do that very thing. If you take those negroes, you must take them by force.

General Vaughan's artillery was then brought to bear on our lines, his cavalry being in our rear and on our right flank. A detachment then advanced and possessed themselves of the negroes and children, with their effects. This being done, Lieutenant-Colonel Hayes was placed in arrest by General Vaughan, and ordered to report to General Curtis, at Saint Louis, on the 15th of December, 1862. Major Kennedy then took command of the Twelfth Regiment, and marched it for the headquarters, at Paola, Kans. A captain and 12 men of Colonel Penick's command escorted the regiment to the State line.

As we returned, we came upon a deserted camp of bushwhackers. Three persons belonging to the camp were killed, and 20 horses taken. The command arrived at Paola, Kans., on the 2d day of December, 1862.

—

E.

Statement of Lieutenant [M. L.] Town.

The Twelfth Kansas Volunteers started from camp at Paola on the 20th of November. I knew nothing of the object of the expedition, nor of the information upon which it was based. We passed through Kansas City and Independence, Mo. We took rebel property whereever we found it. Some of the property was returned upon presentation of enrollment papers from whom it was taken. Quite a number of slaves came within our lines; they came of their own accord. We did not find any party of the enemy. While encamped at Pink Hill, General Vaughan, Enrolled Missouri Militia, came up with about 400 men and examined our camp; said he understood we were a band of jayhawkers and Indians; said he did not propose fighting us, as we carried the Stars and Stripes; said they had no doubt the property we had taken belonged to secesh, but that they had orders to take it, and must do so. They then took all the property, and even some that we had taken with us from our camp. They also demanded the negroes. I know nothing of the conversation which took place between Colonel Adams and General Vaughan. Colonel Adams was placed in arrest, and Lieutenant-Colonel Hayes took command of the regiment. Soon after, General Vaughan sent and took from us all the property and the negroes that had come into our camp. I heard a number of officers and men express themselves dissatisfied with the course General Vaughan had pursued. Before starting for Kansas City, Lieutenant-Colonel Hayes was arrested, and Major Kennedy took command of the regiment. We then marched back to the State line, escorted by a portion of General Vaughan's command.

—

F.

Statement of Captain [G. W.] Ashby.

Colonel Adams left camp at Paola on the 20th of November with about 210 men. The object of the expedition, as I understood it, was to pursue bushwhackers. I have heard the statement of Lieutenant Town, and agree with him in his statement. The facts there stated are correct, to the best of my knowledge. I have nothing to add to his statement.

G.

Statement of Lieut. Col. Josiah E. Hayes.

I know nothing of the information upon which the late expedition of the Twelfth Kansas Volunteers was based.

After we had started, Colonel Adams informed me that we were going to Lexington, to capture parties of guerrillas and punish parties harboring them. We left camp on about the 20th of November, passed through Kansas City, and encamped on the Blue. In the night a man, representing himself as coming from Colonel Penick, came into camp and inquired what command we were, and where we were going. Said he had been sent by Colonel Penick to order us out of the State, but he would modify the order, and request us to leave. Colonel Adams told him he would pass through Independence, and would call and see Colonel Penick. I do not think Colonel Adams called on Colonel Penick. As we passed through Independence, we did not stop in town. We encamped that night at Blue Mills. We lay all next day at Blue Mills. The next day we moved on toward Lexington. While at Blue Mills, a number of horses, said to belong to rebels, were brought into camp. Some of the horses were returned upon presentation of enrollment papers by the parties from whom they were taken. The men were not allowed to take anything from houses. A negro came into camp that night, and reported that there were 12 men concealed about 5 miles from our camp. Colonel Adams and myself started in the night with a party to try and capture them. We succeeded in finding their camp, but did not find the men. We got 10 horses, with bridles and saddles complete. The next night we camped near Pink Hill. About 3 o'clock in the afternoon a negro came into camp and reported that the Enrolled Missouri Militia was after us, and was going to clear us out. The men of the command were drawn up in line, and I went out to ascertain what force was in our front. When I ascertained that it was General Vaughan's command, I returned and informed Colonel Adams of the fact, and he rode forward to meet the officers of General Vaughan's command. I know nothing about what passed between Colonel Adams and General Vaughan. Colonel Adams was soon after placed in arrest, and I assumed [command] of the regiment. Next morning a demand was made upon me to deliver over all the property we had taken from citizens of Missouri. I replied that the order should be complied with. Major Briggs [Biggers] was to receive the property. I ordered Lieutenant Shively to turn over all the property to Major Briggs [Biggers]. While it was being turned over I received notice that the order before received was intended to include negroes. I replied that I did not consider negroes as property, and should not give them up; that if they took the negroes it must be by force. General Vaughan then ordered me placed in arrest. Major Kennedy then took command of the Twelfth Regiment. I do not know how General Vaughan got possession of the negroes. They took them from our lines.

Nothing of interest transpired on our way back to Kansas. We arrived at Olathe on the 29th of November.

H.

Statement of Col. Charles W. Adams.

On the 19th of November I received information that a party of guerrillas was between Lexington and Independence, Mo.

In pursuance to special orders (herewith inclosed, marked I) from

General Blunt, I marched on the 20th of November from Paola, Kans., with 250 men of my command. I passed through Kansas City and camped on the Blue. The same evening a man came into camp, representing that he had been sent by Colonel Penick to ascertain the character of the force then marching into Missouri, its destination, and object. He showed me no orders, nor did he wear any uniform. I stated my orders to him, and told him I would call on Colonel Penick as I passed through Independence. I expected to meet a cordial reception from Colonel Penick, but when I saw no evidence of anything of the kind, I passed through without stopping. I did not like to halt my men in the town. I encamped that night at or near Blue Mills. I was here informed that a small party of bushwhackers were concealed a short distance from my camp, and determined to try and capture them. I had their camp surrounded, and found 10 horses and quite a lot of camp equipage, but no men. One of the men was afterward shot by Colonel Penick's command. I next camped at Pink Hill. General Vaughan, Enrolled Missouri Militia, came up with 400 men soon after I got into camp, and demanded that I should turn over to him all the property I had taken from citizens, and turn the negroes out of camp, and leave the State forthwith. I told General Vaughan that I would comply with the demand, except that part which referred to negroes; told him as they came into my lines of their own free will, I should not drive them out. He then stated that all his demands must be complied with. I told him I was subject to arrest from him, and would prefer trial by court-martial rather than disobey an order from the War Department. I was then placed in arrest, and Lieutenant-Colonel Hayes assumed command of the regiment.

—

I.

HEADQUARTERS DISTRICT OF KANSAS,
In the Field, October 9, 1862.

Col. C. W. ADAMS,
Commanding Twelfth Regiment Kansas Volunteers:

SIR: Immediately on receipt of this, you are directed to dispose the forces under your command so as to cover the eastern border of the State, from the Kansas to the Osage Rivers. It is confidently believed that you can, by a system of patrols and signals, prevent the ingress of bands of Missouri guerrillas who have heretofore been devastating that portion of the State, and by activity and courage drive them from their hiding places in the border counties of Missouri. You will carefully instruct your men that the persons, property, and rights of the people of Kansas, and the loyal people of Missouri, should be held sacred, and any infraction should be promptly and severely punished. Parties sent into Missouri should be placed under prudent and active officers, with instructions to pursue bushwhackers to the death. After you have matured your plans and disposed your forces, you should issue a proclamation to the citizens of Johnson and other border counties of Kansas and Missouri who have fled their homes to return thereto, promising them safety and protection. To you and the troops under your command is intrusted the delicate and important duty of restoring peace to the border between the points named. You should communicate frequently with the military authorities at Fort Leavenworth and Fort Scott.

Keep your troops well in hand, that they may not be cut off in detail, and that they may be concentrated at any given point without delay or confusion.

Major Henning, Third Wisconsin Cavalry, provost-marshal for the District of Kansas south of the Kansas River, will, from time to time, issue such orders to you as he may deem necessary in relation to the disposition of your forces, &c.

You will immediately, on receipt of this order, report by letter to Major Henning, stating your force, station, &c.

By order of Brigadier-General Blunt:

THOS. MOONLIGHT,
Assistant Adjutant-General.

EXECUTIVE MANSION,
Washington, December 19, 1862—10.10 a. m.

Major-General CURTIS, *Saint Louis, Mo.:*

Hon. W. A. Hall, member of Congress here, tells me, and Governor Gamble telegraphs me, that quiet can be maintained in all the counties north of the Missouri River by the Enrolled Militia. Confer with Governor Gamble and telegraph me.

A. LINCOLN,
President.

SAINT LOUIS, *December* 19, 1862.

President ABRAHAM LINCOLN, *Washington:*

Only two skeleton regiments, United States troops, north of the river. The Governor is absent. Some Enrolled Militia; not so reliable. I will write you.*

SAML. R. CURTIS,
Major-General.

SAINT LOUIS, MO., *December* 19, 1862—1 p. m.
(Received 7 p. m.)

Maj. Gen. H. W. HALLECK,
General-in-Chief:

In answer to yours of yesterday, I proposed to furnish all General Sherman calls for from Helena—12,000—leaving about 13,000 to operate in Arkansas. This last force I propose to move cautiously till the down-river move is accomplished. Blunt's force in Arkansas—about 18,000—is still at the north base of Boston Mountains, scouts extending near to Arkansas River. I wish to draw these forces toward each other as fast as circumstances will permit. A move from Helena will prevent Holmes and Hindman massing forces against Blunt, if nothing more, and must go cautiously, awaiting the move and return of down-river force. Will this plan suit you?

SAML. R. CURTIS,
Major-General.

---

* See p. 853.

HEADQUARTERS DEPARTMENT OF THE MISSOURI,
Saint Louis, Mo., December 19, 1862.

Brig. Gen. W. A. GORMAN, *Helena, Ark.:*

GENERAL: I have just received three letters from you relating to special movements, which I have read with care, but must answer very briefly. All my movements now are in reference to others, which bear upon the force at Helena. The down-river move must be arranged so we can send at any moment about 12,000 troops to Vicksburg without any intermediate delay. My old affection for a post on the island of Armagedden must be matured and accommodated at another time. My Arkansas movements will require the Helena force to move directly west, up White River, I suppose, and trains and boats will have to co-operate. Further particulars will be explained by Colonel Chipman. As to new batteries, I have been urging more and better for the last three months, in vain. Not a gun has been sent to this department, and we must make the very best of what we have. The ordnance bureau is the most immovable affair on this continent. Very recent dispatches from General Sherman seem to call only for infantry in the down-river expedition. If so, it will leave a better force for interior movements, where cavalry and artillery are necessary and can be used even in surplus numbers. But by this sending away infantry only, we must be embarrassed in the proper organization. Blair's brigade has been promised to him as a kind of specialty, but other troops may be arranged, as far as possible, to suit the requisition of the down-river commander, who will desire more infantry. I do not understand how General Hovey gets away so easily. General Osterhaus will soon be here to join you. He will desire his German troops as far as the service will admit, and I hope your organization will accommodate him as far as possible.

I am, general, very truly, yours,

SAML. R. CURTIS,
Major-General.

PILOT KNOB, *December* 19, 1862—8 a. m.

General CURTIS:

I arrived here late last night from my reconnaissance. Forced up this way by the unprecedented high water, and out of supplies. The bridge at Black River, built by Benton, is swept away. I have selected Van Buren as the depot, instead of Patterson, and also as the point of crossing on Current River; and the army is now moving forward to that point. I intend supplying it by the way of Centreville and Barnesville. It is a better road; is the old State road from Saint Louis to Van Buren; is 16 miles shorter than by Patterson, and saves two bridges and one ferry. I shall build a good ferry-boat at Van Buren, as there are two saw-mills near, and timber plenty. I shall keep my cavalry at Barnesville until ready to move, as that country is rich in corn. The new route has the advantage of not being stripped of supplies. The Black River was a great obstacle on the Patterson route, but is now crossed where it has three forks.

Cannot Warren move on to Eleven Points when my troops reach Van Buren? I send up my inspector-general, Major Lippert, with my map, who will explain in person better than a report. Gray tells me you said his regiment could go with me if you had a good one to replace it. I will exchange the Twenty-third Iowa, of my command, for it, as I am compelled to leave two companies of it as a garrison to Patterson, and the regiment is not a hardy one, nor in good health. Shall I order up the Twenty-third Iowa before it moves? Gray authorizes me to say he declines the adjutant-generalship of the State, if he can go with me. I will push everything here but the land-slide.

DAVIDSON,
Brigadier-General.

HEADQUARTERS DEPARTMENT OF THE MISSOURI,
Saint Louis, December 19, 1862.

Brigadier-General HERRON,
Prairie Grove, Ark.:

GENERAL: I am in receipt of your interesting letter of the 12th, which I would like to have published as your report, but I see some remarks concerning General Blunt's being overreached by Hindman and something about Colonel Wright which would not do to publish; besides, I suppose your report will be carefully made out and come through General Blunt, who, in the absence of General Schofield, is the commander of the Army of the Frontier. I hope to get both reports soon, so they may be entered on my battle-book and forwarded to Washington, with such recommendations as I think right in the premises.

Due credit is given to you and Blunt both, although you had the long, hard day's work. It was a signal victory, but I regret exceedingly the trick of Hindman prevented you sending the cavalry to harass the retreating foe. It was a great outrage of the laws of war to cover a retreat by such use of a flag of truce.

General Schofield, having recovered, goes back to take command. He is, of course, deeply mortified at not being in the fight.

You have probably done all you can do until I can move up the Arkansas and White Rivers to co-operate with you. This, I think, cannot be long, but everything has to await the great move down the Mississippi.

I congratulate you again, general, on your success, in which your numerous friends seem delighted.

I remain, general, very truly, yours,

SAML. R. CURTIS,
Major-General.

HEADQUARTERS DEPARTMENT OF THE MISSOURI,
Saint Louis, December 20, 1862.

His Excellency President LINCOLN:

In regard to your telegraphic inquiry as to the propriety of relying entirely on the Enrolled Militia in Northern Missouri, I proceed to enlarge on my telegraphic reply.

We have just driven the rebels out of Missouri, and hold them south by a force almost continuous along the southern border of the State. Their anxiety exists to return to Missouri, where the wealthy secessionists in many neighborhoods are ready to receive and replenish them. In such neighborhoods the pro-slavery influence seeks to exclude the Union troops, hoping to hold their negroes better under the Enrolled Militia, many of whom are commanded by pro-slavery officers. I try to study the surrounding elements, and move troops away just as fast as I think the safety of community will permit, and will probably soon withdraw all or nearly all the volunteers from Northern Missouri. Another trouble, however, intervenes. The Enrolled Militia when in actual service are fed by the United States, and levy contributions from the secessionists to indemnify themselves for losses. It becomes necessary to watch these influences, to prevent feeding unnecessary or false musters, and restrain excesses which avarice or revenge may induce. To check these, I may find it necessary to preserve a small regular volunteer force. As the rebels starve out in Arkansas, they sneak back with recruiting papers into Missouri, and in some instances they have enlisted in Enrolled Militia, who have joined them with muskets furnished by the Governor. General Loan, commanding the Central District (recently elected to Congress), is especially troubled and distrustful in this regard. Our best friends are more afraid of our kindness than our severity. The least clemency shown to prisoners seems to create alarm and remonstrance, and communities require the confinement of several hundred troublesome spirits that have been sent to prison from Northern Missouri. Keep them confined is the sentiment of the people, and the Enrolled Militia are the most desperate in this demand. Force, Mr. President—military power—is still the main dependence, and whether it be United States or State troops that represent that power it does not matter much, as the expense in one way or another mainly falls on the United States Government.

So far I have got along without much difficulty with mixed forces, but I have required of my officers and acted myself with great caution and courtesy toward State troops, for fear of trouble.

The Governor seems to desire the sole control of the Enrolled Militia, and partial control of the 10,000 Missouri State Militia, organized under Orders 96, of last year.

I, and all good Union men, dread the least conflict of sovereignties, which has been the cursed argument that has invoked and fostered this infernal rebellion. As commander of the department, I claim, but have not announced or exercised, the right to control any and all military organizations within my domain whenever they take up arms. In time of war, this paramount sovereignty of the United States should be maintained, to prevent bickerings and possible conflicts.

I suppose Governor Gamble would traverse this, and I am inclined to think so, because, in carrying out your arrangement to make the commander of the department a major-general of militia, he inserted words in my commission confining my functions to the volunteers mustered in under Orders 96, thereby attempting to exclude my authority over the Enrolled Militia. The theory of this is pernicious, as it places forces in my command capable of controlling parts of it; but I have so far had very little trouble, as the general resolve of the masses to stand by the old flag is the battle-cry of all. But as we go on to subdue, and to enroll and arm the militia in the country, the danger of variance will increase, and the question of national sovereignty must, in some way, be so clearly settled as to avoid eternal discord and strife.

The object of all this is to present to Your Excellency the delicacy of my position, and the danger of hasty action favorable to rebels, who seem inspired with ideas of a triumph over acts of generosity. The moment a rebel surrenders I am ready to desist, and wherever a community can maintain the peace with civil laws and the Enrolled Militia, I shall gladly relinquish military authority, and, on all occasions, I shall cordially carry out the wishes of Your Excellency to the best of my ability.

I have the honor to remain, Your Excellency's most obedient servant,

SAML. R. CURTIS,

Major-General.

WASHINGTON, *December* 20, 1862.

Major-General CURTIS:

You can use the forces at Helena as you propose. The troops which join the Mississippi expedition will be temporarily under the general direction of General Grant.

H. W. HALLECK,
General-in-Chief.

HEADQUARTERS DEPARTMENT OF THE MISSOURI,
Saint Louis, Mo., December 20, 1862.

Rear-Admiral DAVID D. PORTER:

DEAR SIR: I am again informed that the Arkansas is rising, and I am sure the White River must be, as the tributaries are flush.

I have quite an army near Van Buren, and wish, if possible, to unite that force with the Helena force, or I want to occupy the rebel force at Little Rock, so as to prevent it from massing against General Blunt, who is in Northwestern Arkansas, near Van Buren.

The least move toward Little Rock will be an advantage, and something may be done without impairing the main move down the river, which we must regard as primary. My object in writing is to ask your co-operation, by furnishing light-draught gunboats to go up either the Arkansas or White River, or both, to help clean them out and frighten the rebels out of Northern Arkansas. I do not expect to finish the job until the force which goes down to Vicksburg may be able to return, but a commencement toward Little Rock will do good, and may deceive the rebels in regard to your down-river move.

General Gorman will confer with you.

I am, sir, very respectfully, your obedient servant,

SAML. R. CURTIS,
Major-General.

HEADQUARTERS DEPARTMENT OF THE MISSOURI,
Saint Louis, December 20, 1862.

Brig. Gen. W. A. GORMAN, *Helena, Ark.*:

GENERAL: I want the interior move toward Little Rock made immediately, but, as I have promised the down-river expedition certain aid, it is to be subordinate to that. Twelve thousand are to go down river; the remainder must hold Helena and move west. I will send down forces to augment the strength. You will move cautiously interior, but try to occupy the attention of Holmes, so as to prevent him from sending his force to Hindman. For this purpose begin to move immediately. There are said to be twelve regiments of rebels at Old Post, eight near Brownsville, and a gun on the railroad, mounted on platform car. I name these as particular objects of attention. There are also eight or ten regiments near Brownsville, and three batteries near Little Rock. It is also said that the Arkansas is high at Van Buren. I suppose you may be able to get Rear-Admiral Porter to co-operate by sending some boats up either White River or the Arkansas, or both. I will write him also. Understand me, I want to co-operate with Blunt, and perhaps with Davidson, but you are to move slowly and cautiously, in view of probable help, which is to return after the Mississippi is cleaned out. At the same time it is not necessary to wait the move down river. Your quartermaster must gather up transport boats of suitable draught, and they must be protected by planking pilot-house and placing bales of hay around boilers and engines. I want to hear from you as soon and often as possible. This immediate move toward Little Rock will perhaps divert from the main move down the Mississippi, besides securing ulterior objects, to which I have alluded. I have just spoken to the quartermaster to send down more light-draught boats to aid your movements up the rivers. I will write again soon.

I am, general, very truly, your obedient servant,

SAML. R. CURTIS,
Major-General.

GENERAL ORDERS, No. 32. } HDQRS. DEPARTMENT OF THE MISSOURI, *Saint Louis, Mo., December* 20, 1862.

The demand for fuel for steamboats engaged in the public and Government service requires that proprietors of wood-yards be specially encouraged to increase their supply of wood on the river banks. Owners and masters of steamboats traversing rivers in the Department of the Missouri will be required to make payment in cash for all wood received by them at any wood-yard on the banks of any river within this department. Such payments, at a reasonable price, must be made on the delivery of the wood. The refusal or neglect to make such reasonable compensation upon receiving the fuel will subject owners and masters of steamboats to arrest and punishment, and their property to seizure and confiscation, at the discretion of the general commanding the department.

By command of Major-General Curtis:

H. Z. CURTIS,
Assistant Adjutant-General.

HELENA, ARK., *December* 22, 1862.

Maj. Gen. SAMUEL R. CURTIS:

DEAR SIR: The advance I wrote to you of a few days ago is being sent forward with commendable zeal. The preparation is large, and yet I think there will be but little fighting to get possession of Vicksburg.

A considerable band of guerrillas still lurk around here, committing all kinds of depredations. Last evening a company of the Sixth Missouri were on picket duty on the Saint Francis road, 26 strong, and were attacked by this band of thieves, and 23 of the 26 killed and wounded, 3 only making their escape.

I still learn from secesh that all the troops in this State are under Marmaduke and Hindman, in the northwest of this State, and contemplate an attack on Missouri. The officers still continue to stimulate their men with the promise of leading them to Saint Louis to winter. Too strict a watch cannot be kept on them, as they will try no doubt to come Steward over the Federal troops by making raids past our lines, as they are very destitute and growing desperate. All kinds of meanness is practiced here, from the value of a jack-knife to a mule, and but for the strict watch that is kept a wholesale business would be done. More anon.

H. J. BROOKS.

HEADQUARTERS DEPARTMENT OF THE MISSOURI,
Saint Louis, December 22, 1862.

Brig. Gen. W. A. GORMAN, *Helena, Ark.:*

GENERAL. I suppose my former letters advise you fully of my plans. Helena must be held as my main river depot, it being the only high land below Cape Girardeau, on the west side of the river. All other points are overflowed and may be so for twenty days, for the rains, thank fortune, are beginning to fall.

I have also explained to you my objects so far as clearing out Northern Arkansas are concerned. Your interior movement is for that purpose. Little Rock may be an incident, but I want to drive the rebels from the north side first of all things, my immediate object being to prevent the Austin force joining Hindman.

General Blair's forces must go with General Sherman's force to make up the 12,000, which is all I can spare if I do anything interior, as I am trying to do. This is the more necessary, as I am now obliged to re-enforce Columbus. Twelve thousand is the whole number to go in down-river column. The remainder must hold Helena, and work west slowly and cautiously, as I wrote you recently, to wait, if need be, other re-enforcements, which I will send; or to fall back and re-enforce down-river or up-river movements, if circumstances require. The rains will probably render the roads bad, and I understand the bridges have been burned west of Helena; still, the teams and artillery will have to move by land, as I cannot get boats enough. I am sending, however, a lot of light-draught boats suitable for White and Arkansas Rivers.

I am, general, in haste, very truly yours,

SAML. R. CURTIS,
Major-General.

GENERAL ORDERS, No. 14. } HDQRS. DEPARTMENT OF TENNESSEE,
Holly Springs, Miss., December 22, 1862.

By direction of the General-in-Chief of the Army, the troops in this department, including those of the Department of the Missouri operating on the Mississippi River, are hereby divided into four army corps, as follows:

1st. The troops composing the Ninth Division, Brig. Gen. G. W. Morgan commanding; the Tenth Division, Brig. Gen. A. J. Smith commanding, and all other troops operating on the Mississippi River below Memphis not included in the Fifteenth Army Corps, will constitute the Thirteenth Army Corps, under the command of Maj. Gen. John A. McClernand.

2d. The Fifth Division, Brig. Gen. Morgan L. Smith commanding; the division from Helena, Ark., commanded by Brig. Gen. F. Steele, and the forces in the District of Memphis, will constitute the Fifteenth Army Corps, and be commanded by Maj. Gen. W. T. Sherman.

* * * * * * *

By order of Maj. Gen. U. S. Grant:

JNO. A. RAWLINS,
Assistant Adjutant-General.

SAINT LOUIS, *December* 23, 1862.

General DAVIES, *Columbus:*

I started two infantry regiments and a cavalry company, with howitzers, last evening; they ought to reach you this evening. Another infantry regiment starts to-day. These troops generally belong to General Fisk's brigade, who will follow in a day or two, and report to you for temporary duty and to care for his troops and complete their organization. How are you as to safety?

SAML. R. CURTIS,
Major-General.

SAINT LOUIS, *December* 23, 1862.

Brigadier-Generals BLUNT, HERRON, and SCHOFIELD:

General Gorman, now commanding at Helena, informs me that McCulloch, with about 8,000 troops, started from Little Rock about the 10th to re-enforce Hindman. Be on the alert. Do not venture too far at present. I am trying to secure a diversion or co-operation. If necessary, fall back toward Crane Creek. General Schofield will join you soon, with full information as to my purposes.

SAML. R. CURTIS,
Major-General.

HEADQUARTERS DISTRICT OF EASTERN ARKANSAS,
Helena, December 23, 1862.

Major-General CURTIS:

GENERAL: General Sherman, with 21,000 men from Memphis, and 13,000 more from here, got off last night from here. All well fitted out, and with thirty days' rations, which made a fleet of seventy steamers. They will land in the mouth of the Yazoo, and go up a few miles before debarking, and then strike at the railroad between Vicksburg and Grenada, cut it, if possible, and hold it; while General Banks is known to be below Vicksburg and above New Orleans. The capture of Holly Springs must be embarrassing to Major-General Grant, but it is believed to be only temporary. I have exhausted my command to fully meet General Sherman's wishes, and I am glad to say that the general has expressed his very high satisfaction at my response. I had every part of the force to be sent from here fully ready and on board when he got here.

I am so weak in forces now that it invites attack. I have only 4,000 effective men (infantry) and 3,000 effective cavalry and twenty-four field pieces; but I am specially requested by General Grant and General Sherman to send one or two regiments of infantry and 2,000 cavalry to Friar's Point; the infantry to hold the place, while the cavalry scout and scour the country from there to the Tallahatchee, and down some distance, and for the purpose of opening communication with General Grant. This I have promised to do, and, in fact, I regard it as highly important that this be done; but this force will not remain longer than a week or ten days, if successful. I hope you have anticipated my situation, and, as you said in your dispatch of the 9th instant, "will urge a supply of new forces." I can only hover on the edge of Helena, and fight guerrillas and Texas cavalry. They drove in my pickets yesterday evening, and again this evening. I have sent a large force after them, but I cannot go far off. This force ought, by all means, to be moved to Napoleon, as I have urged before.

The admiral has not left me even one gunboat, and that invites raids at least.

General Sherman told me that he expected they would attack me here, as he knew it to be their plan ten days since, to come in behind Grant, and behind me, or attack us, and then try to get to Memphis. Therefore, as a matter of caution, and justice to this force and myself, I hope you will order more forces here, say General Davidson's command, and that they come by way of Crowley's Ridge or by Saint Louis. At all events, if I am to do any more than lay here in this wonderfully muddy hole, I must have another division of infantry, when I can go to Post Arkansas and Little Rock, if ordered.

I am, general, yours truly,

W. A. GORMAN,
Brigadier-General, Commanding.

HEADQUARTERS DEPARTMENT OF THE MISSOURI,
Saint Louis, December 23, 1862.

Brig. Gen. W. A. GORMAN, *Helena, Ark.:*

GENERAL: I am in receipt of yours of the 15th instant, giving an account of the assault on and capture of our pickets, 23 in number. I hope it will prove a warning to our pickets, although it cost us dearly. Neighborhoods should be held responsible for such rascality. The citizens must know of such incursions, and, if they conceal, deserve vengeance.

I am also in receipt of yours of the 19th, giving the movements of McCulloch to re-enforce Hindman. I have telegraphed General Blunt to put him on his guard. I understand the down-river move is starting. Celerity of movement is of great importance, but I hope precautions against assaults from the shore will also be carefully provided for. There has been so much newspaper spread-eagle talk about the down-river move, I fear it is anticipated by overwhelming forces. I have been required to re-enforce Columbus, and have, therefore, stopped some of General Blair's and other troops to take care of General Grant's rear. I am really afraid I will be too much crippled to do anything in my own department. Everybody draws on me.

I suppose you are pretty well posted as to my plans. I have now the cordial support of everybody at Washington, according to these moves, but the raid on the railroads in Tennessee may require some change or delay.

Keep me informed of everything, and I will do all in my power to strengthen and support you.

It is still raining and the streams are rising; all which I hope will prosper our down-river movements.

I have not heard from General Blunt for several days, owing to the storms having destroyed the telegraph lines.

Davidson has been delayed because of a great flood, which carried off our bridges, but I am adopting a more favorable line.

I am, general, very truly, yours,

SAML. R. CURTIS,
Major-General.

[DECEMBER 23, 1862.—For Gorman to Grant, in reference to expedition to the Tallahatchee River, Mississippi, see Series I, Vol. XVII, Part II, p. 464.]

WASHINGTON, *December* 24, 1862.

Major-General CURTIS, *Saint Louis, Mo.:*

Columbus is reported as in danger of an attack. Re-enforce it with your available forces. The movement must be prompt.

H. W. HALLECK,
General-in-Chief.

SAINT LOUIS, *December* 24, 1862—4 p. m.

Major-General HALLECK:

I am doing all I possibly can for Columbus.

SAML. R. CURTIS.

HEADQUARTERS DEPARTMENT OF THE MISSOURI,
Saint Louis, December 24, 1862.*

[Maj. Gen. T. H. HOLMES:]

GENERAL: Yours of the 7th instant, containing slips from the Memphis Appeal of the 3d ultimo, containing an account, purporting to be derived from the Palmyra (Missouri) Courier, of the murder of ten Confederate citizens of Missouri, by order of General McNeil, of the U. S. Army, and also saying you are instructed to ascertain from me "whether the facts are as stated," and requesting me to give you "full information in regard to the circumstances related," is duly received.

General McNeil is a State general, and his column was mainly State troops. The matter has therefore never come to my official notice. His proceedings seem to have been a kind of police resentment against citizens of Missouri who had violated paroles and engaged in robbery and murder, and has only been presented by such newspaper reports as you have sent me. I transmit to you a slip from the Palmyra Courier of the 12th instant, signed by William R. Strachan, provost-marshal, which further describes the affair, but I am not so informed of the facts as to say whether the slips are true or false. Being thus explained by the provost-marshal, I am not disposed to meddle with it, and am not therefore authorized to admit or deny, justify or condemn. Neither do I admit that the papers justify you or your President of the Confederate States in any inquiry as to this treatment of disorderly citizens in Missouri, where you have no force and no organization of forces. Porter's gang was raised on the occasion of enrolling the militia, it being mainly persons who wished to resist the State enrollment by a kind of State mutiny.

Persons pretending to hold commissions from the Confederate authorities to recruit, who come without uniforms, concealing themselves within my lines, are spies, and if taken will be shot. Persons in the State, who congregate without commissions of any kind, to steal and rob, under the color of warfare, have deserved death, and, in some instances, after being paroled and taken a second time, they have been summarily disposed of by an indignant and outraged community. Such, I understand, was the case at Palmyra, where the authorities of the State of Missouri are competent to punish her criminals and protect her

---

*The letter actually sent appears to have been that dated December 27, p. 879, which see, as that one is recorded in letter-book of the Department of the Missouri, and a copy of it was forwarded to Washington by General Curtis January 1, 1863. The above was found in the miscellaneous papers of that department, but is not recorded in the letter-book, and may have been the original draught of the letter of December 27.

citizens; and you exert no power, except it may be some encouragement to rogues, who hope to escape from justice by running into your lines.

When persons are condemned to be shot by Federal authority, the proceedings have to be approved by the President, but no case of this sort has arisen under my command.

I have the honor to be, general, very respectfully, your obedient servant,

SAML. R. CURTIS,
Major-General.

[Inclosure.]

Vindication of General McNeil.

HEADQUARTERS PROVOST-MARSHAL,
Palmyra, Mo., December 10, 1862.

To the Editor of the New York Times:

SIR: Noticing in your issue of December 1 an extended extract from foreign papers, accompanied by an editorial, upon the execution of ten rebels at this place, which extract and editorial appear based upon an entire misconstruction of the facts of the case, and thereby casting grave censure upon a meritorious officer, I am led (having by position at the time an opportunity of knowing everything connected with the transaction), out of regard to the truth of history, and to do justice to General McNeil, to address you on the subject. It is very difficult for men removed thousands of miles from the scene of action—men who are placed in a locality where law and order prevail, where loyalty is universal—to begin even to appreciate slightly the deep malice, the enormous crimes, the treacheries, the assassinations, the perjuries that invariably have characterized those, especially in Missouri, who have taken up arms avowedly to destroy their Government.

Now, Mr. Editor, here in Missouri our Government commenced by extending toward the rebels in our midst every kindness, and a degree of clemency that soon caused it to be much safer, in every part of our State, to be a rebel than to be a Union man. Every neighborhood was coerced, whilst the Government was maintaining within the State a large force, at no time less than 50,000 men, and often largely overrunning those figures. Still treason continued rampant, traitors publicly held forth on the clemency with which they were treated, regarding it as proof and confession of the weakness of the Government, that she dare not hurt any one. Union men and their families were forced to leave their homes and their all and fly for protection and for life to the loyal States. I have seen hundreds of wagons on their way to Illinois and other States—families who had lived in independent circumstances forced to live on corn-meal and water and beg their way along. The Union troops, by their kindness, were absolutely offering a premium to treason and to crime. Their presence, under the orders they were forced to act on, became, instead of protection, absolutely a terrible evil. Union men dared not give the troops information; assassination was sure to follow. Things went on from bad to worse. Soon the scoundrels began the innocent pastime of shooting into passenger-cars, of burning railroad bridges, not as a military necessity, but for the sole purpose of murder. Hundreds of non-combatants were crippled and murdered—wives made insane by the enormous outrages they committed. Some of the men perpetrating these hideous crimes were caught. I participated in the action of the commission appointed to try them.

They were proved guilty and sentenced to be shot; the sentence approved by General Halleck, commanding Department of the Mississippi; that sentence delayed in its execution, and not carried out to this day. Some of these miscreants have even been turned loose once more. Such clemency proved to be the most horrid cruelty. The unfortunates of our State who, in their heart of hearts, held that loyalty to their Government was a sacred and holy duty that they could not cast aside, began to look at one another in surprise and horror. Will our Government never understand our situation? Will it continue to strengthen the cause of the robbers and murderers? What is to become of us? Stout-hearted men, whose families would not permit of leaving, sat down in the midst of their household gods and shed tears of hopeless agony. Midnight parties had come round and absolutely disarmed every man of even half-way loyalty. Their horses and wagons, their only available means of transit, were stolen from them. During this time our troops would take prisoner after prisoner. I, myself, acting as provost-marshal-general of the District of Northeastern Missouri, administered the oath of allegiance to several thousand traitors, and took bonds for observance of the oath to the amount of over $1,000,000; still, no stop to the outrages of the rebels. Finally, General Schofield, whom all who know must admit to be a gentleman of remarkable kindness of heart, began to come up to the exigency of the times, and issued General Orders, No. 18, an extract from which appears hereinafter. That order has, I believe, never been countermanded, and is in force to this day.

As a specimen of our situation, let me inform you that an old Baptist preacher, named Wheat, was murdered by a rebel gang within 5 or 6 miles of Palmyra, his body mutilated and his person robbed of some $800; that a farmer named Carter, living in an adjoining county, suspected of having given information which led to the arrest of a notorious bridge-burner and railroad destroyer, was shot in his own dooryard and in the presence of his wife and children; that a Mr. Preston, living but a few miles from the same neighborhood, was taken off by a gang of these men, whom you seem desirous of recognizing as honorable belligerents, and murdered, leaving an amiable wife and four very interesting little children to cry for vengeance upon the assassins of their father. A Mr. Pratt, living a few miles north of Palmyra, a very intelligent farmer, unfortunately an emigrant from Massachusetts, and a man of the very highest moral character, but guilty of being an unswerving Union man, was murdered, leaving a widow and six children to mourn his loss. A Mr. Spires, an aged man, over seventy years, one of the oldest citizens of Shelby County (adjoining the county of which Palmyra is the shire-town), was taken from his house and hung, and his body mutilated. Other citizens of that county, and those of the highest standing, were taken out and hung until life was nearly extinct. A man named Spaight was taken out, stripped, and brutally whipped. A large body of these rebels went into the town of Canton, in Lewis County, a town not garrisoned, and murdered William Carnegy, a leading merchant and universally respected, but tainted to them with the leprosy of loyalty. Porter, at the head of several thousand of these guerrillas, went into Memphis, also not garrisoned, seized a Dr. Aylward, the prominent Union man of that locality, and hung him, with a halter made of hickory bark, until he was dead.

I could give a long list of crimes the most horrid committed by these scoundrels, that would make even fiends in hell shudder. Their robberies and devastations you, in New York cannot even conceive of; but when

I say there were thousands upon thousands of these men; that they had no money; that they subsisted wholly by robbery, you may approximate toward an estimate; and all this in a State that refused to secede from the Union, hundreds of miles inside of the Federal lines. General McNeil with a small force was pursuing them, not like the advance of a force in all the "pomp and circumstance of glorious war," but at the rate of 45 miles per day, often camping at 10 p. m., and breaking camp at 2 a. m. Finally he caught them at Kirksville, and effectually crushed them, the guerrillas losing over 700 men, killed and wounded. The next day 15 men, caught with arms in their hands, murder in their hearts, and the oath of allegiance to the United States Government in their pockets, were tried and shot.

In the particular case of Andrew Allsman, he was a man upward of sixty years of age, taken from his family and murdered. Of the ten men executed, one of them was one of the party who murdered Mr. Pratt, above alluded to. The other nine men were all caught with arms, and all of them had been once pardoned for their former treason by taking the oath of allegiance to the United States, and had deliberately perjured themselves by going out again—the very oath they took expressly stipulating that "death would be the penalty for a violation of this their solemn oath and parole of honor." Now, sir, are such men entitled to the consideration of honorable warfare (as you seem to think in your criticisms), or are they not rather to be treated as outlaws and beyond the pale of civilization? And, sir, living as we do in Missouri, in times of red revolution, assassination, rapine, in violation of all laws, both human and divine, acts of justice necessarily assume the garb of severity, and the more severe to the criminal the more merciful to the community. And now, in view of the facts that I have alluded to, publishing as you do a loyal paper in a loyal State, a thousand miles removed from the scenes of these outrages, can you unthinkingly join in the howl raised by the full-fledged and semi traitors in our midst against such or any other acts that insure the punishment of treason and traitors?

Had one-half the severity practiced by the rebels on the Union men of Tennessee, Arkansas, and Missouri been meted out in return to them, every trace of treason would ere this have been abolished from our land. Good cause have the rebels to grumble at that which blasts at once every prospect they might have had for ultimate success. What is war? Is it anything but retaliation? Must we allow our enemies, the enemies of liberty and republicanism, to outrage all the laws of war, and not take some steps to show them the propriety of adhering to those laws? Emissaries from the rebellious States have come into our midst, forming secret associations, swearing citizens of a State that would not secede from the Union not to respect any oath or obligation made to the Federal Government. Men enjoying the disgrace of a commission from the rebel Government have traveled through our land, hundreds of miles inside of the Federal lines, swearing men, singly and in squads, by stealth and in secret, into the Confederate service, with instructions to go home and wait until called on. These men, thus sworn in, continued day by day to pass themselves on us as loyal citizens, while by night they turned out and harassed their Union neighbors.

Suppose officers from the Confederate Army should go through New York recruiting in the same manner, or suppose Federal officers in disguise should visit Georgia and commence raising bodies of men. ostensibly for Government service, but in reality to create disturbance in the community—to rob, murder, and destroy, what treatment would they receive? Would shooting them or hanging them be considered such a butchery? Was Washington, when he signed the order for the execution of Major André, to be considered the original Haynau?

Mr. Editor, if you could have been a witness to many scenes that attended General McNeil's visit to the various posts of his district, made but two weeks since, when he traversed the whole country on horseback, attended by but two orderlies, when old men would come out of their farm houses, shake hands with the general, call down blessings upon him, ask him to delay so that their wives could come out and thank him for executing justice, which had enabled them to come back once more to their homes, instead of indulging in editorials so harshly condemnatory of that which you did not understand, I think you would have fancied you had just perceived the principle which must prevail to crush this rebellion, and bring back to us our fast wasting prosperity. We here, in the West, have been forced to realize the horrors of revolution. They have been forced on the loyal men of Missouri against their desires and in spite of the efforts of the Federal Government. In addition, we think we are fighting a battle for the world, for humanity, for civilization, for religion, for the honor of our forefathers, for republics, a battle in which the welfare of the myriads of sons of men who are to come after us in every age and country is at stake.

General McNeil has even in the early part of this terrible war been censured from headquarters for being too lenient toward the rebels. Time and experience proved to him that in order to save bloodshed it was necessary to show some examples of severe punishment, and the result, in giving security to persons and property of loyal men in our section, has amply justified the steps taken by him. Do you suppose that a rebellion that in this late day has ventured to employ the scalping knife of the savage in its service, that commenced in fraud, that has sustained itself from the commencement by robbery, that has practiced extermination and banishment and confiscation toward citizens that ventured to remain true to their original allegiance, can be put down without somebody being hurt? Let me ask of you to do justice to a kind and brave officer, who has simply dared to do his duty, and in doing so has obtained the thanks and deepest feelings of gratitude from every loyal man in Northern Missouri. Suppose foreign journals dub him the American Haynau. Let the Government, out of regard for the feelings of a grateful people, emulate the example of Austria, who created Haynau a marshal of the Empire, and give to General McNeil a division, with permission to go down into Dixie and bid Jefferson Davis come and take him. Take my word for it, thousands upon thousands of the hardy sons of the West will flock to his standard, and treason upon the sunny plains of the South will find at last that scourge of God which it so well merits.

This rebellion and its settlement belong exclusively to the American people. Governments that are based upon political principles opposed to our own cannot have the right of interference that disinterestedness would give. The roarings of the British lion, his criticisms and his opinions, are, therefore, alike immaterial. Nations in their political decisions and efforts are rarely governed by anything but their self-interest, no matter how loud they mouth about their virtues. And such articles as those in the London Times, Star, and other English papers come with a bad grace from a Government that justified the lashing of Sepoys to the cannon's mouth and blowing their mangled bodies in fragments through the air—the outrages committed by those Sepoys not being one iota greater than those committed by the rebels in our land; with this difference, that the one was the work of ignorance and a religious fanaticism, performed by an enslaved and half-civilized race, while our rebels and murderers have claimed to be our brothers, are enlightened, enjoyed the same rights and privileges that we have enjoyed, and in a day could, as it were, reinstate themselves and our whole country in the possession and enjoyment not only of peace and harmony, but of all the rights, privileges, and independence that freemen can or should enjoy. These terrible "butcheries" (*i. e.*, the just punishing of guerrillas, assassins, and violators of parole) have finally restored safety here. Since the public execution of the ten men at Palmyra, not a murder nor a single personal outrage to a Union man has been committed in Northeastern Missouri, or since the rebels learned what would be the price of a Union man's life, three months ago, for it is that time since official notice was served on them of what would be done if Allsman was not returned to his home, and that the decimal system would be carried out for each loyal noncombatant that should subsequently be murdered by them, so long as guerrillas could be found in the district. "Verily a tree shall be known by its fruits." A wise punishment has once more enabled the dove of peace to hover over our households, unterrified. Guerrillas in this district found their vocation gone. Traitors began at last to recognize that the oath of loyalty meant something. They scattered for security through Illinois, and even there could not cease their career of crime. It was but yesterday that I delivered to the authorities of Pike County, Illinois, three young men raised in this county, and of very respectable (so far as wealth and intelligence goes), but not loyal, families, sworn-members of Porter's guerrillas, who had been with him in every action. When a proposition is made to them to murder an aged farmer who had generously extended to them the hospitalities of his house, they never shudder, show no indignation, but coolly proceed to commit a murder that for atrocity and horror cannot be exceeded throughout the annals of crime. You will, in the paper publishing this, see the confession of one of these three specimens of Southern chivalry. If the authorities of Illinois proceed to execute these three murderers, in retaliation for the murder of Mr. Pearson, a ratio of three for one, will it be cause for an indignant editorial against those authorities? Say not, Mr. Editor, that the last case will be one of the civil law, for it occurs in Illinois. In Missouri these scoundrels that you object to having punished had by their conduct destroyed the last vestige of civil law. Martial law was the only protection citizens had, and by that law these men were publicly and lawfully executed. For martial law in Missouri, see general orders of this department. Read also the following:

GENERAL ORDERS, No. 2. } HEADQUARTERS DEPARTMENT OF THE MISSISSIPPI, *Saint Louis, March 3, 1862.*

* * * * * * *

III. Evidence has been received at these headquarters that Maj. Gen. Sterling Price has issued commissions or licenses to certain bandits in this State, authorizing them to raise guerrilla forces for the purpose of plunder and marauding. General Price ought to know that such a course is contrary to the rules of civilized warfare, and that every man who enlists in such an organization forfeits his life, and becomes an outlaw. All persons are hereby warned that if they join any guerrilla band, they will not, if captured, be treated as prisoners of war, but will be hung as robbers and murderers. Their lives shall atone for the barbarity of their general.

By command of Major-General Halleck:

N. H. McLEAN,
Assistant Adjutant-General.

Also see General Orders, Nos. 13 and 32, issued by General Halleck, and General Orders, No. 18, issued by General Schofield, of which the following is an extract:

> The Government is willing and can afford to be magnanimous in its treatment of those who are tired of the rebellion, and desire to become loyal citizens and to aid in the restoration of peace and prosperity of the country; but it will not tolerate those who still persist in their wicked efforts to prevent the restoration of peace, where they have failed to maintain legitimate war. The time is passed when insurrection and rebellion in Missouri can cloak itself under the guise of honorable warfare. The utmost vigilance and energy are enjoined upon all the troops of the State in hunting down and destroying these robbers and assassins. When caught in arms, engaged in this unlawful warfare, they will be shot down upon the spot.

In conclusion, Mr. Editor, if you are correct in your denunciations of what you term a "butchery," do not waste your anathemas upon General McNeil alone because he saw proper to teach traitors that the life of an unarmed non-combatant Union man, a loyal citizen of the United States, was a sacred thing—that murderers should not take it with impunity—but bestow some of it upon equally gallant and meritorious officers like General Merrill, who executed ten of those perjured scoundrels at Macon City, and General Schofield, who issued Orders No. 18, or General Halleck, whose orders touching bridge-burners and guerrillas I had supposed until now even the editor of the Times approved of.

WM. R. STRACHAN,
Provost-Marshal, Palmyra.

HEADQUARTERS DISTRICT OF EASTERN ARKANSAS,
Helena, December 24, 1862.

Rear-Admiral D. D. PORTER:

ADMIRAL: I have just received orders from General Curtis, based on dispatches from the General-in-Chief, to move on Little Rock. I am also requested to ask your co-operation. I am directed to attract the attention of General Holmes, that he may not send forces to help General Hindman, or to Vicksburg. General Curtis has ordered movements from the east toward Little Rock, which makes it highly important that I should move on Post Arkansas with my land force, and by gunboats and transports by water up the Arkansas River at once.

At Post Arkansas there are 5,000 infantry, and some sort of earthworks, with eight guns, two large and six small, the large ones said to be 100-pounders. I hope it may be consistent with your inclination and ability, under the circumstances, to send to Napoleon such a number of gunboats as you may judge necessary to take the Post with my land force, and then move on Little Rock, if the water will justify it. I will be in Napoleon in ten days, or less, from this date. You will perceive that this combination of movements is such as to suggest the importance of your co-operation to the extent deemed by you advisable.

I trust, admiral, I may receive your reply by the hands of the bearer of dispatches, and by the return boat, that I may shape my course accordingly. The bearer can give you any further information on the subject that I may have omitted.

I am, admiral, your obedient servant,

W. A. GORMAN,
Brigadier-General, Commanding.

SPRINGFIELD, *December* 24, 1862.

Brigadier-General BLUNT, *Cane Hill*:

General Curtis informs me that McCulloch, with about 8,000 men, started from Little Rock about the 10th instant, to re-enforce Hindman. He must have joined him by this time. Keep your divisions in close supporting distance, and fall back if necessary. Do not risk a battle where you are unless very sure of success. Two or three days' march in this direction will give you great advantage over the enemy. Should you find it necessary to retire, parole all the rebel wounded, and send as many of ours as can be moved to Springfield. I will join you as soon as possible. Please give me at once what information you have from the enemy, and keep me advised of everything. I expect to be at Elkhorn on the 28th.

J. M. SCHOFIELD,
Brigadier-General.

SPRINGFIELD, *December* 24, 1862.

Brigadier-General HERRON,
Prairie Grove, Ark.:

I am on my way to the army; will join you about the 30th. General Curtis informs me that McCulloch left Little Rock about the 10th instant, with 8,000 men, to join Hindman. If this is true, he must be there by this time. Be on the alert, and keep me informed of everything. I have dispatched this information to General Blunt, and directed him not to risk a battle, unless very sure of success. By retiring two or three days' march, we will gain a great advantage over the enemy, and can also get re-enforcements. Your wounded should be sent to Springfield as fast as it can be done with safety.

J. M. SCHOFIELD,
Brigadier-General.

YANKTON AGENCY,
Greenwood, Dak., December 24, 1862.

The PRESIDENT OF THE UNITED STATES:

Little Crow, White Lodge, Sleepy Eyes, Pawn, and Big Head, with from 500 to 1,000 Santee and Yankton warriors, are now on the Missouri River, above Fort Pierre, preparing for an early spring campaign against the whites. They are murdering all the whites in that region. They can be captured this winter if General Cook can have the men and means. Let him be ordered to Washington, to confer with General Pope while there. There is no time to be lost, if they are to be captured.

JAMES S. WILLIAMS,
Associate Justice of Dakota.
W. A. BURLEIGH,
U. S. Indian Agent.
W. JAYNE,
Governor.

GENERAL ORDERS, No. 35. } HDQRS. DEPARTMENT OF THE MISSOURI, *Saint Louis, December* 24, 1862.

I. Provost-marshals within this department will be governed by the following instructions: *

They are referred to General Orders, No. 23, Department of the Missouri, current series, for important regulations as to their practice.

II. They will arrest, and send to Saint Louis, all persons belonging to, or enlisted in, the Confederate service, found within this department. It is represented that there are many persons, officers and privates, at large, who do, or claim to, belong to the rebel army. This is contrary to the orders of the major-general commanding, and such persons should at once be sent forward under guard. This is not to apply to persons who have voluntarily surrendered and taken the oath of allegiance before proper authorities.

III. Provost-marshals will arrest and take evidence against all persons guilty of disloyal conduct, such as giving aid and encouragement to the rebellion, including those, first, who act as spies, and carry on secret correspondence with rebels in arms; second, who furnish supplies to the rebels, whether arms, ammunition, provisions, clothing, horses, forage, money, or other material aid—all such property actually being used in that way will be seized and reported at once to Col. B. G. Farrar, Thirtieth Missouri Volunteers, at Saint Louis; third, who encourage the rebellion by speaking, writing, or publishing any disloyal sentiments, or induce the same in others; fourth, persons in arms against the Government, and those guilty of murder, robbery, theft, pillage, and marauding; and all persons who, in disguise as pretended loyal citizens, encourage disloyalty in others, and oppress Union men.

IV. There is a class of pretended loyal men who, while they have not joined the rebel army, have encouraged their relatives and neighbors to go, and who uphold and support them by secret communications and sending money, clothing, and other assistance; and who associate with men who have been disloyal from the first, and with known sympathizers with the rebellion. These men, while pretending that they are better Union men than those charged with the control of the Government, constantly denounce the Government and all who sustain its policy and measures, as enemies of the Union and of the country; such conduct and language gives strong support and encouragement to those actively engaged in the rebellion, producing the belief in their minds that they have a strong and growing party in the North, by whose agency eventually they will be able to divide the country permanently, and strengthens and prolongs the efforts of the rebels. Men are not entitled to the protection of the Government when their every day conduct shows that they look for its overthrow with hope and pleasure. They choose to range themselves with the enemies of the Government, and will be treated accordingly. They will be arrested, the evidence taken against them, and be proceeded against as criminals.

V. Arms and ammunition will be taken from disloyal men above mentioned, and reported to Col. B. G. Farrar, at Saint Louis.

VI. Persons found harboring or concealing spies, rebel soldiers or officers, marauders, and other criminals will be treated as parties to the crimes, and circumstances may make their failing to give information to the military authorities as gross an act of disloyalty as their active efforts to conceal.

VII. Provost-marshals will arrest notoriously bad and dangerous

---

* See Stanton to Curtis, January 14, 1863, Part II, p. 41.

men, where peace and safety require it, though no specific act of disloyalty can be proven against them; and such may be put under bonds, imprisoned, or required to leave the State.

VIII. And also disloyal preachers who have disgraced their profession by encouraging others to rebel, while they may have committed no other kind of disloyal act. The Government has always given liberal exemption to this class, and if they now in return oppose it in the way of their calling, they should be dealt with as rebellious and disloyal men, and expelled from the State.

IX. The good of society and the safety of the Government require that, during the rebellion, offenses such as those spoken of above should be tried and punished by military power. Many offenses which in time of peace are civil offenses become in time of war military offenses, and are to be tried by a military tribunal, even in places where civil tribunals exist. While treason, as a distinct offense, is defined by the Constitution, and must be tried by courts duly constituted by law, yet certain acts of treasonable character, such as carrying information to the enemy, acting as spies, &c., are military offenses, triable by military tribunals, and punishable by military authority. It is a well-established principle that insurgents not militarily organized under the laws of the State, predatory partisans, and guerrilla bands are not legitimately in arms, and the military name and garb which they have assumed cannot give a military exemption to the crimes which they may commit. They are, in a legal sense, mere freebooters and banditti.

X. It will be the duty, therefore, of provost-marshals, who, upon evidence, find persons guilty of serious crimes above set out, to send them forward to Saint Louis, with the evidence against them, and upon charges preferred.

XI. Provost-marshals will arrest persons guilty of discouraging enlistments in the service of the Government, including those opposing the enrollment ordered by the Governor, and persons guilty of exciting dissatisfaction amongst our troops, and of inducing persons to desert, and also those persons found selling liquor to soldiers, in any city or town, near any camps, or at any other place, and also persons interfering with the execution of any military orders or regulations issued by competent authority.

XII. It having been ordered on the 3d of February, 1862, that no one should be employed on any railroad who had not taken the oath of allegiance, and who also was not loyal, it is the duty of provost-marshals to ascertain that all officers, directors, and employés of all railroads have taken the oath, and are loyal, and to arrest all concerned in violation of said order; and it having been ordered by the major-general commanding the department that no disloyal persons shall command or be employed upon any steamboat or vessel, it is made the duty of all officers to report to the headquarters of the department any violation of said order; and any owner or commander of any such boat or vessel violating said order will be liable to be tried for such disobedience.

XIII. On the 4th of December, 1861, Major-General Halleck, commanding this department, in general orders relating to provost-marshals, declared that it was the province of the military authorities to execute the act of Congress that had then been passed, confiscating the slaves of rebels which had been used in aiding the rebellion, and he forewarned disloyal slave-owners in these words, that "should Congress extend this penalty to the property of all rebels in arms, or giving aid, assistance, or encouragement to the enemy, such provisions will be strictly enforced."

On the 5th of December, 1862, an order was issued by the War Department, directing that the Provost-Marshal-General should proceed to carry out the provisions of the act of Congress of July 17, 1862, below mentioned.

And on the 24th of September, 1862, in General Orders, No. 139, of the War Department, a proclamation by the President of the United States was published for the information and government of the Army, and all concerned, in which the ninth and tenth sections of said act of Congress were set out as follows:

SEC. 9. *And be it further enacted*, That all slaves of persons who shall hereafter be engaged in rebellion against the Government of the United States, or who shall in any way give aid or comfort thereto, escaping from such persons, and taking refuge within the lines of the army; and all slaves captured from such persons, or deserted by them, and coming under the control of the Government of the United States; and all slaves of such persons found on or being within any place occupied by rebel forces, and afterward occupied by the forces of the United States, shall be deemed captives of war, and shall be forever free of their servitude, and not again held as slaves.

SEC. 10. *And be it further enacted*, That no slave escaping into any State, Territory, or the District of Columbia, from any other State, shall be delivered up, or in any way impeded or hindered of his liberty, except for crime, or some offense against the laws, unless the person claiming said fugitive shall first make oath that the person to whom the labor or service of such fugitive is alleged to be due is his lawful owner, and has not borne arms against the United States in the present rebellion, nor in any way given aid and comfort thereto; and no person engaged in the military or naval service of the United States shall, under any pretense whatever, assume to decide on the validity of the claim of any person to the service or labor of any other person, or surrender up any person to the claimant, on pain of being dismissed from the service.

By which order of the War Department, it was published to the Army, and all concerned, that the President did enjoin upon and order all persons engaged in the military and naval service of the United States to observe, obey, and enforce, within their respective spheres of service, the act and sections above recited.

And whereas there are large numbers of slaves in this department that belonged to rebels in arms, and disloyal men who have given them aid and countenance by such acts and conduct as are above specified; and also a large number of men who defy said act of Congress and order of the War Department, by pursuing and attempting to hold as slaves those who, by said act of Congress, are declared to be free of their servitude and captives of war; and as captives are entitled to full protection to their persons from all enemies of the Government and opposers of the law:

XIV. Now, all provost-marshals within this department are hereby commanded to protect the freedom and persons of all such captives or emancipated slaves against all persons interfering with or molesting them; and they will arrest all persons guilty of such conduct.

XV. And whereas it is represented to the major-general commanding that the slaves of disloyal men, emancipated by said act of Congress, are kept imprisoned and confined in both the public and private jails, but not upon criminal charges, it is hereby made the duty of provost-marshals to examine into all such cases and report the facts to the provost-marshal-general.

XVI. And all persons disobeying any proper order of a provost-marshal in relation to emancipated slaves will be arrested, the evidence taken against them, and tried for violation of military orders.

XVII. And that loyal men may not be interfered with in their rights, whenever slaves seek protection, under circumstances provided for in said act of Congress, it shall be the duty of all provost-marshals to take evidence as to the facts; and upon ascertaining that the slave is one of the class emancipated and protected by said ninth and tenth sections of said law, the provost-marshal will give to such slave a paper, signed by himself, in the following form:

In pursuance to General Orders, No. 35, Department of the Missouri, dated Saint Louis, December 24, 1862, and in obedience to the order of the War Department, made 24th of September, 1862, I have ascertained that ———, a negro, ——— color, ——— size, aged about ——— years, is to be considered and treated as a captive of war, and as such is entitled to the protection of all officers of the United States.

Given by me at ———, in the county of ———, State of ———, the ——— day of ———, 186–.

——— ———.

The blanks in said paper to be carefully filled up, so as to state the name, sex, color, size, and age of the negro, and the place where given. It shall be signed by the officer executing the same, and delivered to such negro, and upon the paper, or annexed to it, should be stated the names of the witness or witnesses upon whose testimony such paper is granted, and the place of residence; and no negro holding such paper shall be deprived of it against his will.

Said act of Congress provides as follows:

SEC. 9. 1st. As to persons hereafter engaged in rebellion against the United States.

2d. And as to persons who shall in any way give aid or comfort to the rebellion.

Their slaves shall be deemed captives of war, and shall be forever free of their servitude, and not again held as slaves, under the following circumstances:

1st. Slaves escaping from such persons, and taking refuge within the lines of the Army.

2d. Slaves captured from such persons.

3d. Slaves deserted by such persons, and coming under the control of the Government of the United States.

4th. Slaves of such persons found or being within any place occupied by rebel forces, and afterward occupied by the forces of the United States.

XVIII. Any negro designated in such writing given by a provost-marshal will, by persons in the military service of the Government, be regarded as emancipated by said act of Congress; but no person in military service will regard such paper as justifying him to decide on the validity of the claim of any slaveholder to the service or labor of his slave.

XIX. By said order of the War Department, attention was called to an act of Congress, entitled "An act to make an additional article of war," approved March 13, 1862, as follows:

Be it enacted by the Senate and House of Representatives of the United States of America in Congress assembled, That hereafter the following shall be promulgated as an additional article of war for the government of the Army of the United States, and shall be obeyed and observed as such:

ARTICLE —. All officers or persons in the military or naval service of the United States are prohibited from employing any of the forces under their respective commands, for the purpose of returning fugitives from service or labor, who may have escaped from any persons to whom such service or labor is claimed to be due; and any officer who shall be found guilty by a court-martial of violating this article shall be dismissed from the service.

SEC. 2. *And be it further enacted,* That this act shall take effect from and after its passage.

This, and all other rules and articles of war, should be sustained by provost-marshals, who are specially assigned to duty for the purpose of maintaining the laws of war and the peace of society.

The foregoing rules and regulations are made by command of Major-General Curtis:

F. A. DICK,

Lieut. Col. and Provost-Marshal-General, Dept. of the Missouri.

HEADQUARTERS DISTRICT OF EASTERN ARKANSAS,
Helena, December 25, 1862.

Maj. Gen. SAMUEL R. CURTIS,
Comdg. Department of the Missouri, Saint Louis, Mo.:

GENERAL: In obedience to your orders and suggestions, I have ordered my present command to be ready to move at once.

After a full conference with Generals Sherman, Washburn, and others, all concurring, I have determined to move to Napoleon and abandon this place. This point has no more military advantage than any other on the banks of the river, between Memphis and Napoleon. The large siege guns in the fort must not be intrusted to a small garrison. I have only 5,700 infantry and 3,100 cavalry on paper, as per report sent you four days ago. I will place the siege guns on the ordnance boat and the large wharf boat, and take them to Napoleon and destroy the fort. By being at Napoleon, I am at the mouth of the Arkansas River, while Blunt and Herron are at Van Buren. In moving up the Arkansas, I will have the gunboats on my right flank, followed by the transports and supplies. The moral effect of the gunboats to inspirit our own forces and deter the enemy is known to be tremendous. A disaster cannot occur, and success is certain. But I must have at least 10,000 infantry, 3,000 cavalry, and thirty pieces of artillery, and 1,000 infantry, 500 cavalry, and one battery to be left at Napoleon. Shall tow up the Arkansas River to Old Post one mortar boat, which I have here, and leave one mortar boat at Napoleon. By this move threaten Little Rock from the southeast, while Blunt and Herron threaten it from the northwest. At Napoleon I am midway between Memphis and Vicksburg.

I beg to inform you that General Hurlbut, at Memphis, and General Davies, at Columbus, have taken the responsibility to stop the Iowa and Missouri troops and the battery ordered by you to report to me. Colonel Chipman is here, and fully concurs in my plan of operations. He is writing you fully. I cannot garrison this place and move to any other with my present force.

This plan has my maturest judgment and conviction.

I am, general, very respectfully, your obedient servant,

W. A. GORMAN,
Brigadier-General, Commanding.

SPRINGFIELD, *December* 25, 1862.

Major-General CURTIS, *Saint Louis:*

One of my spies, who left Cotton Plant, on White River, about three weeks ago, has just returned. He heard, at Carrollton, six days ago, a general report that McCulloch was on the way to re-enforce Hindman with 15,000 men. The report was not credited by intelligent men at Carrollton, but, taken in connection with that from Helena, is entitled to considerable weight. I have heard nothing from Generals Blunt or Herron since I left Saint Louis.

I will start for Fayetteville in the morning.

J. M. SCHOFIELD,
Brigadier-General.

HDQRS. FIRST DIV., ARMY OF SOUTHEASTERN MISSOURI,
Camp opposite Van Buren, December 25, 1862.

Brigadier-General DAVIDSON,
Commanding Army of Southeastern Missouri:

I have the honor to report that Boyd and Harding arrived here yesterday, and are now comfortable in camp.

The forage train of Colonel Harris was attacked yesterday about a mile below, at old man Carter's, 3 miles from our camp. The rebels captured 2 men and killed 1 horse. We chased them 9 miles, but failed to punish them in the least. I have reliable information that there is a rebel force, from 500 to 800, at Doniphan, and as many more at Pitman's Ferry, while in the vicinity of Pocahontas there are about 2,000; the former cavalry, and the latter infantry. We are in great need of 1,000 cavalry to protect our flanks.

I find it next to a physical impossibility to construct a boat of the dimensions indicated by you. I can and will build two 12 by 45, which will give more space and be much [more] easily handled in this swift current than one of the size specified. We need two ropes, and nails, and spikes, and calking material for the boats, and a half dozen adzes and as many broad axes would greatly facilitate the construction.

At 8 o'clock yesterday morning, I started 100 wagons from the First Division. Forty more have started this morning from Boyd's, both under strong escorts.

Hearing that there was a rebel force, 600 strong, moving in our rear, I re-enforced the first train with two companies of infantry.

The telegraph is completed here, and I have an officer who is a good operator, but the line will not work. Forage is scarce on this side of the river. I expect the other 50 wagons of the supply train, First Division, in to-day. If they come, I will put down the pontoon and collect all the forage I can get on the other side of the river.

I have the honor to be, very respectfully,

WM. P. BENTON,
Brig. Gen., Comdg. First Div., Army of Southeastern Missouri.

CHRISTMAS MORNING, BEFORE DAYLIGHT,
Near Fort Gibson, C. N., December 25, 1862.

General JAMES G. BLUNT:

SIR: On leaving Cane Hill I proceeded with the forces that had reported to me; marched 20 miles. The Sixth Kansas had not been heard from. Next day rained hard. Sent back after the Sixth, and marched on Tahlequah, 28 miles; stream up; fording difficult. Stopped a short distance from Tahlequah, and undertook to surround a party of secesh in town, but they escaped. The howitzers and ambulance of the Sixth had dropped behind Captain Mefford, took the wrong road at Dutch Mills, went to Oransville, and marched with that part of their command by another road, and reached our camp that night; Captain Mefford reaching camp at this place about 1 o'clock this morning. I marched here yesterday. The enemy have not sent a sufficient force to attack our trains. The largest force that went up returned on the evening before yesterday. The enemy are scattered over the country in small bands of from 100 to 400.

I had a man taken in Fort Gibson last night who left the command at Fort Smith on Monday. His information seems to be reliable, and I hasten to apprise you of it. The rebel force did not go down to Dardanelle. General Hindman sent a force there as picket, as it was reported in their camp that we were going to march down the other way. General Hindman has been relieved from command; General Johnston, of Mississippi, takes his place, and was to reach Van Buren on Tuesday last. Two steamboat loads of corn came up last week. A number of other boats are expected, and the troops at Little Rock with General Holmes, computed at 8,000 strong, have been ordered up, and were expected yesterday or the day before. A part of the enemy's force crossed the river after the battle of Prairie Grove, but were recrossing to Van Buren on Saturday and Sunday, and were all to go over; whether for an attack on you or to resist an expected attack, I cannot say. The former is the report. They are said to be going back again. The forces of General Cooper have been reorganized and partly clothed. General McIntosh is up the Arkansas, about 20 miles above this, with his regiment and 200 Osages. He refused to obey General Cooper's orders to join him on the march to Cane Hill before the battle of Prairie Grove.

Cooper has Worten's [Watie's] regiment, said to be 600 strong. It is scattered over the Nation in parties, the largest of which is under Lieutenant-Colonel [R. C.] Parks. We were hunting it all day yesterday. Bryan's battalion is 20 miles below this. Scamlan's [Scanland's] regiment [company] (Texan) is at Scullyville, with Cooper. Some Choctaws and part of the other Creek regiments are somewhere on Lee's Creek, or down there. Livingston, with some Indian forces, is at Webber's. The Arkansas is not fordable. There are a number of ferries near here, at Gibson; poor things; take one or two days to cross. A battalion of 120 men, with four teams, started from Cooper's quarters to go up Grand River to get the salt kettles at Bryant's Lick, to haul them over Arkansas. They were to cross over this morning. I fear they will have alarm, although I have all the fords or ferries within 10 miles guarded. The scattered condition of the enemy, the rain, swollen condition of streams, and scarcity of forage renders it extremely difficult to carry out the order to clear the enemy out of the country, but I will try. As to moving, families without number wish to leave, but I have no transportation for them. I must move toward Webber's to feel for the enemy, who may concentrate there. Colonel Watie has taken all the horses and wagons out of the country, and the order "to assist those who want to leave" I find it difficult to do, for want of wagons. I may get some, but deem it hardly expedient to cross the Arkansas in its present state with little low ferry-boats, until I know what I am doing or hear again from Van Buren.

Very respectfully, yours,

WM. A. PHILLIPS,
Colonel, Commanding.

CAMP OPPOSITE VAN BUREN,
December 25, 1862.

Brigadier-General DAVIDSON:

The First Division got here on the day before yesterday. Boyd and Harding got in yesterday. We are all right. Jeff. Thompson is at Doniphan. Twenty-five of his men attacked my train yesterday within 3 miles of camp, just below Carter's. They got 2 men and killed 1 horse. We chased them 9 miles, but failed to catch them. They are all around us. We need more cavalry to protect our flanks. The supply trains are on the road to Patterson.

BENTON.

HEADQUARTERS, *Helena, Ark., December* 26, 1862.

Maj. H. Z. CURTIS, *Assistant Adjutant-General:*

MAJOR: Last Thursday week, McCulloch was ordered with 8,000 Arkansas and Texas troops to Vicksburg from his camp at Brownsville, Ark. He started and got as far as Little Rock, when he was turned back by orders from Hindman and Holmes to go to the relief of Hindman, who was being pursued by Blunt and Herron, and threatened by others. Deserters heard that Schofield was also moving toward Little Rock. There are from 5,000 to 10,000 troops at Post Arkansas, with eight guns, of which four are large and four are field pieces, all *en barbette.* Hindman has not to exceed 12.000 men, and they are said to be in bad condition. Some forces have lately arrived at Little Rock from Texas, making about 4,000 at that point. General Hawes is camped about 1 mile from Devall's Bluff, on a lake, with three regiments of cavalry and four pieces of artillery (two 6-pounders rifled and two 6-pounders smoothbore). One regiment, seven days ago, crossed the White River in small boats to this side, which I will take care of; it may come within 30 miles of here. An express came from Vicksburg to Holmes to send all the troops he could spare to that point; but never have been sent, unless it has been within the last seven days. The rebel force in Arkansas has a line of communication between Napoleon, Ark., and Grenada, Miss. This information comes from sources that are undoubtedly reliable.

I am, major, very respectfully, your obedient servant,

W. A. GORMAN,
Brigadier-General.

HEADQUARTERS ARMY OF THE FRONTIER,
Rhea's Mills, Ark., December 26, 1862.

Maj. Gen. SAMUEL R. CURTIS,
Commanding Department of the Missouri:

GENERAL: Your telegram of the 23d, informing me of the movements of rebel troops from Little Rock, is received. I have the same advices from below, from spies and deserters. McCulloch's forces probably reached Van Buren yesterday. Whether they propose to act on the offensive or defensive, I am not advised. It was to guard against this combination of rebel forces, that in my telegram of the 12th instant I requested a force sent to menace Little Rock. I shall move upon Van Buren to-morrow morning with all of my best troops, leaving my transportation this side of the mountains.

I have been somewhat surprised at receiving telegrams from General Schofield, now *en route* from Saint Louis, giving directions relative to the movements of this army. I am in command of the Army of the Frontier, and until General Schofield arrives and assumes command by general orders, I shall direct its movements.

Respectfully,

JAS. G. BLUNT,
Commanding Army of the Frontier.

HEADQUARTERS DEPARTMENT OF THE MISSOURI,
Saint Louis, December 26, 1862.

Col. J. T. K. HAYWARD, *Hannibal, Mo.:*

COLONEL: Yours of the 23d, to General Fisk, is before me. We have got to move very prudently here in Missouri, to avoid new issues and new conflicts. When the Enrolled Militia are not in actual military service they are only citizens, entirely subject to the civil authorities, and, as a posse, I suppose they can act as negro-catchers without infringing on the Federal Government authorities. So long as slavery exists in the State, the Governor will have to give some protection to it, and the General Government should not interfere if such acts of the Governor do not molest our proper military camps, and do not interfere with the freedom of the slaves of rebels.

We must not get up an issue on the right of the Governor to regulate his own appointments, but try to induce him to select such men as can be trusted.

While I command the department, and Merrill commands the district, we have a right to command all military movements within our domain, but, to keep down local insurrection, the Enrolled Militia must be considered a State power, commanded by State officers.

General Merrill is here, and I shall give him your letter, with my views of matters generally.

The Governor is preparing an emancipation message, and I hope the Legislature of Missouri will soon pass a law which will conclude the negro question in this State. Emancipationists and pro-slavery men and secessionists will all mix up or divide on this question. The secessionists will, of course, go with the longest term of emancipation, or with those who go for perpetual slavery. The class with which the secessionists go on this subject must not be treated as a rebel class, for they are not all so, and we would alienate too many for our safety.

We must not, as a National Government, or military power, interfere with the State power in discussing, considering, and determining the emancipation issue, and, keeping these maxims in view, you see how difficult a task is imposed upon all of us who have military authority.

The question of returning slaves from a military camp seems to apply equally to the Enrolled Militia, who are to be governed by the regulations of the Army when in actual service; but, in their places as citizens merely, enrolled, they are not in actual service, and cannot be so considered. I hope your zeal and fidelity will in nowise abate, and I hope the hearts of our good Union men of Hannibal will never flag.

Some trying scenes are transpiring everywhere just now; but at such a time firmness must be the more firm, and fidelity never weary of well doing.

I am, colonel, very truly, your friend,

SAML. R. CURTIS,
Major-General.

GENERAL ORDERS, No. 37. } HDQRS. DEPARTMENT OF THE MISSOURI,
Saint Louis, Mo., December 26, 1862.

The following officers, constituting the staff of the major-general commanding, will be addressed, respected, and obeyed accordingly throughout the department: Col. N. P. Chipman, additional aide-de-camp, chief of staff; Col. A. G. Brackett, Ninth Illinois Cavalry, chief of cavalry; Col. Robert Allen, additional aide-de-camp, chief purchasing quartermaster; Col. Lewis B. Parsons, additional aide-de-camp, chief of transportation; Col. T. J. Haines, additional aide-de-camp, chief purchasing commissary of subsistence; Col. F. D. Callender, Missouri State Militia, chief of ordnance; Surg. Madison Mills, medical director; Maj. N. W. Brown, chief paymaster; Maj. H. Z. Curtis, assistant adjutant-general; Maj. T. I. McKenny, additional aide-de-camp, acting assistant inspector-general; Lieut. Col. C. S. Charlot, Missouri State Militia, assistant adjutant-general; Lieut. Col. F. A. Dick, Missouri State Militia, provost-marshal-general; Lieut. Col. S. S. Curtis, Missouri State Militia, acting assistant inspector-general; Capt. F. S. Winslow, assistant quartermaster, aide-de-camp; Capt. Charles N. Turnbull, Corps of Topographical Engineers, chief of engineers; Capt. W. H. Stark, Twenty-fourth Missouri Infantry Volunteers, acting assistant adjutant-general; First Lieut. J. Guylee, Fourth Iowa Cavalry Volunteers, aide-de-camp; Second Lieut. A. Hodge, Fourth Iowa Cavalry Volunteers, aide-de-camp; Second Lieut. Luke O'Reilly, Thirty-third Missouri Infantry Volunteers, aide-de-camp; First Lieut. R. A. Phelan, First Missouri Cavalry Volunteers, acting aide-de-camp, and Second Lieut. M. P. Owens, Twenty-fourth Missouri Infantry Volunteers, acting aide-de-camp.

By command of Major-General Curtis:

H. Z. CURTIS,
Assistant Adjutant-General.

EXECUTIVE MANSION,
Washington, December 27, 1862.

Major-General CURTIS, *Saint Louis, Mo.:*

Let the order in regard to Dr. McPheeters and family be suspended until you hear from me again.

A. LINCOLN.

HEADQUARTERS DEPARTMENT OF THE MISSOURI,
Saint Louis, December 27, 1862.

His Excellency President ABRAHAM LINCOLN:

I have just received your dispatch suspending Rev. McPheeters. This man is evidently a bad rebel, doing injury here, and his removal is, so far as I can learn, universally approved by Union men. I had heard no murmur of doubt as to the propriety. Some of the most reliable men in the city were here to confer with me on this and other matters just before your dispatch came, and they seemed to have a premonition of your interference. They express surprise at the influence rebel sympathizers have at Washington, and desire to prevent it, and although they do not object to your suspension of the assessment, they regret that certain men come home boasting of a triumph, and sneering at Union men. It is a fact that our Union men are disposed to be very severe, but restraint is to be dealt out with moderation, or we modify and weaken them. I will send you a copy of the paper presented to me a few moments before your dispatch came. I explained the propriety of your action in the assessment matter, which they readily approve, but still regret that a Mr. Thompson, who, they say, refused to take the oath, and boasted of his aid to the rebels last year, should now boast of his taking Mr. Bates and detailing an interview with you, and exulting in his success. The Union men that are [whose names are] inclosed in the accompanying paper express great anxiety. They are your fast, unyielding, uncompromising friends. They sympathize with you in your great trials, and any Saint Louis man will tell you they are all sober, honest, wealthy, leading men, deserving the confidence of Your Excellency.

There is no feeling of resentment, but conviction of utility, that induced the order against McPheeters. There is a Union party and secession party in his congregation, and the Union men side with the Union side, and the peace of society seems to require a conclusion of such strife in favor of the loyal side of the question. They think that a priest that will not pray for you should not pray at you, and I concur. Rebel priests are dangerous and diabolical in society. The provost-marshal was for ousting two or three others, but I urged that a single example might do, and the proper man was selected.

It is my judgment that Rev. McPheeters should be required to leave, as ordered by the provost-marshal, at the end of the other five days now granted him, and most respectfully recommend that you allow the order to be executed.

I have the honor to be, Your Excellency's most obedient servant,

SAML. R. CURTIS,
Major-General.

[Inclosure.]

SAINT LOUIS, *December* 27, 1862.

Major-General CURTIS:

DEAR SIR: At an informal meeting of the following-named citizens of Saint Louis, to wit: John Hoor, James E. Yeatman, Carlos S. Greely, Henry Hitchcock, Henry J. Moor, George P. Story, Giles F. Filley, George Partridge, General Edwards, and James O. Broadhead, the undersigned were appointed a committee to wait on you, and propose to offer you their services in the promotion of the Union cause in Saint Louis, by collecting such information and making such suggestions from time to time as might be deemed advisable by them to secure the object in view, so much desired by all loyal men—the restoration of our city and State to a condition of unqualified loyalty to the Federal Government—and to confer with you on these subjects at such times as your public duties will permit.

Respectfully, your obedient servants,

JAMES O. BROADHEAD.
C. S. GREELY.
JAMES E. YEATMAN.

SAINT LOUIS, MO., *December* 27, 1862.

President LINCOLN:

If you intend to leave the country north of the Missouri to the care of the Enrolled Militia, please direct it immediately, that necessary arrangements may be made. Merrill's Horse, a regiment of Missouri cavalry, should be ordered to General Grant immediately. It is much needed.

H. R. GAMBLE,
Governor of Missouri.

WAR DEPARTMENT,
December 27, 1862.

His Excellency Governor GAMBLE:

I do not wish to leave the country north of the Missouri to the care of the Enrolled Militia, except upon the concurrent judgment of yourself and General Curtis. His I have not yet obtained. Confer with him, and I shall be glad to act when you and he agree.

A. LINCOLN.

WAR DEPARTMENT,
Washington, December 27, 1862.

Major-General CURTIS, *Saint Louis, Mo.:*

General Davies reports Columbus as now entirely safe, but General Hurlbut reports Memphis as not sufficiently strong. Can you not give him re-enforcements for a few days, until he can open communication with General Grant? These raids are probably intended to draw back our troops from Vicksburg. This must be avoided.

H. W. HALLECK.

SAINT LOUIS, MO., *December 27, 1862.*

Major-General HALLECK:

Will send some experienced artillerists to Memphis to operate siege guns. Will do all I can, but will have to draw on Helena, and must have a return of forces soon, or trouble on my side may be apprehended

SAML. R. CURTIS.

[DECEMBER 27, 1862.—For Gorman to Hurlbut, in reference to expedition from Helena, Ark., to the Tallahatchee, Mississippi, see Series I, Vol. XVII, Part II, p. 496.]

COLUMBUS, KY., *December 27, 1862.*

Maj. Gen. SAMUEL R. CURTIS, *Saint Louis, Mo.:*

Columbus is threatened by a large force of rebels. We can hold the post. Ram not arrived. General Davies has ordered Colonel Scott to destroy guns, ammunition, and works at New Madrid, and remove his command to Fort Pillow.

CLINTON B. FISK,
Brigadier-General.

HEADQUARTERS DEPARTMENT OF THE MISSOURI,
*Saint Louis, December 27, 1862.**

Maj. Gen. T. H. HOLMES,
Comdg. Trans-Mississippi Department, C. S. Army:

GENERAL: Yours of the 7th instant, containing a slip from the Memphis Daily Appeal, of the 3d of November, concerning what you denominate "an account of the murder of ten Confederate citizens of Missouri, by order of General McNeil, of the U. S. Army," and asking full information in regard to the "circumstances related," is duly received.

The matters of correspondence between us must be confined to the operations of belligerents and the exchange of prisoners.

The idea of "Confederate citizens of Missouri," in Missouri, is inconsistent with a state of war between opposing sections, and utterly repugnant to the attitude heretofore allowed you as a belligerent, which I have cordially approved, for the sake of preserving the immunities recognized by civilized warfare. You have no military power in Missouri, and have had none in Northern Missouri for a year past, much less a civil organization which would induce any man to call himself a

---

* See note of Curtis to Holmes, December 24, 1862, p. 860.

"Confederate citizen." There is but one class of "citizens of Missouri;" they are Federal citizens, not Confederate. They universally acknowledge allegiance to Federal and State authority. The rights of such citizens cannot be adjudicated by appeal through the military authorities of the so-called Confederate States.

I have no disposition to overlook the conduct of any officer in my command or shift any responsibility which it may attach to me; but while the State of Missouri can guard her own citizens, through the regularly constituted authorities, I cannot, even by implication, justify any interference by you with what, by your own showing, relates to her "citizens in Missouri."

I have the honor to be, general, very respectfully, your obedient servant,

SAML. R. CURTIS,
Major-General.

SAINT PAUL, MINN., *December* 27, 1862.

The PRESIDENT OF THE UNITED STATES:

I have the honor to inform you that the 38 Indians and half-breeds ordered by you for execution were hung yesterday at Mankato, at 10 a. m. Everything went off quietly, and the other prisoners are well secured.

Respectfully,

H. H. SIBLEY,
Brigadier-General.

WAR DEPARTMENT,
Washington, December 27, 1862.

Brigadier-General SIBLEY,
Saint Paul, Minn.:

Funds for the Pay Department left here the 24th. The Secretary of War authorizes the quartermaster to loan funds to the Pay Department, to be repaid on their arrival. All forces you can spare should be sent down the Mississippi River, to report first at Cairo or Columbus for further orders.

H. W. HALLECK,
General-in-Chief.

SAINT PAUL, MINN.,
December 27, 1862—8 p. m.

Maj. Gen. H. W. HALLECK,
General-in-Chief:

The Twenty-fifth Regiment Wisconsin Volunteers has already been dispatched. The Third Regiment Minnesota Volunteers will move to Cairo on the 10th proximo. I cannot spare another man. The Indians of the plains are gathering for a general onslaught as soon as weather permits.

Respectfully,

H. H. SIBLEY,
Brigadier-General.

[DECEMBER 28, 1862.—For Curtis to Hurlbut and Davies, and Davies' reply, see Series I, Vol. XVII, Part II, pp. 499-501.]

EXPEDITION IN THE FIELD,
Fort Gibson, December 28, 1862.

Brigadier-General BLUNT,
Commanding Army of the Frontier:

SIR: Your three dispatches have all arrived just this moment—12.30, on the morning of the 28th. I only got in half an hour ago from the Creek Agency. I drove the enemy toward the Canadian and Red Rivers; crossed Arkansas River, with my whole force, at the Frozen Rock Ford; took and burned Fort Davis, reducing all the barrack and commissary buildings and the whole establishment to ashes. I have entered into negotiation with Colonel McIntosh, and am to meet him to-morrow. I expect to disarm or bring over the whole Creek Nation. I sent messengers to the Choctaw Nation, and was in hopes of opening the gates to Texas through friends. Your order breaks off my negotiations, and I start for the place you ordered me to in one hour. It is 70 miles. I scarcely think I can reach by next midnight (28th–29th), but shall try.

Respectfully, yours,

WM. A. PHILLIPS,
Colonel Third Regiment.

FAYETTEVILLE, *December* 28, 1862—9 p. m.

Major-General CURTIS, *Saint Louis:*

Generals Blunt and Herron started for Van Buren yesterday morning; have not been heard from since. I will push on and join them to-morrow. Holmes was at Van Buren a few days ago; started for Little Rock last Tuesday. It is reported at Van Buren that Holmes is to move from Little Rock to Yellville or Carrollton. This does not seem probable. McCulloch has arrived at Van Buren with troops. His force is reported to be 10,000; doubtless exaggerated.

J. M. SCHOFIELD,
Brigadier-General.

HEADQUARTERS DEPARTMENT OF THE MISSOURI,
Saint Louis, December 28, 1862.

Brig. Gen. BEN. LOAN:

GENERAL: I would not care to state the number of troops formerly or now held in Missouri, as it might give improper intelligence to the rebels. Our friends can make an estimate. The fact is I am taking great risks to keep Grant's rear from being destroyed and the river blockaded, and I have drained my department, sending troops to Columbus, Memphis, and Vicksburg.

Blunt keeps going ahead, and is probably at or near the Arkansas River to-night, if Hindman has not checked him.

In the Regular Army it cost about $1,000,000 a year to keep a regiment, taking everything into account, which would be about $1,000 a man; but a great army costs less per man, and $700, I think, would be a fair average of the annual cost of our army. Our western troops are moving, and we may expect stirring news soon. The raid on the Mississippi railroads has been doing about as much harm to the rebels as to us, and I hope it will induce Grant to adopt the river for his base of operations below, which will, in my judgment, be a great advantage to us. I do hope our Union legislators will feel the vast importance of their position. The election in Missouri has gladdened the hearts of our friends throughout the whole country.

I hope and pray the Legislature will succeed in showing the world that the State of Missouri is for the Union now and forever, and that secession has no hiding place within her borders.

I am, general, very truly yours,

SAML. R. CURTIS,
Major-General.

SAINT LOUIS, *December* 29, 1862.

General DAVIDSON, *Southeastern Missouri:*

Colonel Jackson telegraphs that Jeff. Thompson is in Stoddard County, moving on him. General Davies telegraphs that New Madrid is evacuated. This gives Thompson too much scope. You must fall back to Pilot Knob, or otherwise check him.

SAML. R. CURTIS,
Major-General.

SAINT LOUIS, *December* 29, 1862.

General DAVIES, *Columbus:*

I hope you have not evacuated New Madrid. If taken by rebels, it will give us trouble on the river and trouble elsewhere.

SAML. R. CURTIS,
Major-General.

SAINT LOUIS, *December* 29, 1862.

General DAVIES, *Columbus:*

New Madrid must not be given up to Jeff. Thompson if it can be prevented. I send another regiment to resume possession, and, if necessary, you ought to assist. Thompson has three or four pieces of artillery, which, inside of that fort, will close river navigation. It also opens a line of communication to the Iron Mountain Railroad, which Thompson threatens to attack. He is now in Stoddard County. A move of troops or transports would frighten Jeff. Blunt and Herron have driven the rebels across the Arkansas at Van Buren, taking three steamboats, other stores, and 100 prisoners. It was a signal success.

SAML. R. CURTIS,
Major-General.

SAINT LOUIS, MO., *December* 29, 1862.

Maj. Gen. H. W. HALLECK,
General-in-Chief:

Dispatches from Helena show that General Sherman took more than I expected down river, and General Grant asked and received a force to operate from Friar's Point. I have drained this vicinity to hold Columbus, and General Davies yesterday ordered the force from New Madrid. Jeff. Thompson is coming up with 4,000 to 5,000, and is now in Stoddard County, his advance near Fredericktown. I have sent a regiment to recover New Madrid, and will try to bring General Davidson from Current River to press both sides of Thompson. Is there no force in Illinois or Wisconsin to strengthen Grant's line, without relying entirely on me? New Madrid is just as important as any other river point. I can send no more to Memphis, and need forces on my side of the river.

SAML. R. CURTIS,
Major-General, Commanding.

SAINT LOUIS, *December* 29, 1862.

Commanding Officer of the Army of the Frontier:

The attack on the railroad in rear of General Grant's army has given great trouble and made great demands on me, and prevented the possibility of a move from Helena at present. New Madrid is abandoned, and Thompson is moving into Missouri. General Brown fears a move on Springfield. You have finished the matter in Northwest Arkansas gloriously, and must come nearer supplies and nearer to other dangers.

SAML. R. CURTIS,
Major-General.

HEADQUARTERS DEPARTMENT OF THE MISSOURI,
Saint Louis, December 29, 1862.

Brig. Gen. WILLIS A. GORMAN,
Commanding District of Eastern Arkansas:

GENERAL: Yours of the 23d, informing me of the successful departure of our troops for the down-river expedition, is duly received. You say nothing concerning my orders for an interior move, which induces me to suppose Colonel Chipman had not yet arrived.

I trust General Grant has plenty of force to fight his way to the Mississippi, without drawing any more from my department, which I have terribly weakened for his success. I note your report says you sent 13,000, which is a thousand more than my limit, and just that number more than should have gone. Of several regiments I have started to your point, every one is stopped to accommodate other necessities, which General Halleck, General Davies, and General Hurlbut have advised me of this side of you.

General Blunt moved on Van Buren last Saturday (27th), and his hope was that you had moved so as to occupy the fears of Holmes' forces near Little Rock. I see that the downward pressure on you and the upward pressure on me have weakened us so much you will not be able to do good in a westerly move till matters improve elsewhere.

Since writing the above, Lieutenant Stimpson, with dispatches to the 25th, has arrived. I am glad you stopped the move over toward Grenada just as you did. A little move that way is just as good as a ten-days' move, and you need the force on the west side.

The prompt and powerful force sent south from Helena should certainly satisfy the world that we are not holding back on the great move to open the Mississippi, and this will console me for the hazards I have to take in my own department.

I have elsewhere ordered troops to regard this transfer as temporary, but the embarrassment imposed upon me is harassing.

General Davies telegraphs that he has ordered the commanding officer at New Madrid to destroy his guns and vacate that post. Jeff. Thompson is in that vicinity, with Burbridge and others, threatening me, and I send another regiment to recover the place and hold it till I order my guns spiked.

I will write more fully to-morrow. Lieutenant Stimpson will be detained in procuring blanks, for a day or two, and I will send this by other opportunity.

I am, general, your obedient servant,

SAML. R. CURTIS,
Major-General.

WAR DEPARTMENT.
Washington, December 30, 1862.

Major-General CURTIS, *Saint Louis, Mo.:*

I have ordered down everything from Wisconsin, &c., but they will probably be too late. Is it not possible to withdraw some forces from Kansas? As soon as Vicksburg is taken, we shall have forces to reoccupy all necessary points on the river. Banks' expedition should have joined Sherman before now. The pressure is only temporary, and we must meet it the best we can.

H. W. HALLECK,
General-in-Chief.

HEADQUARTERS DEPARTMENT OF THE MISSOURI,
Saint Louis, December 30, 1862.

His Excellency President ABRAHAM LINCOLN:

It is hardly necessary for me to introduce James E. Yeatman, esq., and G. F. Filley, esq., as I have already said to Your Excellency these are some of our most worthy and devoted friends. They wish a private interview, and I hope you will grant it. They are true to their country, and true to you. They are two of the most prominent citizens of Saint Louis. They belong to no clique or party, and you may implicitly rely on their integrity and honor.

While this department has been eminently favored during the three months of my administration, I think it is mainly owing to a steady application of military power.

I take this occasion, also, to say that I would often prefer to send prisoners South rather than North, but have not felt myself authorized to do so; and in many respects it has been my opinion that a commander of a large and remote department should have more rather than less discretion, especially as to the disposal of persons disloyal and dangerous to the public peace. The wives of rebel officers and avowed secessionists have occasionally been ordered East and North, whereas I think these persons had better go where they devote their affections.

Mr. Yeatman, who goes with this to Washington, deserves special notice. Raised in the South, his inclinations are pro-slavery, but he has cast aside all the ease and comforts of society, and devoted his whole time to suffering humanity and the cause of his unhappy country. Neither of these men belong to the congregation of the Rev. McPheeters, and they can speak to you without prejudice on that subject.

I inclose you a letter of Hon. Judge Bates,* which shows further reason to distrust some of our officers of the Enrolled Militia.

I have the honor to be, Your Excellency's obedient servant,

SAML. R. CURTIS,
Major-General.

---

* Not found.

HEADQUARTERS DEPARTMENT OF THE MISSOURI,
Saint Louis, December 30, 1862.

Col. N. P. CHIPMAN, *Helena:*

COLONEL: I wrote General Gorman yesterday, and sent the letter by Colonel Vandever, who may get ahead of Lieutenant Stimpson, who will carry this.

The river must be kept open, if possible. Grant and Sherman seem to have drawn off their forces so far that others must attend to the rear. It may create great disaster in my command and elsewhere, but we must only look to the necessities of the occasion. Sad havoc has been made with the railroad, and now the river is threatened. If necessary and possible, General Gorman must assist Memphis or any other point where our line of communication is in danger, deferring, if need be, all interior operations from Helena till we are re-enforced by Grant or other arrivals on the river.

Thompson, Jeffers, and others, with a force estimated at 5,000 or 6,000, are in Stoddard County, Missouri, and General Davies has ordered New Madrid given up, destroying guns and magazine. The only redeeming affair is the daring dash of Blunt and Herron on Van Buren, the full particulars of which you will receive from the papers of to-day. The Army of the Frontier will have to fall back for supplies, and wait till we can get strength enough to move up the rivers of Arkansas and hold them. If we can move directly up the Arkansas, of course that is best, and on paper one would so decide. I have no choice in the routes, only to carry out my objects, which are, first, to form junctions of forces north of the Arkansas River, thereby showing to the enemy he has no chance of taking my detachments, and give us quiet possession in Northern Arkansas; second, to secure convenient lines of communication interior from Helena, where we must keep supplies for interior posts.

The practical difficulties are considerable on any interior route; and those on the Arkansas are these (I served a military apprenticeship on that river, and understand them):

1st. The Arkansas is so fickle, up to-day and dry to-morrow, it can hardly be called a navigable stream, especially for gunboats.

2d. The fort at Old Post may check transports till the river falls. It is near the mouth, and no junction could be formed there, either with Blunt's or Davidson's forces. Going right forward, as you suggest, may not be so easy. Yet it would be if we have strong gunboat aid to take Old Post, and the water would hold up.

3d. While such forces are on the lower trunk of the Arkansas, they do not support Helena, and Helena does not support them, whereas forces moving direct west from Helena make closer connections.

All commercial men say the White River is the main dependence and surest stream for permanent connections with interior Arkansas, so that whatever we may do temporarily on the Arkansas River, we must also arrange to hold White River and the railroad from Devall's Bluff, as the safe means to supply posts at Little Rock and above.

I am sending small boats to accommodate any move necessary either up and down the Mississippi or up the Arkansas or White, as the general may conclude under my orders. It will be best for such boats to protect the pilot-house and boilers with plank or something else. A little precaution in this way costs very little, and may save a boat. I am glad to know the general cordially supports me. The tone of official correspondence from Washington is now all kind enough. I have not yet had time to ask explanation of the General-in-Chief concerning his unfortunate withdrawal of troops, defeating important operations in Arkansas.

These mysterious remarks have had some light from information obtained from a speculator, Colonel Compton, who says a speculation was on foot to get the Arkansas Hot Springs on speculation, and certain officials were to have 25 per cent. of a half million affair. The Hot Springs belong to the Government. I do not know that the springs had been made the special object of somebody, but the zeal manifested so suddenly to go that way has a singular connection with Colonel Compton's story. I am very busy, and hope I have written on all necessary matters. Communications are very slow, but I hope you will continue to post me and come back soon.

I am, colonel, very truly, yours,

SAML. R. CURTIS,
Major-General.

STEAMER SUNSHINE, *December* 30, 1862.

General [CURTIS]:

We are on our return to Helena, after having gone below the mouth of White River several miles, but not to Napoleon. About midway of the island we were hailed by two men, and took them aboard. They proved to be of the crew of the steamer Blue Wing, which left Helena a day or two since with two barges of coal in tow, bound downward to the fleet. They report her captured at Cypress Bend, 8 miles below Napoleon, on the Arkansas shore. She was attacked by artillery, and, having no guard or escort or other defense, surrendered. The boat and barges were towed up the Arkansas River. This was confirmed by two conscript refugees whom we picked up on the island. They further said they understood that a piece of artillery was to be sent to Napoleon, and a small detachment of troops. They heard firing in the direction of Napoleon about noon yesterday; sounded like cannonading. As it is about time the Rocket, the dispatch boat sent to Admiral Porter, should return, the general (who concluded to go himself to Napoleon) fears it may have been attacked, but thinks, with a hundred good infantry and two howitzers, she can cut her way through. The general thought it imprudent to go to Napoleon, so we put about, and are Helenaward bound now. From these refugees we learn that there is still a large force at Arkansas Post. They say that the road from Napoleon up the Arkansas River is very bad—I should think impassable for artillery until the bluffs are reached, 20 or 30 miles from Napoleon. They report no large rise in Arkansas. They say that there is about 6 feet on the bars; perhaps little more. The White is in better stage. This is about the amount of our information derived.

The cotton-burners in Mississippi are again on a tour of incendiarism and conflagration. A great deal of cotton, which escaped up to the departure of Sherman's expedition, is now being burned under order of Jeff. Davis.

If you decide to give up Helena, what shall be done with the large surplus of transportation, mules, wagons, &c.? Where shall the siege guns be taken if, as I suspect, Napoleon cannot be fortified to advantage? Where shall the thousand contrabands be sent (the old men, women, and children)? Where the accumulated contraband property, condemned and to be condemned quartermaster and commissary stores and property? A very large quantity of commissary stores is being sent to Captain Taggart. He has filled all his sheds and houses, and is compelled to hold boats for storaging purposes. Either Sherman or Grant, or both, are to be supplied from this depot. I very much doubt, from appearances, whether the giving up of Helena, and placing this depot on wheels, would, at this time, be approved at headquarters. I regard Helena as a more secure place than Memphis; besides, it is much nearer Sherman. If Napoleon will fill all the conditions now filled by Helena, it would not then be objectionable.

HELENA, *December* 31, 1862—9 a. m.

General McClernand is here, *en route* to the army down Mississippi River. I was present during a lengthy interview between him and General Gorman. He (General McClernand) thinks it highly important that Old Post be reduced at the very earliest day, viewing it only as a question bearing upon the Mississippi expedition. I told him very plainly that you had been crippled here by overdrafts upon the Helena army, and by stopping of troops at Columbus and Memphis, and the taking away of every gunboat, until you are now powerless. I further gave it as my opinion that when he got below he would find everybody so absorbed in the river movement that they will not be drawn aside to give the interests of your department consideration; that you had done much more than was originally asked of you, and you, therefore, had a right to claim some reciprocation; and submitted as a consideration of interest to both you and him whether or not Arkansas Post should remain garrisoned by 8,000 troops, menacing you and cutting his line of communication by capture of his supply boats, &c. I am glad to know that General McClernand has had a practical illustration of the insecurity of his rear (though it cost us a boat), and that he fully appreciates the necessity of dislodging the enemy at Old Post, and driving them away from his communications. Self-interest, if no other motive, will impel him to urge Admiral Porter to give you, at least, one gunboat.

Later.—The Rocket has just arrived. I have determined to go to Cairo and communicate with you. Will write more fully *en route*.

Very respectfully,

N. P. CHIPMAN,
Colonel, &c.

PRAIRIE GROVE, *December* 30, 1862.

Major-General CURTIS:

I met the army 8 miles this side of Van Buren, at 10 o'clock last night, returning from a raid. They destroyed several steamboats and a considerable amount of corn and other property. I fear the loss of the boats will be a greater loss to us than to the enemy. We will probably have to supply their places soon. I have not yet seen General Blunt. General Herron thinks Hindman has retreated to Arkadelphia. McCulloch's force does not seem to have arrived; on the contrary, a small force, with some artillery, has gone down as far as Clarksville, perhaps farther. There appears no difficulty in my staying or going where I please, so far as force is concerned. Of this, however, I will not be sure until I get further information. I must move immediately, on account of forage. I propose to take two divisions, at least, into Madison County, north of the mountains.

J. M. SCHOFIELD,
Brigadier-General.

HEADQUARTERS,
Saint Louis, Mo., December 31, 1862.

Maj. Gen. H W. HALLECK,
General-in-Chief:

Jeff. Thompson, overestimated, does not advance. New Madrid reoccupied. Will arrest officer who abandoned it against my orders. Will try to keep every point safe. General Blunt destroyed four rebel steamers and much property at Van Buren, bringing away all he could transport. He falls back for supplies.

SAML. R. CURTIS,
Major-General.

JEFFERSON CITY, MO., *December* 31, 1862.

His Excellency ABRAHAM LINCOLN,
President of the United States:

I have stopped all assessments of Enrolled Militia. Please order by telegraph the suspension of all assessments by United States officers. Great distress is produced.

H. R. GAMBLE,
Governor of Missouri.

Abstract from return of the Department of the Missouri, Maj. Gen. Samuel R. Curtis commanding, for the month of December, 1862; *headquarters Saint Louis, Mo.*

Command.	Present for duty.		Aggregate present.	Aggregate present and absent.	Pieces of artillery.		Aggregate present and absent, last monthly return.
	Officers.	Men.			Heavy.	Field.	
District of Saint Louis, Mo	272	5,319	7,645	8,768			10,236
District of Rolla, Mo	169	3,446	5,232	6,197	4	4	6,532
District of Southwestern Missouri	126	1,813	3,122	3,974			4,059
Army of the Frontier:							
Staff	11		11	11			13
First Division, Col. William Weer	260	6,113	6,767	9,333			8,429
Second Division, Col. D. Huston, jr	99	2,440	3,155	4,178		8	3,897
Third Division, Brig. Gen. F. J. Herron	127	2,718	3,642	5,815		12	5,832
Elkhorn Tavern, Ark	25	431	528	596			
Fayetteville, Ark	53	782	1,138	1,824		4	1,726
Central District of Missouri	109	1,827	2,482	3,089		17	3,004
District of Northeastern Missouri	72	1,542	1,874	2,049		2	2,047
District of Kansas	80	1,349	2,051	2,463	7	10	2,376
District of Colorado	34	935	1,169	1,424		4	1,108
District of Nebraska	26	296	634	705			705
Alton, Ill	21	328	521	586			598
Fort Pillow, Tenn	21	385	539	581			530
District of Eastern Arkansas:							
Staff	8		8	8			8
Second Division	304	5,859	7,480	8,535		22	8,533
Cavalry Division	195	3,147	4,747	6,100		12	6,238
Army of Southeastern Missouri:							
Staff	8		8	8			8
First Division	117	2,245	2,755	3,604			3,460
Second Division	127	2,627	3,654	5,234			5,255
Grand total	2,264	43,602	59,162	75,082	11	95	74,594

Organization of the troops in the Department of the Missouri, Maj. Gen. Samuel R. Curtis, U. S. Army, commanding, December 31, 1862.

ARMY OF THE FRONTIER.

Brig. Gen. JOHN M. SCHOFIELD.

FIRST DIVISION.

Col. WILLIAM WEER.

First Brigade.

Col. WILLIAM R. JUDSON.

11th Kansas, Col. Thomas Ewing, Jr.
9th Wisconsin, Lieut. Col. Arthur Jacobi.
6th Kansas Cavalry, Lieut. Col. William T. Campbell.
9th Kansas Cavalry, Col. Edward Lynde.
3d Wisconsin Cavalry, Lieut. Col. Richard H. White.
1st Kansas Battery, Capt. Norman Allen.
Stockton's battery, Capt. Job B. Stockton.

Second Brigade.

Col. WILLIAM F. CLOUD.

10th Kansas, Maj. Henry H. Williams.
13th Kansas, Col. Thomas M. Bowen.
2d Kansas Cavalry, Lieut. Col. Owen A Bassett.

Third Brigade.

Col. WILLIAM A. PHILLIPS

1st Indian Home Guards, Col. Robert W. Furnas.
2d Indian Home Guards, Lieut. Col. David B. Corwin
3d Indian Home Guards, Col. William A. Phillips.
2d Indiana Battery.*

SECOND DIVISION.

Col. DANIEL HUSTON, JR

First Brigade.

Col. JOHN G. CLARK.

26th Indiana, Lieut. Col. Augustine D. Rose.
7th Missouri Cavalry, Maj. David McKee.
Peoria (Illinois) Battery (1st section), Lieut. Herman Borris.

Second Brigade.

Col. WILLIAM McE. DYE.

37th Illinois, Maj. Henry N. Frisbie.
20th Iowa, Lieut. Col. Joseph B. Leake
6th Missouri Cavalry (2d Battalion).*
1st Missouri Light Artillery, Battery F, Capt. David Murphy.

Escort.

1st Missouri Cavalry (2d Battalion), Maj. Charles Banzhaf.

THIRD DIVISION.

Brig. Gen. FRANCIS J. HERRON.

First Brigade.

Col. JAMES O. GOWER.

20th Wisconsin, Col. Henry Bertram.
1st Iowa Cavalry, Lieut. Col. P. Gad Bryan.
2d Wisconsin Cavalry, 1st Battalion, Maj. William H. Miller.
1st Missouri Light Artillery, Battery L, Capt. Frank Backof.

Second Brigade.

Col. WASHINGTON F. GEIGER.

94th Illinois, Lieut. Col. John McNulta.
19th Iowa, Maj. Daniel Kent.
8th Missouri Cavalry, Maj. John W. Lisenby.
1st Missouri Light Artillery, Battery E, Capt. Nelson Cole.

---

*Commander not of record.

Escort.

1st Missouri Cavalry (1st Battalion), Maj. James M. Hubbard.

GARRISONS.

Fayetteville, Ark.

Col. DUDLEY WICKERSHAM.

1st Arkansas Cavalry, Col. M. La Rue Harrison.
10th Illinois Cavalry, Lieut. Col. James Stuart.
Schofield Hussars (one company), Capt. C. G. E. N. Westerberg.

Elkhorn Tavern, Ark.

7th Missouri State Militia Cavalry, Col. John F. Philips.

ARMY OF SOUTHEASTERN MISSOURI.

Brig. Gen. JOHN W. DAVIDSON

FIRST DIVISION.

First Brigade.

Col. CHARLES L. HARRIS.

33d Illinois, Col. Charles E. Lippincott.
11th Wisconsin, Col. Charles L. Harris.

Second Brigade.

Col. DAVID SHUNK.

8th Indiana, Col. David Shunk.
18th Indiana, Col. Henry D. Washburn.

Unattached.

1st Indiana Battery, Capt. Martin Klauss.
24th Missouri (one company),* Capt. James R. Vanzant.

SECOND DIVISION.

Col. S. H. BOYD.

First Brigade.

Col. CHESTER HARDING, Jr.

23d Iowa, Col. William H. Kinsman.
25th Missouri, Maj. Frederic C. Nichols.

Second Brigade.

Col. ROBERT R. LIVINGSTON.

24th Missouri (six companies), Maj. Eli W. Weston.
1st Nebraska, Col. Robert R. Livingston.

Artillery.

1st Missouri Light Artillery, Battery B, Capt. Martin Welfley.
2d Missouri Light Artillery, Battery M, Capt. Gustave Stange.

CAVALRY BRIGADE.

Col. GEORGE E. WARING.

13th Illinois (four companies), Lieut. Col. Theobald Hartman.
4th Missouri, Lieut. Col. Gustav von Helmrich.
1st Wisconsin, Lieut. Col. Oscar H. La Grange.

---

* Serving as pontoniers.

CENTRAL DISTRICT OF MISSOURI.

Brig. Gen. BEN. LOAN (Missouri Militia).

Butler, Mo.

2d Missouri State Militia Cavalry Battalion, Maj. Frank J. White.

Calhoun, Mo.

6th Missouri State Militia Cavalry, Companies B and D, Capt. William Plumb.

Gasconade, Mo.

23d Missouri, Company A, Lieut. Ephraim L. Webb.

Harrisonville, Mo.

5th Missouri State Militia Cavalry (four companies), Lieut. Col. Philip A. Thompson.

Independence, Mo.

Col. WILLIAM R. PENICK.

5th Missouri State Militia Cavalry (three companies), Maj. Thomas B. Biggers.
Missouri State Militia Artillery (one battery).

Jefferson City, Mo.

Lieut. Col. H. L. BRUNS.

4th Missouri State Militia Cavalry, Company I, Capt. Hannibal B. Davis.
5th Missouri State Militia Cavalry, Company E.*
1st Missouri State Militia Battery, Capt. Albert Wachsman.

Kansas City, Mo.

5th Missouri State Militia Cavalry (one company), Maj. William Drumhiller.

Lexington, Mo.

1st Missouri State Militia Cavalry (six companies), Col. James McFerran.

Osage City, Mo.

23d Missouri, Company D, Capt. John W. Moore.

Pleasant Hill, Mo.

5th Missouri State Militia Cavalry (one company), Capt. John Pinger.

Saint Aubert's, Mo.

23d Missouri, Company I, Capt. Marion Cave.

Sedalia, Mo.

Lieut. Col. ALEXANDER M. WOOLFOLK.

1st Missouri State Militia Cavalry (four companies), Lieut. Col. Alexander M. Woolfolk.
3d Indiana Battery.*

Warrensburg, Mo.

6th Missouri State Militia Cavalry (six companies), Col. Edwin C. Catherwood.

DISTRICT OF COLORADO.†

Col. JOHN M. CHIVINGTON.

Fort Lyon, Colo.

Lieut. Col. THEODORE H. DODD.

2d Colorado Cavalry (six companies), Lieut. Col. Theodore H. Dodd.
1st Colorado Battery, Capt. William D. McLain.
9th Wisconsin Battery, Capt. Cyrus H. Johnson.

---

* Actual commanders at this date not of record.

† The garrisons of camp on Arkansas River, Camp Collins, and Colorado City are not indicated on original return. A return for December 20 reports Lieut. Col. S. S. Curtis commanding at Denver City; Maj. E. W. Wynkoop commanding at Colorado City, and Capt. J. S. Maynard at Camp Collins.

DISTRICT OF EASTERN ARKANSAS.*

Brig. Gen. WILLIS A. GORMAN.

SECOND DIVISION.

Brig. Gen. ALVIN P. HOVEY.

First Brigade.

Col. JAMES R. SLACK.

43d Indiana, Col. William E. McLean.
46th Indiana, Lieut. Col. John H. Gould.
47th Indiana, Lieut. Col. John A. McLaughlin.

Second Brigade.

Col. PETER KINNEY.

24th Iowa, Col. Eber C. Byam.
28th Iowa, Col. William E. Miller.
56th Ohio, Lieut. Col. William H. Raynor
29th Wisconsin, Col. Charles R. Gill.

Third Brigade.

Col. GEORGE F. MCGINNIS.

11th Indiana, Lieut. Col. Daniel Macauley.
24th Indiana, Col. William T. Spicely.
34th Indiana, Col. Robert A. Cameron.

Artillery.

Capt. PETER DAVIDSON.

Peoria Light Artillery,† Lieut. Jacob C. Hansel.
3d Iowa Battery, Capt. Mortimer M. Hayden.
2d Ohio Battery, Capt. Newton J. Smith.
16th Ohio Battery, Capt. James A. Mitchell.

CAVALRY DIVISION.

Brig. Gen. CADWALLADER C. WASHBURN.

First Brigade.

Col. CONRAD BAKER.

5th Illinois, Col. Hall Wilson.
10th Illinois (four companies), Maj. Elvis P. Shaw.
1st Indiana, Lieut. Col. William F. Wood.
1st Missouri (four companies), Col. John F. Ritter.
6th Missouri (six companies), Maj. Bacon Montgomery.

Second Brigade.

Col. CYRUS BUSSEY.

2d Arkansas (two companies).‡
9th Illinois, Maj. Hector J. Humphrey.
3d Iowa, Companies A, B, C, D, I, and K, Maj. John W. Noble.
4th Iowa (ten companies), Lieut. Col. Simeon D. Swan.
5th Kansas (ten companies), Col. Powell Clayton.
2d Wisconsin (eight companies), Col. Thomas Stephens.

---

*Transferred to Thirteenth Army Corps by General Orders, No. 14, Headquarters Department of the Tennessee, December 22, 1862. See Series I, Vol. XVII, Part II, p. 461.

† One section reported as in Army of the Frontier, p. 889.

‡ Actual commanders at this date not of record.

DISTRICT OF KANSAS.

Brig. Gen. JAMES G. BLUNT.

GARRISONS.

Fort Larned.

Lieut. WILLIAM WEST.

2d United States, Company H, Lieut. William West.
9th Wisconsin Battery (one section), Lieut. Watson D. Crocker.

Fort Leavenworth.

Lieut. Col. JOHN T. BURRIS.

8th Kansas, Companies A, C, D, and F, Lieut. Col. James L. Abernathy.
9th Kansas Cavalry, Companies G and I, Capt. Willoughby Doudna.
3d Wisconsin Cavalry, Companies B and H, Capt. Nathan L. Stout.

Fort Riley.

9th Kansas Cavalry, Company C, Capt. John E. Stewart.

Fort Scott.

Maj. BENJAMIN S. HENNING.

1st U. S. Battalion, Capt. Robert H. Offley.
3d Wisconsin Cavalry, Companies C, G, I, and M, Maj. Benjamin S. Henning.
2d Kansas Battery (one section), Maj. Charles W. Blair.

Paoli.

12th Kansas, Maj. Thomas H. Kennedy.

Westport, Mo.

Maj. WYLLIS C. RANSOM.

6th Kansas Cavalry, Company B, Capt. Elijah E. Harvey.

DISTRICT OF NEBRASKA.

Brig. Gen. JAMES CRAIG.

Fort Halleck.

Lieut. HENRY L. KOEHNE.

9th Kansas Cavalry, Company B, Lieut. Robert Madden.
6th Ohio Cavalry, Company A, Lieut. Henry L. Koehne.

Fort Kearny.

10th United States, headquarters and Companies D and K, Col. Edmund B. Alexander.

Fort Laramie.

Capt. JOHN A. THOMPSON.

8th Kansas, Company G, Lieut. Joseph Randolph.
6th Ohio Cavalry, Company C, Lieut. Thomas P. Clark.
4th U. S. Cavalry, Companies F and H, Capt. John A. Thompson.

Along Telegraph Line.

6th Ohio Cavalry, Companies B and D, Lieut. Col. William O. Collins.

DISTRICT OF NORTHEASTERN MISSOURI.

Brig. Gen. LEWIS MERRILL.

Canton, Mo.

2d Missouri State Militia Cavalry, Company D, Capt. Samuel Spangler.

Edina, Mo.

2d Missouri State Militia Cavalry, Company K, Capt. Lewis Sells.

Hannibal, Mo.

2d Missouri State Militia Cavalry, Company F, Capt. Dennis C. McKay.

Kirksville, Mo.

2d Missouri State Militia Cavalry, Company M, Capt. Samuel Shibley.

Lancaster, Mo.

2d Missouri State Militia Cavalry, Company L, Capt. Jacob Gilstrap.

Memphis, Mo.

2d Missouri State Militia Cavalry, Company A, Capt. William Dawson.

Monticello, Mo.

2d Missouri State Militia Cavalry, Company B, Capt. James W. Edwards.

Palmyra, Mo.

Col. JOHN MCNEIL.

2d Missouri State Militia Cavalry (four companies), Lieut. Col. John F. Benjamin.
9th Wisconsin Battery (one section), Lieut. James H. Dodge.

Shelbyville, Mo.

2d Missouri State Militia Cavalry, Company I, Capt. Albert G. Priest.

Warrenton, Mo.

2d Missouri Cavalry, Maj. Garrison Harker.

SAINT LOUIS DISTRICT.

Brig. Gen. EUGENE A. CARR.

Benton Barracks, Mo.

Col. BENJAMIN E. L. BONNEVILLE.

8th Iowa, Col. James L. Geddes.
12th Iowa, Lieut. Col. John P. Coulter.
14th Iowa, Col. William T. Shaw.
23d Missouri, Company K, Capt. Richard H. Brown.
3d Illinois Cavalry (detachment).*
6th Missouri Cavalry (detachment).*

Cape Girardeau, Mo.

Maj. GUSTAVUS A. EBERHART.

32d Iowa (detachment).*
29th Missouri (detachment).*
2d Missouri Light Artillery, Battery D, Lieut. Charles Engan.

Jackson, Mo.

12th Missouri State Militia Cavalry,† Col. Albert Jackson.

Pacific City, Mo.

23d Missouri (six companies), Col. William P. Robinson.

Pilot Knob, Mo.

Col. JOHN B. GRAY.

1st Missouri State Militia, Maj. John N. Herder.
13th Illinois Cavalry, 1st Battalion, Maj. Charles A. Bell.
10th Missouri State Militia Cavalry, Col. Edwin Smart.

Saint Louis, Mo.

Col. HENRY ALMSTEDT.

33d Iowa,‡ Col. Samuel A. Rice.
4th Missouri (seven companies), Col. Robert Hundhausen.
27th Missouri (nine companies), Lieut. Col. Augustus Jacobson.
2d Missouri Light Artillery, Batteries B, E, H, I, and K, Col. Henry Almstedt.

INDEPENDENT POSTS.

Alton, Ill.

77th Ohio, Col. Jesse Hildebrand.

Fort Pillow, Tenn.

32d Iowa, Col. John Scott.

*Actual commander at this date not of record.
†Capt. Anthony Arnold's company at Patterson and Capt. George W. Hummell's company at Fredericktown.
‡Left post "for down river."

DISTRICT OF ROLLA.

Col. WILLIAM M. STONE.

Houston, Mo.

Brig. Gen. F. H. WARREN.

99th Illinois, Col. George W. K. Bailey.
21st Iowa, Col. Samuel Merrill.
22d Iowa, Companies A, H, and I, Maj. Joseph B. Atherton.
3d Iowa Cavalry (six companies), Lieut. Col. Henry C. Caldwell.
3d Missouri Cavalry (six companies), Capt. Thomas G. Black.
2d Missouri Light Artillery, Batteries C, F, and L, Capt. Henry Duncker.

Rolla, Mo.

Lieut. Col. HARVEY GRAHAM.

22d Iowa (six companies), Lieut. Col. Harvey Graham.
3d Missouri Cavalry (four companies), Capt. James T. Howland.

Rolla, Mo.—Continued.

9th Missouri State Militia Cavalry (seven companies), Lieut. Col. John F. Williams.
2d Missouri Light Artillery, Batteries A and G, Maj. Theodore Wilkins.

Salem, Mo.

Capt. TIMOTHY M. WILCOX.

22d Iowa, Company F, Capt. Alfred B. Cree.
3d Missouri Cavalry (one company).*
9th Missouri State Militia Cavalry, Company G, Capt. Thomas B. Reed.

Waynesville, Mo.

13th Missouri State Militia Cavalry (eight companies), Col. Albert Sigel.

DISTRICT OF SOUTHWESTERN MISSOURI.

Brig. Gen. EGBERT B. BROWN (Missouri State Militia).

Cassville, Mo.

14th Missouri State Militia Cavalry, 1st Battalion, Maj. James Sullivan.

Elkhorn Tavern, Ark. †

7th Missouri State Militia Cavalry, Col. John F. Philips.

Greenfield, Mo.

4th Missouri State Militia Cavalry, Col. George H. Hall.

Lebanon, Mo.

8th Missouri State Militia Cavalry, 2d Battalion, Maj. John E. Collins.

Newtonia, Mo.

8th Missouri State Militia Cavalry (one battalion), Maj. Edward B. Eno.

Ozark, Mo.

14th Missouri State Militia Cavalry, 2d Battalion, Capt. Milton Burch.

Springfield, Mo.

Col. BENJAMIN CRABB.

18th Iowa, Lieut. Col. Thomas Z. Cook.
3d Missouri State Militia Cavalry, Col. Walter King.

---

* Commander not of record.
† See also Army of the Frontier, p. 890.

Abstract from return of the Department of the Northwest, Brig. Gen. Washington L. Elliott, U. S. Army, commanding, for December* 31, 1862.

Command.	Present for duty.		Aggregate present.	Aggregate present and absent.	Remarks on original.
	Officers.	Men.			
Department staff	12	7	19	29	
First District	10	98	159	477	
District of Minnesota	169	3,821	4,370	6,546	Large numbers sick, and the measles throughout the district.
State of Wisconsin	50	1,360	1,634	1,882	Does not include two companies of paroled prisoners, about 60 men each.
Total	241	5,286	6,182	8,934	This return is necessarily very incomplete, as full returns have not yet been received from the whole command. The aggregates, however, are nearly, if not quite, correct.

Troops in the Department of the Northwest, December 31, 1862.

FIRST MILITARY DISTRICT.

Brig. Gen. JOHN COOK.

41st Iowa, Maj. John Pattee.
Dakota Cavalry, Company A, Capt. Nelson Miner.
Sioux City Cavalry, Company A, Capt. Andrew J. Millard.

DISTRICT OF MINNESOTA.

Brig. Gen. HENRY H. SIBLEY.

3d Minnesota,† Col. Chauncey W. Griggs.
6th Minnesota, Col. William Crooks.
7th Minnesota, Col. Stephen Miller.
8th Minnesota, Col. Minor T. Thomas.
9th Minnesota, Col. Alexander Wilkin.
10th Minnesota, Col. James H. Baker.
1st Minnesota Mounted Rangers, Col. Samuel McPhaill.

STATE OF WISCONSIN.

Brig. Gen. WASHINGTON L. ELLIOTT.

25th Wisconsin, Col. Milton Montgomery.
30th Wisconsin, Col. Daniel J. Dill.

* In temporary absence of Maj. Gen. John Pope.
† Paroled at Murfreesborough, Tenn. In process of reorganization at Fort Snelling.

CONFEDERATE CORRESPONDENCE, ETC.

HDQRS. FIRST CORPS, TRANS-MISSISSIPPI ARMY,
Camp near Fort Smith, Ark., November 22, 1862.

Brig. Gen. J. S. MARMADUKE,
Commanding Fourth Division:

GENERAL: General Hindman directs that you take position as soon as possible so as to cover his entire front, from the Huntsville road toward the left, far into the Indian country. He is satisfied that the squadron under Dobbin is doing no good, and wishes to relieve it as soon as possible. He desires, therefore, that as soon as you get into position, and post your pickets suitably, you report the fact to him immediately, that he may withdraw that squadron.

Respectfully,

R. C. NEWTON,
Assistant Adjutant-General.

[NOVEMBER 22 and 25, 1862.—For Holmes to Cooper and Seddon, in reference to re-enforcements for Pemberton, see Series I, Vol. XIII, pp. 926, 927.]

WAR DEPARTMENT, C. S. A.,
Richmond, Va., November 25, 1862.

Lieut. Gen. T. H. HOLMES,
Commanding, &c., Little Rock, Ark.:

GENERAL: I have received your letter of the 25th ultimo in reference to the urgent need of money for your command. In addition to the sum of $4,888,567 carried out by Major Carr, the sum of $2,500,000 was sent to him in charge of a special agent, who left this city on October 16, and had not reached your headquarters at the date of your letter. It is hoped that these amounts will be sufficient to meet the most pressing claims, and if more funds are necessary you are requested to forward estimates made out by bonded officers, as no money can legally be paid from the Treasury to any others. The sums mentioned above do not include $1,132,393 lately sent to the quartermaster of General Pike's command. The Quartermaster-General reports that in no instance has the reasonable estimate of any bonded quartermaster been received and not acted on the same day it reached his office.

Your obedient servant,

J. A. SEDDON,
Secretary of War.

HEADQUARTERS TRANS-MISSISSIPPI DEPARTMENT,
Little Rock, November 25, 1862.

Lieut. Gen. J. C. PEMBERTON,
Commanding Mississippi Department:

GENERAL: Mr. Adams has just reported to me. The enemy have threatened me very heavily both in Northwestern Arkansas and from Helena; in the former, they drove my advance of 7,000 men from the border of Missouri back to the Boston Mountains. I have sent General Hindman to reorganize that corps of this army, and to protect that frontier and the Indian country for this purpose. [He] has much the larger part of my force. [Illegible.]——Enemy have a large force, having been re-enforced during the last week by two divisions. On the 20th they attempted to enter the White and Arkansas Rivers, but could not, on account of the low water, sending in conjunction with this expedition a land force reported 8,000 strong across from Laconia, on the Mississippi, to a point on White River, opposite the Post of Arkansas, where alone I have fortifications to resist this force. I have three brigades at Brownsville to cover this place, and I hope competent garrisons for the defenses of Arkansas and White Rivers. If the valley of the Arkansas is lost, this department goes with it, for there is absolutely no other stopping place for an army short of Red River, the whole country between the two rivers being exhausted of supplies. Under these circumstances I cannot send [illegible] when you telegraphed me that troops had left Helena and crossed the Mississippi. Not a soldier has left there, and it is stronger to-day than at any former time. But, in addition to this, if I was not threatened at all, I am distant from you 290 miles, with an intervening country almost destitute of supplies and forage, and the march would require too much time to enable me to be of service to you. I have ordered Sibley's brigade, now at Marshall, Tex., to be increased by two regiments, now at Clarksville, and under General [W. R.] Scurry, to report to you as soon as possible. I regret that I cannot tell you when to expect them.

I am, general, very respectfully, your obedient servant,

TH. H. HOLMES,
Major-General.

WAR DEPARTMENT, C. S. A.,
Richmond, Va., November 26, 1862.

Lieut. Gen. T. H. HOLMES, *Commanding, &c.:*

GENERAL: This department is earnestly urged by Maj. Gen. Sterling Price to transfer him, with his command of Missouri troops—consisting now of six regiments of infantry, one regiment and one battalion of dismounted cavalry, and seven light batteries, making an aggregate present of 3,283—from the command of Lieutenant-General Pemberton to your department. The Department would be pleased to comply with the request, but is apprehensive that the safety of General Pemberton's command might be endangered by the withdrawal of troops from him at this time; but if a like or superior force could be exchanged from your department for General Price and his command, it might prove not disadvantageous to both. You would secure veteran troops and the influence of their commander, potent in the district of your expected operations, while General Pemberton might be compensated by fuller regiments and troops not pining for another sphere of action. You will, therefore, consider the feasibility and expediency of such substitution, and, if deemed by you compatible with the safety of your command, endeavor to accomplish it with General Pemberton. A copy of General Price's letter has been forwarded to General Pemberton, with a recommendation, if deemed by him expedient, to effect such exchange with you.*

Most respectfully, yours,

J. A. SEDDON,
Secretary of War.

---

* For further correspondence on this subject, see Series I, Vol. XVII, Part II.

RICHMOND, [VA.,] *November* 29, 1862.

Lieutenant-General PEMBERTON, *Yocona, Miss.:*

Send the following by most expeditious line:

General HOLMES, *Little Rock:*

Sibley's brigade is not wanted at Vicksburg. Order it to report to General Taylor, in West Louisiana. Send to Vicksburg, without delay, the infantry force which you have been twice telegraphed for. The case is urgent, and will not admit of delay.

S. COOPER,
Adjutant and Inspector General.

Repeated November 30.

HDQRS. FIRST CORPS, TRANS-MISSISSIPPI ARMY,
Near Fort Smith, November 29, 1862—11.30 a. m.

Brig. Gen. J. S. MARMADUKE,
Commanding Fourth Division, at Oliver's Store:

GENERAL: I have to acknowledge the receipt of your dispatch of 26th and two dispatches of 28th; the first received yesterday evening, and the other (on subject of yesterday's engagement with the enemy) received early this morning. Lieutenant-Colonel [R. P.] Crump, with Lane's regiment Texas Cavalry, about 600 strong (effective), was ordered forward to you last night, and has, no doubt, reached you by this time. Six wagons, laden with ammunition for you, left Van Buren at daylight, and ought to reach you during the day. The general still expects you, of course, to watch the enemy vigilantly, and give him information of all his movements. You will keep your eye particularly on the Line road. With the addition of Crump's regiment to your force, you ought to be able to determine the strength of the enemy, if he advances farther, and ascertain certainly all his movements and his probable intentions. Major Crump is advised that you desire forage sent to Dripping Springs, and will have it there to-day, though it is reducing us to a great strait to furnish it to you.

In regard to clothing for your men, you received at the last distribution, besides your own, that which belongs properly to the Texas brigade. Your share under the new distribution is at Van Buren, and Major [John H.] Crump tells me that he has notified you of the fact. You can send your wagons for it.

In regard to the rank of Mr. Lawrence, topographical engineer, I am instructed by General Hindman to say that he has no authority to make such appointments and confer rank, but is expressly prohibited from so doing. He needs such an officer very much, however.

Respectfully,

R. C. NEWTON,
Assistant Adjutant-General.

CAMP NEAR FORT SMITH, ARK.,
November 29, 1862.

Brig. Gen. J. S. MARMADUKE, *Commanding Advance:*

GENERAL: I am to-day crossing my entire effective force, with the intention to find the enemy and attack him. The crossing will be completed to-morrow, and the command will move on Monday at daylight. I shall march moderately, not above 12 or 15 miles a day, if it can be helped, so as not to break the men down before the fight commences.

I wish you to send me immediately, by courier, a diagram of all the roads, so far as known to you, leading to the enemy's camp, on every side, with the distances from Fayetteville, Van Buren, Maysville, and other noted points marked, and such memoranda as you may be able to append, giving information as to passes, mountains, ridges, prairies, &c.

I wish also to have your opinion in full as to the routes of march, the manner of attack, &c.; also whether or not there is any Federal force in Arkansas or within supporting distance of Blunt, except that which he commands, and the probable strength of that in each arm.

To prevent as far as practicable rumors of the movement getting to the enemy, spread the report that Little Rock is threatened, and I am ordered there. This can be done, I hope, without disheartening your men.

Respectfully,

T. C. HINDMAN,
Major-General, Commanding.

[Indorsement.]

Some artillery ammunition was sent you in the train this morning. If you need any more, send your requisition at once, as your batteries must be supplied without delay.

By order:

NEWTON,
Assistant Adjutant-General.

HDQRS. FIRST CORPS, TRANS-MISSISSIPPI ARMY,
Camp near Fort Smith, Ark., December 1, 1862.

Brig. Gen. D. H. COOPER,
Commanding First Brigade, First Division:

GENERAL: General Hindman desires you to move with Stand Watie's Cherokee regiment, and any other troops with you which are in condition to march, in sufficient time and in such manner as will enable you to reach Evansville, or the vicinity, on Friday evening, the 5th instant, and will then immediately establish communication with the pickets of Marmaduke's division (which are of Bryan's Cherokee battalion, on the Line road), communicating to them promptly all information you may gain of the enemy's movements. Bryan's battalion will remain under General Marmaduke's orders until the latter shall notify you that he can dispense with its services and order it back to you.

It is the intention of General Hindman to attack Blunt at Cane Hill early Saturday morning, and you will be in such position at Evansville that, when you hear the battle fairly opened to the east of you on that day, you will attack the enemy's right and rear, harassing him, and impeding him if he attempts to escape on the Cincinnati or any other road, capturing his trains, if possible, and otherwise crippling him in his effort to get away. You will be careful to take possession of the Dutch Mills, if you can do so before the enemy burns it, which it is not improbable he will attempt to do. It is impossible now to give you more specific directions; and, as you will be operating at some distance from the main body and in an important position, General Hindman leaves to your discretion the details in the performance of the duty allotted to you. He relies upon you to strike promptly and with vigor.

Respectfully,

R. C. NEWTON,
Assistant Adjutant-General.

HDQRS. FIRST CORPS, TRANS-MISSISSIPPI ARMY,
Camp near Fort Smith, Ark., December 1, 1862.

Brig. Gen. J. S. MARMADUKE,
Commanding Cavalry Division:

GENERAL: On Wednesday morning, 3d instant, you will move your division from Dripping Spring to Oliver's, and will then immediately place pickets and scouts upon the Frog Bayou, Telegraph, Cove Creek, and Line roads, and on all intermediate roads, so as to effectually prevent all communications with the enemy, and to detect any movements he may make. All persons passing, or attempting to pass, the line so established, and all persons whose conduct may be at all suspicious, are to be at once arrested and sent under guard to the post commander at Van Buren. Any information gained from them is to be dispatched at once to Oliver's. You will assign a capable officer to duty as provost-marshal at Oliver's, giving him a sufficient force, and instructing him to receive dispatches and forward them properly; also to give all possible assistance to the trains moving up with supplies, or going for them, to prevent all interference with the instructions given by Maj. John H. Crump, chief quartermaster, concerning the same, and to arrest all stragglers and disorderly persons. Further instructions will be given you at Oliver's Thursday evening. These headquarters will continue at this place until Thursday, when they will be moved to Oliver's.

By command of Major-General Hindman:

R. C. NEWTON,
Assistant Adjutant-General.

DECEMBER 1, 1862.

Resolved by the General Assembly of the State of Arkansas, That the Governor is hereby invested with authority to destroy such of the public property as cannot be conveniently removed, when, in his judgment, it shall become expedient to do so, to prevent the same from falling into the hands of the public enemy.

Adopted by the House of Representatives in secret session, December 1, 1862.

JOHN A. HARRELL,
Speaker of the House of Representatives.

Adopted by the Senate in secret session, December 1, 1862.

THOS. FLETCHER,
President of the Senate.

Approved, December 1, 1862.

H. FLANIGAN.

RICHMOND, VA., *December* 3, 1862.

General T. H. HOLMES, *Little Rock, Ark.:*

GENERAL: The President has deemed it advisable to establish at some point which you may deem most eligible, as near to the Missouri line as may be judicious, a camp of instruction for the rendezvous and place of training and organizing men coming to enlist in the Confederate service from Missouri. For the more effectual carrying out of this intention, he has seen proper to appoint Judge William C. Price major and assistant adjutant-general, with directions to report to you for duty. You will assign to Major Price such assistant officers as you may deem requisite for the effectual performance of his duties, and generally to facilitate Major Price in the duty allotted him.

By order of the Secretary of War:

Very respectfully, &c.,

E. A. PALFREY,
Assistant Adjutant-General.

HEADQUARTERS TRANS-MISSISSIPPI DEPARTMENT,
Little Rock, Ark., December 6, 1862.

Major-General HINDMAN,
Commanding First Corps, Trans-Mississippi Army:

GENERAL: I am instructed by Major-General Holmes to inform you that all the enemy's forces at Springfield, Mo., left that place on Thursday and Friday of last week, the 27th and 28th ultimo, and moved in the direction of Arkansas on the Cassville road. The Federal force at Forsyth left that point on Friday, the 28th ultimo, going toward Cassville. The person giving this information says the force that left Springfield amounted to from 10,000 to 12,000; the force that left Forsyth between 600 and 1,000.

I am, general, very respectfully, your most obedient servant,

S. S. ANDERSON,
Assistant Adjutant-General.

CAMP ON COVE CREEK, ARK.,
December 9, 1862.

COLONEL: On the morning of the 1st instant, while in the advance of the advance picket, I received instructions to order up and take command of the train. At 12 a. m. my pickets reported that 400 Federals with two small pieces of artillery were in the vicinity of Sulphur Springs. There being no suitable place at Hog-Eye to protect the train, I ordered it back 2 miles to a point where I could place it in position to be defended with the small force then under my command, numbering 100 men. From the sick stragglers and detailed men I collected and armed 150 infantry and about 100 cavalry. At midnight I received an order from General Hindman to move the train with all possible dispatch toward Van Buren. The various quartermasters of the command acted with great coolness and moved their wagons with great caution. I am happy to say I succeeded in reaching this place with the entire train, saving all the Government stores and property.

Respectfully,

A. D. BURNS,
Major First Texas Regiment Partisan Rangers.

SPECIAL ORDERS, } ADJT. AND INSPECTOR GENERAL'S OFFICE,
No. 289. } *Richmond, Va., December* 10, 1862.

* * * * * * *

XIII. Brig. Gen. T. J. Churchill is assigned to duty in the Trans-Mississippi Department. He will repair to Little Rock, Ark., and report for duty to Lieut. Gen. T. H. Holmes.

* * * * * * *

By command of Secretary of War:

JNO. WITHERS,
Assistant Adjutant-General.

Organization of the Army of the Trans-Mississippi Department, Lieut. Gen. Theophilus H. Holmes, C. S. Army, commanding, December 12, 1862.

FIRST CORPS.

Maj. Gen. THOMAS C. HINDMAN.

FIRST DIVISION.

Brig. Gen. JOHN S. ROANE.

First Brigade.

Brig. Gen. DOUGLAS H. COOPER.

1st Cherokee, Col. Stand Watie.
1st Choctaw and Chickasaw.
1st Creek, Lieut. Col. D. N. McIntosh.
2d Creek, Lieut. Col. Chilly McIntosh.
De Morse's (Texas) regiment.
Lane's (Texas) regiment.
Randolph's (Texas) cavalry battalion.
Cavalry (seven companies).
Indian regiments, organizing (2).
Indian battalions, organizing (3).
Howell's (Texas) battery.

*Second Brigade.**

Col. WILLIAM R. BRADFUTE.

20th Texas Cavalry, Col. Thomas C. Bass.
22d Texas Cavalry, Col. J. G. Stevens.
[31st] Texas Cavalry (battalion), Lieut. Col. G. W. Guess.
34th Texas Cavalry, Col. A. M. Alexander.
Etter's (Arkansas) battery.

SECOND DIVISION.

Brig. Gen. FRANCIS A. SHOUP.

First Brigade.

Brig. Gen. JAMES F. FAGAN.

—— Arkansas, Col. A. T. Hawthorn.
22d Arkansas, Col. J. P. King.
29th Arkansas, Col. J. C. Pleasants.
34th Arkansas, Col. W. H. Brooks.
Blocher's (Arkansas) battery.

Second Brigade.

Col. DANDRIDGE MCRAE.

28th Arkansas, Col. D. McRae.
26th Arkansas, Col. A. S. Morgan.
30th Arkansas, Col. A. J. McNeill.
32d Arkansas, Col. C. H. Matlock.
West's (Arkansas) battery.
Woodruff's (Arkansas) battery.

Unattached.

Cheek's battalion, sharpshooters.
Venable's (Arkansas) cavalry.

THIRD DIVISION.

Brig. Gen. M. M. PARSONS.

First Brigade.

Col. ALEXANDER E. STEEN.

7th Missouri, Col. J. H. Caldwell.
8th Missouri, Col. De Witt C. Hunter.
9th Missouri, Col. J. D. White.
10th Missouri, Col. A. E. Steen.
Tilden's (Missouri) battery.

Second Brigade.

Col. R. G. SHAVER.

—— Arkansas, Col. C. W. Adams.
27th Arkansas, Col. James R. Shaler.
33d Arkansas, Col. H. L. Grinsted.
38th Arkansas, Col. R. G. Shaver.
Roberts' (Missouri) battery.

Unattached.

Roberts' (Missouri) cavalry.

---

* Dismounted cavalry.

FOURTH DIVISION.

Brig. Gen. JOHN S. MARMADUKE.

First Brigade.

Col. CHARLES A. CARROLL.

Arkansas Cavalry, Col. C. A. Carroll.
Arkansas Cavalry, Col. J. C. Monroe.
Shoup's (Arkansas) battery.

Second Brigade.

Col. JOSEPH O. SHELBY.

Missouri Cavalry, Col. John T. Coffee.
Missouri Cavalry, Col. B. G. Jeans.
Missouri Cavalry, Col. J. O. Shelby.
Bledsoe's (Missouri) battery.

SECOND CORPS.

FIRST DIVISION.

Brig. Gen. HENRY E. McCULLOCH.

First Brigade.

Col. OVERTON YOUNG.

12th Texas, Col. O. Young.
18th Texas, Col. W. B. Ochiltree.
22d Texas, Col. R. B. Hubbard.
13th Texas Cavalry, Col. J. H. Burnett.

Second Brigade.

Col. HORACE RANDAL.

11th Texas, Col. O. M. Roberts.
14th Texas, Col. Edward Clark.
15th Texas, Col. J. W. Speight.
28th Texas Cavalry, Col. H. Randal.
Gould's (Texas) Cavalry Battalion.

Third Brigade.

Col. GEORGE FLOURNOY.

16th Texas, Col. George Flournoy.
17th Texas, Col. R. T. P. Allen.
19th Texas, Col. Richard Waterhouse.
16th Texas Cavalry, Col. William Fitzhugh.

Artillery.

Daniel's (Texas) battery.

SECOND DIVISION.

Brig. Gen. T. J. CHURCHILL.

First Brigade.

——— ———, commanding.

6th Texas, Col. R. R. Garland.
24th Texas Cavalry, Col. F. C. Wilkes.
25th Texas Cavalry, Col. C. C. Gillespie.
Denson's (Louisiana) cavalry.
Hart's (Arkansas) battery.

Second Brigade.

Col. JAMES DESHLER.

10th Texas, Col. R. Q. Mills.
15th Texas Cavalry, Col. Geo. H. Sweet.
18th Texas Cavalry, Col. N. H. Darnell.
Haldeman's (Texas) battery.

Third Brigade.

Col. J. W. DUNNINGTON.

19th Arkansas, Col. C. L. Dawson.
24th Arkansas, Col. E. E. Portlock, jr.
Crawford's (Arkansas) battalion.
Marine Battery.
Nutt's (Louisiana) cavalry.

Fourth Brigade.

Brig. Gen. J. M. HAWES.

12th Texas Cavalry, Col. W. H. Parsons.
19th Texas Cavalry, Col. N. M. Burford.
21st Texas Cavalry, Col. Geo. W. Carter.
Chrisman's (Arkansas) battalion

Fifth Brigade.

Col. M. J. WHITE.

3d Missouri Cavalry, Col. Colton Greene.
4th Missouri Cavalry, Col. J. Q. Burbridge.

HEADQUARTERS TRANS-MISSISSIPPI DEPARTMENT,
Near Van Buren, Ark., December 21, 1862.

Major-General HINDMAN,
Commanding First Corps, Trans-Mississippi Army:

GENERAL: The major-general commanding department directs me to say that the supplies in the neighborhood of Van Buren and Fort Smith having been exhausted, you will move with your corps, except such part of it as is necessary for the defense of the Indian country, to the neighborhood of Lewisburg, and as soon as General Marmaduke's horses are sufficiently recruited you will order him to some point in the Black or White River Valley, where necessary forage for his animals can be procured, and will direct him to assume command of all the troops that are in or hereafter may be ordered to Northeastern Arkansas. You will give him such instructions relative to the defense of that frontier, the apprehension of deserters, and the enforcement of the conscript law as may be best calculated to effect those purposes. On General Marmaduke's assuming command of Colonel [M. J.] White's force, which will be ordered to report to him, he will order that officer to report to me at Little Rock.

Respectfully, your obedient servant,

JOHN W. HINSDALE,
Captain and Assistant Adjutant-General.

HEADQUARTERS TRANS-MISSISSIPPI DEPARTMENT,
Little Rock, Ark., December 29, 1862.

GENERAL: The political condition of the Indians inhabiting the territory bordering this State on the west and the State of Texas on the north has of late assumed an unsettled and unsatisfactory character. The enemy have left nothing undone to promote disaffection among the various tribes who have heretofore entered into treaty stipulations with the Government of the Confederate States. The civilized Indians of this territory are in great fear and apprehension that their country will be invaded by the wild tribes of the West. In view, therefore, of these facts, and the fixed policy of the Government to maintain friendly relations with both the civilized and wild tribes, the lieutenant-general commanding the Trans-Mississippi Department directs me to say that you will order the officer in command of the Indian frontier of Texas, on the north, to confine his operations entirely to the defense of the frontier settlements, and under no circumstances whatever is an aggressive war against the Indians to be inaugurated. The troops stationed on the frontier of Texas are to be fully impressed with the necessity of preserving peaceful relations with all the bordering Indian tribes. War against the Comanches or other wild tribes must recoil upon our civilized Indian allies, and thus tend much to weaken, if not totally destroy, their allegiance to the Government of the Confederate States. I inclose you herewith copy of a special order* assigning Brig. Gen. W. Steele to command in the Indian Territory, and also *ex officio* Superintendent of Indian affairs.

I am, general, very respectfully, your obedient servant,

S. S. ANDERSON,
Assistant Adjutant-General.

---

*Not found.

HEADQUARTERS SECOND CORPS,
December 30, 1862.

General [JOHN S.] BOWEN:

GENERAL: I am instructed by General Price to say that the President, during his late visit to this place, assured him that he fully appreciated the importance of transferring the Missouri troops to the Trans-Mississippi Department, and that he had already given to the Secretary of War orders (which he would forthwith reiterate) to make the necessary arrangements for sending them thither in time to make the spring campaign in Missouri.* As they could not possibly accomplish any good by going there before spring time, and as their presence here at this time is absolutely necessary to the safety of the republic, the general hopes that every Missourian will remain willingly at the post of duty, and endeavor, under the leadership of our new chieftain, General Joseph E. Johnston, to further illustrate, by a prompt and cheerful obedience to orders in camp and on the field, the proud reputation of the Missouri volunteers.

The general wishes General [M. E.] Green to communicate the President's promises informally to the officers and men of his brigade.

I am, very respectfully, your obedient servant,

THOS. L. SNEAD,
Assistant Adjutant-General.

---

* See General Price's address, December 14, to the Missouri troops, p. 794; Johnston to Davis, December 22, p. 800; and Holmes to Johnston, December 29, p. 810, Series I, Vol. XVII, Part II.

APPENDIX.

Embracing documents received too late for insertion in proper sequence.

JUNE 16–SEPTEMBER 13, 1863.—The Sioux Expedition, Dakota.*

HDQRS. DIST. OF MINNESOTA, DEPT. OF THE NORTHWEST,
In the Field, 60 *miles west of Fort Abercrombie*,
Camp Stevens, August 16, 1863.

MAJOR: My last dispatch of the 7th instant from Camp Carter contained a report of my operations against the hostile Sioux, and of their complete discomfiture in three separate engagements, and their hurried flight across the Missouri River, with the loss of large quantities of provisions, clothing, and other indispensable articles. So severely were they punished also by the fall in battle of many of their bravest and most distinguished warriors, that they made none of their customary attempts to revenge their losses by night attacks, excepting in one case, when encamped on the banks of the Missouri. A volley was fired into my camp about an hour after midnight, without any injury being the result, excepting the killing of 1 mule and wounding of 2 others. The fire was promptly returned by the men on guard, and no further demonstration was made by the savages.

From Camp Carter I proceeded to the intrenched portion of Camp Atchison, and, breaking up the encampment, I took up the line of march with the column toward Fort Abercrombie, and am thus far advanced on the route.

I dispatched Colonel McPhaill, with four companies of Mounted Rangers and a section of mountain howitzers, from Camp Atchison, with the directions to proceed to the mouth of Snake River, a tributary of the James River, where a small but mischievous band of E. Yanktonnais Sioux are supposed to have planted corn, to make prisoners of the adult males, or destroy them, if resistance was made; thence to sweep the country to the head of the Redwood River, and down that stream to the Minnesota River, and proceed to Fort Ridgely and await further orders.

The region traversed by my column between the first crossing of Cheyenne River and the Coteau of the Missouri is for the most part uninhabitable. If the devil were permitted to select a residence upon the earth, he would probably choose this particular district for an abode, with the redskins' murdering and plundering bands as his ready ministers, to verify by their ruthless deeds his diabolical hate to all who belong to a Christian race. Through this vast desert lakes fair to the eye abound, but generally their waters are strongly alkaline or intensely bitter and brackish. The valleys between them frequently reek with sulphurous and other disagreeable vapors. The heat was so intolerable that the earth was like a heated furnace, and the breezes that swept

* See also p. 352.

along its surface were as scorching and suffocating as the famed sirocco. Yet through all these difficulties men and animals toiled on until the objects of the expedition were accomplished.

I could not learn from the Red River half-breeds that any of the Red Lake Chippewas were on the Red River; consequently, in the debilitated condition of the men and the suffering state of the animals, I deemed it improper to make any movement in that direction. I shall, however, on my return, make a demonstration of force toward Otter Tail Lake, and other localities where the Chippewa Indians are usually found, and then post the troops under my command so as to protect the frontier at all points from the few roving Indians who are said to infest it.

Should General Sully take up the pursuit of the Indians at the point on the Missouri River where I was obliged to abandon it, as I trust he will, and inflict further chastisement upon them, it might be consistent with the security of the Minnesota frontier to diminish the force in this military district; otherwise I have the honor to submit that there may and probably will be a further necessity for the use of the whole of it in further operations against these powerful bands should they attempt, in large numbers, to molest the settlements in retaliation for the losses they have sustained during the late engagements.

So soon as I shall reach Fort Abercrombie—in five or six days from this time—I will probably obtain such additional information of the state of things along the border as will enable me to act understand ingly in the disposition of my forces, and will again address you on the subject.

I am, major, very respectfully, your obedient servant,

H. H. SIBLEY,
Brigadier-General, Commanding.

J. F. MELINE,
Acting Assistant Adjutant-General, Milwaukee.

HDQRS. DIST. OF MINNESOTA, DEPT. OF THE NORTHWEST,
In the Field, Camp Hackett, Fort Abercrombie, August 23, 1863.

MAJOR: In my last dispatches to headquarters of the department, I inadvertently omitted to state that, after having left Camp Atchison in pursuit of the hostile Indians, I fell in with some of the half-breed hunters from Red River, who informed me that while the main body of the savages had gone toward the Missouri, a small camp of fifteen or twenty lodges had taken the direction of Devil's Lake, and would be found on its shores. I immediately dispatched orders to Major Cook, dated 22d July, to send Captain Burt, of the Seventh Minnesota Volunteers, with two companies of infantry and one of cavalry, to scour the country in that quarter.

That efficient officer took up the line of march on the 24th July, and during eight days' absence from camp he examined thoroughly the region to the west of Devil's Lake, without discovering any Indians or fresh traces of them, excepting one young man, a son of Little Crow, who was found in a state of exhaustion on the prairie, and was taken prisoner without resistance, and brought into Camp Atchison. He states positively that his father, Little Crow, was killed at some point in the Big Woods on the Minnesota frontier, by shots from white men, while his father and himself were engaged in picking berries; that his father had taken with him this son and 16 other men and 1 woman, and gone from the camp, then at Devil's Lake, several weeks previously, to the settlements in Minnesota, to steal horses, Little Crow stating to his son that the Indians were too weak to fight against the whites, and that it was his intention to secure horses, and then to return and take his family to a distant part of the country, where they would not be in danger from the whites.

He has repeated the statement to me without any material variation, and, as his account corroborates the newspaper reports of the mode in which 2 Indians, who were engaged in picking berries, were approached by a Mr. Lampson and his son, and one of them killed, and the body accurately described, there is no longer any doubt that the originator of the horrible massacres of 1862 has met his death.

I have brought Wo-wi-na-pa, Little Crow's son, with 3 other Sioux Indians, taken prisoners by my scouts, to Fort Abercrombie, where they are at present confined. I have ordered a military commission to convene to-day for their trial, the proceedings of which will be sent you when completed. The scouts took prisoners 7 women and 3 or 4 children, who were in the camp with the 3 men, but I released them on my departure from James River, where they were found. Two of the women were fugitives from the reservation on the Missouri below, being recognized by the half-breed scouts as having passed the winter at Fort Snelling. They stated that they had left the reservation in company with 3 men, who had gone to the main camp on the Missouri.

The result of the expedition under Captain Burt has proved conclusively that there are very few, if any, Sioux Indians between Devil's Lake and the Missouri River, and that all the bands whose haunts are in the immense prairie region between the latter stream and the British possessions, were concentrated in the great camp driven by my forces across the Missouri.

I have organized an expedition, composed of three companies of cavalry, to proceed to Otter Tail Lake, and thence to Fort Ripley, with written instructions to the commanding officer, Major Parker. I shall probably dispatch the Tenth Regiment Minnesota Volunteers to scour the country from Sauk Center to Fort Ridgely, more with a view to reassure the settlers along the Big Woods than because I have a belief that any but a few lurking savages are to be found now on the immediate frontier. I shall march from this post on the 25th with the remainder of my column, and take the route by Alexandria and Sauk Center, taking such measures for the security of the border as I may deem necessary.

The cavalry expedition under Major Parker will pass through the region frequented by the Pillager and other strong bands of Chippewa Indians, and will have a decided moral effect.

I will report my movements as opportunities present themselves.

I am, very respectfully, your obedient servant,

H. H. SIBLEY,
Brigadier-General, Commanding.

J. F. MELINE,
Acting Assistant Adjutant-General Milwaukee.

HDQRS. DIST. OF MINNESOTA, DEPT. OF THE NORTHWEST,
In the Field, Camp Rubles, Sauk Center, September 2, 1863.

MAJOR: I have the honor to report my arrival with the column at this post. A requisition has been made upon me by Senator Ramsey, commissioner on the part of the Government to negotiate a treaty with the Pembina and Red Lake bands of Chippewas, for an escort of two companies of cavalry and one of infantry, or a section of artillery, which I shall, of course, furnish. I shall detach the Tenth Regiment from the column there, with orders to scour the country along the line of posts to Fort Ridgely, and like orders to Colonel McPhaill will be sent him to-morrow, who, with five companies of cavalry detached to sweep the region from James River to Fort Ridgely, has doubtless reached that post, to visit the lines of posts south to the Iowa line.

I have no reason to believe that the Indians will make any immediate raid along the border, but the people fear it, and the steps proposed will at least tend to reassure them.

I have as yet received no dispatch from General Pope or yourself informing me of the receipt of my communications detailing the movements of my immediate command since the engagements with the hostile Indians. I trust to receive one very soon.

Major Camp, commanding Fort Abercrombie, has sent a special messenger to overtake me with information received from Captain Donaldson, who left Pembina on the 27th instant. Standing Buffalo, a Sisseton chief, who has uniformly been opposed to the war, had visited Saint Joseph with a few of his men. He reports that the Indians had recrossed the Missouri, and were now on the Missouri Coteau, near the scene of our first battle; that they intend to winter at Devil's Lake; that they are in a state of utter destitution, and 7 of the chiefs are desirous to make peace, and deliver up the murderers as the price for obtaining it. He represents the Indians to be very much frightened at the results of operations against them. They have, however, murdered 24 miners and 1 woman, who were on their way down the Missouri in a flat-boat. They acknowledge a loss of 30 men in the affair. A child was spared, and retained as prisoner. Standing Buffalo further states that the Indians lost many drowned in crossing the Missouri when we were in chase of them, but they deny that they lost more than 13 in battle. The remarkable dislike to acknowledge how many are killed in action is characteristic of the race. Forty-six dead bodies were found by my command, and doubtless many more were concealed or carried off, and a large number were wounded, who were also transported from the field by their comrades.

No blow ever received by them has created such consternation, and I trust and believe that if General Sully takes their fresh trail inland, and delivers another stroke upon them, they will be for peace at any price.

I would respectfully suggest that Major Hatch's battalion be ordered to garrison a post at Saint Joseph or Pembina. They may do good service there. I shall probably leave the column in three or four days and proceed to Saint Paul, where I will again address you.

I am, major, very respectfully, your obedient servant,

H. H. SIBLEY,
Brigadier-General, Commanding.

J. F. MELINE,
Acting Assistant Adjutant-General, Milwaukee.

HDQRS. DIST. OF MINNESOTA, DEPT. OF THE NORTHWEST,
Saint Paul, Minn., September 12, 1863.

MAJOR: I have the honor to report that the portion of the expeditionary force remaining undetached encamped a few miles above Fort

Snelling last night, and will reach the immediate vicinity of that post to-day, and will go into camp until further orders. It consists of the Sixth and Seventh Regiments of Minnesota Volunteers, and one section each of 6-pounders and mountain howitzers.

I would respectfully suggest for the consideration of Major-General Pope, that at least one-third instead of one-fourth of the officers and men who have participated in the long and tiresome campaign just closed be permitted to visit their homes at the same time, so that opportunity be given to all of them to do so before marching orders. In fact, if one-half were granted immediate leave of absence for a limited period, the whole matter would be much simplified, especially as the residence of many of the officers and men is remote from this point.

I have carefully perused General Pope's dispatch of 29th ultimo, relative to the disposition of the forces to remain in the State during the approaching winter.

I would respectfully rècommend that at least two regiments of infantry in addition to the mounted men of Hatch's battalion and those contemplated to be re-enlisted from the Mounted Rangers be retained for the protection of the border.

The Upper Sioux are desirous to have re-established their former amicable relations with the Government, and I think may be made to deliver up, as the price of peace, those of the lower bands who were actors in the tragedies of 1862. But they are in constant intercourse with the Red River half-breeds, and would promptly be informed of the reduction of the force in this district through them, and, if impressed with an idea that the diminution was so great as to prevent the Government from further chastising them in case it became necessary, they might be emboldened to continue the war, and thereby necessitate another expedition for their complete subjugation.

As a measure of economy, therefore, I do not think it would be prudent at the present crisis to weaken too much the military force in this district.

So soon as the requisite information can be obtained, I will dispatch to you a full statement of the arrangements proposed to be made for the defense of the frontier, for the consideration of the major-general commanding.

I beg leave to state that Fort Abercrombie is already inclosed with a stockade sufficient for defensive purposes, and that earthworks have been erected at Fort Ridgely for the security of that post. The defenses at Fort Ripley are also in good condition, a stockade having been built on all sides, excepting on the river front, where Colonel Thomas does not deem one necessary.

I would respectfully request that none of the regiments to be ordered south receive marching orders before the 15th October, by which time all will have had opportunity to visit their homes, and the season for apprehending Indian raids will have passed. As instructed by General Pope, I will indicate in a very few days the regiment or regiments to be posted in this State.

I am, major, very respectfully, your obedient servant,

H. H. SIBLEY,
Brigadier-General, Commanding.

J. F. MELINE,
Acting Assistant Adjutant-General, Milwaukee.

HDQRS. DIST. OF MINNESOTA, DEPT. OF THE NORTHWEST,
Saint Paul, Minn., September 16, 1863.

GENERAL: I have the honor to report for your information certain facts which have lately transpired, that may, and probably will, have a most important bearing upon the future relations between the Government and the upper bands of Sioux inhabiting the country on the north and east of the Missouri River.

My previous dispatches have fully advised you of the great concentration of Indian warriors, to oppose the column under my command in penetrating the immense prairies between the Red River of the North and the Missouri River, and their utter rout and retreat across the latter stream, with the loss of their subsistence, clothing, and means of transportation, which fell into my hands and were destroyed.

The state of destitution in which they found themselves and their utter inability to contend with our disciplined troops in the open field have so terrified the large majority of these savages that they have expressed a fervent desire to re-establish peace with the Government at any price.

Standing Buffalo, a leading chief of the Sisseton Sioux, and who has been consistent in his opposition to the hostilities initiated by the Minday, Wakomton, and Wakpeton bands in 1862, lately visited Saint Joseph, near the British line, accompanied by several deputies from the other upper bands, and held a conference with Father André, a Catholic priest, who is held in high estimation alike by the half-breed hunters and by the Sioux Indians. So far as I can ascertain, these deputies represented all those powerful bands not immediately implicated in the murders and outrages perpetrated on the Minnesota frontier during the past year, but who participated with the refugees from Wood Lake in the engagements with the expeditionary force under my command in the month of July last. In fact, in the communication made to me by Father André, he distinctly states as one of the happy results of the expedition, that "judging from the anxiety displayed by these men (the deputies), the greater portion of the Sioux are desirous of an opportunity to offer their submission, and the murderers, once abandoned by the other Indians, can be easily reduced."

The combination of Indians defeated by my column in the late engagements may be thus classified: Minnesota River bands, remnants, 250 warriors; Sisseton Sioux, 450 warriors; E. Yanktonnais, 1,200 warriors; other straggling bands, including Teton Sioux, from the west side of the Missouri River, probably 400 warriors; making an aggregate force of from 2,300 to 2,500 warriors. These constitute the full strength of the Dakota or Sioux Indians inhabiting the prairies on the east side of the Missouri River, with few and insignificant exceptions. The small number of those who succeeded in effecting their escape after the decisive conflict of Wood Lake, and whose crimes against humanity preclude any hope of pardon on the part of the Government, when deserted by the great bands they hoped to complicate inextricably in their hostilities against the whites will be rendered powerless for evil, as justly remarked by Father André.

That gentleman, in the communication referred to, gives the substance of the appeal of Standing Buffalo for peace:

> He wished me to assure you that neither he nor his men had taken any part in the war against the whites; that he was prepared now, as he always had been, to submit to such disposition as would be satisfactory to the Government, and he regretted very much that he could not meet you in your camp to give you this assurance.

He further stated his desire to deliver himself up to the Government with his band at such time and place as I might designate, only receiving the assurance that they would not be held as prisoners or removed to a greater distance, referring to the reservation on the Missouri to which the families of Sioux captives have been transferred.

Since the news of General Sully having fallen upon a Sioux camp and destroyed it reached me, I feel sanguine that these bands will be even more than ever disposed to submit, and, with the view of opening communication with them, I respectfully ask that I may be instructed to employ Father André, and such other competent persons as may be deemed necessary, to visit the Indians, and proffer such conditions of peace as you may deem proper to accord under the circumstances.

I would also respectfully suggest that these conditions should embrace the expulsion or delivery of the murderers, and the confining of these bands to the limits at such a safe distance from the settlements in Minnesota as would effectually dissipate all apprehensions of renewed raids on the frontier.

If properly managed, I have every reason to believe that the Indian war will soon be terminated and the quiet of the border entirely restored.

I am, general, very respectfully, your obedient servant,

H. H. SIBLEY,
Brigadier-General, Commanding.

Maj. Gen. JOHN POPE,
Milwaukee.

DECEMBER 16-31, 1863.—Scout from Fayetteville, Ark., including skirmishes (23d) at Stroud's Store and (25th) on Buffalo River.*

FAYETTEVILLE, ARK.,
January 1, 1864.

SIR: The scout under command of Capt. John I. Worthington, First Arkansas Cavalry, which left this place December 15, will be in this evening.

Captain Worthington and Lieutenant Thompson returned yesterday evening. They report more or less skirmishing nearly every day, and hard fighting on the 23d, 24th, and 25th. Met a force of about 200 on the 23d, near Marshall's Prairie, Carroll County, and fought them over two hours, routing them completely and killing several.

On the 24th, attacked about the same number, again routing them and driving them in confusion.

On the 25th, in Searcy County, on Richland [Creek], a foraging party, under Lieutenant Jernigan, First Arkansas Cavalry, were attacked about noon by 200 of the enemy, and were obliged to retreat in confusion. Lieutenant Jernigan was wounded, and several of our men taken prisoners, and afterward stripped and shot.

From this time until dusk there was continual skirmishing and picket fighting. At dark, the enemy were found to have been re-enforced, numbering at least 800, and completely surrounding our party. About dark, an attempt was made by 200 to capture our howitzer, which was gallantly frustrated by Lieutenant Thompson, commanding

* See also p. 779.

the piece, who double shotted it, and fired among the enemy when not more than 30 paces distant, killing many and causing them to fall back.

After hard fighting, our boys succeeded in cutting their way out, and retreated in good order.

The enemy lost at least 30 killed, besides many wounded. Our loss was 6 killed, 7 or 8 wounded.

Lieutenant Jernegan was wounded in the thigh, not badly. Two Government wagons were abandoned on account of the roads; the teams were all saved. Official report will be forwarded as soon as possible.

T. J. HUNT,
Major, Commanding.

Brigadier-General SANBORN,
Commanding District of Southwest Missouri.

---

*ALTERNATE DESIGNATIONS OF ORGANIZATIONS MENTIONED IN THIS VOLUME.**

* References are to index following.

Barry's (W. T.) **Cavalry.** See *Missouri Troops, Confederate.*
Bass' (Thomas C.) **Cavalry.** See *Texas Troops, 20th Regiment.*
Bassett's (B. S.) **Artillery.** See *Henry Hopkins' Artillery.*
Bassett's (Owen A.) **Cavalry.** See *Kansas Troops, 2d Regiment.*
Bateman's (M. M.) **Cavalry.** See *A. S. Dobbin's Cavalry.*
Baumer's (William) **Infantry.** See *Nebraska Troops, 1st Regiment.*
Beardsley's (Ezra M.) **Infantry.** See *Illinois Troops, 126th Regiment.*
Bell's (Charles A.) **Cavalry.** See *Illinois Troops, 13th Regiment.*
Bell's (C. O.) **Artillery.** See *Missouri Troops, Confederate.*
Bell s (S. S.) **Infantry.** See *Arkansas Troops, Confederate, 37th Regiment.*
Benjamin's (John F.) **Cavalry.** See *Missouri Troops, Union, 2d Regiment, State Militia.*
Bennett's (G. W. C.) **Cavalry.** See *Emmett MacDonald's Cavalry.*
Benter's (N. L.) **Infantry.** See *Kansas Troops, 12th Regiment.*
Benton's (Thomas H., jr.) **Infantry.** See *Iowa Troops, 29th Regiment.*
Berry's (C. E.) **Infantry.** See *Arkansas Troops, Union, 2d Regiment.*
Bertram's (Henry) **Infantry.** See *Wisconsin Troops, 20th Regiment.*
Biggers' (Thomas B.) **Cavalry.** See *Missouri Troops, Union, 5th Regiment, State Militia (old).*
Biscoe's (C. N.) **Infantry.** See *Arkansas Troops, Confederate, 39th Regiment.*
Bishop's (A. W.) **Cavalry.** See *Arkansas Troops, Union, 1st Regiment.*
Black's (James W.) **Infantry.** See *Missouri Troops, Union, 51st Regiment, Enrolled Militia.*
Black's (John Charles) **Infantry.** See *Illinois Troops, 37th Regiment.*
Black's (Thomas G.) **Cavalry.** See *Missouri Troops, Union, 3d Regiment.*
Blacknall's (T. H.) **Infantry.** See *Arkansas Troops, Confederate, 37th Regiment.*
Blair's (Charles W.) **Artillery.** See *Kansas Troops, 2d Battery.*
Bledsoe's (Joseph) **Artillery.** See *Missouri Troops, Confederate.*
Blocher's (William D.) **Artillery.** See *Arkansas Troops, Confederate.*
Boone's (Squire) **Infantry.** See *Arkansas Troops, Confederate.*
Borris' (Herman) **Artillery.** See *Illinois Troops, 2d Regiment, Battery A.*
Bowen's (Thomas M.) **Infantry.** See *Kansas Troops, 13th Regiment.*
Bowles' (John) **Infantry.** See *Kansas Troops, 1st Regiment (Colored).*
Box's (Richard M.) **Cavalry.** See *Missouri Troops, Union, 7th Regiment, State Militia.*
Boyd's (Marcus) **Infantry.** See *Missouri Troops, Union, 74th Regiment, Enrolled Militia.*
Bradford's (James B.) **Cavalry.** See *Wisconsin Troops, 2d Regiment.*
Brawner's (Milton H.) **Cavalry.** See *Missouri Troops, Union, 7th Regiment.*
Bredett's (Eliphalet) **Cavalry.** See *Missouri Troops, Union, 7th Regiment.*
Brooks' (Iverson L.) **Infantry.** See *Arkansas Troops, Confederate, 26th Regiment.*
Brooks' (W. H.) **Infantry.** See *Arkansas Troops, Confederate, 34th Regiment.*
Brown's (L. T.) **Artillery.** See *Arkansas Troops, Confederate.*
Brown's (Richard H.) **Infantry.** See *Missouri Troops, Union, 23d Regiment.*
Brown's (William) **Cavalry.** See *Arkansas Troops, Confederate.*
Brush's (Daniel H.) **Infantry.** See *Illinois Troops, 18th Regiment.*
Brutsche's (John D.) **Infantry.** See *Missouri Troops, Union, 9th Regiment, Provisional Enrolled Militia.*
Bryan's (J. M.) **Indians.** See *Indian Troops, Confederate, 1st Battalion, Cherokee.*
Bryan's (P. Gad) **Cavalry.** See *Iowa Troops, 1st Regiment.*
Bull's (John P.) **Cavalry.** See *R. C. Newton's Cavalry.*
Bunner's (Lafayette) **Cavalry.** See *Missouri Troops, Union, 7th Regiment.*
Burbridge's (John Q.) **Cavalry.** See *Missouri Troops, Confederate, 4th Regiment.*
Burch's (Milton) **Cavalry.** See *Missouri Troops, Union, 8th Regiment, State Militia;* also *14th Regiment, State Militia.*
Burford's (N. M.) **Cavalry.** See *Texas Troops, 19th Regiment.*
Burner's (John D.) **Artillery.** See *Ohio Troops, 5th Battery.*
Burnett's (J. H.) **Cavalry.** See *Texas Troops, 13th Regiment.*

Burns' (S. P.) **Infantry.** See *De Witt C. Hunter's Infantry.*
Burrows' (Amos L.) **Cavalry.** See *Missouri Troops, Union, 1st Regiment.*
Byam's (Eber C.) **Infantry.** See *Iowa Troops, 24th Regiment.*
Caldwell's (Henry C.) **Cavalry.** See *Iowa Troops, 3d Regiment.*
Caldwell's (J. H.) **Infantry.** See *Missouri Troops, Confederate.*
Caldwell's (Joseph W.) **Cavalry.** See *Iowa Troops, 1st Regiment.*
Calkins' (E. A.) **Cavalry.** See *Wisconsin Troops, 3d Regiment.*
Cameron's (Robert A.) **Infantry.** See *Indiana Troops, 34th Regiment.*
Campbell's (L. A.) **Cavalry.** See *Missouri Troops, Confederate, 3d Regiment.*
Campbell's (L. C.) **Cavalry.** See *Missouri Troops, Confederate, 3d Regiment.*
Campbell's (William T.) **Cavalry.** See *Kansas Troops, 6th Regiment.*
Carpenter's (Robert) **Cavalry.** See *Wisconsin Troops, 3d Regiment.*
Carroll's (Charles A.) **Cavalry.** See *Arkansas Troops, Confederate.*
Carter's (George W.) **Cavalry.** See *Texas Troops, 21st Regiment.*
Catherwood's (Edwin C.) **Cavalry.** See *Missouri Troops, Union, 6th Regiment, State Militia.*
Cave's (Marion) **Infantry.** See *Missouri Troops, Union, 23d Regiment.*
Chandler's (John L.) **Cavalry.** See *Missouri Troops, Union, 7th Regiment.*
Chase's (Jonathan) **Infantry.** See *Minnesota Troops, 9th Regiment.*
Cheek's Sharpshooters. Official designation unknown. See **Cheek, ——.**
Chrisman's (F. M.) **Cavalry.** See *Arkansas Troops, Confederate.*
Clark's (Charles S.) **Cavalry.** See *Kansas Troops, 9th Regiment.*
Clark's (Edward) **Infantry.** See *Texas Troops, 14th Regiment.*
Clark's (John B., jr.) **Infantry.** See *Missouri Troops, Confederate.*
Clark's (John G.) **Infantry.** See *Indiana Troops, 26th Regiment.*
Clark's (Thomas P.) **Cavalry.** See *Ohio Troops, 6th Regiment.*
Clarkson's (T. S.) **Artillery.** See *Missouri Troops, Union, 2d Regiment, Battery K.*
Clayton's (Powell) **Cavalry.** See *Kansas Troops, 5th Regiment.*
Clinton's (George O.) **Cavalry.** See *Wisconsin Troops, 1st Regiment.*
Cloud's (William F.) **Cavalry.** See *Kansas Troops, 2d Regiment.*
Coffee's (John T.) **Cavalry.** See *Missouri Troops, Confederate, 6th Regiment.*
Cole's (Nelson) **Artillery.** See *Missouri Troops, Union, 1st Regiment, Battery E;* **also** *2d Regiment.*
Coleman's (Charles F.) **Cavalry.** See *Kansas Troops, 9th Regiment.*
Coleman's (W. O.) **Partisans.** See *Missouri Troops, Confederate.*
Collins' (John E.) **Cavalry.** See *Missouri Troops, Union, 8th Regiment, State Militia.*
Collins' (Richard A.) **Artillery.** See *Joseph Bledsoe's Artillery.*
Collins' (William O.) **Cavalry.** See *Ohio Troops, 6th Regiment.*
Cook's (R. E.) **Infantry.** See *Kansas Troops, 2d Regiment (Colored).*
Cook's (Thomas Z.) **Infantry.** See *Iowa Troops, 18th Regiment.*
Cooper's (Samuel F.) **Infantry.** See *Iowa Troops, 40th Regiment.*
Corley's (Samuel) **Cavalry.** See *A. S. Dobbin's Cavalry.*
Corwin's (David B.) **Infantry.** See *Indian Troops, Union, 2d Regiment, Home Guards.*
Coulter's (John P.) **Infantry.** See *Iowa Troops, 12th Regiment.*
Crawford's (Samuel J.) **Cavalry.** See *Kansas Troops, 2d Regiment.*
Crawford's (W. A.) **Cavalry.** See *Arkansas Troops, Confederate.*
Cree's (Alfred B.) **Infantry.** See *Iowa Troops, 22d Regiment.*
Creek Indians. See *Indian Troops, Union, 2d Regiment, Home Guards.*
Crittenden's (Thomas T.) **Cavalry.** See *Missouri Troops, Union, 7th Regiment, State Militia.*
Crocker's (Watson D.) **Artillery.** See *Wisconsin Troops, 9th Battery.*
Crook's (William) **Infantry.** See *Minnesota Troops, 6th Regiment.*
Crump's (R. P.) **Cavalry.** See *Texas Troops, 1st Regiment, Partisan.*
Curran's (S. M.) **Infantry.*** See *S. M. Curran.*
Daniel's (James M.) **Artillery.** See *Texas Troops.*
Darnell's (N. H.) **Cavalry.** See *Texas Troops, 18th Regiment.*

* Improvised.

* **Improvised.**

Freeman's (Thomas R.) **Partisans.** See *Missouri Troops, Confederate.*
Frisbie's (H. N.) **Infantry.** See *Illinois Troops, 37th Regiment.*
Furnas' (Robert W.) **Cavalry.** See *Nebraska Troops, 2d Regiment.*
Furnas' (Robert W.) **Infantry.** See *Indian Troops, Union, 1st Regiment, Home Guards.*
Gallaher's (William) **Infantry.** See *Indian Troops, Union, 3d Regiment, Home Guards.*
Galloway's (Charles) **Cavalry.** See *Arkansas Troops, Union, 1st Regiment.*
Gardner's (John) **Cavalry.** See *Kansas Troops, 2d Regiment.*
Garland's (R. R.) **Infantry.** See *Texas Troops, 6th Regiment.*
Garrett's (J. M.) **Cavalry.** See *Missouri Troops, Confederate, 5th Regiment.*
Gatlin's Texas Rangers. Official designation unknown. See *Captain Gatlin.*
Geddes' (James L.) **Infantry.** See *Iowa Troops, 8th Regiment.*
Geiger's (Washington F.) **Cavalry.** See *Missouri Troops, Union, 8th Regiment.*
Gentry's (Henry C.) **Cavalry.** See *Missouri Troops, Union, 2d Regiment, State Militia.*
Gentry's (William) **Infantry.** See *Missouri Troops, Union, 5th Regiment, Provisional Enrolled Militia.*
George's (Solomon A. M.) **Cavalry.** See *Missouri Troops, Union, 8th Regiment, State Militia.*
Gibson's (H. D.) **Infantry.** See *Iowa Troops, 33d Regiment.*
Giddings' (D. C.) **Cavalry.** See *Texas Troops, 21st Regiment.*
Gilbert's (James I.) **Infantry.** See *Iowa Troops, 27th Regiment.*
Gilkey's (C. A.) **Cavalry.** See *Beal G. Jeans' Cavalry.*
Gill's (Charles R.) **Infantry.** See *Wisconsin Troops, 29th Regiment.*
Gillespie's (C. C.) **Cavalry.** See *Texas Troops, 25th Regiment.*
Gillett's (L. E.) **Cavalry.** See *Texas Troops.*
Gilstrap's (Jacob) **Cavalry.** See *Missouri Troops, Union, 2d Regiment, State Militia.*
Glaze's (Henry S.) **Cavalry.** See *Missouri Troops, Union, 9th Regiment, State Militia.*
Glover's (Albert D.) **Cavalry.** See *Missouri Troops, Union, 3d Regiment.*
Glover's (John M.) **Cavalry.** See *Missouri Troops, Union, 3d Regiment.*
Gordon's (B. F.) **Cavalry.** See *Missouri Troops, Confederate, 5th Regiment.*
Gordon's (George P.) **Cavalry.** See *Missouri Troops, Confederate, 5th Regiment.*
Gould's (John H.) **Infantry.** See *Indiana Troops, 46th Regiment.*
Gould's (Robert S.) **Cavalry.** See *Texas Troops.*
Gower's (James O.) **Cavalry.** See *Iowa Troops, 1st Regiment.*
Graham's (Harvey) **Infantry.** See *Iowa Troops, 22d Regiment.*
Gray's (John B.) **Infantry.** See *Missouri Troops, Union, 1st Regiment, State Militia.*
Green's (P. T.) **Infantry.** See *Missouri Troops, Union, 73d Regiment, Enrolled Militia.*
Greene's (Colton) **Cavalry.** See *Missouri Troops, Confederate, 3d Regiment.*
Gregg's Cavalry. See *W. C. Quantrill's Cavalry.*
Griggs' (Chauncey W.) **Infantry.** See *Minnesota Troops, 3d Regiment.*
Grinsted's (H. L.) **Infantry.** See *Arkansas Troops, Confederate, 33d Regiment.*
Griswold's (D. B.) **Artillery.** See *Missouri Troops, Confederate.*
Guess' (G. W.) **Cavalry.** See *Texas Troops.*
Guitar's (Odon) **Cavalry.** See *Missouri Troops, Union, 9th Regiment, State Militia.*
Hadley's (Julius L.) **Artillery.** See *Ohio Troops, 25th Battery.*
Haines' (W. W.) **Artillery.** See *John W. Rabb's Artillery.*
Haldeman's (Horace) **Artillery.** See *Texas Troops.*
Hall's (George H.) **Cavalry.** See *Missouri Troops, Union, 4th Regiment, State Militia.*
Hansel's (Jacob) **Artillery.** See *Illinois Troops, 2d Regiment, Battery A.*
Harker's (Garrison) **Cavalry.** See *Missouri Troops, Union, 2d Regiment.*
Harnden's (Henry) **Cavalry.** See *Wisconsin Troops, 1st Regiment.*
Harrell's (John M.) **Cavalry.** See *Arkansas Troops, Confederate.*
Harris' (Charles L.) **Infantry.** See *Wisconsin Troops, 11th Regiment.*
Harris' (David M.) **Artillery.** See *Joseph Bledsoe's Artillery.*
Harrison's (Isaac F.) **Cavalry.** See *Louisana Troops, 15th Battalion.*
Harrison's (M. La Rue) **Cavalry.** See *Arkansas Troops, Union, 1st Regiment.*
Harvey's (Elijah E.) **Cavalry.** See *Kansas Troops, 6th Regiment.*
Hart's (R. A.) **Infantry.** See *Arkansas Troops, Confederate, 39th Regiment.*

Johnson's (B. A.) **Cavalry.** See *Timothy Reves' Cavalry.*
Johnson's (Cyrus H.) **Artillery.** See *Wisconsin Troops, 9th Battery.*
Johnson's (Horace B.) **Artillery.** See *Missouri Troops, Union.*
Johnson's (James M.) **Infantry.** See *Arkansas Troops, Union, 1st Regiment.*
Johnson's (J. C.) **Infantry.** See *Arkansas Troops, Confederate, 37th Regiment.*
Johnson's (J. J.) **Cavalry.** See *Arkansas Troops, Union, 1st Regiment.*
Johnson's (J. W.) **Infantry.** See *Missouri Troops, Union, 26th Regiment, Enrolled Militia.*
Johnson's (William S.) **Artillery.** See *Arkansas Troops, Union.*
Johnston's (J. A.) **Cavalry.** See *Charles A. Carroll's Cavalry.*
Jones' (B. S.) **Cavalry.** See *Iowa Troops, 3d Regiment.*
Jones' (John) **Artillery.** See *Minnesota Troops, 3d Battery.*
Judson's (William R.) **Cavalry.** See *Kansas Troops, 6th Regiment.*
Kane County Cavalry. See *Illinois Troops.*
Kauffman's (Albert B.) **Cavalry.** See *Missouri Troops, Union, 11th Regiment.*
Kelly's (George W.) **Cavalry.** See *Missouri Troops, Union, 4th Regiment, State Militia.*
Kennedy's (Thomas H.) **Infantry.** See *Kansas Troops, 12th Regiment.*
Kent's (Daniel) **Infantry.** See *Iowa Troops, 19th Regiment.*
Killen's (T. P.) **Cavalry.** See *Kansas Troops, 9th Regiment.*
King's (Austin A., jr.) **Cavalry.** See *Missouri Troops, Union, 6th Regiment, State Militia.*
King's (J. P.) **Infantry.** See *Arkansas Troops, Confederate.*
King's (Walter) **Cavalry.** See *Missouri Troops, Union, 3d Regiment, State Militia (old).*
King's (Walter) **Cavalry.** See *Missouri Troops, Union, 4th Regiment, State Militia.*
Kinsman's (William H.) **Infantry.** See *Iowa Troops, 23d Regiment.*
Kitchen's (S. G.) **Cavalry.** See *Missouri Troops, Confederate.*
Kittredge's (Charles W.) **Infantry.** See *Iowa Troops, 36th Regiment.*
Klauss' (Martin) **Artillery.** See *Indiana Troops, 1st Battery.*
Knowles' (Daniel C.) **Artillery.** See *Kansas Troops, 2d Battery.*
Koehne's (Henry L.) **Cavalry.** See *Ohio Troops, 6th Regiment.*
Krez's (Conrad) **Infantry.** See *Wisconsin Troops, 27th Regiment.*
La Boo's (D.) **Cavalry.** See *Nebraska Troops, 2d Regiment.*
La Fayette County Militia. See *Missouri Troops, Union, 71st Regiment, Enrolled Militia.*
La Grange's (O. H.) **Cavalry.** See *Wisconsin Troops, 1st Regiment.*
Lane's (W. P.) **Cavalry.** See *Texas Troops, 1st Regiment, Partisan.*
Langen's (Edward) **Cavalry.** See *Missouri Troops, Union, 4th Regiment.*
Lawther's (Robert R.) **Cavalry.** See *Missouri Troops, Confederate.*
Lazear's (Bazel F.) **Cavalry.** See *Missouri Troops, Union, 1st and 12th Regiments, State Militia.*
Leake's (Joseph B.) **Infantry.** See *Iowa Troops, 20th Regiment.*
Lee's Militia. Official designation unknown. See *Lieutenant-Colonel Lee.*
Lee's (Roswell W.) **Artillery.** See *Texas Troops.*
Leeper's (William T.) **Cavalry.** See *Missouri Troops, Union, 3d Regiment, State Militia (new).*
Leflar's (Samuel) **Artillery.** See *Indiana Troops.*
Lemon's (Joseph K.) **Infantry.** See *Illinois Troops, 63d Regiment.*
Lennon's (John A.) **Cavalry.** See *Missouri Troops, Union, 3d Regiment.*
Leonard's (Reeves) **Cavalry.** See *Missouri Troops, Union, 9th Regiment, State Militia.*
Lesueur's (A. A.) **Artillery.** See *C. B. Tilden's Artillery.*
Lewis' (L. M.) **Infantry.** See *J. H. Caldwell's Infantry.*
Lindsay's (James) **Artillery.** See *Missouri Troops, Union.*
Lindsay's (James) **Infantry.** See *Missouri Troops, Union, 68th Regiment, Enrolled Militia.*
Lindsay's (John G.) **Infantry.** See *Kansas Troops, 11th Regiment.*
Lines' (E. C. D.) **Cavalry.** See *Kansas Troops, 2d Regiment.*
Linn County Militia. See *Kansas Troops.*

Meeker's (Stephen M.) **Infantry.** See *Illinois Troops, 62d Regiment.*
Mefford's (David) **Cavalry.** See *Kansas Troops, 6th Regiment.*
Meisner's (Charles P.) **Artillery.** See *Missouri Troops, Union, 2d Regiment, Battery D.*
Mentzer's (J. M.) **Cavalry.** See *Kansas Troops, 2d Regiment.*
Merrill Horse. See *Missouri Troops, Union, 2d Regiment (Cavalry).*
Merrill's (Samuel) **Infantry.** See *Iowa Troops, 21st Regiment.*
Millard's (Andrew J.) **Cavalry.** See *Sioux City Cavalry;* also *Iowa Troops, 7th Regiment.*
Miller's (John) **Indians.** See *J. M. Bryan's Indians.*
Miller's (J. J.) **Cavalry.** See *Arkansas Troops, Confederate.*
Miller's (Stephen) **Infantry.** See *Minnesota Troops, 7th Regiment.*
Miller's (William E.) **Infantry.** See *Iowa Troops, 28th Regiment.*
Miller's (William H.) **Cavalry.** See *Wisconsin Troops, 2d Regiment.*
Mills' (Roger Q.) **Infantry.** See *Texas Troops, 10th Regiment.*
Miner's (Nelson) **Cavalry.** See *Dakota Troops, 1st Battalion.*
Missouri Seventh Infantry (Confederate). See *J. H. Caldwell's Infantry.*
Missouri Eighth Infantry (Confederate). See *De Witt C. Hunter's Infantry.*
Missouri Ninth Infantry (Confederate). See *J. D. White's Infantry.*
Missouri Tenth Cavalry (Confederate). See *R. R. Lawther's Cavalry.*
Missouri Tenth Cavalry (Confederate). See *S. G. Kitchen's Cavalry.*
Missouri Tenth Infantry (Confederate). See *A. E. Steen's Infantry.*
Mitchell's (James A.) **Artillery.** See *Ohio Troops, 16th Battery.*
Mitchell's (Greenville M.) **Infantry.** See *Illinois Troops, 54th Regiment.*
Mix's (Edward H.) **Infantry.** See *Iowa Troops, 32d Regiment.*
Monroe's (J. C.) **Cavalry.** See *Arkansas Troops, Confederate, 1st Regiment, Trans-Mississippi Department.*
Montgomery's (Bacon) **Cavalry.** See *Missouri Troops, Union, 6th Regiment.*
Montgomery's (Milton) **Infantry.** See *Wisconsin Troops, 25th Regiment.*
Montgomery's (Samuel) **Cavalry.** See *Missouri Troops, Union, 6th Regiment.*
Moonlight's (Thomas) **Infantry.** See *Kansas Troops, 11th Regiment.*
Moore's Infantry. See *Missouri Troops, Union, 2d Regiment, Provisional Militia.*
Moore's (Amaziah) **Cavalry.** See *Kansas Troops, 2d Regiment.*
Moore's (Frank) **Cavalry.** See *Illinois Troops, 2d Regiment.*
Moore's (John W.) **Infantry.** See *Missouri Troops, Union, 23d Regiment.*
Moore's Scouts. Official designation unknown. See *Captain Moore.*
Morgan's (A. S.) **Infantry.** See *Arkansas Troops, Confederate, 26th Regiment.*
Morgan's (C. L.) **Cavalry.** See *Texas Troops.*
Morgan's (Wick) **Infantry.** See *Missouri Troops, Union, 7th Regiment, Provisional Enrolled Militia.*
Morris' (E. J.) **Infantry.** See *Missouri Troops, Union, 7th Regiment, Provisional Enrolled Militia.*
Morton's (Quinn) **Infantry.** See *Missouri Troops, Union, 23d Regiment.*
Mullins' (Alexander W.) **Cavalry.** See *Missouri Troops, Union, 1st Regiment, State Militia.*
Murphy's (David) **Artillery.** See *Missouri Troops, Union, 1st Regiment, Battery F.*
Murphy's (Richard) **Cavalry.** See *Missouri Troops, Union, 5th Regiment, State Militia (new).*
Neill's (Henry) **Infantry.** See *Missouri Troops, Union, 5th Regiment, Provisional Enrolled Militia.*
Neill's (Henry) **Infantry.** See *Missouri Troops, Union, 71st Regiment, Enrolled Militia.*
Newgent's (B. F.) **Artillery.** See *Missouri Troops, Union, 1st Battery, State Militia.*
Newton's (Robert C.) **Cavalry.** See *Arkansas Troops, Confederate.*
Nichols' (Frederic C.) **Infantry.** See *Missouri Troops, Union, 25th Regiment.*
Noble's (John W.) **Cavalry.** See *Iowa Troops, 3d Regiment.*
Noble's (S. M.) **Cavalry.** See *Texas Troops, 12th Regiment.*
Norris' (W. W.) **Infantry.** See *Indiana Troops, 43d Regiment.*

Reeder's (F. W.) **Cavalry.** See *Missouri Troops, Union, 12th Regiment, State Militia.*
Reves' (Timothy) **Cavalry.** See *Missouri Troops, Confederate.*
Rice's (Samuel A.) **Infantry.** See *Iowa Troops, 33d Regiment.*
Rich's (Josephus G.) **Cavalry.** See *Missouri Troops, Union, 8th Regiment.*
Richardson's (John M.) **Cavalry.** See *Missouri Troops, Union, 14th Regiment, State Militia.*
Richardson's (R. V.) **Cavalry.** See *Tennessee Troops, Confederate.*
Richardson's (S. B.) **Cavalry.** See *Missouri Troops, Union, 5th Regiment, State Militia (new).*
Richey's Rangers. Official designation unknown. See *Captain Richey.*
Ritter's (John F.) **Cavalry.** See *Missouri Troops, Union, 1st Regiment.*
Robbins' (Josephus) **Cavalry.** See *Missouri Troops, Union, 2d Regiment, State Militia.*
Roberts' (L. D.) **Cavalry.** See *Missouri Troops, Confederate.*
Roberts' (O. M.) **Infantry.** See *Texas Troops, 11th Regiment.*
Roberts' (Westley) **Artillery.** See *Missouri Troops, Confederate.*
Robinson's (William P.) **Infantry.** See *Missouri Troops, Union, 23d Regiment.*
Rogers' (Jabez B.) **Cavalry.** See *Missouri Troops, Union, 2d Regiment.*
Rogers' (N. T.) **Cavalry.** See *Missouri Troops, Union, 1st Regiment, State Militia.*
Rose's (Augustine D.) **Infantry.** See *Indiana Troops, 26th Regiment.*
Rowell's (Lyman D.) **Cavalry.** See *Colorado Troops, 2d Regiment.*
Ruark's (Ozias) **Cavalry.** See *Missouri Troops, Union, 8th Regiment, State Militia.*
Ruffner's (S. T.) **Artillery.** See *Westley Roberts' Artillery.*
Sadler's (J. O.) **Cavalry.** See *Charles A. Carroll's Cavalry.*
Sands' (Frank C.) **Artillery.** See *Ohio Troops, 11th Battery.*
Scanland's (John) **Cavalry.** See *Texas Troops.*
Schaurte's (Frederick W.) **Infantry.** See *Indian Troops, Union, 2d Regiment, Home Guards.*
Schmitz's (Joseph) **Infantry.** See *Missouri Troops, Union, 25th Regiment.*
Schofield Hussars Cavalry. See *Missouri Troops, Union.*
Schriner's (Philip) **Infantry.** See *Missouri Troops, Union, 8th Regiment, Provisional Enrolled Militia.*
Scott's* (John) **Cavalry.** See *Charles A. Carroll's Cavalry.*
Scott's (John) **Infantry.** See *Iowa Troops, 32d Regiment.*
Scudder's (Thomas W.) **Cavalry.** See *Kansas Troops, 5th Regiment.*
Searle's (E. J.) **Infantry.** See *Arkansas Troops, Union, 1st Regiment.*
Sells' (Lewis) **Cavalry.** See *Missouri Troops, Union, 2d Regiment, State Militia.*
Shaler's (James R.) **Infantry.** See *Arkansas Troops, Confederate, 27th Regiment.*
Shanks' (David) **Cavalry.** See *Missouri Troops, Confederate.*
Shaver's (R. G.) **Infantry.** See *Arkansas Troops, Confederate, 38th Regiment.*
Shaw's (Elvis P.) **Cavalry.** See *Illinois Troops, 10th Regiment.*
Shaw's (William T.) **Infantry.** See *Iowa Troops, 14th Regiment.*
Shelby's (Joseph O.) **Cavalry.** See *Missouri Troops, Confederate, 5th Regiment.*
Sheppard's (Henry) **Infantry.** See *Missouri Troops, Union, 6th Regiment, Provisional Enrolled Militia;* also *72d Regiment Enrolled Militia.*
Shibley's (Samuel) **Cavalry.** See *Missouri Troops, Union, 2d Regiment, State Militia.*
Shipman's (S. V.) **Cavalry.** See *Wisconsin Troops, 1st Regiment.*
Shoup's (James C.) **Artillery.** See *Arkansas Troops, Confederate.*
Shunk's (David) **Infantry.** See *Indiana Troops, 8th Regiment.*
Sigel's (Albert) **Cavalry.** See *Missouri Troops, Union, 13th Regiment, State Militia.*
Sims' (W. L.) **Infantry.** See *Arkansas Troops, Confederate, 26th Regiment.*
Sink's (George B.) **Artillery.** See *Indiana Troops, 2d Battery.*
Sioux City Cavalry. See *Iowa Troops.*
Smart's (Edwin) **Cavalry.** See *Missouri Troops, Union, 3d and 10th Regiments, State Militia (new).*
Smith's Militia. Official designation unknown. See *Captain Smith.*

* Temporarily commanding.

Waldschmidt's (William) **Artillery**. See *Missouri Troops, Union, 2d Regiment, Battery L.*

Walker's (Tandy) **Indians**. See *Indian Troops, Confederate, 1st Regiment, Choctaw and Chickasaw.*

Ward's (S. J.) **Cavalry**. See *Missouri Troops, Confederate, 8th Regiment.*

Washburn's (Henry D.) **Infantry**. See *Indiana Troops, 18th Regiment.*

Waterhouse's (Richard) **Infantry**. See *Texas Troops, 19th Regiment.*

Watie's (Stand) **Indians**. See *Indian Troops, Confederate, 1st Regiment, Cherokee.*

Wattles' (Stephen H.) **Infantry**. See *Indian Troops, Union, 1st Regiment, Home Guards.*

Wear's (W. D.) **Infantry**. See *Missouri Troops, Union, 9th Regiment, Provisional Enrolled Militia.*

Webb's (Ephraim L.) **Infantry**. See *Missouri Troops, Union, 23d Regiment.*

Welfley's (Martin) **Artillery**. See *Missouri Troops, Union, 1st Regiment, Battery B.*

Wells' (Samuel T.) **Infantry**. See *Indiana Troops, 50th Regiment.*

West's (Henry C.) **Artillery**. See *Arkansas Troops, Confederate.*

West's (William) **Infantry**. See *Union Troops, Regulars, 2d Regiment.*

Westerberg's (C. G. E. N.) **Cavalry**. See *Schofield Hussars.*

Western's (H. H.) **Artillery**. See *Minnesota Troops, 3d Battery.*

Weston's (Eli W.) **Infantry**. See *Missouri Troops, Union, 24th Regiment.*

Whipple's (John C.) **Artillery**. See *Minnesota Troops 3d Battery.*

White's (Calvert C.) **Infantry**. See *Wisconsin Troops, 28th Regiment.*

White's (Frank J.) **Cavalry**. See *Missouri Troops, Union, 2d Battalion, State Militia.*

White's (James D.) **Infantry**. See *Missouri Troops, Confederate.*

White's (Richard H.) **Cavalry**. See *Wisconsin Troops, 3d Regiment.*

Whybark's (Levi E.) **Cavalry**. See *Missouri Troops, Union, 5th Regiment, State Militia (new).*

Wickersham's (Dudley) **Cavalry**. See *Illinois Troops, 10th Regiment.*

Wilkes' (F. C.) **Cavalry**. See *Texas Troops, 24th Regiment.*

Wilkin's (Alexander) **Infantry**. See *Minnesota Troops, 9th Regiment.*

Wilkins' (Theodore) **Artillery**. See *Missouri Troops, Union, 2d Regiment.*

Williams' (Henry H.) **Infantry**. See *Kansas Troops, 10th Regiment.*

Williams' (James M.) **Infantry**. See *Kansas Troops, 1st Regiment (Colored).*

Williams' (John F.) **Cavalry**. See *Missouri Troops, Union, 9th Regiment, State Militia.*

Wilson's (Aristarchus) **Artillery**. See *Kansas Troops, 2d Battery.*

Wilson's (David S.) **Cavalry**. See *Iowa Troops, 6th Regiment.*

Wilson's (Hall) **Cavalry**. See *Illinois Troops, 5th Regiment.*

Wilson's (James) **Cavalry**. See *Missouri Troops, Union, 3d Regiment, State Militia (new).*

Wimer's (John M.) **Cavalry**. See *Missouri Troops, Confederate, 4th Regiment.*

Witherspoon's (J. L.) **Cavalry**. See *Arkansas Troops, Confederate.*

Wood's (Robert C.) **Cavalry**. See *Missouri Troops, Confederate.*

Wood's (William F.) **Cavalry**. See *Indiana Troops, 1st Regiment.*

Woodruff's (William E., jr.) **Artillery**. See *Arkansas Troops, Confederate.*

Woodson's (Richard G.) **Cavalry**. See *Missouri Troops, Union, 3d Regiment, State Militia (new).*

Woolfolk's (Alexander M.) **Cavalry**. See *Missouri Troops, Union, 1st Regiment, State Militia.*

Woosley's (James) **Cavalry**. See *Arkansas Troops, Confederate.*

Worthington's (John I.) **Cavalry**. See *Arkansas Troops, Union, 1st Regiment.*

Wright's Cavalry. Official designation unknown. See *Captain Wright.*

Wright's (Melvil C.) **Artillery**. See *Iowa Troops, 3d Battery.*

Yarnell's (H. A.) **Infantry**. See *Missouri Troops, Union, 9th Regiment, Provisional Enrolled Militia.*

Yates (Henry) **Infantry**. See *Illinois Troops, 106th Regiment.*

Young's (M. L.) **Cavalry**. See *Missouri Troops, Confederate.*

Young's (Overton) **Infantry**. See *Texas Troops, 12th Regiment.*

INDEX.

Brigades, Divisions, Corps, Armies, and improvised organizations are "Mentioned" under name of commanding officer; State and other organizations under their official designation. (See Alternate Designations, pp. 914–926.)

* Howitzers attached to 1st Arkansas Cavalry.

* Afterward Company H, 15th Illinois Cavalry.

* Battery attached to 1st Indiana Cavalry.

† Afterward Company I, 7th Iowa Cavalry.

* Attached to 1st Kansas Colored Infantry.
† Attached to 2d Kansas Cavalry; afterward 3d Kansas Battery.
‡ Howitzers attached to 9th Kansas Cavalry.
§ Howitzers attached to 2d Kansas Cavalry.
‖ Battery attached to 5th Kansas Cavalry.
¶ Became 11th Kansas Cavalry in August, 1863.

* Also called Ruffner's Battery.
† Organized as a regiment July 9, 1863.

* Arm of service and official designation cannot be determined.

† Battery attached to 1st Missouri State Militia Cavalry.

‡ Attached to 68th Regiment Enrolled Militia.

§ Howitzer Battery attached to 2d Missouri Cavalry.

‖ Howitzer Battery attached to 2d Missouri State Militia Cavalry.

¶ Batteries designated when practicable.

** Afterward Company I, 5th Missouri State Militia Cavalry (new).

* Also called Stockton's Battery.

* Afterward designated the 11th.